lonely planet

Rocky Mountains

Mason Florence

Marisa Gierlich

Andrew Dean Nystrom

LONELY PLANET PUBLICATIONS
Melbourne • Oakland • London • Paris

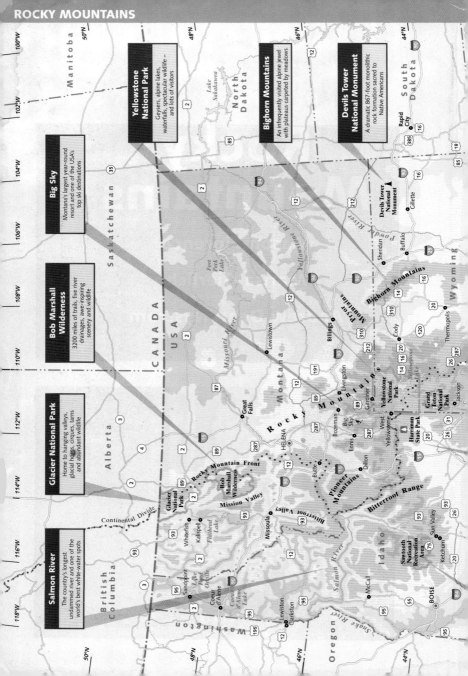

Salmon River
The country's longest undammed river and one of the world's best white-water spots

Glacier National Park
Home to hanging valleys, glacial hugs, cirques, tarns and abundant wildlife

Bob Marshall Wilderness
3200 miles of trails, five river drainages, awe-inspiring scenery and wildlife

Big Sky
Montana's largest year-round resort and one of the USA's top ski destinations

Yellowstone National Park
Geysers, alpine lakes, waterfalls, spectacular wildlife – and lots of visitors

Bighorn Mountains
An infrequently visited alpine jewel with plateaus carpeted by meadows

Devils Tower National Monument
A dramatic 867-foot monolithic rock formation sacred to Native Americans

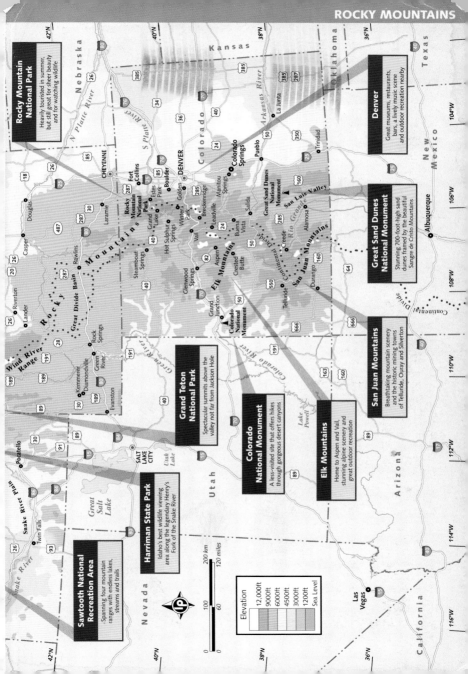

Rocky Mountain National Park
Heavily touristed in summer, but still great for sheer beauty and for watching wildlife

Denver
Great museums, restaurants, bars, a lively music scene and outdoor recreation nearby

Great Sand Dunes National Monument
Stunning 700-foot-high sand dunes framed by the beautiful Sangre de Cristo Mountains

San Juan Mountains
Breathtaking mountain scenery and the historic mining towns of Telluride, Ouray and Silverton

Grand Teton National Park
Spectacular summits above the valley not far from Jackson Hole

Colorado National Monument
A less-visited site that offers hikes through gorgeous desert canyons

Elk Mountains
Home to Aspen and Vail, stunning alpine scenery and great outdoor recreation

Harriman State Park
Idaho's best wildlife viewing area along the legendary Henry's Fork of the Snake River

Sawtooth National Recreation Area
Spanning four mountain ranges with endless lakes, streams and trails

Elevation
12,000ft
9000ft
6000ft
4500ft
3000ft
1200ft
Sea Level

200 km
120 miles
0 60 100

Kansas
Nebraska
Colorado
Oklahoma
Texas
New Mexico
Utah
Nevada
Arizona
California
Wyoming

DENVER
CHEYENNE
SALT LAKE CITY

Fort Collins
Boulder
Golden
Breckenridge
Leadville
Vail
Aspen
Crested Butte
Estes Park
Grand Lake
Winter Park
Hot Sulphur Springs
Steamboat Springs
Glenwood Springs
Grand Junction
Telluride
Durango
Alamosa
Creede
Buena Vista
Salida
Manitou Springs
Colorado Springs
Pueblo
Trinidad
La Junta
Albuquerque
Las Vegas
Twin Falls
Pocatello
Lander
Riverton
Casper
Douglas
Laramie
Rawlins
Rock Springs
Green River
Kemmerer
Diamondville
Evanston

N Platte River
S Platte River
Arkansas River
Rio Grande
Green River
Colorado River
Snake River
N Platte River
Wind River Range
Great Divide Basin
Rocky Mountains
Elk Mountains
San Juan Mountains
Sangre de Cristo
San Luis Valley
Continental Divide
Great Salt Lake
Utah Lake
Lake Powell
Snake River Plain
Great Sand Dunes National Monument
Colorado National Monument
Rocky Mountain National Park

42°N
40°N
38°N
36°N
104°W
106°W
108°W
110°W
112°W
114°W
116°W

Rocky Mountains
3rd edition – August 2001
First published – October 1995

917.8

Published by
Lonely Planet Publications Pty Ltd ABN 36 005 607 983
90 Maribyrnong St, Footscray, Victoria 3011, Australia

Lonely Planet Offices
Australia Locked Bag 1, Footscray, Victoria 3011
USA 150 Linden St, Oakland, CA 94607
UK 10a Spring Place, London NW5 3BH
France 1 rue du Dahomey, 75011 Paris

Photographs
Many of the images in this guide are available for licensing from
Lonely Planet Images.
email: lpi@lonelyplanet.com.au

Front cover photograph
Mountain biking in the Rockies (Chris Mellor)

Title page photographs
Colorado (Richard Cummins)
Wyoming (John Elk III)
Montana (Rob Blakers)
Idaho (Woods Wheatcroft)

ISBN 1 86450 327 0

text & maps © Lonely Planet 2001
photos © photographers as indicated 2001

Printed by The Bookmaker International Ltd
Printed in China

Contents – Text

WESTERN COLORADO 321

EASTERN PLAINS 351

WYOMING 364

MONTANA 490

IDAHO 618

Contents – Maps

6 Contents

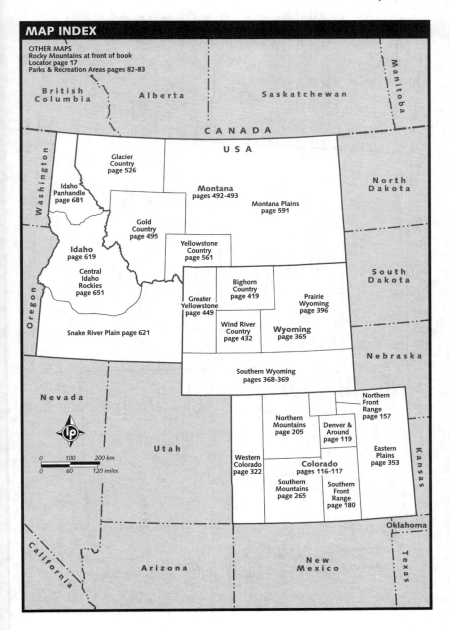

MAP INDEX

OTHER MAPS
Rocky Mountains at front of book
Locator page 17
Parks & Recreation Areas pages 82-83

British Columbia

Alberta

Saskatchewan

Manitoba

CANADA

USA

Washington

Glacier Country page 526

Idaho Panhandle page 681

Montana pages 492-493

Montana Plains page 591

North Dakota

Gold Country page 495

Idaho page 619

Yellowstone Country page 561

Central Idaho Rockies page 651

Oregon

South Dakota

Greater Yellowstone page 449

Bighorn Country page 419

Prairie Wyoming page 396

Wind River Country page 432

Wyoming page 365

Snake River Plain page 621

Nebraska

Southern Wyoming pages 368-369

Nevada

Northern Front Range page 157

Northern Mountains page 205

Denver & Around page 119

Utah

Western Colorado page 322

Colorado pages 116-117

Eastern Plains page 353

Kansas

0   100   200 km
0   60   120 miles

Southern Mountains page 265

Southern Front Range page 180

Oklahoma

California

Arizona

New Mexico

Texas

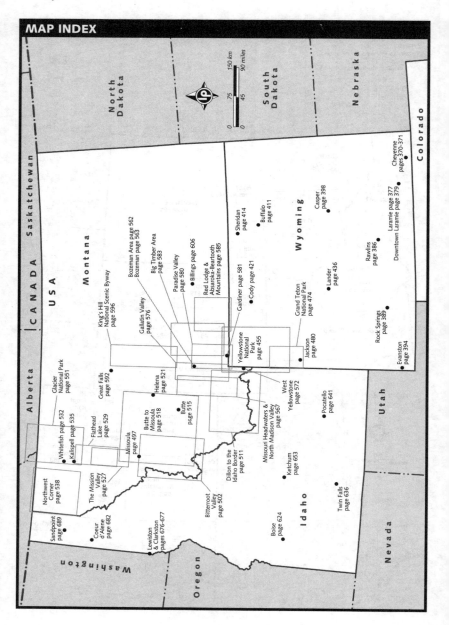

MAP INDEX

MAP INDEX

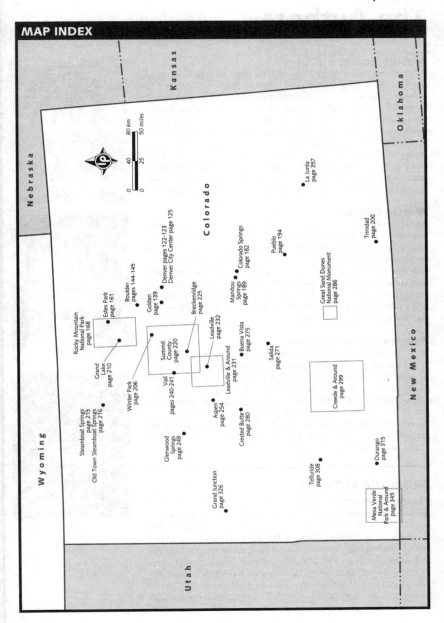

Kansas

Oklahoma

Nebraska

Colorado

0 40 80 km
0 25 50 miles

La Junta
page 357

Trinidad
page 200

Pueblo
page 194

Colorado Springs
page 182

Manitou
Springs
page 189

Denver pages 122–123
Denver City Center page 125

Great Sand Dunes
National Monument
page 286

Boulder
pages 144–145

Golden
page 139

Breckenridge
page 225

Estes Park
page 161

Rocky Mountain
National Park
page 168

Grand
Lake
page 210

Summit
County
page 220

Leadville
page 232

Buena Vista
page 275

Salida
page 271

Winter Park
page 206

Vail
pages 240–241

Leadville & Around
page 231

Creede & Around
page 299

Steamboat Springs
page 215
Old Town Steamboat Springs
page 216

Aspen
page 254

Crested Butte
page 280

Glenwood
Springs
page 249

Grand Junction
page 326

Telluride
page 308

Durango
page 315

Mesa Verde
National
Park & Around
page 345

New Mexico

Wyoming

Utah

The Authors

Mason Florence

A native New Yorker, Mason migrated to Boulder, CO, to pursue a college degree while soaking up the great outdoors. When not indulging his chronic addiction to skiing and mountain biking, he worked hard to realize his lifelong childhood dream of becoming a cowboy, foolishly joining the University of Colorado Rodeo Team. After being flung from horseback one time too many, he graduated (barely), traded in his spurs for a Nikon and a laptop and relocated to Japan. Now a Kyoto-based photojournalist, he spends about half the year traveling and free moments restoring a 300-year-old thatched-roof farmhouse in rural Shikoku. In addition to *Rocky Mountains*, Mason has written for Lonely Planet's *South-East Asia, Japan, Kyoto, Hanoi* and *Ho Chi Minh City (Saigon)*.

Marisa Gierlich

Marisa was born and raised in Hermosa Beach, CA. Thanks to adventurous parents, she began traveling at age seven and hasn't stopped for more than eight months since. She earned an English degree at the University of California, Berkeley, where she began writing for *The Berkeley Guides* – an employ that took her to France, Sweden, Italy and Alaska. She has written for all three editions of Lonely Planet's *Rocky Mountains* as well as *California & Nevada, Hiking in the USA, California Condensed* and *Cycling USA – West Coast*. Marisa leads hiking and biking tours for Backroads, and runs, skis and surfs with her husband Paul.

Andrew Dean Nystrom

Born a mile high in Colorado, Andrew began traveling in the womb and hasn't slowed down since. His parents' US travels introduced him to the Midwest (Detroit, MI, and Cincinnati, OH), the South (Dallas, TX) and the far West (Los Angeles, CA). He finally settled at the University of California, Berkeley, and graduated with a geography and education degree. His earliest childhood memories include picnicking at Denver's now paved-over prairie-dog town and frolicking barefoot in his grandparents' corn silo in Ames, IA. When not out rambling, he works for Lonely Planet's New Media unit in Oakland, CA.

FROM THE AUTHORS

Mason Florence I'm grateful to Nicko Goncharoff and Eric Kettunen, my predecessors on the Colorado chapters, for all of their thorough research. My patient mother, Michelle, was a brave and faithful travel partner in southern Colorado. Denver natives Brandon and Lucy shared their hospitality and insight about what makes things tick at 5280. In Boulder, thanks go to GORP outdoors guru Blake Catlin. In Aspen, infamous ski patrolman Timmy La Croix provided a local's perspective, while David Eckardt and Ken Murphy were great sources for Colorado rafting facts. Muchas gracias to Chris and Sigrid Cotrell in Crested Butte, starving artist Steve Smalzel in Salida, Wyatt Phipps in Steamboat and Richard Milgrim in Grand Junction. Thanks also to the countless staff at regional tourist offices who suffered brain damage from my hundreds of nit-picking questions. Finally, a big tip of the hat to my fellow authors Andrew and Marisa, and to Rachel and the entire Rockies crew at LP for making the adventure a pleasure.

Marisa Gierlich Joan and Jim continue to bless my trips to Montana with stimulating conversation, unselfish friendship and a warm place to stay. Without the gracious hospitality of Bobby and the wonderful Sanders crew, my stay in (and knowledge of) Helena would not be nearly as satisfying. The folks at the Scott deserve hearty thanks for sharing their passion for Butte and its history. Didi and Ursula get special mention for their openness in welcoming people to the Yellowstone and ability to show up in the most unusual places! Thanks to Kelly and Melissa for always being there when I roll into West Yellowstone, and many thanks to Mary and the sisters of Delta Gamma for providing entertainment and accommodations in Missoula.

Last but never least go thanks to the uncontested home team who make traveling do-able and coming home worth anticipating: Paul, Mom, Dad, Marla, Brittney, Kurt, Jim, the Mocks, Sara, Sarah, Kathleen, Sharron, Baty, Amy, Bob and Steiner the Cat.

Andrew Dean Nystrom In inimitable Idaho, thanks to all the incognito hot-springs hounds; Robert Tullis in Stanley; Kristina at the Red Fish Lake Visitors Center; Buhl's dairymen; the McCall Smokejumper's Base Camp; the Craters of the Moon staff; Joyce, Auntie Rachel, Victor and the Scotts in Kellogg; the Smiths at Three Rivers Resort in Lowell; Dugout Dick; Noel and Betty Stone at the River's Fork Inn in North Fork; Julie Fanselow for the Lewis and Clark reading; Gary for my first snow-machine lesson; and the entire Wight family for graciously allowing me to overstay my welcome.

In wide-open Wyoming, a tip of the beanie to Gina in Sheridan; the sheriff who let me go in Buffalo; the Ucross Ranch artists-in-residence; Joyce Speidel for sharing her panoramic view at the Warren Peak Fire Lookout; the fine folks at Pinedale Online, Irv at Lozier's Box R Ranch and Pinedale mayor Rose Skinner; the cards at the bar in Medicine Bow and Atlantic City for the cowpoke poetry; Steve at Louis Lake Lodge; Eleanor Carrigen at Crimson Dawn; Gary Rolland; Casey and Amy at the Sundance Inn in Jackson; and Monte and Maxine for teaching me the importance of establishing a rapport with wildlife.

Back in wild and woolly West Oakland, thanks to backcountry connoisseur Don Root; ace boss Scott McNeely and the entire New Media crew for tending to the flock; my main lobsterman Andy Rebold for the mapping muscle; sourdough senior editor Tom Downs for helping me saddle up; and Mariah Bear for corralling this greenhorn his first LP project. Kudos to Mason Florence for circling the wagons.

Finally, much love to my family, and to Morgan for the shared laughs – without y'all the long haul would have been impossible.

This Book

Mason Florence was the coordinating author of this 3rd edition. He updated the introductory chapters and all of the Colorado chapters. Marisa Gierlich covered Montana and Andrew Dean Nystrom handled Wyoming and Idaho.

The 2nd edition of this book was written by Nicko Goncharoff, Kimberley O'Neil, Eric Kettunen and Marisa. The original version was penned by Wayne Bernhardson, Robert Raburn and Marisa, with contributions by Bill McRae.

FROM THE PUBLISHER

This edition of *Rocky Mountains* was edited by Rachel Bernstein, Paul Sheridan and Kevin Anglin in Oakland, with gianormous editorial contributions by Tom Downs, Wade Fox and Suki Gear. Erin Corrigan, Gabi Knight, Vivek Waglé, Rachel and Paul proofed the book. Ken DellaPenta created the index. Thanks go to Erin for her helping hand and Kate Hoffman for her support and wisdom.

The skillful cartographic team, led by unflappable Patrick 'Peaches' Phelan, included Carole Nuttall, Andrew Rebold, Kat Smith, Matthew DeMartini, Buck Cantwell, Patrick Huerta, Christopher Howard, John Culp, Justin Colgan, Rachel Driver, Gina Gillich, Molly Green, Mary Hagemann, Graham Neale, Don Patterson, Tessa Rottiers, Herman So and Ed Turley. Monica Lepe, Tracey Croom and Alex Guilbert kept all that map-making under control.

Lora Santiago designed the lovely color pages and Paul wrote the captions. Margaret Livingston, Anne Mavromatis and Lora laid out *Rocky Mountains* and Margaret ensured that the whole layout process went smoothly. Beca Lafore was on the illustration tip along with Hugh D'Andrade, Hayden Foell, Justin Marler, Henia Miedzinski, Anthony Phelan, Anne and Lora. Joshua Schefers designed the cover. Susan Rimerman oversaw all things design-related with her typical good cheer.

Many thanks to authors Mason, Andrew and Marisa for their easy natures, flexibility and excellent work.

Foreword

ABOUT LONELY PLANET GUIDEBOOKS

The story begins with a classic travel adventure: Tony and Maureen Wheeler's 1972 journey across Europe and Asia to Australia. Useful information about the overland trail did not exist at that time, so Tony and Maureen published the first Lonely Planet guidebook to meet a growing need.

From a kitchen table, then from a tiny office in Melbourne (Australia), Lonely Planet has become the largest independent travel publisher in the world, an international company with offices in Melbourne, Oakland (USA), London (UK) and Paris (France).

Today Lonely Planet guidebooks cover the globe. There is an ever-growing list of books, and there's information in a variety of forms and media. Some things haven't changed. The main aim is still to help make it possible for adventurous travelers to get out there – to explore and better understand the world.

At Lonely Planet we believe travelers can make a positive contribution to the countries they visit – if they respect their host communities and spend their money wisely. Since 1986 a percentage of the income from each book has been donated to aid projects and human-rights campaigns.

Updates Lonely Planet thoroughly updates each guidebook as often as possible. This usually means there are around two years between editions, although for more unusual or more stable destinations the gap can be longer. Check the imprint page (following the color map at the beginning of the book) for publication dates.

Between editions, up-to-date information is available in two free newsletters – the paper *Planet Talk* and email *Comet* (to subscribe, contact any Lonely Planet office) – and on our website at www.lonelyplanet.com. The *Upgrades* section of the website covers a number of important and volatile destinations and is regularly updated by Lonely Planet authors. *Scoop* covers news and current affairs relevant to travelers. And, lastly, the *Thorn Tree* bulletin board and *Postcards* section of the site carry unverified, but fascinating, reports from travelers.

Correspondence The process of creating new editions begins with the letters, postcards and emails received from travelers. This correspondence often includes suggestions, criticisms and comments about the current editions. Interesting excerpts are immediately passed on via newsletters and the website, and everything goes to our authors to be verified when they're researching on the road. We're keen to get more feedback from organizations or individuals who represent communities visited by travelers.

Lonely Planet gathers information for everyone who's curious about the planet – and especially for those who explore it first-hand. Through guidebooks, phrasebooks, activity guides, maps, literature, newsletters, image library, TV series and website, we act as an information exchange for a worldwide community of travelers.

Research Authors aim to gather sufficient practical information to enable travelers to make informed choices and to make the mechanics of a journey run smoothly. They also research historical and cultural background to help enrich the travel experience and allow travelers to understand and respond appropriately to cultural and environmental issues.

Authors don't stay in every hotel because that would mean spending a couple of months in each medium-size city and, no, they don't eat at every restaurant because that would mean stretching belts beyond capacity. They do visit hotels and restaurants to check standards and prices, but feedback based on readers' direct experiences can be very helpful.

Many of our authors work undercover; others aren't so secretive. None of them accept freebies in exchange for positive write-ups. And none of our guidebooks contain any advertising.

Production Authors submit their raw manuscripts and maps to offices in Australia, the USA, the UK or France. Editors and cartographers – all experienced travelers themselves – then begin the process of assembling the pieces. When the book finally hits the shops, some things are already out of date, we start getting feedback from readers and the process begins again....

WARNING & REQUEST

Things change – prices go up, schedules change, good places go bad and bad places go bankrupt – nothing stays the same. So, if you find things better or worse, recently opened or long since closed, please tell us and help make the next edition even more accurate and useful. We genuinely value all the feedback we receive. Julie Young coordinates a well-traveled team that reads and acknowledges every letter, postcard and email and ensures that every morsel of information finds its way to the appropriate authors, editors and cartographers for verification.

Everyone who writes to us will find their name in the next edition of the appropriate guidebook. They will also receive the latest issue of *Planet Talk*, our quarterly printed newsletter, or *Comet*, our monthly email newsletter. Subscriptions to both newsletters are free. The very best contributions will be rewarded with a free guidebook.

Excerpts from your correspondence may appear in new editions of Lonely Planet guidebooks, the Lonely Planet website, *Planet Talk* or *Comet*, so please let us know if you *don't* want your letter published or your name acknowledged.

Send all correspondence to the Lonely Planet office closest to you:

Australia: Locked Bag 1, Footscray, Victoria 3011
USA: 150 Linden St, Oakland, CA 94607
UK: 10a Spring Place, London NW5 3BH
France: 1 rue du Dahomey, 75011 Paris

Or email us at: talk2us@lonelyplanet.com.au

For news, views and updates, see our website: www.lonelyplanet.com

HOW TO USE A LONELY PLANET GUIDEBOOK

The best way to use a Lonely Planet guidebook is any way you choose. At Lonely Planet, we believe the most memorable travel experiences are often those that are unexpected, and the finest discoveries are those you make yourself. Guidebooks are not intended to be used as if they provided a detailed set of infallible instructions!

Contents All Lonely Planet guidebooks follow the same format. The Facts about the Country chapters or sections give background information ranging from history to weather. Facts for the Visitor gives practical information on issues like visas and health. Getting There & Away gives a brief starting point for researching travel to and from the destination. Getting Around gives an overview of the transport options available when you arrive.

The peculiar demands of each destination determine how subsequent chapters are broken up, but some things remain constant. We always start with background, then proceed to sights, places to stay, places to eat, entertainment, getting there and away, and getting around information – in that order.

Heading Hierarchy Lonely Planet headings are used in a strict hierarchical structure that can be visualized as a set of Russian dolls. Each heading (and its following text) is encompassed by any preceding heading that is higher on the hierarchical ladder.

Entry Points We do not assume guidebooks will be read from beginning to end, but that people will dip into them. The traditional entry points are the list of contents and the index. In addition, however, some books have a complete list of maps and an index map illustrating map coverage.

There may also be a color map that shows highlights. These highlights are dealt with in greater detail later in the book, along with planning questions. Each chapter covering a geographical region usually begins with a locator map and another list of highlights. Once you find something of interest in a list of highlights, turn to the index.

Maps Maps play a crucial role in Lonely Planet guidebooks and include a huge amount of information. A legend is printed on the back page. We seek to have complete consistency between maps and text, and to have every important place in the text captured on a map. Map key numbers usually start in the top left corner.

Although inclusion in a guidebook usually implies a recommendation, we cannot list every good place. Exclusion does not necessarily imply criticism. In fact, there are a number of reasons why we might exclude a place – sometimes it is simply inappropriate to encourage an influx of travelers.

Introduction

With its towering peaks and lush mountain valleys, the magnificent Rocky Mountain range is home to some of the USA's most stunning natural beauty. Each year millions of people flock to these awesome mountains and their nearby plains to enjoy the scenery, outdoor recreation, historical sites and some of the world's best skiing. In addition to the nature, there are countless small towns and villages throughout the region – a legion of charming, friendly stopovers for visitors making their ways from one impressive site to the next.

The Rockies, acting as North America's spine, split the USA along the Continental Divide. Eastward-flowing rivers cross the plains to join the great Mississippi. The arid western drainage snakes through imposing mountain ranges to reach the Pacific via the mighty Columbia River or to dwindle away on the sands of the southern Colorado Desert.

A fascinating range of topography awaits travelers visiting the Rocky Mountain region. In addition to the peaks themselves, some of which reach above 14,000 feet, there are fertile river valleys, sprawling reaches of semidesert, alpine plateaus, plunging canyons and even massive sand dunes. This variety means that often the trip to a destination is just as rewarding as seeing the place itself. As with much of the USA, public transportation is relatively limited and by far the best way to explore the region is by private car or, if you have the time, by bicycle.

Early Spanish explorers were the first Europeans to reach the area, and rugged

mountain folk and fur traders pioneered the European exploration of the northern Rockies. The Rockies soon became identified with the 'Wild West' of brawling, rough and ready mining camps, long-distance cattle drives and gunfighters.

European settlement displaced or supplanted the native peoples who had inhabited the region for millennia, leaving them socially sidelined and impoverished – if they even survived. Despite this grim, unfortunate history, the indigenous presence has not disappeared and, in some ways, is becoming more visible; Native Americans are being voted into public office and powwows are popular community events.

Colorado is the region's economic powerhouse and Denver, Colorado's capital, is the only true metropolis in the four states. Idaho, Montana and Wyoming, almost exclusively rural, are among the least populated states in the country.

This book does not cover the entirety of the Rocky Mountains, which transcend state and national boundaries – see also Lonely Planet's *Southwest* for Utah, New Mexico and Arizona and *Canada* for the mountains' northern reaches.

Facts about the Rocky Mountains

HISTORY

Nearly 20,000 years ago, when the accumulated ice of the great polar glaciers of the Pleistocene epoch lowered sea levels throughout the world, the ancestors of American Indians crossed from Siberia to Alaska via a land bridge over the Bering Strait. Over millennia, subsequent migrations distributed the population southward through North and Central America and down to the southern tip of South America.

The first inhabitants of North America were nomadic hunter-gatherers who lived in small bands, and this type of society existed on the continent into recent times. In the northern plains, from about 16,000 years ago the early Clovis complex consisted of hunters who eventually exterminated megafauna like mammoths and *Bison antiquus*, forerunner of the modern buffalo by about 12,000 years. The slightly later Folsom complex, near the Colorado–New Mexico border, occupied rather larger sites.

Late Paleo-Indian artifacts of the Cody cultural complex indicate reliance on the modern bison, while around 7500 years ago some peoples switched to hunting smaller game – a likely indicator of human population pressure on the declining bison. Petroglyphs along the canyon walls of central Idaho's mighty rivers testify to more than 8000 years of human habitation. The most complex societies in North American antiquity, however, were the agricultural pueblos of the Colorado Plateau, where Anasazi cliff dwellers left behind impressive ruins in areas like Mesa Verde near Cortez, CO.

Native Americans at Contact

Many different Native American groups occupied the Rocky Mountain region at the time of European contact. In the harsh landscapes of Oregon and Idaho's southern desert, nomadic tribes like the Shoshone and Paiute became fearsome warriors and hunters after the 18th century, when horses – stolen from Spanish California –

gave them easy mobility. With horses, the Shoshone-Bannocks quickly became one of the dominant Indian groups in the West, ranging across the Rockies onto the Great Plains to hunt buffalo and onto the Columbia Plateau to trade and plunder.

The Shoshone were most amenable to the foreign presence. Numbering about 2000 in 1800, they were concentrated in the western Wyoming drainage of the Green, Snake, Bear and Columbia Rivers; their population fell from a peak of 3000 in 1840 to only 800 by 1900. Staple foods included bison, elk, beaver, mule deer, fish, berries and wild roots. Most Shoshone now reside on the Wind River Reservation in central Wyoming, but smaller numbers live at Fort Hall, ID, and at Duck Valley, which straddles the Idaho-Nevada border.

Also friendly to traders were the Crow or Absaroka who lived at the headwaters of the Yellowstone, Powder, Bighorn, Platte and Wind Rivers. They numbered about 4000 in 1800. The Blackfeet, by contrast, resented and resisted the European invaders to their territory in the upper Missouri, Milk and Marias Rivers and the Judith Basin. Their population peaked at about 30,000 before the smallpox epidemic of 1837.

The Utes consisted of six eastern bands in Colorado and five western bands in Utah; their Colorado territory stretched from the Uinta Mountains and the Yampa River in the north to the San Juan River in the south, and as far east as the Front Range. They are now confined to the Ute Mountain Indian Reservation in southern Colorado and northern New Mexico, the Southern Ute Indian Reservation adjacent to it in southern Colorado, and the Uintah-Ouray Reservation in northern Utah. The Utes accommodated trappers, even attending the various rendezvous, but eventually came into conflict with settlers on the Western Slope. The Nez Percé, while based in what is now Idaho, also participated in the fur trade and rendezvous in present-day Wyoming.

The Lewis & Clark Expedition

When Jefferson made the decision in 1803 to explore the western part of the country to find a water passage to the Pacific, he enlisted his young protégé and personal secretary, Meriwether Lewis, to lead an expedition. Lewis, then 29, had no expertise in botany, cartography or Indian languages and was known to have bouts of 'hypochondriac affections' – a euphemism for schizophrenia – but he couldn't resist the opportunity. Lewis in turn asked his good friend William Clark, already an experienced frontiersman and army veteran at the age of 33, to join him. In 1804, they left St Louis, Missouri, and headed west with an entourage of 40, including 27 bachelors, Clark's African-American servant, York, and a dog.

They traveled some 8000 miles in about two years, documenting everything they came across in their journals with such bad spelling that it must have taken historians a few extra years just to sort out what they wrote. In an almost biblical fashion they named some 120 animals and 170 plants, including the grizzly bear and the prairie dog. While Clark's entries are the more scientific, Lewis was known to explore alone and write pensive, almost romantic, accounts of the journey.

Despite encountering hostilities, the group faired quite well, in part because they were accompanied by Sacagawea, a young Shoshone woman who had been married off to a French trapper. Her presence, along with her child's, and her ability to liaise between the explorers and some Indians eased many potential conflicts. York also eased tensions between the group and the locals – his color and stature of six feet and 200 pounds being both fascinating and intimidating.

Lewis and Clark returned to a heroes' welcome in St Louis in 1806 and were soon appointed to high offices. In 1808 Lewis was appointed governor of the Louisiana Territory, but died a year later, purportedly during a 'fit' in which he either committed suicide or was murdered. Clark dealt with his new fame a bit better, and was appointed superintendent of Indian Affairs in the Louisiana Territory and governor of the Missouri Territory. He died at the age of 68.

Exploration & Settlement

The first Europeans to see the Rocky Mountain area were Spaniards moving north from Mexico. They founded the city of Santa Fe at the end of the 16th century, and established land grants as far north as the Arkansas River in present-day Colorado. In the search for overland routes to California, the Domínguez-Escalante Expedition of 1775–76 explored the Colorado Plateau well into northern Colorado, but concentrated on what is now Utah.

In the early 18th century French explorers and fur traders converged on the northern plains from eastern Canada, but by the early 19th century Spanish influence extended throughout the western half of present-day Colorado, the southwestern corner of Wyoming, and even shared, at least formally, occupation of parts of Montana with the British. Virtually all of

New Mexico, Arizona, California, Utah and Nevada were under Spanish authority, but another player in the imperial game would soon supersede them.

In 1803 the upstart USA, under the presidency of Thomas Jefferson, took advantage of a surprising French proposal, known as the Louisiana Purchase, to purchase an ill-defined area including the coveted port of New Orleans. The area also included virtually all of present-day Montana, nearly three-quarters of Wyoming and the eastern half of Colorado. Shortly after the 830,000-sq-mile purchase, which guaranteed that the USA would come into conflict with Spain, Jefferson took steps to assess the resources of this enormous acquisition by inviting army captain Meriwether Lewis to command an exploratory expedition; Lewis in turn invited his colleague William Clark to serve as co-commander.

The official rationale for Lewis and Clark's Corps of Discovery was to benefit American commerce by seeking a 'Northwest Passage' to the Pacific Ocean, but Jefferson made it clear that the expedition was to make serious scientific observations on flora, fauna, climate and the inhabitants of the region. (See 'The Lewis & Clark Expedition' for details.)

Lewis and Clark's was the most successful of early US expeditions to the west; others ended in disaster. After a foray into Colorado in 1806–07, Zebulon Pike was arrested in New Mexico by Spanish police, perhaps because of machinations of General James Wilkinson, the governor of Louisiana Territory who took Spanish money in exchange for information on US troop movements. Pike, who was described by historian Herman J Viola as 'a poor explorer with a knack for getting lost,' never climbed the famous peak that bears his name.

Major Stephen Long attempted to organize an expedition to establish a fort on the Yellowstone River in 1819, but failed miserably because of a series of logistical bungles – among other problems, the steamboats carrying their supplies were unable to ascend the shallow Missouri. Long did manage to explore the Front Range of the Rockies, and others in his party even scaled Pikes Peak, but like Pike he produced incomplete and misleading accounts that described the West as a 'Great American Desert,' discouraging settlement for decades.

The Fur Trade & the Emigrant Trails

As knowledge of the American West grew, so did interest in its exploitable resources. One of these resources was the beaver, whose pelts became fashionable hats favored by European gentlemen. For a brief time, the fur trade made a contribution to the settlement of the West. The first white explorers in southern Idaho were fur trappers. The first European to explore the Idaho Panhandle was David Thompson, a fur trader and cartographer who crossed the Rocky Mountains and in 1809 established Kullyspell House on Lake Pend Oreille, where he traded with and maintained friendly relations with the tribes.

Another pioneer fur trader in the Rocky Mountains was Manuel Lisa, a Spaniard who built a fort at the mouth of the Bighorn River and recruited John Colter, who had split off from the Lewis and Clark Expedition (with permission) to explore the Yellowstone region and was, arguably, the first of the legendary 'mountain men.' Colter and others like Kit Carson, Jim Bridger, Jim Beckwourth (a free African-American) and Thomas Fitzpatrick knew the Rockies backcountry better than anyone except the Indians, with whom many of the mountain men had good relationships.

Their annual summer rendezvous, attended by suppliers, Indians and even early tourists, were celebrations of the year's accomplishments.

But the romantic image of the mountain man is an exaggeration; rather than rugged individualists selling their catch to the highest bidder, most of the trappers were company men who were on salary and sometimes advanced a year's supplies. In 1823, for example, William Ashley of St Louis advertised for 100 men to trap beaver in the Rocky Mountains for $200 a year. The trade collapsed by 1840, as silk hats replaced beaver in urban American and European fashion.

The lasting contribution of the mountain men was their local knowledge of the terrain and of routes through and across the mountains, which paved the way for later emigrants all the way to Oregon and California. Their close relations with the Native Americans were another plus – many mountain men married, or at least fathered children by, Native American women, and could pass freely through areas where strangers might draw suspicion. After the fur trade failed, Jim Bridger (who had a Shoshone wife) opened a trading post and guided emigrants over South Pass in south central Wyoming and across the Great Basin.

Even into the 20th century, hundreds of thousands of emigrants followed the

Women on the Trail

Between 1840 and 1870, about 250,000 people crossed the USA to claim 'free land' in the Oregon and California territories and to try their luck at mining. It was generally the men who made the initial decision to embark on the overland journey, and once a woman's husband, father or brother decided to go, there was little recourse for her to stay at home.

While historians and feminists idealize the sense of liberation on the trail, the majority of first-hand accounts tell of resentment of being thrust into an unfamiliar world. Women often clung to their traditional roles, making them bastions of civility in the wild. As Nannie Alderson writes in her memoirs, *A Bride Goes West*, 'I believe we stuck all the more firmly to our principles of etiquette, because we were so far from civilization. We could still stand on ceremony though our floors were dirt.'

The journey often entailed six to eight months of travel in a rickety wagon on a bumpy trail. Typically, women washed the clothes, prepared meals and attended the children, while men drove the team, garnered the meat for meals and tended the herd. Yet in order to survive along the trail, women often found themselves performing tasks traditionally reserved for the men.

Undoubtedly the heaviest burden women bore on the trail was child-rearing. Pregnant women were often without assistance, and many women died during childbirth. Lillian Schlissel reports in *Women's Diaries of the Westward Journey*, 'One out of every five women was seized by some stage of pregnancy, and virtually every married woman traveled with small children.' Children were especially prone to illness and disease, and often were injured in accidents such as falling out of the wagon or getting lost in a herd.

Male pioneers mostly wrote of the ferocity and danger of Native Americans, while women often found them friendly and even helpful. Women's diaries question the value of sacrifices made along the way and describe the personal struggles.

Some women found the trail a welcome break from the boredom of everyday life. Susan Perrish wrote that 'we were a happy carefree lot of young people, and the dangers of hardships found no resting place on our shoulders. It was a continuous picnic and excitement was plentiful.' For others it was a horrible trip. Elizabeth Smith Greer wrote of her 1847 journey from Indiana to Oregon:

> It rains and snows. We start this morning around the falls with our wagons…I went ahead with my children and I was afraid to look behind for fear of seeing the wagons turn over into the mud…there was not one dry thread on one of us – not even my babe…I have not told you half we suffered. I am not adequate to the task.

Oregon Trail up the Missouri River to the North Platte and across the Continental Divide to South Pass, where they split up to various destinations, including Oregon, California and Utah. The latter was where the Mormons, persecuted in New York and the Midwest, found a place to practice their religion. In the late 1860s, completion of the Transcontinental Railroad across southern Wyoming slowed, but did not halt, the inexorable march of wagon trains.

At the same time, explorers continued to seek other routes across the mountains. The ambitious John C Frémont, who became known as the Great Pathfinder, spent much of the 1840s wandering the West for the Corps of Topographical Engineers, thanks in part to the political influence of his father-in-law, Senator Thomas Hart Benton of Missouri. While Frémont's effort at mapping the best route to Oregon and his shadowy attempt at undermining Mexican rule in California were successful, two expeditions to find a route across the southern Rockies failed miserably, costing the lives of many of his men. Nevertheless, Frémont was a political success, becoming a senator from California and the Republican nominee for president in 1856.

Dismantling Mexico

The exploration of the American West had major political consequences, most notably with Mexico, which had gained independence from Spain in 1821. That same year, the USA acknowledged Mexico's hegemony over most of the West, as far north as the present-day northern state lines of California, Nevada and Utah, including southwestern Wyoming, perhaps three-quarters of Colorado, Arizona, New Mexico, Texas and even small parts of Kansas and Oklahoma.

Mexico's independence led to an active settlement strategy in which the Mexican government offered land grants in the southern area to civilians and retired military personnel. In 1822, trade caravans began to travel along the Santa Fe Trail, which stretched between St Louis and Santa Fe (then part of Mexico). William Bent's fort on the Arkansas River provided an important outpost for this commerce from 1833 to 1849. The 1843 land grant to fur traders Cornelio Vigil and Ceran St Vrain, between the Purgatoire and Arkansas Rivers, attracted the likes of Jim Beckwourth, Kit Carson, Thomas Boggs and William Bent. In 1851, Mexican settlers founded San Luis – Colorado's oldest community – on the Sangre de Cristo Grant.

The fledgling Mexican state, however, was weak and unable to hold Texas as Anglo settlers moved into the territory; as early as 1836 Texas had declared independence. The continued movement of American settlers into Mexican territory, and the later warfare over border placement at the Rio Grande, led to huge territorial gains in the Mexican cession of 1848. This land grab expanded US boundaries almost to their present size and incorporated Native American and Spanish-speaking peoples into the Union. Especially in southern Colorado, these communities have proven resilient and culturally distinct.

Mexico was not the only power to lose territory to the expanding USA. After some complex diplomatic maneuvering and threats of war, in 1846 the British and US governments agreed to divide the Oregon Country, an area of land from the Pacific Ocean to the Rocky Mountains that had been under joint occupancy, along the 49th parallel. Sections of Montana and Wyoming were included in the part that became US territory.

The Fate of the Native Americans

In contrast with Hollywood's depiction of wagon trains being regularly ambushed by Native Americans, most crossings of the Oregon Trail were relatively uneventful; the heavily laden emigrants frequently had to abandon many of their prized possessions on the side of the trail, a far more common trauma than Indian attacks. The region's first inhabitants certainly viewed the passing travelers with skepticism, and sometimes reactions were more violent. Seeing increasing numbers of white emigrants treading upon their homeland, the Shoshone and Bannock mounted bolder and bloodier attacks during the 1850s. In response, the US Army built a number of military forts along the Oregon Trail, including a new Fort Hall and Fort Boise. In one engagement in 1863, US Army cavalry units ambushed and slaughtered some 400 Shoshone near Preston. Shortly thereafter, the Shoshone and Bannock were confined to Fort Hall Indian Reservation.

The US government also signed an endless series of treaties to defuse Native American objections, promising that white settlers would not venture beyond certain homeland boundaries, such as Wyoming's North Platte River. These treaties established huge reservations, such as the Shoshone's on Wyoming's Wind River, and a system of government rations to compensate Native Americans for their loss of hunting territory. Under pressure from miners and other emigrants, the federal government continually reduced the reservations' size and even shifted them to less desirable areas.

The Real Wild West

The romantic notion of the Wild West, one of the most misleading images in US history, suggests a principled universe of law and order opposing chaos and anarchy, good guys confronting bad guys, cowboys versus Indians and progress against reaction. These oversimplifications conceal a more complex and interesting reality.

The Wild West is traditionally linked to individuals who stood their ground against challenges to their honor, even against overwhelming odds, such as the hero of Owen Wister's landmark novel *The Virginian*. Wister's protagonist, who tamed the frontier against the anarchy represented by his unsavory adversary, Trampas, was the fictional counterpart to real-life figures like Wyatt Earp, Doc Holliday and Wild Bill Hickok, who faced their enemies in the street.

While these battles often – but not always – took place between individuals or small groups of men, they represented something much greater and more notable: a struggle over control of Western resources between incompatible sectors of society. The hired guns of merchants, mining czars and cattle barons conflicted with the outcast champions of little guys like homesteaders, mineworkers and mavericks – the latter also were called 'rustlers' by those who claimed the unmarked calves they branded. Walter van Tilburg Clark's famous novel *The Ox-Bow Incident* tells the story of powerful men who mistakenly hang an accused but innocent rustler.

Figures like the legendary Butch Cassidy, whose Wild Bunch audaciously robbed the Union Pacific Railroad that dominated Wyoming political and economic life, proved difficult or impossible to apprehend because many ordinary citizens admired or sympathized with their exploits and protected them from authority. It may or may not be true that Cassidy once rode 120 miles in bitter winter to obtain medicine for a sick child, or that he tipped bartenders with $20 gold pieces, but persistent accounts of such generosity imply the high regard with which local people held an individual widely admitted to be a rustler.

The Hollywood legacy of cowboys and Indians, imitated for decades in children's games, shows how one-sided American interpretation of history can be. It's only recently been acknowledged by non-Native historians that cowboys were invaders on Native American lands as cattle herds replaced bison on plains and prairies. The same is true of the US Army: Romantically viewed as heroic defenders of pioneer emigrants and settlers, the ill-trained or vengeful enlistees often were responsible for butchery like the notorious 1861 Sand Creek Massacre, in which the 3rd Colorado Volunteers attacked, slaughtered and mutilated at least 150 sleeping Cheyenne men, women and children.

Of course, Native Americans also committed atrocities, often in response to military or settler provocations. Even though they were viewed as a unified force against the invaders, they were, in fact, a variety of peoples often no more similar than Spaniards and Swedes, and often were bitter rivals. The Pawnee, for instance, often served as US Army scouts against the Lakota, their traditional enemies. Nor were these the only ethnic conflicts: Others took place between whites and Hispanics, Mormons and non-Mormons and between the Chinese and European miners, the former used as strikebreakers by manipulative mining companies. All these disputes embodied ethnic components not usually acknowledged in traditional histories of the West.

Revisionist historians have effectively presented such analyses in recent years, and even popular culture has begun to take a more discriminating view of the Wild West.

On the northern plains, gold miners' incursions into Native American territory en route to gold fields in Montana and the Black Hills, exacerbated by the US Army building a string of forts along the Bozeman Trail, ignited a series of wars against the Lakota (Sioux), Cheyenne, Arapaho and others. As the centennial year of 1876 approached, the Lakota and their allies stunned the country by obliterating Lieutenant Colonel George Armstrong Custer's 7th Cavalry at the Little Bighorn valley (in Montana), but the army's greater resources eventually prevailed – their virtually unlimited supplies arrived by rail, while the Lakota had to hunt the declining bison to get their families through the winter.

Catastrophic for the Indians, the near extinction of the bison was a function of several interrelated factors. The most direct was uncontrolled hunting, as the government implemented a deliberate policy of eliminating the most important subsistence resource on the continent. Professional riflemen took more than four million hides on the southern plains in the early 1870s; incompetent skinners wasted many of these, and nearly all the meat rotted. Facilitated by the arrival of the railroad, the same history recurred on the northern plains in the 1880s, but bison numbers had fallen even before this slaughter because of drought, habitat destruction, competition from introduced livestock such as horses and cattle, and new diseases like tuberculosis and brucellosis. All of these elements contributed to the marginalization of the peoples who depended on them for their livelihood.

In Colorado, Ute territorial sovereignty survived a bit longer due to the tribe's isolated mountain domain. But with the influx of silver miners west of the Divide in the 1870s, Chief Ouray had little option but to sign a series of treaties relinquishing traditional hunting grounds. In 1879, the White River Band of Utes attacked federal troops and White River Indian Agent Nathan Meeker and his family near the present-day town of Meeker. All Utes suffered from the vicious American reaction. By 1881, Utes not removed to forsaken lands in Utah were left with a narrow 15-mile-wide strip of plateau land in southwestern Colorado.

Water & Western Development

While Oregon filled with settlers and the California Gold Rush faded, Americans began to think of occupying the area between the coasts, rather than viewing it simply as a transit corridor. Mining attracted only transitory residents, while extensive land uses like ranching could support only a small population. The lingering image of the Great American Desert, a myth propagated by explorers like Pike and Long who used the humid east coast as a standard of comparison, deterred agricultural settlers and discouraged urban development.

Water was a limiting factor as Denver, Cheyenne and other cities began to spring up at the base of the Front Range and utopians like Horace Greeley, who saw the Homestead Act of 1862 as the key to agrarian prosperity, planned agricultural experiments on the nearby plains. This act envisioned the creation of 160-acre family farms to create a rural democracy on the Western frontier. These plots of land were subdivided based on the General Land Survey, which created a checkerboard pattern of square-mile sections of land still visible from the air today.

Government agents encouraged settlement and development in their assessments of the region, but differed on how to bring it about. Two of the major figures in this process were Frederick V Hayden of the United States Geological Survey (USGS) and John Wesley Powell, first of the Smithsonian Institute and later of the USGS. Hayden, who surveyed the Yellowstone River area and played a major role in having it declared a national park, was so eager to promote economic development in the West that he exaggerated the region's agricultural potential on the optimistic but mistaken assumption that 'rain follows the plow' – that is, that planting and cultivating could change the climate. Unlike Pike and Long, who saw no potential in the plains, Hayden saw too much.

Powell, a great figure in Western and American history, made a more perceptive assessment of the potential and limitations of the region. Famous as the first man to descend the Colorado River through the Grand Canyon, Powell knew that the region's salient feature was aridity, that its limited water supply depended on the snowpack that fell in the Rockies and could vary dramatically from year to year, and that the 160-acre ideal of the Homestead Act of 1862, devised in the humid East and liable to corruption and manipulation, was inappropriate to the terrain and environment of the West. His masterful *Report on the Lands of the Arid Regions of the United States* challenged the tendency toward unbridled exploitation of the region's minerals, pastures and forests, and proposed classifying and distributing the land according to its suitability for irrigation.

Powell's report recommended the construction of dams, canals and ditches to create an integrated, federally sponsored irrigation system administered by democratically elected cooperatives. Unfortunately, his vision collided with the interests of influential cattle barons who wanted to maintain their access to lands and water. Nor did it appeal to boosters and real estate speculators who seemed convinced that the West could absorb an unlimited number of farmers from an overpopulated East. These interests united to undermine Powell's blueprint; what survived was the idea that water development was essential to the West.

It took time to create the technology, but 20th-century development took the form of megaprojects like the mammoth Glen Canyon Dam on the Colorado River, and water transfers from Colorado's Western Slope to the Front Range and the plains via a tunnel under the Continental Divide. These, in turn, provided subsidized water for large-scale irrigators and electrical power for users far from their source – effectively inverting Powell's goals and creating a landscape of dams, reservoirs, canals, tunnels and hydroelectric facilities that would characterize the region as much as, if not more than, its dwindling wildlands.

Statehood

Colorado American expansion in the West spread to Colorado with the discovery of gold in the mountains west of Denver in 1859. In 1861, the boundaries of Colorado Territory were defined, and President Lincoln appointed William Gilpin the first governor.

In 1870 two sets of railroad tracks reached Denver, ending Colorado's isolation: The Denver Pacific Railroad connected Denver with the Union Pacific's transcontinental line at Cheyenne, WY, and the Kansas Pacific arrived from Kansas City, MO. That same year, General William Palmer began planning the Denver & Rio Grande's narrow-gauge tracks into the mountain mining camps. The mining emphasis shifted from gold to silver during the 1870s as mountain smelter sites, like Leadville and Aspen, developed into thriving population centers almost overnight.

National political expedience led to Colorado statehood in 1876, the centennial of United States independence.

Wyoming Construction of the Transcontinental Railroad in the 1860s really opened up the Wyoming territory, which had its boundaries officially designated in 1868. The impetus behind this came from the Union Pacific Railroad (UP), whose westward progress demanded a closer and more responsive government. Cheyenne became the territorial capital, and the powerfully paternalistic and politically influential UP acquired the nickname 'Uncle Pete.'

Wyoming's first legislators enacted an extraordinary statute in 1869 granting all women 21 years of age and older the right to vote and hold office. Unprecedented in its time, Wyoming's action drew praise from Susan B Anthony, the great women's suffrage crusader, and when Wyoming obtained statehood in 1890, it became known as the 'Equality State.' In fact, Wyoming may not have deserved quite the credit it got. While some legislators saw it as an issue of principle, others voted for it because Wyoming had so few women. They thought the resulting publicity would attract more emigrants: In the 1870 census, men older than 21 outnumbered women six to one.

Montana Gold was discovered in Bannack's Grasshopper Creek in 1863, just as rushes in California, Nevada, Colorado and Idaho were petering out. The intense population increase and large sums of money flowing out of Bannack (which was part of Idaho Territory) caused Sidney Edgerton, Chief Justice of Idaho Territory, to petition Congress for a new territory east of the Rocky Mountains. On May 26, 1884, Montana became a territory and Edgerton its first territorial governor.

Gold strikes continued – notably in Last Chance Gulch (Helena) and Alder Gulch (Virginia City). Just as electricity was becoming available to the public and creating an enormous demand for copper wire, Marcus Daly struck the world's largest and purest vein of copper in Butte, which would continue to be mined for the next 100 years. Montana was obviously here to stay, and in 1889 it became the 41st state of the Union.

Idaho Real settlement of Idaho did not come until gold was discovered at Pierce on Orofino Creek in 1860; the following year, gold was discovered in the Boise basin. Miners rushed to the Idaho mountains, establishing gold camps and trade centers like Lewiston and Boise. By 1863 Idaho was declared a US territory.

Rich silver and lead veins spurred the growth of communities such as Wallace, Mullan and Kellogg, which boomed as smelters lined the banks of the river and railroads competed to transport the region's mineral wealth. By 1890 Idaho was granted statehood, and 10 years later the homesteading boom brought more permanent settlers to central Idaho valleys.

The Contemporary Rockies

In all four states, the extractive industries of mining, grazing and timber played a major role in economic development. These highly capitalized industries, with low labor requirements, encouraged the growth of cities and towns to provide financial and industrial support. They also subjected the region to boom and bust cycles as they exhausted those resources in an unsustainable manner, and left a legacy of environmental disruption not likely to disappear any time soon.

From its earliest days the West was, and still is, the country's most urbanized region; when Colorado became a state in 1876,

more than a third of its residents lived in Denver. Even though Wyoming, Montana and Idaho are much less urbanized than fast-growing Colorado, most residents of those states live in cities or small towns amid a very thinly populated countryside.

In part this urbanization was a function of the tourist economy, as Americans, who had flocked to the national parks during the economic boom after WWII, began to appreciate the Rockies as a place to live rather than just to visit. The federal government played a role by providing employment, thanks in large part to investment in Cold War military installations like NORAD, a Dr Strangelove–like facility near Colorado Springs, and Warren Air Force Base, the command center for a series of dispersed missile silos near Cheyenne, WY. Urbanization accelerated as the wealthy beneficiaries of the economic policies of the Reagan era built opulent vacation homes in Aspen, Sun Valley and similarly prestigious resort areas. Others relocated to once remote towns like Telluride, CO, as the communications and information revolution decentralized some sectors of the economy.

Development and urbanization had beneficial effects as well, as increasingly well-educated locals and emigrants shared the environmental concerns of the late 1960s and early 1970s. Practices such as strip mining, overgrazing and clear-cutting came under scrutiny from local chapters of influential environmental organizations such as the Sierra Club, Friends of the Earth and the Wilderness Society, as well as from regional groups including the Greater Yellowstone Coalition and the Wyoming Outdoor Council. Military facilities, such as the Rocky Mountain National Arsenal near Colorado Springs and the Rocky Flats nuclear weapons facility near Denver, came under attack by activists concerned with environmental contamination, and were declared priority cleanup sites under the federal Environmental Protection Agency's Superfund program.

Tourism is now an economic mainstay in the Rockies. While the region's natural attractions have drawn curious visitors since the establishment of Yellowstone National Park in 1872, for most of that time only wealthy travelers with time and money could see the backcountry. But after WWII, general prosperity and the improvement of roads brought larger numbers of middle-class tourists into the national parks.

Colorado, which had also been luring tourists since the late 19th century, wasted little time in tapping this new source of revenue. Promoters offered auto routes over the Royal Gorge, up Pikes Peak and Mt Evans and across the alpine tundra of Rocky Mountain National Park. Skiing started to draw adherents in 1927 when the opening of the Moffat Tunnel brought Winter Park within easy reach of Denverites traveling on the D&RG Railroad. More distant ski resorts had to wait for air service or the opening of the Eisenhower Tunnel on I-70 to bring the crowds to them. To keep the rooms filled during the off-season, in the late 1940s Aspen initiated its widely mimicked cultural festivals.

In 1936, a group of investors associated with the Union Pacific developed a European ski resort near the old smelter town of Ketchum, ID. Called Sun Valley, the resort was soon another early recreational foothold in the region and it became the playground of Hollywood stars and the wealthy elite.

However, Idaho, along with Montana and Wyoming, didn't feel the full effects of tourism until the 1980s. Now that it's begun there seems little chance of turning back. Small towns once known as lumber or agricultural centers are now filled with mountain bike and raft shops, and a new generation of ranchers scramble to entice outsiders to fish or float on their property – a far cry from the isolationist ethic of yesteryear.

GEOGRAPHY

While complex, the physical geography of the Rocky Mountain region divides conveniently into two principal features: the Rocky Mountains proper and the Great Plains. Extending from Alaska's Brooks Range and Canada's Yukon Territory all the way to the Mexican border, the Rockies trend northwest to southeast, sprawling from the steep escarpment of Colorado's Front Range westward to Nevada's Great Basin. Their towering peaks and ridges form the Continental Divide: To the west, waters flow to the Pacific Ocean; to the east, toward the Atlantic Ocean and the Gulf of Mexico.

At the eastern base of the Rockies, the plains extend more than 2500 miles from the delta of Canada's Mackenzie River, draining into the Arctic Ocean, to the coast of southern Texas on the Gulf of Mexico. Toward the east, the plains stretch for hundreds of miles toward the Mississippi River Valley and the Great Lakes.

Colorado A total area of 103,730 sq miles makes Colorado the eighth largest state in the USA. Its lowest point is 3400 feet above sea level where the Arkansas River flows into Kansas; at 14,433 feet above sea level, Mt Elbert near Leadville is the other extreme. Overall, Colorado has more than 1000 peaks of elevations higher than 2 miles, and 54 of the nation's 69 summits higher than 14,000 feet.

Colorado is divided into three general landform provinces: the Eastern Plains, the Rocky Mountains and on the west, the Colorado Plateau. Each of these north-south strips is interrupted by local landform variations. In southwestern Colorado, the San Juan Mountains are thrust up from plateau lands and are out of key with the mountain and plateau provinces typified by high, flat mesas.

Wyoming A total area of 97,105 sq miles makes Wyoming the ninth largest state, and it ranges in elevation from the Belle Fourche River (3100 feet) in the Black Hills to Gannett Peak (13,804 feet) in the Wind River Range.

The Eastern Plains region includes the Powder River and North Platte River basins, the Black Hills, and the Laramie and Medicine Bow Mountains, near the Wyoming-Colorado state line. Western Wyoming has high desert basins west of the Continental Divide, including the huge

Dinosaurs & Their Habitat

The sparse grasslands and fierce winters of Wyoming and western Colorado seem an improbable setting for a diverse subtropical region. But 150 million years ago, this area was covered with shallow lakes and marshes where the great dinosaurs roamed, feeding on aquatic plants, ferns, rushes, cattails – and sometimes on each other. As the climate changed, or, according to other accounts, after a catastrophic meteor struck the planet, these beasts disappeared, but the sediments in which they died preserved their skeletons and over time fossilized them. The resulting sandstones and shale were eventually exposed at the earth's surface by erosion.

Since the 1878 discovery of Como Bluff, near Rawlins, the region has been one of the most important areas for dinosaur research in the world. Further discoveries, like the one at Green River in what is now Dinosaur National Monument, have been numerous. Over time, dinosaurs have worked their way into the popular consciousness, so much so that the Wyoming legislature asked school children to choose an official state dinosaur (as opposed to merely a state fossil) from among *Triceratops, Apatosaurus* (brontosaurus), *Diplodocus* and *Megalosaurus*. They chose *Triceratops*.

The fossil record of dinosaurs is biased toward size, so that the remains of relatively small animals like the ostrichlike *Coelurosaurs,* which walked upright and left birdlike tracks, deteriorated more rapidly and may be underrepresented. This was less the case with carnosaurs, the large, upright meat eaters like *Tyrannosaurus rex;* prosauropods, forerunners of the four-footed vegetarian behemoths like *Apatosaurus* and *Brachiosaurus;* stegosaurs (plated dinosaurs); ankylosaurs (armored dinosaurs); three-toed duckbills and hadrosaurs; and ceratopseans (horned dinosaurs).

Dinosaur enthusiasts visiting the Rocky Mountain states have a host of sites and museums at which to indulge their interests, including Dinosaur National Monument in northwestern Colorado; the Dinosaur Valley Museum in Fruita and several other quarry sites in and around Grand Junction; Picket Wire Canyon near La Junta (in Colorado's Eastern Plains); Como Bluff near Rawlins, WY; Western Wyoming College in Rock Springs; and the University of Wyoming Geological Museum in Laramie. Visitors intending to explore the dinosaur country of western Colorado might obtain Walter R Averett's *Guidebook for Dinosaur Quarries and Tracksites Tour: Western Colorado and Eastern Utah* (Grand Junction Geological Society, 1991).

One good general source for further reading is Ron Stewart's *Dinosaurs of the West* (Missoula, Montana: Mountain Press, 1988). For some of the more controversial ideas on dinosaurs, including the notion that dinosaurs were social animals, see Robert T Bakker's *The Dinosaur Heresies: New Theories Unlocking the Mystery of the Dinosaurs and Their Extinction* (Morrow, 1986).

Finally, be wary of people selling jewelry made of dinosaur fossils; recently people have been blasting the sites where there are fossils in order to collect the pieces. In no way should this be encouraged.

Class of 65 million BC

Green River Basin and the smaller Great Divide and Washakie Basins. Along the Utah and Idaho state lines, the Overthrust Belt is a zone of jumbled sedimentary features. The granitic Teton Range and Jackson Hole line the Wyoming-Idaho state line, with the Yellowstone Plateau in the northwest, the Wind River Range and its expansive basin to the south, and the Bighorn Basin and Mountains trending south from the Wyoming-Montana state line.

Montana With a total area of 145,556 sq miles, Montana is the fourth largest state in the USA. The lowest point in Montana, 1820 feet, is on US 2 at the Montana-Idaho border, the highest is Granite Peak in the Beartooth Range at 12,799 feet.

Montana's three geographic zones are: the plains, which stretch across the eastern two-thirds of the state; the Middle Rocky Mountains, which include part of the Yellowstone Plateau and the Absaroka and Beartooth ranges; and the Northern Rocky Mountains, which make a 200-mile-wide band of northwest-southeast trending ranges from Glacier National Park to Yellowstone National Park.

Montana's main river is the Missouri, which drains from the eastern side of the Continental Divide and eventually flows to the Gulf of Mexico and the Atlantic. Rivers on the western side of the Divide flow into the Pacific via the Clark Fork and Kootenai Rivers.

Idaho Its total area of 82,751 sq miles places Idaho 11th on the state size roster. Its highest point is the 12,662-foot Borah Peak; at the other end of the spectrum is Lewiston at 783 feet.

There are essentially two different geographic areas to Idaho. The Rocky Mountains dominate the Panhandle area – the narrow arm squeezed between Washington and Montana – and the deep mountain canyons of central Idaho. As the mountains rise higher approaching the central spine of the Continental Divide, just across the border in Montana more rainfall is wrung out of the prevailing easterly airflows, supporting both deep forests and mighty rivers. Much of central Idaho is comprised of the highly contorted Salmon and Clearwater River drainages. These rivers both drain directly into the Snake River in its famed Hells Canyon, the deepest gorge in North America.

Nearly all of the broad southern base of Idaho is part of the arid Snake River basin. Although the Snake River rises in Yellowstone National Park, the majority of the river's traverse of Idaho is across a relentless lava plateau. Most of the land paralleling the river through the bottom third of the state is flat and dusty, while to the south rise mirage-like fault block mountains thinly clad with vegetation.

GEOLOGY

In the late Cretaceous Period about 65 million years ago, tectonic movements known as the Laramide Revolution disturbed the broad sediments of western North America. This uplift, accompanied by volcanic activity and subsequent folding and faulting, created the mountainous landscape of much of modern Colorado, Wyoming, Montana and Idaho. The granitic peaks of the Front Range rise nearly 10,000 feet above the adjacent plains; the highest point is Colorado's 14,433-foot Mt Elbert. The sedimentary peaks farther north are slightly lower, but their clearly defined strata add color and variety to the landscape.

Behind the Front Range lie several scattered mountain ranges and broad plateaus; their most notable geological feature is the spectacular Rocky Mountain Trench, a fault valley 1100 miles long that crosses northern Montana into Canada. The Colorado Plateau, in the southwestern part of the state near the borders with Utah, New Mexico and Arizona, has been heavily eroded by the Colorado River and its tributaries. Active volcanism also distinguishes the region, notably in Wyoming's Yellowstone National Park where earthquakes are quite common. Ancient lava flows cover many other areas, punctuated by extinct volcanoes like the Spanish Peaks of southwestern Colorado.

Successive glaciations also altered the face of the land. The Laurentide Ice Sheet, which covered most of eastern North America, scoured much of the Great Plains as far south as Nebraska and westward to the foothills of the Rockies, leaving deep sediments as it receded into the Arctic during the warming of the Quaternary Era. A separate cordilleran system of glaciers formed at higher altitudes in the Rockies, covering the uplands but leaving many moraines, lakes, cirques and jagged alpine landforms as they melted. Remnants of these glaciers survive only at the highest elevations; at the same time, the rivers formed by their melting deposited extensive sediments on the piedmont, at the base of the Front Range.

CLIMATE

The climate of the Rocky Mountain states depends on two major factors: elevation and topography. Nearly all of Colorado, Wyoming and Montana consists of relatively high terrain more than a mile above sea level. Idaho, which has more varied terrain, is somewhat different. Distant from the warming influence of the oceans and at latitudes mostly above 40°N, such elevations may enjoy warm summer days but almost always experience cool nights (and sometimes frosts). Winters can be truly severe in the semidesert areas east of the Rockies, which are vulnerable to dry polar continental air masses that bring sub-zero temperatures and occasional blizzards. Chinooks are powerful seasonal winds that lose their moisture on crossing the mountains and heat up as they descend, and they bring occasional relief from even the coldest weather. The cordillera of the Rockies blocks or slows the penetration of relatively warm, damp air masses from the northern Pacific Ocean; by the time Pacific storms reach the Rockies, they have already passed over several mountain ranges and have lost much of their moisture, and the snow that falls on the western slopes and other favored locations is often the dry champagne powder so favored by skiers. Because of the Rockies' fragmented terrain, there

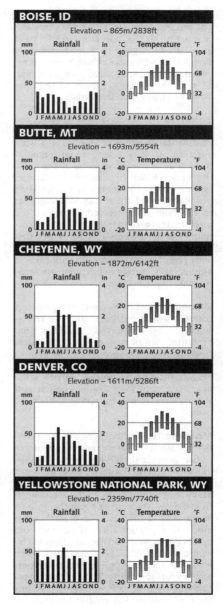

can be great local variation in temperature and precipitation, depending on factors like orientation to the sun and wind. In most areas the brief growing season lasts only from June to September, although a few micro-climates experience a slightly longer period. Most of the region is subject to brief but violent summer thunderstorms.

Colorado The state's climate is influenced by two major factors. First, its mid-continental location accounts for a wide variation in daily and seasonal tempera-tures and the overall semiarid character of the state. Most of Colorado averages between 10 and 18 inches of precipitation per year. Second, the Rocky Mountains act as a barrier that intercepts much of the moisture that arrives from the west – particularly on the higher western slopes that receive an average of 220 inches of snowfall each year. Temperatures drop with gains in altitude, and weather in the mountain areas is highly unpredictable.

Wyoming Most of Wyoming is high desert country where extremes are the rule – summer temperatures can exceed 100°F but nighttime temperatures can fall below freezing, and July snowstorms in Yellow-stone National Park are not unusual. One characteristic of Wyoming's climate is the nearly incessant wind. Chinooks often melt the snow and relieve the winter chill on the plains.

Montana The weather here can bring any-thing at any time, but summer temperatures usually hover in the 80s west of the Rockies, in the 100s on the Eastern Plains. In winter (which can begin in October and last until May) temperatures stay in the 20s, though tremendous winds often bring them down below zero in the east. The plains receive much less precipitation than does the mountainous west, and they are targeted by winds coming unchecked from the north across the Canadian plains. January temper-atures average 11°F to 22°F, July tempera-tures are 64°F to 93°F with thunderstorms most afternoons. The coldest temperature

ever recorded in the USA was in 1954 at Rogers Pass, near Helena, when it dropped to -70°F.

Idaho In southern Idaho's Snake River Plain, winters tend to be milder than in the north. Winter low temperatures hover in the teens, but even in winter most days are sunny. Summer weather can be oppressively hot, especially when combined with the hu-midity from the irrigation projects. Temper-atures can exceed 100°F for days at a time in July and August when evening tempera-tures rarely drop below 80°F. Early summer is a bit cooler. Rainfall is scant in southern Idaho. In the valley bottom, rainfall can be as low as 8 inches annually; Boise, set against the foothills, receives 12 inches.

Rain and snowfall is greatest in the deep forests of the Panhandle, where upwards of

Chinook Winds

Chinook is a regional term for the warm, dry *föhn* wind that can occur on the leeward side of a mountain anywhere in the world. As air masses descend the Front Range of the Rockies, warming and compressing with the decreased elevation, the result is a hot, dry wind that can cause temperatures to rise as much as 50°F in less than an hour. In 1980 a chinook caused the temperature in Nevada City, MT, to rise 47°F in seven minutes.

To ranchers, farmers and cowboys of the Eastern Plains, chinook winds have a special significance. When a chinook blows down from the Rockies in the dead of winter, it brings temperatures that liberate the land, cattle and people from a substantial blanket of snow and ice. Cattle can graze and ranch-ers can increase the animals' feed rations for the rest of the winter. In an area that needs all the climatic help it can get, chinook winds are a boon, a blessing and a mysterious friend. However, for tourists an unexpected chinook can mean the start of the mud season.

60 inches of precipitation is possible. The weather during summer is usually clear and balmy, with highs above 90°F. In winter, storms surge down out of Canada, blanketing the area with snow and low temperatures. Temperatures below 0°F are not unusual.

The mountains and canyons of central Idaho experience much of the same cold, winter weather as the north, but summer temperatures are notably warmer. In the steep canyons of the Snake and Salmon Rivers, summer days can be airless and oppressively hot. Lewiston in August can see daily highs near 100°F, but by evening, temperatures tend to drop.

ECOLOGY & ENVIRONMENT

Though each state can point to its own particular issues and conflicts, all four face the same basic quandary: how to balance the need to live off the land with the need to preserve for current and future generations.

The spectacular environmental bounty of the Rocky Mountain states is coveted by numerous competing interests. Timber and mining companies have drawn enormous wealth from the land, while farmers must partly thank dams on the mighty rivers for increasingly greater harvests. Ranchers are proponents of 'open space,' but only when it's grazed by their cattle. Facing this coalition of 'mixed-use' supporters are those who call for no more exploitation of natural resources: Leave the land to animals and low-impact humans, such as hikers.

Obviously a balance needs to be struck: Humans may like the idea of untouched wilderness, but they also enjoy having food, fossil fuels and conveniences, like cars. None would be possible without farms, oil wells or mines. In the Rockies, a series of debates, verbal altercations and compromises may be defining ways that Americans can utilize the land without losing it.

Already there has been a marked drop in traditional methods of exploiting natural resources. Removing ill-conceived dams, slowing clear-cutting and road building, and limiting open-pit mining are some of the efforts now underway.

Other debates focus on the role of the US Forest Service. Is it here to protect, or to develop, the land it regulates? In Colorado and Montana, the forest service has tried repeatedly to sell off parcels of land to timber or energy firms, and in many cases has been caught between powerful business interests and extremely vocal and angry environmental groups. The agency has yet to define its mission.

Wildlife issues are also highly controversial. Reintroduction of grizzly bears in Montana's Selway-Bitterroot Wilderness and of gray wolves in Yellowstone National Park has kindled debate between animal rights activists and ranchers. Local recreationists, who have neither political nor economic stake in the debates, are generally divided between those who want to see the animals in their original habitats and those who fear the potential harm to humans.

There are many organizations committed to protecting and enhancing the Rockies, including Alliance for the Wild Rockies (☎ 406-721-5420), 415 N Higgins Ave, Missoula, MT 59802, which has a far-reaching and very active political agenda focused on saving the Northern Rockies bioregion from habitat destruction. Web site: www.wildrockiesalliance.org

FLORA & FAUNA

The natural environments of the Rocky Mountain states consist of high mountains, plateaus and plains, each with its own distinctive biota. Many of these lands enjoy varying levels of protection from local, state and federal agencies. See the Activities chapter for information on national parklands, forests and wilderness areas.

Flora

The vegetation of the Rocky Mountain region is closely linked to climate, which in turn depends on rainfall and elevation. Vegetation at certain altitudes varies depending on exposure and availability of water.

Sparse piñon-juniper forests cover the Rockies' lower slopes from about 4000 to 6000 feet above sea level, while ponderosa pines indicate the montane zone between 6000 and 9000 feet, where alders, aspens, willows and the distinctive blue spruce flourish in damper areas. In the sub-alpine zone above 9000 feet, Engelmann spruce largely replace pine (though some stands of lodgepoles grow higher) while colorful wildflowers like columbine, marsh marigold and primrose colonize open spaces. In the alpine zone above 11,500 feet, alpine meadows and tundra supplant stunted trees, commonly known by the German term *krummholz*, which can grow only in sheltered, southern exposures.

East of the Rockies, the Great Plains are an immense grassland of short and tall grasses, interrupted by dense gallery forests of willows and cottonwoods along the major rivers. Those arid zones closest to the Rockies consist of shorter species like wheatgrass, grama and buffalo grass, which grow no higher than about 3 feet.

Fauna

Like the flora, the fauna of the Rockies divides into characteristic assemblages correlated with elevation, but the relative abundance of the more mobile animals varies seasonally. In the alpine zones, for instance, small rodents like pikas inhabit rock-falls throughout the year, but larger mammals like Rocky Mountain elk *(Cervus elaphus)* and bighorn sheep are present only in summer. The Great Plains have their own singular fauna, like pronghorn antelope and prairie dogs that rarely enter the mountains, while species like mule deer and coyotes range over a variety of zones from the plains to the peaks. The solitary, lumbering moose, *Alces alces shirasi,* prefers riparian zones.

The most famous animal of the plains, of course, was the magnificent buffalo or bison that grazed the prairies in enormous herds until its near extinction. The bison survives in limited numbers, but some ambitious conservationists have proposed the elimination of domestic livestock and the restoration of a 'Buffalo Commons' where up to 60 million of this distinctive species may once again graze.

The swift pronghorn *Antilocarpa americana* grazes short-grass plains nearest the mountains, while the prairie dog neither inhabits the prairies, nor is it a dog: Related to the squirrel, it lives in sprawling burrows known as prairie dog 'towns.'

Probably the most notorious animal in the Rockies is the grizzly bear, *Ursus arctos horribilis,* whose notoriety may be inversely proportional to its numbers. The smaller, less aggressive black bear, *Ursus americanus,* is far more widespread.

Bighorn Sheep Colorado's Rocky Mountain National Park (see the Northern Front Range chapter) is a special place: 'Bighorn Crossing Zone' is not a sign you are likely to encounter anywhere else in the world. From late spring through summer, three or four volunteers and an equal number of rangers provide traffic control on US 34 at Sheep Lakes Information Station, 2 miles west of the Fall River Entrance Station. Groups of up to 60 sheep – typically only ewes and lambs – move from the moraine ridge north of the highway across the road to Sheep Lakes in Horseshoe Park. Unlike the big under-curving horns on mature rams, ewes grow swept-back crescent-shaped horns that reach only about 10 inches in length. The Sheep Lakes are evaporative ponds ringed with tasty salt deposits that attract the ewes in the morning and early afternoon after lambing in May and June. In August they rejoin the rams in the Mummy Range.

To see bighorn sheep on rocky ledges you will need to hike or backpack. The estimated 200 animals in the Horseshoe Park herd live permanently in the Mummy Range. On the west side, an equally large herd inhabits the volcanic cliffs of the Never Summer Mountains. A smaller herd can be seen along the Continental Divide at a distance from the rim of the Crater near Milner Pass. Three miles west of the Alpine Visitors Center on Trail Ridge Rd, Crater Trail follows a steep course for 1 mile to the observation point. Crater Trail is closed during spring lambing from May to mid-July.

Elk One highlight of visiting Rocky Mountain National Park is seeing North American elk, or wapiti, grazing in their natural setting. (The Native American term 'wapiti' means 'white,' a reference to the animal's white tail and rump.) According to NPS surveys about 2000 elk winter in the park's lower elevations, while more than 3000 inhabit the park's lofty terrain during summer months. The summer visitor equipped with binoculars or a telephoto lens is almost always rewarded by patiently scanning the hillsides and meadows near the Alpine Visitors Center. Traffic jams up as motorists stop to observe these magnificent creatures near the uppermost Fall River Rd or Trail Ridge Rd. Visitors are repeatedly warned by signs and park rangers not to harass, call to or come in contact with the animals.

Mature elk bulls may reach 1100lb, cows weigh up to 600lb – both have dark necks with light tan bodies. Like bighorn sheep, elk were virtually extinct around Estes Park by 1890 – wiped out by hunters. In 1913 and 1914, before the establishment of the park, people from Estes Park brought in 49 elk from Yellowstone. The elk's natural population increase since Congress' 1915 establishment of Rocky Mountain National Park is one of the NPS' great successes, directly attributable to the removal of the human predator.

During the elk rut in September and October, most large meadows are closed to off-trail travel 5 pm to 7 am.

Beaver The beaver is nature's hydraulic engineer, building dams and hollow island lodges. With four front teeth capable of felling a mature lodgepole pine or aspen, the beaver looks at deciduous woody plants as either food or construction material.

Beavers mate for life, one pair per colony, where offspring born each May or June may stay for two years. A mature beaver can reach 60lb – the largest rodent in North America – and is distinguished from the smaller muskrat by its flat hairless tail and bulbous body. Muskrat add to this identity confusion by sometimes living next to a beaver lodge.

Beaver ponds occur throughout the Rocky Mountain National Park's lower streams. To see the animal, remember that it rarely wanders from its aquatic habitat. Lodges can be found along Mill Creek in Hollowell Park, 2 miles south of the Park Museum.

Other Mammals You are likely to encounter mule deer in Rocky Mountain National Park – the only deer species in the park, so-named for their large mule-like ears – as they browse on leaves and twigs from shrubs at sunny lower elevations. Most moose sightings occur in the Kawuneeche Valley, but don't count on seeing moose

Dances with Llamas

One of nature's creatures you won't likely find roaming in the wild with the elk and bison is the enchanting llama. Millions of these domesticated beasts of burden inhabit South America, and approximately 100,000 llamas are found throughout the US and Canada (the Rockies being home to a substantial number of them, which undoubtedly bolster the local tourist trade). Llamas are one of the four members (along with the alpaca, guanaco and denizen) of the camel (*camelid*) family, believed to have originated in North America before migrating to Asia, Africa and South America. Remarkably brawny yet adorable, shaggy llamas are raised for their wool, in addition to making great pack animals, and even guards!

One place to soak up an authentic llama experience is the Buckhorn Llama Company (☎ 970-667-7411), 7220 N County Rd 27, Loveland, CO 80538. Visitors can arrange for guided tours of the Buckhorn Ranch facilities near Masonville, or just poke around to see how these curious animals look. More intrepid travelers can join an interpretive day hike (you do the walking; the llamas pack your gear) for a chance to interact in nature with the llamas.

Web site: www.llamapack.com

without some effort, as this large dark-colored animal can be surprisingly elusive.

Howling coyotes commonly serenade winter campfires – lucky visitors may spy a coyote stalking small rodents in the montane meadows. Other large carnivores like the bobcat and mountain lion are very rarely seen. Small but ferocious long-tailed weasel hunt near their streamside dens at night; in the winter the weasel's camouflage changes from brown to white, and the animal is called an ermine.

A considerable population of black bears and grizzly bears once inhabited the park area. Only about 30 black bears have survived predation by hunters and 'game management' techniques by federal officials, overanxious to protect visitors and other fledgling species. Two grizzlies were killed in 1951, and the last documented grizzly in Colorado was killed in 1979.

GOVERNMENT & POLITICS

The Rocky Mountain West is generally conservative in its politics, usually supporting the Republican party in presidential elections, but there are enclaves of liberal and even radical politics. Colorado is the most diverse and liberal state.

Political battles are often influenced by powerful business interests supporting natural resource development, such as large-scale agriculture, mining, energy and ranching. This impact is particularly powerful in the less populous states, where business and political ties run deep.

In recent years, political groups outside the mainstream have drawn more than their share of media attention. Northern Idaho has become notorious for its enclaves of neo-Nazis, white supremacists and the militia movement preparing for what it sees as an inevitable war against the federal government. In Montana the Freemen militia group invited a government siege that sparked a media quest to document every quirky, radical group in the state: There was plenty of material. Even Colorado, long considered fairly mainstream, has now become the base for numerous right-wing groups promoting some rather extreme agendas.

ECONOMY

The economies of Colorado, Wyoming and Montana have many features in common, mostly their dependence on natural resources such as minerals and energy, soils and pasture and extensive forests. Gold, of course, spurred early settlement in the 19th century, but silver and copper soon superseded it as corporations replaced the individualistic miner – the cheaply worked open-pit copper mines of Montana drove those of Michigan out of business by the 1880s.

The copper pits have mostly closed, but lesser minerals like lead, zinc and coal remain important. The region's petroleum and natural gas fields are also very productive. While oil shale resources drew considerable attention in the early 1970s, the energy crisis associated with the OPEC oil embargo and falling oil prices has since made their exploitation economically impractical.

The region's marked aridity limits agricultural possibilities, however with more than 100,000 sq miles in national forests and commercial timberland, the four states occupy an important timber industry.

The spectacular mountain scenery and, in some areas, its equally appealing cultural resources, have contributed to the region's flourishing tourist industry. Tourism, which is becoming one of the top earners in each state, may be one way the region can avoid the constant boom-and-bust cycles that afflict economies based heavily on natural resources.

Denver, the region's only sizable city, has been at the forefront of Colorado's development as a center of high-tech and service industries.

Wyoming's economy is less diverse, depending mainly on mining, tourism and agriculture, including ranching. As it becomes more apparent that massive harvesting and extraction of natural resources is unsustainable, Wyoming, like other Rocky Mountain states, is working to halt the erosion of its greatest natural resource – its breathtaking beauty – by promoting both tourism and recreation.

Tourism is now Montana's number one industry, followed by real estate. Ranchers are finding it increasingly profitable to divide their holdings and sell them, parcel by parcel, to developers. Mining is still important, though Canadian companies now control most of Montana's mining operations, the largest being Pegasus, Inc, which has the Zortman and Landusky gold mines in the Little Rocky Mountains. Surveys suggest a wealth of minerals remain below Montana's surface, but environmental concerns have stifled most mining proposals during the past decade.

Agribusiness is by far the largest segment of the Idaho economy, and the state produces one-third of the nation's potatoes and most of its peas, onions and processed vegetables. But high-technology employment has skyrocketed in recent years, and now accounts for twice the number of jobs as the once huge timber sector and almost as many jobs as agriculture.

POPULATION & PEOPLE

The area is thinly populated in contrast to much of the US, but its population is growing rapidly. Colorado, with the area's only truly metropolitan population (in and around Denver and the Front Range), is by far the largest of the four states in population. Idaho and Montana are also growing quickly, but Wyoming remains the second least populated state in the country.

Colorado has the broadest ethnic mix in the region, thanks to a large Latino population concentrated in Denver and the San Luis valley, an African-American population mostly in Denver, and substantial numbers of Native Americans. Colorado's population of 3,822,676 (as of 1996) is still largely white, though Latinos have long held significant influence in the state – particularly in the south – and make up 14% of the overall population. African-Americans represent 4.3% and Native Americans and Asian are both less than 1% of the total. More than half the state's population is concentrated in the Denver Metro area, and about another half million are spread up and down along the Front Range.

Wyoming's 1998 population was 495,930, of which 94% were white, 2.2% Native American and a mere 0.8% and 0.6% African-American and Asian, respectively. Growth into the 21st century is projected at less than 1% annually. Wyoming's largest city is Cheyenne; of the other cities, only Casper and Laramie have more than 20,000 inhabitants. Nearly 60% of the population lives in communities of fewer than 10,000 people. Indicative of a transitory population, more than 20% of the state's housing units are mobile homes or trailers.

The 1996 census showed 879,372 people living in Montana – about six persons per square mile. Montana's population today reflects the makeup of its early northern European settlers. Along with the dominant white population are Native Americans (6%), Latinos (1.5%), Asians (0.5%) and African-Americans (0.3%). Most people of color live in Billings. More than half of the population lives in urban centers, with Billings' population of 85,000 being the largest. Great Falls, Helena, Missoula and Kalispell are close behind (in that order) with Bozeman making fast strides.

Idaho's population was 1,189,251 in 1996; 94% white, 5% Latino, and 1% Native American. Idaho's average annual state growth rate is 3%, the third highest in the US. Boise with a 3.4% annual growth rate is the fastest growing US city. Most people live in the Snake River Plain, although 43% of the population lives on farms or in rural districts.

EDUCATION

Colorado, Wyoming, Montana and Idaho all have state universities, the most prestigious of which is the University of Colorado at Boulder. State universities are tax-supported and generally less expensive than private colleges, many of which are church-affiliated. Other major institutions of higher learning in Colorado are Colorado State University in Fort Collins, the University of Northern Colorado in Greeley and the privately run Denver University. The state is also home to the Colorado Mountain College in Gunnison, which focuses on natural sciences specifically related to alpine environments. Another esoteric university is the Colorado School of Mines in Golden, with its top-rated geology and mineral research curriculum.

Wyoming's only major school is the University of Wyoming in Laramie. Other institutes of higher learning include Casper College in Casper and Central Wyoming College in Riverton.

Montana's two biggest universities are the University of Montana in Missoula, whose forestry and creative writing programs are among the USA's best, and Montana State University in Bozeman, which is known for its strong agribusiness department. Montana College of Mineral Science and Technology (Montana Tech) in Butte has an important mining technology school and mineral science research center. Dillon is home to Western Montana College, which educates about 80% of the teachers in the state.

Idaho's major school is the University of Idaho, located in Moscow. Others include Boise State University, Idaho State University in Pocatello and College of Southern Idaho in Twin Falls.

ARTS

Underestimated because of its isolation and small population, the West has nevertheless inspired generations of artists and writers. The earliest, of course, were the Native Americans who left petroglyphs and pictographs in the canyons of the Colorado Plateau and other regions. Artists accompanied the early expeditions of Lewis and Clark and Stephen Long, and even attended the fur traders' rendezvous of the early 19th century, leaving records that were not just historically valuable but also artistically enduring.

During the Great Depression of the 1930s, the federal government built many new public buildings, usually post offices and courthouses, which became architectural landmarks.

In recent years, resort towns like Jackson, Aspen and Cody have become centers for the arts. Denver and Boulder, CO, have gained national recognition for their performing arts programs. But the spread of culture has gone farther afield. Casper, WY, remodeled a power plant and lumber yard into a delightful facility for local and traveling art exhibitions. Gillette, WY, best known for open-pit coal mining, is one of several unlikely sites, with modern music and theater venues.

Music

Thanks to the region's prevailing cowboy culture, country & western music (which actually originated in the South) is the most widespread musical style in the Rocky Mountain states. Bluegrass is also popular, particularly in Colorado where celebrated bands like Hot Rise and Leftover Salmon formed.

Classical and contemporary music also make themselves heard in the Rockies. This is in part a legacy of the ostentatious opera houses built in mining camps by wealthy silver barons. The tradition of performing arts in the isolated mountain communities is maintained by today's ski resorts – in part as a strategy to attract visitors during the summer off-season.

Telluride's film festival and bluegrass festival draw visitors from around the world. Breckenridge, Aspen and Vail have strong summer schedules featuring renowned classical and jazz artists. Steamboat Springs offers a summer chamber music series. In Wyoming, Jackson's Grand Teton Music Festival attracts classical performers from throughout the country and around the world. Idaho summers see music festivals come to Sandpoint and Boise, and the National Fiddlers contest is held in Weiser.

Literature

Fiction, both literature and pulp, established characters that would be parodied in numerous television films and motion pictures. Owen Wister, a Pennsylvanian, first drew attention to the region with *The Virginian* in 1902. Zane Grey followed suit with *Riders of the Purple Sage* in 1912, which became hugely popular and paved the way for the formula Western novel.

Cowboy Poetry

That such a thing as cowboy poetry even exists is a small puncture in the media stereotype of the American cowboy. Always portrayed as the strong, silent type, the typical Western hero (or heroine) is not the sort you picture reciting Shakespeare as s/he rides off into the sunset.

Cowboy poetry, regular in meter and simple in rhyme, tells stories of what they knew and what surrounded them: unruly cattle, wide-open spaces, dramatic weather and incurable isolation. The poetic language, riddled with shur-nuffs, buckaroos and yonders, reflects their subject matter and poetic intent completely. Unlike their contemporaries, original cowboy poets had no literary training (usually no formal education at all), no mentors to copy and no styles to duplicate. Their easily memorized poems obviously were meant to be recited and repeated. Take Allen McCanless's *The Cowboy's Soliloquy* first published in 1885:

> Not even a dog to run by my side
> My fire I kindle with chips gathered round
> And boil my coffee without being ground.
> Bread lackin' leaven' I bake in a pot
> And sleep on the ground for want of a cot
> I wash in a puddle, and wipe with a sack
> And carry my wardrobe all on my back.
> My ceiling the sky, my carpet the grass
> My music the lowing of herds as they pass
> My books are the brooks, my sermon the stones
> My parson's a wolf on a pulpit of bones.

Cowboy poetry made its first major public appearance in 1908 in Howard (Jack) Thorp's *Songs of the Cowboys* and in 1910 in John Lomax's *Cowboy Songs and other Frontier Ballads*. In the 1970s and '80s, a cowboy poetry revival began to brew and has been gaining popularity ever since. In 1985 the first Cowboy Poetry Gathering met in Elko, NV, and drew a crowd of 10,000. Today there are more than a hundred similar gatherings spread throughout the country, and the Elko event now draws crowds of up to 50,000 people.

Modern cowboy poets, however, are an entirely different breed: While they may write with the sky overhead and earth below, they can't re-create the sense of space and isolation that is lost in today's world. One of the most talented poets is Baxter Black, a frequent contributor on National Public Radio's *Morning Edition*. His recordings, such as *Live at the Grange*, are always amusing and reveal modern urban and rural life in the West.

Several good anthologies of cowboy poetry have been published, including *Cattle, Horses, Sky, and Grass* (Northland Publishing, 1994), edited by Warren Miller, and *Cowboy Poetry: A Gathering* (Gibbs M Smith Inc, 1985).

The dime novel of the early 20th century helped create the epic myths and legends that now haunt the tourist towns of the Rocky Mountain states. Louis L'Amour (1908–1988) once supported himself as a deputy sheriff in North Dakota and wrote very popular pulp fiction; his first Western novel, *Hondo*, published in 1953, was an instant success. He went on to write 80 more, including *How the West Was Won* and *The Quick and the Dead*.

Colorado mining camps inspired Anne Ellis to write her biographical account of hardships among the working class in *The Life of an Ordinary Woman*. Colorado's dean of nature writing, Enos Mills, published

16 books of careful nature observation from his cabin near Estes Park before his untimely death in 1922. His *Adventures of a Nature Guide* contains an excellent sampling of his work.

Black Elk, born in Wyoming's Powder River Basin, is famous for *Black Elk Speaks: Being the Life Story of a Holy Man of the Oglala Sioux*, an autobiographical classic still widely read in university courses. Caroline Lockhart, transplanted from Illinois, became a newspaper editor in Cody and wrote several novels with local settings; most notably *The Lady Doc*. Novelist and essayist Gretel Ehrlich, originally from California, is probably the state's best known contemporary writer.

Idaho claims Ezra Pound, the poet, born in Hailey in 1885, and Ernest Hemingway, who made his home in Ketchum. Novelist and essayist Vardis Fisher chronicled Idaho during the 1930s and '40s and is remembered for *Idaho: A Guide in Word & Picture*, the WPA guide to Idaho.

The Big Sky (1947), by AB Guthrie, Jr, gave Montana its most popular nickname. Dorothy Johnson's *Man Called Horse* (1953) includes the story 'The Man Who Shot Liberty Valance' – the epitome of early Western literature. Spike Van Cleve captured the essence of cowboy curmudgeonry and storytelling in *A Day Late and a Dollar Short*.

Other modern writers, like Wallace Stegner, Ivan Doig and Thomas McGuane have taken Western literature in very different directions, avoiding the stereotypes and breaking the myths. (McGuane's *Something to Be Desired* is a good contemporary choice.) In this realm, Montana's literary tradition has always enjoyed a position of respect. The University of Montana (U of M) in Missoula continually produces gifted writers. *The Last Best Place* (University of Washington Press, 1991), edited by Annick Smith and William Kittredge, is a 1200-page anthology encompassing the entire range of Montana literature, from Native American stories to journal entries of early homesteaders to excerpts of works by popular contemporary writers.

Visual Arts

Colorado's spectacular landscapes have attracted many talented painters and photographers, but few Colorado natives have attained national fame from their own backyard.

Painters and photographers have found Wyoming fertile ground for their crafts ever since Alfred Jacob Miller accompanied Scottish nobleman William Drummond Stewart to the Green River Rendezvous in 1837. Albert Bierstadt, Thomas Moran, Frederic Remington, Carl Rungius and others all interpreted Wyoming landscapes, wildlife and people on canvas, while photographers William Henry Jackson and Charles J Belden both left memorable legacies depicting the state's wild landscapes and peoples. Cody-born abstract painter Jackson Pollock is undoubtedly the best-known artist to hail from Wyoming.

Charles M Russell is undeniably Montana's most celebrated artist. His oil paintings, watercolors and illustrated stories portray virgin Montana scenes – early encounters between Indians and Europeans, buffalo on the plains and cowboys with their herds. Although reproductions of his work are emblazoned on everything from greeting cards to pillowcases, the bulk of his original work is in Great Falls and Helena.

SOCIETY & CONDUCT

By reputation and ideology, the West is the most individualistic region of an individualistic country. It is also a socially conservative area. That conservatism is heightened by constant change and threats to the 'old way of life.' Even in the most progressive cities of the Rocky Mountain states you will encounter people whose lives depend (now or generations hence) on mining, logging and ranching. Change is coming quickly through younger generations, yet these are still the traditional cornerstones of the region's economy and need to be accepted if not necessarily agreed with.

Visitors to the rural areas of the Rockies will most often find the locals extremely friendly and polite. You are, however, most likely to encounter strong conservatism in such areas, especially in areas that rely on agriculture, oil, ranching or logging. Visitors should try to be aware of local political issues; don't broadcast your animal rights convictions in a bar full of hunters or denounce clear-cutting in a mill town, for example, without having some understanding of your audience and their experiences and upbringing.

RELIGION

The oldest religions in North America are Native American religions, some greatly changed since contact with Europeans; some, like the Native American Church, which uses hallucinatory peyote buttons as a sacrament, are in part pan-Indian responses to encroachment by the Judeo-Christian culture. Scattered throughout the region, sacred sites like Devils Tower and the Medicine Wheel (both in Wyoming) draw worshippers from Native American communities throughout the region.

The oldest European religion in the Rockies is Roman Catholicism, the legacy of early Spanish incursions into New Mexico and the San Luis Valley of southwestern Colorado. Catholicism and various Protestant denominations are the most important religions in numbers of adherents.

Both Catholic and Protestant missionaries accompanied early fur traders and traveled the Oregon Trail to evangelize among Native American peoples. Many Indians nominally converted to Christianity or a hybrid form of it. A significant symbol of a settled community, as opposed to a roughshod frontier town, was construction of a permanent church.

Similar in many ways to the Mennonites in Canada, long-standing groups of Hutterites in Montana live simply and practice both pacifism and communism. Because of their strong faith and community orientation, few venture away to join the modern ways – a rare feat among religious communities.

The Hutterites

In the 17th century many brotherhoods of Hutterites (a brethren descended from the Moravian Anabaptists) lived in Moravia, but persecution drove them east to resettle in Russia. Facing further persecution, a group of Hutterites, along with Russian Mennonites, emigrated to the USA in 1874. President Grant offered them sizable land grants in South Dakota, agreeing to their proposal that they pay land tax, but not go to war. They eventually moved west and north to settle also in Montana and Canada. Once these groups had settled, more Hutterites emigrated from Russia. Similar in many ways to the Mennonites in Canada, they live simply and practice both pacifism and communism.

Hutterite communist principles are based on Acts 4:32–35 in the Bible, which say 'neither said any of them that ought of the things which he possessed was his own; but they had all things in common.' The theory that an individual is to be subordinated to the will of the community (*Gelassenheit*) is reinforced in their educational system. Because of their strong faith and community orientation, they have stayed together (few venture away to join the modern ways) – a rare feat among religious communities.

Unlike the Mennonites or Amish, the Hutterites accept farm machinery and vehicles and invite technical improvements. They have always been very efficient farmers and continue to buy more land. Such practices have not sat well with the people of the prairie states, angered that these non-communicative neighbors buy up the land but don't support the economy through consumerism. Apathy, however, seems to be the main reaction to these communities. When asked about their Hutterite brethren, local Montanans generally give a passive 'I don't know or really care' shrug, and move on to another topic of conversation.

Throughout the Rockies are outliers and enclaves of the Church of Jesus Christ of Latter Day Saints (LDS), more commonly known as the Mormons. Though their strongest influence is in neighboring Utah, Mormons are numerous in communities like Wyoming's Star Valley and Powell, near the Wyoming-Montana state line. The Mormon church is also one of Idaho's largest organized religions, and is concentrated in the southeast. Mormon strictures on activities like gambling and alcohol consumption are very influential in these areas, and it is unquestionably the most cohesive religious group in the region.

The most recent religious development in the region is the growth of New Age communities like Crestone, CO (home of actress Shirley MacLaine), which has a Zen Center, Ashram Temple and Spiritual Life Institute. In Montana, where Jesuit missionaries and Lutheran ministers once dominated, one can now go to Buddhist meditation groups and Hindu-based Sidda Yoga meetings, especially in Missoula, Bozeman, Hamilton and Kalispell.

Darker variants of this new spiritualism are millennial groups like Elizabeth Claire Prophet's Church Universal and Triumphant, a heavily armed cult occupying a fortress compound near Gardiner, MT (the northern entrance to Yellowstone National Park). Paramilitary groups, some of whom rationalize their beliefs on religious grounds, also inhabit some rural areas, but visitors are unlikely to come in contact with them.

Facts for the Visitor

HIGHLIGHTS

Without a doubt, the main reason to visit the Rockies is to soak in the magnificent natural beauty that comes in a stunning array of color, terrain and atmosphere. From the desert canyons of western Colorado to the lush alpine splendor of Glacier National Park, this region offers visitors almost unrestricted access to breathtaking nature, the type that defies verbal description and makes one thankful to be part of this amazing world.

But the Rockies' appeal is not limited to natural sights. The region's friendly residents and wealth of historic, well-preserved 19th-century towns also add to the visitor's experience.

Below are some of the authors' choices for best things to see and do in the various states. While these include sights that would make any tourist brochure, there are a few places where you'll find you're mixing mostly with the locals.

Colorado

Arapahoe Basin Enjoy some of the best, and latest, steep skiing in Colorado at this bare-bones ski area that manages to ward off the glitz and haughtiness that have invaded other resorts such as Aspen, Telluride and Vail.

Boulder Hang out on the rooftop deck of the West End Tavern, having a drink and watching the sun set behind the majestic Flatirons.

Colorado National Monument Take advantage of easy access to stunning sandstone canyons from the interstate highway.

Fruita Join the fat tire madness on some of the best mountain-bike trails in the Rockies.

San Luis Experience the distinct Hispanic culture against the backdrop of the Sangre de Cristo Mountains.

The Million Dollar Highway Witness the awe-inspiring alpine scenery around the historic mining towns of Silverton, Ouray and Telluride.

The Peak to Peak Highway Drive this easily reached, stunning stretch of road from Nederland (west of Boulder) to Estes Park.

Wyoming

Bighorn Canyon National Recreation Area Make the detour between Yellowstone and Devils Tower for a glimpse of a vertigo-inspiring 2200-foot gorge and native wildlife.

Devils Tower Make the drive out to this majestic national monument, a Native American sacred site and a popular challenge for rock climbers.

Fort Laramie National Historic Site Soak up the frontier atmosphere of eastern Wyoming's Fort Laramie, the last chance for supplies on the Oregon Trail during the 19th century.

Grand Teton National Park Photograph the breathtaking Tetons from a distance – then walk their trails.

Laramie Spend the afternoon wandering this gracious city's historic district.

Medicine Wheel Take in the awesome views over the Bighorn Basin from this Native American sacred site atop the Bighorn Mountains.

Snowy Range Ramble just west of Laramie for scenic hiking and spectacular views from this high, yet accessible mountain range.

Wind River Range Explore the superb network of trails on Wyoming's highest mountain range, along and across the Continental Divide.

Yellowstone National Park Escape the crowds at the world's first national park by getting out of your car and onto the trails.

Montana
Absaroka-Beartooth Highway Traverse stark tundra-covered plateaus passing jagged granite peaks and glacial lakes; excellent hiking trails lead into this wilderness.

Big Hole Battlefield National Monument Learn about the flight of Chief Joseph and the Nez Percé Indians, a particularly sad episode in US history.

Billings Go cowboy dancing!

Bitterroot Range Choose from 29 canyons lined with prime trails to high mountain lakes in this glacially formed range.

Butte Explore the remnants of Butte's opulent mining history.

Ennis Wet your line in the nearby Madison River.

Glacier National Park Head up Going-to-the-Sun Rd *after* the first week in November, when it's closed to motor traffic and runners and skiers take over.

Makoshika State Park Be one of the few to enjoy grand views of the stunning badlands scenery amid peace and quiet.

Missoula Spend the morning at the Second Thought Cafe or (in summer) outside at Bernice's Bakery.

Museum of the Rockies Experience this Bozeman treasure, featuring Montana's finest natural history exhibits and hauntingly lifelike dinosaur replicas.

Red Lodge Barhop or shop your way around this historic mining town.

Idaho
Boise Check out the hip, lively mix of cultural activity and nightlife, or jump off here to explore the rivers and lakes of southwestern Idaho.

Schweitzer Mountain & Panhandle Lakes Seek solitude or water sports at the pristine Coeur d'Alene, Pend Oreille and remote Priest Lakes; Schweitzer Mountain is among the state's premier year-round mountain resorts.

Salmon River Set out for a day trip or multi-day run down one of the world's top 10 white-water rivers.

Sawtooth National Recreation Area Discover the magnificent high mountain ranges and the countless rivers, lakes and streams.

Sun Valley Spoil yourself amid old-world grandeur, newfangled glitter and deep powder skiing.

SUGGESTED ITINERARIES
Travel options in the Rocky Mountains are vast, depending, of course, on how you hit the road. Long-distance public transportation is limited, but if you've got your own wheels the possibilities are endless and even a short drive is worthwhile. Travelers on a short trip tend to stick to major routes and attractions like Rocky Mountain National Park and Yellowstone National Park. More adventuresome souls with the time and wanderlust can opt for more remote, less-visited sites that are often as scenic and worthwhile (if not more) than the 'must-sees.' Road tripping not only earns you freedom and flexibility, but is ideal for those seeking to surround themselves in nature, camp and enjoy outdoor activities.

A one-week road trip would give you just enough time to scratch the surface, but get a good taste of the mountains. Two or three weeks would allow for further exploration, and time for outdoor enthusiasts to soak up a healthy sampling of Mother Nature's offerings. One month or more is ample time to zigzag around the four states featured in this book, and even slide into southern Utah to check out the stunning geological formations and outdoor opportunities. For leads on the most scenic and interesting road routes in the Rockies, see 'Road-Tripping the Rockies.'

By flying around the region (most regional flights connect in Denver), it is quick and easy, if expensive, to reach worthwhile destinations like the ski resorts of Telluride and Aspen, CO, Wyoming's Jackson Hole, Big Sky in Montana and Idaho's Sun Valley. Most ski areas offer great year-round attractions, activities and outdoor recreation. For more on air travel in the Rockies, see the Getting Around chapter and relevant state and regional chapters.

PLANNING
When to Go

For many travelers, the Rocky Mountain region is a summer destination, but the winter ski season also draws large numbers of visitors. Some prefer the fall, when the aspens flaunt their autumn gold, or the spring wildflower season.

It starts to feel like summer in the Rocky Mountains around June, and the warm weather lasts until about mid-September. While winter weather doesn't usually settle in until late November, snowstorms can start hitting the mountain areas as early as September. Winter usually lasts until March or early April.

Due to the mountain terrain, high altitude and dry climate, the one constant in the weather is that it can always change quickly. The trick is to be prepared and keep an eye on weather conditions in the area you're traveling to. For phone numbers you can call to check on road conditions in each state, see the Emergencies section later in this chapter.

In nearly all parts of the Rockies summer is the high season, which means more crowds and usually higher lodging rates. In areas where winter recreation is well established (mainly ski resorts) peak season rates and conditions also apply.

Traveling in the off-season can be rewarding since you don't have to contend with crowded roads, shops and visitors centers, and places to stay offer more affordable room rates. The downside is that tours and guided activities have limited schedules if they function at all, and restaurants are often vacant, or shut for the season. The best off-season time is the middle of September through October, as the weather usually stays warm and services aren't yet totally shut down. For details on weather and temperatures in the four states, see the Climate section in Facts about the Rocky Mountains.

Maps

Good maps are widely available in the US, making it easy to find your way around. Most tourist offices offer free local and regional maps. The relevant destination chapters have information on maps specific to each area, including those designed for activities such as hiking and mountain biking. Area bookstores and outdoor equipment specialists carry a wide selection of topographic maps.

The *Rand McNally Road Atlas* ($11) covers all 50 US states, as well as Canada and Mexico, and has useful additional features such as driving time and distance charts, and details on state driving laws.

The American Automobile Association (AAA) issues dependable highway maps, which are free to its members (see the Useful Organizations section, later) and also available for a reasonable price to nonmembers.

What to Bring

The Rocky Mountain region is mostly temperate, mid-latitude country whose climate resembles that of northern Europe (but at generally higher elevations). Carry seasonally appropriate clothing, but be prepared for changeable weather, including flash thunderstorms and frosts even in the middle of summer.

Excellent outdoor gear and clothing is available at reasonable prices throughout the region, but the selection is better and

Road-Tripping the Rockies

The ultimate way to travel around the Rocky Mountain states is on your own wheels. The following is a condensed guide to the authors' top picks for roads made for rambling. Routes are chosen for both their scenic beauty and the destinations they lead to. Most routes are prime to travel in either direction.

Colorado

- **To the Plains**: Denver – I-25 to Colorado Springs and/or Manitou Springs (overnight) – I-25/US 50 to La Junta and/or Bents Old Fort – Santa Fe Trail (US 350) to Trinidad (overnight) – Hwy 12 to La Veta. *Duration*: 3 to 5 days. *Highlights*: astonishing rock formations, pioneer history, solitude

- **Rocky Mountain High**: Boulder – Hwy 119 to Nederland – Peak to Peak Highway to Estes Park (overnight) – through Rocky Mountain National Park via Trail Ridge Rd (closed in winter) to Grand Lake (overnight). *Duration*: 3 to 5 days. *Highlights*: breathtaking mountain views, wildlife viewing, outdoor recreation

- **Straddling the Continental Divide**: Denver – I-70 to Glenwood Springs – Hwy 82 to Aspen (overnight) – Hwy 82 over Independence Pass (closed in winter) – US 24 north to Leadville, or south to Buena Vista and Salida. *Duration*: 3 to 6 days. *Highlights*: white-water rafting, hot springs, skiing

- **The Million Dollar Highway**: Telluride – Hwy 145/62/550 to Ouray (overnight) – Million Dollar Hwy to Silverton (overnight) – Hwy 550 to Durango. *Duration*: 3 to 5 days. *Highlights*: mining towns, stunning mountain scenery, hair-raising roads

- **Latin Connection**: Alamosa – US 160 to Fort Garland – Hwy 159 to San Luis – Hwy 142/US 285 to Antonito and Conejos – Hwy 17 south to New Mexico. *Duration*: 2 to 5 days. *Highlights*: Hispanic history, culture and flavors, spectacular steam train ride

Montana

- **Quick Hit**: Missoula – Hwy 93/43/County Rd 278 through Bitterroot Valley to Dillon (via Jackson) – I-15 to Butte. *Duration*: 3 to 5 days. *Highlights*: hiking, hot springs, historic battlefields

- **History & Fish Under the Big Sky**: Butte – I-90/Hwy 287 to Ennis – Hwy 287 to West Yellowstone – Hwy 191 to Bozeman. *Duration*: 3 to 5 days. *Highlights*: rich history, ample trout streams, nature and outdoor recreation

- **Old West Meets New West**: Billings – Hwy 78 to Red Lodge – Beartooth Hwy (closed in winter) to Yellowstone National Park- Hwy 191 to Bozeman – Hwy 84/Hwy 287 to Ennis – Hwy 287/41 to Dillon – Hwy 287/Pioneer Mtns National Scenic Byway to Butte (via Pioneer Mtns) – I-15 to Helen or I-90 to Missoula (optional). *Duration*: 6 to 11 days. *Highlights*: cowboys, historic towns, high alpine scenery

- **Montana Sampler**: Missoula – US 93 to Flathead Lake – US 93 to Whitefish – Hwy 40 to Glacier National Park – Going-to-the-Sun Rd/Hwy 89 to Rocky Mountain Front – Hwy 89/Hwy 287 to Helena – I-15 to Butte or Hwy 287/I-90 to Bozeman (optional). *Duration*: 5 to 10 days. *Highlights*: major sites, backpacking, Going-to-the-Sun Rd

- **Backwoods Delight**: Helena – Hwy 287 to Rocky Mountain Front – Hwy 89 to Glacier National Park – Going-to-the-Sun Rd/North Fork Rd to Polebridge – US 2/Hwy 40 to Whitefish – US 93 to Eureka – Hwy 37 to Libby – Hwy 2/US 93 to Flathead Lake – US 93 to Missoula. *Duration*: 10 to 15 days, including hiking days. *Highlights*: museums, fishing, trees, trees and trees

- **I Want to Do It All!**: Missoula – US 93/Hwy 43/County Rd 278 through Bitterroot Valley to Dillon – I-15/Red Rock Pass Rd to Red Rock Lakes National Wildlife Refuge – Hwy 87/Hwy 287 to Ennis – Hwy 84 to Bozeman – Hwy 85 to Big Sky – US 191 to Yellowstone National Park – Beartooth Hwy (closed in winter) to Red Lodge – Hwy 78/I-90/US 89/US 12 to Helena – US 287/US 89 to Glacier National Park (via Rocky Mountain Front). *Duration*: minimum 12 days. *Highlights*: all of the above!

Idaho

- **Sawtooth See & Ski Loop**: Boise – Hwy 21 through Boise Front and Idaho City to Stanley (overnight) – Hwy 75 to Sun Valley (overnight) – Hwy 75/US 93 to Twin Falls – US 30 loop back to Boise. *Duration*: 2 to 5 days. *Highlights*: mining camps, wilderness trails, hot springs, hiking, biking and skiing

- **Highways & Canyons to Hell**: Boise – Hwy 55 to McCall (overnight) – US 95 to Riggins to Hells Canyon (overnight) – US 95 to Coeur d'Alene and/or Sandpoint. *Duration*: 3 to 5 days. *Highlights*: wildlife viewing, Palouse panoramas, endless lakefront vistas

- **Lake of the Woods**: Coeur d'Alene – US 95 to Sandpoint – US 2 to Flathead Lake, MT, and Glacier National Park. *Duration*: 4 to 7 days. *Highlights*: solitude, open roads, primeval forest, mining towns, big blue lakes, rare wildlife

- **Snake River Plain**: Snake River Plain via I-80 in either direction: Boise – I-84 to Mountain Home – US 30 to Hagerman Valley and Twin Falls – US 26 to Craters of the Moon (overnight) – US 26 to Idaho Falls – US 20 to Henry's Fork and/or Harriman State Park (overnight) – US 20 to Yellowstone National Park (overnight). *Duration*: 3 to 7 days. *Highlights*: wildlife viewing, fertile argicultural panoramas, sci-fi landscapes, national parks

Wyoming

- **Classic Yellowstone Grand Loop**: The Grand Loop in Yellowstone National Park, a 142-mile figure-8 past most of the park's major attractions. *Duration*: 5 to 7 days. *Highlights*: abundant wildlife, scenic mountain passes, awesome views, geysers, alpine lakes

- **Wyoming's Greatest Hits**: Jackson Hole – US 191/89/287 to Grand Tetons and Yellowstone National Park – US 14/16/20 to Cody. *Duration*: 5 to7 days minimum. *Highlights*: all of the above laced with Wild West flavor

- **Bighorn Blitz**: US 14/14A/16/20 Bighorn Scenic Byways – US 14 to Sheridan and/or Buffalo – US 14/16/I-90 to Devils Tower. *Duration*: 3 to 5 days. *Highlights*: Wild West museums, meadow-carpeted plateaus, sacred sites, unique geology

- **The Emigrant Route**: Flaming Gorge – I-80/US 30/State Rd 130 to Snowy Range Scenic Byways – State Rd 130 to Laramie – State Rd 210 to Cheyenne. *Duration*: 3 to 5 days. *Highlights*: pioneer history, outdoor recreation at every turn, Wild West attitude

- **Smack Dab in the Middle of Nowhere**: Cheyenne – US 85/18 north to Sundance via Newcastle and Thunder Basin National Grassland (overnight) – US 14 to Devils Tower National Monument. *Duration*: 2 to 3 days. *Highlights*: open road, amazing sunsets, solitude, natural wonders

prices are generally lower in large cities. If you're bringing your own camping gear, be sure to include an all-weather tent and warm sleeping bags: Even in summer, temperatures in the mountains can drop to freezing at night.

Basic supplies like toiletries are readily available. Due to the high altitude, sunblock should be carried, even in winter. See the Activities chapter for a more detailed list of what to bring on hikes and outdoor trips.

RESPONSIBLE TOURISM

Travelers should maintain a healthy awareness of the local environment and consider our impact, such as the environmental effects of car travel. Although the relative lack of public transportation in the Rockies makes long-distance travel by private car most practical, you can take advantage of local public transportation, especially in and around cities of the region, and often opt for bicycling or walking locally as an alternative.

When traveling into natural areas, tread lightly. Backcountry regions are composed of fragile environments and cannot support an inundation of human activity, especially insensitive and careless activity. A code has evolved to deal with the growing numbers of people in the wilderness. Most conservation organizations and hikers' manuals have their own backcountry codes that outline the same important principles: minimizing the impact on the land, leaving no trace and taking nothing but photographs and memories. Above all, *stay on the main trail*; shortcutting causes severe erosion.

Recycling centers can be found in most larger towns. Materials accepted are usually plastic and glass bottles, aluminum and tin cans and newspapers. Some campgrounds and a few roadside rest areas also have recycling bins next to the trash bins. When hiking and camping in the wilderness, take out everything you bring in – this includes *any* kind of garbage you may create.

Respect the native cultures of the region, especially when visiting Native American sacred sites or attending public gatherings like powwows. In addition, overcome temptation and stay off land that is marked with a 'No Trespassing' or 'Private Property' sign – the more people ignore these signs, the more resentful and dogmatic land owners become toward visitors, not to mention the legal consequences you may face.

As more and more national chains are steadily forcing the 'little guy' under, make some effort to shop in locally owned stores and buy locally grown and produced food and other products.

More information on responsible travel specific to area attractions and activities can be found dispersed throughout this book.

TOURIST OFFICES

Information on state tourist offices can be found in the introductory sections for each state. Local tourist offices are listed under the relevant destination.

The USA currently has no government-affiliated tourist offices in other countries. For region-specific information, ask your travel agent.

VISAS & DOCUMENTS

All foreign visitors (other than Canadians) must bring their passport. Visitors should also bring their driver's license and any health insurance or travel insurance cards. Canadians must have proper proof of Canadian citizenship, such as a citizenship card with photo ID or a passport.

You'll need a picture ID to show that you are older than 21 to buy alcohol or gain admission to bars or clubs. It's a good idea to make a photocopy of your passport and international ID to carry around instead of the original.

The US State Dept's Bureau of Consular Affairs Web site (www.travel.state.gov) has excellent info on visa, passport and customs requirements.

Visas

Apart from Canadians, and those entering under the Visa-Waiver Pilot Program (see below), all foreign visitors need to obtain a visa from a US consulate or embassy. In most countries the process can be done by mail or through a travel agent.

Your passport should be valid for at least six months beyond your intended stay in the USA, and you'll need to submit a recent photo (37 x 37 mm) with the application. Documents of financial stability and/or guarantees from a US resident are sometimes required, particularly for visitors from developing countries.

Visa applicants may be required to 'demonstrate binding obligations' that will ensure their return back home. Because of this requirement, those planning to travel through other countries before arriving in the USA are generally better off applying for their US visa while they are still in their home country, rather than while on the road.

The most common visa is a Non-Immigrant Visitor's Visa, B1 for business purposes, B2 for tourism or visiting friends and relatives. A visitor's visa is good for one or five years with multiple entries, and it specifically prohibits the visitor from taking paid employment in the USA. The validity period depends on what country you're from. The length of time you'll be allowed to stay in the USA is ultimately determined by US immigration authorities at the port of entry. If you're coming to the USA to work or study, you will probably need a different type of visa, and the company or institution to which you're going should make the arrangements. Allow six months in advance for processing the application.

Visa Waiver Pilot Program Citizens of certain countries may enter the USA without a US visa, for stays of 90 days or less, under the Visa Waiver Pilot Program. Currently these countries are Andorra, Argentina, Australia, Austria, Belgium, Brunei, Denmark, Finland, France, Germany, Iceland, Ireland, Italy, Japan, Liechtenstein, Luxembourg, Monaco, the Netherlands, New Zealand, Norway, Portugal, San Marino, Singapore, Slovenia, Spain, Sweden, Switzerland and the UK. Under this program you must have a roundtrip ticket that is nonrefundable in the USA, and you will not be allowed to extend your stay beyond 90 days. Check with the US

embassy in your home country for any other requirements.

Visa Extensions & Reentry If you want, need or hope to stay in the USA longer than the date stamped on your passport, go to the local INS office (☎ 800-755-0777, or look in the local white pages telephone directory under US Government) *before* the stamped date to apply for an extension. Anytime after that will usually lead to an unamusing conversation with an INS official who will assume you want to work illegally. If you find yourself in that situation, it's a good idea to bring a US citizen with you to vouch for your character. It's also a good idea to have some verification that you have enough money to support yourself.

Travel Insurance

No matter how you're traveling, make sure you take out travel insurance. This should cover you not only for medical expenses and luggage theft or loss, but also for cancellations or delays in your travel arrangements. Everyone should be covered for the worst possible case, such as an accident that requires hospital treatment and a flight home. Coverage depends on your insurance and type of ticket, so ask both your insurer and your ticket-issuing agency to explain the finer points. Ticket loss is usually covered by travel insurance. Make sure you have a separate record of all your ticket details – or better still, a photocopy of it. Also make a copy of your policy, in case the original is lost. STA Travel and Council Travel offer travel insurance options at reasonable prices.

If you're planning to travel a long time, the insurance might seem very expensive, but if you can't afford it, you certainly won't be able to afford a medical emergency in the USA.

Driver's License & Permits

An International Driving Permit is a useful accessory for foreign visitors in the USA. Local traffic police are more likely to accept it as valid identification than an unfamiliar document from another country. Your national automobile association can provide one for a small fee. The permits are usually valid for one year.

Hostel Cards

Most hostels in the USA are members of Hostelling International-American Youth Hostel (HI-AYH), which is affiliated with the International Youth Hostel Federation (IYHF). You can purchase membership on the spot when checking in, although it's probably advisable to purchase it before you leave home. Most hostels allow non-members to stay but will charge them a few dollars more.

Student & Youth Cards

If you're a student, get an international student ID or bring along a school or university ID card to take advantage of the discounts available to students, often offered for films and performances.

Seniors Cards

All people older than 65 get discounts throughout the USA. All you need is ID with proof of age should you be carded. There are organizations such as AARP (see Senior Travelers) that offer membership cards for further discounts and extend coverage to citizens of other countries.

Automobile Association Membership Cards

If you plan on doing a lot of driving in the USA, it would be beneficial to join your national automobile association. See Useful Organizations, later, for information.

Copies

All important documents (passport data page and visa page; credit cards; travel insurance policy; air, bus and train tickets; driver's license, etc) should be photocopied before you leave home. Leave one copy with someone at home and keep another with you, separate from the originals.

It's also a good idea to store details of your vital travel documents in Lonely Planet's free online Travel Vault in case you lose the photocopies or can't be bothered with them. Your password-protected Travel Vault is accessible online from anywhere in the world – you can get started at www.ekno .lonelyplanet.com.

EMBASSIES & CONSULATES
US Embassies & Consulates Abroad

US diplomatic offices abroad include:

Australia
(☎ 2-6270 5000)
21 Moonah Place, Yarralumla ACT 2600
(☎ 2-9373 9200)
Level 59 MLC Center 19–29 Martin Place, Sydney NSW 2000
(☎ 3-9526 5900)
553 St Kilda Rd, Melbourne, Victoria

Canada
(☎ 613-238-5335)
490 Sussex Dr, Ottawa, Ontario K1P 5T1
(☎ 604-685-4311)
1095 W Pender St, Vancouver, BC V6E 2M6
(☎ 514-398-9695)
1155 rue St-Alexandre, Montreal, Quebec

France
(☎ 01-43 12 22 22)
2 avenue Gabriel, 75008 Paris

Germany
(☎ 228 33 91)
Clayallee 170, 14195 Berlin

Ireland
(☎ 1-668 7122)
42 Elgin Rd, Dublin 4

Israel
(☎ 3-510 3822)
1 Ben Yehuda St, Tel Aviv
(☎ 2-625 5755)
19 Keren Hayesod, Jerusalem

Japan
(☎ 3-3224 5000)
10-5 Akasaka 1-chome, Minato-ku, Tokyo

Netherlands
(☎ 70-310 9209)
Lange Voorhout 102, 2514 EJ The Hague
(☎ 20-310 9209)
Museumplein 19, 1071 DJ Amsterdam

New Zealand
(☎ 4-722 068)
29 Fitzherbert Terrace, Thorndon, Wellington

Norway
(☎ 22-44 85 50)
Drammensveien 18, 0244 Oslo

Your Own Embassy

It's important to realize what your own embassy – the embassy of the country of which you are a citizen – can and can't do to help you if you get into trouble. Generally speaking, it won't be much help in emergencies if the trouble you're in is remotely your own fault. Remember that you are bound by the laws of the country you are in. Your embassy will not be sympathetic if you end up in jail after committing a crime locally, even if such actions are legal in your own country.

In genuine emergencies you might get some assistance, but only if other channels have been exhausted. If you need to get home urgently, a free ticket home is exceedingly unlikely – the embassy would expect you to have insurance. If all your money and documents are stolen, it might assist you with getting a new passport, but a loan for onward travel is out of the question.

Some embassies used to keep letters for travelers or have a small reading room with home newspapers, but these days most of the mail-holding services have been stopped and even newspapers tend to be out of date.

Sweden
(☎ 8-783 5300)
Dag Hammarskjolds, Vag 31,
SE-115 89 Stockholm

Switzerland
(☎ 31-357 70 11)
Jubilaumsstrasse 93, 3005 Berne
(☎ 22-798 16 05)
World Trade Center, IBC-Building,
29 rte de Pre-Bois, Geneva
(☎ 1-422 25 66)
Dufourstrasse 101, 3rd floor, Zurich

UK
(☎ 20-7499 9000)
20 Grosvenor Square, London W1
(☎ 31-556 8315)
3 Regent Terrace, Edinburgh EH7 5BW
(☎ 232-328 239)
Queens House, 14 Queen St, Belfast BT1 6EQ

Embassies & Consulates in the USA

Addresses and phone numbers of foreign diplomatic representatives can be found in the yellow pages telephone directory under 'Consulates.' To find out the telephone number of your embassy or consulate in Washington, DC, call ☎ 202-555-1212.

In the Rockies, Denver is the only city that has foreign consulates; see the Denver & Boulder chapter.

CUSTOMS

US Customs allows each person older than 21 to bring one liter of liquor and 200 cigarettes duty-free into the United States. US citizens are allowed to import, duty-free, $400 worth of gifts from abroad, while non–US citizens are allowed to bring in $100 worth.

US law permits travelers to bring in, or take out, as much as $10,000 in US or foreign currency, traveler's checks or letters of credit without formality. All larger amounts must be declared to customs by travelers.

MONEY
Currency

The US dollar is divided into 100 cents (¢). Coins come in denominations of 1¢ (penny), 5¢ (nickel), 10¢ (dime), 25¢ (quarter) and the seldom seen 50¢ (half dollar) and $1. Quarters are the most commonly used coins in vending machines, parking meters and laundry machines, so it's handy to have a stash of them with you. Notes, commonly called bills, come in $1, $2, $5, $10, $20, $50 and $100 denominations – $2 bills are rare, but they are perfectly legal.

Exchange Rates

Outside the cities, most banks throughout the Rocky Mountain region will probably not have facilities for exchanging cash or traveler's checks in major foreign currencies. So it's best to take care of this before heading out to the outlying areas. Thomas Cook, American Express and exchange windows in airports offer exchange (although you'll usually get a better rate at a bank).

At press time, exchange rates were:

country	unit		US$
Australia	A$1	=	US$0.51
Canada	C$1	=	US$0.65
euro	€1	=	US$0.93
France	FF10	=	US$1.42
Germany	DM1	=	US$0.48
Hong Kong	HK$10	=	US$1.28
Japan	¥100	=	US$0.84
New Zealand	NZ$1	=	US$0.42
United Kingdom	UK£1	=	US$1.47

Exchanging Money

Cash & Traveler's Checks Though carrying cash is more risky it's still a good idea to travel with some for the convenience; it's useful for paying all those tips, and some smaller, more remote places may not accept credit cards or traveler's checks. The big advantage of traveler's checks is greater protection from theft or loss, and in many places they can be used as easily as cash. American Express and Thomas Cook are widely accepted and have efficient replacement policies.

Keeping a record of the check numbers and the checks you have used is vital when it comes to replacing lost checks. Keep this record separate from the checks themselves.

You'll save yourself trouble and expense if you buy traveler's checks in US dollars. The savings you *might* make on exchange rates by carrying traveler's checks in a foreign currency don't make up for the hassle of exchanging them at banks and other facilities.

ATMs These machines are a convenient way of obtaining cash 24 hours a day from a bank account back home (within the USA or from abroad). The number of ATMs has soared in recent years, and even small-town banks in the middle of nowhere have them.

An insidious practice adopted by US banks is to levy a $1 to $2 fee for using a 'non-web' ATM, that is one not directly run by your own bank. For travelers, this means virtually every ATM, so you may wish to withdraw larger amounts less often.

For a nominal service charge, you can also withdraw cash from an ATM using a credit card or a charge card. Credit cards usually have a 2% fee with a $2 minimum, but using bank cards linked to your personal checking account is usually far cheaper. Check with your bank or credit card company for exact information.

Credit & Debit Cards Major credit cards are accepted at hotels, restaurants, gas stations, shops and car rental agencies throughout the USA. In fact, you'll find it hard to perform certain transactions such as renting a car or purchasing tickets to performances without one.

Even if you loathe using credit cards and prefer to rely on traveler's checks and ATMs, it's a good idea to carry one in case of emergencies.

Places that accept Visa and MasterCard may also accept debit cards. Unlike a credit card, a debit card deducts payment directly from the user's checking account. Instead of an interest rate, users might be charged a minimal fee for the transaction.

Carry copies of your credit card numbers separately from the cards. If you lose your credit cards or they get stolen, contact the company immediately. Following are toll-free numbers of the main credit card companies for reporting lost or stolen cards. Contact your bank if you lose your ATM card.

American Express	☎ 800-992-3404
Diners Club	☎ 800-234-6377
Discover	☎ 800-347-2683
MasterCard	☎ 800-826-2181
Visa	☎ 800-336-8472

International Transfers You can instruct your bank back home to send you a draft. Specify the city, bank and branch to which you want your money directed, or ask your home bank to tell you where a suitable one is, and make sure you get the details right. The procedure is easier if you've previously authorized someone back home to access your account.

Money sent by telegraphic transfer should reach you within a week; by mail allow at least two weeks. When it arrives it will most likely be converted into local currency – you can take it as cash or buy traveler's checks. This type of transfer carries higher fees than sending a bank draft.

You can also transfer money by American Express, Thomas Cook or Western Union.

Security

Carry your money (and only the money you'll need for that day) somewhere inside your clothing (in a money belt, a bra or your socks) rather than in a handbag or an outside pocket. Put the money in several places. Most hotels and hostels provide safekeeping, so you can leave your money and other valuables with them. Hide or don't wear any valuable jewelry. A safety pin or key ring to hold the zipper tags of a daypack together can help deter theft.

Costs

In the Rocky Mountain states, costs are fairly reasonable, especially when compared to expensive US destinations like New York or California. Colorado is generally the most expensive state in the region, followed by Montana, and finally Wyoming and Idaho, two of the cheapest states to live and travel in the US.

As expected, larger cities and resort areas are the most overpriced. Rural areas and college towns tend to be the best places to look for bargains; in the case of the latter, students demand to be fed well, and for a good price.

Cost for accommodations varies seasonally, between the cities and the countryside, and between resorts and everywhere else. Generally rates are higher in summer, between Memorial Day and Labor Day.

The cheapest motel rates will usually be in the $30 to $40 range, with fancier places charging from $40 to $60. Camping on national or state land is generally inexpensive, between $5 to $10 per night, while private sites offering facilities like hot showers and laundry charge anywhere from $10 to $20.

Winter rates at big ski resorts are often ridiculously high, with average motel rooms starting at $70, and upscale hotel rooms at around $200! Ski-accommodation-airfare packages can help bring costs down though.

Food is affordable. The occasional splurge at a first-rate restaurant will cost anywhere between $25 and $50 a head depending on where you are, but good restaurant meals can be found in almost any town or city in the region for $10 – half that for some lunch specials. If you purchase food at markets you can get by even more cheaply.

Except for within cities, public transportation is generally both expensive and limited. In many areas a car is the best way of getting around; fortunately rentals are fairly inexpensive in large cities, and gasoline costs a fraction of what it does in Europe and most of the rest of the world. For more information on purchasing and operating a car, see the Getting Around chapter.

Tipping

Tipping is expected in restaurants and better hotels, and by taxi drivers, hairdressers and baggage carriers. In restaurants, waitstaff are paid minimal wages and rely upon tips for their livelihoods. Tip 15% unless the service is terrible (in which case a complaint to the manager is warranted) or 20% if the service is great. Never tip in fastfood, take-out or buffet-style restaurants where you serve yourself.

Taxi drivers expect 10% and hairdressers get 15% if their service is satisfactory. Baggage carriers (skycaps in airports, attendants in hotels) get $1 for the first bag and 50¢ for each additional bag.

Taxes & Refunds

Almost everything you pay for in the USA is taxed. Occasionally, the tax is included in the advertised price (eg, plane tickets, gas, drinks in a bar and entrance tickets). Restaurant meals and drinks, accommodations and most other purchases are taxed, and this is added to the advertised cost. When inquiring about hotel or motel rates, be sure to ask whether taxes are included or not. Sales and service tax rates are set by state and local governments, and thus vary from place to place.

Unless otherwise stated, the prices given in this book don't reflect local taxes.

POST & COMMUNICATIONS
Postal Rates
Postage rates increase every few years. Currently, rates for 1st-class mail within the USA are 34¢ for letters up to 1oz (21¢ for each additional ounce) and 20¢ for postcards.

International airmail rates to Canada and Mexico are 50¢ for a postcard, or 60¢ for a 1oz letter. To all other countries, postcard rates are 70¢, or 80¢ for a 1oz letter. Aerogrammes are 70¢.

The cost for parcels airmailed anywhere within the USA is $4 for 2lb or less, increasing by a little more than $1 per pound up to $7.50 for 5lb. For heavier items, rates differ according to the distance mailed. Books, periodicals and computer disks can be sent by a cheaper 4th-class rate.

Sending Mail
If you have the correct postage, you can drop your mail into any blue mailbox. However, to send a package 16oz or larger, you must bring it to a post office. If you need to buy stamps or weigh your mail, go to the nearest post office. The address of each town's main post office is given in the text. Usually, post offices in main towns are open weekdays from 8 am to 5 pm, and Saturday 8 am to 3 pm.

Receiving Mail
You can have mail sent to you c/o General Delivery at any post office that has its own zip (postal) code. Mail is usually held for 10 days before it's returned to sender; you might request your correspondents to write 'hold for arrival' on their letters. Or have mail sent to the local representative of American Express or Thomas Cook, which provide mail service for their customers.

Telephone
All phone numbers within the USA consist of a three-digit area code followed by a seven-digit local number. If you are calling long-distance either from within the United States or from another country, dial 1 + the three-digit area code + the seven-digit number. To call Canada, simply dial 1 + the area code.

For local directory assistance dial ☎ 411. For directory assistance outside your area code, dial ☎ 1 + the three-digit area code of the place you want to call + 555-1212. Be aware that directory assistance calls can cost up to 90¢ a call! To obtain directory assistance for a toll-free number, dial ☎ 1-800-555-1212; these calls are free.

Area codes for places outside the region are listed in telephone directories. Be aware that some metropolitan areas are being divided into multiple new area codes.

The 800, 888, 877, 866 and 855 area codes are designated for toll-free numbers within the USA, and sometimes from Canada as well. These calls are free, although if you are dialing locally, the toll-free number is sometimes not available.

The 900 area code is designated for calls for which the caller pays at a premium rate – phone sex, horoscopes, jokes, etc.

Local calls usually cost 25¢ or 35¢ at pay phones, although occasional private phones may charge more. Long-distance rates vary depending on the destination and which telephone company you use – call the operator (☎ 0) for rate information. Don't ask the operator to put your call through, however, because operator-assisted calls are much more expensive than direct-dial calls. Generally, nights (11 pm to 8 am) and weekends are the cheapest times to call. Evenings (5 to 11 pm, Monday to Friday) are mid-priced. Weekday calls from 8 am to 5 pm are full-priced calls within the USA.

International Calls To make an international call direct, dial ☎ 011, then the country code, followed by the area code and the phone number. International rates vary depending on the time of day and the destination. Call the operator (☎ 0) for rates.

Hotel Phones Many hotels (especially the more expensive ones) add a service charge of 50¢ to $1 for each local call made from a room phone and they also have hefty surcharges for long-distance calls. Public pay phones, which can be found in most lobbies, are always cheaper. You can pump in quarters, use a phone credit card or debit card, or make collect calls from pay phones.

Phone Debit Cards A popular long-distance alternative is phone debit cards, which allow purchasers to pay in advance, with access through a toll-free number. In amounts of $5, $10, $20 and $50, these are available from Western Union, supermarkets, convenience stores and other sources.

There's a wide range of local and international phonecards. Lonely Planet's eKno Communication Card (see the insert at the back of this book) is aimed specifically at independent travelers; see below.

eKno Communication Service

Lonely Planet's eKno global communication service provides low-cost international calls – for local calls, you're usually better off with a local phone card. eKno also offers free messaging services, email, travel information and an online travel vault, where you can securely store all your important documents. You can join online at www.ekno.lonelyplanet.com, or by phone from the Rockies by dialing ☎ 800-707-0031. To use eKno from the Rockies once you have joined, dial ☎ 800-706-1333.

Once you have joined, check the eKno Web site for the latest access numbers for each country and for updates on new features.

Fax & Telegram

Fax machines are easy to find in the USA, at shipping companies like Mail Boxes Etc, photocopy services like Kinko's and hotel business service centers, but be prepared to pay high prices (more than $1 a page). Telegrams can be sent from Western Union (☎ 800-325-6000).

Email & Internet Access

Email is quickly becoming a preferred method of communication. If you don't have a laptop and modem that can be plugged into a telephone socket, as well as a local dial-up, you'll have to rely on public Internet access.

Some hotel business service centers provide Internet connections, as do chains like Kinko's. These days a growing number of trendy restaurants and cafes also offer Web access for a nominal fee, and some public libraries have free Internet access.

INTERNET RESOURCES

The World Wide Web is a rich resource for travelers. You can research your trip, hunt down bargain airfares, book hotels, check on weather conditions and chat with locals and other travelers about the best places to visit (or avoid!).

There's no better place to start your Web explorations than the Lonely Planet Web site (www.lonelyplanet.com). Here you'll find succinct summaries on traveling to most places on earth, postcards from other travelers and the Thorn Tree bulletin board, where you can ask questions before you go or dispense advice when you get back. You can also find travel news and updates for many of our most popular guidebooks, and the subWWWay section links you to the most useful travel resources elsewhere on the Web.

Each of the state governments and tourist offices in the Rockies have Web sites, usually with hyperlinks allowing you to access more specific and detailed information on destinations, accommodations, attractions, etc. In addition, each state has hundred of sites and homepages, run by local chambers of commerce, attractions, resorts and small businesses. Site addresses are listed throughout this book with the particular destination or organization.

If you want to do some predeparture research or planning online, log on to one of the various search engines (Yahoo! seems to be one of the best for recreation and tourism) and do a keyword search for your destination or activity. Remember that combining terms to narrow your search (eg, Breckenridge+mountain biking) can prevent you from facing a list of several hundred search items, some of which may only be marginally related to your area of interest.

BOOKS

Most books are published in different editions by different publishers in different countries. As a result, a book might be a hardcover rarity in one country but readily available in paperback in another. Fortunately, bookstores and libraries can search by title, author or ISBN, so your local bookstore or library is the best place to advise you on the availability of the following recommendations.

The western USA has long been a popular subject for writers. In recent years, the focus has shifted from cowboys-and-Indians stereotypes to more complex and sophisticated assessments of the region and its place in national history and politics. Such topics as women's history, urban development and environmental degradation through mining, forestry and agriculture have crept into the forefront.

Previously only large cities and university towns in the Rockies had good bookstores, but in recent years many small towns have acquired better outlets. Noteworthy bookstores are listed in this book under the Information heading for most towns or cities.

Many of the titles below, as well as excellent selections of books and maps on flora, fauna, and local and regional subjects, are available throughout the region. Visit local bookstores, as well as those associated with the NPS, USFS and BLM visitors centers and museums.

Lonely Planet

Southwest covers in detail the nearby US states of Arizona, New Mexico and Utah.

Hiking in the USA will guide you onto popular and seldom-taken trails with tips for hikers of all abilities.

Travel

The Smithsonian Guide to Historic America: The Rocky Mountain States by Jerry Camarillo Dunn is rich in detail and awash with color photographs; it covers Colorado, Wyoming, Montana and Idaho.

Traveling the Oregon Trail by Julie Fanselow is worth consideration for those following the historical pathways across the region.

History & Politics

The Oxford History of the American West, edited by Clyde Milner II, Carol A O'Connor and Martha A Sandweiss, critically reevaluates the stereotyped Western experience of cowboys and Indians, and provides new perspectives in topics like environmental and labor history, Western literature and popular culture.

It's Your Misfortune and None of My Own: A New History of the American West is another revisionist view of the modern West, by Richard White.

Exploring the West by Herman J Viola traces the routes and recounts the experiences of Lewis and Clark, Pike, Frémont, Powell, King and many others.

Isabella L Bird's account of her 1873 climb up Long's Peak in *A Lady's Life in the Rocky Mountains* (University of Oklahoma Press, 1982) is a valuable vignette on that period.

For a comprehensive history on Colorado's best-known park, turn to Curt Bucholtz's *Rocky Mountain National Park: A History* (Colorado University Press, 1983).

Geography, Environment & Natural History

The Great Gates is a comprehensive geographic history of Rocky Mountain passes by one of Western America's best storytellers, Marshall Sprague.

Handbook of Rocky Mountain Plants by Ruth Ashton Nelson is a good source on Rocky Mountain flora.

Rocky Mountain Mammals is a definitive work by David M Armstrong.

Native Americans

Indian Country is a modern classic by one of America's most eloquent writers on Native American issues, Peter Matthiessen.

Indian Tribes of the Northern Rockies by Adolf and Beverly Hungry Wolf is a small but interesting collection of narratives and tales.

FILMS

Though many westerns have been filmed in the dramatic canyon and desert scenery of

Utah, other productions have been shot farther north. In recent years the Rockies have served as locations for a range of films that step out of the Western, and sometimes even Hollywood, mold.

Anthony Mann's *The Naked Spur* (1953) tells the tale of an embittered Civil War veteran who joins up with two dubious partners on a bounty hunt for a murderer. Nominated for an Oscar for best screenplay, the film was shot in Durango and stars Jimmy Stewart, Janet Leigh and Robert Ryan. Filmed in Montrose and Durango, Nery Hathaway's *True Grit* (1969) stars John Wayne as the gruff Rooster Cogburn, who aids a young girl in her search to find the man who killed her father.

Moving to more contemporary Hollywood offerings, Ridley Scott's *Thelma & Louise* (1991), starring Susan Sarandon and Geena Davis as two small-town women who trade in their domestic lives for an odyssey of adventure and violence on the road, includes a good amount of Colorado scenery. Stanley Kubrick directed *The Shining* (1980) based on Stephen King's best-selling novel. Starring Jack Nicholson, this horror classic was filmed largely at Estes Park's famed Stanley Hotel. Veering a bit away from the mainstream, *Things to Do in Denver When You're Dead* (1995), directed by Gary Fleder, is a well-made film noir/gangster flick that chooses the unlikely setting of Colorado's capital, and stars Andy Garcia, Christopher Walken and Treat Williams.

George Steven's *Shane* (1953), starring Alan Ladd, is a classic tale of an embattled gunfighter defending homesteaders from an evil cattle baron. Shot around Jackson Hole, it may now seem a bit clichéd, but it's beautifully filmed and still holds its place as a classic Western. Steven Spielberg's *Close Encounters of the Third Kind* (1977) prominently features Wyoming landmark Devils Tower. Richard Lang's *Mountain Men* (1980), starring Charlton Heston and Brian Keith, is a rather dull film about trappers and Indians, but gives a good feel for the beauty of the Grand Tetons. For a look at Wyoming's 'alien' landscape, check out the high-budget (but sometimes silly) *Starship Troopers,* Paul Verhoeven's 1997 sci-fi film about war between humans and interstellar insects, shot in Hell's Half Acre, near Casper.

The influence of Montana on the national popular imagination extends to Hollywood, where directors have turned many a tale of the Old West into showcases for Jimmy Stewart or John Wayne. Thomas McGuane's comic novel *Rancho Deluxe* (1975), about modern-day rustlers, was made into a film starring Jeff Bridges and Harry Dean Stanton. A more offbeat Western is Arthur Penn's delightful *Little Big Man* (1970), starring Dustin Hoffman as Jack Crabb, who at age 100 recounts his life as Indian captive, gunslinger and scout for General George Custer at Little Big Horn. In the past few years, fishing poles have replaced guns and Montana's rivers have replaced Main St as the site of the final showdown. Robert Redford directed a 1992 film adaptation of Norman Maclean's short story *A River Runs Through It,* which exposed the deep-seated truth that fishing is intertwined in all facets of Montana's existence, including the arts. *The River Wild* (1994), directed by Curtiss Hanson, highlights a rather dangerous version of whitewater rafting. *Powwow Highway* (1989), directed by Jonathan Wacks, takes a sometimes hard-edged look at the challenges of Native Americans trying to preserve their cultural identity in modern America. Though also shot in New Mexico and Sheridan, WY, the story is set (and was partially filmed) on Montana's Northern Cheyenne Reservation.

King Vidor's *Northwest Passage* (1940), starring Spencer Tracy, Robert Young and Walter Brennan, is a typical cowboys and Indians story, filmed in and around McCall. While the clichés may be offensive, the cinematography (which won an Oscar in 1941) is excellent. Clint Eastwood's 1985 *Pale Rider* somewhat redresses the cultural imbalance with its revisionist look at frontier mining life. Though set in California, some filming was done in the Sawtooth National Recreation Area. Starring River Phoenix and Keanu Reeves, Gus Van Sant's 1991 film *My Own Private Idaho,* an offbeat tale of two young male hustlers, was shot in the state and is popular with fans of arty, non-mainstream film.

In the touching comedy *City Slickers* (1993), Billy Crystal and two friends head west from New York City in search of a midlife-crisis remedy; the cure comes in the adventurous form of driving a herd of cattle from New Mexico to Colorado.

Based on the popular novel by Nicholas Evens, the critically acclaimed *The Horse Whisperer* (1998) takes place under the 'big sky' of rural Montana. The film stars Robert Redford, who, endowed with the gift of curing troubled horses, expands his talents to help heal the physical and emotional scars of a young girl who lost her leg in a riding accident.

NEWSPAPERS & MAGAZINES
Colorado
Although the *Denver Post* is generally acknowledged to be the most influential paper in the region, the tabloid-format *Rocky Mountain News* is Colorado's oldest newspaper, founded in 1859.

Westword, a free weekly, contains witty information on events and entertainment in Denver.

Wyoming
The only statewide newspaper is the influential *Casper Star-Tribune.* It does a good job of covering the state, especially in its 'Border to Border' section, and can be critical of politicians. The next largest newspaper is the Cheyenne-based *Wyoming Tribune-Eagle.*

Montana
There are three large-circulation newspapers: the *Billings Gazette, Great Falls Tribune* and the *Missoulian.* Each has an opinionated following. Billings' paper reflects the conservative attitudes of ranchers and oil industry leaders, as does the Great Falls daily, though the former does a better job of covering national and international events. The *Missoulian,* influenced by the

city's progressive university community, has been labeled 'eco-facist' by its eastern counterparts, and is known for its good state news coverage.

Published quarterly, *Big Sky Journal* features articles by Montana natives covering history, art, wildlife and modern problems facing Montanans.

Idaho
The Boise-based *Idaho Statesman* is the mainstream daily newspaper.

RADIO & TV
All rental cars have car radios. Most radio stations have a range of less than 100 miles. In and around major cities, scores of stations crowd the airwaves with a wide variety of music and entertainment. In rural areas, be prepared for a predominance of country & western music, local news and talk radio.

National Public Radio (NPR) features a more level-headed approach to discussion, music and sophisticated news on the FM band. Public radio stations carrying news-oriented NPR are listed in the 'National Public Radio' boxed text.

All the major TV networks have affiliated stations throughout the USA. These include ABC, CBS, NBC, FOX and PBS. Most motels and hotels also offer cable TV stations such as CNN News and movie channel HBO (Home Box Office).

VIDEO SYSTEMS
The USA uses the National Television System Committee (NTSC) color TV standard, which is not compatible with other standards (PAL or SECAM) used in Africa, Europe, Asia and Australia unless converted.

PHOTOGRAPHY & VIDEO
Film & Equipment
Print film is widely available at discount drugstores and supermarkets. Black-and-white and slide film are rarely sold outside of major cities.

Film can be damaged by excessive heat, so don't leave your camera and film in the car on a hot summer's day and avoid placing your camera on the dash while you are driving. It's worth carrying a spare battery to avoid disappointment if your camera dies in the middle of nowhere.

Drugstores are a good place to get your film cheaply processed. If you drop it off by noon, you can usually pick it up the next day. You can find pricier one-hour processing services listed in the yellow pages under 'Photo Processing.'

Restrictions

About the only places you'll find limits on photography are military installations and at Native American rituals. In the case of the former you really needn't worry unless there are specific warning signs: If not, go ahead and snap a shot of that missile silo or jet fighter taking off. If you wish to photograph or videotape Native American powwows and ceremonial dances, special permits often must be obtained from a local

National Public Radio

National Public Radio (www.npr.org) covers most of the Rocky Mountain states region, thanks to repeater transmitters in mountainous areas.

Colorado NPR Stations

Alamosa	KRZA, 88.7 FM	Grand Junction	KPRN, 89.5 FM
Aspen	KAJX, 91.5 FM	Greeley	KUNC, 91.5 FM
Boulder	KGNU, 88.5 FM	Ignacio	KSUT, 91.3 FM
Carbondale		Montrose	KPRN, 91.9 FM
(Glenwood Springs)	KDNK, 90.5 FM	Paonia	KVNF, 90.9 FM
Colorado Springs	KRCC, 91.5 FM	Pueblo	KCFP, 91.9 FM
Cortez	KSJD, 91.5 FM	Telluride	KOTO, 91.7 FM
Crested Butte	KBUT, 90.3 FM	Vail	KPRE, 89.9 FM
Denver	KCFR, 90.1 FM		
	KUVO, 89.3 FM		

Wyoming NPR Stations

Afton	KUWA, 91.3 FM	Laramie	KUWR, 91.9 FM
Buffalo	KBUW, 90.5 FM	Pinedale	KUWX, 90.9 FM
Casper	KUWC, 91.3 FM	Powell/Cody	KUWP, 90.1 FM
Douglas	KDUW, 91.7 FM	Rawlins	KUWR, 89.1 FM
Dubois	KUWR, 91.3 FM	Riverton	KUWR, 90.9 FM
Evanston	KUWR, 93.5 FM	Rock Springs	KUWZ, 90.5 FM
Gillette	KUWG, 90.9 FM	Sheridan	KSUW, 91.3 FM
Jackson	KUWJ, 90.3 FM	Torrington	KUWR, 89.9 FM

Montana NPR Stations

Billings	KEMC, 91.7 FM	Harlem	KGVA, 88.1 FM
Bozeman	KBMC, 102.1 FM	Havre	KNMC, 90.1 FM
Fort Belknap	KGVA, 88.1 FM	Miles City	KECC, 90.7 FM
Great Falls	KGPR, 89.9 FM	Missoula	KUFM, 89.1 FM

Idaho NPR Stations

Boise	KBSU, 90.3 FM	Rexburg	KRIC, 100.5 FM
	KBSX, 91.5 FM	Twin Falls	KBSW, 91.7 FM
Cottonwood	KNWO, 90.1 FM		

tribal council office, and at the least you must ask permission of the individuals you'd like to photograph.

Airport Security
All passengers on flights have to pass their luggage through X-ray machines. Technology as it is today doesn't jeopardize lower speed film. If you are carrying high speed (1600 ASA and above) film, then you may want to carry film and cameras with you and ask the X-ray inspector to visually check your film.

TIME
Colorado, Wyoming and Montana are all on Mountain Standard Time, seven hours behind GMT/UTC. Most of Idaho also lies within the mountain time zone except for parts of northern Central Idaho and the Panhandle, which are on Pacific time, eight hours behind GMT/UTC. All four states switch to Mountain Daylight Time (or Pacific Daylight Time), one hour later, from the first Sunday of April to the last Saturday of October.

ELECTRICITY
In the USA voltage is 110V and the plugs have two (flat) or three (two flat, one round) pins. Plugs with three pins don't fit into a two-hole socket, but adapters are easy to find at hardware or drugstores.

WEIGHTS & MEASURES
Distances are in feet, yards and miles. Three feet equals 1 yard (.914 meters); 1760 yards or 5280 feet are 1 mile. Dry weights are in ounces (oz), pounds (lb) and tons (16oz are 1lb; 2000lb are 1 ton), but liquid measures differ from dry measures. One pint equals 16 fluid ounces; two pints equals one quart, a common measure for liquids like milk, which is also sold in half gallons (two quarts) and gallons (four quarts). Gasoline is dispensed by the US gallon, which is about 20% less than the Imperial gallon. Pints and quarts are also 20% less than Imperial ones. Refer to the chart on the inside back cover to make conversions to metric measurements.

LAUNDRY
There are self-service, coin-operated laundry facilities in most towns of any size and in better campgrounds. Washing a load costs about $1.50 and drying it another $1.50 to $2. Some laundries have attendants who will wash, dry and fold your clothes for you for an additional charge.

HEALTH
For most foreign visitors no immunizations are required for entry, though cholera and yellow fever vaccinations may be required of travelers from areas with a history of those diseases. There are no unexpected health dangers, excellent medical attention is readily available, and the only real health concern is cost: A collision with the medical system can cause severe injuries to your financial state.

Hospitals and medical centers, walk-in clinics and referral services are easily found throughout the region.

In a serious emergency, call ☎ 911 for an ambulance to take you to the nearest hospital's emergency room.

Predeparture Planning
Make sure you're healthy before you start traveling. If you are embarking on a long trip, make sure your teeth are in good shape. If you wear glasses, take a spare pair and your prescription. If you require a particular medication, take an adequate supply and bring a prescription in case you lose your medication.

Health Insurance A travel insurance policy to cover theft, lost tickets and medical problems is a very good idea, especially in the USA where some hospitals will refuse you care without evidence of insurance. There are a wide variety of policies and your travel agent will have recommendations. International student travel policies handled by STA Travel and other student travel organizations are usually a good value.

Some policies specifically exclude 'dangerous activities' like scuba diving, motorcycling and even trekking. Check the fine print, and if these activities are on your agenda, avoid this sort of policy. Also check whether the policy covers ambulance fees or an emergency flight home.

You may prefer a policy that pays doctors or hospitals directly, rather than you having to pay first and claim later. If you have to claim later, keep *all* documentation, and check to see what type of details your insurance provider will require, which sometimes includes proof of the currency exchange rate on the day of your medical visit. Some policies ask you to call back (reverse charges) to a center in your home country for an immediate assessment of your problem.

Food & Water
Care in what you eat and drink is the most important health rule; stomach upsets are the most common travel health problem but the majority of these upsets will be relatively minor. American standards of cleanliness in places serving food and drink are very high.

Bottled drinking water, both carbonated and noncarbonated, is widely available in the USA. Tap water is almost always OK to drink; ask locally.

Everyday Health
Normal body temperature is 98.6°F or 37°C; more than 4°F or 2°C higher indicates a 'high' fever. The normal adult pulse rate is 60 to 80 per minute (children 80 to 100, babies 100 to 140). You should know how to take a temperature and a pulse rate.

Respiration (breathing) rate is also an indicator of illness. Count the number of breaths per minute: Between 12 and 20 is normal for adults and older children (up to 30 for younger children, 40 for babies). People with a high fever or serious respiratory illness (like pneumonia) breathe more quickly than normal.

Environmental Hazards
Altitude Sickness This is something to particularly watch out for in this region. Acute mountain sickness (AMS) occurs at high altitudes and can be fatal. In the thinner atmosphere of the high mountains,

Medical Kit Check List

The following is a list of items you should consider including in your medical kit – consult your pharmacist for brands available in your country.

❑ **Aspirin or paracetamol** (acetaminophen in the USA) – for pain or fever

❑ **Antihistamine** – for allergies (eg, hay fever); to ease the itch from insect bites or stings; and to prevent motion sickness

❑ **Cold and flu tablets, throat lozenges and nasal decongestant**

❑ **Multivitamins** – consider for long trips, when your dietary vitamin intake may be inadequate

❑ **Antibiotics** – consider including these if you're traveling well off the beaten track; see your doctor, as they must be prescribed, and carry the prescription with you

❑ **Loperamide or diphenoxylate** – 'blockers' for diarrhea

❑ **Prochlorperazine or metaclopramide** – for nausea and vomiting

❑ **Rehydration mixture** – to prevent dehydration, which may occur, for example, during bouts of diarrhea; particularly important when traveling with children

❑ **Insect repellent, sunscreen, lip balm and eye drops**

❑ **Calamine lotion, sting relief spray or aloe vera** – to ease irritation from sunburn and insect bites or stings

❑ **Antifungal cream or powder** – for fungal skin infections and thrush

❑ **Antiseptic (such as povidone-iodine)** – for cuts and grazes

❑ **Bandages, Band-Aids (plasters) and other wound dressings**

❑ **Water purification tablets or iodine**

❑ **Scissors, tweezers and a thermometer** – note that mercury thermometers are prohibited by airlines

❑ **Syringes and needles** – in case you need injections in a country with medical hygiene problems; ask your doctor for a note explaining why you have them

lack of oxygen causes many individuals to suffer headaches, nausea, nose bleeds, shortness of breath, physical weakness and other symptoms that can lead to very serious consequences, especially if combined with heat exhaustion, sunburn or hypothermia. Most people recover within a few hours or days. If the symptoms persist it is imperative to descend to lower elevations. For mild cases, everyday painkillers such as aspirin will relieve symptoms until the body adapts. Avoid smoking, drinking alcohol, exercising strenuously or eating heavily.

There is no hard and fast rule as to how high is too high: AMS has been fatal at altitudes of 10,000 feet, although it is much more common above 11,500 feet. It is always wise to sleep at a lower altitude than the greatest height reached during the day. A number of other measures can also prevent or minimize AMS:

- Ascend slowly and have frequent rest days, spending two to three nights at each rise of 1000m. If you reach a high altitude by trekking, acclimatization takes place gradually and you are less likely to be affected than if you fly directly to high altitude.
- Drink extra fluids. Mountain air is dry and cold and you lose moisture as you breathe.
- Eat light, high-carbohydrate meals for more energy.
- Avoid alcohol, which may increase the risk of dehydration.
- Avoid sedatives.

Heat Exhaustion Dehydration or salt deficiency can cause heat exhaustion. This can especially be a problem during the dry, hot summer in the Rocky Mountain region, particularly the lower elevations.

Take time to acclimatize to high temperatures and make sure that you get enough liquids. Salt deficiency is characterized by fatigue, lethargy, headaches, giddiness and muscle cramps. Salt tablets may help. Vomiting or diarrhea can also deplete your liquid and salt levels. Always carry and use a water bottle on long trips.

Heatstroke Long, continuous periods of exposure to high temperatures can leave you vulnerable to this serious, sometimes fatal, condition, which occurs when the body's heat-regulating mechanism breaks down and body temperature rises to dangerous levels. Avoid excessive alcohol intake or strenuous activity when you first arrive in a hot climate.

Symptoms include feeling unwell, lack of perspiration and a high body temperature of 102°F to 105°F (39°C to 41°C). Hospitalization is essential for extreme cases, but meanwhile get out of the sun, remove clothing, cover with a wet sheet or towel and fan continually.

Hypothermia Changeable weather at high altitudes can leave you vulnerable to exposure. After dark, temperatures in the mountains or desert can drop from balmy to below freezing; likewise, a sudden soaking and high winds can lower your body temperature too rapidly. If possible, avoid traveling alone; partners are more likely to avoid hypothermia successfully. If you must travel alone, especially when hiking, be sure someone knows your route and when you expect to return.

Seek shelter when bad weather is unavoidable. Both woolen clothing and synthetics, which retain warmth even when wet, are superior to cottons. A quality sleeping bag is a worthwhile investment. Carry high-energy, easily digestible snacks like chocolate or dried fruit.

Get hypothermia victims out of the wind or rain, remove their clothing if it's wet and replace it with dry, warm clothing. Give them hot liquids – not alcohol – and high-calorie, easily digestible food. In advanced stages it may be necessary to place victims in warm sleeping bags and get in with them. Do not rub victims but place them near a fire or, if possible, in a warm (not hot) bath.

Sunburn In the Rocky Mountains' high altitude areas it can take as little as 10 minutes to get a painful sunburn. Be sure to take along a powerful sunscreen and apply to any exposed areas before hiking, biking, skiing or engaging in any outdoor activities. A hat is also a good idea, and zinc cream offers extra protection for your nose and lips.

Infectious Diseases

Diarrhea A change of water, food or climate can cause the runs; diarrhea caused by contaminated food or water is more serious, but it's unlikely in the USA. Despite all your precautions you may still have a mild bout of traveler's diarrhea from unfamiliar food or drink. Dehydration is the main danger with any diarrhea, particularly for children, who can dehydrate quite quickly. Fluid replacement remains the mainstay of management. With severe diarrhea, a rehydrating solution is necessary to replace minerals and salts. Such solutions, like Pedialyte, are available at pharmacies.

Giardiasis Commonly known as Giardia, this intestinal parasite is present in contaminated water. Giardia routinely contaminates apparently pristine rushing streams in the backcountry, so avoid drinking from them unless you have an advanced filter system: it's just not worth the risk.

Symptoms are stomach cramps, nausea, a bloated stomach, watery, foul-smelling diarrhea and frequent gas. Giardia can appear several weeks after exposure to the parasite; symptoms may disappear for a few days and then return, a pattern that may continue. Tinidazole, known as Fasigyn, or metronidazole (Flagyl) are the recommended drugs for treatment. Either can be used in a single treatment dose. Antibiotics are useless.

Hepatitis This is a general term for inflammation of the liver. There are many causes of this condition: Poor sanitation, contact with infected blood products, drug and alcohol use and contact with an infected person are but a few. The symptoms are fever, chills, headache, fatigue and feelings of weakness and aches and pains, followed by loss of appetite, nausea, vomiting, abdominal pain, dark urine, light-colored feces and jaundiced skin. The whites of the eyes may also turn yellow. Hepatitis A is the most common strain. You should seek medical advice, but there is not much you can do apart from resting, drinking lots of fluids, eating lightly and avoiding fatty foods and alcohol.

HIV/AIDS The Human Immunodeficiency Virus (HIV) develops into AIDS, Acquired Immune Deficiency Syndrome, which is almost always a fatal disease. Any exposure to infected blood, blood products or body fluids may put the individual at risk. The disease is most often transmitted through sexual contact with an infected person or from dirty needles – vaccinations, acupuncture, tattooing and body piercing can be potentially as dangerous as intravenous drug use.

Fear of HIV infection should never preclude treatment for serious medical conditions. A good resource for help and information is the US Centers for Disease Control AIDS hotline (☎ 800-342-2437, 800-344-7432 in Spanish). AIDS support groups are listed in the front of phone books.

Cuts, Bites & Stings

Bites & Stings Bee and wasp stings and nonpoisonous spider bites are usually more painful than dangerous. Calamine lotion will give relief, and ice packs will reduce the pain and swelling. Bites are best avoided by not using bare hands to turn over rocks or large pieces of wood.

Cuts & Scratches Skin punctures can easily become infected in the backcountry, especially if you're sweating or getting dirty. Treat any cut with an antiseptic such as Betadine. When possible avoid bandages, which can keep wounds wet.

Poison Oak Just brushing past this plant while on a hike can cause a blistery and extremely itchy rash on bare skin, which should be washed with a strong soap immediately after exposure. Cortisone creams can lessen the itching in minor cases. Poison oak, related to poison ivy, is a tall, thin shrub with shiny three-part leaves that grows in shady, moist areas.

Rattlesnakes These are common in the desert, the plains and even in some elevated forest areas. To minimize chances of being bitten, always wear boots, socks and long trousers when walking through undergrowth where snakes may be present. Keep your hands out of holes and crevices, and be cautious when collecting firewood.

Though painful, rattlesnake bites do not cause instantaneous death and rarely kill healthy adults, and antivenin is usually available. Keep the victim calm and still, wrap the bitten limb tightly, as you would for a sprained ankle, and then attach a splint to immobilize it. Seek medical help; tourniquets and sucking out the poison are now discredited methods.

Ticks These parasitic arachnids may be present in brush, forest and grasslands, where hikers often get them on their legs or in their boots. Always check your body for ticks after walking through a high grass or thickly forested area. The adults suck blood from hosts by burying their head into skin, but they are often found unattached and can simply be brushed off. However, if you try to brush one off but leave the head in your skin, it increases the likelihood of infection or disease.

If you do find a tick on you, remove it immediately. Using a pair of tweezers, grab it by the head and gently pull it straight out – do not twist it. (If no tweezers are available, use your fingers, but protect them from contamination with a piece of tissue or paper.) Do not touch the tick with a hot object like a match or a cigarette – this can cause it to regurgitate noxious gut substances or saliva into the wound. And do not rub oil, alcohol or petroleum jelly on it. If you get sick in the next couple of weeks, consult a doctor.

The Colorado Tick Fever virus is spread by the Rocky Mountain wood tick, which, despite the name of the disease, may be found outside of Colorado. Anywhere from one to 300 cases are reported each year. The sickness has a three- to five-day incubation period and lasts five to 10 days on average for those ages eight to 30, and up to three weeks for those older than 30. Symptoms include head and body aches, lethargy, nausea and vomiting, sensitivity to light, abdominal pain and a skin rash (rare). There is no vaccine, treatment is by antibiotics, and 20% of cases require hospitalization if lasting as long as three weeks.

Rocky Mountain Spotted Fever is rare in Colorado, but may be found in outlying areas and is caused by *Rickettsia rickessii* bacteria carried by the Rocky Mountain wood tick. A two- to four-day incubation period will result with symptoms like fever, spotted rash on the wrists, ankles or waist that may spread over the entire body, headache, nausea, vomiting and abdominal pain. All symptoms but fever may or may not occur, and muscle cramping is also possible. More severe problems can also develop. Treatment consists of doses of antibiotics and 20% of cases left untreated end in death. If symptoms appear after 12 hours of being in the woods, seek medical attention immediately.

WOMEN TRAVELERS

Women often face different situations when traveling than men do. Women, especially those traveling alone, need a little extra awareness of their surroundings.

The US is such a diverse and varied country that it is impossible to give advice that fits every place and every situation. People are generally friendly and happy to help travelers, and women travelers usually have a wonderful time unmarred by dangerous encounters.

Safety Precautions

Exercise more vigilance in neighborhoods and areas that are reported to have high crime rates. When you go into or through 'unsafe' areas, it is best to travel in a private vehicle (eg, car or taxi). Traveling is more dangerous at night, but crimes do occur in the daytime. Always look confident and act as if you know where you are going.

The threat of sexual assault exists both in cities and in rural areas. Some men might see you as vulnerable if you are drinking, using drugs or traveling alone, so you might choose not to do those things. Try to avoid hiking or camping alone, especially in unfamiliar places. Exercise common sense and communicate honestly, assertively and clearly.

Men may interpret a woman drinking alone in a bar as a bid for male company, whether you intend it that way or not. If the company is unwelcome, most men respect a firm, but polite, 'No thank you.' Be aware of Rohypnol or 'roofies,' a drug that can be slipped into drinks and cause blackouts.

Do not hitchhike alone, and do not pick up hitchhikers when driving alone. If you get stuck on the road and need help, it is a good idea to have a premade sign to signal for help. Avoid getting out of your car to flag down help. Stay inside, lock the doors, turn on the hazard lights and wait for the police to arrive. Carry the telephone number for AAA emergency road service if you are a member. When traveling in remote areas where help may not be readily available, you may want to carry a cellular telephone.

To deal with potential dangers, many women protect themselves with a whistle, mace, cayenne pepper spray or some sort of self-defense training. Remember to have a 'get-away' plan in your head at all times. If you decide to carry a spray, contact the local police to find out about regulations. Airlines do not allow sprays on board; carrying them is a federal felony because of their combustible design.

If despite all precautions you are assaulted, you can call the police or ☎ 911, which connects you with the emergency operator. Larger towns and cities usually have rape crisis centers and women's shelters that provide help and support.

Organizations & Resources

The headquarters for the National Organization for Women (NOW; ☎ 202-628-8669), 733 15th St NW, 2nd floor, Washington, DC 20005, is a good resource and can refer you to state and local chapters.
Web site: www.now.org

Planned Parenthood (☎ 212-541-7800), 810 7th Ave, New York, NY 10019, gives referrals to their nationwide clinics and offers advice on medical issues.
Web site: www.plannedparenthood.org

Alternatively, check the yellow pages under 'Women's Organizations & Services' for local telephone numbers and additional resources.

GAY & LESBIAN TRAVELERS

In US cities and on both coasts it is easier for gay men and women to live their lives with a certain amount of openness. As you travel into the middle of the country it is much harder to be open. With the conservatism that prevails in the Rockies, attitudes towards gay people can sometimes be rather primitive. Gay travelers should be careful, *especially* in the rural areas where just the sight of two men or two women holding hands can be received with verbal abuse, or even result in you being bashed.

Gay and lesbian groups are still targeted by conservative groups in Colorado, especially right-wing religious organizations. Violent incidents, such as the 1998 murder of University of Wyoming student Matthew Shepard in Laramie, WY, are reminders that even the more open college towns are not predictable. But at the same time awareness and attitudes have improved, especially in the Denver area, which is home to a vibrant gay community (including the daughter of US Vice President Dick Cheney).

You may search in vain for gay bars in Wyoming, Montana or Idaho, but you will find meetings and events hosted by gay, lesbian, bisexual and transgender groups. These are often associated with universities, so you're most likely to find such groups in college towns like Laramie, Bozeman and Missoula, and Moscow and Boise.

Organizations & Resources

An array of gay and lesbian travel guides are published by Damron Company (☎ 415-255-0404, 800-462-6654), PO Box 422458, San Francisco, CA 94142-2458. Its Web site, www.damron.com, also boasts extensive listings and links. Ferrari Guides is another player in the gay and lesbian travel guide market; look at www.ferrariguides.com.

A useful community resource is the *Gay Yellow Pages* (☎ 212-674-0120), PO Box 533, Village Station, NY 10014-0533, which has a national edition and also regional editions; look for information at www.glyp.com. Other regional Web sites include www.gayrockymountains.com and www.gaycolorado.com.

In Denver (and some other cities in the Rockies) you can pick up copies of the lesbian and gay *Pink Pages,* which lists gay-supportive businesses in the region. You can also find the list at www.pinkweb.com. Another business directory for the gay-friendly community is the *Rainbow List,* published by Rainbow Planet Inc (☎ 303-443-7768), PO Drawer 2270, Boulder, CO 80306-2270; the directory's Web site is www.rainbowpgs.com.

Equality Colorado (☎ 303-839-5540, 888-557-4441), PO Box 300476, Denver, CO 80203, is more political in nature, and administers the Anti-Violence Project, aimed at curbing both domestic abuse and hate crimes.
Web site: www.equalitycolorado.org

DISABLED TRAVELERS

Public buildings (including hotels, restaurants, theaters and museums) are required by law to be wheelchair accessible and to have accessible restroom facilities. Public transportation services (buses, trains and taxis) must be made accessible to all, including those in wheelchairs, and telephone companies are required to provide relay operators for the hearing impaired. Many banks now provide ATM instructions in Braille and you will find audible crossing signals, as well as dropped curbs, at busier roadway intersections.

Some government agencies and organizations, including the National Park Service, have TTY telephone services for hearing- or speech-impaired persons.

Larger private and chain hotels have suites for disabled guests. Some car rental agencies offer hand-controlled models at no extra charge. All major airlines, Greyhound buses and Amtrak trains allow service animals to accompany passengers, and frequently sell two-for-one packages when attendants of seriously disabled passengers are required.

Visitors to national parks and campgrounds can cut costs greatly by using the Golden Access Passport (see National Parks Passes in the Activities chapter).

Organizations & Resources

A number of organizations and tour providers specialize in the needs of disabled travelers:

Access-Able – This online resource provides useful information for disabled travelers and extensive national and regional links to travel-related organizations and companies.
Web site: www.access-able.com

Mobility International USA – (☎/TTY 541-343-1284, fax 541-343-6812, info@miusa.org), PO Box 10767, Eugene, OR 97440
Web site: www.miusa.org

Moss Rehabilitation Hospital's Travel Information Service – (☎ 215-456-9600, TTY 215-456-9602), 1200 W Tabor Rd, Philadelphia, PA 19141-3099
Web site: www.mossresourcenet.org

Society for the Advancement of Travel for the Handicapped – (SATH; ☎ 212-447-7284), 347 Fifth Ave, No 610, New York, NY 10016
Web site: www.sath.org

SENIOR TRAVELERS

Though the age where benefits begin varies with the attraction, travelers from 50 years and up can expect to receive cut rates and benefits. Be sure to inquire about such rates at hotels, museums and restaurants.

Visitors to national parks and campgrounds can cut costs greatly by using the Golden Age Passport (see National Parks Passes in the Activities chapter).

Organizations & Resources

Some national advocacy groups that can help in planning your travels include the following:

American Association of Retired Persons (AARP; ☎ 800-424-3410), 601 E St NW, Washington, DC 20049
An advocacy group for Americans 50 years and older and a good resource for travel bargains.

US residents can get one-year/three-year memberships for $10/27. Citizens of other countries can get one-year memberships for $10.
Web site: www.aarp.org

Elderhostel (☎ 617-426-8056), 75 Federal St, Boston, MA 02110-1941
A nonprofit organization that offers seniors the opportunity to attend academic college courses throughout the USA and Canada. The programs are open to people 55 years and older and their companions.
Web site: www.elderhostel.com

Grand Circle Travel (☎ 617-350-7500, 800-221-2610, fax 617-350-6206), 347 Congress St, Boston, MA 02210
Offers escorted tours and travel information in a variety of formats and distributes a free useful booklet, 'Going Abroad: 101 Tips for Mature Travelers.'
Web site: www.gct.com

National Council of Senior Citizens (NCSC; ☎ 301-578-8800), 8403 Colesville Rd, suite 1200, Silver Spring, MD 20910-3314
Membership in this group (you needn't be a US citizen to apply) gives access to added Medicare insurance, a mail-order prescription service and a variety of discount information and travel-related advice.
Web site: www.ncscinc.org

TRAVEL WITH CHILDREN

The tourist and visitor market in the four states, especially Colorado, has long catered to families. As a result, there are plentiful attractions and 'family style' restaurants that don't frown upon vocal youngsters and offer children's menus. Smaller motels are generally equipped with extra beds and sometimes cribs, and some of the larger places even have daycare facilities.

Most sights and attractions in the region discount admission for children. If visiting national parks see National Parks Passes in the Activities chapter. During winter, all ski resorts offer children's lift tickets, group lessons for kids and, at larger places, good daycare facilities.

There isn't much of a break for air transportation, although most airlines allow kids younger than 2 years of age to fly free if they sit on a parent's lap. Car rental agencies are not required by law to provide car seats, but if you're traveling with infants,

renting them is highly recommended. Seats cost around $7 to $10 per day.

For information on enjoying travel with the young ones, read *Travel With Children* (1995) by Lonely Planet cofounder Maureen Wheeler.

USEFUL ORGANIZATIONS

For information on state-specific groups, check under the information section of the relevant state chapters.

American Automobile Association

For its members, AAA ('Triple A') provides great travel information, distributes free road maps and guide books, and sells American Express traveler's checks without commission. The AAA membership card will often get you discounts for accommodations, car rental and admission charges. If you plan to do a lot of driving – even in a rental car – it is usually worth joining AAA. It costs around $65 for the first year and $45 for subsequent years.

Members of other auto clubs, like the Automobile Association in the UK, are entitled to the same services if they bring their membership cards and/or a letter of introduction.

AAA also provides emergency roadside service to members in the event of an accident, breakdown or locking your keys in the car. Service is free within a given radius of the nearest service center, and service providers will tow your car to a mechanic if they can't fix it. The nationwide toll-free roadside assistance number is ☎ 800-222-4357. All major cities and many smaller towns have a AAA office where you can sign-up for membership, or you can join via its Web site at www.aaa.com.

Nature Conservancy

With a mission to protect the rarest living things for future generations, the Nature Conservancy has purchased many Rocky Mountain properties with unique natural attributes. Most of the sites are accessible to visitors and offer organized field tours; some offer accommodations as well. The Colorado office for the Nature Conservancy

(☎ 303-444-2985) is at 1881 Ninth St, suite 200, Boulder, CO 80302. The Wyoming Field Office (☎ 307-332-2971) is at 258 Main St, suite 200, Lander, WY 82520. In Montana (☎ 406-443-0303) they are at 32 S Ewing, Helena, MT 59601. The Idaho Field Office (☎ 208-726-3007) can be reached at PO Box 165, Sun Valley, ID 83353.
Web site: www.tnc.org

DANGERS & ANNOYANCES
Personal Security & Theft
Although street crime is a serious issue in large urban areas, visitors need not be obsessed with security. Taking a few sensible precautions should help ensure your safety and prevent theft.

Always lock cars and put valuables out of sight, whether you are in a town or in the remote backcountry. Be aware of your surroundings and who may be watching you. Avoid walking on dimly lit streets at night, particularly when alone. Walk purposefully. Avoid unnecessary displays of money or jewelry. Divide money and credit cards to avoid losing everything.

In hotels, don't leave valuables lying around your room. Use safety-deposit boxes or at least place valuables in a locked bag. Don't open your door to strangers.

Street People The USA has a lamentable record in dealing with its most unfortunate citizens, who often roam the streets of large cities in the daytime and sleep by storefronts, under freeways or in alleyways and abandoned buildings.

This problem is less acute in the Rocky Mountain states compared with urban areas on both coasts, but it is certainly not absent. Street people and panhandlers may approach visitors in the larger cities and towns; nearly all of them are harmless. It's an individual judgment call whether it's appropriate to offer them money or anything else. Some Americans, if they decide to give, choose to offer food to ensure their donation won't be spent on drugs or booze.

Guns The USA has a widespread reputation, partly true but also propagated and ex-

aggerated by the media, as a dangerous place because of the availability of firearms. It is true that many rural residents in the Rocky Mountain states carry guns (sometimes displayed on a rack mounted inside the rear window of their pickup truck), but they most often target animals or isolated traffic signs, rather than humans, so don't be too alarmed. However, care should be taken when hiking during the hunting season (see Hunting in the following section).

Recreational Hazards
In wilderness areas the consequences of an accident can be very serious, so inform someone of your route and expected time of return.

Wildlife As more and more people spend time in the backcountry or impinge on wildlife habitat, attacks on humans and pets are becoming more common especially in Colorado, where tourism and immigration are both booming. Black bears, grizzly bears and pumas (mountain lions) are the most serious hazards, but seemingly placid and innocuous beasts like bison and mule deer are equally capable of inflicting serious injury or even fatal wounds on unsuspecting tourists. Keep your distance from all wild animals – even prairie dogs and squirrels, both of which can transmit disease.

Mining Ruins Many recreational areas, including parts of some national parks, were once mining sites and may contain a variety of hazards, including but not limited to open mine shafts, deadly gases, decayed timbers, hazardous chemicals and radioactivity. Such hazards are usually, but not invariably, posted against trespass. Err on the side of caution.

Hunting One needs to be extra alert when heading into the backcountry during hunting season, generally between late September and early December. During this time hunters from all across the country descend on the Rocky Mountain states to hunt, mainly for deer and elk. While locals are usually quite skilled, visiting hunters

Bears

Travelers in the Rocky Mountain states need to beware of bears, which can be unpredictable and potentially dangerous animals when humans invade their habitat. Whether camping in a developed site or hiking in the backcountry, visitors to this region need to avoid contact with both black and grizzly (brown) bears.

It can be helpful to learn the difference between brown bears and black bears since the two do not behave in exactly the same way (adult grizzlies, for example, can't climb trees very well, but black bears can). You can't rely on color alone – black bears also come in various shades of brown, and some brown bears look almost black. Instead, look for the distinguishing hump on the grizzly's shoulder as well as long claws and the wide, dish-shaped face. Grizzlies also tend to be quite a bit bigger than black bears.

The main causes of human-bear conflict arise from the animal's instinctual protection of its young, the presence of food and surprise encounters.

Bears do not see well. However, they have an extremely keen sense of smell and are attracted not just to food, but to other potentially pungent items such as toothpaste, lotions, perfumes and deodorants. When camping, clean up and pack out garbage and spilled food, use bear-proof canisters for storage, and 'bear-bag' your food and toiletries by suspending them from a tree limb away from your sleeping area, at least 10 feet from the ground and 4 feet from the trunk. In some national parks and USFS wilderness areas, there are simple food and meat storage facilities – usually a pole between two trees that backpackers can use to hang food. Backpackers should carry a 50-foot length of cord or rope in order to take advantage of these facilities. Some developed campgrounds provide barrels or bear-resistant metal boxes, but in other areas campers should always lock their food safely within the car.

Bears live a sedentary life and will typically avoid contact if given sufficient warning of approaching individuals. Make noise, stay out of prime habitat and always make every effort to avoid placing yourself between a sow and her young. The largest bear populations are found in areas of Gambel oak and aspen and near chokecherry and serviceberry bushes, whose berries are well liked by bears.

With the increasing popularity of mountain biking, the odds of surprising a bear are that much greater. Bear bells have been the favorite noisemaking deterrent for many years, but rangers report that the human voice is also effective (show tunes seem to work especially well).

There are several theories, none of them guaranteed, as to what to do if you encounter a bear. Back away slowly out of the bear's path, avoiding eye contact, and wave your hands above your head slowly (humans are the only creatures, besides apes, able to do this) to let the bear know you aren't another animal.

Another tactic is to leave something on the ground (a hat, backpack, water bottle) between you and the bear to distract it if it charges. If a bear does charge, do not run (bears can sprint up to 40mph for short distances), and *do not scream* (that may frighten the bear, making it more aggressive). Drop to the ground and crouch into a ball, covering the back of your neck with your hands, and your chest and stomach with your knees. Do not resist the bear's inquisitive pawing – it may get bored and go away.

If a bear comes to your camp at night or any other time move your camp immediately. Climbing a tree is one alternative. Red pepper spray (or capsicum) is sold as a mace-like self-defense weapon against bears.

The above guidelines are by no means complete and cannot cover every possible bear situation. For more information, contact the NPS or the USFS.

who get out only once a year can be jumpy, and less selective in their targets than one might hope.

Most hunting takes place on national forest or BLM land. During hunting season always wear bright colors when in the backcountry, and be sure to check with local forest rangers to see if there are any areas best avoided.

Natural Hazards

Flash floods are a serious hazard in the desert backcountry and even on paved highways. If bad weather is threatening, seek high ground away from watercourses, which can fill instantly with runoff. Wait for low water before you attempt to cross any swollen stream. If your vehicle becomes stuck under such conditions, abandon it rather than risk drowning.

While the Rocky Mountain region is less famous for seismic activity than is California, earthquakes are not unknown. Montana's 1959 Hebgen Lake quake, which altered many of the main thermal features in Yellowstone National Park, measured a powerful 7.5 on the Richter scale.

Avalanches The Rocky Mountain region, particularly Colorado, witnesses dozens of avalanches every winter. Even if you've had avalanche training and are equipped with locator beacons, chances of surviving a big slide are minimal. Check with local authorities and the forest service before heading out to do any backcountry skiing, snowshoeing or camping.

Lightning Electrical storms are common in the Rocky Mountain high country, especially in summer. Lightning strikes humans fairly rarely, but it is a serious hazard. When in exposed areas, always keep an eye on the weather to see if any storms are developing, and bear in mind the distance and route to more sheltered terrain.

EMERGENCIES

Throughout the USA dial ☎ 911 for emergency service of any sort. This is a free call from any phone.

Each state also maintains telephone numbers for road conditions, traffic information and other emergencies, including the following:

Colorado State Patrol	☎ 303-239-4501
Colorado Road Report	☎ 303-639-1234
Wyoming State Patrol	☎ 307-777-4321, ☎ 800-442-9090 (in-state only)
Wyoming Road Report	☎ 307-733-9966, ☎ 800-332-6171 (in-state only)
Montana State Patrol	☎ 800-525-5555
Montana Road Report	☎ 800-226-7623
Idaho State Patrol	☎ 208-334-2900
Idaho Road Report	☎ 208-336-6600, ☎ 888-432-7623 (in-state only)

Carry a photocopy of your passport separately from your passport. Copy the pages with your photo and personal details, passport number and US visa. If it is lost or stolen, this will make replacing it easier. In this event, you should call your embassy. See Copies under Visas & Documents, earlier.

Similarly, carry copies of your traveler's check numbers and credit card numbers separately.

LEGAL MATTERS

If you are stopped by the police for any reason, bear in mind there is no system of paying fines on the spot. For traffic offenses, the police officer will explain your options to you. Attempting to pay the fine to the officer may compound your troubles by resulting in a charge of bribery.

If you are arrested for more serious offenses, you are allowed to remain silent. There is no legal reason to speak to a police officer if you don't wish to, but never walk away from an officer until given permission. All persons who are arrested are legally allowed (and given) the right to make one phone call. If you don't have a lawyer or family member to help you, call your embassy. The police will give you the number upon request.

Driving Laws

Each state has its own laws; what is legal in one state may be illegal in others.

Some general rules are that you must be at least 16 years of age to drive. Speed limits are generally 65mph to 75mph on interstates and freeways unless otherwise posted. Speed limits on other highways are 55mph or less, and in cities can vary from 25 to 45mph. You can drive 5mph over the limit without much likelihood of being pulled over, but if you're doing 10mph over the limit, you'll be caught sooner or later. Watch for school zones, which can be as low as 15mph during school hours – these limits are strictly enforced. Seat belts and motorcycle helmets must be worn in most states.

You could incur stiff fines, jail time and other unpleasant penalties if caught driving under the influence of alcohol.

Trespassing

Most landowners will enforce their own trespassing laws without getting the police involved. If you refuse to leave their land it's another story. Fines for trespassing usually don't exceed $500 and imprisonment in the county jail for the offense will not be longer than six months, but usually you'll just get fined $100 and escorted out of the county.

Landowners are required by law to mark no-trespassing zones by posting a notice or painting in fluorescent paint on a post, structure or natural object.

BUSINESS HOURS

Shops, offices and restaurants generally stay open from 9 am to 5 pm, but there are certainly no hard and fast rules. In some large cities, certain supermarkets and restaurants are open 24 hours. Shops are usually open from 9 or 10 am to 5 or 6 pm (often until 9 pm in shopping malls), except Sunday when hours are noon to 5 pm.

Post offices are open weekdays from 8 am to 4 or 5:30 pm, and some are open from 8 am to 1 pm on Saturday. Banks are usually open weekdays from 9 am to 5 or 6 pm. A few banks are open from 9 am to 2 or 4 pm on Saturday. Basically hours are decided by individual branches, so if you need specifics call the relevant branch.

PUBLIC HOLIDAYS & SPECIAL EVENTS

On national public holidays, banks, schools and government offices are closed and transportation, museums and other services are on Sunday schedules. Holidays falling on weekends are usually observed the following Monday.

January

New Year's Day, January 1

Dr Martin Luther King Jr Day, 3rd Monday of the month

February

Presidents' Day, 3rd Monday of the month

April

Easter, on a Sunday usually in early April, sometimes in late March

May

Memorial Day, last Monday of the month

July

Independence Day, July 4

September

Labor Day, 1st Monday of the month

October

Columbus Day, 2nd Monday of the month

November

Veterans' Day, November 11

Thanksgiving Day, 4th Thursday of the month

December

Christmas Day, December 25

Besides the above public holidays, the USA celebrates a number of other events linked to culture, religion or society. Here are some of the most widely observed ones:

February

Valentine's Day, February 14. Lovers and spouses celebrate romance with greeting cards, gifts and romantic dinners.

March

St Patrick's Day, March 17. The patron saint of Ireland is honored by all those who feel the Irish in their blood, are inclined to don green garb or down beer.

April

Passover, either in April or March, depending on the Judaic calendar. Families join to honor persecuted forebears and partake in the symbolic seder dinner.

May

Cinco de Mayo, May 5. The day the Mexicans wiped out the French Army in 1862 is now occasion for Americans to eat Mexican food and drink margaritas.

October

Halloween, October 31. Kids and adults dress in costumes: The former go 'trick-or-treating' for candy, the latter to parties to act out their alter egos.

November

Day of the Dead, November 2. Mexicans honor dead relatives.

Election Day, 2nd Tuesday in November.

December

Hanukkah, spans eight days of the month as set by Judaic calendar.

Kwanzaa, December 26 to 31. African-American celebration to give thanks for the harvest.

New Year's Eve, December 31.

Throughout the year, but especially in summer, residents of the Rockies celebrate a variety of local and regional cultural festivals. Some of the more worthwhile are listed here.

Dates for the following events may vary from year to year – local tourist information offices will have exact dates. For details on each event, see individual geographical entries.

Colorado

January

The *Ullr Fest* and the *International Snow Sculpture Championship* are held in Breckenridge. The *National Western Stock Show & Rodeo* takes place in Denver.

February

Steamboat Springs Winter Carnival takes place in Steamboat Springs.

March

The *American Ski Classic* is held in Vail.

April

Taste of Vail happens in Vail.

May

The *Kinetic Conveyance Parade and Challenge* takes place in Boulder. *Cinco de Mayo* festivities happen in Boulder, Denver, Fort Collins, Grand Junction, Greeley, Pueblo and Trinidad. The *Iron Horse Bicycle Classic* is held in Durango. *Bluegrass on the River* occurs in Pueblo.

June

It's a busy month with the *Aspen Music Festival* in Aspen, the *Colorado Brewers Festival* in Fort Collins, the *Colorado Stampede Rodeo* in Grand Junction, the *Greeley Independence Stampede* in Greeley, *FIBArk Boat Race* in Salida, the *Telluride Bluegrass Festival* in Telluride and the *Santa Fe Trail Festival* in Trinidad.

July

Mid-summer events include *Dance Aspen* in Aspen, the *Colorado Shakespeare Festival* in Boulder, the *Breckenridge Festival of Music* and *Jazz in July* in Breckenridge, *Pikes Peak International Hill Climb* (an auto race) in Colorado Springs, *Aerial Weekend* and *Fat Tire Bike Week* in Crested Butte, *Steamboat Cowboy Roundup Days* and *Steamboat Springs Rainbow Weekend* in Steamboat Springs and *Bravo! Colorado Music Festival* in Vail.

August

Events held in August include *Pikes Peak or Bust Rodeo* and *Pikes Peak Marathon* in Colorado Springs, *New West Fest* in Fort Collins, *Mesa County Fair* in Grand Junction, *Boom Days Celebration* in Leadville, the *Rockygrass Bluegrass Festival* in Lyons, the *Colorado State Fair* in Pueblo, *Steamboat Vintage Auto Race* in Steamboat, the *Telluride Jazz Celebration* in Telluride and *Jazz in the Sangres* in Westcliffe.

September

Summer winds down with the *Aspen Filmfest* in Aspen, the *Breckenridge Festival of Film* in Breckenridge, *A Taste of Colorado* in Denver and the *Colorado Mountain Winefest* in Grand Junction. *Oktoberfest* festivities begin in Breckenridge, Fort Collins and Glenwood Springs.

October

Oktoberfest is celebrated in La Veta and other towns.

Wyoming

January & February

The 12-day *International Rocky Mountain Stage Stop Sled Dog Race* starts in late January. *Cutter races* on ice take place in Afton all winter long.

July

Summer events include the *Central Wyoming Fair & Rodeo* in Casper, *Cheyenne Frontier Days* in June and July in Cheyenne, the *Cody Stampede* in Cody, the *International Climbers' Festival* in Lander, *Laramie Jubilee Days* in Laramie, the *Green River Rendezvous* in Pinedale, the *1838 Mountain Man Rendezvous* and the *Hot Air Balloon Rally* in Riverton, *Desert Balloon Extravaganza* in Rock Springs and the *Grand Teton Music Festival* at Teton Village.

August

Buffalo Bill Festival takes place in Cody. The *Wyoming State Fair* is held in Douglas. The *Gift of the Waters Pageant* is in Thermopolis.

September

Events include the *Fort Bridger Mountain Man Rendezvous* at Fort Bridger State Historic Site, and the *Jackson Hole Fall Arts Festival* in Jackson.

October

PRCA Rodeo Finals are held in Casper.

Montana

February

St Patrick's Day Parade and festivities are held in Butte.

April

The *International Wildlife Film Festival* takes place in Missoula.

May

The *Miles City Bucking Horse Sale* is a highlight in Miles City.

June

The *Lewis and Clark Festival* comes to Great Falls, and *Little Bighorn Days* happens in Hardin.

July

Events include *Bannack Days* in Bannack, *Libby Logger Days* in Libby (third weekend), the *Miles City Hot Air Balloon Round-Up* in Miles City and the *Home of the Champions Rodeo* in Red Lodge on the weekend closest to July 4th. The *Flathead Valley Music Festival* comes to Flathead Valley in late July through mid-August.

August

The *Festival of Arts* is held in Big Fork. The *Crow Fair & Rodeo* is in Crow Agency on the third weekend. The *Montana Cowboy Poetry Gathering* comes to Lewistown. The *Festival of Nations* takes place in Red Lodge. The *Commemoration of the Battle of Big Hole* in Big Hole is on the second Saturday.

October

The *Bald Eagle Migration* can be seen in Helena in late October and early November.

Idaho

January & February

The *McCall Annual Winter Carnival* takes place in late January and early February. The *Lionel Hampton Jazz Festival* comes to Moscow in late February.

June

The *National Old Time Fiddlers Contest* is held in Weiser during the third full week of June. The *Boise River Festival* happens in late June.

July

The *San Inazio Basque Festival* is in Boise.

August

Events include the *Western Idaho Fair* in Boise, the *Shoshone-Bannock Indian Festival* on the Fort Hall Indian Reservation and the *Festival at Sandpoint* in Sandpoint.

September

The *Lewiston Roundup* takes place in Lewiston.

WORK

Plenty of seasonal work is possible in national parks and other tourist sites, especially ski areas; for information, contact park concessionaires or local chambers of commerce.

Some of the best places to hunt for seasonal work in the Rocky Mountain states are the larger resort towns (like Aspen, CO; Big Sky, MT; Jackson Hole, WY; and Sun Valley, ID) and heavily visited gateway towns to the popular national parks, such as Estes Park, CO; West Yellowstone, MT; and Whitefish, MT.

If you're not a US citizen, you'll need to apply for a work visa from the US embassy in your home country before you leave. Although in practice many foreigners get work in the US illegally, be forewarned that if caught the penalties can be quite severe: deportation at the very least, and possibly a stiff fine as well.

ACCOMMODATIONS

The spectrum of accommodations in the Rockies ranges from campgrounds and hostels to simple motels, B&Bs and five-star luxury hotels, as well as that uniquely Western institution, the 'guest' or 'dude' ranch. You should be able to find something reasonably priced in most areas.

Camping

Camping is the cheapest, and in many ways the most enjoyable, approach to a vacation. Visitors with a car and a tent can take advantage of hundreds of private and public campgrounds and RV parks at prices of $10 per night or even less.

Public Campgrounds These are on public lands such as national forests, state and national parks and BLM lands. Free dispersed camping (meaning you can camp almost anywhere) is permitted in many public backcountry areas. Sometimes you can camp right from your car along a dirt road, especially in BLM and national forest areas. In other places, you can backpack your gear into a cleared campsite.

Information and detailed maps are available from many local ranger stations or BLM offices (addresses and telephone numbers are given in the text) and may be posted along the road. Sometimes, a free camping permit is required, particularly in national parks, less so in forests and BLM areas.

When camping in an undeveloped area choose a campsite at least 200 yards from water and wash up at camp, not in the stream, using biodegradable soap. Dig a six-inch deep hole to use as a latrine and cover and camouflage it well when leaving the site. Burn toilet paper, unless fires are prohibited. Carry out all trash. Use a portable charcoal grill or camping stove; don't build new fires. If there already is a fire ring, use only dead and downed wood or wood you have carried in yourself. Make sure to leave the campsite as you found it.

Developed areas usually have toilets, drinking water, fire pits (or charcoal grills) and picnic benches. Some don't have drinking water. At any rate, it is always a good idea to have a few gallons of water when camping. These basic campgrounds usually cost about $5 to $10 a night. Some areas have showers or RV hookups and often cost $8 to $20. Costs given in the text for public campgrounds are per site.

National forest and BLM campgrounds are usually less developed, while national park and state park campgrounds are more likely to have more amenities. The less developed sites are often on a 'first-come, first-served' basis, so plan on an early arrival, preferably during the week, as sites fill up fast on Friday and weekends. More developed areas may accept or require reservations; details are given in the text.

Gas, Food, Lodging

When coming into a city on the highway you will notice signs that say 'Gas Food Lodging' followed by something like 'Next Three Exits.' Don't assume these exits will lead you directly into the city center – they won't. You'll end up traveling along strips of chain motels, fast-food restaurants and gas stations with small grocery stores. If you have no intention of staying in town, but would rather catch a few hours' sleep and head out early on the road, these establishments do provide a cheap alternative to downtown and they are a bit of true Americana.

Private Campgrounds These are on private property and usually are close to or in a town. Most are designed with RVs in mind; tenters can camp but fees are at least several dollars higher than in public campgrounds. Fees given in the text are most often for two people per site with a fee of $1 to $3 for each additional person. Some places charge just per vehicle.

Facilities can include hot showers, coin laundry, swimming pool, full RV hookups, games area, a playground and a convenience store. Kampgrounds of America (KOA) is a vast national network of private campgrounds with sites usually ranging from $12 to $22, depending on hookups. You can purchase the annual directory of KOA campgrounds ($4) at any KOA, or by calling or writing: KOA (☎ 406-248-7444, fax 406-248-7414), PO Box 30558, Billings, MT 59114-0558.

Web site: www.koa.com

Reservations During peak months of June through September reservations are a good idea, especially at popular national parks like Grand Teton, Rocky Mountain or Yellowstone. To make a reservation, you must pay with a credit card. For sites in national forests call ☎ 800-280-2267. For sites in national parks call the National Park Reservation Service at ☎ 800-365-2267.

Hostels

The US hostel network is less widespread than in Canada, the UK, Europe and Australia and is predominately in the north and coastal parts of the country. Not all hostels are directly affiliated with Hostelling International-American Youth Hostels (HI-AYH). Those that are offer discounts to HI-AYH members and usually allow non-members to stay for a few dollars more. Dormitory beds cost about $10 to $15 a night. Rooms cost $20 to $30 for one or two people.

HI-AYH hostels expect you to rent or carry a sheet or sleeping bag to keep the beds clean. Dormitories are segregated by sex and curfews may exist. Kitchen and laundry privileges are usually available in return for light housekeeping duties. There

are information and advertising boards, TV rooms and lounge areas. Alcohol and smoking may be banned.

Several Rocky Mountain towns sport hostels, mostly in Colorado.

Colorado – Breckenridge, Colorado Springs, Conejos River, Crested Butte, Denver, Durango, Estes Park, Glenwood Springs, Grand Junction, Grand Lake, Nederland, Pitkin, Silverthorne

Wyoming – Jackson, Teton Village

Montana – Bozeman, Cooke City, East Glacier Park, Kalispell, Missoula, Polebridge, St Ignatius, West Yellowstone

Idaho – Gooding, Kellogg, Naples

Reservations are accepted and strongly advised during the high season – there may be a limit of a three-night stay then. You can call HI-AYH's national office (☎ 202-783-6161) to make reservations for any HI-AYH hostel, or use their code-based reservation service at ☎ 800-909-4776 (you need an access code to use this service, available from any HI-AYH office or listed in its handbook).

B&Bs

European visitors should be aware that North American B&Bs aren't usually the casual, inexpensive sort of accommodations found on the Continent or in Britain. While they are usually family-run, many B&Bs in the Rocky Mountain states require advance reservations, though most will be happy to oblige drop-in guests if they have space.

B&B prices include breakfast. The cheapest establishments, with rooms in the $30 to $50 range, may have clean but unexciting rooms with a shared bathroom. Pricier places ($50 to $150 range) have rooms with private baths and sometimes fireplaces and balconies. They may be in historical buildings, quaint country houses or luxurious urban townhouses.

A large majority of B&Bs prohibit smoking.

Motels

Motel accommodations in the Rocky Mountain states run from basic to very comfortable, with a wide range of prices. It's not impossible to find acceptable motel accommodations for as little as $25 per night in towns along I-80 in southwestern Wyoming, but in tourist destinations like Aspen or Jackson even budget chains charge around $60 per night. In general, summer is the peak season and prices can as much as double; the major ski resorts are also expensive in winter.

In general expect to pay $30 to $50 for a double room in most locations; this will usually include telephone, cable TV and a private bathroom with shower or bathtub. Some places even have swimming pools and hot tubs.

Beware of making phone calls directly from your room. Some places charge around 75¢ for local calls versus 25¢ at a pay phone. Long-distance rates are often surcharged by 100 to 200%!

Be prepared to add room tax to quoted prices. Children are often allowed to stay free with their parents, but rules for this vary.

Hotels & Lodges

The best hotel accommodations are in large cities and resort areas. Amenities include restaurants and bars, swimming pools, Jacuzzis, exercise rooms, saunas, room service and concierges.

Dude Ranches

In his book *Dude Ranches and Ponies,* Lawrence B Smith applies the term 'dude' to 'an outsider, city person, or tenderfoot; one who came from another element of society; in short, a stranger as far as the American West and its ways are concerned.' Most people (men and women) who visit dude ranches today are 'dudes' in the truest sense, looking for an escape from a fast-paced, high-tech world.

Dude ranch history dates back to the late 19th century, when the Eaton brothers established a hay and horse ranch near Medora, North Dakota, 80 miles east of Glendive, MT. Family and friends who came from the East by train stayed for months at a time and helped in all of the everyday ranch chores and cattle activities. When one guest asked if he could pay for his room and board, the Eatons saw the potential for a business venture. In 1904 they moved the first dude ranch to the mountains of Wolf, WY, where Eatons' Ranch is currently run by third, fourth and fifth generation family members.

Soon other ranchers got wind of the Eatons' success, and dude ranches sprang up all over the West.

These days you can find anything from a working-ranch experience (smelly chores and 5 am wake-up calls included) to a Western Club Med. Typical weeklong visits start at over $100 per person per day, including accommodations, meals, activities and equipment. A few B&Bs offer dude-ranch experiences, often allowing shorter stays at considerably lower rates.

While the centerpiece of dude ranch vacations is horseback riding, many ranches feature swimming pools and have expanded their activity lists to include fly-fishing, hiking, mountain biking, tennis, golf, skeet-shooting and cross-country skiing. Accommodations range from rustic log cabins to cushy suites with whirlpools and cable TV; meals range from family-style spaghetti dinners to four-course gourmet meals.

For listings, descriptions and contact information for dude ranches throughout the Rockies, try the Dude Ranchers' Association (☎ 970-223-8440), PO Box F-471, Laporte, CO 80535; the association's Web site is www.duderanch.org. For ranches within Colorado, contact the Colorado Dude & Guest Ranch Association (☎ 970-887-3128), PO Box 2120, Granby, CO 80446 or online at www.coloradoranch.com.

In national parks, accommodations are limited to either camping or park lodges. Lodges are often rustic looking but usually quite comfortable. National park lodges are not cheap, with most rooms going for close to $100 for a double during the high season, but they are your only option if you want to stay inside the park without camping. Many lodges are fully booked months in advance, especially during the high season and around holidays, so reserve as soon as your plans are set.

Long-Term Rentals

Houses or condominiums can be rented for anywhere from two days to two months. This type of lodging is most often found in resort areas and almost always includes kitchens and living rooms. Several people can lodge for the same price so long-term can be more economical than motels or hotels on a per person basis for a larger group, especially since you can cook your own food. The chambers of commerce in resort towns will have information on condominium listings and can give advice on renting.

Reservations

The cheapest budget places may not accept reservations, but at least phone from the road to see what's available.

Chain hotels take reservations days or months ahead. Cancellation policies vary – inquire when you book.

Make sure to let the hotel know if you plan on a late arrival – many motels will give your room away if you haven't arrived or called by 6 pm.

Some places, especially B&Bs and some cabins, don't accept credit cards.

FOOD
Mealtimes

Usually served between about 6 am and 10 am, American breakfasts are large and filling, often including eggs, bacon or ham, fried potatoes, toast with butter and jam and coffee or tea. Budget breakfast specials at diner-style places average around $3; fancier spots can run $5 to $8.

Lunch is available from 11 am to 2 pm, when fixed-price specials for as little as $5 are common. Mid-range places average anywhere from $7 to $10, and top-end lunch spots $10 to $15.

Dinners, served anytime between about 5 and 10 pm, are more expensive but often still reasonably priced, and portions are usually large. Budget dinners are around $8; mid-range $10 to $15; top-end $20 to $40 per person.

Regional

Outside urban areas and tourist centers, much of the Rocky Mountain region is a culinary desert dominated by greasy spoon cafes and monotonous chain restaurants. Montana and Wyoming, in particular, are cattle country, where vegetarians may have to hire a detective to find anything besides conventional meat and potatoes.

Buffalo (bison) meat is an increasingly popular alternative to beef for several reasons, one of which is unquestionably its novelty and tourist appeal. At the same time, the bison is a native range animal well adapted to the prairies and plains, as opposed to ecologically exotic beef cattle. Its fat and cholesterol content is also lower than that of beef, making it a healthier dietary choice.

Another regional specialty, Rocky Mountain oysters, is an 'appetizer' that may cause some men to squirm upon learning precisely what a castrated bull has contributed to this dish. Despite the distance from the coast, seafood lovers will delight in the flavor of local freshwater trout, found on menus throughout the region.

Ethnic Fare

A benefit of the great melting pot of the United States is a diversity of ethnic cuisines. Mexican food, of course, predates the US Constitution, and Chinese restaurants have long served the region, but Thai, Vietnamese, Cambodian, Japanese and other Asian foods are more recent arrivals. Italian food is common, while French and similar Continental cuisines are available in some areas.

The most diverse fare is to be found in large cities like Denver and resorts like Steamboat Springs and Aspen, but there are many surprises in unexpected places.

The Hispanic influence – particularly in southern Colorado, in the large cities and in the agricultural areas that attract itinerant Mexican labor – is responsible for a vibrant, flavorful cuisine termed either Mexican, Tex-Mex or Southwest. There are many Mexican cuisines, but the most popular dishes in the Rocky Mountains are derived from the Mexican interior – with a few Southwestern adaptations.

Fruit

Fresh local fruit is a summer and autumn treat. Because of the high altitude and fero-cious winters, hardy fruits like apples and pears are most common, but the more temperate Grand Valley and surrounding areas on the western Colorado Plateau produce excellent peaches, grapes, apricots and cherries.

Self-Catering

Nearly every town of any size has a super-market with a wide variety of fresh and pre-pared foods at reasonable prices; these are good places to stock up on supplies for camping trips, rather than outlying conven-ience stores that may inflate prices.

Some towns have produce or farmers' markets that offer a good selection of fresh fruits and vegetables at very reasonable prices.

Vegetarians in Cattle Country

If you plan on sticking to a strict vegetarian diet while traveling in the Rocky Mountain states, you'll have to get used to two things: grudging looks from local ranchers and baked potatoes. Cattle ranching constitutes much of this area's economy, and if all at once the world turned vege-tarian, many family ranches – in operation for multiple generations – would be left high and dry.

Because most people in the Eastern Plains were raised on beef, many don't understand vege-tarianism. If you ask for a menu item to be made without meat, a server may look at you quizzi-cally, then suggest something like chicken strips or fish as a 'meat-free' alternative. Terms like 'tofu' and 'tempeh' are as foreign to Eastern Plains folk as the soybean products they describe. In big cities, and the western part of the Rocky Mountain states where tourists and college students shed an alternative light on the culinary scene, the options are more plentiful. Pizza parlors are always a good standby, since most offer vegetable pizza toppings.

When a restaurant's menu revolves around beef, often the only option for a veg-etarian is to order a melange of side dishes: salad (ie, a heap of iceberg lettuce topped with a few cherry tomatoes and croutons), potatoes, fried mushrooms, coleslaw. Most soups contain beef or chicken stock, so be sure to ask before laying into a bowl. The surefire dish, available at most restaurants, full of carbohydrates and low in fat (if you refrain from using heaps of butter and sour cream), is the all-American baked potato. People won't even look at you weirdly if that's all you order.

DRINKS

Parts of the Rocky Mountain states were formerly 'dry' and in some Colorado counties only relatively weak 3.2% beer is available. In Wyoming, only bars or liquor stores may sell alcohol; supermarkets may not legally sell beer or wine. The usual hard liquors (spirits), like whisky and gin, are widely available at both bars and liquor stores.

In the past decade the Rocky Mountain states, Colorado in particular, have played an active role in the revival of small breweries and brewpubs. Foreign visitors who still think all American beer is watery should take the time to try some of these microbrews.

Colorado is the only Rocky Mountain state to boast a substantial wine industry, with wineries in and around the town of Palisade, in the Grand Valley, near the city of Grand Junction.

Persons younger than the age of 21 (minors) are prohibited from consuming alcohol in the USA. Carry a driver's license or passport as proof of age to enter a bar, order alcohol at a restaurant, or buy alcohol from a store.

ENTERTAINMENT

The distinction between bars and nightclubs can be academic, but in general a bar is an establishment that serves alcohol (beer, wine and spirits) and may offer live music on occasion, while a nightclub is a more formal venue that depends on live entertainment.

While the video revolution has certainly driven some movie theaters out of business, towns as small as Paonia, CO (population 1400), have managed to keep their cinemas open. The widest selection of movies, however, is available in large cities and resort towns.

The greatest range of theatrical productions is staged in Denver and in university towns like Boulder. Tourist destinations like Jackson, WY, and Creed and Central City, CO, have small local companies and may support summer performances by repertory groups.

SPECTATOR SPORTS

Baseball

The Denver-based Colorado Rockies play on Coors Field, a downtown baseball-only park. The regular season lasts from early April to early October.

Minor league baseball, the Major Leagues' training ground, is also popular. Colorado Springs Sky Sox, the Rockies' top minor league affiliate, play in the Class AAA Pacific Coast League, while several Major League organizations field teams in the short-season Pioneer League, which consists entirely of first-year professionals. Four of the Pioneer League's eight franchises are in Montana: Butte, Billings, Great Falls and Helena. In many ways, the small, intimate parks provide an ideal environment for viewing the sport and seeing future stars on the way up.

Basketball

America's most popular international sport is organized at the professional level as the National Basketball Association (NBA), which has a prolonged season lasting from late October to mid-June. The region's only NBA team is the Denver Nuggets, but university and high school teams attract many spectators in local communities.

Football

American football draws enormous crowds in the fall. The Denver Broncos of the National Football League (NFL) have the region's largest and most fanatical following. The University of Colorado at Boulder is a major college power, and other state universities in Colorado, Wyoming, Montana and Idaho also field teams. Like basketball, high school football is extraordinarily popular in local communities.

Hockey

The Colorado Avalanche, based in Denver, is one of the top-ranked teams in the National Hockey League (NHL).

Soccer

Also Denver-based, the region's major league soccer team is the Colorado Rapids.

Activities

The national parklands, forests and wilderness areas of the Rockies offer some of the world's greatest opportunities to experience natural beauty and native flora and fauna.

This chapter introduces the national parks in the region, and explains other federally regulated areas like national forest and Bureau of Land Management (BLM) lands. Following that is a list of the major outdoor activities that can be enjoyed in this amazing part of the USA.

As well as federal lands, each of the Rocky Mountain states maintains its own system of parks, wildlife areas and reserves that are generally smaller and less diverse than those in the national system. However, they can contain some surprisingly beautiful scenery, and often make for good camping options. Details on state parks are included within the regional and state chapters.

Outdoor Areas

Many visitors find the USA's national parks a major reason for visiting the country. The now global idea of setting aside large, scenic natural areas for posterity dates from the creation of Wyoming's Yellowstone National Park in 1872. The National Park Service (NPS), an agency of the Dept of the Interior, administers several categories of reserves with differing degrees of protection: national parks, national monuments, national recreation areas and national historic sites.

Created only by acts of Congress, national parks are generally large areas that surround spectacular natural features and cover hundreds of square miles. Commercial activities and development within national parks are, in theory, severely restricted. National monuments, by contrast, may be created by presidential order but do not enjoy the same level of protection as national parks; mining and grazing are allowed within them, though such activities generally are regulated. National recreation areas are usually sites with exceptional natural features that have been severely altered, usually by dam projects and large reservoirs. National historic sites are places of special cultural and historical significance, also administered by the National Park Service.

Travelers with little hiking experience will appreciate the well-marked, well-maintained trails in national parks, often with restroom facilities at either end and interpretive displays along the way. To really escape the crowds, head into the more remote backcountry. Most US national parks require overnight hikers to carry backcountry permits, available from visitors centers or ranger stations.

See Organized Tours in the Getting There & Away chapter for information on tours that target the great outdoors.

National Parks Passes

Several types of pass granting unlimited access to fee-charging national parks can be purchased. The passes admit a private vehicle and its passengers, or the passholder, spouse and children at parks where per person fees are imposed.

An annual **National Parks Pass** costs $50 and can be applied for at any fee-charging national park, by calling ☎ 888-GOPARKS (☎ 888-467-2757), or by sending a $50 check or money order (plus $3.95 for shipping) made out to the National Park Service to National Parks Pass, 27540 Avenue Mentry, Valencia, CA 91355. You can also apply online at www.nationalparks.org.

A **Golden Eagle Hologram** (which you affix to your pass) costs an additional $15 and extends access into sites administered by the US Fish & Wildlife Service, the US Forest Service and the Bureau of Land Management. **Golden Age Passports** carry a one-time fee of $10 and allow US residents 62 years and older (and accompanying passengers in a private vehicle) unlimited entry to all sites in the national park system, with 50% discounts on camping and other fees. **Golden Access Passports** offer the same benefits to US residents who are blind or permanently disabled.

Accommodations

A range of places to stay can be found in and around national parks. Campground and reservations information can be obtained by calling the National Park Reservation System (☎ 800-365-2267) or writing to National Park Service Public Inquiry, Dept of Interior, PO Box 37127, Washington, DC 20013-7127. Online information is available at www.nps.gov.

NATIONAL PARKS & OTHER FEDERAL LANDS
Colorado

The following are scenic areas administered by the NPS in Colorado.

Bent's Old Fort National Historic Site In southeastern Colorado, on the north bank of the Arkansas River, this small site was an early prairie trading post for settlers. For more information, see the Eastern Plains chapter.

Black Canyon of the Gunnison National Park The Gunnison River cut this deep, narrow and scenic western Colorado gorge nearly 2500 feet below the adjacent plateau. Its 13,000 acres also feature forests of ancient piñon pines. See the Western Colorado chapter.

Curecanti National Recreation Area Upstream from the Black Canyon of the Gunnison, several reservoirs have flooded the Gunnison River and its tributaries to create this recreational area. For more information, see the Western Colorado chapter.

National Park Services & Activities

This chart includes accommodations, services and activities available within the region's six national park boundaries. Though not included here, other options are often close by at gateway towns. In addition to facilities listed, all parks have visitors centers and handicapped-accessible toilets.

national park	accommodations	food	activities
Black Canyon of the Gunnison	camping	food market	hiking, biking, fishing
Glacier	camping, chalets, lodges	restaurants, food market	biking, fishing, hiking, horseback riding, cross-country skiing
Grand Teton	camping, cabins, lodges	restaurant, food market	biking, boating, climbing, fishing, hiking, horseback riding, cross-country skiing
Mesa Verde	camping, lodges	restaurant, food market	nature hikes, NPS guided tours
Rocky Mountain	camping	restaurant	biking, climbing, fishing, hiking, horseback riding, cross-country skiing
Yellowstone	camping, cabins, lodges	restaurant, food markets	biking, boating, fishing, hiking, horseback riding, cross-country skiing

PARKS & RECREATION AREAS

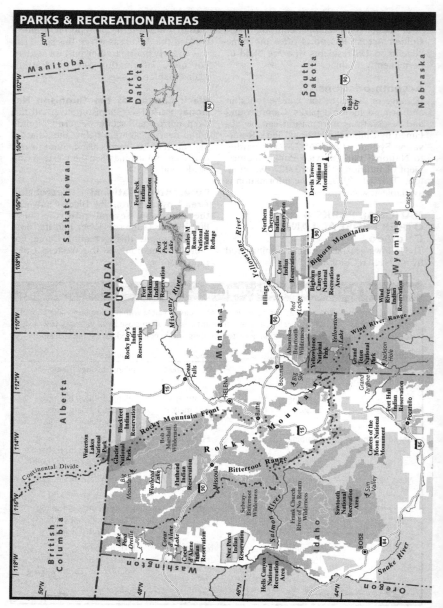

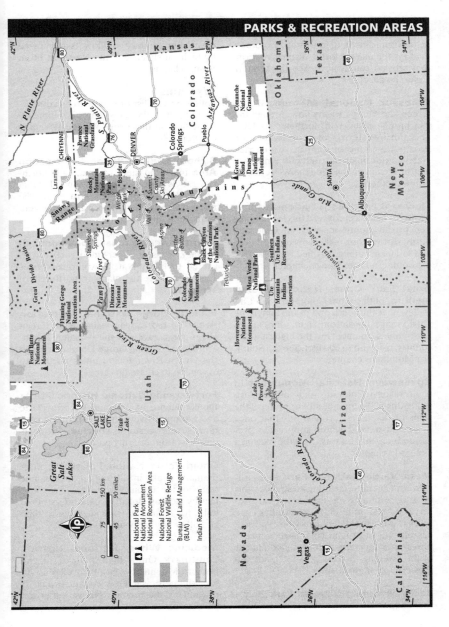

PARKS & RECREATION AREAS

Colorado National Monument Once dinosaur country, this 18,000-acre reserve near Grand Junction, in western Colorado, displays the most colorful, distinctive forms that erosion can achieve. See the Western Colorado chapter.

Dinosaur National Monument The Green and Yampa Rivers flow through this 298-sq-mile reserve in northeastern Utah and northwestern Colorado, where dinosaur fossils lie in impressive quarries. Native American petroglyphs embellish nearby scenic canyons. See the Western Colorado chapter.

Florissant Fossil Beds National Monument Volcanic ash covered this former lake bed in the mountains west of Colorado Springs, preserving 6000 acres of fossil flora and fauna, including petrified sequoias. See the Southern Front Range chapter.

Great Sand Dunes National Monument In south central Colorado's San Luis Valley, near the south end of the Sangre de Cristo range, the shifting sand dunes at this 56-sq-mile monument are the highest in the country, rising up to 800 feet. See the Southern Mountains chapter.

Hovenweep National Monument In southwestern Colorado and southeastern Utah, this 300-acre monument protects the ruins of defensive fortifications that once protected a vital water supply for pre-Columbian inhabitants. See the Western Colorado chapter.

Mesa Verde National Park In southwestern Colorado, covering 80 sq miles, this park is primarily an archaeological preserve. Its elaborate cliffside dwellings are relics of Ancestral Puebloans who evolved a complex social structure that lasted for centuries until their mysterious abandonment of the dwellings around AD 1300. See the Western Colorado chapter.

Rocky Mountain National Park Only a short hop from Denver, this park straddles the Continental Divide offering 395 sq miles of alpine forests, lakes and tundra covered by summer wildflowers and grazed by bighorn sheep. See the Northern Front Range chapter.

Wyoming

Following is a list of scenic areas administered by the NPS in Wyoming. For more information on these sites, see the Wyoming chapter.

Bighorn Canyon National Recreation Area In southeastern Montana and north-central Wyoming, the Yellowtail Dam drowned the Bighorn River to create the reservoir known as Bighorn Lake, the centerpiece of this 188-sq-mile area.

Devils Tower National Monument This solitary, massive sheer-sided rock tower, sacred to many Native Americans, rises 1200 feet above the plains in northeastern Wyoming.

Flaming Gorge National Recreation Area The red canyon walls of the Green River gorge gave this site its name. Northern Utah's Flaming Gorge Dam submerged the Green River for 90 miles north into Wyoming to create this area.

Fort Laramie National Historic Site At the confluence of Wyoming's North Platte and Laramie Rivers, this 836-acre site contains several restored structures from its days as a frontier army post.

Grand Teton National Park The most dramatic peaks in the region, the granitic spires of the Tetons tower 7000 feet above nearby Jackson Hole. The park offers 148 sq miles for hiking, climbing, viewing wildlife and other recreational activities.

Medicine Wheel National Historic Landmark On a high plateau in the Bighorn Mountains east of Lovell, this 70-foot diameter sacred medicine wheel is revered by the region's Native American peoples.

John D Rockefeller Jr Memorial Parkway Rockefeller purchased and then donated more than 55 sq miles of land to Grand Teton National Park. In recognition of his contribution, the US Congress named the 7½ miles of road between Yellowstone and Grand Teton National Parks the John D Rockefeller Jr Memorial Parkway.

Yellowstone National Park The world's first national park (and the region's most popular tourist destination) is a wonderland of volcanic geysers, hot springs, alpine lakes, forested mountains, waterfalls and the most spectacular wildlife in North America outside the Arctic.

Montana

Following are scenic areas administered by the NPS in Montana. For more information on these sites, see the Montana chapter.

Bighorn Canyon National Recreation Area In southeastern Montana and in northern Wyoming, the Yellowtail Dam drowned the Bighorn River to create the reservoir known as Bighorn Lake, the centerpiece of this 188-sq-mile area.

Big Hole National Battlefield In western Montana, this historical site covers 655 acres where in 1877 the US army surprised an encampment of Nez Percé, starting a bloody battle that lasted two days.

Glacier National Park Montana's only national park (excluding a sliver of Yellowstone), Glacier comprises 1558 sq miles of high sedimentary peaks, alpine lakes, small glaciers and imposing fauna, including the grizzly bear.

Grant-Kohrs Ranch National Historic Site Near Deer Lodge, this was the center of one of the largest open-range ranches in the country.

Little Bighorn Battlefield In southeastern Montana, this 765-acre monument memorializes a confrontation on the eve of the nation's centennial in 1876 when the Lakota Sioux took charge of their territory by wiping out General George Armstrong Custer's 7th US Cavalry.

Idaho

Following are scenic areas administered by the NPS in Idaho. For more information on these sites, see the Idaho chapter.

The City of Rocks National Reserve Remote, clean granitic spires attract mostly climbers to this reserve, but these evocative spires fascinate all who visit, including Oregon Trail pioneers who left their names on Register Rock.

Craters of the Moon National Monument Otherworldly barren black basalt, cinder cones and lava tubes at Craters of the Moon National Monument give a glimpse of volcanic activity that ceased only 2000 years ago.

EBR-1 National Historic Landmark The world's first nuclear power plant is known as EBR-1. Electricity from splitting the atom first became a reality here and nearby Arco was the world's first atomic-powered community, almost 50 years ago.

Hagerman Fossil Beds National Monument The world's best upper Pliocene-era fossil beds, from when this was marsh-covered grassland, are close to I-84 near Twin Falls.

Hells Canyon National Recreation Area The Snake River carves the deepest canyon in North America through Hells Canyon; see it from the river via rafts or jet boats, or from the Heavens Gate Lookout on the rim – a stunning view down into the canyon.

Nez Percé National Historic Park The tragic story of the dramatic flight for freedom of the Nez Percé, and their marvelous creation myth, are embodied in the vast landscape of the Nez Percé National Historic Park, adjacent to the Nez Percé Indian Reservation.

Sawtooth National Recreation Area In the heart of Idaho, this recreation area centers on the granitic Sawtooth Mountains, with fabulous Sun Valley to the south and the meadows, forests, lakes and rivers of the Stanley Basin to the east and north.

NATIONAL FORESTS

The US Forest Service (USFS) is under the US Dept of Agriculture and administrates the use of forests. Many of the most scenic areas in the Rocky Mountains are under USFS jurisdiction. National forests are less protected than parks, being managed under the concept of 'multiple use,' which includes timber cutting, watershed management, wildlife management and recreation.

Current information about national forests can be obtained from ranger stations, listed in the text. National forest campground and reservations information can be obtained by calling ☎ 800-280-2267, 800-879-4496 TTY. An $8.65 service charge applies regardless of the number of nights reserved.

Web site: www.fs.fed.us/

For more information on national forests, see the regional and state chapters.

WILDERNESS AREAS

If you want to leave the 'civilized world' behind, these wilderness areas, which are inaccessible to mechanized travel, are the places to go. The general philosophy behind them is to 'take only photographs, leave only footprints.'

The NPS, USFS and BLM all manage wilderness areas in the Rocky Mountain states. Restrictions on certain wilderness areas are imposed by requiring entry permits, limiting group sizes, limiting or prohibiting campfires and regulating camping sites and length of stay. Many wilderness areas have no developed campsites.

Some of the most hikable USFS wilderness areas are the Indian Peaks, Flat Tops and Maroon Bells in Colorado, the Bridger-Teton, Popo Agie and Cloud Peak in Wyoming and the Bob Marshall, Anaconda-Pintler and Selway-Bitterroot in Montana.

For more information on wilderness areas, see the regional and state chapters.

BUREAU OF LAND MANAGEMENT

The BLM manages public use of federal lands. This is no-frills camping, often in untouched settings. There are few restrictions on activity in BLM lands, which means often one can camp, hike or bike wherever one chooses. A downside to this for those who seek quiet is that this laissez-faire approach also attracts off-road drivers and motorcyclists.

Each state has a regional office located in the state capital. Look in the blue section of the local white pages directory under US Government, Interior Dept, call the Federal Information Center (☎ 800-688-9889) or visit www.blm.gov.

FISH & WILDLIFE SERVICE

Each state has a few regional Fish & Wildlife Service (FWS) offices that can provide information about viewing local wildlife. Check the blue section of the local white pages directory under US Government, Interior Dept, call the Federal Information Center (☎ 800-688-9889) or visit www.fws.gov.

For national wild and scenic rivers see Rafting, later.

Outdoor Activities

If you love the great outdoors, the Rockies is as good as it gets. Whether it be for hiking, biking, climbing, camping, fishing, rafting, kayaking or even hot-air ballooning, there is no shortage of ways to convene with Mother Nature.

Web heads surfing for information on outdoor activities in the Rockies should start their search at the extensive Great Outdoor Recreation Pages (GORP), www.gorp.com.

For details on all of the following activities, see the regional and state chapters.

HIKING & BACKPACKING

There is perhaps no better way to appreciate the beauty of the Rocky Mountain states – their lofty glacial peaks, peaceful dense forests, remote mountain meadows and high alpine lakes – than on the trail. Leaving the highway for a few days (or even a few hours) to explore the great outdoors can refresh road-weary travelers and give a heightened appreciation of the scenery that goes whizzing past day after day.

See the regional and state chapters for more information on hiking. Also, please read Responsible Tourism in the Facts for the Visitor chapter, and tread lightly!

Safety

The major forces to be reckoned with while hiking and camping are the elements and your own frame of mind. Be prepared for the Rockies' unpredictable weather – you may go to bed under a clear sky and wake up to two feet of snow, even in mid-August. Carry a rain jacket and a light pair of long underwear at all times, even on short afternoon hikes. Backpackers should have a pack-liner, a full set of rain gear and food that does not require cooking.

Highest safety measures suggest never hiking alone, but regardless, the most important thing is to always let someone know where you are going and how long you plan to be gone. Use sign-in boards at trailheads or ranger stations. Travelers who are looking for hiking companions can inquire or post notices at ranger stations, outdoor equipment stores, campgrounds and hostels.

People with little hiking or backpacking experience should not attempt to do too much, too soon, or you might end up being non-hikers for the wrong reasons. Know your limitations, know the route you are going to take and pace yourself accordingly. Remember, there is absolutely nothing wrong with turning back or not going as far as you originally planned.

What to Bring

Equipment The following is meant to be a general guideline for backpackers. Know yourself and what special things you may need on the trail; consider the area and climatic conditions you will be traveling in. Note that this list is inadequate for snow country or winter.

- Boots – Light to medium are recommended for day hikes, while sturdy boots are necessary for extended trips with a heavy pack. Most importantly, they should be well broken-in and have a good heel. Waterproof boots are preferable.
- Alternative footwear – Thongs (flip-flops), sandals or running shoes are best for wearing around camp, and canvas sneakers for crossing streams.
- Socks – Heavy polypropylene or wool will stay warm even if it gets wet.
- Colors – Subdued colors are recommended, except during hunting season when bright blaze orange is a necessity.
- Shorts, light shirt – Good for everyday wear; heavy cotton takes a long time to dry and is very cold when wet.
- Long-sleeve shirt – This should be light cotton, wool or polypropylene. A button-down front makes layering easy and can be left open when the weather is hot and your arms need protection from the sun.
- Long pants – Heavy denim jeans take forever to dry. Sturdy cotton or canvas pants are good for trekking through brush, and cotton or nylon sweats are comfortable to wear around camp.
- Wool or polypropylene or polar fleece sweater or pullover – Layering is essential in chilly or cold weather.
- Rain gear – Light, breathable and waterproof is the ideal combination.
- Hat – Wool or polypropylene is best for cold weather, while a cotton hat with a brim is good for sun protection.
- Bandana or handkerchief – This is your best bet for a runny nose, dirty face, picnic lunch and flag (especially a red one).
- Small towel – These are indestructible and will dry quickly.
- First-aid kit – Include self-adhesive bandages, disinfectant, antibiotic salve or cream, gauze, small scissors and tweezers.
- Knife, fork, spoon and mug – A double-layer plastic mug with a lid is best.
- Pots and pans – Aluminum cook sets are best.
- Stove – Lightweight and easy to operate is ideal. Most outdoors stores sell and rent propane or butane stoves.
- Water purifier – This is optional but nice to have; water can be purified by boiling for at least 10 minutes.
- Matches or lighter – Waterproof matches are good.

- Candle or lantern – Candles are easy to operate, but can be hazardous inside a tent.

- Flashlight – Each person should have their own and be sure its batteries have plenty of life left.

- Sleeping bag – Goose-down bags are warm and lightweight, but worthless if they get wet.

- Sleeping pad (optional) – Use a sweater or sleeping bag sack stuffed with clothes as a pillow.

- Tent – It should be waterproof, or with a waterproof cover; know how to put it up *before* you reach camp.

- Camera and binoculars – Don't forget extra film and waterproof film canisters.

- Compass and maps – Each person should have their own.

- Eyeglasses – Contact-lens wearers should always bring a back-up set.

- Sundries – Remember toilet paper, small sealable plastic bags, insect repellent, sun screen, lip balm, moleskin for foot blisters, sunglasses, deck of cards, pen or pencil, notebook, books and nature guides.

Food Keeping your energy up is important, but so is keeping your pack light. Backpackers tend to eat a substantial breakfast and dinner and snack heavily in between.

Some basic staples are packaged instant oatmeal, bread, rice or pasta, instant soup or ramen noodles, dehydrated meat (jerky), dried fruit, energy bars, chocolate, trail mix, and peanut butter and honey or jam (in plastic jars or squeeze bottles).

Books & Maps

There are quite a few good how-to and where-to books on the market. They are usually found in outdoors stores, or bookstores' Sports & Recreation or Outdoors sections.

A good map is essential for any hiking trip. Getting to the backcountry can often be a trying tangle of switchback roads and unmarked forest service roads. For this

Wilderness Camping

Camping in undeveloped areas is rewarding for its peacefulness, but presents special concerns. Take care to ensure that the area you choose can comfortably support your presence, and leave the surroundings in better condition than on arrival. The following list of guidelines should help:

- Camp below timberline, since alpine areas are generally more fragile. Good campsites are found, not made. Altering a site shouldn't be necessary.

- Camp at least 200 feet (70 adult steps) away from the nearest lake, river or stream.

- Bury human waste in cat holes dug 6 to 8 inches deep, at least 200 feet from water, camp or trails. The salt and minerals in urine attract deer; use a tent-bottle (funnel attachments are available for women) if you are prone to middle-of-the-night calls by Mother Nature. Camouflage the cat hole when finished.

- Use soaps and detergents sparingly or not at all, and never allow their residue to enter streams or lakes. When washing yourself (a backcountry luxury, not a necessity), lather up (with biodegradable soap) and rinse yourself with cans of water 200 feet away from your water source. Scatter dish water after removing all food particles.

- Carry a lightweight stove for cooking and to use as a lantern instead of a fire.

- If a fire is allowed and appropriate, dig out the native topsoil and build a fire in the hole. Gather sticks no larger than an adult's wrist. Do not snap branches off live, dead or downed trees. Pour wastewater from meals around the perimeter of the campfire to prevent the fire from spreading, and thoroughly douse it before leaving or going to bed.

- Establish a cooking area at least 100 yards away from your tent and designate cooking clothes to leave in the food bag, away from your tent.

- Burn cans to get rid of their odor, remove them from the ashes and pack them out.

- Pack out what you pack in, including all trash – yours *and* others'.

reason it is recommended that you obtain a topographic map and a USFS map of the area you intend to traverse. Both NPS and USFS ranger stations usually stock various maps. In the absence of a ranger station, try the local book, stationery or hardware store.

For more general information on maps, see that entry in Facts for the Visitor; for information regarding maps of specific forests, wilderness areas or national parks, see the regional and state chapters.

BICYCLING

The Rocky Mountain states offer superb road-biking opportunities for both long- and short-haul rides. Bike-friendly cities where you can ditch the car and ride to museums and other attractions on a network of routes include Missoula, Denver, Boulder, Fort Collins, Durango, Pueblo and Colorado Springs.

The Rockies are also a mecca for mountain bikers. The mountains around Aspen and Crested Butte, the hills of the Northern Front Range and trails near Fruita (starting point of the celebrated Kokopelli Trail) are among the top spots for mountain biking in the region.

Multiple-day mountain bike tours are available using the San Juan Hut System that extends from Telluride across the Colorado Plateau to Moab, Utah. Campers can travel the 500-mile Colorado Trail. Mountain biking is becoming increasingly popular in Montana. Big Sky and the Big Mountain (Whitefish) offer lift-serviced trails, while West Yellowstone has an excellent network of trails both in and outside Yellowstone National Park. There are also good single tracks in the Absaroka and Gallatin ranges accessible from the Paradise Valley. Bozeman is the state's mountain-biking hub, largely due to its young and fearless population.

Idaho's Taft Tunnel Bike Trail follows a converted rail line through mountain tunnels and over high railway trestles, across the state line to Montana. The centerpiece of the trail is the 8771-foot-long Taft Tunnel, constructed in 1909.

Leads on bicycling routes in Wyoming, Montana and Idaho can be found on www.great-trails.com.

Backroads (☎ 800-462-2848) leads organized bike tours with camping and inn options ($1000 to $2000) through southwest Colorado, Glacier National Park and Idaho's Sun Valley and Sawtooth Mountains.
Web site: www.backroads.com

Colorado

The nonprofit group Bicycle Colorado (☎ 719-530-0051), PO Box 698, Salida, CO 81201, offers a useful information packet (free) including the handy 'Colorado Bicycle Manual,' a summary of state laws, bicycle resources and guide books. Its Web site, www.bicyclecolo.org, is an excellent source for information on bicycling in the state.

The Colorado Bicycle Pedestrian Program Manager (☎ 303-757-9982) at the Colorado Dept of Highways, 4201 E Arkansas Ave, No 225, Denver, CO 80222, sells helpful maps of suggested touring routes.

Information about state parks with off-road trails is available from Colorado State Parks (☎ 303-866-3437), 1313 Sherman St, No 618, Denver, CO 80203.

Wyoming

The Wyoming Dept of Transportation (☎ 307-777-4719), 5300 Bishop Blvd, PO Box 1708, Cheyenne, WY 82003, publishes the 'Wyoming Bicycle Guidance Map,' which shows statewide routes, significant grades, prevailing winds, average daily summer traffic volume, designated mountain bike routes, campsites, elevations and towns with bike shops. This compact, easy-to-read map is a vital planning tool for cyclists.

Montana

General vehicle traffic-volume maps of the state are available from the Bicycle/Pedestrian Coordinator (☎ 406-444-6118), Montana Dept of Transportation, 2701 Prospect St, Helena, MT 59620.

Adventure Cycling (☎ 406-721-1776), PO Box 8308, Missoula, MT 59807, publishes maps and guides to favorite rides in and around Montana. One popular route is from Missoula up through the Swan Valley (Hwy 83) to Glacier National Park.
Web site: www.adv-cycling.org

Idaho

The Idaho Transportation Dept offers bicycling data, weather information and road reports on its Bicycle Transportation Web site at www.idoc.state.id.us/ITD/bike.html.

Cyclevents organizes an annual 'ride across the land of potatoes' called SPUDS – Cycling Around Idaho (☎ 888-733-9615).
Web site: www.spuds.cyclevents.com

For information on mountain biking in the southwest part of the state, surf onto www.geocities.com/Pipeline/1765/.

Laws & Regulations

Throughout the Rocky Mountains, bikes are restricted from entering designated wilderness areas and national park trails, but may otherwise ride on national forest and BLM single-track trails. Trail etiquette requires that cyclists yield to other users. Helmets should always be worn to reduce the risk of head injury, but they are not mandated by law.

Cyclists may use about 80% of Colorado's rural interstate routes, all but a few short urban sections in Wyoming and all of Montana's broad-shouldered interstate highways. Montana's incomparable Going-to-the-Sun Rd, which goes through Glacier National Park, has midday bicycle access restrictions.

Books & Maps

A wide variety of regional travel guides and maps for both road and mountain biking can be found at area bookstores, as well as bicycle and outdoors shops. DeLorme publishes a topographic *Atlas & Gazetteer* for each state – good tools for planning trail rides. Descriptions of off-road bike trails in national forests are generally available by contacting the forest supervisor's office in the area.

SKIING

The Rocky Mountain states, Colorado in particular, are home to some of the USA's most popular ski destinations. High mountains and reliable snow conditions have attracted investors and multimillion dollar ski resorts, equipped with the latest in chair-lift technology, snow-grooming systems and facilities. Along with the big-name places like Aspen, Vail, Jackson Hole, Big Sky and Sun Valley are small operations with a handful of lifts, cheaper ticket prices and terrain that often is as challenging as that of their glitzier neighbors.

In addition to downhill skiing, snowboarding has swept the nation's ski culture and taken on a following of its own. Growing numbers of snowboarders are seen on Rocky Mountain slopes. Most resorts offer introductory snowboarding lessons.

There are ample opportunities in the Rockies for cross-country and backcountry skiing. The USFS often maintains summer hiking trails as cross-country trails during the winter, offering great opportunities to experience wilderness areas that teem with people in the summer. Many places specialize in cross-country skiing and offer weekend or weeklong packages that include lodging, meals and equipment rentals. Downhill areas also frequently have cross-country areas, and in the winter golf courses often have terrain suited to beginners.

Ski areas are generally well equipped with places to stay, places to eat, shops, entertainment venues, child-care facilities (both on and off the mountain) and transportation. At major ski areas, lift tickets cost anywhere from $35 to $65 for a full day or about half that for a half-day (usually starting at 1 pm). Three-day or weeklong lift passes are more economical, especially if they do not need to be used on consecutive days. Equipment rentals are available at or near even the smallest ski areas.

Downhill Skiing & Snowboarding

The Rockies offer some of the USA's most skiable downhill terrain. Colorado alone boasts 26 ski resorts and there are significant ski mountains in Wyoming, Montana and Idaho.

Colorado The nation's ski scene is dominated by Colorado, which attracts more than 10 million skiers and snowboarders every year.

Convenient access counts: The center of Colorado's ski industry lies about 80 miles west of Denver in Summit County. This is North America's most popular ski destination with four ski areas – Breckenridge, Arapahoe Basin, Keystone and Copper Mountain – that offer something for everybody, from families at Keystone to extreme skiers at A-Basin.

If you have only one day to ski in Colorado, most agree that Vail is the place to go. Aspen and Crested Butte follow in the voting. Nightlife is lively at Aspen, Telluride, Crested Butte and Breckenridge – all historic mining towns with ski slopes. Winter Park's renowned bumps and unique access from Denver on the Ski Train give it a special appeal as a day trip. Families appreciate the beginner and intermediate slopes at Snowmass and Buttermilk, plus the large corps of instructors that teach the kids while mom and dad slip away on the bus to more difficult slopes at nearby Aspen. When snow is in short supply, or you want to extend your ski season into late spring, head for Steamboat Springs, which receives deep snows annually. A-Basin's high elevation on the Continental Divide makes it another late-season favorite.

Information on 23 of Colorado's 26 mountains is available from Colorado Ski Country USA (☎ 303-837-0793), 1560 Broadway, suite 2000, Denver, CO 80202 (www.skicolorado.org). For a report of snow conditions at resorts across the state, call the Snow Report (☎ 303-825-7669).

Wyoming Jackson Hole Mountain Resort in Teton Village is the largest resort in Wyoming, offering a world-class variety of skiing. Other nearby resorts are the Snow King Resort in Jackson and Grand Targhee Ski & Summer Resort in Alta.

Montana Big Sky is Montana's premier resort, 33 miles south of Bozeman. With a tram, gondola, nine chair lifts, 4180 feet of vertical drop and ever-increasing resort developments at the foot of the slopes, Big Sky beats Montana's other ski hills hands down. However, there are other areas near towns where you can soak up some real Western color at night. The Big Mountain has a full resort at its base but is only 11 miles from the lively town of Whitefish, and is also close to Glacier National Park. Red Lodge Mountain is increasing in popularity; besides being next to a great party town, it has a good network of cross-country trails nearby.

Bridger Bowl is where Bozeman locals and MSU students go. It's humble in both size and amenities but has some great chutes and bowls above the area served by the lift. Locals also head toward Snowbowl near Missoula.

Idaho The state's finest skiing is at Sun Valley Resort, where powder-dry snow and steep descents have been attracting celebrity skiers for decades to Bald Mountain and Dollar Mountain. In Idaho's Panhandle, Schweitzer Mountain Resort near Sandpoint and Silver Mountain Resort near Kellogg offer great facilities. Southwestern Idaho's best areas are Bogus Basin, close to Boise, and Brundage Mountain, near McCall.

Cross-Country & Backcountry Skiing

Nordic, or cross-country, skiing offers a chance to get exercise, experience natural beauty at close quarters and save a few dollars by not needing to buy a downhill lift ticket. National parks, notably Yellowstone, close their roads during the winter and maintain cross-country trails into the parks' interiors.

The relatively new sport of backcountry skiing takes its roots from its Nordic cousin. The difference lies in the equipment and the terrain. Special telemark bindings, boots and skis now allow winter skiers not only to travel cross country but also to tackle steep slopes or bowls that lie along their paths. This is one of the most difficult types of skiing to learn, and the best place to first try it is at a ski resort or local snow slopes – not deep in the wilderness.

Modeled after European traditions, yurt or hut systems have made their way into the USA's backcountry landscape. Huts are placed three to four hours (about 15 miles) apart, and provide beds, cooking utensils, stoves, firewood and plenty of camaraderie and conversation. The idea is to ski from hut to hut, spending the night at each one, to make a complete loop of five to 10 days. People with less time or energy can ski into a hut from the initial trailhead, spend the night and ski out again the next day. Most huts enforce a two-night maximum and take reservations up to one month in advance. Each hut system, usually with at least three huts, operates independently. Often terrain between huts can be challenging and may require some strong backcountry skiing skills, so check with hut operators to see what you might be facing.

NPS, USFS, BLM and private lands support hundreds of miles of cross-country trails, some operated under special-use permits by private industries. The following is a list of some of the more popular areas.

Colorado Although many resorts in Colorado offer cross-country facilities adjacent to alpine slopes, most Nordic skiers prefer to avoid the downhill crowds by visiting dedicated Nordic areas and backcountry trails on public park and forest lands. Perhaps the premier scenic skiing opportunities are available at Rocky Mountain National Park, Mesa Verde National Park and Black Canyon of the Gunnison National Park. Among the better, uncrowded cross-country centers are Twin Lakes between Leadville and Aspen, Red Feather Lakes northwest of Fort Collins and also the Fairplay Nordic Ski Center. The Frisco Nordic Center features an exclusive trail area on a peninsula jutting into Dillon Reservoir in Summit County.

Backcountry tourists can set off from high-altitude trailheads at Montezuma.

Ashcroft Ski Touring near Aspen offers groomed trails, plus backcountry trails over Pearl Pass to Crested Butte, where Big Mine Park offers groomed trails, lessons and backcountry guides. Near Vail Pass, Shrine Pass Rd is a popular touring route with a nearby restaurant.

The ultimate backcountry touring is available using the system of 12 huts strategically located along trails in the Aspen-Leadville-Vail area by the renowned 10th Mountain Division Hut Association. Near Lake City, the Hinsdale Haute Route offers three huts along the Continental Divide leading to Creede. Also in the Colorado Plateau, the San Juan Hut System is set up in the vicinity of Telluride, Ridgway and Ouray on the Mt Sneffles Wilderness border. Details and contact information for these hut systems can be found under the relevant destination entries. For a complete list of Colorado's huts, check out Brian Litz's *Colorado Hut to Hut* listed in Books & Magazines, below.

Wyoming Yellowstone National Park provides excellent backcountry access. One fun trip is taking a snow coach to the Snow Lodge near Old Faithful and spending a few days skiing around geyser basins, the Grand Canyon of the Yellowstone and up Mt Washburn. The Snowy Range Ski Area, near Centennial, also has Nordic facilities and the White Pine Recreation Area, near Pinedale, is an area that's not overrun with tourists in the winter. Almost all of Jackson Hole is also skiable.

Montana Most of Montana's groomed cross-country trail systems are on national forest land and maintained by local ski clubs. For this reason there's usually no fee, nor any amenities. The best of these are Rendezvouz Cross-Country Ski Trails (West Yellowstone), Chief Joseph Cross-Country Trails (on the Montana-Idaho border at the southern end of the Bitterroot Valley), Silver Crest Ski Trails (between Great Falls and Livingston), Seeley Lake Ski Trails (in the Swan Range near Seeley Lake and the Bob Marshall Wilderness), Blacktail Ski

Trails (on the west shore of Flathead Lake) and MacDonald Pass Trail System (15 miles west of Helena).

One of the most charming cross-country ski places is the Izaak Walton Inn (in Essex, near Glacier National Park). Trails start from an old railroad lodge; there's a good restaurant and old railroad cars have been made into cozy accommodations. Chico Hot Springs (in the Paradise Valley) is another spot where the lodge atmosphere is as good as the skiing. The Lone Mountain Ranch (at Big Sky) is similar, but less isolated.

Bohart Ski Ranch, near Bozeman, is an old log cabin that acts as a base lodge for an excellent 18-mile trail system. There are also good backcountry trails into Glacier National Park.

Idaho Sun Valley and Galena Lodge in Sawtooth National Recreation Area are the most popular cross-country ski areas. On the west side of the Grand Tetons, near Victor, Rendezvous Ski Tours operates three huts accessible to backcountry skiers at elevations ranging from 8000 to 8800 feet. All can be reached via 4-mile trails that are skiable for anyone with basic cross-country skills.

Books & Magazines

In *Rocky Mountain Skiing,* Claire Waller gives information on ski resorts, accommodations and special ski programs throughout the region.

Brian Litz's *Colorado Hut to Hut* covers backcountry skiing, hiking and mountain biking around Colorado's extensive hut systems (see Cross-Country & Backcountry Skiing, earlier). Another good resource is Richard DuMais' *Fifty Colorado Ski Tours,* which caters more to Nordic skiers. The same author wrote *Fifty Ski Tours in Jackson Hole & Yellowstone.* Another guide to this excellent Nordic ski area is *Cross-Country Skiing Yellowstone Country* by Ken and Dena Olsen and Steve and Hazel Scharosch.

Ski and *Skiing* are both year-round magazines available in most newsstands, airports and sporting goods stores.

ROCK CLIMBING & MOUNTAINEERING

Opportunities for rock climbing and mountaineering are almost unlimited in the Rockies – Colorado alone has 54 peaks over 14,000 feet above sea level, more than the rest of the USA combined. In 1868, the year before his celebrated descent of the Colorado River, the legendary John Wesley Powell and publisher William Byers became the first to sit atop one of these 14ers when they scaled 14,255-foot Longs Peak. In 1916, when Albert R Ellingwood and Eleanor S Davis climbed 14,294-foot Crestone Peak in the Sangre de Cristo Mountains, the last of the 14ers had been conquered.

Some of the world's great mountaineers have learned or polished their skills in the Rockies. Climbing and mountaineering are demanding activities requiring top physical condition. An understanding of the composition of various rock types and their hazards as well as other hazards of the high country are needed too, as is familiarity with a variety of equipment, including ropes, chocks, bolts, carabiners and harnesses. Many climbers prefer granite, like that found in the Teton Range, because of its strength and frequent handholds, but some climbers prefer limestone for a challenge. Some sedimentary rock is suitable for climbing, but crumbling volcanic rock can be very difficult.

Safety

Climbing is potentially a hazardous activity and climbers should be aware of dangers that can contribute to falls, serious injury or death. Weather is an important factor, as rain makes rock slippery and lightning can strike an exposed climber; hypothermia is an additional concern. In dry weather, lack of water can lead to dehydration.

Environmental Concerns

To preserve the resource on which their sport relies, many climbers are now following guidelines similar to those established for hikers. These include concentrating impact in high-use areas by using established roads, trails and routes for access; dis-

US Climbing Ratings

In the US, climbing and mountaineering routes are generally classified using the Yosemite Decimal System (YDS), which has five classes. Class 1 is hiking, while Class 2 involves climbing on unstable materials like talus and may require use of the hands for keeping balance, especially with a heavy pack. Class 3 places the climber in dangerous situations, involving exposed terrain (the Sierra Club uses the example of a staircase on a high building without handholds – scary but not difficult), with the likely consequences of a fall being a broken limb. Ideally one should have climbing rope on hand, just in case.

Class 4 involves steep rock, smaller holds and great exposure, with obligatory use of ropes and knowledge of knots and techniques like belaying and rappelling; the consequences of falling are death rather than injury. Class 5 divides into a dozen or more subcategories based on degree of difficulty and requires advanced techniques, including proficiency with rope.

For serious climbers from outside the US, the following are some comparisons of US Class 5 ratings with those of other international systems.

system	rating	
YDS	5.2 – 5.9	5.10 – 5.14a+
UIAA	I – VI	VI+ – X+
Australian	11 – 18	19 – 33
French	1 – 6a	6a+ – 8c

persing use in pristine areas and avoiding the creation of new trails; refraining from creating or enhancing handholds; and eschewing the placement of bolts wherever possible. Climbers should also take special caution to respect archaeological and cultural resources, such as rock art, and refrain from climbing in such areas. Some climbers even use chalk that's specially colored to blend in with the rock in the area they're climbing.

Sites

So much of the Rocky Mountain region offers superb rock climbing that entire books are devoted to relatively small areas around climbers' meccas like Jackson Hole and Estes Park, the access points to Grand Teton and Rocky Mountain National Parks.

There are good Colorado spots at Penitente Canyon near La Garita in the San Luis Valley, Taylor Canyon near Crested Butte, Greenhorn Reservoir in Summit County and the Gore Range near Kremmling. Lesser known but locally popular areas include Eldorado Canyon State Park and the Flatirons near Boulder, the Snowy Range sites along the Wyoming-Colorado border and Vedauwoo Rocks near Laramie, WY.

Wyoming's Wind River Range, especially the Cirque of the Towers, is another exceptional choice for both general mountaineering and rock climbing. The nearby Lander region attracts climbers with its world-class rock. Devils Tower National Monument, in the Black Hills of northeastern Wyoming, is a popular stop on the summer climbing circuit.

The stable rock and many uncharted climbs of Hyalite Canyon, near Bozeman, make it a rock and ice climbing magnet in Montana. Pine Creek, in the Paradise Valley, is known for the Blue and Green Gullies – featured in Yvon Chouinard's book *Climbing Ice*. Another good spot that is less developed is Humbug Spires, south of Butte; it takes an hour or so on the trail to reach the spires. For mountaineering, many people head to the Bob Marshall Wilderness, which has many great one-day peak climbs. Glacier National Park also offers good peak climbing, but routes are much less documented and thus require advanced trip research and good map and compass skills. For nontechnical peaks, head to the Bitterroot Range or the Gallatin Valley where trails are well marked.

Idaho's Sawtooth Mountains offer great mountaineering and high-quality rock like Elephant Perch. Remote City of Rocks, south of Burley, is a fun place to climb.

Books

A good general introduction to climbing can be found in *Mountaineering: The Freedom of the Hills* by the Mountaineers in Seattle, Washington.

For Colorado, Stewart M Green's *Rock Climbing Colorado* covers some 1500 climbing routes throughout the state. For hitting the big peaks, there's Walter R Borneman's and Lyndon J Lampert's *A Climbing Guide to Colorado's Fourteeners*.

Titles for Wyoming include *Teton Classics: Fifty Selected Climbs in Grand Teton National Park* by the prolific climbing writer Richard Rossiter, *Sinks Canyon Rock Climbs 1994* by Greg Collins and *Free Climbs of Devils Tower* by Dingus McGee.

Falcon Press (Helena, MT) publishes *Rockclimbing Montana* and *The Climber's Guide to Glacier National Park*. *Big Sky Ice,* by renowned Montana climber Ron Brunckhorst, is the state's definitive guide to ice climbing.

HORSEBACK RIDING & PACK TRIPS

Given the western USA's cowboy heritage, horseback riding is naturally a very popular summer activity throughout the Rockies, usually, but by no means always, associated with guest (dude) ranches. Visitors enjoying guest-ranch vacations will often enjoy unlimited access to riding and may even join in cattle drives à la *City Slickers,* the popular film starring Billy Crystal. Another option you may come across is a llama.

More casual riders will find horseback riding an expensive activity, as visitors during the short summer tourist season end up paying for the cost of feeding these hay burners over the winter: Rates for recreational horseback riding start around $15 per hour or $25 for two hours, though the hourly rate falls rapidly thereafter; full-day trips cost around $75 with a guide. Guided trips usually require a minimum of two persons. Backcountry pack trips, again with a guide, cost upward of $100 per person per day, and usually involve some related activity, such as fly-fishing. A new variation on

this theme is the llama pack trip, which substitutes the less predictable horse with these more docile South American animals.

Stables are almost ubiquitous throughout the West, but are most numerous near major resort areas like Aspen, Estes Park and Grand Lake, CO; Jackson and Yellowstone National Park, WY; and Glacier National Park, MT. Experienced riders may want to let the owners know, or else you may be saddled with an excessively docile stable nag.

RAFTING

The Rocky Mountains offer a myriad of alternatives for one of the most exhilarating outdoor activities possible. Commercial outfitters in all four states provide whitewater experiences ranging from inexpensive half-day trips to overnight and multiple-day expeditions; those on NPS, USFS and BLM lands operate under permits from the appropriate agency, but individuals and groups with their own equipment do not need permits. Those not ready for white-water excitement can try more sedate float or tube trips.

River trips are classified on a scale of one to six, according to difficulty; Class I is virtually placid enough for an inner tube, while Class VI is 'unraftable.' On any given river, classifications can vary over the course of the year depending on the water level. Higher water levels, usually associated with spring runoff, can make a river trip either easier or more difficult, by covering up hazards or increasing the velocity of the river. Lower water levels can expose hazards like rocks and whirlpools, making the river more exciting. Some, if not most, rivers depend on water releases from upstream dams.

White-water trips take place in either large rafts seating 12 or more people, or smaller rafts seating 6; the latter are more interesting and exciting because the ride over the rapids can be rougher and because everyone participates in rowing. For multiple-day trips advance reservations are almost always essential. Full-day trips usually run anywhere from $50 to $90 depending on where you are, while overnights can cost $100 to $200. Trips in Colorado are generally more expensive than in the other states.

White-water trips can involve any of a variety of boats, depending on the type of trip you want and the equipment used by the operator. The smallest craft are one- or two-person inflatable or fiberglass kayaks. For group trips, there's the paddle raft, usually 14 feet long and carrying four to eight passengers paddling; the rear-mounted oar raft, with guide and passengers paddling; and the center-mounted oar rafts, in which the guide paddles and passengers just ride. These latter are usually 16 feet long: There are 18- to 22-foot models, but these can take the ride out of rapids. The opposite of these is the dory – a hard-hulled (wood or steel) boat, rowed by a guide, that gives a surprisingly fun 'roller-coaster' ride on the whitewater.

White-Water Ratings

The US rapid-rating system, similar to that used in Europe, is:

Class I – very easy
small regular waves and riffles; few or no obstacles, little maneuvering required
Class II – easy
small waves with some eddies, low ledges, and slow rock gardens; some maneuvering required
Class III – medium
numerous high and irregular waves, strong eddies, narrow but clear passages that require expertise in maneuvering; shore scouting necessary
Class IV – difficult
long rapids with powerful, irregular waves, dangerous rocks and boiling eddies; precise maneuvering and shore scouting imperative
Class V – very difficult
long rapids with wild turbulence and extremely congested routes that require complex maneuvering
Class VI – limits of navigation

While white-water trips are not without danger, and it's not unusual for participants to fall out of the raft in rough water, serious injuries are rare and the vast majority of trips are without incident. All trip participants are required to wear US Coast Guard–approved life jackets, and even nonswimmers are welcome. All trips have at least one river guide trained in lifesaving techniques.

Rivers

Congressional legislation establishes certain criteria for the preservation of rivers with outstanding natural qualities and categorizes them as National Wild & Scenic Rivers. Many of these are the best places for white-water rafting and canoeing. Wild rivers are, simply speaking, free-flowing and remote, while scenic rivers enjoy relatively natural surroundings and are free of impoundment, but have better access by road. Recreational rivers are more developed and usually have roads close by.

In Colorado, good rafting choices are the Arkansas River between Buena Vista and Cañon City, the undammed Yampa River west of Steamboat Springs, the Lake Fork of the Gunnison River, the Rio Grande near Creede and the Cache la Poudre and North Platte Rivers near the Wyoming border.

Popular Wyoming rivers include the Snake River between Hoback Junction and Alpine south of Jackson, Shoshone River west of Cody and the Wind River south of Thermopolis.

Just outside the Yellowstone National Park boundary near Gardiner, MT, the Yellowstone River is the longest free-flowing river in the entire country. The Gallatin and Stillwater Rivers in Montana are also popular choices. The stretch of the Clark Fork River that goes through Alberton Gorge, 35 miles west of Missoula, is considered western Montana's best whitewater with Class III and IV rapids.

Popular Idaho rivers include the Upper Salmon River east of Stanley; Upper Salmon River near the towns of Salmon and North Fork; Lower Fork Salmon River near Riggins; Moyie River and St Joe National Wild & Scenic River in the Panhandle; the

Aspen skyscrapers, CO

Beargrass in bloom

Gunnison County, CO

Angelic prairie coneflowers and Devils Tower, WY

Columbines flower in Grand Teton National Park, WY.

Autumn near Telluride, CO

ANDREW PEACOCK

'You look so familiar....' Prairie dogs, WY

ROB BLAKERS

Mountain goat ponders the return trip.

MASON FLORENCE

Elks will be elks. Estes Park, CO

MASON FLORENCE

They ain't called bighorn sheep for nothing.

JOHN ELK III

So cute they stop traffic; bison in Yellowstone National Park, WY

Snake River near Twin Falls, which heads through the Snake River Birds of Prey Natural Area, through the Hagerman Valley and near Boise; and the Payette River.

Books & Maps

Several excellent guides to white-water and float trips are in print covering the entire Rocky Mountain states region. Look for Doug Wheat's *The Floater's Guide to Colorado*, Dan Lewis' *Paddle & Portage: The Floater's Guide to Wyoming Rivers*, Curt Thompson's *Floating & Recreation on Montana Rivers* and Hank Fischer's *Floating Guide to Montana*.

Maps of wild and scenic rivers are more useful for the actual trip and are usually available at USFS offices and some bookstores. The maps provide very detailed description of rapids and historic and cultural sites along the way, and sensibly, they're also waterproof!

CANOEING

While white-water rafting is the most popular water sport in the Rocky Mountain states, many raft-laden rivers are just as good for canoeing. The best canoe rental resources are often small operations that usually double as campgrounds and summer resorts on the shore of a calm body of water.

Montana's tranquil waters offer some good canoeing opportunities. Swan and Seeley Lakes both have a handful of lakeside lodges with canoe rentals. The Red Rock Lakes National Wildlife Refuge (near West Yellowstone) has a canoe trail connecting several marshy lakes, though rental equipment is nonexistent. The historic Missouri River Breaks, near Fort Benton, MT, offers nearly 160 miles of this federally designated wild and scenic river suitable for canoe travel. The section of the river near Great Falls is a good destination for canoeists with limited experience.

FISHING

The Rocky Mountains have long been a mecca for freshwater anglers. In the mid-1990s thousands of novices were drawn to the sport of fly-fishing after watching Robert Redford's popular motion picture, *A River Runs Through It*, set on Montana's Blackfoot River.

Colorado

The fishing season is year-round, and special regulations apply to many waters in the state. An annual resident license costs $20.25 (nonresidents pay $40.25). Both residents and nonresidents can purchase either a one-day license ($5.25) or a five-day license ($18.25). For licensing information contact the Colorado Division of Wildlife (DOW; ☎ 303-297-1192), 6060 Broadway, Denver, CO 80216.
Web site: www.dnr.state.co.us/wildlife/

Wyoming

With local exceptions on a few lakes, Wyoming offers year-round fishing. Anglers may take no more than six trout or most other cold-water sport fish per day. Fishing licenses cost $6 a day (or $3 for Wyoming residents) and $65 a year ($15 for Wyoming residents). Licenses and regulations are available from the Wyoming Game & Fish Dept (☎ 307-777-4600), 5400 Bishop Blvd, Cheyenne, WY 82006-0001.
Web site: http://gf.state.wy.us/

Montana

Most Montana lakes and reservoirs are open year-round, but the stream and river sport-fishing season runs from the third Saturday in May to the end of November. Special regulations apply to many waters in the state.

You can buy a Montana fishing license at any Fish, Wildlife & Parks office, most ranger stations, sporting goods shops and general stores. (To get a license you must first have a $5 conservation license – good for the rest of your life – available where fishing licenses are sold.) A seasonal license costs $45 and is good for one year; a two-day stamp costs $10. For more information contact Montana Fish, Wildlife & Parks (☎ 406-444-4720), PO Box 200701, Helena, MT 59620-0701.
Web site: www.fwp.state.mt.us/

Idaho

Local vendors and the Idaho Dept of Fish & Game (☎ 208-334-3700), 600 S Walnut, Boise, ID 83707-0025, issue fishing licenses. A license costs $10.50 for the first day, and $4 for additional consecutive days; for the full season it costs $74.50 ($23.50 for Idaho residents). A three-day salmon/steelhead permit costs $28.50.

Web site: www.state.id.us/fishgame

GOLF

Recent decades have seen a proliferation of golf courses throughout the Rocky Mountain states. Even many small towns have nine- or 18-hole courses open to the public at reasonable prices, while the more established resorts have deluxe courses with very high green fees.

WINDSURFING

It's tempting to write that there's plenty of wind but no surf, but one of the few benefits offered by the massive water projects of the Rocky Mountain states is the opportunity for this sport, especially in blustery Wyoming. Most of Wyoming's state parks, like Buffalo Bill State Park near Cody, Pathfinder Reservoir near Rawlins and Glendo State Park near Douglas, are centered around artificial reservoirs, as are Flaming Gorge and Bighorn Canyon. (Flaming Gorge is partly in Utah and Bighorn Canyon is mostly in Montana, but both are accessible from Wyoming.) Along Colorado's Northern Front Range, Horsetooth Reservoir in Ft Collins is another spot where you can take to the wind-blown waters.

CAVING

Experienced spelunkers can explore caves in several areas of limestone bedrock, mostly but not exclusively in Wyoming. The highest altitude limestone cave in North America is Colorado's Marble Cave, 11,000 feet above sea level in the Sangre de Cristo Wilderness of the San Isabel National Forest. The main cave sites in Wyoming are around Bighorn Canyon National Recreation Area, near Lovell, Sinks Canyon State Park near Lander and Shoshone Cavern on Cedar Mountain (Spirit Mountain) near Cody. Montana's Azure Cave, south of the Fort Belknap Indian Reservation on BLM land in the Little Rocky Mountains between Zortman and Landusky, is another possibility.

Two limestone cave areas are open to casual visitors for guided tours, without need of equipment or experience: Lewis & Clark Caverns State Park, near Whitehall, MT, and the tacky and commercial Cave of the Winds, near Manitou Springs, CO.

Because of the delicate and tightly circumscribed subterranean environments, cavers must make special efforts to respect the ecosystem and its inhabitants by leaving no trace of human presence, avoiding contact with sensitive formations and refraining from disturbing bats and other animals. Cavers should also travel in groups, with a minimum of three persons. Hazards associated with caving that you might encounter include poisonous gases and dangerous spores.

Cave maps are available from the Wyoming Geological Survey, PO Box 3008, University Station, Laramie, WY 82070.

HOT-AIR BALLOONING

Floating above the Rockies has its attractions, given the scenery, but it's not cheap at the relatively few locations that offer it commercially. At Jackson, WY, and Steamboat Springs, CO, figure about $80 for a half-hour flight above the mountains, $150 to $200 for an hour or a bit longer. The views are incomparable. Balloon flights that take in the vistas of Glacier National Park are available out of Whitefish, MT.

Getting There & Away

This chapter focuses on getting to transport hubs in the Rocky Mountain states from key US ports of entry and other parts of the world. Because there are so many routes into, out of and within the USA, along with constant changes in routings and ticket prices, much of this information is general.

AIR

US domestic air fares vary tremendously depending on the season you travel, the day of the week you fly, the length of your stay and the flexibility the ticket allows for flight changes and refunds.

While airlines don't maintain set low- and high-season rates, prices rise from mid-June to mid-September (summer), when 90% of Americans go on vacation. It's also expensive to travel around Thanksgiving (the last Thursday in November) and the busy week before and after Christmas.

Airports & Airlines

Denver International Airport (DIA) is the only major airport in the region and is the principal gateway for the Rockies. From here you can get flights to destinations in Colorado, Wyoming, Montana and Idaho. Salt Lake City, Utah, is the only other airport in the region that sees a large amount of national traffic and offers connections to western Colorado, Wyoming, Montana and Idaho. Rapid City, South Dakota, also has connections to Wyoming. Most Montana and Idaho air connections run east-west, between major international airports at Minneapolis–St Paul, Minnesota, to the east and Seattle, Washington, and Portland, Oregon, to the west.

Major international airlines that have service to the Rocky Mountain states include the following:

Air Canada	☎ 800-776-3000
Air France	☎ 800-237-2747
Air New Zealand	☎ 800-262-1234
American Airlines	☎ 800-624-6262
British Airways	☎ 800-247-9297
Canadian Airlines	☎ 800-426-7000
Continental Airlines	☎ 800-525-0280
Japan Air Lines	☎ 800-525-3663
KLM	☎ 800-374-7747
Northwest Airlines	☎ 800-447-4747
Qantas Airways	☎ 800-227-4500
TWA	☎ 800-221-2000
United Airlines	☎ 800-538-2929
US Airways	☎ 800-428-4322
Virgin Atlantic	☎ 800-862-8621

Major domestic airlines that have service to the Rocky Mountain states include the following:

AirTran Airlines	☎ 800-247-8726
Alaska Airlines	☎ 800-426-0333
America West	☎ 800-235-9292
American	☎ 800-433-7300

Continental	☎ 800-525-0280
Delta	☎ 800-221-1212
Hawaiian Airlines	☎ 800-367-5320
Northwest	☎ 800-225-2525
Southwest	☎ 800-435-9792
TWA	☎ 800-892-4141
United	☎ 800-241-6522

Buying Tickets

The plane ticket will probably be the single most expensive item in your budget, so it is always worth putting aside a few hours to research the current state of the market. Rather than just walking into the nearest travel agent or airline office, it pays to do a bit of research and shop around. Start shopping for a ticket early – some of the cheapest tickets must be bought months in advance, and some popular flights sell out early.

Most major newspapers in the US produce weekly travel sections with numerous travel agents' ads. You may decide to pay more than the rock-bottom fare by opting for the safety of a better-known travel agent. Established firms like STA Travel (☎ 800-777-0112) and Council Travel (☎ 800-226-8624) are valid alternatives and offer good prices to most destinations. Both have offices in major cities nationwide; STA has a Web site at www.statravel.com and Council Travel is at www.counciltravel.com.

Those coming from outside the US might start by perusing travel sections of magazines like *Time Out* and *TNT* in the UK, or the Saturday edition of newspapers like the *Sydney Morning Herald* and *The Age* in Australia.

Phoning a travel agent is still one of the best ways to dig up bargains. However, airlines have started to cater more to budget travelers and can sometimes offer the same deals you'll get with a travel agent. Airlines often have competitive low-season, student and senior citizens' fares. Find out not only the fare, but the route (is it direct or are there lots of stops?), the duration of the journey (how long are the layovers?) and any restrictions on the ticket (does it cost to change the dates?).

Use the Internet to hunt for low fares. Cheap Tickets (www.cheaptickets.com) and Travelocity (www.travelocity.com) are two services that can help. To buy a ticket via the Web you'll need a credit card.

Some airlines now offer special deals on the Internet. United Airlines offers e-fares, a program in which tickets for selected routes and dates are released every Wednesday at substantial discounts. These tickets are snapped up almost as soon as

Sample Fares to US Cities

city	low season	high season
Auckland to:		
LA	NZ$1730	NZ$1880
NYC	NZ$2120	NZ$2270
Denver	NZ$2120	NZ$2270
Frankfurt to:		
LA	DM1599	DM1119
NYC	DM 979	DM599
Denver	DM1099	DM1029
London to:		
LA	£467	£259
NYC	£305	£168
Denver	£550	£330
Paris to:		
LA	2400FF	4070FF
NYC	1650FF	3217FF
Denver	2550FF	4383FF
Sydney to:		
LA	A$1349	A$1799
NYC	A$1599	A$2049
Denver	A$1650	A$1850
Tokyo to:		
LA	US$860	US$1040
	¥125,474	¥151,736
NYC	US$900	US$1185
	¥131,310	¥172,891
Denver	US$1050	US$1185
	¥153,195	¥172,891
Toronto to:		
Denver	C$1474	C$1503
Vancouver to:		
Denver	C$1883	C$1902

they are released, so you'll need to log on to United's Web site (www.ual.com) early Wednesday. To purchase these tickets you'll need to register with United and also be a member of its Mileage Plus frequent-flyer program (call ☎ 605-399-2400 to sign up).

Ticket conditions are highly inflexible, so read the directions and requirements carefully.

The cheapest tickets are often nonrefundable and require an extra fee for changing your flight. Many insurance policies will

Air Travel Glossary

Alliances Many of the world's leading airlines are now intimately involved with each other, sharing everything from reservations systems and check-in to aircraft and frequent-flyer schemes. Opponents say that alliances restrict competition. Whatever the arguments, there is no doubt that big alliances are the way of the future.

Courier Fares Businesses often need to send urgent documents or freight securely and quickly. Courier companies hire people to accompany the package through customs and, in return, offer a discount ticket that is sometimes a bargain. However, you may have to surrender all your baggage allowance and take only carry-on luggage.

Fares Airlines traditionally offer 1st-class (coded F), business-class (coded J) and economy-class (coded Y) tickets. These days, there are so many promotional and discounted fares available that few passengers pay full fare.

Lost Tickets If you lose your airline ticket, an airline will usually treat it as a travelers check and, after inquiries, issue you another one. Legally, however, an airline is entitled to treat it as cash, so if you lose it, then it could be gone forever. Take very good care of your tickets.

Onward Tickets An entry requirement for many countries is that you have a ticket out of the country. If you're unsure of your next move, the easiest solution is to buy the cheapest onward ticket to a neighboring country or a ticket (from a reliable airline) that can later be refunded if you do not use it.

Open-Jaw Tickets These are return tickets used to fly out to one place but return from another. If available, this can save you from having to backtrack to your arrival point.

Overbooking Since every flight has some passengers who fail to show up, airlines often book more passengers than they have seats. Usually excess passengers make up for the no-shows, but occasionally somebody gets 'bumped' onto the next available flight. Who is it most likely to be? The passengers who check in late. If you do get 'bumped,' you are normally offered some form of compensation.

Reconfirmation Some airlines require you to reconfirm your flight at least 72 hours prior to departure. Check your travel documents to see if this is the case.

Restrictions Discounted tickets often have various restrictions on them – such as mandatory advance payment and penalties for alterations or cancellations. Others have restrictions on the minimum and maximum period you must be away.

Ticketless Travel Airlines are gradually waking up to the realization that paper tickets are unnecessary encumbrances. On simple one-way or return trips, reservations details can be held on computer, and the passengers merely show identification to claim their seats.

Transferred Tickets Airline tickets cannot be transferred from one person to another. Travelers sometimes try to sell the return half of their tickets, but officials can ask you to prove that you are the person named on the ticket. On an international flight, the name on the ticket is compared with the name on the passport.

cover this loss if you have to change your flight for emergency reasons. Roundtrip (return) tickets usually work out cheaper than two one-way fares – often *much* cheaper.

Once you have your ticket, remember to write down its number, together with the flight number and other details, and keep the information somewhere separate from the originals but still accessible. If the ticket is lost or stolen, having this information readily available will help you get a replacement ticket.

Special Fares for Foreign Visitors Most domestic carriers offer Visit USA passes to non-US citizens. The passes are actually a book of coupons – you redeem one coupon for each flight. Typically, the minimum number of coupons is three or four and the maximum is eight or 10, and they must be purchased in conjunction with an international airline ticket anywhere outside the USA except Canada or Mexico. Coupons cost anywhere from $100 to $160, depending on how many you purchase.

Most airlines require you to plan your itinerary in advance and to complete your flights within 60 days of arrival, but rules can vary between individual airlines. A few airlines may allow you to use coupons on standby, in which case you should call the airline a day or two before the flight and make a standby reservation. Such a reservation gives you priority over all other travelers who just appear and hope to get on the flight the same day.

Round-the-World Tickets RTW tickets have become very popular in recent years. They are often real bargains and can work out to be no more expensive or even cheaper than an ordinary return ticket. Your best bet is to find a travel agent that advertises or specializes in RTW tickets. Prices start at about UK£850, A$1800 or US$1300. These are for 'short' routes such as Los Angeles-New York-London-Bangkok-Honolulu-Los Angeles. As soon as you start adding stops south of the equator, fares can go up to the US$2000 to US$3000 range.

RTW tickets are usually put together by a combination of two or more airlines, and they permit you to fly anywhere you want on their route systems as long as you do not backtrack. Usually you must book the first sector in advance, and cancellation penalties apply. There may be restrictions on the number of stops permitted, and tickets are usually valid from 90 days up to a year. An alternative RTW ticket is one put together by a travel agent combining discounted tickets.

Travelers with Special Needs

If you have special needs of any sort – a broken leg, dietary restrictions, dependence on a wheelchair, responsibility for a baby, severe fear of flying – you should let the airline know as soon as possible so it they can make arrangements accordingly. Airports and airlines can be surprisingly helpful, but they do need advance warning. You should remind them when you reconfirm your booking (at least 72 hours before departure) and again when you check in at the airport.

Most international airports can provide escorts from check-in desk to plane where needed, and there should be ramps, lifts, accessible toilets and reachable phones. Aircraft toilets, on the other hand, are likely to present a problem; travelers should discuss this with the airline at an early stage and, if necessary, with their doctor.

Guide dogs for the blind will often have to travel in a specially pressurized baggage compartment with other animals, away from their owner, though smaller guide dogs may be admitted to the cabin. Guide dogs are not subject to quarantine as long as they have proof of being vaccinated against rabies.

Deaf travelers can ask for airport and inflight announcements to be written down for them.

Children under two travel for 10% of the standard fare (or free, on some airlines), as long as they don't occupy their own seat. 'Skycots' should be provided by the airline if requested in advance; these will take a child weighing up to about 22lb. Strollers can often be taken on as hand luggage.

Baggage & Other Restrictions

On most domestic and international flights you are limited to two checked bags and one carry-on. There could be a charge if you bring more or if the size of the bags exceeds the airline's limits. It's best to check with the individual airline if you are worried about this. On some international flights the luggage allowance is based on weight, not size or number of bags; again, check with the airline.

If your luggage is delayed upon arrival (which is rare), some airlines will give a cash advance to purchase necessities. If sporting equipment is misplaced, the airline may pay for rentals. Should the luggage be lost, it is important to submit a claim. The airline doesn't have to pay the full amount of the claim, rather it can estimate the value of your lost items. It may take anywhere from six weeks to three months to process the claim and pay you.

Smoking is prohibited on all domestic flights within the USA. Many international flights are following suit. Most airports in the USA also restrict smoking.

Arriving in the USA

Even if you are continuing immediately to another city, the first US airport that you land in is where you must carry out immigration and customs formalities. If your luggage is checked from, say, London to Denver, and your flight first lands in New York City, you will have to take your bags through customs there. For more information on customs requirements and limits look under US Customs in Facts for the Visitor.

If you have a non-US passport, with a visa, you must complete an Arrival/Departure Record (form I-94) before you approach the immigration desk. It's usually handed out on the plane, along with the customs declaration. To answer 'Address while in the United States,' give the address

of the location where you will spend the first night.

The staff of the Immigration & Nationalization Service (INS) can be less than welcoming. Their main concern is to exclude those who are likely to work illegally or overstay, so visitors will be asked about their plans, and perhaps about whether they have sufficient funds for their stay. If they think you're OK, a six-month entry is usually approved.

It's a good idea to be able to list an itinerary that will account for the period for which you ask to be admitted, and to be able to show you have $300 or $400 for every week of your intended stay. These days, a couple of major credit cards will go a long way toward establishing 'sufficient funds.' Don't make too much of having friends, relatives or business contacts in the USA – the INS official may decide that this will make you more likely to overstay.

Departure Tax

Airport departure taxes are normally included in the cost of tickets bought in the USA, although tickets purchased abroad may not have this included.

The USA

Buy domestic air tickets in the USA as early as possible, since this is the main way to get the cheapest fares. The lowest priced tickets are 21-day advance purchase, followed by 14-day and seven-day advance purchase. Tickets between major destinations (like New York to Denver) that are purchased within seven days of departure can become ridiculously expensive, usually ranging from $1000 to $1300, compared to $250 to $500 if you buy three weeks in advance.

For information on where to hunt down bargain fares and buy tickets see Buying Tickets, earlier. Following are some sample roundtrip fares (based on 21-day advance purchase) and approximate direct flying times between major US airports and Denver International Airport (DIA), the hub for air travel to the Rockies region. Note that direct flights often cost more, so if you get a bargain ticket you may be facing one or more stopovers and thus a longer flight.

city	fare	duration
Chicago	$250	2¼ hours
Los Angeles	$200	2½ hours
Miami	$500	3¾ hours
New York	$300	3½ hours
San Francisco	$200	2¾ hours

Canada
Travel CUTS (☎ 888-838-2887) has offices in all major cities; check with them online at www.travelcuts.com. The Toronto *Globe and Mail* and *Vancouver Sun* carry travel agents' ads.

Australia & New Zealand
STA Travel (www.statravel.com) and Flight Centre International (www.flightcentre .com.au) are major dealers in cheap air fares; check the travel agents' ads in the yellow pages and call around. Qantas flies to Los Angeles from Sydney, Melbourne (via Sydney or Auckland) and Cairns. United flies to San Francisco from Sydney and Melbourne (via Sydney) and also flies to Los Angeles.

The cheapest tickets have a 21-day advance-purchase requirement, a minimum stay of seven days and a maximum stay of 60 days. Flying with Air New Zealand is slightly cheaper, and both Qantas and Air New Zealand offer tickets with longer stays or stopovers, but you pay more.

The UK
Check the ads in magazines like *Time Out,* plus the *Evening Standard* and *TNT.* Also check the free magazines widely available in London – start by looking outside the main railway stations.

London is arguably the world's headquarters for bucket shops, which are well advertised and can usually beat published airline fares. Good, reliable agents for inexpensive tickets in the UK are Trailfinders (☎ 020-7628-7628), 1 Threadneedle St, London, EC2R 8JX, with a Web site at www.trailfinder.com; Council Travel (☎ 020-7437-7767), 28a Poland St, London, W1; and STA Travel (☎ 020-7581-4132), 86 Old Brompton Rd, London SW7 3LQ.

Continental Europe
In Amsterdam, NBBS (☎ 624 09 89) at Rokin 38 (and other locations throughout the city) is a popular travel agent. In Paris, Council Travel (☎ 01 44 55 55 65) is at 22, rue des Pyramides, 75001. For student fares, contact USIT Voyages (☎ 01 43 29 69 50), 85, Bd Saint Michel, 75005 Paris.

The most common route to the Rocky Mountain states from Europe is west via New York, but other gateway cities like Miami and Atlanta are alternatives. If you're interested in heading east with stops in Asia, it may be cheaper to get a Round-the-World ticket instead of returning same way.

Asia
Hong Kong and Bangkok are the region's two best spots to buy discount airplane tickets, but some bucket shops can be unreliable. Ask the advice of other travelers before buying a ticket. STA Travel, which is dependable, has branches in Hong Kong, Tokyo, Singapore, Bangkok, Manila and Kuala Lumpur.

Of all the carriers serving the US from Asia, United Airlines and Northwest Airlines have the largest number of routes and flights. Some of the lowest fares are offered by Malaysia Airlines and Korean Airlines, which serve southeast and northeast Asia, respectively, as well as Hong Kong.

Central & South America
Most flights from Central and South America go via Miami, Houston or Los Angeles, though some fly via New York. Most countries' international flag carriers (like Aerolíneas Argentinas and LAN-Chile) as well as US airlines (like United and American) serve these destinations, with onward connections. Continental has flights from about 20 cities in Mexico and Central America, including San Jose, Guatemala City, Cancún and Mérida.

LAND

Unless you're one of the few who travel by train, you'll probably be using one of several interstate highways to reach the Rockies by land. Interstates 70 and 80, both of which run nearly the entire length of the USA, pass through central Colorado and southern Wyoming, respectively. Interstate 25 runs north-south from New Mexico through Colorado and ends at a junction with I-90 in northern Wyoming. I-90 in turn runs north and then heads west to span most of southern Montana before continuing on through northern Idaho and on to Seattle, Washington. Southern Idaho is linked to Portland, Oregon, by I-84 while I-15 connects southeast Idaho and western Montana with Salt Lake City, Utah, and Las Vegas, Nevada.

Bus

Greyhound (www.greyhound.com), the only nationwide bus company, has reduced local services considerably, but still runs cross-country buses between San Francisco and New York via Wyoming, Denver and Chicago; between Seattle and New York via Minneapolis–St Paul and Chicago; and between Los Angeles and New York via Las Vegas, Denver and Chicago. There are also bus services from other eastern seaboard cities like Philadelphia and Washington, DC, and southern cities like Atlanta and Miami.

Because buses are so few, schedules can be inconvenient. Fares are relatively high and bargain air fares can undercut buses on long-distance routes; on shorter routes it can be cheaper to rent a car than to ride the bus. However, very long-distance bus trips are often available at bargain prices by purchasing or reserving tickets three days in advance. For more details, see the Bus entry in the Getting Around chapter.

Train

Amtrak (☎ 800-872-7245, 800-523-6590 TTY) provides cross-country passenger service between the West Coast and Chicago; travelers to or from the East Coast must make connections in Chicago. Routes are limited, fares can be expensive and trains often run behind schedule, so only dedicated train travelers will care to take on the adventures of Amtrak travel. The train is an even worse option for getting around within the Rocky Mountain states (as opposed to getting to them); due to service cutbacks, Amtrak trains serve only a few destinations besides Denver.

The northernmost route is the daily *Empire Builder,* which runs from Seattle through northern Montana to Minneapolis and Chicago. The *Empire Builder* makes 12 stops in Montana (including East Glacier and Whitefish) and one stop in Idaho at Sandpoint.

The daily *California Zephyr* from San Francisco (via Emeryville, California) passes through Colorado en route to Chicago. Stops in Colorado include Denver, Fraser-Winter Park, Glenwood Springs and Grand Junction.

The *Southwest Chief* goes from Los Angeles via Albuquerque and the southern Colorado towns of Trinidad, La Junta and Lamar to Kansas City and Chicago. There is no passenger train service in Wyoming or southern Idaho.

Amtrak tickets may be purchased aboard the train without penalty if the station is not open 30 minutes prior to boarding. Rail travel is generally cheaper if you purchase tickets in advance. Roundtrips are the best bargain, but even these are usually as expensive as air fares, if not more so.

A good overall value is the 30-day **North America Rail Pass**, which enables US, Canadian and international passengers unlimited travel in the US (on Amtrak) and Canada (on VIA Rail Canada). This costs $459 (off peak) for adults; during peak travel dates (between June 1st and October 15th) the cost is $656. A 10% discount is available to seniors (over 60), children (ages 2 to 18) and students (with Student Advantage Card in the US or ISIC card in Canada).

For non-US citizens, Amtrak also offers a **USA Rail Pass,** which comes in three types and must be purchased outside the US; check with your travel agent or Amtrak's Web site at www.amtrak.com.

Another travel package is **Amtrak Air Rail** (☎ 800-437-3441), a partnership with United Airlines that allows you to take the train one-way and travel the other way by air. It's a bit limited, as you must start and end your journey from the same city.

For further travel assistance, call Amtrak, surf its Web site or ask your travel agent. Note that most small train stations don't sell tickets; you have to book them with Amtrak over the phone. Some small stations have no porters or other facilities, and trains may stop there only if you have bought a ticket in advance.

Car & Motorcycle

Drivers of cars and riders of motorbikes will need to have the vehicle's registration papers, liability insurance and an international driver's permit in addition to their domestic license. Canadian and Mexican driver's licenses are accepted. Customs officials along the entry points between Canada and Montana can be strict and wary of anything that doesn't look straight-laced.

For information on buying or renting a car, or using a drive-away (driving a car for someone else) see the Getting Around chapter.

ORGANIZED TOURS

Tours of the USA are so numerous that it would be impossible to attempt a comprehensive listing; for overseas visitors, the most reliable sources of information on the constantly changing offerings are major international travel agents.

Probably those of most interest to the general traveler are coach tours that visit the national parks and guest ranch excursions; for those with limited time, package tours can be an efficient and relatively inexpensive way to go. In addition to traditional package tours, there are a variety of outdoors and nature trips available, as well as study and environmental tours to the Rocky Mountain states.

An excellent place to search for unique outdoor trips is the Great Outdoors Recreation Pages (GORP; www.gorp.com), which lists tours from reputable operators.

Green Tortoise (☎ 415-956-7500, 800-867-8647), 494 Broadway, San Francisco, CA 94133, offers alternative bus transportation with stops at places like hot springs and national parks. Meals are cooperatively cooked, and you sleep on bunks on the bus or camp. It's not luxury travel, but it's fun.
Web site: www.greentortoise.com

Trek America (☎ 973-983-1144, 800-221-0596), PO Box 189, Rockaway, NJ 07866, offers roundtrip camping tours to different areas of the country. In England, they are at 4 Water Perry Court, Middleton Rd, Banbury, Oxon OX16 8QG (☎ 01295-256777, fax 01295-257399). These tours last from one to nine weeks and are designed for small, international groups of 18- to 38-year-olds. Tour prices vary with season, with July to September being the most expensive.
Web site: www.trekamerica.com

American Adventures/Road Runner (☎ 800-873-5872, 800-864-0335), 1050 Hancock, Quincy, MA 02169, organizes one- and two-week treks in conjunction with Hostelling International to different parts of the Rockies and across the USA.

Elderhostel (☎ 877-426-8056), 75 Federal St, Boston, MA 02110, is a nonprofit organization offering international educational programs and active trips for those ages 55 and above, and has programs throughout the West.
Web site: www.elderhostel.org

Outdoor Adventure River Specialists (OARS; ☎ 209-736-4677, 800-346-6277), PO Box 67, Angels Camp, CA 95222, runs river rafting and kayak trips on Wyoming's Snake River, Jackson Lake and Yellowstone Lake, Colorado's Yampa and Green Rivers near the border with Utah (including Cataract Canyon), as well as Idaho's Salmon River.
Web site: www.oars.com

Bicycling, hiking and walking, running and multisport tours are another possibility. Two good outfits for this kind of activity are Backroads (☎ 510-527-1555, 800-462-2848), 801 Cedar St, Berkeley, CA 94710 and The World Outside (☎ 303-413-0938, 800-488-8483), 2840 Wilderness Place, suite F, Boulder, CO 80301. Check out their respective Web sites at www.backroads.com and www.theworldoutside.com.

The University of California Research Expeditions Program (☎ 530-752-0692), at the University of California, Davis, runs volunteer work-study expeditions assisting scholars in the field with research projects, some of which occasionally take place in the Rocky Mountain region.

Web site: www.urep.ucdavis.edu

Try Gray Line Tours (☎ 303-433-9800) for standard package bus tours of Rocky Mountain sights. Discover Colorado Scenic Tours (☎ 303-277-0129, 800-641-0129), 2401 East St, No 204, Golden, CO 80401, offers unique, historic and scenic tours.

Getting Around

The states in the Rocky Mountain region are fairly well connected by commuter flights, although the cost may deter most travelers from using this option. On the ground, public transportation in the region leaves much to be desired, and travelers without their own vehicles need to be patient and flexible to take advantage of the limited possibilities.

AIR

Denver International Airport (DIA) is the main air hub for the Rockies, and from here you can get flights to destinations in all four states covered in this book. For information on DIA, see Getting There & Away in the Denver section of the Denver & Boulder chapter.

Most of the short flights within the region carry high price tags. The best way to cut down the cost is to link your regional flight with your flight into Denver or Salt Lake City, UT, in which case the commuter connection is often a fraction what it would cost to book it separately.

Colorado

There are commercial airports at Alamosa, Aspen, Colorado Springs, Cortez, Durango, Fort Collins, Grand Junction, Gunnison (near Crested Butte), Lamar, Montrose, Pueblo, Telluride, Vail (Eagle County) and Yampa Valley (serving Steamboat Springs). All of these destinations are served by flights out of Denver, and Grand Junction also has flights to Salt Lake City, UT. During ski season, the resort airports offer direct flights to major cities around the United States.

Wyoming

Airports around this state are at Casper, Cheyenne, Cody, Gillette, Jackson Hole, Laramie, Riverton, Rock Springs, Sheridan and Worland. Most of Wyoming's airports are not connected to each other, but are instead served by flights out of Denver, CO.

Montana

Commercial airports are at Billings, Bozeman, Glacier National Park (between Whitefish and Kalispell), Great Falls, Helena, Lewistown, Missoula, West Yellowstone and Miles City. Most airports are connected with out-of-state destinations like Salt Lake City or Seattle, Washington, and some airports have in-state flights, such as Helena–Great Falls or Missoula-Kalispell.

Idaho

The main airport is in Boise. Airports at Challis, Hailey, Lewiston, McCall, Salmon and Stanley have connections to Boise. Idaho Falls, Pocatello and Twin Falls airports have flights to Boise, Denver and Salt Lake City.

BUS

Since Americans rely so much on their cars and usually take planes for long-distance trips, bus transport is less frequent than is desirable, but some good deals are available. Greyhound, the main bus line for the region, has extensive fixed routes and its own terminal in most central cities. The company has an excellent safety record, and the buses are comfortable and usually on time.

Other regional bus lines operate in the area. TNM&O (Texas–New Mexico & Oklahoma Coaches, Inc) is affiliated with Greyhound and serves the same lines through Colorado and parts of Wyoming. Powder River Coach USA primarily serves eastern Wyoming, but it also goes to Denver; Billings, Montana; and Rapid City, South Dakota. Rim Rock Stages serves Montana destinations.

Greyhound tickets can be bought over the phone or online with a credit card (American Express, MasterCard or Visa) and mailed if purchased 10 days in advance, or picked up at the terminal with proper identification. Discounts apply to tickets purchased 14 or 21 days in advance.

Greyhound terminals also accept traveler's checks and cash. All buses are nonsmoking, and reservations are made with ticket purchases only.

To contact Greyhound International about fares, promotions, ticketing and routes, call ☎ 800-231-2222 or ☎ 800-246-8572, or log on to www.greyhound.com.

Special Fares

Greyhound occasionally introduces a mileage-based discount fare program that can be a bargain, especially for very long distances, but it's a good idea to check the regular fare anyway.

Ameripass

Greyhound's Ameripass is potentially useful, depending on how much you plan to travel, but the relatively high prices may impel you to travel more than you normally would simply to get your money's worth. There are no restrictions on who can buy an Ameripass; it costs $185 for seven days of unlimited travel, $235 for 10 days, $285 for 15 days, $335 for 21 days, $385 for 30 days, $419 for 45 days and $509 for 60 days. Children under 12 travel for half price, and discounts (with proper ID) are also offered to college students and seniors (over 62). You can get on and off at any Greyhound stop or terminal, and the Ameripass can be bought at any terminal or can be purchased online (at least 14 days in advance).

International Ameripass

This can be purchased only by non–US citizens. Prices options include $135 for a four-day Greyhound pass for unlimited travel, $155 for seven days, $209 for 10 days, $235 for 15 days, $285 for 21 days, $335 for 30 days, $355 for 45 days and $449 for 60 days; children under 12 travel for half price. Those buying an International Ameripass must complete an affidavit and present a passport or visa (or waiver) to the appropriate Greyhound officials.

The International Ameripass can be bought abroad at a travel agency, online (at least 21 days in advance) or at the Greyhound International office (☎ 212-971-0492) in the Port Authority Bus Terminal in New York City, 625 8th Ave at 41st St.

TRAIN

Rail service within the Rocky Mountains region is very limited. Amtrak's long-distance trains are few and serve only a small number of destinations. For more information, see the Land section in the Getting There & Away chapter.

Tourist trains, which are essentially day trips, include the weekend *Ski Train* from Denver's Union Station to Winter Park, CO; the Durango & Silverton Narrow Gauge Railroad in southern Colorado; the Georgetown Loop out of Georgetown, CO; the Cumbres & Toltec Scenic Railroad from Antonito, CO, to Chama, New Mexico; and the Pike's Peak Cog Railway in Manitou Springs, CO. Although they are tourist trains, the Durango and Cumbres lines allow backpackers and anglers access to wilderness areas at their water stops. In Montana, Rockies Rail Tours runs luxury trips between Billings or Bozeman and Sandpoint, ID (with bus transfer on to Spokane, WA), as well as trips that go through Livingston, the Paradise Valley and Yellowstone National Park.

On many of these trains it's imperative that you make reservations or buy advance tickets. For regional fares and specifics on tourist trains, check the destination listing in the text.

CAR & MOTORCYCLE

The US highway system is extensive, and, since distances are great and buses can be infrequent, auto transport is well worth considering despite the expense. Foreigners will need an International or Inter-American Driving Permit to supplement your national driver's license.

Rental

Major international rental agencies like Avis, Budget, Hertz and National have offices throughout the Rocky Mountain region, but there are also local agencies. To rent a car, you must have a valid driver's license, be at least 25 years of age and

Mileage Chart

Following are distances between major cities in the Rocky Mountain states:

Boise to	
Denver	814 miles

Bozeman to	
Kalispell	324 miles
Missoula	201 miles
West Yellowstone	89 miles

Cheyenne to	
Jackson	436 miles
Sheridan	329 miles

Coeur d'Alene to	
Boise	454 miles

Denver to	
Cheyenne	100 miles
Grand Junction	246 miles
Salt Lake City	512 miles

Missoula to	
Coeur d'Alene	168 miles

Sheridan to	
Bozeman	269 miles

present a major credit card or a large cash deposit.

Many rental agencies have bargain rates for weekend or weeklong rentals, especially outside the peak summer and ski seasons. Prices vary greatly in relation to region, season and type or size of the car you rent. If you belong to any frequent-flyer programs, ask what discounts they entitle you to.

Basic liability insurance, which will cover damage that you may cause to another vehicle, is required by law in some states, in which case it is included in the price of renting the car. In other states you have the option of whether or not to purchase liability insurance, which is also called third-party coverage. While it can cost you an extra $10 per day, it may be well worth it: The fee is nothing compared to what a lawsuit in the litigation-happy USA could do to your finances.

Collision insurance, also called the Collision Damage Waiver (CDW), is optional; it covers the full value of the vehicle in case of an accident. You don't need to buy this waiver to rent the car. If you have collision insurance on your personal auto insurance policy, this may also cover rental cars. Again, check with your insurance company to find out.

Some credit-card companies will cover certain types of insurance if you charge the full cost of rental to your card; check with your credit-card company for details.

Agencies also tack on a daily fee per each additional driver in the car (usually around $5 per day).

The following is a list of some of the major car rental agencies:

Alamo	☎ 800-327-9633
Avis	☎ 800-831-2847
Budget	☎ 800-527-0700
Dollar	☎ 800-800-4000
Enterprise	☎ 800-325-8007
Hertz	☎ 800-654-3131
Thrifty	☎ 800-367-2277

Purchase

If you're spending several months in the USA, purchasing a car is worth considering; a car is more flexible than public transport and likely to be cheaper than rentals, but buying one can also be complicated and requires plenty of research.

If you want to purchase a car, contact AAA (☎ 800-222-4357) for general information. Then contact the state's Dept of Motor Vehicles to find out about registration fees and insurance, which can be very confusing and expensive.

Inspect the title carefully before purchasing the car; the owner's name that appears on the title must match the identification of the person selling you the car.

While insurance is not obligatory in every state in the US, all states have financial responsibility laws and insurance is highly desirable; without it, a serious accident could leave you a pauper. (Liability insurance is mandatory in the four states

Accidents Do Happen

In such an auto-dependent country as the USA, accidents do happen. It's important that a visitor know the appropriate protocol when involved in a 'fender-bender' (or worse).

- *Don't try to drive away!* Remain at the scene of the accident; otherwise you may spend some time in the local jail.

- Call the police (and an ambulance, if needed) immediately, and give the operator as much specific information as possible (your location, if there are any injuries involved, etc). The emergency phone number is ☎ 911.

- Get the other driver's name, address, driver's license number, license plate and insurance information. Be prepared to provide any documentation you have, such as your passport, international driver's license and insurance documents.

- Tell your story to the police carefully. Refrain from answering any questions until you feel comfortable doing so (with a lawyer present, if need be). That's your right under the law. The only insurance information you need to reveal is the name of your insurance carrier and your policy number.

- Always comply to an alcohol breathalyzer test. If you take the option not to, you'll almost certainly find yourself with an automatic suspension of your driving privileges.

- If you're driving a rental car, call the rental company promptly.

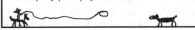

covered in this book.) In order to get insurance, some states require that you have a US driver's license and that you have been licensed for at least 18 months. If you meet those qualifications, you may still have to pay anywhere from $300 to $1200 a year for insurance, depending on the state and where the car is registered. The minimum term for a policy is usually six months, but some insurance companies will refund the difference on a prorated basis if the car is sold and the policy voluntarily terminated. Collision coverage has become very expensive, with high deductibles, and is generally not worthwhile unless the car is somewhat valuable. Regulations vary from state to state but are generally becoming stringent throughout the USA.

Holders of foreign driver's licenses may have difficulty finding insurance firms that will sell you a policy. AAA may be able to help.

Drive-Aways

When a car-owner can't drive their car to a specific destination but is willing to allow someone else to drive it for them, they might use a drive-away service. For example, if somebody moves from Boston to Denver, they may elect to fly and leave the car with a drive-away agency. The agency will find a driver and take care of all necessary insurance and permits. If you happen to want to drive from Boston to Denver and have a valid license and a clean driving record, you can apply to drive the car. Normally, you have to pay a small refundable deposit. You pay for the gas (though sometimes a gas allowance is given).

You are allowed a set number of days to deliver the car – usually based on driving eight hours a day. You are also allowed a limited number of miles, based on the best route and allowing for reasonable side trips, so you can't just zigzag all over the country. However, this is a cheap way to get around if you enjoy long-distance driving and meet eligibility requirements.

Drive-away companies are listed in the yellow pages of telephone directories under 'Automobile Transporters & Drive-Away Companies.' You need to be flexible about dates and destinations when you call.

Safety

Drivers should be aware that much of the Rocky Mountain region is open-range country in which cattle and, less frequently, sheep forage along the highway. A collision with a large animal (including game animals like deer or moose) can wreck a car and severely injure or kill the driver and passengers, not to mention the animal, so pay attention to the roadside – especially at night. Seat belts are obligatory for the driver and all passengers in all four states.

During winter months, especially at the higher elevations, there will be times when tire chains are required on snowy or icy roads. Sometimes roads will be closed to cars without chains or 4WD, so it's a good idea to keep a set of chains in the trunk. Other cold-weather precautions include keeping a wool blanket, warm clothing, extra food, a windshield ice-scraper, a snow shovel, flares and an extra set of gloves and boots in the trunk for emergencies.

Some states have motorcycle helmet laws. Colorado doesn't, but Wyoming stipulates that riders under the age of 19 must wear helmets, while Montana and Idaho require helmets on those under 18. Use of a helmet is *highly* recommended regardless of your age.

Weather is a serious factor throughout the Rocky Mountain states, especially in winter. All four states provide road and travel information as well as state highway patrol information by telephone; for these numbers, see the Emergency section in the Facts for the Visitor chapter and Information for each regional and state chapter.

To avert theft, do not leave expensive items such as purses, compact discs, cameras, leather bags or even sunglasses visibly lying about in the car. Tuck items under the seat, or even better, put them in the trunk. Don't leave valuables in the car overnight.

TAXI

Minivans or taxis connect some popular tourist destinations (notably ski areas), like Denver and Winter Park, CO, or Jackson and Pinedale, WY. Taxis are especially expensive for long distances, but aren't so outrageous if shared among two or three people. Check with the service before setting out regarding fares per person, return-trip fees and taxes. Check the yellow pages under 'Taxi' for phone numbers and services. Drivers often expect a tip of about 10% of the fare.

BICYCLE

Cycling is an interesting, inexpensive and increasingly popular way to travel in the USA, and in the Rocky Mountain states especially. Roads are good, shoulders are usually wide and there are many good routes for mountain bikes as well. The changeable weather can be a drawback, especially at high altitudes where thunderstorms are frequent. Cyclists should carry at least two full bottles and refill them at every opportunity. Spare parts are widely available and repair shops are numerous. Some cities require helmets, others don't, but they should always be worn.

Bicycles can be transported by air, but always check the specific rules with the airline well in advance. For more details, see the Bicycling section in the Activities chapter.

HITCHHIKING

It is never entirely safe to hitchhike in any country in the world, and we don't recommend it. Travelers who decide to hitch should understand that you are taking a small but potentially serious risk. People who do choose to hitch will be safer if you travel in pairs and let someone know where you are planning to go.

Because public transport is so limited in parts of the Rocky Mountain states, especially in Wyoming, Montana and Idaho, some visitors may be tempted to hitchhike to areas that are difficult to access. Should you hitch, keep a close watch on your possessions; there have been instances of 'friendly' drivers absconding with an innocent hitchhiker's possessions while the latter visited the toilet during a gasoline stop.

In Colorado, hitchhiking is illegal and pedestrians on the highway must walk in the opposite direction of traffic. It is legal in Montana and Wyoming, though restricted in areas near state prisons in Montana. Hitchhiking in Idaho is illegal on interstates, though it's allowed on all other roads.

Colorado

Facts about Colorado

The best known of the Rocky Mountain states, Colorado owes its fame to the mountains that soar to majestic heights and create unrivaled vistas and recreation opportunities. This wealth of alpine scenery means that during the peak summer season when millions of tourists flood the state, visitors still can find solitude at a remote mountain lake or meadow or atop a craggy summit. Even Rocky Mountain National Park, the state's premier attraction, offers dozens of backcountry hikes and campgrounds that see few visitors (see the Northern Front Range chapter). The hiking, climbing and mountain biking found in Colorado's high country are among the best in the USA. During winter these areas are home to some of the world's most famous ski resorts.

But there is more than just mountains. Western Colorado has beautiful desert canyons and mesas, and areas like the sprawling San Luis Valley that open up to reveal farms and ranchlands. Rivers, including the Arkansas, Colorado and Rio Grande, snake throughout the state, offering outstanding white-water rafting, kayaking and canoeing. East of the Rockies the prairie lands of the Eastern Plains stretch far beyond the horizon.

Colorado's urban attractions mostly are located along the Front Range, the foothills that mark the eastern edge of the Rocky Mountains. Long derided as a glorified cowtown, Denver developed into a lively city with good entertainment, dining and culture. Nearby, the university town of Boulder draws visitors with its beautiful natural setting and progressive intellectual atmosphere.

Though not as homogeneous as Montana, Colorado is not very socially diverse. However, visits to the southern section of the state, particularly the San Luis Valley, reveal some nearly intact preserves of Hispanic culture (see the Southern Mountains chapter). Some Native Americans still live in the Ute Mountain and Southern Ute Indian reservations in southwest Colorado, which lie near the fascinating ruins of Mesa Verde National Park (see the Western Colorado chapter). Native American tribes used to inhabit large areas of the state until they were pushed back by European settlers in the late 19th century. Signs of these 'frontier days' are readily found throughout the state, particularly in historic mining towns such as Telluride, Creede and Crested Butte.

INFORMATION
State Tourist Offices

The Colorado Travel & Tourism Authority (☎ 800-COLORADO, 303-296-3384), PO Box 3524, Englewood, CO 80155, publishes useful summer and winter state vacation guides and offers regional information packages. It also operates Colorado Welcome Centers in Burlington, Cortez, Dinosaur, Fort Collins, Fruita, Julesburg, Lamar and Trinidad, where you'll find free state highway maps and a wealth of other travel information. Call ☎ 800-265-6723 to have a vacation guide sent to you. Its extensive Web site, www.colorado.com, features travel tips, itinerary planning and useful links. The Colorado Vacation & Adventure

Guides offers useful information on destinations, accommodations and suggested itineraries; visit www.coloradovacation.com.

Information is also available from the statewide Colorado Division of Wildlife (DOW; ☎ 303-297-1192) at 6060 Broadway, Denver, CO 80216.
Web site: www.dnr.state.co.us/wildlife/

For USFS information on the state, call the USFS Rocky Mountain Region headquarters (☎ 303-275-5350), 740 Simms St in Golden; its mailing address is PO Box 25127, Lakewood, CO 80225. For information about its 40 state parks and recreation areas, call ☎ 303-866-3437.
Web site: www.coloradoparks.org

See the Activities chapter for a list of the state's national parks and recreation areas.

To check on road conditions call ☎ 303-639-1234, or log onto the Colorado Dept of Transportation Web site, www.cotrip.org, which is loaded with useful travel and transport information.

Useful Organizations

Most of the many environmental and conservation groups in Colorado belong to the Colorado Environmental Coalition (CEC; ☎ 303-534-7066), 1536 Wynkoop St, No. 5C, Denver, CO 80202. CEC has field offices in Grand Junction and Durango.
Web site: www.ourcolorado.org

Area Codes

Originally covering the entire state, the telephone area code ☎ 303 now includes only the metropolitan Denver, Boulder and Golden areas. It has been replaced by ☎ 970 in the expansive northern and western regions, which stretch from Fort Collins all the way out to Grand Junction, and by ☎ 719 in the southeastern area of the state, which includes Colorado Springs and Pueblo.

Road Rules

Speed limits on state highways range from 55 to 65mph, and go as high as 75mph on interstate highways I-25 and I-70. Limits in cities are generally 25mph to 35mph. In general, Colorado is less tolerant of speeding than other Western states, and if you're consistently flaunting the speed limit you stand a good chance of meeting a representative of the highway patrol.

Seat belts are required for the driver and front seat passenger and for all passengers on highways and interstates. On motorcycles, helmets are required for anyone under 18.

Far more serious are the consequences (legal and otherwise) of drinking and driving. Driving while impaired (DWI) will probably land you in jail and definitely earn you heavy fines. Don't do it.

Taxes

Sales taxes are generally around 3% throughout Colorado, though the exact amount varies with each town. Many towns have a lodging tax of 2% or less, except in Denver where lodging tax is 12%. Denver also levies a dining tax on prepared food and beverages of 4%.

COLORADO

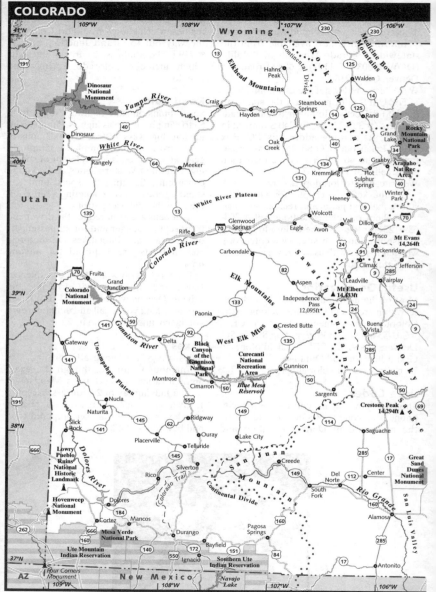

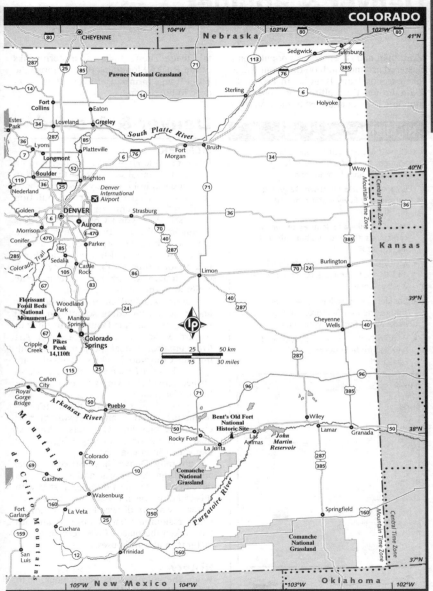

Denver & Boulder

More than half of Colorado's population is clustered around a hub on the Front Range that extends from Boulder in the north, south through the multitude of suburbs surrounding Denver and west to the Continental Divide. The foothills and eastern peaks of the Rocky Mountains that comprise the Front Range form a beautiful western backdrop to the region.

Highlights

- Denver Museum of Nature & Science – some of the USA's best wildlife, geological and dinosaur exhibits

- LoDo – lower downtown Denver, a surprisingly lively restaurant and nightlife hub

- 16th St Mall – a wide array of shops, cafes, bars and good restaurants make for a great stroll

- Mt Evans – amazing views from a 14,264-foot summit, a one-hour drive west of Denver

- Boulder – a hip college town offering culture and excellent hikes in its mountain parks at the foot of the Rockies

- Peak to Peak Hwy – the slowest and prettiest route between Boulder and Estes Park

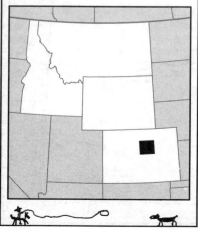

Denver & Around

DENVER

Denver's 'Mile High City' moniker is more than mere symbolism – one of the steps to the State Capitol is exactly 5280 feet above sea level. Metro Denver (population 2,152,000) represents an economic realm that extends beyond Colorado's borders throughout the Rocky Mountain region. Denver harbors the corporate headquarters for mining, oil and rail-transportation firms, plus regional offices for nearly every branch of the federal government. It is also the major air terminal for the region.

Visitors will find an array of museums and galleries, including some of national stature, such as the Denver Museum of Nature & Science and the Denver Art Museum. Professional sports teams, including the Colorado Rockies baseball team and the Denver Broncos football team, also attract a loyal following whose enthusiasm borders on mania.

Denver is a town for the outdoors-oriented. Flat terrain and a network of trails encourage bicycling. Of course, skiing at nearby mountain resorts is a big part of Denver's winter character.

Culturally, Denver has also come alive, and a vibrant local music and art scene has developed in the past decade. In step with this trend has been the revival of Denver's lower downtown district, known as 'LoDo,' where restaurants, bars, shops and galleries have taken the place of obsolescent manufacturers and warehouses.

History

When the gold seekers began flocking to the South Platte River Valley in 1859,

DENVER & AROUND

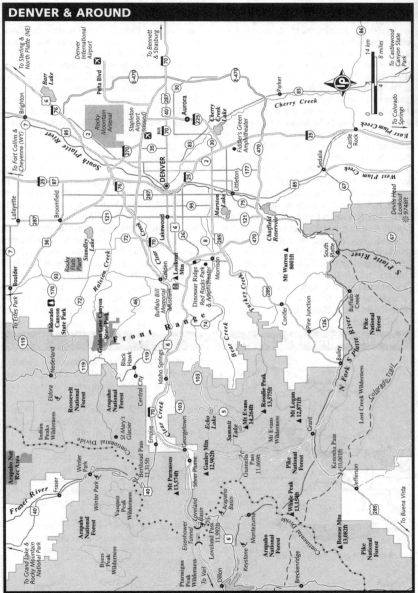

Arapaho and Cheyenne buffalo hunters already occupied hundreds of camps in the area. Urban development threatened the wilderness resources that Native Americans relied upon, and the new arrivals had little concern for the rights or welfare of the prior inhabitants.

By proposing to name the new town Denver, General William H Larimer made a shameless attempt to sway Kansas Territorial Governor James W Denver into granting Larimer and his partners a township at the confluence of Cherry Creek and the South Platte River. It worked, and the Denver City Township Company was set up in late 1859. On the west bank of Cherry Creek, another party had already laid out Auraria in 1858. Nevertheless, local claims of mineral riches were greatly exaggerated by the land promoters and many gold seekers became 'go-backers,' proclaiming the Pikes Peak gold claims to be nothing but humbug. New discoveries in 1859 on Clear Creek, west of Denver, which flows through present-day Golden, and in the South Park interior area, brought a resurgence of people to the human tide at the Front Range.

The gold rush led to increased overland freight and passenger business via horse and wagon, focusing on Denver. Its position at the foot of the Rocky Mountains was as convenient as any Front Range location for the shipments and financial operations that served mining areas in the mountains. But without water or rail transportation, Denver's overnight rise soon stagnated. Its isolated position south of the Transcontinental Railroad, opened in 1869 through Cheyenne, threatened to curtail all growth.

By 1881, Union Station opened to consolidate passenger traffic for five railroads. This Italian Romanesque station burned in 1894 and was replaced with the neoclassical Union Station, which anchored 17th St as the prominent location for banks and hotels, including the Oxford and Brown Palace. Finally in 1928 the Moffat Tunnel was opened to bring transcontinental rail traffic through Denver. At the pre-WWII height of railroad travel, 60 to 80 trains arrived or departed daily, carrying more than a million passengers each year. By 1954, train service was decreased by one-

---

The Life & Times of a Legend

William F 'Buffalo Bill' Cody gained his colorful sobriquet while working as a buffalo hunter for the Kansas Pacific Railroad in 1867. Prior to that he'd been a Pony Express rider and received the Medal of Honor as an Indian scout.

At his famous Wild West Show, which opened in 1883, Cody presented a cast of performers demonstrating shooting, riding and acting skills. His cast reflected racial and ethnic diversity not found in today's rodeo events (also see Cody in the Bighorn Country section of the Wyoming chapter). A featured performer was sharpshooter Miss Annie Oakley. Native Americans, including Chief Sitting Bull, were presented as proud and honorable people in reenacted battles. Russian cossacks and Mexican vaqueros were also part of the program.

'If Cody hadn't lived, we would've had to invent him,' joked Bill Carle, the park concessionaire whose family operated the Pikes Peak summit store from 1893 to 1992 and the Mt Evans Crest House from 1956 to 1979.

Early 'riot grrl' Annie Oakley

half, and passenger service is now limited to one Amtrak train daily.

Economic 'boom and bust' cycles have been common elements in Denver's past. The initial boom continued until 1893 when the Silver Panic destroyed the city's economy and threw the entire state into a depression. The following year discovery of rich gold deposits in Cripple Creek rejuvenated Denver's stature as a center of finance and commerce. Following the Great Depression, WWII brought wartime jobs at hastily built munitions and chemical warfare plants in and around the city. In 1952, Denver's 12-story height limit was repealed in the downtown area, excepting the historic districts. Denver's skyline sprouted high-rises (there are presently more than 20), but many of these suffered during the mid-1980s when an office construction boom suddenly turned into a glut. The cycle reversed yet again in the 1990s, and by the millennium Denver had become a hub for computer, telecommunication and other high-technology firms and service providers, which now underpin the local economy.

Several of Denver's dot-coms were affected by the post-millennium bubble-burst, but relative to other parts of the country (New York, California, Seattle, etc) the region weathered the storm well. Denver is heavier, in fact, with established high-technology companies than with actual dot-com start-ups, and though there have been some layoffs, most were administrative as opposed to tech-related jobs.

Orientation

Denver is on the flat plains abutting the eastern slope of the Rocky Mountains. The city's layout of streets and avenues follows a compass-oriented grid pattern outside of the diagonal blocks downtown.

Most of Denver's sights are in the downtown district, which roughly comprises a square defined to the south and east by Colfax Ave and Broadway. The 16th St Mall is the focus of most retail activity, and is close to some of the top-end hotels. Lower downtown, or 'LoDo,' which includes historic Larimer Square near Union Station, is the heart of Denver's restaurant and nightlife scene and arguably the most interesting urban district.

Information

Tourist Offices Denver's Convention & Visitors Bureau (☎ 303-892-1112) is in the Tabor Center, 1668 Larimer St. It's open 8 am to 5 pm Monday to Saturday, 10 am to 2 pm Sunday; the 'concierge desk' at the Lawrence St entrance of the Tabor Center keeps extended hours. Both offer free visitors' guides and myriad information on Denver. In addition to local sights, you can get information on most Colorado destinations here, or by logging onto www.denver.org.

For statewide lodging reservations, call ☎ 800-645-3446.

Money Among the larger banks with downtown offices, Wells Fargo Bank (☎ 303-861-8811) is at 1740 Broadway. For foreign currency exchange, head to Thomas Cook Currency Services (☎ 303-571-0808), 1625 Broadway, or American Express (☎ 303-298-7100), 555 S 17th St.

Post & Communications The Denver downtown post office at 951 20th St is open weekdays; the zip code is 80201. A convenient postal annex sits at the corner of 16th and Wynkoop Sts.

Kinko's operates numerous 24-hour outlets in Denver offering copy, email and fax services; near downtown try the location at 1509 Blake St (☎ 303-623-3500). Common Grounds (☎ 303-296-9248), a popular coffee house near Union Station at 1601 17th St, also offers Internet access ($2/hour).

Travel Agencies AAA Colorado (☎ 303-753-8800), 4100 E Arkansas Ave (four blocks north of Colorado Blvd and I-25), offers maps and guides for members and full travel services for nonmembers. American Express Travel (☎ 303-383-5050) is at 555 17th St. Council Travel (☎ 303-571-0630), 900 Auraria Pkwy, suite 267 (on the UC Denver Auraria campus), is a good place for cheap air tickets.

COLORADO

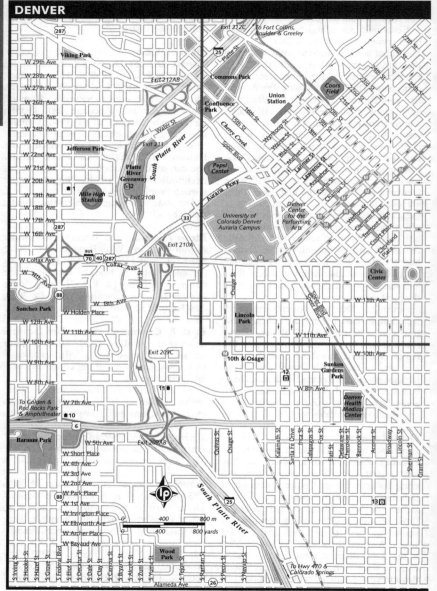

DENVER

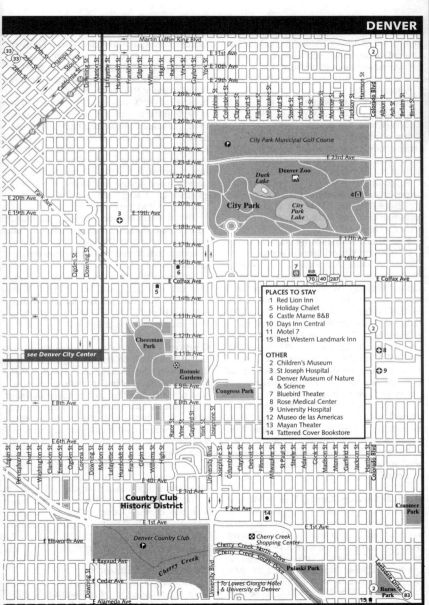

DENVER

PLACES TO STAY
1 Red Lion Inn
5 Holiday Chalet
6 Castle Marne B&B
10 Days Inn Central
11 Motel 7
15 Best Western Landmark Inn

OTHER
2 Children's Museum
3 St Joseph Hospital
4 Denver Museum of Nature & Science
7 Bluebird Theater
8 Rose Medical Center
9 University Hospital
12 Museo de las Americas
13 Mayan Theater
14 Tattered Cover Bookstore

see Denver City Center

Bookstores & Publications Johnny's Newsstand (☎ 303-825-6397), in the basement level at 1555 Champa St (below Mc-Donald's), carries a worthwhile selection of foreign newspapers in addition to hard-to-find environmental papers such as *High Country News.*

Tattered Cover Bookstore (☎ 303-322-7727), 2955 E 1st Ave, just north of the Cherry Creek Shopping Center, has four floors of shelves containing an awesome array of new volumes and regional maps. Its LoDo branch (☎ 303-436-1070), 1628 16th St, is at the corner of Wynkoop St.

A good used bookstore with steady turnover and reasonable prices is Capitol Hill Books (☎ 303-837-0700), at the intersection of Grant St and Colfax Ave near the State Capitol.

Hue-Man Experience (☎ 303-293-2665), 911 Park Ave W, specializes in books by and about African-Americans; it's open 10:30 am to 6:30 pm weekdays, 10 am to 5 pm Saturday. Women's and gay- and lesbian-interest books can be found at The Book Garden (☎ 303-399-2004), 2625 E 12th Ave. It's open 10 am to 6 pm Monday to Saturday, 12 to 5 pm Sunday. Cultural Legacy Books/Libros (☎ 303-964-9049), 3633 W 32nd Ave, specializes in Latino-interest and Spanish titles. It's open 10 am to 6 pm Monday to Thursday (to 9 pm Friday, to 5 pm Saturday).

At most restaurants and bars in town you can pick up a copy of *Westword,* an irreverent weekly entertainment newspaper that has great listings for music, theater, art and restaurants. The state's two largest newspapers are the *Denver Post* and the *Rocky Mountain News.*

Medical Services Denver Health Medical Center (☎ 303-436-6000) is at 777 Bannock St. The name is a recent change, so you'll still hear locals refer to it as 'DG' (Denver General). Denver's University Hospital (☎ 303-399-1211) is at 4200 E 9th Ave at Colorado Ave. Rose Medical Center (☎ 303-320-2121) is nearby at 4567 E 9th Ave. St Joseph Hospital (☎ 303-837-7111) is at 1835 Franklin St.

Denver Museum of Nature & Science

Located in spacious City Park, Denver Museum of Nature & Science (☎ 303-322-7009, 800-925-2250), 2001 Colorado Blvd, is one of the premier natural history museums in the country. It features excellent wildlife, geological and dinosaur exhibits. Also housed in the complex is an **IMAX Theater**, the giant-screen (4½ stories high) movie experience that stuns audiences with documentary films on nature and other topics. Another attraction is the **Gates Planetarium**, featuring a laser light show that takes guests on entertaining tours of distant galaxies. The T-Rex Cafe serves inexpensive sandwiches and tasty hot meals.

The museum is open 9 am to 5 pm daily. Admission costs $7/4.50 adults/children. The entrance fee for the IMAX theater is separate, though discounted combination tickets are available.

To get to the museum from downtown, take eastbound bus Nos 20 or 32 from 17th and Blake Sts. Also, see Bus under Getting Around, later.

Web site: www.dmns.org

Denver Zoo

In the event you do not see bighorn sheep in the wild, the Denver Zoo (☎ 303-376-4800), 2300 Steel St in City Park, is the next best place to go. The zoo features indigenous species like Rocky Mountain bison, goats, elks, moose and wolves. About 600 species from around the world are also represented – the Tropical Discovery exhibit is a major attraction.

The zoo is open 9 am to 6 pm daily April to September, 10 am to 5 pm October to March. Admission costs $8/4 adults/children.

Eastbound bus No 20 connects the zoo with downtown Denver (17th and Blake Sts). Also, see Bus under Getting Around, later.

Web site: www.denverzoo.org

Denver Art Museum

Resembling a modern high-rise jail, the Denver Art Museum (☎ 303-640-4433), 100 W 14th Ave, houses one of the largest

DENVER CITY CENTER

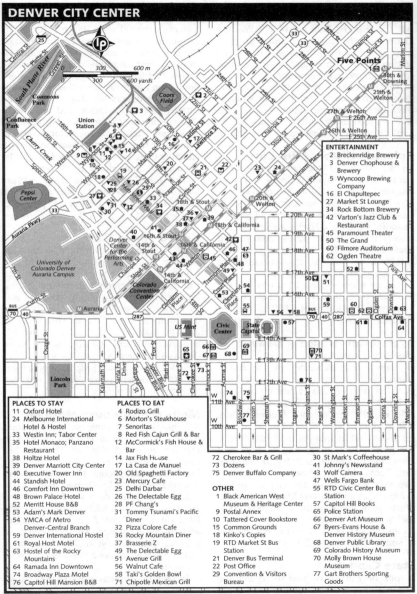

Five Points

ENTERTAINMENT
2 Breckenridge Brewery
3 Denver Chophouse & Brewery
5 Wyncoop Brewing Company
16 El Chapultepec
27 Market St Lounge
34 Rock Bottom Brewery
42 Varton's Jazz Club & Restaurant
45 Paramount Theater
50 The Grand
60 Filmore Auditorium
62 Ogden Theatre

PLACES TO STAY
11 Oxford Hotel
24 Melbourne International Hotel & Hostel
33 Westin Inn; Tabor Center
35 Hotel Monaco; Panzano Restaurant
38 Holtze Hotel
39 Denver Marriott City Center
40 Executive Tower Inn
44 Standish Hotel
46 Comfort Inn Downtown
48 Brown Palace Hotel
52 Merritt House B&B
53 Adam's Mark Denver
54 YMCA of Metro Denver-Central Branch
59 Denver International Hostel
61 Royal Host Motel
63 Hostel of the Rocky Mountains
64 Ramada Inn Downtown
74 Broadway Plaza Motel
76 Capitol Hill Mansion B&B

PLACES TO EAT
4 Rodizo Grill
6 Morton's Steakhouse
7 Senoritas
8 Red Fish Cajun Grill & Bar
12 McCormick's Fish House & Bar
14 Jax Fish House
17 La Casa de Manuel
20 Old Spaghetti Factory
23 Mercury Cafe
25 Delhi Darbar
26 The Delectable Egg
28 PF Chang's
31 Tommy Tsunami's Pacific Diner
32 Pizza Colore Cafe
36 Rocky Mountain Diner
37 Brasserie Z
49 The Delectable Egg
51 Avenue Grill
56 Walnut Cafe
58 Taki's Golden Bowl
71 Chipotle Mexican Grill

72 Cherokee Bar & Grill
73 Dozens
75 Denver Buffalo Company

OTHER
1 Black American West Museum & Heritage Center
9 Postal Annex
10 Tattered Cover Bookstore
15 Common Grounds
18 Kinko's Copies
19 RTD Market St Bus Station
21 Denver Bus Terminal
22 Post Office
29 Convention & Visitors Bureau

30 St Mark's Coffeehouse
41 Johnny's Newsstand
43 Wolf Camera
47 Wells Fargo Bank
55 RTD Civic Center Bus Station
57 Capitol Hill Books
65 Police Station
66 Denver Art Museum
67 Byers-Evans House & Denver History Museum
68 Denver Public Library
69 Colorado History Museum
70 Molly Brown House Museum
77 Gart Brothers Sporting Goods

COLORADO

Native American art collections in the USA, displaying work from tribes throughout the country. Non-native US Western artists are also featured, and European masters are well-represented. A sizable selection of books on art and Western Americana is offered in the gift shop.

The museum is open 10 am to 5 pm Tuesday to Saturday (until 9 pm Wednesday), noon to 5 pm on Sunday. Admission is free on Saturday, otherwise $4.50/2.50 adults/students and seniors.

Colorado History Museum

Unlike the myriad local museums throughout the state displaying bedpans, you won't find the Colorado History Museum (☎ 303-866-3682), 1300 Broadway in the Civic Center area, a tedious experience. There are beautiful exhibits of Native American rugs, mostly from Pueblo tribes from farther south and New Mexico. Technological innovations in mining and transportation are also displayed in life-size exhibits.

The museum is open 10 am to 4:30 pm Monday to Saturday, noon to 4:30 pm Sunday. Admission costs $4.50/2.50 adults/children (six to 16).

Byers-Evans House & Denver History Museum

William Byers, publisher of the *Rocky Mountain News,* built the two-story brick mansion Byers-Evans House (☎ 303-620-4933) at 1310 Bannock St in 1883. It was sold in 1889 to another Denver scion, William Gray Evans. The Colorado Historical Society offers tours of the house featuring period furnishings and a short film about the two families. Entry to the adjacent Denver History Museum, with interactive videodisks about the city as well as exhibit cases and drawers filled with city artifacts, is included in the admission price; $3/1.50 adults/children (six to 16). Byers-Evans House is open 11 am to 3 pm Tuesday to Sunday (last tour at 2 pm).

State Capitol

It took only 200oz of gold to replace the original copper dome of the 1886 State Capitol (☎ 303-866-2604), at the corner of Broadway and E Colfax Ave. In many aspects, especially the large rotunda, its layout mimics the national capitol. Drop by the governor's reception room on the 1st floor. Access to public galleries for the House and Senate chambers is on the 3rd floor. Don't miss the stained-glass portraits honoring pioneers like Barney Ford, the former slave who influenced the state's Constitution to protect the civil rights of minorities. These are in the **Colorado Hall of Fame** near the top of the dome (well worth climbing up to take in the view, but start by 3 pm as the dome closes at 3:30 pm).

The State Capitol is open 7 am to 5:30 pm weekdays; free 45-minute tours are offered hourly between 9:30 am and 2:30 pm. Meet tour guides at the north (Colfax) entrance.

United States Mint

In 1869, the federal government opened the Denver Mint (☎ 303-405-4761), 320 W Colfax Ave, a branch of the US Mint, to transform Colorado's mineral riches into bullion. However, no coining was done until 1906, two years after the present building was completed. The Denver Mint is one of three gold depositories in the USA. Six gold bars, each weighing 400 troy ounces, are on display there, and it produces more than 5 billion coins each year. Free 20-minute tours are offered on a first-come, first-served basis 8 am to 3 pm weekdays.

Molly Brown House Museum

Although on a first-name basis with Eastern society, Molly Brown was snubbed in Denver. A social climber, she and her husband James prospered from the Leadville mining boom. However, she was not acknowledged by Denver high society until her good deeds toward poor immigrant women on a lifeboat following the 1912 sinking of the *Titanic* brought her acclaim as a heroine. The well-received musical from the 1960s, *The Unsinkable Molly Brown,* immortalized her rags-to-riches story.

In 1894 the Browns moved to the elaborate sandstone-trimmed Victorian home at

1340 Pennsylvania St. Today, costumed guides (Molly liked big hats) give 45-minute guided tours every 30 minutes (first-come, first-served or reserve ahead) and serve visitors afternoon tea. The museum (☎ 303-832-4092) is open 10 am to 3:30 pm Tuesday to Saturday, from noon to 3:30 pm Sunday. Admission costs $6/2 adults/children (six to 12).

Black American West Museum & Heritage Center

'We tell it like it was' is the motto of the Black American West Museum & Heritage Center (☎ 303-292-2566), 3091 California St in the Five Points neighborhood north of downtown. Although a few notable African-American pioneers arrived with the onset of Colorado's mining boom in the early 1860s, it was after the Civil War that most black professional and working-class people arrived in the state. Black cowboys were particularly important – almost a third of the Western range workers were African-American. The museum, dedicated to correcting former versions of history, is housed in the home of Dr Justina Ford, Denver's first black physician.

Take the light rail to the stop at 30th and Downing Sts. The museum is open 10 am to 2 pm weekdays (closed Monday and Tuesday in winter), 10 am to 5 pm weekends. Admission costs $4/3 adults/children and students.

Children's Museum of Denver

Hands-on exhibits at the Children's Museum of Denver (☎ 303-433-7444), across from Mile High Stadium at 2121 Crescent Dr (23rd and I-25), include a mini television studio, a supermarket and a bank. Kids (at least those up to 8) are guaranteed to have a ball. It's open 9 am to 4 pm Tuesday to Friday, 10 am to 5 pm weekends. Admission costs $6.50 ages three to adult; $3.50 up to age two.

Museo de las Americas

Southeast of downtown Denver, this engaging museum (☎ 303-571-4401), 861 Santa Fe Dr, focuses on Latino art and history and Latinos' contribution to the southwestern United States. It's a good way to appreciate the extensive role played by Latino culture in the development of this part of the country, which has often been obscured or 'written out' by traditional white historians. The neighborhood around the museum is mostly Latino and offers many opportunities to sample authentic Mexican and Latin American cuisine.

It's open 10 am to 5 pm weekdays, 10 am to 4 pm on Saturday. Admission costs $3/1 adults/children and students (under eight free). From downtown Denver catch the light rail to 10th and Osage Sts, walk four blocks east on 10th Ave to Santa Fe, then turn right and head another block to the museum.

Denver Botanic Gardens

A quiet respite from urban sounds and hard-edged terrain is available east of downtown at the Denver Botanic Gardens (☎ 303-331-4000), 1005 York St. In addition to indigenous plants in the Plains Garden and Xeriscape Demonstration Garden, imported species are featured in the Tropical Conservatory, Water Garden and Japanese Garden.

It's open 9 am to 5 pm daily. Admission to the serene pathways and trails costs $5.50/3 adults/children. From Broadway and Colfax Sts, take the eastbound No 10 bus to York St, then walk two blocks south to the gardens. Also, see Bus under Getting Around, later.

Bicycling

Denver's flat terrain and wide streets make utilitarian bicycle trips easy, but you can also find plenty of easy recreational trails. Especially popular trails follow the Platte River Greenway and Cherry Creek from **Confluence Park**. The Colorado Division of Parks and Recreation (☎ 303-866-3437) publishes a useful map and trail guide for the Denver Metro Area that is usually available from the Denver Convention & Visitors Bureau (see Information, earlier).

Golf

The Denver Dept of Parks & Recreation (☎ 303-964-2563) runs a few municipal courses charging reasonable greens fees; call for details, or inquire at the Convention & Visitors Bureau in the Tabor Center (see Information, earlier).

Special Events

Kicking off the new year in mid-January is the two-week **National Western Stock Show & Rodeo** (☎ 303-297-1166), held at Brighton Rd and I-70 exit 275B. This is the largest show of its kind in the country. Mexico's victory at the Battle of Puebla is celebrated with two days of festivities at the 16th St Mall during **Cinco de Mayo**. The first weekend in July is the **Cherry Creek Arts Festival** at Cherry Creek North, one of the country's largest arts and crafts shows. Bring a healthy appetite to **A Taste of Colorado**, a showcase of the region's top restaurant talent held on Labor Day weekend in September at the Civic Center.

Places to Stay

Denver has dozens of places to stay, a select sampling of which you'll find below. If you need further help booking accommodations, you can call Denver Metro Convention and Visitors Bureau Area Reservations at ☎ 800-462-5280. (Call ☎ 800-645-3446 for lodging reservations in other parts of the state.)

Budget Denver has three hostels, all of which offer fairly convenient access to downtown.

The cheapest beds in town are at the **Denver International Hostel** (☎ 303-832-9996, 630 E 16th Ave). More than 100 beds are distributed through dorms with a maximum of six beds each, for the amazing price of $8.60. Linen rental is $1 per week. Separate dorm rooms for females and families are available, and there's also a library, game room and coin laundry. The office is open from 8 to 10 am and 5 to 10:30 pm.

The basic but clean **Melbourne International Hotel & Hostel** (☎ 303-292-6386, 607 22nd St) is east of the bus terminal and

Union Station. The female guests' dorm has its own bathroom. Other pluses include bicycle storage and a coin laundry. Dorm beds cost $12 for HI-AYH members, $15 for nonmembers. There are private rooms with shared bath for $27/34. Guests are limited to a two-day stay, and reservations are necessary between April and September.

The **Hostel of the Rocky Mountains** (☎ 303-861-7777, 1530 Downing St), a bit farther east from the Denver International Hostel, has 80 beds divided into two- and four-bed dorm rooms. Each bed costs $15; private rooms with shared bath are available for $36/40. Each room comes equipped with a mini kitchen and cable TV. A laundry and bike rentals are available. Office hours are 8 am to 11 pm. The hostel also offers free pickup from the bus and train stations.

Centrally located is the **YMCA of Metro Denver – Central Branch** (☎ 303-861-8300, 25 E 16th Ave), where rooms with common bath cost $37; rooms with private bath are $44. The **Standish Hotel** (☎ 303-534-3231, 1530 California St) may not look impressive on the outside, but is cheap and convenient to the 16th St Mall. Singles/doubles with shared bath are $38/43; $40/47 with private bath. Weekly rates are available at both of the above places.

In Broomfield, a suburb 15 miles north of the city, **Denver North Campground** (☎ 303-452-4120, 800-851-6521, 16700 N Washington), is one of the closet places to camp near Denver. Tent sites are fairly steep at $20 in winter (more in summer); RV sites with water and electric hookup are $27. There is a pool and a convenience store on the grounds. Take I-25 north to exit 229 and turn right.

While there are lots of trucker and budget motels scattered outside the city, most are too far away to be of practical value for visiting Denver. One exception is **Motel 7** (☎ 303-592-1555, 930 Valley Hwy) at 8th Ave, at the intersection of US 6 and I-25 exit 209C; basic singles/doubles are $38/46.

There are no budget accommodations right next to Denver International Airport, but there are a few places in the nearby

JOHN ELK III

CHARLES COOK

Peace and quiet on the Yellowstone River, WY

Upper Falls, Yellowstone River, WY

JIM WARK

Chasing white water on the Arkansas River, CO

LEE FOSTER

BRENT WINEBRENNER

Cross-country in Keystone, CO

Bunny slope, here we come. Breckenridge, CO

Small horse or big chair? Denver Art Museum

A cowboy who never falls off, Colorado Springs

The silver lady, Colorado style

Buffalo Bill shines on in Golden, CO.

Chaps and map in Colorado Springs, CO

Crested Butte's take on David and Goliath, CO

RICHARD CUMMINS

RICHARD CUMMINS

WOODS WHEATCROFT

RICHARD CUMMINS

RICHARD CUMMINS

MASON FLORENCE

suburb of Aurora near the junction of Colfax Ave and I-225, about a 20-minute drive from DIA. *Family Motel* (☎ 303-344-9150, 13280 E Colfax Ave) has rooms with full kitchens for $45/50 as well as a hot tub and swimming pool. Shuttle vans and taxis to DIA are easily arranged.

A slew of hotels and motels were left high and dry when Stapleton Airport closed to make way for DIA, 14 miles away. In the budget range there's *Motel 6 Denver East* (☎ 303-371-1980, 12020 E 39th Ave), which offers spartan singles/doubles for $48/55. Similar rooms at *Super 8* (☎ 303-371-0551, 3850 Peoria St) are $43/47. Getting from the Stapleton area to DIA will cost you $10 by Super Shuttle, or around $25 by taxi.

Mid-Range In the city center, the drab *Royal Host Motel* (☎ 303-831-7200, 930 E Colfax Ave) is a bit dodgy looking, but cheap with singles/doubles for $40/45. The nearby *Ramada Inn Downtown* (☎ 303-831-7700, 800-542-8603, 1150 E Colfax Ave) isn't a bad off-season deal at $72/82 for singles/doubles, though summer rates increase to $82/99. A better bet is *Broadway Plaza Motel* (☎ 303-893-0303, 1111 Broadway), where singles/doubles go for $55/59. It's reasonably close to city center attractions and restaurants.

Near the upper end of the mid-range category is the high-rise *Comfort Inn Downtown* (☎ 303-296-0400, 401 17th St), where rooms cost $129. At this price you're really just paying for location and may want to consider spending just a bit more for one of the more affordable top-end spots.

Another option is the weekend special at *Executive Tower Inn* (☎ 303-571-0300, 800-525-6651, 1405 Curtis St). Rooms that normally cost $89 to $99 are offered for $85 Friday to Sunday and include access to the health club. Daily parking costs $9.

Out of the city center, two miles west of downtown is the *Red Lion Inn* (☎ 303-433-8331, 800-388-5381, 1975 Bryant St), west of I-25 exit 210B. Rooms are not a bad deal at $69 when you throw in the free shuttle to downtown, fitness center and swimming pool. A bit more downmarket is *Days Inn*

Central (☎ 303-571-1715, 620 Federal Blvd) on US 6 west of downtown. Average singles/doubles cost $49/59 during the week, but jump to $59/69 on weekends.

One place worth trying east of downtown is *Holiday Chalet* (☎ 303-321-9975, 1820 E Colfax Ave). This mansion, built in 1896, features 10 bright rooms with private baths and mini kitchen. Rates range from $94 to $160, including breakfast.

South of Cherry Creek Shopping Center, *Best Western Landmark Inn* (☎ 303-388-5561, 455 S Colorado Blvd) boasts an indoor pool, fitness room and hot tub, and some rooms have nice mountain views. Rates start at $79.

There are only two hotels genuinely next to Denver International Airport, both offering comfortable, upscale rooms. The *Fairfield Inn DIA* (☎ 303-576-9640, 800-228-2800, 6851 Tower Rd) has rooms from $59. Singles/doubles at the nearby *Hampton Inn DIA* (☎ 303-371-0200, 6290 Tower Rd) are $69/79. Both places offer free Continental breakfasts and 24-hour airport shuttles.

Nearby along the hotel row near the defunct Stapleton Airport, *Quality Inn & Suites* (☎ 303-320-0260, 800-677-0260, 4590 Quebec St), just north of I-70, offers singles/doubles for $65/70 along with an outdoor pool and fitness center. In Aurora, *Best Western Executive Hotel* (☎ 303-373-5730, 4411 Peoria St), near I-70 exit 281, has well-appointed rooms for $89 and a swimming pool. Both places offer airport shuttle service.

Top End In the city center *Hotel Monaco* (☎ 303-296-1717, 800-397-5380, 1717 Champa St) boasts a bright, modern, Art Deco interior and sees to all the details (including complimentary national newspapers, morning coffee and evening wine). Traveling alone? Not to worry, upon request guests can take 'Lily,' the hotel's mascot Jack Russell terrier, for a walk and even adopt goldfish for in-room company. Rates range from $125 to $175.
Web site: www.monaco-denver.com

The *Adam's Mark Denver* (☎ 303-893-3333, 1550 Court Place) is in a great location for seeing downtown Denver and offers high-end amenities including a fitness room, sauna, heated outdoor pool, full business center and two restaurants. Rooms are a good value at $89/199.

Capitol Hill Mansion B&B (☎ *303-839-5221, 800-839-9329, 1207 Pennsylvania St)* features balconies and fireplaces on the upper floors of a turreted red sandstone mansion. Listed in the National Register of Historic Places, this is one of the top-rated B&Bs in the country. All rooms offer private baths and range in price from $90 to $175, the latter including an in-room Jacuzzi and either balcony or fireplace. Its Web site is at www.capitolhillmansion.com. Another fine historic B&B near downtown is the 10-room *Merritt House* (☎ *303-861-9009, 877-861-5230, 941 E 17th Ave)*. Guests at this charming 1889 Victorian mansion are greeted at check-in with cookies! Rates are $90 to $150 and the pricier rooms are equipped with Jacuzzis.

Denver's oldest hotel, the luxurious *Oxford Hotel* (☎ *303-628-5400, 800-228-5538, 1600 17th St)*, opened in 1891 near Union Station. Rooms range from $209 to $500, though weekend specials can lower the price.
Web site: www.theoxfordhotel.com

Another excellently maintained historic landmark is the distinguished *Brown Palace Hotel* (☎ *303-297-3111, 800-321-2599, 1600 17th St)*, where rooms range from $195 to $350. Though not equipped with as many modern touches (health clubs, etc), the hotel consistently retains its four-star rating for its outstanding atmosphere, decor and service.
Web site: www.brownpalace.com

For a more modern place, *Westin Inn/Tabor Center* (☎ *303-572-9100, 800-937-8461, 1672 Lawrence St)* is a good bet for decor, service, location and facilities, including a heated indoor/outdoor pool. Rates range from $89 to $250. Also conveniently located, the *Denver Marriott City Center* (☎ *303-297-1300, 1701 California St)* has a full range of guest facilities. Rooms cost $189 upward.

The central *Holtze* (☎ *303-607-9000, 800-422-2092, 818 17th St)* is a rather stately,

business-oriented choice with rates from $109 to $179.
Web site: www.holtze.com

Away from the city center *Castle Marne B&B* (☎ *303-331-0621, 800-926-2763, 1572 Race St)* is a stunning three-story masonry mansion listed on the National Register of Historic Places. It offers nine elegant rooms, all with private bath, ranging from $95 to $250 for the Presidential Suite featuring an in-room hot tub and private balcony.
Web site: www.castlemarne.com

South of Cherry Creek Shopping Center, the isolated black tower of *Lowes Giorgio Hotel* (☎ *303-782-9300, 800-345-9172, 450 E Mississippi Ave)* is in an unlikely (noncentral) location for a luxury hotel catering to business travelers. Elaborate Italian decor resembles Milan's finest lodgings. Rooms cost $154 to $224, but $79/89 (city view/mountain view) weekend rates are a relative bargain.
Web site: www.loweshotels.com

Places to Eat

Downtown Denver is overrun with restaurants of all types. In addition to those listed below, you might want to check the places listed in the *Westword* weekly.

For breakfast, *Dozens* (☎ *303-572-0066, 236 13th Ave)*, south of the Capitol, offers egg breakfasts for about $6, or fresh muffins and cinnamon rolls, in a smoke-free dining room. The nearby *Cherokee Bar & Grill* (☎ *303-623-0346, 1201 Cherokee St)*, is a favorite with courthouse employees, whose sketches grace the walls. Try the Acoma omelet with roasted chilies or, for lunch, the 'Verdict Burger' with cheddar and bacon. Other popular breakfast and lunch spots include *Walnut Cafe* (☎ *303-832-5108, 338 E Colfax Ave)*, and both locations of the health-conscious bistro, *The Delectable Egg* (☎ *303-572-8146, 1642 Market St; ☎ 303-892-5720, 1625 Court Place)*.

If all you need is a caffeine fix, espresso is available on many corners – you shouldn't have to look hard to find a coffee shop. One spot catering to both locals and Larimer Square visitors is *St Mark's Coffeehouse* (☎ *303-446-2925, 1416 Market St)*. *Common*

Grounds (☎ 303-296-9248, 1601 17th St), at the corner of Wazee, does great gourmet coffees and offers a library of books, as well as Internet access. Afternoon tea is served noon to 4 pm daily in the atrium lobby at the *Brown Palace Hotel* (☎ 303-293-9204, 321 17th St).

For cheap lunches, it's hard to beat *Taki's Golden Bowl* (☎ 303-832-8440, 341 E Colfax Ave), where you can get generous rice bowls, yakisoba or udon soup for $3 to $5. On the other side of town, *Mercury Cafe* (☎ 303-294-9281, 2199 California St) offers what *Westword* magazine perfectly describes as 'healthy hippie fare.'

Adding a nice touch of Old West style to the corner of 18th and Stout Sts is *Rocky Mountain Diner* (☎ 303-293-8383, 1800 Stout St), a comfortable Western-style eatery with a modern menu, including such items as buffalo meatloaf and roast duck enchiladas, along with more traditional fare.

If you want to go really Western, the *Denver Buffalo Company* (☎ 303-832-0880, 1109 Lincoln St), a few blocks south of the Capitol, specializes in lean buffalo burgers, steaks and sausages from its own Colorado ranch.

Reasonably priced Italian meals in a casual atmosphere are available at a few downtown establishments. *Pizza Colore Cafe* (☎ 303-534-6844, 1512 Larimer St) is open late with ample outdoor seating and serves delicious vegetarian lasagna with a cream sauce for $8. *The Old Spaghetti Factory* (☎ 303-295-1864, 1215 18th St), in the former cable-car building, offers large plates of spaghetti for around $8. For upscale Italian, *Panzano Restaurant* (☎ 303-296-3525, 909 17th St) on the ground floor of the Hotel Monaco is divine.

If you're looking for Mexican food, locals reckon *La Casa de Manuel* (☎ 303-295-1752, 2010 Larimer St) is one of the better choices. Also recommended is *Chipotle Mexican Grill* (☎ 303-623-5432) at the corner of 13th Ave and Pennsylvania St.

Indian-food fans should enjoy *Delhi Darbar* (☎ 303-595-0680, 1514 Blake St), a popular spot with Denverites. The $6 lunch buffet is a good value.

Red Fish Cajun Grill & Bar (☎ 303-595-0443, 1701 Wynkoop St) is an entertaining Cajun restaurant-cum-blues bar adjacent to Union Station. Nearly across the street is *Senorita's* (☎ 303-298-7133, 1700 Wynkoop St), known for its authentic Mexican cantina cooking.

Tommy Tsunami's Pacific Diner (☎ 303-534-5050, 1432 Market St) is a funky Japanese eatery offering various Asian-inspired delights and good sushi specials. Slightly more stylish is *PF Chang's* (☎ 303-260-7222, 1415 15th St), which earns good marks for nouvelle Chinese fare and atmosphere.

McCormick's Fish House & Bar (☎ 303-825-1107, 1659 Wazee St) offers fresh oysters – not the Rocky Mountain variety, but extremely fresh ocean harvests from around the globe. The menu changes daily to reflect what's available. Just across the road is another unexpected seafood haven, *Jax Fish House* (☎ 303-292-5657, 1539 17th St).

Brasserie Z (☎ 303-293-2322, 815 17th St) is unique in that it offers good US nouvelle cuisine at affordable prices.

The popular *Avenue Grill* (☎ 303-861-2820, 630 E 17th Ave) serves a wide array of US standards from burgers to pasta and has a great wine list to match. Slightly more up-market, *Rodizo Grill* (☎ 303-294-9277, 1801 Wynkoop St) is a fashionable gathering point for Denver's business set.

If you're really in the mood to splurge, head to the *Palace Arms* (☎ 303-297-3111, 321 17th St) in the Brown Palace Hotel. The menu is an interesting mix of East-West fusion and traditional European fare. For a top-notch steak experience, *Morton's Steakhouse* (☎ 303-825-3353, 1710 Wynkoop St) is unforgettable.

Entertainment

To find out what's happening in music, theater and other performing arts, pick up a copy of the weekly *Westword* (free). *Out Front* carries informative articles about the local gay scene.

Denver Center for the Performing Arts

Denver's regional leadership in cultural events is undeniable. The Denver

Bi-ways, Transplants & Homos on the Range

If the Rockies were to elect a gay capital, Denver would win hands down. The city has a thriving gay scene evidenced by a wide range of gay, lesbian, bisexual, transgender and questioning community organizations and some 30 gay bars that attract travelers from around Colorado and surrounding states. The next closest metropolis with a noteworthy gay scene is Utah's reserved Salt Lake City; other than that, it's a long ride south to Dallas, Texas. Denver's largest gay event is the annual Pride Parade in late June.

In the mid-1990s, Denverites stood at the forefront of a long-fought battle over the highly controversial Amendment 2. Put forth by Colorado's religious right, the legislation was aimed at stripping gay men, lesbians and bisexuals of protective laws against discrimination based on sexual orientation. After being declared unconstitutional by the Colorado Supreme Court, the case was appealed to the US Supreme Court and was again voted down in May 1996. The media blitz surrounding Amendment 2, however, tarnished Colorado's image and led to a widespread gay boycott of the state. And while memories of Amendment 2 still lead to misconceptions that Colorado is anti-gay, Denver and Boulder, as well as resort towns like Vail and Aspen, are helping the state earn back its gay-friendly reputation.

The following Web-based Denver city guides are chock-full of information on queer events, venues, organizations and activities:

www.cafevivid.com
www.denvergay.com
www.thinkgay.com/den.html
www.milehighnights.com
www.outindenver.com

At Tattered Cover Bookstore Bookstore (☎ 303-322-7727), 2955 E 1st Ave, or any local gay venue, pick up *Quest*, a free gay and lesbian news and lifestyle magazine, and *H*, Denver's leading monthly gay bar rag. *Out Front*, a biweekly queer newspaper, has been covering local, national and international news for more than 25 years.

On the tube, watch for *Colorado Outspoken*, a TV program with news for the gay and lesbian community, at 11 pm Sunday on Channel 12. Music lovers can check out the Denver Gay Men's Chorus; visit http://members.tde.com/dgmc/ for information. Metropolitan Community Church of the Rockies offers services for the GLBTQ community; its Web site is www.mccrockies.org.

Denver's most gay-friendly accommodations choice is the charming **Victoria Oaks Inn** (☎ 303-355-1818, 800-662-6257, fax 303-331-1095, vicoaksinn@aol.com, 1575 Race St), 1 mile east of downtown between City Park and Cheesman Park, a restored 1886 Victorian mansion tastefully furnished with antiques. Rates are reasonable at $60 to $95.
Web site: www.victoriaoaks.com

The Rockies being outdoors heaven, sports fans should check out Colorado Outdoor and Ski/Board Association, which specializes in gay and lesbian skiing, snowboarding and outdoor sports. Its Web site is http://members.tde.com/cosa/index1.htm. The Kneelers, also known as Blizzard Boys from Hell, is a gay men's Nordic skiing and snowshoeing group. Visit www.members.aol.com/kneelers/index.htm for more. Bicycle Boys from Hell is for those who do it on two wheels; find out more on www.members.aol.com/bbfhco/index.htm. Colorado Gay Ice Hockey Association is pucking heaven; it has a Web site at www.climaxhockey.org, and Colorado Squid Swim Team is a gay, lesbian, bi, and straight-friendly masters swim team; check it out at www.members.tde.com/squid/. And to top them all, there's the International Gay Rodeo Association at www.igra.com. How much more Western can you get?

Center for the Performing Arts complex (☎ 303-893-4300, 303-893-4100 box office) is the world's largest performing arts center (under one roof), occupying almost four city blocks south of 14th St between Arapahoe and Champa Sts.

See Bus under Getting Around, later, for trolley service between the Center and other attractions.

Cinemas Denver has more than enough mega-multiplex movie chains, which you can find through the local papers. However, it might be more fun to check out the **Mayan Theater** (☎ 303-744-6796, 110 Broadway) for good old, garish movie-house atmosphere.

Don't miss the 4½-story-tall **IMAX** screen in the Denver Museum of Nature & Science (☎ 303-370-6300), mentioned earlier.

Brewpubs Denver's first brewpub, **Wyncoop Brewing Company** (☎ 303-623-9518) is a lively spot at the corner of 18th and Wynkoop Sts. The 2nd floor is littered with billiard tables, and it's a hopping scene on weekend nights.

Another place that sees a lot of action on weekends is **Rock Bottom Brewery** (☎ 303-534-7616, 1001 16th St), which generally draws a 'prettier' crowd than the other brewpubs. The beer is good, and the patio seating on the pedestrian mall is a plus.

Near Coors Field baseball stadium, **Breckenridge Brewery** (☎ 303-297-3644, 2200 Blake St) has some outstanding beer selections that you can sip on the outdoor patio. The nearby **Denver Chophouse & Brewery** (☎ 303-296-0800, 1735 19th St) is also good, though it's perhaps better known for steak than beer.

Bars The brewpubs mentioned above are some of Denver's most popular bars, but for variety take a stroll through Larimer Square, where there are bars to suit just about any personality.

The Art Deco **Cruise Room Bar** (☎ 303-628-5400), in the Oxford Hotel, was designed to resemble the 1st-class bar on the

Queen Mary. Cigar or scotch aficionados may want to stop by the **Churchill Bar** in the Brown Palace Hotel (☎ 303-297-3111).

If you're looking for a younger, more raucous atmosphere, **Wazoo's** (☎ 303-297-8500, 1819 Wazee) fits the bill.

Live Music & Clubs There's always some musician playing somewhere in Denver's surprisingly lively music scene. Westword is your best guide.

Market Street Lounge (☎ 303-893-6754, 1417 Market St) books plenty of local bands. Occasional headliners such as Warren 'Werewolves of London' Zevon appear at the **Ogden Theatre** (☎ 303-830-2525, 935 E Colfax Ave).

El Chapultepec (☎ 303-295-9126, 1962 Market St), near the ballpark (Coors Field), is a cozy venue for top jazz performers; music begins nightly at 9 pm with no cover charge. More sedate is **Varton's Jazz Club and Restaurant** (☎ 303-399-1111, 1800 Glenarm Place).

The Grand (☎ 303-839-5390, 538 E 17th), a stylish piano and martini bar, is perhaps Denver's hottest gay hangout.

Denver's **Botanic Garden Amphitheater** (☎ 303-331-4000, 1005 York St) hosts a summer evening series of classical, jazz and world music concerts.

In town, the main venues for national acts are the **Paramount Theater** (☎ 303-534-8336, 1631 Glenarm Place) and **Filmore Auditorium** (☎ 303-837-0360, 1510 Clarkson St). East of downtown, the **Bluebird Theater** (☎ 303-322-2308, 3317 E Colfax) also gets the occasional big-name performer along with good local bands.

Fiddler's Green Amphitheater (☎ 303-220-7000, 6350 Greenwood Plaza Blvd) and the wonderful **Red Rocks Amphitheater** (☎ 303-964-2500) host headline performers, as does Denver's largest venue for rock music, **The Pepsi Center** (☎ 303-405-1111) near Mile High Stadium. Most concert tickets are available from Ticketmaster (☎ 303-830-8497). Its Web site is at www.ticketmaster.com.

For country & western entertainment, head for **Grizzly Rose** (☎ 303-295-2353,

5450 N Valley Hwy), where headliners like Marshall Tucker, the Charlie Daniels Band and Jerry Lee Lewis helped earn the club an award from the Country Music Association as the best venue in the nation.

Spectator Sports

Baseball The Colorado Rockies play downtown at Coors Field. For information, tickets and schedules call ☎ 303-262-0200, 800-388-7625.

Basketball The Denver Nuggets are in the National Basketball Association's Midwest Division and play at The Pepsi Center (☎ 303-405-1111). Take westbound bus No 31 from downtown and get off at Federal Blvd (Rte 287) and 17th; walk east 5 minutes. Better yet, walk 10 minutes from the downtown visitors center. Parking costs $10, so it's better to walk even if you have a car. For ticket information call ☎ 303-830-8497.

Hockey The Colorado Avalanche, a top-rated National Hockey League team, play at The Pepsi Center (see above).

Football The Denver Broncos attract some of the most fanatic, rabid fans in the National Football League. Games are played at Mile High Stadium near The Pepsi Center, west of downtown. To get there see Basketball, above. For ticket information call ☎ 303-649-9000.

Soccer The Colorado Rapids, a major league team, play at Mile High Stadium (see above); for ticket information call ☎ 303-299-1570.

Shopping

Denver Convention & Visitors Bureau (☎ 303-892-1112), in the Tabor Center, will happily supply you with shopping guides to nearly every corner of the city. Following is a brief summary of the main areas where consumers cluster.

Larimer Square The 1400 block of Larimer St presents an appealing array of boutiques, galleries, restaurants and night-clubs, making up a vibrant activity center. Restaurants can get you started in the morning, and the clubs let you wind down from a day of shopping and exploring the historic district.

Most businesses in Larimer Square (☎ 303-534-2367) are open 10 am to 7 pm weekdays, 10 am to 6 pm Saturday and noon to 5 pm Sunday. See Bus under Getting Around, later, for trolley service between the Square and other attractions.

16th St Mall Denver's 16th St Mall, the primary downtown retail street, has been sensibly redesigned to accommodate pedestrians, not cars. The mix of shops – upscale, downscale, you name it – makes for a nice change from most pedestrian malls. Be sure to stop and admire the restored clock mechanism in the **D&F Tower** at Arapahoe St. Free shuttle transit operates between the RTD Civic Center bus terminal on Broadway and the RTD Market St Station at the north end.

About 65 upscale specialty shops and a dozen-plus restaurants are in the two-block glass-enclosed **Tabor Center** (☎ 303-572-6866), next to 16th St at the north end between Larimer and Arapahoe Sts. **Writer Square** (☎ 303-628-9056), 1512 Larimer St, is yet another city block of frivolous boutiques and restaurants near the north end of the 16th St Mall.

Cherry Creek Shopping Center The mall, 3000 E 1st Ave, is Denver's single largest attraction. There are top-end comparison-shopping opportunities at 125 specialty shops and restaurants plus an eight-screen cinema. Also, Tattered Cover Bookstore is nearby (see Bookstores & Publications under Information, earlier). The shopping center is open 10 am to 9 pm weekdays, 10 am to 7 pm Saturday and noon to 6 pm Sunday.

Film & Photography Wolf Camera (☎ 303-623-1155), in the historic Denver Dry Goods Building at 1545 California St (corner of 15th St), is the Rockies' largest camera store.

Sporting Goods Denver is a sporting goods bazaar with many giant stores offering a multitude of gear for every imaginable recreational activity. Among the most amazing is Gart Brothers Sporting Goods Company (☎ 303-861-1122), 1000 Broadway, a retail sports palace housed in a handsome neo-Gothic–style three-story building.

Getting There & Away

Air DIA is served by about 20 airlines, connecting it to nearly every major US city. The most flights are run by United Airlines, which has made Denver one of its two main US hubs. See the Getting There & Away chapter for airline telephone numbers.

Information on airline connections, schedules, ground transportation and parking is available from DIA (☎ 303-342-2000, 800-247-2336). Tourist and airport information is available 6 am to midnight from a booth at the north end of the terminal's central hall, near the top of the escalators from the subway train. Information on ground transport is available from a booth at the south end of the hall. Also see To/From the Airport under Getting Around, below.

Denver International Airport (DIA), 24 miles from downtown, is connected with I-70 exit 238 by the 12-mile-long Peña Blvd. The facility has an automated subway that links the terminal to three concourses and 94 gates. Concourse C is almost a mile from the terminal, hence the need for automated transport of people and baggage, and a little extra time for finding your way around.

Bus Greyhound and affiliate TNM&O offer frequent buses on routes along the Front Range and on transcontinental routes. All buses stop at the Denver Bus Terminal (☎ 303-293-6555) at the corner of 19th and Arapahoe Sts in downtown Denver; open 6 am to midnight.

Powder River Coach USA (☎ 800-442-3682), offering service north to Cheyenne, WY, and on to Montana and South Dakota, also runs from the Denver Bus Terminal.

Train Amtrak's *California Zephyr* runs daily between Chicago and the San Fran-

cisco Bay Area (Emeryville) via Denver. Trains arrive and depart from Denver's **Union Station** at the corner of 17th and Wynkoop Sts. The Amtrak ticket office (☎ 303-825-2583) at the station is open 7 am to 9 pm. For recorded information on arrival and departure times, call ☎ 303-534-2812. Amtrak agents (☎ 800-872-7245) can also provide schedule information and train reservations.

Denver's *Ski Train* (☎ 303-296-4754) to Winter Park operates on weekends throughout the ski season. It also departs from Union Station.

Web site: www.skitrain.com

Car At the intersection of I-70 and I-25, Denver is pretty hard to miss: Even the poorest navigators should have no trouble finding this place.

If you're 21 or over, Auto Driveaway Co (☎ 303-757-1211, autodriveaway@quest.net), 5777 E Evans Ave south of downtown, may be able to provide free transportation in exchange for vehicle delivery – get a driveaway just like Jack Kerouac did in *On the Road*! Be prepared to post a substantial deposit that will be forfeited if you damage the car (as Kerouac did).

Also check the ride boards at the hostels (see Places to Stay) or at the north wing of Driscoll University Center at the University of Denver, which is connected to the main campus by the pedestrian walkway over E Evans Ave.

Getting Around

To/From the Airport A complete Ground Transportation Center is centrally located on the 5th level of DIA's terminal, near the baggage claim. All transportation companies have their booths here and passengers catch vans, shuttles and taxis outside the doors.

Complimentary hotel shuttles represent the cheapest means of getting to or from the airport. Courtesy phones for hotel shuttles are available in the Ground Transportation Center.

Regional Transit District (RTD; ☎ 303-299-6000, 800-366-7433) buses are available

COLORADO

outside door 506 in the West Terminal and door 511 in the East Terminal. Travel time is typically less than an hour to or from the city and fares cost $6, or $10 roundtrip – exact fare only. Buses (routes AS, AF and AB) run every 15 minutes between DIA and Stapleton Airport, providing access to lodging and budget parking ($2 per day). The fare is $4. For DIA-Boulder travelers, fares for the 1½-hour trip cost $8, $13 roundtrip.

Web site: www.rtd-denver.com

There are a number of airport shuttle van and limousine services. Super Shuttle (☎ 303-370-1300, 800-258-3826) and Denver Express Shuttle (☎ 303-342-3424, 800-448-2782) offer frequent van service to downtown hotels for $15. If you need door-to-door service, try Shuttle King (☎ 303-363-8000), which charges $20 to $35 for rides to destinations in and around Denver. Airport shuttles to the Front Range and mountain/ski areas are also not hard to come by (see Getting Around in the relevant chapter).

Taxi service to downtown Denver costs a flat fare of $43, excluding tip.

Bus The RTD (see above) provides public transportation throughout the Denver and Boulder area. Local fares are $1.25 during peak weekday hours (6 to 9 am, 4 to 6 pm), 75¢ during off-peak hours. Free **shuttle buses** operate along the 16th St Mall, closed to automobile traffic since 1980.

Buses to Boulder (route B) carry bicycles in the cargo compartment and offer frequent service from the Market St Station at the corner of 16th and Market Sts. The Denver to Boulder one-way RTD fare is $3. To reach Golden, take the Nos 16 or 16L buses that stop at the corner of 15th and California Sts.

From Memorial Day to Labor Day, visitors to the Museum of Nature & Science, the Zoo, Larimer Square, the Botanic Gardens and other attractions can board the RTD's special **Cultural Connection Trolley** with the purchase of an all-day ticket for $3. Self-guided tours aboard the trolley provide an excellent orientation that takes less than an hour. The trolley leaves the Denver Center for the Performing Arts at 14th and Curtis Sts every half-hour 9:30 am to 5:30 pm.

Light Rail RTD's light rail line serves 16 stations on a 12-mile route that passes through downtown; NB (northbound) trains run on California St, while SB (southbound) trains follow Stout St. The northern end of the line follows Welton St through the Five Points neighborhood to the Black American West Museum & Heritage Center at the corner of 30th and Downing Sts. The southern end passes the Auraria Campus and terminates at Santa Fe and Mineral Sts. Trains operate between 4:30 am and 1:30 am and run every five minutes during peak periods. Fares are the same as for local buses. Bikes may board during off-peak hours with permit only.

Car & Taxi Nearly all the major car rental firms have counters in the baggage claim level at DIA – the cars, however, are 5 miles away, so allow extra time. There are complimentary shuttle buses for all rental car companies. Several agencies also have offices in downtown Denver, including: Avis, Budget, Enterprise and Hertz (see the Getting Around chapter).

If you don't have a credit card, A-Courtesy Rent A Car (☎ 303-733-2218, 800-441-1816) accepts cash deposits, but its vehicles cannot be driven outside Colorado.

Three taxi companies offer door-to-door service in Denver: Metro Taxi (☎ 303-333-3333), Yellow Cab (☎ 303-777-7777) and Zone Cab (☎ 303-444-8888).

DENVER MOUNTAIN PARKS & SOUTH PLATTE RIVER

In 1912, Denver voters approved spending public money to acquire the distant Mountain Parks land. That same year, Frederick Law Olmsted, the esteemed planner of New York City's Central Park, recommended the purchase of Genesse Mountain and construction of a road up Lookout Mountain west of Golden. The system currently includes 27 parks, beginning 15 miles west of Denver at an elevation of 5700 feet and rising to Echo Lake and Summit Lake on the flank of 14,264-foot Mt Evans – 60 miles from Denver. Red Rocks Park was acquired in 1927, and the skiers' playground at Winter Park, west of the Continental Divide over Berthoud Pass, was acquired in 1933 (see Winter Park & Fraser in the Northern Mountains chapter).

Today there are a surprising number of open space parks within a short drive of downtown Denver. The visitors information center in the Tabor Center (see Information at the beginning of this chapter) can provide brochures and more information on area parks and other quick escapes to the great outdoors.

Reynold's Park

Southwest of the city center, the 1260-acre Reynold's Park makes a fine choice for hiking, jogging or mountain biking along the park's 4½ miles of trails. Camping is free at the *Idylease Camp*, though a permit must be obtained from Jefferson County Open Space Parks (☎ 303-271-5925), 700 Jefferson County Pkwy, suite 100, Golden; the office is open 7:30 am to 5:30 pm weekdays.

Morrison

At an elevation of 5800 feet, Morrison (population 465) is a National Historic District 32 miles southwest of Denver on Hwy 8, set amid spectacular upturned red rocks on the banks of Bear Creek. Excavations of what is called the Morrison Formation began in 1877 and have yielded fossils of more than 70 dinosaur species. You can view dinosaur footprints by taking a self-guided tour of **Dinosaur Ridge** (☎ 303-697-3466), about 2 miles north of Morrison along Hwy 26. A visitors center, open 9 am to 4 pm, is on the east side of the ridge near the C-470 highway.

Morrison's restaurants are popular destinations for cyclists following the Bear Creek Greenway and Platte River Greenway from downtown Denver. A former drugstore and soda fountain is now a fun Mexican restaurant-bar called the *Morrison Inn* (☎ *303-697-6650, 301 Bear Creek Ave*). Historic photos of early Morrison line the restaurant walls.

Red Rocks Park & Amphitheater

The park is a 600-acre section of Denver's Gateway Mountain Parks. North of Morrison, it's open 5 am to 11 pm daily. From 1936 to 1941, members of the Civilian Conservation Corps worked on constructing the outdoor amphitheater, set between 400-foot-high red sandstone rocks with splendid natural acoustics, which has since featured a variety of concert performances. Climbing on the stunning formations is prohibited. However, 250-plus steps lead to the top of the 9000-seat theater, offering views of the park and of Denver, miles off to the east.

South Platte River

Pressure from nearby urban populations is evident everywhere you look in this part of the Pike National Forest southwest of the Chatfield Reservoir. Maps and information are available at the USFS (United States Forest Service) South Platte Ranger Station (☎ 303-275-5610), on US 285, 6½ miles west of the exit from highway C-470 and about 5 miles from Morrison.

Starting at Chatfield Reservoir, the 500-mile-long **Colorado Trail** (USFS Trail 1776) enters the Rocky Mountains along the South Platte River on its way to Durango. It crosses eight mountain ranges, seven national forests, six wilderness areas and five river systems. The lower section of the trail through Platte Canyon to Strontia Springs Reservoir is used heavily during the day. The Colorado Trail Foundation (CTF), PO Box 260876, Lakewood, CO 80226-0876, offers maps and books that describe the trail.

In the **Buffalo Creek Mountain Bike Area** the USFS South Platte Ranger District offers about 40 miles of bike trails, including the Colorado Trail, in the Buffalo Creek Mountain Bike Area. There are two access points: The busiest is 3½ miles south of Buffalo Creek where Jefferson County Rd 126 (S Deckers Rd) intersects the Colorado Trail. Another option is the Miller Gulch trailhead reached from Bailey by taking Park County Rd 68 for 5 miles, then veering left on Park County Rd 70 for another mile before taking a left on USFS Rd 553. Miller

Gulch Rd (USFS 554) will be on your right within half a mile. The USFS South Platte Ranger Station (☎ 303-275-5610) can provide you with a free pamphlet outlining some of the rides.

Southwest of Denver, **Devil's Head Lookout** (elevation 9748 feet) is on the highest summit in the forested Rampart Range. Although the area offers USFS *campsites* ($9), they are typically full and sometimes more noisy than relaxing. Picnics and day hikes, however, are highly recommended. In a little over a mile, you can climb almost 1000 feet to the fire lookout, which offers a commanding 360° view of Spanish Peaks to the south, Mt Evans to the north, South Park to the west and the eastern plains.

To get there from Denver, follow US 85 south to Sedalia then take Hwy 67 west for 10 miles to Rampart Range Rd, which leads 9 miles to the Devils Head National Recreation Trail and picnic grounds.

GOLDEN

This city (population 15,800; elevation 5674 feet) has earned a place on the map largely due to the Coors Brewery, which calls the town home. While this fact attracts many visitors, it deters those who are understandably unimpressed with the watery beer or its controversial manufacturer. But there's a bit more to Golden than brewery tours. The town has a small historic district, a few interesting museums and the highly regarded Colorado School of Mines. Some may find Golden an interesting day trip, but it probably doesn't warrant on overnight stay, particularly since accommodations are fairly expensive.

Golden was founded in 1859 at the mouth of Clear Creek Canyon, after prospectors discovered gold in the stream that flows through town. From 1862 to 1867, Golden served as the Colorado Territorial capital. You can win plenty of bar bets with visitors who assume Golden is named for the glinting yellow mineral – the seat of Jefferson County was named for Thomas L Golden who camped near the creek in 1858.

Information

The Golden Chamber of Commerce/Visitor Center (☎ 303-279-3113, 800-590-3113), at the corner of 10th St and Washington Ave, is open 8:30 am to 5 pm weekdays, 10 am to 4 pm weekends. In addition to maps and museum and hotel info, it can provide you with a walking tour guide to the 12th St historic district.
Web site: www.goldencochamber.org

Wells Fargo Bank (☎ 303-279-4563) has a 24-hour ATM at 1301 Jackson St. The post office is at 619 12th St; the zip code is 80402.

Bent Gate Mountaineering (☎ 303-271-9382), 1300 Washington Ave, stocks a wide range of outdoors gear, as well as books and maps; it's closed Saturday.
Web site: www.bentgate.com

Astor House Hotel Museum & Clear Creek History Park

Built from native stone quarried in Golden, the 1867 Astor House Hotel Museum (☎ 303-278-3557), at 822 12th St, is a fine example of a late Victorian Western hotel and is listed on the National Register of Historic Places. It's open from 10 am to 4:30 pm Tuesday to Saturday. Admission costs $3/1 adults/children.

Nearby at 11th and Arapahoe Sts, the intriguing Clear Creek History Park (☎ 303-278-3557) provides a taste of frontier life in the 19th century. The park features a collection of reconstructed period buildings, including a blacksmith shop, smokehouse and an 1876 schoolhouse. Visitors can learn about traditional ways such as gold panning, wool spinning and even lasso throwing!
Web site: www.clearcreekhistorypark.org

The park is open May through October, and 45-minute tours usually start on the hour between 11 am and 4 pm. During winter months tours can be pre-arranged. Admission costs $3/2 adults/children; at $4.50/2.50 the combined ticket for the two sites is a worthy value.

Golden Pioneer Museum

Established in 1939, the Golden Pioneer Museum (☎ 303-278-7151) at 923 10th St focuses on memorabilia from Golden's

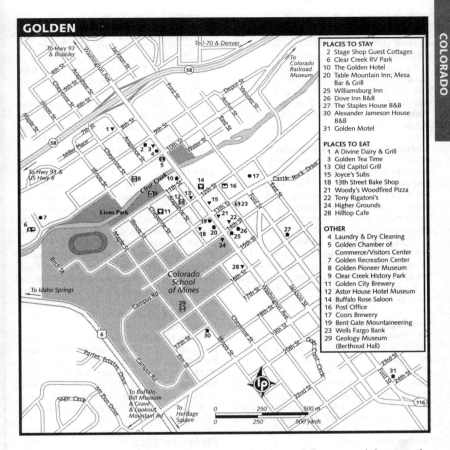

GOLDEN

PLACES TO STAY
2 Stage Shop Guest Cottages
6 Clear Creek RV Park
10 The Golden Hotel
20 Table Mountain Inn; Mesa
   Bar & Grill
25 Williamsburg Inn
26 Dove Inn B&B
27 The Staples House B&B
30 Alexander Jameson House
   B&B
31 Golden Motel

PLACES TO EAT
1 A Divine Dairy & Grill
3 Golden Tea Time
13 Old Capitol Grill
15 Joyce's Subs
18 13th Street Bake Shop
21 Woody's Woodfired Pizza
22 Tony Rigatoni's
24 Higher Grounds
28 Hilltop Cafe

OTHER
4 Laundry & Dry Cleaning
5 Golden Chamber of
   Commerce/Visitors Center
7 Golden Recreation Center
8 Golden Pioneer Museum
9 Clear Creek History Park
11 Golden City Brewery
12 Astor House Hotel Museum
14 Buffalo Rose Saloon
16 Post Office
17 Coors Brewery
19 Bent Gate Mountaineering
23 Wells Fargo Bank
29 Geology Museum
   (Berthoud Hall)

Territorial Capital years, 1859 to 1930. Exhibits include regional artifacts, photos, Indian dolls, mining tools, period clothing and furniture, military accessories and Golden's first galvanized bath tub! It's open 10 am to 4:30 pm Monday to Saturday. Admission is free.

Buffalo Bill Memorial Museum & Mountain Parks

Four and a half miles west of Golden on Lookout Mountain Rd, **Lookout Mountain Park** is the gateway to the Denver Mountain Park system. The summit offers great views

of Golden and Denver and features the Buffalo Bill Memorial Museum (☎ 303-526-0747), near the site where Buffalo Bill Cody was buried in 1917.

Like Buffalo Bill's 19th-century Wild West Show, the museum is an engaging presentation. Find out more on its Web site at www.buffalobill.org. It's open 9 am to 5 pm daily in summer (in winter to 4 pm and closed Monday); admission costs $3/1 adults/children (six to 15).

Short trails through scenic wildflower meadows and ponderosa forest are nearby at the **Lookout Mountain Nature Center**

(☎ 303-526-0594), part of the Jefferson County Open Space Parks, about 2 miles west of the museum. The center is open 10 am to 4 pm Tuesday to Sunday.

Continuing west on Lookout Mountain Rd from the museum, turn right onto US 40 and follow the road west to the I-70 overpass (exit 254) leading to Denver's **Genesee Park**, a favorite place to view elk and bison herds.

Colorado Railroad Museum

A surefire winner for the railroad buff, this museum housed in an old depot provides a comprehensive history of Colorado railroads and street rail companies. Indoor exhibits and model trains, some 50 locomotives and cars, comprise the impressive collection of 'railroadania.'

The Colorado Railroad Museum (☎ 303-279-4591) is 2 miles east of Golden at 17155 W 44th Ave; take 10th St from downtown. It's open 9 am to 5 pm daily; extended hours to 6 pm June through August. Admission costs $6/3 adults/children (under 16).

Geology Museum

Set below the giant 'M' on Mt Zion, the Colorado School of Mines, founded in 1874, is the nation's second oldest institution devoted to minerals. On the 2nd floor of Berthoud Hall at the corner of 16th and Maple Sts, the school's geology museum (☎ 303-273-3815) features mining exhibits and mineral and fossil displays. It's open 9 am to 4 pm Monday to Saturday, 1 to 4 pm Sunday; free.

Coors Brewery Tour

Water – now pumped from below ground rather than drawn from the roiling muddy waters of Clear Creek – is what Coors claims makes its beer distinctive. Tours of the brewery (☎ 303-277-2337) cover the history of Adolph Coors after his arrival in the USA from Wuppertal, Germany, in 1847, though it omits his family's reported links to fascist groups earlier in this century.

The great copper vats are impressive, as is the scale of the entire operation. The plant visit, however, accounts for only 30 minutes of the 1½-hour tour; the rest is little more than a tedious promotion followed by tastings (for adult visitors only). Free tours are offered Monday to Saturday, every 15 minutes from 10 am to 4 pm. To arrange tours in languages other than English, call ☎ 303-277-2552.

From Washington Ave, Coors Brewing Company is only three blocks east on 12th St; walk past the hops growing on the plant fence to the giant copper kettle at the entrance, where tours begin.

Bicycling

Nearby parks offer plenty of opportunity for off-road rides, and road riders will find a number of loops beginning in Golden. Immediately south of I-70 along Hwy 26, **Matthews/Winters Park** has trail access to the Mt Vernon townsite, which in 1859 was the capital of the provisional Territory of Jefferson. East of Matthews/Winters Park and Hwy 26, the **Dakota Ridge Trail** follows the spine of Hogback Park south for 2 miles before crossing Hwy 26 near Morrison to **Red Rocks Trail**, which returns to Matthews/Winters Park.

If you're in good shape and don't mind a steep climb, try **White Ranch Open Space Park**, which has miles of challenging single-track and fire-road rides. There are two trailheads: one just off Hwy 93 on the way to Boulder, the other 15 miles up Golden Gate Canyon Rd en route to Golden Gate Canyon State Park.

Places to Stay

As the name suggests, *Clear Creek RV Park* (☎ *303-278-1437*), only a few blocks west of downtown on 10th St, caters mainly to vehicle camping but does have three tent sites that are little more than patches of grass and dirt next to a chain-link fence. Sites are pricey at $20 but include access to showers. Far nicer campsites are available 16 miles out of town at *Golden Gate Canyon State Park* (☎ *303-470-1144, 800-678-2267*), featuring 19 sq miles of camping and hiking among beautiful rocky peaks and aspen-filled meadows. Backcountry sites cost $6, while more than 130 developed sites with showers and laundry cost $10. From Hwy 93, a half-mile north of Golden, turn left on Golden Gate Canyon Rd and continue 15 miles to the visitors center. Daily park fees are $4 per vehicle.

The cheapest motel lodgings reasonably near the Golden downtown area are at *Golden Motel* (☎ 303-279-5581, *510 24th St*). Fairly basic singles/doubles cost $44/48.

Don't confuse the above with *The Golden Hotel* (☎ 303-279-0100, 800-233-7214, 800 11th St), a plain-on-the-outside but pleasing-on-the-inside brick building, set on the edge of Clear Creek. Well-appointed rooms cost from $99 to $169 for the Presidential Suite (featuring mountain views, a wet bar, fireplace and Jacuzzi). Web site: www.golden-hotel.com

Rooms at the motel-like *Williamsburg Inn* (☎ 303-279-7673, 1407 Washington Ave) are more expensive at $105/120, but the furnishings are cozy, the rooms clean and the owners amiable. The *Table Mountain Inn* (☎ 303-277-9898, 800-762-9898, 1310 Washington Ave) is an upscale Santa Fe–style hotel with rooms for $99/109 and suites for $138 and $168.

The friendly *Dove Inn B&B* (☎ 303-278-2209, 711 14th St), a handsome Victorian home built between 1878 and 1886, offers rooms with private bath and TVs with VCRs from $69 to $99. It has a Web site at www.doveinn.com. *The Staples House B&B* (☎ 303-271-1891, 1523 Ford St) dates from the 1890s and represents Queen Anne–style Victorian architecture. Rooms with private bath rent for $80. Its Web site is www.stapleshouse.com.

Period antiques furnish *Alexander Jameson House B&B* (☎ 303-278-0200, 888-880-4448, 1704 Illinois St), reminiscent of an English country inn. Rooms cost $80 and $90, and suites with a private hot tub and fireplace go for $110 to $130.
Web site: www.jamesonhouse.com

The rustic *Stage Shop Guest Cottages* (☎ 303-279-2667, 807 9th St) is a designated historical site (circa 1860) where guests can stay in a southwestern-style, stucco-walled cottage or the '1873 House.' Rates are $80.

Places to Eat

Freshly made, light bistro fare (soup, sandwiches, gourmet pizzas and salads) is the scene at the *Hilltop Cafe* (☎ 303-279-8151, 1518 Washington Ave). *A Divine Dairy & Grill* (☎ 303-278-7311, 720 Arapahoe St) does burger and sandwich lunches for around $3. Another good sandwich spot in town is *Joyce's Subs* (☎ 303-277-2460, 1250 Washington Ave).

The *Mesa Bar & Grill* (☎ 303-277-9898, 1310 Washington Ave), in the Table Mountain Inn, offers fine Southwest cooking.

At the site of the former Territorial Capitol Building, *Old Capitol Grill* (☎ 303-279-6390, 1122 Washington Ave) features pleasant 'modern Old West' decor. Lunch sandwiches are about $6 and Old West platters like chicken-fried steak are $8 to $10.

The rustic *Woody's Woodfired Pizza* (☎ 303-277-0443, 1305 Washington Ave) serves great Italian food, has a salad and soup bar and attracts customers with its pool tables and full bar. *Tony Rigatoni's* (☎ 303-277-9020, 710 14th St) has an appealing menu of pizza and pasta items; lunch specials go for about $6 and dinner items range from $7 to $12.

For an eye-opening caffeine jolt, check out the patio overlooking Golden at *Higher Grounds* (☎ 303-271-9998, 803 B 14th St) at the corner of Washington Ave. Don't miss the three-story cobblestone Armory Hall, built in 1913, which now houses the *13th Street Bake Shop* (☎ 303-278-2225, 1301 Arapahoe St), at the corner of 13th. *Golden Tea Time* (☎ 303-271-3650, 908 Washington Ave) is a charming little Victorian tea house and also sells nostalgic bric-a-brac.

Entertainment

Featuring retro-rock acts such as Leon Russel, Edgar Winter and Dr Hook, *Buffalo Rose Saloon* (☎ 303-279-5190, 1119 Washington Ave) is one of the more entertaining venues in Colorado for the genre.

Dwarfed by Coors, the delightful *Golden City Brewery* (☎ 303-279-8092, 920 12th St), in a Victorian doctor's home, is proud to be the number-two brewery in Golden. It offers half-gallon jugs of its various ales, bitters and stouts for $7. The front section houses a cozy mini-brewpub where light lunches are available along with pints of beer for $2, one of the best bargains you'll find anywhere in Colorado.

Getting There & Away

RTD (☎ 303-299-6000) connects Golden with downtown Denver (at the corner of 15th and California Sts). The easiest route by car from Denver is I-25 north to I-70, then I-70 to exit 265 where you can catch Hwy 58 west into town. From downtown Denver to Golden is about 16 miles.

IDAHO SPRINGS & GEORGETOWN

Just west of Denver along I-70, Idaho Springs (20 miles west of Denver) and Georgetown (15 miles farther west) were founded as mining towns in the 19th century and still have an historical feel about them. Both towns have a spread of antique shops, galleries and restaurants as well as the dramatic backdrop of the rising Rocky Mountains.

For tourist information, visit the Idaho Springs visitors center and museum (☎ 800-685-7785) at 2060 Miner St, or its Web site at www.idahospringschamber.com. Historic Georgetown visitors center (☎ 888-569-0750), at exit 228 off I-70, also has a Web site: www.georgetowncolorado.com.

Indian Springs Resort

Once advertised as Radium Hot Springs, later Soda Creek, the Indian Springs Resort (☎ 303-989-6666), south of I-70 at 302 Soda Creek Rd, features geothermal caves, an enclosed pool and 'Club Mud.' Rates are reasonable, and it's open 7:30 am to 10:30 pm year-round (see Places to Stay & Eat, below).

Argo Gold Mill

In 1910 a 22,000-foot tunnel was completed by Samuel Newhouse connecting Idaho Springs with Central City. It was used to transport ore to the Argo Mill (☎ 303-567-2421), 2350 Riverside Dr, where it was processed to recover gold. Half-hour tours

of the mill (9 am to 6 pm daily, May 1 to September 30) cost $9/5 for adults/children. Note the boulder filled with holes at the entrance, which was used in a drilling contest. Web site: www.historicargotours.com

Georgetown Loop Railroad

From late May to early October you can ride an historic steam engine train through the mountains between Devil's Gate (Georgetown) and the town of Silver Plume. The roundtrip takes 70 minutes and costs $12.95/8.50 adults/children under 15. Look for more information at the Old Georgetown station (☎ 303-569-2403, 800-691-4386), 1106 Rose St (exit 228 off I-70). Web site: www.georgetownloop.com

St Mary's Glacier

If you like the idea of skiing year-round, head to this 11,000-foot, 10-acre permanent snowfield. Two miles west of Idaho Springs take I-70 exit 238 and follow the Fall River Rd for 12 miles to the trailheads at the glacier.

Places to Stay & Eat

Hot-spring buffs will appreciate *Indian Springs Resort (☎ 303-989-6666, 302 Soda Creek Rd)* in Idaho Springs (see Indian Springs Resort, above). Pleasant doubles cost $55 to $79, and campsites are $18. Web site: www.indianspringsresort.com

Georgetown's *Red Ram Restaurant & Saloon (☎ 303-569-2300, 606 6th St)* offers tempting menu selections including slow-cooked prime rib. Live entertainment is featured on weekends.

MT EVANS

The pinnacle of many visitors' trips to Colorado is a drive to the alpine summit of Mt Evans (elevation 14,264 feet) – less than an hour west of Denver's skyscrapers. In 1930, the state added a new meaning to the term 'highway' when it opened the **Mt Evans Hwy**. From I-70 exit 240 at Idaho Springs, Mt Evans Hwy takes you through a 6725-foot elevation change. Near the exit in Idaho Springs, the USFS Clear Creek Ranger Station (☎ 303-567-2901), open

8 am to 5 pm daily, offers information and a good selection of books and topo maps of the area.

The lower portion of the road travels through a montane ecosystem for 13 miles to **Echo Lake**, where the University of Denver's High Altitude Lab is situated in the sub-alpine ecosystem at 10,700 feet. Reservable USFS campsites at *Echo Lake Campground* (☎ 800-280-2267) get plenty of use and cost $10, plus the $8.65 reservation fee. Freezing temperatures can be experienced here throughout the year – the lab once recorded a low of -52°F.

The last vestiges of forest before ascending to the alpine tundra, the gnarly bristle-cone pine, can be visited on foot at the **Mt Goliath Natural Area**. Four miles above Echo Lake, take the Alpine Gardens Trail for just over a mile downhill and back. Continuing on the road past Summit Lake, which freezes solid in winter, you are likely to encounter Rocky Mountain goats and bighorn sheep. From the end of the highway it's a 200-foot scramble to the summit.

The area is typically open from Memorial Day to Labor Day. The onset of cold temperatures returns Mt Evans' slopes to their rightful inhabitants.

EMPIRE
I-70 now carries most of the traffic toward the Continental Divide, while Empire (population 401) sits astride US 40, the historic route toward scenic 11,315-foot Berthoud Pass. When dedicated in 1938, US 40 was the first hard-surfaced transcontinental route. Summer traffic bound for Granby or Winter Park on the western slope over Berthoud Pass continues to follow US 40, and in the winter Empire (elevation 8614 feet) plays host to many skiers returning from Winter Park. (Drivers take heed: Empire is a prime hideout for the highway patrol ready to ambush those who flout the town's 35mph speed limit.)

Top-end dining and lodging is offered at the historic *Peck House* (☎ 303-569-9870, 83 Sunny Ave). Established in 1862, it's the oldest hotel in Colorado. The well-planned lack of in-room TVs or telephones helps guests to step back in time. Excellent dinners cost between $17 and $27. One shared-bath double costs $50; most rooms with private baths cost $60 to $95.
Web site: www.thepeckhouse.com

LOVELAND SKI AREA
Set against the Continental Divide above the I-70 Eisenhower Tunnel, Loveland Basin Ski Area (☎ 800-736-3754) is only 56 miles west of Denver. Convenient access to Denver and reasonable lift tickets make Loveland a popular day trip. Its base elevation is 10,600 feet and the summit is 12,280 feet. About half of the 836 skiable acres are intermediate, while the remainder of the trails are evenly divided between beginner trails and expert runs such as Avalanche Bowl and Tigers Tail, served by the No 1 lift. Loveland averages around 340 inches of snow a year, and some glorious powder days can be had here. It also has a cozy, unassuming atmosphere that makes for a nice change from some of Colorado's snobbier resorts.

Access to Denver is via I-70 (exit 216). Lift tickets cost $41/17 adult/child.
Web site: www.skiloveland.com

Boulder & Around

BOULDER
This city (population 95,000; elevation 5430 feet) has traditionally been considered a unique community within Colorado. In a largely conservative state, Boulder has long been a bastion of liberal politics, alternative lifestyles and progressive social attitudes. While most other towns in postwar Colorado worried about boosting their economies, the City of Boulder focused more on quality-of-life issues, spending money to acquire mountain parks and other open space areas and putting caps on business growth. This is reflected in the human scale of the Pearl St Mall, Boulder's excellent network of bicycle routes and the surrounding greenbelt that has preserved a place for people to enjoy the natural environment near their homes, a successful model for other cities and counties.

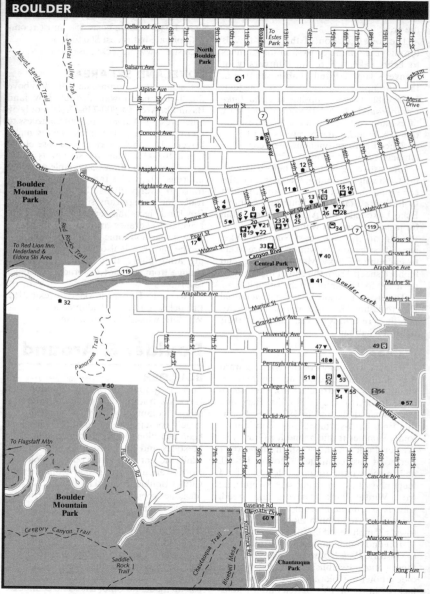

BOULDER

BOULDER

COLORADO

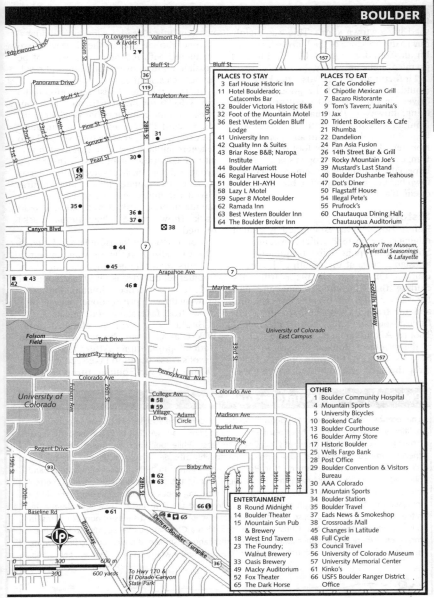

PLACES TO STAY
3 Earl House Historic Inn
11 Hotel Boulderado;
   Catacombs Bar
12 Boulder Victoria Historic B&B
32 Foot of the Mountain Motel
36 Best Western Golden Bluff
   Lodge
41 University Inn
42 Quality Inn & Suites
43 Briar Rose B&B; Naropa
   Institute
44 Boulder Marriott
46 Regal Harvest House Hotel
51 Boulder HI-AYH
58 Lazy L Motel
59 Super 8 Motel Boulder
62 Ramada Inn
63 Best Western Boulder Inn
64 The Boulder Broker Inn

PLACES TO EAT
2 Cafe Gondolier
6 Chipotle Mexican Grill
7 Bacaro Ristorante
9 Tom's Tavern; Juanita's
19 Jax
20 Trident Booksellers & Cafe
21 Rhumba
22 Dandelion
24 Pan Asia Fusion
26 14th Street Bar & Grill
27 Rocky Mountain Joe's
39 Mustard's Last Stand
40 Boulder Dushanbe Teahouse
47 Dot's Diner
50 Flagstaff House
54 Illegal Pete's
55 Prufrock's
60 Chautauqua Dining Hall;
   Chautauqua Auditorium

ENTERTAINMENT
8 Round Midnight
14 Boulder Theater
15 Mountain Sun Pub
   & Brewery
18 West End Tavern
23 The Foundry;
   Walnut Brewery
33 Oasis Brewery
49 Macky Auditorium
52 Fox Theater
65 The Dark Horse

OTHER
1 Boulder Community Hospital
4 Mountain Sports
5 University Bicycles
10 Bookend Cafe
13 Boulder Courthouse
16 Boulder Army Store
17 Historic Boulder
25 Wells Fargo Bank
28 Post Office
29 Boulder Convention & Visitors
   Bureau
30 AAA Colorado
31 Mountain Sports
34 Boulder Station
35 Boulder Travel
37 Eads News & Smokeshop
38 Crossroads Mall
45 Changes in Latitude
48 Full Cycle
53 Council Travel
56 University of Colorado Museum
57 University Memorial Center
61 Kinko's
66 USFS Boulder Ranger District
   Office

Boulder was also an intellectual and cultural center long before Denver started to shed its cowtown status. This was mainly due to the presence of the University of Colorado-Boulder, or 'CU,' Colorado's premier public university.

Unfortunately, crowds flocking to Boulder in search of the good life have driven up property and retail prices. One thing, however, that hasn't changed is Boulder's mania for outdoor recreation, kept alive by the large student population, Boulder's location at the foot of the Front Range and the excellent open space system. Especially in summer it seems as if half the town has taken the day off to bike, hike, run or climb a mountain.

History

Before Boulder was established as a small mining center in 1858, Chief Niwot and the Southern Arapaho tribe frequented the artesian springs at the mouth of Eldorado Canyon. Other nomadic plains tribes, including the Cheyenne, Comanche and Kiowa, were also noted by the few explorers and fur trappers who entered the area. English-speaking Chief Niwot intercepted Thomas Aikens and a party of gold seekers at the mouth of Boulder Canyon in 1858. Niwot's request that the miners leave Arapaho land was rebuffed and he was

helpless in stopping the advance of the armed intruders. Chief Niwot is said to have subsequently placed a curse on Boulder – anyone who sets eyes on the place will be so enamored with it that leaving will not be possible. In turn, overpopulation will result in the area's demise.

In 1875 the state legislature offered the city $15,000 for the construction of a university, on the condition that Boulder's citizens contribute an equal amount. Construction of Old Main followed and two teachers initiated instruction at the University of Colorado in fall 1877. In 1898, a group of Texas teachers selected Boulder as the spot to emulate the summer cultural haven for music and art at Lake Chautauqua in New York. A year later, Texado Park (now called Chautauqua Park) opened.

Construction of the Boulderado Hotel in 1909 capitalized on the growing popularity of tours to the mountains west of town. Boulder set out to make itself a destination and soon the system of Mountain Parks was growing through private donations and purchases from federal and state agencies.

Boulder's growth accelerated after WWII, as GI loans helped to swell the student population. After 1951, Chief Niwot's curse began to take seed when the 27-mile Denver-Boulder turnpike (now

---

Politically Correct – Intellectually Awry

The recent surge in numbers of upper-middle-class residents and Boulder's history as an outspoken, politically active community have resulted in a strange mix: a town that bickers over petty social issues and gets hung up on what's 'politically correct.' While 'political correctness' – the idea of speaking in a such a way that no one on earth is possibly offended – has afflicted much of the US, it's put down particularly firm roots in Boulder. An example: In 1995 a local high school band planned to play the Christmas carol 'Silent Night' during the school's holiday festivities. Letters poured into the local *Daily Camera* newspaper expressing shock that Christian music should be imposed on the community in such a manner. Proposed solutions included students humming, rather than singing, the tune, so the offensive words wouldn't harm the ears of non-Christians. In this silly debate, the fact that Christmas is by definition a Christian holiday seemed to have been forgotten. Where Boulder once embraced the radical and outspoken, it now seems to have swung in another, less inspiring direction: trying to build a community where no one's feathers get ruffled.

– **Nicko Goncharoff**

US 36) opened, making metropolitan commuting feasible. Now some 140 years later, many believe Niwot's curse has finally become reality.

Orientation

Central Boulder is bordered by the mountains to the west, 28th St to the east, Baseline Rd to the south and Valmont Rd to the north. Numbered streets are aligned roughly north-south; street numbering begins at the foothills with 3rd St.

Boulder's two major districts of interest to the visitor are the Pearl St Mall downtown and the University Hill district that rises to the south. The two areas are separated by east-west Boulder Creek, a 9-mile corridor for pedestrians and bicyclists. Canyon Blvd (Hwy 119), which intersects 28th St, heads west to skirt the southern edge of downtown before entering Boulder Canyon and continuing to Nederland, Eldora Ski Area and the Peak to Peak Hwy. The University Hill area is adjacent to the main CU campus.

Information

Tourist Offices The Boulder Convention & Visitors Bureau (☎ 303-442-2911), 2440 Pearl St at Folsom St, offers maps, brochures and assistance 9 am to 5 pm weekdays.
Web site: www.bouldercoloradousa.com

There is also an information cart toward the west end of Pearl St Mall near the courthouse. Motorists arriving from Denver on US 36 can stop at the Davidson Mesa Information Center a few miles south of town to pick up brochures and maps. This spot gives a great view of Boulder, the Flatirons and, on a clear day, the Rocky Mountains.

For information and self-guided tour maps of the CU campus, head to the reception desk at University Memorial Center, on campus at the intersection of Broadway and Euclid Ave. For guided tour information call ☎ 303-492-6301.

For information about the Arapaho and Roosevelt National Forests, stop by the USFS Boulder Ranger District Office (☎ 303-444-6600), 2995 Baseline Rd.

Boulder's Beautiful Backdrop

Boulder's most distinguishing physical feature is the Flatiron Rock Formation. Lending a strong scenic emblem to the town, the Flatirons are part of the Fountain formation seen at Denver's Red Rocks Park and Colorado Springs' Garden of the Gods. With the uplift of the Rocky Mountains beginning about 65 million years ago, the Fountain formation sediments were tilted upward. Subsequent erosion has carved the broken edges of the strata into jagged ridges. Over the past 1½ million years, cooling has resulted in glaciers scouring the deep U-shaped canyons in the terrain above the Flatirons. The general warming trend over the past 10,000 years has caused the glaciers to retreat to the highest ridges on the Continental Divide. One of these, Arapaho Glacier, is owned by the City of Boulder to provide water, considered by many (mostly Boulderites) to be the tastiest in the country.

In addition to providing a stunning scenic backdrop to the town, the Flatirons are popular with hikers and climbers. Trails up and around the Flatirons lead to nice views of the Eastern Plains and to the west the gorgeous peaks of the Continental Divide. The first and second Flatirons can be attempted without ropes, though serious accidents have resulted when some free-climbers got too careless. Free-climbing the third Flatiron is not a wise idea at all.

Money An ATM is in the downstairs lobby of the building at the corner of 13th St and College Ave on University Hill, and another one is at University Memorial Center, on campus. Just one block south of the Pearl St Mall on 13th St is a Wells Fargo Bank ATM. The bank branch itself (☎ 303-442-0351) is at 1242 Pearl St and offers complete banking services.

Post & Communications The central post office is at 1905 15th St; the zip code for the post office is 80304. Kinko's (☎ 303-494-2622, fax 303-494-0879), near the south end of campus at 2616 Baseline Rd, can handle email, fax and copy needs 24 hours a day.

Travel Agencies On University Hill, Hostelling International-American Youth Hostels (HI-AYH; ☎ 303-442-1166), 1310 College Ave, can issue a membership card and help you plan your itinerary. AAA Colorado (☎ 303-753-8800), 1933 28th St, offers travel-planning services for members and the general public. Council Travel (☎ 303-447-8101), 1138 13th St, caters to student and budget travelers. Among the larger agencies is Boulder Travel (☎ 303-443-0380), 1655 Folsom St.

Bookstores The Bookend Cafe (☎ 303-447-2074), 1107 Pearl St Mall, has a great selection of books and an adjacent coffee shop.

Rue Morgue Bookshop (☎ 800-356-5586), 946 Pearl St, is good for mystery titles. Word Is Out Women's Bookstore (☎ 303-449-1415), 1731 15th St, is open 10 am to 6 pm Tuesday to Saturday, 12 to 5 pm Sunday. Other more general bookstores include, Boulder Book Store (☎ 303-447-2074) at 1107 Pearl St, Stage House Books (☎ 303-447-1433), 1039 Pearl St and Bookworm (☎ 303-449-3765), 2850 Iris Ave.

For travel books and maps check out Changes in Latitude (☎ 303-786-8406), 2416 Arapahoe Ave (in a strip mall between 28th and Folsom Sts). The Boulder Army Store (☎ 303-442-7616), 1545 Pearl St, offers a selection of outdoors books and topo maps. There's also Boulder Map Gallery (☎ 303-444-1406) at 1708 13th St.

Out-of-town and foreign newspapers are available at Eads News & Smokeshop (☎ 303-442-5900), 1715 28th St.

Medical Services Boulder Community Hospital (☎ 303-440-2273) is at 1100 Balsam Ave at N Broadway.

Pearl St Mall
Along Pearl St between 11th and 15th Sts, Pearl St Mall is a welcome change from the conformity of the bland, enclosed shopping

malls typically found in US towns. It's more like a European shopping district with crowds of people making up a significant part of the overall show. Sit back on a bench and observe the mix of people, listen to street musicians playing flutes, guitars and even sitars and catch a whiff of patchouli oil or clove tobacco. Posters and bills on public information kiosks list upcoming events. The mall even has that US rarity, public restrooms, at 13th St.

Historic Boulder
Guided and self-guided tours of Boulder's historic homes and downtown buildings are available from the Historic Boulder (☎ 303-444-5192) organization, based in the 1877 Arnett-Fullen House at 646 Pearl St. Nearby is Mapleton Hill, home to Boulder's oldest and most magnificent homes. Historic Boulder is open 9 am to 4 pm weekdays.

University of Colorado Museum
Exhibits in the museum (☎ 303-492-6892), on 15th St at Broadway, focus on the geology, biology, human prehistory and native cultures of the Rocky Mountain region. It's open 9 am to 5 pm weekdays, 9 am to 4 pm Saturday and 10 am to 4 pm Sunday. Admission is free, but donations are welcome.

Naropa Institute
'New Age' is not what this small, Buddhist-inspired institute of higher learning would care to add to its list of attributes, though most people would think of it that way. Instead, the Naropa Institute (☎ 303-444-0202), 2130 Arapahoe Ave, promotes itself as a fully accredited, nonsectarian liberal arts college (called Naropa University) that is 'colorful, unconventional and photogenic.' Beat poet Allen Ginsberg and writer Ann Waldman founded Naropa's Jack Kerouac School of Disembodied Poetics, a writing and poetics MFA program.

The institute, established 25 years ago by Chögyam Trungpa Rinpoche to blend Western logic with Eastern intuition, offers traditional degrees as well as continuing education courses. It's held in high regard

internationally and has even played host to the Dalai Lama. The Naropa Institute also hosts a number of lectures, performances and workshops throughout the year.
Web site: www.naropa.edu

Leanin' Tree Museum of Western Art

In an industrial park off the Diagonal Hwy, Leanin' Tree Museum (☎ 303-530-1442), 6055 Longbow Dr, is also the corporate headquarters for Leanin' Tree, publishers of Western-art greeting cards. The museum features more than 200 original Western paintings and 80 bronze sculptures. It's open 8 am to 4:30 pm weekdays, 10 am to 4 pm weekends. Admission is free.
Web site: www.leanintree.com

Celestial Seasonings Tour of Tea

Boulder-based herbal tea maker Celestial Seasonings (☎ 303-581-1202) offers absorbing, 45-minute tours – including tea tasting, of course – of the factory (northeast of town) on a first-come, first-served basis. Tours are on the hour between 10 am and 3 pm daily (no 10 am tour on Sunday, however); free. Celestial Seasonings is on Sleepytime Dr, off Hwy 119.

Hiking & Backpacking

Years ago, hikers used to climb to the Crags Hotel, 800 feet above South Boulder Creek in Eldorado Canyon (see Rock Climbing, below) and could even flag the D&RG Western train as it passed on its way toward Moffat Tunnel. Nowadays, when the **Rattlesnake Gulch Trail** is not closed to protect raptor nesting sites (February 1 to July 31), you can hike about 1½ miles to the ruins of the hotel and continue another half-mile to wave to passengers on Amtrak's *California Zephyr*. Below the entrance to Eldorado Canyon, the **Mesa Trail** enters the City of Boulder Open Space, and the **Towhee Trail** leads through chokecherry canyon bottoms, frequented by black bears in late summer, before rejoining the Mesa Trail on the uplands where mule deer roam. The relatively easy Mesa Trail continues north for 7 miles to Chautauqua Park, offering access to

more difficult routes such as the **Shadow Canyon**, **Fern Canyon** and **Bear Canyon Trails**. These three trails lead to the top of Bear Peak (8461 feet), a steep climb that rewards you with spectacular views of the plains to the east and the Rockies to the west.

From the Chautauqua Park area, trails head in many directions. An easy trail that introduces hikers to Boulder's natural environment, the **McClintock Nature Trail** leads to a stunning view of the Flatirons and Boulder from its starting point behind the Chautauqua Amphitheater in the park. By continuing south on the **Enchanted Mesa Trail** and returning on the Mesa Trail, you can hike an easy 2-mile loop.

Also at the Chautauqua site is the **Boulder Mountain Parks Ranger Cottage** (☎ 303-441-3408), open 8:30 am to 5 pm weekdays and irregular hours on weekends, with information on trails leading across the broad sloping meadow to the climbing areas on the first, second and third Flatirons. Information about areas of the City of Boulder Open Space (☎ 303-441-4142) is also available at this station, but the 'Space Rangers' are on patrol elsewhere.

To start your hike from higher-elevation trailheads, continue west on Baseline Rd past Chautauqua Park. Baseline Rd becomes Flagstaff Rd as it follows a switchback course to the trailheads from Realization Point or the Summit Amphitheater. Hikers on **Flagstaff Mountain** (6872 feet) look directly down on Boulder. Slightly longer and more difficult loops start from the **Gregory Canyon Picnic Area**, reached from a turnoff to the left at the top of Baseline Rd.

Bicycling

The 9-mile **Boulder Creek Trail** is the main bicycle route in town for commuters, students and visitors. West of downtown, the Boulder Creek Trail follows an unpaved streamside path up and back to Four Mile Canyon. An easy optional spur along this route heads north to Mt Sanitas. Those seeking a challenge can join the locals riding up Flagstaff Rd to the top of **Flagstaff Mountain**, a 4-mile ride that should give you more than enough exercise.

Most trails in the Boulder Mountain Parks are off-limits to riders; exceptions include intermediate-level trails in **Doudy Draw** near Eldorado Springs and **Marshall Mesa** off Marshall Rd south of town. Far more technically challenging is the 10-mile loop at **Walker Ranch**, west of Flagstaff Mountain about 10 miles from Boulder along Flagstaff Rd.

Bike rentals are available from University Bicycles (☎ 303-444-4196), at the corner of 9th and Pearl Sts. On University Hill, try Full Cycle (☎ 303-440-7771), 1211 13th St. Books and maps for road and mountain biking are available at both shops.

Rock Climbing

Whether you climb or just want to watch others practice traditional climbing techniques, the vertical rock faces at Eldorado Canyon State Park (☎ 303-494-3943), 7 miles south of Boulder, are certain to provide plenty of entertainment.

This is one of the most popular climbing areas in the country, offering Class 5.6 to 5.9 climbs. Peregrine and prairie falcons nest on the walls; be sure to stay 100 yards from any nesting sites. The park is closed from February to August to protect the raptor habitat. No-bolt sport climbing is available on the three Flatirons, reached via hiking trails from Chautauqua Park (see Hiking & Backpacking, above).

The entrance is on Eldorado Springs Dr, 3 miles west of Hwy 93. Admission costs $4 for motor vehicles, $2 for hikers and cyclists.

Mountain Sports (☎ 303-442-8355), 2835 Pearl St and 821 Spruce St, offers gear, books, maps, climbing lessons and guide service.

Special Events

The **Kinetic Conveyance Parade and Challenge** for human-powered vehicles takes place in late April and early May. The parade takes place downtown; the race (challenge) takes place at the Boulder Reservoir.

From June to September **Chautauqua Summer Festival** (☎ 303-449-2413) performances are held in the Chautauqua Auditorium, a national landmark. The free **Forum Lecture Series** is held in the Chautauqua Community House on summer weekdays.

From late June to mid-August the **Colorado Shakespeare Festival** (☎ 303-492-0554) is presented on the CU campus.

In early August, the three-day **Rocky Mountain Bluegrass Festival** (☎ 303-449-6007), also called 'Rockygrass,' is held in Lyons, 12 miles north of Boulder.

Places to Stay

Camping & Hostels For camping near town try *Boulder Mountain Lodge* (see Motels, below). The campground offers 15 spaces shaded by pines and cottonwood trees for $14.

In the University Hill district, the *Boulder International Youth Hostel* (☎ *303-442-0522, 1107 12th St*) offers men's and women's dorms with plenty of showers for each. There is a three-day stay limit in the dorms, which are open only to out-of-state guests. Dorm beds cost $15, with up to a $4/night surcharge for linens. Private rooms with shared bath are available in 13 adjacent buildings for $36/day, $170/week, $290/fortnight and $540/month. Web site: www.boulderhostel.com

Motels Unfortunately Boulder is an expensive place to stay, especially during the long peak season that lasts from May to October. During winter months you can expect discounts of 15% or more.

North of the CU campus, singles/doubles cost $115/130 (peak season) and $75/85 (off-peak) at the *Quality Inn & Suites* (☎ *303-449-7550, 888-449-7550, 2020 Arapahoe Ave*). Facilities include an indoor pool, hot tub, coin laundry and free 24-hour Internet access. Rates include a full breakfast. It has a Web site at www.qualityinnboulder.com. Cheaper (and less noteworthy) is the *University Inn* (☎ *303-442-3830, 1632 Broadway*), near campus. Rooms start at $85/95 (peak), $67/77 (off-peak).

Near the entrance to Boulder Canyon, cozy (though somewhat small) wood-paneled rooms are available during summer for $65/80 at *Foot of the*

Mountain Motel (☎ 303-442-5688, *200 Arapahoe Ave*). Winter rates are $50/65. If you really want to be in the mountains, motel-style rooms (some with kitchenettes) are $52 to $68 at *Boulder Mountain Lodge* (☎ 303-444-0882, *91 Four Mile Canyon Rd*), set in a shady canyon 4 miles west of Boulder on Hwy 119. You can also camp here (see above).

There is a string of motels (largely similar) east of the CU campus on 28th St, including the following:

Best Western Boulder Inn (☎ 303-449-3800, 800-233-8469, *770 28th St*), $64 to $109, pool, sauna, free Continental breakfast
Web site: www.boulderinn.com

Best Western Golden Buff Lodge (☎ 303-442-7450, 800-999-2833, *1725 28th St*), $64 to $114, pool, health club, hot tub
Web site: www.goldenbluff.com

Lazy L Motel (☎ 303-442-7525, 800-525-1444, *1000 28th St*), $56 to $116, pool, kitchenettes

Ramada Inn (☎ 303-443-3322, 800-542-0304, *800 28th St*), $75 to $115, indoor pool, sauna, Jacuzzi

Super 8 Motel Boulder (☎ 303-443-7800, 800-800-8000, *970 28th St*), $55 to $150, pool

Hotels The *Regal Harvest House* (☎ 303-443-3850, 800-222-8888, *1345 28th St*) is an upmarket, business-oriented hotel with rooms in winter/summer from $99/169.
Web site: www.regal-hotels.com/boulder

The historic *Boulder Broker Inn* (☎ 303-444-3330, 800-338-5407, *555 30th St*) has a definite Old-World feel to it, but lacks the elegance (and prime location) of the Boulderado (see below). Rates are $118 to $138 per night in Victorian-inspired rooms.
Web site: www.boulderbrokerinn.com

The *Boulder Marriott* (☎ 303-440-8877, 888-238-2178, *2660 Canyon Blvd*) offers modern top-end rooms starting from $149 (including breakfast).

The well-situated and beautifully restored brick *Hotel Boulderado* (☎ 303-442-4344, 800-433-4344, *2115 13th St*), a block from Pearl St Mall, first opened in 1909. All of the rooms are furnished with antiques and remain true to the hotel's original elegance. Summer rates range from $159 to

$234, and $130 to $229 in winter.
Web site: www.boulderado.com

B&Bs The 1890s brick *Briar Rose Bed & Breakfast* (☎ 303-442-3007, *2151 Arapahoe Ave*) offers nine unique rooms ranging from $129 to $169 in summer, $99 to $154 in winter. Top-end rooms have fireplaces.

The well-appointed, 1882 *Earl House Historic Inn* (☎ 303-938-1400, *2429 Broadway*) is a lovely, Gothic Revival stone mansion with six guest rooms (each with steam shower or Jacuzzi) and two carriage houses. Rates are from $129 to $189.
Web site: www.bouldervictoria.com/earl.html

The *Boulder Victoria Historic Bed & Breakfast* (☎ 303-938-1300, *1305 Pine St*) is a beautifully restored mansion close to downtown. Its seven rooms range from $119 to $215 in summer, $99 to $169 in winter.
Web site: www.bouldervictoria.com

Cottages and lodge rooms are available from Memorial Day to Labor Day at *Chautauqua Park* (☎ 303-442-3282, *900 Baseline Rd*), a city-owned historic district on 26 beautiful acres at the base of the Flatirons. Rates range from $57 to $123.

Places to Eat
Boulder has around 300 restaurants, an enormous number given the population.

A cheap way to get started is to take advantage of the 7 to 9 am early bird special at *Dot's Diner* (☎ 303-447-9184, *1333 Broadway)*; eggs, hash browns and toast costs $2.50. Another good breakfast spot is the long-standing *Rocky Mountain Joe's* (☎ 303-442-3969, *1410 Pearl St*), where two eggs with two side dishes costs $3.75. This is also a good spot for lunch. You can still see some of the more colorful local characters at a favorite downtown coffee shop, *Trident Booksellers & Cafe* (☎ 303-443-3133, *940 Pearl St*). For more upscale breakfasts and lunches there's *Cafe Louie* (☎ 303-449-8402, *825 Walnut St*), a cozy, European-style bistro serving gourmet fare and decadent desserts.

Pan Asia Fusion (☎ 303-447-0101, *1175 Walnut St*) serves up an eclectic selection of

Pacific Rim specialties in an atmosphere of chic, minimalist decor. The $6 lunch specials are a good value. Down the street, *Dandelion* (☎ 303-443-6700, 1011 Walnut St) is another stylish place serving contemporary US cuisine and fine wine.

Rhumba (☎ 303-442-7771, 950 Pearl St) specializes in Caribbean-inspired fare like Jamaican jerk chicken and conch fritters. The *14th Street Bar & Grill* (☎ 303-444-5854, 1400 Pearl St) does amazingly good, gourmet wood-fired pizzas, plus superb pastas, salads and soups.

Jax (☎ 303-444-1811, 928 Pearl St), Boulder's premier seafood spot, is known for its raw bar happy hour (4 to 6 pm). *Bacaro Ristorante* (☎ 303-444-4888, 921 Pearl St), another upmarket spot, cooks up northern Italian fare.

Chipotle Mexican Grill (☎ 303-544-9383, 919 Pearl St) is an in place for nouvelle Mexican. For a more casual south-of-the-border meal, try *Juanita's* (☎ 303-449-5273, 1043 Pearl St). Just next door, *Tom's Tavern* (☎ 303-443-3893), at the corner of 11th and Pearl Sts, has been serving celebrated hamburgers since 1962. Or if it's a hot dog you're craving, march over to *Mustard's Last Stand* (☎ 303-444-5841, 1719 Broadway).

Up on University Hill, *Prufrock's* (☎ 303-443-7461, 1322 College Ave) offers wholegrain baked goods, vegetarian foods and espresso at reasonable prices. Next door, *Illegal Pete's* (☎ 303-444-3055, 1320 College Ave) has won rave reviews from locals for its excellent oversized burritos.

Homestyle Italian pastas and seafood dinners typically run $8 to $12 at *Cafe Gondolier* (☎ 303-443-5015, 2845 28th St) near Valmont Rd; on Tuesday and Wednesday, try the all-you-can-eat spaghetti dinner for $3.50.

All Boulder visitors should experience the 1898 *Chautauqua Dining Hall* (☎ 303-440-3776, 900 Baseline Rd) at the end of 9th St. The menu on the veranda overlooking the expansive grounds features gourmet US cuisine with breakfasts around $8, lunches $10 and dinners $20. The restaurant is open May to October only.

For something totally different, *Boulder Dushanbe Teahouse* (☎ 303-442-4993, 1770 13th St) is an authentic, traditional Tajik teahouse presented by Boulder's Russian sister city, Dushanbe.

Among the many top-end restaurants in town, the most spectacular is probably the *Flagstaff House* (☎ 303-442-4640, 1138 Flagstaff Rd). Perched on the north side of Flagstaff Mountain, it offers great views of Boulder and the Front Range along with excellent Continental dishes and some local game offerings. Another upscale spot definitely worth visiting is the *Red Lion Inn* (☎ 303-442-9368), about 2½ miles up Boulder Canyon Dr west of town. Specializing in German fare and wild game, this place oozes with character and warmth.

Entertainment

Pick up a free copy of the *Boulder Weekly* for the calendar of events. The *Boulder Planet* has an easy-to-read chart of music and other cultural events happening around town in the Arts & Entertainment section.

Bars & Brewpubs Again, there's plenty of these on hand. For billiards and brews, head to *The Foundry* (☎ 303-447-1803, 1109 Walnut St), a cavernous place with nearly a dozen full-size pool tables and a fine selection of draught beer, whiskey and cigars. Bands also play here on weekend nights. Next door, *Walnut Brewery* (☎ 303-447-1345, 1123 Walnut St) has fairly refined decor and attracts an older, professional crowd.

The lively *Oasis Brewery* (☎ 303-449-0363, 1095 Canyon Blvd) has billiards and games and draws a younger, collegiate crowd. Just east of Pearl St Mall, *Mountain Sun Pub & Brewery* (☎ 303-546-0886, 1535 Pearl St) hosts a more down-to-earth crowd: Long hair, dreadlocks and tie-dye are the norm here. Live music happens on Sunday night.

Round Midnight (☎ 303-442-2176, 1005 Pearl St) also has a few pool tables but the action centers on the dance floor. The nearby *West End Tavern* (☎ 303-444-3535, 926 Pearl St) is perfect in the late afternoon, when you can enjoy a beer and a burger on the rooftop deck and take in the outstanding view of the Flatirons.

The Dark Horse (☎ 303-442-8162, 2922 Baseline Rd) is a rustic, barn-like pub where the walls are covered with car license plates and movie memorabilia. In addition to cold beer, it serves decent pub grub (chicken wings, burgers, etc).

Live Music In the University Hill Area, the *Fox Theater (☎ 303-447-0095, 1135 13th St)* is a good place to catch popular local and touring bands; likewise for the *Boulder Theater (☎ 303-786-7030)*, at 14th and Pearl Sts. Nearby, *Catacombs Bar (☎ 303-443-0486)*, in the basement of the Hotel Boulderado, often has local blues bands.

The University of Colorado regularly schedules performances of classical music, either at the Gothic *Macky Auditorium* or *Grusin Music Hall* in the Imig Music Building. For concert schedules and information call ☎ 303-492-8008.

Getting There & Away
Public ride boards are posted in the Boulder International Youth Hostel, 1107 12th St, and on the CU campus in University Memorial Center.

Regional Transit District (RTD; ☎ 303-299-6000) buses (route B) operate between Boulder Station (corner of 14th and Walnut Sts) and Denver's Market St Station. Express buses make the journey in 45 minutes; normal service takes about an hour. All buses carry bikes in the luggage compartment. The one-way fare is $3.

By car Boulder is 27 miles northwest of Denver via I-25 to US 36.

Getting Around
To get to and from Denver International Airport RTD's (☎ 303-299-6000) Skyride bus route AB offers hourly service (1½ hours) daily for $8 one-way. The bus makes stops at the Boulder Station and along Broadway at Euclid St, Regent St and Baseline Rd.

Frequent door-to-door shuttle service between the Boulder area and Denver

International Airport is available from Super Shuttle (☎ 303-444-0808), which provides service from Boulder hotels for $18 or from private addresses for $22. Call ahead to book a reservation.

RTD buses provide fairly frequent service in and around Boulder. Car rental companies include Avis, 4800 Baseline Rd, and Dollar at 30th St and Arapahoe Ave in Crossroads Mall (see the Getting Around chapter for more car rental companies). Boulder Yellow Cab (☎ 303-442-2277) operates around the clock.

NEDERLAND
Heading west 17 miles up scenic Boulder Canyon will bring you to the lively and sometimes gritty town of Nederland (founded 1871). Nederland (population 1100; elevation 8236 feet) has a certain rugged charm, as well as several worthwhile restaurants and bars. For most visitors, however, the town serves as a gateway to Eldora Ski Area, hiking and camping in Indian Peaks Wilderness Area and the Peak to Peak Hwy.

The Nederland Visitors Center (☎ 303-258-3936) is downtown diagonally opposite The Village shopping mall.

Places to Stay
The grubby *Nederland International Hostel (☎ 303-258-7788, 8 W Boulder St)*, a blue and white building across the road from The Village shopping mall, offers foam mattresses and one bathroom for two dorms that can house four men and four women. Dorm beds are $16, private singles/doubles cost $27/40.

The next cheapest option is *Nederhaus Motel (☎ 800-422-4629, 686 Hwy 119 S)*, a half-mile west of the town center near the turnoff for Eldora Ski Resort. The motel has fairly unexciting singles/doubles from $79/89.

A better value for the standard is the woodsy *Best Western Lodge at Nederland (☎ 303-258-9463, 800-279-9463, 55 Lakeview Dr)*, opposite The Village shopping mall. Nicely appointed singles/doubles/triples start at $85/95/105.

Places to Eat

A great place for morning coffee and fresh pastries is ***Laura's Mountain Bakery*** (☎ 303-258-7346, 229 E Hwy 119). Another good breakfast spot is ***Whistler's Cafe*** (☎ 303-258-7871), behind the Nederland Visitors Center. It closes around 2 pm. Nearby ***Neapolitan's Italian Restaurant*** (☎ 303-258-7313, 1 W 1st St) has fairly standard Italian fare, but it's a fun place and portions are huge.

The best food in town is served at ***Tungsten Grill*** (☎ 303-258-9231, 155 Hwy 119 S), diagonally opposite the Nederland Visitors Center. The eclectic menu has an interesting blend of American and European dishes.

Entertainment

Nederland has in recent years become a small center for live music, mostly of the acoustic variety. One place that regularly books nationally known acts is ***Acoustic Coffeehouse*** (☎ 303-258-3209, 95 East 1st St). Most of the music takes place Thursday through Saturday nights, but look for the daytime front-porch bluegrass sessions on Sunday.

The long-standing ***Pioneer Inn*** (☎ 303-258-7733, 15 1st St) is a woodsy saloon with live music on Thursday and Friday nights (plus some Saturdays). A few doors from the PI, ***Wolf Tongue Brewery*** (☎ 303-258-7001, 35 E 1st St) is Nederland's first and only brewpub. Live folk and bluegrass start some nights around 10 pm.

Getting There & Away

Nederland is reached via Hwy 119, also known as Boulder Canyon Dr. If you're relying on public transportation, the RTD (☎ 303-299-6000) bus N from Boulder goes to Nederland and on to the Eldora Ski Area for only $2.

ELDORA SKI AREA

Four miles west of Nederland, Eldora Ski Area (☎ 303-440-8700) primarily gets day visitors who take advantage of its convenience and inexpensive lift tickets ($42). Though a fairly small facility with around 500 skiable acres, there is some interesting terrain, and a few expert trails in the Corona Bowl boast a 1400-foot vertical drop.
Web site: www.eldora.com

The Eldora Rossignol Nordic Center offers about 27 miles of machine-set tracks and some backcountry trails. A lift ticket ($12) is required on the Nordic ski trails.

INDIAN PEAKS WILDERNESS AREA

Forming the impressive backdrop to Nederland, the Indian Peaks area offers many fine hiking and camping opportunities. Especially nice is the hike up to 12,000-foot **Arapaho Pass**, accessed from the Fourth of July campground. It's a gentle ascent but be prepared to spend the entire day – if the altitude doesn't slow you down, the scenery should.

For more information on Indian Peaks check at the Nederland Visitors Center (see Nederland, earlier), which has maps and guidebooks. In the mall, the Ace Hardware store also sells topographic and USGS maps for the Indian Peaks area and issues camping permits (required June to September 15) as well as hunting and fishing licenses.

PEAK TO PEAK HIGHWAY

Stretching some 40 miles between Nederland and Estes Park, this north-south route takes you past a series of breathtaking mountains, including the 14,255-foot Long's Peak, lush valleys and grassy meadows. You can break up the ride by stopping at one of the little towns along the way. These include **Ward**, a center for alternative living and '60s throwbacks, **Peaceful Valley**, notable for the little onion-domed church perched above the village and tiny **Ferncliff** and **Allenspark**, which lie near some stunning mountain vistas.

Just opposite the turnoff for Ward is the road leading up to **Brainard Lake**. The lake itself is tiny but is in a gorgeous setting, and there are some great hiking trails leading from it. If hiking around here works up your appetite, stop in at the ***Millsite Inn***, just north of the turnoff to Ward. The food is nothing special, but it's an interesting place for a bite to eat or a beer, with plenty of local color.

There are national forest *campgrounds* near Peaceful Valley and Allenspark, as well as the *Long's Peak Campground*, which is part of Rocky Mountain National Park. There are also places to stay in Peaceful Valley, Ferncliff, Allenspark and south of Estes Park, mostly in the form of lodges, cabins and B&Bs; prices range from $50 to $90.

At the southern end, the Peak to Peak Hwy starts from Nederland as Hwy 72. It then turns into Hwy 7 W just north of Allenspark and continues from there to end at Estes Park.

Northern Front Range

COLORADO

Once a refuge from the rapid growth of Denver, and Boulder, the northern reaches of the Front Range are now being targeted for development, particularly the college town of Fort Collins. The primary attraction of the Northern Front Range, however, is Rocky Mountain National Park, worth visiting any time of year. Though the summer crowds can be oppressive at the gateway town of Estes Park, if the prospect of hiking into the backcountry sounds appealing you can leave most

Highlights

- Rocky Mountain National Park – sheer beauty and abundant wildlife abound despite tourist hordes
- Long's Peak – a strenuous though popular hike that rewards you with views from 14,256 feet
- Fort Collins – entertaining bars and restaurants in Old Town, with fine hiking and biking nearby
- Cache la Poudre River – 75 miles of protected river canyon, home to elk, moose and bighorn sheep

of your fellow visitors behind. In any case, equally beautiful scenery and outdoor activities can be found both north and south of the park boundaries.

FORT COLLINS

Fort Collins (population 108,000; elevation 5004 feet) lies 65 miles northwest of Denver, at the northern end of the Front Range. This formerly staid farming community has developed into a vibrant city, especially near the Colorado State University (CSU) campus and refurbished historical buildings of Old Town. Daytime cultural attractions include the Fort Collins Museum and Avery House Museum, and by nightfall Fort Collins' ubiquitous bars and brewpubs come to life. Suds aficionados assemble in Old Town Square for two days in late June for the Colorado Brewers Festival, a major event for microbreweries. The school semester's start in mid-August is marked by a three-day carnival, New West Fest, the city's biggest bash with food and craft booths and continuous performances. Yet more celebration of ales, porters and stouts takes place during Oktoberfest in mid-September.

Proximity to the Rocky Mountains and 'Poudre' River also contribute to Fort Collins' appeal, and make it a good jumping-off point for wilderness excursions. The city's extensive bike paths provide a pleasant tour of Fort Collins' waterways and parks, while nearby Horsetooth Mountain Park and Reservoir attracts mountain bikers, campers, hikers and cross-country skiers. The Cache la Poudre River offers serious white-water challenges for rafters and kayakers.

The Fort Collins Convention and Visitors Bureau operates a small downtown tourist information counter in the centrally located police station on Walnut St, but for more extensive information head for the outstanding Colorado Welcome Center (☎ 970-491-3388, 800-274-3678), 3545 E Prospect Rd, just off the Prospect Rd exit of I-25. It's

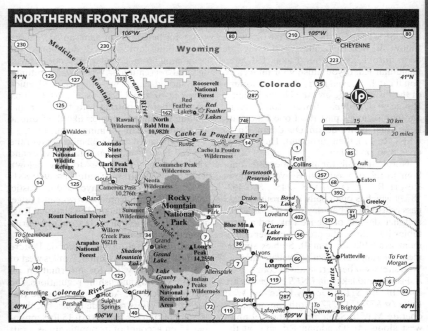

NORTHERN FRONT RANGE

well stocked with books, maps and pamphlets on recreational and cultural activities in the area, as well as information on area camping, lodging, restaurants and entertainment (including interesting local brewery tours). Found at the same address, Colorado State Parks (☎ 970-491-1168) has information about access to local recreational areas and campsites.

The USFS headquarters for the Arapaho and Roosevelt National Forests and the Pawnee National Grassland is at 240 W Prospect Rd and Colorado Blvd. Its information center (☎ 970-498-2770), 1131 S College Ave, offers maps and trail information for an extensive recreational area.

RED FEATHER LAKES

Secluded fishing lakes, good hiking and a Nordic recreation area attract year-round visitors to this forested area of the Lone Pine Creek drainage about 50 miles northwest of Fort Collins. Take US 287 north for

21 miles, turn left (west) at Livermore on Larimer County Rd 74E for 24 miles to Red Feather Lakes Ranger Station (☎ 970-881-2937), 274 Dowdy Lake Rd, which is operated by the Roosevelt National Forest. It's open 8:30 am to 5 pm Memorial Day to Labor Day only; in winter contact the USFS in Fort Collins for off-season information. Both offices provide trail maps and information on hiking, biking, cross-country skiing and camping.

About 8 miles from the junction of US 287 and County Rd 74E, on the north side, is the Lone Pine Cherokee Park unit trailhead, offering good single-track mountain biking and equestrian opportunities. It's a pretty trail and mostly moderate, though there are some steep sections and technical areas for bikers.

Pleasant, ambling hikes can be had along the Lone Pine Trail, which passes by North Bald Mountain and ascends Middle Bald Mountain. From the latter you can loop back along a jeep road to come out just west of the trailhead. Maps are available from the USFS. To get to the Lone Pine trailhead, follow 74E west for 6 miles. On the way 74E turns into Red Feather Lakes Rd, then Deadman Rd. If you finish your hike early, you'll catch an even more scenic panorama of the Front Range and the Never Summer Range at Deadman Tower (10,710 feet), another 10 miles past the Lone Pine trailhead. Just continue on Deadman Rd to USFS Rd 170, then turn right. The tower is open 8:30 am to 4 pm.

Nordic ski trails for all abilities offer one-hour to full-day loops at Beaver Meadows Resort Ranch (☎ 970-881-2450, 800-462-5870), which is open daily year-round. A ski pass costs $10/15 half-day/full-day for adults and includes use of the ice rink and a snow tubing hill (inner tube provided; other equipment available for rental). Stables supplement the range of activities available here. Web site: www.beavermeadows.com

Fishing and lakeside *USFS campsites* are available for $11 at Dowdy Lake and West Lake (☎ 877-444-6777). Both campgrounds operate May to September. About 9 miles west along 74E/Deadman Rd, sites at the *North Fork Poudre Campground* cost $9. It's open June to November.

Beaver Meadows Resort Ranch (see above) also has lodge rooms from $52, cabins from $63 and condos from $75. Package deals including skiing and meals are also available. To get there from the Red Feather Lakes Ranger Station, take 74E west for about 2 miles and turn right (north) on County Rd 73C (gravel) for 5 miles to Beaver Meadows.

CACHE LA POUDRE RIVER

From the mouth of the Cache la Poudre (rhymes with 'neuter') River Canyon at Laporte – site of an Overland Stage Station in 1862 – to Walden 92 miles west, Hwy 14 travels through some of Colorado's most scenic country. Mule deer, elk and bighorn sheep inhabit many parts of the canyon and adjacent wilderness areas. The Wild & Scenic Rivers Act protects 75 miles of the Cache la Poudre River from new dams or

diversions. Thirty miles of the river meet the highest standards and are designated as 'wild' for being free of dams and diversions and having undisturbed shorelines; the remaining 45-mile protected section is designated 'recreational.' White-water enthusiasts should check with experienced guide services or the USFS (see Fort Collins, earlier) before putting into the river and finding unrunnable rapids, like the frothing Narrows, or a dam looming up ahead.

The village of **Rustic**, 32 miles west of the US 287-Hwy 14 junction, offers services and cabin lodging (see Places to Stay, below). The USFS Visitors Center (☎ 970-881-2152), 34484 Poudre Canyon Rd in Rustic, occupies the handsome Arrowhead Lodge, built in 1935 and listed on the National Register of Historic Places. It's open 9 am to 5 pm daily in summer.

Stop at the self-service Cache la Poudre Visitors Information Center, 3 miles west of US 287 on Hwy 14, for information on wildlife viewing and fishing regulations. The Picnic Rock River Access opposite the visitors center offers riverside tables, but there is a $4 parking fee from April 15 to September 15 on account of its popularity as a raft take-out point. Watch for bighorn sheep on the steep slopes along a 35-mile section of the north bank from Mishawaka to **Poudre Falls**, a series of picturesque roaring cascades. The USFS recently developed a particularly good bighorn sheep viewing site equipped with telescopes and explanatory plaques at **Big Bend**, 41 miles west of the US 287-Hwy 14 junction.

After Hwy 14 branches away from the river it ascends Cameron Pass (10,276 feet), where the stunning 12,485-foot **Nohku Crags** form the northernmost peaks of the Never Summer Range.

Fishing

Two sections of the Poudre River, a 10-mile stretch from Pingree Park Rd upstream to the Hombre Ranch west of Rustic and another section between Black Hollow Creek and Big Bend, are specially managed wild trout waters. Catches are limited to two fish over 16 inches long per person, and anglers are required to use artificial flies and lures. The remaining sections are stocked with rainbow trout.

A few nearby lakes offer unique fishing for distinctive species. Mackinaw up to 20lb can be taken in **Chambers Lake** 53 miles up the canyon. You will have to hike about 6 miles to fish for wild brook trout at **Browns Lake** in the Comanche Wilderness. In 1951, a wild early summer–spawning rainbow species (like the Arctic grayling), called emerald lake rainbow, was introduced to Zimmerman Lake near Cameron Pass on the border of the Neota Wilderness.

Hiking & Backpacking

Many backcountry activities in the Cache la Poudre, Comanche Peak, Neota and Rawah Wilderness Areas can be accessed via trailheads from the Poudre River. Trails from the Comanche Wilderness lead into Rocky Mountain National Park. The USFS pamphlet 'Cache La Poudre – A Wild & Scenic River' has a map showing the various trailheads and campsites along the river. The USFS Fort Collins office also can provide more detailed information on hiking trails.

Nine miles from the US 287-Hwy 14 junction, the **Greyrock National Recreation Trail** climbs about 2000 feet to the summit of Greyrock Mountain, offering spectacular views of the Front Range. From the trailhead 3 winding miles west of the filtration plant at the North Fork, you can choose either a 3½-mile up-and-back route, or add a 2-mile loop through adjoining Greyrock Meadow.

At the other extreme, just east of Cameron Pass, hikers start at an elevation of 9500 feet and continue 5 miles along USFS Trail 959 through sub-alpine forests to **Alpine Blue Lake** (10,800 feet) in the extensive Rawah Wilderness. The trailhead begins 55 miles west of US 287 on the north side of Hwy 14, opposite the turnoff to Long Draw Reservoir and Rocky Mountain National Park.

Places to Stay

Camping The USFS operates about a dozen primitive *campgrounds* (pit toilets,

no showers) along Hwy 14. All are available on a first-come, first-served basis, except for *Chambers Lake* and *Mountain Park* (☎ 877-444-6777). The campgrounds are often full in summer, so try and get in early. The USFS Tom Bennett Campground, south of of the Poudre Canyon on Larimer Country Rd 63E, is a popular staging point for Comanche Peak Wilderness users. Listed below are the USFS Poudre Canyon campgrounds in order of distance in miles (west) from US 287:

campground	miles	fee	number of sites
Ansel Watrous	13	$10	19
Stove Prairie	17	$11	9
Narrows	21	$10	13
Mountain Park	22	$13	52
Kelly Flats	26	$11	29
Big Bend	41	$10	6
Sleeping Elephant	45	$10	15
Big South	50	$8	4
Aspen Glen	51	$9	8
Chambers Lake	53	$13	51

The *North Park KOA* (☎ 970-723-4310) at Gould on Hwy 14, 72 miles west of US 287 and 20 miles southeast of Walden, offers wooded tent sites for $15 and fresh-baked cinnamon rolls every morning.

Also around Gould are a number of campgrounds run by the Colorado State Forest. Access to the state forest costs $4 per day, and a camping pass is an additional $6.

Cabins Most accommodations are grouped around Rustic. The *Rustic Resort* (☎ 970-881-2179, 31443 Poudre Canyon Rd) has cabins on the river ranging from $50 to $85, tent sites for $10 and RV sites for $15. There is a decent restaurant here as well. A bit farther west is *Archer's Poudre River Resort* (☎ 970-881-2139, 33021 Poudre Canyon Rd). One-bedroom cabins are $90, two-bedroom units are $110; see them at www.poudreriverresort.com. There are more cabin operations farther west along the river, most with similar conditions and prices.

COLORADO

Yurts Within the Colorado State Forest, *Never Summer Nordic* (☎ *970-482-9411*) operates a system of Mongolian-style yurts: circular tents with an inner frame. Each yurt sleeps between five and nine people, and is sited to act as a base for mountain biking, hiking, climbing or fishing in the beautiful Never Summer wilderness. Amenities include wood-burning stoves, complete kitchens and padded bunks. Visitors supply their own food and sleeping bags. Getting to most of the yurts requires a hike of at least 1½ miles. There are trails linking the yurts, allowing you to plan a backcountry excursion. Summer rates for yurts are $55/65 weekdays/weekends; in winter prices rise to $85/105. Reservations are advised, and can be made by phone or on the Web at www.neversummernordic.com. For more information, write to Never Summer Nordic, PO Box 1983, Fort Collins, CO 80522. Access to the yurts is off of Hwy 14, about 72 miles west of US 287, not far from the North Park KOA Campground.

ARAPAHO NATIONAL WILDLIFE REFUGE

Nearly 200 species of birds frequent the summer sagebrush and wetlands of the USFWS' Arapaho National Wildlife Refuge, 105 miles west of Fort Collins by the Cache la Poudre-North Park Scenic Byway (Hwy 14). The star of the show is the sage grouse and its spring mating ritual, the lek. The Refuge Headquarters (☎ 970-723-8202), PO Box 457, Walden, CO 80480, is 8 miles south of Hwy 14 via Hwy 125, then 1 mile east on Jackson County Rd 32.

If you are visiting the refuge or its surrounding backcountry, Walden is the nearest town of note. North-south Main St is the principal thoroughfare and business district in Walden, and nearly all the town's motels and restaurants can be found here. A good detailed Jackson County road map is available for 75¢ at the North Park Chamber of Commerce in Walden (☎ 970-723-4600), 416 4th St, open 9 am to 5 pm, Monday to Friday.

The USFS Routt National Forest North Park Ranger Station (☎ 970-723-8204), 100 Main St, is at the north end of town. It's open 7:30 am to 4:30 pm Monday to Friday and has detailed trail information for hikes and biking in the Routt National Forest, including the eastern side of the Mt Zirkel wilderness.

There's a self-guided auto tour pamphlet available; look for information at the North Park Chamber of Commerce. In late April and early May, the chamber's Sage Grouse Tours brings people to view the ritual lek.

ESTES PARK

The eastern gateway to Rocky Mountain National Park, Estes Park (population 10,000; elevation 7522 feet) depends on a steady flow of tourists for its economic survival. The town's population explodes to between 25,000 and 30,000 on any given summer weekend.

The flood of tourism supports countless motels, craft shops, kitschy souvenir stores and restaurants. Visitors expecting immediate views of the pristine beauty of Rocky Mountain National Park may be disappointed to find themselves in bumper-to-bumper traffic on E Elkhorn Ave, the town's artery to both park entrances. However, there are ways to bypass this tourist traverse (see Orientation, below).

Despite its popularity, Estes Park has a certain charm, especially in the off-season, and has nearly any convenience or service a traveler might need. The soaring peaks that form the town's backdrop also help make up for the mundane spread of motels and mini shopping malls.

Orientation

Estes Park occupies the valley at the confluence of the Big Thompson and Fall Rivers, just a few miles east of Rocky Mountain National Park. US 36 follows the Big Thompson River out of town to park headquarters and the Beaver Meadows entrance station; US 34 leads upstream to the Fall River entrance station. South of town, Hwy 7 provides access to the national park at Lily Lake, Twin Sisters Peaks, Long's Peak and Wild Basin. To the north, MacGregor Ave leads to the historic MacGregor Ranch (see

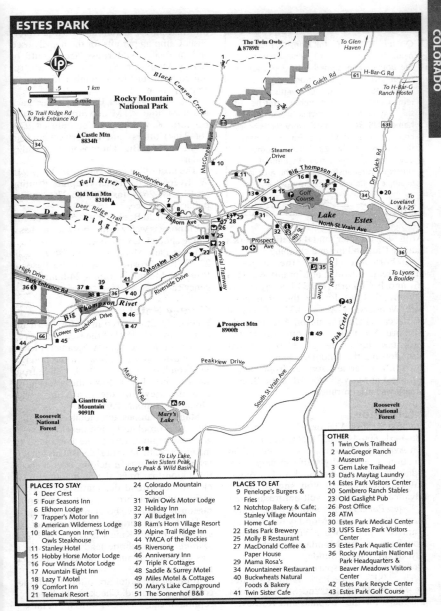

ESTES PARK

PLACES TO STAY
4 Deer Crest
5 Four Seasons Inn
6 Elkhorn Lodge
7 Trapper's Motor Inn
8 American Wilderness Lodge
10 Black Canyon Inn; Twin Owls Steakhouse
11 Stanley Hotel
15 Hobby Horse Motor Lodge
16 Four Winds Motor Lodge
17 Mountain Eight Inn
18 Lazy T Motel
19 Comfort Inn
21 Telemark Resort

24 Colorado Mountain School
31 Twin Owls Motor Lodge
32 Holiday Inn
37 All Budget Inn
38 Ram's Horn Village Resort
39 Alpine Trail Ridge Inn
44 YMCA of the Rockies
45 Riversong
46 Anniversary Inn
47 Triple R Cottages
49 Miles Motel & Cottages
50 Mary's Lake Campground
51 The Sonnenhof B&B

PLACES TO EAT
9 Penelope's Burgers & Fries
12 Notchtop Bakery & Cafe; Stanley Village Mountain Home Cafe
22 Estes Park Brewery
27 Molly B Restaurant
27 MacDonald Coffee & Paper House
29 Mama Rosa's
34 Mountaineer Restaurant
40 Buckwheats Natural Foods & Bakery
41 Twin Sister Cafe

OTHER
1 Twin Owls Trailhead
2 MacGregor Ranch Museum
3 Gem Lake Trailhead
13 Dad's Maytag Laundry
14 Estes Park Visitors Center
20 Sombrero Ranch Stables
23 Old Gaslight Pub
26 Post Office
28 ATM
30 Estes Park Medical Center
33 USFS Estes Park Visitors Center
35 Estes Park Aquatic Center
36 Rocky Mountain National Park Headquarters & Beaver Meadows Visitors Center
42 Estes Park Recycle Center
43 Estes Park Golf Course

Big Thompson Canyon

On July 31, 1976, following a four-hour deluge that dumped 12 inches of water in the upper basin around Estes Park, raging waters from the Big Thompson Canyon swept 145 people to their deaths. The torrential waters scoured narrow stretches of the canyon floor, destroying businesses and homes. US 34 became history. Emergency crews recovered victims from the broad floodplain nearly 23 miles southwest, beyond the canyon near Longmont. The subsequent reconstruction of the area is an example of stalwart Western resolve.

Around Estes, later) and the national park's Lumpy Ridge hiking and climbing area.

Elkhorn Ave (US 34), the congested main street, is divided at Moraine Ave (US 36) into E Elkhorn (US 34/US 36) and W Elkhorn (US 34). East of the intersection with Wonderview Ave and US 36, US 34 also is called Big Thompson Ave. To avoid Elkhorn Ave traffic on your way to the park, take either the US 34 bypass that turns toward the landmark Stanley Hotel just off Wonderview Ave, or from Hwy 7 turn west at Mary's Lake Rd to the Beaver Meadows park entrance.

Information

The Estes Park Visitors Center (☎ 970-586-4431, 800-443-7837), 500 Big Thompson Ave (US 34) is just east of the US 36 junction. The friendly staff can help book lodgings, but most are chock-full throughout the summer so you should make advance reservations well before arriving in Estes Park. During summer the center is open 8 am to 8 pm Monday to Saturday, 9 am to 6 pm Sunday. Winter hours are from 8 am to 5 pm Monday through Saturday, 10 am to 4 pm Sunday.
Web site: www.estesparkresort.com

The USFS Estes Park Visitors Center (☎ 970-586-3440), 161 2nd St, sells books and maps for the Arapaho and Roosevelt National Forests and has camping and trail information for hikers and off-road bicyclists. Camping permits for the heavily used Indian Peaks Wilderness Area, south of Rocky Mountain National Park, are required from June to September 15 and cost $5 per person.

The First National Bank of Estes Park has a 24-hour ATM downtown at 334 E Elkhorn. Key Bank of Colorado (☎ 970-586-2364) offers banking services and an ATM at 541 Big Thompson in Stanley Village.

The post office (zip code 80517) is at 215 W Riverside Dr. Master Graphics Printing (☎ 970-586-2679, fax 970-586-2366) offers public fax service.

MacDonald Books (☎ 970-586-3450), 152 E Elkhorn, is well worth a browse and has a coffee shop annex out back.

Estes Park Medical Center (☎ 970-586-2317), 555 Prospect Ave at the base of Prospect Mountain, offers 24-hour emergency care.

Stanley Hotel

Freelan O Stanley, co-inventor (with his twin brother) in 1897 of the steam-powered car known as the Stanley Steamer, picked an amazing spot for his sprawling hotel at 333 Wonderview Ave in 1909. Visible from almost everywhere in town, the hotel enjoys stunning views of the peaks in Rocky Mountain National Park.

Stanley's famous automobile was gradually made obsolete by the development of gasoline engines, though he continued to manufacture them until 1925. But his longer-lasting impact was in helping spur a social revolution that freed the recreational traveler from railroad destinations. Fleets of Stanley Steamers brought visitors to his outrageously expensive hotel in the wilderness.

The hotel is perhaps best known for inspiring Stephen King's horror novel *The Shining,* the psychotic lead role of which was later fleshed out on the screen by Jack Nicholson.

Tours of the hotel are offered daily, according to demand. Check at the hotel reception or call ☎ 970-577-4018 for details.

Aerial Tramway

In the time you wait to be herded aboard a tram to the top of Prospect Mountain, you could have climbed Lily Mountain (see Rocky Mountain National Park, later). The Aerial Tramway (☎ 970-586-3675), 420 E Riverside Dr, operates 9 am to dusk daily Memorial Day to Labor Day; the fare is $10/5 adults/children under 12.

Activities

The USFS Crosier Mountain Trail, a strenuous loop through beautiful meadows near Glen Haven, comes highly recommended by locals. Another favorite is the combination of USFS Pierson Park Rd and Lion Gulch Trail in the vicinity of Homestead Meadows south of Estes Park. Pick up maps and information from the USFS Estes Park Visitors Center. Colorado Bicycling (☎ 970-586-4241), 184 E Elkhorn Ave, rents bikes and can help with tips on trails in the area.

Two golf courses are available. The Estes Park Golf Course (☎ 970-586-8146) offers an 18-hole course at 1080 S St Vrain Ave, or try the nine-hole Lake Estes Executive Golf Club (☎ 970-586-8176) at 690 Big Thompson Ave.

Long's Peak Scottish-Irish Festival

Four days of Celtic activities (☎ 970-586-6308) take place at the fairgrounds in early September. You can purchase a three-day weekend pass, or a ticket package for shows and pub nights for around $60.

Places to Stay

Warning: Lodgings fill up *very* fast during the peak July and August period. Do not travel west of Greeley without a reservation during the summer. Off-season rates may be up to one-half of summer prices, and many accommodations simply close for the winter. Most of the cheaper motels (which still aren't that cheap) are located east of town along US 34 or Hwy 7.

The multi-purpose Estes Park Center at the **YMCA of the Rockies** (☎ 970-586-3341, 800-777-9622) is set on 860 acres on the out-skirts of town. This massive, family-oriented facility offers forest campsites ($17 to $21), more than 530 lodge rooms ($64 to $92), plus around 200 cabins and vacation homes ($116 to $279). Activities include everything from horseback riding and tennis to hands-on craft making. The Y is one of the few accommodations in the area offering guests Internet access.

Web site: www.ymcarockies.org

Camping Tent sites/RV hookups are $22/31 for two persons at the **Estes Park KOA** (☎ 970-586-2888), 1 mile east of Estes Park. **National Park Resort** (☎ 970-586-4563, 3501 Fall River Rd), near the Fall River Park entrance, has wooded tent sites and RV hookups at similar rates. **Mary's Lake Campground** (☎ 970-586-4411, 2120 Mary's Lake Rd) offers 40 tent sites for $22 for two people as well as RV spaces for $27. Five miles southeast of Estes Park at the end of Hwy 66, near the boundary of Rocky Mountain National Park, **Estes Park Campground** (☎ 970-586-4188) caters to tent campers for $23 for two people per site.

Hostels Perhaps the best lodging deal in Estes Park is the **Colorado Mountain School** (☎ 970-586-5758, 351 Moraine Ave), close to both the park and town center. Beds with full linen, soap and towels in comfortable, sparkling clean dorm rooms are $20. There's lockable storage and the staff is quite helpful and friendly.

Motels Estes Park has more than 40 motels to choose from. There aren't any real bargains, especially during summer. One of the least expensive places is **Lazy T Motel** (☎ 970-586-4376, 1340 Big Thompson Ave). Though not exciting, it has all the amenities, even a pool and sauna! Rooms range from $45 to $70.

Most of the town's motels are remarkably similar: shag carpet and fairly small rooms with television and refrigerator, though some places also boast pools, hot tubs and saunas. Following is a selection of mid-range offerings; rates quoted are for double occupancy during peak season.

All Budget Inn (☎ 970-586-3485, 945 Moraine Ave), $74 to $93, kitchens

Alpine Trail Ridge Inn (☎ 970-586-4585, 927 Moraine Ave), $66 to $141, swimming pool, kitchens

Comfort Inn (☎ 970-586-2358, 1450 Big Thompson Ave), $80 to $95, swimming pool, hot tub

Four Winds Motor Lodge (☎ 970-586-3313, 1120 Big Thompson Ave), from $61, swimming pool, hot tub, sauna, kitchens

Hobby Horse Motor Lodge (☎ 970-586-3336, 800 Big Thompson Ave), $70 to $85, swimming pool

Mountain Eight Inn (☎ 970-586-4421, 1220 Big Thompson Ave), $80, swimming pool

Saddle & Surrey Motel (☎ 970-586-3326, 1341 S St Vrain Ave), $55, swimming pool, hot tub, kitchens

Trapper's Motor Inn (☎ 970-586-2833, 553 W Elkhorn Ave), from $50

Twin Owls Motor Lodge (☎ 970-586-4471, 700 St Vrain Ave), $55 to $90, swimming pool

The *Holiday Inn* (☎ 970-586-2332, 800-465-4329, 101 S St Vrain Ave), at US 36 and Hwy 7, asks at least $144 per room in the summer. Facilities include a pool, fitness room and whirlpool, but for the money you're probably better off at a B&B.

American Wilderness Lodge (☎ 970-586-4403, 481 E Elkhorn Ave), offers nicely appointed rooms from $95 to $175. It's walking distance from the town center and includes amenities such as fireplaces, kitchens, sauna, Jacuzzi and an indoor pool. Web site: www.estesparkco.com/awlodge.htm

Hotels The landmark *Stanley Hotel* (☎ 970-577-4018, 800-976-1377, 333 Wonderview Ave), is the grand dame of northern Colorado's historic resort hotels. Set on 35 acres, the 133-room hotel features white-pillared Georgian architecture and commands stunning mountain views. The Stanley also offers gourmet dining, as well as seasonal theater and musical performances. Room rates range from $165 to $250. Also see the Stanley Hotel section, earlier.

South of Estes Park near Lily Lake, the *Baldpate Inn* (☎ 970-586-6151, 4900 Hwy 7) is a unique lodge and restaurant with 12 modest rooms. Rooms cost $75 with shared

bath, $90 with private bath, including full breakfast. Built in 1917, the comfortable inn features a rustic, 2nd-story veranda and handmade lodgepole pine furniture. Guests with bicycles are welcome and the knowledgable staff can offer local trail tips.

Tucked down a dead-end dirt road overlooking the Big Thompson River, *Riversong* (☎ 970-586-4666, 1765 Lower Broadview Dr) offers nine rooms with private bath in a Craftsman-style mansion for $150 to $295 depending on the room's furnishings and amenities (like spa tubs). The minimum stay is two nights. West of town take Moraine Ave, turn onto Mary's Lake Rd then take the first right.
Web site: www.romanticriversong.com

In the same section of town, the *Anniversary Inn* (☎ 970-586-6200, 1060 Mary's Lake Rd) is an 1890s log house with four rooms, each with private bath, where prices range from $95 to $160.

Cottages, Cabins & B&Bs Though the facilities can sometimes be basic, cottages generally offer more scenic locations and privacy than motels and often are cheaper as well.

Miles Motel & Cottages (☎ 970-586-3185, 1250 S St Vrain Ave) is a good smoke-free choice with spacious grounds and a swimming pool; some units are wheelchair accessible. Summer rates start at $104.
Web site: www.estes-park.com/miles

Studio cottages cost $55/65 and one-room cottages are $80 at *Triple R Cottages* (☎ 970-586-5552, 1000 Riverside Dr). *Telemark Resort* (☎ 970-586-4343, 800-669-0650, 650 Moraine Ave) has two-person cottages from $90, most of which are located on the Big Thompson River.

Knotty-pine interiors, full kitchens and a riverside hot tub are among the features of the cabins at *Blackhawk Lodges* (☎ 970-586-6100, 1750 Fall River Rd); prices start at around $100. On the boundary of Rocky Mountain National Park, *Glacier Lodge* (☎ 970-586-4401, 2166 Hwy 66) is a lodge and conference center with more than 20 meticulously maintained hillside and riverside cottages spread over 15 acres. Rates range from $125 to $210.

The **Elkhorn Lodge** (☎ 970-586-4416, 877-586-4416, 600 W Elkhorn Ave) has been in operation since 1824, but the heated pool is a more recent addition. Lodge rooms (double/triple/quad) go for $100/110/130. Cabins cost $95, and cottages for three to eight guests start at $102. It also rents 'alpine homes' for $150 to $250, plus a deluxe four-bedroom spread (with a private hot tub on the deck) for $400. Traveling in a group? Its nine-bedroom/seven-bathroom coach house goes for a cool $900.

Deer Crest (☎ 970-586-2324, 800-331-2324, 1200 Fall River Rd), northwest of town on Hwy 34 (near the north entrance to the national park), boasts a riverside setting and has rates from $94 to $135. View the facilities at www.deercrest.net. The nearby **Four Seasons Inn** (☎ 970-586-5693, 800-779-4616, 1130 W Elkhorn Ave) also rents woodsy cabins (with private hot tub) from $95 to $138. Its Web site is www.estes-park.com/4seasons.

A cozy two-room getaway set amid the trees, **The Sonnenhof B&B** (☎ 970-577-7528, 650 Lakewood Court) is just a 10-minute drive from the park and town. The inn provides great views and has rates ranging from $115 to $160.
Web site: www.sonnenhofestespark.com

A fine place to splurge is the lovely **Black Canyon Inn** (☎ 970-586-8113, 800-897-5123, 800 MacGregor Ave), a secluded 14-acre property offering luxury suites (one/two/three bedrooms from $160/225/385) and rustic log cabins from $160.
Web site: www.blackcanyoninn.com

Another nice upmarket option, this one closer to the main road, is the **Ram's Horn Village Resort** (☎ 970-586-4338, 800-229-4676, 1565 Colorado Hwy 66). Handsome new wood cabins, each with two bedrooms and two baths, rent for $269, and there is a four-night minimum stay.
Web site: www.ramshornvillageresort.com

Places to Eat
Like lodgings, restaurants in Estes Park often shift to shorter hours, close for several days of the week or shut down altogether in the off-season. If you're visiting between September and May it's wise to call ahead.

One of the best spots in town for tasty and healthy food is **Notchtop Bakery & Cafe** (☎ 970-586-0272) in Stanley Village. The bread and pastries are delicious and the kitchen also dishes up fine lunches and dinners. Just a few doors down, late-risers can try **Mountain Home Cafe** (☎ 970-586-6624), which serves breakfast 7 am to 2:30 pm. The **Mountaineer Restaurant** (☎ 970-586-9001, 540 S St Vrain Ave) also does a great all-day breakfast (omelets for around $5.50), plus sandwiches and full dinners.

On the Riverwalk, **MacDonald Coffee & Paper House** (☎ 970-586-3450, 152 E Elkhorn) offers topographic maps and guidebooks to examine while you sip a cappuccino. A good place to stock up on trail foods or get freshly made cinnamon rolls, muffins and healthy sandwiches is **Buckwheats Natural Foods & Bakery** (☎ 970-586-5658, 870 Moraine Ave). Just across the road, the **Twin Sister Cafe** (☎ 970-586-4822, 865 Moraine Ave) makes for a pleasant spot to pull over for a light meal.

Estes Park Brewery (☎ 970-586-5421, 470 E Riverside Dr) serves up some fairly good beer along with its own 'brewery pizza.' Pool tables and a big deck make this a fun spot to go for a snack and a beer. **Mama Rosa's** (☎ 970-586-3330, 338 E Elkhorn Ave) offers outdoor seating and an attentive staff serving family-style Italian lunches and dinners daily.

Molly B Restaurant (☎ 970-586-2766, 200 Moraine Ave) has hearty, reasonably priced dishes for both vegetarians and carnivores. It shouldn't take a rocket scientist to determine what's cooking at **Penelope's Burgers & Fries** (☎ 970-586-2277, 229 Elkhorn). It also has great hot dogs and sandwiches.

For top-end dining, make a reservation at the **Twin Owls Steakhouse** (☎ 970-586-9344, 800 MacGregor Ave), north of town at the historic Black Canyon Inn. They specialize in steak and wild game, but also do superb fresh seafood; most dinner entrees are priced at more than $20.

Entertainment

The casual **Old Gaslight Pub** (☎ 970-586-7302), across the road from the Colorado Mountain School on Moraine Ave, features a pleasant outdoor beer garden.

For a more 'civilized' atmosphere, the **Stanley Hotel** (☎ 970-577-4018, 800-976-1377) offers summer theater performances, big-band music and orchestral concerts. Admission generally ranges between $10 and $20. The schedule changes yearly, so check with the hotel.

Getting There & Away

From Denver International Airport, Estes Park Shuttle (☎ 970-586-5151, 800-950-3274) provides four daily trips year-round to Estes Park for $39/75 one-way/roundtrip. Emerald Taxi (☎ 970-586-1991) also runs DIA shuttles.

Estes Park is 34 miles west of Loveland via US 34, which you can access from I-25 exit 257. Many visitors also come up by way of Boulder along US 36, passing through Lyons. A slower but more scenic route is the spectacular Peak to Peak Hwy, which comprises Hwys 72 and 7 and runs north from Nederland to Estes Park. (See Around Boulder in the Denver & Boulder chapter.)

Getting Around

Emerald Taxi (☎ 970-586-1992) provides 24-hour taxi service, as well as guided tours.

Bicycling is a great way to get around the area, though few visitors seem to use this mode of transport (of course the altitude does make for some huffing and puffing). Mountain bikes can be rented from Colorado Bicycle (☎ 970-586-4241), 184 E Elkhorn Ave.

AROUND ESTES PARK
Enos Mills' Cabin

A naturalist who led the struggle to establish Rocky Mountain National Park, Enos Mills (1870–1922) succeeded due to, undoubtedly, his infectious enthusiasm and willingness to share nature information. His daughter Enda Mills Kiley continues to share the incredible history of her father with visitors to his tiny cabin, built in 1885.

The Mills family maintains an interpretive nature trail leading from the parking lot to the cabin, where news clippings and photographs recount Mills' advocacy to protect nature.

Reprints and vintage copies of many of Mills' 16 books are available for sale at the cabin, in addition to an outstanding collection of his writings edited by Enda, *Adventures of a Nature Guide* (New Past Press, 1990). Worth reading is the short 1917 classic *The Story of Early Estes Park: Rocky Mountain National Park and Grand Lake;* a self-published 5th edition (1980) is available here or by post from Enda Mills Kiley, Long's Peak Route, Estes Park, CO 80517.

Enos Mills' Cabin (☎ 970-586-4706), 10 miles south of Estes Park on Hwy 7, is open 10 am to 5 pm daily Memorial Day to Labor Day; free.

MacGregor Ranch Museum

In 1872 AQ and Clara MacGregor arrived in Estes Park and settled beside Black Canyon Creek near Lumpy Ridge. Their granddaughter Murial MacGregor bequeathed the ranch as an educational trust upon her death in 1970.

The MacGregor Ranch, 1 mile north of Estes Park on Devils Gulch Rd, is a living museum featuring original living and working quarters; the ranch still raises Black Angus cattle. An NPS scenic and conservation easement helps fund the operation (admission is free) and provides trail access to Lumpy Ridge. It's open 9 am to 6:30 pm daily mid-May to mid-September.

Glen Haven

The North Fork of the Big Thompson River flows through Glen Haven, 7 miles east of Estes Park on Devils Gulch Rd. Another scenic approach follows the narrow canyon road for 8 miles northwest from US 34 at Drake, site of the North Fork's confluence with the main channel in Big Thompson Canyon. Handsome picnic grounds at Glen Haven on the narrow banks of the tumbling North Fork beckon travelers to stop. If you forgot to pack a lunch, drop in at the **Glen Haven General Store**, open 9 am to 6 pm daily in summer, for baked goods and deli items. In winter it's open 'from 9 am to whenever we feel like it!'

The prime attraction, however, is *The Inn of Glen Haven* (☎ 970-586-3897, 7468 County Rd 43), an effete lair of the English gentry, offering delightful B&B rooms and fine dining. The six top-end rooms cost between $85 (shared bath) and $145. Web site: www.innofglenhaven.com

ROCKY MOUNTAIN NATIONAL PARK

Rocky Mountain National Park exemplifies the dual – and often conflicting – purposes Congress intended when it established the park in 1915 to promote recreational use while protecting the environment for future generations. Federal action to perpetually reserve the park's more than 400 sq miles of scenic wilderness successfully replenished previously decimated populations of elk, bighorn sheep, moose and beaver. Recent efforts have begun to reestablish native greenback and cutthroat trout in 50 of the park's 147 lakes. The NPS also has succeeded at promoting public recreation – almost too well. Some 3 million visitors enter the park each year – many attracted solely to the park's crowded Trail Ridge Rd through spectacular alpine tundra environments. However, you don't have to hike or camp with everyone else. Those who venture on foot into areas away from the road corridor will be rewarded with superlative scenery and wildlife viewing, and even solitude.

Aspen and lodgepole pines are pioneering trees in the montane and higher sub-alpine forests; they are the first to establish themselves following disturbances like fire, timber cutting, avalanche or glacial retreat. The sight and sound of 'quaking' aspen leaves and radiant fall color displays – ranging from golden yellow to red – enhance most visits to the area. Above the montane forests and meadows, between about 9000 and 11,000 feet at treeline, deep lingering snows and a short growing season permit the Englemann spruce and sub-alpine fir to dominate the sub-alpine ecosystem.

Toward the upper limit of the sub-alpine zone, brutal weather stunts tree growth, creating the stark beauty of the Krummholz, a German word for 'crooked timber.' In this transition zone from the sub-alpine forest to treeless alpine tundra, you can admire how the wind and cold have shaped Englemann spruce, sub-alpine fir and limber pine into shortened, bizarre forms.

Above the treeline is the alpine tundra. Winter burn effectively prunes woody growth that extends into exposed areas above rocks. The hairy leaves of rydbergia – a showy, large yellow sunflower that always faces east – help reduce water loss in the dry climate and enable the plant to survive the years it takes to produce its first and only flower. Avoid trampling nature's fragile carpet – the dwarf clover's pink flowers may be more than 200 years old! Stepping on the purple-flowered sky pilot will acquaint you with why it's also called skunkweed. Fall is heralded by the Arctic gentian's late blooming greenish-white trumpet.

The Rocky Mountains' spine cleaves its namesake park from north to south only 25 miles from the eastern Great Plains. Long's Peak is the highest peak in the park – its 14,256-foot crest acts as a sentinel to travelers on the plains. West of the Continental Divide, the Colorado River begins its southwestward journey to the Gulf of California while the headwaters of the Cache la

COLORADO

ROCKY MOUNTAIN NATIONAL PARK

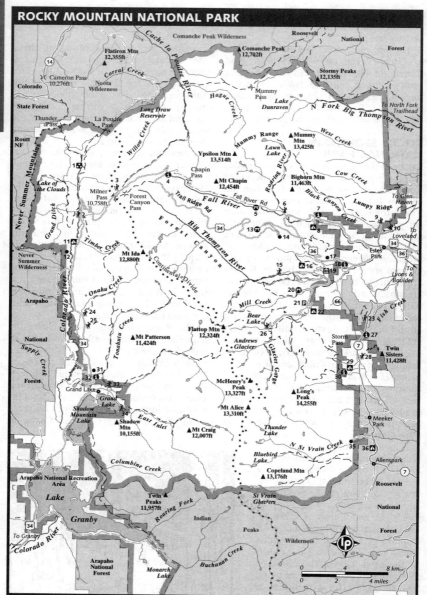

ROCKY MOUNTAIN NATIONAL PARK

CAMPGROUNDS
8 Aspenglen Campground
11 Timber Creek Campground
16 Moraine Park Campground
22 Glacier Basin Campground
29 Long's Peak Tent
   Campground
36 Olive Ridge Campground

TRAILHEADS
2 Colorado River Trailhead
3 Crater Trailhead
6 Lawn Lake Trailhead
9 Twin Owls/Black Canyon
   Trailheads
10 Gem Lake Trailhead
15 Fern Lake Trailhead

23 Lily Mountain Trailhead
24 Onahu Creek Trailhead
25 Green Mountain Trailhead
26 Bear Lake/Glacier
   Gorge/Flattop Mountain
   Trailheads
28 Twin Sisters Trailhead
33 Tonahutu/North Inlet
   Trailheads
34 East Inlet Trailhead

OTHER
1 Lulu City Ruins
4 Alpine Visitors Center
5 Endovalley Picnic Area
7 Fall River Visitors Center
12 Never Summer Ranch

13 Hidden Valley Picnic Area
14 Many Parks Curve
17 Beaver Meadows Entrance
   Station
18 Park Headquarters; Beaver
   Meadows Visitors Center
19 Moraine Park Museum
20 Hollowell Park
21 Bear Lake Shuttle Bus Parking
27 Lily Lake Visitors Center
30 Long's Peak Ranger Station
31 Grand Lake Entrance Station
32 Kawuneeche Visitors Center
35 Wild Basin Entrance Station

Poudre and Big Thompson Rivers originate in the alpine peaks on the east side.

Most light-colored granite peaks in the park were exposed during a regional geologic uplift that began 60 million years ago and ended 5 to 7 million years ago. Volcanic activity during the past 30 million years added other distinctive features to the park: the conical Estes Cone, massive flat-topped lava cliffs along Trail Ridge Rd and the Never Summer Mountains.

Upon this rocky palette, water and ice carved the jagged peaks, cutting canyons and depositing debris on the plains and great mountain parks and meadows. Hikers climbing a glacial trough will typically encounter a steep head wall and semicircular basin containing a cirque lake – these are remnants of the glacier's steady excavation.

Weather in the park – as in all mountainous areas – is variable. Summer days often reach 70°F to 80°F, yet a sudden shift in the weather can bring snow to the peaks in July! Nevertheless, the climate follows broad predictable patterns based on season, elevation, exposure and location east or west of the Continental Divide. Strong winds are common above the treeline. July thundershowers typically dump two inches of rain on the park, while January is the driest month – Bear Lake (9400 feet) normally has a January snow base of 25 inches. The Continental Divide causes a pronounced rain-shadow effect: Grand Lake (west of the Divide) annually averages 20 inches of moisture, while Estes Park receives only about 13 inches yearly.

Careless campfire habits at the beginning of the 20th century led to major burns in the Bear Lake and Glacier Creek areas. Yet long-term fire suppression has caused the forests to grow dense and more susceptible to great conflagrations, like the one that decimated Yellowstone Park in 1988. In 1992, the park adopted a cautious policy to allow two types of fire: Certain lightning-caused fires may burn under careful monitoring, and park staff may prescribe burning in areas that accumulate fuel such as dry underbrush, leaves and such.

One of the major attractions at Rocky Mountain National Park is the opportunity to view a diversity and abundance of wildlife rarely encountered outside the park's sanctuary. Policies against hunting, harassing and feeding animals, as well as against other disturbing activities, have helped to save many species from the brink of extinction. Most visitors are attracted to viewing the larger mammals, like elk, bighorn sheep and moose, but the various smaller animals and birds should not be overlooked. For details about some of the unusual animals you'll find here, see

COLORADO

Roaring Floods

In contrast with the gradual geologic forces, occasional catastrophic events, most commonly avalanches and floods, bring sudden change to the park's landscape. On July 15, 1982, the failure of Lawn Lake Dam, built in 1903, sent a 25-foot-high wall of water racing down the narrow Roaring River Valley. And roar it did! The flood uprooted trees and swept earth and giant boulders 5 miles over Horseshoe Falls, where the incredible mass crashed to the valley floor, damming Fall River. The mass of mud and debris advanced down the valley, covering Elkhorn Ave in Estes Park to a depth of 6 feet before the floodwaters were absorbed in Lake Estes Reservoir almost 3½ hours later. Within that time, three campers were killed and the alluvial debris created a lake. Visitors to the alluvial fan climb over boulders weighing as much as 452 tons that were deposited by the flood.

Flora & Fauna in Facts about the Rocky Mountains.

Among the 260 bird species is the white-tailed ptarmigan, which changes color to blend with its seasonal environment. Raptors like the redtail hawk, prairie falcon and the endangered peregrine falcon frequently seek out rocky nest sites in the Twin Owls area of the park. The endangered bald eagle also visits the park – this national symbol is now making a strong comeback in Colorado. The open rocky scree above the timberline provides visitors with opportunities to see yellow-bellied marmots, a large rodent also called a 'whistle pig' and the tailless, mouse-like pika.

History

Members of the Ute tribe once were numerous throughout Middle Park but they avoided Grand Lake because of its spirits. Legend is that Arapahos and Cheyennes attacked a Ute camp next to Grand Lake, killing many warriors. Before the legendary

battle, Ute women and children were placed on a raft and sent out on the lake for safety, but a fierce wind overturned the raft and all aboard drowned. The tale reflects the tragic history of the Arapaho and Cheyenne. After losing their plains hunting grounds to pioneer advances, members of the two tribes were driven into the mountains where they were notorious for their raids on Ute horses grazing in the meadows.

In 1819, Major Stephen H Long's government exploration party on the S Platte River noted 'a high peake was plainly to be distinguished towering above all the others…' but they continued south without entering the area of his namesake summit. Joel Estes arrived with his family in 1860, but left after six years and his cabin was converted into a lodge for visitors, primarily hunters.

Using hired hands to make fraudulent claims on 160-acre homesteads in his behalf, English earl Lord Dunraven assembled a private hunting estate covering 23½ sq miles of land within a few years of his 1873 arrival. World-famous landscape artist Albert Bierstadt painted his rendition of Estes Park in 1877 and reportedly selected the site for Dunraven to build a hotel.

Construction of the hotel and road-building in the park prompted Enos Mills to begin his campaign in 1909 to protect the area from 'unrestricted tourist development' as the Estes National Park and Game Preserve. In his own words, 'for six years there was not a day that I failed to work or plan for it.' Mills' allies in advocacy included John Muir, the great naturalist of the Sierra Nevada; J Horace McFarland, President of the American Civic Association; and George Horace Lorimer of the *Saturday Evening Post*. Strong opposition to the plan came from private grazing and timber interests. Mills noted that the USFS was a particular foe to the formation of national parks.

After devoting years to the campaign, Mills emerged victorious when Congress approved the bill creating Rocky Mountain National Park in early 1915. To reach the celebration and tribute to Mills held on January 26, 1915, attendees from the west side of the newly created park arrived in Estes Park after hiking across the Continental Divide in snowshoes.

Workers completed Fall River Rd over the Divide in 1920, and the Trail Ridge Rd opened in 1932 to provide an alternative route traversing 10 miles of treeless alpine tundra.

Orientation

The park lies between Comanche Peak and Neota Wilderness Areas in the Roosevelt National Forest to the north, Indian Peaks Wilderness on the south and between the towns of Grand Lake to the west and Estes Park to the east. (For more on Grand Lake see the Northern Mountains chapter). The Continental Divide runs northwest to southeast to exit at the south-central end of the park.

Trail Ridge Rd (US 34) is the only east-west through the park; the US 34 eastern approach from I-25 and Loveland follows the Big Thompson River Canyon. The most direct route from Boulder follows US 36 through Lyons to the east entrances. Another approach from the south, mountainous Hwy 7, passes by Enos Mills' Cabin and provides access to campsites and trailheads (including Long's Peak) on the east side of the Divide. Winter closure of US 34 through the park makes access to the park's west side dependent on US 40 at Granby.

There are two entrance stations on the east side, Fall River (US 34) and Beaver Meadows (US 36). The Grand Lake Station (also US 34) is the only entry on the west side. Three of the park's five visitors centers are located outside park entrances: the Park Headquarters Visitors Center is on US 36 between Estes Park and Beaver Meadows Entrance Station, Lily Lake is 6 miles south of Estes Park on Hwy 7 and Kawuneeche is north of Grand Lake on US 34. Year-round access is available through Kawuneeche Valley along the Colorado River headwaters to Timber Creek Campground. The main centers of visitor activity on the park's east side are the Alpine Visitors Center high on Trail Ridge Rd and Bear Lake Rd, which leads to campgrounds, trailheads and the Moraine Park Museum.

North of Estes Park, Devils Gulch Rd leads to MacGregor Ranch and Lumpy Ridge hiking trails. Farther out on Devils Gulch Rd, you pass through the village of Glen Haven to reach the trailhead entry to the park along the North Fork of the Big Thompson River.

Information

Tourist Offices Park Headquarters and the Beaver Meadows Visitors Center (☎ 970-586-1206, TTY 970-586-1319), 2½ miles west of Estes Park on Hwy 36, is the park's main information facility and is open daily year-round. Audiovisual programs are presented in the auditorium and a bookstore is operated by the Rocky Mountain Nature Association. The center is open 8 am to 5 pm daily (9 pm in summer).

Kawuneeche Visitors Center (☎ 970-627-3471), at the southwest entrance of the park 1 mile north of the town of Grand Lake, is open year-round. It has a small museum, a bookstore and audiovisual programs and it issues backcountry permits (see Fees & Permits, below).

Straddling the park boundary with adjacent USFS lands, the Lily Lake Visitors Center, 6 miles south of Estes Park on Hwy 7, offers a small exhibit and a bookstore. It's not worth a special trip unless you plan to stroll around Lily Lake, the park's most recent addition, or make the short hike up Lily Mountain.

Moraine Park Museum and Visitors Center, 5 miles west of Estes Park on Bear Lake Rd, has natural history exhibits along with park history displays and film presentations (see Moraine Park Museum, later). Park at the museum and take a shuttle bus to the campgrounds or trailheads along Bear Lake Rd (see Getting Around).

Alpine Visitors Center (closed in winter), 25 miles west of Estes Park on Trail Ridge Rd, has excellent exhibits of alpine geology and flora and fauna, but the crowds seeking shelter from frequent lightning storms can be overwhelming. From the observation

COLORADO

deck visitors can often spot grazing elk on nearby hillsides.

The Fall River Visitors Center, located in the northeast part of the park, features wildlife displays and viewer guidelines.

NPS rangers provide a variety of organized summer activities (mostly free) for visitors, ranging from fireside chats to visitors center lectures and short interpretive hikes which change from year to year. Check a recent issue of *High Country Headlines,* the free newspaper given to visitors, or contact the Interpretive Ranger Supervisor (☎ 970-586-1226) for current programs and schedules.

In the winter, rangers present weekly Saturday evening programs at the park headquarters.

Fees & Permits For private vehicles, the park entrance fee is $10, valid for seven days. Individuals entering the park on foot, bicycle, motorcycle or bus pay $5 each. All visitors receive a free copy of the park's information brochure, which contains a good orientation map and is available in English, German, French, Spanish and Japanese.

Backcounty permits ($15) are required for overnight stays (May through October) outside of developed campgrounds. Reservations can be made by phone, mail or in person. Phone reservations (☎ 970-586-1242) can be made only from November to April. Reservations by mail are accepted via the Backcountry Office, Rocky Mountain National Park, Estes Park, CO 80517. Permits can be obtained in person at Park Headquarters, Kawuneeche Visitors Center, and (in summer only) at the Long's Peak and Wild Basin Ranger Stations.

Money, Post & Communications The park has no banking or postal services; for these you'll need to head to either Estes Park or Grand Lake. Public phones are found at visitors centers and all campgrounds except Long's Peak.

Medical Services There are no care facilities in the park, but most rangers are trained to give emergency treatment. Emergency

telephones (☎ 911, 970-586-1399 at headquarters) are at Long's Peak and Wild Basin Ranger Stations, as well as at the Bear Lake, Deer Ridge Junction and Lawn Lake trailheads.

Dangers & Annoyances With the onset of warmer spring weather, hikers should take precautions to avoid bites from wood ticks, which can transmit Colorado tick fever. (For more about ticks see Health in Facts for the Visitor.)

Moraine Park Museum

Built in 1910 as the Moraine Lodge, this structure offers a splendid example of Craftsman-style architecture, intended to blend with nature through the use of native building materials. The park service purchased the lodge during the Depression and it has since served as a visitors center and museum. Featured exhibits portray the park's natural history along with the history of tourism in the park. The geology exhibits provide especially good interpretation of local textbook examples like South Lateral Moraine or the Taylor and Tyndall glaciers visible from the front steps.

The Moraine Museum, 5 miles west of Estes Park on Bear Lake Rd, is open 9 am to 5 pm daily May to mid-October; free.

Never Summer Ranch

On the west side of the park, just south of Timber Creek Campground and reached by a 1-mile trail, Never Summer Ranch is an early dude ranch now preserved as a cultural landmark. It's open 9 am to 5 pm daily.

Hiking & Backpacking

With more than 300 miles of trail, the park is suited to every hiking ability, traversing all aspects of the park's terrain. Families might consider the easy hikes in the Wild Basin to Calypso Falls or to Gem Lakes in the Lumpy Ridge area. At the other extreme is the strenuous hike to Long's Peak, which should be attempted only by those in good physical condition. Spend at least one night at 7000 to 8000 feet prior to setting out to allow your body to adjust to the elevation. Before July, many trails are snowbound and high water runoff makes passage difficult. The following trail descriptions are only a representative selection of the many possible hikes in the park. Dogs and other pets are not allowed on the trails. All overnight stays in the backcountry require permits (see Information earlier).

A useful organization, the Colorado Mountain Club's local Shining Mountain Group (☎ 970-586-6623) offers some 600 outings each year in the area, many of which are open to the public. To learn more about the group's schedule of activities – and conservation and service work – drop by the Estes Park Public Library at 335 E Elkhorn Ave.
Web site: www.cmc.org

Long's Peak You need not worry about being alone on this 15-mile roundtrip to the lofty summit of Long's Peak (14,255 feet) – during the summer peak you're likely to find a line of more than 100 parked cars snaking down the road from the East Long's Peak trailhead (9400 feet). After the initial 6 miles of moderate trail to the Boulder Field (12,760 feet) the path steepens at the start of the Keyhole Route to the summit, which is marked with yellow and red bulls-eyes painted on the rock. Even superhuman athletes are slowed by the route's ledge system, which resembles a narrow cliffside stairway without a handrail. Scramble the final 'homestretch' to the summit boulders. The roundtrip hike takes anywhere from 10 to 15 hours.

Remember that safety is more important than the transient goal of reaching the summit. Hikers should immediately turn back in the event of afternoon lightning storms, the first indication of altitude sickness or hypothermia. Many climbers make the trail approach in early predawn hours after overnighting at Long's Peak Campground. The Keyhole Route is generally free of snow mid-July to October – otherwise you will need technical climbing skills and equipment to reach the summit.

The trailhead is at Long's Peak Ranger Station, 11 miles south of Estes Park on

Hwy 7; the station is open 8 am to 4:30 pm daily in summer.

Chasm Lake High on the east side of Long's Peak, Chasm Lake (11,800 feet) is a cirque fed by Mills Glacier. About 3 miles from the start of the East Long's Peak Trail, a backcountry toilet marks a branch to the south (left) over the Mills Moraine to Columbine Falls and Chasm Lake, 1 mile from the junction. The final part of the trail before reaching Chasm Lake involves traversing a rock ledge.

Twin Sisters Peaks This up-and-back hike provides an excellent warm-up to climbing Long's Peak; in addition, the 11,428-foot summit of Twin Sisters Peak offers unequaled views of Long's Peak. It's an arduous walk, gaining 2300 feet in just 3.7 miles. Erosion-resistant quartz rock caps the oddly deformed rock at the summit and delicate alpine flowers (plenty of mountain harebell) fill the rock spaces near the stone hut. The trailhead is near Mills Cabin, 10 miles south of Estes Park on Hwy 7.

Lily Mountain One of the easiest climbs in the area, Lily Mountain sits on the park border 6 miles south of Estes Park on Hwy 7. A 1½-mile trail goes up almost 1000 feet to the summit for an outstanding panorama that includes the Mummy Range, Continental Divide, Long's Peak, Estes Park and Estes Cone.

Wild Basin From the Wild Basin Ranger Station, 15 miles south of Estes Park to the turnoff on Hwy 7, easy day hikes lead to cascading waterfalls, beaver ponds and wildflowers in what is also referred to as 'Ouzel country.' Near the trailhead is Copeland Falls; Calypso Cascades appears in less than 2 miles; and in another mile you reach Ouzel Falls and a nearby overlook of Long's Peak. Hikers can continue another mile to a junction with the Bluebird Lake Trail that follows Ouzel Creek, or take the north branch to Thunder Lake in the upper St Vrain Creek. Both trails offer campsites and reach timberline at the 6-mile mark.

Fern Lake Trailhead Forested Fern Lake, 4 miles from the trailhead in Moraine Park, reached by shuttle bus, is dominated by craggy Notchtop Peak. You can complete a loop to the Bear Lake shuttle stop in 8½ miles for a rewarding day hike. With a back-country camping permit, you can spend more time exploring the countless pristine lakes and waterfalls in the upper Fern Creek drainage before returning by foot via the Mill Creek Basin-Cub Lake routes, or aboard a shuttle from the Bierstadt Lake trailhead.

Bear Lake Trailhead A sub-alpine inter-pretive nature trail circles the lake, and a 1-mile hike takes you past Nymph Lake to beautiful Dream Lake, a small gem sur-rounded by Englemann spruce below massive Hallett Peak. From here, one trail follows the Tyndall Glacier Gorge, crossing the terminal moraine that separates Dream Lake from Emerald Lake less than a mile upstream. The trail south from Dream Lake passes upstream of Chaos Canyon Cascades and continues to Loch Vale, past Glacier Falls and Alberta Falls, before emerging at Glacier Gorge Junction trailhead. Bear Lake is served by the Glacier Basin–Bear Lake shuttle. An emergency telephone is located at the trailhead.

Flattop Mountain Trail Surprisingly, this is the only hiking trail in the park to link the east and west sides. Reaching the Divide on Flattop Mountain from the Bear Lake trail-head entails a strenuous 4½-mile climb, gaining 2800 feet in elevation. From the summit, you have two equidistant options for continuing to Grand Lake: Tonahutu Creek Trail or the North Inlet Trail. Both offer plenty of backcountry campsites on the east side.

Glacier Gorge Junction Trailhead hikes in this busy area of trails range from the easy stroll to Alberta Falls to more strenuous 5-mile trips either up Glacier Gorge, past Mills Lake and many glacial erratics to Black Lake, or Loch Vale to Andrews Glacier on the Divide. The trailhead is served by the Glacier Basin–Bear Lake shuttle.

Lawn & Gem Lakes Strenuous hikes into the Mummy Range climb abruptly from the alluvial fan in Horseshoe Park. Although trails to Ypsilon Lake (4½ miles) and Lawn Lake (6 miles) are up and back excursions, it's possible to continue down Black Canyon to Lumpy Ridge.

Easy hikes of about 2 miles in the Lumpy Ridge area lead to Gem Lake from trail-heads at either the MacGregor Ranch or below the Twin Owls formations on Devils Gulch Rd, 1 or 2 miles north of Estes Park, respectively.

North Fork Trailhead The North Fork of the Big Thompson River flows from the park through the Comanche Wilderness Area in the Roosevelt National Forest and appeals to families interested in easy hiking along the river, or accomplished backpack-ers who want a more extensive trail network. The North Fork Trail enters the Comanche Wilderness and follows the river-side path for 4½ miles to the park boundary, eventually reaching Alpine Lost Lake at the 7½-mile mark and Lake Dunraven.

Backpackers can hike a branch trail over Stormy Peaks Pass into the Comanche Wilderness or take a cross-country route to Mummy Pass. To get to the North Fork trail-head from Estes Park, take Devils Gulch Rd for 9 miles east over the scenic divide through Glen Haven and past some picnic areas along the North Fork to a bridge marked 'Dunraven Forest Access' on your left (east), then proceed 2½ miles to the trailhead.

Milner Pass The Trail Ridge Rd crosses the Divide at Milner Pass (elevation 10,759 feet), where trails head southeast to Mt Ida, the most accessible view peak on the west side of the park. The trail climbs 2000 feet in 4 miles, steeply at first through dense forest, before emerging onto an exhilaratingly open tundra zone with fabulous views of the valleys below. At about the 3-mile point the trail peters out, but the route is still easy to follow. Figure about three hours to the summit, and about 2½ hours to return. Because the route is so exposed, there is real danger during thunderstorms.

Colorado River Trailhead About 1½ miles north of Timber Creek Campground, this trail follows the Colorado River to the deteriorating ruins of Lulu City, a former mineral boomtown 3½ miles from Trail Ridge Rd. It's possible to make this a loop via the slightly longer Red Mountain Trail.

North & East Inlets The North Inlet trail climbs gradually to Cascade Falls, then more steeply to Lakes Nokoni and Nanita. You can reach it by a short spur from the Kawuneeche Visitors Center north of Grand Lake on US 34, or from the road near Shadowcliff Lodge in Grand Lake. It's possible to continue east across the Divide.

At the east end of Grand Lake in Grand Lake Village, the East Inlet trail climbs gradually and then steeply toward the Divide, passing several glacial lakes.

Rock Climbing

Many climbers head to Lumpy Ridge, a sub-alpine outcrop of many rock faces only 2 miles north of Estes Park that offers outstanding short climbs and attracts climbers of all abilities. Two trailheads provide access to Lumpy Ridge climbing areas from Devils Gulch Rd: Twin Owls trailhead begins at the MacGregor Ranch, and about 1 mile east of the ranch is the Gem Lake trailhead. To protect the nests of birds of prey, some climbing routes are closed mid-April to mid-July.

A quality alpine face with a short approach is the Englishman's Route up Hallett Peak (12,713 feet), the wedge-shaped monolith seen from Bear Lake. This Class 5.8 climb on a sunny, south-facing slope is reached from the Bear Lake/Glacier Gorge trailhead. Another recommended climb is the Sidetrack Route up Sundance Mountain, a Class 5.9 climb. Trail Ridge Rd passes over Sundance Mountain and the Fall River Rd follows the glacial

valley north of this tremendous glacially carved remnant.

Many of the park's alpine climbs are long one-day climbs or require an overnight stay on the rock face. Often the only way to accomplish a long climb and avoid afternoon thundershowers is to begin climbing at dawn – this can mean an approach hike beginning at midnight! An alternative is to bivouac at the base of the climb. (A bivouac is defined as a temporary open-air encampment – no tents – established in designated zones between dawn and dusk.) Free bivouac permits are issued only to technical climbers and are mandatory for all overnight stays in the backcountry.

To minimize the environmental impact of backcountry use, the Rocky Mountain National Park Backcountry Office (☎ 970-586-1242) allows only a limited number of people to bivouac at four popular climbing areas. Phone reservations may be made March to May 20 for the following restricted zones: Long's Peak area, including Broadway below Diamond, Chasm View, Mills Glacier and Meeker Cirque; Black Lake area (Glacier Gorge), encompassing McHenry Peak, Arrowhead, Spearhead and Chiefshead/Pagoda; the base of Notchtop Peak; and the Skypond/Andrews Glacier Area, including the Taylor/Powell Peaks and Sharkstooth Peak. Reservations are not needed nor accepted for other bivouacs.

For climbing gear try Estes Park Mountain Shop (☎ 970-586-6548) at 358 E Elkhorn in Estes Park. A small stock of climbing gear also is available from Colorado Mountain School (☎ 970-586-5758), 351 Moraine Ave in Estes Park, where you can also sleep in a dorm for $20, shower after a climb for $2 or enroll in a climbing course. Advanced expeditions also are available.

Mountain Biking

A splendid way to see the park and wildlife is to mountain bike on park roads, though you are restricted to paved roads and to one dirt road, Fall River Rd.

Climbing the paved Trail Ridge Rd has one big advantage over Fall River Rd: You can turn around should problems arise. (Fall River Rd is a 9-mile one-way climb of more than 3000 feet.) The pleasant summer weather at lower elevations can suddenly become unmercifully cold at higher altitudes – especially when descending from the park's alpine peaks. Hypothermia is an emergency experienced by many unprepared bicyclists each month: Change into a dry shirt, full gloves and a warm, water-repellent outer shell before you get above treeline and into the wind. The only shelter from lightning is at Alpine Visitors Center. Yet another unpleasantness is the altitude sickness and subsequent dehydration that strikes many people unaccustomed to the 12,000-foot elevation reached on Trail Ridge Rd.

Less daunting climbs and climes are available on the park's lower paved roads. A popular 16-mile circuit is the Horseshoe Park/Estes Park Loop. For a bit more of a climbing challenge you can continue to Bear Lake Rd, an 8-mile long route that rises 1500 feet to the high mountain basin.

If you are not up to climbing either Trail Ridge or Fall River Rds, Colorado Bicycling Adventures (☎ 970-586-4241, 800-607-8756), 184 E Elkhorn in Estes Park, offers tours of Rocky Mountain National Park. It also rents bikes.

Fishing

This is not the primary attraction at Rocky Mountain National Park. Solid freeze and other natural factors at 42 of the 156 lakes in the park limit the number of reproducing populations of fish. In the past, the NPS stocked many lakes and streams with non-native species to appease sport fishing demands, but today only native greenback cutthroat trout and Colorado River cutthroat trout are stocked. The endangered greenback cutthroat is a major focal point of restoration efforts. Fishing regulations further encourage replenishment of native fish and removal of exotic species. To abide by these rules, you must be able to identify each species of fish taken. A list of current regulations, open lakes, closed waters and catch-and-release areas is available at park visitors centers and ranger stations.

For supplies, information or fly-fishing classes, stop by the Estes Angler (☎ 970-586-2110), 338 W Riverside Dr in Estes Park. Scot's Sporting Goods (☎ 970-586-2877), 2325 Spruce Ave, also offers equipment and guided trips outside park boundaries. Two more Estes Park outfits running guided trips are Rocky Mountain Adventures (☎ 970-586-6191, 800-858-6808) and Renegade Outfitters (☎ 877-904-0333). Also see Ice Fishing, later.

Horseback Riding & Pack Trips

Pack animals are permitted on approximately 80% of the park's trails – mostly outside the heavily used east-side zones. Even so, trails in the vicinity of the YMCA Conference Center and up Twin Sisters Peaks are overcrowded with equestrians. Check the park brochure 'Horses & Other Pack Animals' for trails open to pack animals. The park's Backcountry Guide identifies campsites suited for livestock.

A large number of livery stables rent horses and most have permits for leading trips into the park. Hi Country Stables has facilities within the park at Glacier Basin (☎ 970-586-3244) and Moraine Park (☎ 970-586-2327). Other operations include Sombrero Ranch Stables (☎ 970-586-4577), 1 mile east of Estes Park on Hwy 34, which offers hourly rides and overnight packtrips, as well as 'breakfast rides' and 'steak dinner rides.'

Driving Tours

Most of the park's three million annual visitors get no farther than the windshield tour along **Trail Ridge Rd** (US 34) over the Continental Divide, which usually opens in late May and is closed at Many Parks Curve on the east side by mid-October. The ridgetop route, formerly a Ute trail over Milner Pass, was surveyed by federal road builders in 1927 to replace Fall River Rd. Allow at least three hours to travel the 47 miles between Estes Park and Grand Lake, depending on the length of your stops at the short Tundra Nature Trail, Crater Trail, Alpine Visitors Center and various overlook sites.

Have four quarters ready to purchase a guide booklet from a dispenser at the start of Fall River Rd, a one-way uphill route near the Endovalley Picnic Area. The 9-mile unpaved road looks much as it did when completed in 1920 and usually opens in July. Views are obscured for most of the trip by forested slopes along the Fall River, but Chasm Falls and frequent elk sightings in the tundra near the Alpine Visitors Center are exceptional attractions. If you're heading up in late September or October check with the visitors center for road conditions: By that point in the season some large ruts can develop.

Snowshoeing & Cross-Country Skiing

The ratio of wildlife to people greatly increases during winter months, though the park also is becoming more popular as a winter destination. Elk, mule deer and bighorn sheep frequent the meadows and plowed roadways. The tracks of coyotes, porcupines, weasels and other small mammals crisscross the blanket of snow. This abundant wildlife further attracts migrating falcons and eagles.

From December into May, the high valleys and alpine tundra of Rocky Mountain National Park offer cross-country skiers unique opportunities to view wildlife and the winter scenery undisturbed by crowds. January and February are the best months for dry, powdery snowpack – spring snows tend to be heavy and wet. Most routes follow summer hiking trails, but valley bottoms and frozen streambeds typically have more snow cover and are less challenging. In fact, most of the park should be considered 'backcountry skiing' rather than 'cross-country.' Avalanche hazards are greatest on steep, open slopes in mountainous terrain. Overnight trips require permits, and the USFS NPS will have a list of closed trails.

On the east side, the Bear Lake trailheads offer short or long routes suitable for all skiing abilities, from beginner to experienced. The easiest trail for a short one- or two-hour roundtrip leads to Nymph Lake, but experienced skiers can continue to Dream and Emerald Lakes. Another beginner trail starts at Glacier Gorge Junction and leads to Alberta Falls before continuing as an intermediate route to the Loch Vale–Glacier Gorge Trail junction. From here, a snowy streambed alternative to the summer trail takes you to the Loch Trail, an all-day roundtrip.

Other extended tours are possible from the Bear Lake area; for these, you should be equipped for an emergency bivouac. A 10-mile out-and-back tour to Fern Lake generally follows Mill Creek after crossing the low divide from Bear Lake on the summer trail. This route is scenic and protected from the harshest winds commonly encountered by skiers on the alternate approach from Moraine Park, which passes the appropriately named Windy Gulch. Likewise, the exposed Trail Ridge Rd (US 34), closed to vehicles west of Many Parks Curve in the winter, also is subject to high winds and blowing snow and makes a poor choice for enjoyable touring.

Rangers lead weekend snowshoe hikes in the east side of the park from January to April, depending on snow conditions. Trailhead locations and times are available from the park headquarters.

NPS visitors centers (see Information, earlier) can provide additional route suggestions. Adventurous skiers planning on overnight backcountry stays also need to obtain free camping permits and information about areas open to overnight stays.

Snowshoe and ski rentals are available at the Estes Park Mountain Shop (☎ 970-586-6548), 358 E Elkhorn in Estes Park.

Winter Hiking

Snow depth to 35 feet on the peaks precludes winter hiking, yet elevations below 8700 feet on the east side often are snow-free. Note that an easy or moderate summer day hike becomes a strenuous affair in deep snow, and roundtrip circuits at lower elevations may be blocked. A few suggestions for up-and-back winter hikes include the Fern Lake Trail to the Pool and the Cub Lake Trail. Both are reachable from Moraine

Park and provide short hikes with opportunities to view wildlife. The closed Fall River Rd also beckons foot travel to Chasm Falls. Lumpy Ridge north of Estes Park is another winter hiking area – try the Gem Lake Trail from Devils Gulch Rd.

Ice Fishing

Ice fishing is allowed at many of the park's frozen lakes. The same restrictions and regulations apply as in warmer months – check at the visitors center for open waters and suggestions for winter access; monitor ice conditions carefully and take every caution.

Places to Stay

The only overnight accommodations in the park are at campgrounds; the majority of motel or hotel accommodations are around Estes Park (see earlier) or Grand Lake (see the Northern Mountains chapter).

The park's five formal campgrounds provide campfire programs, have public telephones and a seven-day limit during summer months; all except Long's Peak take RVs (no hookups). Camping fees are $16, or $10 in winter (when the water supply is off).

You will need a backcountry permit to stay outside developed park campgrounds (see Information, earlier). None of the campgrounds feature showers, but they do have flush toilets in summer and outhouse facilities in winter. Sites include a fire ring, picnic table and one parking spot.

In the east side of the park, Moraine Park and Long's Peak campgrounds are open

year-round. The location of **Long's Peak Tent Campground**, 12 miles south of Estes Park on Hwy 7, is intended to provide Long's Peak hikers with an early trail start. It has 26 tent sites available on a first-come, first-served basis for seven-day stays. **Aspenglen**, 5 miles west of Estes Park on US 34, also has 54 first-come, first-served sites early May to early September.

Moraine Park (247 sites) and **Glacier Basin** (150 sites) accept reservations (with Visa or MasterCard) up to five months in advance through the National Park Reservation Center (☎ 800-365-2267), PO Box 85705, San Diego, CA 92186-5705, and via the Internet: http://reservations.nps.gov. Both campgrounds are served by the shuttle buses on Bear Lake Rd. Glacier Basin is open June to September.

At the southeast boundary of the park near Wild Basin, the USFS **Olive Ridge Campground** (☎ 877-444-6777) has 56 heavily used sites for $12; it's open from mid-May to November.

In the west side of the park seven miles north of Grand Lake, **Timber Creek** remains open in winter and has 100 sites (no reservations).

Getting Around

A free shuttle bus provides frequent summer service from the Glacier Basin parking area to Bear Lake. During the summer peak, a second shuttle operates between Moraine Park campground and the Glacier Basin parking area. Shuttles run on weekends only from mid-August through September.

Southern Front Range

A swath of development spreads along the Rockies' eastern edge from Denver down to Colorado Springs, the best-known destination along the southern Front Range. Within the city there are some nice hiking and biking trails. But outside the Springs area the crowds thin out and the scenery picks up. To the west, the Florissant Fossil Beds National Monument offers an interesting look at Colorado's ancient past as well as some nice hiking and wildflower viewing. To the south, the industrial city of Pueblo is not too pretty, but farther down Trinidad offers a nice mix of frontier history and Mexican-American culture. West of Trinidad, the meadows and alpine forests around La Veta and Cuchara offer a chance to take a scenic tour that's a bit off the beaten path.

The area code for telephone numbers in this area is ☎ 719.

COLORADO SPRINGS

Beneath the famous summit of Pikes Peak, Colorado Springs (population 345,000; elevation 6035 feet) is the state's second-largest city, a curious mix of military installations, evangelical conservatives and tourists. Highlights include the Pioneer Museum, Pikes Peak Toll Rd (see Around Manitou Springs, later) and the Garden of the Gods. Cashing in on the steady crowds are numerous tourist traps like the Ghost Town Wild West Museum, Mollie Kathleen Gold Mine and the Cave of the Winds.

The city is pleasant enough, and parts of Old Colorado City feature some interesting architecture, notably some exquisite Victorian homes along Cascade and Nevada Aves.

Orientation

At the northern border of the city, just west of I-25, is the US Air Force Academy. The interstate bisects the metropolitan area: To the east is the central Colorado Springs business district, and to the west is Old Colorado City, the Garden of the Gods and the pleasant town of Manitou Springs.

Referred to as the 'West Side' of Colorado Springs, Old Colorado City stretches along the north side of Colorado Ave just south of 30th St. Its historic district is found along W Colorado Ave between 24th and 27th Sts, where the 1859 Pioneer County Office is located in Bancroft Park.

To get to the cog railway that travels up Pikes Peak, turn west onto Ruxton

Highlights

- Garden of the Gods – spectacular sandstone formations nestled at the edge of Colorado Springs

- Florrisant Fossil Beds National Monument – a rich collection of flora and fauna dating back 35 million years

- La Veta – a tiny artists' community enlivened by scenic splendor and Latino heritage

- Trinidad – a compact city with a wealth of historic sights and a friendly atmosphere

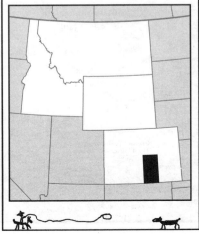

COLORADO

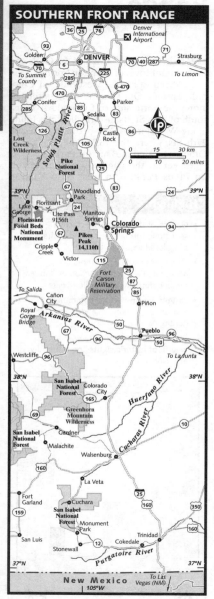

SOUTHERN FRONT RANGE

Ave from Manitou Ave in Manitou Springs. A panoramic view of Pikes Peak with the Garden of the Gods in the foreground is available from Mesa Rd, just off 30th St.

Colorado Springs is on I-25, 68 miles south of Denver and 44 miles north of Pueblo.

Information

At the Colorado Springs Visitor Information Center (☎ 719-635-7506, 800-368-4748), on the corner of Cascade and Colorado Aves, you can examine a photo album of B&Bs and stock up on brochures. The center, open from 8:30 am to 5 pm daily (only weekdays in winter), offers on-line information at www.coloradosprings-travel.com.

There are ATM machines throughout the downtown area. A convenient one is at the Wells Fargo Bank, 90 S Cascade Ave, at the intersection with Colorado Ave, opposite the visitors center.

The post office is at 201 E Pikes Peak Ave; the zip code is 80903. Opposite the post office, Kinko's Copies (☎ 719-633-6683, fax 633-7046), 214 E Pikes Peak Ave, offers email, fax and copy services.

The impressive Chinook Bookstore (☎ 719-635-1195), 210 N Tejon St, and Gateway Books (☎ 719-635-4514), 119 E Bijou St, are both across from Acacia Park. McKinzey-White Booksellers (☎ 719-590-1700), 4201 Centennial Blvd, is open 9:30 am to 9 pm Monday to Saturday, 11 am to 6 pm Sunday.

Memorial Hospital (☎ 719-356-5000), 1400 E Boulder St, offers adult and pediatric care in the Emergency & Trauma Center (☎ 719-365-5221).

Colorado Springs Pioneer Museum

Occupying two floors of the 1903 El Paso County Courthouse building, this pioneer museum (☎ 719-385-5990), at 215 S Tejon St, is well worth a visit if time allows. In addition to taking in the fine exhibits and displays (nearly a century in the making), visitors can admire the restored Main Courtroom and ride the Otis 'Birdcage Elevator.'

The Springs' Founders

The soda-water springs at the foot of Pikes Peak once were sacred sites for Native Americans. Each winter, the Utes camped in the Garden of the Gods at Camp Creek in the present Glen Eyrie estate. Their annual migration from the Rocky Mountains to the plains buffalo-hunting grounds by the Ute Pass Trail is among the best-documented journeys of any Native American group. The Utes created paths that became the mountain highways pioneers would one day follow.

In 1859 Colorado City, then part of Kansas Territory, gained prominence as the supply center for the gold camps of the South Park area that used the Ute Pass Trail. This was a center of activity, where miners patronizing the saloons and brothels rubbed shoulders with tuberculosis patients seeking cures in the area's mineral water.

By 1869 General William Jackson Palmer arrived following his release from the Union Army. Palmer envisioned a resort around the springs that wouldn't have the rough character of most early Western towns. His vision was an attempt to coerce his sheltered young Long Island bride, Queen Mellen, to settle with him in Colorado, since her father's investment would fund Palmer's D&RG Railroad. In 1871 Palmer founded the Fountain Colony, which struggled at first but was rescued by the unlikely combination of tourists and tuberculosis sufferers. Those partaking in the evils of drink weren't welcomed in Palmer's strict society, but they could easily slake their thirst in nearby Colorado City.

Palmer's infatuation with British customs led to the creation of his Glen Eyrie estate, as well as forming the basis of friendships with several gentlemen from the United Kingdom. Among the first to move to Fountain Colony with Palmer's prompting was Dr William Bell, who founded Villa La Font (now Manitou Springs) around 1872. Another was Dr Samuel Edwin Solly, who promoted the health benefits of smelly, foul-tasting soda water. William Blackmore renamed Villa La Font (Fountain Village) 'Manitou' after the Algonquin spirit of Longfellow's epic poem. Rose Kingsley, the daughter of famed poet Charles Kingsley, also came to reside here.

Americans took on British affectations for formal teas and old-world sports – Fountain Colony began to be called Little London. All this helped Palmer's endeavor to succeed, yet his wife, Queen, remained dissatisfied and returned to the East Coast.

Seeking to improve her health in 1873, author Helen Hunt Jackson was also an early settler in Colorado Springs. In 1881 she published *A Century of Dishonor,* an impassioned appeal for honorable treatment of the native tribes by the US government. With no improvement in her health, in 1885 she left for the moderate climate of San Francisco, where she died that same year.

In 1911 the elderly Chipeta, widow of Chief Ouray, rode with other tribal members to mark the historic Ute Pass Trail in an event that commemorated Colorado Springs' establishment.

The museum is open 10 am to 5 pm Tuesday to Saturday and also 1 to 5 pm Sunday May to October; free.

US Olympic Training Complex

Formerly an Air Defense Command site, since 1978 the training center has evolved to support more than half of the sports on the Olympic program, including swimming, cycling, basketball and gymnastics. Visitors may get training schedules to watch the gymnasts and swimmers from large viewing windows.

The visitors center (☎ 719-578-4618), 1750 E Boulder St, offers free video and walking tours of the training complex from 9 am to 5 pm Monday to Saturday and from 10 am to 5 pm on Sunday. A mile south of the training center, the banked-track velodrome in Memorial Park offers bicycle-racing thrills under the lights on weekday evenings throughout the summer.

COLORADO

COLORADO SPRINGS

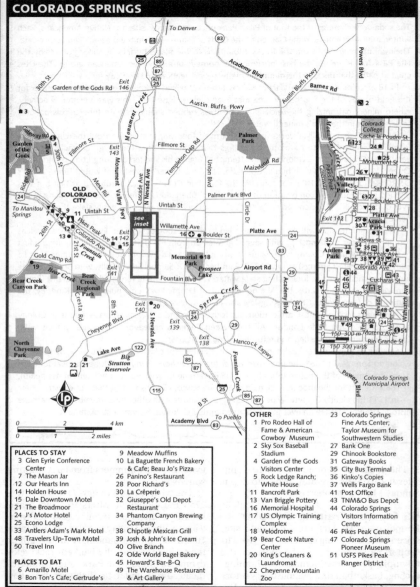

Western Museum of Mining & Industry

Much of the historic mining equipment on display at this museum still works, and visitors will learn more about mining here from the many exhibits and hands-on displays than by taking every mine tour offered in the state.

The accredited Western Museum of Mining & Industry (☎ 719-488-0880) occupies 27 acres east of I-25 via exit 156A. Open 9 am to 4 pm Monday to Saturday and noon to 4 pm Sunday; $6/3 adults/children.

US Air Force Academy

The academy is one of Colorado Springs' more popular attractions. No guided tours are offered, but a self-guided tour map is available from the visitors center (☎ 719-333-2025), open 9 am to 5 pm daily. The center also has exhibits on cadet life and the history of the institution. Some of the more notable stops along the self-guided route include a B-52 bomber near the north entrance and the spires of the stunning **Cadet Chapel**. The grounds are open from 9 am to 5 pm. To get to the visitors center from I-25 take exit 156B and turn onto Northgate Blvd, which turns into Academy Dr.

Colorado Springs Fine Arts Center

This pueblo-style Art Deco facility is listed on the National Register of Historic Places. Galleries in the Fine Arts Museum feature the finest work of Native American, Mexican-American and other painters and sculptures. The center (☎ 719-634-5581), 30 W Dale St, is also home to the Taylor Museum for Southwestern Studies. The galleries and museum are open 9 am to 5 pm Tuesday to Friday, Saturday they open at 10 am and Sunday at 1 pm. Admission costs $4, with discounts for seniors and children.

Pro Rodeo Hall of Fame & Museum of the American Cowboy

To find out how ranch work led to competitive rodeo events, see the film and exhibits at the Pro Rodeo Museum (☎ 719-528-4764),

Chamber Pots

Careful readers may have noted that museums throughout Colorado are inclined to include an inconspicuous chamber pot or two in their Victorian displays. No such display currently exists at the 1st-class Pioneer Museum, but the amused curators provided a valuable bit of information on the topic by sharing a poem on the porcelain bowl that is not a cookie jar. A brief excerpt from *The Thunder-Mug*, written in 1974 by Owen Sanders, follows:

> When tub and privy moved indoors
> To occupy a closet,
> The thunder-mug lay silent
> And received no more deposit.

Museums that display the chamber pot are the Rosemont Museum in Pueblo, which has a fine example, the Glenwood Springs Frontier Historical Museum and Fairplay's South Park City Museum, among others.

101 Pro Rodeo Dr near I-25 exit 147. It's open 9 am to 5 pm daily; $6/3 adults/children.

Van Briggle Pottery

Artus Van Briggle was a leading potter in the early-20th-century Arts and Crafts movement who moved to Colorado Springs in 1899 for health reasons. Here he perfected the Chinese matte glaze, a lost art for 400 years, combining it with art nouveau shapes to create prizewinning pottery. Some of the finest examples are on display in the Pioneer Museum, but the tradition continues and free tours are offered at Van Briggle Pottery (☎ 719-633-7729), 600 S 21st St.

Cheyenne Mountain Zoo

Billed as America's only 'mountain zoo' (starting at 6800 feet), this excellent facility (☎ 719-633-9925) southwest of the city center is home to some 150 species and more than 500 animals. Don't miss the remarkable rotating wolf exhibition; the habitat is fitted with one-way windows and wolves are fed through slots so they never establish visual contact with humans. The zoo is open 9 am to 6 pm daily (5 pm in winter); admission costs $8.50/5 adults/children.

Hiking & Backpacking

Early accounts of life in the area note that before the advent of roads, cogs and bicycle shuttles, large numbers of tenderfoot hikers flocked to Pikes Peak each day, following the 17-mile **Bear Creek Trail** built by the Army Signal Corps in 1873. The lower portion is a regional park trail that offers easy streamside hiking on a route from the 21st St trailhead, a mile south of Old Colorado City. The Bear Creek Nature Center (☎ 719-520-6387) is about a mile west, at 245 Bear Creek Rd.

By the 1880s, locals constructed shorter routes that first advanced up the steep slope of Mt Manitou. The most popular route since 1921 has been the tough 12½-mile **Barr Trail** (USFS Trail 620). From the trailhead just above the Pikes Peak Cog Railway Depot on Ruxton Ave in Manitou Springs, the path climbs 7300 feet to the 14,110-foot summit. Fit hikers should reach the top in about eight hours – the return takes around four hours. If you're not adjusted to the altitude, the USFS recommends making it a two-day trip, with an overnight stay at Barr Camp (☎ 719-630-3934), 7 miles from the trailhead ($10). You can also stay in a shelter at timberline, about 8½ miles from the trailhead. An emergency shelter is available at the summit, but don't plan to camp there. An additional option is to walk only partway: One-way tickets on the Cog Railway to the summit, or to the halfway point on Mountain View Trail, are available on a limited basis.

For maps, books and hiking information about the Pike National Forest, which surrounds the springs and the South Platte River, contact the Pikes Peak Ranger District office (☎ 719-636-1602), 601 S Weber St.

Bicycling

Road bikes are a good means of getting around near the Colorado College campus north of downtown, along Pikes Peak Ave through Old Colorado City and in Manitou Springs. Also, consider visiting Garden of the Gods (see that section, later) on a bike – good bike access exists along 30th St on the park's east side and along El Paso Blvd on the south side. Bijou St provides bicycle access over I-25 and Monument Creek.

The 14-mile **Santa Fe Hiking Trail** passes the Air Force Academy and Western Museum of Mining & Industry on the west side of I-25, north of Colorado Springs between trailheads near Southgate Blvd and Palmer Lake, and is accessible on mountain bike. In Colorado Springs, the Pikes Peak Greenway will eventually connect with the Santa Fe Trail to form the 40-mile Spine Trail. For now, the trail follows **Monument Valley Park** north 5 miles from the Bijou St trailhead to Roswell Park near Fillmore St, and south 1 mile to the power plant on Fountain Creek. The hills surrounding Fountain Valley offer a few good trails for mountain bikes to follow, like Bear Creek Trail, west of the Bear Creek Nature Center.

Special Events

Every July 4 the Pikes Peak Hwy becomes the course for the **Pikes Peak International Hill Climb**, an auto race that started in 1916. In August, the **Pikes Peak or Bust Rodeo** (☎ 719-635-3548) provides 1st-class professional rodeo entertainment, and the Triple Crown of Running (☎ 719-473-2625) organizes the **Pikes Peak Ascent**, a 13½-mile run to the summit of Pikes Peak. It also coordinates the **Pikes Peak Marathon** in August.

Places to Stay

Rates really get out of hand in summer, and rooms can also be scarce during the peak travel months. For nearby accommodations in more pleasant surroundings, see Manitou Springs later in this chapter.

Camping A few trees have been thrown in for consolation at the *Garden of the Gods Campground* (☎ *719-475-9450, 800-248-9451, 3704 W Colorado Ave)*, where tent/RV spaces for $27/33 are provided in a large, paved area. It also has small, ultra-basic cabins that sleep four, $40 for two people and $5 for each additional person, including bedding. Bathrooms are outdoors, and laundry, showers, a pool and a spa are available; see the Manitou Springs map.

Motels The *Amarillo Motel* (☎ 719-635-8539, 2801 W Colorado Ave), offers rooms for $50 in summer, $35 in winter. It's on the site of the first cabin in Old Colorado City.

Rooms at *J's Motor Hotel* (☎ 719-633-5513, 820 N Nevada Ave) are a bit plain, but reasonable at $45/55 a single/double in summer, about $15 less in winter. Amenities include a heated pool and satellite TV. Similar facilities and rates can be found nearby at the *Econo Lodge* (☎ 719-636-3385, 800-553-2666, 714 N Nevada Ave).

At the south end of downtown, the *Travelers Up-Town Motel* (☎ 719-473-2774, 220 E Cimarron St) and the *Travel Inn* (☎ 719-636-3986, 512 S Nevada Ave) both offer plain singles/doubles for about $55/65 in summer, $32/42 in winter.

Just west of downtown the *Dale Downtown Motel* (☎ 719-636-3721, 620 W Colorado Ave) may not look all that elegant, but it's not a bad value at $35/40 for singles/doubles in summer. There's a heated pool, and kitchenette units are available.

The *Maple Lodge* (☎ 719-685-9230, 9 El Paso Blvd), located near the Garden of the Gods (see the Manitou Springs map), has a heated pool, patio area and well-kept rooms starting from $50 in summer, $34 in winter.

Hotels & B&Bs General Palmer would not recognize the lavish high-rise that replaced the 1st-class Antlers Hotel he established in the late 19th century. The rooms at the modern *Antlers Adam's Mark Hotel* (☎ 719-473-5600, 800-222-8733, 4 S Cascade Ave) start around $120 for a double in summer, $90 in winter.

Our Hearts Inn (☎ 719-473-8684, 2215 W Colorado Ave) is a Victorian home where all four rooms have private bath; some have fireplaces or Jacuzzis. Rates range from $65 to $150.

Another Victorian B&B, *Holden House* (☎ 719-471-3980, holdenhouse@worldnet.att.net, 1102 W Pikes Peak Ave) has gotten good reviews from travelers and features private baths in all rooms; rates are $125 to $145.

At the foot of Cheyenne Mountain, 5 miles southwest of downtown Colorado Springs, stands Colorado's one and only five-star resort. *The Broadmoor* (☎ 719-473-5600, 800-444-2326, 4 S Cascade Ave) ranks among the country's most elite establishments. Tourists come to gawk at the grounds and the 550-room hotel, which was opened by Spencer Penrose in 1918 to rival the Antlers Hotel. Doubles range from $310 to $460 in summer and $190 to $340 in winter. Suites soar to $2585 a night! Special packages are also available.
Web site: www.broadmoor.com

At the *Glen Eyrie Conference Center* (☎ 800-944-4536), just up the road from Garden of the Gods, guests can stay in a 19th-century English Tudor castle or in lodges on the historic estate. Rates range from $50 to $140. Glen Eyrie draws a steady stream of day-trippers for its **castle tours** ($5), offered daily at 1 pm. For an extra $3 you can sip Glen Eyrie Teas in the castle. A special English Cream Tea ($8) is served Monday to Saturday at 2:30 pm (plus mornings at 10:30 am from May to September). A Victorian Tea ($11.50) is held on Sunday from 11:30 am.
Web site: www.gleneyrie.org

Places to Eat
Colorado Springs Metro Area A good health-conscious place is the *Olive Branch* (☎ 719-475-1199, 23 S Tejon St). It's a favored breakfast spot offering omelets, low-fat French toast and fresh-fruit smoothies. The lunch and dinner menus are also appealing and include a good selection of salads.

Giuseppe's Old Depot Restaurant (☎ 719-635-3111, 10 S Sierra Madre St) is housed in a former D&RG train station, with live tracks in back and an historic steam engine displayed in front. Hearty Italian and American lunches cost between

$6 and $8, while dinner prices start at $10. The salad bar and desserts are excellent.

Since the mid-1970s, *Poor Richard's* (☎ 719-632-7721, 324½ N Tejon St) has served vegetarian meals, pizza and beer to a hip crowd that enjoys the selection of alternative press materials and bulletin board advertisements.

La Crêperie Restaurant (☎ 719-632-0984, 204 N Tejon St) features a mouthwatering selection of dessert crepes for $3, or you can have a crepe entree for about $6. On Friday and Saturday nights, the crowd at *Panino's Restaurant* (☎ 719-635-7452, 604 N Tejon St) spills out into the street. For $5 you get homemade dough rolled with fillings of cheese, vegetables and beans or lean meats, served with a salad.

Take the kids for a handcrafted draft root beer at the *Phantom Canyon Brewing Company* (☎ 719-635-2800, 2 E Pikes Peak Ave), where fine microbrews are also on tap. The menu includes some tasty entree salads and hearty pub fare.

Howard's Bar-B-Q (☎ 719-473-7427, 114 S Sierra Madre St) dishes up killer ribs; even former president Bill Clinton stopped in for some! Early risers can sample its tasty egg-filled 'Railroad Wrap' ($2.50) for breakfast, 6 to 10 am. The *Chipotle Mexican Grill* (☎ 719-632-4311, 19 S Tejon St) does fantastic gourmet burrito wraps and other Mexican standards.

Colorado's answer to Ben & Jerry's is *Josh & John's Ice Cream* (☎ 719-632-0299, 111 E Pikes Peak Ave), located near the city bus terminal. Nearby, at the corner of Colorado and Nevada Aves, the *Olde World Bagel Bakery* (☎ 719-527-9651) whips up fresh, New York–style bagels and gourmet coffee.

The Warehouse Restaurant & Art Gallery (☎ 719-475-8880, 25 W Cimarron St) is a combination restaurant, gallery and brew pub. Microbrews are handcrafted on the premises using gravity-fed machinery (one of only three such systems in the US), and the fusion dishes are excellent.

Old Colorado City A bright, spacious eatery, *La Baguette French Bakery & Cafe* (☎ 719-577-4818, 2417 W Colorado Ave)

opens at 7 am and serves espresso. Next door, *Beau Jo's Pizza* (☎ 719-442-0270, 2415 W Colorado Ave) features a good pizza buffet, while *Bon Ton's Cafe* (☎ 719-634-1007, 2601 W Colorado Ave) serves breakfast and lunch to a casual crowd on its large patio.

The *Mason Jar* (☎ 719-632-4820, 2925 W Colorado Ave) boasts attentive service and inexpensive American fare for breakfast, lunch or dinner.

Gertrude's (☎ 719-471-0887, 2625 W Colorado Ave) offers a good choice of sandwiches, salads and pastas for lunch and dinner, with a lot of veggie options. Ditto for *Meadow Muffins* (☎ 719-633-0583, 2432 W Colorado Ave).

Entertainment

Colorado Springs has a fairly lively music and theater scene. Pick up a copy of *Go!*, a free entertainment newspaper, at the Colorado Springs visitors center.

The *Colorado Springs Sky Sox* (☎ 719-597-3000) is the Triple A minor-league farm club for the Major League Colorado Rockies. From April to September the Sky Sox play 72 home games at the Sky Sox Baseball Stadium.

Getting There & Away

Though not served by as many flights or airlines, the Colorado Springs Municipal Airport (☎ 719-550-1900) offers a viable alternative to Denver International Airport, especially if you're headed to southern Colorado destinations.

The TNM&O Bus Depot (☎ 719-635-1505) is at 120 Weber St.

Getting Around

The Yellow Cab (☎ 719-634-5000) fare from the Colorado Springs Airport to the city center is around $20 to $25.

The City Bus Terminal (☎ 719-475-9733), 127 E Kiowa St, offers schedule information and route maps for all 13 transit lines in the Colorado Springs area.

Alamo, Avis, Budget, Hertz and National all rent cars at the Colorado Springs Airport.

Call Yellow Cab for local transportation.

GARDEN OF THE GODS

With its spectacular sandstone formations, Garden of the Gods attracts some two million visitors each year and provides a scenic introduction to the geologic history of the Colorado Front Range. The most interesting way to experience the area and avoid the crowd is to take to one of the park trails, as most visitors prefer the windshield tour. Wildlife in the park includes 60 or so bighorn sheep, as well as less docile creatures like bears, bobcats and mountain lions.

Garden of the Gods is northwest of Old Colorado City, about 4½ miles west of downtown Colorado Springs on US 24. Begin your tour at the visitors center (☎ 719-634-6666) on the park's eastern border at Gateway Rd and 30th St. Here you'll see the exhibits on the natural and social history of the rock formations. Special presentations and free 45-minute ranger-led nature walks are scheduled at 10 am and 2 pm. During summer months the visitors center is open 8 am to 8 pm daily; winter hours are from 9 am to 5 pm.

Don't miss the high-tech 12-minute history and geology video presentation ($2/1 adults/children), shown every 30 minutes.

The park covers 2 sq miles and has a 7-mile, one-way driving loop. The loop road is well suited for bicyclists (with moderate climbing). Visitors also can choose to leave their cars at the visitors center and take a tram for a small fee. The closure of the road passing between Gateway Rocks allows unobstructed viewing of the famous scene toward Pikes Peak, photographed by William Henry Jackson. This route is now a trail that leads to the former Hidden Inn curio shop (where rest rooms are available), where you will see a stunning view of Cathedral Valley and possibly observe daring rock climbers in action. An option from the loop route follows Garden Dr past additional formations to another park entrance near US 24 in Manitou Springs.

Garden of the Gods is open 5 am to 11 pm (9 pm from November to March) and is artificially lit at night.

MASON FLORENCE

The gods must be crazy.

Rock Ledge Ranch

Ornithologist Dr William Slater, author of *History of the Birds of Colorado,* taught at Colorado College and built the Cape Town Dutch–style White House in 1907. Guides at the living-history site wear period dress as they show visitors around a restored 1867 homestead, working ranch and blacksmith shop. From the Garden of the Gods visitors center, take Gateway Rd and take the first left onto Ranch Rd. The Rock Ledge Ranch (☎ 719-578-6777) is open 10 am to 4 pm daily from June to December; $5.

Activities

The vertical faces of the sandstone formations are not suitable for amateur climbers. Technical climbers must follow established routes and register at the visitors center.

Academy Riding Stables (☎ 719-633-5667, 888-700-0410), on the park's south edge at 4 El Paso Blvd (see the Manitou Springs map), offers one- and two-hour rides into the park.

Web site: www.arsriding.com

MANITOU SPRINGS

A collection of seven soda-water springs (plus one particularly nasty-tasting sulfur-water spring) is located in Manitou Springs (population 5000; elevation 6500 feet), a short drive from Colorado Springs. The water has a high mineral content, and some locals prefer to drink it by mixing it with lemonade. The downtown area has a nice historical feel to it, though summer's throngs of tourists can drown it out.

Orientation & Information

Manitou Springs, founded in the narrow canyon of Fountain Creek, sits at the base of Pikes Peak on the southern border of Garden of the Gods, just west of I-25. The core historic district is along Manitou Ave near the intersection with Canon Ave.

The Manitou Springs Chamber of Commerce (☎ 719-685-5089, 800-642-2567), 354 Manitou Ave, offers friendly service and has well-organized information on local attractions, lodging and restaurants. It's open 9 am to 5 pm daily.

Web site: www.manitousprings.org

Things to See & Do

Community volunteers lead free one-hour tours of the historic mineral springs. You can contact the chamber of commerce (see above) for reservations or pick up a map and set out on your own. If you have a bike, consider taking your water bottle along to visit all eight springs on the map.

Don't miss the handsome gazebo at **Seven Minute Spring**, next to Memorial Park, or the **Ute sculpture fountain** at the Ute Chief Spring. Just upstream on Fountain Creek is the Ute Pass shelf road to the gold fields, built in 1860, that follows the old Ute Trail. From the switchback on Serpentine Rd you can follow the old route to **Rainbow Falls**, only a short distance from the paved roadway.

The **Italian Town Clock** at the intersection of Canon and Manitou Aves was a gift from Jerome Wheeler in 1899.

From the junction of Manitou and Ruxton Aves, it's a stiff climb up Ruxton Ave to the 46-room **Miramont Castle**, 9 Capital Hill Ave, built between 1892 and 1895. Tours of the castle and its exhibits are available for $4/1 adults/children.

Pikes Peak Cog Railway

Tourists have been making this trip since 1891, but newer Swiss-built trains operate like clockwork on the 3¼-hour roundtrip journey, which includes a 40-minute orientation at the top. Bring a jacket or plan on wasting your time in the summit restaurant and gift shop.

Trains leave the Cog Railway Depot (☎ 719-685-5401), 515 Ruxton Ave, daily from May to November. Ticket prices are $23.50 for adults and $12 for children. Reservations are essential.

Web site: www.cograilway.com

Places to Stay

Many of the small lodgings close for the winter, and their rates attempt to make up for it during peak summer months. But

MANITOU SPRINGS

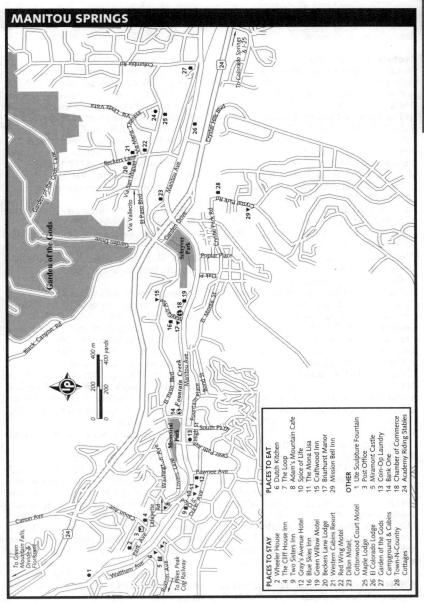

PLACES TO STAY
2 Wheeler House
4 The Cliff House Inn
9 Two Sisters Inn
12 Gray's Avenue Hotel
16 Blue Skies Inn
19 Green Willow Motel
20 Beckers Lane Lodge
21 Western Cabins Resort
22 Red Wing Motel
23 Dillon Motel;
   Cottonwood Court Motel
25 Maple Lodge
26 El Colorado Lodge
27 Garden of the Gods
   Campground & Cabins
28 Town-N-Country
   Cottages

PLACES TO EAT
6 Dutch Kitchen
7 The Loop
8 Adam's Mountain Cafe
10 Spice of Life
11 The Mona Lisa
15 Craftwood Inn
17 Briarhurst Manor
29 Mission Bell Inn

OTHER
1 Ute Sculpture Fountain
3 Post Office
5 Miramont Castle
13 Coin-Op Laundry
14 Bank One
18 Chamber of Commerce
24 Academy Riding Stables

COLORADO

prices aren't really higher than those in Colorado Springs, and the surroundings are generally more pleasant.

Motels If you want to do your own cooking, *Western Cabins Resort* (☎ 719-685-5755, 106 Beckers Lane) has fairly spacious cabins with kitchens, available as singles/doubles for $70/80.

The *Town-N-Country Cottages* (☎ 719-685-5427, 800-366-3509, 123 Crystal Park Rd) are away from the traffic on Manitou Ave and offer cozy adobe cottages and duplex-style units from $79.
Web site: www.townncountryc.com

The quiet and shady *Beckers Lane Lodge* (☎ 719-685-1866, 115 Beckers Lane) has rooms for around $45 in summer, though sometimes it takes only weekly rentals ($185 to $200). If so, the *Red Wing Motel* (☎ 719-685-5656, 800-733-9547, 56 El Paso Blvd) has plain but well-kept rooms from $50 in summer, $30 in winter.

There's a slew of motels along the heavily trafficked Manitou Ave; several feature classic, 1940s-style private carports. One of the more charming spots is *Cottonwood Court Motel* (☎ 719-685-1312, 120 Manitou Ave). Rooms are a bit small, but most are set back from the road among shade trees, and start at $50 in summer, $35 in winter. The nearby *Dillon Motel* (☎ 719-685-1139, 134 Manitou Ave) has a heated pool and similar rates. The *Maple Lodge* (☎ 719-685-9230, 9 El Paso Blvd), nestled among the pine trees, offers a variety of rooms costing $40 to $140.

A nice summer option is the cozy *Green Willow Motel* (☎ 719-685-9997, 328 Manitou Ave). Cabin-style rooms sit back from the road around a grassy courtyard area. Rooms with kitchenettes are available and rates start around $50. Historic *El Colorado Lodge* (☎ 719-685-5485, 800-782-2246, 23 Manitou Ave) is a Southwest-style motel with adobe units featuring beamed ceilings and fireplaces. Rates range from $98 to $105 in summer (from $65 in winter).

Hotels The no-smoking (and no telephones in rooms) *Wheeler House* (☎ 719-685-4100,

800-685-2399, 36 Park Ave) is peaceful and rustic. A wide range of efficiency and one- and two-bedroom units rent from $68 to $143.
Web site: www.wheelerhouse.com

Up the street, a grand, historic landmark building, *The Cliff House Inn* (☎ 719-685-3000, 888-212-7000, 306 Canon Ave), is the recent recipient of an extensive, $9 million restoration. Past guests include Teddy Roosevelt, Thomas Edison, Clark Gable and Buffalo Bill. Guests can enjoy the hotel's lavish Victorian ambiance and gourmet dining. Studios go for $119 to $189, and suites rise from $169 to $400.
Web site: www.thecliffhouse.com

B&Bs A lovely Gothic revival inn, *Blue Skies Inn* (☎ 719-685-3899, 800-398-7949, 402 Manitou Ave) has a definite artistic touch. Each room is unique – and with names like Deep Blue, Dot Matrix and Starlight, they should be. Rates range from $125 to $225.
Web site: www.blueskiesbb.com

The charming, rose-colored *Two Sisters Inn* (☎ 719-685-9684, 800-274-7466, 10 Otoe Place) dates from 1919 and features four quaint Victorian bedrooms. The congenial proprietors see to all the details.
Web site: www.twosisinn.com

Built in 1886, the three-story Queen Anne–style *Gray's Avenue Hotel* (☎ 719-685-1277, 711 Manitou Ave) offers rooms with private bath ranging from $65 to $85, including full breakfasts.
Web site: www.pikespeakmall.com/GraysB&B

Places to Eat

Inexpensive *Dutch Kitchen* (☎ 719-685-9962, 1025 Manitou Ave) has been serving its famous corned-beef sandwiches and homemade pies since 1959; closed Friday. Set in a cozy Victorian dining room, *Adam's Mountain Cafe* (☎ 719-685-4370, 110 Canon Ave) is an exceptional choice for a moderately priced lunch or dinner. It offers fabulous fusion cooking, everything from Southwestern to Asian, with an emphasis on fresh organic local ingredients and vegetarian dishes.

The Mona Lisa (☎ *719-658-0277, 733 Manitou Ave*) offers a romantic, candlelit setting and possibly the best fondue in the Rockies. You'd be wise to reserve ahead; dinner only.

Spice of Life (☎ *719-685-5284, 727 Manitou Ave*) is a cozy little cafe dealing in gourmet tea and coffee, as well as an extraordinary selection of organic spices and herbs. Specializing in California-style Mexican dishes, *The Loop* (☎ *719-685-9344, 965 Manitou Ave*) offers a few window seats opening onto the busy sidewalk. Daily lunch specials are a good deal, and dinner combination platters are also reasonable. The adobe-style *Mission Bell Inn* (☎ *719-685-9089, 178 Crystal Park Rd*) specializes in more traditional Mexican meals.

For top-end dining, superb game entrees range from wild boar to exotic caribou at the *Craftwood Inn* (☎ *719-685-9000, 404 El Paso Blvd*). The *Briarhurst Manor* (☎ *719-685-1864, 404 Manitou Ave*) offers outstanding cuisine in a masonry home built in 1876 by Dr William Bell, founder of Manitou Springs.

AROUND MANITOU SPRINGS
Pikes Peak Toll Road
From the town of Divide, west of Manitou Springs on US 24, you can drive the Pikes Peak Toll Rd to the summit. Built in 1915 by Spencer Penrose, the road is open from 7 am to 7 pm in the summer, 9 am to 3 pm the rest of the year. The trip costs $6 per person. Road conditions and directions are available by calling ☎ 719-635-7506 or ☎ 719-684-9383.

Green Mountain Falls
Bypassed by the new US 24 alignment, the town of Green Mountain Falls (population 700) is on the old highway. Its imposing wooden **Church in the Wildwood**, with a bell tower and elaborate stained glass, dates from 1889 – few wooden structures of such antiquity have avoided fire in this area. A 3-mile loop hike from the small lake, the central focus of the town, leads to **Catamount Falls** and **Crystal Falls**. A trail map is available from a booth at the lake.

Near the lake, the *Pine Gables Tavern* (☎ *719-684-2555*) has a rustic mountain atmosphere and offers live entertainment on Friday and Saturday nights. At the upper end of the lake, the *Pantry Restaurant* has earned a reputation for good breakfasts. It's conveniently located next to the peaceful *Falls Motel* (☎ *719-684-9745*), which has doubles from $50 in summer, $40 in winter. Amenities include an outdoor hot tub and a picnic area.

FLORISSANT FOSSIL BEDS NATIONAL MONUMENT
In 1873, Dr AC Peale, part of the USGS Hayden expedition, was on his way to survey and map the South Park area, when he reputedly discovered these ancient lake deposits, which were buried by the dust and ash from a series of volcanic eruptions. The highlight of the site is the ancient, enormous **petrified tree stumps**. Subsequent excavations revealed some 1200 insect species and 150 plant species, plus several fish, birds and small mammal species, including the tapirlike oreodont and the mesohippo. In 1969 the triumvirate of renowned paleobotanist Dr Estella Leopold, wildflower authority Dr Beatrice Willard and activist Vim Crane Wright succeeded in gaining national monument protection for the fossils of 35 million-year-old Lake Florissant.

Orientation & Information
The monument is located about 35 miles west of Colorado Springs via US 24. The place to start is the visitors center (☎ 719-748-3253), in the center of the monument on Teller County Rd 1, 2 miles south of US 24. Museum-quality fossil exhibits are on display, and rangers provide guides to nearby trails and conduct daily interpretive programs. Special presentations and guided walks are scheduled each summer – call ahead for a calendar of events. It's open 8 am to 7 pm daily from Memorial Day to Labor Day; otherwise, 8 am to 4:30 pm. Admission is $2 per individual older than 16 years of age, or $4 for three or more in a family.

Hornbeck House

Adeline Hornbeck settled the first 160-acre homestead in the valley in 1878 with her four children. The outbuildings include a bunkhouse, carriage shed, barn and root cellar. All of the buildings have been restored or rebuilt by the NPS.

Florissant Heritage Museum

The striking old Grange Hall, with its bell tower, schoolhouse and outhouse, sits in a field of flowers next to US 24 in Florissant. The 'museum' is rarely open, but it really doesn't matter – it's just pretty to look at. Nearby, the mound-shaped rock formation at Fortification Hill was a favorite Ute campsite.

Hiking

The park has 14 miles of trails through open meadows and rolling hills – all can be reached on foot from the visitors center. No one should miss the **Walk Through Time Nature Trail**, a half-mile loop. The 1-mile **Petrified Forest Loop** leads to several petrified stumps, including the remains of a giant sequoia measuring 38 feet in circumference. Interpretive brochures are available for both trails.

Signs of deer and elk often are seen along the southeastern segment of the **Hornbeck Wildlife Loop**, which crosses the highway in front of the visitors center. After a mile it intersects **Shootin' Star Trail**, which leads to the Barksdale Picnic area, near Lower Twin Rock Rd.

Between late June and mid-August, visitors make special trips to Florissant (French for 'blooming') for ranger-guided walks held at 10:30 am Friday. Admire, but please don't pick.

Places to Stay

No overnight stays are allowed in the monument. The nearest accommodations are in Lake George (4 miles west) and Woodland Park (15 miles east). Both towns are located on US 24. In Lake George the *11 Mile Motel* (☎ *719-748-3931, 38122 US 24*) has cabins with mountain views from around $60 in summer, $50 in winter. *Elwell's Guest Cabins* (☎ *719-687-9838, 2220 Lee Circle Dr),* in Woodland Park, has five cabins spread over 5 acres. Rates start at $75.

PUEBLO

Once considered the Pittsburgh of the West, Pueblo was based on a smokestack economy that waned after WWII. Whereas Pueblo (elevation 4695 feet) was Colorado's second-largest city during the first half of the 20th century, its present population of 104,000 makes it only the sixth largest. Pueblo hosts the Colorado State Fair from mid-August to Labor Day. Other notable events each year include bluegrass music performances during **Bluegrass on the River** in May. Cinco de Mayo (May 5th) is a lively time to be in town. Local attractions include the recently completed Riverwalk of Pueblo – a 26-acre waterfront park in the Union Avenue Historic District – and a few museums, but there is little more to attract visitors – for most, Pueblo is just a place to overnight after a long day on the road.

Orientation

Downtown Pueblo's jumbled street pattern is the result of the consolidation of four separate towns. Santa Fe Ave is the north-south commercial artery. From downtown, Union Ave takes a diagonal path southwest across the Arkansas River to the Mesa Junction area.

Pueblo is 112 miles south of Denver at the crossroads of I-25 and US 50.

Information

The Pueblo Chamber of Commerce (☎ 719-542-1704, 800-233-3446), 302 N Santa Fe Ave, can provide maps, lodging information and walking-tour directions 8 am to 5 pm weekdays.

Web site: www.pueblo.org

The USFS headquarters office (☎ 719-545-8737) for the Pike and San Isabel National Forests is north of US 50 at 1920 Valley Dr. This is a good place to get maps, wilderness hiking gear and camping information for the forests of Colorado's southern Front Range.

Battle of Cuerno Verde

Recorded history of the Pueblo area begins with the battle of Cuerno Verde (Green Horn) on September 2, 1779. The Comanche tribe had acquired firearms from French trappers in the first half of the 18th century to strike fear into other tribes, as well as into the Spanish. In fact, the Ute word *komantica* (Comanche) means 'constant adversary.' Comanche raiders drove the Apache from the plains and battled Utes for horses and control of the Arkansas River basin. In the 1760s New Mexican pueblos and Spanish colonies also suffered from fierce Comanche raids, led by a daring chief the Spaniards called Cuerno Verde.

Juan Bautista de Anza, appointed governor of New Mexico in 1777 after founding San Francisco, vowed to stop the raids. De Anza left Santa Fe in August 1779 with a force of 600 mounted men consisting of some regular soldiers, but mostly Spanish and Pueblo community volunteers. Seeking to surprise, they headed north into the San Luis Valley before turning east toward the plains. On the way they defeated a small band of Comanche and learned from captives that Cuerno Verde was returning from a raid in New Mexico to a camp south of the Arkansas River, below present Greenhorn Mountain. Ute and Apache warriors anxious to combat the Comanche reportedly joined de Anza's corps in ambushing the returning Comanche party. With numerical superiority, the Spaniards killed Cuerno Verde and his son, along with four of his war chiefs, a medicine man and a number of warriors. Although several years passed before the Spanish formally negotiated peace with the Comanche, de Anza's work led to a generation of stability.

Accounts differ about how Cuerno Verde was named. One story suggests the Spanish called the leader of the raids Cuerno Verde because he wore a green-painted buffalo-horn headdress. Another legend claims that the young chief earned the name because he was fearless, like the young bull elk when his antlers are still green. His nickname lives on in nearby Greenhorn Mountain and Greenhorn Creek, both named after the battle.

The Pueblo Bank & Trust (☎ 719-545-1834), in the central district at 301 W 5th St, and Wells Fargo Bank (☎ 719-544-5090), at 201 W 8th St, have ATMs. The midtown post office is at 1005 W 4 St, and the zip code is 81003.

Just north of the central area, Parkview Episcopal Medical Center (☎ 719-584-4000), 400 W 16th St, provides 24-hour emergency services.

Rosemont Museum

Pueblo's premier historic attraction is the three-story, 37-room Victorian mansion, constructed in 1893 of pink rhyolite stone. It contains elaborate stained glass and elegant, original furnishings. The top floor features an Egyptian mummy and other assorted booty from Andrew McClelland's global travels during the early 20th century.

The Rosemont Museum (☎ 719-545-5290), 419 W 14th St at Grand Ave, is open 10 am to 3:30 pm Tuesday to Saturday and 2 to 3:30 pm Sunday June through August. The remainder of the year, with the exception of January, when it's closed for the entire month, it's open 1 to 3:30 pm Tuesday to Saturday and 2 to 3:30 pm Sunday. Admission is $5, with discounts for seniors and children.

Other Museums

El Pueblo Museum (☎ 719-583-0453), 324 W 1st St, houses historical exhibits representing the crossroads of culture and rich, diverse heritage in the region, including Indian and Mexican life. It's open 10 am to 4:30 pm Monday to Saturday; $2/1 adults/children.

The delightful Buell Children's Museum (☎ 719-543-0130) at the Sangre de Cristo

COLORADO

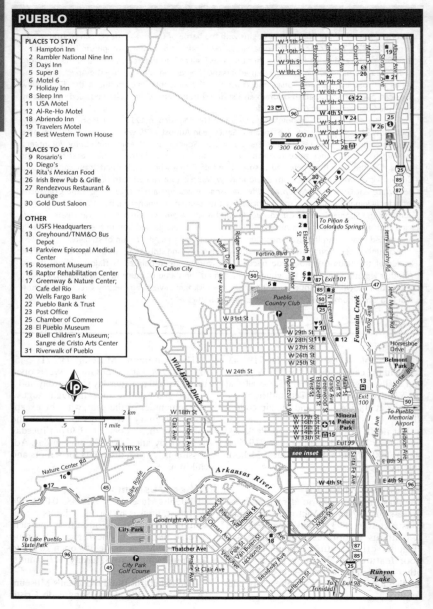

PUEBLO

PLACES TO STAY
1 Hampton Inn
2 Rambler National Nine Inn
3 Days Inn
5 Super 8
6 Motel 6
7 Holiday Inn
8 Sleep Inn
11 USA Motel
12 Al-Re-Ho Motel
18 Abriendo Inn
19 Travelers Motel
21 Best Western Town House

PLACES TO EAT
9 Rosario's
10 Diego's
24 Rita's Mexican Food
26 Irish Brew Pub & Grille
27 Rendezvous Restaurant & Lounge
30 Gold Dust Saloon

OTHER
4 USFS Headquarters
13 Greyhound/TNM&O Bus Depot
14 Parkview Episcopal Medical Center
15 Rosemont Museum
16 Raptor Rehabilitation Center
17 Greenway & Nature Center; Cafe del Rio
20 Wells Fargo Bank
22 Pueblo Bank & Trust
23 Post Office
25 Chamber of Commerce
28 El Pueblo Museum
29 Buell Children's Museum; Sangre de Cristo Arts Center
31 Riverwalk of Pueblo

Arts Center beside the chamber of commerce, is a technical marvel and an excellent hands-on place to visit if you're traveling with kids. Open 11 am to 4 pm Monday to Saturday; $4/3.

Greenway & Nature Center

Riverside trails, reptile displays, picnic and playground areas and a raptor center attract visitors to the Greenway & Nature Center (☎ 719-549-2414), 5200 Nature Center Rd, beneath the cottonwoods on the Arkansas River. Particularly interesting is the Raptor Rehabilitation Center (☎ 719-549-2327), 4828 Nature Center Rd, which was started in 1981 to assist the Dept of Wildlife in rehabilitating injured birds of prey.

Visitors are welcome to stop by between dawn and dusk Tuesday to Saturday, as well as Sunday from Memorial Day to Labor Day; the offices and rest rooms are open only from 9 am to 5 pm. The Raptor Rehabilitation Center is open 11 am to 4 pm Tuesday to Sunday year-round. The turnoff for Nature Center Rd is 3 miles west of downtown, north of the Pueblo Ave Bridge.

Places to Stay

You will need to make a room reservation during the state fair in late August and early September, when rates can soar above those quoted below.

Camping At its Northern Plains campground, *Lake Pueblo State Park* (☎ 719-561-9320, 800-678-2267 for reservations) offers fully developed campsites that include flush toilets, showers and laundry facilities. It's accessible from the North Gate entrance and the Arkansas Point Campground, off Hwy 96 south of the Pueblo dam. Sites with electric hookups cost $14 and are closed in winter. Primitive sites are also available on the north side for $6. Camping fees do not include the park's daily admission pass of $4. Reservations may be needed in summer. The state park headquarters is located just north of Hwy 96 (4th St in the city) about 13 miles west of I-25 exit 101.

Motels For those who don't mind the blaring roar of I-25, *Al-Re-Ho Motel* (☎ 719-542-5135, 2424 N Freeway) offers rooms from $25. Rooms at the *Travelers Motel* (☎ 719-543-5451, 1012 N Santa Fe Ave) aren't very cheerful, but with rates like $31/36 for singles/doubles, it's hard to beat.

Along US 50 W at the junction with I-25 (exit 101) is a string of national franchise motels, including *Motel 6* (☎ 719-543-6221, 4103 N Elizabeth St), with singles/doubles for $35/41. Rooms start at $40/45 at the *Rambler National Nine Inn* (☎ 719-543-4173, 4400 N Elizabeth St). The *Super 8* (☎ 719-545-4104, 1100 US 50 W) rents rooms from $36/42; the *Days Inn* (☎ 719-543-8031, 4201 N Elizabeth St) charges $60/65. The relatively upscale *Sleep Inn* (☎ 719-583-4000, 3626 N Freeway) is a good value at around $60/70. The latter two motels have swimming pools.

The *USA Motel* (☎ 719-542-3268, 414 W 29th St) is a friendly spot with an outdoor pool and rooms for $45/50. Rooms cost $50/55 at the central *Best Western Town House* (☎ 719-543-6530, 730 N Santa Fe Ave).

Hotels & B&Bs Rooms at the *Holiday Inn* (☎ 719-543-8050, 4001 N Elizabeth St) are around $100/80 during summer/winter. Facilities include an indoor swimming pool and sauna, cafe and sports bar. Rates are similar at the *Hampton Inn* (☎ 719-544-4700, 4701 N Freeway); a Continental breakfast comes with the clean and comfortable, but otherwise utilitarian, rooms.

Hang out on the veranda at the elegant *Abriendo Inn* (☎ 719-544-2703, 300 W Abriendo Ave). All seven rooms in this mansion, built in 1906 by the owner of Walter's Brewery, have private baths. Rates start at $69 and increase to $125 for rooms with whirlpool tubs.

Places to Eat

Those staying on motel row (US 50 W and I-25) are faced with choosing among various national chain eateries. However, a short hike down to *Rosario's* (☎ 719-583-1823, 2930 N Elizabeth St) will reward you with an excellent Italian lunch or dinner.

Nearby, *Diego's* (☎ 719-744-0414, 2928 N Elizabeth St) is a stylish Mexican eatery with creative dishes; try the tasty lime chipotle smoked-salmon quesadilla ($7). For a more casual scene, try the hearty, home-style meals at *Rita's Mexican Food* (☎ 719-542-4820, 302 N Grand Ave). Combination platters for around $5 are enormous.

Since 1944 the *Irish Brew Pub & Grille* (☎ 719-542-9974, 108 W 3rd St) has been anything but a traditional Irish pub. Until 11 pm nightly it serves excellent minestrone soup for about $3, in addition to full gourmet meals for $7 to $15.

Gold Dust Saloon (☎ 719-545-0741, 217 S Union Ave) is a popular dig for hearty sandwiches and salads and Pueblo's best burgers. Locals recommend the *Rendezvous Restaurant & Lounge* (☎ 719-542-2247, 218 W 2nd St) for more upscale lunches and dinners.

For a patio lunch shaded by huge cottonwoods on the Arkansas River, go to the excellent *Cafe del Rio* (☎ 719-549-2009), a Southwest-adobe-style restaurant at the end of Nature Center Rd at the Nature Center.

Getting There & Away

Pueblo Memorial Airport (☎ 719-948-3355) is 8 miles east of central Pueblo on US 50/Hwy 96. United Express offers daily commuter flights to Denver and Alamosa.

The Greyhound/TNM&O bus depot (☎ 719-543-2775) is at 1080 Chinook Lane, near I-25 exit 100.

Getting Around

The Pueblo Transit System (☎ 719-542-4306) provides weekday commuter service every 30 minutes on seven routes depicted on a map in the telephone directory.

At Pueblo Memorial Airport, rental cars are available from Avis, Budget and Hertz.

City Cab Company (☎ 719-543-2525) provides local transportation.

LA VETA

La Veta (population 800, elevation 6100 feet) is the gateway to the Cuchara Valley and the Spanish Peaks' Great Dikes, from which the town takes its Spanish name, meaning 'the vein.' From the streets of this tiny town visitors can admire the scenic Spanish Peaks. Artists and writers have been drawn to La Veta's splendor; their works are featured at the cooperative gallery and in local theater performances by the Fort Francisco Players.

Orientation & Information

It would take effort to get lost in La Veta – its compass-oriented grid is divided by north-south Main St (Hwy 12). Most businesses are at the north end near the old narrow-gauge railroad. The Cucharas River flows along the western edge of town just a block west of Main St.

The La Veta/Cuchara Chamber of Commerce (☎ 719-742-3676), 131 E Ryus Ave, is on the web at www.ruralwideweb.com. Visitors to the office are greeted with a display of local artists' work and offered maps and information 10 am to 4 pm weekdays. The San Isabel National Forest Ranger Station (☎ 719-742-3681), 103 E Field St, has maps and information on hiking near the Great Dikes of the Spanish Peaks and Culebra Range.

Fort Francisco Museum

Partially surrounding the town's original plaza are the Spanish-style adobe fort buildings built in 1862. Additional buildings on the museum grounds house coal-mining exhibits, a school, a blacksmith shop, a post office and a saloon.

An exhibit on 1914's Ludlow Massacre (see 'Ludlow Massacre Monument,' later) shows how mine owners and state militia made life miserable for the foreign-born laborers who came to work in the coal mines. The exhibit features a rare display of Penitente carved and painted religious items, known as *santos,* which provide an opportunity to understand this locally important aspect of Mexican-American culture.

A gift shop sells souvenirs and local crafts. Fort Francisco Museum is open 10 am to 4 pm Wednesday to Saturday, 1 to 4 pm Sunday from Memorial Day to Oktoberfest weekend; $2/1.

The Gallery

More than two dozen artists display paintings, pottery, glasswork and weavings at The Gallery (☎ 719-742-3074), 132 W Ryus St, built in 1983 by the Friends of the Art Guild as a cooperative exhibition space for local artists. It's open 10 am to 3 pm Tuesday to Saturday and is a two-minute walk east of La Veta Inn.

Bicycling & Horseback Riding

Between Walsenburg and north La Veta Pass (9413 feet), Hwy 160 has a good shoulder for bicyclists. Old La Veta Pass is a 4-mile-long alternative that's also worth exploring. From just west of the pass, mountain bicyclists can experience a long descent down Pass Creek Pass north to lodging at Malachite, about 12 miles from Hwy 160. The total La Veta–Malachite distance is 27 miles. From Malachite you can ride to hiking trailheads leading west through the Sangre de Cristo Wilderness to Great Sand Dunes National Monument.

Shorter mountain-bike rides near La Veta include a 4-mile trip beside the Cucharas River on Valley Rd northeast of town; a visit to Sulfur Springs and nearby trails, 4 miles southwest of town past the Goemmer Butte volcanic plug on Huerfano County Rd 420; and a climb to the Wahatoya Camp, where the trail to the Spanish Peaks begins. To reach Wahatoya Camp, which is 6 miles south of La Veta, from Hwy 12 south of town, turn left on Huerfano County Rd 361 and go 1 mile. Then turn left on County Rd 360 a short distance across School Creek and turn right 5 miles from the trailhead.

Dark Horse Outfitters (☎ 719-742-3652) offers an 'Elk Express' horseback ride including tag games and galloping up to an elk ranch north of La Veta. Half- and full-day rides into the mountains are also available.

Special Events

During the 4th of July weekend the **Art in the Park** festival includes booths, food and entertainment. Nearby Cuchara holds the **Cuchara Hermosa Art Festival** on the last weekend in July. Another regional art and

brew festival, **Oktoberfest**, is held in La Veta on the first Saturday in October.

Places to Stay

The congenial owner of *Circle the Wagons* (☎ 719-742-3233, 124 N Main St), at the north edge of La Veta, offers tent sites and RV hookups for $20. If you need just a shower after a day on the trail, it costs $3. He also rents out singles/doubles for $40/50 in spacious, immaculate double-wide mobile homes.

Posada de Sol y Sombra (☎ 719-742-3159, 113 W Virginia) is a short walk from the center of activity and offers two home-style rooms with shared bath for $45/50. The owners of **Hunter House** (☎ 719-742-5577, 115 W Grand St) do their best to cater to guests' recreation and dietary needs. They have three rooms starting at $70.

Charming *La Veta Inn* (☎ 719-742-3700, 103 W Ryus St) has 18 uniquely decorated rooms with private bath that rent for $70 a double.
Web site: www.lavetainn.com

Places to Eat

You can get started with a hearty breakfast burrito at *La Veta Inn* (see above); it also serves excellent home-cooked lunches and dinners. The neighboring *Ryus Avenue Bakery* (☎ 719-742-3830) has scones, muffins and sandwiches on Tuesday, Thursday and Saturday mornings.

Silver Spoon Restaurant (☎ 719-742-3764, 16984 Hwy 12) is a place for fine rural dining. It does great steaks, chicken, seafood and pasta dishes. In the summer you can eat outdoors on its 'river island.'

Entertainment

Since 1979 the Fort Francisco Players (☎ 719-742-3676) have staged performances at the *Fort Francisco Center for the Performing Arts*, a 100-year-old theater.

Getting There & Away

La Veta is 19 miles west of I-25 via US 160 and Hwy 12. The Great Sand Dunes National Monument in the San Luis Valley lies 74 miles east over La Veta Pass via US 160.

COLORADO

AROUND LA VETA
Great Dikes of the Spanish Peaks

Some of the Kapota band of the Ute tribe aptly expressed their infatuation with the striking volcanic Spanish Peaks southeast of La Veta by regarding them as 'breasts of the earth.' Spanish and American travelers relied on these twin sentinels to guide their approach to the Front Range across the eastern Great Plains.

On closer inspection, you'll find hundreds of magnificent rock walls radiating like fins from the peaks. Called 'dikes,' they were formed from fissures surrounding the volcanic core, where molten rock was injected into the earth's crust and cast into solid rock as it cooled. Subsequent erosion has exposed the dikes, leaving a peculiar landscape of abrupt perpendicular rock formations protruding from the earth.

For an opportunity to see wildlife and wildflowers instead of cattle, you can explore the Great Dikes of the Spanish Peaks on foot by following the Wahatoya Trail (USFS Trail 1304) along the saddle between the East and West Spanish Peaks. The trailhead begins at Wahatoya Camp, 6 miles south of La Veta on Huerfano County Rd 360, or from the road over scenic Cordova Pass (11,743 feet). Cordova Pass is on USFS Rd 415, 6 miles east of Cucharas Pass on Hwy 12, 17 miles south of La Veta. Trail information, maps and a wildflower brochure are available at the USFS ranger station in La Veta (☎ 719-742-3681).

Cuchara

On Hwy 12, 11 miles south of La Veta, Cuchara (elevation 8650 feet) is a charming Old West–style, one-street hamlet that comes to life in winter when it serves patrons of the nearby Cuchara Mountain Ski Resort (☎ 877-282-4272); get skiing information at www.cuchara.com. Aside from the post office and a few shops, there's the nicely appointed **Cuchara Inn** (☎ 719-742-3685), with rooms from $75 to $160. A quieter bet is the nearby **River's Edge B&B** (☎ 719-742-5169, rebb@rmi.net), a cozy wooden building with a delightful riverside

setting and very friendly owners; visit www.ruralwideweb.com/rebb.htm. Comfortable rooms feature log beds and cost $85 to $138.

Pizza, steaks, booze and occasional live entertainment attract revelers and their dogs to the **Boardwalk Saloon** (☎ 719-742-3450). At the other end of the spectrum, **The Timbers** (☎ 719-742-3838) is an upscale restaurant somewhat modeled on La Veta's food-art-music theme.

Monument Park

Evergreen forests surround Monument Park, 29 miles south of La Veta and 36 miles west of Trinidad on Hwy 12. The park is named for a rock formation rising from the waters of an attractive mountain reservoir. Numerous summer activities are offered, including fishing on the trout-stocked lake, horseback riding and mountain biking. A $4 park entrance fee is charged.

Trailheads at nearby USFS campgrounds lead to Trinchera Peak (13,517 feet). North of Monument Park on Hwy 12, turn left (west) onto USFS Rd 411 to the trailhead at **Purgatoire Campground** (9700 feet), where USFS Trail 1309 leads to the peak about 6 miles away. Another shorter trail from **Blue Lake Campground** (10,500 feet) involves less climbing; it's reached by USFS Rd 413 north of Cucharas Pass.

The popular **Monument Lake Resort** (☎ 719-868-2226, 800-845-8006, 4789 Hwy 12) has $10 campsites for RVs and tents, as well as showers and coin-op laundry. Southwestern furnishings distinguish the lodge rooms and cabins, which can be rented from $63 to $83. The resort's restaurant serves well-prepared, home-style American food. The **Road to Ruin Bar** features live entertainment and dancing on Friday and Saturday nights. The resort is closed in winter. West of the resort, the San Isabel National Forest (☎ 719-742-3681) offers five primitive **campgrounds** on the flanks of the Sangre de Cristo range.

TRINIDAD

Trinidad (population 9800; elevation 6025 feet) sits on the Purgatoire River where it flows down from the heights of the Sangre de Cristo Mountains out to the Eastern Plains. The town's past is documented in several good museums and on the brick-paved streets in **Corazon de Trinidad**, the 'heart' of downtown, which has been designated a National Historic District. Visitors will also find Trinidad a good place to pick up on the outstanding scenery of the upper Purgatoire River and Cucharas Pass (elevation 9994 feet) in the San Isabel National Forest. History buffs might consider spending a day or two to take in the museums, but outdoor enthusiasts will probably want to keep heading west.

Trinidad is also unofficially credited with being the sex-change capital of the USA. However, you won't find much

---

Ludlow Massacre Monument

Cruel tragedy visited the Ludlow coal miners' camp, 12 miles northwest of Trinidad, during the early 20th century. Feudal working conditions in the Huerfano and Las Animas County coal mines led John Lawson and Mary Harris 'Mother' Jones to make demands in Trinidad for union recognition, wage scales and eight-hour workdays. The mine owners refused to meet these demands, prompting workers to call a strike on September 23, 1913, against domination by the Colorado Fuel & Iron Company and others. The mining companies evicted the mostly foreign-born miners from company housing, and the displaced laborers formed large tent colonies. Some 1200 people ended up in the Ludlow tent colony. As the strike wore on, tempers flared into violent clashes between striking workers and mine guards. Governor Elias Ammons called on the Colorado National Guard to help quell the clashes.

The militia sided with the mine guards. One individual in particular, Lieutenant Linderfelt, openly demonstrated his bitterness and on April 20, 1914, a battle between Linderfelt's troops and strikers erupted, causing Ludlow residents to seek shelter from government machine guns and rifles. The militia ransacked and burned the tent city.

While the town was under militia guard, three strikers were killed, including Louis Tikas, leader of the Greek workers. Huddled amid the charred rubble were the bodies of two women and 11 children – victims of asphyxiation.

Inquiries by President Woodrow Wilson's US Commission on Industrial Relations found that the Colorado National Guard had been misused as 'an instrument of suppression maintained for the purpose of intimidating and crushing workmen who go on strike.' In a court-martial, however, Linderfelt was merely demoted in rank. Strikers did not return to work until December and their grievances were still unresolved. However, federal and state legislation eventually led to protection of workers from abuses like those suffered in the southern Colorado coal mines.

The monument at Ludlow, 1 mile west of I-25 exit 27, was dedicated by the United Mine Workers in 1918 to tell the story of this tragic chapter in American labor history.

Mary Harris 'Mother' Jones

gender swapping among the local population, only at the local physicians' cash-only practices.

Orientation

The Purgatoire River marks the division between the old Corazon de Trinidad south of the river and the grid plan to the north. The railroad and elevated I-25 further accentuate this division. Although the Corazon was established as a grid incorporating the Catholic Church and Santa Fe Trail (now Main St or US 350), the hilly terrain and river together create an interesting – and sometimes confusing – street pattern.

Main St is reached by I-25 exit 13B and is divided between east and west addresses at Commercial St, which crosses the river to the rail depot.

Trinidad is only 14 miles north of the border with New Mexico at Raton Pass and about 200 miles south of Denver on I-25.

The town is at the junction of Hwy 12 (designated the Scenic Hwy of Legends), leading into the Sangre de Cristo Mountains, and US 350, the historic Mountain Branch of the Santa Fe Trail.

Information

The Trinidad–Las Animas County Chamber of Commerce (☎ 719-846-9285) shares space with the Colorado Welcome Center at 309 Nevada Ave, near I-25 exit 14A; it's open 8 am to 6 pm daily (5 pm in winter). Guides to the Corazon de Trinidad National Historic District and hundreds of other maps and brochures to help plan your stay or entire Colorado vacation are handed out at no cost.

Web site: www.trinidadco.com

The post office is at 301 E Main St. Email access is free at the Carnegie Public Library (corner of Church and Animas Sts).

Bob's Books (☎ 719-846-3672), 249 N Commercial St, is open from 9 am to noon

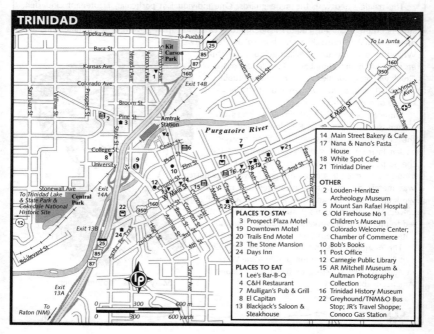

TRINIDAD

PLACES TO STAY
3   Prospect Plaza Motel
19 Downtown Motel
20 Trails End Motel
23 The Stone Mansion
24 Days Inn

PLACES TO EAT
1   Lee's Bar-B-Q
4   C&H Restaurant
7   Mulligan's Pub & Grill
8   El Capitan
13 Blackjack's Saloon & Steakhouse

14 Main Street Bakery & Cafe
17 Nana & Nano's Pasta House
18 White Spot Cafe
21 Trinidad Diner

OTHER
2   Louden-Henritze Archeology Museum
5   Mount San Rafael Hospital
6   Old Firehouse No 1 Children's Museum
9   Colorado Welcome Center; Chamber of Commerce
10 Bob's Books
11 Post Office
12 Carnegie Public Library
15 AR Mitchell Museum & Aultman Photography Collection
16 Trinidad History Museum
22 Greyhound/TNM&O Bus Stop; JR's Travel Shoppe; Conoco Gas Station

Monday to Saturday and 1 to 5:30 pm 'most of the time,' as the sign says.

The Mount San Rafael Hospital (☎ 719-846-9213), 410 Benedicta Ave, is south of E Main St (US 350).

Trinidad History Museum

If you're going to pick one museum to visit in Trinidad, make it this one. Two of Trinidad's most prominent families, the Bacas and the Blooms, lived in these homes overlooking the Santa Fe Trail; together the buildings are operated by the Colorado Historical Society as a complex that includes the Pioneer Museum.

Informed tour guides will show you through the houses and discuss local history. The museum complex (☎ 719-846-7217), 300 E Main St, is open 10 am to 4 pm daily Memorial Day to Labor Day; $4/2. During the rest of the year call for appointments.

For a closer look at Trinidad's natural history, head for the free **Louden-Henritze Archeology Museum** (☎ 719-846-5508), on the Trinidad State campus.

AR Mitchell Museum

Cowboy artist and illustrator Arthur Roy Mitchell contributed to the romantic image of the American West with his leathery cowboy characters created for pulp fiction. Mitchell (1889–1977) painted more than 160 covers for Western action and adventure magazines, most during the 1920s and 1930s. Mitchell's illustrations and oil paintings are featured here along with his contemporaries' works.

The museum also houses the **Aultman Photo Collection**. Oliver E Aultman established his photo studio in Trinidad in 1889. His photos captured the life and struggles of early residents, depicting the broad ethnic diversity that characterized Trinidad from the late 1800s onward.

The AR Mitchell Museum and the Aultman collection (☎ 719-846-4224) are at 150 E Main St. An added highlight is the **Hispanic Folk Art Exhibit**. The museum is open 10 am to 4 pm Monday to Saturday, April through September; $2.

Old Firehouse No 1 Children's Museum

Old Firehouse No 1 (☎ 719-846-8220), built in the 1880s at 314 N Commercial St, also housed city officials upstairs and criminals in the dungeonlike jail cells in the basement. Horse-drawn fire-fighting equipment and a fire truck are the museum's highlights. In addition, a model train depicts the railroad system in Las Animas County. The Children's Museum is open noon to 4 pm Monday to Saturday, June through August; free.

Special Events

A country-music showdown is featured at the **Santa Fe Trail Festival**, held over a weekend in early June. The **Las Animas County Fair** in late August and early September is a week of rodeo, cowboy poetry, music and dancing capped off by the **Labor Day Parade**.

Places to Stay

Trinidad is a popular spot for overnight stays, and peak summer rates often remain in effect until October as demand warrants. The closest tent camping is off Hwy 12 in Trinidad State Park (see Around Trinidad, later).

Motels One of the better choices in town is the ***Trails End Motel*** (☎ *719-846-4425, 616 E Main St),* which offers convenient access to downtown. Rooms with handmade Southwestern-style furniture are $33/40 single/double. The ***Prospect Plaza Motel*** (☎ *719-846-4422, 416 State St)* charges $38 for basic rooms. The ***Downtown Motel*** (☎ *719-846-3341, 526 E Main St)* has rooms from $42 ($32 in winter).

Near I-25 exit 13B and the foot of W Main St, the ***Days Inn*** (☎ *719-846-2271)* has rooms facing away from the freeway for $84 in summer ($62 in winter). Facilities include a pool, spa, exercise room, restaurant and coin-op laundry.

At the ***Holiday Inn*** (☎ *719-846-4491),* south of town off I-25 exit 11, rooms start around $100 in summer. Among the amenities are a heated indoor pool and a hot tub and exercise room. Also south of town, a landmark oil derrick marks the picnic area at the **Budget Host Inn Trinidad** (☎ 719-846-3307, 10301 Santa Fe Trail Dr), at I-25 exit 11. It features coin-op laundry and rooms starting at $46/53 in summer ($33/40 in winter).

B&Bs An elegant Victorian shingle-style building, **The Stone Mansion** (☎ 719-845-1625, 877-264-4279, 212 E 2nd St) was completed in 1904. Tastefully decorated with period furniture and museum-quality oil paintings, the inn offers comfortable guest rooms and public areas. Rooms cost $75 with shared bath, $90/95 with a private bath.

Places to Eat
The excellent **Main Street Bakery & Cafe** (☎ 719-846-8779, 121 W Main St) serves excellent fresh breads and pastries, deli sandwiches, pizzas, pastas and salads. The $3 breakfast specials are a good value.

At the **C&H Restaurant** (☎ 719-846-3851, 443 N Commercial St), if you start the day at 6 am with a veggie omelet for $5, you'll need to burn plenty of calories before returning for lunch to eat a humongous 'All Day Burger.' Good Mexican lunch entrees and killer green chili are also available at low prices.

Mulligan's Pub & Grill (☎ 719-846-1400, 516 Elm St), in the old Elm St Depot, makes an interesting choice for a burger, a juicy slab of prime rib or some ultra-spicy buffalo wings.

Take a step back to the 1950s at the **White Spot Cafe** (☎ 719-846-9957, 500 E Main St), a refurbished neon-lit roadside diner open for all meals, with your choice of counter seating or vinyl booths. A bit farther out is the **Trinidad Diner** (☎ 719-846-7798, 734 E Main St), which offers Greek gyros in addition to burgers and sandwiches for less than $5. Yet another popular drive-in cafe is **Lee's Bar-B-Q** (☎ 719-846-7621, 825 San Pedro Ave), across from Kit Carson Park. Choose from curb service, inside tables or takeout orders. Grill your own steak or seafood in an 1890 saloon atmosphere at **Blackjack's Saloon & Steakhouse** (☎ 719-846-9501, 225 W Main St).

Italian entrees are featured at **Nana & Nano's Pasta House** (☎ 719-846-2696, 418 E Main), open for dinner Tuesday to Saturday. You can choose between Italian or Mexican dishes for lunch and dinner at **El Capitan** (☎ 719-846-9903, 321 State St).

If you're driving out of town on Hwy 12 toward the lake, in about a mile look for **Bob & Earl's**, famous for its breakfast burritos and green chili.

Getting There & Away
Greyhound/TNM&O buses stop at JR's Travel Shoppe (☎ 719-846-6390), 639 W Main St, a Conoco gas station near I-25 exit 13B.

Amtrak's Southwest Chief passes through Trinidad on its daily Chicago–Los Angeles route.

AROUND TRINIDAD
Trinidad Lake & State Park
Three miles west of the city off Hwy 12, Trinidad State Park (☎ 719-846-6951) sits on a bluff above the Purgatoire River downstream from the reservoir dam. Facilities here include tent pads, fire rings, rest rooms and drinking water. There are additional campsites about a mile west of the dam at **Carpios Ridge Campground** (☎ 800-678-2267 for reservations) that have flush toilets, showers and coin laundry, along with 62 sites for RVs ($16) and tents ($10). Hiking, wildlife viewing, an interpretive nature trail, fishing and boating on the reservoir are available. Vehicle passes cost $4 per day.

Campfire Programs Events at the amphitheater on Carpios Ridge feature local speakers and slide presentations during the summer on weekend evenings. Check the Friday issue of Trinidad's Chronicle-News 'Focus' section for scheduled speakers. Admission is free, but a state-park day pass is required for each vehicle entering the park.

Hiking The 5-mile trail from Carpios Ridge to Cokedale National Historic Site passes a site where Utes once camped and left tepee rings. On the south side of the reservoir, **Long's Canyon Watchable Wildlife Area** is a good place to view many species, including mule deer, collared lizards, cottontail rabbits, hummingbirds and coyotes. You can reach Longs Canyon by the 2½-mile South Shore Trail from the picnic grounds on the south side of the reservoir.

Cokedale National Historic Site

Remnants of 350 coke ovens that once lit the night sky sit beside Hwy 12, 7 miles west of Trinidad. Cokedale is now a National Historic Site that visitors can tour.

James M John State Wildlife Area

Colorado acquired the 128-sq-mile area on top of Fishers Peak Mesa, southeast of Trinidad, for wildlife protection. Trails for hikes and mountain bikes provide the only access to this rich habitat for birds, elk, mule deer and black bear. Nearby, Lake Dorothy SWA is open for cold-water lake and stream fishing with flies or artificial lures. At Lake Dorothy, a trail leads northwest 4 miles to the Fishers Peak Mesa. Camping is permitted at least 200 yards from the water, except in designated areas with rest-room facilities.

To get to James M John SWA you first must go to Raton, New Mexico, 23 miles south of Trinidad on I-25. From Raton, drive 7 miles northeast on New Mexico Hwys 72 and 526, then head north up Sugarite Canyon 12 miles to Lake Dorothy.

Northern Mountains

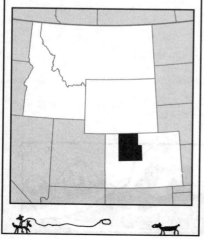

With some of the state's most impressive alpine scenery and outstanding ski resorts, Colorado's northern Rockies are a mountain-lover's dream. But downhill skiing isn't the only thing that draws travelers to the northern mountains in the winter – backcountry skiing, hut camping and snowshoeing also entice outdoor enthusiasts.

In the spring, summer and autumn, hiking and biking in state and national

parks, national forests and even the ski resorts continue to draw visitors. There's also top-notch fishing, rafting and kayaking, weathered ghost towns to explore, horseback riding, camping and touring the mountains until well after autumn turns the aspens to gold.

Highlights

- Steamboat Springs – a laid-back and attractive ski town that's graced by some of Colorado's deepest powder

- Winter Park – outstanding mountain-bike trails and great, unpretentious skiing

- Arapahoe Basin – no-nonsense, steep, deep skiing for true powder-hounds

- Breckenridge – an historic mining town, now known for partying, skiing and mountain biking

- Elk Mountains – the glitter of Aspen and Vail humbled by gorgeous alpine scenery

Middle Park

Colorado's Middle Park includes parts of Rocky Mountain National Park and other federal lands, among them Arapaho National Forest and Arapaho National Recreation Area. Its main attractions are the Winter Park and Steamboat Springs ski resorts, but this major recreation area is not just a winter destination. Hundreds of miles of alpine trails offer excellent chances to delve into Middle Park's gorgeous backcountry.

WINTER PARK & FRASER

At the southern limit of the Middle Park area, these twin Fraser Valley communities (population 1400; elevation 9000 feet) form one of Colorado's most reasonable, most convenient and least pretentious ski resorts. The surrounding area is also a focus for summer activities like hiking and camping, and has one of the state's best mountain-biking trail systems.

Orientation & Information

Winter Park is 67 miles northeast of Denver via I-70 exit 232, then north about 8 miles beyond Berthoud Pass on US 40. Most services are along US 40, which runs the length of both Winter Park and Fraser and continues to Granby (the turnoff for Rocky Mountain National Park), Hot Sulphur Springs, Kremmling and Steamboat Springs.

Winter Park's visitors center (☎ 970-726-4118, 800-903-7275) is on US 40 across from Gasthaus Eichler; the office is open 8 am to 5 pm daily. The Winter Park Resort (www.winterparkresort.com) and Winter

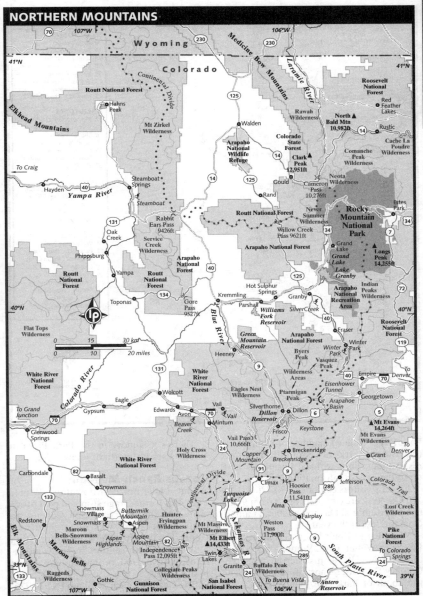

COLORADO

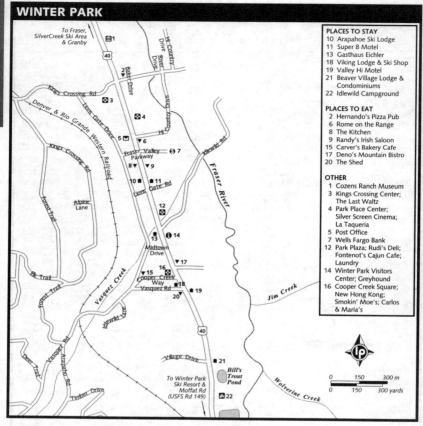

WINTER PARK

PLACES TO STAY
10 Arapahoe Ski Lodge
11 Super 8 Motel
13 Gasthaus Eichler
18 Viking Lodge & Ski Shop
19 Valley Hi Motel
21 Beaver Village Lodge &
    Condominiums
22 Idlewild Campground

PLACES TO EAT
2   Hernando's Pizza Pub
6   Rome on the Range
8   The Kitchen
9   Randy's Irish Saloon
15 Carver's Bakery Cafe
17 Deno's Mountain Bistro
20 The Shed

OTHER
1   Cozens Ranch Museum
3   Kings Crossing Center;
    The Last Waltz
4   Park Place Center;
    Silver Screen Cinema;
    La Taqueria
5   Post Office
7   Wells Fargo Bank
12 Park Plaza; Rudi's Deli;
    Fontenot's Cajun Cafe;
    Laundry
14 Winter Park Visitors
    Center; Greyhound
16 Cooper Creek Square;
    New Hong Kong;
    Smokin' Moe's; Carlos
    & Maria's

Park/Fraser Valley Chamber of Commerce (www.winterpark-info.com) offer online reservations, links to local businesses and up-to-date resort information.

Fraser's visitors center (☎ 970-726-8312), 120 US 40 (Zerex Ave), is open from 9 am to 6 pm Memorial Day to October, 11 am to 6 pm the rest of the year.

Wells Fargo Bank has an ATM just off US 40 in Winter Park. Winter Park's post office is on US 40 just across from Hi Country Dr. Fraser's post office is on US 40 just south of Park Ave. Winter Park's zip code is 80482; Fraser's is 80442.

There's a laundry in the Park Plaza in Winter Park just north of Idlewild Rd.

Cozens Ranch Museum

About a mile north of downtown Winter Park, this former stage stop and post office is named for William Zane Cozens, an early settler who was once sheriff of Central City. It offers an interesting look back at 19th-century life in the mountains, with period rooms and historical photographs.

The Cozens Ranch Museum (☎ 970-726-5488) is open 11 am to 5 pm daily Memorial

Day to October; winter hours are 11 am to 4 pm Wednesday to Saturday, and noon to 4 pm on Sunday. Admission is $4/2 adults/children.

Skiing
Winter Park Ski Resort (☎ 970-726-5514, 800-525-2466), Denver's most convenient world-class ski resort and highly popular among Coloradans, covers over 2 sq miles on four mountains. The season runs from November to mid-April; high season (early December to early April) lift tickets are $54/30 adults/children, with a two-day minimum. Seniors age 70 and over and children under five ski free. Discount lift tickets are available on the Ski Train from Denver, which has a convenient stop near the mountain.
Web site: www.winterparkresort.com

Viking Lodge & Ski Shop (☎ 970-726-8885), at the corner of US 40 and Vasquez Rd in the Viking Lodge in Winter Park, offers affordable ski rental packages.

Devil's Thumb Ranch (☎ 970-726-5632) located north of Fraser, offers a scenic 65-mile network of groomed cross-country trails. Lessons and rentals are available. Visit www.devilsthumbranch.com. Snow Mountain Ranch (☎ 970-887-2152) has 62 miles of trails for all abilities, including some lighted track for night skiing and ice-skating.

Bicycling
Winter Park advertises itself as 'Mountain Bike Capital, USA,' and with more than 45 miles of expertly designed lift-accessible trails connecting to a 600-mile trail system running throughout the valley, it's a title that's well earned. The Zephyr Express lift ($6 per trip or $18 per day) gives riders a 1700-foot lift to some of the best trails on the mountain – from the easy and scenic Lower Roof of the Rockies/Fantasy Meadow Loop to the extreme 3-mile Mountain Goat Trail, one of the most 'technical' trails around. Be advised that helmets are required and riders must stay on the trails.

Viking Lodge & Ski Shop (☎ 970-726-8885) rents high quality bicycles – see Skiing, above.

Horseback Riding
Grand Adventures (☎ 970-726-9247, 800-726-9247), just south of downtown Winter Park, arranges horseback rides in Arapaho National Forest, as well as special breakfast and dinner rides throughout the week. Winter activities include snowmobiling, sleigh riding and dog sledding.
Web site: www.grandadventures.com

Special Events
Winter Park's first major summer event is the **American Red Cross Fat Tire Classic** held in late June. The annual **Alpine Art Affair** takes place in late July, along with the **Winter Park Jazz Festival**. The annual **Wine & Food Festival** and the **King of the Rockies Mountain Bike Race** take place in early and mid-August, respectively.

Fraser Valley Railroad Days follows in early September, around the same time as the **Famous Flamethrowers High Altitude Chili Cookoff** at Winter Park Resort.

The local **High Country Stampede Rodeo** takes place, rain or shine, at 7:30 pm Saturday in July and August at the John Work Arena in Fraser.

Places to Stay
Winter Park Central Reservations (☎ 970-726-5587, 800-453-2525) is the area's central booking agent.

The USFS *Idlewild Campground* ($10), at the south end of Winter Park just before the Moffat Rd turnoff, is the closest camping area to town. It has only 26 sites, however, and can fill up early. Five miles south of Winter Park, also on US 40, *Robbers Roost Campground* offers another 11 sites.

The *Viking Lodge* (☎ 970-726-8885, 800-421-4013), on US 40 between Vasquez Rd and Cooper Creek Way, offers doubles that range from $65 to $105. This friendly skiers' lodge has a ski and bike shop, hot tub and sauna. Across US 40, the *Valley Hi Motel* (☎ 970-726-4171, 800-426-2094) has doubles for as little as $65 during peak ski season.

Beaver Village Lodge & Condominiums (☎ 970-726-5741, 800-666-0281), off US 40 downtown, offers hotel rooms and multi-bedroom condos and has a pool and sauna. In summer hotel rooms range from $50 to $80 and a one-bedroom condo goes for $95, but these rates roughly double during winter ski season.

Doubles at the *Arapahoe Ski Lodge* (☎ 970-726-8222), on US 40 just north of Lions Gate Rd, are $65 in summer (including breakfast). During ski season rates are $178 (including dinner and breakfast). *Super 8 Motel* (☎ 970-726-8808, 800-541-6130), on US 40 near Lions Gate Rd, has clean doubles starting at $44 in the off-season. There's an indoor hot tub and a free Continental breakfast during ski season.

At the *Raintree Inn* (☎ 970-726-4211, 800-726-3340), across from Winter Park Ski Resort, doubles start at $49 in summer, $115 during ski season. The pseudo-Swiss *Gasthaus Eichler* (☎ 970-726-5133, 800-543-3899, 78786 US 40), across from Idlewild Rd near Vasquez Creek, has doubles from $79 summer, $120 winter; winter rates include a full breakfast and dinner.

Probably the most luxurious place in town is the *Vintage Resort Hotel* (☎ 970-726-8801, 800-472-7017), at Winter Park Ski Resort, where midsummer doubles start at $75 but rise to $185 in the peak Christmas season. The *Iron Horse Resort* (☎ 970-726-8851, 800-621-8190), at the entrance to Winter Park, has lodge rooms and one-bedroom condos for $89/115 in the off-season, $129/240 during regular ski season.

Engelmann Pines (☎ 970-726-4632, 800-992-9512, 1035 Cranmer Ave), in Fraser, charges $75 to $95 for a double – some rooms feature private Jacuzzi baths and fireplaces. The *Pines Inn* (☎ 970-726-5416, 800-824-9127), walking distance from Winter Park Ski Resort, offers singles/doubles from $100/110 in summer, $70/120 in ski season.

Places to Eat

Winter Park has a wide variety of gourmet food, but Fraser is a bit cheaper and more down to earth. Many of Winter Park's shopping centers house restaurants.

Winter Park's *The Kitchen* (☎ 970-726-9940) on US 40 in the middle of town, warns customers, 'If you're in a hurry, eat some-

where else,' but the breakfast specialties are worth the wait. *Carver's Bakery Cafe* (☎ 970-726-8202, 93 Cooper Creek Way) also has superb, reasonably priced breakfasts and lunches with large portions.

Deno's Mountain Bistro (☎ 970-726-5332), across from Cooper Creek Square, is a popular dining and watering hole for skiers and bikers. *Randy's Irish Saloon* (☎ 970-726-5402), near Lions Gate Rd, is a local favorite for meat and potatoes (washed down with a Guinness). *New Hong Kong* (☎ 970-726-9888), in Cooper Creek Square, features Szechuan and Mandarin dishes made with lighter and healthier ingredients.

Rudi's Deli (☎ 970-726-8955), in Park Place Center on US 40, has excellent sandwiches but is not cheap. *Smokin' Moe's* (☎ 970-726-4700), in Cooper Creek Square, serves up 'darn good Oklahoma-style barbecue,' while *Carlos & Maria's* (☎ 970-726-9674), in the same building, serves Mexican food and has a daily happy hour between 3:30 and 6:30 pm. *The Last Waltz* (☎ 970-726-4877), in Kings Crossing Center, features a variety of sandwiches and Mexican and vegetarian specialties. Located at the north end of town, *Hernando's Pizza Pub* (☎ 970-726-5409) serves pizza, pasta and a selection of imported and domestic beers.

Rome on the Range (☎ 970-726-1111), across from the post office, is a massive eatery and saloon decorated with Western art and antiques. It's known for excellent steaks, ribs and wild game. Downtown, chef-owned *Gasthaus Eichler* (☎ 970-726-5133, 78786 US 40) features an extensive German menu specializing in veal. *Fontenot's Cajun Cafe* (☎ 970-726-4021), in Park Place Center, serves moderately priced sandwiches, pasta and entrees with a Cajun flavor. *The Shed* (☎ 970-726-9912), near the corner of US 40 and Vasquez Rd, is a popular grill and cantina serving respectable southwestern fare. For spicy Mexican delights, look for *La Taqueria* (☎ 970-726-0280) in Park Place Center.

Visitors can take the Zephyr Express chairlift, at the base of Winter Park Ski Resort, to the popular *Lodge at Sunspot* (☎ 970-726-8155), a restaurant and bar high above the resort.

In Fraser, the **Fraser Brazier** (☎ 970-726-8490, 406 US 40), across from the Crooked Creek, has inexpensive sandwiches, burgers, ice cream and Mexican food.

Entertainment
A popular local hangout in Fraser is **Crooked Creek Saloon** (☎ 970-726-9250, 401 US 40). **The Derailer** (☎ 970-726-5514), at the base of Winter Park, is the place where après-ski nightlife begins, with live music during the ski season most nights. **The Slope** (☎ 970-726-5727), between town and the mountain, is another popular après-ski venue.

Getting There & Away
Greyhound (☎ 800-231-2222) stops at the visitors center on US 40 in Winter Park and also makes a flag stop in front of Fraser's Crooked Creek Saloon.

Home James Transportation Services (☎ 970-726-5060, 800-359-7536) charges $39 per passenger for van rides between Winter Park and Denver International Airport. Schedules and prices may vary seasonally and reservations are essential.
Web site: www.homejames-shuttle.com

Reservations are required for the scenic Ski Train (☎ 303-296-4754), which drops Denver passengers at Winter Park Resort just outside the Moffat Tunnel. It runs Saturday and Sunday mid-December to early April, Friday from early February to late March; same-day roundtrip fares are $38 in coach class, $65 in the club car, which includes Continental breakfast, beverages and après-ski snacks. Departure time is 7:15 am from Denver, arriving in Winter Park at 9:30 am; the returning train leaves Winter Park at 4:15 pm and arrives in Denver at 6:30 pm. In summer the Ski Train runs from mid-June to mid-August.

Amtrak (☎ 800-872-7245) stops daily in Fraser at the unmanned depot on the corner of Fraser and Railroad Aves.

Getting Around
Winter Park's frequent free shuttle (☎ 970-726-4163) carries skiers around Winter Park and Fraser; it runs every 10 to 15 minutes in winter, hourly in summer. The free Smart

Shuttle serves local restaurants and bars 10:30 pm to 2 am Friday and Saturday nights and takes passengers right to their doorsteps.

THE MOFFAT ROAD & ROLLINS PASS
In the mid-1860s, JA Rollins established a toll wagon-road over this 11,660-foot pass from Nederland/Rollinsville, and early in the 20th century David H Moffat's Denver, Northwestern & Pacific Railway crossed the Continental Divide here. First known as Boulder Pass, then Rollins Pass, it also earned the appellation 'Corona' as railroad workers considered it the crown at the 'top of the world.' Until 1928, when the Moffat Tunnel made the route superfluous, there existed a railroad station, hotel, restaurant and workers' quarters on the summit.

At the south end of Winter Park, just beyond the USFS Idlewild Campground, Moffat Rd (also known as Corona Rd, Rollins Rd and USFS Rd 149) to Rollins Pass is a good dirt road usually open by late June. The upper stretches before Rollins Pass are poorly maintained and a high clearance vehicle is desirable, though 4WD is not necessary. Before driving it, try to find the self-guided auto tour pamphlet 'The Moffat Road,' available for $1 from the chambers of commerce in Winter Park or Fraser. The most interesting roadside attraction is the **Loop Trestle & Tunnel** at the 11-mile point, where the train, emerging from a tunnel, circled 1½ miles to gain just 150 feet in elevation.

From the parking lot at the summit of the pass, the High Lonesome Trail II, a segment of the Continental Divide National Scenic Trail, enters the Indian Peaks Wilderness to the north. Offering superb views of the Divide, the trail drops 2000 feet to intersect the High Lonesome Trail, which continues north to Junco Lake, Monarch Lake and beyond to Rocky Mountain National Park.

Another hiking possibility is the Rogers Pass Trail, which leaves Rollins Pass Rd near the Loop Trestle; its continuation, the James Peak Trail, climbs to 13,294 feet and is named for Dr Edwin James, who made

COLORADO

the first recorded ascent of Pikes Peak. The total length is 3½ miles, with the last half-mile largely unmarked.

For maps and guides, go to the USFS Sulphur Ranger District Office (see below) in Granby.

GRANBY

At the junction of US 40 and US 34, Granby (population 1200) is a crossroads service center convenient to Rocky Mountain National Park and several other nearby recreation and ski areas. The USFS Sulphur District Ranger Office (☎ 970-887-3331) for the Arapaho National Forest is at 62429 US 40 at the east end of town. It has useful hiking brochures for the Continental Divide National Scenic Trail, the Never Summer Wilderness Area and the Winter Park-Fraser-Tabernash area. It is also the place to get permits for back-country camping in the Indian Peaks Wilderness.

GRAND LAKE

The western gateway to Rocky Mountain National Park, Grand Lake (population 400; elevation 8400 feet) was an early mining zone but soon got into the tourist game, establishing a yacht club by 1901. It has since become 'Estes Park West,' a tourist trap with very little to recommend it except a few decent restaurants and one of the cheapest and best accommodations alternatives in the state, the Shadowcliff Lodge hostel. Grand Ave, the main drag, is a jumble of souvenir shops, T-shirt stores and restaurants along a hokey boardwalk. The beautiful lake, however, lives up to its name.

Orientation & Information

On the north shore of its namesake, the largest natural lake in the state, Grand Lake Village is a mile east of the Grand Lake junction of US 34 and W Portal Rd. It is 14 miles north of Granby and only a mile south of the western entrance to Rocky Mountain

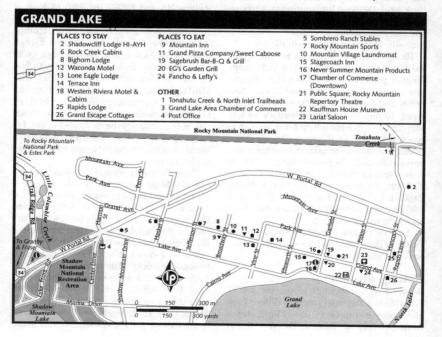

GRAND LAKE

PLACES TO STAY
2 Shadowcliff Lodge HI-AYH
6 Rock Creek Cabins
8 Bighorn Lodge
12 Waconda Motel
13 Lone Eagle Lodge
14 Terrace Inn
18 Western Riviera Motel & Cabins
25 Rapids Lodge
26 Grand Escape Cottages

PLACES TO EAT
9 Mountain Inn
11 Grand Pizza Company/Sweet Caboose
19 Sagebrush Bar-B-Q & Grill
20 EG's Garden Grill
24 Pancho & Lefty's

OTHER
1 Tonahutu Creek & North Inlet Trailheads
3 Grand Lake Area Chamber of Commerce
4 Post Office

5 Sombrero Ranch Stables
7 Rocky Mountain Sports
10 Mountain Village Laundromat
15 Stagecoach Inn
16 Never Summer Mountain Products
17 Chamber of Commerce (Downtown)
21 Public Square; Rocky Mountain Repertory Theatre
22 Kauffman House Museum
23 Lariat Saloon

National Park; US 34 crosses the high tundra of the park as Trail Ridge Rd. The main drag of the village's compact grid is Grand Ave.

The Grand Lake Area Chamber of Commerce (☎ 970-627-3402, 800-531-1019) is at the junction of US 34 and W Portal Rd; it's open 9 am to 5 pm Monday to Saturday, 10 am to 4 pm Sunday in summer. The chamber's winter hours are 9 am to 5 pm Friday and Saturday, 10 am to 4 pm Sunday, Monday and Thursday (closed Tuesday and Wednesday). The downtown information office, upstairs at 928 Grand Ave (enter from the Garfield Ave side), is more helpful. Web site: www.grandlakechamber.com

The post office is at 520 Center Dr; Grand Lake's zip code is 80447. The Mountain Village Laundromat is located on Grand Ave between Broadway and Vine Sts.

Kauffman House Museum
The Ezra Kauffman House, 407 Pitkin St between Lake Ave and Grand Ave, is an 1892 log building that operated as a hotel until 1946. Now on the National Register of Historic Places and operated by the Grand Lake Historical Society (☎ 970-627-3351), it contains period furniture and other artifacts and is open 1 to 5 pm daily in summer.

Activities
The Grand Lake Metro Recreation District (☎ 970-627-8328) publishes a 'Grand Lake Mountain Bike Trail Map' of routes in the Arapaho National Forest west of town; rides are color-coded according to difficulty. Rocky Mountain Sports (☎ 970-627-8124), 711 Grand Ave, rents and sells bikes.

Never Summer Mountain Products (☎ 970-627-3642), 919 Grand Ave, carries rock climbing and mountaineering equipment, clothing and topographic maps.

Several Rocky Mountain National Park trailheads are just outside the town limits, including those to the Tonahutu Creek Trail and the Cascade Falls/North Inlet Trail, both near Shadowcliff Lodge.

The Sombrero Ranch Stables (☎ 970-627-3514), 304 W Portal Rd, offers a wide array of trail ride options, plus a large

number of fishing and hunting trips. Web site: www.sombrero.com

Monarch Guides (☎ 970-627-2409, 888-463-5628), 1028 Grand Ave, runs half-day, full-day and overnight white-water rafting trips on both the upper Colorado and Eagle Rivers.

Grand Lake is a popular snowmobile center with hundreds of miles of trails around town and in Rocky Mountain National Park. Inquire at the visitors center about snowmobile rentals and guided tours.

Special Events
Winter's main event is **Winter Carnival**, held in mid-January, while the annual **Ice Fishing Derby** happens in early February.

Grand Lake's annual **Festival of Arts & Crafts** takes place in late June, and in late July boaters clog the waters during the **Grand Lake Regatta**.

Places to Stay
Since Grand Lake is not a ski resort per se, summer is the high season but seasonal price variations are relatively small.

Camping RVs can park at the vacant city lot at the corner of Park Ave and Hancock St, but it's less than scenic and there are no facilities.

Elk Creek Campground (☎ 970-627-8502, 800-355-2733), on Golf Course Rd (Grand County Rd 48) just west of US 34 and just south of the entrance to Rocky Mountain National Park, stays open year-round and charges around $20. Facilities include a store, laundry and recreation room.

Winding River Resort (☎ 970-627-3215), reached via Grand County Rd 491 opposite the NPS Kawuneeche Visitors Center, has tent sites for $18, and full hookup sites for $20. It also has cabins from $70 to $90.

Hostels Overlooking the town and the lake from Summerland Park Rd just north of W Portal Rd, the nonprofit *Shadowcliff Lodge HI-AYH* (☎ 970-627-9220), open late May to late September, is one of the best budget alternatives anywhere in the state.

Spotless, comfortable hostel accommodations cost $11 for HI-AYH members, $13 for nonmembers, but it also has cabins with kitchens (see below). Hostel guests should bring sheets or a sleeping bag and, in keeping with the hostelling tradition, must perform a small chore.

Lodges & Cabins Private singles/doubles at *Shadowcliff Lodge* (☎ 970-627-9220) are $25/30. Shadowcliff also has a limited number of cabins for $65 to $80 for five persons (linen $2 extra per bed); reservations are essential and there is a six-day minimum.

With an ideal setting next to the Tonahutu River, *Rapids Lodge* (☎ 970-627-3707, 209 Rapids Lane) offers six cozy, uniquely decorated rooms in a historic building for $65 to $105, plus cabins and condos for around $80. Check it out at www.rapidslodge.com. *Grand Escape Cottages* (☎ 970-627-3410), on the east end of Grand Ave at Hancock St, has rustic cabins ranging from $60; it's open from mid-May to early October. *Rock Creek Cabins* (☎ 970-627-8019, 416 Grand Ave), has basic cabins that can sleep four to eight starting at $80/double.

The historic *Grand Lake Lodge* (☎ 970-627-3967, 15500 US Hwy 34), a National Register of Historic Places landmark, is reached via an eastward lateral a half-mile north of Grand Lake junction. It has cabins with views ranging from $70/double to $550 for an eight-bedroom cabin with kitchen for up to 25 people. It's open early June to mid-September only.
Web site: www.grandlakelodge.com

Motels The *Waconda Motel* (☎ 970-627-8312, 725 Grand Ave) is a good bet with doubles starting at $65, $70 for rooms with a fireplace. *Lone Eagle Lodge* (☎ 970-627-3310, 800-282-3311, 712 Grand Ave) has one- or two-bedroom cabin-style rooms from around $50 to $80, while the *Bighorn Lodge* (☎ 970-627-8101, 888-315-2378, 613 Grand Ave) ranges from $55 to $110. The lakeside *Western Riviera Motel & Cabins* (☎ 970-627-3580, 419 Garfield St) has

economy units for $68; most motel rooms go for $70-plus; cabins with kitchenettes are around $100.

The *Terrace Inn* (☎ 970-627-3079, 813 Grand Ave) downtown charges $45 to $125 for a double, Continental breakfast included. Web site: www.grandlaketerraceinn.com

Places to Eat
The best dining experience in Grand Lake is at *Rapids Lodge*. With a reasonably priced gourmet Italian menu served in a charming restaurant overlooking the gently flowing rapids of the Tonahutu River, this is a nice place for a romantic dinner.

EG's Garden Grill (☎ 970-627-8404, 1000 Grand Ave) has a festive beer garden, serves varied cuisine from interesting salads to seafood and occasionally has live music. The *Grand Pizza Company/Sweet Caboose* (☎ 970-627-8390, 717 Grand Ave) has standard and specialty pizzas, while *Pancho & Lefty's* (☎ 970-627-8773, 1120 Grand Ave) dishes up a commendable mix of American and Mexican classics.

The *Mountain Inn* (☎ 970-627-3385, 612 Grand Ave), in the historic Humphrey's building, serves steaks and burgers after 5 pm. Another worthy option for carnivores is the *Sagebrush Bar-B-Q & Grill* (☎ 970-627-1104, 1101 Grand Ave).

Entertainment
The *Lariat Saloon* (☎ 970-627-9965, 1121 Grand Ave) is the main live music venue in town with shows Wednesday through Sunday. The *Stagecoach Inn* (☎ 970-627-8079, 920 Grand Ave) has occasional live country & western bands.

Rocky Mountain Repertory Theatre (☎ 970-627-3421) continues its 30-year tradition on Grand Ave in the Public Square. The company culls actors from across the USA to present live musicals, comedies and other family entertainment. The season runs June through August.

Getting There & Away
Home James Transportation Services (☎ 970-726-5060, 800-359-7536) charges $58 per person for door-to-airport minivan service

to/from Grand Lake and Denver International Airport. Reservations are required. Web site: www.homejames-shuttle.com

ARAPAHO NATIONAL RECREATION AREA

Between Granby and Grand Lake, the USFS-managed Arapaho National Recreation Area (ANRA) abuts Rocky Mountain National Park and Arapaho National Forest's Indian Peaks Wilderness. Part of the Colorado–Big Thompson Reclamation Project, a massive water transfer from the Western Slope to arid northeastern Colorado, the ANRA encompasses several reservoirs, including Lake Granby, pumping stations, canals and the Alva B Adams Tunnel through the Rockies.

The ANRA is largely an uninviting place best left to RVs and motorboats, but it does provide good access to the Indian Peaks Wilderness Area from the Monarch Lake trailhead at the east end of Lake Granby. Note that backcountry camping in Indian Peaks requires a permit from the USFS at Monarch Lake or in Granby. One interesting crossing of the Front Range is the Cascade Creek Trail over 12,000-foot Pawnee Pass, but the north-south Continental Divide National Scenic Trail also passes through the area. Four major *campgrounds* (☎ 877-444-6667) within the ANRA cost $10.

HOT SULPHUR SPRINGS

Denver Post editor William Byers first promoted Hot Sulphur Springs (population 480; elevation 8200 feet) as a tourist destination in the 19th century. At one time its rivalry with Grand Lake was so serious that a struggle over which town would be the Grand County seat led to a fatal shoot-out between elected officials; Hot Sulphur Springs prevailed politically, but fortunately it has never suffered the tourist invasion that has made Grand Lake so ticky-tacky. Of all the hamlets along US 40, Hot Sulphur Springs most deserves a stopover.

Orientation & Information

At the foot of 12,804-foot Byers Peak, Hot Sulphur Springs is midway between Granby and Kremmling on US 40 and wedged between Routt National Forest to the north and Arapaho National Forest to the south. It has no formal tourist office, but Grand County Museum (see below) is a good source of information.

The post office is at 506 Grand St; the zip code is 80451.

Greyhound (☎ 800-231-2222) will make a flag stop in Hot Sulphur Springs if it's arranged in advance.

Fishing

Local hunting and fishing guide Dave Perry (☎ 970-725-3531) leads summer fly-fishing trips (beginners welcome) on several of the region's best rivers. Call well in advance to make arrangements.

Grand County Museum

One of the Rockies' better rural museums, the former Hot Sulphur School dates back to 1924. Well-arranged exhibits deal with the evolution of settlement in the area since the time of the Paleo-Indians, the development of area frontier communities, the rise of winter sports, construction of the Moffat Tunnel and German POW camps at Fraser. Outside is a collection of relocated historic buildings, including the original county courthouse, the jail, a blacksmith shop and the Horseshoe Ranger Station.

At 110 Byers Ave just off US 40 at the east end of town, the museum (☎ 970-725-3939) is open 10 am to 5 pm daily Memorial Day to Labor Day, and 11 am to 4 pm Wednesday to Saturday in the low season.

Places to Stay & Eat

There's no official campground but tent campers and RVs can take advantage of the shade and good fishing at *Pioneer Park* on the north bank of the river, where there's not even anyone to pester you for money. Get drinking and cooking water from the standpipe across from the Riverside Hotel near the bridge; there are portable toilets, but to clean up try the pools at Hot Sulphur Springs Resort & Spa (see below).

The *Canyon Motel* (☎ *970-725-3395, 221 Byers Ave*) is an affordable choice with singles/doubles for $36/40. The **Riverside Hotel** (☎ *970-725-3589, 509 Grand St*) is housed in a historic building with a first-rate restaurant. Rooms rent for $36/47. The **Ute Trail Motel** (☎ *970-725-0123, 800-506-0099, 120 E US 40*) has rates of $42/48.

Hot Sulphur Springs Resort & Spa (☎ *970-725-3306, 5617 County Rd 20*), the town's original spa, dates back to 1894. Nightly rates range from $74 to $108, which includes use of outdoor pools. The pools are also open daily to nonguests for $13.50/11.50 adults/children, including access to showers. A full range of massage, body wraps, and facials are available for an additional charge. Open year-round, the resort is two blocks west of town and so close to the railroad tracks that light sleepers may fear an earthquake when a train passes.

Casa Milagro B&B (☎ *970-725-3640, 13628 County Rd 3*) is a secluded, log cabin–style inn on the Williams Fork River, about a 20-minute drive from the hot springs. Rates are $140 to $160, with a two-night minimum.

Web site: www.casamilagro.com

The **County Seat Grill** (☎ *970-726-3309, 517 Byers Ave*) is Sulphur Spring's most popular eatery. They do great burritos, steaks, burgers and pizza.

KREMMLING

A popular base for hunters and snowmobilers, Kremmling (population 1500; elevation 7411 feet) has recently made efforts to encourage mountain biking. It is a service center at the junction of US 40 and Hwy 9 about 100 miles west of Denver, 32 miles north of Silverthorne on Hwy 9 and 53 miles southeast of Steamboat Springs.

The USFS Middle Park Ranger District Office (☎ 970-724-9004), 210 S 6th St (Hwy 9), is open weekdays. Kremmling Memorial Hospital (☎ 970-724-3442), 214 S 4th St, is the only such facility in Grand County.

If you want to spend the night, the **Eastin Hotel** (☎ *970-724-3261, 800-546-0815, 105 S 2nd St*) has singles with 1930s shared bathrooms from $30, or $39 for a private bath. Showers are available to nonguests for $5.

Cliffside Pizza (☎ *970-724-9219, 276 Central Ave*) does a great pepperoni pie. For juicy steaks, head to **The Quarter Circle** (☎ *970-724-9601*), just across the road.

STEAMBOAT SPRINGS

One of Colorado's more appealing high-class ski resorts is Steamboat Springs (population 6700; elevation 6728 feet). Far from the glitter of Vail and Aspen and despite the sprawling Steamboat Village built to service skiers, the town retains some of its original low-rise character and charm in a delightful natural setting. Many consider it the most laid-back of the major ski resorts. Summer is almost as popular, with hiking, backpacking, white-water rafting, mountain biking and other outdoor activities.

Orientation & Information

Steamboat Springs consists of two major areas: the relatively regular grid of central Old Town which straddles US 40, and the newer warren of winding streets at Steamboat Village, centered around the Mt Werner Ski Area at the southeast end of town. US 40 is known as Lincoln Ave through Old Town.

The Steamboat Springs Chamber Resort Association runs a visitors information center (☎ 970-879-0880, 800-922-2722), 1255 S Lincoln Ave, facing Sundance Plaza.

Web site: www.steamboat-chamber.com

The USFS Hahn's Peak Ranger Office (☎ 970-879-1870), 925 Weiss Dr (at the southeast end of town), has information on hiking, mountain biking, fishing and other activities in the area, including the Mt Zirkel Wilderness.

Wells Fargo Bank has an ATM located at 320 Lincoln Ave. The main post office is at 200 Lincoln Ave; the zip code is 80477. Off the Beaten Path Bookstore & Coffeehouse (☎ 970-879-6830), 56 7th St, is a great place to browse for books, magazines and newspapers; if you buy something, you can read it over pastries and coffee in the cozy cafe.

Spring Creek Laundromat (☎ 970-879-5587) is at 235 Lincoln Ave.

Routt Memorial Hospital (☎ 970-879-1322) is at 80 Park Ave.

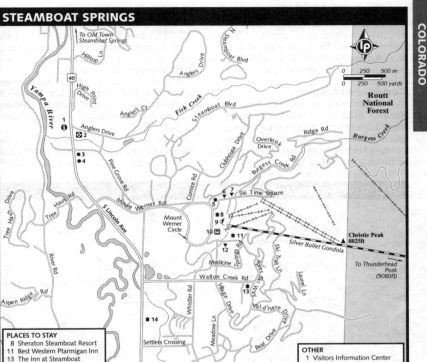

STEAMBOAT SPRINGS

Routt
National
Forest

PLACES TO STAY
8 Sheraton Steamboat Resort
11 Best Western Ptarmigan Inn
13 The Inn at Steamboat
14 Holiday Inn Steamboat

PLACES TO EAT
6 Tugboat Grill & Pub;
Cat House Cafe
7 Mattie Silks
12 La Montaña Restaurant

OTHER
1 Visitors Information Center
2 Sundance Plaza; Post Office;
Sundance Laundromat
3 Ski Haus
4 Safeway Supermarket
5 Steamboat Trading Company
9 Steamboat Ski Area
10 Steamboat Springs Transit

├─┼─┼─┤ Chairlift

Trail of the Pioneers Museum

Dedicated to early Steamboat Springs, exhibits in this beautifully maintained Victorian house recreate a period bedroom, kitchen, parlor and dining room, plus a ski gallery, a Western room and a room dedicated to Colorado Utes. The museum (☎ 970-879-2214), 800 Oak St, is open 11 am to 5 pm daily. Admission is $4/1 adults/children.

Mineral Springs

Most of Steamboat's numerous springs are warm rather than hot, and some have been damaged by highway construction. Probably the nicest spring is 3 miles from Old Town at Strawberry Park: it's open until midnight and you can actually bathe in it. Most of the others are in the area around 13th St on both sides of the river; look for the map and brochure 'A Walking Tour of the Springs of Steamboat' for more information.

To try the waters in town, head for the Steamboat Springs Health & Recreation Center (☎ 970-879-1828), 135 Lincoln Ave, a modern facility on the site of the old hot springs. It has an Olympic-size swimming pool, hot mineral pools, a water slide, weight room and saunas. It's open 5:30 am to 10 pm weekdays (from 8 am weekends). Admission to the pool and sauna is $6/4/2.50 adults/teens/children (three to 12) and seniors (62 and older). The water slide costs an additional $4 for 10 rides, and the weight room and exercise classes are also extra.

Gondola Rides

In summer, visitors can take Steamboat Village's Silver Bullet Gondola to the 9080-foot Thunderhead complex for hiking or mountain biking. Service runs late June to Labor Day. The one-way fare is $13/7 adults/children (six to 12).

Skiing

Steamboat Ski Area (☎ 970-879-6111, 800-922-2722) is a world-class resort that has earned a reputation for having consistently good powder, some of the lightest (and most abundant) in Colorado.

The season starts around Thanksgiving and runs until Easter; lift tickets are $50/30 adults/children, though multiple-day discount tickets can reduce the bite to some degree.

If you'd rather cross-country ski, the Steamboat Ski Touring Center (☎ 970-879-8180) uses the Sheraton Steamboat Resort

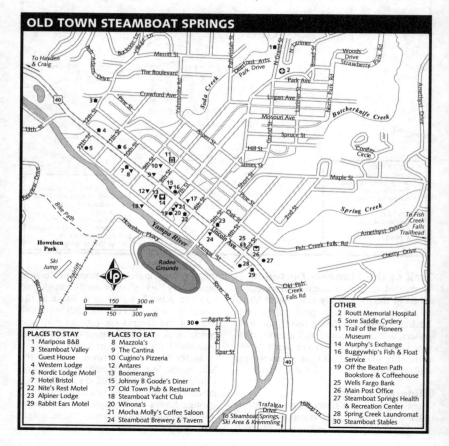

OLD TOWN STEAMBOAT SPRINGS

PLACES TO STAY
1 Mariposa B&B
3 Steamboat Valley Guest House
4 Western Lodge
6 Nordic Lodge Motel
7 Hotel Bristol
22 Nite's Rest Motel
23 Alpiner Lodge
29 Rabbit Ears Motel

PLACES TO EAT
8 Mazzola's
9 The Cantina
10 Cugino's Pizzeria
12 Antares
13 Boomerangs
15 Johnny B Goode's Diner
17 Old Town Pub & Restaurant
18 Steamboat Yacht Club
20 Winona's
21 Mocha Molly's Coffee Saloon
24 Steamboat Brewery & Tavern

OTHER
2 Routt Memorial Hospital
5 Sore Saddle Cyclery
11 Trail of the Pioneers Museum
14 Murphy's Exchange
16 Buggywhip's Fish & Float Service
19 Off the Beaten Path Bookstore & Coffeehouse
25 Wells Fargo Bank
26 Main Post Office
27 Steamboat Springs Health & Recreation Center
28 Spring Creek Laundromat
30 Steamboat Stables

COLORADO

Golf Course in winter, but there are many other cross-country sites, such as the Yampa River Trail, Spring Creek Mountain Park and Rabbit Ears and Dunkley Passes.

Mountain Biking

The 'Steamboat Trails Map' shows mountain bike routes around town, in Stagecoach and Pearl Lake State Parks and the Mt Zirkel Wilderness. It's available at the visitors information center (see Orientation & Information, above). Steamboat Ski Area (☎ 970-879-6111) promotes biking on Mt Werner, allows bikes on the Silver Bullet Gondola and rents them at the Thunderhead lift.

Steamboat Trading Company (☎ 970-879-0083), 1850 Ski Time Square, rents mountain bikes. Other rental places include Ski Haus (☎ 970-879-0385), 1450 S Lincoln Rd, and Sore Saddle Cyclery (☎ 970-879-1675), 1136 Yampa St, which also offers tours of Routt National Forest.

Other Activities

Buggywhip's Fish & Float Service (☎ 970-879-8033, 800-759-0343), 720 Lincoln Ave, offers white-water rafting trips on the Yampa, Colorado, Eagle and Arkansas Rivers.

Steamboat Stables/Sombrero Ranch (☎ 970-879-2306), southeast of the rodeo grounds, offers one-hour horseback rides, plus breakfast and dinner rides and pack trips.

Places to Stay

Steamboat Central Reservations (☎ 970-879-4074, 800-922-2722) is a clearinghouse for accommodations, especially condominiums.

Camping The *Steamboat Springs KOA Campground* (☎ 970-879-0273), on US 40 about 2 miles west of downtown, is one of the best such facilities in the Rocky Mountain states. For $19, tent campers get the benefit of quiet, shady sites on a small island in the Yampa River. Sites with full hookups are $25. All guests have access to the hot tub and other facilities. (For other camping options see Around Steamboat Springs, later.)

Motels Steamboat's best value is probably the *Nordic Lodge Motel* (☎ 970-879-0531, 800-364-0331, 1036 Lincoln Ave). The highest winter rates are singles/doubles for $80/95 but during most of the season you should be able to get a room for between $50 and $60. The rooms are sparkling clean and amenities include a hot tub, sauna and cable TV.

Western Lodge (☎ 970-979-1050, 800-622-9200, 1122 Lincoln Ave) is an undistinguished but moderately priced motel at the west end of town; in winter singles/doubles cost around $70/80, about $20 less in off-peak periods. The *Nite's Rest Motel* (☎ 970-879-1212, 800-828-1780, 601 Lincoln Ave) with a good location in the heart of town, has rooms that are a bit dark and small but otherwise not too bad. Singles/doubles are around $80/90 during winter. *Rabbit Ears Motel* (☎ 970-879-1150, 800-828-7702, 201 Lincoln Ave) is a bit nicer and offers discount passes to the Steamboat Springs Health & Recreation Center across the street. Winter rates average around $95/120, and drop about $20 in the off-season.

Another centrally located 'economy' choice is *Alpiner Lodge* (☎ 970-879-1430, 424 Lincoln Ave), which has winter rates of around $90.

Hotels One of the nicer choices is Old Town's *Hotel Bristol* (☎ 970-879-3083, 800-851-0872, 917 Lincoln Ave), a warm, nicely appointed place that has 22 rooms with either shared or private bath. Winter rates generally range from $75 to $120.

To be near the slopes, you can't do much better than the *Best Western Ptarmigan Inn* (☎ 970-879-1730, 800-538-7519, 2304 Apres Ski Way). It's located right next to the Silver Bullet gondola. Singles/doubles range from $99/110 to $120/135 during ski season (plunging to around $60 in summer). Also right on the slopes is *Sheraton Steamboat Resort* (☎ 970-879-2220, 2200 Village Inn Court), with luxuries such as a full-size heated pool, private balconies, saunas and the like. The lowest winter rate of $115 gets you a ground-floor room with no view, and even this modest accommodation will cost more than $200 between December and February.

Out on Hwy 40, *Holiday Inn Steamboat* (☎ 970-879-2250, 3190 S Lincoln Ave) charges less than the Sheraton but is also several miles from the slopes and is not as luxurious.

The Inn at Steamboat (☎ 970-879-2600, 800-872-2601, 3070 Columbine Dr), near Walton Creek Rd, has winter rates anywhere from $50 in November to $150 during Christmas.

B&Bs In Old Town, *Steamboat Valley Guest House* (☎ 970-870-9017, 800-530-3866, 1245 Crawford Ave), is a wooden ski lodge affair with rooms from $80 to $125 during ski season.
Web site: www.steamboatvalley.com

Mariposa B&B (☎ 970-879-1467, 800-578-1467, 855 N Grand St) is a Southwest-style adobe home set back in a quiet residential area. Doubles are around $90 in winter, $80 in summer.

Places to Eat
Steamboat Springs has such a variety of restaurants that it's hard to give more than a representative sample, but in general the quality is high. Caffeine boosts (as well as healthy meals: breakfast, lunch and dinner) are offered at *Mocha Molly's Coffee Saloon* (☎ 970-879-0587, 635 Lincoln Ave). One of the best eating deals in town is *Johnny B Goode's Diner* (☎ 970-870-8400, 738 Lincoln Ave).

Cugino's Pizzeria (☎ 970-879-5805, 825 Oak St) has an appealing Italian menu and atmosphere. *Mazzola's* (☎ 970-879-2405, 917 Lincoln Ave) is a little more expensive but is quite popular.

Winona's (☎ 970-879-2483, 617 Lincoln Ave) is a friendly little deli-bakery with good breakfast and lunch specials. At the upmarket end of the spectrum, *Antares* (☎ 970-879-9939, 57½ 8th St) serves creative 'new world cuisine' and offers an excellent selection of fine wines.

The *Steamboat Brewery & Tavern* (☎ 970-879-2233), at 5th and Lincoln, has great food and the beer brewed on the

premises is excellent. *Boomerangs* (☎ 970-879-3131, 50 8th St) is known locally for its steaks and seafood.

The Cantina (☎ 970-879-0826, 818 Lincoln Ave) has reasonably priced Mexican lunch and dinner specials. Considered the best Mexican-Southwestern place in town, *La Montaña* (☎ 970-879-5800, 2500 Village Dr), in Steamboat Village, is considerably more expensive.

The *Tugboat Grill & Pub* (☎ 970-879-7070, 1860 Ski Time Square) does a good mix of Mexican and American standards, while the adjacent *Cat House Cafe* (☎ 970-879-2441) is known for creative California cooking. Nearby *Mattie Silks* (☎ 970-879-2441, 1890 Ski Time Square) is one of Steamboat's most highly regarded restaurants for continental cuisine, steaks and seafood. The *Steamboat Yacht Club* (☎ 970-879-5570, 811 Yampa St) is another well-rated steak and seafood place.

Entertainment
Murphy's Exchange (☎ 970-879-2022, 703 Lincoln Ave) often has live music and can be one of the rowdier spots in town. The *Old Town Pub & Restaurant* (☎ 970-879-2101, 600 Lincoln Ave) also has live music on weekends.

Getting There & Away
Steamboat Springs is served by the Yampa Valley Regional Airport (☎ 970-276-3669) near Hayden, 22 miles west.

Alpine Taxi/Limo (☎ 970-879-2800, 800-232-7433) runs several shuttles daily between Steamboat and Denver International Airport.

Greyhound's US 40 service between Denver and Salt Lake City inconveniently stops at the Phillips 66 gas station about a mile west of town at 30475 Hwy 40. There is also an old Steamboat Springs Transit bus stop about 30 feet west of the gas station where you can catch a bus into town.

Steamboat Springs is 157 miles from Denver, 196 miles from Grand Junction and 339 miles from Salt Lake City. It lies along US 40 which connects with I-70 to the south, the most commonly used route.

There's also an intersection with Hwy 14 that then takes you east to Fort Collins and the Front Range.

Getting Around
Alpine Taxi/Limo (see above) and Steamboat Express (☎ 970-879-3400, 800-545-6050) both provide van service to Yampa Valley Regional Airport.

Steamboat Springs Transit (☎ 970-879-5585) runs a free bus service along Lincoln Ave from 12th St in the west to Walton Creek Rd in the east. It also goes up Mt Werner Rd to the gondola.

AROUND STEAMBOAT SPRINGS
Stagecoach State Park
Sixteen miles south of Steamboat Springs via US 40, Hwy 131 and Routt County Rd 14, Stagecoach State Park (☎ 970-736-2436) is the nearest inexpensive camping to Steamboat Springs; sites cost $8 to $12. There's fishing and a handful of hiking trails.

Mt Zirkel Wilderness
Famed mountaineer Clarence King, first director of the USGS, named 12,180-foot Mt Zirkel for a German petrologist when the two reconnoitered the country in 1874. The most popular entry points to this 250-sq-mile roadless area of the Routt National Forest are in the vicinity of Steamboat Springs, though it's also approachable from Walden or Clark. Detailed maps and information on hiking, mountain biking, fishing and other activities in this beautiful area are available at the Hahn's Peak Ranger Station (☎ 970-978-1870), 925 Weiss Dr, in Steamboat Springs.

Trails Illustrated publishes *Hahn's Peak/Steamboat Lake* and *Clark/Buffalo Pass* maps, while Jay and Therese Thompson describe the walks in *The Hiker's Guide to the Mt Zirkel Wilderness*.

Hahn's Peak
This picturesque quasi-ghost town, 27 miles north of Steamboat Springs via Elk River Rd (Routt County Rd 129), was once the terminus of the railroad from Wyoming. It's

an unfrequented destination that still has a handful of residents and a couple of interesting junk and crafts shops. Nearby Steamboat Lake State Park and Pearl Lake State Park (☎ 970-879-3922) are really reservoirs that offer shoreline camping ($10, plus $4 day pass) as well as fishing and boating.

Summit County

Locals joke that there are four seasons in Summit County – winter, late winter, Fourth of July and early winter. Reached by I-70 via the Eisenhower Tunnel, this mountain playground is just more than an hour's drive from Denver and is home to four ski mountains: Arapahoe Basin Ski Area, Keystone, Breckenridge and Copper Mountain.

SummitNet is the official Web site of the Summit County Chamber of Commerce (☎ 970-668-5800) and has information on accommodations, restaurants, activities, events, shopping and transportation for all of the towns and resorts within the county, and an online reservation service.
Web site: www.summitnet.com

Bighorn Rentals (☎ 970-668-1666, 800-826-7706), on W Main St in Frisco, is a good local source for lodging and vacation rentals in Frisco, Breckenridge, Keystone, Dillon and Silverthorne, as well as for tour arrangements.
Web site: www.bighornrentals.com

ARAPAHOE BASIN SKI AREA
Near the Continental Divide where US 6 crosses 11,992-foot Loveland Pass, 6 miles east of Keystone Resort and 90 miles west of Denver, Arapahoe Basin (☎ 970-468-0718, 888-272-7246) is Summit County's oldest ski area.

Locals call it 'A-Basin' and it's a favorite with experts who enjoy using one lift to get to the good stuff. Arapahoe is often still open in mid-June, giving it the longest ski season of any Colorado resort.

Lift passes are $40/32/12 for adults/teens/children (six to 14). Children under six and seniors 70 and over ski free.
Web site: www.arapahoebasin.com

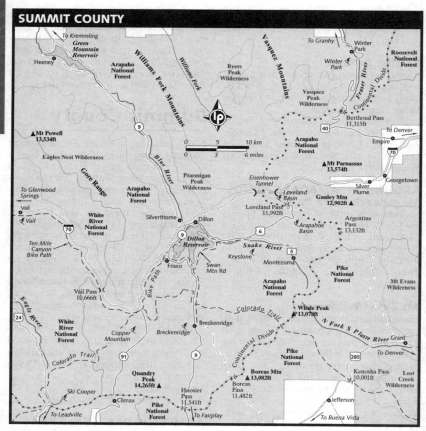

KEYSTONE SKI RESORT

In operation since 1970, Keystone is a family-oriented resort on the Snake River 5 miles east of Dillon on US 6. It attracts downhill and cross-country skiers as early as mid- to late-October, while other ski areas are still waiting for snow. Keystone is definitely a resort in that all the accommodations, restaurants and services are owned and operated by a single company. As a result, while the base area lacks the character and variety of real ski towns like Breckenridge and Aspen, Keystone has been well planned and it is easy to book

reservations and get information by calling one number (☎ 970-496-2316, 800-258-9553).

For summer visits, Keystone offers about 100 miles of bike trails through some amazing scenery, accessed by gondola for $10/day. Bike rentals, tours and lessons can be arranged by calling the Activities Center (☎ 800-354-4386), also the place to inquire about summer sports like golfing, horseback riding and hayrides, rafting, fly-fishing and a variety of children's programs.

Web site: www.keystoneresort.com

MONTEZUMA

Interested in what life is like in the highest town in the USA? The silver mining town of Montezuma (population 70; elevation 10,400 feet), 5 miles east of Keystone on Montezuma Rd, has little in common with trendy neighboring resorts. Folks here post homemade signs asking motorists to slow down, but even at 10mph a visit to Montezuma doesn't take long. Cross-country skiers and mountain bikers will want to explore the nearby trails, especially to the old mining town of Saints John, or up Peru Creek to the huge Pennsylvania Mine or on to Argentine Pass on the Continental Divide.

South of town near the Swan River crossing is the secluded *Western Skies Lodge B&B* (☎ *970-468-9445, 5040 Montezuma Rd*). You can stay in one of three cabins with a kitchen, or one of four doubles in the main lodge. Rates range from $60 to $130 and include breakfast and use of the wood-fired outdoor hot tub.

By day, the lodge doubles as a *coffee shop* serving light meals, soup and sandwiches. For dinner out, most head to Keystone. Check out its Web site at www.westernskies-keystone-cabins.com.

DILLON

Dillon (population 750; elevation 9017 feet) serves mainly as a place for day-skiers to pick up a bag lunch before heading to Keystone or A-Basin. It also offers some (relatively) cheaper accommodations that are still fairly close to the ski areas.

The Dillon Marina (☎ 970-468-5100) rents fishing boats, touring kayaks and sailboats at reasonable rates.

The *Best Western Ptarmigan Lodge* (☎ *970-468-2341, 800-842-5939, 652 Main St*) is in the center of Dillon. It's clean, well maintained and has a pool, sauna and whirlpool. Rates start around $75 in the high season and climb to more than $100 during peak holidays and weekends. *Spinnaker at Lake Dillon* (☎ *970-468-8001*) offer nightly rates for studios beginning at $50 in the summer and $100 during the winter, use of the pool,

sauna and garage included. Each unit has a fully equipped kitchen and laundry.

The *Arapahoe Cafe & Pub* (☎ *970-468-0873, 626 Lake Dillon Dr*) began in the 1940s as a roadside cafe and motel. In the summer, breakfast – granola, fresh fruit, yogurt and juice for about $6 – and lunch are served on the deck. Dinners of trout, roast duck and vegetarian pasta entrees are served inside. *Ristorante Al Lago* (☎ *970-468-6111, 240 Lake Dillon Dr*) features Italian entrees for $12 to $20, while *Pug Ryan's* (☎ *970-468-2145*), at the corner of Lake Dillon Dr and Village Place, is the most popular steakhouse in the area.

Drop by the *Corona Street Grill* (☎ *970-262-1122, 154 Dillon Mall*) for occasional live music and a lively happy hour.

Dillon is 85 miles west of Denver via I-70 to exit 205, then 1 mile south on US 6. The nearest Greyhound bus stop is in Silverthorne (see below).

SILVERTHORNE

Silverthorne (population 3100; elevation 9000 feet) is between Dillon and Frisco north of I-70. The earthfill dam that backs up Dillon Reservoir looms 230 feet above its glitzy clutter of shops. Silverthorne took a turn for the worse when numerous factory outlet stores opened, bringing metropolitan-like congestion and uncharacteristic urban development to the rustic setting at the base of the Gore Mountains.

The USFS visitors center for the Arapaho National Forest's Dillon Ranger District (☎ 970-468-5400), 680 Blue River Pkwy (Hwy 9), offers information and books on hiking and camping in the area. The Summit County Chamber of Commerce operates an information booth at the US 6/Hwy 9 junction.

Activities

Hiking is a draw. Silverthorne is wedged between Eagles Nest Wilderness Area to the west and Ptarmigan Peak Wilderness Area to the east. Both offer backcountry solitude away from vehicles and bikes, but trails directly from Silverthorne are heavily used. The Ptarmigan Wilderness is only a mile wide and 12 miles long, following the treeless ridge of the Williams Fork Mountains. A good day hike in the Ptarmigan Wilderness, with outstanding views of the Gore Range, is the Ute Pass Trail. It's a 4½-mile hike from Ute Pass (9558 feet) to 12,303-foot Ute Peak. To get to the trailhead, follow Hwy 9 north for 12 miles to Ute Pass Rd and continue to the trailhead west of the cattle guard at the pass.

A 'Summer Trailhead Guide,' available from the USFS or Summit County Chamber of Commerce, lists suggestions for other hikes. The USFS Dillon District Map is available at the USFS visitors center (see earlier in Silverstone section).

Rocky Mountaineering Guides (☎ 970-468-9646) offers guided hiking, trekking and rock climbing in Summit County.

Thirty-four miles of the Blue River between Dillon Dam and the Colorado River is designated Gold Medal water, rich for fishing. For guided fishing trips on the Blue River try Columbine Outfitters (☎ 970-262-0966), 191 Blue River Pkwy.

Places to Stay & Eat

One thing that Silverthorne does have going for it is the *Alpen Hütte Lodge* (*☎ 970-468-6336, 471 Rainbow Dr*), one of the best-run HI-AYH facilities in Colorado. Its dorms feature bunks with innerspring mattresses and built-in storage lockers, and the Blue River can be heard from an open window. Guests may rent mountain bikes for $10. Beds are $28 through the ski season ($25 during the holidays in December and March) and $18/20 in the off-season. HI-AYH members receive a $2 discount per night.

Other standard chain accommodations can be found along Silverthorne Lane, including: *Days Inn* (*☎ 970-468-8661*), *Hampton Inn* (*☎ 800-321-3509*) and *Luxury Inns & Suites* (*☎ 800-742-1972*).

To start the day, the *Blue Moon Baking Company* (*☎ 970-468-1472, 253 Summit Place*), in the City Market shopping center, offers espresso drinks, smoothies, fresh bagels, apple strudel and stuffed croissants. Its lunch menu of salads and sandwiches on

fresh breads is also appealing. *Sunshine Cafe* (*☎ 970-468-6663*), across from City Market, is open daily for breakfast, lunch and dinner and is a local favorite for good food and low prices.

Grill your own steak or seafood dinner at the rustic *Historic Mint* (*☎ 970-468-5247, 347 Blue River Pkwy*). Dinners range from $8 to $16 and the bar offers a good selection of beer. If you feel like kicking up your heels, head for the *Old Dillon Inn* (*☎ 970-468-2791, 321 Blue River Pkwy*), with inexpensive Mexican food and country & western music in a rustic decor. *Matteos's* (*☎ 970-262-6508, 122E W 10th*), on the north end of town at Hwy 9, has a great happy hour and good salads, pasta and pizza by the slice.

Getting There & Away

Greyhound buses (☎ 970-468-1938, 800-231-2222) stop at the Alpen Hütte between Denver and Grand Junction. Use the free Summit Stages buses (☎ 970-453-1339), which carry skis and bikes, to get to Copper Mountain, Keystone or Breckenridge.

Resort Express (☎ 970-468-0330, 800-334-7433), 273 Warren Ave, provides service between Denver International Airport and Summit County for $49/98 one-way/roundtrip.

Web site: www.resort-express.com

FRISCO

This is a convenient base for enjoying Summit County's summer and winter activities. Frisco (population 3150; elevation 9100 feet) offers a good selection of accommodations, restaurants and shops in a compact area. Copper Mountain, Breckenridge, Keystone and Arapahoe are 20 minutes away, as are some of the country's best white-water rafting, kayaking and fly-fishing waters, and miles and miles of road- and mountain-biking trails.

Information

Maps and tourist information about the county and towns are available from the Summit County Chamber of Commerce (☎ 970-668-5800, 800-424-1554),

COLORADO

11 S Summit Blvd at Main St. The chamber is open 9 am to 5 pm daily.
Web site: www.townoffrisco.com

Summit County Central Reservations (☎ 970-468-6222, 800-365-6365) arranges lodging, transportation, lift tickets and activities for winter or summer visitors.

The Colorado Community First National Bank (☎ 970-668-3333) is at 1000 N Summit Blvd. The Safeway next door has an ATM. The post office is at 65 W Main St; the zip code is 80443.

The Daily Planet Bookstore (☎ 970-668-5016) offers a good selection of travel guides and local history books and sells topo maps. Frisco's Washtub Laundromat (☎ 970-668-3552) is at 406 Main St. Frisco Medical Center (☎ 970-668-3003) is at the corner of Hwy 9 and School Rd.

Frisco Historic Park
Frisco's proliferation of vintage log cabins – many of which are still inhabited – reflects the historical character of this former mining camp. Aficionados of log construction techniques will appreciate the double-dovetail joints at the 1890 Dills Ranch House and the 1895 Bailey House. Inside the Trappers Cabin, visitors will find the kind of pelts that once sustained the area's meager economy prior to mining. Small windows mark the four cells of the 1881 jail next to the Frisco School House Museum (☎ 970-668-3428), 120 Main St. The one-room school, complete with bell tower, is on its original site; it arose in 1890 as a saloon where backwoods chemists practiced fermentation using a copper still. It's open 11 am to 4 pm Tuesday to Sunday in summer, Tuesday to Saturday in winter.

Bicycling
Summit County's network of paved paths provide one of the nation's finest systems for bicycle travel, connecting Frisco with Dillon (5 miles), Breckenridge (10 miles), Copper Mountain (8 miles), Keystone (12 miles) and Ten Mile Canyon over Vail Pass (14 miles). On the Dillon Dam Trail is an overlook and telescope to view an osprey nest. From Frisco Historic Park, ride south

on 2nd St to Farmers Korner, where trails lead to all destinations except Dillon. Restrooms and water are available at the Blue River inlet to Dillon Reservoir. Cyclists are not the only ones to benefit from the trails – Nordic skiers and skaters also enjoy them in winter.

The gear stores in Frisco can equip you for these outdoor activities and they even rent bike trailers for the kids. Antlers Ski & Sport Shop (☎ 970-668-3152), 900 N Summit Blvd, has fishing and camping supplies, topo maps and bike and ski rentals. Also try Pioneer Sports (☎ 970-668-3668), 842 N Summit Blvd, for ski, bike or skate rentals.

Cross-Country Skiing
The Frisco Nordic Center (☎ 970-668-0866) offers about 20 miles of set cross-country ski trails on the Dillon Reservoir peninsula east of Frisco. Lessons and rentals are available. The main trailhead and parking is off Hwy 9 a mile east of Frisco, or you can reach the center from the Frisco Marina parking area at the foot of Main St. Once the snow arrives, the center is open 9 am to 4 pm daily. Adult/child passes are $15/8.

Boating
Whether you want to fish or just cruise Dillon Reservoir, Osprey Adventures (☎ 970-668-5573, 888-780-4970), 900 E Main St at Frisco Bay Marina, offers canoe, sailboat and outboard motorboat sales and rentals.

Places to Stay & Eat
Four large USFS-run Arapaho National Forest campgrounds (☎ 970-468-5400) line the shores of Dillon Reservoir. Seventy-two pleasant sites shaded by lodgepole pines can be found at *Heaton Bay* (☎ 877-444-6777), about a mile east of N Summit Blvd on Dam Rd or reached by the bike path from Frisco. Also reservable are the 79 sites at *Peak One*, only a mile east of town on Hwy 9. Fees at both campgrounds are $12.

First-come, first-served sites are available at *Pine Cove*, with 50 sites ($9) or at *Prospector*, 109 sites ($11); both are on the south shore.

Doubles start at $45/59 in summer/winter at the unexciting but centrally located *Snowshoe Motel* (☎ 970-668-3444, 800-445-8658, 521 Main St).

Built in 1885, Summit County's oldest lodging, *Frisco Lodge* (☎ 970-668-0195, 800-279-6000, 321 Main St) once served as a railroad inn. Its rustic rooms with shared bath are the cheapest in town and include breakfast. Lockable storage for bikes and skis is available, as well as an outdoor hot tub. Singles/doubles with shared bath cost from $35/45 during summer.
Web site: www.friscolodge.com

Woods Inn (☎ 970-668-2255, 877-664-3777, 205 S Second Ave), one block off Main St, is a great value. It includes a pine-log building constructed in 1938 and now provides economical B&B accommodations with shared bath from $25. There's also a newer building that has standard rooms from $75 to $95 and suites from $125 to $265. Amenities include a cozy living area with a fireplace and a hot tub.
Web site: www.woodsinnbandb.com

If you're willing to spend a bit more, the *Galena Street Mountain Inn* (☎ 970-668-3224, 800-248-9138, galenast@aol.com), at First Ave and Galena St, is the place to stay. Each of its uniquely decorated 14 rooms has a private bath, cable TV, and phone; the shared amenities include a comfortable living and dining room, a sun deck, hot tub and sauna. Summer rates range from $75 to $95; $110 to $140 in winter.

Also downtown, the modern *Twilight Inn* (☎ 970-668-5009, 800-262-1002, 308 Main St) offers 12 rooms with a variety of decor, from Victorian frills to Mission-style furnishings, plus an enclosed hot tub, laundry and storage/work area for skis and bicycles. Four 3rd-floor rooms share two bathrooms. A simple buffet breakfast is included with the shared/private rooms that rent from $50/70 during summer, $90/128 in winter.

Butterhorn Bakery & Deli (☎ 970-668-3997, 408 W Main St) is the place to 'carb-up' for a day on the slopes or trails.

For mountain haute cuisine, head for the award-winning *Uptown Bistro* (☎ 970-668-4728, 304 Main St).

Getting There & Around

The closest Greyhound bus stop on the way to Frisco is at the Alpen Hütte in Silverthorne.

Resort Express (☎ 970-468-7600, 800-334-7433) offers service between Denver International Airport and Summit County for $49/98 one-way/roundtrip.
Web site: www.resort-express.com

From Denver, take I-70 west 95 miles to exit 203. Frisco lies just southeast of the interstate on Hwy 9.

Summit Stage (☎ 970-668-0999) operates local buses 6 am to 11 pm from the Frisco Transit Center, next to the WalMart on N Summit Blvd. Free buses leave Copper Mountain, Keystone, Breckenridge and Silverthorne at the top of the hour and meet in Frisco on the half-hour.

BRECKENRIDGE

The high point of any visit to Summit County, the small town of Breckenridge is largely a National Historic District. It's also home to Breckenridge Ski Resort, one of the state's more pleasant ski areas.

Orientation

Breckenridge (population 1700) is on the Blue River south of Frisco and the Dillon Reservoir. Farther south, Hwy 9 and the narrow river valley rise to 11,541-foot Hoosier Pass, leading to the South Park Basin and its surrounding five 14,000-foot peaks. The ski resort is centered around the Breckenridge Village and Beaver Run complexes south of S Park Ave. The four mountain ski areas, arrayed along the west side of the valley from north to south, are Peaks 7 through 10.

Information

Run by the Breckenridge Resort Chamber, the Breckenridge information center (☎ 970-453-6018), 309 N Main St in the 1914 Gaymon House, and the activity center (☎ 970-453-5579), 137 S Main, offer assistance with lodging reservations and provide free copies of *Breckenridge Magazine*, which contains a self-guided walking tour of the historic town. You can also purchase tickets from the Summit Historical Society to take guided tours of the Edwin Carter Museum, Lomax Placer Mine, Washington Mine or the Breckenridge Historic District. Web site: www.breckenridge.com

The Community First National Bank operates two branches in Breckenridge: 106 N French St (☎ 970-453-2521) and 600 S Ridge St (☎ 970-453-9288). The 1stBank (☎ 970-453-1000), 200 Ski Hill Rd, has an ATM.

The post office is at 300 S Ridge; the zip code is 80424. Mail Boxes Etc (☎ 970-453-8080) offers package shipping next to City Market shopping center at 400 N Park Ave.

Weber's Books & Drawings (☎ 970-453-4723), 100 S Main St, carries a good stock of titles on Colorado history, Native American culture and a very good selection of local and international guidebooks. It also sells topo maps.

Norge Laundry (☎ 970-453-2426), 105 S French St, is open daily and offers drop-off service. The Breckenridge Recreation Center (☎ 970-453-1734), 880 Airport Rd, has showers for $4.

Should you have an emergency, the Medical Center (☎ 970-453-9000) is in the Village Plaza II at 555 S Park St.

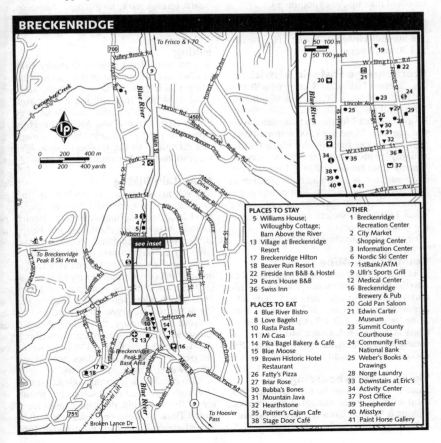

BRECKENRIDGE

PLACES TO STAY
5 Williams House;
  Willoughby Cottage;
  Barn Above the River
13 Village at Breckenridge
  Resort
17 Breckenridge Hilton
18 Beaver Run Resort
22 Fireside Inn B&B & Hostel
29 Evans House B&B
36 Swiss Inn

PLACES TO EAT
4 Blue River Bistro
8 Love Bagels!
10 Rasta Pasta
11 Mi Casa
14 Pika Bagel Bakery & Café
18 Blue Moose
19 Brown Historic Hotel
  Restaurant
26 Fatty's Pizza
27 Briar Rose
30 Bubba's Bones
31 Mountain Java
32 Hearthstone
35 Poirrier's Cajun Cafe
38 Stage Door Café

OTHER
1 Breckenridge
  Recreation Center
2 City Market
  Shopping Center
3 Information Center
6 Nordic Ski Center
7 1stBank/ATM
12 Medical Center
16 Breckenridge
  Brewery & Pub
20 Gold Pan Saloon
21 Edwin Carter
  Museum
23 Summit County
  Courthouse
24 Community First
  National Bank
25 Weber's Books &
  Drawings
28 Norge Laundry
33 Downstairs at Eric's
34 Activity Center
37 Post Office
39 Sheepherder
40 Misstyx
41 Paint Horse Gallery

Edwin Carter Museum

Edwin Carter arrived in Breckenridge in 1868 from Oneida, New York. Often addressed as 'Professor' Carter, he was a self-taught naturalist who sought to protect the local flora and fauna from the consequences of placer mining. He was also a collector who, by 1875, had built this log museum to house his specimens. The collection grew to more than 10,000 specimens by 1898, when Carter negotiated to transfer the collection to the newly formed State Museum of Natural History and was appointed the first curator. Carter passed away in 1900 before he could take up the appointment.

The museum is at the corner of Wellington Rd and Ridge St. Tours are offered by the Summit Historical Society (see below) at 1:30 and 3 pm weekdays.

Breckenridge Historic District

The Summit Historical Society (☎ 970-453-9022), 309 N Main St, offers a 10 am two-hour walking tour of the well-preserved historic district Monday to Saturday during the summer. More than 200 historic buildings are in the four-by-four-block district roughly centered on the 1909 **Summit County Courthouse** at 200 E Lincoln Ave. Purchase tickets for $6/3 adults/children at the Breckenridge information center or activities center. Call ahead or look online for other Historical Society activities (including gold mine tours).
Web site: www.summithistorical.org

Country Boy Mine

This underground tour takes you 1000 feet into the mine where there are working drills and 100-year-old ore carts and dynamite demonstrations. The 1887 Country Boy Mine (☎ 970-453-4405), 2 miles northeast of town at 542 French Gulch Rd, is open in summer and winter; admission $10/5 adults/children. Phone ahead for seasonal hours.

Skiing & Snowboarding

Since 1961, Breckenridge has expanded to a total of four interconnected mountains, making it Summit County's largest ski area in both area and number of visitors.

Regular lift tickets cost $53/21 adults/children 12 and under. The $168 three-day ticket is good for one day at either Vail or Beaver Creek, and any Breckenridge ticket can be used at Keystone and Arapahoe Basin. For recorded snow information, call ☎ 970-453-6118.

Breckenridge Nordic Ski Center (☎ 970-453-6855), at the Whatley Ranch at 1200 Ski Hill Rd, about a half-mile from Peak 8 on the free shuttle route, offers more than 17 miles of groomed cross-country trails, lessons and equipment rental.

Breckenridge features a 6-acre snowboard terrain park, including a half-pipe, located on Peak 9. Snowboarding lessons are offered through the ski school.

Hiking

Southwest of Breckenridge, **Quandry Peak** (14,265 feet) offers one of the easier walkups if you have a 4WD to reach the trailhead. A 4-mile trail follows an exposed ridgeline to the summit that looks over South Park County and Mt of the Holy Cross. The ranger station in Dillon has maps and directions to the trailhead, as well as suggestions for other routes in the area.

Mountain Biking

There's no shortage of backroads and single-track trails around Breckenridge. A good loop for intermediate riders begins midway between Breckenridge and Frisco at the Gold Hill trailhead. Take the paved Blue River path down the valley for a warm-up; the single-track Gold Hill Trail is on your left (west) immediately after crossing the river. It climbs 3 miles to the Peaks Trail, which takes you 6 miles back to the top of Ski Hill Rd above Breckenridge.

From Breckenridge, the Boreas Pass Rd follows an old railroad alignment and climbs 1925 feet in 11 miles to the 11,482-foot top of the pass. As the gradient does not exceed 5%, however, it's considered 'easy.'

Also consider a loop through Keystone. Use both Keystone gondolas to get to the top of the mountain, descend 2 miles from North Peak to Keystone Gulch Rd, then ascend about 2 miles up West Ridge Trail and turn left at the Colorado Trail to Tiger Run Rd along the Swan River, back to Hwy 9 north of Breckenridge.

The free *Summit County Mountain Bike Guide*, available at bike shops and information offices, covers all of the major biking trails and lists degrees of difficulty. A more descriptive guide is Laura Rossetter's *The Mountain Bike Guide to Summit County Colorado*, available at local bookstores and bike shops. The Breckenridge Fat Tire Society (☎ 970-453-5548) runs a 'Mountain Bike Hotline' (☎ 970-453-4636 ext 3288) with information on ride activities.

Mountain Outfitters (☎ 970-453-2201), 112 S Ridge St, and Great Adventure Sports Center (☎ 970-453-0333), 400 N Park St, are two places to go for equipment, advice and maps.

Other Activities

Early-season half-day white-water rafting trips on the Blue River below Silverthorne are not why people come to Summit County. Nevertheless, scenic views of the Gore Range and about 2 miles of Class III whitewater make the convenient trip worthwhile. River trips are offered by Performance Tours (☎ 970-453-0661, 800-328-7238), 110 Ski Hill Rd; visit www.performancetours.com.

Breckenridge Stables (☎ 970-453-4438), at the base of Peak 9, offers 90-minute horseback rides on the Breckenridge Trail, as well as daily breakfast rides.

Jackson Streit's Mountain Angler (☎ 970-453-4665, 800-453-4669), 311 S Main St, is a full-service fish and tackle store and Summit County's longest-running fishing guide service; visit www.mountainangler.com. Blue River Anglers (☎ 970-453-9171, 888-453-9171), 209 N Main Street, also offers guide services; its Web site is www.blueriveranglers.com.

Many golfers appreciate the added advantage of the thin air at the 9300-foot high Breckenridge Golf Course (☎ 970-453-9104), on Tiger Run Rd 3 miles north of Breckenridge. The course was designed by Jack Nicklaus.

Special Events

In late January the **Ullr Fest**, celebrating the Norse god of winter, is a wild parade and four-day festival featuring a twisted version of the Dating Game, an ice-skating party and a kids concert. Also in January, the **International Snow Sculpture Championship** provides decorations for the River Walk and Bell Tower Mall. A month-long spring skiing celebration in April, **Beach Daze** features BBQs, races and great deals on lift tickets and accommodations after Easter. On the weekend after the Fourth of July, **Jazz in July** (☎ 970-453-6018) features top regional performers at the Maggie Pond in the Village at Breckenridge Resort. The Riverwalk Center hosts more than 50 orchestral concerts and chamber recitals each summer in its Breckenridge Festival of Music series. For a concert schedule call the Breckenridge Music Institute & National Repertory Orchestra (☎ 970-453-2120).

The 'Kingdom of Breckenridge' was declared after it was discovered that the 1300 sq miles surrounding Breckenridge were not positively part of the USA. The early **August No Man's Land Celebration** celebrates this 'independence' with gold panning and woodcarving contests and historic walking tours. During the third week of September, the **Breckenridge Festival of Film** (☎ 970-453-6200) attracts well-known celebrities, writers and producers to premiere screenings at six theater sites in Summit County. It's followed by a lively **Oktoberfest** with plenty of German beer and oompah music.

Places to Stay

Most of the pillows in Breckenridge are in condominiums. A standard one-bedroom unit for four costs between $100 and $150 during winter. Breckenridge Resort Central Reservations (☎ 970-453-6678, 877-234-3981), 311 S Ridge St, can help find a condo. Web site: www.gobreck.com

The rundown *Fireside Inn B&B & Hostel* (☎ 970-453-6456, 114 N French St) is the only Hostelling International lodging in town. It has beds for $23 in summer, $25 to $30 in winter; breakfast is available at an additional charge. Private rooms at the inn range from $50 to $150. Storage for bikes and skis is available and there is a hot tub.

At the base of the Peak 9 lifts, huge top-end resorts dwarf the historic town and are separate, self-contained enclaves offering deluxe hotel rooms and suites. The *Breckenridge Hilton* (☎ 970-453-4500, 550 Village Rd) has 208 rooms beginning at $90/165 summer/winter. *Beaver Run Resort* (☎ 970-453-6000, 800-288-1282, 620 Village Rd) has more than 500 rooms with two queen beds for $115/195 summer/winter or more expensive studios and large suites with spas; visit online at www.beaverrunresort.com. Slightly smaller rooms range from $75 to $220 at *Village Hotel*, part of the enormous *Village at Breckenridge Resort* (☎ 970-453-2000, 800-800-7829, 655 S Park Ave), which covers over 18 acres; visit www.breckresort.com.

The clean and well-run *Swiss Inn* (☎ 970-453-6489, 888-794-7750, 205 S French St) is the budget traveler's best bet in Breckenridge. A bed in an eight-person mixed-gender dorm costs $39, including breakfast. Or you can stay in one of four late 19th-century Victorian rooms that range from $69 to $156. The dormitory is adjacent to a beautiful garden solarium with a hot tub.

Rates for the comfortable rooms with shared bath at the 1886 *Evans House B&B* (☎ 970-453-5509, 102 S French St) start at $68/100 summer/winter; $77/114 with attached bath.
Web site: www.coloradoevanshouse.com

The historic *Williams House* (c 1885), *Willoughby Cottage* (c 1880), and the newer *Barn Above the River* (c 1997) form a collective known as Bed & Breakfasts on North Main Street (☎ 970-453-2975), 303 N Main St. They all offer antique furnishings and private baths and start at $89, $169 and $119 respectively.

Places to Eat

Good places to get started with caffeine, muffins, guidebooks and maps are *Mountain Java* (☎ 970-453-1874, 118 S Ridge St)

and the *Stage Door Café* (☎ 970-453-6964, 213 S Main St), with a full range of coffees plus breakfast burritos and deli sandwiches. Whole-wheat pancakes are a bargain at *Blue Moose* (☎ 970-453-4859, 540 S Main St), open until 2 pm only.

A bagel fix can be had at *Pika Bagel Bakery & Café* (☎ 970-453-6246, 500 S Main St) or *Love Bagels!* (☎ 970-547-1115, 325 S Main St).

Reggae will be playing as you enter the colorful *Rasta Pasta* (☎ 970-453-7467, 411 S Main St). Try the Natural Mystic – pasta with jerk chicken and pineapple curry – but get there early because the place is usually jammin'. For Mexican dinners, try *Mi Casa* (☎ 970-453-2071, 600 S Park Ave). Its adjacent cantina features margaritas by the liter.

Blue River Bistro (☎ 970-453-6947, 305 N Main St) offers lunch selections such as pastas, salads, sandwiches and burgers. At *Fatty's Pizza* (☎ 970-453-9802, 106 S Ridge St) you can enjoy pizza and pasta on an up-stairs deck. *Bubba's Bones* (☎ 970-547-9942, 110 S Ridge St) is the locals' favorite for real Southern-style BBQ; lunches are around $5 or $6, dinners from $7 to $13.

The Brown Historic Hotel Restaurant (☎ 970-453-0084, 208 N Ridge St) is appealing with its $5 stuffed shrimp with red beans and rice dinner special. Most of the varied menu offerings served in the Victorian dining room, however, cost between $10 and $20. Innovative American cooking is featured at *Hearthstone* (☎ 970-453-1148, 130 S Ridge St) which has starters like grilled portobello mushrooms and smoked seafood, and main courses including wild mushroom–stuffed chicken, rack of elk and crab-stuffed trout.

Poirrier's Cajun Cafe (☎ 970-453-1877, 224 S Main) has it all, from a simple bowl of N'awlins red beans and rice for $4 to catfish Atchafalaya for $17. It offers special early dinner deals. Elegant to the extreme, the *Briar Rose* (☎ 970-453-9948, 109 E Lincoln Ave) features steak, game and seafood at top-end prices in an historic building complete with none other than a trophy lounge.

Entertainment

John Wayne would look just right sidled up to the bar at the *Gold Pan Saloon* (☎ 970-453-5499, 105 N Main St), established in the 1870s. At *Downstairs at Eric's* (☎ 970-453-1401, 111 S Main St) you can choose from about 120 beers and swap stories with the mountain bikers and climbers who gather there. Also check out *Breckenridge Brewery & Pub* (☎ 970-453-1550, 600 S Main St), which offers several fine brews made on the premises.

Ullr's Sports Grill (☎ 970-453-6060, 401 S Main St) offers cheap drinks on Tuesday.

From the month of July to September the *Backstage Theatre* (☎ 970-453-0199), on Maggie Pond in the Village at Breckenridge Resort, presents nightly plays at 8 pm.

Shopping

The Breckenridge Gallery features original paintings and limited-edition bronzes by local and international artists. For locally made sheepskin apparel, stop by the Sheepherder (☎ 970-453-1181), 211 S Main St. For fine antique Navajo weavings and Western memorabilia, visit the Paint Horse Gallery (☎ 970-453-6813), 226 S Main St. Locally made furniture can be found at High Country Furniture & Gallery (☎ 970-453-2816), 13217 Hwy 9, 2½ miles north of town. For unusual jewelry and hair accessories, check out Misstyx (☎ 970-547-0202), 311 S Main St.

Getting There & Around

Resort Express (☎ 800-334-7433) offers service between Denver and Summit County for $49/98 one-way/roundtrip. Web site: www.resort-express.com

Breckenridge is 104 miles west of Denver via I-70 exit 203, then Hwy 9 south.

The local free Downtown Trolley operates 9 am to midnight June to September and November to April. Free shuttles (☎ 970-453-5000) to the lifts travel in both directions on French St, Lincoln Ave and Park Ave. Summit Stage buses leave the Bell Tower in Breckenridge at the top of the hour, from the recreation center seven minutes later, arriving at the Frisco Transfer Center on the half hour.

COPPER MOUNTAIN SKI RESORT

West of Dillon Reservoir at I-70 exit 195, Copper Mountain Resort (☎ 970-968-2882, 800-458-8386) opened in 1973, the last ski area to crowd into Summit County. Lift tickets at Copper Mountain cost $55/19 adults/children.
Web site: www.ski-copper.com

Summer Activities

During summer, business is so slow that the resort offers free chairlift rides to a mid-mountain barbecue and USFS ranger-led nature hikes. You can choose between a tundra trek or forest hike that's geared for all abilities and ages; sign up at the activities desk or the welcome center. Also in summer, cyclists can bring their mountain bikes on the lift for $10 per day.

Places to Stay

Rooms at the 600-unit *Copper Mountain Resort* (☎ 970-968-2882, 800-458-8386) start at $185 in winter. Accommodations range from basic hotel rooms to deluxe suites and condominiums that can sleep up to 10 people.

Club Med (☎ 970-968-2161, 800-258-2633) offers various seven- and eight-day accommodations and ski packages for around $1400 that include a six-day lift ticket, ski and snowboard instruction, meals and nightly entertainment.

Getting Around

A free shuttle service in the Village runs every 10 minutes 8 am to 10 pm during ski season. The free Summit Stage shuttle leaves every half hour from the Mountain Plaza at Copper Mountain and serves Breckenridge and other Summit County destinations.

LEADVILLE & AROUND

Nicknamed 'Cloud City' for its altitude, Leadville (population 2900; elevation 10,430 feet) attracts visitors curious about the enormous mining operations and characters that once made it Colorado's second-largest city. Poor living conditions make this Colorado's

COLORADO

'Appalachia.' Few would confuse Leadville with other Colorado mountain towns that have readily traded their mining past for resort status.

Visitors who are not attracted to Leadville's bawdy past are most likely interested in the area's outdoor activities. Quickly scaling the two highest peaks in Colorado is a popular feat. But some may find greater satisfaction in slowly taking in the extensive alpine environment of the stunning terrain surrounding Leadville.

Dee Hive Tours & Transportation (☎ 719-486-2339), 506 Harrison Ave, offers 4WD tours of old mines and ghost towns.

Orientation

The principal route through town, US 24, follows a dogleg course from Harrison Ave in the south to E 9th St before continuing north on Poplar St.

Three historic mining areas east of Leadville are easy excursions. Take E 7th St from Harrison Ave to the Fryer Hill mining district, site of the Matchless Mine. This route continues east over 13,186-foot Mosquito Pass (4WD required). The Carbonate Hill mining district is reached by following E 5th St out to Stray Horse Gulch. To reach California Gulch, where Oro City's mines played out before Leadville's founding, take E 2nd St and turn right on Toledo St to the gulch.

Information

At the visitors center (☎ 719-486-3900, 800-939-3901), 809 Harrison Ave, you can pick up maps and brochures; visit www.leadvilleusa.com. The Leadville Chamber of Commerce presents a 30-minute multimedia show, 'The Earth Runs Silver: Early Leadville,' daily at the New Fox Theater (☎ 719-489-0979), 115 W 6th St. The USFS Leadville Ranger Station (☎ 719-486-0749), at the north end of town at 2015 Poplar St, has information, books and topo maps on the Mt Massive Wilderness Area and other forest sites like the crowded Turquoise Lake Reservoir. It's open 7:30 am to 4:30 pm weekdays, 8 am to 4:30 pm Saturday.

People's Bank (☎ 719-482-0420) is at 400 Harrison Ave. Safeway grocery store (☎ 719-486-0795), 1900 N US 24, provides an ATM and Western Union money transfers.

The post office is at 130 W 5th St; the zip code is 80461. The Aspen Leaf (☎ 719-486-3244, fax 719-486-2693), 711 Harrison Ave, offers fax service.

The Book Mine (☎ 719-486-2866), 502 Harrison Ave, has books on local history and outdoor activities.

Showers with towel cost $4.50 at the Laundromat (☎ 719-486-0551), at the corner of Poplar St and Mountain View Dr. Showers with towel cost $3, or $6 including

The Triumphs & Tribulations of Horace Tabor

Horace Tabor arrived in Leadville in 1877 and had the good fortune to grubstake Rische and Hook's successful exploration, receiving half of their discovery for a reported investment of $17. Then he hit the jackpot again by purchasing the Matchless Mine. The millions he made were invested locally and helped launch a political career that eventually led him to a US Senate seat.

However, in 1883, while he was serving in the senate, Horace and Augusta Tabor divorced and Horace married a young divorcée, Mrs Elizabeth McCourt Doe, known as Baby Doe. This created a national scandal. The nationwide Silver Panic of 1893 led to widespread mine closures and struck Leadville with a vengeance. Tabor lost his fortune and property holdings but kept the closed Matchless Mine. From his deathbed in 1899, he instructed Baby Doe to 'Hang on to the Matchless. It will make millions again.'

Like others before and after her, Baby Doe clung to the dream until 1935, when her frozen body was found in a cabin at the mine.

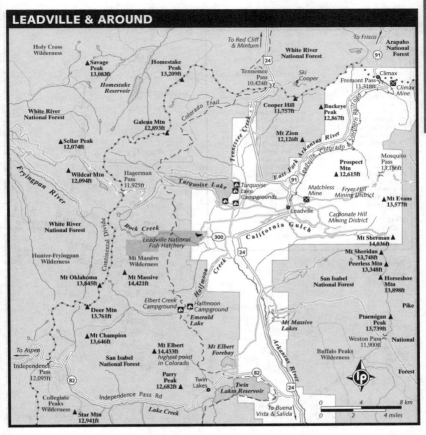

LEADVILLE & AROUND

use of the center's other facilities, at the Leadville Recreation Center (☎ 719-486-0917), 1000 W 6th St.

St Vincent General Hospital (☎ 719-486-0230) is at 822 W 4th St.

Walking Tour

Start from the small picnic area on W 10th St near the summit of Harrison Ave. On your right you can see the solid mass of tailings on Fryer Hill to the east – site of the Matchless Mine – with the Mosquito Range in the background. To the left are the slopes of Mt Massive, Colorado's second-highest peak.

At the base of the hill, Horace Tabor oversaw the completion of the imposing **Tabor Grand Hotel**, 711 Harrison Ave. Drop into the Cloud City Coffee House at the hotel to admire the marblework and high-ceiling skylight. Continue past the Lake County Courthouse on the west side of Harrison Ave.

The **Western Hardware Company**, at the corner of Harrison Ave and 5th St, has displays of antique tools and hardware plus a collection of early ski equipment. Continue to the **Silver Dollar Saloon**, built in 1879 at 315 Harrison Ave, where antique decor and

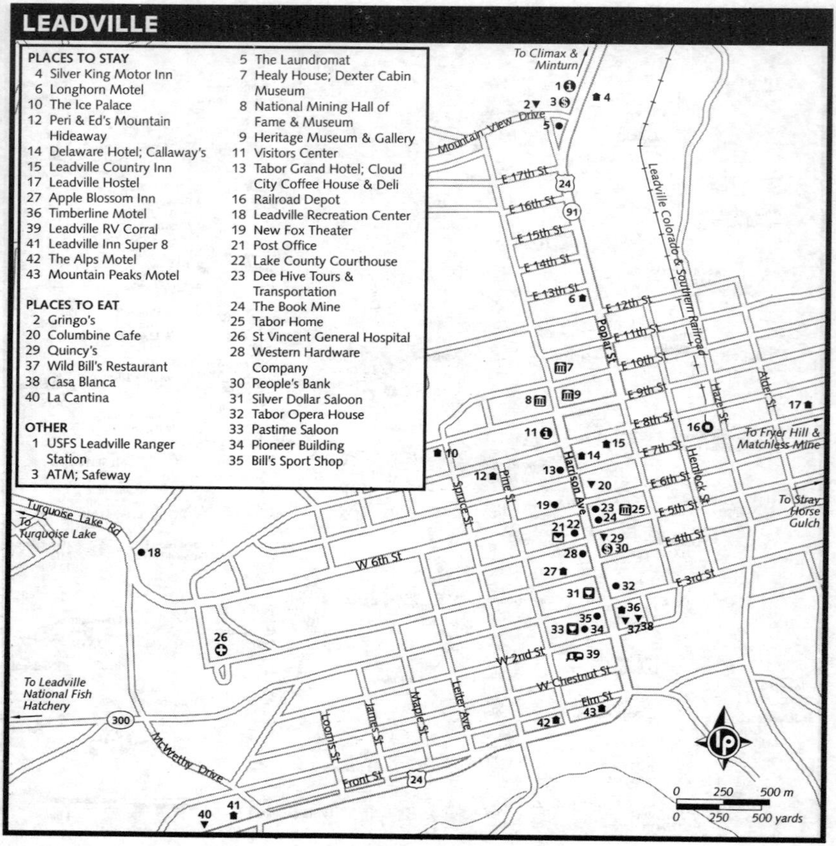

LEADVILLE
PLACES TO STAY
4 Silver King Motor Inn
6 Longhorn Motel
10 The Ice Palace
12 Peri & Ed's Mountain Hideaway
14 Delaware Hotel; Callaway's
15 Leadville Country Inn
17 Leadville Hostel
27 Apple Blossom Inn
36 Timberline Motel
39 Leadville RV Corral
41 Leadville Inn Super 8
42 The Alps Motel
43 Mountain Peaks Motel
PLACES TO EAT
2 Gringo's
20 Columbine Cafe
29 Quincy's
37 Wild Bill's Restaurant
38 Casa Blanca
40 La Cantina
OTHER
1 USFS Leadville Ranger Station
3 ATM; Safeway
5 The Laundromat
7 Healy House; Dexter Cabin Museum
8 National Mining Hall of Fame & Museum
9 Heritage Museum & Gallery
11 Visitors Center
13 Tabor Grand Hotel; Cloud City Coffee House & Deli
16 Railroad Depot
18 Leadville Recreation Center
19 New Fox Theater
21 Post Office
22 Lake County Courthouse
23 Dee Hive Tours & Transportation
24 The Book Mine
25 Tabor Home
26 St Vincent General Hospital
28 Western Hardware Company
30 People's Bank
31 Silver Dollar Saloon
32 Tabor Opera House
33 Pastime Saloon
34 Pioneer Building
35 Bill's Sport Shop
To Climax & Minturn
Mountain View Drive
Leadville Colorado & Southern Railroad
E 17th St
E 16th St
E 15th St
E 14th St
E 13th St
E 12th St
E 11th St
E 10th St
E 9th St
E 8th St
E 7th St
E 6th St
E 5th St
E 4th St
E 3rd St
Poplar St
Hazel St
Alder St
Hemlock St
Harrison Ave
Spruce St
Pine St
W 6th St
W 2nd St
W Chestnut St
Elm St
Loomis St
James St
Maple St
Leiter Ave
Front St
McWethy Drive
Turquoise Lake Rd
To Turquoise Lake
To Fryer Hill & Matchless Mine
To Stray Horse Gulch
To Leadville National Fish Hatchery
0 250 500 m
0 250 500 yards

early photographs are on display. At W 2nd St, the vacant **Pioneer Building**, built in 1892, and the lively **Pastime Saloon** are remnants of an area that was once so rowdy it was off limits to Camp Hale military personnel during WWII.

From 1877 to 1881, Horace and Augusta Tabor resided at 116 E 5th St. The **Tabor Home** is now operated as a museum displaying the period furnishings and recounting the story of the scandal surrounding Horace's second marriage to 'Baby Doe.'

National Mining Hall of Fame & Museum

The mining museum (☎ 719-486-1229), 120 W 9th St, part of a three-story Victorian schoolhouse built in 1896, is undoubtedly the premier museum in Leadville. The hall of fame on the 3rd floor honors the nation's foremost earth scientists such as John Wesley Powell, famous prospectors like Paddy Martinez, who discovered New Mexico's uranium deposits, and the kingpins of the US mining industry such as the Comstock Lode's Adolf Sutro. The museum is open 9 am to 5 pm daily May to November, 10 am to 2 pm weekdays the rest of the year. Admission is $4/3.50/2 adults/seniors (62 and over) and children (6 to 12).

Healy House & Dexter Cabin Museum

The saltbox-style Healy House (☎ 719-486-0487), 912 Harrison Ave, was built in 1878 by August Meyer, a mining engineer from St Louis. The rough-hewn exterior of the adjacent Dexter Cabin, built by James V Dexter in 1879 and since relocated from W 3rd St, gives no hint of the sumptuous interior used exclusively by Dexter for entertaining and gambling. Daily tours of these antique-filled buildings at 912 Harrison Ave are offered by the Colorado Historical Society (☎ 719-486-0487) from 10 am to 4:30 pm Memorial Day to Labor Day. Admission is $3.50/2 adults/children.

Heritage Museum & Gallery

This Carnegie Library, built in 1904 at the corner of 9th St and Harrison Ave, now houses the Heritage Museum & Gallery (☎ 719-486-1878), a local history collection. From Memorial Day to October, you can view early dioramas of Leadville and learn about the 10th Mountain Division, which trained 10,000 troops for alpine warfare near Tennessee Pass during WWII. Kids enjoy panning for gold. Admission is $3.50/2.50 adults/children.

Tabor Opera House

Horace and Augusta Tabor reinvested their mining riches in Leadville by opening the opulent 880-seat opera house (☎ 719-486-1147), 308 Harrison Ave, in 1879. Before the Tabors lost the opera house in 1893, it attracted top New York stage talent to the 'Silver Circuit.' Since 1955, Evelyn Furman has offered tours ($4/2 adults/children) of

---

The Rise & Fall of Leadville

In the spring of 1878, August Rische and George Hook established the Little Pittsburg Mine on Fryer Hill, which led to a silver bonanza that eclipsed earlier findings at nearby Oro City. Soon after the ore discovery, Leadville vaulted to a financial position surpassed only by Denver. By 1879 Leadville's character during the silver boom was reflected in its new cultural institutions: four churches, 120 saloons and 188 gambling houses! The 1880 census counted nearly 15,000 residents, five times as many as in Colorado's next largest city, Pueblo. With 15 silver-lead smelters, Leadville could boast that it was the nation's largest smelting center.

As an army of prospectors overturned the mountains in search of ore, speculative investors and profiteers, including Horace Tabor, hauled in exaggerated riches. Others reaped a financial harvest from the sales of staple commodities that they struggled to bring to the isolated mining outpost – often by pack burro. Early freight rates from Denver exceeded the cost of shipping freight from New York to San Francisco around Cape Horn.

Technical innovation focused on the mining district and its accompanying physical isolation. Telephone wires crossed 13,186-foot Mosquito Pass from Fairplay in 1878. The following year, a 'High Line' wagon road over Loveland Pass brought the Georgetown railroad terminal within 60 miles of Leadville. In 1880 the D&RG Railroad entered Leadville from the Arkansas Valley. The UP Railroad opened a connection with the South Park area in 1884 over Fremont and Boreas Passes. But the most remarkable accomplishment was the construction of the standard-gauge Colorado Midland Railroad through Arkansas Valley in 1887. Its route followed a difficult alignment avoided by the D&RG.

In 1893 the Silver Panic decimated the mining economy, leaving Leadville to dwindle in importance as the population plummeted to fewer than 4000 by 1930.

COLORADO

the building to finance maintenance and restoration. It's open 8:30 am to 5 pm daily throughout summer.

Leadville, Colorado & Southern Scenic Railroad

From Leadville's red-brick railroad depot, built in 1893 at 326 E 7th St, the Leadville, Colorado & Southern Railroad (☎ 719-486-3936) offers 2½-hour scenic excursions to Fremont Pass. The diesel train and open passenger cars ascend the 21-mile route by backing up past old mines lining the East Fork of the Arkansas River before reaching the giant scar left by the defunct Climax Mine – once the nation's only source for molybdenum. Don't forget your coat, as Climax sees only 35 to 40 frost-free days a year. The train operates daily Memorial Day to early October, with a few special geology and wildflower excursions scheduled each year. Tickets cost $22.50/12.50 adults/children four to 12.
Web site: www.leadville-train.com

Hiking & Backpacking

The 44-sq-mile **Mt Massive Wilderness Area** has Mt Massive (14,421 feet) as its focal point. From the Elbert Creek Campground, follow the Colorado Trail (USFS Trail 1776) north almost 3 miles to the junction with USFS Trail 1487, which continues almost 3 miles to the top. South of the campground, the Colorado Trail leads to USFS Trail 1481 up Mt Elbert. Also consider visiting the many high lakes along Rock Creek on USFS Trail 1382, which intersects the Colorado Trail about 10 miles north of Elbert Creek Campground. Another trailhead for the Rock Creek Lakes begins at Willow Creek near the fish hatchery west of town. More extended backpacking trips cross the Continental Divide into the adjacent Hunter-Fryingpan Wilderness Area to the west.

When the Leadville National Fish Hatchery opened in 1889, fish were transported throughout the state in milk cans by wagon and rail from the sandstone building, once a social center for Leadville. Three-day hikes ranging from less than 2 miles to 6 miles

begin at the fish hatchery, the oldest in the West. It's 5 miles west of town on 3rd St, or 2 miles west on Hwy 300 from US 24 south of town. Timberline Lake in the Holy Cross Wilderness Area west of Turquoise Lake Reservoir is a favorite destination for day-hikers and anglers. Timberline Lake offers catch-and-release fishing of native greenback and cutthroat trout. To get there, hikers climb about 1000 feet in a little more than 2 miles from the trailhead west of the May Queen Campground.

Mountain Biking

Mosquito Pass presents a unique opportunity to ride above 13,000 feet in treeless alpine scenery. This extremely challenging 7-mile ascent follows E 7th St from Leadville.

Another good destination where you can enjoy panoramic vistas is Hagerman Pass (11,925 feet) west of Leadville. Riders follow a relatively easy railroad grade on USFS Rd 105 for 7 miles to Hagerman Pass from the junction on the south bank of Turquoise Lake Reservoir. On the way you pass **Skinner Hut** (☎ 970-925-5775), maintained by the 10th Mountain Division Hut Association; cyclists and hikers can call for reservations from July to October at the rate of $25 per person per night. The 10th Mountain's system of 12 huts is ideally suited to mountain-bike tours, as they are all accessible by USFS roads and trails outside the wilderness areas (where mountain biking is prohibited).

An easy ride follows the shoreline trail on the north side of Turquoise Lake Reservoir for 6 miles between Sugar Loaf Dam and May Queen Campground. Another follows the Colorado Trail north from Tennessee Pass for 2½ miles to Mitchell Creek. For other suggestions, pick up a map from the USFS Leadville Ranger Station.

Daily bike rentals can be had at Bill's Sport Shop (☎ 719-486-0739), 225 Harrison Ave, which also sells topo maps.

Skiing

Ski Cooper (☎ 719-486-2277), 9 miles north of Leadville, offers 460 acres of skiable terrain and a dedicated snowboard terrain park. Lift tickets cost $29/18 adults/children (12 and under) – the lowest regular lift price in the state.

The Ski Cooper/Piney Creek Nordic Center (☎ 719-486-1750) offers 24km of machine-set tracks for backcountry and cross-country skiing. While there you can ski about a mile to the Tennessee Pass Cookhouse for lunch or come back at night for a gourmet five-course meal.

More than 300 miles of backcountry ski trails are served by the 10th Mountain Division Hut Association (☎ 970-925-5775). Its 12 huts sleep 16 each. Membership in the association costs $25 and entitles you to priority reservations.

Places to Stay
Camping & Hostels The USFS *Halfmoon* and *Elbert Creek* campgrounds in the Halfmoon Creek area, 10 miles southwest of Leadville, offer sites for $8 with access to stream and lake fishing. The Elbert Creek Campground is a peak-bagger's Shangri-la, located on the Colorado Trail midway between Colorado's tallest peaks – Mt Massive to the north and Mt Elbert to the south. Be sure to get there early as these 10,000-foot sites are available only on a first-come, first-served basis.

Of the six USFS campgrounds on Turquoise Lake Reservoir, you can make reservations (☎ 877-444-6777) for the $12-sites at *Silver Dollar*, *Molly Brown*, *Baby Doe* or *Father Dyer* campgrounds. All are within a 2-mile stretch of USFS Rd 104 along the eastern shore. Near the Lake Fork tributary on the reservoir's western tip, *May Queen* has 27 sites available for $11.

The private *Sugar Loafin' Campground* (☎ 719-486-1031), 4 miles west of town on Lake County Rd 4, offers tent areas under the trees away from RVs for $19 for two people. The proprietors offer nightly slide presentations and there is a coin-operated laundry. Showers for nonguests cost $4. Or pitch your tent and take a shower in town for $15/18 at the *Leadville RV Corral* (☎ 719-486-3111, 135 W 2nd St).

If you're on a budget and feeling adventurous try the *Leadville Hostel* (☎ 719-486-9334, 500 E 7th St). It's a bit worn down but costs only $20 a night.

Motels The *Mountain Peaks Motel* (☎ 719-486-3178, 1 Harrison Ave) advertises 'steam heat' and offers budget singles/doubles for $30/35. Funky trailers form the *Longhorn Motel* (☎ 719-486-3155, 1515 Poplar St), where rooms cost $32/40. The *Alps Motel* (☎ 800-818-2577, 207 Elm St) is the best motel in town with clean, modern rooms for $39/45. If you don't mind lodgings that resemble a 1950s elementary school, the *Timberline Motel* (☎ 719-486-1876, 216 Harrison Ave) is a better budget choice with rooms for $57/65.

Rooms start at $45 at the *Leadville Inn Super 8* (☎ 719-486-3637, 25 Jack Town Place), south of town on US 24, which has a sauna. The *Silver King Motor Inn* (☎ 719-486-2610, 2020 N Poplar St) offers laundry facilities and modern singles/doubles for $44/46.

B&Bs *Peri & Ed's Mountain Hideaway* (☎ 719-486-0716, 201 W 8th St) offers eight cozy rooms for $45 to $90. The Victorian *Leadville Country Inn* (☎ 719-486-3637, 800-748-2354, 127 E 8th St) offers 10 rooms with breakfast ranging from $57/67 singles/doubles to a top-end room with high-post bed and whirlpool tub for $118/142. All rooms have private bath and guests may use the outdoor hot tub. You can't miss the *Delaware Hotel* (☎ 719-486-1418, 800-748-2004, 700 Harrison Ave). Built in 1886, this Victorian gem features an elegant oak-paneled lobby lit by crystal chandeliers. Its 36 rooms with private bath include breakfast; doubles go for $55 to $120. *The Ice Palace* (☎ 719-486-8272, 800-754-2840, 813 Spruce St) dates from 1899 and offers rooms from $79 to $139.

The *Apple Blossom Inn* (☎ 719-486-2141, 800-982-9279, 120 W 4th St), built in 1879, offers rooms with shared bath or rooms with fireplaces and private baths. There are also private rooms in the former library. Rates range from $89 to $144.

Places to Eat

Loitering is encouraged with gallery exhibits, music and good coffee and food at *Cloud City Coffee House & Deli* (☎ *719-486-1317, 711 Harrison Ave)* in the Tabor Grand Hotel. The *Columbine Cafe* (☎ *719-486-3599, 612 Harrison Ave)* serves hearty breakfasts and lunches at very reasonable prices.

Callaway's (☎ *719-846-1418)*, in the Delaware Hotel, is an exceptional value and offers simple egg breakfasts for less than $4; large charbroiled burgers on the lunch menu cost less than $6. Dinner prices range from $7 to $15 and entrees like fettuccine and prime rib are weekend specials.

La Cantina (☎ *719-486-9927)*, 1 mile south of town at 942 US 24, is the local favorite for authentic Mexican food. Daily lunch specials (11 am to 4 pm) cost less than $6. *Casa Blanca* (☎ *719-486-9969, 188 E 2nd St)* has the best margaritas in town, while *Gringo's* (☎ *719-486-3227, 102 Mountain View Dr)* offers speedy drive-through service.

Quincy's (☎ *719-486-9765, 416 Harrison Ave)* is a cozy tavern serving great steaks, including locally known filet mignon dinners for around $10.

Wild Bill's Restaurant (☎ *719-486-0533, 200 Harrison Ave)* is the place to go for 99¢ flame-broiled hamburgers and ice cream.

Entertainment

The *Pastime Saloon* (☎ *719-486-9986, 20 W 2nd St)* is the last saloon on a street that held 64 bars in Leadville's wilder days. For more historic atmosphere and walls lined with Baby Doe memorabilia, drop into the garish *Silver Dollar Saloon* (☎ *719-486-9914, 315 Harrison Ave)*.

Getting There & Around

Dee Hive Tours & Transportation (☎ 719-486-2339), 506 Harrison Ave, charges $61 one-way to Denver with a four-passenger minimum (more per person if there are fewer passengers).

At the northernmost headwaters of the Arkansas River, Leadville is 24 miles south of Summit County and I-70 via Hwy 91 over Fremont Pass. From Vail, Leadville is 38 miles south via I-70 and US 24 over Tennessee Pass.

Dee Hive Tours & Transportation also welcomes hikers, skiers and bicyclists in need of local shuttle transportation. Rides to trailheads or ski areas cost $10 to $15 per person for groups of four to six.

Rental cars (including 4WDs) are available at the Leadville Airport (☎ 719-486-2627), a couple of miles south of town.

FAIRPLAY & AROUND

Flanked by the Mosquito Range to the west and the Tarryall Mountains to the east, the extensive South Park area is an outdoor paradise. Fairplay (population 550) represents South Park's only 'urban' center – and the human inhabitants are probably outnumbered by the bison at Hartsel to the south.

Lord of the prairie

In the courthouse square, you will find a small monument to 'Shorty, age 45, 1951'; on Front St there's a memorial to 'Prunes, A Burro 1867–1930.' These revered beasts of burden carried supplies to the mines and returned down the slopes loaded with ore. Since 1949, Fairplay has celebrated **Burro Days** on the last weekend of July, featuring Colorado's indigenous sport – pack-burro racing. Racers run beside a loaded burro over a 30-mile course up Mosquito Pass (13,186 feet) and back.

Information

Visitor information is available from the South Park Chamber of Commerce

(☎ 719-836-3410), which runs a new visitors center next door to the South Park City Museum.

The USFS South Park Ranger Station (☎ 719-836-2031) is open daily 7:30 am to 4:30 pm during summer. Helpful rangers offer plenty of information and maps for wildflower excursions, hiking and biking trails and camping.

People's Bank (☎ 719-836-2797), at the intersection of US 285 and Hwy 9, has a 24-hour ATM. The post office is at 517 Hathaway St behind the Fairplay Hotel. The zip code is 80440.

The Company Store at South Park City Museum (☎ 719-836-2387), at 4th and Front Sts, offers a good selection of books on the area's history.

Fairplay is 23 miles south of Breckenridge on Hwy 9 but is most often approached from Denver 90 miles east on US 285, or else from Colorado Springs on US 24 over scenic Wilkerson Pass, then north on Hwy 9.

South Park City Museum
Over 35 relocated historical buildings, and a few still in their original sites, make up the fictional (but highly photogenic) South Park City. Each contains an exhibit representing economic or social life during the 1860 to 1900 mining era, including one on burro pack trains.

The museum (☎ 719-836-2387), 100 4th St on Hwy 9 toward Breckenridge near the caboose, is open 9 am to 5 pm May 15 to October 15, until 7 pm during peak summer season. Admission costs $5/2 adults/seniors and children.

Como
The historic railroad town of Como, 8 miles north of Fairplay on US 285, has the feel of an early Clint Eastwood movie (cue theme music) with its stark, treeless setting on the slope of Little Baldy Mountain. The Como Roundhouse, built in 1881 by the Denver, South Park & Pacific Railroad company, features six masonry engine bays that are presently undergoing restoration.

B&B lodging is available between April and mid-November at the old *Como Depot* (☎ *719-836-2594),* an interesting architectural design with its symmetrical towers. Singles/doubles start at $32/46; it's closed Tuesday. It also has a restaurant open 8 am to 8 pm Wednesday to Monday.

Windy Ridge Bristlecone Pines
During the 5th century BC, Colorado's oldest living trees sprouted from seed. By counting and measuring the annual tree rings on the bristlecone pines, dendrochronologists not only know their age but also can make inferences about past climatic conditions. The 11,000-foot Windy Ridge grove of limber and bristlecone pines is stunning for the stark beauty of the wind-bent trees against the backdrop of Mt Silverheels across the South Platte River headwaters.

From Alma, 5 miles north of Fairplay, turn left (west) at the Alma Fire House & Mining Museum and continue about 3 miles to the Paris Mine. Turn right on USFS Rd 415 and continue another 3 miles to an old metal ore-loading chute, following a switch-back and park. Cross Dolly Varden Creek on foot and continue up the steep road less than a mile to a snake-style rail fence and interpretive sign at the entry to the ridge.

Hiking & Backpacking
The Buffalo Peaks Wilderness Area, established in 1993 southwest of Fairplay, features volcanic terrain that differs from the other glacially carved ranges in the area. From the USFS Weston Pass Campground, USFS Trail 616 follows Rich Creek and leads to the Rough & Tumbling Creek or Fourmile Creek Trails, which provide good backcountry hiking loops. Take US 285 11 miles south of Fairplay, turn right (west) onto Park County Rd 22 and continue 12 miles to the trailhead.

In the Tarryall Mountains east of Fairplay, the Colorado Trail passes through the Lost Creek Wilderness Area, crossing US 285 at Kenosha Pass. The Brookside-McCurdy Trail (USFS Trail 607) is the north-south spine and travels 37 miles through the Lost Creek Wilderness Area, between the Glen-Isle resort in the north and the Twin Eagles trailhead in the south. It intersects with several other trails that can be used to plan loop hikes. The Twin Eagles trailhead is north of Tarryall on Park County Rd 77 near USFS Spruce Grove Campground. Another backcountry trailhead, at the USFS Lost Park Campground, is about 20 miles south of US 285 on Park County Rd 56.

Mountain Biking

Many opportunities exist for fat-tire enthusiasts on the USFS roads and nonwilderness trails in the area. Also, Hwy 9 is a signed bike route providing access to the South Platte River's superb fishing sites. From Hoosier Pass, 14 miles north of Fairplay on Hwy 9, a moderate ride of less than 4 miles heads west to Magnolia Mine then cuts north on single-track trail, descends to Crystal Reservoir and returns to the pass. The railroad grade to Boreas Pass from Como is an easy up-and-back 23-mile ride. The Colorado Trail west of Kenosha Pass, north of Como, is a more challenging 13-mile route to Georgia Pass, with a loop option on the 11-mile West Jefferson Trail (USFS Trail 643). Alternatively, you can continue on the Colorado Trail for 12 miles to Breckenridge.

A bit more difficult is the railroad grade up Weston Pass south of Fairplay on Park County Rd 22. From the Rich Creek trailhead (see Hiking & Backpacking, above) it's about 6 miles to the scenic summit, where you can choose between continuing to Mt Massive Lakes and Leadville or turning back for an exhilarating descent.

The USFS South Park Ranger Station (☎ 719-836-2031) can provide more details or suggest additional options.

Fishing

Sections of the Middle and South Forks of the South Platte River are Gold Medal waters, offering trophy rainbow trout with special catch-and-release restrictions. The South Fork section is south of Fairplay between US 285 and the inlet to Antero Reservoir. The designated section of the Middle Fork is on either side of Hwy 9, past the junction with US 24 at Hartsel and the confluence with the Middle Fork. The Colorado Dept of Wildlife (DOW) refers to this section as the Badger Basin Fishing Easement and has developed numerous access points from US 24 in Hartsel and along Park County Rd 439 north of Hartsel. Spinney Mountain Reservoir is also Gold Medal water, harboring huge cutthroat and brown trout. Ice fishing at Antero and Spinney Reservoirs is said to often be quite good.

For additional fishing suggestions you can contact the USFS South Park Ranger Station (☎ 719-836-2031) or the Colorado DOW (☎ 719-836-2521), at 16226 Park County Rd 77 near Lake George.

Cross-Country Skiing

You can cross-country ski on 12 miles of groomed trails at the Fairplay Nordic Center (☎ 719-836-2658), 2 miles north of Fairplay on Beaver Creek Rd (4th St) – it's well-signed from town. Ski instruction and rentals are also offered.

Places to Stay

In town, the *South Park Lodge* (☎ 719-836-3278, 801 Main St) has tent sites for $12, showers included.

Nearby USFS campgrounds are all on a first-come, first-served basis and include *Horseshoe* and *Fourmile*. Drive 1½ miles south of Fairplay via US 285 then turn onto Park County Rd 18 and drive 8 and 9 miles, respectively. Campsites cost $8. Only three sites ($6) are available at the USFS *Beaver Creek* campground, about 6 miles east of Fairplay on USFS Rd 659. The USFS campgrounds *Jefferson Creek* (17 sites), *Aspen* (12 sites) and *Lodgepole* (35 sites) north of Fairplay all cost $10. Above timberline at 12,000-foot elevation *Kite Lake*, 6 miles west of Alma, is the highest USFS campground in the country; sites are $4.

Budget travelers can try the bunkhouse at *South Park Lodge* (☎ 719-836-3278, 801 Main St), where a clean bed and locker costs $20. Singles/doubles are also available for $45/55 in summer, $10 less in winter.

History beckons travelers to the *Fairplay Hotel* (☎ *719-836-2565, 500 Main St), origi*nally established in 1873. Rooms with private bath are a decent value at $49 to $89. Another pleasant upscale option is the *Hand Hotel B&B* (☎ *719-836-3595, 531 Front St),* which offers cozy rooms with modern Western decor from $45 to $60; visit www.handhotel.com.

Places to Eat
The *Fairplay Hotel Restaurant* (☎ *719-836-2565, 500 Main St)* is open for breakfast, lunch and dinner, serving standard American fare. The daily lunch specials are good. The *Ranch Restaurant* (☎ *719-836-2789, 729 Main St)* seems to draw a steady stream of satisfied diners and also has daily specials.

Elk Mountains & Around

This is what most people envision when they think of Colorado. Though the beautiful Elk Mountains make up only a small part of Colorado's Rocky Mountain range, they are home to Aspen and Vail ski resorts, easily the state's most famous destinations. Though both towns have gone upscale to the point of snobbery, the influx of unabashed wealth has not diminished the awesome scenery that rewards hikers, bikers and other outdoors enthusiasts.

VAIL
The nation's largest ski resort, Vail (population 4000; elevation 8120 feet) has a semi-arid climate that makes for gorgeous powder skiing and some of the best runs in Colorado. Vail Village gets mixed reviews at best for its 'Instant Tyrolia' design, though nobody can fault the Village's compact, pedestrian-oriented layout, its slew of excellent restaurants, bars and fashion boutiques.

One of the many local backcountry adventure outfits is Vail-based Paragon Guides (☎ 970-926-5299, 877-926-5299). It organizes a wide array of scheduled and custom-guided trips including backpacking, hiking, mountain biking, rock climbing and llama trekking.
Web site: www.paragonguides.com

Orientation
Vail Village, on the south side of I-70 at exit 176, is the principal center of activity. Motorists must leave their cars at the Vail Transportation Center & Public Parking Garage before entering the pedestrian mall area of lodges, restaurants and shops at the base of the chairlifts. Lionshead is a secondary center and lift about half a mile to the west.

At the extreme ends of the Gore Valley are East Vail, an exclusive residential zone beyond the Vail Golf Course and I-70 exit 180, and West Vail at I-70 exit 173, where most highway-oriented services are located. Farther west at I-70 exit 171, US 24 and the D&RG Western Tracks climb south past Minturn toward Leadville.

Information
Tourist Offices The Vail Visitors Center (☎ 970-479-1394) at the Transportation Center, 231 S Frontage Rd, is open daily and provides maps, lodging and activities information and schedules for Vail's outstanding transit system. The visitors center also has a Lionshead office located in the parking garage (☎ 970-479-1385). The Vail Valley Tourism & Convention Bureau (☎ 800-525-3875), 100 E Meadow Dr, can book rooms, transportation and ski packages Monday to Saturday; the bureau is online at www.visitvailvalley.com.

The Vail Valley Information Network Web site, web.vail.net, is an excellent trip-planning tool for the entire valley, with up-to-date information on accommodations, including reservation services, restaurants, schedule of events, etc. It includes links to many of the area's lodges, hotels and B&Bs, with photographs and updated prices. Another worthy Web site for local goings-on is www.vailsource.com.

The White River National Forest operates a first-class visitors center at the Holy Cross Ranger Station (☎ 970-827-5715), Dowds Junction at the corner of I-70 exit 171 and US 24. You can pick up books and maps as well as information on USFS campgrounds or hiking in the nearby Holy Cross Wilderness Area. In fact, trailheads to the wilderness are located in the parking area.

Money, Post & Communications First Bank of Vail (☎ 970-476-5686) is on Vail Rd near the intersection with W Meadow Dr. WestStar Bank (☎ 970-476-4600) is between Lionshead and Vail Village on S Frontage Rd. Both banks have ATMs.

The post office is in West Vail at N Frontage Rd; the zip code is 81657.

Bookstores Verbatim Booksellers (☎ 970-476-3032), 450 Lionshead Circle, across the street from the transportation center at Lionshead, is a terrific full-service bookstore that has maps and a wide selection of guidebooks.

Medical Services Vail Valley Medical Center (☎ 970-476-8065), 181 W Meadow Dr, provides 24-hour emergency care.

Colorado Ski Museum & Hall of Fame

Even nonskiers will enjoy this excellent museum, where exhibits depict the history of Colorado skiing. The Colorado Ski Museum (☎ 970-476-1876), 231 S Frontage Rd on level three of the Vail Transportation Center, is open 10 am to 5 pm Tuesday to Sunday. Admission is free but donations are recommended.

Skiing

Vail Mountain is so big that skiers never get bored. No matter what your ability, you can always find a new route down the mountain; some say it takes about a week to ski the entire mountain. Vail's four base areas from east to west are Golden Peak, Vail Village, Lionshead and Cascade Village. Call ☎ 970-476-4888 for a snow report.

Lift tickets are $62/41 adults/children. Seniors older than 70 ski free and discounts for other seniors are available. Lift tickets also can be used at the Beaver Creek ski area 9 miles west of Vail on I-70, as well as at Breckenridge, Keystone and Arapahoe

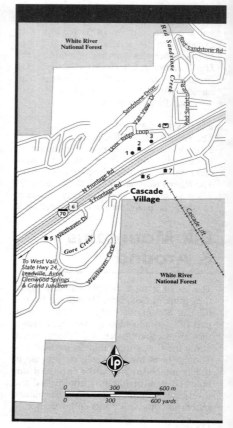

Basin. For information about tickets call Vail Associates (☎ 970-476-5601).

Cross-country and backcountry trails abound. The Nordic Center at the Vail golf course (☎ 970-479-4391), at the eastern end of S Frontage Rd, has 10 km of machine-maintained tracks and is free. Rentals are $18 and you can get there on the free bus from the Transportation Center.

At the base of Chair 6, the Golden Peak Center (☎ 970-476-3239) offers backcountry tours combined with gourmet dining.

About 15 miles west of Vail, the larger Cordillera Nordic Center (☎ 303-926-5100)

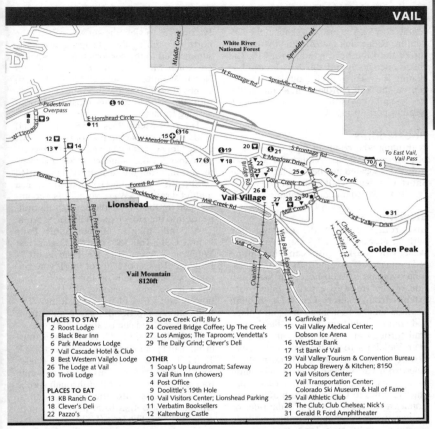

PLACES TO STAY
2 Roost Lodge
5 Black Bear Inn
6 Park Meadows Lodge
7 Vail Cascade Hotel & Club
8 Best Western Vailglo Lodge
26 The Lodge at Vail
30 Tivoli Lodge

PLACES TO EAT
13 KB Ranch Co
18 Clever's Deli
22 Pazzo's

23 Gore Creek Grill; Blu's
24 Covered Bridge Coffee; Up The Creek
27 Los Amigos; The Taproom; Vendetta's
29 The Daily Grind; Clever's Deli

OTHER
1 Soap's Up Laundromat; Safeway
3 Vail Run Inn (showers)
4 Post Office
9 Doolittle's 19th Hole
10 Vail Visitors Center; Lionshead Parking
11 Verbatim Booksellers
12 Kaltenburg Castle

14 Garfinkel's
15 Vail Valley Medical Center;
    Dobson Ice Arena
16 WestStar Bank
17 1st Bank of Vail
19 Vail Valley Tourism & Convention Bureau
20 Hubcap Brewery & Kitchen; 8150
21 Vail Visitors Center;
    Vail Transportation Center;
    Colorado Ski Museum & Hall of Fame
25 Vail Athletic Club
28 The Club; Club Chelsea; Nick's
31 Gerald R Ford Amphitheater

has easy, intermediate and expert terrain and packages that include use of its hot tub, pool and sauna as well as guided tours, lessons, moonlight skiing and snowshoeing.

Check with the USFS Holy Cross Ranger Station (☎ 970-827-5715), I-70 exit 171 at US 24, for information on nearby backcountry trails including **Shrine Pass**, but be aware that many of the nonwilderness routes are infested with noisy snowmobiles. The 10th Mountain Division Hut System (☎ 970-925-5775), 1280 Ute Ave in Aspen, offers a system of trails almost 300 miles long connecting 14 overnight cabins.

Paragon Guides (☎ 970-926-5299, 877-926-5299) uses these huts between Vail and Aspen for guided three- to six-day trips for all ability levels. Guides provide instruction in telemark, backcountry skiing and winter mountaineering skills; visit www.paragonguides.com.

Ice Skating
Skaters can practice their skills year-round at the Dobson Ice Arena (☎ 970-479-2271), on W Meadow Dr near E Lionshead Circle. Daily public skating hours are 11 am to 1 pm and evening hours are 7:30 to 9 pm

Monday, Wednesday, Friday and Sunday. Admission is $5/4 adults/children. Skate rentals cost $2. You also can skate at the Adventure Ridge rink (☎ 970-476-9090) at the top of the Lionshead gondola for $10. The rink is open noon to 10 pm daily. Free public skating is available on the outdoor skating rink at the Vail Nordic Center and at the Eagle-Vail Pavilion (☎ 970-949-1504), weather permitting.

Bobsledding
A thrilling 60 seconds of high-speed fun is offered on a 2900-foot course for $14. Vail Bobsled is located just below Mid-Vail near Short Cut Run. Call the activities desk (☎ 970-476-9090) for additional information.

Bicycling
Bike routes connect the outlying free parking areas with Vail Village. From the West Vail Market you can ride along N Frontage Rd, crossing I-70 at the pedestrian overpass to Lionshead. On the south side of the freeway, a paved bike route extends from W Gore Creek Dr through Cascade Village, Lionshead and Vail Village and continues east on the **10-Mile Canyon Trail** through auto-free road-bike heaven over Vail Pass to Frisco. From the road closure at the east end of Bighorn Rd, 6 miles from Vail Village, it's an 8-mile climb to Vail Pass; there you can turn back or continue 11 miles to Frisco, the hub of Summit County bike trails. Another popular ride, for the hearty rider acclimated to high-altitude exertion, climbs over Tennessee Pass to Leadville on the narrow shoulders of US 24.

Vail Mountain has about 20 well-marked mountain-bike trails crisscrossing the ski runs for cyclists of all abilities. Pick up a free copy of the 'Biking & Hiking Map,' as well as a list of where to rent bikes, at the information office.

Hiking & Backpacking
In 1873 William Henry Jackson discovered and photographed Mt of the Holy Cross (14,005 feet) while with the Hayden Expedition. Along with paintings by Thomas Moran, another member of the expedition, their work symbolized the Colorado wilderness to millions of 19th-century Americans. Pilgrimages to view the snowy cross on the north face during the late spring and early summer led to the construction of a shelter on Notch Mountain in 1924. The difficult **Notch Mountain Trail** (USFS Trail 2000) climbs almost 3000 feet in 5 miles to 13,100-foot elevation – leaving most tenderfeet gasping for air!

The **Half Moon Pass** (USFS Trail 2009) leads to the cross-country approach up Mt of the Holy Cross. Get an early start to complete in a day the 6-mile climb on this overused trail. From the turnoff to Tigawan Rd (USFS Rd 707), 4 miles south of Minturn, a high-clearance (4WD) vehicle is recommended for the 8-mile journey to both trailheads into the Holy Cross Wilderness Area.

A 2-mile hike to 60-foot **Booth Falls** follows USFS Trail 1885 into the Eagles Nest Wilderness Area. The trailhead is off N Frontage Rd west of I-70 exit 180. If you continue beyond the falls on this popular trail, you will encounter meadows filled with wildflowers and views of the Gore Range. The trail continues to Booth Lake, 6 miles from the trailhead, and climbs about 3000 feet.

From the USFS Gore Creek campground, the popular **Gore Creek Trail** (USFS Trail 2015) leads to Gore Lake in the Eagles Nest Wilderness Area. This strenuous 6-mile trail climbs about 2700 feet through spruce and fir forests into the alpine tundra. Another trail option from near the campground is **Two Elk Trail** (USFS Trail 2005), an 11-mile hike that climbs to Two Elk Pass, passing prime elk habitat before leaving the forest and Vail's back bowls at Cemetery Rd in Minturn. Elk bugling during rutting season is best observed in late summer. This hike can be done in a day or as an overnight trip – consider leaving a vehicle at the Minturn trailhead. The east trailhead is at the gate closing the old US 6 frontage road. Do not park in the campground.

Register for a guided naturalist hike that meets on Tuesday and Thursday at the **Vail Nature Center** (☎ 970-479-2291), at 841 Vail Valley Dr. The hikes are 'leisurely in nature' and cost $15. For a short stroll, the four trails at the Nature Center offer excellent interpretive displays on the plants and wildlife along Gore Creek and can be done in under an hour. Shrine Mountain Adventure (☎ 970-827-5363) is a guide service that does not cater to hunters and offers 'alternative backcountry tours.'

Fishing

It's hard to believe that a stream so close to a freeway would be included among Colorado's Gold Medal waters, yet 4 miles of Gore Creek from Red Sandstone Creek to its confluence with the Eagle River is prize trout fly-fishing water. Expect to find rainbow, brook and big brown trout, plus native cutthroat in its tributaries. Regulations permit anglers to take only two fish over 16 inches from the creek. The Eagle River, once too polluted to sustain large mature fish, now yields decent catches, due to EPA Superfund cleanup of the Gilman mill tailings above Minturn. If you're willing to go for a hike, there are nearby mountain lakes and streams offering great fishing opportunities.

Check at the USFS Holy Cross Ranger Station (☎ 970-827-5715) for a complete list of lake- and stream-fishing opportunities in the district. For tackle and supplies, stop by Gorsuch Outfitters (☎ 970-476-2294), 263 E Gore Creek Dr. It offers a variety of float and wading trips. Gore Creek Fly Fisherman, (☎ 970-476-3296), 183 Gore Creek Dr, offers trips at competitive prices.

Rafting & Kayaking

The upper Eagle River near Dowd Junction features a kayak slalom course upstream from I-70. Immediately downstream from I-70 is Dowd Chutes Class IV whitewater rapids. Below Dowd Chutes, the lower Eagle River offers relatively sedate Class II-III floats for about 25 miles. The peak season is in May and wetsuits are necessary. By mid-June the water level is too low for much fun.

Several local companies offer area rafting trips. One outfitter worth trying out is Rock Gardens Rafting (☎ 970-945-6737, 800-958-6737).

Web site: www.rockgardens.com

Alpine Kayak & Canoe (☎ 970-949-3350), 40814 US 6 and US 24 in Avon, is a kayaking school with a full range of programs. Web site: www.alpinekayak.com

Special Events

Throughout the winter and summer you can expect some activity nearly every weekend. A week of ski celebration takes place in early March during the **American Ski Classic**. Gourmets will enjoy sampling the creations of Vail's chefs at the **Taste of Vail**, held on the first weekend in April. On Memorial Day weekend, a kayak competition on the Eagle River is the main event during the Jeep White-Water Festival.

During July and August, free Tuesday night concerts begin at 6:30 pm at the Gerald R Ford Amphitheater (☎ 970-476-2918), 530 S Frontage Rd E, featuring popular rock, soul and jazz artists as part of the Hot Summer Nights series. For information contact the Vail Valley Foundation (☎ 970-476-9500).

On July and August weekends, Vail hosts the **Bravo! Colorado Music Festival**, featuring 60 chamber, orchestral and symphonic programs. For schedules and ticket information contact the festival box office (☎ 970-827-5700), 953 S Frontage Rd suite 104, Vail, CO 81657.

Places to Stay

Aside from camping, don't expect to find any low-end lodging near Vail. Ski season rates reach their peak during the Christmas and New Year's holidays, when most innkeepers quote rates double to triple the amount charged after the snow melts. Ask at the Vail Visitors Center about nightly specials, especially during the off-season.

Camping The forested USFS *Gore Creek Campground* at the east end of Bighorn Rd offers 25 campsites for $8 on a first-come, first-served basis. It's only 6 miles from Vail Village by bike route or bus; it's open from June to Labor Day weekend. Reservations are accepted for the 21 sites at the USFS *Camp Hale Memorial Campground* (☎ 877-444-6777), 15 miles south of Minturn on US 24. Campsites at this former training site for the 10th Mountain Division cost $7. It's near the Colorado Trail in a flat, open valley sparsely forested by lodgepole pines.

Motels Among the least expensive places to stay is the *Roost Lodge* (☎ 970-476-5451, 800-873-3065, 1783 N Frontage Rd) in West Vail. Its plain contemporary rooms sleep four comfortably. Summer/winter rates start at $40/62. Vail's other 'budget' place is the *Park Meadows Lodge* (☎ 970-476-5598, 1472 Matterhorn Circle) on the other side of the freeway. It offers 28 one- and two-bedroom condos starting at $64/119 summer/winter. Both offer summer discounts with a certificate available from the visitors information center.

Only one block from four lifts in Vail Village, the small *Tivoli Lodge* (☎ 970-476-5615, 800-451-4756, 386 Hanson Ranch Rd) features a cozy lounge with fireplace, outdoor heated pool, hot tub, sauna and a guest laundry. The Tivoli is like a traditional European ski lodge – the opposite of a sterile condo. Hotel-style rooms with private bath start at $69/139 summer/winter, single or double occupancy, and include Continental breakfast.

Rooms cost $85/230 summer/winter at the *Best Western Vailglo Lodge* (☎ 970-476-5506, 701 W Lionshead Circle), an elegant small hotel.

The *Vail Cascade Hotel & Club* (☎ 970-476-7111, 800-420-2424, 1300 Westhaven Dr) has its own chairlift, two movie theaters and a full indoor athletic facility. Rates range from $109 to $290 in summer, $300 to $1000 in January; visit www.vailcascade.com. At the extreme top end is *The Lodge at Vail* (☎ 970-476-5011, 800-331-5634, 174 E Gore Creek Dr) at the base of the lifts. It has the most convenient location and more amenities than any other lodge in Vail; rates start at $175/215 summer/winter.

It's not much cheaper, but staying in Avon 9 miles west of Vail is a good option if you're planning to ski at both Vail and Beaver Creek. There's also the terrific Avon Recreation Center (☎ 970-748-4060), 325 Benchmark Rd, with a pool, sauna, steam and hot

tub for $8/5.50 adults/children – the perfect way to unwind after a day on the slopes. One- and three-bed condos start at $99/225 in winter at the *Christie Lodge* (☎ 970-949-7700, 800-551-4326, 47 E Beaver Creek Blvd). Summer rates are $25 less; visit www.christielodge.com. *Season's at Avon* (☎ 970-845-3900, 800-859-8242, 134 W Benchmark Rd) has one- and two-bedroom condos for $180 and $250 during ski season.

B&Bs The *Lazy Ranch* (☎ 970-926-3876, 0057 Lake Creek Rd) has five rooms in a beautifully restored 100-year-old Victorian about 10 miles west of Vail in Edwards. The comfortable rooms go for $95 to $135 in winter, $70 to $90 in summer and include a big hot breakfast. In West Vail, the log *Black Bear Inn* (☎ 970-476-1304, 2405 Elliot Ranch Rd) features a large streamside deck and 12 rooms with private bath from $105 to $115 in summer, $120 to $225 in winter.

The contemporary *Intermountain* (☎ 970-476-4935) has two double rooms and is a couple of miles from town on the free shuttlebus route. Rates are $77/135 winter/summer and a Continental breakfast is included.

Condominiums Vail Central Reservations (☎ 970-476-1000, 800-525-3875), 100 E Meadow Rd, handles most properties in Vail; look at www.visitvailvalley.com. A typical medium-priced condominium complex in Vail Village is *The Willows* (☎ 970-476-2233, 888-945-5697, 74 Willow Rd) which offers a good location near the lifts and standard contemporary furnishings. Double occupancy hotel-style rooms cost $69/150 summer/winter; two-bedroom condos suitable for four people run from $140/400.

Places to Eat
At the top of Bridge St, *The Daily Grind* (☎ 970-476-5856) begins serving muffins and coffee at 6:30 am. If you're too tired to make it up the street you can stop for a caffeine fix at *Covered Bridge Coffee* (☎ 970-479-2883). There's a full range of coffees as well as bagels, pastries and hot breakfasts.

Even if you sleep 'til noon, you can start your day at *Blu's* (☎ 970-476-3113, 193 E Gore Creek Dr), which serves breakfast until 5 pm. At night an eclectic menu features upscale dinners along with 'homestyle' staples like chicken-fried steak or liver and onions. In the same area the *Gore Creek Grill* (☎ 970-476-2828) is notable for fresh seafood and juicy steaks.

Pizza slices, accompanied by reggae and young locals complaining about high rents and low wages, cost about $3 at *Pazzo's* (☎ 970-476-9026), in Vail Village at Willow Bridge Rd and E Meadow Dr. It's open for breakfast at 7:30 am and serves pizza and lasagna until 11 pm.

For Mexican food, *Los Amigos* (☎ 970-476-5847), at the top of Bridge St facing the mountain, has all the classics as well as fish tacos and filling vegetarian black bean soup. Nearby, *The Taproom* (☎ 970-479-0500, 333 Bridge St), near the base of the Vista Bahn chairlift, has won over locals with its inexpensive food and extensive variety of on-tap beverages.

With patio seating facing Gore Creek is *Up the Creek* (☎ 970-476-8141), offering fresh fruit or burgers and sandwiches for lunch and dinner.

Though it bears no resemblance to a ranch, *KB Ranch Co* (☎ 970-476-1937), in Lionsquare Lodge next to the Lionshead gondola, offers unpretentious dinners with a great salad bar for $10 to $15.

A no-nonsense deli, *Clever's Deli* (☎ 970-476-6084), with two locations in Vail Village, serves up tasty submarines and sandwiches.

The upstairs pizza bar at *Vendetta's* (☎ 970-476-5070, 291 Bridge St) is open until 2 am, one of the few late-night dining options in Vail. You can also enjoy their sunny deck.

Entertainment

Nightclub activity centers on Bridge St from the mountain to the covered bridge. At the top of the street, *The Club* (☎ 970-479-0556) is a basement bar featuring rock music. Also at the top of Bridge St, *Nick's* (☎ 970-476-5011), near the bridge, is another nightspot popular with young locals featuring DJ

dance music, while the older crowd at *Club Chelsea* (☎ 970-476-5600) dances to blues and piano music.

In Crossroads Shopping Center you'll find Vail's own Rainbow Trout Stout at the *Hubcap Brewery & Kitchen* (☎ 970-476-5757) and Vail's largest dance floor at *8150* (☎ 970-479-0607), which has both DJs and live music.

If you're in Lionshead, *Garfinkel's* (☎ 970-476-3789), next to the gondola, offers live rock music. Happy hour is 3 to 7 pm every day at *Doolittle's 19th Hole* (☎ 970-479-2911), which is in the Concert Hall Plaza.

Kaltenburg Castle (☎ 970-479-1050), at the base of the Eagle Bahn Gondola, is a giant Bavarian-style brewhouse decked out in full royal decor.

Getting There & Away

Most visitors fly into Denver International Airport and continue to Vail on a shuttle van (see Getting Around, below). During the December to early April ski season, the Eagle County Airport, 35 miles west of Vail, offers a surprising amount of jet service.

Greyhound buses stop at the Vail Transportation Center just off the middle I-70 exit for Vail.

Via I-70, Vail is 107 miles west of Denver and 57 miles east of Glenwood Springs.

Getting Around

Colorado Mountain Express (☎ 970-949-4227, 800-525-6363) offers shuttle service to/from Denver International Airport; visit www.cmex.com. From Eagle County Airport the shuttle costs $35. Also try Vail Valley Transportation (☎ 970-476-8008, 800-882-8872).

Vail has fine public transportation – it's free, it goes where you need to go and it operates at short intervals. Travel by bus is thus faster and more convenient than most car trips. The in-town shuttle runs between the base of Golden Peak and Vail Village and Lionshead from 6:15 to 2:15 am at intervals of less than 10 minutes. From the Transportation Center, Vail Buses (☎ 970-328-8143) serves the local golf course and

Ford Park; West Vail, both North and South; Sandstone; and East Vail. Shuttles and buses stop only at designated stops. Schedules appear in *Vail Valley* magazine.

Thrifty rents cars at the Vail Transportation Center. Dollar offers rentals at the Marriott. Also try Enterprise in Avon, and Hertz at the Eagle County Airport.

Vail Valley Taxi (☎ 970-476-8294) offers 24-hour local taxi service.

MINTURN

Squeezed between the burgeoning luxury condominium and resort developments of Vail and Beaver Creek, Minturn (population 1200) is a nice respite in the heart of Eagle County. This small railroad town next to the Eagle River was founded in 1887 and its shops and homes retain the coziness and charm of a place that really has been around for a while. To get there, go 3 miles west of Vail on I-70 then 2 miles south on US 24.

Up until 1997 Minturn was the base for 'helper' engines that assisted heavy freight trains over the 10,242-foot Tennessee Pass tunnel to Leadville, the highest mainline railroad route in the US. As many as 24 freight trains would pass through town daily. Locals credited these trains with warding developers off Minturn in favor of places farther away from Vail – like Avon and Gypsum – as targets for resort expansion. The line was closed after Union Pacific took over Southern Pacific and opted to run trains via its more efficient rail lines in Wyoming and New Mexico.

Now that the trains are gone the townspeople are getting nervous about Vail's rumored plans to one day connect Beaver Creek and Vail Mountain – via Minturn. Property values have skyrocketed in the last couple of years, so some development looks inevitable. There is also a campaign to turn the rail line into a bike trail as part of the national 'Rails to Trails' program, though nothing was set at the time of writing.

Minturn is gaining a reputation for its galleries and antique stores. Western settlers' and Native American art are featured at Woodwind Galleries (☎ 970-827-9232), 151 N Main St. Across the street, Two Elk

Gallery (☎ 970-827-5307) features cowboy kitsch and lots of branding-iron and antler-style furnishings and lamps. The owners of Battle Mountain Trading Post (☎ 970-827-4191), 1031 S Main St, lure prospective customers inside by offering cheap ice cream cones, then let the crowded rustic appeal of their costly antiques sell themselves. Bring a truck to haul away such things as barbershop poles, old-fashioned gas pumps or more antler furnishings.

Activities

Minturn and Red Cliff (located about 10 miles farther south on US 24), gateways to the Holy Cross Wilderness Area, offer some of the most spectacular hiking and backcountry skiing in the area. Anyone heading up to the region should first check in with the USFS Holy Cross Ranger District (☎ 970-827-5715), 24747 US 24 at the US 24/I-70 junction. They have free maps of all the area trails and campsites as well as complete information about degree of difficulty and trail conditions. Do not head up to the wilderness area without the proper information from the USFS and the appropriate equipment.

Places to Stay & Eat

The *Minturn Inn* (☎ 800-646-8876, 442 Main St) is a delightful B&B housed in a restored 1915 home along the Eagle River, adjacent to the White River National Forest. All 14 rooms are tastefully furnished and comfortable, from those with shared bath to the 'premier' rooms featuring their own fireplaces, vaulted ceilings and two-person Jacuzzis. The friendly owners are longtime residents of the town and have a wealth of knowledge about the area. Rates vary for season and room type – anywhere from $79 to $189 from April 1 to December 21, and $99 to $269 during ski season – but it's well worth it.

Web site: www.minturninn.com

The *Turntable Restaurant* (☎ 970-827-4164, 160 Main St), open 5:30 am to 10:30 pm, is on the site of an old railroad engine turntable and the restaurant is decorated with D&RG Western Railroad memorabilia on the walls. They dish up hearty breakfasts, as well as burgers, tacos and burritos. Prices are reasonable – most meals cost from $4 to $7.

The *Cougar Ridge Cafe* (☎ 970-827-5609, *132 Main St)* is another good spot for lunch or dinner, with great sandwiches, pizza, soups and salads.

The Saloon (☎ 970-827-5954, *146 Main St)* is best known for Mexican dishes and its Western atmosphere.

There's no golf course near the *Minturn Country Club* (☎ 970-827-4114, *131 Main St)*, but you can play shuffleboard after grilling your own steak and making a salad.

RED CLIFF

About 6 miles south of Minturn on US 24, on the way to the Holy Cross Wilderness Area, the turnoff for Red Cliff (population 315) is just before the big green bridge spanning the Eagle River. This genuine Western town began life as a gold-mining center in the mid- to late-1800s before becoming a lumber center. The buildings along Eagle and Water Sts have a definite 'Old West' feel, enhanced by the mountain backdrop. Take a five-minute walk up the switchback trail behind the Red Cliff Lodge for a view of the area, including the hill where the entire town once gathered to defend against a feared Indian attack.

The cozy *Red Cliff Lodge* (☎ 970-827-9109, *206 Eagle St)* has a hostel-style bunkroom with beds renting for $30/39 in summer/winter, and three private rooms (with Jacuzzi baths!) for around $69/105 in summer/winter; visit online at www.redclifflodge.com. The adjacent *Mango's Mountain Grill* serves killer 'backcountry breakfasts' or try its signature dish, the fish taco.

If you're leaving Red Cliff and heading east, consider taking the Shrine Pass Rd. This 12½-mile dirt road cuts through some remarkable countryside before dropping down to the east side of Vail Pass. Be sure to stop at the top to check out the view of Mt of the Holy Cross behind you.

BEAVER CREEK

This is an exclusive gated enclave 8 miles west of Vail from its entrance at Avon and I-70. There's something surreal about the sudden appearance of perfectly maintained grounds and neo-Tyrolean buildings that climb before a truly spectacular ski mountain. Though it feels artificial, the skiing is great and accommodations outstanding (though you pay for what you get).

Beaver Creek was initially conceived as part of Vail's scheme to attract the 1976 Winter Olympics, high hopes that were aborted in 1972. Against the environmental objections of the state's voters, the USFS and two governors, Beaver Creek's enterprising proponents finally gained the necessary permits to develop the wooded terrain on the margins of the Holy Cross Wilderness, and the resort opened in 1980.

Beaver Creek boasts a 3400-foot vertical drop, 14 lifts including five high-speed quad chairs and a wide variety of ski terrain for all abilities. Experts will head to the double black diamonds off the Grouse Mountain Express lift or the Westfall lift with runs every bit as challenging as anything at Vail. Beaver Creek is also the first US resort to offer European-style village-to-village skiing from the main village over to Bachelor Gulch and then to Arrowhead Mountain Village several miles west.

Looking for a cheap room at Beaver Creek in the winter? Don't even bother passing through the front gates unless you're prepared to drop at least a couple hundred dollars a night. For leads, call Vail/Beaver Creek Reservations (☎ 970-845-5745, 800-525-2257).

The **Vilar Center for the Arts** (☎ 970-845-8497, 888-920-2787), 28 Avondale Lane at Beaver Creek Resort, hosts a year-round line-up of top-notch theatre, dance, comedy and music.

Web site: www.vilarcenter.org

GLENWOOD SPRINGS

Next to the Colorado River, Glenwood Springs (population 8200; elevation 5746 feet) has natural hot springs, a mild climate and a range of summer and winter activities.

The springs and large outdoor pool are one of Colorado's most popular vacation destinations. Glenwood Springs also represents an inexpensive 'down-valley' winter alternative to Aspen ski areas and is only about 45 minutes west along I-70 from Vail and Beaver Creek, making it a good base for skiing some of Colorado's best mountains.

Orientation

Since 1896, Grand Ave has crossed the Colorado River and formed the main business street extending due south from the river. The resort spa and pool are north of the river, reached by a highway and pedestrian/bicycle bridge. West Glenwood Springs evolved north of the river along US 6, a route now followed by I-70.

Information

The anteroom visitors center is always open at the Chamber Resort Association (☎ 970-945-6589, 888-445-3696), at the corner of 11th St and Grand Ave. Helpful staff are available 8:30 am to 5 pm weekdays, 9 am to 3 pm weekends.
Web site: www.glenwoodsprings.net

USFS headquarters for the White River National Forest (☎ 970-945-2521), 900 Grand Ave, has maps and information about hiking, biking and Nordic skiing. Offices for both the BLM (☎ 970-945-2341) and the Colorado DOW (☎ 970-945-7228) are in West Glenwood Springs at 50633 US 6.

The centrally located Bank of Colorado (☎ 970-945-7422), at 9th St and Grand Ave, has an ATM. The main post office is at 113 9th St; the zip code is 81601. For magazines and books on Colorado and the Southwest, stop by Book Train (☎ 970-945-7045), 723 Grand Ave.

Valley View Hospital (☎ 970-945-6535) offers 24-hour emergency care at 1906 Blake Ave.

Frontier Historical Museum

For the $3 admission you can learn about the history of the town, from coal mining to Doc Holliday to an exhibit on the Native American Utes. Period exhibits include furnished rooms – and the ubiquitous porcelain bedpan – in the 1905 house now occupied by the Frontier Historical Museum (☎ 970-945-4448) at 1001 Colorado Ave. Opening hours vary, so call ahead.

Glenwood Caverns

From mid-April to early November, experience low-impact spelunking amid the subterranean caverns and grottos of the **Fairy Caves** (☎ 970-945-4228, 800-530-1635), 503 Pine St. The self-proclaimed title 'Eighth Wonder of the World' may be a bit over the top, but those interested in caves will enjoy the two-hour 'family tour' that covers a half mile, or the more extensive and adventurous 'wild tour.'
Web site: www.glenwoodcaverns.com

Swimming & Spas

The **Hot Springs Lodge and Pool** (☎ 970-945-7131, 800-537-7946), 401 N River St, is the big tourist draw. Salty water from Iron Mountain's limestone caverns feeds the large 400-by-100-foot open-air pool, created in 1888 and maintained at 90°F. There's also a smaller therapeutic pool, a children's pool and water slide. Admission is $8.75/5.75 adults/children. Four trips on the water slide costs $3.75. Admission to the athletic club is $15.75. It's open 7:30 am (9 am in winter) to 10 pm daily. Massages start at $39 for half an hour.

At 709 E 6th St, **Yampah Spa and Vapor Caves** (☎ 970-945-0667) features steam baths and spa treatments including massages, facials and herbal wraps. Admission to the caves costs $8.75 and spa treatments start at $34. It's open 9 am to 9 pm daily.

Bicycling

The paved **Glenwood Canyon Trail** follows the Colorado River upstream below the cantilevered I-70 and on the old highway around Horseshoe Bend for 16.2 miles between the Yampah Vapor Caves and Dotsero.

Other local rides are shown on the free topographic *Glenwood Springs Hiking & Mountain Bicycle Trail Map* from the Chamber Resort Association and USFS headquarters.

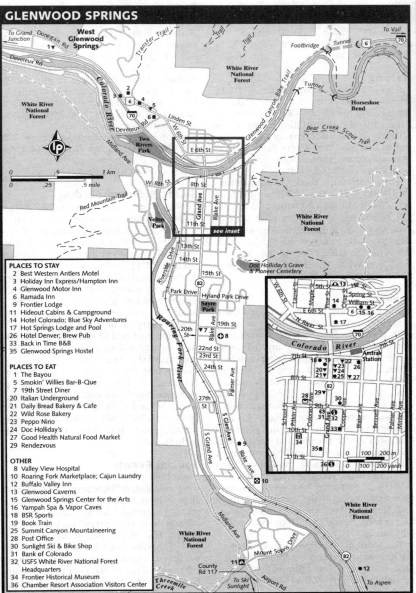

GLENWOOD SPRINGS

PLACES TO STAY
2 Best Western Antlers Motel
3 Holiday Inn Express/Hampton Inn
4 Glenwood Motor Inn
6 Ramada Inn
9 Frontier Lodge
11 Hideout Cabins & Campground
14 Hotel Colorado; Blue Sky Adventures
17 Hot Springs Lodge and Pool
26 Hotel Denver; Brew Pub
33 Back in Time B&B
35 Glenwood Springs Hostel

PLACES TO EAT
1 The Bayou
5 Smokin' Willies Bar-B-Que
7 19th Street Diner
20 Italian Underground
21 Daily Bread Bakery & Cafe
22 Wild Rose Bakery
23 Peppo Nino
24 Doc Holliday's
27 Good Health Natural Food Market
29 Rendezvous

OTHER
8 Valley View Hospital
10 Roaring Fork Marketplace; Cajun Laundry
12 Buffalo Valley Inn
13 Glenwood Caverns
15 Glenwood Springs Center for the Arts
16 Yampah Spa & Vapor Caves
18 BSR Sports
19 Book Train
25 Summit Canyon Mountaineering
28 Post Office
30 Sunlight Ski & Bike Shop
31 Bank of Colorado
32 USFS White River National Forest
    Headquarters
34 Frontier Historical Museum
36 Chamber Resort Association Visitors Center

Look for bike rentals at Canyon Bikes (☎ 970-945-8904), 504 W Harvard Dr, BSR Sports (☎ 970-945-7317), 210 7th St, and Sunlight Ski & Bike Shop (☎ 970-945-9425), 309 9th St at Cooper.

Rafting

Glenwood Canyon offers Class III-IV whitewater below the Shoshone Dam 7½ miles east of town. Families with young children can take shorter float trips at the Grizzly Creek turnoff from I-70, or go during low flow. Two Rivers Park, north of the confluence of the Colorado and Roaring Fork Rivers, is the take-out point.

For guided tours, Rock Gardens Rafting (☎ 970-945-6737, 800-958-6737), east of town on I-70 exit 119 at 1308 Garfield County Rd 129, offers free hot showers after the trip; visit www.rockgardens.com. Also consider Blue Sky Adventures (☎ 970-945-6605), 319 6th St (on the ground floor of the Hotel Colorado), or White-Water Rafting (☎ 970-945-8477), 200 Devereux Rd.

Hiking

The relatively low elevations around Glenwood Springs means that there are no alpine trails above treeline. Numerous trails head north from the Glenwood Canyon Trail, including the 1.2-mile-long **Hanging Lake Trail**, which leads to a breathtaking waterfall-fed pond perched in a rock bowl on the canyon wall. It's a strenuous 1½- to 3-hour roundtrip with a 1020-foot elevation gain – but well worth the work! Keep a sharp lookout for bighorn sheep in Glenwood Canyon. Take the Hanging Lake exit 8 miles east of town on I-70, or make a morning or afternoon of it and bike the Canyon Trail 10½ miles to the Hanging Lake trailhead.

A short half-mile hike to the **Pioneer Cemetery** begins at the corner of 12th St and Bennett Ave where gambling gunfighter John Henry 'Doc' Holliday is reportedly buried.

For hiking, rock climbing and kayak gear, topographic maps and outdoor books and guides, head for Summit Canyon Mountaineering (☎ 970-945-6994), at 1001 Grand Ave.

Fishing

Productive Gold Medal water on the Roaring Fork River has large trout and trophy mountain whitefish, averaging 2 to 3lb, for 12 miles between the Crystal River below Carbondale and the Colorado River. Secluded Veltus Park, near W 8th and 9th Sts, is a pleasant picnic area that provides fishing access and a pier on the west side of the river. Also consider contacting a rafting company to float down the river.

Drop by Roaring Fork Anglers (☎ 970-945-0180), 2022 Grand Ave, for gear and advice.
Web site: www.RFAnglers.com

Skiing & Snowboarding

Serious skiers head 'up-valley' to Aspen, Aspen Highlands and Snowmass, or east on I-70 to Vail. But Sunlight Mountain Resort (☎ 970-945-7491, 800-445-7931), 12 miles south of Glenwood Springs on Garfield County Rd 117, survives by offering good deals to families and intermediate skiers; look at www.sunlightmtn.com. Adult lift passes cost just $30/20 adults/children – among the least expensive in the state. The cross-country ski area features 18 miles of groomed track and snow-skating trails, plus snowshoeing and ice-skating areas. Call for the latest ski, swim and stay packages. There's free transportation to the hill from the corner of 11th and Grand Sts. Equipment and rentals are available at the mountain or in town at Sunlight Ski & Bike Shop (☎ 970-945-9425), 309 9th St. For snowboard rentals, head to BSR Sports (see Bicycling, earlier).

Special Events

Since 1898, residents of Glenwood Springs have celebrated **Strawberry Days** in mid-June, which feature artisans, entertainment, a carnival, bike and track events, a parade and free strawberries and ice cream. For two weeks in late June and early July, **Glenwood Springs Dance Festival** features performances, films and open rehearsals. Contact the Glenwood Springs Center for the Arts (☎ 970-945-2414) for information.

Places to Stay

Camping & Hostels On the way to Sunlight Mountain Resort, *Hideout Cabins & Campground* (☎ *970-945-5621, 800-987-0779, HideoutCO@aol.com, 1293 Garfield County Rd 117*) has shaded tent sites near Threemile Creek for $18, showers included. RV sites are $19 with full hookups and fully furnished cabins with kitchens are $45 to $135.

The *Glenwood Springs Hostel* (☎ *970-945-8545, 800-946-7835, 1021 Grand Ave*) has more than 40 beds and five private rooms. Mountain-bike rentals and all-day kayaking trips are offered to guests. Dorm beds start at $12. Private rooms with shared bath run $20 to $26.

Motels There are about 20 motels and hotels in the Glenwood area and those closest to the city center fill up quickly during the summer season, so make reservations well in advance.

The *Glenwood Motor Inn* (☎ *970-945-5438, 800-543-5906, 141 W 6th St*) is clean, comfortable and close to the center of town. Rates range from $45 to $96. South of town, the *Frontier Lodge* (☎ *970-945-5496, 888-606-0602, 2834 Glen Ave*) is a great value with doubles starting at $50. Just west of the bridge on the north side of the river in Glenwood Springs, the *Best Western Antlers Motel* (☎ *970-945-8535, 171 W 6th St*) is the nicest motel in town and includes a pool and hot tub. It's also a bit more expensive: High-season rates start at $90, off-season rates drop to $65. Across the street and a bit east, the *Ramada Inn* (☎ *970-945-2500, 800-228-2828, 124 W 6th St*) is only a short walk to the resort spa and pool. Doubles start around $100 in summer and go for as little as half that in the off-season.

If you find yourself without a room in June or July your best bet may be one of the dozen or so motels in West Glenwood, 1 to 2 miles from town on US 6. The *Red Mountain Inn* (☎ *970-945-6353, 800-748-2565, 51637 US 6*) features large, modern rooms, a pool and hot tub. Rates are $49 to $125. Just down the road, the *Budget Host* (☎ *970-945-5682, 800-283-4678, 51429 US 6*) offers similar amenities and cheaper rates, from $29 to $69.

The modern *Holiday Inn Express* (☎ *970-928-7800, 501 W 1st St*) offers a wide range of amenities (including an outdoor hot tub), and charges from $49 to $109. *Hampton Inn* (☎ *970-947-9400, 800-426-7866, 401 W 1st St*), just next door, has similar rates and facilities.

Hotels Opposite the railroad depot, the 1906 *Hotel Denver* (☎ *970-945-6565, 800-826-8820, 402 7th St*) is a comfortable and completely renovated hotel in the middle of town with rates from $55 to $150. A pedestrian bridge crosses the river to the pool.

Modeled after the Villa de Medici in Italy, the *Hotel Colorado* (☎ *970-945-6511, 800-544-3998, 526 Pine St*) is an imposing sandstone resort hotel in operation for more than 100 years. It has a rich history that includes presidential guests, gangsters and perhaps a ghost or two! Antique furnishings decorate the rooms, which start at $98.

The *Hot Springs Lodge and Pool* (☎ *970-945-6571, 415 E 6th St*) has nice modern rooms ranging from $67 to $112. Guests get a slight discount on pool or spa services.

B&Bs Housed in a pleasant 1903 Victorian home, *Back in Time B&B* (☎ *970-945-6183, 888-854-7733, 927 Cooper Ave*) is furnished with antiques, old-fashioned clocks and quilts. Nightly singles/doubles start at $55/75.
Web site: www.backintimebb.com

On the way to Sunlight Mountain Resort, the *Four Mile Creek Bed & Breakfast* (☎ *970-945-4004, 6471 County Rd 17*) offers a nice escape to the countryside. Housed in a remodeled farmhouse and log cabin next to a pond and stream, this elegant Western B&B has rates from $85 to $120.
Web site: www.fourmilecreek.com

Places to Eat

Vegetarians can go to *Good Health Natural Food Market* (☎ *970-945-0235, 730 Cooper Ave*), south of the train station, for deli items, organic produce, bulk herbs and

COLORADO

a complete line of natural foods. There's usually a crowd waiting for breakfast at the *Daily Bread Bakery & Cafe* (☎ 970-945-6253, 729 Grand Ave). *Wild Rose Bakery* (☎ 970-928-8973, 310 7th St), across from the train depot, serves delicious muffins, danish, scones and fresh bread.

Carnivores will enjoy the smoked-meat selections at *Smokin' Willies Bar-B-Que* (☎ 970-945-2479, 101 W 6th St). Try *Doc Holliday's* (☎ 970-945-8568, 724 Grand Ave) for great burgers and steaks in a woodsy cowboy saloon.

The *Brew Pub* (☎ 970-945-1276, 402 7th St), next to the Hotel Denver, has delicious sandwiches and salads as well as five hand-crafted beers on tap. Kids can try the home-made root beer. For soda-fountain counter service, check out the *19th Street Diner* (☎ 970-945-9133, 1908 Grand Ave). It serves breakfast all day and has traditional blue-plate specials.

For bargain carbo-loading you can't beat *Italian Underground* (☎ 970-945-6422, 715 Grand Ave), offering heaping pasta dinners for less than $10. *Peppo Nino* (☎ 970-945-9059, 702 Grand Ave) does respectable lasagna and spaghetti dinners.

Rendezvous (☎ 970-945-6644, 817½ Grand Ave) is a cozy little bistro serving excellent French and American cuisine for lunch and dinner. For a zanier atmosphere that befits Cajun food, check out the S&M ('swamp and moo') special at *The Bayou* (☎ 970-945-1047, 52103 US 6) in West Glenwood Springs.

Entertainment
Doc Holliday's (☎ 970-945-8568, 724 Grand Ave) is a favorite watering hole. For good country music, check out the *Buffalo Valley Inn* (☎ 970-945-6967, 3637 Hwy 82).

Getting There & Away
Colorado Mountain Express (☎ 970-949-4227, 800-525-6363) offers shuttle service to/from Denver International Airport.
Web site: www.cmex.com

Greyhound buses between Grand Junction and Denver stop at the Ramada Inn, 124 W 6th St. Amtrak's *California Zephyr*

stops daily at the Amtrak Station (☎ 970-945-9563) on South River St.

Glenwood Springs is 159 miles west of Denver and 90 miles east of Grand Junction along I-70.

Getting Around
Colorado Mountain Express (see above) serves Aspen Airport.

Glenwood Trolley buses operate on the half-hour between the W Glenwood Mall and the Roaring Forks Marketplace at the south end of town. Fares cost 50¢. During ski season, free buses serve Sunlight Mountain Resort from a stop at 11th St and Grand Ave. Roaring Forks Transit Authority (☎ 970-925-8484) offers bus connections with Aspen from the Glenwood Mall.

ASPEN & AROUND
Hedonism reigns in Aspen – host to some of the wealthiest skiers in the world. Instead of mountain-bike mania, you're more likely to see middle-aged men on rented Harley 'hogs,' their thinning hair flying in the breeze, and leather-clad 'mamas' hanging on tight. For many, Aspen (population 5500; elevation 7908 feet) represents a fantasy getaway. For mere mortals not encumbered with payments on one of the private jets parked at Sardy Field, watching the parade of personalities strutting about in garish attire is a bit like peeking at a royal court.

To adjust to the flow of Aspen life, relax and take a seat on one of the reclining benches in front of the Paradise Bakery. Whether it's the end of a winter day of skiing or a midsummer evening, an entertaining spectacle is bound to pass by. Aspen police cruise by in Saabs, but one can only wonder if they'd be driving red Cadillac convertibles if 'gonzo journalist' (and Aspen resident) Hunter S Thompson had succeeded in his 1970 campaign to become the local sheriff.

Highbrow cultural activities dominate Aspen's summer schedule, which nurtures artists, musicians, chefs, directors and great minds. There is also, however, ample opportunity to explore an array of regional outdoor pursuits, from hiking and mountain biking to top-notch river rafting.

Information

For extensive tourist information, be sure to stop at the Aspen Chamber Resort Association (☎ 970-925-9000, 800-262-7736), housed on the bottom floor of the large Aspen Public Parking Garage at 425 Rio Grande Place (near N Mill St). It's open 8 am to 5 pm weekdays. On weekends, ample visitor information is also available at the Wheeler Opera House (☎ 970-920-7148), 320 E Hyman Ave, open 9 am to 5 pm daily. From mid-June through Labor Day, you can also pick up visitor information at the kiosk on the Cooper Street Mall (corner of Galena St); open 10 am to 6 pm daily. Visit the chamber's Web site at www.aspenchamber.org.

The USFS Aspen Ranger Station (☎ 970-925-3445), 806 W Hallam, offers topo maps and information on more than 200 miles of trails in the forest and three wilderness areas surrounding Aspen: Hunter Fryingpan, Maroon Bells–Snowmass and Collegiate Peaks. It's open 8 am to 5 pm daily.

You'll find ATMs at Colorado National Bank (☎ 970-925-1450), 420 E Main St, and Wells Fargo Bank (☎ 970-925-2500), 119 S Mill St.

'When the going gets weird, the weird turn pro.'

The main post office is at 235 Puppy Smith St; the zip code is 81612. Explore Booksellers & Bistro (☎ 970-925-5336), 221 E Main St, is the largest and most comprehensive bookstore in Aspen.

Aspen Valley Hospital (☎ 970-925-1120) is at 401 Castle Creek Rd near Aspen Highlands, southwest of town.

Aspen Center for Environmental Studies

The center (☎ 970-925-5756), 100 S Puppy Smith St, is a 25-acre wildlife sanctuary beside the Roaring Fork River. Take a self-guided tour of the preserve surrounding Hallam Lake. Anglers can study the native cutthroat trout and its food supply in an indoor trout stream. During summer months, the center also conducts guided natural history tours at the top of Aspen Mountain, at Maroon Bells and in Snowmass, as well as Naturalist Field School courses. It's open from 9 am to 5 pm Monday to Saturday. A $2 donation is requested.

Aspen Historical Society Museum

Once the home of silver baron Jerome Wheeler, the faithfully restored Wheeler-Stallard House, built in 1888, now houses the Aspen Historical Society Museum (☎ 970-925-3721), 620 W Bleeker St. Tours through the three-story home are offered in summer, plus changing exhibits and archives in the Carriage House are open daily 9 am to 5 pm. Admission is $3.

Interpretive **walking tours** of Aspen's West End leave from the museum at 9:30 am on Wednesday and Friday, mid-June to mid-September. Downtown walking tours leave from the Wheeler Opera House (see below) at 9:30 am Monday (mid-June to mid-August). You can also snap up a copy of its excellent self-guided walking tour. Web site: www.aspenhistory.org

Wheeler Opera House

For a brief period after opening in 1889, the 500-seat Wheeler Opera House (☎ 970-920-7148), 320 E Hyman Ave attracted top talent on the 'Silver Circuit.' This sandstone

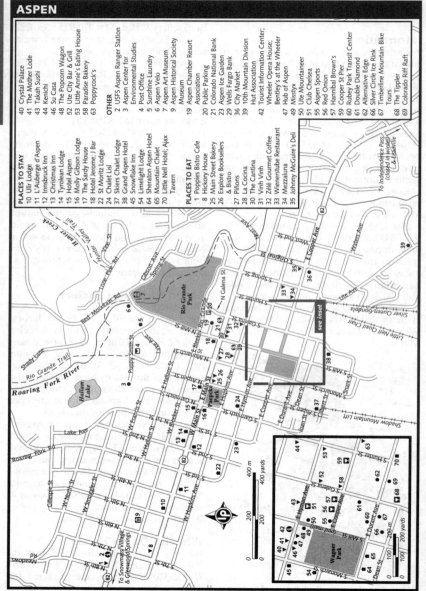

ASPEN

PLACES TO STAY
10 Ullr Lodge
11 L'Auberge d'Aspen
12 Innsbruck Inn
13 Christmas Inn
14 Tyrolean Lodge
15 Hotel Aspen
16 Molly Gibson Lodge
17 The Sardy House
18 Hotel Jerome; J Bar
22 St Moritz Lodge
24 Chalet Lisl
37 Skiers Chalet Lodge
38 Grand Aspen Hotel
45 Snowflake Inn
54 Limelight Lodge
64 Sheraton Aspen Hotel
65 Mountain Chalet
70 Little Nell Hotel; Ajax
   Tavern

PLACES TO EAT
1 Poppies Bistro Cafe
8 Hickory House
25 Main Street Bakery
26 Explore Booksellers
   & Bistro
27 Piñons
28 La Cocina
30 The Cantina
31 Vinh Vinh
32 Zélé Gourmet Coffee
33 Wienerstube Restaurant
34 Mezzaluna
35 Johnny McGuire's Deli

40 Crystal Palace
41 The Mother Lode
43 Takah Sushi
44 Kenichi
46 Su Casa
48 The Popcorn Wagon
52 Ute City Bar & Grill
53 Little Annie's Eating House
58 Paradise Bakery
63 Poppycock's

OTHER
2 USFS Aspen Ranger Station
3 Aspen Center for
  Environmental Studies
4 Post Office
5 Sunshine Laundry
6 Aspen Velo
7 Aspen Art Museum
9 Aspen Historical Society
  Museum
19 Aspen Chamber Resort
   Association
20 Public Parking
21 Colorado National Bank
23 Aspen Ice Garden
29 Wells Fargo Bank
36 City Market
39 10th Mountain Division
   Hut Association
42 Tourist Information Center;
   Wheeler Opera House;
   Bentley's at the Wheeler
47 Hub of Aspen
49 Misstyx
50 Ute Mountaineer
51 Club Chelsea
55 Aspen Sports
56 Red Onion
57 Hannibal Brown's
59 Cooper St Pier
60 Rubey Park Transit Center
61 Double Diamond
62 Alternative Edge
66 Silver Circle Ice Rink
67 Timberline Mountain Bike
   Tours
68 The Tippler
69 Colorado Riff Raft

building reopened after a renovation in 1984. Except during rehearsal for Aspen Music Festival performances, it's open daily for tours.

Aspen Art Museum
From the Art Park, pedestrians cross a 1911 trestle bridge over the Roaring Fork River to the Aspen Art Museum (☎ 970-925-8050), 590 N Mill St near Red Mountain Rd. Rotating exhibits feature nationally recognized artists. The museum is open 10 am to 6 pm Tuesday to Saturday, noon to 6 pm Sunday. Admission is $4/2 adults/seniors and students.

Maroon Bells
One of the most photographed spots in the state overlooks Maroon Lake toward the pair of 14ers known as the Maroon Bells. Part of the Elk Mountain Range, the Maroon Bells are unique among Colorado's major peaks for their sedimentary composition, giving them their distinctive color, tilted layers and sharp angular forms chiseled by glacial action. To the east, Pyramid Peak is a third 14er in the area. The peaks are part of the Maroon Bells–Snowmass Wilderness Area.

Maroon Creek Rd, a 'cherrystem' into the wilderness, is closed between 8:30 am and 5 pm to cars not using the campgrounds. A guided bus tour is the best way to get to Maroon Lake trailheads. Bicycling the 11-mile Maroon Creek Rd is another option – it climbs 1700 feet. Buses leave Aspen's Rubey Park Transit Center every half-hour from 9 am to 4:30 pm, returning between 9:30 am and 5 pm. Roundtrip fare is $4/2 adults/seniors and children (six to 16).

In summer, the Aspen Center for Environmental Studies offers hourly natural history tours from 10 am to 2 pm. The center's telescope may also help you spot bighorn sheep, elk or eagles on the cliffs above the lake. Inquire at the Maroon Bells bus stop information desk.

Ashcroft
For a scenic excursion, especially during fall, visit the historic mining town of Ashcroft.

Check with the Aspen Center for Environmental Studies (see above) about guided nature hikes. An admission fee of $2/1 adults/children is charged by the Aspen Historical Society (see above), which also offers occasional historical walking tours of the town site. To get there, travel west of town a half-mile on Hwy 82 and go left at Castle Creek Rd. Ashcroft is 11 miles ahead.

Gondola Rides
The Silver Queen Gondola (☎ 970-925-1220) starts south of Durant St near Hunter St and runs to the top of Ajax Mountain 9:30 am to 4 pm daily during summer and costs $18/14/7 adults/teens/children ages seven to 12. Kids six and under and seniors over 70 ride free. At the top, naturalists from the Aspen Center for Environmental Studies lead free guided summer nature walks. Two-hour snowshoe tours take place in winter. Call ahead for details.

Skiing
Four ski areas operated by the Aspen Skiing Company dominate daytime activity during winter: Snowmass, 12 miles northwest of Aspen on Hwy 82 (not to be confused with the small town of Snowmass); Buttermilk Mountain, 2 miles west of Aspen; Aspen Highlands, which is about 2 miles southwest of town; and Aspen (Ajax) Mountain, which overlooks the town. All the areas are managed by one company, so its phone numbers (☎ 970-925-1220, 800-525-6200) will connect you with any of the mountains for lift ticket information, accommodations or company-run rental shops. Lift tickets are significantly discounted before December 1.

The best cross-country skiing in the area is at Ashcroft (see above) in the beautiful Castle Creek Valley. It offers more than 20 miles of groomed trails that pass through the ghost town. You can arrange for instruction or guided backcountry day and overnight trips. Be sure to have lunch at the ski-in (or sleigh-in) Pine Creek Cookhouse. The Aspen Cross-Country Ski Center (☎ 970-925-2145) operates 'on the tracks' at the Aspen Golf Course, west of town on

Hwy 82. Nordic skiing at Snowmass is available at the Club Cross-Country Touring Center (☎ 970-923-3148), featuring 20 miles of groomed trails.

The 10th Mountain Division Hut Association (☎ 970-925-5775), 1280 Ute Ave, offers a system of backcountry trails almost 300 miles long connecting 14 overnight cabins. Nearby huts on the margins of the Hunter-Fryingpan and Holy Cross Wilderness Areas are available for $24 per person; these huts are popular – especially over weekends – so it's good to reserve space far in advance. Reservations are accepted June 1 for the following winter and there's a $25 membership fee. These trips do require some backcountry skiing experience and avalanche training is highly recommended.

The office also has information and takes reservations for the Braun Hut System, which covers Aspen, Vail, Leadville and Hunter Creek. There are six cabins and the terrain is generally remote and challenging, mainly meant for experienced backcountry skiers.

Many independent shops in and around Aspen offer rental alternatives to shops run by resorts. For Alpine ski rentals, try Aspen Sports (☎ 970-925-6331), 408 E Cooper Ave.

Snowboard rentals and gear are also available at Alternative Edge (☎ 970-925-8272), 555 E Durant Ave. For snowshoes and cross-country and telemark skis your best bets are Ute Mountaineer (☎ 970-925-2849), at 308 S Mill St and the Hub of Aspen (☎ 970-925-7970), 315 E Hyman Ave.

Ice Skating

Silver Circle Ice Rink (☎ 970-544-0303) has outdoor skating and lessons at Dean and Mill Sts. It's open 9 am to 10 pm; admission is $6/4 adults/children.

The Ice Garden (☎ 970-920-5141), at the corner of S 1st and E Hyman Sts, is an almost full-size indoor ice rink with public skating, hockey, lessons and skate rentals and a full pro shop. Rates are $4/3 adults/children, rentals are $2.

Hiking & Backpacking

Aspen is surrounded by three wilderness areas offering plenty of trails that are typi-cally open from July through early fall, when aspen foliage decorates the land. From Lone Pine Rd in Aspen, the **Hunter Valley Trail** (USFS Trail 1992) follows Hunter Creek northeast about 3 miles through wildflower meadows to the **Sunnyside** and **Hunter Creek** trails into the Hunter-Fryingpan Wilderness Area.

From Maroon Lake, the easy **Maroon Creek Trail** (USFS Trail 1982) is a six-mile streamside route that passes beaver ponds and the avalanche area as it follows a downhill path along Maroon Creek to the valley bottom. A 3-mile option ends at East Maroon Portal, where the bus picks up hikers by the roadside.

Conundrum Hot Springs, west of Castle Peak (14,265 feet), is the reward for 8½ miles of moderate climbing on the **Conundrum Creek Trail** (USFS Trail 1981). You can continue over Triangle Pass and return on **East Maroon Creek Trail** to catch a bus from Maroon Lake back to Aspen. The trailhead is 5 miles south of the Hwy 82 turnoff for USFS Rd 102, immediately west of town.

Other trails in the Hunter-Fryingpan or Collegiate Peaks Wilderness Areas east of Aspen tend to be less used than the Maroon Bells–Snowmass area. From Lincoln Creek Rd 11 miles east of Aspen, **New York Creek Trail** (USFS Trail 2182) climbs 4 steep miles to a 12,000-foot-plus pass.

(For more excursions into this wilderness area, see also Leadville, earlier, and Buena Vista and Crested Butte in the Southern Mountains chapter.)

Mountain Biking

RFTA buses offer racks to carry up to four bikes on a first-come, first-served basis throughout the valley. At Snowmass, bikes are allowed on the Burlingame and Sam's Knob chairlifts. An easy ride for new arrivals is the **Rio Grande Trail** along the Roaring Fork River – it's crowded with joggers, dogs and bicyclists on its 4-mile length on the old railroad grade between Aspen's post office and the Slaughterhouse Bridge.

Mountain bicyclists are restricted from the wilderness trails, but there are still plenty of heavily used routes near town on Aspen Mountain and Smuggler Mountain. **Hunter Valley** and **Sunnyside** trails provide a challenging single-track loop north of town. Once you're acclimated to high altitudes, the **Montezuma Basin** and **Pearl Pass** rides offer extreme cycling experiences well above timberline, south of town from Castle Creek Rd. Trails Illustrated publishes the handy topographic *Aspen Bike Map*.

Look for bike rentals at The Hub of Aspen (☎ 970-925-7970), 315 E Hyman Ave, Colorado Riff Raft (☎ 970-925-5404, 970-925-5405), 555 E Durant Ave, or Aspen Velo (☎ 970-925-1495), 465 N Mill St.

Bike shuttles to trailheads and guided trips with lunch are available from Aspen Bike Tours (☎ 970-920-4059), 1435 Sierra Vista Dr. Timberline Mountain Bike Tours (☎ 970-925-3586, 800-842-2453), 516 E Durant Ave, offers customized tours around Aspen as well as multiple-day hut-to-hut trips using the 10th Mountain Hut System.

Fishing

From McFarlane Creek below the Difficult Campground to upper Woody Creek Bridge, the wild-trout water of the Roaring Fork River is restricted to fly-casting. A catch-and-release program is in effect. Many of the beautiful tributary streams to the Roaring Fork – including Lincoln Creek, Hunter Creek, Castle Creek, Maroon Creek and Snowmass Creek – also offer good fishing. Gold Medal water extends for 14 miles on the Fryingpan River from Ruedi Dam to its confluence with the Roaring Fork River at Basalt.

Fishing gear and information on guide services is available from Aspen Sports (☎ 970-925-6331), 408 E Cooper Ave.

Rafting

White-water action on the Roaring Fork River does not get a lot of attention, partly because of the short season that typically ends by July, but also because of the difficulty of the river. From Slaughterhouse Bridge in Aspen it's Class V (or higher) during high runoff periods. Extensive experience is necessary to handle upper or lower sections of the river.

For equipment and information drop by Ute Mountaineer (☎ 970-925-2849), 308 S Mill St. Colorado Riff Raft (see Mountain Biking, above) offers a variety of rafting trips on the Roaring Fork River and Crystal River. For excellent guided trips around Glenwood Springs and farther afield, contact Rock Gardens Rafting (☎ 800-958-6737); its Web site is www.rockgardens.com.

Horseback Riding

T-Lazy-7 Ranch (☎ 970-925-4614), 3129 Maroon Creek Rd, offers hourly horse rentals and breakfast rides. Its menagerie of animals includes llamas and elk. Snowmass Stables (☎ 970-923-3075), 2737 Brush Creek Rd in Snowmass Village, can also put you on an oat-burner or whisk you away on a dinner sleigh ride.

Special Events

There's *always* something happening in Aspen during the summer months, including season-long music and dance festivals. Check the calendar in *Aspen Magazine*'s 'Travelers Guide' for a comprehensive list of activities.

The **Snowmass Village Rodeo** (☎ 970-923-4433) takes place Wednesday and Saturday night from late June to late August. Web site: www.snowmassrodeo.com

Places to Stay

Aspen Central Reservations, affiliated with the Aspen Chamber Resort Association (☎ 970-925-9000, 800-262-7736), 425 Rio Grande Place, can set you up with accommodations ranging from hotel rooms to houses to condos; visit www.aspen4U.com. Treasures of Aspen (☎ 888-290-1325) is an alternative if you are looking to stay in a small lodge or B&B.

Winter rates peak during the December to early January holidays and are at their lowest in fall and spring (late April and May). Prices rise again in summer, but still average around half of winter peak prices.

Snowmass Central Reservations (☎ 970-923-2000, 800-332-3245), outside of Aspen,

Rodeo: A Western Ritual

Rodeo, from the Spanish word meaning roundup, began with the cowboys of the Old West. As they used to say, 'There was never a horse that couldn't be rode – and never a rider that couldn't be throwed.' Naturally, cowboys riding half-wild horses eventually competed to determine who was the best. The speed with which they could rope a calf also became a competitive skill.

Rodeo as we know it today began in the 1880s. The first rodeo to offer prize money was held in Texas in 1883, and the first to begin charging admission to the event was in Prescott, Arizona, in 1888. Since then, rodeo has developed into both a spectator and professional sport under the auspices of the Professional Rodeo Cowboys Association (PRCA).

For the first-time spectator, the action is full of thrills and spills but may be a little hard to understand. Within the arena, the main participants are cowboys and cowgirls, judges and clowns. Although the clowns perform amusing stunts, their function is to help out the cowboys when they get into trouble. During the bull riding, they are particularly important if a cowboy gets thrown. Then clowns immediately rush in front of the bull to distract the animal, while the winded cowboy struggles out of the arena.

While men are the main contenders in a rodeo, women also compete, mainly in barrel racing, team roping and calf roping. Each rodeo follows the same pattern, and once you know a few pointers, it all begins to make sense. The first order of the day is the grand entry, during which all contestants, clowns and officials parade their horses around the arena, raise the US flag and sing the national anthem. The rodeo then begins, usually including seven events:

Bareback Bronc Riding Riders must stay on a randomly assigned bucking bronco (a wild horse) for eight seconds, which from the back of a crazed horse can seem like an eternity. The cowboy holds on with one hand to a handle strapped around the horse just behind its shoulders. His other hand is allowed to touch nothing but air, otherwise he's disqualified. His spurs must be up at the height of the horse's shoulders when the front hooves hit the ground on the first jump out of the chute, and he must keep spurring the horse during the ride. Two judges give up to 25 points each to the horse and the rider, for a theoretical total of 100. A good ride is one in which the horse bucks wildly and the rider stays on with style – a score of over 70 is good.

Calf Roping This is a timed event. A calf races out of a chute, closely followed by a mounted cowboy with a rope loop. The cowboy ropes the calf (usually by throwing the loop over its head, although a leg catch is legal), hooks the rope to the saddle horn and dismounts, keeping the rope

will do its best to match your price and quality requirements with one of the many hotel rooms or condos in Snowmass Village, or you can ask for a specific hotel by name.

Budget The USFS White River National Forest's Aspen Ranger District (☎ 970-925-3445) operates nine campgrounds in the vicinity of Aspen, but only three are reservable (☎ 877-444-6777): *Silver Bar*, *Silver Bell* and *Silver Queen*, all south of Aspen on Maroon Creek Rd. Together they

account for only 14 sites. The fee is $12 plus a $7.50 reservation fee.

Nearby *Maroon Lake* offers 44 sites ($12) assigned at the Maroon Valley entrance station. Five miles east of town, *Difficult* campground has 47 sites ($12), but finding a vacant site is difficult. Continuing east on Hwy 82 toward Independence Pass, the smaller *Weller*, *Lincoln Gulch* and *Lost Man* campgrounds offer a total of 27 sites ($7). A last resort is the free *Portal* campground, 7 miles south of Lincoln Gulch on Pitkin County Rd 23.

Rodeo: A Western Ritual

tight all the way to the calf. A well-trained horse will stand still and hold the rope taut to make the cowboy's job less difficult. When he reaches the calf, the cowboy throws the animal down, ties three of its legs together with a 6-foot-long 'piggin string' and throws up his hands to show he's done. A good roper can do the whole thing in just a few seconds.

Saddle Bronc Riding This has similar rules to the bareback event and is scored the same way. In addition to starting with the spurs up above the horse's shoulders and keeping one hand in the air, the cowboy must keep both feet in the stirrups. Dismounting from the saddle of a bucking bronco is not easy – watch the two pickup men riding alongside to help the contestant off. This demands almost as much skill as the event itself.

Steer Wrestling In this event (also called bull-dogging), a steer that may weigh as much as 700lb runs out of a chute, tripping a barrier line, which is the signal for two cowboys to pursue the animal. One cowboy – the hazer – tries to keep the steer running in a straight line, while the other cowboy – the wrestler – rides alongside the steer and jumps off his horse trying to grip the steer's head and horns – this at speeds approaching 40mph! The wrestler must then wrestle the steer to the ground. The best cowboys can accomplish this in less than five seconds.

Barrel Racing Three large barrels are set up in a triangle, and the rider must race around them in a clover shape. The turns are incredibly tight, and the racer must come out of them at full speed to do well. There's a five-second penalty for tipping over a barrel. Good times are around 15 to 17 seconds.

Team Roping A team of two horseback ropers pursues a steer running out of the chute. The first roper must catch the steer by the head or horns and then wrap the rope around the saddle horn. The second team member then lassos the steer's two rear legs in one throw. Good times are as low as five seconds.

Bull Riding Riding a bucking and spinning 2000lb bull is wilder and more dangerous than bronc riding, and it is often the crowd's favorite event. Using one heavily gloved hand, the cowboy holds on to a rope that is wrapped around the bull. And that's it – nothing else to hold on to, and no other rules apart from staying on for eight seconds and not touching the bull with your free hand. Scoring is the same as for bronc riding.

Dispersed camping is not permitted except along Lincoln Creek 11 miles southeast of Aspen, and a five-day limit is enforced.

A European-style lodge offering dorms with shared baths for $44/29 winter/summer is *St Moritz Lodge* (☎ 970-925-3220, 334 W Hyman Ave). Rates include Continental breakfast.

The *Tyrolean Lodge* (☎ 970-925-4595, 200 W Main St) offers standard rooms from $70 to $95 in summer, while the *Snowflake Inn* (☎ 970-925-3221, 800-247-2069, 221 E Hyman Ave) charges from $55 to $139.

Rates at both places are close to double during ski season.

Mid-Range Since 1952, the *Skiers Chalet Lodge* (☎ 970-920-2037, 233 Gilbert St) has offered no-frills rooms at the base of the Shadow Mountain Lift. Basic rooms with private bath are between $72 and $105 in summer, about double that in winter. Room prices are slightly more at the *Limelight Lodge* (☎ 970-925-3025, 800-433-0832, 228 E Cooper Ave), which offers a pool and laundry facilities.

The Mountain Chalet (☎ 970-925-7797, 800-321-7813, 333 E Durant Ave) is closest to the lifts and town center. Standard rooms cost $78 to $105 during ski season, less during summer, and there's a pool, sauna and whirlpool. Similar rates and facilities can be found at the **Innsbruck Inn** (☎ 970-925-2980, 233 W Main St).

For couples or groups the **Chalet Lisl** (☎ 970-925-3520, 877-925-3520, 100 E Hyman Ave) is a great deal. Clean, attractive studio apartments with kitchen and one queen and one single bed rent for $128/80 winter/summer. One-bedroom apartments with a twin bed in the living room are $145/85.

If you prefer to stay out of town and want a real Western experience, the **T Lazy Seven** (☎ 970-925-4614, 888-875-6343, 3129 Maroon Creek Rd) may be the place. It's close to Aspen Highlands, just 3 miles down Maroon Creek Rd, and offers comfortable rustic wood cabins. Summer or winter prices range from $90 for studios to $280 for five-bedroom cabins that can sleep 10. There are no TVs or telephones but there is a wonderful outdoor heated pool and whirlpool. In the summer there's horseback riding, and sleigh rides and snowmobiling in the winter. Advance reservations are strongly advised.

The modern **Grand Aspen Hotel** (☎ 970-925-1150, 800-242-7736, 515 S Galena St) is close to the lifts and Rubey Park Transit Center. Its draconian five-night minimum requirement during the regular ski season is balanced with room rates that begin at $150/doubles. During summer, a one-night stay costs around $90, though lower rates may be available.

Not to be confused with the above, **Hotel Aspen** (☎ 970-925-3441, 800-527-7369, 110 W Main St) features a pool and rooms with kitchenettes. Off-season rooms go for $139 to $229, or around 30% more in winter.

A few former motels offer reasonable B&B lodging. At the garish **Christmas Inn** (☎ 970-925-3822, 232 W Main St) rates range from $66 to $100; a simple breakfast is included. The **Ullr Lodge** (☎ 970-925-7696,

520 W Main St) has standard rooms for $90 to $170 during ski season, $50 to $80 in low season, including a full breakfast in the winter and a Continental breakfast in summer.

L'Auberge d'Aspen (☎ 970-925-8297, 877-282-3743, 435 W Main St) is a cozy and unusual place offering cottages with fireplaces in the $80 to $250 range, slightly more in winter. Similar rates apply at the charming **Molly Gibson Lodge** (☎ 970-925-3434, 800-356-6559, 101 W Main St).

Top End In a beautiful, classic Victorian home, **The Sardy House** (☎ 970-920-2525, 800-321-3457, 128 E Main St) has luxury B&B accommodations with pool, sauna, restaurant and bar. Rates range from $115 to $500. Rooms at the venerable **Hotel Jerome** (☎ 970-920-1000, 800-331-7213, 330 E Main St), one of the finest hotels in Colorado, start at $365 during ski season but drop as low as $180 in October.

Little Nell Hotel (☎ 970-942-4600, 888-843-6355, 675 E Durant Ave) is a luxury hotel convenient to the slopes that books up fast. Room amenities include a wet bar, marble bathroom, TV and VCR, king or two queen beds, a fireplace and a balcony overlooking either the town or Ajax Mountain. It's Aspen's only five-star, five-diamond hotel; in peak winter season, a basic room goes for between $430 and $800, while the two-bedroom Pfeifer Suite goes for a mere $3500. In summer, rates begin at $330.

The **Sheraton Aspen Hotel** (☎ 970-920-3300, 315 Dean St), in a beautifully designed red-brick building at the base of Ajax, offers outstanding service, luxury and convenience. Peak winter rates run from $700 to $4000, dropping to as little as $165 in the off-season.

Places to Eat

Since 1965, the Austrian **Wienerstube Restaurant** (☎ 970-925-3357, 633 E Hyman Ave) has offered reasonably priced no-nonsense meals and efficient service. Breakfasts range from oat-bran pancakes to egg dishes. For crêpes and refreshing smoothies try **Poppycocks**

(☎ 970-925-1245, 609 E Cooper Ave). The **Zélé Gourmet Coffee** (☎ 970-925-5745, 121 S Galena St) can get you going quickly with fresh juice and pastries.

Budget diners rely on **The Popcorn Wagon** (☎ 970-925-2718, 305 S Mill St), which has outdoor seating and serves tasty crêpes and sandwiches for less than $5 until 2 am. **Main St Bakery** (☎ 970-925-6446, 201 E Main St) is a good place for dinners such as vegetarian lasagna or chicken pot pie. **Explore Booksellers & Bistro** (☎ 970-925-5336, 221 E Main St) offers vegetarian dinner specials each night on its rooftop patio.

Little Annie's Eating House (☎ 970-925-1078, 517 E Hyman Ave) has a bar and grill atmosphere and offers lunch specials for less than $10, dinner for about $12. For a corned beef on rye or an imaginative 'Tahiti' sandwich (ham, bacon, pinneaple, cream cheese, sprouts and mayo!), **Johnny McGuire's Deli** (☎ 970-920-9255, 730 E Cooper Ave) is the place to go.

For lunchtime burgers or more elaborate late-night fare, drop in to the historic **Bentley's at the Wheeler** (☎ 970-920-2240, 328 E Hyman Ave) in the Wheeler Opera House, which offers moderately priced dinners and a Victorian bar.

Su Casa (☎ 970-920-1488, 315 E Hyman Ave) opposite the Opera House, isn't the most popular Mexican restaurant in town, but its lunches and dinners are unpretentious and relatively inexpensive. More popular (and a bit more expensive) is **The Cantina** (☎ 970-925-3663, 411 E Main St). Also try the New Mexican–style blue-corn enchiladas and a bowl of *posole* at **La Cocina** (☎ 970-925-9714, 308 E Hopkins Ave).

Crowds flock to **The Mother Lode** (☎ 970-925-7700, 314 E Hyman), where they've been serving delectable pasta dishes since 1959. The place to see or be seen during lunch, dinner or après-ski is **Mezzaluna** (☎ 970-925-5882, 624 E Cooper Ave), which has a menu of northern Italian dishes.

The imposing sandstone Ute City Banque building houses the **Ute City Bar & Grill** (☎ 970-925-4373, 501 E Hyman Ave), an upmarket bistro that specializes in wild game, seafood and vegetarian dishes.

Another decent bistro, **Piñons** (☎ 970-920-2021, 105 S Mill St), offers Colorado cuisine that features elk, ahi and pork tenderloin. A less expensive option for meat lovers is the **Hickory House** (☎ 970-925-2313, 730 W Main St), which does great ribs and hickory-smoked chicken dinners, in addition to fluffy breakfast burritos and omelets.

For Japanese, try **Takah Sushi** (☎ 970-945-8588, 420 E Hyman Ave), which has an innovative menu and a lively sushi bar, or **Kenichi** (☎ 970-920-2212, 533 E Hopkins St), a popular and upscale restaurant featuring amazing sushi and innovative dinner combinations. At **Vinh Vinh** (☎ 970-920-4373, 413 E Main St), run appropriately by a couple sharing the name Vinh, they dish-up authentic Vietnamese fare in pleasant surroundings.

An innovative restaurant that gets rave reviews is **Poppies Bistro Cafe** (☎ 970-925-2333, 834 W Hallam St), housed in a cozy Victorian home. Finish the evening with a baked dessert or frozen yogurt at **Paradise Bakery** (☎ 970-925-7585, 320 S Galena Ave), and watch the street activity. Reservations are essential at the **Crystal Palace** (☎ 970-925-1455, 300 E Hyman Ave), a fun theater and dining experience where, after serving you a delicious meal, the waiters perform an original satirical show. The place was named for the elaborate chandeliers that grace the room and it's been doing business for 40 years. Dinner and the meal run around $50 per person, not including appetizers or drinks.

Entertainment

Bars Begin your pub crawl at **Cooper St Pier** (☎ 970-925-7758, 508 E Cooper Ave), a good place to shoot pool or have some pub food before the place gets rowdy – which is early. For a quieter scene, try Hotel Jerome's **J Bar** (☎ 970-920-1000) at Main and Mill Sts, a traditional watering hole where everyone can be comfortable. There's a more historical atmosphere at **Bentley's at the Wheeler** (☎ 970-920-2240, 328 E Hyman Ave). You can round out your history lesson with a visit to Aspen's oldest saloon, the **Red Onion** (☎ 970-925-9043, 420 E Cooper Ave), first opened in 1892 and a long-standing nighttime watering hole of the local ski patrol.

The après-ski crowd hangs out at *Ajax Tavern* (☎ 970-920-9333, 685 E Durant Ave) in the Little Nell Hotel. The deck is strictly see-and-be-seen.

Down-valley about 8 miles, **Woody Creek Tavern** (☎ 970-923-4585, 2 Woody Creek Plaza) is a 'stuff-on-the-walls' hangout for locals that closes at 11 pm. The popular watering hole of gonzo journalist Hunter S Thompson, it offers cheap beer on tap and pool tables – just like the places back home.

Nightclubs Top rock and blues performers are occasionally featured at **Double Diamond** (☎ 970-920-6905, 450 S Galena St). Near the gondola base, **The Tippler** (☎ 970-925-4977, 535 E Dean St) features late-night DJ dancing, while the small dance floor at **Hannibal Brown's** (☎ 970-925-7464, 424 E Cooper Ave) gets hopping with occasional live music.

Club Chelsea (☎ 970-920-0066, 415 E Hyman Ave) is a vast and popular basement-level nightclub with a mellow piano room, a thumpin' dance floor and even segregated smoking rooms to contain the secondary smoke.

Shopping

Aspen's toney shops will not disappoint even the most materialistic shopper. Probably the only items you won't find here are refrigerator magnets and rubber tomahawks (and the T-shirts here are embroidered with sequins). A vintage gas pump is just the thing for that garage addition project you had in mind.

For unusual jewelry and a most eclectic array of hair accessories, check out the selection at Misstyx (☎ 970-544-3842), 400 E Hyman Ave.

For detailed information on local art galleries, pick up a free copy of *Aspen Magazine*'s 'Gallery Guide' from the Chamber Resort Association.

Getting There & Away

Sardy Field (☎ 970-920-5384), 4 miles north of Aspen on Hwy 82, has to be seen to be believed. Confirming the jet-set appeal of Aspen, it's crammed with the most modern aviation equipment and a fleet of private jets in all shapes and sizes.

For those without their own aircraft, Aspen is serviced by United Express, Northwest and Aspen Mountain Air, a feeder for American Airlines.

The Eagle County Airport (☎ 970-524-9490) is 70 miles east of Aspen/Snowmass but has an increasing number of jet flights during ski season. American, Delta, United and Northwest Airlines fly Boeing 757s into Eagle from their hubs in Dallas and Houston, Texas; Miami, Florida; New York; Chicago, Illinois; Los Angeles, California; Atlanta, Georgia; Minneapolis, Minnesota; and Detroit, Michigan.

Colorado Mountain Express (☎ 970-949-4227, 800-525-6363) offers frequent service to Denver International Airport for $100 per person one-way.
Web site: www.cmex.com

Aspen is 41 miles south of Glenwood Springs. From Denver, Aspen is 208 miles via I-70 and Hwy 82. During winter months, Hwy 82 over 12,095-foot Independence Pass to Leadville is closed.

Getting Around

To/From the Airport The Roaring Fork Transit Agency (RFTA) does not operate a designated shuttle to Sardy Field, but the free valley buses stop every half-hour about two blocks from the Airport Business Center, and will take you to Aspen. In the summer there is direct service to the airport leaving from Rubey Park Transit Center every half-hour from 6:30 am to 6 pm.

High Mountain Taxi (☎ 970-925-8294) will take you to and from Sardy Field for $24. It also offers private charter services to/from anywhere in Colorado; get information at www.highmountaintaxi.com. Colorado Mountain Express (see Getting There & Away, above) offers frequent service to Eagle Airport (near Vail) for $60 one-way.

Bus RFTA (☎ 970-925-8484) buses serve Snowmass Village and the valley to El Jebel north of Basalt, on half-hour intervals from

6:15 to 12:15 am. Free in-town shuttles serve the Aspen Highlands Ski Area, Hunter Creek, Mountain Valley, Snowbunny as well as the Music School on Castle Creek Rd. During the music festivals, buses also ply the route to and from the Music Tent.

Car & Taxi Rental agencies with counters at Sardy Field include Alamo, Avis, Budget and Dollar. If you feel a bit roguish, Magic Carpet Rides (☎ 970-544-0699) can rent you a Harley-Davidson motorcycle.

High Mountain Taxi (☎ 970-925-8294) operates meter cabs 24 hours a day.

Southern Mountains

The southern reaches of Colorado's Rockies offer diverse and fascinating terrain. There is plenty of stunning alpine scenery and some world-class ski resorts, like Crested Butte and Telluride. But there is also the sprawling San Luis Valley, a broad swath of agricultural land that is home to the scenic wonders of the Great

Sand Dunes and the Sangre de Cristo Mountains. Toward the southern border of the state, towns like San Luis help preserve the Hispanic culture that first took root in the area 300 years ago. The Rio Grande headwaters and the Arkansas River offer some of the finest white-water rafting and kayaking in the state. Heading west, the San Juan Mountains offer a different landscape from their northern counterparts, boasting craggy peaks, roaring streams and incredibly lush flora: a hiker's paradise.

Highlights

- San Juan Mountains – the breathtaking 'Alps of America,' with volcanic rock formations

- Great Sand Dunes National Monument – Arabian-style sand dunes contrast with the gorgeous Sangre de Cristo Mountains

- San Luis – a charming town that has become a sanctuary for Hispanic culture

- Crested Butte – possibly Colorado's coolest ski town, and home to amazing mountain-bike trails

- Lake City – a small, off-the-beaten-track town that retains its Old West character

- Telluride – hair-raising skiing, excellent hiking and hip nightlife

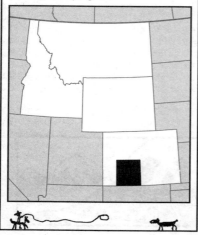

CAÑON CITY & AROUND

Home to the 13 state penitentiaries, Cañon City (population 15,000; elevation 5344 feet) is a popular stop for visitors to the Arkansas River, particularly Colorado's top tourist trap, the Royal Gorge. One good reason for hanging out in Cañon City is to raft down the Arkansas River, for this is a gateway to white-water heaven. And if you're interested, there is also (not surprisingly) a prison museum to check out.

Orientation & Information

Most of Cañon City's services are located on Royal Gorge Blvd (US 50) and on Main St.

The Cañon City Chamber of Commerce (☎ 719-275-2331, 800-876-7922) is in the historic Peabody Mansion (circa 1880), 403 Royal Gorge Blvd, and is open 8 am to 5 pm weekdays. It also operates visitor information booths at either side of town on US 50 (Memorial Day to Labor Day only). Web site: www.canoncitycolorado.com

For details on camping or hiking in the Wet Mountains in the San Isabel National Forest south of Cañon City, stop by the USFS/BLM office (☎ 719-269-8500) east of town at 3170 E Main St; 8 am to 4:30 pm weekdays.

Museum of Colorado Prisons

The Colorado Territorial State Penitentiary (one of the 13 in town, and housing around

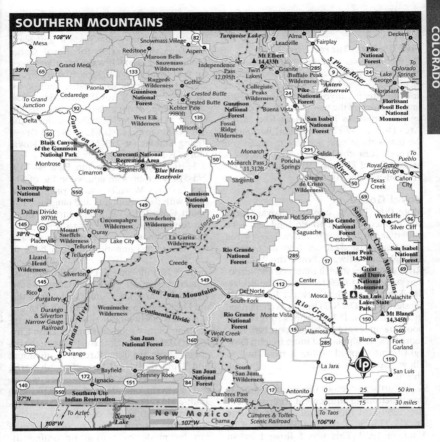

SOUTHERN MOUNTAINS

700 inmates) has been in the incarceration business since 1871.

Not everyone will want to visit this disturbing museum (☎ 719-269-3015) adjacent to the prison that renders a nightmare of life behind bars. Before entering the paid admission area, visitors are confronted with a hulking gas chamber on display in the museum yard. If this gruesome spectacle – last used in 1967 – does not deter you, you can tour the museum cell blocks.

You can't miss the museum; it forms the entire west end of town at 1st St and Macon Ave and is well lit at night. It's open in summer 8:30 am to 6 pm daily and in winter, 10 am to 5 pm Friday through Sunday; adults/seniors/children $5/4/3.

Dinosaur Depot

Housed in an old fire station downtown at 4th St and Hwy 50, Dinosaur Depot (☎ 719-269-7150, 800-987-6379) is a working preparatory lab featuring Jurassic fossils and interpretive displays. Tours of the **Garden Park Fossil Area** (active since 1877 and the world's largest Jurassic graveyard) are offered from 9 am to 5 pm daily in summer, otherwise from 10 am to 4 pm

Tuesday to Saturday.
Web site: www.dinosaurdepot.com

Five Points Recreation Area
On the Arkansas River about 12 miles west of Cañon City, Five Points is a good place to picnic while watching the river for rafters and the steep canyon slopes for bighorn sheep. It's one of the many facilities operated by the Arkansas Headwaters Recreation Area (☎ 719-539-7289 in Salida) but one of the few without boat access – meaning you will not be disturbed by busloads of rafters. A parking fee of $1 per person is also good for other sites on the river.

Royal Gorge
More than 10,000 years ago, Royal Gorge was created when hard Precambrian rock underlying a relatively thin veneer of red sandstone resisted erosion from the tremendous glacial meltwater flows. The Arkansas River continues to etch the steep and turbulent stream bed 1100 feet below the bridge. The Santa Fe and the Denver & Rio Grande Western Rail (D&RG) railroads challenged the gorge in the 1870s, anxious to reach the booming mines at Leadville. Soon, however, tourist traffic supplanted mine freight: Daylight trains stopped on the narrow shelf to allow passengers to get off and view the chasm.

To further promote the Royal Gorge as an attraction, an amusement company built the 1260-foot-long **Royal Gorge Bridge** (☎ 719-275-7507), the world's tallest of its kind, in 1929. This was followed by an incline railway to the bottom of the canyon, an aerial tramway across the gorge, a trolley across the bridge, a miniature train ride, a theatre and nature center. All of these 'scenic wonders' and more are viewable by paying $15/13 adults/children (ages four to 11). The suspension bridge is open 7:30 am to 7:30 pm daily in summer; shorter hours apply the rest of the year.

The savvy traveler who merely wants to see the Royal Gorge can walk to the edge from the parking lot just outside the North Gate entrance on Royal Gorge Rd, 8 miles west of Cañon City. But be warned that

trapping tourists is a well-honed profession in this area. First you must run the gauntlet of other attractions that line the approach, including the **Buckskin Joe Royal Gorge Scenic (miniature) Railway** – often mistaken for the Royal Gorge Bridge entrance by unsuspecting tourists who realize their error only after paying $7 for the train ride to the canyon edge where they see the distant bridge. A one-hour horseback ride to the rim of the gorge costs $12 at **Royal Gorge Riding Stables** (☎ 719-275-4579) on Royal Gorge Rd.

Farther on, **Buckskin Joe Park** (☎ 719-275-5149) requires an admission fee of $13 and features Western movie props, complete with daily gunfights and hangings. The South Gate Rd is another snare awaiting the tourist – this one leads to what effectively becomes an expensive toll crossing for visitors too impatient to turn back to US 50.

In 1999, following a 32-year hiatus, passenger service on the **Royal Gorge Route** (☎ 888-724-5748), a 12-mile segment of the old D&RG train line, was restored. Visitors can make the two-hour ride in carriages or open-air observation cars from Cañon City to Parkdale and back through the majestic gorge. There are departures at 9 am, noon and 3 pm daily mid-May through early October. In winter departures are weekends at noon only. Tickets cost $27/16.50 adult/child (ages 3 to 12), or for $75 you can ride in the cab of one of the locomotives. Advance reservations (recommended) can be made by phone or online at www.royalgorgeroute.com.

Rafting
The best way to see the Royal Gorge is on a raft, but the 7 miles of Arkansas River white water are not for the timid. Tour operators typically require rafters to be over 18 years of age in the early season or over 12 when the flow diminishes by midsummer.

A concentration of rafting guides near the Royal Gorge turnoff, 8 miles west of Cañon City, offers competitive prices and a variety of trips. Most of the following guide services operate May to October:

American Adventure Expeditions (☎ 719-269-9652, 800-288-0675) Royal Gorge Rd near US 50
Web site: www.americanadventure.com

Buffalo Joe River Trips (☎ 719-395-8757, 800-356-7984) Fort Gorge RV Park & Campground

Echo Canyon River Expeditions (☎ 719-275-3154, 800-748-2953) 45000 US 50 W
Web site: www.echocanyonrafting.com

Raft Masters (☎ 800-568-7238) 2315 E Main St
Web site: www.raftmasters.com

For a map and information about river access points contact the BLM (☎ 719-269-8500), which shares its office with the USFS and DOW at 3170 E Main St on the east side of town, or the Arkansas Headwaters State Recreation Area (☎ 719-539-7289) in Salida.

Places to Stay

The *Wet Mountains* in the San Isabel National Forest about 6 miles south of town on Oak Creek Grade Rd (Fremont County Rd 123) offer dispersed camping. *Buffalo Bill's Royal Gorge Campground* (☎ 719-269-3211), near the busy intersection of US 50 and Royal Gorge Rd, is not exactly a wilderness area, but tent sites cost $18 and a coin-op laundry is available. Showers for nonguests cost $3.

Rooms at the aging but well-maintained *Holiday Motel* (☎ 719-275-3317, 1502 Main St) cost $40/50 single/double (summer) and are a good value compared to the national chains.

Rooms cost $55/68 in summer, $30/38 in winter, at *Travel Inn* (☎ 719-275-9125, 2980 E Main St), opposite the Holy Cross Abbey. The rooms are a little frayed around the edges, but still comfortable. There's a lawn area set back from the highway, with a pool and a funky miniature golf course. Near the prison the very plain *Parkview Motel* (☎ 719-275-0624, 231 Royal Gorge Blvd) offers basic rooms for $45/55 in summer, $28/38 in winter, and has a coin-op laundry.

Rooms are priced at $69/79 in summer (add $10 on Friday and Saturday) at the *Best Western Royal Gorge* (☎ 719-275-3377, 1925 Fremont Dr), east of the town center. Facilities include a swimming pool, hot tub, playground and laundry. The attractive

Cañon Inn (☎ 719-275-8676, 3075 E US 50) goes one better with six hot tubs, a pool and two restaurants. Rooms cost $68/73 in summer, $58/63 in winter.

The delightful *St Cloud Hotel* (☎ 719-276-2000), at 7th and Main St, was built in 1879 in Silver Cliff and was moved to Cañon City in 1886. Until it shut down for a period in the 1980s it was said to be Colorado's longest-running hotel. The building is listed on the National Register of Historic Places. On a darker note, it once served as the local headquarters for the Ku Klux Klan during the 1920s. All the same, rooms, costing $75/85 in summer and $49/59 in winter, have a pleasant, antique feel.

Places to Eat

Inside the St Cloud Hotel, *Dr B's Bar & Grill* serves up well-prepared lunches and dinners, including some interesting appetizers. *Old Mission Deli* (☎ 719-275-6780, 1905 Fremont Dr)serves delicious Mexican a la carte specialties; burritos or chimichangas filled with *adobado,* spicy chorizo or *machaca.*

Merlino's Belvedere (☎ 719-275-5558, 1330 Elm Ave), on the old highway (now Hwy 115) 2 miles southeast of the 9th St Bridge, is probably Cañon City's favorite restaurant. The Italian dinners are reasonably priced. Another upscale spot worth trying is *Le Petit Chablis* (☎ 719-269-3333, 512 Royal Gorge Blvd). Locals consider its French cuisine among the best food in town.

Getting There & Away

Greyhound/TNM&O buses running between Pueblo and Grand Junction stop at the Video House (☎ 719-275-0163), 731 Main St.

Cañon City is on US 50, 35 miles west of Pueblo and 48 miles east of Salida.

WESTCLIFFE & SILVER CLIFF

South of the Arkansas River Canyon in the Wet Mountain Valley, Westcliffe and Silver Cliff (combined population 700) lie only a mile apart at elevations of 7888 feet and 7982 feet, respectively. They are surrounded by alpine valley scenery, and within striking distance of the beautiful **Sangre de Cristo Mountains**. Within the towns there are a number of well-preserved historical buildings.

Mountain grassland in the Wet Mountain Valley extends for about 35 miles between the jagged peaks of the Sangre de Cristo Mountains to the west and the Wet Mountains to the east, capped by the granitic summit of Greenhorn Peak (12,347 feet). Access to USFS lands on either side of the valley is limited to a few routes; otherwise, dire signs threaten trespassers on cattle grazing lands with Old West justice. Nevertheless it's fairly easy to reach the magnificent Sangre de Cristo range, which includes five 14ers in the Crestone Peak group. Other 14ers rise to the south around the prominent Blanca Peak.

Information

Pick up a copy of the 'Custer County Visitors Guide' at the Custer County Chamber of Commerce (☎ 719-783-9163, 877-793-3170), 101 N 3rd St in Westcliffe. Web site: www.custerguide.com

For information about the San Isabel National Forest and the Sangre de Cristo Wilderness, check with USFS ranger stations at Cañon City (☎ 719-269-8500) or La Veta (☎ 719-742-3681). For USGS maps, try Valley Ace Hardware, south of Westcliffe on US 69 (toward Walsenburg).

Silver Cliff Museum

The former Town Hall and Fire Station, built in 1879, houses a small museum where you can view relics and photographs of the valley's history. The museum is open 1 to 4 pm Thursday to Sunday from Memorial Day to Labor Day.

Hiking & Backpacking

Climbers use South Colony Lakes as a base camp, yet even if you don't wish to scale peaks, the 12,000-foot tarn lakes beneath the incredibly rugged Crestone Needle are worthy of a visit. Another hiking option in this area traverses the ridge at Music Pass (11,400 feet) leading to Sand Creek Lakes on the west side of the range.

For outstanding views from Comanche and Venable Passes on the crest of the Sangre de Cristo Mountains, plus a waterfall, the **Comanche/Venable Loop Trail** (USFS Trail 1345) is hard to beat.

Fishing

Close to Westcliffe is **Middle Taylor Creek SWA**, where restrooms, open camping and picnic tables are close to fishing spots along the stream. A 4WD road continues to **Hermit Lake** and **Horseshoe Lake** in USFS lands near the 13,000-foot summits of the Sangre de Cristo Mountains.

The regularly stocked DeWeese Reservoir and the Grape Creek, which flows from it, are included in the **DeWeese SWA**; for more information contact the Division of Wildlife (DOW; ☎ 719-561-4909) in Pueblo.

Other Activities

Off-road cyclists will find plenty of opportunities in San Isabel National Forest lands on either side of the Wet Mountain Valley. The most popular rides use portions of the **Rainbow Trail** (USFS Trail 1336), a 100-mile-long route along the Sangre de Cristo foothills between Salida and Music Pass, about 15 miles south of Westcliffe.

Bear Basin Ranch (☎ 719-783-2519), 11 miles east of Westcliffe, offers horseback rides on its extensive ranch property in the Wet Mountains. All-day trips into the mountains are also available.

Among the five jagged 14,000-foot peaks in the Crestone group (Crestone Peak, Crestone Needle, Kit Carson Mountain, Challenger Point and Humboldt Peak), only Humboldt Peak is a nontechnical climb. Gary Ziegler, who owns Bear Basin Ranch (see above), is a local authority on the peaks and can guide climbing trips.

Special Events

A rodeo and dance are the featured events at the **Custer County Fair**, held the last weekend in July. Over the second weekend of August, jazz artists perform both day and night at **Jazz in the Sangres**. Contact the chamber of commerce for details.

Places to Stay

East of Silver Cliff, *Kleine's Trailer Park* (☎ 719-783-2295, 320 Cliff St) is mostly geared for RVs (sites cost $12) but does allow tent camping and has showers and adjacent laundry facilities.

Abundant open sites (not fixed) are found at nearby *Middle Taylor Creek SWA* and *DeWeese SWA* and on USFS lands. Middle Taylor Creek is about 8 miles northeast of Westcliffe; DeWeese is about 4 miles northeast of Westcliffe. The USFS *Alvarado* campground has 47 sites available for $8. Head south from Westcliffe on Hwy 69 for 3 miles and turn right (west) on Custer County Rd 302 (Schoolfield Rd); it's 7 miles to the trailhead. A bit farther out is *Lake Creek*, which has 11 sites for $8 each. Go 15 miles north on Hwy 69 to Hillside (store and post office), turn left on Custer County Rd 198; it's 4 miles to campsites and USFS Trail 300 to Rainbow Lake.

In Westcliffe *Antler Motel* (☎ 719-783-2426), at Main and S 6th St (Hwy 69), has acceptable singles/doubles for $31/35. *The Courtyard Inn* (☎ 719-783-9616, 410 Main St) features featherbeds and down comforters (but no room phones). Rooms cost $70/75, including a Continental breakfast featuring homemade breads and Starbucks coffee. Its Web site is at www.courtyardinn.com.

Westcliffe's charming *Main Street Inn B&B* (☎ 719-783-4000, 877-783-4006, 501 Main St) makes a pleasant choice for couples seeking a quiet weekend as it is not a family-oriented place. The five double rooms, some with whirlpool baths, are tastefully decorated and rent from $95 to $120. Web site: www.mainstreetbnb.com

The nicest accommodations are at the *Westcliffe Inn* (☎ 719-783-9275), at the south end of Westcliffe on Hwy 69 at the intersection with Hermit Rd. Rooms cost $42/48 and include use of the indoor hot tub and sauna to soothe trail-sore muscles.

You will not have any complaints at Silver Cliff's *Yoder's High Country Inn* (☎ 719-783-2656, 700 Ohio St), where rooms cost $37/44, discounted for stays of more than two days.

Places to Eat

Shining Mountain Food & Gifts (☎ 719-783-9143, 212 Main St) is a nonsmoking breakfast and lunch spot that offers soups, sandwiches and a variety of Mexican dishes, with plenty of choices for vegetarians. *Purnell's* (☎ 719-783-2313, 104 Main St), another worthy cafe option for breakfast or lunch, does good gourmet coffees.

For home-style cooking go to Silver Cliff, where *Yoder's High Country Restaurant* (☎ 719-783-2656, 700 Ohio St) offers a complete lunch and dinner menu in a nonsmoking environment from Tuesday to Saturday. The US fare includes soups and baked goods made daily. For something more stylish, *Morgan's* (☎ 719-783-3399, 102 S Adams Blvd), just on the edge of Westcliffe, is perched on a bluff overlooking the Sangre de Cristo Mountains. It offers gourmet menu selections like steak and shrimp scampi in the $12 to $18 range. Pastas and Mexican entrees go for around $9.

In Silver Cliff the *Mining Company Restaurant* (☎ 719-783-9144, 202 Main St) serves varied fare from $4 to $7 and is open 7 am to 9 pm daily. Also in Silver Cliff, *Pizza Madness* (☎ 719-783-9300, 620 Main St) promotes 'better living through pizza.'

Midway between Cañon City and Westcliffe the historic *Oak Creek Grade General Store & Steakhouse* (☎ 719-783-2245), formerly a general store, serves up great steaks in an Old West atmosphere.

Getting There & Away

Westcliffe and Silver Cliff lie on Hwy 96, which continues east through the Wet Mountains to Pueblo 54 miles away. An alternate route from Cañon City, 52 miles away, turns south onto Hwy 69 at the Texas Creek junction with US 50 on the Arkansas River. Hwy 69 offers little traffic through pastoral scenery from the north end of the Wet Mountain Valley to the Huerfano River in the south and on to I-25 at Walsenburg.

SALIDA

Flanked by the soaring 14ers of the Collegiate Range, Salida (population 4100; elevation 7038 feet) enjoys a gorgeous setting and an unusually mild climate, making it one of the more desirable places to live in Colorado. Visitors come to enjoy the hiking, rafting, mountain biking and other outdoor activities in town and nearby areas in Chaffee County. The authentic Western ghost town of **Turret**, 12 miles northeast of Salida, makes for an eye-opening excursion. When you come back from your outings, there is a fairly good choice of accommodations and several fine restaurants.

Orientation & Information

US 50 (Rainbow Blvd) is lined with motels and restaurants, while downtown businesses congregate along F St near the river in the historic district.

The Heart of the Rockies Chamber of Commerce (☎ 719-539-2068), 406 W Rainbow Blvd, provides a free guide to Chaffee County that covers food, lodging and activities in Salida, Buena Vista and Poncha Springs, a walking tour of Salida's historic district and seasonal 'fun guides' that detail outdoor activities and special events. It is open 9 am to 5 pm daily in summer, weekdays in winter. Also visit www.salidachamber.org. Just next door at 406½ W Rainbow Blvd is the interesting little **Salida Museum** (summer only).

The Salida USFS Ranger Station (☎ 719-539-3591), 325 W Rainbow Blvd, sells books and topo maps and provides information on nearby trails and camping.

An ATM is available at Pueblo Bank & Trust (☎ 719-539-6696), 200 F St. The post office is at 310 D St; Salida's zip code is 81201.

Check out the used books and Native American literature at All Booked Up (☎ 719-539-2344), 134 E 1st St. Adventure Media Books & Coffee Bar, 148 F St, sells a good selection of regional titles, as well as high-powered caffeine drinks.

The Laundromat at 14th and E St is open daily, and Band Box Cleaners (☎ 719-539-2426), 119 F St, has drop-off service. Showers cost $3 at the Salida Hot Springs Pool (☎ 719-539-6738), 410 W Rainbow Blvd.

The Regional Medical Center (☎ 719-539-6661), 448 E 1st St, provides 24-hour emergency care.

Hiking

Salida offers hikers convenient access to USFS lands at the Continental Divide intersection of Colorado's two most extensive trails: the **Colorado Trail**, connecting 500 miles of mountain areas between Denver and Durango, and the 100-mile **Rainbow Trail** (USFS Trail 1336) that extends along the east side of the Sangre de Cristo Mountains from the Divide junction south of Marshall Pass to Music Pass. The **South Fooses Creek Trail** is a 6-mile segment of the Colorado Trail that climbs to the Divide beside a trout stream from Chaffee County Rd 225, 13 miles west of Poncha Springs.

A moderate 4-mile hike to Pass Creek Lake (11,600 feet) follows **USFS Trail 1411** from Chaffee County Rds 210 and 212, 2 miles west of Poncha Springs. Mt Shavano (14,229 feet) is a strenuous 4-mile hike on **USFS Trail 1428**.

For further information and descriptions of the trails contact the Salida USFS Ranger Station (see Orientation & Information, above).

Mountain Biking

The most popular ride for experienced cyclists acclimated to high altitudes is the 12-mile **Monarch Crest Trail** (USFS Trail 531) along the Continental Divide south of Monarch Pass (11,386 feet) to Marshall Pass (10,840 feet). To get to the trailhead take US 50 past Monarch Park and turn left on USFS Rd 906.

If you want some help getting to Monarch Pass, High Valley Center (☎ 719-539-6089, 800-871-5145) runs a mountain-bike shuttle service to Monarch Pass, 18 miles west of its location at the Conoco gas station, 305 S Main St, Poncha Springs. The ride costs $15 per person. Cyclists who shuttle to the top can ride the Divide and then choose between three exhilarating descents to Poncha Springs. The easiest route adds 16 miles to the journey and drops from Marshall Pass along old railroad tracks, now the graded Marshall Pass Rd (Chaffee County Rd 200), to US 285 into Poncha Springs. Guided half-day rides with shuttle are offered by American

SALIDA

PLACES TO STAY
1 Woodland Motel
6 The Thomas House B&B
8 The Century House B&B
10 Gazebo Country Inn
11 Piñon & Sage B&B Inn
14 Aspen Leaf Lodge
15 Motel Westerner
16 Travelodge
22 Apple Grove Motel
24 Circle R Motel
26 Budget Lodge
27 Mountain Motel

PLACES TO EAT
3 Bongo Billy's
5 Steam Plant
20 Country Bounty
28 Laughing Ladies Cafe
29 Moonlight Pizza
30 Spaghetti Western; La Frontera
34 First St Cafe
38 Il Vicino

OTHER
2 Absolute Bikes
4 Arkansas Headwaters Recreation Office
7 Regional Medical Center
9 Post Office
12 Arkansas River Fly Shop & Guide Service
13 Division of Wildlife (DOW)
17 Salida Hot Springs Pool
18 Salida Museum
19 Heart of the Rockies Chamber of Commerce
21 Salida USFS Ranger Station
23 Laundry
25 TNM&O Bus Depot
31 Band Box Cleaners

32 Victoria Tavern
33 Otero Cyclery
35 All Booked Up
36 Adventure Media Books & Coffee Bar
37 Pueblo Bank & Trust

Adventure Expeditions (☎ 719-539-4680, 800-288-0675).

Beginning riders enjoy **Garfield Trail**, a scenic forest route that follows the gentle gradient of an abandoned railroad spur for an up-and-back ride of less than 8 miles. The trail starts in the town of Garfield, just off Chaffee County Rd 228.

For more information on the area's many bike trails, pick up a free copy of 'Mountain Bike Guide to the 14ers Region' at the chamber of commerce or the USFS office (see Orientation & Information, above). For bike supplies, service and rental visit

Absolute Bikes (☎ 719-539-9295), 330 W Sackett St, or the Otero Cyclery (☎ 719-539-6704), 104 F St.

Other Activities

The Monarch Ski & Snowboard Area (☎ 719-539-3573, 800-996-7669) offers excellent downhill skiing conditions. A portion of the Old Monarch Pass route is groomed by the resort, which offers 2 miles of cross-country skiing.
Web site: www.skimonarch.com

In contrast to the daring white-water rapids upstream near Buena Vista or in the

Royal Gorge near Cañon City, Salida features rather sedate float trips perfect for families or beginners. For a complete list of all outfits permitted to operate on the Arkansas Headwaters, as well as full information on rafting and fishing opportunities, visit the Arkansas Headwaters Recreation Office (☎ 719-539-7289), 307 W Sackett St.

During the spring and fall anglers can expect good fishing on the Arkansas River for brown and rainbow trout averaging 12 inches. For additional information contact DOW (☎ 719-539-3529), 7405 W Rainbow Blvd.

Fishing supplies and guided trips are available from Arkansas River Fly Shop & Guide Service, just west of the Aspen Leaf Lodge on Rainbow Blvd.

In 1937 the Works Progress Administration (WPA) completed Colorado's largest indoor hot springs pool facility, Salida Hot Springs Pool (☎ 719-539-6738), 410 W Rainbow Blvd. Water temperatures in three separate sections are maintained at between 90°F and 100°F – with lap lanes always available in an 82-foot pool. It is open 1 to 9 pm daily in summer but is closed on Monday and operates shorter hours on winter weekdays. Admission costs $6/4 adults/children. In addition, private European-style hot baths are offered for $6.

Special Events

Salida's annual boat race on the second to last weekend in June, **FIBArk**, features serious kayak and raft races plus the **Hooligan Race**, an event that sees some rather unique craft (such as a brass bed) take to the waters. Late June is also the time for Salida's **Art Walk** through the many galleries and studios in the historic district. Contact the chamber of commerce for details.

Places to Stay

Camping In the vicinity of Salida, the USFS operates four developed campgrounds (most charge $10) and one primitive campground. *O'Haver Lake* (29 sites) is 8 miles southwest of Poncha Springs at US 285 and USFS Rd 243. Traveling on US 50, 7 miles west of Poncha Springs, on the right, is the

turnoff to USFS Rd 240, which follows the North Fork of the South Arkansas River 4 miles to *Angel of Shavano* (20 sites), on the Colorado Trail. Bring your own water and pack out all trash from the primitive *North Fork* campground ($5 fee) at 11,000 feet, another 5 miles up from the beautiful valley. *Garfield* (11 sites) is adjacent to US 50, 12 miles west of Poncha Springs. Another 2 miles up US 50 brings you to the turnoff to *Monarch Park* (36 sites). This campground at 10,500 feet is a good place to get acclimated to the altitude.

Reservations (☎ 877-444-6777) can be made for O'Haver Lake, Angel of Shavano and Monarch Park campgrounds.

Motels The *Motel Westerner* (☎ 719-539-2618, 7335 Rainbow Blvd) is not too fancy, but charges only $25/30 for singles/doubles year-round. *Budget Lodge* (☎ 719-539-6695, 1146 Rainbow Blvd) has very clean rooms for $30/38 in summer, $29/32 in winter.

If you don't mind spending a bit more, there are several places that offer quite a good value. At the east end of town, the attractive *Mountain Motel* (☎ 719-539-4420, 1425 E Rainbow Blvd) has older wood-paneled cabin-style rooms with kitchen and sitting area for $50 in summer, as well as newer rooms for $55. Subtract $10 at other times of the year. Off the beaten track but only seven blocks northwest of downtown, the small *Woodland Motel* (☎ 719-539-4980, 800-488-0456, 903 W 1st St) is another good bet, offering immaculate rooms starting at $40/45 in summer. There's an outdoor hot tub.

There's a shaded picnic area complete with basketball court and horseshoe pit at the older *Apple Grove Motel* (☎ 719-539-4722, 129 W Rainbow Blvd). Rooms with refrigerators and microwave ovens cost $45/50 in summer, $40/45 in the off-season. *Circle R Motel* (☎ 719-539-6296, 800-755-6296, 304 E Rainbow Blvd) looks pretty well worn but does have a hot tub and laundry. Rooms run about $45 in summer, $13 less in the off-season.

Well-maintained rooms cost $60/70 at *Aspen Leaf Lodge* (☎ 719-539-6733, 800-

759-0338, 7350 W Rainbow Blvd), which also has a hot tub. A bit more upscale, the **Travelodge** (☎ *719-539-2528, 800-234-1077, 7310 Rainbow Blvd)* has a heated pool, two hot tubs, sun decks and a backyard overlooking the mountains. Rooms start at $59/69 in summer (around $20 less off-season). Family suites ($95) and rooms with enclosed hot tubs are also available.

B&Bs Outdoor enthusiasts should consider staying at the **Piñon & Sage B&B Inn** (☎ *719-539-3227, 800-840-3156, 803 F St)*, which offers four Southwest-style rooms in a beautifully restored late-Victorian home. Breakfast is made to order and there's a hot tub on the premises. Rooms with shared/private bath go for $60/85 in summer, $55/75 in winter.

Rates start at $50 at **The Century House** (☎ *719-539-7064, 401 E 1st St)*. Built in 1890 as the town doctor's practice, this French Victorian bills itself as a 'Painted Lady' since being redesigned in a seven-color scheme. Another nearby historic property is **The Thomas House** (☎ *719-539-7104, 888-228-1410, 307 E 1st St)*, built in 1888, which has comfortable rooms named for area mountain peaks from $55 to $75; its Buffalo Peaks cottage rents for $100.
Web site: www.thomashouse.com

The Gazebo Country Inn (☎ *719-539-7806, 507 E 3rd St)* is a Victorian house with a white picket fence that offers three rooms with private bath and full breakfast beginning at $80/85 in winter/summer.
Web site: www.gazebocountryinn.com

The River Run Inn (☎ *719-539-3818, 8495 Chaffee County Rd 160)*, northwest of town 3 miles east of US 285, is listed on the National Register of Historic Places and offers six rooms, two with private bath, for $65 to $85. There is also a small dormitory that has beds for $30.
Web site: www.riveruninn.com

Places to Eat
For an early morning coffee stop, the **Country Bounty Restaurant** (☎ *719-539-3546, 413 W Rainbow Blvd)* is a surprise, offering homemade granola with a fresh whole-wheat apple muffin for around $3. **Bongo Billy's** (☎ *719-539-4261, 300 W Sackett St)* is a popular local's spot serving great sandwiches, salads, gourmet coffees and teas. There's a large outdoor sundeck and there's live music on Friday. You can get fresh and healthy food, espresso and draft microbrews at the popular **First St Cafe** (☎ *719-539-4759, 137 E 1st St)*.

For great Italian food and craft-brewed beers, head for the stylish **Il Vicino Wood Oven Pizza & Brewery** (☎ *719-539-5219, 136 E 2nd St)*. For something more casual, check out the choices at **Moonlight Pizza** (☎ *719-539-4277)*, near the corner of 1st and F Sts, or the 'quick draw' pasta menu ($9) at **Spaghetti Western** (☎ *719-530-9909, 122 N F St)*.

Definitely worth a visit is **Laughing Ladies Cafe** (☎ *719-539-6209, 128 W 1st St)*, which offers a great menu of innovative and diverse meals and desserts in a dining room decorated with the work of local artists. For Mexican fare, try **La Frontera** (☎ *719-539-7919, 128 N F St)*, which offers pleasant outdoor patio dining and devilish margaritas.

Out in Poncha Springs the historic **Jackson Hotel** (☎ *719-539-4861, 6340 US 285)* has played host to the likes of Jesse and Frank James, President Ulysses S Grant, Rudyard Kipling and Susan B Anthony. Its boarding days might be over, but it still lives up to its legacy by serving fine US and Mexican lunches and dinners in an appealing Western setting.

Entertainment
A good crowd usually shows up for live music at the **Victoria Tavern** (☎ *719-539-4891, 143 N F St)*. With century-old decor, pool tables and numerous fine brews on tap, the 'Vic,' erected as the Park Saloon in 1886, still has a lot of character.

The **Steam Plant** (*200 W Sackett St)* theater features irregular summer performances by visiting dance groups, jazz musicians and other performing artists. Check with the Heart of the Rockies Chamber of Commerce for current and upcoming events.

Getting There & Away

Daily TNM&O (☎ 719-539-7474) buses serving Denver and Grand Junction stop at 731 Blake St, near Rainbow Blvd (US 50) at the east end of town.

Salida is on the Arkansas River headwaters 135 miles west of Denver via US 285, 20 miles east of the Continental Divide. Access from Colorado Springs, which is 100 miles east, is via US 50 over Monarch Pass (which, at 11,386 feet, makes for dangerous conditions in winter).

BUENA VISTA

Appropriately named but oddly pronounced locally as 'Beyuna Vista,' Buena Vista (population 1800; elevation 7955 feet) is a white-water rafting mecca, complete with a city park boat-launching area. To the west, the 'vista' is the lofty Collegiate Peaks area formed (from north to south) by Mts Oxford (14,153 feet), Harvard (14,420 feet), Columbia (14,073 feet), Yale (14,196 feet) and Princeton (14,197 feet); look for details at www.fourteenernet.com. Mountain bicyclists, anglers and rafters overrun the small town in busy summer months. Sites in town include the 1882 **Buena Vista Herotage Museum** on Main St near Court St.

Orientation & Information

Buena Vista is 122 miles west of Pueblo via US 50, Hwy 291 and US 285. It's 83 miles northeast of Gunnison via US 50 and US 285. Denver is 115 miles northeast by US 24, Hwy 91 and I-70. Cottonwood Creek flows through the center of town and the Arkansas River runs against the cliffs on the eastern side of town. Most travelers pass through on US 24, intersected by E Main St.

The visitors center (☎ 719-395-6612), 343 S US 24, in a former church built in 1880, is open 9 am to 5 pm weekdays and offers seasonal guides detailing outdoor activities and a walking tour guide of historic buildings and sites.

Web site: www.buenavistacolorado.org

The Collegiate Peaks Bank (☎ 719-395-2472), 105 Centennial Plaza, has an ATM. The post office is at 110 Brookdale Ave; the zip code is 81211.

Creekside Books (☎ 719-395-6416), 300 Cedar St, offers a good selection of new books, travel guides and periodicals. Trail guides and maps are available at The Trailhead outdoors shop (☎ 719-395-8001), north of town at 707 US 24.

The laundry at 104 Linderman Ave is open from 7 am to 10 pm daily. Public restrooms with coin-operated showers (25¢ per minute) are open 24 hours daily at the end of E Main St beside the Buena Vista Community Center.

The Mountain Medical Center of Buena Vista (☎ 719-395-8632), 36 Oak St, is located west of US 24.

Rafting

Buena Vista is on the map because of the great white-water opportunities on the Arkansas River. The town lies at one of the most exciting portions of the **Arkansas Headwaters Recreation Area**, a 148-mile-long stretch of state-run recreation facilities and wildlife areas. There are several boat put-ins (including one in River Park), which usually cost $1, and camp sites costing $8. Maps and complete information on the area are available at the visitors center (see above), or check in with the Arkansas Headwaters Recreation Office in Salida (☎ 719-539-7289), 307 W Sackett St.

Buffalo Joe River Trips (☎ 719-395-8757, 800-356-7984), 113 N Railroad St, has a good reputation for safe and enjoyable trips.

At Johnson Village, where US 24/US 285 crosses the river 2 miles south of Buena Vista, you will find Wilderness Aware Rafting (☎ 719-395-2112, 800-462-7238); online it's at www.inaraft.com. Also in Johnson Village is American Adventure Expeditions (☎ 800-288-0675), with a Web site at www.americanadventure.com.

At Nathrop, look for Dvorak's Kayak and Rafting Expeditions (☎ 719-539-6851, 800-824-3795) and Four Corners Rafting (☎ 800-332-7238); www.fourcornersrafting.com.

Fishing

With all the rafts in the water, you might wonder if there is any room left for the fish.

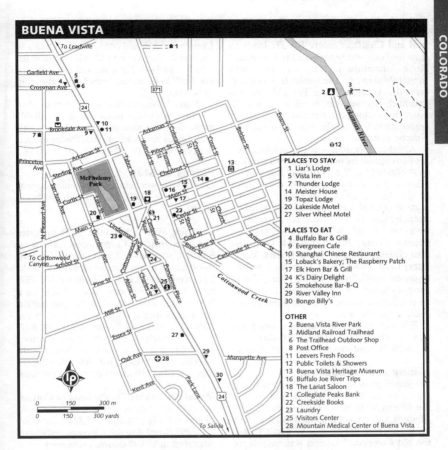

BUENA VISTA

PLACES TO STAY
1 Liar's Lodge
5 Vista Inn
7 Thunder Lodge
14 Meister House
19 Topaz Lodge
20 Lakeside Motel
27 Silver Wheel Motel

PLACES TO EAT
4 Buffalo Bar & Grill
9 Evergreen Cafe
10 Shanghai Chinese Restaurant
15 Loback's Bakery; The Raspberry Patch
17 Elk Horn Bar & Grill
24 K's Dairy Delight
26 Smokehouse Bar-B-Q
29 River Valley Inn
30 Bongo Billy's

OTHER
2 Buena Vista River Park
3 Midland Railroad Trailhead
6 The Trailhead Outdoor Shop
8 Post Office
11 Leevers Fresh Foods
12 Public Toilets & Showers
13 Buena Vista Heritage Museum
16 Buffalo Joe River Trips
18 The Lariat Saloon
21 Collegiate Peaks Bank
22 Creekside Books
23 Laundry
25 Visitors Center
28 Mountain Medical Center of Buena Vista

Yet the Arkansas River has a good supply of fish, mainly wild brown trout. Anglers frequent its banks at the **Buena Vista River Park**, at the foot of Main St. Other nearby fishing spots include the area near the **Midland Tunnels**, 4 miles north on Chaffee County Rd 371 and at **Ruby Mountain**, administered by the Arkansas Headwaters Recreation Area.

For more information, a detailed fishing map is offered for sale by the Collegiate Peak Chapter of Trout Unlimited at The Trailhead outdoors shop (☎ 719-395-8001), 707 N US 24.

Mountain Biking
East of Buena Vista, across the pedestrian and bike bridge at the foot of Main St, the 6-mile **Midland Bike Trail** follows the gentle grade of the old Colorado Midland Railroad. To avoid the initial ¾-mile climb up the steep Whipple Trail to the old depot site, many cyclists begin by shuttling to the end of the Midland Trail. At 5 miles east of Johnson Village turn left on USFS Rd 315. The trailhead is about half a mile from the highway. Many other trail options offering challenging climbs are possible from the Midland Trail.

North along the river from Buena Vista River Park, the combination of riverside trail and Chaffee County Rd 371 leads to three old railroad tunnels and the Elephant Rock formation just beyond the third tunnel. Midway on the 4-mile trip, you will cross the Arkansas River. For a longer out-and-back ride you can continue another 5 miles north along the river to watch white-water fanatics tackle the near-suicidal Numbers section.

Another appealing – yet more difficult – area to explore by bike is the St Elmo ghost town (listed on the National Register of Historic Places) and, farther up, the remains of the Alpine Tunnel. In 1880 it was the highest (11,524 feet) and costliest railroad tunnel built. To get there travel south 9 miles on US 285, then turn right (west) on Chaffee County Rd 162 past Mt Princeton Hot Springs (see Around Buena Vista, later) to St Elmo, about 15 miles from the highway. South from St Elmo the old railroad grade follows USFS Rd 295 for 8 miles to the Alpine Tunnel, passing Romley and Hancock on the way.

For bike rentals and tips on area rides, head for The Trailhead (☎ 719-395-8001), 707 N US 24, an outdoors shop north of town.

Hiking & Backpacking

For superior views of Buena Vista with the Collegiate Peaks in the background, head to the Buena Vista River Park at the foot of Main St and cross the pedestrian and bike bridge to climb the cliffside **Whipple Trail** to the old Colorado Midland Railroad depot on the ridgetop.

North of Cottonwood Canyon, the **Collegiate Peaks Wilderness Area** offers alpine backcountry hiking. After a day or more of acclimation, you can hike to the top of Mt Harvard (14,420 feet), Colorado's third-highest peak, or Mt Yale (14,196 feet). An easy 4-mile, one-way hike to **Kroenke Lake** is a good day trip or the start of a longer backpack trip that includes a scramble up one of the peaks or a crossing of the Continental Divide. From The Trailhead sporting goods store north of town (see Mountain Biking), go west 2 miles on Chaffee County Rd 350, then turn right on Chaffee County Rd 361. After 1 mile turn left on Chaffee County Rd 365 and continue for 5 miles to the North Cottonwood Creek trailhead for USFS Trail 1449. Kroenke Lake is accessed via Trail 1448, which branches south from Trail 1449.

A free hiking guide describing more than 10 other hikes near Buena Vista is available at the visitors center, and detailed topo maps and guides are sold at The Trailhead outdoors shop (☎ 719-395-8001), 707 N US 24.

Places to Stay

On summer weekends, all accommodations in town are likely to be filled, so book ahead.

Camping West of town the USFS operates two campgrounds. *Cottonwood Lake* is on South Cottonwood Creek above Cottonwood Lake, about 5 miles down USFS Rd 344 from the Chaffee County Rd 306 turnoff. Campsites cost $10 and are on a first-come, first-served basis. Mountain goats are often spotted on the way to the camp. The large *Collegiate Peaks* (☎ 877-444-6777) campground on Middle Cottonwood Creek 11 miles west of Buena Vista on Chaffee County Rd 306, also offers campsites for $10 and accepts reservations.

Motels & Cabins On the bank of Cottonwood Creek, cabins cost $64 in summer at *Thunder Lodge* (☎ 719-395-2245, 800-330-9194, 207 Brookdale Ave). In summer/winter rates start at $74/49 double occupancy. Web site: www.thunderlodge.com

The *Vista Court Cabins & Lodge* (☎ 719-395-6557, 1004 W Main St), west of downtown, surround a large grassy area and patio and represent a good value with one/two-bedroom cabins for $80/95 ($55/60 in winter) and lodge rooms starting at $70, $45 in winter.

The rustic log *Silver Wheel Motel* (☎ 719-395-2955, 520 S US 24) has clean singles/doubles for $59/69, $37/45 in winter. Motel rooms are overpriced at $63/75 in summer at the modest *Topaz Lodge* (☎ 719-395-2427), on the corner of US 24 and E Main

St. But rates fall around $20 in winter. Off the busy highway and next to the town park and lake, *Lakeside Motel* (☎ 719-395-2994, *112 Lake St*) has well-scrubbed doubles available for $75 in summer, $35 in winter.

For top-end hotel rooms there's the *Vista Inn* (☎ 719-395-8009, 800-809-3495, *733 N US 24*). Rooms are nicely furnished and there are three outdoor hot tubs that enjoy great mountain views, plus a fitness room. Rooms cost around $100 in summer, or $55/65 for singles/doubles in winter; rates include a generous Continental breakfast.

Five miles west of town at the mouth of Cottonwood Canyon, *Cottonwood Hot Springs Inn* (☎ 719-395-6434) is a lodging smorgasbord offering tepees for $25 per person, dorm beds for $25, rooms for $67 ($77 on weekends) and cabins with private hot tub from $95. Blissful guests can soak all night long in three rock-lined soaking pools.

B&Bs A delightful choice is *Liar's Lodge* (☎ 719-395-3444, 888-542-7756, *30000 County Rd 371*), a handsome log cabin inn just a few hundred yards from downtown, yet in a peaceful, natural setting on the banks of the Arkansas River. It has a friendly family feel. Rates range from $65 to $95 off season, $95 to $105 in the peak. Web site: www.liarslodge.com

The handsome brick *Meister House* (☎ 719-395-9220, 888-395-9220, *414 E Main St*) was built in the 1890s as a hotel and now offers six rooms that start around $80 in summer, $70 in the off season. A full breakfast is served in the open courtyard.

Places to Eat
Since it opened in 1936 *Loback's Bakery* (*326 E Main St*) has had tried-and-true formulas for donuts and shepherds bread. The roadside snack bar *K's Dairy Delight* (☎ 719-395-8695, *223 S US 24*) hasn't changed its menu much either since opening next to the shady streamside picnic grounds. For a more contemporary gourmet take on coffee and baked goods, head for *Bongo Billy's* (☎ 719-395-2634, *713 S US 24*).

Starting at 6:30 am, *Evergreen Cafe* (☎ 719-395-8984, *418 N US 24*) offers a large breakfast menu, including eggs Benedict. It also serves lunch (mainly burgers and sandwiches) and Italian-style dinners. The *Raspberry Patch* (☎ 719-395-4481, *328 E Main St*) is open for breakfast and lunch and features homemade sandwiches, quiche, pastries and pies. Just up the street, *The Lariat Saloon* (☎ 719-395-0284, *E 206 Main St*) has been serving hearty pub grub and stiff whiskey drinks since 1885.

The *Shanghai Chinese Restaurant* (☎ 719-395-4950, *527 US 24*), next to Leevers Fresh Foods, offers perhaps the best dining bargain in Buena Vista. Lunches cost around $4.

The *Elk Horn Bar & Grill* (☎ 719-395-2120, *301 E Main St*) is a local sports bar offering wood-fired grill items as well as pizza, pasta and burgers. Similar fare is served at *Buffalo Bar & Grill* (☎ 719-395-6472, *710 Hwy 24*), while *Smokehouse Bar-B-Q*, across from the tourist office on US 24, does the best hickory-smoked ribs in town.

The *River Valley Inn* (☎ 719-395-0977, *605 S US 24*), decorated with antiques and Western bric-a-brac, does US standards for lunch and dinner, including good soups and a salad bar.

AROUND BUENA VISTA
Mt Princeton Hot Springs Area
The turnoff from US 285 to *Mt Princeton Hot Springs Resort* (☎ 719-395-2361, 888-395-7799, *15870 Chaffee County Rd 162*) is 6 miles south of Buena Vista in Nathrop. Choose between outdoor pools and indoor soaking at the century-old bathhouse. Cliffside rooms look out on the Collegiate Peaks and start at $70/62 in summer/winter. The Princeton Club dining room offers steaks and seafood. If you're not staying you can still access the pools, including makeshift hot tubs on the river's edge, from 9 am to 9 pm. Admission costs $6/3 adults/seniors and children. Web site: www.mtprinceton.com

On beautiful Chalk Creek, the cozy, three-room *Streamside Bed & Breakfast* (☎ 719-395-2553, *18820 Chaffee County Rd 162*) offers doubles with private bath and full breakfast from $79 to $85. This place makes a good base for exploring the surrounding San Isabel National Forest.

On your way to the St Elmo ghost town and Alpine Tunnel (see Buena Vista, earlier), you may see bighorn sheep and mountain goats. You definitely should not miss the short trail to **Agnes Vaille Falls** on your right, opposite Chalk Lake. Three USFS campgrounds – *Mt Princeton*, *Chalk Lake* and *Cascade* – are found within a 1-mile stretch. Each has about 20 campsites that go for $10 each and will most likely require a reservation (☎ 877-444-6777) in the popular summer months.

Twin Lakes

Between Buena Vista and Leadville is Twin Lakes, 7 miles west of US 24 on Hwy 82 (the white-knuckle route over 12,095-foot Independence Pass – closed in winter – to Aspen). It is widely known as the trailhead leading up to **Mt Elbert** (14,433 feet), Colorado's highest peak; follow the Colorado Trail (USFS Trail 1776) for the first 3 miles, then turn left on USFS Trail 1481 to the summit. The once natural Twin Lakes now serve as a pumped storage facility, but anglers couldn't care less as long as they continue to catch giant Mackinaw and smaller rainbow trout. In winter Twin Lakes is a favorite cross-country ski area for well-informed Coloradans.

Three USFS campgrounds have sites for $10. Reservations (☎ 877-444-6777) are accepted at the large lakeside *White Star* campground and *Lakeview*, which offers sites perched on top of a glacial moraine ridgetop overlooking the lakes, only 4 miles west of the junction with US 24. It's also the trailhead for the strenuous 6-mile climb up Mt Elbert. *Parry Peak* and *Twin Peaks* campgrounds are next to Lake Creek, farther up the valley at 10 and 12 miles, respectively, west of the junction. For more information contact the Leadville Ranger Station (☎ 719-486-0749).

For unsurpassed German dishes, stop at the *Nordic Inn* (☎ 719-486-1830, 6435 Hwy 82) in the village of Twin Lakes. The historic inn once served as a stagecoach stop and brothel. Rooms with shared bath and common kitchen cost $48/55 a single/double; $65/75 with private bath. In winter, the lodge is open solely on weekends and holidays.

GUNNISON

The town of Gunnison (population 5000; elevation 7703 feet) is home to the handsome campus of **Western State College**, opened in 1911. A short excursion through the older residential neighborhoods will reveal numerous Victorians and masonry homes, their lawns and trees watered by the unique Gunnison ditch system. However, most folks blast through on their way to Crested Butte.

The Gunnison County Chamber of Commerce visitors center (☎ 970-641-1501, 800-323-2453) is on the east side of town at 500 E Tomichi (US 50). Here you can pick up a self-guided historic walking tour booklet, maps of area mountain-bike trails, as well as lists of accommodations and activities. Web site: www.gunnison-co.com

The USFS has an office at 216 N Colorado Ave, which is open 7:30 am to 4:30 pm weekdays.

The Gunnison Bank & Trust at 232 W Tomichi has an ATM. The post office is at 200 N Wisconsin St. The zip code is 81230.

Places to Stay & Eat

A great place to hang your hat and slip off your boots is the *Cattleman Inn* (☎ 970-641-1061, 888-223-3466, 301 W Tomichi), which offers bargain hotel rooms with private bath for $32/39 a single/double. Reservations are recommended in summer and autumn. Larger, better furnished rooms are available at the *Hylander Inn* (☎ 970-641-0700, 412 W Tomichi), near the visitors center, though they cost more: $62/68 in summer, $40/46 in winter. Nearby, friendly *Bennet's Western Motel* (☎ 970-641-1722, 403 E Tomichi) has slightly cheaper rates.

The main-floor restaurant at the Cattleman Inn doubles as the informal board room for locals each morning, while the downstairs *Beef & Barrel* offers reasonably priced home-style dinner specials.

Getting There & Around

Gunnison County Airport (☎ 970-641-2304) is south of US 50 at 711 Rio Grande Ave. In the ski season Boeing 757 airliners migrate to Gunnison.

Alpine Express (☎ 970-641-5074, 800-822-4844), at the Gunnison County Airport Terminal, meets all commercial flights in winter but requires reservations in summer. Roundtrip fares to Crested Butte cost $40.

TNM&O buses connecting Pueblo with Grand Junction stop at the Gunnison County Airport Terminal (☎ 970-641-0060), 711 Rio Grande Ave.

Gunnison lies on US 50, 65 miles east of Montrose and 34 miles west of Monarch Pass – the highway to the Divide is a scenic route that follows Tomichi Creek.

At the airport, you can rent cars from Budget, Avis or Hertz.

CRESTED BUTTE

On the headwaters to the Gunnison River, the historic mining town of Crested Butte (population 2300; elevation 8867 feet) has a laid-back feel that sets it apart from glamour resorts like Aspen and Vail. The area is surrounded by forests and rugged mountain peaks in the Elk Mountains, plus three wilderness areas: West Elk, Raggeds and Maroon Bells–Snowmass. Perhaps due to Crested Butte's roots as a coal mining town – as opposed to gold or silver – its sense of community and its relative isolation, it has a relaxed, friendly atmosphere that makes it easy to while away days and weeks here.

Orientation & Information

The Crested Butte Chamber of Commerce visitors center (☎ 970-349-6438, 800-545-4505), at Hwy 135 and Elk Ave, is open 9 am to 5 pm daily in summer and winter (weekdays only in late spring and early autumn). There's a smaller visitors center up the hill at the resort for winter visitors. Both locations offer maps, recreation information and a walking-tour guide to the town. The chamber also offers online information on lodging, restaurants and outdoor activities at www.crestedbuttechamber.com. The chamber's reservation center (☎ 970-349-7048, 800-215-2226, cbreserve@rmi.net) can help book lodging, air tickets, rental cars, etc.

Community First Bank (☎ 970-349-6606), with branches at 405 6th St and in Mt Crested Butte's town center, has ATMs. The post office is at 215 Elk Ave, and the zip code is 81224. The Paper Clip (☎ 970-349-7211, fax 970-349-7445), 305 6th St, has fax service. The Book Worm Book Seller (☎ 970-349-6245), 408 3rd St, has a good selection of books about the area.

Things to See & Do

The **Crested Butte Mountain Heritage Museum** (☎ 970-349-1880), 200 Sopris Ave, includes the popular **Mountain Bike Hall of Fame**.

A curious sight is the **two-story outhouse** in the alley behind the Company Store at Elk Ave and 3rd St. Throughout the town is the creative artwork made from chrome car bumpers by Shawn Guerrero and Andy Bamberg.

Skiing

Crested Butte Mountain Resort (☎ 970-349-2333, 800-544-8448) has a base elevation of 9375 feet to go with its healthy average snowfall of 229 inches. Adult lift tickets cost $53, while children five to 16 pay their age in dollars. Lift tickets are $27 at the start and finish of the season, usually late November to mid-December and early to mid-April. Web site: www.skicb.com

About 19 miles of machine-set cross-country track are available at the Nordic Ski Center (☎ 970-349-1707), Big Mine Park at the south end of 2nd St. It offers rentals and lessons and is open 9 am to 5 pm mid-November to mid-April. Trail fees cost $10/5 for adults/children. There's also an ice rink at the center.

Mountain Biking

Crested Butte has earned a reputation as an alpine mecca for mountain bikers, and rightfully so. Recommended rides include the Upper Loop (considered a good 'starter' trail), Strand Hill and 401.

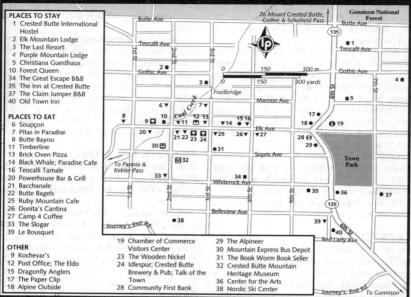

CRESTED BUTTE

PLACES TO STAY
1 Crested Butte International Hostel
2 Elk Mountain Lodge
3 The Last Resort
4 Purple Mountain Lodge
5 Christiana Guesthaus
10 Forest Queen
34 The Great Escape B&B
35 The Inn at Crested Butte
37 The Claim Jumper B&B
40 Old Town Inn

PLACES TO EAT
6 Soupçon
7 Pitas in Paradise
8 Butte Bayou
11 Timberline
13 Brick Oven Pizza
14 Black Whale; Paradise Cafe
16 Teocalli Tamale
20 Powerhouse Bar & Grill
21 Bacchanale
22 Butte Bagels
25 Ruby Mountain Cafe
26 Donita's Cantina
27 Camp 4 Coffee
33 The Slogar
39 Le Bousquet

OTHER
9 Kochevar's
12 Post Office; The Eldo
15 Dragonfly Anglers
17 The Paper Clip
18 Alpine Outside
19 Chamber of Commerce Visitors Center
23 The Wooden Nickel
24 Idlespur; Crested Butte Brewery & Pub; Talk of the Town
28 Community First Bank
29 The Alpineer
30 Mountain Express Bus Depot
31 The Book Worm Book Seller
32 Crested Butte Mountain Heritage Museum
36 Center for the Arts
38 Nordic Ski Center

The best place to head for maps and information is The Alpineer (☎ 970-349-5210, 800-223-4655), near the intersection of Elk St and Hwy 135. The Alpineer rents mountain bikes, and its Web site (www.alpineer.com) is worth checking out. You can also rent bikes at Flatiron Sports (☎ 970-349-6656), in the Treasury Building at the base of Mt Crested Butte.

Other Activities
Hiking trails heading into the Maroon Bells–Snowmass Wilderness Area from either Schofield Pass or Gothic offer scenic alpine hiking. The chamber of commerce offers a simplified map of trails in the area and describes suggested routes. It's only good for planning – be sure to pick up a guidebook, topo maps or the USFS Gunnison Basin Area Map before heading out.

For information about fishing, hatchery tours or viewing wildlife, contact the Colorado DOW (☎ 970-641-0088), 300 W New York Ave in Gunnison. Also there, Gunnison Sporting Goods (☎ 970-641-5022), 133 E Tomichi Ave, sells fishing gear and topo maps. A knowledgeable local fishing guide runs Dragonfly Anglers (☎ 970-349-1228), 132 Elk St in Crested Butte.

Guided rafting trips on the Taylor River booked by Alpine Outside (☎ 970-349-5011), Hwy 135 and Elk Ave, encounter Class III and IV white water.

Special Events
Blossoms abound by mid-July when 'Beauties' (as local residents are called) hold the **Wildflower Festival** in the 'Wildflower Capital of Colorado' – monarch butterflies also brighten the skies on daily hikes throughout the week. The **Fat Tire Bike Week**, held in June or July, is the sport's oldest festival. At the end of July, **Aerial Weekend** features hot-air balloons, skydivers, hang gliders and paragliders. In August 'culcha' creeps in with the **Festival of the Arts** and **Chamber**

Music Festival. Contact the chamber of commerce for details.

Places to Stay

The story is the same here as at other Colorado ski resorts: Prices are steep in summer, soar even higher in winter, and drop to reasonable levels in early fall and late spring. Crested Butte Vacations (☎ 800-544-8448) can help you make reservations and arrange travel-lodging-ski packages.

Camping The Gunnison National Forest's Taylor River Ranger District (☎ 970-641-0471), 216 N Colorado in Gunnison, operates 18 campgrounds north of Gunnison. Most are in Taylor Canyon, southeast of Crested Butte. The closest large campground is *Lake Irwin* (☎ 877-444-6777), west of town before Kebler Pass at the foot of the Ruby Range, which offers 32 reservable sites for $10 plus a reservation fee. Only four sites are available at *Gothic* on a first-come, first-served basis for $8. The turnoff to *Cement Creek Campground* is south of town about 7 miles – it offers 13 sites for $10.

Hostels Budget travelers get a break at *Crested Butte International Hostel* (☎ 970-349-0588, 888-389-0588, hostel@crested-butte.net, 615 Teocalli Ave). Clean and spacious, the hostel has 52 beds ranging from $17 to $28 (supply your own sheets or rent them from the hostel). Facilities include a well-equipped kitchen, public laundry and showers, a library and a large common room with a fireplace. HI-AYH members enjoy reduced rates, and reservations are advised.

Motels & Hotels The ghost of a working girl supposedly visits the former madam's room at the 1881 *Forest Queen* (☎ 970-349-5336, 800-937-1788, 129 Elk Ave). Rooms with shared bath cost $49/59 in the off-peak/peak season, those with private bath are $59/69. Its downstairs bar and restaurant is a comfortable place to relax over a foamy pint of microbrew.

The modern *Old Town Inn* (☎ 970-349-6184), at Hwy 135 near Belleview Ave, can't boast about its noisy roadside location but has relatively decent motel rooms and an outdoor hot tub. Rates are $71/79 single/double in summer, $81/89 in winter. *The Inn at Crested Butte* (☎ 970-349-1225, 800-949-4828, innatcb@rmii.com, 510 Whiterock Ave) offers fairly comfortable doubles and a hot tub. Rates vary greatly month to month but start from around $60 in summer and $85 in winter.

Up on Mt Crested Butte the best deal is *Manor Lodge* (☎ 970-349-5365, 650 Gothic Rd) behind the Sheraton. Rooms are small and basic, offering little more than a place to sleep but only $59 in summer, capping out around $120 in winter. Up the next rung on the budget ladder is *The Nordic Inn* (☎ 970-349-5542, 800-542-7669, 14 Treasury Rd), which has an outdoor hot tub. Doubles start from $72 in summer, $100 in winter. Web site: www.nordicinncb.com

The *Sheraton Crested Butte Resort* (☎ 888-222-2469, 6 Emmons Rd) is near the main chairlifts. Doubles start at $70 in summer, $147 in winter. The area's top hotel is the 261-room *Club Med* (☎ 970-349-8700, 800-258-2633, fax 970-349-4080, 500 Gothic Rd), right at the base of the mountain next to the Silver Queen high-speed quad. Four-star rooms feature all the luxury amenities (including whirlpool baths), and resort facilities include indoor and outdoor hot tubs, a pool, sauna, gym, business center and theater. Call for current rates, or visit www.clubmed.com.

B&Bs For something truly out of the ordinary, book one of the six funky guest rooms at *The Claim Jumper* (☎ 970-349-6471, fax 970-349-7757, 704 Whiterock Ave). This well-kept, museum-like inn is feverishly decorated with colorful paraphernalia and each room is dedicated to an individual theme. A personal favorite is the Coca Cola room, though the marine room (where the legs of a mannequin dangle from the jaws of a shark mounted over the bed) is a close second. Rates go from $99 to $139. The cheerful innkeeper, Jerry Bigelow, has performed more than 500 weddings in his distinguished career and can, consequently, marry you.

COLORADO

Another interesting place with theme rooms (plus heated wood floors and a hot tub) is *The Great Escape B&B* (☎ 970-349-1131, 329 Whiterock Ave). Guests can choose local motifs like the Cowboy Room and Southwestern Room, or go global in the English Room or Indonesian Room. Standard room rates range from $75 to $150 depending on the season, or $175 to $250 for a two-bedroom suite; discounts are usually offered for available last-minute reservations.

Purple Mountain Lodge (☎ 970-349-5888, 800-286-3574, purplemt@rmi.net, 714 Gothic Ave) is a cozy five-bedroom inn featuring down comforters and terrycloth robes to lounge around in before you hit the Jacuzzi. Rates range from $75 to $98.

Elk Mountain Lodge (☎ 970-349-7533, 129 Gothic Ave) is a former boarding house built in 1919. It offers 16 rooms with private bath that start at $100. *The Last Resort* (☎ 970-349-0445, 213 3rd St) at the pedestrian bridge over Coal Creek, features a solarium that heats the energy-efficient building. Four spacious rooms with private bath range from $90 to $110 and come with a hearty breakfast. *Christiana Guesthaus* (☎ 970-349-5326, 800-824-7899, 621 Maroon Ave) offers European-style lodging (including an outdoor hot tub) and breakfasts from $66 in summer, $85 in winter.

Places to Eat

Locals congregate in the morning at *Butte Bagels* (☎ 970-349-2707), on Elk Ave near 2nd St, with indoor and outdoor seating, tasty bagel treats, espresso and smoothies. You can't miss *Camp 4 Coffee* (☎ 970-209-0346, 402½ Elk Ave); the building is *covered* in old car license plates! They serve great coffee and baked goods here, and at the adjacent coffee wagon. Camp 4 Coffee has another location up at the ski resort. Another favorite breakfast spot is *Ruby Mountain Cafe* (☎ 970-349-7280, 302 Elk Ave), serving homemade granola with yogurt and lots of goodies. For heartier (but less healthy) American breakfasts and lunches, try *Paradise Cafe* (☎ 970-349-6233), at 4th St and Elk, which has a nice terrace for warm-weather eating. Nearby,

the basement-level *Black Whale* (☎ 970-349-0480), at 3rd St and Elk Ave, attracts a younger, snowboarder crowd.

For pizza slices, try *Brick Oven Pizza* (☎ 970-349-5044, 313 3rd St). Even New Yorkers concede it's a pretty good slice. *The Slogar* (☎ 970-349-5765, 517 2nd St) does a good job with the standard meat-and-potatoes fare, with dinners priced at around $12. A good après-ski choice for steaks, original pizzas and Southwestern fare is *Casey's* (☎ 970-349-5365), up on Mt Crested Butte at the Manor Lodge (see Motels & Hotels, earlier).

Donita's Cantina (☎ 970-349-6674, 332 Elk St) dishes up good Tex-Mex food, and there's almost no chance you'll complain about either the prices or the portions. The Mexican fare at *Powerhouse Bar & Grill* (☎ 970-349-5494, 130 Elk Ave) is pricier than Donita's, but some prefer it for the lively atmosphere. *Teocalli Tamale* (☎ 970-349-2005, 311½ Elk Ave) is a good lunch choice for burritos, tacos and tamales in the $5 range.

Butte Bayou (☎ 970-349-9761), near the corner of 1st St and Elk Ave, whips up great po-boy sandwiches and spicy Cajun food. *Pitas in Paradise* (☎ 970-349-0897, 313 3rd St) has slow service, but locals agree it's worth the wait for the great gyros and Mediterranean food.

For top-end dining, Crested Butte has some good choices. The *Timberline* (☎ 970-349-9831, 201 Elk Ave) has a creative selection of Continental and US cuisine, while *Le Bousquet* (☎ 970-349-5808), at 6th and Belleview, has earned kudos from locals for its excellent French food. In an alleyway behind Kochevar's bar (see below), *Soupçon* (☎ 970-349-5448) offers a selection of fresh fish, plus beef and game dishes. Dinner seatings at 6 pm and 8 pm require reservations. *Bacchanale* (☎ 970-349-5257, 208 Elk St) is a praiseworthy upper-end Italian restaurant.

The cheapest place to eat at the foot of the ski mountain is *Ted's Hot Dog Cart* – try the amazing meatball sandwiches. For a proper sit-down meal, look for the nearby *Avalanche Bar & Grill* (☎ 970-349-7195) or

Firehouse Grill (☎ 970-349-4666), which both do good burgers, pizzas and sandwiches.

Entertainment
As befits an historic mining town, Crested Butte is loaded with century-old saloons like *Kochevar's* (☎ 970-349-6745, 127 Elk Ave), an 1890s structure built of hand-hewn logs that's listed on the National Register of Historic Places. This is one of the main local watering holes, along with *The Eldo* (☎ 970-349-6125, 215 Elk Ave), which sometimes has live bands and also sports an outstanding 2nd-story deck that's perfect for late-afternoon beers or a burger.

The *Idlespur* (☎ 970-349-5026, 226 Elk Ave) is the home of the Crested Butte Brewery & Pub and often features live entertainment. It also serves great steak, buffalo burgers and elk. Just next door *Talk of the Town* (☎ 970-349-2743) draws a more rookie drinking crowd, evident by the smell of vomit assaulting customers' nostrils. Another long-standing and popular saloon is the *Wooden Nickel* (☎ 970-349-6350, 222 Elk Ave), which also does good bar food.

The *Center for the Arts* (☎ 970-349-7487), south of the Town Park on Hwy 135, offers both summer and winter performances by local groups as well as touring companies.

Getting There & Around
Many visitors take advantage of Crested Butte's air link to the outside world via Gunnison County Airport, located 28 miles south. See the Gunnison Getting There & Around section, earlier.

Alpine Express (☎ 970-641-5074, 800-822-4844), at Gunnison County Airport Terminal, meets all commercial flights in winter but requires reservations in summer. Roundtrip fares to Crested Butte cost $38/24 adults/children.

The free Mountain Express bus (☎ 970-349-5616) connects Crested Butte with Mt Crested Butte hourly between 7 am and 11:40 pm. It carries bikes and skis on exterior racks. The shuttle departs from Old Town Hall, at Elk Ave and 2nd St, and stops at the visitors center before continuing up the hill.

Crested Butte is 28 miles north of Gunnison on Hwy 135 and about 225 miles from Denver via I-25 and US 50.

San Luis Valley

The vast intermountain San Luis Valley is dotted with small towns and farming hamlets. Wetland wildlife sanctuaries, the surrounding craggy peaks and the stark beauty of the Great Sand Dunes provide scenic contrast to the wide plains of the valley floor.

On the east side of the valley rise the jagged 14,000-foot peaks of the Sangre de Cristo Mountains, luring hikers and backpackers to its wilderness. Crestone Peak was the last of Colorado's 14ers to be climbed; wilderness hikers often see large herds of Colorado's state animal, the bighorn sheep, on the rough slopes. To the west lie the volcanic San Juan Mountains, which host many outdoor activities. The Rio Grande's headwaters flow by the historic mining camp at Creede, now a popular tourist site. In the southern reaches of the valley, a landscape dotted with adobe churches and historic Hispanic villages evokes images of New Mexico.

Mexican land grants attracted the first civilian settlers. West of the Rio Grande the Mexican government wasted little time settling the Conejos grant in 1833, yet 10 years later the Utes continued to thwart Mexican attempts at settlement. Mexican pioneers met with better fortune east of the Rio Grande on the Sangre de Cristo grant, where in 1851 they established San Luis, the oldest permanent settlement in Colorado.

In the 1870s most white Americans merely passed through the San Luis Valley on their way to the San Juan Mountain mining districts. In the area's period as a part of the USA's New Mexico Territory, the federal government awarded much of the extensive Conejos grant to the D&RG railroad. The arrival of steel rails in 1878 attracted homesteaders, and since the rail's arrival most of the valley has come under the plow.

CRESTONE

Despite its minute population of 75, Crestone (elevation 7500 feet) is surprisingly well known, due mostly to its reputation as a center of spiritual energy. The tangible evidence lies in the unusual variety of religious and spiritual institutions that have set up shop here. These include the Crestone Mountain Zen Center, the Haidakhandi Universal Ashram, the Spiritual Life Institute, the Sri Aurobindo Learning Center and the San Luis Valley Tibetan Project. Some find Crestone's energy uplifting, though there are others who sense a darker presence. Either way, there is a unique feel to the place. And there's no question about Crestone's setting: The backdrop of the 14,000-foot peaks of the Sangre de Cristo Mountains is truly stunning.

Crestone is on the east side of the San Luis Valley, north of Great Sand Dunes National Monument. From Alamosa, Hwy 17 follows a straight course for 40 miles to Saguache County Rd T, which then heads 13 miles east to Crestone.

The Crestone-Moffat Business Association (☎ 719-256-4110, 719-256-4959) has an information board outside town, next to the turnoff for the Baca Grande housing estate. On it, as well as on www.crestone.org, is a map and list of lodgings, restaurants and businesses in both Crestone and Baca Grande.

Hiking & Backpacking

Two outstanding trails into the high Sangre de Cristo Wilderness Area begin in Crestone's backyard. Hikers on the **South Crestone Creek Trail** travel about 5 miles to South Crestone Lake, a cirque beneath Mt Adams (13,931 feet). This prime bighorn sheep habitat harbors more than 500 sheep that range between Hermit and Music Passes. Begin from the top of Galena St above the post office; within a mile you reach USFS Trail 949, following the north side of South Crestone Creek for 1½ miles to a junction. On the right across the creek is USFS Trail 865 to Willow Creek Lakes (and waterfall); to the left USFS Trail 860 continues to South Colony Lake.

Another option is to go up **North Crestone Creek Trail** to either North Crestone Lake below Fluted Peak (13,554 feet) or to cross the ridge to the east side over either Comanche or Venable Passes. From the North Crestone Creek Campground reached by USFS Rd 950, USFS Trail 744 follows the north side of North Crestone Creek for 1½ miles to a three-way junction: On your right the southernmost trail continues for 3 miles to North Crestone Lake; the middle trail, USFS Trail 746, passes north of Comanche Peak before dropping into the Wet Mountain Valley on USFS Trail 1345; and the northern choice, USFS Trail 747, heads toward Venable Pass (see Westcliffe & Silver Cliff, earlier).

For information about hiking on the west side of the Sangre de Cristo Wilderness Area contact the USFS Saguache Ranger District (☎ 719-655-2547), 46525 State Hwy 114, a quarter mile west of Saguache.

Places to Stay & Eat

Campsites are available for $8 at the USFS *North Crestone Creek Campground*, about 2 miles north of Crestone past the historical Community Center on Alder Terrace Rd.

The *Alder Terrace Inn* (☎ 719-256-4975) offers apartment-style single/double rooms with kitchens for $50/55. It is next to the laundry. If no one is there, inquire at the 21st Amendment Liquor store, one block north. In the Baca Grande area, *Rainbow Bed & Breakfast* (☎ 719-265-4110, 800-530-1992) is a modern home near the mountains with tasteful decor where rooms with shared bath cost $30/40. To get there from Sagauche County Rd T take the turnoff into the Baca Grande estates for 1 mile, then turn left up a dirt road: It's up 350 yards on the left.

In the Baca Grande, *Desert Sage* (☎ 719-256-4402) is open daily and features outstanding breads and other baked goods.

GREAT SAND DUNES NATIONAL MONUMENT

Colorado's sea of sand is an amazing trick of nature. From the air or nearby mountain-tops, the dune field of approximately 55 sq miles stands out starkly from the surrounding terrain. Even more surreal are the fluid shapes and interplay of light on the dunes as you approach by land – particularly when the sun is low on the horizon. Explorers in the dunes lose the perception of depth and scale needed to discern that the tallest dunes rise almost 700 feet. In this beige landscape lacking familiar benchmarks, only other hikers serve as a gauge to judge distance and the size of surrounding dunes.

Orientation
Great Sand Dunes National Monument is northeast of Alamosa. To get here, travel east on US 160 for 14 miles toward prominent Blanca Peak (14,345 feet), named for its light-colored granite, turn left (north) on Hwy 150 and follow the road for 19 miles to the visitors center 3 miles north of the park entrance; access to the dunes is another mile along the road.

Most visitors limit their activities to a narrow juncture where the curious **Medano Creek** (Spanish for 'Dune' Creek) divides the main dune mass from the towering Sangre de Cristo Mountains to the east. The remaining 85% of the monument's area is designated wilderness. From the visitors center, a short trail leads to the Mosca Picnic Area next to Medano Creek, which you must ford to reach the dunes. Across the road from the visitors center, the Mosca Pass Trail enters the Sangre de Cristo Wilderness, and the short Wellington Ditch Trail heads north to campsites and the Little Medano Trail.

North of the visitors center in the piñon pine forest is Pinyon Flats Campground; beyond the campground is the end of the paved road called 'Point of No Return.' From here Little Medano Trail and the Medano Pass Primitive Rd provide access to backcountry campsites that require a permit for overnight wilderness camping.

Information
Visitors receive a guide and map brochure on entry to the park where an NPS ranger collects an admission fee of $3 per person (17 and under free). Before venturing out to the dunes, stop by the visitors center (☎ 719-378-2312) to check out the exhibits, chat with a ranger about hiking or backcountry camping options, or purchase books and maps. Be sure to ask about scheduled nature walks and nightly programs held at the amphitheater near Pinyon Flats. From Memorial Day to Labor Day the center is open 8 am to 6 pm daily; otherwise 8:30 am to 4:30 pm.

A privately run store, campground and lodge at the entrance to the park offers Jeep tours, gas, campsites and cabins for visitors turned away from overflowing park campsites.

Montville Nature Trail
The Montville Store once stood at the foot of Mosca Pass Trail. It was built in the 1830s by fur trader Antoine Robidoux, who used the pass to transport supplies to his posts in western Colorado and eastern Utah. Many miners passed here on their way west to the San Juan Mountains. Today, a short half-mile trail next to Mosca Creek provides a self-guided tour through a variety of ecosystems, leading to a grand view of the San Luis Valley and the dunes. The Montville Nature Trail is opposite the visitors center.

Mountain Biking
Off-road cyclists should plan to slog through some sandy areas before climbing the beautiful narrow valley to **Medano Pass**. The pass is 11 miles from the Point of No Return parking area at the north end of the paved road. A detailed mileage log for the Medano Pass Primitive Rd is available at the visitors center.

For a shorter fat-tire ride, visit the spectacular **Zapata Falls**, south of the monument, which also offers outstanding views of the valley. A consortium of 13 agencies opened 4 miles of trail in the **Zapata Falls Special Recreation Area** on the west flank of Blanca Peak.

Bicycle rentals, repairs and riding information are available at Kristi Mountain Sports (☎ 719-589-9759), 7565 US 160 in

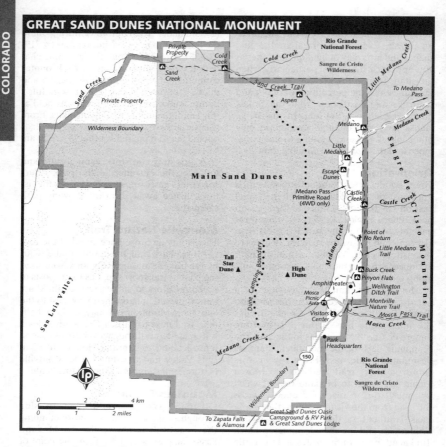

GREAT SAND DUNES NATIONAL MONUMENT

Alamosa, about 1 mile east of the City Market behind the Conoco gas station.

Organized Tours

Throughout the summer NPS rangers lead interpretive nature walks from the visitors center parking lot. Inquire at the center about specific programs and times.

Great Sand Dunes Tours (☎ 719-378-2222) carries passengers past the dunes and partway up the primitive road to Medano Pass in open-air 4WD vehicles from May to November. The trips take about two hours and leave from the Oasis Store on the mon-

ument boundary at 10 am and 2 pm. The cost for the tours is $14 for adults and $8 for children.

Places to Stay & Eat

In the peak months of July and August, visitors often fill the 88 sites ($10) at *Pinyon Flats Campground*, which are available on a first-come, first-served basis. The campground is open year-round and water is available at all times. Backpackers have the option of staying at one of seven designated backcountry campgrounds requiring hikes ranging from less than a mile to Buck

Creek, to more than 10 miles to Sand Creek. In addition, campers may stay in the main dune mass to the west of the most accessible dunes frequented by day-users. You must obtain a backcountry permit, available free of charge from the visitors center, for overnight wilderness stays.

At the entrance to the monument *Great Sand Dunes Oasis Campground & RV Park* (☎ *719-378-2222, fax 719-378-2910, 5400 Hwy 150*) offers showers, laundry and barren tent sites for $12. A few primitive cabins cost $33 double occupancy and typically require reservations. A little farther uphill from the campground, *Great Sand Dunes Lodge* (☎ *719-378-2900*) is open mid-March to mid-November and has rooms with balconies offering fine views of the dunes for $79 in summer, $69 in the off-season. There's also a restaurant and an indoor pool. Reserve a room at www.gsdlodge.com.

A nature preserve owned and operated by the Nature Conservancy (www.tnc.org), the delightful *Inn at Zapata Ranch* (☎ *719-378-2356, 5303 Hwy 150*) is set amid groves of cottonwood trees. The peaceful property contains several historic buildings and offers distant views of the sand dunes. Most rooms in the Main Inn, Bunk House and Steward House range from $150 to $180 from late May to mid-September; in the off season rates drop to the $112 to $135 range. The ranch is closed from November through April. Horseback riding, mountain bike rentals and massage therapy are also on offer.

AROUND GREAT SAND DUNES NATIONAL MONUMENT
San Luis Lakes State Park
At this park (☎ 719-378-2020) the bleak terrain of sand dunes covered with saltbush and rabbitbrush contrasts with the grassy wetlands – the secondary beneficiary of this governmental largesse. Waterfowl, shorebirds and birdwatchers alike enjoy the newly created wetlands and reservoir, just west of the Great Sand Dunes National Monument. The *Mosca Campground* has a bath house, laundry

and drinking fountains and is a convenient alternative to camping in the monument. Campsites cost $10, plus the daily vehicle fee of $4. The park is 8 miles west of Hwy 150 on Alamosa County Rd 6N. To get from Alamosa to the park drive 13 miles north on Hwy 17, then turn right (east) on County Rd 6N for 8 miles.

Blanca
Below 14,345-foot Mt Blanca, at an elevation of 7000 feet, the small farming town of Blanca (population 300) straddles US 160, 5 miles east of Hwy 150. Travelers to Great Sand Dunes National Monument and nearby wildlife areas may conveniently camp at *Blanca RV Park*, where shaded tent sites cost $12 and include hot showers.

The *Mt Blanca Game Bird & Trout Lodge* (☎ *719-379-3825*) is an oasis near the small noncommercial airport 3 miles south of Blanca. Visitors can fish at several stocked ponds on the 9-sq-mile property. Rooms with bath cost $88/99 single/double. It's located 2½ miles down a small dirt road off US 160 just east of Blanca.

The closest that Denver-Albuquerque buses come to Great Sand Dunes National Monument is Blanca. Call the TNM&O terminal at Alamosa (☎ 719-589-4948) for the latest schedule.

Fort Garland
US troops occupied Fort Garland from 1858 to 1883, shortly after the US government fully removed the Utes from the area. Visitor information can be found at the **Fort Garland Museum** (☎ 719-379-3512), on Hwy 159 next to the junction with US 160, where a complete restoration of the fort's buildings and exhibits are maintained by the Colorado Historical Society. From there it's 10 miles east to the Hwy 150 turnoff to Great Sand Dunes National Monument, 26 miles east to Alamosa or 17 miles south to San Luis via Hwy 159. The museum is open 9 am to 5 pm daily April to late October, 8 am to 4 pm Thursday to Monday in winter; $3/1.50 adults/children.

Overnight accommodations are available at *The Lodge* (☎ 719-379-3434), on US 160, a friendly and comfortable place that charges $35/40 single/double year-round. Slightly nicer is *Fort Garland Motor Inn* (☎ 719-379-2993), where rooms start at $45/65. Daily TNM&O buses between Denver and Albuquerque stop just across the street.

ALAMOSA & AROUND

Located in the center of the San Luis Valley, Alamosa (population 8775; elevation 7544 feet) is the largest city in the valley. Established in 1878, it is both an agricultural center and a convenient overnight stop for tourists visiting nearby Great Sand Dunes National Monument or riding the excellent Cumbres & Toltec steam train from Antonito to the south.

Orientation

Most lodgings are found either along US 160 east of the Rio Grande (in East Alamosa) or west of the central district on US 160/US 285.

A short river walk starting at the information depot in Cole Park offers views of Blanca Peak followed by a stroll through tree-lined neighborhood streets to the downtown. Paths follow the Rio Grande on both banks from the information depot, but most walkers and certainly all joggers will prefer the wide, well-drained levee on the east side.

Information

The Alamosa County Chamber of Commerce (☎ 719-589-4840, 800-258-7597) operates an information center at the **Narrow-Gauge Engine, Car and Depot History Center** in Cole Park at 3rd St and the west bank of the Rio Grande.
Web site: www.alamosa.org

First National Bank on Edison Ave at Main St has an ATM. Alamosa National Bank operates an ATM in City Market, west of town on US 160/US 285, which also has money order and Western Union telegram service. The post office is at 505 3rd St; Alamosa's zip code is 81101.

Narrow Gauge Newsstand (☎ 719-589-6712), 602 Main St, features a good selection of books and periodicals on local topics and is open 8 am to 8 pm Monday to Saturday, 10 am to 5 pm Sunday.

Sunshine Laundry on Market St next to City Market west of town on US 160/US 285 has a drop-off service. B&D's Laundromat on La Veta Ave next to Safeway has coin-op machines.

San Luis Valley Regional Medical Center (☎ 719-589-2511), 106 Blanca Ave, is west of Adams State College between Main (US 285) and 2nd Sts.

San Luis Valley History Center

Located behind the Chamber Depot, the San Luis Valley History Center (☎ 719-589-4624) has a small but well-arranged collection of 'then and now' photographs and artifacts from early farm life in the valley. Knowledgeable volunteers answer questions and can help plan excursions to historical sites. An interesting exhibit about the nearby La Jara Buddhist Church tells the story of the Japanese in the valley. The center is open 10 am to 4 pm daily June to September.

Alamosa National Wildlife Refuge

Outside Alamosa a 2½-mile trail along the Rio Grande and a panoramic overlook on the east side of the refuge give visitors views of the wetland marshes, ponds and river corridor. In the spring and fall look for sandhill cranes and whooping cranes (an endangered species); in the early spring visitors see large concentrations of bald eagles. The USFS (☎ 719-589-4021) operates a visitors center, open 7:30 am to 4 pm weekdays. To get here from Alamosa, go 3 miles east on US 160 (to just past the Outhouse restaurant), then south on El Rancho Lane.

Blanca Wetlands

The BLM (☎ 719-589-4975) recently restored the wildlife habitat at Blanca Wetlands, east of Alamosa. Activities include **fishing** for bass or trout in newly created ponds and viewing waterfowl, shorebirds

Native architecture, Mesa Verde National Park, CO

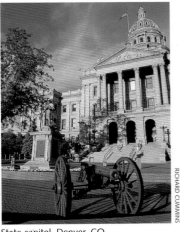
State capitol, Denver, CO

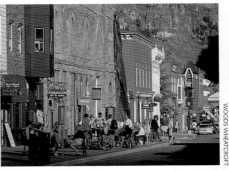
Downtown Telluride, CO

Wall-to-wall license plates, Crested Butte

US Air Force Academy chapel, Colorado Springs, CO

Life on Mars, or perhaps Red Rocks Park, CO

A cow's eye view of the Flatirons, Boulder, CO

Independence Pass, Sawatch Range, CO

and other species. **Hiking** trails lead throughout the many marshes and ponds but are closed in the nesting season from February 15 to July 15. Nevertheless, one 'watchable wildlife area' is open all year. To get here from Alamosa, travel 6 miles east on US 160, then 5 miles north on Alamosa County Rd 116S.

Places to Stay

Camping Campgrounds are found on the east and west sides of Alamosa, and the information center can provide details on camping options around Great Sand Dunes National Monument, the Rio Grande National Forest and San Luis Lakes State Park.

The Alamosa **KOA** (*☎ 719-589-9757, 800-562-9157)* is 3 miles east of town on US 160 then north on Juniper Lane. Open May through October, it has grassy tent sites for $18; RV sites cost $25 for full hookup.

Motels Among the cheapest rooms in town are those at *Sky-Vue Motel* (*☎ 719-589-4945, 250 Broadway)*, which has basic but clean singles/doubles for $36/46 in summer, $25/28 in winter. On the west side of town, *Rio Grande Motel* (*☎ 719-589-9095, 2051 W Main)* has rooms for $42/55 in summer, $40/53 in the off-season.

Singles/doubles cost $50/60 in peak summer season at the modern *Days Inn* (*☎ 719-589-9037)*, in East Alamosa on US 160. The central *Alamosa Lamplighter Motel* (*☎ 719-589-6636, 800-359-2138, 425 Main St)* charges $52/60 in summer, about $20 less in the off-season. The hotel has an annex five blocks away with a pool, hot tub and sauna. On US 160/US 285 at the western edge of town, *Super 8 Motel* (*☎ 719-589-6447, 800-800-8000, 2505 W Main St)* has rooms with hot tubs and also provides a Continental breakfast; $55/68 peak season.

In summer, rooms cost $80/89 single/double at the *Best Western Alamosa Inn* (*☎ 719-589-2567, 800-459-5123, 1919 Main St)*, close to the campus. The motel features an indoor pool, restaurant and lounge.

Hotels & B&Bs An appealing Craftsman-style home (with hot tub) and gracious hosts make the *Cottonwood Inn & Gallery* (*☎ 719-589-3882, 800-955-2623, 123 San Juan Ave)* a fine B&B. Two rooms with shared bath are available for $75, but you can have a private bath for $82/92 or stay in the spacious Art Deco apartment annex next door for $99 (rates are around 30% lower November to February). Learn more about the inn (including the eclectic cooking class offerings) online at www.cottonwoodinn.com.

On US 160 in East Alamosa, the *Holiday Inn* (*☎ 719-589-5833, 333 Santa Fe Ave)* offers rooms for $83/93 and has a restaurant, indoor pool and sauna. Rates fall to around $65/75 in the off-season.

Places to Eat

Breakfasts are good at *Milagro's Coffee House* (*☎ 719-589-6175, 529 Main St)*, which also offers some healthy lunch choices.

Mexican restaurants are as numerous as recipes for salsa. Near the campus, *Monterrey Cafe* (*☎ 719-589-3838, 1406 W Main St)* offers huge breakfast burritos smothered with green chili sauce. *El Charro Mexican Foods* (*☎ 719-589-2262, 421 6th St)* offers entrees like *chilies rellenos* for around $6. *Mrs Rivera's Kitchen* (*☎ 719-589-0277, 1019 6th St)* has a nice atmosphere and a slew of tasty entrees for around $5. For spicy Mexican in an ultracasual, dinerlike atmosphere look for *Taqueria Calvillo*, at Broadway and Hwy 17.

True Grits Steakhouse (*☎ 719-589-9954)*, at Broadway and 1st St, is a sort of shrine to John Wayne that serves all sorts of steak platters. *Oscar's* (*☎ 719-589-9230, 710 Main St)* does a mixture of US and Mexican dishes and offers a generous salad bar. Similar fare is served up the road at *Trujilla's* (*☎ 719-589-9801, 326 Main St)*.

You can select from Colorado microbrews with a burger or sandwich at *St Ives Pub & Eatery* (*☎ 719-589-0711)*, on Main between Edison and San Juan Aves.

Getting There & Around

The Alamosa San Luis Valley Regional Airport, south of the central district on State

Ave, has daily flights on United Express (☎ 719-589-9446) to Denver via Pueblo.

TNM&O buses stop in Alamosa on daily Denver-Albuquerque service at the offices of the local agent SLV Van Lines (☎ 719-589-4948), 8480 Stockton St, on the west side of town south of the railroad tracks.

Alamosa is 73 miles west of Walsenburg on US 160 and 23 miles north of Antonito, near the New Mexico border, on US 285, which turns at Alamosa toward Monte Vista, 31 miles west. L&M Car Rental (☎ 719-589-4651) has its office at the Alamosa San Luis Valley Regional Airport.

SAN LUIS

Tucked into the far southeast margin of the San Luis Valley, the town of San Luis (population 800; elevation 7965 feet), Colorado's oldest settlement, escaped the 'progress' that revoked Hispanic tenure in other parts of the valley following the incursion of the railroad. The town's population is today still 95% Hispanic. It's an appealing, friendly place, and slowing down the pace and staying for a few days might allow you to appreciate the sense of community San Luis still conveys.

The character of San Luis is largely the result of isolation. To Spain, the upper Rio Grande was a lost province best left to the mounted nomadic Native American tribes that Spain was unable to dominate. Mexico encouraged civilian settlement and agriculture with the Sangre de Cristo grant in 1843, yet did not establish a plaza at San Luis until 1851. Under the threat of Ute raids and far from the mercantile and spiritual centers at Taos and Santa Fe, San Luis developed as a self-sufficient outpost.

The San Luis Visitors Center (☎ 719-672-3321), on Main St opposite the intersection with Hwy 142, is open 9 am to 1 pm Thursday to Sunday.

San Luis is 42 miles from Alamosa. By car, first head 26 miles east on US 160 to Fort Garland, then south on Hwy 159 for 16 miles. From Romeo on US 285 between Antonito and Alamosa, Hwy 142 heads east through Manassa (home of the Jack Dempsey Museum) to San Luis.

San Luis Museum & Cultural Center

This handsome museum and gallery chronicles Hispanic culture in southern Colorado and was built to modern solar-heating standards following a plaza design incorporating Old World architecture. Exhibits on the Penitente Brotherhood are especially intriguing for their insight into this formerly secretive local lay religion.

The San Luis Museum (☎ 719-672-3611) is open daily from Memorial Day to Labor Day and weekdays the rest of the year. The movie theater in the Cultural Center is open weekends. It's located on Main St, just south of the visitors center.

Stations of the Cross

For many years, San Luis residents re-enacted the capture, trial and crucifixion of Christ during Holy Week (Easter). There are also pilgrimages to the Stations of the Cross every Friday during Lent. During the Centennial Jubilee of the Sangre de Cristo Parish in 1986, parish members conceived the Stations of the Cross Shrine to formalize this re-enactment. Sculptor Huberto Maestas created 15 dramatic life-size statues stationed along a 1-mile pathway – beginning with Jesus being condemned to death and proceeding to the resurrection. Other volunteers contributed thousands of hours to the shrine.

From the crucifixion on the mesa summit during late afternoon sunsets you can observe the reddish light cast on the Sangre de Cristo Range, including Culebra Peak (14,069 feet), giving the mountains their 'Blood of Christ' name. You can also look out over San Luis and its surrounding fields and pasture. The trailhead to the mesa is located at the junction of Hwys 142 and 159.

Viejo San Acacio

The beautiful Viejo (old) San Acacio is an historic Catholic church where mass is still occasionally held. To get to San Acacio, go 4 miles east of San Luis on Hwy 142, then turn left (south) on Costilla County Rd 15 to the church near Culebra Creek.

San Luis People's Ditch & the Commons

Small tracts of rich bottomlands first lured settlers into the San Luis Valley from Taos. In 1852 colonists dug a 4-mile *acequia* (irrigation ditch) from Culebra Creek, called the San Luis People's Ditch, that's still in use. In addition to individual landholdings, in 1863 San Luis set aside about 1½ sq miles as La Vega, a common crop field and pasture used by all the inhabitants. Community members also held common rights to hunt, fish or gather wood in La Sierra, 120 sq miles of privately held lands in the mountains.

But because Americans tend to view land as a commodity, not a cooperative resource, San Luis residents are now struggling to regain a part of La Sierra. During the 1960s, San Luis residents' use of La Sierra and almost 300 acres of La Vega was restricted as a private owner removed their access rights from the deed and erected fences on the land. Violence erupted when San Luis residents initially attempted to defend their rights. The challenge was recently taken to the courts, where the people of San Luis and neighboring villages hope to regain rights to La Sierra.

Places to Stay & Eat

In winter you may find the only lodging choice is the **San Luis Inn Motel** (☎ 877-672-3331, 138 Main St), which has an indoor hot tub and singles/doubles for $49/59.

Fabian's Bed and Breakfast (☎ 719-672-3794, 125 Main St), at the south end of town, has very friendly owners and single/double rooms with shared bath for $60/75. Breakfast is included in the price of the room and is served at the adjacent **Fabian's Cafe** (☎ 719-672-0322).

Similar rates are offered at **El Convento B&B** (☎ 719-672-4223, 512 Church Place), opposite the church. This unique property, owned by the Sangre de Cristo Parish, was originally built as a school in 1905, and the substantial adobe building later served as a convent. Four luxurious upstairs rooms, each with private bath, are decorated with antiques and handcrafted furniture. Downstairs you can purchase local handmade crafts in the Centro Artesano gallery.

For 50 years, Emma Espinosa has cooked Mexican specialties for lunch and dinner at **Emma's Hacienda** (☎ 719-672-9902), on Main St across from the San Luis Inn Motel. Walking into Emma's is like arriving at a family reunion: As many as four generations of the Espinosa family may be working at any one time. Emma's specialty dish is red and green enchiladas, or you might try a Pancho Villa Burrito.

ANTONITO & AROUND

A dusty, run-down place, the only real attraction in Antonito (population 870) is the northern terminus of the Cumbres & Toltec Scenic Railroad (C&TS), a narrow-gauge railway that winds its way through the mountains to Chama, New Mexico. Nearby is a highway that follows the Conejos River into the Rio Grande National Forest where you can camp, fish, observe wildlife or watch the steam train wind its way through Cumbres Pass.

TNM&O buses to Albuquerque, New Mexico, or Denver can be flagged down daily in front of the Lee's Texaco Store (☎ 719-376-5949), 217 Main St. Antonito is 28 miles south of Alamosa on US 285, and 5 miles north of the border with New Mexico. To the west on Hwy 17 is Chama, New Mexico, some 39 miles away over Cumbres Pass.

The Cumbres & Toltec Scenic Railroad Depot is a mile south of Antonito at the junction of US 285 (Main St) and Hwy 17. The Antonito Visitors Center (☎ 719-376-2049, 800-835-1098) is on US 285 opposite the railroad depot and is only open in summer. For visitor information call the Antonito Chamber of Commerce (☎ 719-376-2277, 800-323-9469).

Cumbres & Toltec Scenic Railroad

In 1880 the Denver & Rio Grande (D&RG) Western Rail completed track over Cumbres Pass, linking Chama, New Mexico, with Denver by way of Alamosa. The twisting mountainous terrain could most easily be breached by using narrow-gauge track, 3 feet wide as opposed to the 4-foot, 8-inch standard gauge. Within a few years the line was extended to Durango, Farmington and the Silverton mining camp, 152 miles away. Railroad buffs encouraged Colorado and New Mexico to buy the scenic Cumbres Pass segment when the Antonito-Farmington line came up for abandonment in 1967. Their efforts led to a compact between Colorado and New Mexico to save the railway as a National Historic Site.

Today, chugging steam engines pull passenger cars up the 10,022-foot Cumbres Pass between Antonito and Chama – the longest and highest narrow-gauge steam line in North America. Along the way, the train follows a precipitous rock ledge 600 feet above the Rio Los Pinos in the Toltec Gorge. At a plodding 12 to 15mph, the 64-mile ride takes slightly more than six hours, including water stops and a lunch stop midway at Osier. You can take a roundtrip to Osier, or a trip to the beautiful Cumbres Pass. The through trip to Chama returns by van in slightly more than an hour. All trips require a full day.

The C&TS can also provide access to the backcountry and prime fishing streams in the USFS lands along the border between Colorado and New Mexico. Backpackers can make reservations for drop-off and later pickup at the water stops. If you wish to camp in Chama, *Rio Chama RV Campground* (☎ 505-756-2303) offers tent sites only two blocks north of the depot.

Trains run daily roughly from Memorial Day to mid-October, during which the Antonito Depot (☎ 719-376-5483) is open 7:30 am to 6 pm. Dress warmly as the unheated cars, both enclosed and semi-enclosed, can get extremely cold.

There are currently 13 different day-trip options to choose from, some require one portion to be traveled by van. Seven options from Antonito cost between $40 and $60 ($99 for a parlor car), and six trips from Chama cost between $29 and $50. Children 11 years and under pay half fare. Call ahead or log-on for current schedules and reservations. Web site: www.cumbrestoltec.com

Places to Stay & Eat

With lodging or campsites available nearby in the beautiful Conejos River Canyon to the west on Hwy 17 – some camps and cabins are only 5 miles away – there's no reason to stay in glum Antonito. If you do get stuck, a short walk from the C&TS Depot is the *Narrow Gauge Railroad Inn* (☎ 719-376-5441, 800-323-9469), a standard motel with clean singles/doubles for $44/54.

Good Mexican food and standard US dishes are available at the *Dutch Mill (401 Main St)*, open 6:30 am to 9 pm daily.

CONEJOS RIVER

Although a few travelers explore historical sites along the lower Conejos River near Antonito, most visitors prefer the upstream portions of the river to the west of Antonito along Hwy 17. The Conejos is a top fishery, and numerous tributaries and nearby high-elevation lakes also provide good fishing. Bighorn sheep, elks and deer can occasionally be observed near the river or on canyon cliffs. On the steep Hwy 17 ascent toward the Cumbres Pass are superb vistas of the Conejos River and sheer face of Black Mountain across the valley. The winding tracks pass the picturesque upland meadow, created by fire in 1879, and an historic wooden water tank at Los Pinos. The volcanic character of the San Juan Range is seen in the vivid, ragged rock outcrops encountered soon after crossing Cumbres Pass.

To reach the Conejos River from Antonito, travel directly west on Hwy 17. Or take a short detour to the north along the river, passing the scrawny county seat at Conejos and Colorado's oldest church – the Nuestra Señora de Guadalupe – before rejoining Hwy 17. Another example of early architecture is the adobe San Pedro y San Rafael Church at Paisaje. This handsome building, topped by an octagonal wooden bell tower, can also be reached by Hwy 17 – turn right on Conejos County Rd 1075, 3 miles west of Antonito.

Hiking & Backpacking
The South San Juan Wilderness Area, within the Rio Grande National Forest, straddles the Continental Divide and is traversed by the Continental Divide National Scenic Trail, which emerges from the backcountry at the Cumbres Pass depot.

Trailheads and campsites are located along the river on USFS Rd 250, northwest of Elk Creek. Near Cumbres Pass USFS Rd 118 leads to Trujillo Meadows Wilderness Area and a USFS campground before reaching a trailhead on the southern boundary of the wilderness.

For maps and information contact the Conejos Peak Ranger District (☎ 719-274-8971), 11 miles north of Antonito (3 miles south of La Jara) on US 285.

Fishing
Specially managed 'Wild Trout Waters' are designated by the Colorado Division of Wildlife on the uppermost Lake Fork, plus sections of the Conejos River next to the South San Juan Wilderness and below the Menkhaven Lodge for 4 miles. These streams support self-sustaining native cutthroat trout populations. The DOW manager in Antonito prepares a map and handout on fishing the Conejos River for each season; it's available at the Antonito visitors center (see Antonito & Around, earlier) and tackle shops. On your way in stop at Cottonwood Meadows Fly Shop (☎ 719-376-5660), 5 miles west of Antonito, for information on fishing conditions and specific regulations for the season. The shop also offers fishing guides for your choice of wading, hiking or horseback trips on the Conejos River and its tributaries from May to November.

Places to Stay & Eat
There's plenty of camping near the river at either USFS campgrounds or privately run sites that often also offer rustic cabins. A few lodges provide very comfortable accommodations. Most places close from late October to April. The following selection is organized by distance from Antonito along Hwy 17.

Only 5 miles from Antonito, Hwy 17 crosses the Conejos River where large cottonwood groves shade nice tent sites at *Mogote Meadow* (☎ 719-376-5774), available with showers for $16. Farther down, *Cottonwood Meadows* (☎ 719-376-5660) offers cabins for around $50 double occupancy.

At the 10-mile mark, heavy wool blankets, feather pillows and breakfasts are provided to HI-AYH members at *Conejos River HI-AYH* (☎ 719-376-2518) for only $9 (non-members pay $12). The two dormitories feature the soothing sound of rushing water from the nearby river. The hostel is open late May to mid-October.

The *USFS Mogote Campground* (☎ 877-444-6777), 13 miles west of Antonito, has popular sites for $10 next to the river or in an upper area shaded by ponderosa pines. A laundry and showers are available 1 mile downstream at *Conejos River Campground*, but the tent sites for $14 are not very appealing. Additional USFS campgrounds upstream on the river include *Aspen* (16 miles) and *Elk Creek* (23 miles), where Hwy 17 leaves the river. Fees at both are $10.

Top-end cabins and B&B accommodations, all with private bath, are available at *Conejos River Guest Ranch* (☎ 719-376-2464), 14 miles west of Antonito. Six fully equipped riverside cabins cost $95 to $115 double occupancy; the eight comfortably furnished lodge rooms include breakfast and range from $85 to $95 depending on the season.

At 22 miles, *Mrs. Rio's Restaurant* (☎ 719-376-5964) is the center of a miniature building boom that detracts from the once pristine landscape. It's open 9 am to 9 pm daily all year and features Southwestern and Mexican dishes. Behind the restaurant *Mountain Home Lodge* (☎ 719-376-5393) is open year-round and has one-bedroom cabins with full kitchens for $70 in summer, $50 in winter. Laundry and showers are available with tent sites for $12 at nearby *Ponderosa Campground*, but the *USFS Elk Creek Campground* is also close by and much prettier.

Rio Grande Headwaters

In the heart of the San Juan Mountains above Creede, far to the west of the San Luis Valley, the Rio Grande begins its 1900-mile journey to the Gulf of Mexico. Most impressions of the Rio Grande come from the final 1800 miles of its path: a deep gorge near Taos, a sere corridor of settlement in New Mexico and an international border renowned for its languid flow that's a foot deep and a mile wide. But the Rio Grande's initial 100 miles – from headwater source to the San Luis Valley floor at Monte Vista – is a turbulent mountain channel of cold, clear water teeming with naturally thriving fish.

MONTE VISTA

Monte Vista (population 5100; elevation 7666 feet) is on the west side of the San Luis Valley floor. Coming east and following the Rio Grande, it is at the intersection of US 160 and US 285 (Gunbarrel Rd) coming from Saguache in the north. The local economy relies on potatoes, barley for the Coors Brewing Co and tourists looking for directions and information on the Rio Grande headwaters. Nearby wildlife areas should appeal to birdwatchers and a few notable lodgings may entice you to spend the night, but most of the tourist flock continues west to roost in the forests along the Rio Grande.

Information

Visitor information is available at the Monte Vista Chamber of Commerce (☎ 719-852-2731, 800-562-7085), 1035 Park Ave. Web site: www.monte-vista.org

The Rio Grande National Forest Headquarters (☎ 719-852-5941), 1803 W US 160 west of town, is the place to get maps and information on public lands in the Rio

Grande headwaters. It's open 8 am to 4:30 pm weekdays.

Birdwatchers and anglers should stop by the Colorado DOW (☎ 719-852-4783) on the east side of town, south of US 160/US 285. Turn right near Haefeli's Honey Farms on to Rio Grande County Rd 1E. Monte Vista Sporting Goods, 831 1st St, has USGS maps for the San Luis Valley and the Rio Grande National Forest.

Monte Vista National Wildlife Refuge

Six miles south of town on Hwy 15, the Monte Vista National Wildlife Refuge (☎ 719-589-4021) features a 2½-mile self-guided driving loop, the Avocet Trail, that provides views of waterfowl. In fall a few endangered whooping cranes may be spotted among the thousands of migrating sandhill cranes.

Places to Stay & Eat

The handsome *Monte Villa Inn* (☎ 719-852-5166, 925 1st Ave), located in the center of town, is listed on the National Register of Historic Places. Singles/doubles cost $54/60. Check out the hotel's dining room, furnished with antiques and heavy chandeliers.

A bit more outlandish is the *Best Western Movie Manor Motor Inn* (☎ 719-852-5921), 2 miles west of Monte Vista, where you can watch movies on a drive-in screen from the picture window of your motel room (sound is piped into the room). All rooms have screen views and cost $79 in summer. Movies are only screened from April to September.

One of the most popular restaurants in the San Luis Valley is *Restaurante Dos Rios* (☎ 719-892-0969), two miles north of Monte Vista on Hwy 285. Provincialism is celebrated at the Dos Rios – the menu displays ads for tractors and irrigation pumps and includes a San Luis Valley baked potato with green chili and cheese. A variety of vegetarian dishes like grilled vegetable fajitas are available, as is a wide selection of salads. The restaurant is open 11 am to 9 pm Tuesday to Saturday.

Another appealing option for Mexican fare is **Ninos** (☎ *719-852-0101*), right on Main St downtown.

LA GARITA

La Garita (Spanish for 'the Overlook') is the scene of outstanding **rock-climbing** opportunities near an historic Hispanic landscape. Here you can also find low adobe root cellars, a former Hispanic workers union hall, identified by the abbreviation 'SPMDTU,' and an offshoot of the Penitente Brotherhood.

Experienced climbers are attracted to the bolted face climbs on the rhyolite rock walls in Penitente Canyon and Rock Canyon. With more than 400 routes in the area, there are plenty of opportunities for all levels of experience and skill. Some climbers consider these among the best short climbing routes in Colorado. You can get more information, maps, guidebooks and climbing gear at Casa de Madera (☎ 719-657-2336), 680 Grande Ave in Del Norte, where the owner, Alex Colville, is a climbing guide. The BLM area has several developed fee campgrounds in the area.

A chapel, known as La Capilla de San Juan Bautista, listed on the National Register of Historic Places, and a cemetery stand in stark splendor on a prominent site above the village. The chapel was originally built in 1861 but was rebuilt in 1924 following a fire. It now houses the **San Juan Art Center**, a cooperative work and display space operated by Artes del Valle (☎ 719-589-4769), an organization that promotes traditional Hispanic folk art.

La Garita Llamas (☎ 719-588-2907) offers extended pack trips in the remote backcountry of the San Juan Mountains. Unlike horseback trips, llamas carry the gear while you hike unencumbered.

The **La Garita Creek Ranch** (☎ *719-754-2533, 800-838-3833, 38145 County Rd E-39*) is southwest of the chapel on Saguache County Rd. Singles/doubles in the modern lodge cost $75/79, while cabin rooms cost $85/89. Ranch amenities include a hot tub and sauna; horseback trail rides and other outdoor pursuits can be arranged. In summer it operates as a full guest ranch; six-night stays start at $1050 (all-inclusive). Web site: www.lagarita.com

To get to La Garita from Monte Vista travel north 20 miles on US 285, turn left (west) at the sign on Saguache County Rd G for 8 miles. Penitente Canyon is southwest from the chapel on County Rd 38.

DEL NORTE

An attractive town, Del Norte (population 1800; elevation 7884 feet) is beside the Rio Grande del Norte, for which it was named, in the foothills west of the San Luis Valley on US 160. One of Colorado's oldest towns, it was founded in 1860 and by 1873 it was a thriving supply point for mining in the San Juan Mountains. Now Del Norte marks the beginning of 'Gold Medal' fishing on the Rio Grande and is a popular jumping-off point (so to speak) for rock climbers (see La Garita above) and mountain bicyclists.

Information

For visitor information call the Del Norte Chamber of Commerce (☎ 888-616-4836) or stop by Casa de Madera (☎ 719-657-2336), 680 Grande Ave (US 160). The USFS Divide District Ranger Station (☎ 719-657-3321) is at 1308 Grande Ave, just past Skaff's Super grocery store at 1215 Grande Ave on the east end of town. There's an ATM machine in Skaff's.

The Los Piños Health Vista Clinic (☎ 719-657-3342) is on the opposite side of Grande Ave.

Rio Grande County Museum & Cultural Center

The museum (☎ 719-657-2847), housed in a modern building at Oak and 6th Sts, features Pueblo and Ute rock art, Hispanic history and early photographs of Monte Vista's 'potato row' wagons loaded high with valley spuds at the turn of the 20th century. Special programs include talks and outdoor excursions led by local historians and naturalists. The museum has information for people who want to visit local **rock art** sites. The museum is open 10 am to 5 pm Tuesday to Saturday in summer, and noon

COLORADO

to 5 pm in winter. Admission costs $1/50¢ adults/children.

Fishing

Gold Medal fishing on the Rio Grande begins a mile upstream at the Farmer's Union Canal. From here to the Hwy 149 bridge at South Fork is one of Colorado's most productive fisheries, producing 16- to 20-inch trout. You access the river and signed public property via the bridges on Rio Grande County Rds 17, 18 and 19, plus the Hwy 149 bridge above South Fork.

Mountain Biking

Fat-tire bikes are permitted on all public trails with the exception of designated wilderness areas. A relatively easy ride heads north about 10 miles to La Ventana, a natural arch 'window' in a volcanic dike. To get there from Del Norte, cross the river and follow Rio Grande County Rd 22 for 8 miles passing the small airport, turn right on USFS Rd 660 for a quarter of a mile, then turn left and follow the road for about 2 miles to the short trail to the volcanic wall.

Another ride recommended by the USFS follows an old stock driveway along an alpine ridge on USFS Trail 700 from Grayback Mountain (12,616 feet) east 7 miles to Blowout Pass (12,000 feet). To reach the Grayback Mountain trailhead, you must travel about 20 miles south of Del Norte on USFS Rd 14, then continue another 5 miles on USFS Rd 330.

Places to Stay & Eat

Two motels on the eastern end of Grande Ave (US 160) offer comparable rooms. *El Rancho* (☎ 719-657-3332, 1160 Grande Ave) has singles/doubles for $32/42, while *Del Norte Motel & Cafe* (☎ 719-657-3581, 800-372-2331, 1050 Grande Ave) is a bit nicer and charges $36/43. The cafe is a good spot for breakfast or lunch.

Stone Quarry Pizza (☎ 719-657-9115, 580 Grande Ave) features a salad bar and outdoor patio and is open daily for lunch and dinner. Authentic Mexican specialties like *menudo* (an offal soup) are featured at *Peppers* (☎ 719-657-3492, 540 Grande Ave).

SOUTH FORK

Founded around a lumber mill, South Fork (population 400; elevation 8300 feet) is not so much a town as a stretch of buildings along US 160, 31 miles west of Monte Vista. However, it lies at the confluence of the South Fork and the Rio Grande Rivers and is a good base from which to fish the Gold Medal waters of the Rio Grande.

In ski season, South Fork provides a lodging alternative to Pagosa Springs for skiers at Wolf Creek (see Pagosa Springs, later). Exceptional backcountry hiking in the Weminuche Wilderness of the Rio Grande National Forest, Colorado's largest pristine area, is readily accessible from trailheads near South Fork. An abundance of nearby campgrounds also attracts vacationers who want to enjoy a forested mountain setting.

Orientation & Information

At South Fork, US 160 turns south from the Rio Grande toward Wolf Creek Pass 18 miles away, and Hwy 149 continues upstream 21 miles to Creede before crossing the Continental Divide to Lake City.

The Silver Thread Interpretive Center (☎ 719-873-5512, 800-571-0881), 28 Silver Thread Lane, is the name of South Fork's visitors center, a reference to the Silver Thread Byway leading to Creede. It has information on outdoor activities and lodging and sells biking and hiking trail maps. It's open 9 am to 5 pm weekdays and 10 am to 4 pm weekends in summer.
Web site: www.southfork.org

Wildlife Viewing

The grassy river benches in the Coller State Wildlife Area attract elks, deer and moose in winter. From South Fork, follow Hwy 149 toward Creede for about 7 miles, and there's a sign on the left; turn there and you enter the area after a couple hundred yards. You can see bighorn sheep throughout the year on the south-facing Palisade cliffs extending from the Coller State Wildlife Area to Wagon Wheel Gap. At the gap, golden eagles soar above the cliff faces and fish the Rio Grande.

Hiking & Backpacking

Named for a band of the Ute tribe, the Weminuche Wilderness Area is the most extensive wilderness in Colorado with an area of more than 700 sq miles. The Weminuche extends west along the Continental Divide from Wolf Creek Pass to the Animas River near Silverton. By early July you can reach Archuleta Lake (11,800 feet) near the Divide by following USFS Trail 839 for about 7 miles from the Big Meadows Reservoir (9200 feet) along Archuleta Creek into the wilderness area.

Along the **Continental Divide National Scenic Trail** (USFS Trail 813) you will find many secluded hiking opportunities as the trail passes through 80 miles of the Weminuche Wilderness between Wolf Creek Pass and Stony Pass. One trail of particular interest leads to an undeveloped natural hot spring west of the Divide. To reach **Rainbow/Wolf Creek Pass Hot Spring** take USFS Trail 560 west from the Divide, descending more than 6 miles through the Beaver Creek drainage on the West Fork headwaters of the San Juan River. The spring of more than 100°F is to the right on USFS Trail 561, about half a mile above the trail junction.

To get to the trailhead at Big Meadows Reservoir, travel south on US 160 for 11 miles to the turnoff on the right (to the west). Proceed to the boat ramp parking area on the north side of the reservoir. You will need maps of both the Rio Grande and San Juan National Forests. Ranger stations for the Rio Grande National Forest are in either Del Norte or Creede; the nearest San Juan National Forest ranger station is in Pagosa Springs (☎ 970-264-2268).

Places to Stay

There are some 300 RV spaces at several private campgrounds within a few miles of South Fork, but not really any appealing tent sites.

Primitive USFS campsites cost $10 in the vicinity of South Fork. The closest are at Beaver Creek, about 4 miles south of South Fork. From South Fork go 2 miles southwest on US 160 and turn left across the South Fork of the Rio Grande to USFS Rd 360. Continue 3 miles to *Lower Beaver Creek* and *Upper Beaver Creek* campgrounds; in another 3 miles you reach Beaver Creek Reservoir Wilderness Area and USFS *Cross Creek Campground*. With 56 camping units, the USFS *Big Meadows Campground*, 11 miles south of South Fork near Wolf Creek Pass, is the largest facility in the area and is at the start of several appealing trails. Eight miles upstream from South Fork on Hwy 149 is the small USFS *Palisade Campground* on the Rio Grande – its 13 sites are nearly always full in summer.

Peak season rates apply in July and August and also in November and December, when the brutal weather makes the nearby Wolf Creek Ski Area an early winter favorite.

One of the first motels to fill up is the *Inn Motel* (☎ 719-873-5514, 800-233-9723), at the junction of US 160 and Hwy 149, where windows open to the river and singles/doubles cost $50 in summer and $32/35 in winter. Also near the highway junction, *Foothills Lodge* (☎ 719-873-5969, 800-510-3897) offers rooms from $35/50 in summer, around $5 more in winter, and has a hot tub.

B&B accommodations with shared bath at the woodsy *Spruce Lodge* (☎ 719-873-5605, 800-228-5605, 29431 W Hwy 160), about 1 mile east of the visitors center, cost $45/60 year-round. Chalet cabins are also available for $55/65. Carnivorous folk will appreciate *Chinook Lodge & Smokehouse* (☎ 719-873-9993, 888-890-9110, cktri@amigo.net, 29666 W Hwy 160), where copious meats are smoked on the premises (sample its amazing beef jerky). Guests stay in rustic, century-old cabins, most with handsome rock fireplaces and kitchens. Budget beds (shared bath) go for $25, or $65/85 for a one/two-bed cabin.

The *Wolf Creek Ski Lodge* (☎ 719-873-5547, 800-874-0416) on US 160 about half a mile west of the junction, offers quite comfortable rooms for $45 to $58, or $55 to $68 with kitchenettes.

Places to Eat

Next to the Rainbow Grocery, *Rockaway Cafe* (☎ 719-873-5581) is a quaint place known mainly for its fine steak, but it also serves seafood, chicken and large salads. Just next door to the Spruce Lodge, *Brown's Cafe (☎ 719-873-2903)* is the place to go for barbecue.

CREEDE & AROUND

Mineral and Hinsdale Counties currently vie for the title of least-populated county in the state: Each has less than 600 people.

Since 1988 all the silver mines of Mineral County have closed, except to visitors who enjoy touring the rugged mining landscape north of town, where tremendous mills cling to spectacular cliffs. Below the vertical-walled mouth of Willow Creek Canyon, narrow Creede Ave is a mix of galleries and shops in historic buildings offering unique gifts.

For scenic beauty, the country surrounding Creede is hard to beat. Relatively untrampled trails into the immense surrounding wilderness areas provide appreciative hikers and backpackers with beauty and solitude, as well as access to unique sights like the bizarre volcanic spires and pinnacles of the Wheeler Geologic Area.

Creede is 23 miles northwest of South Fork on the Silver Thread National Scenic Byway, which follows Hwy 149 for 75 miles between South Fork and Lake City.

Information

At the top of Creede Ave opposite the low-rise Mineral County Courthouse you will find the Creede/Mineral County Chamber of Commerce (☎ 719-658-2374, 800-327-2102), open 8 am to 5 pm Monday to Saturday in summer, 9 am to 5 pm weekdays in winter. Be sure to pick up a walking tour map of historic Creede.
Web site: www.creede.com

The USFS Divide District Ranger Station (☎ 719-658-2556), at 3rd St and Creede Ave, has information on the La Garita and Weminuche Wilderness Areas. It's open weekdays between May and November. On weekends and in winter try the folks at San Juan Sports on Creede Ave for information on outdoor activities.

The First National Bank, about midway along Creede Ave, has an ATM. The post office is on the corner of Wall St and Creede Ave.

The Amethyst Emporium (☎ 719-658-2430) offers a large selection of books on the region.

Creede Museum

Mineral treasures attracted miners by the trainload, but this museum chronicles the more intriguing opportunists and scoundrels who arrived to take advantage of Creede's short-lived prosperity. The former D&RG Railroad Depot, behind City Park, now houses the Creede Museum (☎ 719-658-2303), which is open 10 am to 4 pm Monday to Saturday from Memorial Day to Labor Day. Admission costs $1.

Creede Underground Mining Museum

Opened in 1992, this fascinating museum (☎ 719-658-0811), two blocks north of town on N Main St, was hewn from the ground by mine workers, and the tours, which really bring home the grim reality of life in the mines, are also led by miners. It's a chilling exhibit in more ways than one: With the temperature a steady 51°F year-round, visitors are advised to bring jackets. It's open 10 am to 4 pm daily in summer, 10 am to 3 pm after September, and closed weekends in winter. Admission costs $5/3 adults/children.

Bachelor Historic Tour

No visit to Creede would be complete without bouncing over the 17-mile loop tour of the abandoned mines and town sites immediately north of town. The loop offers outstanding views of La Garita Mountains (San Luis Peak is 14,014 feet) and Rio Grande Valley. Sections of the road are very narrow and steep, but not difficult if the road is dry and you drive slowly enough to avoid destroying your car.

Mountain bikers will note that much of the 2000-foot rise in elevation occurs in the initial 2 miles along West Willow Creek that miners called the **Black Pitch** – some cyclists

---

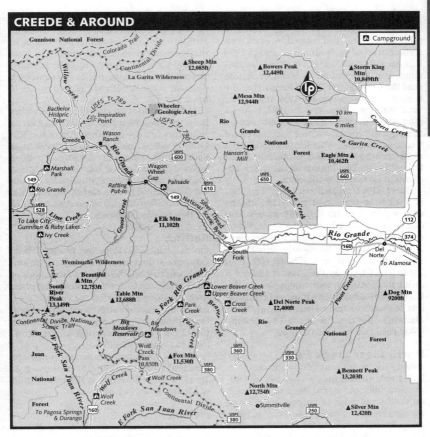

CREEDE & AROUND

may prefer to tour mines along the gentler grades of East Willow Creek. Below the Black Pitch, failed brakes on loaded teamster wagons often pulled unfortunate animals to their end at **Dead Horse Flats**. Above this treacherous section, workers in the **Amethyst**, one of Colorado's richest silver mines, sent ore down the steep canyon to the railroad aboard ore cars on a high rotary tram system. You can see remnants of the tall towers up the steep slope to the east of the Black Pitch.

An excellent illustrated tour booklet prepared by local historians is available for $1 from the Creede Chamber of Commerce, the USFS, the Creede Museum or from a dispenser at the first interpretive stop: West Willow/East Willow Creek junction, immediately north of the rock spires that mark the gateway to Willow Creek Canyon.

You can rent a mountain bike for $18 per day at San Juan Sports (☎ 719-658-2359), 102 Main St. The shop also carries a thorough collection of USGS topographic maps. Guided mountain-bike tours and bike rentals are offered by Mountain Man Rafting & Tours (☎ 719-658-2663).

Wheeler Geologic Area

The dramatic shapes carved by wind and rain into volcanic tuff framed by evergreen forest attracted early attention, and in 1908 this area was declared a national monument. But the remote 11,000-foot setting near the Continental Divide kept all but the hardiest visitors away. By 1950 the monument status was removed. In 1993, 85 years after it was declared a national monument, the bizarre eroded volcanic forms west of Creede called the Wheeler Geologic Area were granted wilderness protection when federal lawmakers approved the area's addition to La Garita Wilderness.

The USFS East Bellows Trail (Trail 790) is a 17-mile roundtrip hike that climbs nearly 2000 feet from the Hanson's Mill campground to the base of the geologic formations. To get to the trailhead, drive southeast along Hwy 149 for slightly more than 7 miles and turn left on USFS Rd 600 (Pool Table Rd). Continue along this road for 9½ miles to Hanson's Mill campground. The trail affords some great views and there are lots of places to camp along the way. From Hanson's Mill there is also a 14-mile-long 4WD road that leads to the area.

North Clear Creek Falls

Twenty-five miles west of Creede and only half a mile from signs on Hwy 149, the impressive falls are visible from an overlook on the fenced edge of a deep gorge. From the parking area a short walk over the ridge away from the falls takes you to another viewpoint above the sheer-walled canyon with Bristol Head in the distance. Far below your feet a metal aqueduct carries Clear Creek away from its natural course to the Santa Maria Reservoir as part of a massive effort to regulate the flow of the Rio Grande headwaters.

Hiking & Backpacking

The Upper Rio Grande Walkers (☎ 719-658-2430) describe several of their favorite walks with a map and brochure that also grades each walk's difficulty. All walks are up and back, but the views are so spectacular and different in each direction that you will not mind retracing your steps. The hike through the upland meadow called Phoenix Park is especially appealing, as it begins at the King Solomon Mill at the top of East Willow Creek Canyon and proceeds past waterfalls and beaver ponds. You can pick up maps at the Amethyst Emporium, 129 N Main St.

Hiking options are nearly limitless within the extensive Weminuche and La Garita Wilderness Areas on either side of the Rio Grande Valley. Colorado's largest wilderness naturally presents many additional options beyond the scope of this book. A good source of information if you wish to explore the Continental Divide east of Stony Pass is Dennis Gebhardt's *A Backpacking Guide to the Weminuche Wilderness*.

Rafting

On the Rio Grande below Wagon Wheel Gap, scenic float trips with a few rapids and quality fishing are the primary attractions of this 20-mile run to South Fork. A good place to put in along Hwy 149 is the Goose Creek Rd Bridge immediately west of the gap. During high water, rafters should beware the closely spaced railroad bridge abutments at Wagon Wheel Gap.

Rafting tours and equipment rental are available from Mountain Man Rafting & Tours (☎ 719-658-2663) at the intersection of Main St and Hwy 149.

Fishing

On the Rio Grande above Wagon Wheel Gap, anglers will find two choice sections of the river with special regulations for catch-and-release on rainbow trout using either artificial fly or lure, and a two-bag limit on brown trout more than 12 inches long. One section between Creede's Willow Creek and Wagon Wheel Gap is mostly private and boat access is necessary. Farther upstream, however, you can fish from public lands on both sides of the Rio Grande at USFS Marshall Park and Rio Grande campgrounds.

The fishing is good at **Ruby Lakes** (11,000 feet) accessible by USFS Trail 815, a 4-mile hike or horseback ride along Fern Creek.

The trailhead is about 1¼ miles along USFS Rd 522, 16 miles southwest of Craig off Hwy 149.

Brown Lakes State Wildlife Area (9840 feet) is stocked by the DOW with rainbow and brook trout, but the large browns and native cutthroat are the real attraction. The lakes are surrounded by spruce and fir forests and are located 2 miles west of Hwy 149 and the USFS Silver Thread Campground, 25 miles west of Creede.

Fishing supplies, information and guide services are available at the Rio Grande Angler (☎ 719-658-2955) in Creede. Guided river fishing is offered by Mountain Man Rafting & Tours (☎ 719-658-2663).

Special Events
On the second weekend in June visitors crowd the street to attend the renowned **Creede Repertory Theater** (☎ 719-658-2540). The theater presents talented casts in well-honed productions until Labor Day.

Although Creede's hard-rock mining days are over, many locals stay in practice – keeping local bars solvent – for the **Days of '92 Mining Competition** leading up to the **Colorado State Mining Championships** during the Fourth of July weekend.

Places to Stay
Camping All of the public forest lands surrounding Creede are open to camping, but 10 USFS campgrounds offering water and restrooms are in the Divide District above Wagon Wheel Gap. On the banks of the Rio Grande's designated Wild Trout Waters is the popular USFS *Marshall Park Campground* (☎ 877-444-6777), only 7 miles southwest of Creede, where campsites cost $10. Book ahead in summer. Nine miles south of Marshall Park, on the Weminuche Wilderness boundary, is the isolated USFS *Ivy Creek Campground* and trailhead. To get there from Marshall Park follow USFS Rd 523 for 4 miles, then turn left on USFS Rd 528 for 3 miles and continue straight on USFS Rd 526. Sites are free.

Plenty of sites are available on the boundary of the Weminuche Wilderness at four campgrounds along USFS Rd 520, 21 miles southwest of Creede on Hwy 149. The largest of the group, *Thirtymile Campground*, offers 33 sites for $10. About 25 miles west of Creede near Clear Creek, *South Clear Creek* and *South Clear Creek Falls* are two USFS campgrounds where sites with scenic views cost the same. The secluded canyon sites at *North Clear Creek Campground* are also worth checking out. All three are near North Clear Creek Falls and Brown Lakes Wilderness Areas. See the Creede & Around map for additional campgrounds in the area.

Motels & B&Bs Peak season rates are in effect in July and August. On the southeast edge of town, clean singles/doubles at the friendly *Snowshoe Motel* (☎ 719-658-2315) cost $56/67 in summer, $32/35 in winter. Rates include a Continental breakfast.

Next to the Repertory Theater, *Creede Hotel B&B* (☎ 719-658-2608) has four rooms with private baths that cost $70/90 single/double. Both the hotel and its excellent restaurant are closed from October to May.

The top-end 1892 *Old Fire House B&B* (☎ 719-658-0212), on Main St, has four fully renovated Victorian rooms and a library lounge. Rates range from $78 to $139, and it's also closed from October to May.

Resorts There are nearly 20 ranches and resorts around Creede, ranging from economical to extravagant. Following are several of the more accessible places: The Creede/Mineral County Chamber of Commerce (see Information) can help further.

Two miles southeast of Creede, the *Wason Ranch* (☎ 719-658-2413) has two-bedroom cabins equipped with kitchenettes for $70 per day (available May through October). Riverside cottages with three bedrooms and two baths are available year-round and cost $175/135 in summer/winter, with a minimum stay of three/two days. The ranch also offers fly-fishing lessons, fishing guides and a dory.

Families are welcome at **Antlers Ranch** (☎ 719-658-2423), 5 miles southwest of Creede, which offers motel-style rooms for $70 and cabins on both banks of the Rio Grande from $600 to $750 weekly.

About 8 miles southwest of Creede is the beautiful **Soward Ranch** (☎ 719-658-2295). Open May to October, it's the only 'centennial' ranch in the area – meaning it's been operated by the same family for more than 100 years. Guests can enjoy fishing from four lakes as well as 4 miles of trout creek on the 1500-acre property. Twelve cabins range in price from $45 to $105 depending on size and amenities. To get there, take Hwy 149 southwest for 7 miles, turn left on Middle Creek Rd, continue for 1 mile and when you get to the fork in the road, bear right, following the signs to the ranch.

San Juan Mountains

Straddling the Continental Divide and covering an extensive area north of Durango and Pagosa Springs, the San Juan Mountains offer scenery that leads admirers to call this range the 'Alps of America.' Volcanic rock formations distinguish these peaks from other Colorado ranges.

LAKE CITY

Residents don't seem to mind their town's status as the 'flyspeck' seat of Hinsdale County. In 1877 Lake City (population 380; elevation 8671 feet) was known as the 'Metropolis of the Mines' and reached its peak population of 5000, but unlike many mining towns, it attracted optimistic settlers rather than itinerants. The Greek and Gothic Revival architecture and tree-lined streets reflect the settlers' nostalgia for earlier eastern cities.

Orientation & Information

Lake City is on Hwy 149 (Gunnison Ave in town), 47 miles south of the intersection with US 50, which in turn leads west to

Gunnison and east to Montrose. It lies west of the Continental Divide at Spring Creek Pass and the giant Slumgullion landslide that dammed the Lake Fork of the Gunnison River to form Lake San Cristobal south of town. To the west rises Uncompahgre Peak and four others more than 14,000 feet in elevation, creating a barrier between Lake City and Ouray, crossed only by the USFS Alpine Byway, which requires 4WD vehicles or mountain bikes. From Lake City it's 50 miles south on Hwy 149 to Creede.

The Lake City/Hinsdale County Chamber of Commerce (☎ 970-944-2527, 800-569-1874), on Silver St in the center of town, also acts as the USFS and BLM visitors center, selling topo maps and offering free trail information. The chamber also sells booklets with maps of local fishing spots for $1. Web site: www.hinsdale-county.com

Slumgullion Slide

In AD 1270 a catastrophic earth flow moved almost 5 miles down the mountainside and dammed the Gunnison River to form Lake San Cristobal, Colorado's second-largest lake. A slower but more persistent flow began about 350 years ago and continues at rates of two to 20 feet per year. This active section of the slide, whose name comes from the yellowish mud's resemblance to the watery miner's stew, is either barren or features forests of crooked trees. It's best viewed in the morning from Windy Point Overlook, south of town off Hwy 149, at 10,600 feet. Another good view is from the top of Cannibal Plateau Trail (USFS Trail 464), the site where prospector Alferd Packer is said to have had his companions for dinner (see 'Colorado's Cannibal King'). The trailhead is below Slumgullion Campground, off Cebolla Creek Rd.

Alpine Loop Byway

After 16 miles up Hensen Creek, this unpaved byway becomes a rugged route over Engineer Pass suited only for Jeeps and mountain bikes headed to Ouray. Another part of the 4WD loop heads south along the

Colorado's Cannibal King

South of town near the junction of Hwy 149 and Lake County Rd 30, a simple plaque in memory of five unfortunate prospectors sits on the spot where they were murdered in 1874.

Ignoring Chief Ouray's warnings about attempting to reach the Breckenridge gold strike in winter weather, six men set out from near present-day Montrose in February, 1874. In April, after severe storms and extreme cold, only one of the men – a fellow named Alferd Packer – emerged near Lake City, without his companions. He told one of the first people he met, Alonso Hartman, of personal hardships and an injury that did not allow him to keep up with the rest of the party. Hartman observed that Packer appeared in remarkably good shape for a man who had endured near starvation. Other parts of his story soon unraveled: His companions were never heard from again, Packer had some of their belongings on his person and Utes found strips of human flesh on Packer's trail.

In June, the five victims were found by a *Harper's Weekly* photographer who noted that one victim had been shot in the back and the others' skulls were crushed. Nearby was a crude cabin where the accused cannibal sat out the storms.

In 1989, Packer's five victims were exhumed for a forensic examination that revealed battered skulls and defensive wounds on their arms and hands. Their remains were reinterred at the site.

Though he protested his innocence, Packer was eventually tried for murder, spent some time in jail and became a vegetarian. He died in 1907 and his grave can be found in Littleton, CO. He has since become somewhat of a legendary figure in the state, inspiring songs, cookbooks, an irreverent 'Alferd Packer Day' at the University of Colorado in Boulder and even a musical!

Lake Fork of the Gunnison River and crosses Cinnamon Pass to Silverton.

Fat-tire bikes are for rent at San Juan Mountain Bikes (☎ 970-944-2274), behind Lake City Market at the north end of town. Cannibal Outdoors (☎ 970-944-2559), 367 S Gunnison Ave, offers trips to Engineer Pass in an open truck. Rocky Mountain Jeep Rental (☎ 970-944-2262), at the Pleasant View Resort, rents Jeeps. The resort is at the south end of Lake City, on Hwy 149 (near mile marker 72).

Hiking & Backpacking

Alpine wildflowers are a prime attraction on the many summer trails in the area. West of Lake City and north of Hensen Creek is the **Big Blue Wilderness Area**, featuring many stunning peaks more than 13,000 feet, including two 14ers: Uncompahgre Peak and Wetterhorne Peak.

Northeast of Lake City, the **Powderhorn Wilderness Area** features the 4-mile-long BLM Trail 3030 to Powderhorn Lakes, crossing a huge alpine meadow loaded with wildflowers.

South of Lake San Cristobal, day hikes in the BLM's Alpine Loop Byway (see above) offer high altitude scenery and peak ascents – but the lower parts of most trails are shared with 4WD vehicles that disperse wildlife and disrupt the solitude.

Rafting

Local white-water enthusiasts enjoy the uncrowded Lake Fork of the Gunnison River stretching from High Bridge Creek, 8 miles north of Lake City, for 30 miles to the BLM Redbridge Campground, where the river is stilled as it enters Blue Mesa Reservoir. On the way, the river passes through the spectacular volcanic columns breached by the river to form **The Gate**, a giant notch visible for miles.

Cannibal Outdoors (☎ 970-944-2559) offers half-day rafting trips that are either scenic floats above The Gate or white-water thrills below it.

Other Activities

Lakeview Guides & Outfitters (☎ 970-944-2401) offers two-hour **horseback rides** for $32, or longer summer pack trips from its stables at Lake San Cristobal.

For **cross-country skiing** the Hinsdale Haute Route (☎ 970-944-2269) is a non-profit organization that maintains four yurts on the Divide between Lake City and Creede. Even novice skiers can enjoy the 2 miles of backcountry travel from Hwy 149 to an overnight stay at the first yurt. The yurts sleep up to eight people, have cooking facilities and are rented to groups for $100 for the first two nights, and $75 thereafter.

For **mountain biking** see Alpine Loop Byway, earlier.

Places to Stay

Camping Two options are available for camping in town. *Lake City Campground* (☎ 970-944-2668), on Bluff St north of 8th St, offers grassy tent sites, showers and laundry for $12, RV sites for $15. *Hensen Creek RV Park* (☎ 970-994-2274) has shower facilities and streamside tent sites for $18.

Dispersed camping is available on USFS lands along Hensen Creek immediately east of town. Free BLM riverside campsites are available at *The Gate*, 20 miles north next to Hwy 149, and at *Gateview* and *Redbridge* along Lake County Rd 25, which continues beside the river where Hwy 149 turns east from the river course.

Nine miles southwest of town immediately below Slumgullion Pass (elevation 11,361 feet), the USFS *Slumgullion Campground* offers 21 campsites for $8.

Additional primitive sites are available by continuing east on Cebolla Creek Rd, where rarely used trails enter La Garita Wilderness Area in the Gunnison National Forest's Cebolla Ranger District (☎ 970-641-0471).

Motels Budget rooms cost $38/48 single/double at *Matterhorn Mountain Lodge* (☎ 970-944-2210, 800-779-8028), on Bluff St on the west side of town. Rooms start at $59/49 (summer/winter) at *Silver Spur*

Motel (☎ 970-944-2231, 800-499-9701, 301 Gunnison Ave), at the corner of 3rd St and Hwy 149. The *Crystal Lodge* (☎ 970-944-2201), 2½ miles south of town on Hwy 149, offers lodge rooms for $60 and cottages for $110 (less in winter). Singles/doubles at the motel-style *Quiet Moose Lodge* (☎ 970-944-2415), on Hwy 149 N at the north end of town, cost $62/72 in summer, $49/55 in winter and feature vaulted ceilings. Rooms in the lower block have balconies and the best mountain views.

B&Bs Open year-round, the restored 1878 *Cinnamon Inn* (☎ 970-944-2641, 800-337-2335, 426 Gunnison Ave) offers comfortable rooms with Victorian antique furnishings. Rooms with shared bath cost $90; from $95 with private bath. Suites range in price from $110 to $140.
Web site: www.lakecityco.com

The *Old Carson Inn* (☎ 970-944-2511, 800-294-0608) is a log inn set in a secluded forest along the Alpine Loop. Each of the seven antique-filled guest rooms are named for area mines and cost from $98 to $128.
Web site: www.oldcarsoninn.com

Places to Eat

The *Mother Lode* (☎ 970-944-5044, 310 Gunnison Ave) offers substantial breakfasts and plentiful lunch and dinner choices. A good lunchtime spot is *Charlie P's Mountain Harvest* (☎ 970-944-2332, 951 N Hwy 149), at the north end of town. It proudly proclaims 'from meat lovers to tree huggers, we have something for everyone,' and it's pretty much right.

The *Crystal Lodge Restaurant* (see Motels, above) features impeccable gourmet food at affordable prices.

OURAY

Pronounced 'you-ray,' Ouray (population 800; elevation 7760 feet) is billed as the 'Switzerland of America.' As the area's favorite son David Lavender wrote of Ouray's spectacular natural setting, 'the best way to see it is to stretch out flat on your back.' Imposing alpine peaks leave barely a quarter mile of valley floor in town. The biggest attractions here are the Ouray Hot Springs, hiking and Jeep trails throughout the surrounding mountains and the scenic 'Million Dollar Highway.'

Ouray is named after the famed chief of the Utes who maintained peace by relinquishing his people's traditional lands to the hordes of miners that invaded the San Juan Mountains. Founded during the silver boom as Uncompahgre City in 1875, Ouray enjoyed a second spurt of activity following Thomas Walsh's discovery of gold in 1896 – his Camp Bird Mine extracted $27 million in ore.

TNM&O buses pass through Ouray northbound for Montrose and southbound for Durango. By car, Ouray is on Hwy 550, 34 miles south of Montrose and 80 miles north of Durango.

The visitors information center (☎ 970-325-4746, 800-228-1876), near the hot springs, has plenty of information on Jeep tours and hiking in the Mt Sneffels and Uncompahgre Wilderness Areas, as well as a walking tour map of Ouray's historic buildings. Web site: www.ouraycolorado.com

Buckskin Trading Co (☎ 970-324-4044), 636 Main St, has books on local history and guides to hiking, rock climbing and mountain biking in the area.

Ouray Hot Springs

Open year-round, Ouray Hot Springs (☎ 970-325-4638), 1200 Main St, offers a 250-foot-by-150-foot swimming pool at 80°F to 85°F, plus a soaking pool at 95°F and a hot pool at 100°F. It's open 10 am to 10 pm daily Memorial Day to Labor Day, and noon to 9 pm the rest of the year. Admission costs $7.

Hiking

Visitors should not miss **Cascade Falls**, a short walk east up 8th Ave. From the USFS Amphitheatre Campground (see below), the **Cascade Trail** (closed to bikes) goes to Chief Ouray Mine and upper Cascade Falls, offering incredible views of Ouray during the last half mile as the trail crosses exposed rock faces. The hike takes two to three hours.

A longer, more strenuous route climbs the **Horsethief Trail** from north of the hot

springs, across US 550 to the Bridge of the Heavens Overlook Area, offering spectacular views. This area is prime bighorn sheep habitat.

Mountain Biking

Bicyclists can follow the Uncompahgre River for 10 miles north to Ridgway on the easy Ouray County Rd 17 that traces the abandoned Rio Grande Southern narrow-gauge railroad bed. The route begins as Oak St on the west side of the Uncompahgre River, reached by the 7th Ave Bridge.

Ice Climbing

The owners of the Ouray Victorian Inn spearheaded the establishment of the **Ouray Ice Park**, the world's first dedicated ice-climbing area. By running pipes from mountain streams they have managed to create some 50 routes. Access is free. For information, guide service or instruction, contact the Ouray Victorian Inn (☎ 800-846-8729), 50 3rd Ave.

Jeep Tours

Old mine trails connect Silverton, Telluride and Lake City with Ouray on perilous routes amid the 14,000-foot San Juan Mountain summits, aerial ore trams and 19th-century mining ghost towns. The 4WD routes are often snowbound well into June. It's best to leave the driving to someone with experience while you enjoy the scenery. Since 1959, San Juan Scenic Jeep Tours (☎ 970-325-4444, 800-325-4385), 824 Main St, has provided specially modified open-top 4WD tours.

Places to Stay & Eat

A glacial headwall forms the backdrop to 30 USFS campsites at *Amphitheatre Campground* (☎ 877-444-6777), more than 700 feet above Ouray and about 1 mile from the south end of town on US 550. The steep and narrow campground road limits trailers to only a few sites. Campsites cost $12 plus the reservation fee of $8.65.

Across the river from town, the *4J+1+1* (☎ 970-325-4418, 790 Oak St) offers shaded tent sites next to the river from $16, with clean showers and a coin-op laundry. It's open mid-May to mid-October.

The friendly **Ouray Victorian Inn** (☎ 970-325-7222, 800-846-8729, 50 3rd Ave) offers a variety of accommodations including cabins, town homes, rooms with kitchenettes, and a mini-ranch. Motel rates range from $45 to $95.

Web site: www.ouraylodging.com

The **Historic Western Hotel** (☎ 970-325-4645, 210 7th Ave) has restored Victorian-style rooms from $35 to $95. The family-run **Ouray Cottage Motel** (☎ 970-325-4370), at the corner of 4th and Main Sts, has knotty-pine doubles for $60 in summer. A nice feature is the telescope pointed toward the nearby cliffs frequented by bighorn sheep.

The pleasant **Box Canyon Lodge & Hot Springs** (☎ 970-325-4981, 800-327-5080, 45 3rd Ave) has attractive motel-style rooms and features four outdoor redwood hot tubs overlooking the mountains. Rates start at $65 to $100, depending on the season. Another place with in-house hot springs is **The Wiesbaden** (☎ 970-325-4347), at the corner of 6th Ave and 5th St. In addition to outdoor tubs and spa, it features a natural vaporcave. Nightly rates start at $120.

A romantic B&B option is **The Christmas House** (☎ 970-325-4992, 888-325-8627, 310 Main St), an 1889 Victorian home featuring private whirlpool tubs in each of the five suites. Rates range from $80 to $150 a night.

The handsomely restored **St Elmo Hotel** (☎ 970-325-4951, 426 Main St) opened in 1898 and offers nine B&B rooms with private baths and period furnishings starting at $100 in summer, less the rest of the year. In 1886 the in-house **Bon Ton Restaurant** (☎ 970-325-4951, 426 Main St) was considered the best establishment in Ouray and still is one of the top spots.

The Groundskeeper Coffee House (☎ 970-325-0550, 524 Main St) has local topographic maps laminated in the table tops for pre-hike study while you sip an espresso over breakfast. Next door **Mountain Garden Restaurant** (520 Main St) offers home-style breakfasts. A good sandwich spot for lunch is **Timberline Deli** (☎ 970-325-4958, 803 Main St).

TELLURIDE

With 300 inches of snow annually, a 3000-foot vertical drop to the ski lifts in town, a dramatic box-canyon setting and a rich mining history, Telluride (population 2500; elevation 8750 feet) is one of Colorado's most popular ski towns. Ever since Telluride was designated a National Historic Landmark in 1964 – well before skiing arrived – conscientious citizens have strictly followed preservation guidelines. Many newer buildings follow Victorian designs so closely that it is sometimes difficult to tell the modern from historic construction.

Orientation

Colorado Ave, also known as Main St, is where you'll find most of the restaurants, bars and shops. The town's small size means you can get everywhere on foot, so you can leave your car at the intercept parking lot at the south end of Mahoney Dr (near the visitors center) or wherever you're staying.

From town you can reach the ski mountain via two lifts and the gondola. The latter also links Telluride with Mountain Village, the true base for the Telluride Ski Area. Located 7 miles from town along Hwy 145, Mountain Village is a 20-minute drive east on Hwy 145, but only 12 minutes away by gondola, which is free for foot passengers.

Ajax Peak, a glacial headwall, rises behind the town to form the end of the U-shaped valley that contains Telluride. To the right (south) of Ajax Peak, Colorado's highest waterfall, Bridal Veil Falls, cascades 365 feet; a switchback trail leads to a restored Victorian powerhouse atop the falls. To the south, Mt Wilson reaches 14,246 feet among a group of rugged peaks that form the Lizard Head Wilderness Area.

Information

Telluride Visitor Services (☎ 970-728-3041, 888-288-7360), 666 W Colorado Ave at the west entrance to town, operates a 24-hour visitors information center complete with restrooms and ATM. The center is staffed 9 am to 5 pm weekdays in winter, until 7 pm daily in summer. In the same building is Telluride Central Reservations (☎ 888-355-8743), which handles accommodations and festival tickets. Online information about lodging, restaurants, skiing and other activities can be found at www.telluride.com and www.telluridemm.com.

Telluride Sports (☎ 970-728-4477), 150 W Colorado Ave, has topo and USFS maps, sporting supplies and information.

The Bank of Telluride (☎ 970-728-2000), 238 E Colorado Ave, offers ATMs at the bank and at the visitors center.

Post offices are at 101 E Colorado Ave and the corner of Willow St and Pacific Ave; the zip code is 81435. Mail Boxes Etc (☎ 970-728-8111, fax 970-728-8128), 398 W Colorado Ave, offers both fax and postal services.

Bookworks (☎ 970-728-0700), 191 S Pine St, is the town's biggest bookstore. Between the Covers (☎ 970-728-4504), 224 W Colorado Ave, offers a good selection of regional history and local maps and guides, plus espresso drinks.

The Washateria, 107 W Columbia Ave, is a coin-op laundry. Hot/cold showers are $1.50/free at the Town Park swimming pool.

Telluride Medical Center (☎ 970-728-3848) is at 500 W Pacific Ave.

Skiing

Telluride Ski & Golf Company (☎ 970-728-7533, 888-288-7360) can answer questions about the downhill ski area. Daily adult/child lift tickets cost $61/33 from mid-December to mid-April – before mid-December tickets cost $40/22. For a snow report call ☎ 970-728-7425.

Web site: www.telluride-ski.com

Public cross-country trails in Town Park facilitate Nordic skiing along the San Miguel River and the Telluride Valley floor west of town. Instruction and rentals are available from the Nordic Center (☎ 970-728-1114).

Experienced skiers will appreciate San Juan Hut Systems' (☎ 970-626-3033) five crude huts linking Telluride with Ouray, separated by backcountry USFS roads and trails 5 to 7 miles in length. Ski between

The hills are alive around Telluride.

MASON FLORENCE

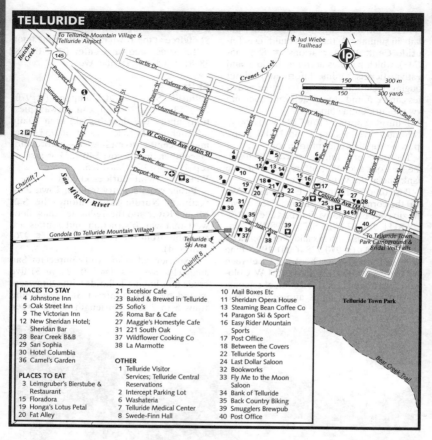

TELLURIDE

PLACES TO STAY
4 Johnstone Inn
5 Oak Street Inn
9 The Victorian Inn
12 New Sheridan Hotel;
   Sheridan Bar
28 Bear Creek B&B
29 San Sophia
30 Hotel Columbia
36 Camel's Garden

PLACES TO EAT
3 Leimgruber's Bierstube &
   Restaurant
15 Floradora
19 Honga's Lotus Petal
20 Fat Alley

21 Excelsior Cafe
23 Baked & Brewed in Telluride
25 Sofio's
26 Roma Bar & Cafe
27 Maggie's Homestyle Cafe
31 221 South Oak
37 Wildflower Cooking Co
38 La Marmotte

OTHER
1 Telluride Visitor
   Services; Telluride Central
   Reservations
2 Intercept Parking Lot
6 Washateria
7 Telluride Medical Center
8 Swede-Finn Hall

10 Mail Boxes Etc
11 Sheridan Opera House
13 Steaming Bean Coffee Co
14 Paragon Ski & Sport
16 Easy Rider Mountain
   Sports
17 Post Office
18 Between the Covers
22 Telluride Sports
24 Last Dollar Saloon
32 Bookworks
33 Fly Me to the Moon
   Saloon
34 Bank of Telluride
35 Back Country Biking
39 Smugglers Brewpub
40 Post Office

huts or establish a base camp to stage day trips into the Mt Sneffels Wilderness Area. You can rent the huts – each provided with eight bunks and cooking facilities – for $22 per person.

Web site: www.sanjuanhuts.com

Mountain Biking

An easy smooth gravel **River Trail** connects Town Park with the Coonskin ski-lift area and continues to Hwy 145 for a total trail distance of about 2 miles. If you want a bit more of a workout, continue up **Mill Creek Trail**, west of the Texaco near where the River Trail

ends – after the initial climb the trail follows the contour and ends at the Jud Wiebe Trail (hikers only) where cyclists turn back.

At the east end of Pine St, **Bear Creek** is an up-and-back ride that climbs 1000 feet in a little more than 2 miles to reach a tiered waterfall.

From Ophir, site of a former railroad loop 7 miles south on Hwy 145, you can follow the **Old Railroad Grade** along the South Fork of the San Miguel River downhill for 8 miles to Ilium where the Ilium Trail returns to the junction of Hwy 145 into Telluride. At Ophir take the USFS Rd 625 to the historic power plant site at Ames, turn left and cross a bridge before continuing on switchbacks to another bridge above the falls that leads to the old railroad grade.

Consider the beauty of taking a week-long backcountry bike tour without a load of camping gear, guides or support vehicles. Riding in its purest form is offered by San Juan Hut Systems (☎ 970-626-3033), where you pick up the keys to huts, stocked with food and sleeping bags, about 35 miles apart over a 205-mile route from Telluride to Moab, Utah. For $395, riders get route descriptions and maps to the huts, plus three meals a day for seven days of remote Colorado Plateau cycling.
Web site: www.sanjuanhuts.com

Easy Rider Mountain Sports (☎ 970-728-4734), 101 W Colorado Ave, is the town's main cycling shop, and has rentals, repairs and sales. You can also try Telluride Sports (see Information, earlier) and Back Country Biking on San Juan Ave. Paragon Ski & Sport (☎ 970-728-4525) has stores at 217 W Colorado Ave in Telluride and the Granita complex in Mountain Village. The complete guide to mountain biking around Telluride is Dave Rich's *Tellurides,* available at the above shops.

Hiking & Backpacking

The **Jud Wiebe Trail**, a 2.7-mile loop from town, offers views after a 1300-foot climb and is the only trail near town dedicated to foot travel. Take Oak St north to Tomboy Rd and continue to the gated road on your left to reach the signed trailhead. The return portion of the loop ends at the north end of Aspen St.

The Bear Creek Trail is slightly more than 2 miles but ascends 1040 feet to a beautiful cascading waterfall. From this trail you can access the strenuous Wasatch Trail, a 12-mile loop that heads west across the mountains to **Bridal Veil Falls**. The Bear Creek trailhead is at the south end of Pine St, across the San Miguel River.

It's a little more than 2 miles to Bridal Veil Falls on the switchback road that gets heavy Jeep traffic to Silverton by midday. Backpackers will find plenty of solitude amid the

14,000-foot summits in nearby Lizard Head and Mt Sneffels Wilderness Areas.

Telluride Sports (see Information, earlier) has topo maps and USFS Uncompahgre Forest maps. If you are traveling through Montrose, stop by the Montrose Public Lands Office (☎ 970-240-5300), 2505 S Townsend Ave, to pick up maps and information.

Fishing

Although the San Miguel River is no Gold Medal fishery, it does offer some excellent dry fly-fishing for rainbow and brown trout from mid-June to December. A DOW fishing easement is less than a mile south of Placerville. Telluride Sports (see Information, earlier) has all the gear you will need and houses Telluride Flyfishers, which offers guides and instruction.

Special Events

Something is going on just about every weekend in Telluride – from the laid-back **Steps to Awareness Festival** in May to intimate gourmet experiences with noted sommeliers at June's **Wine Festival**. Four days of outdoor adventure and environmental films and filmmakers are featured at **Mountainfilm** over Memorial Day weekend.

The **Telluride Bluegrass Festival** is a major late-June event attracting 10,000 visitors. The **Telluride Jazz Celebration** is for one weekend in August, and in late August fungiphiles sprout up at the **Telluride Mushroom Festival**.

The **Telluride Film Festival** over Labor Day weekend offers free open-air films along with many national and international premieres. Blues musicians take the stage while microbrews dominate the stands during the **Brews & Blues Festival** in mid-September.

Places to Stay

Aside from the campgrounds, there really are no cheap places to stay. If you arrive in the off-season (late spring and early fall) you may enjoy considerably lower tariffs. Telluride Central Reservations (☎ 888-288-7360) can provide information on lower-rate periods and ski-free packages.

Camping Right in Telluride Town Park *Telluride Town Park Campground* (☎ 970-728-3071) offers 42 campsites, showers and swimming and tennis from mid-May to October. Developed campsites cost $12 and five primitive sites cost $10, all on a first-come, first-served basis.

Two campgrounds in the Uncompahgre National Forest (☎ 970-327-4261) are within 15 miles of Telluride on Hwy 145 and cost $14. *Sunshine* offers 15 first-come, first-served campsites; facilities at *Matterhorn* include showers and electrical hookups for some of the 27 campsites.

Hotels The *Oak Street Inn* (☎ 970-728-3383, 134 N Oak St) offers the least expensive rooms in town. Spartan rooms with shared bath cost from $42 throughout the year, except during holidays and festivals. The *Victorian Inn* (☎ 970-728-6601, 401 W Pacific Ave) hardly looks Victorian, however it is conveniently close to the Oak St lift and gondola. Doubles start at $73 off-season, and $135 in the peak.

The historic *New Sheridan Hotel* (☎ 970-728-4351, 800-200-1891, 231 W Colorado Ave) replaced the original 1881 hotel in 1895 and has continued to provide lodging ever since. Regular winter rates range from $90 to $275.
Web site: www.newsheridan.com

If you're going to shell out this kind of cash, you might want to consider *Hotel Columbia* (☎ 970-728-0660, 800-201-9505, 300 W San Juan Ave), right across the street from the gondola. Each of the hotel's 21 rooms has a balcony, fireplace and a mountain view. The food and service is excellent. A rooftop hot tub and a library are other nice details. Doubles range from $175 in summer, $225 to $280 in winter. Visit its Web site online at www.columbiatelluride.com. Nearby *The San Sophia* (☎ 970-728-3001, 800-537-4781, 330 W Pacific Ave) is another elegant high-end option. Doubles, including breakfast and après-ski snacks, start at $134 in summer, $195 in winter. Visit www.sansophia.com.

Camel's Garden (☎ 970-728-9300, 888-772-2635, 250 W San Juan) is a modern and luxurious choice located at the base of the gondola. It offers hotel rooms from $230 to $485, and one/two-bedroom condos from $485/595.
Web site: www.camelsgarden.com

B&Bs Right in town the pleasant *Bear Creek B&B* (☎ 970-728-6681, 800-338-7064, 221 E Colorado Ave) features tastefully done rooms, a steam room, sauna and remarkable rooftop hot tub. Winter rates range from $127 to $192.
Web site: www.telluridemm.com/bearcrek/html

The 1891 *Johnstone Inn* (☎ 970-728-3315, 800-752-1901, 403 W Colorado Ave) is another nicely redone Victorian home. It charges $80 in the off-season, rates rise to $140 most of the winter.
Web site: www.johnstoneinn.com

Places to Eat

One affordable standout is the popular *Baked & Brewed in Telluride* (☎ 970-728-4775, 127 S Fir St), which offers baked goods, pizza, delicious daily specials, home-brewed beer and a nice porch from which to catch the morning rays while enjoying breakfast. *Wildflower Cooking Co* (☎ 970-728-8887), right at the base of the gondola, does great freshly baked treats for breakfast and lunch. If you're just looking for a caffeine fix, *The Steaming Bean Coffee Co* (☎ 970-728-0220, 221 W Colorado Ave) has fine brewed coffee, espresso and specialty coffee drinks.

Serving up inexpensive lunches, as well as cheap breakfasts, is *Maggie's Homestyle Cafe* (☎ 970-728-3334, 217 E Colorado Ave). *Sofio's* (☎ 970-728-4882, 110 E Colorado Ave) is recommended for breakfasts, Mexican specialties, smoothies and espresso drinks. Another budget option is *Fat Alley* (☎ 970-728-3985, 122 S Oak St), which has Southern-style barbecue and some good veggie choices.

The *Excelsior Cafe* (☎ 970-728-4250, 200 W Colorado Ave) does pricey breakfasts and Italian lunches and dinners. *Roma Bar & Cafe* (☎ 970-728-3669, 113 E Colorado Ave) is another good spot for fine Italian and pizza.

Honga's Lotus Petal (☎ 970-728-5134, *133 S Oak St*) has become a favorite restaurant for its well-prepared Asian dishes. *Floradora* (☎ 970-728-3888, *103 W Colorado Ave*) has been around since 1974. The Mexican food is good and prices are pretty reasonable.

Nearer the top-end is *Leimgruber's Bierstube & Restaurant* (☎ 970-728-4663, *573 W Pacific*) where Paulaner beer is on draft and meat lovers can stuff themselves on German fare and wild American game. Located in a handsomely restored home, *221 South Oak* (☎ 970-728-9507) is also a good place to splurge on lunch or dinner. Wednesday is 'martini day.'

The seasonal *La Marmotte* (☎ 970-728-6232, *150 W San Juan Ave*), in the historic masonry ice house, offers a nice selection of hors d'oeuvres and gourmet French dinner entrees.

Entertainment
Most of the historic *Sheridan Bar* (☎ 970-728-3911, *231 W Colorado Ave*) survived the waning mining fortunes, while the Sheridan Hotel was busy selling off chandeliers and finely carved furnishings to help pay the heating bills. These days overdressed visitors occupy stools and chat about upcoming film releases next to the occasional old-timer who hasn't been driven out by Telluride's escalating property values.

Two watering holes popular with locals are *The Last Dollar Saloon* (☎ 970-728-4800, *100 E Colorado Ave*), where on cold nights you can sip whiskey in front of the fireplace, and *Swede-Finn Hall* (☎ 970-728-2085, *427 W Pacific*), which has billiards and a fine beer selection.

Smugglers Brewpub (☎ 970-728-0919), at the corner of San Juan Ave and Pine St, sells microbrews and grilled foods.

For live music, the best place in town is *Fly Me to the Moon Saloon* (☎ 970-728-6666, *132 E Colorado*).

The Telluride Repertory Company presents live theater productions and movies at the *Sheridan Opera House* (☎ 970-728-6363), built in 1914.

Getting There & Around
Commuter aircraft serve the mesa-top Telluride Airport (☎ 970-728-5051), 5 miles east of town on Hwy 145. If weather is poor flights may be diverted to Montrose, 65 miles north.

United Express offers daily service to Denver year-round, while America West Express has flights to Phoenix, Arizona. In ski season Montrose Regional Airport (☎ 970-249-3203) has direct flights to and from Denver (on United), Houston and Newark, New Jersey (Continental), Dallas (American) and Phoenix (America West).

Shuttles from the Telluride Airport to town or Mountain Village cost $8. Shuttles between the Montrose Airport and Telluride cost $32. Contact Telluride Express (☎ 970-728-6000, 888-212-8294) or Mountain Limo (☎ 970-728-9606, 888-546-6894).

For car rental, National and Budget both have airport locations.

SILVERTON
An historic mining town 9318 feet up in the San Juan Mountains, Silverton (population 400) is a throwback to another era – the entire town was designated a National Historic Landmark in 1966. Silver and gold miners invaded the area after the Brunot Agreement removed the Ute bands in 1873. Mining activity peaked in the early 1900s, but since 1991, when the Sunnyside mine closed, the economy has been dependent on the tourists riding the seasonal Durango & Silverton Narrow Gauge Railroad from Durango. (See Durango, later, for more on this scenic steam train ride.)

Between Silverton and Ouray, US 550 is known as the **Million Dollar Highway** because the roadbed fill contains valuable ore. The route passes many old mine headframes and some extraordinary alpine scenery. It is a dangerous road in rain and snow, so take extra care.

A visitors center and museum (☎ 970-387-5654, 800-752-4494), south of town at the junction of Greene St and US 550, is open 9 am to 5 pm daily (hours are shorter in winter).

Web site: www.silverton.org

San Juan County Museum

The old county jail, at the corner of Greene and 15th Sts by the turgid waters of Cement Creek, still has bars on the upper-floor cells and now houses the county museum (☎ 970-387-5838) featuring displays on mining and the railroad. The museum is the starting point for a walking tour of the historic district and offers a free map and guide. It's open 9 am to 5 pm daily Memorial Day to early October. Admission costs $2.50; children under 12 free.

Jeep Tours

Old mine roads lead to remote workings above the timberline in many directions around Silverton. A difficult route over Bear Pass leads to Telluride, while the Alpine Loop Byway (see Lake City, earlier), an assemblage of rugged 4WD routes, leads to either Ouray or Lake City. Information about the Alpine Loop Byway is available from the visitors center.

Places to Stay & Eat

Two miles west of town on US 550, USFS Rd 585 leads about 4 miles to **South Mineral Campground**, with 26 USFS campsites available for $10 on a first-come, first-served basis.

The Silverton Hostel (☎ 970-387-0115, 1025 Blair St), a restored 1911 grocery store and bordello, is open year-round. Dorm beds in summer are $10/12 members/nonmembers; $24/28 for a private room.

At the south end of town **Triangle Motel** (☎ 970-387-5780, 864 Greene St) offers comfortable singles/doubles for $50/60 in summer, $25/35 in winter. Nearby the **Prospector Motel** (☎ 970-387-5466, 1015 Greene St) offers similar rates, but it's only open early March to late November.

One of the most interesting and enjoyable places to stay in town is the Victorian **Teller House Hotel** (☎ 970-387-5423, 800-342-4338, 1250 Greene St), where in summer rooms start at $60. The place gives you a real feel for what a late-19th-century boarding house was like.

The 1898 **Inn of the Rockies** (☎ 970-387-5336, 800-267-5336, 220 E Tenth St) has nine unique rooms furnished with Victorian antiques. Its New Orleans–inspired breakfasts and baked treats merit special mention. Rates range from $70 to $150.
Web site: www.innoftherockies.com

Fully restored, the top-end 1902 **Wyman Hotel** (☎ 970-387-5372, 800-609-7845, 1371 Greene St) has beautiful rooms from $95 to $180 in summer; $80 to $160 otherwise. Rates include a full breakfast, afternoon tea and homemade cookies. It's open most of the year, usually closing in March and April – call ahead to check.

Antique furnishings are featured in the imposing 1882 **Grand Imperial Hotel** (☎ 970-387-5527, 800-341-3340, 1219 Greene St), open year-round. Rooms range from $59 to $150, but fall to around half that price between November and April. The Imperial's **Gold King** dining room is worth a visit.

At 7:30 am locals begin dropping in at **Tiki's Place** (☎ 970-387-5658, 1124 Greene St) for good American breakfasts. The interesting **Brown Bear** (☎ 970-387-5630, 1129 Greene St) serves tasty food and the staff is friendly.

Eclectic items hang from the ceiling at **Handlebars** (☎ 970-387-5395, 117 E 13th St), but the breaded and fried Rocky Mountain oysters no longer hang from the bull. It's open in the rail season and offers nightly entertainment.

Getting There & Away

TNM&O buses stop in front of Tiki's Place at 1124 Greene St.

One-way train tickets to Durango or Weminuche Wilderness trailheads on the Durango & Silverton Narrow Gauge Railroad (see Durango, below), as available, can be purchased from the 1882 Silverton Depot (☎ 970-387-5416), open early May to late October. A bus ($15) operated by Durango Transportation (☎ 800-626-2066) leaves for Durango several times daily and allows passengers to board the train back to Silverton.

DURANGO

On the Animas River, Durango (population 15,000; elevation 6512 feet) is a year-round destination for travelers, many of whom flock to ride the steam-driven Durango & Silverton Narrow Gauge Railroad – an especially scenic trip in the colorful fall season. Outdoor enthusiasts enjoy mountain biking and rafting in summer and skiing in winter.

Durango was the brainchild of General William Jackson Palmer, founder of the Denver & Rio Grande (D&RG) Railroad that reached the Animas River in 1881 as it progressed toward the mining camp at Silverton to the north. Durango soon overshadowed a small town immediately north called Animas City, founded in 1876 to serve the miners.

Earlier inhabitants of the area included Ancestral Puebloans – the Falls Creek Caves north of town are among the most important excavation sites for the Basket Maker II period (AD 1 to about AD 500).

Orientation

Most visitor facilities are along Main Ave, including the 1882 D&SNGR Depot (at the south end). Motels are mostly north of the town center. A walking tour guide to Durango's central area, listed on the National Register of Historic Places, is available from the visitors information center. Consider using the trolley (see Getting Around, later) and walking through this area instead of spending $7 to park near the depot.

Animas Overlook has a wheelchair-accessible trail and bathrooms on a mesa 5 miles northwest of Durango (reached from Main Ave by turning west on 25th St to La Plata County Rd 204).

Information

The visitors information center (☎ 970-247-0312, 800-525-8855), 111 S Camino del Rio, south of town at the Santa Rita exit from US 550, offers lots of information on accommodations, restaurants and outdoor activities. It's open 8 am to 6 pm Monday to Saturday (until 5 pm in winter) and from 10 am to 4 pm on Sunday.
Web site: www.durango.org

The San Juan–Rio Grande National Forest Headquarters and BLM office

(☎ 970-247-4874), 15 Burnett Court, offers camping and hiking information and forest maps. It's about a half mile west on US 160 from Camino del Rio; look for the sign reading, 'San Juan Public Land Center,' and turn right there. It's open 8 am to 5 pm weekdays.

First National Bank of Durango (☎ 970-247-3020), 259 W 9th St, has an ATM. Another ATM is available at the City Market at the corner of 9th and Camino Del Rio, which also offers Western Union service.

The post office is at 222 W 8th St; the zip code is 81302. Free Internet access can be found at the library, 118 E 2nd Ave at 12th St. There is a nominal charge to get on-line at the Steaming Bean Coffee Co (☎ 970-385-7901), 915 Main Ave.

Maria's Bookshop (☎ 970-247-1438), 960 Main Ave, is a good general bookstore, open 9 am to 8:30 pm Monday to Saturday; 10 am to 5 pm Sunday. Waldenbooks, beside the D&SNGR Depot, stocks countless regional titles, while overflowing shelves of used books are available at Southwest Book Trader (☎ 970-247-8479), 175 E 5th St.

North Main Coin Laundry (☎ 970-247-9915), 2980 N Main Ave, offers showers for $3. College Plaza Laundromat (☎ 970-247-8255), 509 E 8th Ave, has both coin-op and drop-off services.

Mercy Medical Center (☎ 970-247-4311), 375 E Park Ave, has outpatient and 24-hour emergency care.

Durango & Silverton Narrow Gauge Railroad

The 45 miles of spur track following the scenic Animas River Gorge to Silverton, and the longer Antonito to Chama section, are all that remain of the extensive system of the narrow-gauge D&RG Western Railroad that carried passengers and freight through the Colorado Mountains.

Riding the steam-driven D&SNGR (or a bike) is a great way to visit the isolated mining community of Silverton. Trains to Silverton run early May to late October – in the peak summer months four trains depart from Durango between 7:30 and 9:45 am.

Travel time to Silverton is about 3¼ hours, and passengers spend at least two hours there before reboarding the train for the trip home.

The historic train has a 1st-class parlor car, enclosed coaches and open gondola cars for the cinders-and-ash crowd. Some passengers may elect to layover in Silverton and experience the peace and quiet after the last train departs. The train also stops at Elk Park on the Colorado Trail near Molas Pass.

Touring bicyclists might consider purchasing a one-way ticket (available on a limited basis) and paying to check the bicycle as baggage to Silverton. Because the trains rarely have unoccupied seats, layovers and flag stops require prior arrangement with the Durango ticket office.

With prior arrangements, the train will drop-off at Cascade Canyon, which offers backcountry access on USFS Trails 675 and 504 to Columbine Pass in the Weminuche Wilderness Area.

The D&SNGR ticket office (☎ 970-247-2733, 888-872-4607), 479 Main Ave, urges passengers to purchase tickets at least two weeks prior to their trips. Roundtrip fares are $53/27 adults/children under 12; $88 for the 1st-class parlor car. Other trains that only go 26 miles to a turnaround at Cascade Canyon operate in summer evenings (subject to change), as well as in the late spring and winter (come well dressed!) when trains do not serve Silverton. These trips include a stop for passengers to wander next to the river for an hour and cost $45/22.50 adults/children. Fees include admission to Durango's **Railroad Museum** and the Silverton Freight Yard Museum. Web site: www.durangotrain.com

Bicycling

An easy road ride circles for either 15 or 30 miles around the Animas Valley, north of Durango's 32nd St. On the east side of the Animas River, take La Plata County Rd 250 for 15 miles north to Baker's Bridge – site of the cliff-jumping scene in the film *Butch Cassidy and the Sundance Kid*. Return by crossing the bridge, proceeding around the KOA camp to follow the Hwy 550 shoulder

south to Hermosa, then turn right onto La Plata County Rd 203. This takes you by Trimbles Hot Springs and back to town. The 15-mile route also starts on County Rd 250 but turns left earlier at County Rd 252 (Trimble Lane), crosses Hwy 550 and turns left again on County Rd 203.

Off-road riders can set off for the Animas Overlook, about 5 miles from the corner of 25th St and Main Ave. A 5-mile loop climbs to the mesa top of Animas City Mountain from the trailhead at the north end of W 4th Ave. Near the Durango Mountain Resort ski area there are a number of trail options, including the 8-mile Worlds Cross-Country Course, which you can access via its chairlifts.

Find out about other rides at the San Juan–Rio Grande National Forest Headquarters and BLM office (see Information, earlier), or at Hassle Free Sports (☎ 970-259-3874, 800-835-3800), 2615 Main Ave, which offers bike repairs and rentals. For guided tours, contact Southwest Adventures (☎ 970-259-0370), at 12th St and Camino del Rio, or Durango Single Track Tours (☎ 888-336-8687).

Rafting & Kayaking

Rivers West (☎ 970-259-5077), 520 Main Ave opposite the train depot, offers a one-hour introduction to rafting on the Animas River for $15 and two-hour trips for $26. More adventurous rafters can combine a shuttle trip to Silverton on the D&SNGR train with a trip on the upper Animas. Mountain Waters Rafting (☎ 970-259-4191, 800-748-2507), 108 W College Ave, and Durango Rivertrippers (☎ 970-259-0289, 800-292-2885), 720 Main Ave, offer similar trips.

Horseback Riding & Pack Trips

Colorado Mountain Holidays (☎ 970-375-1250, 877-600-2656) offers a variety of backcountry pack trips in the San Juan and Rio Grande National Forests. Visit online at www.colomntholiday.com. Rapp Guides & Packers (☎ 970-247-8923, fax 970-247-1255) is a highly popular local horseback outfitter and also offers winter snowmobile tours.

COLORADO

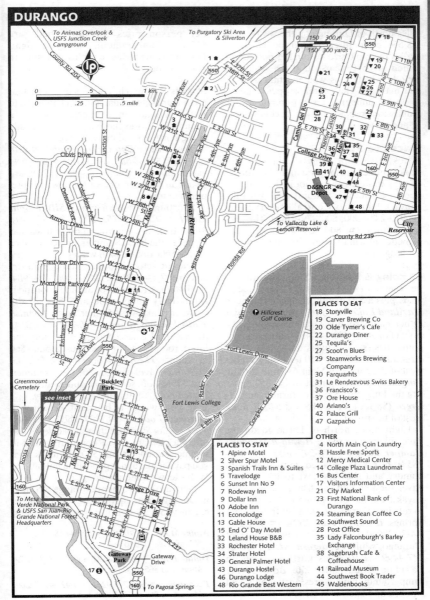

DURANGO

To Animas Overlook &
USFS Junction Creek
Campground

To Purgatory Ski Area
& Silverton

To Vallecito Lake &
Lemon Reservoir

City
Reservoir

Hillcrest
Golf Course

Fort Lewis College

Greenmount
Cemetery

Buckley
Park

see inset

To Mesa
Verde National Park
& USFS San Juan–Rio
Grande National Forest
Headquarters

Gateway
Park

Gateway
Drive

To Pagosa Springs

D&SNGR
Depot

PLACES TO EAT
18 Storyville
19 Carver Brewing Co
20 Olde Tymer's Cafe
22 Durango Diner
25 Tequila's
27 Scoot'n Blues
29 Steamworks Brewing
Company
30 Farquarhts
31 Le Rendezvous Swiss Bakery
36 Francisco's
37 Ore House
40 Ariano's
42 Palace Grill
47 Gazpacho

OTHER
4 North Main Coin Laundry
8 Hassle Free Sports
12 Mercy Medical Center
14 College Plaza Laundromat
16 Bus Center
17 Visitors Information Center
21 City Market
23 First National Bank of
Durango
26 Steaming Bean Coffee Co
26 Southwest Sound
28 Post Office
35 Lady Falconburgh's Barley
Exchange
38 Sagebrush Cafe &
Coffeehouse
41 Railroad Museum
44 Southwest Book Trader
45 Waldenbooks

PLACES TO STAY
1 Alpine Motel
2 Silver Spur Motel
3 Spanish Trails Inn & Suites
5 Travelodge
6 Sunset Inn No 9
7 Rodeway Inn
9 Dollar Inn
10 Adobe Inn
11 Econolodge
13 Gable House
15 End O' Day Motel
32 Leland House B&B
33 Rochester Hotel
34 Strater Hotel
39 General Palmer Hotel
43 Durango Hostel
46 Durango Lodge
48 Rio Grande Best Western

Swimming

Trimble Hot Springs (☎ 970-247-0111), 6 miles north of Durango on the west side of US 550, offers three outdoor pools, including an Olympic-size swimming pool maintained at 85°F year-round. The facilities include private tubs, women's fitness studio and massage. The center is open 8 am to 11 pm in summer, 9 am to 10 pm in winter. Admission costs $8.50/6 adults/children age 12 and under.

Places to Stay

Rates are depressingly high in the peak summer season, and all of Durango's 40-plus motels can be booked up. If you need assistance finding a vacancy, contact Durango Central Reservations (☎ 970-247-8900, 800-979-9742). The visitors center (☎ 800-525-8855) can also provide information and phone numbers for lodgings.

Camping & Hostels USFS campsites can be reserved (☎ 877-444-6777) for a fee of $8.65 plus a $10 nightly campsite charge at *Haviland Lake*, 18 miles north of Durango. Other campgrounds in the San Juan National Forest (☎ 970-247-4874) are on a first-come, first-served basis and include the large *Junction Creek* ($10 fee), only 3 miles west of the corner of Main Ave and 25th St; *Purgatory* ($10 fee), next to US 550 opposite the Purgatory Ski Area turnoff; and *Sig Creek* ($8 fee), on USFS Rd 578, 7 miles west of the resort.

Eight miles north of Durango on the valley plain, the private *Hermosa Meadows Camper Park* (☎ 970-247-3055, 800-748-2853) offers 90 shaded tent sites with laundry and showers next to the Animas River for $20. You can fish or launch your kayak from the campground or rent a bike to ride into Durango or nearby Trimble Hot Springs. *Durango East KOA* (☎ 970-247-0783, 30090 US 160) is 5 miles east of Durango, while *Ponderosa KOA* (☎ 970-247-4499) is 10 miles north of town on La Plata County Rd 250. Both of the campgrounds have stores, restaurants and wooded and open sites for $20.

The *Durango Hostel* (☎ 970-247-9905, 543 E 2nd Ave) offers the bare necessities. Per person rates for dorm beds are $13/15 (members/nonmembers) a night. For the same price, couples can stay in aprivate room.

Motels Durango has dozens of motels that are remarkably similar and all charge $60 to $70 for a double in summer, around $35 in winter. The less-expensive places are mostly at the northern end of Main Ave.

The low-key *End O' Day Motel* (☎ 970-247-1722, 350 E 8th Ave) is one of the best values in town where singles/doubles are $34/42 in summer, one of the lowest motel prices in town.

Sporting a western motif, *Silver Spur Motel* (☎ 970-247-5552, 800-748-1715, 3416 Main Ave), at the northern tip of town, has a pool in the back. Summer singles/doubles cost $65/85, or $40/44 in winter.

The attractive and well laid-out *Sunset Inn No 9* (☎ 970-247-2653, 800-414-5984, 2855 Main Ave) has a hot tub and pool and is a relatively good value at $58/68 in the summer peak. A bit farther north, *Spanish Trails Inn and Suites* (☎ 970-247-4173, 3141 Main Ave) also has a pool, guest laundry and lots of rooms, most of which cost around $60 in summer. *The Adobe Inn* (☎ 970-247-2743, 2178 Main Ave) charges $69/79 in summer, and $39/44 off season. Facilities include a heated pool, hot tub and guest laundry.

If you want to be right downtown, *Durango Lodge* (☎ 970-247-0955, 888-440-4489, 150 5th St) is near the railroad depot and offers a pleasant stay. Rooms are pricey in summer, starting around $80, but that's what you pay for location, a pool and a hot tub. Web site: www.durangolodge.com

Here are some other mid-range offerings in Durango (rates quoted are for double occupancy in peak season):

Alpine Motel (☎ 970-247-4042, 800-818-4042, 3515 N Main Ave) $78 to $84

Dollar Inn (☎ 970-247-0593, 800-727-3746, 2391 Main Ave) $65 to $75

Econolodge (☎ 970-247-4242, 800-424-4777, 2002 Main Ave) $68 to $135 with hot tub, pool

Rodeway Inn (☎ 970-259-2540, 800-752-6072, 2701 Main Ave) $69 to $99 with hot tub, pool, laundry

Travelodge (☎ 970-247-1741, 800-578-7878, 2970 Main Ave) $68 to $88

Hotels & B&Bs The charming *Gable House* (☎ 970-247-4982, ghbb@frontier.net, 805 E 5th Ave) is a splendid 1892 Queen Anne–style Victorian B&B. Rooms with shared bath cost between $75 and $135. The *Leland House B&B* (☎ 970-385-1920, 800-664-1920, 721 E 2nd Ave) is near the town center and has 10 spacious, charming rooms from $139 to $320 in summer; $109 to $299 in winter.

Durango has several intriguing Victorian hotels to choose from, among them the 1898 *General Palmer Hotel* (☎ 970-247-4747, 800-523-3358, 567 Main Ave). This elegant building been restored to near perfection, and rooms start at $98 in summer, $75 in winter, and rise to $275. Along similar lines the *Strater Hotel* (☎ 970-247-4431, 800-247-4431, 699 Main Ave) was built in 1887 and has elaborately furnished rooms from $120 to $250 in summer; $70 to $140 in winter. Film buffs may prefer *Rochester Hotel* (☎ 970-385-1920, 800-664-1920, 726 E 2nd Ave), which has 15 rooms decorated in themes of Western movies filmed in and around Durango. Rates are $139 to $209 in summer; $109 to $179 in winter.

If you're more into creature comforts than atmosphere, the *Rio Grande Best Western* (☎ 970-385-4890, 800-245-4466, 400 E 2nd Ave) has an indoor heated pool, Jacuzzi, fitness room and in-room VCRs. Standard rooms cost $85 to $150; suites go for $169 to $189. Rates include a Continental breakfast and free cocktails!

Places to Eat
As with accommodations, there's a lot to choose from in Durango, although prices aren't quite as steep when it comes to eating. *Sagebrush Cafe & Coffeehouse* (☎ 970-385-4041, 601 E 2nd Ave) is a good spot for an espresso or latte. You can caffeine up *and* surf the Net at *Steaming Bean Coffee Co* (☎ 970-385-7901, 915 Main Ave). For cheap and hearty American breakfasts head for the *Durango Diner* (☎ 970-247-9889, 957 Main Ave), where biscuits and gravy with roasted green chilies can be had for around $3.

Both food and beer are quite good at *Steamworks Brewing Company* (☎ 970-259-9200, 801 E 2nd Ave). The *Carver Brewing Co* (☎ 970-259-2545, 1022 Main Ave) has built up a strong following for its cool outdoor beer garden. *Le Rendezvous Swiss Bakery* (☎ 970-385-5685, 750 Main Ave) also draws a good crowd and offers a slightly more refined menu and atmosphere. Though it can get crowded and smoky, the historic-looking *Olde Tymer's Cafe* (☎ 970-259-2990, 1000 Main Ave) has good lunches and outdoor patio seating.

Francisco's (☎ 970-247-4098, 601 Main Ave) features New Mexico–style lunch and dinner dishes in a large and busy restaurant. For standard, but amazing, Mexican try *Tequila's* (☎ 970-259-7655, 948 Main Ave). If you like it spicier, head for *Gazpacho* (☎ 970-259-9494, 431 E 2nd Ave), which serves good northern Mexican and New Mexican dishes.

The Italian dishes at *Farquarhts* (☎ 970-247-5440, 725 Main Ave) are not all that exciting, but you do get a lot of food for your money. Northern Italian dinner specialties are featured at *Ariano's* (☎ 970-247-8146, 150 E College Dr).

Storyville (☎ 970-259-1475, 1150B Main Ave) does great barbecue and wood-fired pizzas. *Scoot'n Blues* (☎ 970-259-1400, 900 Main Ave) is a virtual hybrid of the House of Blues and Harley Davidson Cafe. Decorated with vintage motorcycles and featuring blues music, tourists come for the huge salads, gourmet burgers and wraps.

The *Ore House* (☎ 970-247-5707, 147 E College Ave) does a fine job with steak and seafood. Among the most respected top-end places in town is *Palace Grill* (☎ 970-247-2018), in the former Palace Hotel next to the train depot: It's known for its excellent aged beef, game and fresh fish dishes.

Entertainment
Farquarhts (see Places to Eat, above) offers live rock music and dancing on weekends and some weeknights as well. *Lady*

Falconburgh's Barley Exchange (☎ 970-382-9664, 640 Main Ave) has a selection of more than 100 beers in addition to its tasty pub grub.

The *Diamond Circle Melodrama* (☎ 970-247-3400), in the Strater Hotel, offers nightly summer theater performances.

Tune in to the local live entertainment scene at *Southwest Sound* (☎ 970-259-5896), a long-standing and praiseworthy record shop at 922 Main Ave. The friendly owners are a gold mine of music information.

Getting There & Away

Durango–La Plata County Airport (☎ 970-247-8143) is 18 miles southeast of Durango via US 160 and Hwy 172. American Airlines offers daily jet service to Dallas in the winter ski season. Otherwise, you are on commuter turbo-prop equipment. United Express has daily flights to Denver, while America West and Rio Grande Airlines have daily flights to Phoenix, Arizona and Albuquerque, New Mexico, respectively.

By bus, Greyhound/TNM&O provide daily service to Montrose, Delta and Grand Junction and Albuquerque, New Mexico. The Bus Center (☎ 970-259-2755), 275 E 8th Ave, has lockers.

Durango lies at the junction of US 160 and US 550, 42 miles east of Cortez, 49 miles west of Pagosa Springs and 190 miles north of Albuquerque.

Getting Around

Durango Transportation (☎ 970-259-4818) operates airport shuttles 24 hours to or from the Durango–La Plata County Airport. The one-way fare is $15 and you must book a seat at least two hours in advance.

Around town, the Durango Lift (☎ 970-259-5438) runs a bus trolley service along Main Ave; the fare is 25¢. There is also a bus service that makes an hourly clockwise circuit of town.

At the Durango–La Plata Airport you can rent cars from Budget, Avis, National, Dollar and Hertz.

AROUND DURANGO
Durango Mountain Resort

Formerly known as Purgatory, the Durango Mountain Resort (☎ 970-247-9000, 800-982-6103) is 25 miles north of Durango on US 550. Besides the ski area, facilities include a cross-country ski center, a ski school for the disabled and a snowboard park.

Web site: www.durangomountainresort.com

Southern Ute Indian Reservation

Unlike their neighbors at the Ute Mountain Indian Reservation, the Southern Utes – primarily composed of the Muache and Capote bands – live on a checkerboard reservation resulting from their sale of individually owned allotments to Hispanic and Anglo farmers and ranchers. The tribal headquarters in the town of Ignacio, on the Los Pinos River 25 miles southeast of Durango, is on Ute land. To get there continue east for 10 miles on Hwy 172 from the Durango–La Plata County Airport, or exit US 160 at Bayfield and travel south on 'Buck Hwy,' La Plata County Rd 521.

This tri-ethnic community with *chili ristras* and adobe buildings is reminiscent of New Mexican villages. The Southern Utes are proud of their integration, and some claim that it has fostered a better business sense than that found on cooperative reservations. On the east bank of the Los Pinos, the Ouray Memorial Cemetery features the gravesites of Chiefs Ouray and Buckskin Charley – prominently located at the center of the Catholic and Protestant sections.

At the Southern Ute Culture Center (☎ 970-563-9583) you can find out about traditional Ute life from the attractive museum displays of artifacts, clothing and ceremonies. Photographs document the Los Pinos Agency, established in 1869 after the Ute chiefs traveled with Kit Carson to Washington, DC, and signed the Treaty of 1868 that relinquished their traditional homeland to the incoming miners. The museum is open 9 am to 6 pm weekdays and 10 am to 3 pm weekends in summer. It's closed Sunday from October 1 to May 15. Admission costs $1.

The **Sky Ute Lodge & Casino** (☎ 970-563-3000, 800-876-7017) is a Ute-owned facility that includes a modern motel and restaurant that caters to guests of the casino. Single/double rooms at the lodge are a pretty good value at $60/70 in summer; $40/50 in winter.
Web site: www.skyutecasino.com

CHIMNEY ROCK ARCHAEOLOGICAL AREA

Here, stunning rock spires house Ancestral Puebloan (Anasazi) ruins overlooking the Piedra River, 42 miles east of Durango on Hwy 131, 3 miles south of the town of Chimney Rock on US 160. Recent research suggests that the site was a Chacoan outlier that may have furnished timber to communities to the south. Another recent discovery suggests the twin pinnacles were used to observe lunar events. By AD 1125 the site, like others in the southwest, was abandoned possibly as a consequence of drought.

Guided tours are the *only* way to visit the hundreds of structures, including the Great Kiva, that once housed between 1200 and 2000 inhabitants. A fire lookout tower offers views of the excavated Chacoan sites perched high on the rock formation. Two-hour walking tours are scheduled at 9:30 and 10:30 am and 1 and 2 pm daily from May 15 to September 30. Admission costs $5/2 adults/children. For more information call Chimney Rock (☎ 970-883-5359) or the San Juan National Forest Pagosa Ranger District (☎ 970-264-2268).

PAGOSA SPRINGS

West of Durango, on US 160 at the junction with US 84 south to New Mexico, the open ponderosa pine forests give way to the tourist billboards of Pagosa Springs (elevation 7079 feet). Pagosa is a Ute term for 'boiling water' and refers to the town's main draw: hot springs that provide heat for some of the town's 1900 residents. The steam rises from many spots along the San Juan River as it flows past volcanic rock formations in the center of town.

The Pagosa Springs Area Chamber of Commerce (☎ 970-264-2360, 800-252-2204)

operates a large visitors center located across the bridge from US 160. More information about Pagosa Springs can be found on the Web at www.pagosa-springs.com and www.pagosasprings.net. Advice about what to do in the San Juan National Forest is available from the USFS Pagosa Ranger Station (☎ 970-264-2268) at the corner of 2nd and Pagosa Sts.

If you're itching to check your email, Pagosa Worldwide (☎ 970-264-6532), 511 San Juan St, offers Internet access for a nominal fee.

Hot Springs

For visitors to Pagosa Springs, soaking in the glorious riverside pools at 'The Springs' (☎ 970-264-4168, 800-225-0934) is de rigueur. The healing, mineral-rich waters are drawn from the Great Pagosa Aquifer, and the 11 different outdoor pools (open 24 hours) overlook the San Juan River within view of US 160. The pools vary in temperature from 94°F to 111°F, with the hottest of them appropriately named 'the lobster pot!' Guests at the adjacent Spring Inn (see below) bathe free, so it's worth considering spending the extra money to stay there and save the $10 nonguest admission fee.

Wolf Creek Ski Area

With an annual snowfall of 435 inches, Wolf Creek (☎ 970-264-5639), 23 miles north of Pagosa Springs, boasts having 'the most snow in Colorado.' Adult/child lift tickets cost $38/25.

For cross-country skiing, many backcountry and groomed trails are available that lead into quiet, pristine forest. Contact the Pagosa Ranger Station for details.
Web site: www.wolfcreekski.com

Places to Stay & Eat

For an economical stay try the **San Juan Motel** (☎ 970-264-2262, 191 E Pagosa St), where singles/doubles cost $58/65 in summer peak. Older rooms are available for $48/55 and there are also cabins for $65, as well as a campground where tent sites cost $15, RV hookups $25. Motel guests have hot tub access. Just across the road from The Spring Inn, **The Spa Motel & RV Resort** (☎ 970-264-5910, 800-832-5523) is far less to look at but has singles/doubles from $50/60, a hot mineral swimming pool and a couple of indoor baths. A few doors down, **Best Western Oak Ridge Lodge** (☎ 970-264-4173, 800-528-1234) offers pleasant rooms from $56 to $79 and has an indoor heated pool, Jacuzzi and sauna.

Guests at **The Spring Inn** (☎ 970-264-4168, 800-225-0934) enjoy all-you-can-soak privileges in the hotel's top-notch hot springs; nonguests pay $10. Rates vary greatly depending on the season, ranging from around $80 to $140.

If you're skiing Wolf Creek, you might want to consider staying in South Fork, 18 miles northeast of the ski area along US 160 (see South Fork, earlier).

Right across from the hot springs entrance gate, **Harmony Works Juice Bar**

(☎ 970-264-6633) sells 'natural products for the body and soul,' including healthy organic sandwiches, fresh fruit smoothies and 'veggie tonics.'

Amore's House of Pasta (☎ 970-264-2822, 121 E Pagosa St) serves excellent pasta dinners from $6. The **Elkhorn Cafe** (☎ 970-264-2146, 438 Pagosa St) is a town stalwart, offering US and Mexican lunches for less than $5 and dinners for $5 to $7. Its signature dish is stuffed sopaipilla.

JJ's Upstream Restaurant (☎ 970-264-9100, 356 E Hwy 160), seven blocks east of downtown on San Juan River, is great for Sunday brunch, soups, salad and does nice dinner entrees.

Three miles east of town (toward Durango), **Paradise Brewpub & Grill** (☎ 970-731-9191, 164 N Pagosa Blvd) brews its own beer and has great gourmet pizza and vegetarian choices.

Snake River slithers toward the Tetons. WY

JOHN ELK III

KIMBERLEY O'NEIL

The Teton Range rises and shines. WY

JOHN ELK III

Satan rocks! Devils Tower, WY

Mammoth Hot Springs, Yellowstone National Park, WY

JOHN ELK III

It's amazing what you can do with elk antlers. Jackson Hole

Back at the ranch, Dubois Badlands, WY

WAGON GULCH

Winter descends on Laramie, WY.

Ain't no mountain high enough. WY

Mud volcano attracts the herds (and bison). WY

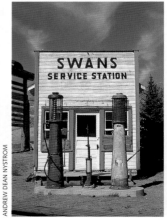

SWANS
SERVICE STATION

All out of gas, Dubois, WY

Western Colorado

Western Colorado's arid landscape of flat-topped mesas and multihued, deeply incised canyons is part of an extensive plateau country. Native Americans refer to this land of multicolored canyon walls as 'the land of frozen rainbows.'

Generally less frequented by visitors, western Colorado nonetheless has plenty of stunning scenery to offer. Probably best known are the fascinating cliff dwellings at Mesa Verde National Park. Near Grand Junction, the scenic Colorado National Monument exemplifies the 'frozen rainbows' that are found along the Colorado Plateau, as does Dinosaur National Monument in the northwest corner of the state. Other highlights include the alpine meadows, forests and streams hidden away atop the 10,000-foot Grand Mesa, the shadowy lure of the plunging Black Canyon of the Gunnison National Park and the little-traveled roads and trails of the Dolores River Canyon.

Northern Plateau

Northwestern Colorado is the state's 'empty' quarter, a thinly populated region of high desert that in remote times was dinosaur country. These days the region's wilderness areas are largely the province of hunters and in autumn the area is overrun with camouflage-clad outdoorsmen. The Northern Plateau includes some beautiful scenery, though not as spectacular as that farther to the south.

CRAIG

Lying on the north bank on the Yampa River between the towns of Meeker and Steamboat Springs, Craig (population 9100; elevation 6185 feet) is more of a pit stop than a destination.

Craig's Moffat County Visitors Center (☎ 970-824-5689, 800-864-4405), 360 E Victory Way, is open from 9 am to 5 pm weekdays, and also offers information online at www.craig-chamber.com.

Stop in at the Bureau of Land Management's Little Snake Resource Area Office (☎ 970-824-4441) at 1280 Industrial Ave.

The **Museum of Northwest Colorado**, 590 Yampa Ave, has excellent displays on local history, fossils and an exhibit on the Denver

Highlights

- Colorado National Monument – gorgeous desert canyons, natural sandstone sculptures and few tourists

- Grand Mesa – an alpine haven of streams and forests overlooking the deserts of the Colorado Plateau

- Black Canyon of the Gunnison National Park – a 2000-foot chasm with little traffic and great views

- Dolores River Canyon – hauntingly beautiful, little-traveled desert canyon with fine biking and rafting

- Mesa Verde National Park – awe-inspiring ancient cliff dwellings of the Ancestral Puebloans

WESTERN COLORADO

Northwestern & Pacific Railroad. It's open 10 am to 5 pm Monday to Saturday; free.

Places to Stay & Eat

Accommodations are reasonably priced but prices typically rise during hunting season, mid-September to late November. One of the best bargains is ***Trav O Tel Motel*** (*☎ 970-824-8171, 224 E Victory Way*), which has small but efficiently designed rooms starting at $25/32 for singles/doubles. Farther east, ***Westward Ho Motel*** (*☎ 970-824-3413, 517 E Victory Way*) has decent rooms for $28/40.

Craig's priciest rooms are at the ***Holiday Inn*** (*☎ 970-824-4000, 300 S Hwy 13*) on the road to Meeker. Doubles start around $79, and amenities include a swimming pool, hot tub, sauna, gym and restaurant.

La Plaza (*☎ 970-824-7345, 994 Yampa Ave*) has respectable Tex-Mex food and shaded patio seating. All in the same building at 420 Yampa Ave (*☎ 970-824-9966*) you'll find ***Mather's Bar***, the ***Cactus Grill*** and more good Mexican dishes at ***Virgina's*** in back. Also popular with locals is the unpretentious ***Golden Cavvy*** (*☎ 970-824-6038, 538 Yampa Ave*), a meat-and-potatoes place.

Getting There & Away

Yampa Valley Regional Airport is midway between Craig and Steamboat Springs (see Steamboat Springs in the Northern Mountains chapter). Greyhound (*☎ 970 824-5161*), 470 Russell St, serves Denver and Salt Lake City.

MEEKER

The cozily picturesque seat of Rio Blanco County, Meeker (population 2400; elevation 6239 feet) takes its name from infamous government agent Nathan Meeker (see 'Greeley: A Utopian Experiment,' in the Eastern Plains chapter), whose arbitrary plowing of a Ute racetrack precipitated a fatal confrontation in 1879 which cost Meeker and several other settlers their lives. Contemporary Meeker is a small town surrounded by sagebrush country where Greek-American sheepherders graze huge

Ike's

Barring the blizzard of the century, no one approaching Craig on US 40 from Steamboat Springs can miss the rolling hillsides covered by something that, according to local yellow pages, is Ike's Automatic Transmission Shop. In fact, Ike's is a sprawling junkyard that may hold more wrecks than there are licensed vehicles in Moffat County. According to local legend, the sight so aggravated Lady Bird Johnson that it prompted her to launch her famous nationwide beautification program during her husband Lyndon's presidency. Ike's is not really photogenic, but it is unforgettable.

flocks for their wool. The tiny but well-preserved downtown includes several buildings of historical and architectural intrigue, plus the interesting **White River Museum**, 565 Park St.

Information

The Meeker Chamber of Commerce (☎ 970-878-5510) maintains an information office at 710 W Market St, and also offers travel information on its Web site: www.meekerchamber.com. The White River National Forest's Blanco Ranger District Office (☎ 970-878-4039) is at 317 E Market St. The BLM's White River Resource Area Office (☎ 970-878-3601) is southwest of town at 73544 Hwy 64.

On the north bank of the White River near the junction of Hwy 13 and Hwy 64, Meeker is 45 miles south of Craig and 42 miles north of Rifle.

Places to Stay & Eat

Meeker gets booked up with hunters from late September to mid-November. Rates are a bit higher on weekends and during hunting season.

Meeker Town Park, at the foot of 4th St, has $5 campsites but no showers. For a shower try the Rustic Lodge (see below), which charges $3 per person. *Stagecoach*

Campground (☎ 970-878-4334), 2 miles south of Meeker at the junction of Hwy 13 and Hwy 64, is a shady riverside facility charging $16 for tent sites, $25 for sites with full hookups.

The congenial *Valley Motel* (☎ 970-878-3656, 723 Market St) has singles/doubles for $32/38, and a hot tub. The *Meeker Hotel* (☎ 970-878-5255, 560 Main St) is a historic building with restored 19th-century rooms. Singles with shared bath are $35, doubles with private bath are $50; suites start around $80. At the east end of town, *Rustic Lodge* (☎ 970-878-3136, 173 1st St) has two-person cabins with kitchenettes for $45, $5 each additional person. There's a hot tub and a restaurant with bar on the premises.

The *Meeker Cafe* (☎ 970-878-5062), next to the Meeker Hotel, has reasonably priced burgers, sandwiches and other lunch and dinner items. *The Bakery* (☎ 970-878-5500, 265 6th St) opens bright and early for pastries and coffee at 6 am.

AROUND MEEKER
Flattops Scenic Byway

This gravel road (Rio Blanco County Rd 8) east of Meeker is a more scenic alternative route to Steamboat Springs than US 40 via Craig. It intersects Hwy 131 near Yampa (snow closes the route in winter) and also provides access to the Rio Blanco National Forest's Flat Tops Wilderness, a 367-sq-mile roadless area with countless alpine lakes favored by hikers and anglers. The scenic and popular **Trapper's Lake** has five developed campgrounds; camping permits are $10. You also can access several nice hikes from here. The USFS ranger station in Meeker has information and maps for the area. The 'Flat Tops Trail Scenic Byway' brochure has a map showing points of interest along the route, which has 17 accessible *campgrounds* ranging from $3 to $14.

Ute Indian Monument

This monument at the Thornburg Battle Ground, 20 miles northeast of Meeker via Rio Blanco County Rd 15, marks the place where the Ute resistance attacked US army Major Thomas Thornburgh's 5th Cavalry, while it was en route to support Nathan Meeker. Thornburg died in the battle, which lasted from September 29 to October 6, 1879. The site also is accessible from Moffat County Rd 45, off Hwy 13 about 5 miles south of Hamilton.

DINOSAUR NATIONAL MONUMENT

Although dinosaurs once inhabited much of the earth, in only a few places have the proper geological and climatic conditions combined to preserve their skeletons as fossils. Paleontologist Earl Douglass of Pittsburgh's Carnegie Museum discovered this dinosaur fossil bed, one of the largest in North America, in 1909. Six years later, President Woodrow Wilson acknowledged the scientific importance of the area by declaring it a national monument.

Today visitors can view Dinosaur Quarry, now completely enclosed within a building to protect the fossils from weathering, in which more than 1600 bones have been exposed. Apart from dinosaur bones, the monument's starkly eroded canyons provide the visitor with scenic drives, hiking, camping, backpacking and river-running.

Orientation & Information

Dinosaur National Monument straddles the Utah-Colorado state line. Monument headquarters and most of the land is within Colorado, but the quarry (the only place to see fossils *in situ*) is in Utah.

There are several drives with scenic overlooks and interpretive signs, leading to a number of trailheads for short nature walks or access to the backcountry.

At the town of Dinosaur, a Colorado welcome center (☎ 970-374-2205) offers maps and brochures for the entire state. Information is available from Dinosaur National Monument Headquarters' visitors center (☎ 970-374-3000), which has an audiovisual program, exhibits and a bookstore. It's open 8 am to 4:30 pm weekdays year-round, plus weekends in summer. There's also a visitors center at Dinosaur Quarry.

Entrance to the monument headquarters' visitors center is free, but entrance to

all other parts of the monument (including Dinosaur Quarry) is $10 per private vehicle, $2 for cyclists or bus passengers.

Dinosaur Quarry

The Jurassic strata containing the fossils give a glimpse of how paleontologists transform solid rock into the beautiful skeletons seen in museums, and how they develop scientifically reliable interpretations of life in the remote past. Ranger-led walks, talks and tours explain the site; information can also be gleaned from brochures, audio-visual programs and exhibits. There is also a gift and bookshop.

Dinosaur Quarry (☎ 435-789-2115) is open 8 am to 7 pm daily from Memorial Day to Labor Day; the rest of the year 8 am to 4:30 pm.

Activities

Both the Yampa and Green Rivers offer excellent river-running opportunities, with plenty of exciting rapids and whitewater amid splendid scenery. From mid-May to early September, trips range from one to five days. Adrift Adventures (☎ 800-824-0150) and Adventure Bound (☎ 970-241-5633, 800-423-4668), in Grand Junction, are two popular rafting outfitters.

Fishing is permitted only with the appropriate state permits, available from sports stores or tackle shops in Dinosaur or Vernal, Utah. Check with park rangers about limits and the best places.

Places to Stay

Dinosaur National Monument's main campground is *Green River*, 5 miles east of Dinosaur Quarry along Cub Creek Rd, with 88 sites. Open May to September, it has bathrooms and drinking water but no showers or hookups. Sites are $5 to $10 per night.

For camping during winter when Green River is closed, try nearby *Split Mountain*, which lacks water but is free (closed in summer). Free camping is also permitted at *Rainbow Park*, *Deerlodge Park*, *Gates of Lodore* and *Echo Park*. Only the latter two have drinking water and all are closed in winter. Call the visitors centers to check on opening dates and availability.

There are designated backcountry campsites only on the Jones Hole Trail; otherwise wilderness camping is allowed anywhere at least one-quarter mile from an established road or trail. Backpackers must register at one of the visitors centers or ranger stations, where you can receive free permits and review the best routes with a ranger.

There are no lodges in the monument but Vernal has a good selection of motels and restaurants, and the town of Dinosaur also has a couple of motels and restaurants.

Getting There & Away

Dinosaur National Monument is 88 miles west of Craig via US 40 and 120 miles east of Salt Lake City, Utah, by I-80 and US 40. Dinosaur Quarry is 7 miles north of Jensen, UT, on Cub Creek Rd (Utah Hwy 149). Monument headquarters is just off US 40 on Harpers Corner Dr, about 4 miles east of the town of Dinosaur.

RANGELY

An isolated coal and oil town on Hwy 64, Rangely (population 2000; elevation 5274 feet) is about 56 miles west of Meeker and about 90 miles north of Fruita and Grand Junction via Hwy 139. Visitors to nearby Dinosaur National Monument may wish to detour through Rangely to access the very fine rock art sites along Hwy 139 just south of town. The Rangely Chamber of Commerce (☎ 970-675-5290) maintains a useful Web site at www.rangely.com.

The excellent **Rangely Outdoor Museum** (☎ 970-675-2612), 434 W Main St, is open 10 am to 4 pm daily in summer, and weekends only in April, May, September and October. There are several notable pre-Columbian rock art sites on nearby BLM lands; look for self-guided tour brochures along Hwy 64 East and West, the Dragon Trail south of Rangely and Cañon Pintado.

Shady **Rangely Camper Park**, a municipal site just north of Main St (Hwy 64) at the east end of town, is a real bargain at $5/10 without/with hookups, including hot

showers. The **4 Queens Motel** (☎ 970-675-5035, 206 E Main St) charges $52 for a double, which includes free swimming passes to the town recreation center. **Budget Motel** (☎ 970-675-8461, 117 S Grand Ave) has clean singles/doubles for $49/52.

The **Cowboy Corral** (☎ 970-675-8986, 202 W Main St), is good for standard American fare, but for the best steaks in town head to **Ace Hi** (☎ 970-675-8574, 616 E Main St). **Magalinos** (☎ 970-675-2321, 124 Main St) has good-value lunches and dinners; **Max's Pizza** (☎ 970-675-2670, 855 E Main St) is a local favorite.

CAÑON PINTADO HISTORIC DISTRICT

Most of the several rock art sites in the area just south of Rangely along Hwy 139 observed by the Domínguez-Escalante Expedition of 1776, date from the Fremont cultures that inhabited the area from about AD 600 to 1300. Later, Utes also made their contributions.

Look for green and white BLM rods that indicate the sites along Hwy 139. The nearest site to Rangely, 1.3 miles south of the junction with Hwy 64, is a panel about 50 yards west of the highway showing several abstract and anthropomorphic shapes. At the 4.1-mile point west of the highway is a conspicuous Fremont ruin that may have served as a watchtower.

At the 10½-mile point on the east side of the highway, **East Fourmile Canyon** requires a short hike along the nearby cliff face on the north side of the canyon, crossing a fairly deep arroyo past a crumbling pioneer cabin and then on toward the east.

At 14.2 miles, the **Philadelphia Draw** site is accessible by a dirt road leading about a mile to the east; look to your left after crossing the second cattle guard. At 15.4 miles on the west side of the highway, the conspicuous **White Birds** site displays what appear to be multicolored chiles.

A half mile south, the main **Cañon Pintado** site includes an image of Kokopelli, a flute-playing figure common in the Ancestral Puebloan art of the Southwest.

COLORADO

Central Plateau

Stretching south from the Colorado River to the San Juan Mountains is the plateau country of Grand Mesa and the lower Gunnison River. This area is home to some excellent geological formations and scenery. Two National Park Service units, the Colorado National Monument near Grand Junction and the Black Canyon of the Gunnison National Park east of Delta and Montrose, are largely underappreciated by visitors and offer great opportunities for tranquil nature exploration, even during the summer peak.

GRAND JUNCTION

Amid one of Colorado's most productive agricultural zones, Grand Junction (population 35,000; elevation 4586 feet) is western Colorado's main urban center. Planners have partially turned downtown Main St into a pleasant pedestrian mall by reducing roads, planting trees, providing benches and placing sculptures at regular intervals throughout. This has helped the city retain something of a small-town atmosphere.

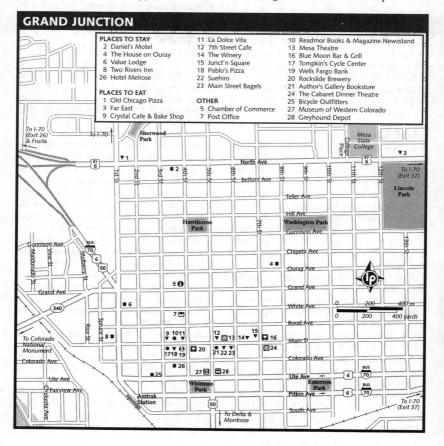

GRAND JUNCTION

PLACES TO STAY
2 Daniel's Motel
4 The House on Ouray
6 Value Lodge
8 Two Rivers Inn
26 Hotel Melrose

PLACES TO EAT
1 Old Chicago Pizza
3 Far East
9 Crystal Cafe & Bake Shop

11 La Dolce Vita
12 7th Street Cafe
14 The Winery
15 Junct'n Square
18 Pablo's Pizza
22 Suehiro
23 Main Street Bagels

OTHER
5 Chamber of Commerce
7 Post Office

10 Readmor Books & Magazine Newsstand
13 Mesa Theatre
16 Blue Moon Bar & Grill
17 Tompkin's Cycle Center
19 Wells Fargo Bank
20 Rockslide Brewery
21 Author's Gallery Bookstore
24 The Cabaret Dinner Theatre
25 Bicycle Outfitters
27 Museum of Western Colorado
28 Greyhound Depot

The Art of Grand Junction

Among downtown Grand Junction's most pleasant features are the 100-plus imaginative sculptures on Main St. Look for *Freewheelin II* between 3rd and 4th Sts, a cyclist in training by James Haire, or *Chrome on the Range*, a silvery bison at the corner of 4th and Main Sts. Art on the Corner (☎ 970-245-2926) can provide more information on the works on display, some of which are for sale.

In addition, the **Western Colorado Center for the Arts** (☎ 970-243-7337), 1803 N 7th St, is a modern facility emphasizing the work of local artists. It's open 9 am to 4 pm Tuesday to Saturday.

Though a nice enough place, for travelers Grand Junction mainly functions as a base for exploring the nearby scenic wonders of the Colorado National Monument and the Grand Mesa. The **Colorado Stampede Rodeo** happens in June, **Dinosaur Days** take place in July and the **Mesa County Fair** in August.

Orientation & Information

The I-70 Business Loop enters town from the west at I-70 exit 26 (River Rd). Hwy 340, the western extension of Grand Ave, crosses the Colorado River and leads to Monument Rd, the eastern approach to the Colorado National Monument. Hwy 340 then continues northwest, paralleling I-70, toward the town of Fruita and the western entrance to the monument.

Grand Junction's Visitors & Convention Bureau Information Center (☎ 970-244-1480, 800-962-2547) is at 740 Horizon Dr (at the junction of I-70). It's open 8:30 am to 5 pm daily (until 8 pm in summer) and has loads of information and maps. Information is also available at the downtown chamber of commerce (☎ 970-242-3214), 360 Grand Ave; visit www.grand-junction.net.

The USFS Grand Junction Ranger District Office (☎ 970-242-8211), 764 Horizon Dr, is open 8 am to 5 pm weekdays. Staff at the BLM Grand Junction Area Office (☎ 970-244-3000), opposite Walker Field Airport at 2815 H Rd, are helpful and it has a good book selection. Hours are 7:30 am to 4:30 pm weekdays.

Wells Fargo Bank has a downtown ATM at 359 Main St. The main post office (zip code 81501) is at 241 N 4th St. Readmor Books & Magazine Newsstand (☎ 970-242-7229), 344 Main St, has a good selection of fiction, nonfiction, newspapers, magazines and USGS maps. Author's Gallery Bookstore (☎ 970-241-3696), 537 Main St, has an extensive collection of used books.

Museum of Western Colorado

This well-arranged museum (☎ 970-242-0971) at 5th and Ute Sts features impressive displays on regional history, as well as various special exhibits and events. Admission is $5/4/3 adults/seniors/children. Hours are 10 am to 4 pm Tuesday to Saturday (plus Monday in summer).

Mountain Biking

Some of Colorado's finest mountain biking areas can be found around Grand Junction. Major trails include the 142-mile Grand Junction to Montrose **Tabegauche Trail** (pronounced 'tab-a-watch'), and the 128-mile **Kokopelli Trail**, which stretches from nearby Fruita to Moab, Utah. While doing the full length of these trails would require extensive preparation, both offer plenty of loops and other shorter ride possibilities.

There are also numerous trails north of the town of **Fruita** (see Around Grand Junction, later in this chapter), one of Colorado's top mountain-biking destinations. In Fruita, the bicycle shop to visit is Over the Edge Sports (☎ 970-858-7220), 202 E Aspen Ave.

Grand Junction bike shops can provide detailed information on bike routes and how to access them. Tompkin's Cycle Center (☎ 970-241-0141), 301 Main St, and Bicycle Outfitters (☎ 970-245-2699), 227 Ute Ave, are two good choices.

COLORADO

Other Activities

Adventure Bound (☎ 970-245-5428, 800-423-4668), 2392 H Rd, offers intriguing single- and multiple-day river-rafting trips throughout western Colorado and Utah. Trip rates average around $125 per day inclusive.
Web site: www.raft-colorado.com

There's some fine climbing to be had nearby, notably in **Unaweep Canyon** and **Monument Canyon** in the Colorado National Monument. Climbers can stop by Summit Canyon Mountaineering (☎ 970-243-2847), 549 Main St, for climbing equipment, books, topographic maps and tips on where to go.

Mt Garfield Stables (☎ 970-464-0246) is located north of town near its namesake mountain, which towers over the airport and I-70. Rides in the scenic areas around Mt Garfield and the Bookcliffs start at $17 per hour. The friendly staff offer free pickup from your hotel with a minimum two-hour ride.

Places to Stay

Grand Junction has abundant accommodations, and downtown is the most interesting area.

There's plenty of good camping on surrounding NPS and BLM lands. Within city limits, try *RV Ranch* (☎ 970-434-6644, 3238 E I-70 Business Loop), reached by I-70 exit 37. Rates are $30 for tents, $32 for full hookups.

The unique *Hotel Melrose* (☎ 970-242-9636, 800-430-4555, 337 Colorado Ave), housed in a restored 1908 building, is the sole survivor of Grand Junction's 12 original hotels. Dormitory beds (four to a room) cost $15 (though open to everyone, HI-AYH members get first priority when space is limited). If you're able to afford more amenities, the hotel also has uniquely furnished single/double rooms in early 20th-century style with shared bath for $30/40; rooms with private bath are $55/65. Internet access is available and the friendly owners are happy to provide tips on sights and activities in the area. Hotel Melrose is conveniently located just several blocks away

from downtown and the Amtrak and Greyhound stations. Reservations (recommended!) can be phoned in.
Web site: www.hotelmelrose.com

One of the cheapest spots near downtown is *Daniel's Motel* (☎ 970-243-1084, 333 North Ave), which has basic but adequate singles/doubles for $35/40. *Value Lodge* (☎ 970-242-0651, 104 White Ave) rents singles/doubles for $35/38, and has a swimming pool.

In the downtown area, *Two Rivers Inn* (☎ 970-245-8585), at 1st and Main Sts, has fairly nice rooms, a pool, hot tub and discount breakfasts; singles/doubles go for $45/50.

Rooms at *The House on Ouray* (☎ 970-245-8452, 760 Ouray Ave), a restored Victorian, all are named for influential Colorado women. Singles/doubles range from $50/60 to $65/75.

Places to Eat

Try the attractive *Crystal Cafe & Bake Shop* (☎ 970-242-8843, 314 Main St) for excellent breakfasts, lunches and baked goods. *Main Street Bagels* (☎ 970-241-2740, 559 Main St) bakes scrumptious NY-style bagels.

The *7th Street Cafe* (☎ 970-245-5194, 504 Main St) features '50s-style soda fountain decor and serves good breakfasts, sandwiches, espresso and Italian sodas.

Pablo's Pizza (☎ 970-255-8879, 319 Main St) was inspired by Picasso and serves steaming pies with names like Dracula's Nemesis, The Cowboy, and Naked Truth.

Junct'n Square (☎ 970-243-9750, 119 N 7th St) also specializes in pizza, as does *Old Chicago Pizza* on the corner of First St and North Ave. For upscale Italian fare, try *La Dolce Vita* (☎ 970-243-3466, 363 Main St).

Suehiro (☎ 970-245-9548, 541 Main St) is one of the few Japanese restaurants in western Colorado, and the sushi is said to be good. *The Winery* (☎ 970-242-4100, 642 Main St), downtown's most upscale restaurant, is a steak and seafood venue open for dinner only.

For the best Chinese in town, the massive *Far East* (☎ 970-255-9800, 1530 North Ave) does great Mandarin and Cantonese dishes.

Entertainment
The *Rockslide Brewery* (☎ 970-245-2111, 401 Main St) has decent food, though locals like it more for the beer. The *Blue Moon Bar & Grill* (☎ 970-242-5406, 120 N 7th St) attracts a boisterous pool hall crowd, but often has good bands on the weekends.

For something more cultural, see what's on at *The Cabaret Dinner Theatre* (970-241-4613, 710 Main St). Touring bands often play at the *Mesa Theatre* (538 Main St).

Getting There & Around
Walker Field, Grand Junction's commercial airport, is 6 miles northeast of downtown.

From the Greyhound depot (☎ 970-242-6012), at 830 S 5th St, there are buses to Denver; Las Vegas, Nevada; and Salt Lake City, Utah. TNM&O runs a daily bus to Montrose and Durango with connections to Albuquerque, New Mexico, and another to Salida and Pueblo with connections to Dallas.

Amtrak's daily *California Zephyr* between Chicago, Illinois, and Oakland, California, stops at the passenger depot (☎ 970-241-2733), 339 S 1st St, next to the old depot; there's a small information booth here.

Hertz, Avis, National and Budget have locations at Walker Field Airport. Grand Junction is on I-70, 248 miles west of Denver via and 30 miles east of the Utah state line.

AROUND GRAND JUNCTION
Fruita
Besides being a mecca for mountain bikers (see Mountain Biking earlier), the pleasant town of Fruita, 13 miles west of Grand Junction, is steadily attracting more visitors. Dinosaur buffs won't want to miss the skeletons, fossils and animated dinosaurs at **Dinosaur Journeys** (☎ 970-858-7282), 550 Jurassic Court, open 9 am to 5 pm daily. Visitors also can catch the Tuesday night **rodeo** during summer months.

Fruita is the gateway to the 550-mile **Dinosaur Diamond Prehistoric Highway**, a recent addition to Colorado's Scenic & Historic Byways network.

For more information on local attractions, lodging and events, call the Fruita Chamber of Commerce (☎ 970-858-3894). Web site:www.fruita.org

Dinosaur Hill
In 1900 paleontologist Elmer Riggs discovered the enormous and previously unknown *Brachiosaurus altithorax* near Grand Junction. He soon followed up with a nearly intact *Apatosaurus excelsus* (brontosaurus) at this site south of the Colorado River near Fruita. The site, which includes Riggs's original quarry and several fossil remnants in place, is now commemorated with a small reserve and interpretive trail. To get there, take Hwy 340 (I-70 exit 19) south from Fruita; the road continues south to Colorado National Monument.

Little Bookcliffs Wild Horse Range
Managed by the BLM, this 47-sq-mile unit is one of only three reserves in the entire country that is dedicated to protecting the descendants of early Spanish horses. About 80 mustangs roam the area. It can be reached by driving north from Grand Junction on 25 Rd. It is also accessible from the ghost town of Cameo (I-70 exit 46, then 10 miles north) or from DeBeque (I-70 exit 62). Hiking, horseback riding and mountain biking are permitted in the area, but most trails are fairly challenging. Camping also is allowed. Contact the BLM Grand Junction Resource Area Office (☎ 970-244-3000) for information and maps.

Wineries
Colorado is less than famous for its wines, but the Grand Valley, particularly nearby Palisade (I-70 exit 32), is home to a cluster of wineries producing both whites (mostly chardonnay) and reds (merlot and pinot noir) that are worth checking out. The visitors center in Grand Junction can provide numerous leads.

COLORADO

GRAND MESA

Towering above the Grand Valley, this 'island in the sky' is a lava-capped plateau rising more than 11,000 feet at its highest point. Its broad summit offers a delightful respite from the Grand Valley's summer heat, beautiful alpine scenery and an interesting four-hour loop drive from Grand Junction via I-70, Hwy 65 and US 50 (with plenty of opportunities for side trips and stopovers). The highway passes through a number of distinct environments as it climbs the 6000-foot mesa, ranging from canyons of sage, piñon pines and junipers through areas of scrub oak and montane forests of Engelmann spruce and Douglas fir to sub-alpine forests and meadows.

There are several visitors centers on and around the mesa: The Grand Mesa Byway Welcome Center (☎ 970-856-3100) is on Hwy 65 in Cedaredge on the southern side of the mesa. Atop the mesa near Cobbet Lake, the Grand Mesa visitors center is at the intersection of Hwy 65 and USFS Rd 121. Land's End visitors center is at the southwest end of Land's End Rd, which leads to Hwy 50 and Grand Junction. All the centers generally operate from late May to mid-October. The USFS also has a ranger station (☎ 970-487-3534) at 218 High St in Collbran on the north side of the mesa.

Maps of trails and campsites and information on accommodations are also available from the visitors center in Grand Junction. 'The Grand Mesa Scenic Byway' is an annual publication that includes maps, important phone numbers, lodging, restaurant and historical information for the area.

Powderhorn Ski Area

Barely half an hour east of Grand Junction, on the northern slopes of Grand Mesa, is the convenient ski center (☎ 970-268-5700, 800-241-6997). Though not the most challenging terrain in the state, it often has excellent quality powder.

Crag Crest National Recreation Trail

Starting about half a mile west of Carp Lake on Hwy 65, this 10-mile loop follows the crest of the mesa before returning via a lower section past a series of attractive lakes; there's also an eastern trailhead from USFS Rd 121, a lateral off Hwy 65 just south of Carp Lake. The trail offers views of the Grand Valley and Uncompahgre Plateau to the west, Battlement Mesa to the north, the Elk Mountains to the east and the San Juan Mountains to the south.

Places to Stay

There are 12 USFS *campgrounds* in the Grand Mesa National Forest, most of which levy fees of $7 to $10. There are also *lodges* at Alexander Lake (☎ 970-856-6700), Grand Mesa (☎ 970-856-3250) and Powderhorn (☎ 970-268-5700). Rates generally range from $35 to $55 for motel or lodge rooms to $65 and $75 for cabins equipped with kitchens. Some lodges close for the winter, so call ahead to check.

COLORADO NATIONAL MONUMENT

From the Uncompahgre Uplift of the Colorado Plateau, 2000 feet above the Grand Valley of the Colorado River, half a dozen or more accessible colorful sandstone canyons precipitously descend to the flatlands. Once dinosaur country, this 32-sq-mile scenic wonder is one of the most rewarding side trips possible from an interstate highway, well worth a detour by car but even better for backcountry exploration. Open all year, the Colorado National Monument is an exceptional area for hiking, camping and road biking.

Over the past 140 million years, erosion exposed the reddish sandstones of the Morrison formation and created freestanding landforms, including Independence Monument, a 450-foot monolith. Despite the aridity of both plateau and canyons, water continues to sculpt the landscape.

A sparse cover of sage, piñon pines and junipers dots the plateaus and canyons of Colorado National Monument, but large mammals like the mule deer, puma, coyote and desert bighorn sheep nevertheless frequent the area. Smaller mammals include desert cottontails, ground squirrels and chipmunks, but you're more likely to see birds such as piñon jays.

Saddlehorn Campground near the visitors center has the only formal sites within the park proper; for $10, you get spectacular views of the canyons and the Grand Valley below.

Orientation & Information
The east entrance to Colorado National Monument is just 4 miles west of Grand Junction; the western entrance is 5 miles south of Fruita (I-70 exit 19, south). The meandering Rim Rock Dr, which links the two entrances, is a popular drive with many exceptional overlooks, and an even better bicycle route. The best way to see the monument is on foot through the canyons.

The Colorado National Monument visitors center (☎ 970-858-3617), on the plateau at the north end of the park, is open 9 am to 5 pm daily (hours are extended in summer). There are brochures, a selection of books and maps and a theater for audiovisual presentations. NPS rangers offer guided hikes throughout the day, as well as campfire programs in the Saddlehorn Campground Amphitheatre. Admission to the park is $5 per automobile, $3 for pedestrians or cyclists.

Hiking & Backpacking
Colorado National Monument contains a variety of hiking trails starting on Rim Rock Drive, most of them relatively short, such as the half-mile **Coke Ovens Trail**. The numerous canyons are more interesting, but the rugged terrain makes loop hikes difficult or impossible; a steep descent from the canyon rim means an equally steep ascent on the return. One alternative is to use either a car or bicycle shuttle, since some trailheads outside the park are reached most easily from Hwy 340, the Broadway/Redlands Rd between Fruita and Grand Junction.

Perhaps the most rewarding trail is the 6-mile **Monument Canyon Trail**, leading from Rim Rock Dr down to Hwy 340 past many of the park's most interesting natural features, including the Coke Ovens, the Kissing Couple and Independence Monument. Another possibility is the less precipitous

Liberty Cap Trail, which links up with the much steeper **Ute Canyon Trail** to form a lengthy 14-mile loop.

The backcountry of Colorado National Monument is open for backpacking, but requires carrying water and camping at least a quarter-mile from any road and 100 yards off all trails. Backcountry permits also are required and can be obtained free of charge at the Saddlehorn visitors center, or at either entrance to the monument.

DELTA
Once known as Uncompahgre, Delta (population 4500; elevation 4890 feet) is the gateway to the north rim of Black Canyon of the Gunnison National Park and is a small but attractive crossroads town. Its downtown historic district is graced by a series of interesting murals along Main St and its cross streets that depict Delta's history, society and environment. The murals are a good reason to stop here for lunch and an afternoon stroll.

The Delta Chamber of Commerce (☎ 970-874-8616), 301 Main St, is open 9 am to 5 pm weekdays and has information on sights in and around town, and a useful Web site at www.deltacolorado.org. The USFS Grand Mesa, Uncompahgre and Gunnison National Forest Headquarters (☎ 970-874-6600) is south of town at 2250 US 50.

Places to Stay
Delta has several convenient campgrounds and RV parks. The shady *Four Seasons River RV Park* (☎ 970-874-9659, 676 N US 50) charges $15/17 for tent sites in winter/summer, $19/23 for full hookups. Across the highway, the *Riverwood Inn* (☎ 970-874-5787, 677 N US 50) is equally shady and costs around the same.

The *El-D-Rado Motel* (☎ 970-874-4493, 702 Main St) has $30/35 singles/doubles. At the *Budget Host South Gate Inn* (☎ 970-874-9726, 800-621-2271, 2124 S Main St), rates start at $40 and include pool and hot tub access. The *Four Seasons River Inn* (☎ 970-874-9659, 676 N US 50) has clean rooms from $32 to $64 in winter, and $42 to $74 in summer. Going slightly upmarket, the **Best Western Sundance** (☎ 970-874-9781, 903 Main St) has rooms starting from $46/51.

Places to Eat

A pleasant soup and sandwich lunch place is **The Eatery** (☎ 970-874-9634, 305 Main St). **Leon's Mexican Restaurant** (☎ 970-874-0309, 420 Main St) has decent, moderately priced food. **North Fork Valley** (☎ 970-874-4222, 1204 Main St) also does respectable Mexican, as well as good salads and steaks. **Daveto's** (☎ 970-874-8277, 520 Main St) is the choice for Italian food.

Getting There & Away

TNM&O/Greyhound (☎ 970-874-9455) buses depart from the depot at 270 E Hwy 92 (1st St) for Montrose, Durango, and Albuquerque, New Mexico, and Montrose, Salida and Pueblo. There also are daily buses to Grand Junction, where you can connect with buses to Denver; Salt Lake City, Utah; and points beyond.

Delta is 40 miles southeast of Grand Junction and 21 miles northwest of Montrose via US 50.

PAONIA

For its size, Paonia (population 1660; elevation 5674) offers a surprising combination of natural beauty, working-class society and liberal culture. Surrounded by the North Fork Valley's charming countryside of farms and wildlands, it also has a bundle of late 19th-century buildings in superb condition and is the home of *High Country News,* one of the country's most outspoken environmental publications. The casual visitor hardly notices that coal mining is still a significant local industry.

The chamber of commerce (☎ 970-527-3886), in the DE Frey office at 124 Grand Ave, usually is open 9 am to 3 pm weekdays. The USFS Paonia Ranger Station (☎ 970-527-4131) is on N Rio Grande Ave eight blocks east of Grand Ave along 3rd St, then one long block north (left).

From July to mid-October, 9 am to 4 pm Tuesday and Friday, North Fork Valley farmers bring fresh and organic produce to the **Paonia Farmers Market** in the mini-park north of the Paradise Theatre. On the 4th of July, **Paonia Cherry Days**, celebrating the season's first fruit to reach the market, also features a rodeo. The **Delta County Fair & Rodeo** takes place in August at nearby Hotchkiss.

Paonia is 29 miles east of Delta via Hwys 92 and then 133, and 72 miles south of Glenwood Springs by Hwy 133.

Historic District & Murals

Downtown Paonia's Grand Ave features interesting early 20th-century buildings, most notably Curtis Co Hardware (1902) and the United Mine Workers Building (1903). Away from Grand Ave there is an excellent selection of Victorian houses, as well as landmarks like the turreted Queen Anne–style Christian Church at the corner of E 3rd St and Box Elder Ave.

An excellent mural of Paonia's history adorns the wall in the mini-park just north of the Paradise Theatre on Grand Ave. An even more imposing five-wall mural at the corner of 3rd St and Grand Ave depicts five successive nightly camps of the Domínguez-Escalante Expedition in August 1776.

West Elk Wilderness

Readily accessible from Paonia via a 4WD road that parallels Minnesota Creek, Gunnison National Forest's expansive West Elk Wilderness is a 900-sq-mile roadless area with a dense 200-mile trail network capped by the 13,035-foot West Elk Peak. There are other points of access along Hwy 133 east of Paonia and from Crawford south of Paonia. Pamphlets with details about the area's various recreational activity opportunities are available at the Paonia and Delta USFS offices.

Places to Stay & Eat

The lack of accommodations helps keep outsiders from overrunning Paonia, but also means that reservations are necessary if you're going there in autumn, when hunters book up all the rooms.

Rates at the friendly family-run **Rocky Mountain Inn** (☎ 970-527-3070), at 3rd and

Niagara Sts, start at $45 for doubles. The *Redwood Arms Motel* (☎ *970-527-4148, 1478 Hwy 133)*, about a mile west of town, has singles/doubles from $42/45.

A restored hotel that first opened in 1906, the *Bross Hotel Bed & Breakfast* (☎ *970-527-6776, 312 Onarga St)*, one block east of Grand Ave, has 10 early–20th-century rooms ranging from $70 to $90. Amenities include a hot tub.

The Diner (☎ *970-527-4774, 203 Grand Ave)*, is a conventional American restaurant open for breakfast, lunch and dinner Monday to Saturday; breakfast and lunch only on Sunday. *Linda's 3rd St Bistro* (☎ *970-527-6146)* is open only Thursday to Saturday, but locals say Linda's Mexican food is definitely worth trying. Next door, *Moonrise Espresso Co* (☎ *970-527-5551)* has tasty baked goods and all sorts of coffees. It's open 7 am to 2 pm weekdays, 8 am to noon Saturday. *The Casa* (☎ *970-527-4343, 312 Grand Ave)* is Paonia's most upscale restaurant, serving Italian, Mexican and vegetarian dishes.

MONTROSE

Montrose (population 13,000; elevation 5974 feet) is an agricultural center and wholesale supply point for Telluride, 65 miles to the south. The Ute Museum in town and the Black Canyon of the Gunnison National Park to the east on Hwy 50, typically visited as a day trip, are the major attractions for visitors.

Information

The Montrose Chamber of Commerce (☎ 970-249-5000, 800-923-5515) is located at 1519 E Main St (Hwy 50). Among other pamphlets, it offers a visitor's guide listing accommodations, restaurants and things to see and do in the area. Hours are 9 am to 5 pm weekdays. There's also a smaller visitors center (☎ 970-249-1726) open 9 am to 4 pm Monday to Saturday at the Ute Indian Museum (see below).

The Montrose Public Lands Office (☎ 970-240-5300) combines the offices of the BLM, NPS and USFS. It's located toward the south edge of town at 2505 S Townsend Ave (Hwy 550, within city limits). The office offers maps and access information for surrounding public lands and is open 7:30 am to 4:30 pm weekdays.

Ute Indian Museum

Near the US 550 bridge over the Uncompahgre River south of town, the Ute Indian Museum (☎ 970-249-3098), 17253 Chipeta Rd, was the homestead site of Chief Ouray and his wife Chipeta. Gallery exhibits of photos, artifacts and clothing highlight and explain Ute ceremonies and the sad chronology of the US occupation of their Colorado lands.

The museum is open 10 am to 5 pm Monday to Saturday, 1 to 5 pm Sunday, year-round. Admission is $2.50/1.50 adults/children.

Places to Stay & Eat

Near the Chamber of Commerce, the *Log Cabin Motel* (☎ *970-249-7610, 1034 E Main St)* is a cozy little place with singles/doubles for $36/46. In the same area, the basic but clean *Canyon Trails Inn* (☎ *970-249-3426, 800-858-5911, 1225 E Main St)* charges around the same.

The *Daily Bread & Bakery Cafe* (☎ *970-249-8444, 346 Main St)* serves tasty breakfasts and lunches as well as fine baked goodies 6 am to 4 pm Monday to Saturday. For lunch or dinner, try *Kokopelli's Southwestern Grille* (☎ *970-252-8100, 647 E Main St)* for creative regional cooking. Near the visitors center, the *Red Barn* (☎ *970-249-9202, 1413 E Main St)* is popular for its steaks and generous salad bar.

Getting There & Around

Passengers to and from Telluride are the primary customers at the Montrose Regional Airport (☎ 970-249-8455), north of town on US 50. Shuttles to Telluride with Telluride Express (☎ 970-249-6993) cost $32 per person.

TNM&O buses stop at the depot (☎ 970-249-6673), 132 N 1st St in the old Coors building, opposite a mural of fighting cocks. Buses serve Grand Junction, Durango and Pueblo.

At the airport you will find Budget and Hertz car rental offices.

BLACK CANYON OF THE GUNNISON NATIONAL PARK

Upgraded to a national park – America's 55th – in 1999, Black Canyon's dark narrow gash above the Gunnison River leads down a 2000-foot-deep chasm, evoking a sense of awe (and vertigo) for most visitors as they look over the edge. In some places, Black Canyon, 12 miles east of Montrose via US 50 and Colorado 347, is narrower than it is deep. The park offers myriad outdoor recreation opportunities year-round.

Orientation & Information

Except as a vista from the South Rim, the remote North Rim has little to offer. From Montrose, it's 8 miles to the Hwy 347 turnoff, then 7 miles to the visitors center on the South Rim. The visitors center (☎ 970-249-1915, 800-873-0244), open year-round, offers detailed displays on the canyon's geology and wildlife. Admission (good for seven days) costs $7 per vehicle or $3 for bikes.

NPS rangers provide information and free permits for camping and technical climbing in Black Canyon.

South Rim Road

The 6-mile-long plateau-top road takes you to the edge of the canyon and to 11 overlooks, some reached by short trails of up to 1½ miles roundtrip.

At the narrowest part of Black Canyon, **Chasm View** is only 1100 feet across yet 1800 feet deep. Rock climbers are frequently seen on the opposing North Wall. Colorado's highest cliff face is the 2300-foot **Painted Wall**.

An ideal way to see the canyon is by cycling along the smooth pavement with a 2000-foot drop by your side – you definitely get a better feel for the place than if you're trapped in a car.

Hiking

The **Rim Rock Trail** connects Tomichi Point with the visitors center only a quarter-mile

away. From the visitors center, the easy 1½-mile loop **Oak Flat Trail**, on the plateau through gambel oak, Douglas fir and aspen, offers good views of Black Canyon. Plan to take the **Warner Point Nature Trail**, a 1½-mile roundtrip at the end of South Rim Rd, before watching the sunset from either High Point or Sunset View overlooks. Rangers can provide information and a backcountry permit if you want to descend one of the South Rim's three unmarked routes on talus to the infrequently visited riverside campsites. From the remote North Rim, the **SOB Trail** heads to the river.

Fishing

From the upstream boundary of the Monument to the confluence with the North Fork is some of the best fishing in Colorado for large numbers of 16- to 25-inch rainbow and brown trout. Whoppers over 5lb are not uncommon in this 26-mile stretch of Gold Medal water.

Within the monument itself, the so-called trails into the canyon are just steep rock chutes that entail a strenuous day of work to complete the roundtrip, difficult if you're laden with fishing gear. Four longer and less strenuous trails reach the lower gorge below the monument from Peach Valley Rd east of Olathe.

Places to Stay

Near the entrance station, *South Rim Campground* has 102 campsites on a first-come, first-served basis and drinking water hauled in by tank truck. Camping is $8 in summer, free in winter. You can camp near the river at the *East Portal Campground*, a part of the Curecanti National Recreation Area, for the same fees. The *North Rim Campground*, accessed by a dirt road beyond the North Rim Ranger Station, also costs $8 per night; closed in winter.

CURECANTI NATIONAL RECREATION AREA

The Gunnison River, once free-flowing through the canyons, is now plugged by three dams to create Curecanti. A more apt and official title is the Wayne N Aspinal

Storage Unit, named for a US representative, in office between 1948 and 1973, who never met a water project he did not like. Many RVs are strangely attracted to the bleak and windy shores of chilly Blue Mesa Reservoir, which the NRA surrounds.

Stunning landforms that survived immersion are the unsinkable Curecanti Needle and Dillon Pinnacles, a volcanic breccia capped by welded tuff.

The Elk Creek visitors center (☎ 970-641-2337 ext 205), on US 50 6 miles west of the junction with Hwy 149 to Lake City, offers topographic maps and exhibits describing the area's cultural and natural history. It's open 8 am to 4:30 pm daily (until 6 pm in summer). There also are information centers at Cimarron and Lake Fork, which only operate from late May to late September.

Curecanti has 10 campgrounds, most of which charge fees of $8 or $9. Some, such as **Elk Creek** and **Lake Fork**, are developed, with showers and flush toilets, while others are more basic. For hikers there are also small campgrounds at the end of the Curecanti Creek Trail (2 miles) and Hermit's Rest Trail (3 miles). The latter descends 1800 feet, so be prepared for a steep climb back out.

Southern Plateau

The southwest section of this region is also known as the 'Four Corners' area, in reference to the point where the borders of Colorado, New Mexico, Arizona and Utah meet. Here the mountains and mesas give way to desert, a stark contrast with the rest of Colorado.

The prime attractions in this area are the many ruins of the pre-Columbian peoples known formally as the Ancestral Puebloans. Together the Mesa Verde National Park and Ute Mountain Tribal Park protect the archaeological remains at hundreds of these prehistoric communities, while providing access to a few of the most spectacular sites.

Nearby towns such as Cortez and Mancos offer places to stay and further information about the Ancestral Puebloans and their legacy. A bit farther north is the sleepy Dolores River Canyon, which offers untrammeled access to desert backcountry hiking, biking and river rafting.

FOUR CORNERS MONUMENT

Some find it entertaining to watch the antics of tourists as they pose on all fours on this inlaid concrete monument to political geography – where the borders of Colorado, Utah, Arizona and New Mexico meet. Then it's your turn!

In addition, Native Americans operate 40 licensed stalls – *ramadas* – that encircle the monument, selling food and handicrafts. Four Corners Monument is 38 miles south of Cortez on US 160. It's open 7 am to 7 pm daily; admission is $1.

DOLORES

In the narrow Dolores River Canyon, Dolores (population 1100; elevation 7000 feet) enjoys a scenic location 11 miles north of Cortez on Hwy 145 (also called Railroad Ave). Housed in a replica of the town's old railroad depot, the Dolores visitors center (☎ 970-882-4018, 800-807-4712), 421 Railroad Ave, has information on lodging and outdoor activities in the area. It's open 9 am to 5 pm Monday to Saturday (10 am to 4 pm Sunday) from May to October, and in winter 8 am to noon Monday to Friday.

Adjacent to the visitors center is the **Galloping Goose Museum**, which has displays and one example of the rather odd-looking gasoline-powered vehicles used by the Rio Grande Southern Railroad to continue rail service into the San Juan Mountains during the economic troubles of the 1930s.

You can find out about nearby camping and hiking opportunities in the San Juan National Forest at the USFS Dolores Ranger Station (☎ 970-882-7296) at the corner of 6th St and Central Ave. It's open 8 am to 5 pm weekdays year-round. To get cleaned up after your outings, the Dolores Laundry & Public Showers, 302 Railroad Ave, offers a shower and towel for about $3.

The **Dolores River RV Park** (☎ 970-882-7761, 18680 Railroad Ave), located about

COLORADO

1½ miles east of town, has pleasantly located tent sites for $12. RV hookups are $20. At the east end of town, the *Outpost Motel* (☎ 970-882-7271, 800-382-4892, 1800 Central Ave) has small but clean singles/doubles for $43/49, as well as cabins for $85/95. Most of the motel rooms have kitchenettes and the courtyard features a pleasant little wooden deck overlooking the Dolores River.

Dolores Mountain Inn (☎ 970-882-7203, 800-842-8113, 701 Railroad Ave), has immaculate modern rooms from around $60 in summer ($45 in winter). The motel's genial owner also offers bike rentals, shuttle service and guided tours.
Web site: www.dminn.com

Near the visitors center and listed on the National Register of Historic Places, the three-story *Rio Grande Southern Hotel* (☎ 970-882-7527, 101 S 1st St) dates from 1893 and has B&B singles/doubles with shared bath for $39/65; rooms with private bath are $50/75.

Get started with a good espresso at the *German Stone Oven Restaurant & Bakery* (☎ 970-882-7033, 811 Railroad Ave). The owners serve delicious Belgian waffles or German pancake breakfasts for around $5.

DOLORES RIVER CANYON

This area used to be bustling with uranium mine activity, reflected in the good condition of Hwy 141 through Unaweep Canyon which was widened in the 1950s by the US Atomic Energy Commission to provide access to the now abandoned mines and mills. The wildflower meadows in the deep canyon are silent now that traditional ranch operations have resumed as the economic mainstay. Most recently, rafting and mountain biking have boosted the local economy.

Stark sandstone formations, mesas covered with dark patches of piñon-juniper and sagebrush valleys, whose primary inhabitants are prairie dogs and ever-watchful raptors, are reminiscent of Utah's canyon lands. The Dolores and San Miguel Rivers beckon some travelers, while the 'Uranium Road' may intrigue others. A great sandstone formation, the **Palisade**, looms as you

follow the winding road down to the isolated Dolores River Canyon and the small community at Gateway.

Hwy 141 is designated a part of the Unaweep/Tabeguache Scenic & Historic Byway. The **Tabeguache Trail** follows the Uncompahgre Plateau through the Uncompahgre National Forest.

Orientation & Information

To travel between Cortez and Grand Junction, you either can combine the winding, twisting, narrow Hwys 145 and 62 through the scenic San Juan Mountains over Lizard Head Pass and Dallas Divide with US 50, or take the winding, twisting, narrow Hwy 141. A brochure describing the sights along these routes is available at the Colorado Welcome Center in either Cortez or Fruita. The Nucla-Naturita Chamber of Commerce (☎ 970-865-2350), 217 W Main St (Hwy 141) in Naturita, and the Dove Creek Chamber of Commerce (☎ 970-677-2245), 128 Hwy 666, also offer information.

Dove Creek

Located on US 666 35 miles north of Cortez and 2 miles south of Hwy 141, Dove Creek (population 710) claims to be the 'Pinto Bean Capital of the World.' Recently, nonirrigated growers have rediscovered the beans grown by the Anasazi (Ancestral Puebloans) and found that they are sweeter, prettier and – most importantly – cause less flatulence than the high-carbohydrate pinto bean. Anasazi beans are marketed by Adobe Milling (☎ 970-677-2620, 800-542-3623) which offers gourmet beans and recipes to visitors.

Rooms at the *Country Inn Motel* (☎ 970-677-2234) start at $38, $28 in winter. Unfortunately, the nearest restaurants serving 'gourmet' beans are in Mesa Verde and Durango, but you can sample a bowl of old-fashioned gas-inducing pinto beans at the *Blue Mountain Cafe* (☎ 970-677-2261), on US 666 at the north end of town.

Naturita

Compared to the surrounding area, friendly Naturita (population 500), situated along

The Sorrows of the Dolores

The loneliest area of Colorado may be the Dolores River Canyon. In 1776 Father Escalante gave the river its Spanish name, Río de Nuestra Señora de los Dolores (River of Our Lady of Sorrows); much later Alfred Castner King provided a poetic interpretation of the 'river of sorrow.' After losing his sight, King published the poem 'Dolores' in a 1907 collection of his work on the San Juan Mountains titled *The Passing of the Storm*. The following lines from 'Dolores' reflect the feeling of solitude that the starkly beautiful red rock landscape evokes:

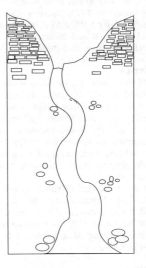

> Long ago, ere the foot of the white man
> Had left its first print on the sod,
> A people, both free and contented,
> Her mesas and cañon-ways trod.
> Then Dolores, the river of sorrow,
> Was a river of laughter and glee…
> As she playfully dashed through the cañons
> In her turbulent rush to the sea.…
> Gone, gone are this people forever,
> Not a vestige nor remnant remains
> To gather the maize in its season
> And join in the harvest refrains;
> But the river still mourns for her people
> With weird and disconsolate flow,
> Dolores, the river of sorrow,
> Dolores – the river of woe.

King's reference to the 'weird flow' rings true in many ways. Paradox Valley is so named because the river cuts across the narrow part of the valley through notches in the rimrock cliffs, rather than flowing along the valley length. The stunning palisade formation at Gateway Palisades marks the entrance to Unaweep Canyon, which slices through the Uncompahgre Plateau. 'Unaweep' is a Ute term meaning 'the canyon with two mouths,' a reference to its curious drainage divided between East Creek, which flows to the Gunnison River, and the West Creek mouth. An 1889 attempt to engineer an elaborate 'hanging flume' on the walls of the Dolores Canyon to deliver water to its intended target, the Lone Tree Placer mine, unfortunately failed through miscalculation.

Another well-regarded author, David Lavender, chronicled his early experiences in the Dolores River Canyon during the 1930s. In a folksy first-person manner, Lavender captures the life of the rancher in this remote corner of Colorado in his 1943 book *One Man's West*. Lavender witnessed the boom-and-bust economy that uranium mining brought to the region, which left the land as forsaken as it had been before mining arrived. Subsequent editions of *One Man's West* note the sudden attention that atomic weapons brought to the haunting canyonlands of the Dolores River during WWII.

Hwy 141 and the San Miguel River 59 miles north of Dove Creek, is a thriving metropolis. The yellow carnotite ore (containing uranium) brought a burst of activity to a region that has since reverted to a largely uninhabited state.

Overlooking the valley, the **Bunkhouse Motel** (☎ *970-865-2893, 118 Hwy 97*) offers singles/doubles for $25/30. Rooms start at $35 at the **Ray Motel** (☎ *970-865-2235, 123 Main St/Hwy 141*). Across the street, **Sandy's Cafe** (☎ *970-865-2599*) is open for breakfast, lunch and dinner and is known for its hamburgers and steak.

Bedrock

An 18-mile side trip on Hwy 90 follows a still-used stock driveway into Paradox Valley to the Dolores River crossing and the solitary **Bedrock Store** (☎ 970-859-7395). Built in 1876, the store's two-story masonry construction makes a visit to the refrigerated cold case a real treat on a hot day. Historic displays of old merchandise make this a unique stop.

At the west end of the Paradox Valley, the La Sal Mountains rise like a forested island amid a desert. From the Hwy 90 turnoff to Paradox, it's 14 miles to Buckeye Reservoir in the Manti–La Sal National Forest in Utah.

Rafting

Although the McPhee Reservoir interrupts the Dolores River, the 150-mile stretch from below the dam to the Utah state line offers springtime runs. The courses here are unequaled for their combination of the beauty and solitude of canyon country with occasional technical whitewater challenges.

If planning your own trip, be sure to purchase Ralph DeVries' and Stephen Maurer's *Dolores River Guide*. Alternatively, Wilderness Aware Rafting (☎ 800-462-7238, www.inaraft.com) and Rocky Mountain Adventures (☎ 800-858-6808, www.shoprma.com) offer exciting multi-day trips that explore the cultural and natural history along the river.

Mountain Biking

A 26-mile trail along the red-rock Dolores River Canyon, from Dove Creek to nearby Slick Rock, offers an easy ride and swimming opportunities during the first 11 miles. The remainder is a more challenging ride involving a potentially dangerous river ford followed by steep climbs. Stop by the Dove Creek Chamber of Commerce (☎ 970-677-2245) for information on river conditions and a map and description of the route.

The 142-mile **Tabeguache Trail**, comprising single-track trails and Divide Rd across the Uncompahgre Plateau, connects Montrose and Grand Junction. For a map and trail log contact the Colorado Plateau Mountain Bike Trail Association (☎ 970-241-9561), PO Box 4602, Grand Junction, CO 81502. Forest maps and camping information for the Dolores Canyon area are available from the USFS Dolores Ranger Station (☎ 970-882-7298) in Dolores, while maps and information for the Tabeguache are available at the USFS offices in Montrose (☎ 970-240-5300) and in Grand Junction (☎ 970-242-8211).

MANCOS

The historic homes and landmark buildings in tiny Mancos (population 900; elevation 7000 feet), between Cortez and Durango, make for a worthwhile stop and a pleasant place to stay while visiting Mesa Verde National Park, only 7 miles west.

Historic displays and a walking tour map are available at the visitors center (☎ 970-533-7434), at the corner of Main St and Railroad Ave (US 160). It also has information on outdoor activities in the area and local ranches that offer horseback rides and Western-style overnight trips.
Web site: www.mancos.org

Places to Stay

At the east end of Grand Ave, the Mancos River runs beside the town's wooded **Boyle Park**. Tent campsites and restrooms are free; a small donation goes to help fund park upkeep. Please register with the park host in the trailer at the park entrance.

The best bet in town is *Old Mancos Inn* (☎ *970-533-9019, fax 970-533-7138, 200 W Grand Ave)*. The hotel's friendly owners, Dean and Greg, have worked hard to renovate the place and provide unique, pleasant rooms for reasonable prices. Twelve rooms with shared bath cost $30/35; three rooms with private bath are $45/50. The outside deck adds yet more value. This is also one of the few truly gay-friendly hotels in Colorado. Greg is the town mayor, one of only five openly gay mayors in the US.

A nice nearby B&B is the historic *Bauer House* (☎ *970-533-9707, 800-733-9707, 100 Bauer Ave)*, an 1880s brick Victorian mansion that has two rooms starting at $95, and two suites (one complete with kitchen and bar) for $125.
Web site: www.bauer-house.com

Comfortable singles/doubles cost $35/45 ($25/30 in winter) at *Enchanted Mesa Motel* (☎ *970-533-7729, 862 W Grand Ave)*. The *Mesa Verde Motel* (☎ *970-533-7741, 191 Railroad Ave)* isn't as cozy but does have a hot tub. Singles/doubles are around $49/59 during high season.

How about spending the night in a former fire lookout tower? Standing 55 feet above a meadow 14 miles north of Mancos at 9800 feet elevation, the *Jersey Jim Lookout* (☎ *970-533-7060)* is on the National Register and is complete with its Osborne fire-finder and topographic map. The tower accommodates up to four adults (bring your own bedding) and must be reserved long in advance: The reservation office opens March 1 and the entire season (usually late May to mid-October) is typically booked within days. The nightly fee is $40, with a two-night maximum.

Places to Eat
The congenial owners of the *Absolute Baking Co* (☎ *970-533-1200, 110 S Main St)* are justified in advertising 'sublime breads...food with integrity.' They bake fresh bread and pastries using only organic flours and grains, and prepare excellent light meals from scrumptious sandwiches ($4) to quiche and quesadillas. The cafe also

doubles as a used bookstore and is open daily for breakfast and lunch, except Wednesday.

For dinner, the *Dusty Rose Cafe* (☎ *970-533-9042, 200 W Grand Ave)* offers tasty dishes like fresh seafood and veal, all made from fresh ingredients. Try the homemade desserts and don't miss the champagne brunch on Saturday and Sunday (8 am to 2 pm).

A popular steak and seafood dinner joint is *Millwood Junction* (☎ *970-533-7338)* at the corner of Main St and Railroad Ave. Folks from miles around come to Mancos on Friday night for the $14 seafood buffet.

CORTEZ
For visitors to Mesa Verde National Park and other nearby Ancestral Puebloan sites, Cortez (population 8900; elevation 6200 feet) is the main lodging spot. Those seeking a more relaxed environment can try Mancos, 17 miles east, or Dolores, 11 miles north.

The Colorado Welcome Center (☎ 970-565-4048), 928 E Main St, is housed in an adobe-style building at the City Park. It has maps, brochures and some excellent pamphlets and maps on local activities such as fishing and mountain biking. Hours are from 8 am to 5 pm (6 pm in summer).

The post office is at 35 S Beech St; the zip code is 81321.

Quality Book Store (☎ 970-565-9125), 34 W Main St, sells travel books and maps and offers a good selection on local history and Native American cultures.

Southwest Memorial Hospital (☎ 970-565-6666), at 1311 N Mildred Rd, has a 24-hour emergency room.

A laundry is at the corner of E Main St and Mildred Rd opposite the City Park and Colorado Welcome Center. M&M Truckstop (☎ 970-565-6511), south of town at 7006 US 160/666, offers showers for $5.

Colorado University Center Museum
Throughout the year this museum (☎ 970-565-1151), 25 N Market St, hosts exhibits on

the Ancestral Puebloans as well as visiting art displays in its gallery.

The **Cultural Park** is an outdoor space where Ute, Navajo and Hopi tribe members share their cultures with visitors through dance and crafts demonstrations. Weaving demonstrations and Ute Mountain art also are displayed and visitors can check out a Navajo hogan.

Summer evening programs feature Native American dances six nights a week at 7:30 pm, followed at 8:30 by cultural programs such as Native American storytellers. The Center Museum is open Monday to Saturday; summer hours are from 10 am to 9 pm, 10 am to 5 pm in winter.

Places to Stay

Sadly, the only campground in town not right next to a highway or dedicated to RVs is the **Cortez-Mesa Verde KOA** (☎ 970-565-9301, 27432 E Hwy 160) at the east end of town. Tent sites are a pricey $20, full RV hookups $25. It's open mid-May to mid-September.

Summer or winter the basic but clean **Ute Mountain Motel** (☎ 970-565-8507, 531 S Broadway) offers singles/doubles for $28 to $45 in summer, and $26 to $32 in winter. Another economy choice is the **Aneth Lodge** (☎ 970-565-3453, 645 E Main St) where high-season rates for fairly large, comfortable rooms are $38/52.

Taking a slight step up in quality, the **Budget Host Bel Rau Inn** (☎ 970-565-3738, 2040 E Main St) has a pool, hot tub and spacious, spotless rooms for $78 in summer; singles/doubles are as low as $32/38 in winter. On the west side of town, the **Sand Canyon Inn** (☎ 970-565-8562, 800-257-3699) is another pleasant spot with a pool, sundeck and laundry. Peak summer rates for singles/doubles are $48/55.

Still farther west, **The Tomahawk Lodge** (☎ 970-565-8521, 800-972-6232, 728 S Broadway) has a pool, 24-hour coffee and tea and singles/doubles from $47/57 (summer rates). The friendly owners of the **Arrow Motor Inn** (☎ 970-565-7778, 800-727-7692, 440 S Broadway) offer clean rooms for $56/79 in summer. Facilities include a pool, hot tub and laundry.

The **Anasazi Motor Inn** (☎ 970-565-3773, 640 S Broadway). It's not bad but rooms are overpriced at $57/71 for singles/doubles; even winter rates are fairly steep.

Fifteen miles west of Cortez, **Kelly Place** (☎ 970-565-3125, 14663 Montezuma County Rd G), in McElmo Canyon, is a unique adobe-style guest lodge on a 100-acre archaeological and horticultural preserve founded by the late George Kelly, botanist and author of many outstanding guides to Rocky Mountains plants. Singles/doubles cost $65/75 and include private bath and breakfast. Cabins with kitchenettes start at $95. Horseback rides, cultural tours and archaeological programs also are offered.

Places to Eat

You can start the day with an espresso and light breakfast at the Quality Book Store's **Earth Song Haven** (☎ 970-565-9125, 34 W Main St), which also serves tasty lunches featuring fresh ingredients.

The **Main Street Brewery & Restaurant** (☎ 970-544-9112, 21 E Main St) serves a mix of Southwestern, Mexican and Italian dishes. Their house-brewed beer is excellent, reason enough in itself to stop by.

Locals nominate **Francisca's** (☎ 970-565-4093, 125 E Main St) as the best Mexican food in town. For standard American family fare, there's **Homesteaders** (☎ 970-565-6253, 45 E Main St), open all day for barbecue dinners and fresh-baked pies and breads.

At the upper end, **Nero's Italian Restaurant** (☎ 970-565-7366, 303 W Main St) is another local favorite. The **Dry Dock Lounge & Restaurant** (☎ 970-564-9404, 220 W Main St) also occupies the higher-end bracket, dishing up steak and seafood platters with a Southwestern flair.

Getting There & Around

Cortez Municipal Airport is served by United Express, which offers daily turboprop flights to Denver. The airport is 2 miles south of town off US 160/666.

In the extreme southwest corner of the state, Cortez is easier to reach from either Phoenix, Arizona, or Albuquerque, New Mexico, than from Denver, 379 miles away by the shortest route. East of Cortez, US 160 passes Mesa Verde National Park on the way to Durango, the largest city in the region, 45 miles away. To the northwest, Hwy 145 follows the beautiful Dolores River through the San Juan Mountains on an old Rio Grande Southern narrow-gauge route over Lizard Head Pass to Telluride, 77 miles distant.

Budget and U-Save Auto Rental (☎ 970-565-9168) operate out of the Cortez Airport.

AROUND CORTEZ
Anasazi Heritage Center
One of the largest archaeological projects in the Four Corners region was undertaken along the Dolores River between 1978 and 1981, prior to the filling of the McPhee Reservoir. The Anasazi Heritage Center (☎ 970-882-4811), 27501 Hwy 184, 10 miles north of Cortez or 3 miles west of Dolores, offers modern displays of Ancestral Puebloan artifacts found during this project and other archaeological work in the area. Hands-on exhibits include weaving, corn-grinding, tree-ring analysis and an introduction to how archaeologists examine potsherds.

Between AD 1 and 1300, Ancestral Puebloans inhabited the hilly sites of the Escalante and Dominguez Pueblos overlooking the Montezuma Valley. A short interpretive nature trail leads to the hilltop Escalante ruin that was discovered in 1776 by Father Francisco Atanasio Escalante and Father Silvestre Vélez Domínguez. Archaeologists believe the Escalante site was linked with the Chaco Culture, an Ancestral Puebloan society that existed nearly 200 miles south in New Mexico.

The BLM operates the museum and the nonprofit museum shop offers a wide variety of books, maps and nature guides ranging from professional reports to introductory materials suited to the general public. It's open 9 am to 5 pm daily (until 4 pm in winter); $3.

Crow Canyon Archaeology Center
The center (☎ 970-565-8975, 800-422-8975), 23390 Montezuma County Rd K, offers a day-long educational program that visits an excavation site west of Cortez. Programs teach the significance of found artifacts and are offered Wednesday and Thursday from June to mid-September. This is an excellent way to learn about Ancestral Puebloan culture first-hand. The fee is $50/25 adults/children under 18.

An adult research program costs $900 and includes southwestern meals and log cabin lodging for a week. Classroom time culminates with visits to the dig site and active participation in excavation. Reservations are required for both programs. Web site: www.crowcanyon.org

Lowry Pueblo Ruins National Historic Landmark
The ruins at Lowry Pueblo, north of Cortez and 9 miles west of Hwy 666 at Pleasant View, underwent heavy stabilization in 1994 to give visitors an opportunity to explore this Ancestral Puebloan site and even enter a central *kiva* (a usually round, ceremonial structure constructed partially underground). Near the pueblo, constructed between AD 1060 and 1170, is one of the largest Great Kivas in the Four Corners region.

Self-guided walking tour brochures are available at the site. Picnicking is permitted but overnight camping is not allowed. For further information contact the Anasazi Heritage Center (see above).

Fishing
The 11-mile stretch of the lower Dolores River below McPhee Dam to the Bradfield Bridge is a state-designated quality water stream where a catch-and-release program is in effect. To reach the area, turn east off US 666 onto Montezuma County Rd DD a mile north of Pleasant View. Follow the signs for 6 miles to the Bradfield Bridge and USFS campground; from the bridge, the Lone Dome Rd follows the east bank of the river to the dam.

If trolling is your preference, McPhee Reservoir offers both warm- and cold-water species in the recently flooded Dolores River Canyon. Perhaps to make amends for drowning Ancestral Puebloan ruins, burial sites and untold artifacts, the reservoir is kept well stocked for the visiting angler.

Pick up the 'Guide to Fishing in Mesa Verde Country' at the Colorado Welcome Center for additional information.

Bicycling

The Four Corners area offers some outstanding mountain bike trails among piñon-juniper woodland and over 'slickrock' mesa trails. The dispersed ruins at Hovenweep National Monument (see that section, later) are ideal riding destinations. In fact, the roads are often better suited for bikes than cars.

A good ride begins at the Sand Canyon archaeological site west of Cortez and follows a downhill trail west for 18 miles to Cannonball Mesa near the state line. If you're looking for a shorter ride, at the 8-mile mark the Burro Point overlook of Yellow Jacket and Burro Canyons is a good place to turn back. Fat-tire enthusiasts should not miss the 26-mile trail from Dove Creek to Slick Rock along the Dolores River (see Dolores River Canyon, earlier).

Pick up a copy of 'Mountain and Road Bike Routes' for the Cortez-Dolores-Mancos area, available at the Colorado Welcome Center in Cortez and at local chambers of commerce. It provides maps and profiles for several road and mountain bike routes. The booklet 'Bicycle Routes on Public Lands of Southwest Colorado' also describes area rides in good detail. It's available for $7 from the USFS Dolores Ranger Station (☎ 970-882-7296), 100 N 6th St in Dolores. Contact the Colorado Plateau Mountain Bike Trail Association (☎ 970-241-9561) for even more routes and information.

In Cortez, Kokopelli Bike & Board (☎ 970-565-4408), at 30 W Main St, rents mountain bikes for $20 per day, including helmet, air pump, water bottle and tools. They also can provide information about trails in the area.

Places to Stay

A few walk-in tent sites are available for $8 at the USFS *McPhee Campground* (☎ 970-882-9905, 800-280-2267), but most of the 70 reservable campsites are set up for RVs and cost $12. The sites look out over the Montezuma Valley and are convenient to McPhee Recreation Area and reservoir fishing 14 miles north of Cortez on Hwy 184.

Below McPhee Dam to the reservoir, the USFS operates three campgrounds on a first-come, first-served basis: *Bradfield*, *Cabin Canyon* and *Ferris Canyon*. Tent sites are $8 at each. To reach them from US 666, travel 1 mile north of Pleasant View (20 miles north of Cortez), turn east on Montezuma County Rd DD and follow the signs for 6 miles to the bridge. The Bradfield site is a half-mile downstream from the bridge; the other two are within 6 miles to your right (south) on USFS Rd 504. For more camping locations in the San Juan National Forest contact the USFS Dolores Ranger Station (☎ 970-882-7296), or visit www.fs.fed.us/r2/sanjuan.

MESA VERDE NATIONAL PARK

Among national parks, Mesa Verde is unique for its focus on preserving cultural relics so that future generations may continue to interpret the puzzling history of its settlement and then abandonment by early inhabitants.

Ancestral Puebloan sites are found throughout the canyons and mesas of Mesa Verde, a high plateau south of Cortez and Mancos. If you have time for only a short visit, check out the Chapin Mesa Museum and try a walk through the Spruce Tree House, where you can climb down a wooden ladder into the cool chamber of a kiva. Mesa Verde rewards travelers who set aside a day or more to take the ranger-led tours of Cliff Palace and Balcony House, explore Wetherill Mesa, linger in the museum or participate in a campfire program.

The people of Mesa Verde have been commonly referred to as Anasazi, a term archeologists borrowed from a Navajo word thought to mean 'the Ancient Ones.' However, in recent years a number of conflicts have arisen surrounding this term. Primarily, Native American tribes in Arizona and New Mexico who count the Puebloans among their ancestors recently pointed out

Ancestral Puebloan Settlement

Why the Ancestral Puebloans entered Mesa Verde is a subject for speculation. Habitations in Mesa Verde evolved greatly between AD 450, when the earliest simple structures were constructed, and AD 1300, when the great cities were mysteriously left behind.

The earliest period of settlement, the so-called Modified Basketmaker phase that extended to about AD 750, found the Ancestral Puebloans dispersed across the mesatops in small clusters of permanent pithouse dwellings – semi-subterranean structures with posts supporting low-profile roofs.

During the Developmental Pueblo Period, up to AD 1100, Ancestral Puebloans built surface houses with simple shared walls – like row-house apartments – forming small hamlets surrounded by fields of maize, beans and squash.

The following Classic Pueblo phase, to AD 1300, saw the Mesa Verde Ancestral Puebloans elaborate on the earlier structures using masonry building materials. Their efforts housed a peak population of perhaps several thousand in pueblo villages, the precursors to cities. Greater clusters of people created opportunities for united accomplishments and perhaps a rudimentary division of labor, social organization, political control and even organized raids on neighboring villages. During this period the Ancestral Puebloans developed subsurface roundrooms, or kivas – for decades believed by archaeologists to be only for ceremonial use, but more recently seen to have more basic functions as well. At this time the Ancestral Puebloans also developed hydraulic schemes to irrigate crops and provide water for villages.

There is mounting evidence of regular communication between Mesa Verdeans and Chaco Canyon peoples in northwestern New Mexico during this period. Some researchers suggest that the political, economic and social influences extended from even farther afield in Mesoamerica (present-day Mexico and Central America).

The Puebloans suddenly moved to the alcoves of the cliff faces around AD 1200. Community size depended on available cliff space, so while small cavities may have contained only a few compartments, there were many larger communities with more than 200 compartments, including elaborate blocks or rooms, cantilevered balconies, sunken round rooms and even tower structures – many connected with internal passageways.

Ancestral Puebloans inhabited the cliff dwellings for less than a century before disappearing in accord with a regional demographic collapse that is the greatest unexplained event of the era. Death, disease, invasion, internal warfare, resource depletion and climatic change are among the hardships that these peoples faced. Tree-ring chronologies offer proof of a widespread drought from AD 1276 to 1299, yet this explanation fails to account for the earlier population decline at Chaco Canyon or Mesa Verde's survival of earlier droughts. Population movements did occur and it is probable that many Ancestral Puebloans migrated south to the Pueblos of present-day New Mexico and Arizona.

Although archaeologists adopted the Navajo term Anasazi during the 1930s to refer to these early inhabitants of the American Southwest, they have often mistaken it to mean 'ancient people.' Instead, and much to the chagrin of modern Pueblo peoples of Ancestral Puebloan heritage, it can be translated as 'enemy ancestors' in the Navajo tongue.

period	chronology
Hunter-Gatherer	5500 BC
I Basketmaker	AD 1–450
II Modified Basketmaker	450–750
III Developmental Pueblo	around 750 to 1100
IV Classic Pueblo	around 1100 to 1300

that since the latter were not related to the Navajo, using the name 'Anasazi' is inappropriate. Also, the correct translation for 'Anasazi' is not agreed upon and many translate it as 'enemy people' rather than 'ancient people.' The National Park Service has since begun calling them 'Ancestral Puebloans.' In addition, the commonly used term 'ruins' is gradually being substituted with the seemingly more respectful term 'sites.'

Preserving the Ancestral Puebloan sites while accommodating ever-increasing numbers of visitors continues to challenge the National Park Service. The NPS strictly enforces the Antiquities Act, which prohibits removal or destruction of any such items and also prohibits public access to many of the approximately 4000 known sites.

History

A US army lieutenant recorded the spectacular cliff dwellings in the canyons of Mesa Verde in 1849–50. The large number of sites on Ute tribal land, and their relative inaccessibility, protected the majority of these antiquities from pot-hunters.

The first scientific investigation of the ruins in 1874 failed to identify Cliff Palace, the largest cliff dwelling in North America. Discovery of the 'magnificent city' occurred only when local cowboys Richard Wetherill and Charlie Mason were searching for stray cattle after a December 1888 snowfall. The cowboys exploited their 'discovery' for the next 18 years by guiding both amateur and trained archaeologists to the site, particularly to collect the distinctive black-on-white pottery.

The shipping of artifacts overseas motivated Virginia McClurg of Colorado Springs to embark on a long campaign to preserve the site and its contents. McClurg's efforts led Congress to protect artifacts on federal land with passage of the Antiquities Act and to establish Mesa Verde National Park in 1906.

Orientation

The North Rim summit at Park Point (8571 feet) towers more than 2000 feet above the Montezuma Valley. From Park Point the mesa gently slopes southward to 6000-foot elevation above the Mancos River in the Ute Mountain Tribal Park. The mesa-top is dissected by parallel canyons, typically 500 feet below the rim, which carry the drainage southward. Mesa Verde National Park occupies 81 sq miles of the northernmost portion of the mesa and contains the largest and most frequented cliff dwellings and surface sites.

The park entrance is off US 160 midway between Cortez and Mancos. From the entrance it's about 21 miles to park headquarters, Chapin Mesa Museum and Spruce Tree House. Along the way are Morefield Campground (4 miles), the panoramic viewpoint at Park Point (8 miles) and the Far View Visitors Center opposite the Far View Lodge and Restaurant (about 11 miles). Towed vehicles are not allowed beyond Morefield Campground.

Chapin Mesa contains the largest concentration of sites in the area. South from park headquarters, Mesa Top Rd consists of two one-way circuits. Turn left about one-quarter mile from the start of Mesa Top Rd to visit Cliff Palace and Balcony House on the east loop. Take the west loop by continuing straight to mesa-top sites and many fine cliff-dwelling vantages. Taking the west loop first allows you to roughly follow the Ancestral Puebloan chronology in proper sequence.

At Wetherill Mesa, the second-largest concentration of sites, visitors may enter stabilized surface dwellings and two cliff dwellings. From the junction with the main road at Far View Visitors Center, the 12-mile mountainous Wetherill Mesa Rd snakes along the North Rim, acting as a natural barrier to tourbuses and indifferent travelers. The road is open only from Memorial Day to Labor Day.

Information

Far View Visitors Center (☎ 970-529-4543) is open 8 am to 5 pm, late spring through early autumn. More comprehensive information is available at the Chapin Mesa Museum, but visitors must first stop at Far

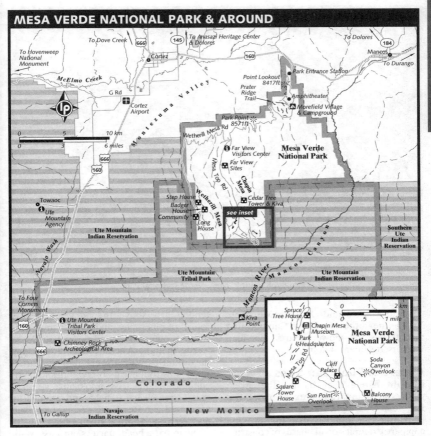

MESA VERDE NATIONAL PARK & AROUND

View to obtain the required tickets ($1.75) for tours of Cliff Palace or Balcony House.

Park headquarters (☎ 970-529-4461) is open weekdays during park hours. For additional information write Mesa Verde National Park, CO 81330. The Chapin Mesa Museum (☎ 970-529-4475) is open 8 am to 5 pm daily (to 6:30 pm in summer) and provides information on weekends when park headquarters is closed.

The park entry fee is $10 per each vehicle passenger, $5 for bicyclists, hikers and motorcyclists, and is valid for seven days. The combined brochure and map handed to each visitor also is available in French, Spanish and German. Park roads are open 8 am to sunset, except Wetherill Mesa Rd, which closes at 4:30 pm. Winter vehicle travel on Mesa Top Rd is subject to weather conditions. You may snowshoe or cross-country ski on the roadway when conditions permit.

The post office is at park headquarters in Chapin Mesa; the zip code is 81330. The Mesa Verde Museum Association (☎ 970-529-4445), located in the Chapin Mesa Museum, has an excellent selection of materials on the Ancestral Puebloan and modern tribes in the American Southwest.

MARK PARKES

Petroglyph Point in Mesa Verde National Park

From May to mid-October, Morefield Village, near the Morefield Campground turnoff, has 10¢ showers and $1 per load washers. It's open 24 hours.

Ancestral Puebloan Sites

Chapin Mesa There is no other place where so many remnants of Ancestral Puebloan settlement are clustered together, providing an opportunity to see and compare examples of all phases of construction – from pithouse to pueblo villages to the elaborate multiroom cities tucked into cliff recesses. Pamphlets describing most excavated sites are available at either Far View Visitors Center or Chapin Mesa Museum.

On the upper portion of Chapin Mesa are the **Far View Sites**, perhaps the most densely settled area in Mesa Verde after AD 1100. The large walled pueblo sites at Far View House enclose a central kiva and planned room layout that originally was two stories high. To the north is a small row of rooms and attached circular tower that likely ex-

tended just above the adjacent 'pygmy forest' of piñon pine and juniper trees. This tower is one of 57 found throughout Mesa Verde that the Ancestral Puebloans may have built as watchtowers, religious structures or astronomical observatories for agricultural schedules. They also built a system to divert streamwater to fields and into nearby Mummy Lake Reservoir – a masonry ditch also led toward Spruce Tree House.

Near park headquarters, an easy walk without ladders or steps leads to **Spruce Tree House**. This sheltered alcove, more than 200 feet wide and almost 90 feet deep, contains about 114 rooms and eight kivas and once housed about 100 people. One kiva has a reconstructed roof and ladder for entry. During the winter when many portions of the park are closed, access to this site is by ranger-led tours only. Spruce Tree House is open 9 am to 5 pm daily.

South from park headquarters, the 6-mile Mesa Top Rd circuit connects 10 excavated mesa-top sites, three accessible cliff dwellings and many vantages of inaccessible cliff dwellings from the mesa rim. It's open 8 am to sunset. Perhaps the most photographed site in the park is the secluded four-story **Square Tower House** on the west loop of Mesa Top Rd. Among the excellent late afternoon views of many cliff dwellings from **Sun Point** is the vista of Cliff Palace, sighted by Richard Wetherill in 1888. The mesa-top sites on the west loop of Mesa Top Rd also feature the astronomically aligned **Sun Temple**.

On the east loop of Mesa Top Rd, you must have a ticket to take part in the one-hour guided tours of either **Cliff Palace** or **Balcony House**, open 9 am to 5 pm daily (closed in winter).

Foot access to Cliff Palace, the largest site in the park, resembles the approach taken by the Ancestral Puebloans – visitors must climb a stone stairway and four 10-foot ladders. This grand representative of engineering achievement, with 217 rooms and 23 kivas, provided shelter for as many as 250 people. However, the inhabitants were without running water – springs across the canyon below Sun Temple were the most likely water sources. Use of small 'chinking' stones between the large blocks is strikingly similar to Ancestral Puebloan construction employed at distant Chaco Canyon.

The residents of Balcony House had outstanding views of Soda Canyon, 600 feet below the sandstone overhang that served as the ceiling for 35 to 40 rooms. Panoramic views, however, were apparently secondary either to concerns for security (entry was via a narrow tunnel) or to the attraction of two reliable springs. Today, visitors enter the obviously stabilized sites by a 32-foot ladder to see the cantilevered balcony and enjoy clambering throughout the tunnel and dwelling.

Wetherill Mesa The less frequented western portion of the park offers a comprehensive display of Ancestral Puebloan relics. From Memorial to Labor Day, the winding Wetherill Mesa Rd is open 8 am to 4:30 pm daily. The **Badger House Community** consists of a short trail between four excavated surface sites depicting various phases of Ancestral Puebloan development. For a complete chronological circuit, continue on the trail to **Long House**, the second largest cliff dwelling in Mesa Verde (for this you'll first need a $1.75 ticket purchased at the Far View Visitors Center). The nearby **Step House**, initially occupied by Modified Basketmaker peoples residing in pithouses, later became the site of a Classic Pueblo period masonry complex of rooms and kivas. Stairways and indentations in the rocks provided access to the partially irrigated crops in the terraces on the mesa top.

Park Point

The fire lookout at Park Point (8571 feet) is the highest elevation in the park and accordingly offers panoramic views. To the north are the 14,000-foot peaks of the San Juan Mountains; in the northeast can be seen the 12,000-foot crests of the La Plata Mountains; to the southwest, beyond the southward sloping Mesa Verde plateau, is the distant volcanic plug of Shiprock; and to the west is the prone humanlike profile of Sleeping Ute Mountain.

Hiking

Backcountry access is specifically forbidden within Mesa Verde National Park. However, there are several marked trails open to hikers.

From park headquarters and adjacent Chapin Mesa Museum, two trail loops, each less than 3 miles in length, are accessed from the short path to Spruce Tree House. All hikers must first register at park headquarters. While you're there, pick up pamphlets for the **Petroglyph Point Trail** and the self-guided tour of Spruce Tree House.

From the museum overlook of Spruce Tree House, follow the path to the canyon floor. Return via Petroglyph Point Trail to view the petroglyphs etched into the naturally varnished rock surface and interpret the uses of native plants. After climbing about 300 feet back to the rim, either return directly to park headquarters or continue to the left on another loop, the **Spruce Canyon Trail**.

From the amphitheater parking area near Morefield Campground, a spur trail climbs to **Point Lookout** about 2 miles away, where you may witness a fabulous sunset over Sleeping Ute Mountain (9884 feet). The 8-mile **Prater Ridge Trail** loop starts at the Hopi group area in Morefield Campground. Neither trail requires a permit.

Bicycling

Finding convenient parking at the many stops along Mesa Top Rd is not a problem for those on bikes. Only the hardiest cyclists, however, will want to enter the park by bike and immediately face the grueling 4-mile ascent to Morefield Campground, followed by a narrow tunnel, to reach the North Rim. An easier option is to unlimber your muscles and mount up at Morefield, Far View Visitors Center or park headquarters.

If you choose to cycle, note that the NPS prohibits bicyclists from Wetherill Mesa Rd, and throughout the park secure bicycle parking is rare. Ride *only* on paved roadways.

Organized Tours

ARAMARK Mesa Verde, the park concessionaire, offers guided tours to excavated pit homes, views of cliff dwellings and the Spruce Tree House daily from May to mid-October.

Introductory three-hour tours ($31/21 adults/children) depart from Morefield Campground at 8:30 am and from Far View Lodge at 9 am. Afternoon tours ($33/23) include the Balcony House and depart the Far View Lodge *only* at 1 pm.

A full-day tour ($51/41 adults/children) includes the morning tour sites, and then goes on to examine later architecture and social developments, also taking in the Cliff Palace. For further information contact ARAMARK Mesa Verde (☎ 970-529-4421), PO Box 277, Mancos, CO 81328.

Places to Stay

Although there are plenty of mid-range places to stay nearby in Cortez and Mancos, within the national park the visitor must choose between two extremes: camping or staying at a high-end lodge. An overnight stay in the park allows convenient access to the many sites during the best viewing hours, participation in evening programs and the sheer pleasure of watching the sun set over Ute Mountain from the quiet of the mesa top.

With 445 campsites only 4 miles from the park entrance, *Morefield Campground* (☎ 970-529-4421), open May to mid-October, has plenty of capacity for the peak season. Grassy tent sites at Navajo Loop are conveniently near Morefield Village (with a general store, gas station, restaurant, showers and laundry) and cost $18. Full hookups are available for $25. Free evening campfire programs are Memorial Day to Labor Day nightly at the Morefield Campground Amphitheater; for information contact the NPS (☎ 970-529-4631).

The nonsmoking *Far View Lodge* (☎ 970-529-4421), 15 miles from the park entrance, perched on the mesa top, has rooms with Southwestern furnishings, private balconies and outstanding views. Rooms are available mid-April to the third week in October; the off-peak rate is $90; Memorial Day to Labor Day it's $107. Compared to top-end lodging in Cortez, the Far View Lodge is a good value and offers a memorable visit (with no TVs or phones to disturb guests).

Places to Eat

The self-service *Far View Terrace*, immediately south of the visitors center, serves reasonably priced meals 7 am to 8 pm (closed during winter months). Near the Chapin Mesa Museum, the *Spruce Tree Terrace* serves sandwiches, salads and the like 10 am to 5 pm daily.

The *Metate Room* (☎ 970-529-4421), at the Far View Lodge, is the nearest restaurant to Dove Creek serving gourmet Anasazi beans (a variegated pinto bean). Open 5 to 9:30 pm nightly, the Metate Room also serves steak, seafood, game specialties and good Mexican dishes.

HOVENWEEP NATIONAL MONUMENT

Hovenweep, meaning 'deserted valley' in the Ute language, is a remote area of former

Ancestral Puebloan settlements straddling the Colorado/Utah border, 42 miles west of Cortez via McElmo Canyon Rd from US 160. This was once home to a large population before drought forced people out in the late 1200s. Six sets of unique tower ruins are found here, but only the impressive ruins in the Square Tower area are readily accessible.

Three easy- to moderate-loop hiking trails (none longer than 2 miles) leave from near the ranger station and pass a number of buildings in the Square Tower area. The trails give both distant and close-up views of the ancient sites whose fragile unstable walls are easily damaged – please stay on the trail and don't climb on the sites. Visitors are reminded that all wildlife is protected – including rattlesnakes – but you are more likely to see the iridescent collared lizard scampering near the trail. Brochures are available for the self-guided tours and also describe plant life along the trails.

The Hovenweep National Park Service Ranger Station (☎ 970-749-0510) is open 8 am to 5:30 pm daily. Rangers answer questions and sell maps and interpretive booklets. You can also call ☎ 970-526-4282 for further information.

Biting gnats are a problem mid-May to July. Wear long sleeves and pants.

Places to Stay
The NPS *campground* is about a mile from the ranger station and is open year-round on a first-come, first-served basis. The 31 sites rarely fill, but are busiest in summer. There are toilets and picnic facilities; the fee is $10. Spring water is available when weather permits, usually from April to October only.

Getting There & Away
From US 160/US 666 south of Cortez, turn at the sign for the Cortez Airport onto Montezuma County Rd G, which follows McElmo Canyon east through red-rock country north of Sleeping Ute Mountain and Ute tribal lands. At the Utah border you cross onto the Navajo Reservation and can expect sheep, goats or even a cattle

drive on the road. A signed road to the monument turns right (north) from McElmo Creek.

UTE MOUNTAIN INDIAN RESERVATION
The Weminuche band of Utes objected to the dispersed allotments offered by the US government and left their Mouache and Capote cousins in the Southern Ute Reservation to establish a tribal camp in the shadow of Sleeping Ute Mountain in 1895. Towaoc (population 700), 12 miles south of Cortez, is the tribal center for the Ute Mountain Ute Reservation. The formerly nomadic peoples retain a more communal lifestyle than their dispersed Navajo and Southern Ute neighbors. Nevertheless, intermarriage is not uncommon, and the Bear Dance in early June attracts single people from other tribes to participate in the ritual of seeking a mate.

Dramatic changes have followed the opening of the popular **Ute Mountain Casino** (☎ 970-565-8800, 800-258-8007), 11 miles south of Cortez on US 160/US 666. Since Congress enacted the Indian Gaming Regulatory Act in 1988, casinos have brought jobs and money to the tribal governments; this is the first federal economic program to do so. The casino is open 20 hours daily, 8 am to 4 am, and attracts a steady stream of 'donors' of Cortez residents and visiting tourists.

Traditional Ute handicrafts focused on beadwork, baskets and leatherwork articles used in a nomadic existence. Since 1970, Ute Mountain Pottery (☎ 970-565-8548), on US 160/US 666, has welcomed visitors to watch Ute artists produce reasonably priced original designs.

Ute Mountain Tribal Park
Spectacular cliff dwellings and other unstabilized sites exist here in a secluded and undeveloped setting. A Ute Mountain Tribal Park guide must accompany all nontribal members who want to enter this portion of the Ute Mountain Reservation.

Tribal members lead full-day tours of surface sites, cliff dwellings and Ute pictographs. Visitors should be prepared to drive 80 miles on unpaved roads and hike about 3 miles. Tour rates are on a sliding scale: Parties of fewer than 10 pay $30 per person, those of more than 10 pay $25/person. Nonmotorists may travel with the tour guide for an additional $5. Half-day tours are also available for $17/person. Tours leave daily at 8:30 am from the Ute Mountain Park Tribal Park Visitors center, 20 miles south of Cortez at the junction of US 160 and US 666. The impressive spire of Chimney Rock provides a nearby landmark.

Mountain-bike tours, overnight backpack hikes and photographic tours also can be arranged. Information and reservations are obtained at the visitors center (☎ 970-565-9653, 800-847-5485).

Places to Stay

Behind the Ute Mountain Casino, *Sleeping Ute RV Park & Campground (☎ 970-565-8800, 800-889-5072)* is open year-round with an indoor pool, laundry, showers and game room. Sites with full hookups are $14. *Ute Mountain Tribal Park*, the park's no-frills campground along the Mancos River, costs $10 per vehicle and requires advance reservations and joining a tour. Food and drinking water are not available in the park.

Eastern Plains

Before the arrival of European settlers in the 1820s, the Eastern Plains were home to several tribes: the Apache, Pawnee and Comanche in the south and the Cheyenne and Arapaho in the north.

Most visitors blast through the Eastern Plains on their way to the Rocky Mountains, and with good reason. While making your way slowly across the plains offers a slice of small-town USA, few spots are genuinely worth a special trip. A good case might be made for visiting the displays of nature and wildlife at Pawnee National Grassland or rock art on the canyon walls beside the Purgatoire River in the Comanche National Grassland. Keen history buffs may also enjoy tracing the path of pioneer travelers along the Santa Fe Trail, including a stop at Bent's Old Fort National Historic Site.

GREELEY

The largest city in the Eastern Plains, Greeley (population 76,000; elevation 4658 feet) is 50 miles east of Estes Park via US 34 and slightly more than 50 miles north of Denver via US 85. The city was founded as a cooperative agricultural colony along the railroad, and since the initial arrival of educated colonists, the performing arts have been popular in Greeley. The University of Northern Colorado (UNC) campus is renowned for its jazz and summer theater programs.

The Greeley Convention & Visitors Bureau (☎ 800-449-3866, 970-352-3566), 902 7th Ave in the former Union Pacific Railroad Depot, has maps, lists of accommodations and restaurants and a large supply of brochures on area attractions. Web site: www.greeleycvb.com

Tourist drawing cards include the charming **Meeker Home Museum** and **Centennial Village Museum**, a diverse collection of 28 historic structures and exhibits. **Greeley Independence Stampede** presents two weeks of rodeo and entertainment on July 4 at Island Grove Park, culminating in fireworks.

PAWNEE NATIONAL GRASSLAND

Stretching across the plains northeast of Greeley, 193,000 acres of stark, tallgrass prairie have been spared the plow. Amid the solitude of this far-reaching preserve and raptor nesting site are the scenic Pawnee Buttes. This area is best known among birdwatchers, who flock here in the spring and early summer to observe the wide variety of raptors and other feathered creatures.

Highlights

- Greeley – Horace Greeley's utopian experiment, now home to farmers, ranchers and symphony musicians

- Pawnee National Grassland – 193,000 acres of stark, tall-grass prairie, home to raptors and the stunning Pawnee Buttes

- Bent's Old Fort National Historic Site – an impressive restoration that recreates life on the Santa Fe Trail in the 1840s

Greeley: A Utopian Experiment

New York Tribune editor Horace Greeley coined the phrase, 'Go west, young man, go west!' in the 1870s. His promotion was a pragmatic appeal for workers to help build a cooperative colony based on large-scale irrigation. His articles sought settlers who 'practiced temperance,' had $1000 in savings and belonged to an organized religion. He misrepresented the site as a forested area in the shadows of the Rocky Mountains – causing many of the first arrivals in 1870 to promptly turn back. Still, the colony took hold.

Greeley chose Nathan Meeker to be his western representative. Meeker then located Union Colony in the fertile wedge immediately upstream from the confluence of the Cache la Poudre and South Platte Rivers. The newly opened Denver Pacific Railroad provided another compelling attraction and sold the land to the colony for the townsite which was platted with streets wide enough to allow a team of horses and wagons to make a U-turn. Each colonist received a 5-acre agricultural plot near town, or an 80-acre tract farther away, in addition to a city lot. The colonists soon prospered with harvests of truck crops, fruit, potatoes and wheat.

Eventually, temperance lost favor when Greeley went 'wet' in 1977. Now the wide streets leave plenty of room for a network of bike lanes throughout the town. Agricultural products and services still lead all employment categories, but Eastman Kodak and Hewlett Packard operate plants nearby.

Orientation

The grassland is divided into two extensive tracts: In the west is the Crow Valley Area and the hamlet of Briggsdale; to the east is the Pawnee Area and a store at Raymer. The highlight for most visitors is the panoramic view of Pawnee Buttes, north of the map speck called Keota. A checkerboard pattern of public and private ownership in the area requires care to avoid trespassing.

Access to the area is via Hwy 14 which forms the start of the Pawnee Pioneer Trails, a route of paved and gravel roads that weaves in and around the grassland before heading east to Sterling.

Information

It's strongly recommended to stop first at the USFS Pawnee National Grassland Ranger Station (☎ 970-353-5004), 660 East O St, which is actually 34 miles southeast of the grassland in northern Greeley. A detailed USFS map of the grassland is available for $6; birding tour guides, larger scale maps to the Pawnee Buttes and other information are also on offer. You'll need the maps to make your way around the confus-

ing warren of roads crisscrossing the grassland. The ranger station is open 8 am to 4:30 pm weekdays.

Web site: www.fs.fed.us/arnf/png/

Grover Grassland Museum

The 110-year-old wooden depot housing the museum (☎ 970-895-2349) on the east end of the small town of Grover on the now defunct Chicago, Burlington & Quincy Railroad, is listed on the National Register of Historic Places. Opening hours are not set, so it's best to call ahead and schedule a visit.

Pawnee Buttes

Standing 300 feet above the plains, the Pawnee Buttes are a stunning variation in an otherwise level landscape. Over time, sudden afternoon downpours have carved the vertical cliffs of the buttes and bluffs, wearing away the soft sandstone and undercutting the cap rock (don't stand too close to the edge!). Note the formation of new steepsided buttes north of the overlook, which one day may also become an isolated butte.

Once your ears become accustomed to the silence of the prairie, listen for wildlife. The cliff faces of the bluff provide nesting

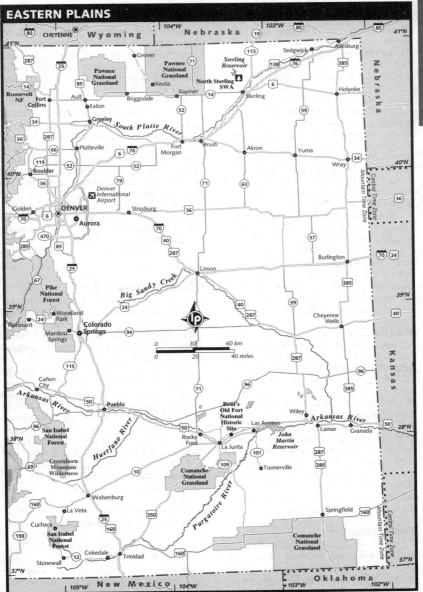

EASTERN PLAINS

habitat for many bird species, including the ferruginous hawk and the prairie falcon. The chestnut-collared longspur, mountain plover, American avocet and burrowing owl also call this treeless land home. The overlook cliffs are closed to visitors from March to July to protect nesting activity. Binoculars and a telephoto lens are the only ways to get close-up views of nest areas.

From the bluff you might also observe an unsuspecting coyote stalking small game or playing. Spring hikes have the added reward of abundant fields of wildflowers among the grasses. Yucca and prickly pear cactus dot the land – often invading once overgrazed areas. Climbing the crumbling cliffs is not recommended and would disturb endangered bird species.

The limited number of signs directing visitors over the gravel roads to Pawnee Buttes makes it essential that you carefully study the map to avoid getting lost; it's 11 miles north from Keota to Pawnee Buttes. Take water and a hat. An easy 1½-mile trail leads to the base of the Buttes from the signs near the overlook entrance gate. Mountain bikes are not permitted on the trail.

Missile Silo

An active Minuteman III silo is located near the route to Pawnee Buttes. From Keota drive north 3 miles on Weld County Rd 105, then turn right onto Weld County Rd 104 and go a little more than 2 miles; Silo 08 is on the left. It is one of more than 200 Minuteman silos dispersed a minimum of 4.2 miles apart in an extensive field covering a large area of southeastern Wyoming, southwestern Nebraska and a small part of northeastern Colorado. There may be no one around but don't try hopping the barbed-wire fence for a closer look – you will likely soon have company in the form of US Air Force military police.

Birdwatching

Make sure to pick up the self-guided birdwatching tour route and map at the USFS office in Greeley (see Information, above). Bird lists are also available. If you did not pick up these materials before entering the Grass-

land, you could try the USFS Briggsdale Work Center (☎ 970-656-3532), about half a mile north of the **Crow Valley Recreation Area**, where the 36-mile tour begins. Call ahead to be sure the lone ranger is on duty. The recreation area is located about half a mile north of the town of Briggsdale. During wet weather, travel on the unpaved roads by passenger automobile is not recommended.

The best time for birdwatching is February to July, after which activity dies down. Remember to be very careful as you observe: Birds are particularly vulnerable to any human interference and just strolling up for a closer look can cause adults to flee, leaving their chicks exposed to the environment and predators.

The birdwatching tour can be enjoyed by bicycle, too. You may want to modify the counterclockwise circuit to return on Weld County Rd 96 rather than Hwy 14. Be prepared for possible afternoon cloudbursts in summer months.

Places to Stay & Eat

The only developed campground in the entire grassland area is the USFS *Crow Valley Recreation Area* (☎ 970-353-5004), immediately north of Hwy 14 on Weld County Rd 77, a half-mile from Briggsdale. It has shaded $8/12 single/double sites.

In the friendly, tiny town of Grover, *The Plover Inn* (☎ 970-895-2275, 223 Chatoga St) is a B&B that mostly caters to birders. It has four suites that can accommodate a total of 16 people. Rates range from $60 to $90 for two people. *West Pawnee Ranch* (☎ 970-895-2482), northwest of Grover near the intersection of Weld County Rds 130 and 59, is a working ranch that offers accommodations in its 'Ranch House' or two-room 'Prairie House' for between $60 and $100.
Web site: www.bbonline.com/co/pawnee/

Grover has two small cafes, one of which also has a small grocery store. If you're planning to camp or picnic it's probably best to do your shopping in Greeley or some other larger town. You may also be able to pick up snack items at the Briggsdale Market.

Getting There & Away

To get to the grassland from the USFS Ranger Station in Greeley, head north 10 miles on US 85 to Ault and the Hwy 14 intersection. Turn right toward Briggsdale, 24 miles away. From Briggsdale it's another 22 miles to Grover and then a further 20 miles or so east to the Pawnee Buttes.

FORT MORGAN

Though not really a destination in itself, there are some nice diversions if you decide to stay overnight in Fort Morgan (population 10,250; elevation 4330 feet), including the **Fort Morgan Museum**, which, along with Western history displays, has exhibits on the town's most famous native, WWII-era Big Band leader Glenn Miller. The pleasant **Riverside Park**, a 240-acre wildlife preservation area along the South Platte River, encompasses wetlands, swimming pools, sports fields and a nature trail where you may see deer, turkeys, eagles, herons and foxes. Fort Morgan is about 80 miles northeast of Denver on I-76, about 40 miles southwest of Sterling.

For more information on the town, stop by the Fort Morgan Chamber of Commerce (☎ 970-867-6702, 800-354-8660), 300 Main St, or visit www.fortmorganchamber.org.

Fort Morgan's handsome **Riverside Park** has a number of free wooded tent sites and restrooms in an area beyond the popular picnic grounds near the east parking lot. Parking for RVs is available near the children's playground. Showers are available during summer months at the park's swimming pools. The small and basic **Fort Morgan Motel** (☎ 970-867-8264, 525 W Platte Ave) has singles/doubles for $30/35. Similar rates are available at **The Deluxe Motel** (☎ 970-867-2459, 817 E Platte Ave). The **Central Motel** (☎ 970-867-2401, 201 W Platte Ave) has quiet and clean rooms with microwave ovens and refrigerators for $43/49. The **Best Western Park Terrace** (☎ 970-867-8256, 725 Main St) has a swimming pool, hot tub and restaurant; rates are $54/60.

Breakfast is served all day at **Memories Restaurant** (☎ 970-867-8205) in the Best Western. It's a popular spot serving fresh fruit pies and Mexican and standard US entrees 6 am to 9 pm daily. Similar fare can be found at **Strohs** (☎ 970-867-6654, 901 W Platte Ave), though the menu is less extensive. Carnivorous Americana reigns at **Country Steakout** (☎ 970-867-7887, 19592 E 8th Ave), a lunch and dinner restaurant east of Main St. The Steakout is the best restaurant in town, renowned for quality steaks; seafood and spaghetti are also on the menu.

Greyhound (☎ 970-867-8072) buses stop in front of Pets Are People Too, 835 E Platte Ave. There are daily buses to Denver and Omaha, Nebraska. Amtrak's *California Zephyr*, which serves Chicago–San Francisco (Emeryville) via Denver, stops daily at the depot on Ensign St south of Railroad Ave.

STERLING

The main claim to fame of Sterling (population 10,700; elevation 3939 feet) is its collection of imaginative (and sometimes bizarre) tree carvings of animals, people and surreal characters from fables that can be seen from sidewalks around town. Sterling is also home to the **Overland Trail Museum** (☎ 970-522-3895), on US 6 just a mile east of town on the south bank of the South Platte River, where excellent exhibits bring to life the hardships and experiences of early pioneers and the region's history. The museum is open 9 am to 5 pm Monday to Saturday (10 am to 4 pm Tuesday to Saturday in winter). A park near the museum is a convenient rest stop for weary travelers contemplating the 125-mile journey southwest to Denver.

Detailed information on Sterling is available at the Logan County Chamber of Commerce (☎ 970-522-5070, 800-544-8609), in the restored Union Pacific Depot at Front and Main Sts.
Web site: www.sterlingcolo.com

The city-owned **Pioneer Park**, on the western edge of town next to Hwy 14, offers free camping and restrooms. Small singles/doubles at **Crest Motel** (☎ 970-522-3753, 516 S Division St), at 3rd St, are a good value for $30/35. Basic, clean singles/doubles are available at **Colonial**

Motel (☎ *970-522-3382, 915 S Division St)* for $29/34. Another centrally located place is the *Oakwood Inn* (☎ *970-522-1416, 810 S Division St)*, which has well-kept rooms equipped with refrigerators and microwave ovens for $30/35.

TJ Bummers (☎ *970-522-8397, 203 Broadway)* is a pleasant surprise; breakfast, lunch and dinner are served 5:30 am to 9 pm daily in smoke-free surroundings. The 'Hobo Dinner,' a foil-baked stew, costs $5 and a full rack of baby back ribs with side dishes is $11. *Delgado's Dugout* (☎ *970-522-0175, 116 Beech St)*, in the basement of the former First Baptist Church, serves inexpensive Mexican lunches and dinners daily except Monday. *Fergie's West Inn Pub*, (☎ *970-522-2492, 324 W Main St)*, between 3rd and 4th Aves, offers a selection of beers and deli sandwiches. For mouth-watering steaks in pleasant surroundings, look for *Atwood Steakhouse*, near I-76 mile marker 115, about 10 miles west of town.

Greyhound (☎ 970-522-5522) buses stop at the Days Inn Motel, 12881 Hwy 61, an inconvenient freeway location about 2 miles south of Sterling. There are daily buses to Denver and Omaha, Nebraska.

JULESBURG

In the extreme northeastern corner of Colorado on the South Platte River, Julesburg was once known as the 'Wickedest City in the West,' an end-of-the-line outpost packed with brothels and bars. Today its main feature for visitors is the Colorado Welcome Center (☎ 970-474-2054), at the junction of I-76 and US 385 (I-76 exit 180), open 8 am to 5 pm daily. Julesburg proper is about 3 miles beyond the Welcome Center across the river and a modern rail overpass – this is where road-weary travelers will find a place to spend the night.

Free primitive camping on the south bank of the South Platte River is available at *Lions Park*, immediately south of Julesburg on US 385. The two-story *Grand Motel* (☎ *970-474-3302, 220 Pine St)*, across 3rd St from the courthouse, has a coin laundry on the premises and clean singles/doubles with phone and cable TV for

$28/36. Another budget option is the *Holiday Motel* (☎ *970-474-3371)*, on the western edge of town at the junction of US 138 and US 385; rooms cost $26/36. A little more expensive is the *Platte Valley Inn* (☎ *970-474-3336, 800-562-5166)*, next to the freeway exit, where rooms cost $43/48.

I-70 CORRIDOR

Between Denver and the Kansas border, I-70 runs through some of the state's blandest landscape. The only reason to stop in this area is if you're in danger of falling asleep at the wheel.

Some travelers bound for Denver have found themselves too frazzled by the endless drive through the plains of Kansas and have sought shelter in the motels of Limon, 86 miles east of the Colorado capital. Most of the accommodations in this little agricultural town are in the downtown area accessed by exit 361. At the *KOA* (☎ 719-775-2151), adjacent to I-70 exit 361, grassy tent sites cost $15, but you must endure the freeway noise. The three-story *Midwest Country Inn* (☎ *719-775-2373, 795 Main St)* is a comfortable place: Rooms have attractive quilt bedspreads and some antique furnishings and cost $38/42 singles/doubles. The nearby *Safari Motel* (☎ *719-775-2363, 637 Main St)* has a swimming pool, coin laundry and rooms for $32/38 (higher in summer). Near exit 361 is *Preferred Motor Inn* (☎ *719-775-2385)* with swimming pool and hot tub; rooms cost $35/40.

Just 12 miles from the Kansas border, 163 miles east of Denver, the town of Burlington boasts several motels and a Colorado Welcome Center (☎ 719-346-5554) at the I-70 exit, along with its Thursday cattle auctions. If you're in town for any length of time, venture north of the railroad tracks off 15th St to the 1905 Kit Carson County Carousel, which sports 46 hand-carved animals.

Campland (☎ *719-346-8763)*, on the east side of town at the corner of 4th St and Senter Ave, has RV sites available for $12. The brick *Western Motor Inn* (☎ *719-346-5371)*, at the corner of Rose Ave and Lincoln St, has clean, quiet singles/doubles for $28/33. An enclosed pool and children's play area are added amenities at *Sloan's Motel* (☎ 719-346-5333, 800-362-0464, 1901 Rose Ave); rooms go for $30/38.

LA JUNTA

At an elevation of 4100 feet, La Junta (mispronounced 'La Hunt-ah'; population 8000) is Spanish for 'The Junction,' namely the junction once here between the main line and Denver branch of the Santa Fe Railroad. For the few travelers who roam the Eastern Plains, it's still a junction of sorts, lying between Bent's Old Fort National Historic Site to the northeast and the Comanche National Grassland to the south. La Junta, while not stunning, offers a pleasant snapshot of small-town US life yet to be overrun by freeways, shopping malls and tourist kitsch. Ranchers from the Rocky Mountains to the far corners of the Eastern Plains come to La Junta's livestock auctions to market their range-fed animals, lending the town a distinctive Western flair.

Orientation

Through traffic on US 50 follows east-west 1st St through town, south of the Arkansas River and the railroad. Colorado Ave is the main business artery, extending south from the rail depot at 1st St. On the east side of town, Hwy 109 crosses the Arkansas River, going north to connect with Hwy 194 leading to Bent's Old Fort, 6 miles away.

Information

The La Junta Chamber of Commerce (☎ 719-384-7411), 110 Santa Fe Ave on US 50 opposite the Amtrak Depot, has useful maps and information and is open 9 am to 5 pm weekdays. Its Web site is at www.lajunta.net. The USFS Comanche National Grassland Ranger Station (☎ 719-384-2181), 1420 E 3rd St, has detailed information on the grassland (see Comanche National Grassland, later).

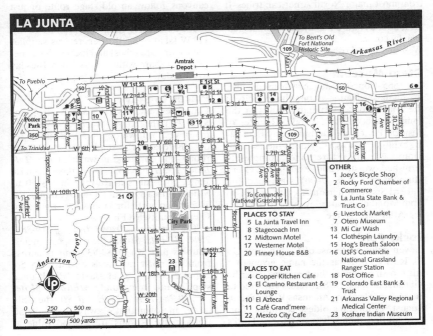

LA JUNTA

PLACES TO STAY
5 La Junta Travel Inn
8 Stagecoach Inn
12 Midtown Motel
17 Westerner Motel
20 Finney House B&B

PLACES TO EAT
4 Copper Kitchen Cafe
9 El Camino Restaurant & Lounge
10 El Azteca
11 Café Grand'mere
22 Mexico City Cafe

OTHER
1 Joey's Bicycle Shop
2 Rocky Ford Chamber of Commerce
3 La Junta State Bank & Trust Co
6 Livestock Market
7 Otero Museum
13 Mi Car Wash
14 Clothespin Laundry
15 Hog's Breath Saloon
16 USFS Comanche National Grassland Ranger Station
18 Post Office
19 Colorado East Bank & Trust
21 Arkansas Valley Regional Medical Center
23 Koshare Indian Museum

ATMs are located at the Colorado East Bank & Trust, 405 Colorado Ave, and La Junta State Bank & Trust Co near the corner of Colorado Ave and 1st St. The Spanish-style post office, which is on the National Register of Historic Places, is at the corner of 4th St and Colorado Ave. The Clothespin Laundry (☎ 719-384-9812), 717 E 3rd St, offers a drop-off service; closed Sunday.

The Arkansas Valley Regional Medical Center (☎ 719-384-5412) is at 1100 Carson Ave at the corner of 10th St.

Koshare Indian Museum

The Koshare tribe is actually a La Junta Boy Scout group locally famous for performing tribal dances in June and July. The dancers literally go through hoops of fire in their own kiva-like auditorium built in 1949. The museum (☎ 719-384-4411), 115 W 18th St, also has an extensive collection of Native American artifacts that includes examples from most major North American tribes. It is open 10 am to 5 pm daily. Admission costs $2/1, adults/children. Dances, when staged, usually cost $5.

Web site: www.koshare.org

Otero Museum

An 1865 Concord stagecoach used along the Santa Fe Trail is among the exhibits in the coach house. Other buildings in the complex are on the National Register of Historic Places and contain many interesting exhibits, such as a doctor's office, schoolroom, grocery store and completely furnished two-story adobe home. The Otero Museum (☎ 719-384-7406) is between 2nd and 3rd Sts at Anderson Ave. It's open 1 to 5 pm Monday to Saturday, June to September. Admission is free.

Rocky Ford

Eleven miles northeast of La Junta on US 50, Rocky Ford was the name given to a safe crossing point in the Arkansas River by Kit Carson. Since 1878, revelers attracted to the Melon Pile at the **Arkansas Valley Fair** in August, Colorado's oldest continual fair, have stuffed themselves on Rocky Ford's delicious honeydew melons, watermelons and cantaloupes. When residents of the 'Melon Capital of the World' dedicated the small general aviation field south of town, they appropriately named it 'Melon Field.' The Rocky Ford Chamber of Commerce (☎ 719-254-7483), in the restored Santa Fe Depot at 105 N Main, has maps showing more than 30 produce farms and markets open to the public.

Bicycling

You can ride to Rocky Ford on the paved country backroads from La Junta. A 32-mile counterclockwise loop crosses the Arkansas River to N La Junta on Hwy 109, then turns left (west) on Hwy 266 to Rocky Ford. Return by traveling south on Hwy 71 to Hawley where a left turn (east) on Hwy 10 heads back to La Junta. The wide-open spaces of the Comanche National Grassland (see below) invite fat-tire enthusiasts to explore the unexpected greenness of its canyons, follow an old stage route or just cruise the gravel roads across the plains.

Joey's Bicycle Shop (☎ 719-384-6575), 112 W 1st St (US 50), offers rentals, supplies (take extra tire tubes) and local riding experience to share with visitors; open Tuesday to Saturday.

Places to Stay

Grassy tent and RV sites are available for $16/19 at the *KOA* (☎ *719-384-9580),* 2 miles west of town on US 50. A bit farther out, there are free shaded sites with rest rooms but no drinking water at the *Holbrook Reservoir SWA.* To get there from La Junta, go 5 miles northwest on US 50 to Swink, turn right onto Otero County Rd 24.5 and go north for 3 miles, then right onto Otero County Rd FF.

The *La Junta Travel Inn* (☎ *719-384-2504, 110 E 1st St)* has the cheapest singles/doubles in town at $30/39, but is across from the noisy rail yards on busy US 50. Popular cowboy poet Baxter Black once slept at the immaculate *Midtown Motel* (☎ *719-384-7741, 215 E 3rd St),* the only motel in town that's away from US 50 traffic noise. Rooms are a good value at

$30/40. The **Westerner Motel** (☎ 719-384-2591, 1502 E 3rd St), near the USFS office on the east side of town, has comfortable rooms for $30/40. Old toy collectors will want to check out the collection in the front office. The 1960s cinderblock **Stagecoach Inn** (☎ 719-384-5476), on the west side of town at the intersection of US 50 and US 350, has amiable staff, a swimming pool and clean rooms for $40/45.

Finney House B&B (☎ 719-384-8758, 606 Belleview Ave) is an attractive inn dating from 1899. It's listed with the National Register of Historic Places and features original oak moldings and stained glass windows. The friendly owner rents her charming rooms for $45 to $75 (an excellent value).

Places to Eat

The **Copper Kitchen Cafe** (☎ 719-384-7508, 116 Colorado Ave) has friendly service, breakfast specials from $3 and overflowing dinner plates.

A testament to its large Hispanic population, La Junta has quite a few Mexican restaurants. **El Camino Restaurant & Lounge** (☎ 719-384-2871, 816 W 3rd St) offers good Mexican dishes for lunch and dinner; closed Sunday and Monday. **Mexico City Cafe** (☎ 719-384-9518, 1617 Raton Ave), in a residential neighborhood, is a popular spot with combo plates for around $5, though it caters to a more mainstream US palate. A third option is **El Azteca** (☎ 719-384-4215), across from the Otero Museum on 3rd St. It's been in business since 1950.

The **Hog's Breath Saloon** (☎ 719-384-7879, 808 E 3rd St) is a local cowboy hangout that does hearty steaks, burgers, seafood and sandwiches. You can catch live music here on weekends.

Cafe Grand'mere (☎ 719-384-2711, 408 W 3rd St), perhaps the only gourmet eatery on the Eastern Plains, is a most unexpected surprise. Expert chef Ron Charlton prepares creative, yet authentic French cuisine in a lovely former carriage house. It's open for lunch 11 am to 2 pm weekdays and for dinner from 5:30 pm to 9 pm Thursday to Saturday.

Getting There & Away

TNM&O buses stop at the Mi Car Wash (☎ 719-384-9288), 619 E 3rd St. Tickets are available for daily westbound buses to Pueblo and beyond and eastbound buses to either Wichita, Kansas or Dallas, Texas.

The Amtrak **Southwest Chief** serves Chicago and Los Angeles daily and stops at the Amtrak Depot (☎ 719-384-2275) on 1st St (US 50) at the corner of Colorado Ave.

La Junta is 50 miles west of Lamar and 64 miles east of Pueblo on US 50 along the Arkansas River, and 81 miles northeast of Trinidad along the old Santa Fe Trail route followed by US 350.

BENT'S OLD FORT NATIONAL HISTORIC SITE

An impressive restoration and preservation effort went into the site surrounding this fort, a hub of commerce on the Santa Fe Trail from 1833 to 1849. Parking is relegated to an area some distance from the fort so visitors can appreciate the historic authenticity of approaching on foot. Upon entering the front gate, the pioneer trader was greeted, as are visitors today, by a bustle of commotion within the compound. It is all the more impressive to consider that this fort was reconstructed in 1976 from little more than a foundation and a few drawings.

At the fort you can view a 20-minute film, take a 45-minute tour with a ranger dressed in period costume or simply walk through the rooms on your own. Demonstrations of frontier skills like blacksmithing, carpentry or the preparation of hides are presented during summer months.

Bent's Old Fort (☎ 719-383-5010, 719-383-5032 TTY) is on Hwy 194, 8 miles east of La Junta or 13 miles west from Las Animas. It's open 8 am to 5:30 pm Memorial Day to Labor Day, 9 am to 4 pm the rest of the year. Admission is $2 adults; children under five free.

COMANCHE NATIONAL GRASSLAND

Southeastern Colorado suffered greatly from the drought and economic depression of the 1930s. The Dust Bowl disaster in the same decade, an environmental collapse caused by poor soil management, led the federal government to purchase land and protect it from plowing and overgrazing. Since 1954, the Comanche National Grassland has been managed by the USFS. It currently consists of two extensive management units: the Timpas Unit south of La Junta, which includes readily accessible portions of the Santa Fe Trail and the many scenic, historic and archaeological sites along the Purgatoire River; and the Carrizo Unit, an even larger but more isolated area near Springfield south of Lamar. Information and trail descriptions are available from the USFS Comanche National Grassland Ranger Station (☎ 719-384-2181), 1420 E 3rd St in La Junta.

Vogel Canyon

This small tributary to the Purgatoire River is an ideal picnic area. Four short hiking and mountain-bike trails wind down to the canyon bottom, an oasis of lush vegetation and springs, and back up to the juniper trees and shortgrass prairie of the mesa top. Between 300 and 800 years ago, Native Americans lived near the springs in the canyon and etched petroglyphs on the canyon walls. A few recent vandals have added their work as well. To reach Vogel Canyon from La Junta, travel south on Hwy 109 for 13 miles. At the Vogel Canyon sign turn right (west) for a mile, then left (south) for 2 miles to the parking area.

Picket Wire Canyon

Due to Anglos' inability to pronounce 'Purgatoire,' the canyon's name eventually degraded to 'Picket Wire.' In stark contrast to the shortgrass prairie, buckhorn cholla and sparse juniper woodland of the plains surrounding Picket Wire Canyon, the Purgatoire River cuts an oasis corridor along its path. Access to Picket Wire Canyon is not easy, but few other places in this region offer so much to the hiker or cyclist. The suggested 11-mile roundtrip trek to the Dinosaur Tracks is best accomplished on a

mountain bike. There are four other hikes ranging from 2 to 18 miles.

The **Dinosaur Tracks**, found in the limestone rock about 5 miles from the trailhead, comprise the largest track site in North America. Nearby are the ruins of **Dolores Mission & Cemetery**, built between 1871 and 1889, when Mexican pioneers established the first modern settlement in the canyon.

To reach the Picket Wire Canyon trailhead from La Junta, travel south on Hwy 109 for 13 miles. At the Vogel Canyon sign turn right (west) on Otero County Rd 802 and continue for 8 miles. Turn left (south) on Otero County Rd 25 and continue for 6 miles before turning left (east) where a corral and bulletin board mark the very poor USFS Rd 500. Passenger cars should park here. Bicyclists or high-clearance vehicles may continue ¾ mile east to a wire gate (please keep closed) and another 2 miles to the locked pipe gate at the trailhead. If you have a high-clearance 4WD vehicle you can participate in all-day jeep tours led by the USFS, which run April to July and September to October; inquire at the Comanche National Grassland Ranger Station.

SANTA FE TRAIL

In 1821, Mexico achieved independence from Spain, opening up trade opportunities between the new country and the USA. The conduit for this commerce became the Santa Fe Trail, linking St Louis, Missouri, with Mexico's northern center at Santa Fe in what is now New Mexico. At the outset in 1822, the Santa Fe Trail was a pack trail following a path where animals would find grass. Later the freight capacity of the trail was increased with the development of wagon routes over the difficult terrain at Raton Pass and Apache Cañon in New Mexico.

You can visit three historically significant Santa Fe Trail sites within 27 miles of La Junta along Hwy 350. No services or drinking water presently exist along the 80-mile La Junta–Trinidad route, so gas up and bring supplies.

At 13 miles, turn right (north) on Hwy 71 for a half-mile to the **Sierra Vista Overlook**, where the first views of the Rocky Mountains represented a major milestone in the journey across the plains from the east. From the bluff you can share the same distant view and see the fenced corridor marking the trail for hikers wishing to follow a 3-mile segment to the **Timpas Creek Picnic Area**. Timpas Creek was the first source of water for Santa Fe Trail travelers after leaving the Arkansas River. From 1861 to 1871 the Metcalf Ranch, previously located here, served as a stagecoach station.

Timpas Creek Picnic Area is 16 miles southeast of La Junta on the right (west) side of the highway: Take Otero County Rd 16.5 across the railroad tracks and turn right to the parking lot.

You can see wagon ruts at the **Iron Spring** water stop on the Santa Fe Trail. This site was also a stagecoach station from 1861 to 1871. At 27 miles southwest of La Junta on US 350, turn left (south) onto Otero County Rd 9 and proceed 1 mile.

LAMAR

If your mind is numb from hours of driving through Kansas wheat fields, Lamar (population 10,000; elevation 3640 feet) might make for a good overnight stop. The town is 32 miles west of the Kansas border. If you stop early, or just want to stroll around after lunch, check out the **wooden windmills**, said to be among the finest examples in the entire state. One is across from the railroad depot and the other is in the front yard of the president of the Colorado Windmill Society at 900 S Main St.

You can also pick up information for your Colorado vacation at the Colorado Welcome Center (☎ 719-336-3483), in the restored railroad depot at Main and Beech Sts. It's open 8:30 am to 5 pm daily.

Places to Stay & Eat

The **Mike Higbee State Wildlife Area**, 4 miles east of Lamar on US 50, offers free unimproved campsites along the Arkansas River. Free overnight camping is also allowed at **Lamar Roadside Park** at the Prowers County Fairgrounds at the south entrance to town.

The cheapest rooms in town are at **Stockmens Motor Inn** (☎ 719-336-2271), at the corner of Olive and Main Sts, with $25 doubles. The hotel's location (right above a local bar!), however, may deter some travelers. The conveniently located **Passport Inn** (☎ 719-336-7746, 113 N Main St) is a friendly place with clean singles/doubles for $36/44, including Continental breakfast. Rooms at **Blue Spruce Motel** (☎ 719-336-7454, 1801 S Main St) have soundproof brick walls; $32/44.

The top spot in town is the ***Best Western Cow Palace Inn*** (☎ *719-336-7753, 800-678-0344, 1301 N Main*). Rooms cost $74/79, and facilities include an indoor heated pool, hot tub, lounge and restaurant.

Cheap and hearty breakfast specials start from around $3 at the ***Main Cafe*** (☎ *719-336-5736, 114 S Main),* open 6:30 am to 9 pm daily. Reasonably priced sandwiches, burgers, Mexican dishes and steaks are found on the lunch and dinner menus. The ***Hickory House*** (☎ *719-336-5018, 1115 N Main)* is the top-end steak house featuring baby back ribs. ***Blackwell Station*** (☎ *719-336-7575, 1301 S Main St)* also does respectable steaks and has a commendable salad bar.

Getting There & Away

United Express has flights to Denver from Lamar Municipal Field, 4 miles southwest of town.

The TNM&O/Greyhound Bus Station (☎ 719-336-5291) is across from the courthouse at 401 S Main St. There are daily buses to Denver, Amarillo and Dallas and Wichita, Kansas. The Amtrak *Southwest Chief,* serving Los Angeles and Chicago, stops daily at the depot (☎ 719-336-3483) on US 50 and Beech St, which also houses the Colorado Welcome Center.

Lamar is 50 miles east of La Junta and 32 miles west of the Kansas border on US 50.

Wyoming

Wyoming

Facts about Wyoming

From the Black Hills and Devils Tower to the geysers of Yellowstone National Park and the granite summits of the Teton and Wind River ranges, wild Wyoming (population 485,000) is a state of physical contrasts, where broad arid basins and sagebrush plains rump up against forested mountains.

More than 150 million years ago this landscape was a tropical marshland ruled by dinosaurs. Subsequent volcanoes and glaciation shaped the topography, and now a rich fossil record and huge coal and oil deposits are the legacy of those past epochs. Today's tall forests and open plains support bountiful wildlife. Pronghorn antelope herds abide in the high desert, and moose, elk and bear roam the high country. Trout spawn in most every stream and rare birds revel in diverse habitats. Such remarkable physical contrasts provide one of America's best outdoor sports arenas, from fishing and hunting to climbing, camping, skiing and spelunking.

Modern Wyomingites inherit a colorful history of pioneer migration and settlement, underlain by the enduring presence of the Shoshone and Arapaho people, who today live on the Wind River Indian Reservation. The Wild West legacy is indelibly imprinted on the culture. Almost every town has a rodeo, and the era of mountain men and Indians is reenacted in pageants statewide. Each summer, more than 3 million visitors come to see Yellowstone and Grand Teton National Parks, and every winter, skiers flock to world-famous Jackson Hole. All this adds up to make tourism the state's second biggest economic booster, after resource extraction.

INFORMATION
State Tourist Offices

The Wyoming Division of Tourism shares a building with the Frank Norris Jr Wyoming Information Center (☎ 307-777-7777, 800-225-5996); take I-25 exit 7 to College Dr in Cheyenne. The Division of Tourism's Web site is www.wyomingtourism.org. Other Wyoming Information Centers are at

Highlights

- Medicine Bow Mountains – a popular year-round outdoor playground, capped by the scenic Snowy Range
- Devils Tower National Monument – an otherworldly volcanic rock formation sacred to Native Americans
- Cody – the heart of the Bighorn Basin, where Buffalo Bill and other Wild West legends live on
- Yellowstone National Park – the world's first national park and home to North America's most spectacular concentration of wildlife, a wonderland of geysers, hot springs, forested mountains, Alpine lakes and waterfalls
- Grand Teton National Park – jagged granite spires towering over scenic lakes and hiking trails

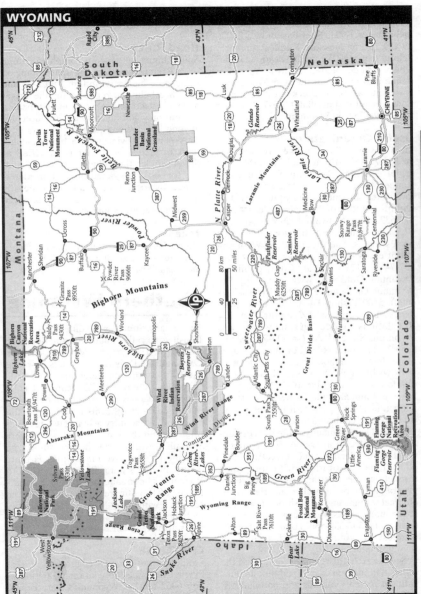

various gateways: I-80 in Pine Bluffs, I-80 in Evanston, I-80 9 miles east of Laramie, I-90 in Sundance, I-90 in Sheridan and US 26/US 89/US 191 in Jackson. Request the very helpful seasonal 'Wyoming Vacation Guide,' which includes a state highway map. For online info, check out the state Web site at www.state.wy.us. To check on road conditions across the state, dial ☎ 307-772-0824 or ☎ 888-996-7623 in Wyoming.

Useful Organizations

The Division of State Parks & Historic Sites (☎ 307-777-6323) is at 122 W 25th St, Herschler Building, 1st floor E, Cheyenne. Request their 'Wyoming State Parks & Historic Sites' brochure. The State Board of Outfitters and Professional Guides (☎ 307-777-5323, 800-264-0981), 1750 Westland Rd, Cheyenne, publishes a directory of licensed professionals. The independent Wyoming Outfitters & Guides Association (☎ 307-527-7453), 1716 8th St, Cody, publishes 'Wyoming Outdoors'; www.wyoga.org. The Wyoming Game and Fish Dept (☎ 307-777-4600), 5400 Bishop Blvd, Cheyenne, publishes the annual 'Wyoming Fishing Regulations' guide; gf.state.wy.us. The Wyoming State BLM (☎ 307-775-6256), 5353 Yellowstone Rd, Cheyenne, manages more than 18 million acres of public land; www.wy.blm.gov. Wyoming Homestay & Outdoor Adventures (☎ 307-237-3526) publishes an annual guide to B&Bs, inns and guest ranches; you can visit its Web site at www.wyomingbnb-ranchrec.com.

Several important environmental organizations are based in Lander. The National Outdoor Leadership School (NOLS) is an educational institution with programs throughout the West and overseas. NOLS programs combine intellectual rigor with physical training and acquisition of practical backcountry skills. Its international headquarters (☎ 307-332-5300) is at 288 Main St. Request a course catalog online at www.nols.edu.

See the Activities chapter for a list of the state's national parks, national monuments, national recreation areas and national historic sites.

Area Code

Wyoming's only area code is ☎ 307.

Road Rules

Speed limits range from 55mph to 65mph on most state highways, and up to 75mph on some state highways and on I-80, I-25 and I-90. Seatbelts are required for the driver and passengers on highways and interstates. On motorcycles, helmets are required for anyone 19 years or younger.

A person driving with a blood alcohol limit of 0.10% or higher is classified as driving under the influence (DUI). Penalties for those convicted of DUI are determined by local courts, and are generally quite severe – but drive-thru 'package liquor' stores are commonplace!

Taxes

State sales tax is 4%; county sales tax ranges from zero to 2%. State lodging tax is no more than 8%.

Southern Wyoming

Historically, Southern Wyoming has been a transit zone rather than a destination in its own right. The Oregon, Mormon Pioneer, Overland and Pony Express Trails, as well as the transcontinental telegraph, Overland Stage and Union Pacific Railroad (UP; 'Uncle Pete') passed through. Today, when not closed by snowstorms, I-80 traverses this hardscrabble country, where gusting winds often exceed the speed limit. Southeastern Wyoming, with its reliance on subsidized agriculture and government jobs, is more economically stable than southwestern Wyoming's boom-and-bust resource extraction belt. The entire region is politically conservative, with many Mormon communities looking toward Salt Lake City for cultural and spiritual guidance.

CHEYENNE

Straddling the western edge of the Great Plains, Cheyenne (population 55,000; elevation 6062 feet) is Wyoming's state capital and the state's largest city. Historically a cattle and railroad town and famous for Cheyenne Frontier Days celebrations, Cheyenne features an economy that is supported mainly by the state government and a large air force base. The well-preserved historic downtown is surrounded by worthwhile cultural attractions, parks and museums. For visitors from the east and south, Cheyenne is the gateway to most Wyoming destinations.

History

Cheyenne owes its development to the US military and the UP. In 1865, surveying possible transcontinental railroad routes through the Laramie Mountains under orders from President Abraham Lincoln, General Grenville Dodge chanced upon a gentle eastward grade near Lone Tree Creek. This slope, known as the 'gangplank,' was the only Front Range pass that required no tunnels or switchbacks to continue westward. Its discovery enabled the UP to follow the coal-rich southern Wyoming route. Returning two years later, Dodge named the new UP terminus 'Cheyenne'; the military base established to protect it was Fort DA Russell.

Early Cheyenne was a lawless 'hell on wheels' full of lowlifes and speculators. But with military assistance, the railroad soon asserted its dominance over Cheyenne and other southern Wyoming towns. The Romanesque grandeur of the UP depot, facing the Wyoming State Capitol at the opposite end of Capitol Ave, symbolized the railroad's influence in the state. The railroad also spurred the growth and influence of the

WYOMING

Cattle Barons & the 'Cowboy State'

The removal of the Native American 'threat' opened Wyoming's plains to ranchers who pastured cattle where enormous bison herds once roamed. Wyoming later became the 'Cowboy State,' but it really was the cattle barons' state, as the powerful Wyoming Stock Growers Association (WSGA) controlled the politicians in Cheyenne.

The cattle barons lived in luxury in Cheyenne or even back east, while their employees did the hard work of running unsustainable numbers of cattle on the arid prairies. The ferocious winter of 1886–87 killed much of their stock and made them vulnerable to small-time ranchers, whom they accused of being rustlers, and to homesteaders, who were known pejoratively as 'nesters.'

While the cattle barons remained a powerful factor in Wyoming politics – even passing legislation excluding the smaller ranches from acquiring stock except on WSGA approval – the disaster of 1886–87 marked a turning point. The WSGA's foolish attempt to drive out Powder River homesteaders with a mercenary Texan army in 1892 largely discredited the organization, though it never

entirely disappeared. The unsuitability of most of Wyoming for homesteading allowed relatively large cattle ranches to return in some areas.

The cowboy was more an icon than a reality. Rather than the independent, self-reliant individual depicted in romantic literature, he was an ordinary employee of large enterprises like the legendary Swan Land and Cattle Company, which controlled hundreds of thousands of acres of pastureland. The few lucky enough to establish their own herds emulated the men for whom they had worked.

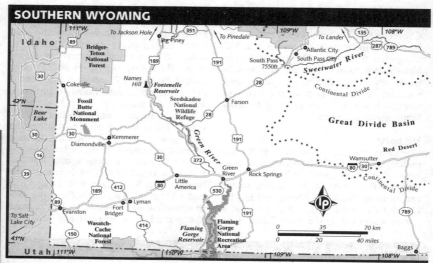

SOUTHERN WYOMING

great open-range ranchers, who built extravagant mansions and the opulent Cheyenne Club downtown. The bitter 1886–87 winter devastated livestock and marked the beginning of the decline of the cattle barons, as smaller ranchers and sheepmen gradually acquired lands grazed without title.

During the 20th century, Cheyenne grew through state government and the military. Fort DA Russell, renamed Fort Warren (now Warren Air Force Base), grew enormously after WWII with construction of nuclear missile sites nearby.

Orientation & Information
Lincolnway (US 30, I-80 Business), which replaces 16th St, is the main east-west thoroughfare. The railroad tracks run along the south side of Lincolnway, and downtown is north of the tracks. The main north-south routes are Central Ave (southbound) and Warren Ave (northbound); at various points these avenues also form parts of US 87 Business, US 85, I-80, I-25 Business and Greeley Hwy. Grocery stores and fast-food restaurants are north of the airport along Dell Range Blvd.

The Cheyenne Area Convention & Visitors Bureau (☎ 307-778-3133, 800-426-5009), 309 W Lincolnway, publishes a free vacation guide; look on its Web site at www.cheyenne.org. The state Travel Info Center at I-25 exit 7 is open 8 am to 5 pm daily. ATMs are downtown on Carey and Capitol Aves. The post office is in the Federal Center at 2120 Capitol Ave. United Medical Center (☎ 307-634-2273) is at 300 E 23rd St.

Historic District Walking Tour
To get a feel for Cheyenne, begin a walking tour at the Plains Hotel (1911) on the corner of Lincolnway and Central Ave. One block west at 1518 Capitol Ave, the Phoenix Block (1882) has housed a hotel, stores and offices. The sandstone blocks of the imposing Romanesque 1886 Union Pacific (UP) depot, 121 W 15th St, house a free transportation museum (☎ 307-637-3376), open 10 am to 4 pm weekdays. Two blocks west is the Hofmann Building (1880), 316 W 15th St; note the cast-iron facade of this former saloon. One block north, the turreted Dinneen Building, 400 W Lincolnway, has

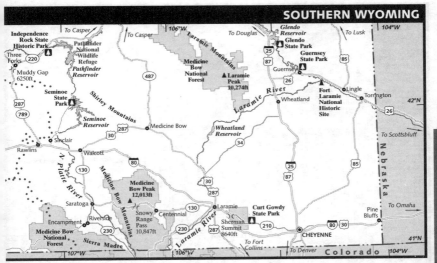

been an automobile showroom since it opened in 1927. The superbly restored Queen Anne Tivoli (1892), 301 W Lincolnway, was once a brothel.

The well preserved 200 block of W Lincolnway includes the Commercial Building (1883 – note the Moorish details), the First National Bank Building (1882) and the Hynds Building (1922). Across the street, the Atlas Theatre (1887), 211 W Lincolnway, was redesigned as a playhouse in 1908.

One block west and three blocks north is the Greek Revival City and County Building (1917), 319 W 19th St, with Ionic columns. Two blocks east is the Masonic Temple (1901), 1820 Capitol Ave. Nearby are the Gothic Revival St Mark's Episcopal Church (1893), 1908 Central Ave, and the First United Methodist Church (1894), at 18th St and Central Ave, a Romanesque and Gothic Revival red sandstone combo.

East of Warren Ave, the leafy residential Rainsford District has several historic houses you might like to stroll among, including the Queen Anne Lane House (1881), 1721 Warren Ave, and the Corson House (1884), 209 E 18th St. Several interesting Queen Anne houses are another block east of 18th St on Evans Ave. The Italianate Victorian Whipple House (1883), 300 E 17th St, belonged to the founder of the Wyoming Stock Growers Association (WSGA). One block farther west, merchant Erasmus Nagle built two houses of note: the Romanesque Nagle-Warren Mansion (1888), 222 E 17th St, and the earlier Nagle House (1880), 216 E 17th St, now both part of a B&B.

Wyoming State Capitol

The gold-leaf dome of the Wyoming State Capitol (☎ 307-777-7220 for group tours), on 24th St at Capitol Ave, tops an imposing sandstone structure (1888), a national historic landmark. The impressive interior rotunda is crowned by blue and green stained glass. The House and Senate chambers, completed in 1917 with murals by artist Allen True, flank the rotunda and have unique stained-glass ceilings. *Wyoming, the Land, the People,* a mural by Mike Kopriva, was added in 1982. Visitors can watch the legislature's deliberations from balconies. The State Capitol is open 8 am to 5 pm weekdays.

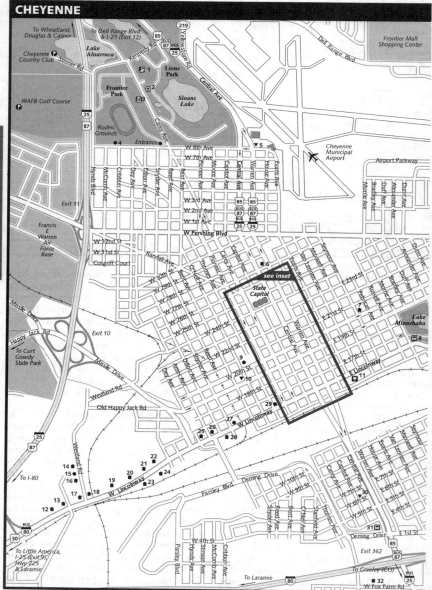

CHEYENNE

CHEYENNE

PLACES TO STAY
6 Avenue Rose B&B
7 Porch Swing B&B
12 Econolodge
13 La Quinta Inn
14 Luxury Inn
16 Motel 6; Sanford's Grub & Pub
17 Days Inn
18 Super 8
19 Lincoln Court
20 Best Western Hitching Post Inn
21 Atlas Motel
22 Frontier Motel
23 Stage Coach Motel
24 Wyoming Motel
25 Guest Ranch Motel
26 Sands Motel
28 Ranger Motel
32 Holiday Inn
46 Rainsford Inn B&B
48 Nagle-Warren Mansion B&B
55 Plains Hotel

PLACES TO EAT
5 Cloud 9
10 Dynasty Cafe
30 Los Amigos Mexican Restaurant
42 Twin Dragon
44 Chloe's Java Joint
47 Lexie's
49 Botticelli Ristorante Italiano

OTHER
1 Municipal Pool
2 Botanic Gardens
3 Frontier Days Old West Museum
4 Frontier Park Ticket Office
8 CTP Transfer Station
9 Cheyenne Civic Center
11 Green Door
15 Wyoming State Board of Outfitters & Professional Guides
27 Enterprise Rent-a-Car
29 Dinnen Building
31 Greyhound; TNM&O; Powder River Coach USA Bus Depot
33 Wyoming Arts Council
34 Supreme Court; State Library
35 Wyoming State Museum
36 United Medical Center
37 Post Office
38 Historic Governors' Mansion
39 US Bank
40 American National Bank
41 Community First National Bank
43 Manitou Gallery
45 Wells Fargo
50 Hofmann Building
51 Saturday Farmers' Market
52 Crown Bar
53 Cheyenne Club
54 Gallery West
56 Lincoln Movie Palace
57 Queen Anne Tivoli
58 Cheyenne Area Convention & Visitors Bureau
59 Chamber of Commerce
60 Atlas Theatre
61 The Wrangler; Phoenix Block

WYOMING

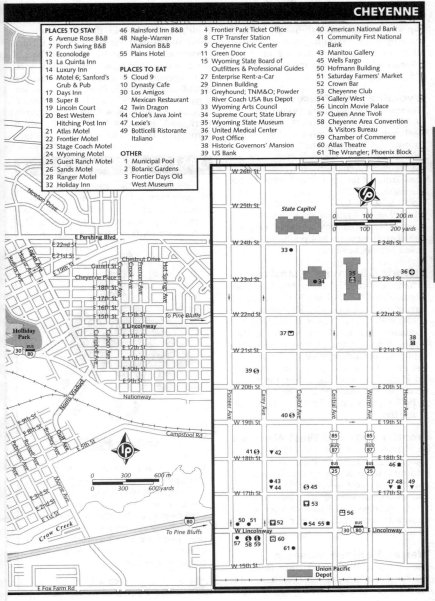

Wyoming Arts Council

This small gallery (☎ 307-777-7742), 2320 Capitol Ave, features high-quality work by contemporary Wyoming artists. It also offers presentations by scholars and living histories by performance artists. Open 8 am to 5 pm weekdays.

Wyoming State Museum

This respectable but unexceptional museum (☎ 307-777-7022 weekdays, ☎ 307-777-7024 weekends) occupies most of the ground floor of the Barrett State Office Building, 2301 Central Ave. The best attractions are the frequently changing traveling exhibitions from other institutions, such as the Smithsonian and the Library of Congress. Open 8:30 am to 5 pm weekdays year-round, 9 am to 4 pm Saturday and 1 to 4 pm Sunday Memorial Day to Labor Day. It's also open from noon to 4 pm Saturday, but closed Sunday, in winter.

Historic Governors' Mansion

In a pleasant residential neighborhood, this mansion (☎ 307-777-7878), 300 E 21st St, is a three-story brick Georgian Revival building (1904) with Corinthian columns. Originally a comfortable residence for the state's highest official, it was far more modest than the homes of Cheyenne's cattle barons. The last governor to occupy the mansion was Ed Herschler, Wyoming's only three-term executive. The mansion became a museum in 1977. Open 9 am to 5 pm Tuesday to Saturday; free.

Frontier Days Old West Museum

This museum (☎ 307-778-7290), 4501 N Carey Ave, at Frontier Park (I-25 exit 12, Central Ave to Kennedy Rd) records the early history of Cheyenne, Frontier Days and its rodeos since 1897. Open 9 am to 5 pm weekdays and 10 am to 5 pm weekends with extended summer hours; $4/2 adults/students.

Warren Heritage Museum

The Francis E Warren Air Force Base, the US Air Force's oldest base, claims to be 'home to the most powerful missile wing in the free world.' Established in 1867 to protect laborers on the Transcontinental Railroad, the base grew dramatically during WWI and in 1930 was renamed for former senator and governor FE Warren. The US Air Force acquired the base after WWII, and it became the Strategic Air Command's first all-missile base in 1958. It retains many original red-brick Colonial Revival buildings, one of which now houses the Warren Heritage Museum (☎ 307-773-2980), which chronicles local and regional military

---

The Cowboy Myth

Owen Wister's *The Virginian*, the most popular book in America when published in 1902, invented and established the Western hero. Wister created the archetype for all later cowboys from Hopalong Cassidy to

Roy Rogers and John Wayne. A Harvard-educated Philadelphia aristocrat, Wister was a college chum and lifelong friend of Teddy Roosevelt, with whom he shared a romanticized passion for the West. At a time when the West was an alien place to most Americans, Wister captured the character of the cowboy, creating a myth that persists in the popular imagination.

history. Open 8 am to 4 pm weekdays; free. Enter the base via Gate 1 (I-25 exit 11, Randall Ave); look for the conspicuous Atlas warheads.

Organized Tours
The Cheyenne Historic Trolley runs two-hour tours of downtown, the FE Warren Air Force Base and the Old West Museum mid-May to mid-September. Tours ($8/4) depart from the corner of Lincolnway and Capitol Ave 10 am and 1:30 pm Monday to Saturday and 1:30 pm Sunday.

Cheyenne Frontier Days
When Cheyenne 'realized it was through living the real thing,' as historian Earl Pomeroy wrote, 'it turned to playing the Wild West.' So began Cheyenne Frontier Days in 1897. Wyoming's biggest special event (beginning the last full week in June) features 10 days of rodeos (concerts, parades, dances, air shows, pancake breakfasts, chili cookoffs and 'most every other sorta shindig. Cheyenne's Frontier Park, 4501 N Carey Ave, is the center of activities. To secure rodeo seats ($11 to $22), drop in to the ticket office (☎ 307-778-7222, 800-227-6336), on 8th Ave at Frontier Park, or visit www.cfdrodeo.com.

Places to Stay
It's hard to escape the continual noise from the railroad tracks anywhere along Lincolnway. Reservations are essential during Cheyenne Frontier Days, when everything within a 50-mile radius is booked and rates typically double even as far away as Laramie and Greeley, CO. Rates (and temperatures!) drop a few degrees in the dead of winter.

Camping Cheyenne's nicest RV park is *AB Camping* (☎ 307-634-7035, 1503 W College Dr), off I-25 exit 7. Near a busy road, it's comfortable and well landscaped. Tent sites cost $13, RV hookups $20; open March to October. East of town at *Cheyenne KOA* (☎ 307-638-8840, 800-562-1507, 8000 I-80 E Service Rd), I-80 exit 367, tent sites cost $16 to $20, RV hookups $27, kabins $35. *Terry*

Bison Ranch (☎ 307-634-4171), off I-25 exit 2, 7 miles south of town and 2 miles north of the Colorado state line, has tent sites ($12), basic cabins and other amusements. The closest public camping is 25 miles west in Curt Gowdy State Park (see Around Cheyenne, later).

Motels Several motels line W Lincolnway (take I-25 exit 9). Prices for doubles at the following establishments range from $25 to $50:

Atlas Motel
  (☎ 307-632-9214, 1524 W Lincolnway)
Frontier Motel
  (☎ 307-634-7961, 1400 W Lincolnway)
Guest Ranch Motel
  (☎ 307-634-2137)
Ranger Motel
  (☎ 307-634-7995, 909 W Lincolnway)
Wyoming Motel
  (☎ 307-632-8104, 1401 W Lincolnway)

North of W Lincolnway are *Motel 6* (☎ 307-635-6806, 1735 Westland Rd), with rates of $45/50, and *Luxury Inn* (☎ 307-638-2550, 1805 Westland Rd), which goes for $35/45. Singles/doubles are $60/70 at the *Quality Inn* (☎ 307-632-8901, 800-876-8901, 5401 Walker Rd), off I-25 exit 12. There are several more budget places along E Lincolnway. The *Home Ranch Motel* (☎ 307-634-3575, 2414 E Lincolnway) is one of the best for $28/30. Otherwise, try the *Cheyenne Motel* (☎ 307-632-5505) or the adjacent *Firebird Motel* (☎ 307-632-5505, 1905 E Lincolnway) for $30/35.

There are several good if unexciting mid-range lodgings at I-25 exit 9, including *Econolodge* (☎ 307-632-7556, 2512 W Lincolnway) and *Super 8* (☎ 307-635-8741, 1900 W Lincolnway), both for $50. Others are *Sands Motel* (☎ 307-634-7771, 1022 W Lincolnway) for $35/40; *Stage Coach Motel* (☎ 307-634-4495, 1515 W Lincolnway), which charges $40/50; and *Lincoln Court* (☎ 307-638-3302, 1720 W Lincolnway) with rates of $50 to $65.

W Lincolnway is also home to some pricier spots. *La Quinta Inn* (☎ 307-632-7117,

2410 W Lincolnway) and **Days Inn** (☎ 307-778-8877, 2360 W Lincolnway) charge $50 to $80. Deluxe quarters at the **Best Western Hitching Post Inn** (☎ 307-638-3301, 800-221-0125, 1700 W Lincolnway) start at $80.

Hotels Good-value refurbished rooms start at $35/45 in downtown's historic **Plains Hotel** (☎ 307-638-3311, 1600 Central Ave), at Lincolnway. Sprawling **Holding's Little America Hotel** (☎ 307-775-8400, 800-445-6945, 2800 W Lincolnway), west of I-25, starts at $75/85. The **Marriott Fairfield Inn** (☎ 307-637-4070, 1415 Stillwater Ave), near Frontier Mall, is north of the airport and costs $55 to $80. Slots at the **Holiday Inn** (☎ 307-638-4466, 204 W Fox Farm Rd), on I-80 at US 85, are $90.

B&Bs There are four B&Bs within walking distance of downtown. Three rooms at the homey **Porch Swing B&B** (☎ 307-778-7182, 712 E 20th St) fetch $50/60 for rooms with shared/private bath. Seven rooms at the **Rainsford Inn B&B** (☎ 307-638-2337, 219 E 18th St) range from $75 to $95. Both places are nonsmoking. The two rooms at **Avenue Rose B&B** (☎ 307-635-2400, 100 E 27th St) share a bathroom; each goes for $65. The historic **Nagle-Warren Mansion B&B** (☎ 307-637-3333, 800-811-2610, 222 E 17th St), at $105 to $135, is the classiest option.

North Cheyenne options include **Howdy Pardner B&B** (☎ 307-634-6493, 1920 Tranquility Rd), for $65 to $95, and the gay-friendly **Storyteller Pueblo B&B** (☎ 307-634-7036, 5201 Ogden Rd), charging $50 to $75.

Places to Eat

Friendly **Chloe's Java Joint** (☎ 307-638-7332, 1711 Carey Ave) offers breakfast (good pastries, muffins and espresso) and light lunches (vegetarian options) in funky downtown digs. Nonsmoking **Lexie's** (☎ 307-638-8712, 216 E 17th St) has an appealing menu of reasonably priced sandwiches, burgers and Italian and Mexican dishes. It's open all day (closed Sunday and Monday) and has a pleasant deck. **Sanford's**

Grub & Pub (☎ 307-634-3381, 115 E 17th St) features hearty eats and a good selection of beers. **Los Amigos Mexican Restaurant** (☎ 307-638-8591, 620 Central Ave) is south of the railroad tracks. **Dynasty Cafe** (☎ 307-632-4888, 600 W 19th St) has Chinese and Vietnamese food. **Twin Dragon** (☎ 307-637-6622, 1809 Carey Ave) specializes in Mandarin, Szechuan and seafood. Both have cheap lunch buffets and veggie options. **Botticelli Ristorante Italiano** (☎ 307-634-9700, 300 E 17th St) is the best choice for pizza and pasta. Locals agree that **Cloud 9** (☎ 307-635-1525, 300 E 8th Ave), near the Municipal Airport, prepares the best beef in town.

Entertainment

Cheyenne's bar scene is lively, the live music scene less so, except during Frontier Days, when all C&W hell breaks loose. The **Cheyenne Club** (☎ 307-635-7777, 1617 Capitol Ave) entertains off-base air force enlistees with DJ-spun dance hits. Dare to enter the **Green Door** (☎ 307-634-4141, 301 E Lincolnway) and alter your perception of the locals with a few longnecks. The **Crown Bar** (☎ 307-778-9202, 222 W Lincolnway) is an 80-proof watering hole. At the Best Western, the **Hitching Post Inn Lounge** (☎ 307-638-3301, 1700 W Lincolnway) is a quiet spot for a casual drink. South of town on Hwy 85, try **Cowboy Lanes** (☎ 307-638-0455, 312 S Greeley Hwy) for slick alleys, weeknight happy-hour specials and honky-tonk weekends.

On the tamer side, the **Little Theatre Players** (☎ 307-638-6543) produce amusing summertime melodramas at the Atlas Theatre (☎ 307-635-0199, 211 W Lincolnway). The **Cheyenne Symphony Orchestra** (☎ 307-778-8561) plays the Civic Center, 510 W 20th St, September through May. The classic **Lincoln Movie Palace** (☎ 307-637-7469, 1615 Central Ave) projects second-run flicks on giant screens and has cheap weekend matinees.

Shopping

The Wrangler (☎ 307-634-3048), 1518 Capitol Ave, is one of Wyoming's biggest

Western-wear emporiums. Gallery West (☎ 307-632-1258, 800-786-2258), 1601 Capitol Ave, deals in Western art, as does Manitou Gallery (☎ 307-635-0019), 1715 Carey Ave. There are several other galleries along W Lincolnway. Sierra Trading Post (☎ 307-775-8090, 800-713-4534), 5025 Campstool Rd, off I-25 exit 364 or I-80 exit 384, has good deals on quality outdoor gear; take a look at the Sierrra Trading Post Web site, www.sierratradingpost.com.

The *farmers' market* convenes 8 am to 1 pm Saturday in summer in the parking lot at Lincolnway and Carey Ave.

Getting There & Away

Air Cheyenne Municipal Airport (☎ 307-634-7071), 200 E 8th Ave, has daily United Express (☎ 800-241-6522) flights to Denver. However, it can be cheaper to fly into Denver International Airport (DIA) and rent a car or catch the Armadillo Express DIA Shuttle (☎ 307-632-2223, 888-256-2967). The shuttle ($28 one-way) picks up several times daily at the Best Western Hitching Post Inn and the Holiday Inn.

Bus All bus lines use the depot at 222 E Deming Dr (on US 85 at I-80 exit 362). Greyhound (☎ 307-634-7744) has two daily northbound departures to Billings, MT, six daily southbound runs to Denver, three eastbound to Chicago and three westbound to San Francisco. Daily TNM&O buses (☎ 307-634-7744) go to Denver three times daily via Fort Collins and Greeley, CO, with connections southbound to Dallas and El Paso, Texas, as well as eastbound to Chicago. Powder River Coach USA (☎ 307-635-1327, 800-442-3682) goes to Denver ($24 one-way) twice daily. Daily buses also follow two routes to Billings, MT. One route goes through the Bighorn Basin and the other route, which requires a change of bus in Douglas, goes via Gillette, Buffalo and Sheridan. The one-way fare on both routes is $68. Cheyenne is northeast of the junction of east-west I-80 and north-south I-25. North-south US 85 passes through Cheyenne, leading south to Greeley and north to Torrington, Lusk, Newcastle and

the Black Hills. Cheyenne is 100 miles north of Denver, CO, and 50 miles east of Laramie.

Getting Around

The Cheyenne Transit Program (CTP; ☎ 307-637-6253) operates buses 6:30 am to 5 pm weekdays. All routes depart hourly (15 minutes after the hour) from the CTP Transfer Station on E Lincolnway at Morris Ave, 1½ miles east of downtown. Passengers can flag down a bus anywhere along its route. Schedules and routes may vary during Cheyenne Frontier Days. Avis (☎ 307-632-9371), Dollar (☎ 307-632-2422) and Hertz (☎ 307-634-2131) are at the airport. Other options include Enterprise (☎ 307-632-1907), 800 W Lincolnway, and the cheaper Affordable Rent-A-Car (☎ 307-634-5666, 800-711-1564), 701 E Lincolnway. Stalwart AA Taxi (☎ 307-634-6020) is on call 24-7.

AROUND CHEYENNE

Happy Jack Rd (Hwy 210) leads west from Cheyenne toward Vedauwoo Glen into the Medicine Bow National Forest (see that section later in this chapter). This lovely rural area has three nice B&Bs charging $65 to $225. The modern *Windy Hills Guest House* (☎ 307-632-6423, 877-946-3944, 393 Happy Jack Rd) is at www.windyhillswyo.com online. *Drummond's Ranch* (☎ 307-634-6042, 399 Happy Jack Rd) is on 120 luxurious acres; and the *Bit-O-WYO* guest ranch (☎ 307-638-8340, 470 Happy Jack Rd) can be glimpsed at www.bitowyo.com.

Scenic **Curt Gowdy State Park** (☎ 307-632-7946), off Happy Jack Rd (Hwy 210), 25 miles west of Cheyenne (I-25 exit 10B) and 23 miles east of Laramie, is named for a Wyoming-born sportscaster. Historically, bison roamed these plains and Native Americans (Shoshone, Crow, Pawnee and Comanche) camped here during the hunt. Today its two reservoirs, Granite Springs and Crystal Lake, offer boating, summer fishing and winter ice fishing (for rainbow, brown and lake trout and Kokanee salmon), waterskiing, hiking and camping, but no swimming. Migratory waterfowl, including trumpeter swans, visit the area April to May. Day use is $5. The *campground* ($9) has separate areas for backpackers and for those traveling with horses. (See Around Laramie, later, for other nearby activities.)

LARAMIE

High-altitude Laramie (population 25,000; elevation 7165 feet) lies between the Medicine Bow Mountains to the west and the Laramie Mountains to the east, surrounded by the inviting and accessible Medicine Bow National Forest. Most towns along the I-80 corridor are only for passing through, but Laramie is the place to linger. Laramie owes its prosperity to the stately University of Wyoming (UW – 'Go Buffs!'), which employs many residents. Laramie is also Wyoming's cultural capital, with several museums and a thriving historic downtown.

History

Prior to the arrival of settlers, several Native American nations – Shoshone, Crow, Arapaho, Cheyenne and (Sioux) Oglala and Brulé – contended for Laramie Plains resources. By the early 19th century, trappers like French-Canadian Jacques LaRamie were chasing pelts in the area. The obscure LaRamie died at the hands of the

Shoshone, but somehow left an improbable legacy in the place names of a city, county, river, mountain range and conspicuous 10,274-foot peak.

Decades after the fur trade declined, the US army built Fort Sanders to protect Overland Trail emigrants, but the UP's 1868 arrival was what really spurred Laramie's growth. In the early years, though, the UP brought rabble-rousers and speculators, lending the town an unsavory reputation it undoubtedly deserved. The new territorial prison quickly filled with those gamblers and gunfighters (including Jesse James) who had not been lynched in the streets. Eventually a more genteel Laramie attracted individuals like humorist and newspaper editor Bill Nye. Laramie registered the nation's first female voters and the world's first female jurists in 1870. Landing UW in 1887 was a major coup that helped transform the town into the 'Gem of the Plains.'

Orientation

Most of Laramie is northeast of I-80 and east of the Laramie River. The main north-south road is 3rd St. Grand Ave is the main east-west road. US 30/US 287 and I-80 Business follow 3rd St through most of Laramie. They diverge at Grand Ave; US 30 and I-80 follow Grand Ave east, and US 287 continues south along 3rd St. Grocery stores and fast-food restaurants are along Grand Ave east of 30th St.

Information

The Chamber of Commerce (☎ 307-745-7339) and the Albany County Tourism Board (☎ 307-745-4195, 800-445-5303) are at 800 S 3rd St. An information center in an old yellow UP caboose at 3rd St and Boswell Dr (I-80 exit 313) is open 8 am to 5 pm weekends in summer. The UW Visitors Information Center (☎ 307-766-4075), 1406 Ivinson Ave, is open 8 am to 5 pm weekdays and 9 am to 1 pm Saturday; visit online at www.uwyo.edu. The USFS Medicine Bow–Routt National Forest & Thunder Basin Grassland Forest Headquarters (☎ 307-745-2300), 2468 Jackson St, is at the Hwy 230/130 junction; open 7:30 am to

---

Beaver Fever

Beaver pelts (also known as 'hairy dollars') were the focus of the Wyoming fur industry from 1820 to 1840. Individuals as well as companies trapped beavers whose pelts were shipped as far as St Louis and New York City to make men's hats. During this heyday, trappers, Native Americans and traders frequently rendezvoused where 'beaver pelts were gold.' By the 1840s, the beaver population had declined and the hats had gone out of style. The unemployed trappers became guides, scouts or businessmen at trading posts along the emigrant trails.

LARAMIE

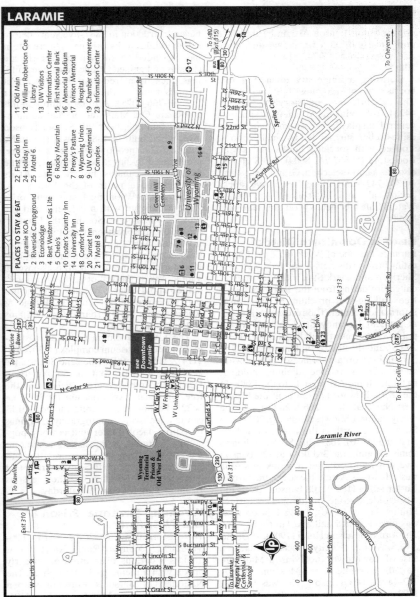

5 pm weekdays year-round and 7:30 to 11:30 am Saturday in summer. ATMs are downtown off Ivinson Ave and 3rd St. The post office is at 152 N 5th St. Ivinson Memorial Hospital (☎ 307-742-2141) is at 255 N 30th St.

Befitting a university town, Laramie boasts some of Wyoming's best bookstores. The delightful Second Story (☎ 307-745-4423), 105 Ivinson Ave, has a spacious general display area, which includes an espresso bar, surrounded by smaller rooms stocked with specialty books. Chickering Bookstore (☎ 307-742-8609), 203 S 2nd St, also has a good selection. Grand Newsstand (☎ 307-742-5127), 214 E Grand Ave, stocks periodicals and bestsellers. At Muddy Waters Cafe (see below) you can trade used books.

Historic Downtown District

Laramie has one of Wyoming's most interesting historic districts (bounded by 1st, 5th, Sheridan and Clark Sts), with Victorian architecture dating from the 1860s. Pick up a free walking-tour brochure at the visitors information center. The restored UP depot at 1st and Kearney Sts is closed to the public. The Jensen Building (1890), 313 S 2nd St, and the nearby building at 305 S 2nd St both have ornate cornices. The brickwork at 220 S 2nd St and the adjoining buildings as far as Grand Ave all date to the 1880s. In the 1870s, Edward Ivinson built the former First National Bank, 206 S 2nd St, and the nicely painted Midwest Building, 202 S 2nd St. A block north is the neoclassical Elks Building (1910), 103 S 2nd St. According to some accounts, the 3rd floor at 123 Ivinson Ave was removed after it shook in strong westerly winds. Across the street, the former Kuster Hotel (1869), 108 Ivinson Ave, is the city's oldest stone building. The former Phillips Hotel (1890), 107½ Ivinson Ave, was once a dance hall and later a brothel. The former Johnson Hotel (1900), at Grand Ave, was once the city's social center. Just east of downtown, the Ivinson Mansion, now the Laramie Plains Museum (☎ 307-742-4448), 603 Ivinson Ave, was built in 1892 and occupies an entire block.

University of Wyoming

Wyoming's only four-year university (UW) began instruction in 1887, five years before statehood. From its original 17-acre site it has expanded to an inviting, tree-shaded campus of dignified Gothic sandstone buildings. Pick up a free map and ask about campus tours at the information center (☎ 307-766-4075). Among campus landmarks are Old Main, the present administration building, near 9th St and Ivinson Ave. When built in 1887, it was the entire campus. The meadow of Prexy's Pasture, crisscrossed by paved walkways, is still the focus of the campus' historic core. At its southeast edge, north of the 13th St entrance, is the Wyoming Union, a favorite student hangout with a cafeteria and the university bookstore. South of the Union is the William Robertson Coe Library. The UW Fine Arts Center (☎ 307-766-6666) hosts concerts and art exhibits. The UW Planetarium (☎ 307-766-6150) is also worth a look. Ask at the visitors center for information about other UW collections, including the Entomology Museum, Range & Rocky Mountain Herbaria and Williams Botany Conservatory.

The UW Centennial Complex, a strikingly modern museum complex (☎ 307-766-4114), 2111 Willett Dr (the 22nd St entrance is off Grand Ave), contains the American Heritage Center research facility and the free University Art Museum (☎ 307-766-6622). Permanent exhibits include 20th-century landscape photography, paintings by Alfred Jacob Miller and cowboy pop-culture material. A downstairs restaurant serves lunch. Summer hours are 10 am to 7 pm weekdays, 10 am to 5 pm Saturday and noon to 5 pm Sunday; in other seasons 10 am to 5 pm Monday to Saturday.

Wyoming Territorial Prison & Old West Park

This historical site (☎ 307-745-6161, 800-845-2287), 975 Snowy Range Rd (I-80 exit 311), is a curious restoration of an early prison with a theme park atmosphere. The National US Marshals' Museum is open 9 am to 6 pm daily May to October; $10/7

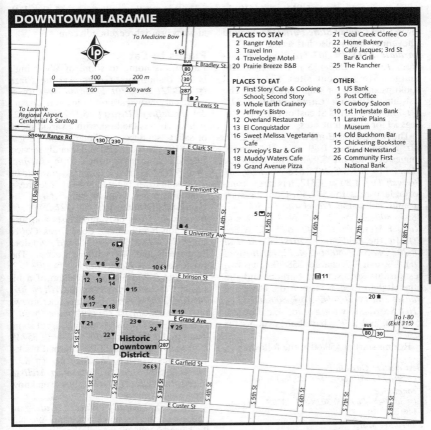

DOWNTOWN LARAMIE

PLACES TO STAY
2 Ranger Motel
3 Travel Inn
4 Travelodge Motel
20 Prairie Breeze B&B

PLACES TO EAT
7 First Story Cafe & Cooking
    School; Second Story
8 Whole Earth Grainery
9 Jeffrey's Bistro
12 Overland Restaurant
13 El Conquistador
16 Sweet Melissa Vegetarian
    Cafe
17 Lovejoy's Bar & Grill
18 Muddy Waters Cafe
19 Grand Avenue Pizza

21 Coal Creek Coffee Co
22 Home Bakery
24 Café Jacques; 3rd St
    Bar & Grill
25 The Rancher

OTHER
1 US Bank
5 Post Office
6 Cowboy Saloon
10 1st Interstate Bank
11 Laramie Plains
    Museum
14 Old Buckhorn Bar
15 Chickering Bookstore
23 Grand Newsstand
26 Community First
    National Bank

WYOMING

adults/children (six to 12). Admission to
Wyoming Frontier Town, open 10 am to
6 pm daily Memorial Day to Labor Day, is
$5/4. The laughable Horse Barn Dinner
Theatre is held at 6 pm Thursday to Saturday June to August, Wednesday to Saturday
in July and Friday and Saturday in September. Admission is $30/20 (reservations
required).

Special Events
Dial ☎ 307-721-7345 for the Laramie Area
Events Hot Line. The **Laramie River Night
Rodeo** starts in June. The **Mountain Man**
Rendezvous is the fourth weekend in June.
The weeklong **Laramie Jubilee Days** kick
off on July 4th. In August, the **Albany
County Fair** features 'action, action, action'
and demolition derby.

Places to Stay
Laramie has good, moderately priced accommodations. Reservations are recommended (and rates are much higher) for
UW graduation (mid-May), Independence
Day (July 4), Cheyenne Frontier Days (the
last full week in July) and fall UW football
weekends.

The best options are **USFS sites** ($10) in the Pole Mountain area, 10 miles east of town. **Curt Gowdy State Park** (see Around Cheyenne, earlier) also has scenic sites. The **Laramie KOA** (☎ 307-742-6553, 800-562-4153, 1271 W Baker St), I-80 exit 310, charges $15 for tent sites, $22 for full hookups and $30 for klapboard kabins. The last-ditch **Riverside Campground** (☎ 307-721-7405), on Curtis St east of I-80 exit 310, begs $9 for bleak tent sites.

The best deal is **Motel 6** (☎ 307-742-2307, 621 Plaza Lane), I-80 exit 313, where singles/doubles are $38/45. The sprawling **Motel 8** (☎ 307-745-4856, 888-745-4800, 501 Boswell Dr), I-80 exit 313, has large, comfortable rooms for $42/50. Doubles start around $40 at the **Travel Inn** (☎ 307-745-4853, 800-227-5430, 262 N 3rd St) and **Ranger Motel** (☎ 307-742-6677, 453 N 3rd St). In the mid-range, **First Gold Inn** (☎ 307-742-3721, 800-642-4212, 421 Boswell Dr), I-80 exit 313, charges $58/70. It has two restaurants, one serving burgers and the other Italian food. Nearby is the attractive **Sunset Inn** (☎ 307-742-3741, 800-308-3744, 1104 S 3rd St) with a pool and hot tub ($50/56), and a few bare-bones rooms for $20/25.

Rooms start at $50/60 at the following:

Best Western Gas Lite
(☎ 307-742-6616, 800-942-6610, 960 N 3rd St)

Econolodge
(☎ 307-745-8900, 800-303-6851, 1370 McCue St), I-80 exit 310

Travelodge Motel
(☎ 307-742-6671, 800-942-6671, 165 N 3rd St)

University Inn
(☎ 307-721-8855, 800-869-9466, 1720 Grand Ave)

The **Comfort Inn** (☎ 307-721-8856, 800-228-5150, 3420 Grand Ave), I-80 exit 316, starts at $60/70. **Foster's Country Inn** (☎ 307-742-8371, 800-526-5145, 1561 Snowy Range Rd), I-80 exit 311, asks $80 to $100. Rooms at the **Holiday Inn** (☎ 307-742-6611, 800-526-5245, 2313 Soldier Springs Rd), I-80 exit 311, are $80. Downtown, Victorian **Prairie Breeze B&B** (☎ 307-745-5482, 800-840-2170, 718 Ivinson Ave), which charges $60 to $80, is within walking distance of the UW campus; for more information, look online at www.prairiebreezebandb.com.

Places to Eat

Laramie is home to some of Wyoming's better restaurants. **Grand Avenue Pizza** (☎ 307-721-2909, 301 E Grand Ave) tosses great cheesy wheat-crust pies, but doesn't deliver. **Jeffrey's Bistro** (☎ 307-742-7046, 123 Ivinson Ave) is the best, with a varied menu of salads, sandwiches, dinners (entrees less than $10), great desserts and friendly service. Elsewhere in Wyoming, **Café Jacques** (☎ 307-742-5522, 216 E Grand Ave) would be the best in town, but it falls short of Jeffrey's. Adjoining it is the **3rd St Bar & Grill**. The **Overland Restaurant** (☎ 307-721-2800, 100 Ivinson Ave) has tasty breakfasts and also serves lunch and dinner. **Coal Creek Coffee Co** (☎ 307-745-7737, 110 E Grand Ave) does light meals and offers Internet access. The sweet goods at **Home Bakery** (☎ 307-742-2721, 304 S 2nd St) are excellent, if a bit sugary. Casual **Lovejoy's Bar & Grill** (☎ 307-745-0141, 101 Grand Ave) has microbrews on tap. Mexican **El Conquistador** (☎ 307-742-2377, 110 Ivinson Ave) is good, but some locals prefer **Chelo's** (☎ 307-745-5139, 357 W University Ave), west of the railroad tracks. Carnivores worship **The Rancher** (☎ 307-742-3141, 309 S 3rd St). At **Sweet Melissa Vegetarian Café** (213 1st St), they even know what 'vegan' means.

The cozy **Muddy Waters Cafe** (no phone), on the 100 block of Grand Ave, has it all: used books, vintage clothes, live music, strong joe and good comfort food. For bulk goods and imported gourmet items, visit the **Whole Earth Grainery** (☎ 307-745-4268, 800-368-4268, 111 Ivinson Ave). The **First Story Cafe & Cooking School** (☎ 307-745-4423, 307-745-5444 for reservations, 101 Ivinson Ave) offers gourmet cooking classes and fancy dinners twice a month.

Entertainment

The **Old Buckhorn Bar** (☎ 307-742-3554, 114 Ivinson St) is a favorite with rowdy university students, while the **Cowboy Saloon** (☎ 307-721-3165, 108 S 2nd St) attracts country & western diehards and agile line dancers.

Getting There & Around

Laramie Regional Airport (☎ 307-742-4164) is off Hwy 230 4 miles west of I-80 exit 311. Daily United Express (☎ 307-742-5296) flights serve Denver, CO, though, as with Cheyenne, it may be cheaper to fly into Denver International Airport (DIA) and rent a car or catch the frequent Armadillo Express DIA Shuttle (☎ 307-632-2223, 888-256-2967), which stops on the UW campus and at the Holiday Inn, 2313 Soldier Springs Rd (I-80 exit 311). The one-way fare is $52.

Bus lines share the depot at the Tumbleweed Express gas station, 4700 Bluebird Lane off E Grand Ave (I-80 exit 316), at the east end of town. Greyhound (☎ 307-742-5188) eastbound buses stop four times daily; westbound buses stop five times daily. Powder River Coach USA (☎ 800-442-3682) departs for Denver ($30 one-way) twice daily.

Laramie is along the north side of I-80, 50 miles west of Cheyenne and 99 miles east of Rawlins. US 287 leads 121 miles south to Denver via Ft Collins, CO. Hwy 130 (Snowy Range Scenic Byway) leads west across the Snowy Range to Saratoga in the Platte Valley. Hwy 230 heads southwest toward Walden, CO.

Avis (☎ 307-745-7156), Dollar (☎ 307-742-8805) and Enterprise (☎ 307-721-9876) are at the airport. Laramie Auto Rental (☎ 307-742-8412, 800-982-5935) may be cheaper. Hail Laramie Cab (☎ 307-745-8294) if you're stranded.

AROUND LARAMIE
Laramie Plains

West of Laramie and east of the Sheep Mountain Game Refuge, lakes and reservoirs dot the Laramie Plains, interspersed by roads, ranches and national wildlife refuges at Bamforth, Mortenson Lake and Hutton Lake. The area boasts excellent fishing and wildlife viewing. On Hwy 130, 11 miles west of Laramie, are **trail ruts** from the Overland Trail, the major pioneer route across the Laramie Plains from 1862 to 1868.

Pole Mountain Area

I-80 crosses Sherman Summit (8640 feet) between Laramie and Cheyenne, about 12 miles southeast of Laramie. The Summit Information Center (☎ 307-721-8040), 150 Happy Jack Rd (I-80 exit 323), is open 9 am to 7 pm daily May to October. Adjacent to the building and picnic area is the imposing **Abraham Lincoln Memorial** bust. US 30 (Lincoln Hwy) was named to commemorate the former president's support of the Transcontinental Railroad.

Vedauwoo Glen

Freestanding granite formations tower above the high plains and the surrounding juniper-dotted slopes of picturesque Vedauwoo ('VEE-dah-voo') Glen. Three unique and easily accessible rock formations (Vedauwoo Rocks, Devil's Playground and Turtle Rock), formed in the Ice Age, are along the Middle Crow Creek. The area attracts picnickers, photographers, campers and rock climbers. The name Vedauwoo means 'earthborn spirits,' and Native Americans believe the rock formations were created by playful humans and animals. The site is in the Sherman Mountains, 13 miles southeast of Laramie (I-80 exit 329) on USFS Rd 700. (Scenic USFS Rd 700 is unpaved north of the recreation area, and connects to Happy Jack Rd.) *Camping* costs $5; day use is $2.

MEDICINE BOW NATIONAL FOREST

The 11,000-foot summits of the Snowy Range cap the rugged Medicine Bow Mountains west of Laramie and south of I-80. Southwest are the Sierra Madre and the Continental Divide. The Medicine Bow National Forest extends across both mountain ranges. Between them is the North Platte River valley, where the hot-springs resort of Saratoga is the main settlement. The twin towns of Riverside and Encampment are the gateways to the Sierra Madre. The 79-mile **Snowy Range Scenic Byway** (Hwy 130) traverses the Snowy Range at Snowy Range Pass (10,847 feet) between Laramie and Saratoga. The byway (open

WYOMING

Memorial Day to October, depending on snow) provides easy access to this popular recreational area with lovely scenic overlooks, trails, fishing areas and campgrounds.

CENTENNIAL

Site of an 1875 gold rush, Centennial (elevation 8076) is an agreeable little town in the prairie grassland at the eastern base of the Snowy Range, on Hwy 130, 33 miles west of Laramie. Its year-round population is just 50; the population rises up to 100 with visitors. Rail enthusiasts will enjoy the **Nici Self Museum** (☎ 307-742-7158), open 1 to 4 pm weekends June to Labor Day.

Rooms at the **Old Corral Motel** (☎ 307-745-5918, 800-678-2024), which boasts a popular restaurant, cost $40/60, including breakfast. **Friendly Motel** (☎ 307-742-6033) has basic rooms for $37/45 and six-person cabins for $75. The **Trading Post Restaurant** (☎ 307-721-5074) serves steaks and seafood, and has live music on weekends and rustic cabins with kitchenettes ($50).

MEDICINE BOW MOUNTAINS

The impressive Medicine Bow Mountains extend 90 miles between Elk Mountain (Hwy 72 at I-80) to the north and Colorado's Cameron Pass to the south. From open tundra above the treeline (11,000 feet) streams descend through aspen forests to semiarid prairies at 5500 feet. The mountains have been inhabited for 12,000 years, since Native Americans began coming here in summer to hunt and to cut mountain mahogany for making bows. The name Medicine Bow derives from their annual bow-making gatherings and ceremonial disease-curing powwows.

Information

Maps and trail, fishing and campground information are available from two friendly USFS Medicine Bow–Routt National Forest stations on Hwy 130. The year-round Centennial Visitors Center (☎ 307-742-6023) is 1 mile west of town. The Brush Creek Visitors Center (☎ 307-326-5562), 20 miles east of Saratoga, is open Memorial Day to September, depending on weather.

Snowy Range

This dramatic range rises above the Medicine Bow Mountains treeline, west of Snowy Range Pass. The entire area is subject to windy, cold and very changeable weather, with snowfall possible anytime. The area is popular for **hiking, mountain biking** and numerous winter activities.

The USFS 'Snowy Range Trails' brochure helps plan outings. From the Libby Flats Observation Lookout on Hwy 130, 13 miles west of Centennial, superb views extend south into Colorado and west toward the Continental Divide. The **Libby Flats Wildflower Trail** introduces the flora – alpine phlox, bluebell, cinquefoil, rose clover and yarrow – that gives the alpine tundra its summer color.

The rocky **Medicine Bow Peak Trail** leads to the summit (12,013 feet) of the Snowy Range's highest peak. From the Lake Marie trailhead (10,600 feet) hike 3.6 miles one-way (two to 2½ hours) to the top. Retrace your steps from the summit, or descend along the **Lake Trail** past Lookout Lake to the Mirror Lake Picnic Area, and walk back along the road to the Lake Marie trailhead. From Lewis Lake trailhead, beyond Sugarloaf Campground northeast of the Lake Marie trailhead, a steeper route to the summit skirts behind Sugarloaf Mountain (11,398 feet).

Kennaday Peak Lookout

East of Saratoga is Kennaday Peak (10,808 feet), one of Wyoming's last functioning fire lookouts. Originally sited here in the 1930s, it was rebuilt in 1964 to include a ground-level visitors center, typically open 8 am to 5 pm Friday to Tuesday July to Labor Day. From Hwy 130, take USFS Rd 100 (North Brush Creek Rd) north 6 miles from the Brush Creek Visitors Center, and follow USFS Rd 215 another 6 miles to the summit.

Skiing & Snowboarding

The Snowy Range Ski and Recreation Area (☎ 307-745-5750, 800-462-7669) is off Hwy 130, 5 miles west of Centennial or 32 miles west of Laramie, a few miles east of Snowy

Range Pass. Downhill skiers and snowboarders enjoy its maximum 990-foot vertical drop. Base elevation is 9000 feet. Four lifts serve 25 runs; the longest is 1.8 miles. Daily lift tickets cost $30 for adults, $15 for seniors over 59 and $11 for children six to 12. Half-day passes are $22. Easily accessible USFS trails provide good cross-country skiing. There's a cafeteria, and instruction and rentals are available. Open 9 am to 4 pm daily Thanksgiving to Easter.

Places to Stay
The *Sugarloaf* and *Nash Fork* USFS campgrounds ($10) are east of Snowy Range Pass and typically are open whenever the pass is. The picturesque *Silver Lake Campground* is on Hwy 130, 2 miles west of the Lake Marie trailhead. Other pleasant campgrounds are near Corner Mountain and Barber Lake Rd. *Snowy Mountain Lodge* (☎ *307-742-7669*) is 2 miles west of the ski area. Beds in the bunkhouse cost $15; two- to eight-person cabins range from $50 to $150. There's also a restaurant and bar.

SARATOGA & AROUND
This up-and-coming bedroom community and resort town (population 1800; elevation 6786 feet) 'where trout leap on Main St' occupies a sagebrush plain along the North Platte River at the western base of the Medicine Bow Mountains. The noisy Louisiana Pacific's sawmill still operates all night, but tourism is increasingly important, especially the 'executive retreat' sort. The town's free mineral baths draw visitors from around the state. Motels are reasonable, restaurants are decent and quaint downtown has nice Western shops. The North Platte River offers top-notch fly-fishing and floating and also serves as a gateway for excursions into the surrounding mountains and wilderness areas.

History
Saratoga's hot springs were a favorite retreat for Native Americans until the arrival of settlers. William Cadwall built a rustic bathhouse here in 1878, when it was known as Warm Springs. The current name was adopted to imitate New York state's fashionable Saratoga Springs resort. Construction of the Wolf Hotel (on the National Register of Historic Places) in 1893 was a step in this direction. Saratoga relied, however, on mining and timber for most of the 20th century.

Orientation & Information
Hwy 130 (1st St in town) is the main north-south road. Many businesses are downtown on Bridge Ave. The USFS Medicine Bow–Routt National Forest Brush Creek–Hayden Ranger Station (☎ 307-326-5258) is on the east side of Hwy 130 just south of the Hacienda Motel (see Places to Stay, below). The kiosk outside has useful after-hours information. ATMs are downtown on 1st St. The post office is at 105 W Main Ave.

Municipal Pool & Hot Springs
On the banks of the North Platte River at the east end of Walnut Ave, this former state park reverted to local control in 1982. Its famous **Hobo Pool** (117°F–128°F) is free and open 24 hours daily year-round. The municipal pool (nominal admission), which is not a mineral spring, is open 11 am to 4 pm and 6 to 9 pm daily Memorial Day to Labor Day. Bathing suits are required in both pools.

Saratoga Museum
The free Saratoga Museum (☎ 307-326-5511), 104 Constitution Ave, in the former UP depot (1915), features railroad memorabilia and Native American artifacts. On the attractively landscaped grounds are a mint condition UP boxcar and caboose, a vintage sheepherder's wagon and an older log cabin. Open 1 to 5 pm daily Memorial Day to Labor Day and noon to 4 pm Tuesday to Saturday in winter.

Grand Encampment Museum
This free museum (☎ 307-327-5308), on Barrett St near 6th St on the south side of the town of Encampment, concentrates an excellent collection of furnished historic buildings transported from their original

sites. Its main building is jammed with regional artifacts. Several towers from the aerial tram, complete with cables and ore buckets, stand nearby along with a USFS fire lookout tower. The outbuildings include several provocative false fronts and are open only for 90-minute guided tours. The museum is open 11 am to 5 pm Sunday to Tuesday and 10 am to 5 pm Wednesday Memorial Day to Labor Day, and weekends September and October.

Activities

To arrange **floating** and **fishing** trips, contact Medicine Bow Drifters (☎ 307-326-8002), 120 E Bridge St; Hack's Tackle & Outfitters (☎ 307-326-9823), 407 N 1st St; Platte Valley Outfitters (☎ 307-326-5750), 112 S 1st St; or Great Rocky Mountain Outfitters (☎ 307-326-8750, 800-326-5390), 216 E Walnut Ave. Two nearby **rock climbing** sites, southeast of Hwy 130/230 junction, are Baggett Rocks and Bennett Peak (8312 feet).

Places to Stay

Deer Haven RV Park (☎ 307-326-8746, 706 N 1st St) is just north of the bridge. Grassy tent sites cost $5; full hookups are $10. The shaded but forlorn *Saratoga RV Park* (☎ 307-326-8870, 116 W Farm Ave) is closer to town and has showers. Tent sites cost $10; full hookups $16.

The closest *USFS campground* ($10) is 20 miles east off Hwy 130 near the Brush Creek Visitors Center.

The historic *Wolf Hotel* (☎ 307-326-5525, 101 E Bridge Ave) is the best value. Rooms with shared bath start at $30/35, suites run $75 and the restaurant and bar are highly regarded. Tidy, renovated *Riviera Lodge* (☎ 307-326-5651, 104 E Saratoga Ave) charges $35 to $90 for suites. *Silver Moon Motel* (☎ 307-326-5974, 412 E Bridge Ave) asks $37/45, while the comparably priced *Sage & Sand Motel* (☎ 307-326-8339, 304 S 1st St) has some kitchenettes. *Hacienda Motel* (☎ 307-326-5751), on Hwy 130 south of the airport, charges $50/60. Upscale *Saratoga Inn* (☎ 307-326-5261), east of the river on E Pic Pike Rd, is a favorite of re-treating corporate execs, with a spa, tennis courts, golf course and private fishing. Rates start at $100.

Places to Eat

Mom's Kitchen (☎ 307-326-5136, 402 S 1st St) is the local breakfast favorite. *Stumpy's Eatery* (☎ 307-326-8132, 218 N 1st St) is worth a try for moderately priced all-American lunches and dinners. Bodacious *Bubba's Bar-B-Que* (☎ 307-326-5427, 119 N River St) is part of a popular chain. *Lollypops* (☎ 307-326-5020, 107 E Bridge Ave) serves basic breakfasts, espresso, sandwiches and homemade ice cream. The *Saratoga Inn* and *Wolf Hotel* both offer more elaborate meals; don't miss the Wolf's Sunday prime-rib dinner. The *Rustic Bar* (☎ 307-326-5965, 124 E Bridge Ave) occasionally has live country & western music on weekends.

Getting There & Away

Saratoga is on Hwy 130, 20 miles south of I-80 and 79 miles west of Laramie. It's 18 miles north of Riverside and Encampment and 45 miles from the Wyoming-Colorado state line via Hwy 230.

RAWLINS

Boom-and-bust Rawlins (population 8750; elevation 6755 feet) is the only sizable town along I-80 between Laramie and Rock Springs in what's known as the Great Divide Basin. Like most southern Wyoming towns, it owes its origin to the railroad and its cyclical prosperity to oil and minerals – particularly the coal that gives Carbon County its name. The area around Rawlins is also one of the world's finest for jade, and the color of the soil lends it the name Red Desert. The region, which appears desolate at first glance, is actually rich in natural beauty and wildlife. Rawlins' major attraction is the Wyoming Frontier Prison. Otherwise, the hardworking town is somewhat indifferent to tourism.

History

Named for President Grant's war secretary General John Rawlins, Rawlins grew quickly, suffering the usual disorder in its early years. In 1878, for instance, railroad employees foiled a robbery attempt by Big Nose George Parrott and Dutch Charlie Burris, but lawmen tracking the escaped desperadoes were ambushed and shot dead. After their capture in Montana a year later, Rawlins vigilantes lynched Burris on arrival but waited to dispatch the brutal Parrot until after his murder conviction. Even after his death, Parrott continued to make the news (see Carbon County Museum, below). Following incorporation in 1886, Rawlins became the county seat, with an economy dependent on ranching and resource extraction. Like the rest of southern Wyoming, Rawlins boomed in the 1970s, but the 1980s oil bust devastated the town and by 1990 its population had fallen by nearly 20%. Today the town appears to be on the rebound.

Orientation & Information
The main east-west roads are Cedar St (I-80 exit 215) and Spruce St (I-80 exit 211), which together form US 30 Business. North-south 3rd St (US 287/Hwy 789) links Spruce and Cedar Sts. Downtown is bounded by Walnut St, the railroad tracks, 10th St and 3rd St. Higley Blvd, at the east end of Cedar St, is also the US 287 S Bypass.

The Rawlins/Carbon County Chamber of Commerce (☎ 307-324-4111, 800-228-3547), 519 W Cedar St, is open 9 am to noon and 1 to 5 pm weekdays. The BLM Rawlins District office (☎ 307-328-4200) is at 1300 N 3rd St. ATMs are downtown on Buffalo St. The post office is at 106 5th St. The Memorial Hospital of Carbon County (☎ 307-324-2221) is at 2221 Elm St.

Historic District
Rawlins' interesting buildings are in the area bounded by the railroad tracks and 6th, Walnut and 2nd Sts. The Queen Anne Ferris Mansion (1903), 607 W Maple, was an early mine-owner's residence. The Shrine Temple (1909), at 5th and Pine Sts, is well preserved despite several stuccoed lower windows. South and east of the prison are many Neoclassical, Art Deco and Gothic Revival examples of early-20th-century architecture. The France Memorial Presbyterian Church (1882) is at W Cedar and 3rd Sts. One block south of the church is Front St, site of the former UP depot (1901), mothballed when passenger service was terminated in 1983.

Wyoming Frontier Prison
The original Wyoming State Penitentiary, authorized in 1886 and completed in 1901, operated for more than 80 years. When the prison moved to its current location in 1981, the 'old pen' was turned into the Wyoming Frontier Prison (☎ 307-324-4422), 500 W Walnut St at 5th St. This free and ghoulishly fascinating museum is on the National Register of Historic Places. Crowned by turrets on its distinctive Romanesque exterior, the grim building overlooks downtown. After confronting unheated cell blocks, the forbidding shower room, maximum-security cells, death row and the gallows and gas chamber, one leaves with a sense of unease. Its walls are covered by peeling murals painted by one-armed prisoner Art Orcutt. In 1988 the B-movie horror flick *Prison* was filmed here. Unlike the sanitized Wyoming Territorial Prison in Laramie, this is the real deal.

The prison is open 8 am to 7 pm in summer. Worthwhile half-hour guided tours ($4.50; $4 for seniors and children, and $15 for families) depart 8:30 am to 6:30 pm daily Memorial Day to Labor Day and by reservation the rest of the year. For an even creepier experience, join a nighttime tour on summer weekends.

Carbon County Museum
This free museum (☎ 307-328-2740), 904 W Walnut St, holds such grisly artifacts as Big Nose George Parrott's death mask and a pair of shoes made from his skin by physician (and future Wyoming governor) John Osborne. Osborne, who later became a US congressman and then a State Dept official under President Woodrow Wilson, gave Big Nose George a postmortem lobotomy but found nothing abnormal about his cerebrum. The museum also contains noteworthy

WYOMING

RAWLINS

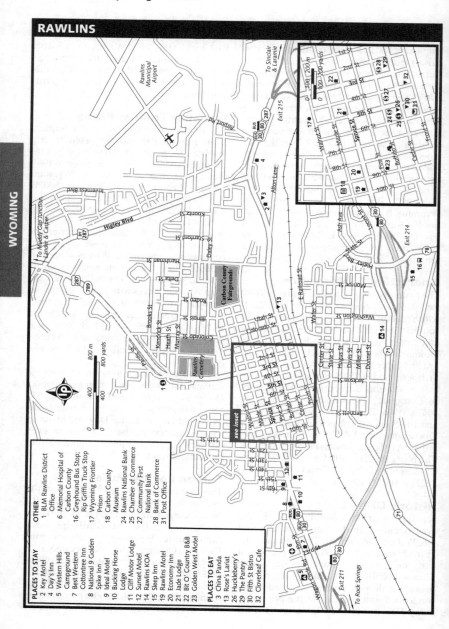

PLACES TO STAY
2   Key Motel
4   Day's Inn
5   Western Hills
    Campground
7   Best Western
    Cottontree Inn
8   National 9 Golden
    Spike Inn
9   Ideal Motel
10 Bucking Horse
    Lodge
11 Cliff Motor Lodge
12 Sunset Motel
14 Rawlins KOA
15 Sleep Inn
19 Rawlins Motel
20 Economy Inn
21 Jade Lodge
22 Bit O' Country B&B
23 Golden West Motel

PLACES TO EAT
3   China Panda
13 Rose's Lariat
26 Huckleberry's
29 The Pantry
30 Fifth St Bistro
32 Cloverleaf Cafe

OTHER
1   BLM Rawlins District
    Office
6   Memorial Hospital of
    Carbon County
16 Greyhound Bus Stop;
    Rip Griffin Truck Stop
17 Wyoming Frontier
    Prison
18 Carbon County
    Museum
24 Rawlins National Bank
25 Chamber of Commerce
27 Community First
    National Bank
28 Bank of Commerce
31 Post Office

exhibits on Native American pottery and basketry, sheep wagons and historic photographs. Open 10 am to 5 pm May to September, otherwise 1 pm to 5 pm.

Places to Stay

Rawlins has abundant, reasonably priced lodgings along Cedar and Spruce Sts; the latter tend to be cheaper. Rates drop slightly in winter.

Both campgrounds are barren and shadeless and often windy and dusty, but have showers and laundry. *Western Hills Campground* (☎ 307-324-2592, 888-568-3040, 2500 Wagon Circle Rd) has tent sites ($12) and full hookups ($18). *Rawlins KOA* (☎ 307-328-2021, 800-562-7559, 205 E Hwy 71), I-80 exit 214, is open mid-June to October ($18/27). The closest public campgrounds are 17 miles south at *Teton Reservoir* (free; open summer only) and 28 miles north of Sinclair in *Seminoe St Park* ($9).

These establishments range from $25 to $35:

Economy Inn
    (☎ 307-324-4561, 713 W Spruce St)

Golden West Motel
    (☎ 307-324-4452, 822 W Pine St)

Ideal Motel
    (☎ 307-324-3451, 1507 W Spruce St)

Jade Lodge
    (☎ 307-324-2791, 415 W Spruce St)

Rawlins Motel
    (☎ 307-324-3456, 905 W Spruce St)

Doubles start at $35 at the following:

Bucking Horse Lodge
    (☎ 307-324-3471, 1720 W Spruce St)

Cliff Motor Lodge
    (☎ 307-324-2905, 1500 W Spruce)

Key Motel
    (☎ 307-324-2728, 1806 E Cedar St)

National 9 Golden Spike Inn
    (☎ 307-328-1600, 1617 W Spruce)

Sunset Motel
    (☎ 307-324-3448, 800-336-6752, 1302 W Spruce)

Of the more expensive places, the best is the comparatively new *Sleep Inn* (☎ 307-328-1732, 1400 Higley Blvd), I-80 exit 214, with a sauna ($53/63). *Day's Inn* (☎ 307-324-6615, 2222 E Cedar St), with rooms for $60/70, and *Best Western CottonTree Inn* (☎ 307-324-2737, 800-662-6886), at 23rd and W Spruce Sts ($80/90), were both recently renovated.

Rawlins' only B&B is the relaxing *Bit O' Country B&B* (☎ 307-328-2111, 888-328-2111, 221 E Spruce St), priced at $60/80.

Places to Eat

Fifth St Bistro (☎ 307-324-7246, 112 5th St) features homemade baked goods, sandwiches, chai and milk shakes. For coffee, juice and ice cream, try *Huckleberry's* (☎ 307-324-5233, 509 W Cedar St). The Mexican food at friendly, hole-in-the-wall *Rose's Lariat* (☎ 307-324-5261, 410 E Cedar St) is authentic and appealing. Downtown, *Cloverleaf Cafe* (☎ 307-324-9841, 113 4th St) serves Navajo tacos. Bamboo shoots are only the beginning at *China Panda* (☎ 307-324-2198, 1810 E Cedar St). In the atmospheric Victorian Italianate Blake House (1881), *The Pantry* (☎ 307-324-7860, 221 W Cedar St) has the most diverse menu in town. In nearby Sinclair, the Mexican seafood dishes at *Su Casa Cafe* (☎ 307-328-1745, 705 Lincoln) draw out-of-town crowds for lunch and dinner.

Getting There & Away

The Greyhound depot (☎ 307-328-2103), 1400 S Higley Blvd, is at the Rip Griffin Truck Stop (I-80 exit 214). Eastbound and westbound buses stop twice daily. Rawlins is along the north side of I-80, 94 miles west of Laramie and 106 miles east of Rock Springs. US 287/789 goes northwest to Muddy Gap Junction (46 miles). US 287/789 then heads west for Lander (82 miles), and Hwy 220 leads northeast to Casper (73 miles).

ROCK SPRINGS

Founded in 1868, Rock Springs (population 19,500; elevation 6271 feet) owes its gritty character to the UP and the coal-mining industry. The railroad brought a multicultural mishmash of mostly European immigrant

WYOMING

laborers to town. In 1875 the miners went on strike, only to be replaced by Chinese scabs who were willing to toil for lower wages. By 1885 widespread resentment toward them culminated in the burning of Rock Springs' Chinatown. Eventually the UP brought Chinese laborers back and the US government paid a claim to the Chinese government for damages. During the 1970s energy boom, Rock Springs enjoyed a notorious prosperity that also brought drugs, violence, prostitution and corruption. Fortunately, Rock Springs has more to offer than this list of unsavory incidents would suggest; the town prefers to be known as the gateway to Flaming Gorge National Recreation Area (see later).

Orientation

Downtown Rock Springs is a warren of narrow streets that were once footpaths which led to coal mines within the town boundaries. South of the tracks, which bisect the town, streets follow a more conventional pattern. Elk St/US 191 (I-80 exit 104) is the main north-south road, but most businesses are along Dewar Dr (I-80 exit 102) and Center St (I-80 Business/US 30 Business). Bitter Creek parallels Center St, except downtown, where it disappears beneath pavement.

Information

The brochure-filled lobby at the Rock Springs Chamber of Commerce (☎ 307-362-3771), 1897 Dewar Dr, is open 24 hours daily. Pick up the rather interesting 'Rock Springs Historic Downtown Walking Tour' pamphlet. The BLM Rock Springs District Office/Green River Resource Area (☎ 307-352-0256), 280 US 191 N, is on the north side of town. ATMs are at North Side State Bank, 601 N Front St; the Community First National Bank is at 200 N Center St, and there are several banks in the malls along Dewar Dr. The main post office is at 2829 Commercial Way, north of I-80 and east of Dewar Dr off Foothill Blvd; the downtown branch is at 422 S Main St. Memorial Hospital of Sweetwater County (☎ 307-362-3711) is at 1200 College Dr.

Walking Tour

For an interesting historic tour, start at the pedestrian underpass at C St, where the former **Park Hotel**, at Elk and N Front Sts, was the center of Rock Springs' social life from the hotel's opening in 1914 until the late 1950s. Continue northeast along Front St, where most of the buildings were saloons until the advent of Prohibition in 1919. Turn onto K St, then onto Pilot Butte Ave trending northeast from K St. Here, the second stories of the buildings and the irregular street pattern give a sense of what the area was like when Butch Cassidy supposedly worked here as a butcher. Turn west on Bridger Ave to the **North Side Catholic Church** (1925). **Slovenski Dom** (1913), at Tisdel St, is a reminder of immigrant Slovenians. At Soulsby St turn south to shady **Bunning Park**.

Rock Springs Historical Museum

This free museum (☎ 307-362-3138), 201 B St, built in 1894 of distinctive red sandstone, was Rock Springs' city hall. It opened as a museum in 1988 and is now on the National Register of Historic Places. It's southwestern Wyoming's only remaining Richardson Romanesque building. Open 10 am to 5 pm Tuesday to Saturday in summer and noon to 5 pm Wednesday to Saturday in winter.

Community Fine Arts Center

Next door to the main library, the free Community Fine Arts Center (☎ 307-362-6212), 400 C St, has permanent exhibits by local and state artists and a major mural of the 1885 massacre. The center hosts special exhibitions and events as diverse as cowboy poetry readings, ballet and children's theater. Open 10 am to 5 pm Monday to Saturday with extended hours some weekday evenings.

Special Events

In summer, Rock Springs simply rocks. Mid-May brings the **All-Girl Rodeo**. The three-day **Desert Balloon Extravaganza** floats into town the second week of July. Residents barely have time to recover from the rollicking **Red Desert Round Up** rodeo the last

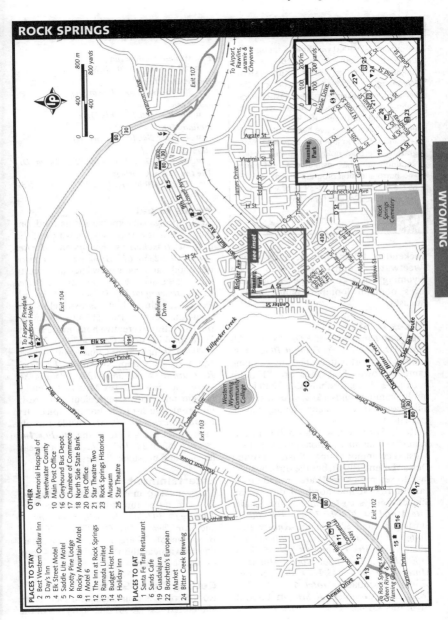

ROCK SPRINGS

PLACES TO STAY
2   Best Western Outlaw Inn
3   Day's Inn
4   Elk Street Motel
5   Saddle Lite Motel
7   Knotty Pine Lodge
8   Rocky Mountain Motel
11 Motel 6
12 The Inn at Rock Springs
13 Ramada Limited
14 Budget Host Inn
15 Holiday Inn

PLACES TO EAT
1   Santa Fe Trail Restaurant
6   Sands Cafe
19 Guadalajara
22 Boschetto's European
    Market
24 Bitter Creek Brewing

OTHER
9   Memorial Hospital of
    Sweetwater County
10 Main Post Office
16 Greyhound Bus Depot
17 Chamber of Commerce
18 North Side State Bank
20 Post Office
21 Star Theatre Two
23 Rock Springs Historical
    Museum
25 Star Theatre

WYOMING

Wild Horses

Approximately 3000 wild horses, thought to be partly descended from 16th-century Spanish mustangs, roam southwestern Wyoming. Herds are easily seen (look for the telltale long, unkempt manes) east of Rock Springs along I-80 and along the west side of US 191 between Rock Springs and Boulder. The horses have been protected by law since 1971. In an effort to reduce overgrazing, the BLM holds annual Red Desert Roundups and has instigated a wild horse and burro adoption program. Phone ☎ 406-657-6262 or ☎ 800 370-3936 or visit www.adoptahorse.blm.gov for details.

weekend in July before the early-August **Sweetwater County Fair.** The **Great Wyoming Polka & Heritage Festival** features oompah loompah bands in late August.

Places to Stay

The bleak ***Rock Springs KOA*** (☎ 307-362-3063, 800-562-8699, 86 Foothill Blvd), I-80 exit 99, is unfortunately the only camping game in town. Tent sites are $17; full hookups $22; kozy kabins $32. The closest public campgrounds ($12) are nearly 30 miles south of town near Flaming Gorge (see later).

Rock Springs has reasonably priced motels with minimal seasonal rate variation. Most accommodations cluster around Dewar Dr and Elk St, but the dirt-cheapest (ask to see rooms first!) are around 9th St east of Elk St and north of downtown. Singles/doubles cost $19/24 at the ***Saddle Lite Motel*** (☎ 307-362-1846, 1411 9th St). Starting around $28 are the ***Knotty Pine Lodge*** (☎ 307-362-4515, 1234 9th St) and friendly ***Elk Street Motel*** (☎ 307-362-3705, 1100 Elk St). The older ***Rocky Mountain Motel*** (☎ 307-362-3443, 1204 9th St) charges $25/35. Dependable ***Motel 6*** (☎ 307-362-1850, 2615 Commercial St), off Foothill Blvd, asks $39/45.

The following mid-range places charge $50 to $90 for a double:

Best Western Outlaw Inn
(☎ 307-362-6623, 1630 Elk St)
Budget Host Inn
(☎ 307-362-6673, 1004 Dewar Dr)
Day's Inn
(☎ 307-362-5646, 1545 Elk St)
Holiday Inn
(☎ 307-382-9200, 1675 Sunset Dr)
Ramada Limited
(☎ 307-362-1770, 888-307-7890, 2717 Dewar Dr)
The Inn at Rock Springs
(☎ 307-362-9600, 800-442-9692, 2518 Foothill Blvd)

Places to Eat

Rock Springs isn't known for its food, but there are a few surprises. Downtown, the deli at ***Boschetto's European Market*** (☎ 307-382-2350, 617 Broadway St) churns out good barbecue sandwiches and hearty lunch specials. Across the street, ***Bitter Creek Brewing*** (☎ 307-362-4782, 604 Broadway St) produces high-viscosity chili and semi-gourmet pub grub ($12 all-you-can-eat ribs) to buffer its creative homemade brews. Hard-drinkin' ***Sands Cafe*** (☎ 307-362-5633, 1549 9th St) has cheap Chinese and American fare. The popular ***Santa Fe Trail Restaurant*** (☎ 307-362-5427, 1635 Elk St) serves rather bland Tex-Mex and pseudo-Navajo fare, but its ingredients are fresh. For real south-of-the-border spice, try ***Guadalajara*** (19 Elk St), inside the old Park Hotel. Locals prefer the ***Outlaw Inn*** (☎ 307-362-6623, 1630 Elk St) for cheap lunches and big steak dinners.

Entertainment

There are two movie theaters downtown that screen first-run Hollywood flicks: ***Star Theatre*** (☎ 307-362-2101, 618 Broadway St) and ***Star Theatre Two*** (☎ 307-382-9707, 591 Broadway St). There are several dive bars downtown near the railroad tracks – look for the neon signs.

Getting There & Around

Rock Springs is connected with Denver by United Express (☎ 307-382-5887) out of the

Rock Springs/Sweetwater County Airport (☎ 307-382-4580), 382 Hwy 370 (I-80 exit 111), 7 miles east of Rock Springs. Greyhound (☎ 307-362-2931) buses depart from the depot at 1655 Sunset Dr (next to Burger King) several times daily for Salt Lake City, Cheyenne and Denver. Rock Springs sprawls along the north and south sides of I-80, 101 miles west of Rawlins and 7 miles east of Green River. US 191 leads north to Farson, Pinedale and Jackson, or south to Flaming Gorge National Recreation Area. Hwy 430 leads southward to the Wyoming-Colorado border and Dinosaur National Monument (see the Western Colorado chapter).

STAR Transit (☎ 307-382-7827) shuttles between Green River and Rock Springs. Avis (☎ 307-362-5599), Enterprise (☎ 307-362-8799) and Hertz (☎ 307-382-3262) are at the airport. Wayne's Car Rental (☎ 307-362-6970), 1539 Foothill Blvd, provides more personalized (and perhaps cheaper) service. Hail a City Cab (☎ 307-382-1100) when you're tired of bumming rides.

FLAMING GORGE NATIONAL RECREATION AREA

Flaming Gorge was named by surveyor John Wesley Powell for the fiery red sandstones he saw during his first descent of the Green and Colorado Rivers in 1869. Between 1957 and 1964, the Bureau of Reclamation built Flaming Gorge Dam, which backed up the Green River for more than 90 miles to form the Flaming Gorge Reservoir, with a 375-mile shoreline. The Flaming Gorge NRA (elevation 6040 feet), established in 1968 and administered by the USFS Ashley National Forest, is almost equally divided between Wyoming and Utah. But the better scenery, campgrounds and recreational opportunities are found on the Utah side.

The reservoir's prime attractions are boating and year-round, record-setting fishing. It's stocked with more than half a million fish annually. Visitors come for picnicking, hiking, backpacking and camping in summer, and cross-country skiing, snowshoeing and snow camping in winter. Moose, elk, pronghorn antelope and mule deer are common; bighorn sheep, black bear and mountain lion make infrequent cameos. There are more than two dozen campgrounds in and around Flaming Gorge, most of them operated by private concessionaires.

Write in advance to District Ranger, Flaming Gorge NRA, USDA Forest Service, Box 278, Manila, UT 84046, for information. The Flaming Gorge NRA Headquarters (☎ 435-784-3445), at the Hwy 43/44 junction, is open 8 am to 4:30 pm weekdays year-round and also weekends in summer; its Web site is www.fs.fed.us/r4/ashley.

Flaming Gorge NRA is southwest of Rock Springs via US 191 (east side) and south of Green River via Hwy 530 (west side). South of the Wyoming-Utah border Hwy 530 becomes Utah Hwy 44, which intersects US 191 at Greendale Junction. Six miles north on US 191 is the Flaming Gorge Dam.

The Utah section in Lonely Planet's *Southwest* guide is a detailed resource for visiting Flaming Gorge.

GREEN RIVER

This working-class railroad town, 7 miles west of Rock Springs and 86 miles east of Evanston, was the staging point for John Wesley Powell's epic descent of the Colorado River in 1869. Today it's one of the Flaming Gorge National Recreation Area's primary gateways. Founded in 1868, Green River (population 13,000; elevation 6100 feet) is overshadowed by the prominent sandstone Castle Rock.

Orientation

Downtown Green River is just south of I-80 and north of the railroad tracks and the river. A pedestrian overpass and Uinta Dr provide river access. Flaming Gorge Way (I-80 Business/US 30 Business) bisects downtown (from I-80 exit 89 or 91); its eastern end intersects Uinta Dr (Hwy 530), the main north-south road. Newer businesses and residential areas are along Uinta Dr south of the river.

Information

The Green River Chamber of Commerce (☎ 307-875-5711) shares its location with the

WYOMING

USFS Flaming Gorge Information Center (☎ 307-875-2871), 1450 Uinta Dr; both are open 8 am to 5 pm weekdays and 8 am to 4:30 pm weekends in summer (weekdays only in winter). The Wyoming Game & Fish Dept office (☎ 307-875-3223) is at 351 Astle Ave. There is an ATM at First Security Bank, 125 W Flaming Gorge Way at N 1st St W. The post office, 350 Uinta Dr at River View Dr, is south of the river. The Castle Rock Medical Center (☎ 307-875-6010) is at 1400 Uinta Dr.

Historic Buildings

The Green River Historic Preservation Commission publishes the detailed 'Self-Guided Tour of Historic Green River,' but many of the buildings it describes have been either razed or altered beyond recognition. Highlights include the wood-frame St John's Episcopal Church (1892), W 2nd St N, and the gabled Third School/Masonic Building (1891), on Flaming Gorge Way at N 1st St E. The best view of the UP depot (1910) is from the pedestrian overpass to Expedition Island. Three blocks of Railroad Ave, N 2nd E to N 1st St W, retain vintage buildings, including the restored Green River Brewery (1901), 50 W Railroad Ave, an eccentric National Register of Historic Places landmark.

Sweetwater County Historical Museum

This free museum (☎ 307-872-6435), 80 W Flaming Gorge Way, features a valuable display of 'ledger art.' These are paintings and drawings with indigenous themes created by 19th-century Plains Indians using imported materials like pencils and crayons on appropriated accounting ledgers. Open from 9 am to 5 pm weekdays year-round and 1 to 5 pm Saturday July to August.

Places to Stay

Tex's Travel Camp (☎ *307-875-2630*) is on Hwy 374 west of town (I-80 exit 85 or 89). Sites start at $16; the few tent sites have some grass and there's a store, laundry and showers ($5 for nonguests). Motels are more expensive than in nearby Rock Springs, and trains trundle through town all night long.

The following places offer rooms for $30 to $50 (ask to see them first!):

Coachman Inn Motel
    (☎ *307-875-3681, 470 E Flaming Gorge Way*)
Flaming Gorge Motel
    (☎ *307-875-4190, 316 E Flaming Gorge Way*)
Mustang Motel
    (☎ *307-875-2468, 550 E Flaming Gorge Way*)
Super 8
    (☎ *307-875-9330, 280 W Flaming Gorge Way*)
Western Motel
    (☎ *307-875-2840, 890 W Flaming Gorge Way*)

Little America

It's hard to miss Little America, a neon oasis in the high desert on the north side of I-80 (exit 68), between Green River and Bridger Valley. The world's largest truck stop, a microcosm of American transience, materializes like a welcome hallucination, with a 150-room motel, a 24-hour coffee shop and surprisingly good restaurant, a deli and convenience store, a bar and even a post office with its own zip code (82929).

Little America was the brainchild of sheepherder SM Covey, who, after weathering a night stranded in a fierce winter storm, envisioned a shelter in the area. In 1930 Covey recalled photographs of Admiral Byrd's desolate 'Little America' Antarctic base. The original Little America, an unassuming landmark literally 'in the middle of nowhere' smoldered to the ground in 1948, but was resurrected as this extravagant phoenix now visited by more than a million passersby annually. It has been successfully reproduced, with siblings in Cheyenne; Salt Lake City, Utah; San Diego, California; Flagstaff, Arizona; and Sun Valley, ID. Singles/doubles at Little America (☎ 307-875-2400, 800-634-2401) start at $65/70. Hot showers and hospitality are free with a full tank of gas.

Fort Bridger State Historic Site & Mountain Man Rendezvous

This 1987 reconstruction of trapper Jim Bridger's Trading Post (☎ 307-782-3842) is a worthwhile detour, 3 miles east of I-80 exit 34. Built in 1846, the original trading post became a US military outpost in 1858 and was crucial to the Pony Express and Overland Trail. The well-restored Commanding Officer's quarters (1883) contains period furniture, and the museum features exhibits on Native Americans, mountain men and local military history.

The site is open 9 am to 5:30 pm daily Memorial Day to Labor Day and 9 am to 4:30 pm weekends in April and October. Admission is $2; youth under 18 get in free. One-hour ($2) and two-hour ($3) guided tours are scheduled 9 am to 4 pm daily; tours cost $1 for children 11 and under. Reservations are recommended for August moonlight tours.

Every Labor Day weekend, the fort is the site of Wyoming's biggest annual rendezvous, the **Fort Bridger Mountain Man Rendezvous**. This hugely popular event includes primitive firearms shoots, tomahawk throwing, crafts trading and Native American dancing. Contact the Fort Bridger Rendezvous Association (☎ 307-782-3272), PO Box 198, Fort Bridger, WY 82933, for more information.

The two top-end places are the UP-friendly **Oak Tree Inn** (☎ 307-875-3500, 1190 W Flaming Gorge Way), I-80 exit 91, with rates of $45/50; and **Sweet Dreams Inn** (☎ 307-875-7554, 1420 Uinta Dr), for $50/60, which is farthest from the railroad tracks and has a bowling alley and karaoke lounge.

Places to Eat

Embers (☎ 307-875-9983, 95 E Railroad Ave) is a popular steak house and breakfast spot. The **Red Feather** (☎ 307-875-6625, 211 E Flaming Gorge Way) has a varied and fairly sophisticated menu. For ethnic food, try **China Garden** (☎ 307-875-3259, 190 N 5th St E) or **Trudel's Gasthaus** (☎ 307-875-8040, 520 Wilkes Dr), which specializes in Mexican food and the occasional German dish. **Don Pedro's Mexican Family Restaurant** (☎ 307-875-7324, 520 Wilkes Dr) is more authentic. **Penny's Diner** (☎ 307-875-3500, 1170 W Flaming Gorge Way) serves UP workers 24 hours a day. There are several hard drinkin' bars along Railroad Ave.

EVANSTON

Only 5 miles east of the Wyoming-Utah state line and 80 miles from sin-starved Salt Lake City, Evanston (population 12,000; elevation 6748 feet) is the Uinta County seat and Wyoming's westernmost town along I-80. Established on the Transcontinental Railroad in 1868, it has experienced several boom-and-bust cycles, most recently during the 1970s energy explosion. With a rejuvenated downtown, access to Utah's nearby Uinta Mountains and many affordable motels, Evanston is experiencing an economic renaissance. For information about the Uinta Mountains, take a look at Lonely Planet's *Southwest* guide.

Orientation & Information

Downtown Evanston is north of I-80. Its main roads are Bear River Dr (I-80 exit 6), Front St (I-80 exit 5) and Harrison Dr (I-80 exit 3), which replaces 11th St between Front and Lombard Sts. At Evanston's west end, Harrison Dr is called W Lincoln Hwy.

The Evanston Chamber of Commerce (☎ 307-789-2757, 800-328-9708), 36 10th St, shares a building with the Uinta County Museum (see below); it's open 9 am to 5 pm weekdays. Call to hear its entertaining recorded events hot line. The Bear River Information Center (☎ 307-789-6540), 601 Bear River Dr (I-80 exit 6), has a good selection of maps and brochures; open 8 am to 5 pm daily. The USFS Wasatch-Cache National Forest Evanston Ranger District (☎ 307-789-3194), 1565 Hwy 150 S, has info on the High Uintas Wilderness; it's open 8 am to 4 pm weekdays.

ATMs are downtown on Front and Main Sts. The post office is on Harrison Dr between Front and Main Sts. Bear River Books (☎ 307-789-5111, 888-641-2665), 1008 Main St, has a thoughtful selection of books. IHC Evanston Regional Hospital (☎ 307-789-3636, 800-244-3537) is at 190 Arrowhead Dr.

Historic Buildings

Among Evanston's restored buildings is the brick UP depot (1900) at the north end of 10th St. Not far away, the Beeman Cashin Implement Depot (1883) is a restored frame building that was relocated here in 1984. Alongside it, the Joss House, 920 Front St, is a replica of the temple that served Evanston's once-populous Chinatown. There are several interesting churches along Center St between 7th and 10th Sts. The Uinta County Courthouse (1873), 225 9th St, was drastically modified in 1904, but is nevertheless the state's oldest courthouse. The Blyth & Fargo Building, 927 Main St (1872–87), is a former department store.

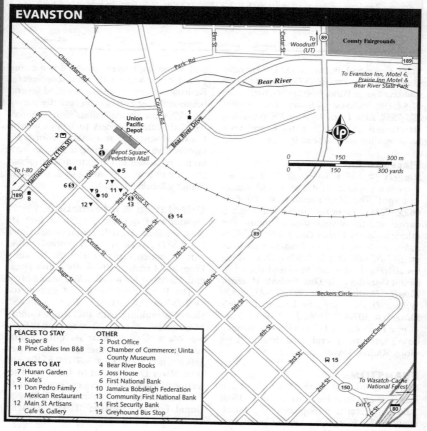

EVANSTON

PLACES TO STAY
1 Super 8
8 Pine Gables Inn B&B

PLACES TO EAT
7 Hunan Garden
9 Kate's
11 Don Pedro Family
    Mexican Restaurant
12 Main St Artisans
    Cafe & Gallery

OTHER
2 Post Office
3 Chamber of Commerce; Uinta
    County Museum
4 Bear River Books
5 Joss House
6 First National Bank
10 Jamaica Bobsleigh Federation
13 Community First National Bank
14 First Security Bank
15 Greyhound Bus Stop

Uinta County Museum

This free cluttered historical repository (☎ 307-789-2757), 36 10th St, is in the former Carnegie Library (1906). Among its many displays are artifacts from Evanston's once-substantial Chinese community. Ask here for the informative 'Evanston, Wyoming: A Walking Tour' brochure. The museum is open 9 am to 5 pm weekdays year-round and 10 am to 4 pm weekends in summer.

Bear River State Park

The 300-acre Bear River State Park (☎ 307-789-6547), I-80 exit 6, is open for day use only and has picnic areas, 3 miles of foot and bike paths along the Bear River and small captive bison and elk herds. In winter, trails are groomed for cross-country skiing, and the pond becomes an ice rink. The paved Bear Parkway greenbelt trail network links the park to downtown.

Places to Stay

The friendly and well maintained *Phillips RV & Trailer Park* (☎ 307-789-3805, 800-349-3805, 225 Bear River Dr), I-80 exit 6, has shaded tent sites ($16) and full hookups ($18); open April to October.

Evanston motels have reasonable rates year-round. Several places cluster at the east end of Evanston along Bear River Dr. The spacious and comfortable *Prairie Inn Motel* (☎ 307-789-2920, No 264) has singles/doubles for $35/45. The well-run *Motel 6* (☎ 307-789-0791, No 261) has a laundry ($37/42). Rooms (some with kitchenettes) at the *Evanston Inn* (☎ 307-789-6212, No 247) cost $25/30.

Within walking distance of downtown are *Super 8* (☎ 307-789-7510, 70 Bear River Dr), with rooms for $37/43, and the distinctive 1883 *Pine Gables Inn B&B* (☎ 307-789-2069, 800-789-2069, 1049 Center St), for $45 to $70; you can take a look online at www.cruising-america.com/pinegables.

At the west end of town are superior *Best Western Dunmar Inn* (☎ 307-789-3770, 800-654-6509, 1601 Harrison Dr), with rates of $70/110; and basic *Hillcrest DX Motel* (☎ 307-789-1111, 1725 Harrison Dr), for $22/28. Nearer to I-80 exit 3 are *Weston*

Super Budget Inn (☎ 307-789-2810, 800-255-9840, 1936 Harrison Dr), which starts at $45/50, and more upscale *Weston Plaza* (☎ 307-789-0783, 1983 Harrison Dr) for $65/70.

Places to Eat

Evanston's restaurants are average at best. Artsy *Main St Artisans Cafe & Gallery* (☎ 307-789-4991, 927 Main St) hints at the direction Evanston is headed, with espresso, lite lunch and homemade desserts. Popular *Lotty's* (☎ 307-789-9660, 1925 Harrison Dr) has big breakfasts, salad bar and burgers for lunch and surf 'n' turf and all-you-can-stand dinner buffets. The authentic *Don Pedro Family Mexican Restaurant* (☎ 307-789-2944, 909 Front St) is Evanston's best, with pleasant atmosphere and tasty dishes. *Hunan Garden* (☎ 307-789-1256, 933 Front St) serves Chinese and American food. Drop into *Kate's* (☎ 307-789-7662, 936 Main St) for a friendly beer.

Getting There & Away

Greyhound (☎ 307-789-2810) stops at McDonald's, 212 Front St (I-80 exit 5). Evanston is along I-80, at the junction of northbound Hwy 89 and southbound Hwy 150, 3 miles east of the Wyoming-Utah state line and 86 miles west of Green River. Kemmerer and Diamondville are on US 189, 49 miles northeast of Evanston.

Prairie Wyoming

Northeastern Wyoming's vast prairie is bounded by the southern Laramie Mountains, the western Bighorn Mountains and the Black Hills along the Wyoming–South Dakota state line. The picturesque valleys of the North Platte, Belle Fourche and Powder Rivers course through an arid sage-covered landscape whose appeal is often subtle. Driving between popular destinations like Devils Tower National Monument and Fort Laramie presents continual opportunity for visiting historic sites and viewing wildlife. The region's stark beauty is accentuated by herds of pronghorn antelope and white-tailed

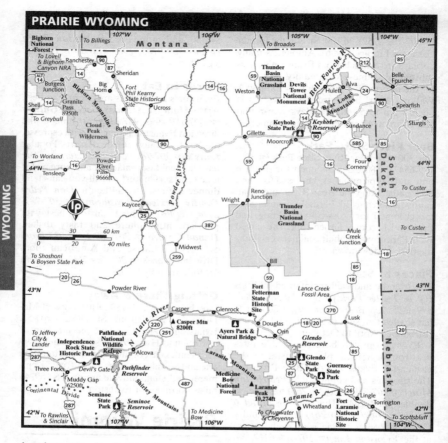

deer that outnumber the friendly people who live here.

CASPER

The North Platte River flows east from Casper (population 49,000; elevation 5338 feet), where Oregon Trail pioneers, who had followed this river valley across eastern Wyoming, set out through central Wyoming. Towns and historic sites cluster along the river, and thick coal seams and oil fields underlie the region.

The 1941 WPA Guide's description of Casper as an 'industrialized cow-town' still fits Wyoming's most centrally located and second-largest city. Today, Casper is an inviting way station for travelers interested in pioneer history. The Natrona County seat is a mercantile powerhouse whose primary products – cattle, sheep, coal and oil – make it an economic rival to Cheyenne. Casper has surprising cultural resources too, including the Nicolaysen Art Museum and performing arts centers. Downtown Casper is gradually being resuscitated, and only 30 minutes away, the scenic Casper Mountain offers opportunities for outdoors enthusiasts (see below).

History

Before Europeans arrived, the Shoshone and Lakota frequented the North Platte River valley. From the 1840s, Oregon-bound travelers crossed the river on Mormon ferries here en route to South Pass. The first permanent settlement was Louis Guinard's trading post, which became the US Army's Platte Bridge Station. Lakota and Cheyenne resistance in 1865 led to a major confrontation between Native American forces under Red Cloud and the US Cavalry at Platte Bridge. This battle led to the death of Lieutenant Caspar Collins, in whose honor the fort was renamed.

Casper's present name resulted from a misspelling by officials the Fremont, Elkhorn & Missouri Railroad, a subsidiary of the Chicago & Northwestern, which arrived in 1888. Around this time Philip Shannon drilled his first well at Salt Creek Oil Field, near Midwest, 40 miles north of Casper. Shannon's Pennsylvania Oil & Gas Company sold lubricants to the railroad and erected a small refinery, and early 1900s gushers produced one of Wyoming's biggest fields. 'Black gold' remains the region's economic linchpin.

Orientation

Most of Casper is south of the North Platte River and I-25. Downtown Casper is bounded roughly by I-25 on the north, Beverly St on the east, Poplar St (Hwy 252) on the west and 15th St on the south. Downtown exits include E Yellowstone Hwy (I-25 exits 185 and 186), Center St (I-25 exit 188A) and Poplar St (I-25 exit 188B). Grocery stores, fast-food chains and other eateries are along CY Ave. Downtown, tree-lined 2nd St, nicknamed 'Snake Alley,' curves between David and Durbin Sts. The paved Platte River Pkwy parallels the river.

Information

The Casper Area Chamber of Commerce (☎ 307-234-5362, 800-852-1889), 500 N Center St, is south of I-80 exit 188A; open 8 am to 5 pm weekdays year-round and 9 am to 6 pm weekends in summer. The

'I was born a Lakota and I shall die a Lakota.'
– Red Cloud

BLM Casper District office (☎ 307-261-7600) is at 1701 E 'E' St. There are several ATMs downtown on Wolcott and E 1st Sts. The post office is at 150 E 'B' St. Browse periodicals at Westerner News (☎ 307-235-1022), 245 S Center St. Blue Heron Books & Espresso (☎ 307-265-3774, 800-585-3774), 201 E 2nd St in the Atrium Plaza, serves espresso and pastries. The Book Exchange (☎ 307-237-6034), 323 S Center St, has a huge used selection. Wyoming Medical Center (☎ 307-577-7201) is at 1233 E 2nd St.

Downtown Casper

Downtown Casper is less distinguished than Laramie or Sheridan, not for lack of historic buildings but because newer facades conceal their classic features. To get a feel for historic Casper, walk the alley on the south side of 2nd St. The **Kistler Building**, 245–249 S Center St, has housed a post office, saddle shop and tent factory. Across the street, the building (1907) at **240 S Center St** has spectacular tilework that was added in 1924. The **Natrona County Courthouse** (1940), 200 N Center St, is a limestone WPA gem. The exterior friezes are striking examples of New Deal art: On one, a Native American bison hunter and a cowpoke roping a steer advance from opposite directions toward an oil derrick; on another, Conestoga pioneers and a settler's plow team converge on a city on the plains. Elsewhere, in opposite niches, a Native American chieftain confronts a US cavalryman. The abandoned **Townsend Hotel** (1923), 115–117 N Center St, retains its exterior integrity, with handsome cornices and columns. At 137–141 S Center St, the five-story **Oil Exchange Building** (1917), later renamed the Con Roy Building, is on the National Register of Historic Places; the upper four floors are exceptionally well preserved.

Fort Caspar National Historic Place

Reconstructed Fort Caspar, on the North Platte River west of downtown, was a 1930s WPA project. It portrays life at an Oregon Trail outpost. Few artifacts remain, but the ruins of Louis Guinard's toll bridge are worth a look. Other structures include the blacksmith's shop, a corral, the Overland Stage station, the commissary storehouse, the Guinard trading post and a carriage shed. The outpost was abandoned in 1867 with the construction of Fort Fetterman. The free **Fort Caspar Museum** (☎ 307-235-

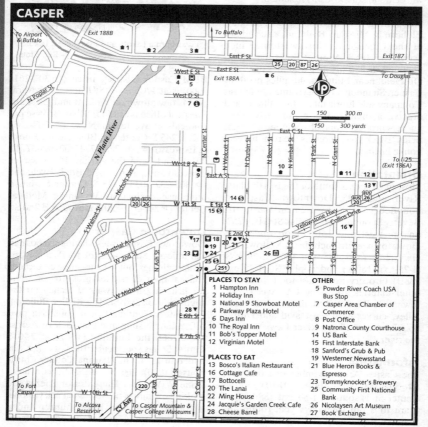

CASPER

PLACES TO STAY
1 Hampton Inn
2 Holiday Inn
3 National 9 Showboat Motel
4 Parkway Plaza Hotel
6 Days Inn
10 The Royal Inn
11 Bob's Topper Motel
12 Virginian Motel

PLACES TO EAT
13 Bosco's Italian Restaurant
16 Cottage Cafe
17 Bottocelli
20 The Lanai
22 Ming House
24 Jacquie's Garden Creek Cafe
28 Cheese Barrel

OTHER
5 Powder River Coach USA Bus Stop
7 Casper Area Chamber of Commerce
8 Post Office
9 Natrona County Courthouse
14 US Bank
15 First Interstate Bank
18 Sanford's Grub & Pub
19 Westerner Newsstand
21 Blue Heron Books & Espresso
23 Tommyknocker's Brewery
25 Community First National Bank
26 Nicolaysen Art Museum
27 Book Exchange

8462) has interesting photos of African-American cowboys (one in four cowboys was African-American). It's open 8 am to 7 pm Monday to Saturday and noon to 7 pm Sunday mid-May to mid-September, and 8 am to 5 pm weekdays and 1 to 4 pm Sunday in winter. To reach the site, take I-80 exit 188B to Wyoming Blvd or head west on W 13th St from downtown.

Nicolaysen Art Museum

The 'Nic' (☎ 307-235-5247), 400 E Collins Dr, is in a former power plant. The 1920s brick building that is now home to contemporary art galleries once housed three diesel generators beneath its 30-foot ceilings. It later served as a lumberyard, then sat vacant for several years before being refurbished in 1990 to the tune of $2.6 million. The **Discovery Center** is a big hit with kids. Open 10 am to 5 pm Tuesday to Sunday and 5 to 8 pm Thursday, Memorial to Labor Day; admission $2/1 adults/children.

Casper College Museums

Casper College, a junior college with a few four-year programs, is Casper's top cultural resource. Its free **Tate Geological Museum** (☎ 307-268-2447), off Casper Mountain Rd at the south end of the campus, hosts both permanent and special exhibitions of fossils (including a preparation lab open to the public), Wyoming jade, meteorites and minerals; open 9 am to 5 pm weekdays and 10 am to 3 pm Saturday. The free **Werner Wildlife Museum** (☎ 307-268-2108), 405 E 15th St, is essentially an homage to taxidermy.

Special Events

The **Cowboy State Games** pit cowpokes against each other each June. Celebrate the summer solstice (June 21) on Caspar Mountain (see later) at **Midsummer's Eve**. The **Central Wyoming Fair & Rodeo** takes over the fairgrounds in July.

Places to Stay

Casper has a large choice of accommodations off I-25 at E Yellowstone Hwy, Center St and Poplar St. Seasonal rate changes are negligible, and rates here are some of the state's lowest.

The year-round **Fort Caspar Campground** (☎ 307-234-3260, 888-243-7709, 4205 Fort Caspar Rd), I-25 exit 188B, beyond the Fort Caspar Museum, offers little shade but good river access, laundry and showers ($11/16). Farther out, Bar Nunn's **Antelope Campground** (☎ 307-577-1664, 1101 Prairie Lane), I-25 exit 191 off Salt Creek Hwy, has an indoor pool, hot tub, laundry and showers ($12/18); open April to October. Good public campgrounds are 10 miles south of town atop Caspar Mountain (see later).

Book ahead for clean, spacious rooms ($30/40) at Casper's best budget deal, the popular **Royal Inn** (☎ 307-234-3501, 800-967-6925, 440 E 'A' St). If it's full, take your chances at one of the following dirt-cheap downtown options, but take a peek at a few rooms before settling in: **Ranch House Motel** (☎ 307-266-4044, 1130 E 'F' St); **Virginian Motel** (☎ 307-266-3959, 830 E 'A' St), with rates of $25/30, or the similarly priced **Bob's Topper Motel** (☎ 307-237-8407, 888-262-8677, 728 E 'A' St). Rooms cost $35/45 at **National 9 Showboat Motel** (☎ 307-235-2711, 800-524-9999, 100 W 'F' St). There are several other cheapies along Yellowstone Hwy east of downtown.

Casper's pleasant **Super 8** (☎ 307-266-3480, 888-266-0497, 3838 CY Ave), at $45/50, is one of the chain's best in Wyoming. The **Kelly Inn** (☎ 307-266-2400, 800-635-3559, 821 N Poplar St) has a whirlpool and sauna and rates of $45 to $55. Rooms at the **1st Interstate Inn** (☎ 307-234-9125), on I-25 at Wyoming Blvd, are $40/50. Rooms are $55/65 at the **Days Inn** (☎ 307-234-1159, 301 E 'E' St). Rooms fetch $55 to $80 at the **Parkway Motel** (☎ 307-234-2162, 5102 W Yellowstone Hwy).

The **Parkway Plaza Hotel** (☎ 307-235-1777, 800-270-7829, 123 W 'E' St), I-25 exit 188A, has a pool and restaurant with room rates of $60/65. Within walking distance of downtown, the **Antique B&B** (☎ 307-265-2304, 939 S Wolcott St) costs $65. Other options include the **Hampton Inn** (☎ 307-235-6668, 400 W 'F' St), I-25 exit 188B, for

$70 to $85, and ***Holiday Inn*** (☎ *307-235-2531, 300 W 'F' St)*, from $120.

Places to Eat
For breakfast, lunch and sushi dinners, try ***Jacquie's Garden Creek Cafe*** (☎ *307-265-9018, 251 S Center St)*. ***Cottage Cafe*** (☎ *307-234-1157, 116 S Lincoln St)* is popular for soup and salad. ***Cheese Barrel*** (☎ *307-235-5202, 544 S Center St)* has a good deli. ***La Casacita*** (☎ *307-234-7633, 633 W Collins Dr)* is a popular Tex-Mex joint. For Chinese try ***Ming House*** (☎ *307-265-1838, 233 E 2nd St)*. ***The Lanai*** (☎ *307-237-7516, upper level 201 E 2nd St)* isn't authentically Polynesian, but has good sandwiches and tasty 'Island Lunches' like Hawaiian chicken salad. ***Bosco's Italian Restaurant*** (☎ *307-265-9658, 847 E 'A' St)* is also good; reservations are recommended. Upscale ***Botticelli*** (☎ *307-266-2700, 129 W 2nd St)* is a romantic Northern Italian *ristorante*. ***Tommyknocker's Brewery*** (☎ *307-472-7837, 256 S Center St)* offers pub grub and good microbrews.

Entertainment
Three movie theaters downtown (near the corner of 2nd and Center Sts) screen mainstream Hollywood releases; tickets are only $3. ***Sanford's Grub & Pub*** (☎ *307-234-4555, 241 S Center St)* is a lively sports bar. The ***Casper Events Center*** (☎ *307-577-3030, 1 Events Dr)*, north of I-25 via Poplar St, hosts many concerts. The ***Casper Planetarium*** (☎ *307-577-0310, 904 N Poplar St)* runs family-oriented programs in summer; admission is $2/5 for adults/families.

Getting There & Away
Casper is served by SkyWest/Delta and United Express out of the Natrona County International Airport (☎ 307-472-6688), 6 miles west of downtown off US 20/US 26. Note the Richard Jacobi **Casper Centennial Mural** inside the terminal. SkyWest/Delta Connection flies daily to Salt Lake City, while United Express serves Denver daily.

Powder River Coach USA (☎ 307-266-1904, 800-442-3682) is at the Parkway Plaza

Hotel at 123 W 'E' St. Twice daily, buses depart Casper for Douglas and Cheyenne; the evening bus continues to Denver. One daily bus departs for Cody and another for Billings, MT, via the Bighorn Basin, and for Billings via Buffalo and Sheridan.

Casper is along the south side of I-25, 178 miles northwest of Cheyenne and 112 miles south of Buffalo. US 20/US 26 leads west to Shoshoni (94 miles). Hwy 220 leads southwest to Muddy Gap Junction (73 miles) where it meets US 287/Hwy 789, which leads west to Lander (82 miles) or south to Rawlins (46 miles).

Getting Around
Avis (☎ 307-237-2634), Budget (☎ 307-266-1122) and Hertz (☎ 307-265-1355) are at the airport. Enterprise (☎ 307-234-8122) is at 535 N Beverly. Try Aries (☎ 307-234-3501), 440 E 'A' St at the Royal Inn, or Price King (☎ 307-472-7378), 3280 E Yellowstone Hwy, for cheaper rates. Reliable RC Cab (☎ 307-235-5203) is always on call.

CASPER MOUNTAIN
The prominent peak to the south of Casper, Casper Mountain (8200 feet) offers ample recreation. Head south from Casper on Casper Mountain Rd (Hwy 251). Camping ($5) is possible Memorial Day to mid-October at several county-run areas on top of the mountain.

Hogadon Basin Ski Area
Nine miles south of Casper, the modest Hogadon Basin Ski Area (☎ 307-235-8499) offers downhill and cross-country skiing. The 600-foot vertical drop to the base elevation of 7500 feet is suitable for beginner and intermediate downhill skiers. The area also boasts 15 miles of groomed cross-country trails and 60 miles of snowmobile trails. Full-day lift tickets are $20/17/15; half-day tickets (9 am to 12:30 pm or 12:30 to 4 pm) are $15 for all ages. The ski season is Thanksgiving to April; call ☎ 307-235-8369 for a snow report. For rentals, try Mountain Sports (☎ 307-266-6904) or Hogadon Ski Rentals (☎ 307-265-0399), both on the mountain.

Crimson Dawn Cabin & Museum

This free mountaintop homesteader's museum (☎ 307-235-1303) is the bequest of longtime Casper Mountain resident Neal Forsling, a painter and storyteller who spent nearly 50 years here with her husband, daughters and the mystical creatures who populate her stories and paintings. If you happen to be in the area for the summer solstice, June 21, don't miss the **Midsummer's Eve** celebration of local spirits. Open 11 am to 7 pm Saturday to Thursday mid-June until either the last yellow leaf falls or the first big snowstorm hits (typically mid-October). The museum and the USFS *Tower Hill Campground* are both off unpaved East End Rd.

DOUGLAS

Founded when the Fremont, Elkhorn & Missouri Valley Railroad extended through central Wyoming in 1886, Douglas (population 5725; elevation 4815 feet) provided access to the region's early mining and ranching zones. It was named for Illinois Senator Stephen Douglas – best known as Abraham Lincoln's debate opponent – and became known as the 'Gateway City' for the railroad. Douglas, 46 miles east of Casper, is the seat of Converse County, in which the major industries are ranching, coal mining and oil.

The open-air **Railroad Interpretive Center** at Center St and Brownfield Rd is a worthwhile stop for anyone, but especially for railroad enthusiasts. The renovated former Chicago & Northwestern Railroad Depot is on the National Historic Register. East of Douglas, the USFS Medicine Bow–Routt National Forest and USFS Thunder Basin National Grassland Douglas Ranger Station (☎ 307-358-4690), 2250 Richards St, is open 7:30 am to 4:30 pm weekdays. (See 'Thunder Basin' under Gillette, later, for information about the grassland.)

The original business district and most **historic buildings** are on N 2nd St. On the National Register of Historic Places are the original Douglas City Hall (1915), 130 S 3rd St, and the College Inn Bar, a prefab built in Chicago in 1906 and assembled here on the original site of Pringle's Saloon (1886). The intriguing Odd Fellows' Hall, on S Riverbend Dr, served as part of a WWII POW camp that housed mostly Italians.

The free **Wyoming Pioneer Memorial Museum** (☎ 307-358-9288), at the Wyoming State Fairgrounds, has a large collection of weapons emphasizing local participation in foreign wars and an exhibit of barbed wire dating as far back as 1868. The original bar from the La Bonte Inn is worth a look. Open 8 am to 5 pm weekdays and 1 to 5 pm Saturday.

Since 1905 Douglas has hosted the annual **Wyoming State Fair**. With agricultural and livestock displays, rodeos, a carnival, live entertainment and more, the fair runs one week in mid-August. In June Douglas celebrates **Jackalope Days**, claiming the fictitious jackrabbit with antlers as its own. The Wyoming State **High School Rodeo Finals** take place in late June at the fairgrounds, while the annual **Senior Pro Rodeo** is held in early August.

Powder River Coach USA (☎ 307-358-4484) stops at Plains Cafe (☎ 307-358-4489), 628 Richards St. Daily buses depart Douglas for Billings, MT, via Gillette; Billings via Casper and the Bighorn Basin; and Cheyenne and Denver, CO.

FORT LARAMIE NATIONAL HISTORIC SITE

The tiny town of Fort Laramie (population 250) is on US 26, 21 miles northwest of Torrington and 13 miles east of Guernsey (28 miles from I-25 exit 92). Tourist information is in a log building on US 26. Camping (three days max) is free at the *Municipal Campground* on S Laramie Ave south of US 26 and the railroad tracks. *Chuckwagon RV Park* is near US 26. There are several modestly priced motels and decent restaurants.

Founded as a frontier trading post by fur trader William Sublette in 1834, sold to the American Fur Company in 1836 and acquired by the US army in 1849, **Fort Laramie** is an important Oregon Trail landmark and eastern Wyoming's most worthwhile historic site. The well-restored buildings are filled with period artifacts. The NPS conducts park tours, living-history presentations and historic-weapons demonstrations. On the north side of the park, directly behind Old Bedlam, is a shady picnic area. The site is 3 miles southwest of town on Hwy 160.

History

Even before 1849, Fort Laramie (originally known as Fort William, then Fort John) played a critical role in the opening of the frontier to emigrants, who streamed across the plains en route to Oregon and California. After acquiring the post, the army began construction of substantial buildings. This was the last major opportunity for transcontinental emigrants to resupply, repair their wagons and change horses or oxen.

Fort Laramie was a rendezvous point for the Lakota as well, but this changed as increasing numbers of emigrants violated Native American lands. Outright warfare developed in the 1860s and 1870s, as the USA broke a series of treaties that guaranteed the northern Plains Indians their hunting grounds north of the North Platte River and, later, the Black Hills of northeastern Wyoming and South Dakota. In both cases the invasive miners provoked the Native American response. In the case of Red Cloud's War (1866–68), the army built several posts along the Bozeman Trail to facilitate the passage of miners, in deliberate violation of previous territorial agreements.

Fort Laramie was the base for the US army's Great Sioux Campaign (1876), ordered by President Ulysses S Grant. This campaign, which included the battles of Rosebud Creek (June 17) and the Little Bighorn (June 24), ultimately broke Sioux resistance. Fort Laramie continued as an army center, while the northern Plains Indians were gradually forced onto reservations. By 1890, having outlived its usefulness, the fort was abandoned. For a time, squatters inhabited the buildings, but the state acquired the property in 1936 and transferred it to the NPS two years later.

The grounds are open 8 am to dusk daily. The museum and visitors center (☎ 307-837-2221) are open 8 am to 7 pm daily in summer (until 4:30 pm in winter). A library containing 25,000 computerized records of travelers who passed through Fort Laramie in the 19th century is on the 2nd floor of the Cavalry Barracks; open 9 am to 4:30 pm weekdays. Admission to the site is $2 (youth 16 and under are free) and includes a brochure depicting the fort as it was in 1888, with current buildings indicated by number.

Walking Tour

The best starting point for a self-guided walking tour is the visitors center, formerly the Commissary Storehouse (1884). Directly to the south is the still-functioning Old Bakery (1876). At the southwest corner of the parade ground, the New Guardhouse (1876) was for disciplining rowdy soldiers. A short distance upstream, the Old Guardhouse (1866) detained serious prisoners in a solitary-confinement dungeon. At the parade ground's west end, the Captain's Quarters (1870) was a duplex for junior officers. On its north side is Old Bedlam (1849), Wyoming's oldest surviving military building. At the east end of the parade ground, the Post Surgeon's Quarters (1875) is a Victorian officers' duplex. Immediately to its east are the relatively modest Lieutenant Colonel's Quarters (1884) and the Post Trader's Store (1849, but restored to appear as in 1876). Duck into its Enlisted Men's Bar (an 1883 addition) for an ice-cold sarsaparilla. Continue east to the sprawling Cavalry Barracks (1874), which served as a store, saloon and dance hall after the fort closed in 1890. On the slope to its north are ruins of the hospital (1873).

SUNDANCE

In remote northeastern Wyoming, the Black Hills span the Wyoming–South Dakota state line. Rumped up against the Black Hills, Sundance (population 1275; elevation 4750 feet) is known for its rich history, ranching tradition and natural beauty. Sundance Mountain (see below) lends its name to the town, the Crook County seat.

Founded in 1879 and incorporated in 1887, the town is probably most famous for giving Butch Cassidy's companion Harry Longabaugh his nickname ('Sundance Kid') after the Pennsylvania teenager spent 18 months in the town's jail for horse theft. White-tailed deer share the plains with pronghorn antelope and the occasional buffalo. The town's pleasant atmosphere and its convenient I-90 location make it a good base for exploring Devils Tower National Monument and the surrounding Black Hills.

Orientation & Information

Cleveland Ave (US 14) is the main east-west road. Main St parallels it one block north. The main north-south road is S 6th St (Hwy 585). There's a tiny tourist information building (☎ 307-283-2440) at the I-90 exit 189 rest area; open 8 am to 7 pm daily in summer and 8 am to 5 pm in October. The USFS Black Hills National Forest Bear Lodge Ranger District (☎ 307-283-1361), 1 mile east of town on US 14E, has copious information. The post office is at 2nd and Main Sts. Crook County Memorial Hospital (☎ 307-283-3501) is at 713 Oak St.

Crook County Museum & Art Gallery

Harry Longabaugh's court records are the pride of the free Crook County Museum (☎ 307-283-3666), in the Crook County courthouse basement on Cleveland between 3rd and 4th Sts. Other exhibits include a diorama of the Vore Buffalo Jump (see Around Sundance, below), Native American artifacts, a country store and pioneer memorabilia. Most interesting is the tribute to Bob Brislawn, a packer and teamster for the USGS Topographic Survey who also identified and bred Spanish mustangs. Open 8 am to 8 pm weekdays June to August, otherwise 8 am to 5 pm weekdays.

Sundance Mountain

The prominent 5829-foot peak south of Sundance was called the 'Temple of the Sioux' by Plains Indians, who held one of their most significant ceremonies here, the sacred and secretive Sun Dance. Contact landowner Cecil Cundy (☎ 307-283-2193) for permission to access the private trail.

Places to Stay & Eat

Thinking of visiting Sundance during the Bike Rally in nearby Sturgis, South Dakota, in early August without a reservation? Fahgetaboutit! Prices rise dramatically and many lodgings are booked up to a year in advance. Motel rates drop by as much as 30% in winter. See Around Sundance, below, for information on nearby USFS campgrounds.

Year-round *Mountain View Campground* (☎ 307-283-2270, 800-792-8439), on Government Valley Rd 1 mile east of town, has little shade but is well maintained, with a pool, laundry and rates of $13/18. *Deane's Pine View Motel* (☎ 307-283-2262, 117 N 8th St) has basic rooms ($45) and kitchenettes ($55). Clean rooms are $50/60 at the *Arrowhead Motel* (☎ 307-283-3307, 800-456-6016, 214 Cleveland Ave). Next door is the *Bear Lodge Motel* (☎ 307-283-1611, 800-341-8000, 218 Cleveland Ave), for $57/65. The remodeled *Sundance Mountain Inn* (☎ 307-283-3737, 888-347-2794), on US 14E (I-90 exit 189), asks $80 to $90. The *Best Western Inn at Sundance* (☎ 307-283-2800, 800-238-0965, 121 S 6th St), I-90 exit 187, charges $60 to $100.

Sundance's restaurants are friendly and inexpensive, if unexciting. *Higbee's Cafe* (☎ 307-283-2165, 101 N 3rd St) serves breakfast all day. The *Log Cabin Cafe* (☎ 307-283-3393, 1620 Cleveland Ave) is a good choice for all meals. The fancier *Aro Family Restaurant* (☎ 307-283-2000, 205 Cleveland Ave) serves steak and seafood. The *Country Cottage* (☎ 307-283-2450, 423 Cleveland Ave) offers sub sandwiches and frozen yogurt.

Getting There & Away

Powder River Coach USA (☎ 800-442-3682) stops at the Bear Lodge Motel, 218 Cleveland Ave. Daily buses depart for Rapid City, South Dakota; and Gillette. Sundance is along the north side of I-90, 18 miles west of the Wyoming–South Dakota state line and 33 miles east of Moorcroft. Devils Tower, on Hwy 24, is 27 miles northwest of Sundance via US 14. Hwy 585 leads south to Four Corners (28 miles), where it meets US 85. US 85 continues 18 miles south to Newcastle.

AROUND SUNDANCE
Vore Buffalo Jump

This is one of the most important archaeological sites in North America. Over a 350-year period, pre-Columbian peoples drove more than 20,000 bison into this sinkhole, which filled slowly with sediment, thus preserving bones and stone artifacts that offer insight into early Plains cultures, as well as data on climatic and environmental changes. The University of Wyoming is collaborating with the private Vore Buffalo Jump Foundation (☎ 307-283-1192) to excavate the site. Visitors may view ongoing excavation in early summer. The site is northeast of Sundance, near the Wyoming–South Dakota state line. Take I-90 exit 199, then go 3 miles east on US 14.

Bearlodge Mountains & Black Hills

North of Sundance, the Bearlodge Mountains are bounded by US 14, Hwy 24, Hwy 11 and I-90, while the Black Hills extend from South Dakota into northeastern Wyoming. The area offers plentiful year-round recreational opportunities, but the USFS occasionally closes some roads to protect elk and wild turkeys.

Warren Peak Lookout

Take US 14 west from Sundance to Warren Peak Rd (USFS Rd 838) and continue to the Warren Peak Lookout (☎ 307-283-1525). From this working forest-fire lookout tower (6656 feet), four states, Devils Tower and the Bighorn Mountains are visible. The drive takes 30 minutes. While USFS Rd 838 is not paved beyond the lookout, the well-graded road continues through aspen groves, known as the 'Emerald Forest,' toward Cook Lake. Alternatively, head west on scenic USFS Rd 847 and down Lytle Creek Valley (on County Rd 196) to Devils Tower.

Cook Lake Recreation Area

North of Cook Lake, cliff swallows build nests in the limestone bluffs that tower above the pine and aspens in picturesque Beaver Creek Valley. Keep an eye out for wildlife when you hike, fish or birdwatch around the lake, including beaver dams along a 2-mile section of the perennial creek in the aspen forest below. Popular loop trails include a walk around Cook Lake and the Cliff Swallow Trail, which begins from the northwest end of the Cook Lake campground. Take USFS Rd 838 north from US 14 west of Sundance or south from Hwy 24 east of Alva.

Hiking & Horseback Riding

The **Bearlodge Trails** lead through the Bearlodge Mountains. The 50-mile **Sundance Trail System** starts from the USFS Sundance Campground, and the 6-mile **Carson Draw Trails** start from the USFS Reuter Campground. Both trail systems also can be reached by USFS roads. Corrals are at the USFS Sundance Campground. **Beaver Creek Trail**, east of Four Corners at the junction of US 85 and Hwy 585, is excellent.

Places to Stay

A few minutes' drive from Sundance are three reservable USFS campgrounds. *Sundance Campground* ($10), off Government Valley Rd, 3 miles north of Sundance, is open April to November. En route to Warren Peak Lookout, the USFS *Reuter Campground* ($8), off USFS Rd 838, is open year-round. The USFS *Cook Lake Campground* ($6 to $10) is along the southeast shore of the lake off USFS Rd 843. Camping is free at the USFS *Bearlodge Campground*, on Hwy 24 between Alva and Aladdin. The remote USFS *Beaver Creek Campground* ($8) lies at 6500 feet, a few miles east of the US 85/Hwy 585 junction at Four Corners, 28 miles southeast of Sundance.

DEVILS TOWER NATIONAL MONUMENT

Lakota leader Arvol Looking Horse described Devils Tower as 'the heart of every-

unique hazards include everything from spiny plants to poisonous snakes, wasps and falcons. Some routes may be closed mid-March to midsummer to protect nesting falcons. Consider the voluntary June climbing ban when planning your trip. For instruction and guided climbs, contact Tower Guides (☎ 307-467-5589, 888-345-9061), www.towerguides.com, at the Base of Tower; or Sylvan Rocks (☎ 605-574-2425), www.sylvanrocks.com, in Hill City, South Dakota.

Places to Stay & Eat
Camping is permitted in the Bearlodge Mountains and Black Hills and in Sundance (see Sundance, earlier). The nearest motels are in Hulett, Sundance and Moorcroft.

A half-mile inside the park, the **Belle Fourche Campground** is open April to late October. Sites cost $12 and fill up early. Open year-round, **Fort Devils Tower** (☎ 307-467-5655, 601 Hwy 24) has tent sites ($12) and full hookups ($15). Showers are $3 for noncampers. At the entrance station, **Devils Tower KOA** (☎ 307-467-5395) is open mid-May to mid-September and has a pool, cafe and ATM ($22/28).

Devils Tower Trading Post (☎ 307-467-5295) sells some groceries, but it's best to bring your own. Ten miles north of Devils Tower on Hwy 24 is Hulett, the nearest town, with meager motels and restaurants.

Getting There & Away
Devils Tower is on Hwy 24, 6 miles north of Devils Tower Junction at US 14, which is 26 miles northeast of Moorcroft (I-90 exit 154), 22 miles northwest of Sundance (I-90 exit 185) and 125 miles west of South Dakota's Mount Rushmore National Monument.

GILLETTE & AROUND
The Powder River flows through the sagebrush prairies north of Casper, between the snowcapped Bighorn Mountains to the west and the Thunder Basin Grassland and the Black Hills to the east. Historically, the Bozeman Trail and the Deadwood Stage from Cheyenne passed through this area,

igniting conflicts between white migrants and Native Americans, who viewed these incursions as threats to their territory. Today the region's economy depends largely on ranching and coal mining. Sightings of busloads of Japanese tourists stopping along the roadside to snap photos 'of nothing' are not uncommon.

In 1974, a *New York Times* reporter described the mineral boomtown of Gillette as

…a raw jumble of rutted streets and sprawling junkyards, red mud and dust, dirty trucks and crowded bars, faded billboards and sagging utility lines, and block after block of house trailers squatting in the dirt like a nest of giant grubs….

Thus, it is all the more startling that down-but-not-out Gillette (population 20,000; elevation 4538 feet) received a Lady Bird Johnson Roadside Beautification Award in 1992.

Gillette, Wyoming's fourth-largest city and the seat of Campbell County (where folks proudly insist that there are more pronghorn antelope than people!), is the region's most economically important city, and has a Northern Wyoming Community College campus. An onslaught of shopping malls and fast-food franchises, the consequence of Gillette's coal-fueled prosperity, is overwhelming the area. Many businesses have fled downtown for the malls. The scale of downtown's newer buildings, such as City

Thunder Basin

South of Gillette sprawls the enormous Thunder Basin National Grassland. Hwy 59 between Douglas and Gillette is the main north-south road through the region. It's often uttered in this wide-open country that 'you can watch your dog run away for three days.' No services or campgrounds exist, although free dispersed camping is permitted. Detailed information is available from the USFS in Douglas (☎ 307-358-4690), 2250 Richards St; open 7:30 am to 4:30 pm weekdays.

Hall and the multistory First Interstate Bank, seems exaggerated for this two-lump town.

History

Once called Donkey Town after nearby Donkey Creek, then Rocky Pile for a local landmark, Gillette inherited its present name from Weston Gillette, a surveyor and civil engineer who helped bring the CB&Q Railroad in 1891. Local ranchers made Gillette the largest shipping point on the CB&Q, with stockyards harboring up to 40,000 sheep and 12,000 cattle. Coal, however, is what stokes the economy. East of town, the massive **Wyodak Mine** contains a 70-foot seam worked since 1922, when it may have been the world's largest strip mine. Petroleum and uranium are also found, but the area's relatively clean-burning, low-sulfur coal remains in high demand, and a majority of the Campbell County population works in resource extraction.

Orientation & Information

Downtown Gillette is north of I-90 and south of US 14/16 (2nd St), the main east-west road; 2nd St turns into Hwy 51 east of Hwy 59. Douglas Hwy (Hwy 59), the main north-south road, bisects Gillette. Many motels and restaurants are along 2nd St, but the newer ones are along Douglas Hwy (I-90 exit 126).

The Gillette Information Center (☎ 307-686-0040, 800-544-6136), 1810 S Douglas Hwy, is next to the Flying J Travel Plaza near I-90 exit 126. It's open 8 am to 5 pm daily in summer, otherwise 8 am to 5 pm weekdays. Their extensive cache of information includes useful nuggets about coal mines and tips on wildlife viewing. The BLM Survey Project office (☎ 307-686-6750) positively radiates at 1901 Energy Court, suite 160.

First Interstate Bank has an ATM at 222 S Gillette Ave. Wells Fargo dispenses cash at 500 S Douglas Hwy. The post office is downtown at 311 Kendrick St. Daniels Books (☎ 307-682-8266) is at 320 S Gillette Ave. Campbell County Memorial Hospital (☎ 307-682-8811) is at 501 S Burma Rd.

Campbell County Rockpile Museum

In the shadow of Gillette's most unmistakable natural feature, this popular free museum (☎ 307-682-5723), 900 W 2nd St, displays an interesting collection of Native American and pioneer artifacts. Open 9 am to 8 pm Monday to Saturday and 12:30 to 6:30 pm Sunday from June to August, otherwise 9 am to 5 pm Monday to Saturday.

Strip Mines & Power Plants

Fourteen mines around Gillette produce 25% of the USA's coal. Several mines and related industries are open for free one-hour tours, usually 8 am to 3 pm daily in summer, otherwise by appointment. Contact the Gillette Information Center or the Wyodak Mine (☎ 307-682-3410) for details. Views of the area's largest strip mine are possible from the **Wyodak Overlook**, 5 miles east of Gillette off US 14/16 (I-90 exit 132). Half of this output fuels the nearby 330-megawatt **Wyodak Power Plant** (☎ 307-686-1248); call for free tour reservations.

Durham Buffalo Ranch

South of Gillette on Hwy 59 is Durham Buffalo Ranch (☎ 307-939-1271), one of the country's largest buffalo ranches. Tours are by appointment only.

Special Events

Mid-June's **Cowboy Days** and July's **National High School Rodeo Finals** (one of Wyoming's biggest events) draw enthusiastic crowds. The traveling **PRCA Rodeo** in August is another big whoop-de-do.

Places to Stay

Gillette has abundant lodgings at reasonable, sometimes rock-bottom, prices. Rates may drop slightly after October 1 but are jacked up in early August during the motorcycle rally in Sturgis, South Dakota.

Green Tree's shady *Crazy Woman Campground* (☎ 307-682-3665, 1001 W 2nd St) has showers and a hot tub. Campsites command up to a whopping $20; full hookups fetch as much as $30. The *High Plains Campground* (☎ 307-687-7339,

160 S Garner Lake Rd), I-90 exit 129, is barren and less appealing; campsites cost $12. Both have laundry.

The hotels listed below charge from $30 to $100 for double rooms; they're given in increasing order of price:

Arrowhead Motel
(☎ 307-686-0909, 202 S Emerson Ave)

Mustang Motel
(☎ 307-682-4784, 922 E 3rd St)

Motel 6
(☎ 307-686-8600, 2105 Rodgers Dr)

Budget Inn Express
(☎ 307-686-1989, 800-709-6123, 2011 Rodgers Dr)

Circle L
(☎ 307-682-9375, 401 E 2nd St)

Days Inn
(☎ 307-682-3999, 800-329-7466, 910 E Boxelder Rd)

Ramada Limited
(☎ 307-682-9341, 800-272-6232, 608 E 2nd St)

National 9 Inn
(☎ 307-682-5111, 1020 Hwy 51 E)

Quality Inn
(☎ 307-682-2616, 800-228-5151, 1002 E 2nd St)

Econolodge
(☎ 307-682-4757, 409 Butler Spaeth Rd)

Best Western Tower West Lodge
(☎ 307-686-2210, 800-762-7375, 109 N US 14/US 16), I-90 exit 124

Places to Eat

Lula Belle Coffee Shop (☎ 307-682-9798, 101 N Gillette Ave) is Gillette's favorite breakfast spot, specializing in colossal sweet rolls. *Coffee Friends* (☎ 307-686-6119, 320 S Gillette Ave) serves espresso, bagels and sandwiches. *Bailey's Bar & Grill* (☎ 307-686-7678, 301 S Gillette Ave) is a stylish restaurant with appealing sandwiches and dinner options. *The Goings* (☎ 307-682-6805, 113 S Gillette Ave) serves dinner that tastes better after a few drinks. Where's the beef? At the popular *Prime Rib Restaurant* (☎ 307-682-2944, 1205 S Douglas Hwy), of course. *Hong Kong Restaurant* (☎ 307-682-5829, 1612 W 2nd St) has cheap lunch and dinner specials. *Casa del Rey* (☎ 307-682-4738, 409 W 2nd St) is the reigning king of local Mexican munchies. Querida *Aunt*

Chilotta (☎ 307-682-0610, 400 W 2nd Ave) is one notch above Taco Hell.

Entertainment

The sprawling *Cam-Plex* (☎ 800-358-1897, 307-682-8802 ticket office, 1635 Reata Dr), at Garner Lake (I-90 exit 129) and Boxelder Rds, covers more than 1½ sq miles. The Cam-Plex Heritage Center includes a fine arts theater for live performances, films and lectures. Its art gallery is open 8 am to 5 pm weekdays and during events. Cam-Plex Morningside Park is home to decidedly less cultured to-dos: rodeo, demo derby and horse racing at whimsical Energy Downs. Several down-home dive bars line S Douglas Hwy – look for the neon macrobrew signs.

Getting There & Around

By air, Gillette is connected with Denver, CO, and Sheridan by United Express (☎ 307-685-2280) out of the Gillette–Campbell County Airport (☎ 307-686-1042), 5 miles north of Gillette off US 14/16 exit 124.

The Powder River Coach USA (☎ 307-682-0960, 800-442-3682) bus depot is at 1700 E US 14/16 (I-90 exit 128). Buses go twice daily to Sheridan; Billings, MT; Casper; Cheyenne; and Denver; and once daily to Rapid City, SD.

By car Gillette is along the north side of I-90, 68 miles east of Buffalo and 63 miles west of Sundance. Hwy 59 leads south to Douglas (115 miles) via Wright (37 miles). US 14/16 leads 26 miles east to Moorcroft and north and west to Sheridan, although I-90 is a more direct route.

Avis (☎ 307-682-8588) and Hertz (☎ 307-686-0550) are at the airport. Try A&A Auto Rental (☎ 307-686-8250), 1200 E 2nd St, or Enterprise (☎ 307-686-5655) for better rates.

BUFFALO

Settlers founded the Johnson County seat of Buffalo (population 3750; elevation 4645 feet) after the US Army forced the Lakota Sioux onto reservations in the Black Hills. This town literally bears the brand of Wyoming's ranching heartland – ranchers'

WYOMING

marks cover the benches in the pleasant riverside park downtown over Clear Creek. Cattle and sheep graze its placid prairies at the eastern foot of the Bighorn Mountains, but late-19th-century Johnson County was the arena for the bitter conflict known as the Johnson County War. For many decades this conflict was so sensitive it could hardly be brought up in public, but it's been kosher ever since the First National Bank sponsored two bronze statues by local sculptor Mike Thomas depicting a 'rustler' and a

ranch foreman catching him in the act of mavericking. Today Buffalonians rustle more tourists than cattle while promoting their town as a base for Bighorn excursions.

Orientation & Information

The Powder River tributary of Clear Creek flows through the center of town. Main St (US 87), the business loop between I-90 exit 56A and I-25 exit 298, is the main north-south road. East of N Main St, Hart St (US 16) leads to I-90 and north towards Ucross. West of Main St, Fort St (US 16 W) becomes the Cloud Peak Scenic Byway.

The visitors center (☎ 307-684-5544, 800-227-5122), 55 N Main St, is open 8 am to 6 pm in summer; otherwise 8:30 am to 4:30 pm. You can find its Web site at www.buffalowyoming.org. The USFS Bighorn National Forest Buffalo Ranger District and the BLM Buffalo Resource Area (☎ 307-684-1100), 1425 Fort St (US 16 W), have extensive information; open 8 am to 4:30 pm. Drive-up ATMs are conspicuous along Main St. The post office is at 193 S Main St. The Johnson County Memorial Hospital is on the corner of Lott St and Desmet Ave (off Fort St).

Historic District

The Main St historic district, between Fort St on the north and Angus St on the south, retains an early 20th-century ambiance. Among the notable buildings are **Gatchell's Drug Store** (1904), 76 S Main St, named for pharmacist and collector Jim Gatchell (see below); the neoclassical **Johnson County Courthouse** (1884), 76 N Main St; and the **Carnegie Library** (1909), 90 N Main St, now part of the museum. The **Occidental Hotel** (1910), 10–30 N Main St, is celebrated as the site where Owen Wister's Virginian faced his adversary in a classic shoot-out (see 'The Cowboy Myth' in the Southern Wyoming section).

Jim Gatchell Memorial Museum

Despite its lustrous reputation, this museum (☎ 307-684-9331), 100 Fort St at Main St, is a somewhat haphazard and quixotic collection of Indian artifacts and Bozeman Trail

A Well-Known Son of a Gun

Tom Horn (1860–1903) was 'probably the best tracker, most experienced man hunter and one of the deadliest killers in the West,' according to Western historian Lauran Paine. Horn left his home in Missouri at age 15 and drifted west to settle among the Apache Indians of the Arizona Territory. He stayed for 10 years, serving as a US Army scout during the Apache wars, and was instrumental in arranging the great warrior chief Geronimo's surrender. Later Horn worked as a Pinkerton agent and deputy US marshal out of Denver.

His dispassionate ability to hunt and shoot men made him a feared legend as a stock detective for the cattle outfits of the unfenced range. Always on the side of the cattle barons and against the 'sodbusters,' Horn served the powerful Wyoming Stock Growers Association in the bloody Johnson County War. With the eruption of the Spanish-American War in 1898, Horn, along with other Wild West types, joined Teddy Roosevelt's Rough Riders in Cuba. After the war Horn returned to Wyoming, but the Wild West was dying as industry and farming took over. He worked as an executioner for the cattlemen in their last efforts to stave off the inevitable, but in 1903 Horn's life ended when he was hanged from the gallows for the murder of Willie Nickell, a sheepherder's son. (See 'Johnson County War.')

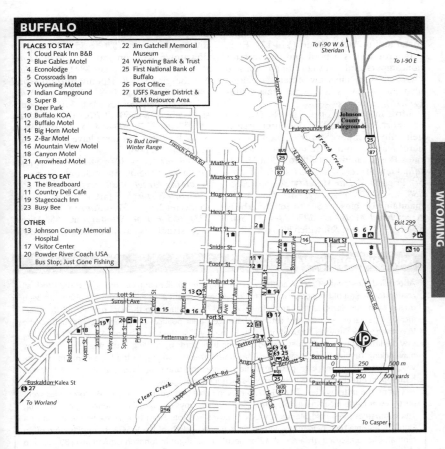

BUFFALO

PLACES TO STAY
1 Cloud Peak Inn B&B
2 Blue Gables Motel
4 Econolodge
5 Crossroads Inn
6 Wyoming Motel
7 Indian Campground
8 Super 8
9 Deer Park
10 Buffalo KOA
12 Buffalo Motel
14 Big Horn Motel
15 Z-Bar Motel
16 Mountain View Motel
18 Canyon Motel
21 Arrowhead Motel

PLACES TO EAT
3 The Breadboard
11 Country Deli Cafe
19 Stagecoach Inn
23 Busy Bee

OTHER
13 Johnson County Memorial
   Hospital
17 Visitor Center
20 Powder River Coach USA
   Bus Stop; Just Gone Fishing

22 Jim Gatchell Memorial
   Museum
24 Wyoming Bank & Trust
25 First National Bank of
   Buffalo
26 Post Office
27 USFS Ranger District &
   BLM Resource Area

WYOMING

memorabilia. Its best exhibits are dioramas, documents and other materials dealing with the Johnson County War. The video on local history playing in the Carnegie Wing is worth a look. It's open 8 am to 8 pm daily May to October; call for winter hours. Admission is $2 (under 15 free).

Special Events

Powder River Roundup Days fill the first weekend in July. The **Johnson County Fair & Rodeo** (☎ 307-684-7357) occupies a week in early August. August's other notable event is the **Basque Festival**, which honors de-

scendants of sheepherders who arrived in the early 20th century.

Places to Stay

Three private campgrounds are near I-25 exit 299 and I-90 exit 58. ***Indian Campground*** (☎ *307-684-9601, 660 E Hart St*) is shady and well maintained ($16/21 campsite/full hookup). ***Deer Park*** (☎ *307-684-5722, 800-222-9960, 146 US 16 E*) is the next-best option ($15/21). ***Buffalo KOA*** (☎ *307-684-5423, 800-562-5403, 87 US 16 E*) has shadeless sites ($15/21) and kabins ($38). Two miles west of Main St the ***Big***

Horn Mountains Campground (☎ 307-684-2307, 8935 US 16 W) is friendly and comfortable, but lacks shade ($14/17). Each campground has a pool and showers for noncampers and is usually open April to October. Mountain View Motel (see below) also has a few year-round grassy sites ($15/18).

Most motels are on E Hart St (US 16) and Fort St (US 16 W); the latter area is generally cheaper. Summer rates (listed here) may be up to 50% more than winter rates. Rustic cabins cost $40 to $75 at *Mountain View Motel (☎ 307-684-2881, 585 Fort St)*. Friendly *Z-Bar Motel (☎ 307-684-5535, 888-313-1227, 626 Fort St)* has well-maintained cabins for $45 to $60. Nearby is *Arrowhead Motel (☎ 307-684-9453, 800-824-1719, 749 Fort St)*, which charges $40 to

$65. Acceptable *Canyon Motel (☎ 307-684-2957, 800-231-0742, 997 Fort St)* is about as low as you can go ($36 to $55). Nearest to downtown is revamped *Big Horn Motel (☎ 307-684-7822, 800-936-7822, 209 N Main St)*, charging $60/70. Roomy *Buffalo Motel (☎ 307-684-5230, 888-684-0753, 370 N Main St)* has kitchenettes for $45 to $70. Spic-and-span cabins ($40/60) at *Blue Gables Motel (☎ 307-684-2574, 800-684-2574, 662 N Main St)* lack phones but some have kitchenettes, and there's a pool.

Econolodge (☎ 307-684-2219, 333 E Hart St) charges $45/50 single/double. Bunks at *Wyoming Motel (☎ 307-684-5505, 800-666-5505, 610 E Hart St)* start at $65, and family rooms fetch up to $130. *Super 8 (☎ 307-684-2531, 655 E Hart St)* starts at $65. Across the street is remodeled *Crossroads*

Johnson County War

Also called the Powder River War, this was one of many similar conflicts throughout the West, all related to the end of the open-range tradition. After the Native Americans and the bison had been driven from the plains, cattle barons freely grazed their animals on the vast prairie. But the ever-increasing smaller ranchers and settlers challenged their political and economic supremacy. The Wyoming Stock Growers Association (WSGA), run by absentees like Thomas Sturgis of New York, saw the little guys as cattle thieves who acquired their herds by rustling (changing of brands) or by mavericking (unauthorized branding of newborn calves belonging to the large companies). The WSGA used its influence to pass legislation preventing branding except at the annual WSGA roundup, in effect creating a government-sanctioned monopoly.

During the bitter winter of 1886–87, 3 million cattle starved and many cattle companies went bust. Fewer cattle meant unemployment, so more cowboys engaged in mavericking and rustling. The companies hired cold-blooded stock detectives like Tom Horn (see 'A Well-Known Son of a Gun') to enforce their hegemony. Judges were in the pockets of the WSGA, but juries were often sympathetic to accused rustlers – all 13 prosecutions brought in Johnson County in 1889 failed to obtain convictions. Consequently, the WSGA often took matters into its own hands. In 1892, stock growers Frank Walcott and William Irvine hired a group of Texan gunslingers to teach the Johnson County 'rustlers' a lesson.

Arriving by special train in Casper and carrying a hit list of their opponents, the Texans ambushed the Kaycee Ranch, 50 miles south of Buffalo. Nick Ray and Nate Champion, two notorious rustlers, were there. Ray was killed, but Champion's determined resistance enabled news to get to other settlers. Champion died at the ranch, but the settlers rallied to surround the Texans at the TA Ranch, just south of Buffalo. The 6th US Cavalry intervened, ostensibly to arrest the mercenaries, and moved them to Fort Fetterman and Cheyenne, where Johnson County was responsible for their upkeep. Unable to pay the costs of lengthy incarceration and an expensive trial, the county declined to prosecute and all the accused went free.

Inn (☎ 307-684-2256, 800-852-2302, 75 N Bypass), which asks $80/90; it has some kitchenettes. Within walking distance of downtown, *Cloud Peak Inn B&B (☎ 307-684-5794, 800-715-5794, 590 N Burritt Ave)* has a hot tub and roomy rooms ($60 to $85).

West of Buffalo off US 16 within 20 miles of town are a few good lodges. Most offer horseback riding ($25/hour, $75/half-day and $125/day) and pack trips ($200/day) in the surrounding Cloud Peak Wilderness Area. They are *South Fork Inn (☎ 307-684-9609), Bear Track Lodge (☎ 307-684-2528)* and *Pines Lodge (☎ 307-684-5204)*.

Places to Eat
Buffalo's restaurants are unexceptional. Alongside Clear Creek since 1928, the lively *Busy Bee (☎ 307-684-7544, 2 N Main St)* fills its stools for breakfast and lunch, and also does dinner. *Country Deli Cafe (☎ 307-684-5446, 386 N Main St)* is an early-riser breakfast venue (open 5:30 am). *The Breadboard (☎ 307-684-2318, 190 E Hart St)* is a decent sandwich shop. *Stagecoach Inn (☎ 307-684-2507, 845 Fort St)* has $2 all-u-can-eat pancakes and hearty buffet meals from $7.

Getting There & Away
Powder River Coach USA stops at Just Gone Fishing, 777 Fort St at Spruce St. Buses go twice daily to Sheridan; Billings, MT; Casper; and Cheyenne.

Buffalo is at the junction of I-90 and I-25, 31 miles south of Sheridan, 68 miles west of Gillette, and 109 miles north of Casper. US 16 leads west across the Bighorn Mountains via Powder River Pass (9666 feet) to Worland.

SHERIDAN
The region's most interesting town, Sheridan (population 15,000; elevation 3725 feet) is also the seat of the eponymous county, where both coal and cattle contribute to the economy and sometimes come into conflict. At the eastern foot of the Bighorn Mountains in the Big Goose Valley, Sheridan boasts a wealth of historic buildings that make for an interesting visit. All-night coal trains rumble on the Burlington Northern Railroad's tracks, yet Sheridan is not a gritty mining town, and the historic downtown is nicely restored.

History
Plains Indians kept settlers out of the northern Bighorns until 1877, and some of the earliest transplants were British horse breeders. Colonization proceeded slowly until John Loucks purchased the isolated Mandel post office in 1882 and named the new settlement after his Civil War commander, General Philip Sheridan. Sheridan and the surrounding area seceded from neighboring Johnson County to form a separate county in 1888. The turning point in its history, however, was the arrival of the railroad, which spurred development of local coal fields. These attracted Eastern European immigrants, who left an enduring cultural legacy, including the annual autumn polka festival. In the late 1930s, disgruntled residents upset with politics in Cheyenne called for northern Wyoming to secede and form the new state of Absaroka. The capital's attention to the locals' grievances smoothed over the problem, although not before Sheridan's street commissioner had declared himself governor of aspiring Absaroka.

Orientation & Information
US 87 and US 14 combine with I-90 Business just west of I-90 exit 25 to form Coffeen Ave. North of Burkitt St, they become north-south Main St and continue north to I-90 exit 20. South of Burkitt St, Main St becomes Hwy 332 until College Ave, where Hwy 332 turns 1 block west to Big Horn Ave and heads south toward the airport.

The Wyoming Information Center (☎ 307-672-2485, 800-453-3650) is at Valley View Dr (Hwy 336 at I-90 exit 23). It's open 8 am to 7 pm daily mid-May to mid-October, otherwise 8 am to 5 pm. Across the road is the Wyoming Game & Fish Dept (☎ 307-672-2790), with interesting exhibits on wildlife habitat and fauna; open 8 am to 5 pm daily. The USFS Bighorn National Forest Headquarters/Sheridan District

WYOMING

SHERIDAN

PLACES TO STAY
1 Bramble Motel
2 Super 8
3 Trail's End Motel
4 Stage Stop Motel
6 Guest House Motel
7 Sundown Motel;
  Aspen Inn
8 Super Saver Inn
15 Evergreen Inn
18 Best Western Sheridan
  Center
21 Old Croff House B&B
22 Rocktrim Motel
24 Holiday Inn;
  Rent-A-Wreck
25 Parkway Motel
26 Mill Inn
27 Days Inn

PLACES TO EAT
5 Golden Steer
9 Pablo's
11 Silver Spur Cafe
13 The Caboose
19 Main St Bagel
  Company
30 The Chocolate Tree
35 Java Moon Cafe
39 Ciao Bistro

41 Paolo's Pizzeria
46 Melinda's

OTHER
10 Memorial Hospital of
  Sheridan County
12 Sheridan Inn
14 Powder River Coach
  USA Bus Stop
16 Wyoming Information
  Center
17 Wyoming Game & Fish
  Department Visitor
  Center

20 Carriage House Theater;
  Trail End State Historic Site
23 USFS Headquarters;
  District Ranger Station
28 Back Country Bicycles
29 Sanford's Grub & Pub
31 Centennial Theaters (C5)
32 Art Galleries
33 Sheridan Stationery,
  Books & Gallery
34 Fly Shop of the Bighorns
36 King's Saddlery; Hangin
  Tree Gallery
37 Mint Bar

38 Foothills Gallery
40 Beaver Creek Saloon
42 The Book Shop
43 Best Out West Antiques
  & Collectibles Mall
44 WYO Theater
45 Community First
  National Bank
47 Sheridan State Bank
48 Post Office
49 Ye Olde Book Knook
50 Sheridan County
  Courthouse
51 US Bank

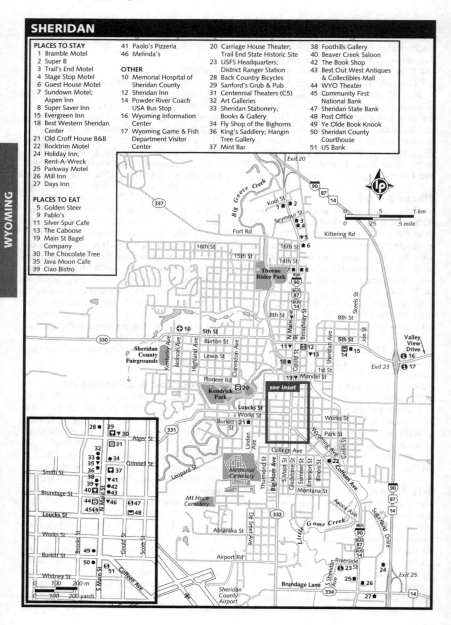

Office (☎ 307-672-0751) and Tongue River District Ranger Station are at 1969 S Sheridan Ave. They have useful information for the Bighorns and Cloud Peak Wilderness Area.

ATMs are strung out along Main St. The post office is at E Loucks and Gould Sts, one block east of N Main. The Book Shop (☎ 307-672-6505), 117 N Main St, is a bright, cheerful place with a good Western selection. Sheridan Stationery, Books & Gallery (☎ 307-674-8080), 206 N Main St, is also worth a visit. Ye Olde Book Knook (134 S Main) deals in dog-eared titles. Memorial Hospital of Sheridan County (☎ 307-672-1000) is at 1401 W 5th St.

Historic District

The six blocks along Main St between Burkitt and Mandel Sts form one of Wyoming's more interesting historic districts. The most impressive public building is the **Sheridan County Courthouse** (1904, with 1913 additions), 224 S Main St. To the south sit gracious Victorian houses in a tranquil, shaded neighborhood. Note the renovated Pueblo-style **Western Hotel** (1900), 104-112 Main St. **Hospital Pharmacy** (1883), 15 Main St, features the only remaining wooden false front in town, with a mural of the original streetscape. **Beaver Creek Saloon**, 112-120 N Main St, was the original firehouse (1893).

Sheridan Inn

Buffalo Bill Cody was a partner and occasional resident of this reputedly haunted hostelry, 856 Broadway at 5th St, which was described as the 'finest hotel between Chicago and San Francisco' in its heyday. This elaborately gabled structure (built in 1893 for $25,000) was based on a Scottish hunting lodge by architect Thomas Kimball, and lured many celebrities with its enormous ballroom, restaurant and saloon. It was the first building in town with running water, electricity and a telephone. The hotel closed in 1965 and narrowly averted the wrecker's ball in 1967. It sat empty for several years, but is now gradually being restored as a B&B under the aus-

pices of the Sheridan Heritage Center (☎ 307-674-5440).

Trail End State Historic Site

Locally known as the Kendrick Mansion, this lavish three-story Flemish Revival residence (☎ 307-674-4589), 400 Clarendon Ave, was designed by architect Glenn Charles McAllister at the behest of John Kendrick, a cattle baron who served Wyoming briefly as governor and nearly 30 years as US senator. Exterior building materials include Wyoming granite, Indiana limestone and Kansas brick. The interior features exquisite oak and mahogany woodwork, an Italian marble fireplace and early luxuries like an elevator and a built-in vacuum system. Perhaps its most dazzling feature is the spacious 3rd-floor ballroom, with a maple dance floor and an orchestra loft. Open 9 am to 6 pm daily June to August, otherwise 1 to 4 pm; $2 (kids under 18 and picnicking on the well-manicured grounds are both free).

Special Events

At the west end of 5th St, the Sheridan County Fairgrounds are the venue for most special events: mid-June's **North American Cowboy Roundup**; July's **WYO Rodeo**, a key stop on the professional circuit; and August's **Sheridan County Rodeo**.

Places to Stay

Open May to October, *Sheridan/Big Horn Mountains KOA* (☎ 307-674-8766, 800-562-7621, 63 Decker Rd), I-90 exit 20, is north of town ($16/20 campsite/full hookup). It has a pool, hot tub, laundry and nightly barbecue.

Rates for the following budget motels range from $25 to $40 and drop by up to 30% in winter:

Aspen Inn
  (☎ 307-672-9064, 1744 N Main St)
Bramble Motel
  (☎ 307-674-4902, 2366 N Main St)
Guest House Motel
  (☎ 307-674-7496, 800-226-9405, 2007 N Main St)
Parkway Motel
  (☎ 307-674-7259, 2112 Coffeen Ave)

WYOMING

Rocktrim Motel
(☎ 307-672-2464, 449 Coffeen Ave)

Stage Stop Motel
(☎ 307-672-3459, 2167 N Main St)

Super Saver Inn
(☎ 307-672-0471, 1789 N Main St)

Renovated rooms at **Trail's End Motel** (☎ 307-672-2477, 800-445-4921, 2125 N Main St) start at $45. **Evergreen Inn** (☎ 307-672-9757, 800-771-4761, 580 E 5th St) charges $55/65 single/double. The historic ex-flour **Mill Inn** (☎ 307-672-6401, 888-357-6455, 2161 Coffeen Ave) has free breakfast and charges $60/70. **Sundown Motel** (☎ 307-672-2439, 1704 N Main St) has comparable rates.

Rooms start at $65 at **Super 8** (☎ 307-672-9725, 2435 N Main St), I-90 exit 20. **Days Inn** (☎ 307-672-2888, 800-329-7466, 1104 Brundage Lane) has a pool ($75 to $110). **Holiday Inn Holidome** (☎ 307-672-8931, 1809 Sugarland Dr) starts at $100. Downtown **Best Western Sheridan Center** (☎ 307-674-7421, 612 N Main St) is the fanciest option ($70 to $90).

Also downtown, **Old Croff House B&B** (☎ 307-672-0898, 508 W Works St) is open June to September. Twin-bed rooms range from $65 to $75; the suite costs $90. The luxurious 550-acre **Ranch Willow B&B** (☎ 307-674-1510, 800-354-2830, 501 US 14), I-90 exit 25, is located 5 miles east of I-90 ($80 to $90).

Places to Eat

The **Main St Bagel Company** is at Main and Dow Sts. **Melinda's** (☎ 307-674-9188, 57 N Main St) is a popular lunch spot. Nearby, cheery **Paolo's Pizzeria** (☎ 307-672-3853, 123 N Main St) has authentic pastas and salads. **Java Moon Cafe** (☎ 307-673-5991, 176 N Main St) is a nice spot for espresso, salads and hummus sandwiches. **Silver Spur Cafe** (☎ 307-672-2749, 832 N Main St) offers conventional Western breakfasts and lunches. **The Chocolate Tree** (☎ 307-672-6160, 5 E Alger St) serves breakfast, burgers and decadent desserts. **Pablo's** (☎ 307-672-0737, 1274 N Main St) has decent Mexican food. Carnivores enjoy the **Golden Steer** (☎ 307-674-9334, 2071 N Main St). For some atmosphere, try **The Caboose** (☎ 307-674-0700, 841 Broadway), in the old brick railroad depot across from the Sheridan Inn.

Casual yet sophisticated **Ciao Bistro** (☎ 307-672-2838, 120 N Main St) is one of Wyoming's best restaurants outside Jackson Hole. Imaginative salads, sandwiches, pasta and fine California wines are reasonably priced. Lunch is first-come, first-served, although waiting is not unusual; dinner reservations are recommended.

Entertainment

Centennial Theaters (☎ 307-672-5797, 36 E Alger St) shows Hollywood flicks. The restored **WYO Theater** (☎ 307-672-9084, 38 N Main St) presents a variety of live music year-round. The **Beaver Creek Saloon** (☎ 307-674-8181, 112 N Main St) is the nicest downtown bar; take a look at the old photographs. The **Mint Bar** (☎ 307-674-9696, 151 N Main St) is a local favorite. **Sanford's Grub & Pub** (☎ 307-674-1722, 1 E Alger St) has tons of brews of tap.

Shopping

For Western wear, King's Saddlery (☎ 307-672-2702, 800-443-8919), 184 N Main St, is unsurpassed. A free museum at the rear of the store has an astonishing collection of cowboy memorabilia. Best Out West Antiques & Collectibles Mall (☎ 307-674-5003), 109 N Main St, includes both the Lannan and the Medicine Wheel galleries (☎ 307-672-0124). Other downtown galleries include the Foothills Gallery (☎ 307-672-2068), 134 N Main St; Hangin Tree Gallery (☎ 307-674-9869), 142 N Main St; Wagner's Art Supply & Gallery (☎ 307-672-2454), 214 N Main St (original art and jewelry); and Bozeman Trail Gallery (☎ 307-672-3928), 214 N Main St (19th- and 20th-century Western art and Indian beadwork). Most shops are closed on Sunday.

Getting There & Away

The Sheridan County Airport (☎ 307-674-4222) is at the south end of town via Big Horn Ave (Hwy 332). Daily United Express

(☎ 307-674-8455) flights depart for Denver, CO, with some continuing to Gillette.

Powder River Coach USA (☎ 307-674-6188) stops at the Evergreen Inn, 580 E 5th St. Buses depart twice daily northbound to Billings, MT, and southbound to Cheyenne (and Denver) via Buffalo, Gillette, Casper and Douglas.

By car, Sheridan is along the west side of I-90, 31 miles north of Buffalo and 25 miles south of the Wyoming-Montana state line. US 14 leads east to Gillette via Ucross, although I-90 is a more direct route. US 14 leads west from Ranchester, 15 miles north of Sheridan, across the Bighorn Mountains via Granite Pass (8950 feet) and to Greybull. Avis (☎ 307-672-2226) and Enterprise (☎ 307-672-6910) are at the airport. Rent-A-Wreck (☎ 307-674-0707), 1809 Sugarland Dr, is often cheaper.

AROUND SHERIDAN
The North Tongue River, north of Sheridan, is popular for trout fishing. For gear, including a wide selection of specialty flies, visit Fly Shop of the Bighorns (☎ 307-672-5866), 227 N Main St, Sheridan. The battle of the Tongue River was fought between the US Army and the Arapaho at **Connor Battlefield State Historic Site**. Today the site, near Ranchester north of Sheridan, offers fishing and camping. **Mountain biking** is a major attraction, and Sheridan has several good bicycle shops. Visit Back Country Bicycles (☎ 307-672-2453), 334 N Main St, for sales, rentals, repairs and information.

BIGHORN MOUNTAINS
The Bighorn Mountains are a jewel that should not be missed by those traveling to or from Yellowstone and Grand Teton National Parks. The three scenic east-west roads across the mountains are US 16 (Cloud Peak Skyway) between Buffalo and Worland via Powder River Pass (9666 feet); US 14 (Bighorn Scenic Byway) between Ranchester, north of Sheridan, and Greybull via Granite Pass (8950 feet); and US 14 Alternate (Medicine Wheel Passage) between Burgess Junction and Lovell via Baldy Pass (9430 feet).

Along these roads are numerous trailheads, picnic areas, scenic overlooks and dozens of inviting USFS and BLM campgrounds. Pick up the free USFS 'Bighorn Bits and Pieces,' an informative guide to trails and campgrounds in the Bighorn National Forest available from offices in Buffalo and Sheridan. All this open country, much within the Bighorn National Forest, means easy wildlife viewing. A few private lodges offer basic accommodations, campsites and services. (See Bighorn Mountains in the Bighorn Country section.)

Scenic Drives
Three short scenic drives are in the Bighorns west of Buffalo and east of Powder River Pass off US 16. The 10-mile Pole Creek Rd (USFS Rd 31) leaves US 16 about 20 miles west of Buffalo and rejoins it below the Powder River Pass; look for mule deer. Nearby is **Sheep Mountain Lookout**. Continue 2 miles west on US 16 to Sheep Mountain Rd (USFS Rd 28), and follow this road 5 miles to its end; the Powder River Pass and Cloud Peak can be seen from the lookout. To reach stunning **Crazy Woman Canyon**, head west 25 miles on US 16 from Buffalo, look for the well-signed Crazy Woman Canyon Rd, then turn east and follow the road down the scenic canyon to Hwy 196. Continue north on Hwy 196 for 10 miles to Buffalo.

Cloud Peak Wilderness Area
The 295-sq-mile Cloud Peak Wilderness Area, with more than 250 lakes and 150 miles of maintained trails, stretches along the backbone of the Bighorn Mountains between US 14 and US 16. The area is named for glacially formed, often obscured **Cloud Peak** (13,175 feet), the Bighorns' highest summit. The epic 53-mile **Solitude Loop** trail circles the entire wilderness area. All day-use and overnight visitors must register at nearby USFS offices.

Trailheads on its four sides access the wilderness area. The main trailheads from the east side, each with campgrounds, are **Hunter Corral**, 13 miles west of Buffalo via US 16 and then 3 miles west on USFS Rd 19 and USFS Rd 394; and **Circle Park**, 15 miles southwest of Buffalo via US 16 and USFS Rd 20.

From the south, **Mistymoon Trail** is the most direct route to Cloud Peak's summit. From US 16 near the head of Tensleep Canyon, west of Powder River Pass, turn north onto USFS Hwy 27 and continue 7½ miles to its end at West Tensleep Lake (9100 feet) and the Mistymoon trailhead. The hike takes three days and two nights, usually camping at Mistymoon Lake both nights. The nontechnical route follows the southwest ridge to the summit. Snow and ice remain until midsummer. Wilderness rock climbing is possible near Cloud Peak and adjacent Black Tooth Mountain. Contact the USFS in Buffalo for climbing information.

From the west side of the range, the main trailhead is for **Shell Creek Trail**. Two miles east of Shell Falls on US 14, turn southeast on USFS Hwy 17 and USFS Rd 271 to Adelaide Lake and the trailhead.

From the north side, follow Hwy 335 from Sheridan and Big Horn to USFS Rd 26, and then USFS Rd 293 to Cross Creek Campground and **Coffeen Park** trailhead. An alternative route is the **Twin Lakes** trailhead, 12 miles farther west from the Coffeen Park turnoff via USFS Rd 26 and USFS Rd 285.

Bighorn Country

Bighorn Country encompasses the watersheds of the Shoshone and Bighorn Rivers, north of the Owl Creek, east of the Absaroka and west of the Bighorn Mountains. South of the Wyoming-Montana state line, this region is bordered by Yellowstone National Park to the west and the Wind River Country to the south. South of Thermopolis, the Bighorn River emerges from the Wind River Canyon and flows north across the barren Bighorn Basin, where prehistoric dinosaurs once trod, hot springs still hint at the underlying volcanism and traditional ranching has metamorphosed into a symbol for tourism.

CODY

The brash Wild West bluster of Cody (population 9000; elevation 5095 feet) contrasts with sleepy agricultural towns hiding out in the surrounding Bighorn Basin's riparian zones. A popular Yellowstone stopover, it rivals Jackson as Wyoming's premier tourist town, at least in summer. Rather than erecting new faux-Western facades, local businesses have retained or restored their original storefronts, giving Cody a veneer of greater authenticity. Its major attraction is the Buffalo Bill Historical Center. In addition to tourist-wrangling, Cody's economy depends on resource exploitation, agriculture and small industry.

History

The town of Cody is inextricably linked to the self-promoting vanity of William (Buffalo Bill) Cody, who gladly lent his surname to real-estate speculator George Beck's newly minted town in 1901. Beck and his backers milked Cody's fame as a Pony Express rider and Wild West showman to promote settlement, attract the railroad and lobby for a massive dam on the Shoshone River. The town's ultimate blessing turned out to be its proximity to Yellowstone National Park. Wild Bill himself built the landmark Irma Hotel (named for his daughter) to take advantage of this closeness. Its imported French cherry-wood bar cost more ($100,000) than the hotel itself ($80,000). In 1910 the town became the seat of newly constituted Park County. Oil gushers in the Elk Basin north of Cody spurred further growth.

Orientation & Information

Cody's principal commercial strip, east-west Sheridan Ave (US 14/16/20), snakes south at 8th St and then west at Yellowstone Ave. Five blocks north of Sheridan Ave, 16th St splits into Hwy 120 and US 14 Alternate. South of Sheridan Ave, 17th St divides into US 14/16/20 and Hwy 120.

The useful visitors center (☎ 307-587-2777), 836 Sheridan Ave, in a 1927 lodgepole-pine cabin, is open 8 am to 6 pm daily. The USFS Shoshone National Forest

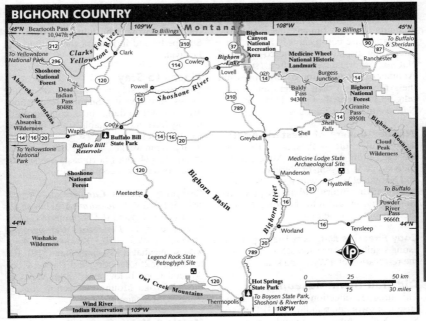

BIGHORN COUNTRY

Wapiti Ranger District (☎ 307-527-6921), 203A Yellowstone Ave, is open 8 am to 4:30 pm weekdays. The BLM office (☎ 307-587-2216), 1002 Blackburn St, is east of downtown. The Wyoming Game & Fish Dept (☎ 307-527-7125) is at 2820 Hwy 120.

There are several ATMs on Sheridan and Yellowstone Aves. The post office occupies 1301 Stampede Ave. Cody Newsstand (☎ 307-587-2843), 1121 13th St, has a good selection of periodicals and Western books. Swap dog-eared tomes at the quirky Wyoming Well Book Exchange (☎ 307-587-4249), 1902 E Sheridan Ave. West Park Hospital (☎ 307-527-7501, 800-654-9447) fronts 707 Sheridan Ave.

Buffalo Bill Historical Center

Sometimes called (with considerable hyperbole) the 'Smithsonian of the West,' this tour-bus mecca (☎ 307-587-4771), 720 Sheridan Ave, consists of four museums and the Harold McCracken Research Library. In total, it's an homage to male Anglo-Saxon Western myths, which Buffalo Bill's promotion of the Wild West molded into the enduring image of the region. The center hosts special events and offers daily Western film programs. Open 7 am to 8 pm daily June to mid-September; call for off-season hours. Tickets are valid for two consecutive days and cost $10/6 adults/students and seniors over 62. Children cost $4 (free under six). Web site: www.bbhc.org

Buffalo Bill Museum The Historical Center's original collection began in 1927 as a record of the life of William F Cody and presents a wealth of fascinating, if uncritical, information about his Wild West shows.

Plains Indian Museum This large museum includes a substantial exhibit entitled 'The People Today' that suggests that Native Americans have adapted to modern life without forfeiting their distinctive identities, although most items date from the late 19th and early 20th centuries, and accounts of urban Indians and life on the reservation are conspicuously absent. One interesting display details the co-opting of Native Americans and their symbols. Another excellent exhibit covers tepees and the symbolism of their designs and Indian religion, including the Ghost Dance and the Native American Church.

Whitney Gallery of Western Art This major collection of Western artists like George Catlin, Alfred Jacob Miller, Alfred Bierstadt, CM Russell, Frederic Remington and Nathaniel Wyeth, with portraits of well-known 19th-century Indian leaders, provides visual insight into the complexity of the Western experience.

Cody Firearms Museum The most interesting exhibit in this inventory of guns is the re-creation of a Wyoming stage stop.

Old Trail Town Museum

This unique collection of log cabins and false-front wooden buildings, 1831 Demaris St off Yellowstone Ave, includes a trading post, stage stop and saloon. Many buildings were relocated here from the old stage road between Fort Washakie and Red Lodge, MT. The museum (☎ 307-587-5302) is open 9 am to 6 pm daily mid-May to mid-September; admission is $5/4 adults/children (free under 12). Follow the unpaved road past the museum through the gravel pit for a free peek at the impressive Shoshone Canyon.

Cody Nite Rodeo

Cody's wildly popular rodeo (☎ 307-587-5155) is held 8:30 pm nightly June to August at Stampede Park, 421 W Yellowstone Ave. Tickets are $10/4 adults/children for grandstand seating and $12/6 for Buzzard's Roost seating, closer to the action. Admission is free for children under seven.

Special Events

Cody hosts a variety of special events: in February, the Buffalo Bill Birthday Ball; in April, the Cowboy Poetry & Range Ballads; in June the Frontier Festival and Plains Indian Powwow; from July 1 to 4 the Cody Stampede; and in August, the Buffalo Bill Festival.

Places to Stay

Summertime rates rise by up to 50%; many places close in winter. Summer reservations are recommended, but campgrounds usually have sites available. Call Cody Area Central Reservations (☎ 888-468-6996) 9 am to 5 pm weekdays for assistance. Prices in Powell (24 miles northeast) are slightly lower for similar accommodations.

Camping *Gateway Campground* (☎ 307-587-2561, 203 W Yellowstone Ave) has shady campsites ($12) and RV hookups ($17). Cyclists prefer the ***Ponderosa Campground*** (☎ 307-587-9203, 1815 Yellowstone Ave), with somewhat noisy campsites ($19), RV hookups ($25), laundry and showers. See Around Cody below and Wapiti Valley in the Absaroka Mountains section for the closest USFS campgrounds.

Motels & Hotels Several places begin at less than $50: the friendly ***Uptown Motel*** (☎ 307-587-4245, 1562 Sheridan Ave), **Big Bear Motel** (☎ 307-587-3117, 139 W Yellowstone Ave) and ***Rainbow Park Motel*** (☎ 307-587-6251, 800-341-8000, 1136 17th St). The nonsmoking ***Carriage House*** (☎ 307-587-2572/3818, 800-531-2572, 1816 8th St) has log cabins on attractive grounds for $50 to $65 and six-person suites for $85 to $135. The slightly more expensive ***Gateway Motel*** (☎ 307-587-2561, 203 Yellowstone Ave) also has cozy cabins.

Most chain options fall in the top-end category, at least in terms of price. ***Western 6 Gun Motel*** (☎ 307-587-4835, 800-231-6486, 433 Yellowstone Ave) starts around $70. Rooms at the homey ***Buffalo Bill Village*** (☎ 307-587-5544, 800-527-5544, 1701 Sheridan Ave) are $70 to $100. Nearest the Buffalo Bill Historical Center is **Best Western Sunrise Motor Inn** (☎ 307-587-5566, 1407 8th St), charging from $85, and ***Best Western Sunset Inn*** (☎ 307-587-4265,

CODY

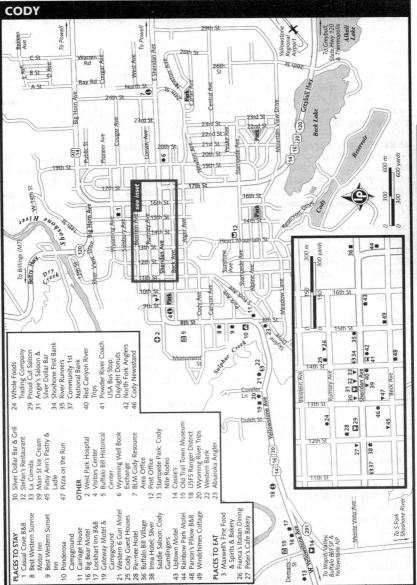

PLACES TO STAY
1 Casual Cove B&B
8 Best Western Sunrise Motor Inn
9 Best Western Sunset Inn
10 Ponderosa Campground
11 Carriage House
16 Big Bear Motel
17 Lockhart Inn B&B
19 Gateway Motel & Campground
21 Western 6 Gun Motel
25 Cody Guest Houses
28 Pa'vnee Hotel
36 Buffalo Bill Village
38 Irma Hotel; Silver Saddle Saloon; Cody Gunslingers
43 Uptown Motel
44 Rainbow Park Motel
48 Parson's Pillow B&B
49 Windchimes Cottage

PLACES TO EAT
3 Maxwell's Fine Food & Spirits & Bakery
26 Franca's Italian Dining
27 Peter's Cafe Bakery

30 Silver Dollar Bar & Grill
32 Stefan's Restaurant
33 La Comida
39 Main St Ice Cream
45 Patsy Ann's Pastry & Ladle
47 Pizza on the Run

OTHER
2 West Park Hospital
4 Visitors Center
5 Buffalo Bill Historical Center
6 Wyoming Well Book Exchange
7 BLM Cody Resource Area Office
12 Post Office
13 Stampede Park; Cody Nite Rodeo
14 Cassie's
15 Old Trail Town Museum
18 USFS Ranger District
20 Wyoming River Trips
22 Western Bank
23 Absaroka Angler

24 Whole Foods Trading Company
29 Proud Cut Saloon
31 Angie's Saloon & Silver Dollar Bar
34 Shoshone First Bank
35 River Runners
37 Community 1st National Bank
40 Red Canyon River Trips
41 Powder River Coach USA Bus Stop; Daylight Donuts
42 North Fork Anglers
46 Cody Newsstand

WYOMING

4-2727, 1601 8th St), which charges from $110.

The friendly, century-old **Pawnee Hotel** (☎ 307-587-2239, 1032 12th St) is remodeled and has a nice garden ($32/36 single/double). Smoky rooms with shared bathrooms start at $29. Buffalo Bill's atmospheric **Irma Hotel** (☎ 307-587-4221, 800-745-4762, 1192 Sheridan Ave) has rooms in the original hotel (from $100) and less appealing annex ($65).

B&Bs The least expensive is three-room **Casual Cove B&B** (☎ 307-587-3622, 1431 Salisbury Ave), at $50 to $65. **Parson's Pillow B&B** (☎ 307-587-2382, 800-377-2348, 1202 14th St), $65 to $85, is in a 1902 church. **Windchimes Cottage** (☎ 307-527-5310, 800-241-5310, 1501 Beck Ave) asks $80. **Lockhart Inn B&B** (☎ 307-587-6074, 800-587-8644, 109 W Yellowstone Ave) is unfortunately close to the noisy main drag ($75 to $100). **Cody Guest Houses** (☎ 307-587-6000, 800-587-6560, 1401 Rumsey Ave) rents rooms in local Victorians, lodges and cottages.

Places to Eat

Whole Foods Trading Company (☎ 307-587-3213, 1239 Rumsey Ave) has natural bulk and camping foods. **Patsy Ann's Pastry & Ladle** (☎ 307-527-6297, 1243 Beck Ave) bakes tasty pastries and from-scratch soups and sandwiches. **Peter's Cafe Bakery** (☎ 307-527-5040, 1191 Sheridan Ave) specializes in buffalo burgers and has espresso. **Main St Ice Cream** (☎ 307-587-9084, 1320 Sheridan Ave) also doles out soup and sandwiches.

Proud Cut Saloon (☎ 307-527-6905, 1227 Sheridan Ave) is big on beef, but the lax service doesn't always cut the mustard. **Silver Dollar Bar & Grill** (☎ 307-587-3554, 1313 Sheridan Ave) deals mostly in burgers. **Pizza on the Run** (☎ 307-587-5550, 1302 Sheridan Ave) delivers prefab pies. **La Comida** (☎ 307-587-9556, 1385 Sheridan Ave) has authentic but overpriced Mexican food and patio seating. **Maxwell's Fine Food & Spirits** (☎ 307-527-7749, 937 Sheridan Ave) has a nice selection of salads, sandwiches and bistro dinners. Their adjacent bakery serves good espresso. Upscale newcomer **Stefan's** (☎ 307-587-8511, 1367 Sheridan Ave) aims to impress with 'contemporary American cuisine.'

In a class by itself is **Franca's Italian Dining** (☎ 307-587-5354, 1421 Rumsey Ave), open Wednesday to Sunday in summer for dinner only (reservations required). Fixed multicourse dinners ($18 to $30) and pasta entrees ($15) are superb.

Entertainment

The rodeo and its related events are the primary post-sunset summertime attractions. Happy hour at the Irma Hotel's **Silver Saddle Saloon** is a blast after the Gunslingers shoot their summer shtick at 6 pm daily. Other options include **Angie's Saloon & Silver Dollar Bar** (☎ 307-587-3554, 1313 Sheridan Ave) for comedy, rump-shaking and live rock, and **Cassie's** (☎ 307-527-5500, 214 Yellowstone Ave) for heavy swilling and swingin' country & western tunes.

Getting There & Around

SkyWest/Delta connects Cody with Salt Lake City, Utah, daily flights out of Yellowstone Regional Airport (☎ 307-587-5096), 1 mile east of Cody at the US 14/16/20 and Hwy 120 junction.

Powder River Coach USA (☎ 800-442-3682) buses stop at Daylight Donuts, 1452 Sheridan Ave, en route to Casper and Billings, MT, and also offer daylong guided Yellowstone tours ($50).

By car, Cody is at the junction of US 14/16/20 and Hwy 120. US 14/16/20 leads east to Greybull (47 miles) and west to Yellowstone National Park's East Entrance (51 miles). US 14 Alternate leads northeast to Lovell (47 miles) via Powell. Hwy 120 leads north to Hwy 296 and Yellowstone's Northeast Entrance (70 miles) and south to Thermopolis (85 miles). Avis (☎ 307-587-5792) and Hertz (☎ 307-587-2914) are at the airport. Other car rental companies include Budget (☎ 307-587-6066), 3227 Duggleby Dr; Rent-A-Wreck (☎ 307-527-5549, 800-452-0396), 2515 Greybull Hwy; and Thrifty (☎ 307-587-8855), 3001 Duggleby Dr.

Phidippides (☎ 307-527-6789) provides regional airport and taxi services.

AROUND CODY
South Fork Shoshone River
Hwy 291 heads southwest from US 14/16/20 just beyond the USFS office at the west end of Cody and follows South Fork Rd (Hwy 291) along the river. The waterless but free USFS *Deer Creek Campground* is 47 miles southwest of Cody on USFS Rd 479. Trails lead west into the Teton Wilderness Area and southeastern Yellowstone National Park.

Buffalo Bill State Park
Six miles west of Cody along US 14/16/20, this popular local recreation area centers on the Buffalo Bill Reservoir and Dam (☎ 307-587-9227). Having acquired water rights to irrigate 266 sq miles in the Bighorn Basin, but lacking the capital to develop adequate storage, Buffalo Bill and his associates convinced the US Bureau of Reclamation to build the 328-foot Shoshone Dam. Begun in 1905, it was the world's highest dam upon completion in 1910. Renamed 'Buffalo Bill Dam' by President Truman in 1946, it's a national civil-engineering landmark. The dam provides drinking water for Cody as well as hydroelectricity. It also makes possible fishing and water sports on the reservoir.

The Buffalo Bill Dam visitors center (☎ 307-527-6076) is open 8 am to 6 pm daily May to September. Day use costs $5. Along the banks of the reservoir are the shadeless and windy *North Shore Bay* and *North Fork* campgrounds ($9). Several nearby ranches offer horseback-riding and fishing trips.

Rafting & Kayaking
The North Fork Shoshone River is a favorite of white-water rafting aficionados. Elk, Bighorn sheep and moose are often seen from the river. The rafting season is mid-May to mid-September in the Red Rock and Lower Canyons, and Memorial Day to late July for the North Fork. Floating Red Rock Canyon takes two hours ($20). A three-hour trip through the geologically interesting Lower Canyon downstream of Red Rock Canyon costs $26. Half-day North Fork trips are $50. Outfitters in Cody include Red Canyon River Trips (☎ 307-587-6988, 800-293-0148), 1374 Sheridan Ave; River Runners (☎ 307-527-7238, 888-236-6716), 1491 Sheridan Ave; and Wyoming River Trips (☎ 307-587-6661, 800-586-6661), 233 Yellowstone Ave.

Fishing
In Cody, North Fork Anglers (☎ 307-527-7274), 1438 Sheridan Ave, and Absaroka Angler (☎ 307-587-5105), 754 Yellowstone Ave, sell gear and offer backcountry fly-fishing excursions.

LOVELL
'LOVE-uhl' (population 2350; elevation 3814 feet) is the gateway to the Bighorn Canyon National Recreation Area at the northwestern base of the Bighorn Mountains. This Mormon agricultural settlement with a significant Hispanic population produces sugar beets and is home to several major mining outfits.

Information
The Information Center (☎ 307-548-7552), 287 E Main St, is open 9 am to 5 pm daily. The USFS Bighorn National Forest Medicine Wheel Ranger District (☎ 307-548-6541), 604 E Main St, is on the east end of town. Ask here about visiting the Medicine Wheel National Historic Landmark (see the Bighorn Mountains section, later). The Bighorn Canyon National Recreation Area visitors center (☎ 307-548-2251), at the confluence of Hwys 14A and 310, is nearby. Its Web site is at www.nps.gov/bica/.

Places to Stay & Eat
Camping and showers are free at shady *Lovell Camper Park* (two or three days maximum, sheriff's mood depending), off Quebec Ave between 1st and 2nd Sts. Alternatively, the shadeless *Camp Big Horn RV Park* (☎ 307-548-2725, 595 E Main St) cowers behind the Super 8; tithe for campsites ($7) and full hookups ($12) at the motel's front desk.

The tidy *Western Motel* (☎ 307-548-2781, *180 W Main St*) has rooms from $30. The nicer *Cattlemen Motel* (☎ 307-548-2296, *470 Montana Ave*) and *Horseshoe Bend Motel* (☎ 307-548-2221, 800-548-2850, *375 E Main St*) both charge around $39/45 single/double. Sensible *Super 8* (☎ 307-548-2725, *595 E Main St*) undercuts a wee bit at $35/40.

The *Rose Bowl Cafe* (☎ 307-548-7121, *483 Shoshone Ave*) is the local breakfast and lunch hangout. The popular *Big Horn Restaurant* (☎ 307-548-6811, *605 E Main St*) is large but mediocre. *Hot Stuff Pizza* (☎ 307-548-2888, *127 E 3rd St*) doesn't pull any punches. When pressed, locals will admit to heading to Cody for a fancy night out.

Getting There & Away

Powder River Coach USA (☎ 307-548-7231, 800-442-3682) halts daily near Rexall Drug, 164 E Main St, before proceeding to Greybull-Thermopolis-Casper and Billings, MT. Lovell is 26 miles east of Powell, 50 miles northeast of Cody and 100 miles west of Sheridan on US 14 Alternate and US 310/Hwy 789. US 310/Hwy 789 leads south to Greybull (32 miles); US 310 goes north to Billings (90 miles); and US 14 Alternate, the **Medicine Wheel Passage**, heads east to Burgess Junction.

BIGHORN CANYON NATIONAL RECREATION AREA

The Bighorn River carved a canyon 2500 feet deep and 71 miles long through the desert, and Montana's Yellowtail Dam created Bighorn Lake, the centerpiece of this stunning but little-visited area. The Bighorn Canyon NRA encompasses the river, lake and surrounding land. This narrow corridor straddles the Wyoming-Montana state line northeast of Lovell, between the Pryor Mountains to the west and the Bighorn Mountains to the east. The NRA covers approximately 120,000 acres, 64,000 of which are open for public use.

Bighorn Canyon environments range from desert shrubland inhabited by feral horses, snakes and rodents to juniper woodlands with large mammals like coyotes, deer and bighorn sheep. Canyonside pine and fir forests harbor mountain lions, bears, elk and mule deer, while short-grass prairie once fed grazing bison. The area hosts large numbers of raptors.

At the south end of the NRA, 6 miles east of Lovell, the **Yellowtail Wildlife Habitat Management Area** is wetlands managed jointly by the NPS and the Wyoming Game & Fish Dept. Besides cottonwood riparian and permanent and seasonal pool environments, it contains cultivated lands that support wildlife.

History

Inhabited more than 10,000 years ago, Bighorn Canyon was controlled by the Crow Indians when trappers first saw it in the early 19th century. In 1864, the US Army built Fort CF Smith on the east side of the canyon to protect miners traveling on the Bozeman Trail, but pulled out in 1868 following the Fort Laramie Treaty. Still, whites continued to chip away at Indian territory, and open-range cattle ranching became a way of life, supplemented by early dude ranches.

Regional water management began with the Crow, who had 54 sq miles under irrigation by 1904, but it really got going in 1966 with the completion of the 525-foot Yellowtail Dam near Fort Smith, MT. This was the centerpiece of the Bureau of Reclamation/US Army Corps of Engineers scheme, combining flood control, navigation, hydroelectricity and irrigation, that created Bighorn Lake. In recent years, however, the flow into the reservoir has fallen dramatically because of drought. Many other factors may be involved, but if this continues, the recreational attributes of the NRA will, quite literally, evaporate.

Orientation

Bighorn Canyon NRA is divided into the South and North districts. The South District is accessible only from Wyoming, the North District from Hardin, MT. Hwy 37, the only road through the South District, is 3 miles east of Lovell off US 14 Alternate.

Six miles from the entrance there's a junction to Horseshoe Bend, which has a marina and campground. Hwy 37 enters Montana 4 miles beyond the junction and continues to Barry's Landing, another reservoir access point, where it dead-ends.

Information

The Bighorn Canyon NRA visitors center (☎ 307-548-2251) is at the east end of Lovell, 2 miles east of the US 310/Hwy 789 junction. It features interesting displays on the area's ecology, geology, archaeology and Native Americans, and its solar design provides 70% of its heat even in harsh winters. Open 8:30 am to 5 pm daily. The NPS ranger station at Crooked Creek also has information. The NPS also distributes the 'Canyon Echoes' newsletter, published infrequently. No permits are required for overnight backcountry trips; day use is $5.

Pryor Mountain Wild Horse Range

Feral mustangs, descendants of the original Spanish breeds brought to Mexico in the 16th century, roam the BLM-managed 38,000-acre Pryor Mountain Wild Horse Range, established in 1968. The range overlaps the NRA from Horseshoe Bend north to Layout Creek. Sightings are common along the west side of Hwy 37 between Devil Canyon Overlook and Mustang Flat. The animals have multiplied so prolifically that the BLM runs a public adoption program. See 'Wild Horses' in this chapter.

Devil Canyon Overlook

About 3 miles north of the Wyoming-Montana state line, reached by a paved 1-mile lateral off the main highway, the Devil Canyon Overlook peeks 1000 feet into Bighorn Canyon for impressive views, excellent yo-dee-lay-hee-hooing and resident raptor sightings.

Hillsboro

This abandoned early 20th-century homestead was by turns a mine, post office and dude ranch; several buildings remain stand-ing. It's 1 mile east of Hwy 37 above Barry's Landing and accessible only on foot via a short hiking trail.

Lockhart Ranch

Where Hwy 37 descends to Barry's Landing, a dirt road heads 2 rough miles north toward pioneering journalist Caroline Lockhart's L Slash Heart Ranch, a 7000-acre retreat that makes for an intriguing picnic spot. Visiting the abandoned ranch requires a short downhill hike. The main house, sod-roofed storage cabins, a storage shed cooled by a subterranean spring, stables and garage and a chicken coop are all that remain of this isolated homestead.

Activities

For **boating**, Horseshoe Bend Marina (☎ 307-548-7230) is open 8 am to 10 pm daily Memorial Day to Labor Day. Boat rentals (pedal, fishing and pontoon) range from $3/hour to $40/hour. Charters to Devil Canyon ($40 minimum) and Barry's Landing ($75 minimum) also depart from Horseshoe Bend Marina.

Good **fishing** can be had at Bighorn Lake, which the Montana and Wyoming Game & Fish Depts stock with brown and lake trout, as well as ling and perch, but locals go gaagaa for walleye. State fishing licenses are obligatory.

Places to Stay & Eat

Campgrounds are at the barren, RV-friendly *Horseshoe Bend* and the shadier, more tent-friendly *Barry's Landing*. The boat-in or hike-in campground at *Medicine Creek*, 2 miles north of Barry's Landing, lacks drinking water. Reservations are probably not necessary; a nominal camping fee will be charged beginning in 2001. Free backcountry camping in the southern NRA outback is an appealing option. The *Horseshoe Bend Marina* has a small cafe and basic beer-and-snacks grocery store.

THERMOPOLIS

The resort town of Thermopolis (population 3200; elevation 4326 feet) is the home of the world's largest mineral hot springs.

Dr Julius Schuelke first coined the name in the late 1890s, cleverly combining the Latin *thermae* (hot springs) with the Greek *polis* (city). The town is north of the Owl Creek Mountains and straddles the Bighorn River, which emerges from the Wind River Canyon south of town.

History

The Shoshone and Arapaho ceded the hot springs to the US government in 1896, severing it from the northeast corner of the Wind River Indian Reservation in exchange for $60,000 in cattle and rations. Shoshone Chief Washakie stipulated that the healing waters remain free of charge, and in 1899 the state legislature honored the chief's request by establishing Hot Springs State Park (see below). In its early years, the remote area was frequented by Hole-in-the-Wall Gang outlaws, but the 1913 arrival of the CB&Q Railroad from Billings put Thermopolis on the map. Thanks to the healing waters and medical institutions like the Gottsche Rehabilitation Center, tourism has steadily flourished and now eclipses oil prospecting and ranching as the area's economic mainstay. Washakie's grant of the Bah Guewana (Smoking Waters) is celebrated in Thermopolis' **Gift of the Waters Pageant**, which was begun in 1925 and is held annually the first weekend in August.

Orientation

The main streets are north-south 6th St (US 20) and east-west Broadway (Hwy 120) on the west bank of the river. Hot Springs State Park is along the east bank, reached by bridges on Broadway and Park St.

Hot Springs State Park

Along the east bank of the Bighorn River, Hot Springs State Park is Wyoming's first and most popular state park, especially with families and retired folks. The 3000 gallons of water that surge from **Big Horn Spring** every minute average 127°F, making it one of the world's largest mineral springs. Visitors can relax free of charge in the comfortable 104°F waters of the nearby **State Bath House** (☎ 307-864-3765); rental towels and

bathing suits (required) are available for a nominal fee. Open 8 am to 5:30 pm Monday to Saturday and noon to 5:30 pm Sunday.

Other sights include the **Rainbow Terraces**, formed by lime and gypsum secreted from the mineral waters and encircled by a boardwalk; the nearby **Swinging Bridge** over the Bighorn River; the gurgling **Black Sulphur Spring**; and the 1000-acre **Buffalo Pasture**, where a small herd of bison roams. The park's expansive lawns and its massive shade trees make for a nice picnic spot. Within the park, the private Hellies Tepee Spa (☎ 307-864-9250) has a pool and water slide. The private Star Plunge (☎ 307-864-3771) also has water amusements.

The park headquarters (☎ 307-864-2176), 220 Park St, are open 7:30 am to 4 pm weekdays. The park is open 6 am to 10 pm daily. Camping is not permitted.

Hot Springs Historical Museum

This cultural center (☎ 307-864-5183), 700 Broadway, has a spacious museum and a large open-air section on local farm economy and Thermopolis' role as a transportation hub. Inside the museum is the original cherry-wood bar from the Hole in the Wall Saloon, once frequented by Butch Cassidy and the Sundance Kid. Open 8 am to 5 pm Monday to Saturday; $3/2 adults/children.

Wyoming Dinosaur Center

This profit-seeking venture (☎ 307-864-2997, 800-455-3466) offers a behind-the-scenes look at paleontological prospecting. Punters join professional fossil seekers on guided tours of nearby quarries. There's also a museum full of fossils, casts and skeletons. Open 8 am to 8 pm daily in summer, 10 am to 5 pm in winter. Admission is $12/8 adults/children; $6/$3.50 museum only or $10/7 dig site only.

Places to Stay

The shady *Grandview Trailer Park* (☎ 307-864-3463, 120 US 20 S) has campsites ($13), full hookups ($16) and laundry and showers for nonguests ($3) from March to November. Comparably priced with similar amenities is the pleasant **Eagle RV Park** (☎ 307-864-5262, 204 US 20 S), which also has basic cabins ($20) and is open April to October. The closest public campgrounds are 18 miles south of town at Boysen St Park.

Motels, though abundant, can still be crowded in summer, when rates rise up to 30%. The basic **Hot Springs (Bahgue Wana) Motel** (☎ 307-864-2303, 401 Park St) charges $30/40 single/double but doesn't have phones. The renovated **Coachman Inn** (☎ 307-864-3141, 888-864-3854, 112 US 20 S) has a shady garden ($40/50). The comparable **Cactus Inn** (☎ 307-864-3155, 605 S 6th St) costs $35/45. **Jurassic Inn** (☎ 307-864-2325, 888-710-3466, 501 S 6th St) charges $35 to $45. **El Rancho Motel** (☎ 307-864-2341, 800-283-2777, 924 Shoshoni St) asks $45/55. Friendly **Roundtop Mountain Motel** (☎ 307-864-3126, 800-584-9126, 412 N 6th St) is $60/65; their rustic-looking but comfortable cabins with full kitchenettes ($69) are worth the extra bucks. **Best Western Moonlighter** (☎ 307-864-2321, 600 Broadway) has a pool and charges from $60. **Holiday Inn of the Waters** (☎ 307-864-3131, 115 E Park St) starts around $100 (ask about off-season discount packages) and prominently displays the owner's astonishing big-game trophy collection in its swank Safari Club restaurant.

Places to Eat

Gourmet options are limited, but fast food is plentiful. **Granny's Donuts & Ice Cream** (☎ 307-864-2809, 200 N 6th St) boasts a dozen different burgers. **Pumpernick's** (☎ 307-864-5151, 512 Broadway) is popular with the local business-lunch crowd; its shady patio offers alfresco dining and is a good spot for a quick sandwich or quiet beer. Nearby, all-American **Manhattan Inn** (☎ 307-864-2501, 526 Broadway) serves breakfast all day. **Don's IGA** (☎ 307-864-5576, 225 S 4th St) is your best bet for groceries.

Entertainment

Heavy metal dominates the jukebox at headbanging **One Eyed Jack's Bar** (☎ 307-864-9919, 633 Broadway). **The Ritz** (☎ 307-864-3118, 309 Arapahoe St) screens first-run Hollywood flicks.

Getting There & Away

Powder River Coach USA (☎ 307-864-2858) stops at Larry's Small Engine Repair, 421 Warren St. Buses go to Casper and Douglas via Shoshoni; and to Billings, MT, via Worland, Greybull and Lovell. Thermopolis is on US 20/Hwy 789 at the junction of Hwy 120. US 20/Hwy 789 leads north to Worland (35 miles) and south to Shoshoni (32 miles). Hwy 120 leads northwest to Cody (85 miles).

MEETEETSE

Facing the plains from the eastern escarpment of the Carter Mountains, Meeteetse ('mee-TEET-see'; population 385; elevation 6000 feet) is a delightful little village along the Greybull River. Remarkably for its size, it has a couple of excellent museums. The conspicuous Meeteetse Mercantile (1899), 1946 State St, still serves as the general store.

Meeteetse is on Hwy 120, 31 miles southeast of Cody and 52 miles northwest of Thermopolis.

Things to See & Do

The fine **Town Hall Museum** (☎ 307-868-2423), 942 Mondell Ave, pays homage to cowboy culture; it is open 10 am to 4 pm Monday to Saturday and 1 to 4 pm Sunday in summer. The **Meeteetse Bank Museum** is in the handsome old brick Hogg, Cheeseman & McDonald's Bank (1901) building at 1033 Park Ave; open 9 am to 5 pm Tuesday to Saturday in summer, with limited winter hours. Admission to both museums is by donation.

Places to Stay & Eat

There are two free **USFS campgrounds** (open June to November) southwest of town off Hwy 299 at the end of Wood River Rd (also known as Rd 4DT and FR 200). The superior summer-only **Vision Quest Motel** (☎ 307-868-2512, 2207 State St) charges $36/46 single/double and has kitchenettes. **Oasis Motel** (☎ 307-868-2551, 1702

WYOMING

State St) asks $26/36. It also has cabins with kitchenettes ($46) and a few campsites ($12). ***Broken Spoke Cafe*** *(☎ 307-868-2362, 1943 State St)* serves hearty meat-and-potatoes meals and rents out a couple of basic B&B rooms ($25/35) over the restaurant. Nearby, there's ***Outlaw Pizza Parlor*** *(☎ 307-868-2585, 1936 State St)* in the intriguing Cowboy Bar, and ***Elk Horn Bar & Grill*** *(☎ 307-868-9245, 1916 State St),* with occasional live country & western tunes.

BIGHORN MOUNTAINS

The Bighorn Mountains, marking the eastern extent of the Bighorn Basin, are crossed by three scenic east-west roads: US 14 is the **Bighorn Scenic Byway** from Greybull to Ranchester, north of Sheridan, via Granite Pass (8950 feet); US 14 Alternate is the **Medicine Wheel Passage** between Lovell and Burgess Junction via Baldy Pass (9430 feet); and US 16 is the **Cloud Peak Skyway** between Worland and Buffalo via Powder River Pass (9666 feet).

Burgess Junction is the junction of US 14 and US 14 Alternate, midway between Lovell and Ranchester. It has a visitors center with information, exhibits, and books and maps for sale; there's also an interpretive trail. A few private lodges near Burgess Junction offer basic accommodations, campsites and services (also see Bighorn Canyon National Recreation Area in the Montana chapter).

Medicine Wheel National Historic Landmark

At nearly 10,000 feet, on the western slope of Medicine Mountain, is the Medicine Wheel, a circular arrangement of irregularly shaped flat stones with 28 spokes radiating from its center. The Medicine Wheel is profoundly sacred to the Northern Cheyenne, Crow, Shoshone, Lakota and other Native American tribes that frequent the site and revere the Bighorn Mountains. It was constructed sometime between AD 1200 and 1700, but who made it and what it means are matters of some speculation. It may represent a likeness of the Sun Dance Lodge of Crow legend. The sunrise of the summer solstice aligns with the Medicine Wheel and Duncum Mountain to the east, suggesting astronomical significance.

Circle the Medicine Wheel clockwise, staying on the marked path. Respect it as you would any place of worship, and do not touch the religious offerings left at the site. (A fence actually surrounds the Medicine Wheel to protect it from vandals.) The north-

JOHN MOCK

The Medicine Wheel, sacred and mysterious

facing trail can be snow-covered into June, and weather is changeable and often blustery above timberline. USFS rangers staff the site and the parking lot 8 am to 6 pm daily mid-June to October. The site is closed for a few days around the summer solstice and may be closed for brief periods without notice for Native American ceremonies, but otherwise it is open round the clock.

From Lovell follow US 14 Alternate east for 27 miles, or from Burgess Junction follow US 14 Alternate west 30 miles to the USFS Hwy 12 turnoff. Drive with caution, as US 14 Alternate between Big Horn Lake and Baldy Pass is a 10% grade over 10 miles with 3600 feet elevation change. Follow the unpaved USFS Hwy 12 north to the parking lot. All visitors must then walk on the road the last 1½ miles to the site.

Camp near the Medicine Wheel at any of the three campgrounds along US 14 Alternate east of Big Horn Lake and west of Baldy Pass. The BLM *Five Spring Falls Campground* ($6; open May to September) is on the north side of US 14 Alternate at the base of the 10% grade, about 12 miles (by road) from the site. It's possible to hike from this campground to the Medicine Wheel; follow the steep trail from the campground to USFS Hwy 12 west of Medicine Mountain. One mile east of the USFS Hwy 12 turnoff is the USFS *Porcupine Campground*, north of US 14 Alternate. USFS *Bald Mountain Campground* is an eighth of a mile farther east, south of US 14 Alternate. Both are scenic campgrounds set in pine forest open from the end of June to the beginning of September ($10/night).

Shell Canyon
US 14 rises from the Bighorn Basin town of Greybull into Shell Canyon, where colorful layers of sedimentary rock and dinosaur fossils are found. Cliffs tower 2,000 feet over the highway. The canyon and the 120-foot **Shell Falls** take their name from some of the earliest fossils of hard-shelled creatures found in the remaining sandstone and limestone that capped most of the Bighorn Mountains hundreds of millions of years ago. Copman's Tomb is the distinctive peak

rising to the north above Shell and Cedar canyons.

The Shell Falls Interpretive Site, on US 14 east of Shell (population 50), has a summer-only information center, a bookstore, short trails and overlooks of the falls.

Several guest ranches are east of Shell. The seasonal *Shell Campground & RV Park* (☎ 307-765-9924) is at the west end of town.

East of upper Shell Canyon below Granite Pass is Antelope Butte (☎ 307-655-9530), a popular **downhill skiing** area with a base elevation of 8200 feet, 18 runs and a maximum 1000-foot vertical drop. Several trailheads lead into the Bighorns. Nearby USFS campgrounds include *Paintrock Rd*, east of US 14.

US 14 continues across Granite Pass to Burgess Junction; from there you can drive east to Ranchester or loop back to Lovell in the Bighorn Basin via US 14 Alternate.

ABSAROKA MOUNTAINS
At the western extent of the Bighorn Basin are the Absaroka Mountains, an eroded volcanic range named by the Crow Indians. The enormous Shoshone National Forest, part of the Yellowstone Timberland Reserve (the country's first, established by President Benjamin Harrison in 1891), covers the mountains, and the Shoshone River cuts a dramatic course through them along the Wapiti Valley, providing access to Yellowstone National Park's East Entrance.

For information on access to the Absarokas from Montana, see the Yellowstone Country section in the Montana chapter.

Wapiti Valley
The North Fork (Shoshone River) Scenic Byway (US 14/16/20) leads 50 miles west from Cody to the East Entrance of Yellowstone National Park, tracing the scenic Wapiti Valley. *Wapiti* is an Algonquin Indian word meaning 'pale white'; they used it to differentiate the lighter-colored elk from darker-colored moose. Hemmed in by the rugged Absaroka Mountains and the Shoshone National Forest, the North Fork wends its way through a picturesque

WYOMING

canyon. The North Absaroka Wilderness Area to the north and the Washakie Wilderness Area to the south are home to bears, deer, elks, moose, bighorn sheep and a few buffalo. An extensive network of trails leads through the wilderness areas along trout streams, past hidden lakes and into Yellowstone National Park.

The highway narrows to provide up-close views of the valley's dramatic rock formations at **Shoshone Canyon**, a beautiful place to picnic en route to or from Yellowstone National Park. One of Wapiti Valley's most scenic areas is **Holy City**, a cluster of eerie volcanic landforms north of the Shoshone River, just west of the Wapiti Wayside Exhibit.

The Wapiti Valley Visitors Center (☎ 307-587-3925), 29 miles west of Cody next to the Wapiti Wayside Exhibit, offers detailed information on the valley's frequent grizzly bear sightings; open 8 am to 8 pm weekdays and 8:30 am to 5 pm weekends from Memorial Day to Labor Day. Built in 1903, the adjacent Wapiti Ranger Station is a national historic landmark. It offers free tours 9 am to 4 pm weekdays. Lodges East of Yellowstone Valley (☎ 307-587-9595), PO Box 21, Wapiti, WY 82450, provides information on the valley's numerous family-owned member dude ranches and lodges; the Web site is at www.yellowstone-lodging.com.

Hiking & Horseback Riding

In the **Washakie Wilderness Area** two main trailheads with corrals are near the USFS Elk Fork and Eagle Creek campgrounds. The Elk Fork Trail follows the Elk Fork and then Rampart Creek up steadily to Overlook Mountain (11,869 feet).

At the USFS Blackwater Pond Picnic Area, USFS Rd 435 heads south and crosses the Shoshone River over a bridge. It climbs a short distance past the Blackwater Creek Ranch, following Blackwater Creek, to a trailhead. After 1 mile the trail divides. The Memorial Trail climbs south and east to Clayton Mountain and a monument to smoke jumpers who died in the Blackwater Fire of 1937. The Natural Bridge Trail continues south, climbing steadily through

dense forest before emerging onto the meadows of Sheep Mesa, beneath Fortress Mountain (12,085 feet).

From Eagle Creek, the trail crosses a pass beneath Eagle Peak (11,358 feet) and descends to the Thorofare Trail in Yellowstone; it leads across Two Ocean Plateau north to the east shore of Yellowstone Lake or south to the Teton Wilderness Area.

In the **North Absaroka Wilderness Area** a trail follows Clearwater Creek for views of Sleeping Giant Mountain. The main trailhead is at Pahaska Tepee. Here the Pahaska-Sunlight Trail heads north, branching northeast to the Sunlight Basin, west to Yellowstone's Pelican Valley, or continuing north to Yellowstone's Lamar Valley.

Skiing

Four miles east of Yellowstone's east gate, the **Sleeping Giant Ski Area** (☎ 307-587-4044) has a base elevation of 7000 feet with a maximum vertical drop of 500 feet. Lift tickets are $20/10 adults/children. Its Web site is at www.skisleepinggiant.com.

North Fork Nordic Trails (☎ 307-527-7701), which connects Pahaska Tepee Resort and Sleeping Giant Ski Area, offers 25 miles of groomed cross-country trails.

Places to Stay

Nine USFS campgrounds ($9 overnight/$3 day use) are in the Wapiti Valley (5900 feet to 6700 feet) along US 14/16/20, 28½ miles to 48½ miles west of Cody. Forested *Wapiti*, *Elk Fork*, *Clearwater* and *Newton Creek* campgrounds are farthest from the road. All campgrounds are along the river, offering easy access to trout fishing. Most campgrounds are open mid-May to September (a few into October), but can be closed at any time due to grizzly bear activity.

Wapiti Valley's lodges and dude ranches make a great base for exploring Yellowstone National Park or Cody, and most offer fishing, hiking, rock climbing, guided horseback rides ($20/one hour, $30/two hours, $45/half-day and $90/full day) and overnight horsepacking trips (from $125). South of US 14/16/20 is *Blackwater Creek Ranch* (☎ 307-587-5201, 888-243-1607). From east to west, all along the north side of US 14/16/20 are year-round **Absaroka Mountain Lodge** (☎ 307-587-3963); **Elephant Head Lodge** (☎ 307-587-3980), with cabins starting at $75 in the off-season; **Shoshone Lodge** (☎ 307-587-4044); and the historic year-round **Pahaska Tepee** (☎ 307-527-7701, 800-628-7791), Buffalo Bill's hunting lodge, the best deal with doubles starting at $85/55 peak-season/off-season. Many offer weekly rates, but luxury in proximity to the park doesn't come cheap.

Clarks Fork Canyon

The Clarks Fork of the Yellowstone River, Wyoming's only National Wild & Scenic River, runs along much of the Chief Joseph Scenic Hwy (Hwy 296) and US 212 linking Cody (via Hwy 120 north) with Yellowstone National Park's Northeast Entrance, 62 miles away. The 1200-foot gorge of the Clarks Fork separates the 50-million-year-old volcanic rock of the Absaroka Mountains from the 2-billion-year-old granite of the Beartooth Plateau.

Take Hwy 120 16 miles north of Cody to the start of Hwy 296. It heads northwest, climbing to Dead Indian Pass (8048 feet). Indians used to wait here and ambush game that migrated through the pass between summer pastures in the mountains and winter ranges in the plains. At the western base of the Dead Indian Pass is the primitive USFS **Dead Indian Campground** ($9/night).

Nearby, Hwy 296 crosses Sunlight Creek. Here USFS Rd 101 heads southwest into the breathtakingly beautiful Sunlight Basin. Hwy 296 continues northwest to the junction of US 212. Along this stretch of Hwy 296 are a few guest ranches and other basic USFS campgrounds, including **Hunter Peak** (6,500 feet) and the lovely, forested **Lake Creek** (6,900 feet), both $9/night.

Two main trailheads from Hwy 296, Dead Indian and Sunlight Creek, lead southwest into the North Absaroka Wilderness Area. A trail also follows much of Clarks Fork north of Hwy 296. Two USFS ranger stations along Hwy 296, Sunlight and Crandall, have information on area trails and campgrounds.

Near the junction of Hwy 296 and US 212 is a popular rock-climbing area. US 212 west of this junction dips into Montana toward Yellowstone with huge Absaroka views. Several more USFS campgrounds are en route to the entrance, the best of which are **Crazy Creek** and **Fox Creek** (elevation 6900 and 7100 feet, respectively), both $9 per night.

Beartooth Range

US 212 east of the junction with Hwy 296 enters the Beartooth Mountains and is known as the Beartooth Scenic Byway. It leads northeast toward Billings, MT, via Red Lodge, MT. The Wyoming section of US 212 crosses Beartooth Pass (10,940 feet) just south of the Wyoming-Montana state line. North of US 212 is the Absaroka-Beartooth Wilderness Area. Watch for mountain goats on crags and in alpine plateaus.

The **hiking** is excellent: Two trails worth investigating are the Beartooth Loop National Recreation Trail, which begins east of the pass and heads south, looping back to US 212 west of the pass; and Beartooth High Lakes, which begins west of the pass, heading north from US 212.

Easily accessible USFS campgrounds along US 212 are **Lily Lake**, **Beartooth Lake** and **Island Lake**.

Wind River Country

The glaciated Wind River Range, which dominates this region and marks the Continental Divide, comprises Wyoming's highest mountains. The cultural legacy of the Native Americans – Shoshone, Gros Ventre, Bannock, Sheepeater and Crow – who roamed the range when European trappers and explorers like Benjamin Bonneville and John C Frémont arrived in the early 19th century, is almost as dominant as the range. The region's other prominent feature is the Wind River Indian Reservation, home to the Shoshone and Arapaho.

In the latter half of the 19th century, the Oregon Trail and its Lander Cutoff led more travelers to the region. Much of the

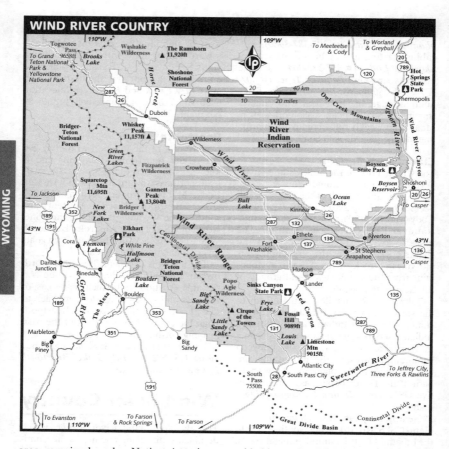

WIND RIVER COUNTRY

area remained under Native American control, but increasing numbers of immigrants settled here and took up cattle ranching. After the arrival of the railroad, the Lander-Riverton area was placed under irrigated agriculture. Later, timber and minerals became economic mainstays. With the boom and bust of these industries, however, tourism has become more important, growing rapidly by taking advantage of the region's spectacular natural assets. But even though tourism has a long history in the area – the first 'dude,' Scottish nobleman William Stewart, paid William Sublette to guide him to the Green River Rendezvous in the 1830s – small communities like Pinedale and Dubois are ambivalent about their increasing popularity.

RIVERTON

Northeast of the confluence of the Big and Little Wind Rivers, Riverton (population 10,250; elevation 4956 feet) was carved out of the Wind River Indian Reservation after promises of irrigation water persuaded the Shoshone and Arapaho to relinquish some of their lands in 1906. The town has little tourist appeal, other than as a way station.

There's a long-standing rivalry with its neighbor Lander, whose old-money inhabitants look down on Riverton's nouveaux riches.

Agriculture is a major industry, with malt barley (sold to Colorado's Coors Brewery), hay, corn and sugar beets the main crops. Over most of the 20th century, Riverton farmers have expanded onto reservation lands, which presently may be leased but not sold to non–Native Americans. Land and water usage continue to be sensitive issues. Trona (soda ash) transport also employs a number of people.

Orientation & Information

Newer chain outlets, motels and fast-food franchises line north-south Federal Blvd (US 26/Hwy 789). East-west Main St (US 26), which begins at Federal Blvd, is the main drag. Visitor information is available at the Riverton Chamber of Commerce (☎ 307-856-4801, 800-325-2732), 102 S 1st St, as well as the former railroad depot (same ☎), 8 am to 5 pm weekdays. For regional information, contact the Wind River Visitors Council (☎ 800-645-6233).

There are several ATMs on Main St. The post office, with an exceptional indoor mural titled *Lambing Time*, is at 501 E Main St. Books & Briar (☎ 307-856-1797), 313 E Main St, carries a large selection of books on Wyoming and Native American history and also stocks magazines and topo maps. Riverton Memorial Hospital (☎ 307-856-4161, 800-967-1646) is at 2100 W Sunset Dr, northwest of downtown.

Riverton Museum

This free museum (☎ 307-856-2665), 700 E Park Ave, has interpretive exhibits on Native American lands and water, displays of a frontier school, a general store and well-preserved horse carriages. Don't miss the stuffed bucking bronco in the basement. The museum is open 10 am to 4 pm Tuesday to Saturday.

Special Events

Riverton's major spring event is **Native American Week & Central Wyoming College Powwow**. The weeklong **1838**

Mountain Man Rendezvous (☎ 307-856-7306), held in early July on the Little Wind River at the east end of Monroe Ave, includes a rodeo. Late July brings the colorful **Hot Air Balloon Rally**. The **Fremont County Fair & Rodeo** is held over five days in early August. In October, all comers to the **Cowboy Poetry Gathering** prove the juice is worth the squeeze. Contact the Wind River Visitors Council (☎ 800-645-6233) for exact dates of events.

Places to Stay

Most motels are on or near Federal Blvd; others are on W Main St. Rates vary little seasonally. Low-budget places (around $30) include *Mountain View Motel* (☎ 307-856-2418, 720 W Main St), *Jack Pine Motel* (☎ 307-856-9251, 120 S Federal Blvd) and *Driftwood Inn* (☎ 307-856-4811, 800-821-2914, 611 W Main St).

The following mid-range options charge from $42 to $55 for doubles:

El Rancho Motel
 (☎ 307-856-7455, 800-650-7455,
 221 S Federal Blvd)
Hi-Lo Motel
 (☎ 307-856-9223, 800-492-9223,
 414 N Federal Blvd)
Paintbrush Motel
 (☎ 307-856-9238, 800-204-9238,
 1550 N Federal Blvd)
Thunderbird Motel
 (☎ 307-856-9201, 888-498-9200,
 302 E Fremont Ave)
Tomahawk Motor Lodge
 (☎ 307-856-9205, 800-637-7378, 208 E Main St)

Top-end places include *Sundowner Station Motel* (☎ 307-856-6503, 800-874-1116, 1616 N Federal Blvd), which charges $50 and up; *Super 8* (☎ 307-857-2400, 1040 N Federal Blvd), at $50/55; *Days Inn* (☎ 307-856-9677, 909 W Main St), near the airport, which charges $60/65; and *Holiday Inn* (☎ 307-856-8100, 900 E Sunset Dr) at $89.

Places to Eat

Friendly *Splitrock Coffee & Bagels* (☎ 307-856-4334, 219 E Main) has espresso and an extensive healthy lunch menu. Next door, *Wind River Mercantile* (☎ *307-856-0862, 221 E Main St)* stocks organic produce and bulk natural foods. *Country Cove* (☎ *307-856-5451, 309 E Main St)* does reliable breakfasts. At the airport, the *Airport Cafe* (☎ *307-856-2838)* is another good early-morning bet. *Breadboard Sub Shop* (☎ *307-856-7044, 124 E Washington Ave)* builds good sandwiches, while the *Mad Greek* (☎ *307-856-5007, 719 E Main St)* offers sanity-restoring gyros, burgers and shakes. The fanciest option is *The Broker* (☎ *307-856-0555, 203 E Main St),* with plush booths and good Mexican-American for lunch and surf 'n' turf for dinner at about $25 a head.

Entertainment

Good Time Charlie's (☎ *307-856-4285, 502 E Main St)* has live country-rock music weekends. *Central Wyoming College Arts Center* (☎ *307-855-2002, 2660 Peck Ave),* off US 26 west of town, hosts a wide variety of performances and exhibitions.

Getting There & Around

Riverton Regional Airport is 3 miles northwest of Riverton off US 26. United Express (☎ *307-856-1307)* operates daily flights to and from Denver.

The Wind River Transportation Authority (WRTA; ☎ *307-856-7118)* runs buses between Riverton, Lander and the Wind River Indian Reservation. WRTA stops on Federal Blvd at Monroe Ave and in front of Central Wyoming College's Activity Center.

By car, Riverton is along US 26/Hwy 789. US 26 leads east to Casper (119 miles) via Shoshoni (22 miles), and west across the Wind River Indian Reservation over Togwotee Pass (9658 feet) to Jackson (168 miles) via Grand Teton National Park. Hwy 789 leads southwest to Lander (25 miles) and southeast to Rawlins (123 miles). Avis (☎ *307-856-5052)* and Hertz (☎ *307-856-2344)* are at the airport. Courteous Cowboy Taxi (☎ *307-856-7444)* is always on call.

WIND RIVER CANYON

The Wind River carved a dramatic 2500-foot canyon through the Owl Creek Mountains, south of Thermopolis and north of Boysen Reservoir. Markers along US 20/Hwy 789, which hugs the eastern riverbank, display the age and type of the exposed sedimentary rock, ranging from Precambrian rocks (2.9 billion years old) to relatively youthful Triassic (a mere 200 million years old).

Boysen Dam tames the Wind River, creating Boysen Reservoir, the centerpiece of mostly barren Boysen State Park ($5 day use). There's a marina (☎ *307-876-2772)* at its north end with some surprisingly attractive campsites not far off US 20/Hwy 789. The nicest is *Lower Wind River Campground* ($9), near the tunnel.

Below the dam the Wind River has Class III–IV rapids and some tamer sections. Half-/full-day trips start at $25/65 per person. Contact Wind River Canyon Whitewater (☎ 307-864-9343 or ☎ 888-246-9343 in summer, ☎ 307-486-2253 in winter). The season is April to October; reservations are necessary April and May. Its Web site is at www.windrivercanyonraft.com.

SHOSHONI

Shoshoni (population 500; elevation 4820 feet) epitomizes boom gone bust, in this case the short-lived romance with uranium and nuclear power in the 1980s. Dusty Main St (don't look too hard for a street sign, there isn't one) is a ghost town, but elsewhere there are some faint signs of a resurfacing civic pride. Over Memorial Day weekend Shoshoni hosts the **Wyoming State Fiddle Championships**.

If you get stuck here, the *Desert Inn Motel* (☎ *307-876-2273, 605 W 2nd St)* has some dirt-cheap rooms, as does the *Shoshoni Motel* (☎ *307-876-2216, 503 W 2nd St).* The air-conditioned *Yellowstone Drug Company* (☎ *307-876-2539, 127 Main St),* open 10 am to 7 pm daily, does brisk business in 50 flavors of fantastic malts and shakes – pass on the mediocre short orders. On the north end of town, *Patti's Cafe* promises 'world famous biscuits and gravy' that'll raise your cholesterol significantly, or your money back – *and* 'leaches, minnows and worms.' Quite the deal, eh?

Powder River Coach USA (☎ 307-876-2561, 800-442-3682) buses stop at the Conoco Trail Town Supply, 107 W 2nd St. Buses go to Casper-Douglas and Billings, MT, via the Bighorn Basin. Contact WRTA (☎ 800-439-7118) for buses to Riverton and other Wind River Country destinations. Shoshoni is at the junction of US 20/Hwy 789 and US 26 at the southeastern tip of Boysen Reservoir, 15 miles northeast of Riverton and 32 miles south of Thermopolis.

LANDER

Genial Lander (population 7500; elevation 5357 feet) straddles the Middle Fork of the Popo Agie ('pah-poh-sha') River, a southern tributary of the Wind River. At the foot of the Wind River Range, Lander is the perfect base for backcountry forays. The presence of the National Outdoor Leadership School (NOLS) lends a college-town atmosphere, and the miniparks and comfy wooden benches along Main St invite visitors to linger. Off Main St, broad tree-lined streets shelter gracious older houses and offer pleasant strolls to attractive parks.

History

Though its namesake was Colonel Frederick W Lander, surveyor of the Lander Cutoff to the Oregon Trail in 1857–58, the town of Lander owes its existence to the Wind River Indian Reservation. In 1869, at the request of Chief Washakie, the US Army established Camp Augur to protect Shoshone lands from settlers. Ironically, the camp attracted even more immigrants to the area. Then, after the Bannock tribe voluntarily moved to Idaho in 1872, the US government carved half a million additional acres from the remaining Shoshone Reservation to encourage more settlement in the Popo Agie Valley. Lander then became the seat of Fremont County, which comprised almost one-quarter of the state's territory, and nearly became the state capital in 1904. In 1884 Wyoming's first oil well was drilled a few miles east of town, and the railroad arrived in 1906 (and stopped coming in 1972).

Orientation & Information

Main St (US 287) runs west of the river; newer suburbs sprawl east. From Main St, S 5th St leads to westbound Fremont St, Sinks Canyon Rd (Hwy 131) and Sinks Canyon State Park (see Around Lander, later).

The helpful Lander Area Chamber of Commerce (☎ 307-332-3892, 800-433-0662), 160 N First St, is open 9 am to 8 pm weekdays early June to mid-August, otherwise 9 am to 5 pm weekdays. Its Web site is at www.landerchamber.org. The USFS Shoshone National Forest Washakie District Ranger Station (☎ 307-332-5460), 333 Hwy 789 S, east of Buena Vista Dr, has good information on the Popo Agie Wilderness Area. Other useful contacts are the BLM Lander Resource Area (☎ 307-332-8400), 1335 Main St, and the Wyoming Game & Fish District (☎ 307-332-2688), 260 Buena Vista Dr.

ATMs dot Main St. The post office is at 230 Grand View Dr. Main St Books (☎ 307-332-7667), 381 W Main St, has the largest selection in town as well as coffee and email access. Lander's oldest bookseller, the Booke Shoppe (☎ 307-332-6221, 800-706-4476), 160 N Second St, carries a good selection of field guides and hiking maps and has a shady garden. Cabin Fever Books (☎ 307-332-9580), 163 S 5th St, trades used books. To reach Lander Valley Medical Center (☎ 307-332-4420, 307-856-1420), 1320 Bishop Randall Dr, head east across the river to Buena Vista Dr and go south past the golf course.

Historic Buildings

On First St just north of Main St, along the Popo Agie River, sits the former Chicago & Northwestern Railroad depot (1908); Lander was the end of the line, 'where the rails end and the trails begin.' The town's most imposing historic landmark, the little-changed Lander Mill (1888), 129 Main St, is still a feed dealer. On the north side of Main St, at the back of the lot between 144 and 166, is an 1876 log cabin. Centennial Park, just down the block, is a pleasant spot to relax. The ground floor of the largely unchanged Odd Fellows Hall (1886), 202 Main

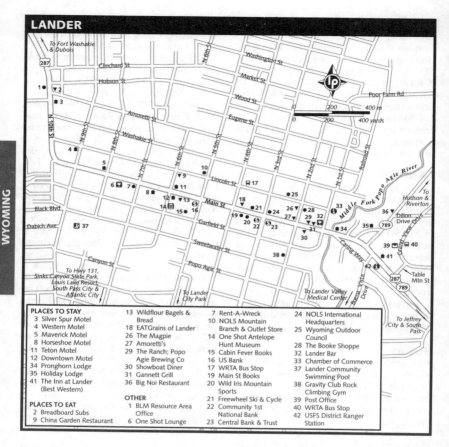

LANDER

PLACES TO STAY
3 Silver Spur Motel
4 Western Motel
5 Maverick Motel
8 Horseshoe Motel
11 Teton Motel
12 Downtown Motel
34 Pronghorn Lodge
35 Holiday Lodge
41 The Inn at Lander (Best Western)

PLACES TO EAT
2 Breadboard Subs
9 China Garden Restaurant

13 Wildflour Bagels & Bread
18 EATGrains of Lander
26 The Magpie
27 Amoretti's
29 The Ranch; Popo Agie Brewing Co
30 Showboat Diner
31 Gannett Grill
36 Big Noi Restaurant

OTHER
1 BLM Resource Area Office
6 One Shot Lounge

7 Rent-A-Wreck
10 NOLS Mountain Branch & Outlet Store
14 One Shot Antelope Hunt Museum
15 Cabin Fever Books
16 US Bank
17 WRTA Bus Stop
19 Main St Books
20 Wild Iris Mountain Sports
21 Freewheel Ski & Cycle
22 Community 1st National Bank
23 Central Bank & Trust

24 NOLS International Headquarters
25 Wyoming Outdoor Council
28 The Booke Shoppe
32 Lander Bar
33 Chamber of Commerce
37 Lander Community Swimming Pool
38 Gravity Club Rock Climbing Gym
39 Post Office
40 WRTA Bus Stop
42 USFS District Ranger Station

St, is now a restaurant. The former Fremont Lumber Company (1887), 159 N Second St, has been restored and is home to The Magpie (see below), a delightful cafe.

One-Shot Antelope Hunt Museum

Rub broad shoulders with influential National Rifle Association (NRA) members at the One-Shot Antelope Hunt Museum (Evans-Dahl Memorial Museum; ☎ 307-332-8190), 545 W Main St, a revealing peek inside a unique good-old-boys club. Every September, guided teams mar-

shaled by the governors of Wyoming and Colorado head out into the wilds in funny outfits to take a very prestigious single shot at an antelope.

Activities

The rugged areas surrounding Lander are popular with rock-climbing, mountaineering and mountain-biking enthusiasts. Wild Iris Mountain Sports (☎ 307-332-4541, 888-284-5968), 333 Main St, is the climbers' mecca. The Gravity Club (☎ 307-332-6339), 221 S 2nd St, has an indoor wall and offers hot showers. Freewheel Ski & Cycle (☎ 307-

332-6616, 800-490-6616 in Wyoming), 378 W Main St, rents mountain bikes.

Lander is home to NOLS (see Useful Organizations in the Facts about Wyoming section). Check the NOLS' bulletin board for folks seeking rides or climbing and hiking partners. The NOLS Outlet Store (☎ 307-332-1421), 502 Lincoln St, hawks quality trail-tested outdoors gear.

Special Events
The annual **International Climbers' Festival** (☎ 307-332-8662) in early July attracts craghounds from around the world; visit its Web site at www.climbersfestival.org. The lively **Taste of Lander Fine Arts Festival** happens every September. You can call the chamber of commerce for further details.

Places to Stay
Camping is free (three-night maximum) at **Lander City Park** (☎ 307-332-4647, 405 Fremont St), off 3rd St, but count on meeting rowdy teenagers. Holiday Lodge (see below) is the best in-town tenting option. The closest public campsites are at Sinks Canyon State Park (see later) and Ray Lake (see Wind River Indian Reservation, later).

Many motels offer kitchenettes and family rooms for a few bucks extra. Seasonal rate fluctuations are minimal. **Western Motel** (☎ 307-332-4270, 151 N 9th St) is the cheapest, at $28/30 single/double. At $35/50 are **Downtown Motel** (☎ 307-332-3171, 800-900-3171 in Wyoming, 569 Main St); **Horseshoe Motel** (☎ 307-332-4915, 685 Main St); **Silver Spur Motel** (☎ 307-332-5189, 800-922-7831, 1240 Main St); **Teton Motel** (☎ 307-332-3583, 592 Main St), where some rooms are nicer than others; and friendly **Maverick Motel** (☎ 307-332-2300, 877-622-2300, 808 Main St), with a surf 'n' turf restaurant.

Holiday Lodge (National 9) (☎ 307-332-2511, 800-624-1974, 210 McFarlane Dr) charges $40/50 and has a hot tub. It also has riverfront campsites ($5/person), including hot-tub use and showers ($3 for nonguests). **Pronghorn Lodge (Budget Host)** (☎ 307-

332-3940, 800-283-4678, 150 E Main St) charges $55 to $70 for suites that sleep four. Rooms at **The Inn at Lander (Best Western)** (☎ 307-332-2847, 260 Grand View Dr) command $50 to $80.

Blue Spruce Inn B&B (☎ 307-332-8253, 888-503-3311, 677 S 3rd St) is on a quiet residential street and charges $70/80. Its Web site is at www.bluespruceinn.com. **The Bunk House** (☎ 307-332-5624, 800-582-5262, 2024 Mortimore Lane), which sleeps five comfortably ($75), is five minutes south of town at the Lander Llama Ranch; visit www.landerllama.com. Ten minutes west of town in a rural setting is **Piece of Cake B&B** (☎ 307-332-7608, 2343 Baldwin Creek Rd), asking $80/90.

Places to Eat
Grains of Lander grocery (☎ 307-332-5966, 388 Main St) has a good health-food selection. **The Magpie** (☎ 307-332-5565, 159 N 2nd St) is the best spot in town for pastries, espresso or a light lunch. **Wildflour Bagels & Bread** (☎ 307-332-9728, 545 Main St) is the best bakery. **Showboat Diner** (☎ 307-332-2710, 173 Main St) serves cheap breakfast and lunch. **Breadboard Subs** (☎ 307-332-6090, 1350 Main St) makes good moderately priced sandwiches.

For a change of pace, try **China Garden Restaurant** (☎ 307-332-7666, 162 N 6th St). Another pleasant surprise is **Big Noi Restaurant** (☎ 307-332-3102, 280 N Hwy 789), featuring surf 'n' turf and some of Wyoming's only Thai food. **Gannett Grill** (☎ 307-332-8228, 126 Main St), next to the Lander Bar, sustains the outdoors crowd with good pizzas, burgers, sandwiches and salads. **The Ranch** (☎ 307-332-7388, 148 Main St) does Texas barbecue and is home to the **Popo Agie Brewing Co** brew pub. The new upscale continental **Amoretti's** (☎ 307-335-8500, 202 Main St) looks promising and has a nice bar.

Two popular Slavic 'supper clubs,' 10 miles northeast of Lander off Hwy 789 in the tiny hamlet of Hudson, draw crowds from miles around: Democratic **Club El Toro** (☎ 307-332-4627, 132 S Main St) and Republican **Svilar's** (☎ 307-332-4516,

175 Main St) face off on opposite sides of Main St and specialize in full, fine, main, meaty mains and homemade raviolis. Satiated diners head to the **Union Bar** to hash out their differences.

Entertainment

In the former Lander Hotel, the **Lander Bar** (☎ *307-332-7009, 126 Main St)* is good for a casual, if not exactly quiet, drink. Other watering holes include **Gannett Grill** (see above) and **One Shot Lounge** (☎ *307-332-2692, 695 Main St)*. The **Hitching Rack** (☎ *307-332-4322)* is just south of town on Hwy 287.

Getting There & Around

Wind River Transportation Authority (WRTA; ☎ 307-856-7118) provides both regularly scheduled weekday and on-demand bus service between Lander and the Wind River Reservation, Riverton, Dubois and Rock Springs. It also serves Riverton Regional Airport ($13). WRTA's Lander stops are at 9th and Main St and at the Alco Discount Store, 275 Grand View Dr.

Lander is at the junction of US 287 and Hwy 789, 9 miles northwest of the junction of US 287/Hwy 789 and Hwy 28. US 287 leads northwest through the Wind River Indian Reservation over Togwotee Pass (9658 feet) to Grand Teton National Park. Hwy 789 leads northeast to Riverton (24 miles) and southeast to Rawlins (128 miles). Rock Springs is 126 miles southwest via Hwy 28 and US 191. Haggle with Rent-A-Wreck (☎ 307-332-9965, 888-332-9965), 715 E Main St, for a local car rental.

AROUND LANDER

According to an enthusiastic native, the best thing about Lander is 'You can grab a bucket o' chicken downtown, head for the hills and have a picnic in the wilderness while it's still warm.'

Sinks Canyon State Park

This park was once named one of the USA's top 50 state parks by *National Geographic Traveler*. The Middle Fork of the Popo Agie River flows through the narrow canyon, disappearing into the soluble Madison limestone called The Sinks and emerging with increased volume and higher temperature a quarter-mile downstream in a trout-filled pool called The Rise. The sudden disappearance of the copious flow intrigues a steady stream of visitors. **Fishing** is not permitted in The Rise, but is allowed at **Popo Agie Campground**.

Pick up a brochure describing the area's wildlife, flora and fauna at the park's visitors center (☎ 307-332-3077); open daily 8 am to 7 pm summer only. It also offers information on easily accessible rock-art sites and occasional caving tours of Wind River Grotto. Day use is free.

The two park campgrounds ($9), **Sawmill**, north of the visitors center, and **Popo Agie**, south of it, fill up early and are open May to October. Both campgrounds are along the Popo Agie River in open forest but are dusty and close to the road. Other USFS campgrounds are nearby (see The Loop, below).

The park is off Sinks Canyon Rd (Hwy 131) 6 miles south of Lander and is also accessible from Hwy 28, just north of South Pass City, via Louis Lake Rd (USFS Rd 300), an unpaved 27-mile route to the south entrance.

The Loop

'The Loop' refers to Sinks Canyon Rd (Hwy 131), which leads southwest from Lander through Sinks Canyon State Park, past Frye Lake, to where it meets Louis Lake Rd (USFS Rd 300). The Loop continues southeast on Louis Lake Rd past Fiddlers and Louis Lakes, through Grannier Meadows, to Hwy 28. The area offers rock climbing, mountain biking, hiking, backpacking, fishing and boating.

Four USFS campgrounds ($6 to $8) are along the Loop. **Sinks Canyon Campground**, 10 miles south of Lander, is open May to October. The other three are open July to mid-September: **Worthen Meadows**, 16 miles from Lander to Frye Lake plus 2½ miles on USFS Rd 302 to the reservoir; **Fiddlers**, 23½ miles from Lander; and **Louis Lake**, 28 miles from Lander. The charming

Resort at Louis Lake (☎ 307-332-5549, 888-422-2246), on USFS Rd 300 about 10 miles northwest of Hwy 28, has rustic log cabins starting at $65, campsites ($15) and hot showers ($3). It rents gear, outfits pack trips and is a good source of information about area activities; visit its Web site at www.louislake.com.

Popo Agie Wilderness Area
South of Sinks Canyon State Park, at the southeast end of Shoshone National Forest, is the readily accessible 158-sq-mile Popo Agie Wilderness Area. Popo Agie Falls Trail offers an easy morning's hike to several waterfalls and attractive swimming pools. Both the Popo Agie Trail and the Stough Creek Lakes Trail, at the end of USFS Rd 302, lead into the high country on the east side of the Continental Divide. They offer opportunities for loop trips to the area's many lakes and extended backpacking trips toward Boulder or Pinedale.

ATLANTIC CITY & SOUTH PASS CITY
These twin historic sights, just a few miles apart, make for a nice day trip from Lander.

Atlantic City
Don't pay no mind to the 'Welcome to Atlantic City: We don't give a rotten rodent's rectum how you did it back home' signs – this feisty little tourist-savvy town (population 'about 57'; elevation exactly 7905 feet) extends visitors a friendly welcome. Founded in 1868 by miners from South Pass, it once boasted an opera house and the first brewery in the territory. By the 1950s it was nearly a ghost town, but enjoyed a minor revival a decade later when US Steel developed an open-pit mine at Iron Mountain along Hwy 28. The mine closed in the 1980s, but the town retains a handful of historic buildings in its scenic Rock Creek surroundings. **St Andrew's Episcopal Church** (1911) has a woodstove dated 1883. The **Gratrix Cabin** (circa 1860) was the residence of a justice of the peace who claimed to have lived in three counties (Carter, Sweetwater and Fremont), two territories

(Dakota and Wyoming) and one state (Wyoming) without ever moving.

South Pass City State Historical Site
North of the strategic South Pass (see below), South Pass City served passing migrants and, in the late 1860s, boomed with gold strikes at the Carissa Lode, Atlantic City and Miners Delight. Like many early mining camps, South Pass City experienced a brief period of lawlessness, with Native American raids and general disorder. At the same time, the town claimed its place in history by championing the cause of women's suffrage, thanks to local legislator William Bright's sponsorship of a bill to grant women the right to vote. The town languished after the mining boom went bust in 1873, but the state acquired the site in 1966 and restored 27 of the original log, frame and stone buildings.

The visitors center, a former 1890 dance hall, has video presentations and a bookstore, while the **Smith Store** (1874) contains interpretive exhibits. Among the other intriguing structures are the **Smith-Sherlock Store** (1896), the nicely outfitted **Blacksmith Shop** (1915), the **South Pass Hotel** (1868) and the ore-crushing **Franklin Mine Stamp Mill** (1869). The **Variety Theater** hosts plays, films, musicals and special events.

Continental Divide Trail
Crossing the divide five times, the controversial Continental Divide Snowmobile Trail consists of 365 miles of continuous, groomed trails at 9000 feet, from Atlantic City, Lander and Pinedale via Dubois and Togwotee Pass to Grand Teton and Yellowstone National Parks and West Yellowstone, MT. The trip usually takes two to four days, December to April, with overnight stops in Pinedale and Dubois. Snowmobilers must register at state park offices, snowmobile dealers or service stations. Maps are available from USFS or BLM offices.

This BLM-administered site (☎ 307-332-3684) is open 9 am to 6 pm daily May 15 to September 30; $2, free for children under 18.

Activities

Behind the Rock Shop Inn on Hwy 28, 35 miles south of Lander, **cross-country skiing** trails begin. An access trail follows Willow Creek north of Hwy 28, while four loops wind through aspens. Other activities include **fly-fishing** in nearby Sweetwater River and **mountain biking** on the extensive network of backcountry roads.

Places to Stay & Eat

Open June to October, two pleasant BLM campgrounds ($6) in mixed forest are 2 miles north of Atlantic City, 2 miles off Hwy 28: *Atlantic City*, where many Wild Iris (a rock climber's mecca full of white limestone crags 45 minutes south of Lander) climbers camp, is in an aspen grove on Fremont County Rd 237; and *Big Atlantic Gulch* (no water) is a half-mile east on BLM Rd 2324.

Atlantic City Mercantile (☎ 307-332-5143, 888-257-0215), in the former Giessler Store & Post Office (1893), has a steak house and saloon along with full RV hookups (June to October; $10) and summer cabins ($55) that sleep up to six. Call for details about their monthly seven-course Basque dinners ($25; reservations required). Next door to the 'Merc,' the *Sagebrush Saloon & Cafe* (☎ 307-332-7404), also known as 'the Dredge,' has a general store and offers family buffalo-burger dining. Cabins are $60 and upstairs rooms start at $75 at the year-round *Miner's Delight Old West B&B* (☎ 307-332-0248, 888-292-0248), the former Carpenter Hotel (1904). It was for sale at the time of writing.

Getting There & Away

Atlantic City and South Pass City are along unpaved Fremont County Rd 237, off Hwy 28 about 35 miles south of Lander. Atlantic City is 3 miles south of Hwy 28 and 4 miles north of South Pass City. The paved Fremont County Rd 479 connects Hwy 28 directly to South Pass City, which is 2 miles east.

SOUTH PASS NATIONAL HISTORIC LANDMARK

South Pass (7550 feet) is on Hwy 28, 10 miles southwest of South Pass City. Between 1843 and 1912, nearly half a million emigrants, miners and trappers crossed South Pass, the gentlest route across the Continental Divide. Farther west is the **Parting of the Ways**, where the Oregon and Mormon Pioneer trails split: The Oregon Trail headed west to Oregon and California, and the Mormon Pioneer Trail turned southwest to Utah.

WIND RIVER INDIAN RESERVATION

Home to more than 2500 Eastern Shoshone and more than 4500 Arapaho, the 3594-sq-mile Wind River Indian Reservation is Wyoming's only Native American reservation. Under the US Constitution, the reservation is an autonomous political entity, operating its own tax and court systems, game and fish department, and public transportation, and monitoring its own water quality. Oil, gas and grazing royalties finance many of these services. The reservation is not as picturesque as the postcard photographs of events like powwows would suggest, but a visit can offer an interesting glimpse into Native American life. Nearby communities like Lander and Riverton have minimal contact with the reservation. Despite high infant mortality and substance abuse problems, the reservation is a positive symbol of cultural identity. Cultural centers promote the study of Native American languages and participation in traditional religious events like sun dances.

History

The Wind River Indian Reservation reveals the complexity of the relationships of Native Americans to non–Native Americans, and the relationships between groups of Native Americans with distinct interests. Ironically the Shoshone, who were once allied with the US government, now share the same reduced territory with the defeated Arapaho. The Shoshone had always been friendly to settlers, and the Treaty of

Fort Bridger in 1863 granted the Shoshone a large area consisting of parts of present-day Colorado, Utah, Idaho, Montana and Wyoming. After the treaty proved impossible to enforce, the famed Shoshone Chief Washakie obtained, by the second Treaty of Fort Bridger in 1868, an area stretching from the Popo Agie Valley (comprising the core of the current reservation) to South Pass.

But gold strikes at South Pass chipped away at the reservation's south margin. For a cash indemnity and the promise of government protection, Chief Washakie accepted the further reduction of the reservation. After the end of the Plains Indians wars of the 1870s, the US government asked the Shoshone to share the reservation temporarily with their traditional adversaries, the Arapaho. Chief Washakie reluctantly agreed, and the arrangement soon became permanent. Today the Arapaho outnumber the Shoshone by almost two to one.

In 1906 the Riverton Project usurped even more land from the reservation, forming a prosperous white enclave surrounded by reservation lands. In 1989, however, US Supreme Court rulings upheld Native American water rights, placing the Shoshone and Arapaho in a much stronger position with Riverton farmers.

Much of the enmity between the Shoshone and Arapaho dissipated during the 20th century, but the two peoples retain distinct identities, and intermarriage is uncommon. Missionary activity may have contributed to this: Jesuits evangelized the Arapaho in the late 19th century, while Episcopalians converted the Shoshone. Between 1910 and 1917, the Episcopalians also constructed St Michael's Mission at Ethete.

Orientation & Information

The reservation consists of several small towns, the most important of which are the administrative center of Fort Washakie, primarily a Shoshone town, and the Arapaho settlements of St Stephens and Ethete ('EEE-thuh-tee').

Contact the Shoshone Tribal Cultural Center (☎ 307-332-9106) in Fort Washakie for dates of upcoming events. The year-round center has self-guiding tour maps and historic and cultural exhibits. It's usually open 9 am to 4 pm weekdays; $1. The North American Indian Heritage Center in St Stephens is open 9 am to 5 pm weekdays, April to December. Check the weekly *Wind River News*, published in Lander, for rez news.

The Tribal Fish and Game Dept (☎ 307-332-7207, 800-284-6857 in Wyoming) has a brochure listing outfitters and mapping the reservation's excellent fisheries. Wyoming fishing licenses are not valid here; nonresident reservation licenses are $25/65 per day/week. Even hikers must have a license, which includes use of designated public campgrounds.

Sales tax is not collected on the reservation.

Things to See & Do

Part of the historic St Michael's Mission complex at Ethete, the **Arapaho Cultural Museum** (☎ 307-332-2660) has displays of fine artifacts plus a superb collection of

The Resting Places of Legends

On the north side of North Fork Rd west of US 287, the fenced **Washakie Graveyard** has the remains of the great Shoshone Chief Washakie. The headstone on his grave reads 1804–1900, but Washakie ('Always loyal to the government and his white brothers') may well have been more than 100 years old when his remarkable life ended.

West of US 287 and Fort Washakie via South Fork Rd and Dushell Lane, the **Sacagawea Cemetery** purportedly holds the remains of Lewis and Clark's famous Shoshone guide. Episcopal missionary John Roberts claimed Sacagawea died on the reservation in 1884, but an alternative account is that she met her end in South Dakota in 1912.

photographs of reservation residents. Unfortunately, the building is inadequate and exhibits unexplained. The museum is typically open 10 am to 6 pm Monday to Saturday from May to October. Visitors, however, may have to locate the Episcopal vicar (a Shoshone) to gain admission. If possible, call for an appointment.

St Stephens Jesuit Mission, founded in 1884, is in the village of Arapahoe a few miles southwest of Riverton. The mission church is embellished with geometric Arapaho designs.

The **Wind River Trading Co** (☎ 307-332-3267) and **Gallery of the Wind** (☎ 307-332-4321), both next to Hines General Store in Fort Washakie, market tribal arts and crafts of varying quality.

Three miles east of Fort Washakie, the **Chief Washakie Plunge** (☎ 307-332-4530) complex has an outdoor swimming pool fed by 110°F sulfur mineral springs. Open noon to 8 pm Wednesday through Sunday April to October; admission is $5/2.50 and worth every penny.

Special Events

Dates for the numerous annual reservation events vary from year to year; confirm them with the cultural centers or the Riverton Chamber of Commerce (☎ 307-856-4801, 800-325-2732). Non–Native Americans are welcome at religious ceremonies, but cameras, video equipment and tape recorders are not.

Since **Powwows** are more social than religious gatherings, cameras are generally allowed, but ask permission. Likewise, etiquette requires standing for the grand entry, and rising during the singing of an honor song, dropping of a feather or men's traditional dancing. Follow the lead of Native Americans. Alcohol and drugs are prohibited. Important gatherings include:

United Tribes Powwow
  Central Wyoming College, Riverton (May)
Yellow Calf Memorial Powwow
  Ethete (May or June)
Big Wind Powwow
  Crowheart (June)
Arapaho Community Powwow
  Arapahoe (June)
Shoshone Treaty Day Celebration
  Fort Washakie (June)
Shoshone Indian Day Powwow & Rodeo
  Fort Washakie (June)
Eastern Shoshone Sundance Ceremony
  Fort Washakie (July)
Ethete Powwow
  Ethete (July)
Northern Arapaho Sun Dance
  Ethete (August)
Labor Day Powwow
  Ethete (September)
Northern Arapaho Powwow (September)

Places to Stay & Eat

Two campgrounds are usually open May to October. Grassy ***Rocky Acres Campground*** (☎ *307-332-6953, 5700 US 287*), 5 miles northwest of Lander, charges $10/13.50 for tent/RV sites and has laundry and showers. The friendly ***Ray Lake Campground*** (☎ *307-332-9333, 39 Ray Lake Rd*), off US 287, 8½ miles north of Lander, charges $7/13, or $15 for four-person teepees. There's also a cafe. ***Red Rock Lodge*** (☎ *307-455-3272*), on US 26/US 287 near Crowheart 25 miles east of Dubois, has double rooms for $25 and RV sites for $15; tepees and campsites cost $5, including showers. It's open in summer only and has a bar and restaurant.

Getting There & Away

The Wind River Transportation Authority (WRTA; ☎ 307-856-7118, 800-439-7118) provides regular weekday and on-demand bus service between Fort Washakie, Ethete, Kinnear, Lander, Hudson, Arapahoe and Riverton. Regular stops include the Hines General Store in Fort Washakie, the stoplight intersection in Ethete and Z's Country Corner in Kinnear. You can also flag down buses en route. WRTA goes to the Rock Springs/Sweetwater County Airport for $45 as needed; reservations are required. The nearest Powder River Coach USA bus stop is in Shoshoni (see Shoshoni earlier in this chapter).

Fort Washakie is along US 287, 15 miles northwest of Lander. Ethete is 5 miles east of Fort Washakie at Ethete Rd and Hwy 132. St Stephens is on Rendezvous Rd (Hwy 138), 3 miles southwest of Riverton. US 26 and US 287 join south of the Wind River, 16 miles north of Fort Washakie, and run together to Grand Teton National Park via Dubois.

Upper Wind River Valley

The Wind River headwaters descend from the eastern slopes of Togwotee Pass. South of the river the glacially carved granitic Wind River Mountains carry the Continental Divide for more than 100 miles. To the north of Wind River are the forested volcanic Absaroka Mountains. The enormous Shoshone National Forest covers parts of both mountain ranges. The name 'Wind' comes from the warm winter chinook winds that limit snow accumulation. Dubois is the only town in the upper valley, east of which is the semiarid red sandstone Dubois badlands. Hiking, climbing, fishing, horseback riding and snowmobiling are the most popular activities. Several dude ranches are in the area. The short summer season lasts August to September.

FITZPATRICK WILDERNESS AREA

Access to the 311-sq-mile Fitzpatrick Wilderness Area is southeast of Dubois, south of US 26/US 287. At the end of USFS Rd 257 (Trail Lake Rd) by the head of the Torrey Valley, 8 miles south of US 26/US 287, the **Glacier Trail** begins. The two-hour hike to Lake Louise starts here, as does one of two equally popular trails for towering **Gannett Peak** (13,804 feet), Wyoming's highest. This approach to Gannett Peak is drier, hotter, longer and tougher than the approach from Elkhart Park (see Around Pinedale later in this chapter), but the summit day is easier. The longer **Dinwoody Trail** joins the Glacier Trail approach to Gannett Peak. Llamas and horses frequently pack gear for ex-

tended backcountry trips; numerous outfitters are in Dubois.

The largest glaciers in the lower 48 states descend from the Winds. Many technical summits range up to 5.10; snow and ice routes lead to Gannett's summit. For instruction and guided climbs in the Wind River Range, contact Exum Mountain Guides (☎ 307-733-2297), Box 56, Moose, WY 83012.

Web site: www.exumguides.com

DUBOIS & AROUND

Picturesque Dubois ('DEW-boys'), originally settled by Scottish and Slavic immigrants, is a small farming and ranching community (population 1000; elevation 6917 feet) between the Wind River Indian Reservation and Grand Teton National Park. An old beaver-trapping area, Dubois for years supplied railroad ties for the CB&Q Railroad, though nowadays tourism is replacing the waning timber economy, and trophy heads and stuffed game animals serve only as reminders of a fading way of life.

Orientation & Information

US 26/US 287, the main road, enters Dubois from the southeast as S 1st St, then turns sharply west to become Ramshorn St, which runs east-west through town. Horse Creek Rd (USFS Rd 285), which heads north from Dubois just west of the creek, is the dividing line for east-west street addresses. The Wind River flows south of US 26/US 287.

The Dubois Chamber of Commerce (☎ 307-455-2556, 800-645-6233) is at 616 W Ramshorn St. The USFS Shoshone National Forest Wind River Ranger Station (☎ 307-455-2466), 1403 W Ramshorn St, is 1 mile west of downtown. There are a couple of ATMs on Ramshorn St. The post office is at 804 W Ramshorn St. Two Ocean Books (☎ 307-455-3554), 128 E Ramshorn St, has a small but excellent selection of Western writers and natural history.

National Bighorn Sheep Interpretive Center

This center (☎ 307-455-3429, 888-209-2795), 907 W Ramshorn St, is dedicated to the conservation of the Rocky Mountain bighorn sheep and its habitat. It offers a series of videos along with exhibits on other threatened species and environments, and is open 9 am to 8 pm daily Memorial Day to Labor Day, otherwise 9 am to 4 pm Thursday to Monday. Admission is $2/75¢ for adults/children, $5 for families.

Whiskey Basin Wildlife Habitat Area

Whiskey Basin has one of the USA's densest concentrations of bighorn sheep, with Torrey Valley, beneath Whiskey Peak (11,157 feet), being the winter range for 900 bighorn sheep as well as other mammals and waterfowl. Turn onto Fish Hatchery Rd off US 26/US 287 about 4½ miles east of Dubois and turn immediately left onto USFS Rd 257 (Trail Lake Rd), then follow signs. The 8-mile Trail Lake Rd along Torrey Creek passes Julia, Torrey, Ring and Trail Lakes. Bring binoculars for excellent roadside wildlife viewing. The National Bighorn Sheep Interpretive Center offers five-hour weekend tours ($20) mid-November to April.

Wind River Historical Center

This well-organized museum (☎ 307-455-2284), 909 W Ramshorn St, displays unique facets of life in the Dubois region, including a fine diorama of hunting drives, the history of the now-vanished Sheepeater branch of the Shoshone, tie-hack camps (including WWII German POWs), a relief map of the Dubois area and full mounts of bighorn sheep. The museum also contains a noteworthy collection of pioneer outbuildings. Pick up the 'Self-Guided Tour of Tie-Hack Country' handout to inspire further exploration. Open 10 am to 5 pm mid-May to mid-September; nominal admission fee. The Headwaters Community Art Gallery is upstairs.

Fishing

For fishing gear, maps and information, you can contact the Wind River Fly Shop (☎ 307-455-2140), 211 W Ramshorn St; Whiskey Mountain Tackle (☎ 307-455-

2587), 102 W Ramshorn St; or Welty's General Store (☎ 307-455-2377), 113 W Ramshorn St.

Places to Stay

Dubois, a prime Yellowstone stopover, gets crowded and expensive in summer; reservations are recommended. Some places close for the winter after Thanksgiving. The riverfront *Circle-Up Camper Court* (☎ 307-455-2238, 225 W Welty St) has shady campsites ($14) and barren RV hookups ($19). They also have hot showers ($4), six-person tepees ($17) and four-person cabins ($25) without bedding. The USFS *Horsecreek Campground* ($8), 12 miles north of town off Horse Creek Rd (USFS Rd 285), is open June to October.

Three miles east of town, the friendly *Riverside Inn & Campground* (☎ 307-455-2337, 5810 US 26) has tranquil kitchenette rooms with no phone or TV ($36/40 single/double) and tent ($15) and RV ($20) sites. A mile west of town, the *Bald Mountain Inn* (☎ 307-455-2844, 800-682-9323, 1342 W Ramshorn St) has upgraded kitchenette rooms for $55. Historic *Twin Pines Lodge & Cabins* (☎ 307-455-2600, 800-550-6332, 218 W Ramshorn St) charges $45/55. Other comparably priced options include the renovated *Trail's End Motel* (☎ 307-455-2540, 511 W Ramshorn St), *Wind River Motel* (☎ 307-455-2611, 519 W Ramshorn St) and *Pinnacle Buttes Lodge & Campground* (☎ 307-455-2506, 3577 US 26).

Rooms at the riverside *Black Bear Country Inn* (☎ 307-455-2344, 800-873-2327, 505 W Ramshorn St) are $45/50. Slightly more is the *Super 8* (☎ 307-455-3694, 1414 Warm Springs Dr), which charges $50/55. Next to Horse Creek is the attractive *Stagecoach Motor Inn* (☎ 307-455-2303, 800-455-5090, 103 E Ramshorn St), with a pool and nightly summer outdoor cookout ($47/60). The *Branding Iron Motel* (☎ 307-455-2893, 800-341-8000, 401 W Ramshorn St) has cabins (from $50) and kitchenette rooms for a bit more. Half a mile east of town, the Western-style *Chinook Winds Mountain Lodge* (☎ 307-455-2987, 800-863-0354, 640 S 1st St) ranges from $50 to $80.

Places to Eat

The Dubois diet is pretty much meat-and-potatoes, with a few revelations. *Daylight Donuts & Village Cafe (☎ 307-455-2122, 515 W Ramshorn St)* is a daybreak coffee shop that transforms into a passable steak house after dark. *The Hang-Out (☎ 307-455-3800, 8 Stalnaker St)* has bagels, espresso, soups, sub sandwiches and salads. For hardscrabble chuck-wagon grub, try the family-oriented *Cowboy Cafe (☎ 307-455-2595, 115 E Ramshorn St)* or the *Rustic Pine Tavern & Steakhouse (☎ 307-455-2772, 119 E Ramshorn St)*. The *Ramshorn Inn (☎ 307-455-2400, 202 E Ramshorn St)* has lighter breakfasts and lunches. The *Outlaw Cafe & Saloon (☎ 307-455-2387, 204 W Ramshorn St)* has a bit more dinner variety.

Getting There & Away

Dubois is on US 26/US 287, 78 miles west of Riverton, 75 miles northwest of Lander and 55 miles east of Moran Junction via Togwotee Pass. The Wyoming Centennial Scenic Byway follows US 191 and US 287 between Dubois and Pinedale via Grand Teton National Park.

DUBOIS TO TOGWOTEE PASS

The dramatic Pinnacle Buttes loom over the grizzly bear habitat of the upper Wind River valley northwest of Dubois. Horse Creek Rd (USFS Rd 285) leads 12 miles north of Dubois to the **Ramshorn Basin**, above which towers The Ramshorn (11,920 feet). Here trails begin that cross passes such as Shoshone Pass into the 1100-sq-mile **Washakie Wilderness Area**. From Ramshorn Basin, USFS Rd 285 continues as Wiggins Fork Rd for 17 miles to the Frontier Creek trailhead; 4WD is recommended. USFS campgrounds ($6) in the area are *Horse Creek* (at 7500 feet) in Ramshorn Basin and *Double Cabin* (at 8053 feet) at the Frontier Creek trailhead.

The scenic **Brooks Lake Recreation Area**, 5 miles north of US 26/US 287 on Brooks Lake Rd (USFS Rd 515), is popular for fishing and camping. From the northwest shore of Brooks Lake meanders the very pleasant Jade Lakes Trail, while the Yellow-stone Trail leads north into the Teton Wilderness Area. Other trails circle Pinnacles Buttes via Kissinger Lakes east of Brook Lake. Kissinger Lakes are also accessible via Long Creek Rd (USFS Rd 659) north of US 26/US 287. The USFS campgrounds ($9) nearby are *Falls* (at 8000 feet), on US 26, 23 miles west of Dubois, and *Pinnacles* and *Brooks Lake*, on opposite sides of Brooks Lake (at 9200 feet).

Nearby, luxurious year-round *Brooks Lake Lodge (☎ 307-455-2121, 458 Brooks Lake Rd)*, on the National Register of Historic Places, features fishing and horseback riding in summer and cross-country skiing and hearty midday meals (reservations required) in winter.
Web site: www.brookslake.com

Wind River Mountains – Southwest Side

The steep southwest side of the Wind River Mountains contrasts dramatically with the gentle, forested slopes on the northeast. Dozens of creeks and rivers flow through the Bridger-Teton National Forest, where more than 1000 lakes offer great fishing. Fremont Lake, just north of Pinedale, is the largest; to the east are Half Moon, Burnt and Boulder Lakes; and farther north are Willow, New Fork and Green River Lakes. Many trails follow the creeks and rivers that feed these lakes up into the 669-sq-mile **Bridger Wilderness Area**, where meadows, high plateaus and secluded valleys teem with wildlife. Pinedale, just north of a vast, natural-resource-rich sagebrush plateau called The Mesa, is the premier gateway for backcountry excursions into the Winds.

PINEDALE

On the Wind River Range's southwest slope, the Sublette County seat (affectionately known as 'the nation's ice box' due to its harsh winters) is a year-round outdoor-activities mecca. The friendly ranching and

WYOMING

government service center is slowly but surely embracing tourism and extends visitors an amiable welcome. Pinedale (population 1400; elevation 7175 feet) has always been off the beaten path – there isn't a single stoplight in the entire county, and the post office is one of the nation's farthest from a railroad – and although the town entertains many folks who are headed for the Greater Yellowstone area, it shows few signs of becoming 'another Jackson.'

Orientation

Pine Creek flows south through the town's two inviting parks. US 191 (Pine St) is the main drag and runs east-west through town. East of Bridger Ave, US 191 turns south and Fremont Lake Rd (Skyline Dr) heads north for the popular Elkhart Park trailhead.

Information

The helpful Pinedale Area Chamber of Commerce (☎ 307-367-2242), 32 E Pine St, is open 9 am to 5 pm weekdays in summer and less frequently in winter. The USFS Bridger-Teton National Forest Pinedale Ranger District (☎ 307-367-4326) is at 29 E Fremont Lake Rd. The BLM Pinedale Resource Area office (☎ 307-367-4358), 432 E Mill St, is on the east end of town. The Wyoming Game and Fish Dept (☎ 307-367-4352), 117 S Sublette Ave, publishes a free Bridger Wilderness Area pocket fishing guide. The Web site at www.pinedaleonline.com offers a wealth of local information.

Both banks on Pine St have ATMs. The post office is at 413 W Pine St. The superb public library (☎ 307-367-4414), 155 S Tyler Ave, has speedy, free Internet access. Friendly Moosely Books (☎ 307-367-6622), 7 W Pine St, stocks a thoughtful selection of Western books. The Cowboy Shop (☎ 307-367-4300, 877-567-6336), 137 W Pine St, is an incomparable Western wear outfitter; its Web site is at www.cowboyshop.com. Pinedale Medical Clinic (☎ 307-367-4133), 619 E Hennick St, is off Fremont Lake Rd.

Special Events

The **International Rocky Mountain Stage Stop Sled Dog Race** (☎ 307-734-1163), a qualifier for the prestigious Alaskan Iditarod, mushes into town in early February. Find out more on its Web site at www.wyomingstagestop.org. The annual **Green River Rendezvous**, held the second weekend of July, is one of Wyoming's biggest events. It's a reenactment of the arrival of settlers in the upper Green River, their interactions with the Native Americans and the establishment of the fur trade. The rendezvous is much more than a pageant: It includes living-history presentations, live entertainment, rodeos and the Pelt & Plew Social (an inexpensive buffalo feed); contact the museum (see below) for a full schedule.

Museum of the Mountain Man

This exceptional 15,000-sq-foot museum (☎ 307-367-4101), 700 E Hennick Ave, half a mile northeast of town off Fremont Lake Rd, may be the finest of its kind, with critical interpretations of early European exploration of the West, the fur trade and pioneer settlement in western Wyoming. Open 10 am to 6 pm daily, May through September and by appointment; $4/3/2 adults/seniors/children six to 12.

Places to Stay

Northbound travelers may find that Pinedale is where rates rise, due to its proximity to Jackson and Yellowstone. Reservations are recommended in summer, especially during the Green River Rendezvous in July.

The shadeless but friendly *Pinedale Campground* (☎ 307-367-4555, 204 Jackson Ave), 2 blocks south of Pine St, is the only in-town campground. Grassy campsites cost $11; full RV hookups cost $18. Showers for nonguests cost $4. The USFS *Fremont Lake Campground* (see Around Pinedale, below) is 7 miles northeast of town near several osprey nests.

Rooms at attractive creekside *Rivera Lodge* (☎ 307-367-2424, 442 W Marilyn St) start at $50. The snug cabins are clean but don't have telephones; many have kitchenettes. The well-maintained, historic *Log Cabin Motel* (☎ 307-367-4579, 49 E Magno-

lia St) starts at $45/55 single/double. Comparably priced is the remodeled *Half Moon Motel* (☎ 307-367-2851, 46 N Sublette Ave). Rooms that sleep six at the *Sun Dance Motel* (☎ 307-367-4336, 800-833-9178, 148 E Pine St) fetch $60 to $90. The roomy *Wagon Wheel Motel* (☎ 307-367-2871, 407 S Pine St) asks $40 to $85. The newer *Best Western Pinedale Inn* (☎ 307-367-6869, 800-528-1234, 850 W Pine St) has $90/100 rooms and all the chain amenities.

A mile west of Pinedale, the modern *Window on the Winds B&B* retreat (☎ 307-367-2600, 888-367-1345, 10151 US 191) has a hot tub and doubles for $75. Its Web site is at www.windowonwinds.com. Beds at the remodeled *Chambers House B&B* (☎ 307-367-2168, 800-567-2168, 111 W Magnolia St) go for $50 to $105. Three miles south of town, the rustic *Pole Creek Ranch B&B* (☎ 307-367-4433, 244 Fayette Pole Creek Rd) charges $55 per 'married couple.' Visit online at www.bbonline.com/wy/polecreek for details.

There are many fine guest ranches around Pinedale, including the *Fort William Guest Ranch* (☎ 307-367-4670), with a popular restaurant (visit www.forwilliam.com); and the century-old *Lozier's Box R Ranch* (☎ 307-367-4868, 800-822-8466), in nearby Cora. Its Web site is at www.boxr.com.

Places to Eat

Tastes in Pinedale are slowly evolving beyond traditional cowboy cuisine. *Moose Creek Trading Company* (☎ 307-367-4616, 44 W Pine St) has excellent sandwiches on homemade bread, as well as espresso, steaks for dinner and a pleasant bar. The *Fremont Peak Restaurant* (☎ 307-367-2259, 20 W Pine St) prepares excellent German food from scratch. *Wrangler Cafe* (☎ 307-367-4233, 905 W Pine St) is a cheap, no-nonsense local favorite, as is the *Patio Grill & Dining Room* (☎ 307-367-4611, 35 W Pine St). *LaVoie Brewery* (☎ 307-367-2337, 406 W Pine St) caters to the anti-macrobrew crowd. Upscale *McGregor's Pub* (☎ 307-367-4443, 21 N Franklin Ave) has a diverse surf 'n' turf menu and a shady patio.

The huge *Faler's General Store* (☎ 307-367-2131, 341 E Pine St) sells groceries (and everything for avid outdoors enthusiasts).

Entertainment

Several bar/restaurants feature live country & western on summer weekends: *Calamity Jane's*, also known as the *World Famous Corral Bar* (☎ 307-367-2469, 30 W Pine St); the *Cowboy Bar* (☎ 307-367-4520, 104 W Pine St); Moose Creek Trading Co's *Sweet Tooth Saloon*; and *Stockman's Bar & Steak Pub* (☎ 307-367-4563, 117 W Pine St), which also has a good salad bar.

Getting There & Away

Pinedale is on US 191, which leads northwest to Jackson (77 miles) and south to Rock Springs (100 miles). The Wyoming Centennial Scenic Byway follows US 191 and US 287 between Pinedale and Dubois via Grand Teton National Park. The private, noncommercial Pinedale Municipal Airport is jet-ready. Pinedale Taxi (☎ 307-360-8313) provides airport and trailhead transport.

AROUND PINEDALE
Fremont Lake

Four miles north of Pinedale via Fremont Lake Rd (also known as Skyline Dr) is the south shore of pristine, glacial Fremont Lake (7400 feet), the region's largest body of water. The lake has a 22-mile shoreline and is 600 feet deep. Sandy Beach picnic area, at its south end, is good for swimming. Fishing for grayling, brook and golden trout is popular.

The USFS *Fremont Lake Campground* (open mid-May to late September; $7) is 7 miles north of Pinedale, midway up the lake's eastern shore. At the south end, *Lakeside Lodge Resort & Marina* (☎ 307-367-2221) has a good restaurant, campsites ($10), RV hookups ($20), rustic cabins and motel rooms ($60 to $70) and new lakefront cabins ($120/130). The marina rents canoes and fishing boats. Open May 15 to mid-October. Visit its Web site at www.lakeside-lodge.com. The luxurious *Half Moon Lake Resort* (☎ 307-367-6373) and restaurant are a bit farther up Fremont Lake Rd. Visit www.halfmoonlake.com.

White Pine Ski Area

Along Fremont Lake Rd 10 miles northeast of Pinedale, the revamped White Pine Ski Area (☎ 307-367-6606) has a base elevation of 8480 feet, a new lift serving more than 900 vertical feet and extensive, groomed cross-country trails. The USFS brochure 'Skyline Drive Nordic Touring Trails' details several loop routes (which are also popular for hiking and mountain biking) around Fortification Mountain, Lower Sweeney Lake and Elkhart Park (see below). Check www.whitepineski.com for rates and snow conditions.

Elkhart Park

At the north end of the scenic 15-mile Skyline Dr is Elkhart Park (9480 feet), a popular Wind River trailhead. The volunteer-staffed visitors center is open 9 am to 6 pm daily June 1 to Labor Day. Nearby is the USFS *Trails End Campground* (9100 feet; $7). The best day hike is the 4-mile **Pole Creek Trail** through spruce and pine forest to Photographer's Point (10,340 feet), for a spectacular view of Gannett Peak and the Continental Divide. The trail continues north toward Jackson, Fremont and Gannett Peaks. This approach to Gannett Peak is higher, shorter and easier – but the summit day harder – than the Glacier Trail approach from Dubois (see Fitzpatrick Wilderness Area, earlier).

Fishing

Blue-ribbon fishing sites are unlimited around Pinedale, from the Green and New Fork Rivers of the lowlands to expansive Fremont Lake in the foothills and more than a thousand smaller backcountry lakes in the Bridger Wilderness. Ice fishing is also popular. Randall's Fishing Guide Service (☎ 307-367-4857), 118 S Maybell Ave, specializes in fly-fishing trips. Two Rivers Emporium (☎ 307-367-4131, 800-329-4353), 211 W Pine St, knows trout inside and out; visit www.2rivers.net.

Hiking & Backpacking

The major Wind River trailheads are Green River Lakes (see below), New Fork Lakes, Willow Creek Guard Station and Spring Creek Park northwest of Pinedale; Boulder Lake, Scab Creek and Big Sandy southeast of Pinedale; and Elkhart Park (see above).

In Pinedale, the Great Outdoor Shop (☎ 307-367-2440), 332 W Pine St, and Faler's General Store (see Pinedale, earlier) sell essential gear. Several outfitters arrange backcountry trips, many with pack animals; contact the chamber of commerce or the Wyoming Outfitters & Guides Association (☎ 307-527-7453) for details. The latter's Web site is at www.wyoga.org/.

GREEN RIVER LAKES

The upper Green River was once a prime tie-hacks area. Railroad ties were cut in winter and floated 130 miles south during the spring runoff to the town of Green River. Today these lakes are the westernmost trailhead for the Wind River Range and are reached by driving 6 miles west of Pinedale on US 191 and then 40 miles (first 25 miles paved) north on Hwy 352. En route, watch for **Kendall Dace** on USFS Rd 10091, beyond Hwy 352, along the Green River. Here endemic 2-inch-long freshwater fish live their entire lives in the 84.4°F Kendall Warm Springs. Breeding males are purple; females green.

When hiking around the lower of the two Green River Lakes, take the warm southfacing slope on the north side in the morning; return via the shady north-facing slope in the afternoon. The frequently photographed **Square Top Mountain** (11,695 feet) is a massive landmark butte.

A good day hike to **Clear Creek Natural Bridge**, where the creek has cut a channel through weak limestone, is the easy twohour walk from the Highline Trail at the north end of Green River Lakes, through a burned lodgepole forest. A mile before you reach the natural bridge, a log bridge crosses the creek to a spur trail to Slide Lake, which features a natural water slide. The Lakeside Trail returns to the USFS *Green River Lakes Campground* (8000 feet;

$6) on the west side of the lake, which has a few spots with panoramas of the Winds. The Highline Trail is also the starting point for traversing the 100-mile crest of the Wind River Range to Little Sandy Lake.

Greater Yellowstone

The Greater Yellowstone ecosystem, a 43,750-sq-mile area in Wyoming, Montana and Idaho, encompasses Yellowstone and Grand Teton National Parks, seven national forests and three national wildlife refuges. Conservationists consider this area an intact natural ecosystem, with rivers, forests, prairies and abundant wildlife best managed as a sustainable entity. In the 1990s a 12% annual population growth rate pressured the ecosystem's finite resources. Yellowstone National Park is the area's main attraction, and the area's history is largely the history of the park and its development.

History

Hunter-gatherers occupied the Yellowstone plateau for more than 8500 years after the region's last glaciers melted. In 1807, when John Colter was the first white man to visit the area, the only inhabitants were Tukudikas or 'Sheepeaters,' a Shoshone-Bannock people who hunted bighorn sheep. The Crow and Blackfeet also visited the area. Other Native American tribes occasionally passed through Yellowstone country even after its declaration as a national park. One of the most extraordinary historic episodes was the 1877 flight of the Nez Percé, led by Chief Joseph, who fled their ancestral lands in Oregon to avoid persecution by the US Army. In crossing Yellowstone, the Nez Percé briefly seized several tourists before continuing north up the Clarks Fork River toward Canada. They were eventually captured in Montana.

Mountain men in search of furs came after Colter from 1820, but the fur trade hit the skids by 1840. Miners inspired by gold strikes in Montana came in the early 1860s, but the results were disappointing. Then

reports of Yellowstone's extraordinary geothermal features, at first dismissed as tall tales, brought increased scientific interest. This led to a series of expeditions, culminating in the US Geological and Geographical Survey (USGS), headed by FV Hayden, in 1871. Hayden's scientific work was fairly pedestrian, but two members of his party, landscape painter Thomas Moran and photographer William Henry Jackson, produced works of art that excited interest in the area. This led to, with lobbying from the Northern Pacific Railroad, the designation of Yellowstone as a national park in

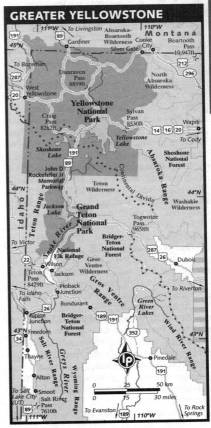

1872 – in large part because the US Congress could not imagine any other use for this remote area.

At first the US Congress failed to fund direct protective activities. The US Cavalry managed the park from 1886 until after the creation of the NPS in 1918. Under the US Army, the park's features were largely maintained in their existing state, but with the changeover to the newly formed NPS, policies of predator eradication, habitat destruction in the name of development and unregulated hunting outside park boundaries led to the creation of an artificial and ultimately unsustainable ecology.

The NPS now admits that efforts to exterminate predators were misguided. The intensive development of a small area (about 1%) of the park for tourism, however, continues to raise controversy. The park's 370 miles of narrow roads are crowded, and the more than 2000 buildings are seen by some as an artificial distraction from the park's natural splendor. The NPS sees it as meeting public demand. Historian Richard White has argued that rather than being a vestige of wild America, Yellowstone is 'a petting zoo with a highway running through it.' Nevertheless, in 1972, Yellowstone became a United Nations Biosphere Reserve and in 1978 it was designated a World Heritage Site. It's estimated that 95% of visitor use is concentrated in developed areas – join the minority and explore the seldom-seen backcountry!

Overly protective of the park's spectacular features, the NPS was unprepared for the major 1988 wildfires. Under the influence of immutable 'Smokey the Bear' policies, the NPS had suppressed virtually all forest fires since the 1940s. Since many tree species, such as lodgepole pines, depend on the heat from minor fires to open their reproductive cones, fire suppression resulted in extensive stands of older trees and a dangerous tinderstick buildup. The dense forest canopy also rendered the shady understory a biological desert that provided little sustenance for wildlife.

By the mid-1970s, the NPS had switched to a more realistic 'let-burn' policy, which

acknowledged the importance of fire in the ecosystem but failed to recognize that what remained was not a natural ecosystem but an unsustainable, artificial one. Smaller prescribed burns might have restored the natural balance over time, but lightning strikes in the dry, windy summer of 1988 ignited major wildfires that incinerated the artificially maintained forests and threatened historic structures. Only early September snows extinguished the fires, which had begun in May.

Even so, the 1988 fires were more a public relations disaster than an environmental catastrophe. Barely a third of the park's surface burned, and not even half of that was a canopy fire – though many heavily charred areas are still visible from the Grand Loop Rd. Only a few large mammals, mostly elk, died. Small mammals, on the other hand, perished in large numbers because they were unable to outrun the fires and proved more vulnerable to predators afterward due to reduced shelter. Nearby commercial interests, which suffered short-term losses from decreased tourism, unfairly criticized the essentially sound NPS policy of allowing natural fires to burn.

Since 1988, ecological developments have been encouraging. In many of the burned areas, the open understory has flourished with new grasses, wildflowers, shrubs and tree seedlings providing more diverse wildlife habitat. This developing mosaic may lack the appeal of pure stands of coniferous forest, but discriminating visitors may find the recovering Yellowstone a more rewarding experience.

Today, Yellowstone faces several questions. One is how to accommodate growing numbers of visitors (up from 1 million to more than 4 million over the last decade) while repairing the deteriorating infrastructure, all within a meager annual budget of $24 million. Another is what to do about an invasion of nonnative trout, illegally introduced into Yellowstone Lake, which are eating the native Yellowstone cutthroat trout on which black and grizzly bears, bald eagles, pelicans and otters feed. Yet another

Slaughtering a National Symbol

Revered by Native Americans and a national symbol, the Yellowstone mountain bison are the country's last wild herd. Despite protection within Yellowstone National Park, the herd's existence is threatened. Harsh winters cause bison to forage outside the park and many stray north toward Gardiner, MT.

During the 1996–97 winter, ranchers around Gardiner slaughtered over 1000 to prevent the spread of brucellosis, a bacterium that causes domestic cows to abort their calves. Brucellosis spreads from the park's abundant elk population to the bison, which are themselves unaffected by the bacteria. Whether or not brucellosis can actually spread from bison to cattle is unknown, as scientific studies have yet to be conducted. But public outrage soared upon viewing footage of the 1996–97 bison slaughter, filmed by the Missoula, MT–based group Cold Mountain, Cold Rivers.

No policy to halt continuing bison slaughter has been implemented, but a long-term management plan is being studied that would allow bison to stray outside the park into designated safe foraging areas, limit the maximum number of bison inside the park and/or vaccinate bison against brucellosis. Yellowstone's chief bison specialist does not believe brucellosis can be eradicated, however, because of the park's high elk concentration. Snowmobiling in the park also affects winter bison movement and is being studied as part of the problem. To lend support, contact the National Parks Conservation Association (☎ 800-628-7275), which launched the 'Bison Belong' campaign, calling for an end to the bison slaughter, or visit www.npca.org.

---

question is the management of the park's bison herds: Flourishing in part because of earlier NPS efforts to exterminate predators like cougars and wolves (see 'Return of the Wolf,' later), they are now causing friction with ranchers outside the park.

Climate

Yellowstone has a humid continental climate with lots of unpredictable and extreme weather. Wind, rain and lightning storms are common and can occur at any time: The park has had huge snowstorms on July 4, and has recorded a January temperature of 50°F. Visitors should check current weather conditions and be prepared for any type of weather at any time of year. Most visitors come in summer, when daylight remains until about 9:30 pm, allowing ample time for late-afternoon and evening excursions. However, Yellowstone has much to offer in any season.

Average high temperatures in April and May range from 40°F to 50°F, with low temperatures ranging from 0°F to -20°F. In late May and June average high temperatures are from 60°F to 70°F. Summer high temperatures at lower elevations are usually around 70°F, and occasionally reach 80°F, with low temperatures ranging from 40°F to 30°F. Temperatures are 10°F to 20°F cooler at high elevations. The mean monthly temperature, however, is 50°F.

Average high temperatures in fall are 40°F to 60°F, with low temperatures ranging from 20°F to 0°F. Winter high temperatures average 0°F, but occasionally rise to 20°F, with low temperatures ranging from 0°F to subzero. Occasionally a warm chinook westerly wind blows in over the Rockies and raises winter high temperatures to 40°F, melting the snowpack. More often the wind-chill factor intensifies because of cold winter winds.

The annual rainfall varies with the park's topography, ranging from 10 inches in the north to about 80 inches in the southwest. Snow lingers into April and May. June is usually rainy. July and August are drier, but afternoon thunderstorms are not uncommon. In fall and winter, snowstorms occur with increasing frequency. The average winter snowfall is 150 inches, with 200 to 400 inches at the higher elevations.

Flora

Yellowstone's wide variety of habitats supports a diversity of plants. More than 900 native (and 185 nonnative) plant species have been identified in the park. Aquatic grasses and plants thrive in the marshes, rivers and lakes. A large community of algae, along with plants like the yellow monkey flower, flourishes in and around geothermal features. The sparsely vegetated northern desert (around Mammoth Hot Springs) supports grasses, sagebrush and Rocky Mountain juniper. Lower-elevation mixed sagebrush and grasslands (such as the Hayden and Pelican valleys) are filled with wildflowers, grasses and shrubs and have relatively warm, dry weather.

Douglas fir, quaking aspen, shrubs and berry bushes blanket the mixed forests from 6000 to 7000 feet between Mammoth Hot Springs and Roosevelt Junction. Lodgepole pine forests, which range from 7600 to 8400 feet (for example, along Yellowstone Lake), cover 60% of the park's broad plateaus and compose 80% of the park's forests. At elevations of more than 8400 feet (at the base of Mt Washburn and along Yellowstone Lake) the forests are predominantly Engelmann spruce and sub-alpine fir, mixed with lodgepole pine, which shades the spruce and fir.

Above the tree line, at more than 10,000 feet (Mt Washburn's summit), is alpine tundra that supports lichen, sedges, grasses and flowers like alpine buttercup and phlox.

Fauna

The Greater Yellowstone ecosystem sustains the largest concentration of free-roaming native wildlife in the lower 48 states. The park is home to 50 mammal species, including seven species of native hoofed mammals (ungulates): persistent Yellowstone bison (buffaloes), bugling Rocky Mountain elks, drooling moose, hardy Rocky Mountain bighorn sheep, long-eared mule deer, fleet-footed pronghorn antelope and spry mountain goats. Burly black bears and around 350 endangered grizzly bears also call Yellowstone home. Other notable species include red foxes, at least 13 recovering packs of gray wolves, threatened Canadian lynx, wily coyotes and stealthy mountain lions.

The spectacular Rocky Mountain trumpeter swans, the most notable of Yellowstone's 311 documented feathered species, are hardy enough to winter here, but their numbers are declining. It has proved difficult to wean them from winter feeding, and Canadian trumpeter populations have crowded them out. Other large birds include ospreys, resurgent peregrine falcons, majestic great blue herons, sandhill cranes, golden eagles, recovering bald eagles, honking Canada geese and white pelicans. Smaller birds like flighty ouzels (dippers), pesky magpies and yellow-headed blackbirds abound.

In marshland and aquatic areas look for bald eagles, beavers and moose, and trout in fast-flowing streams. Moose favor flat meadows near streams with protective cover like pine forest and willow shrubs. Such areas include Canyon Country and the Lewis River south of Lewis Lake. Bison, elks and mule deer frequent geothermal areas. Bison are found in three main areas of the park: Lamar Valley, Pelican Valley at the north end of Yellowstone Lake, and the corridor over Mary Mountain between Hayden Valley and Lower Geyser Basin along the Firehole River. August is rutting season.

The northern desert teems with bighorn sheep, elks, mule deer and pronghorn antelope. The sagebrush and grasslands support pronghorn antelope, elks, bison, badgers, Uinta ground squirrels, pikas and yellow-bellied marmots. Coyotes, elks, mule deer and bobcats roam in mixed forests. Elks also roam along the edge of forests; the largest herd is west of Madison Campground and September to mid-October is their rutting season. In lodgepole forests look for bears, squirrels, snowshoe hare and porcupines. The last two also inhabit the spruce and fir forests. Grizzly bear habitat is open meadows and grasslands near whitebark and lodgepole pines. Stay alert throughout the park and recognize when you are in bear habitat. Yellow-bellied

Return of the Wolf

Gray wolves (Canis lupus), the ultimate symbol of wilderness, have been a barometer of the NPS wildlife-management policy in Yellowstone National Park. At first strongly protected, they were then deliberately eradicated, then reintroduced in 1995 under considerable controversy and, at the time of this writing, have multiplied and spread and are denning in Grand Teton National Park. They are often spotted in Jackson National Elk Refuge, where they feast on elk carcasses.

The gray wolf flourished in the late 19th century when livestock replaced bison herds in the Great Plains ecology, thereby increasing the wolves' food supply. Wolves continued to inhabit the Greater Yellowstone region after the creation of the national park in 1872 and the institution of US Army administration. The US Army protected the park's fauna, including predators like the wolf and puma. The creation of the NPS in 1916 paradoxically led to the wolf's extinction within a few years under misguided predator control policies intended to protect game like elk. The last gray wolf den was destroyed near Tower Falls in 1923. Under these policies, armed NPS rangers eradicated wolves and pumas, thereby allowing game populations to increase to unsustainable levels. The size of elk herds was controlled only by starvation or by farcical (if not tragic) approaches like the slaughter at Gardiner, MT, where hunters waited just outside the park boundary to blast away as the unwary animals left protected territory.

Recognizing the need for a natural sustainable control regime, the NPS made plans to introduce Canadian wolves. Ranchers in the surrounding region were predictably suspicious of reintroduction, claiming that the carnivore would reduce game populations and that adequate compensation for livestock killed by wolves was unlikely. They also argued that the wolf had already returned to the park, though some reported sightings may have been mistaken. The gray wolf, 26 to 34 inches high at the shoulder, 5 to 6 feet long (from nose to tail) and 70 to 120 lbs, is much more imposing than the smaller coyote, but inexperienced viewers could easily confuse the two from a distance.

The USFWS, NPS and USFS proposed a compromise, revising the wolves' status from 'endangered' to 'threatened,' thereby giving ranchers the right to shoot any wolves attacking their livestock. In February 1995, they introduced 14 wolves in acclimation pens in the Lamar Valley. As of December 2000, at least 25 wolf packs totaling more than 200 animals were resident in Yellowstone National Park, north-central Idaho and western Montana. The organization Defenders of Wildlife continues to reimburse ranchers for livestock depredation. By 2001 the gray wolf population stabilized and is soon to be removed from the list of threatened species.

marmots and bighorn sheep live in the alpine tundra.

YELLOWSTONE NATIONAL PARK

Established on March 1, 1872, this was the world's first national park. It was created to preserve the area's unique geologic features: the geothermal phenomena, the Grand Canyon of the Yellowstone, the fossil forests and Yellowstone Lake. Yellowstone also harbors the largest concentration of wildlife in the lower 48 states, and its alpine lakes, rivers and waterfalls are world renowned.

Five distinct regions comprise the 3472-sq-mile park (starting clockwise from the north): Mammoth, Roosevelt, Canyon, Lake and Geyser Countries. In 1912 National Geographic published its first article about Yellowstone, recommending that visitors allow 5½ days to visit. The same holds true today, although it's easy to spend more time. This cornucopia of natural features attracts up to 30,000 visitors daily, and more than 3 million visitors annually. Ironically, the park's great appeal threatens to destroy the very features that attract such numbers.

Yellowstone National Park is in northwestern Wyoming, with small portions extending into eastern Idaho and southwestern Montana. The park is circumscribed by the Gallatin Range and Gallatin National Forest to the northwest, the Madison Plateau and the Targhee National Forest to the southwest, the Teton Range and Grand Teton National Park to the south, the Bridger-Teton and Shoshone National Forests to the southeast, the Absaroka Mountains to the northeast and the rugged Absaroka-Beartooth Wilderness to the north.

The Continental Divide zigzags through the southwest quadrant of the park, trending east-west. Areas north of the Continental Divide drain into the Yellowstone River, areas south into the Snake River. The lowest point is near the North Entrance (5314 feet), the highest point is Eagle Peak (11,358 feet), on the eastern boundary. Yellowstone's large Central Plateau (mostly above 7000 feet) is in one of the world's largest volcanic calderas, bisected by the Yellowstone River.

Volcanic activity characterizes Yellowstone National Park: Catastrophic eruptions occurred here about 2 million, 1.2 million and most recently about 590,000 years ago. The last eruption emptied an underground magma chamber, spewing 240 cubic miles of debris. The resulting collapse of the chamber created the 28-mile by 47-mile **Yellowstone caldera** in the central and southern portions of the park. Lava eventually filled the caldera. Other lava flows created numerous lakes and the 20-mile-long **Grand Canyon of the Yellowstone**. The canyon was later blocked three times by glaciers. Each time melting glaciers created outburst floods that deepened the canyon. It reached its present form only about 10,000 years ago.

The Yellowstone River now flows through the canyon, which ranges from 800 to 1200 feet in depth and 1500 to 4000 feet in width. Its yellowish volcanic-rock walls are comprised mainly of rhyolite, the lava form of granite. **Yellowstone Lake** is one of North America's highest freshwater lakes,

at 7733 feet. It's also one of the world's largest alpine lakes, at 136 sq miles, covering part of the Yellowstone caldera. It has 110 miles of shoreline and its greatest depth is 390 feet. Volcanic activity also created unique fossil forests, some as old as 50 million years, in the northern portion of the park.

The park has some 10,000 geothermal features, including 200 to 250 active geysers, more than all other geothermal areas on the planet combined. Magma, the earth's molten rock, is closer to the surface here than anywhere else on earth – just 3 to 5 miles underground. Its heat fuels these geothermal features. The role of this and similar hot spots in mountain building, plate tectonics and the extinction of the dinosaurs is the subject of considerable research and speculation. The bulging of twin magma chambers on the rim of the Yellowstone caldera indicates possible future eruptions – but not for another 10,000 years or so.

Orientation

The park has five entrance stations. The historic arched North Entrance (5314 feet), on US 89 near Gardiner, MT, is the only one open year-round. The other four are typically open early May to late October, weather permitting: the Northeast Entrance (7365 feet), on US 212 near Cooke City, MT; the East Entrance (6951 feet), on US 14/16/20 at the head of the Wapiti Valley; the South Entrance (6886 feet), on US 89/191/287 north of Grand Teton National Park; and the West Entrance (6667 feet), on US 20/191/287 near West Yellowstone, MT. Roads named for each entrance lead from it to the main road through the park, the Grand Loop Rd.

USGS topographic maps ($5) are readily available, but hikers may prefer either the Trails Illustrated 1:168,500 *Yellowstone National Park* ($3) from Earthwalk Press (☎ 800-828-6277) or the 1:106,250 *Hiking Map & Guide: Yellowstone National Park* ($10), both with 80-foot contour intervals. Both maps indicate areas burned in the 1988 fires, but Earthwalk Press' map divides these areas into canopy and mixed burns.

YELLOWSTONE NATIONAL PARK

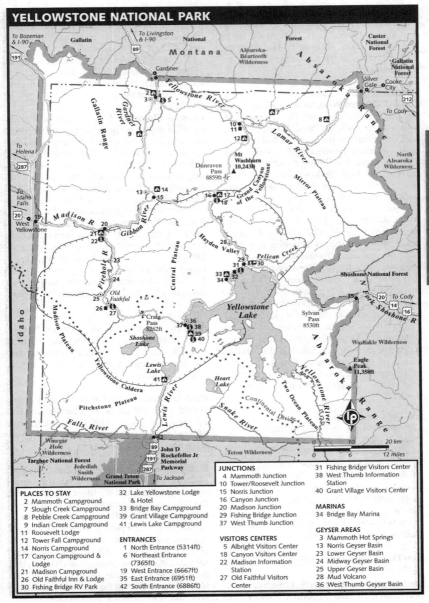

PLACES TO STAY
2 Mammoth Campground
5 Slough Creek Campground
8 Pebble Creek Campground
11 Indian Creek Campground
11 Roosevelt Lodge
12 Tower Fall Campground
14 Norris Campground
17 Canyon Campground & Lodge
21 Madison Campground
26 Old Faithful Inn & Lodge
30 Fishing Bridge RV Park
32 Lake Yellowstone Lodge & Hotel
33 Bridge Bay Campground
39 Grant Village Campground
41 Lewis Lake Campground

ENTRANCES
1 North Entrance (5314ft)
6 Northeast Entrance (7365ft)
19 West Entrance (6667ft)
35 East Entrance (6951ft)
42 South Entrance (6886ft)

JUNCTIONS
4 Mammoth Junction
10 Tower/Roosevelt Junction
15 Norris Junction
16 Canyon Junction
20 Madison Junction
29 Fishing Bridge Junction
37 West Thumb Junction

VISITORS CENTERS
5 Albright Visitors Center
18 Canyon Visitors Center
22 Madison Information Station
27 Old Faithful Visitors Center

31 Fishing Bridge Visitors Center
38 West Thumb Information Station
40 Grant Village Visitors Center

MARINAS
34 Bridge Bay Marina

GEYSER AREAS
3 Mammoth Hot Springs
13 Norris Geyser Basin
23 Lower Geyser Basin
24 Midway Geyser Basin
25 Upper Geyser Basin
28 Mud Volcano
36 West Thumb Geyser Basin

The Trails Illustrated map is available in English, German, French, Spanish and Japanese. Other Trails Illustrated maps (1:83,333) cover Mammoth Hot Springs, Old Faithful, the Tower/Canyon area and Yellowstone Lake.

Information

Tourist Offices Write to the National Park Service, Visitor Services Office, Box 168, Yellowstone National Park, WY 82190, for a park information packet. The Yellowstone National Park headquarters (☎ 307-344-7381 for office and 24-hour recorded information), at Fort Yellowstone, Mammoth Hot Springs, is open 9 am to 6 pm daily; their Web site is at www.nps.gov/yell.

Amfac Parks & Resorts (☎ 307-344-7311), Reservations Dept, Box 165, Yellowstone National Park, WY 82190-0165, is the concessionaire for park activities, as well as camping and accommodations.
Web site: www.travelyellowstone.com

Yellowstone's visitors centers and information stations are usually open 9 am to 6 pm daily, with extended hours from 8 am to 8 pm in summer. Most are closed or are open only for shortened hours Labor Day to Memorial Day; Albright Visitors Center is open year-round and Old Faithful Visitors Center is open in winter. Check the park newspaper for current hours of operation. The visitors centers and information stations are:

Albright Visitors Center
   Mammoth Country (☎ 307-344-2263)
Canyon Visitors Center
   Canyon Country (☎ 307-242-2550)
Fishing Bridge Visitors Center
   Lake Country (☎ 307-242-2450)
Grant Village Visitors Center
   Lake Country (☎ 307-242-2650)
Old Faithful Visitors Center
   Geyser Country (☎ 307-545-2750)
Madison Information Station
   Geyser Country
West Thumb Information Station
   Lake Country

Daily ranger-led activity schedules are posted on their bulletin boards. Visitors with

disabilities should pick up a park brochure describing accessible facilities and attractions, or contact the Special Populations Coordinator (☎ 307-344-2019).

The West Yellowstone Chamber of Commerce (☎ 406-646-7701) has a helpful national-park counter where you can purchase entrance permits.

Fees & Permits All park entrances are open 24 hours daily, although some roads and entrances are closed to motor vehicles in winter (see Road & Weather Conditions, below). Entry reservations are not necessary, but a park entrance permit is. Permits, available at all five park entrance stations (credit cards accepted) and valid for seven days for both Yellowstone and Grand Teton National Parks, cost $20/private (noncommercial) vehicle, $15/person for individuals entering by motorcycle or snowmobile and $10/person for individuals entering by bicycle, skis or on foot. Keep the entrance fee receipt for reentry. An annual Yellowstone and Grand Teton National Parks pass costs $40.

Money ATMs are at the Canyon Lodge, Lake Yellowstone Hotel and Old Faithful Inn. The front desks of all park accommodations exchange foreign currency 8 am to 5 pm weekdays.

Post & Communications The only year-round post office is at Mammoth Hot Springs (zip code 82190). Seasonal post offices are at Canyon, Lake and Grant Villages and Old Faithful.

Bookstores The nonprofit Yellowstone Association (☎ 307-344-2293) supports educational, historical and scientific programs via the Yellowstone Institute. Annual memberships start at $30. It operates bookstores (usually 9 am to 5 pm) at the park's visitors centers, information stations and Norris Geyser Basin that sell books, maps and various informative pamphlets (50¢) on the park's main attractions; these are also available in weatherproof boxes at the sites.
Web site: www.yellowstoneassociation.org

Showers & Laundry Canyon Village, Fishing Bridge RV Park and Grant Village (see Places to Stay, later) have laundry and showers; Old Faithful Lodge has showers only; and Lake Lodge has laundry only. All facilities close in winter. Showers cost $3.50, towel and soap included.

Road & Weather Conditions Dial ☎ 307-344-2114 to check road and weather conditions prior to your visit, as road construction, rock or mud slides and snow can close park entrances and roads at any time. Entrances and roads are generally closed to motor vehicles in winter (mid-November to mid-March). However, the North Entrance is open year-round, as is the Grand Loop Rd between Mammoth and Tower-Roosevelt junctions and the Northeast Entrance Rd between Tower-Roosevelt Junction and Cooke City, MT. (US 212, however, closes mid-October to Memorial Day between Cooke City and Red Lodge, MT.)

The first roads to open, in mid-April, are the West Entrance Rd and the following sections of the Grand Loop Rd: Mammoth Hot Springs to Norris Junction, Norris Junction to Madison Junction and Madison Junction to Old Faithful. The South and East entrances, the Grand Loop Rd over Craig Pass (8262 feet) between West Thumb Junction and Old Faithful and the East Entrance Rd typically open in early May. The Grand Loop Rd between Tower and Canyon junctions over Dunraven Pass (8859 feet) usually opens by Memorial Day.

Publications The *Yellowstone Journal* (☎ 307-332-2323, 800-656-8762) is an independent tourist-oriented publication that provides extensive information; check it out at www.yellowstonepark.com. Amfac's free *Yellowstone Guide* has current activity, accommodations and other vital visitor information. *Inside Greater Yellowstone*, published by the Bozeman-based Greater Yellowstone Coalition (☎ 406-586-1593), advocates regional environmental protection and restoration; its Web site is at www.greateryellowstone.org. Browsing the *Yellowstone Net News* is a good way to survey the scene from a safe distance; www.yellowstone.net/newspaper.

Upon entry, visitors receive a free map and copy of the park's seasonal newspaper, *Yellowstone Today*, with a useful orientation map and schedule of the ranger-led activities, special events, exhibits and educational activities.

Medical Services Yellowstone Park Medical Services operates three clinics: Mammoth Hot Springs Clinic (☎ 307-344-7965), Old Faithful Clinic (☎ 307-545-7325) and Lake Hospital (☎ 307-242-7241), near the Lake Yellowstone Hotel, the latter of which offers 24-hour services. All are open 8:30 am to 5 pm daily in summer; Mammoth Hot Springs Clinic is open year-round. NPS emergency medical technicians and medics (☎ 307-344-2132) are on call 24 hours a day, year-round.

Dangers & Annoyances Most hiccups in Yellowstone stem from inappropriate visitor behavior around wildlife. Some folks don't realize that all of Yellowstone's animals are wild and potentially dangerous. Mom says: Do not harass, feed or approach wildlife. Stay at least 100 yards away from bears and at least 25 yards away from other wildlife; it's illegal to approach any closer. The wise learn to recognize bear habitat and exercise extreme caution – every year the cute grizzlies maul a few cute visitors. Keep campsites spotless. Lock all foods out of sight inside your vehicle or in bearproof containers. Otherwise, suspend food from trees out of the bears' reach. Do not hike alone or after dusk, stay on designated trails and make noise to alert bears to your presence. (See 'Bears' in the Facts for the Visitor chapter and 'Please Don't Feed the Bears' in the Montana chapter.) Bison, which can weigh 2000 pounds and sprint at 30mph, actually injure (gore) more visitors than bears do. Read *Death in Yellowstone,* by park archivist Lee Whittlesey (Court Wayne Press, 1995) for all the gory (ouch!) details.

WYOMING

Stay on existing boardwalks and maintain a safe distance from all geothermal features. Thin crusts can break, giving way to boiling water. Keep children and pets, where permitted, on a short leash. If either fall in, don't go after them!

Burned in the 1988 and 2000 fires, many dead trees, or 'snags,' remain standing. Snags tend to fall down when it's windy. Avoid leaning against damaged trees, and watch and listen for falling timmmmm-ber in campgrounds and when hiking through burned areas.

Safe driving is as essential as safe sex. Rubbernecking (and gabbing on the cell phone) while watching wildlife is a common cause of traffic jams. Pull completely off the road if you must gawk. Needless to say, don't abandon your vehicle in the middle of the road while in hot pursuit of that rutting elk snapshot. The park's speed limit is generally 45 mph, but your results may vary. Tumble dry low, steam iron.

Grand Loop Road Scenic Drive

Conceived by Lt Daniel C Kingman in 1886 and named by writer Harry W Frantz in 1923, the 142-mile, figure-8 Grand Loop Rd passes most of the park's major attractions. The 12-mile Norris-Canyon Rd links Norris and Canyon junctions, dividing the Grand Loop Rd into two shorter loops: the 96-mile Lower (South) Loop and the 70-mile Upper (North) Loop. Allow at least a day to drive the loop, if not two or more.

A clockwise drive from the North Entrance begins at Mammoth Hot Springs (6239 feet). Head east to Tower-Roosevelt Junction, then go south and cross the Dunraven Pass (8859 feet) to Canyon Junction. Dunraven Pass offers awesome views of the Absaroka and Teton ranges and the Grand Canyon of the Yellowstone. Continue south along the Yellowstone River through Hayden Valley to Fishing Bridge Junction (7792 feet), skirt Yellowstone Lake's northern shore to West Thumb Junction, then head west and cross Craig Pass (8262 feet) to Old Faithful. Turning north, follow the Firehole River to Madison Junction (6806 feet). The road heads northeast through the

Gibbon River Canyon to Norris Junction, where it turns north to Mammoth Hot Springs. (See Organized Tours, later, for Grand Loop Rd sightseeing tours.)

Activities

The following paragraphs provide introductory information, including permits and regulations, for activities that are possible in the geographic areas of Yellowstone National Park. Refer to the respective sections for details. The pamphlets mentioned are free from any visitors center.

Backpacking Backpackers, as well as those traveling by canoe and on horseback, can explore Yellowstone's backcountry from almost 100 trailheads that give access to 1200 miles of trails. The 150-mile Howard Eaton Trail, named for a famous Bighorn Mountain guide, is the park's longest trail. A free backcountry use permit, available at visitors centers and ranger stations, is required for overnight trips. Backcountry camping is allowed in some 300 designated sites. The backcountry use permit is site specific and states where you must camp. About half of backcountry sites can be reserved by mail (see Information, earlier); a $15 reservation fee applies regardless of the number of nights. Backcountry use permits are issued no more than 48 hours in advance on a first-come, first-served walk-in basis for the remaining backcountry sites. At higher elevations, trails are often snow-covered until late July.

Hiking & Pack Trips Horsepacking parties must obtain a backcountry use permit (see Backpacking, above) for overnight trips. For day trips a day horse-use permit, also available at most ranger stations, is required. The 'Horsepacking in Yellowstone' pamphlet details regulations.

Corrals at Mammoth Hot Springs (near the Lower Terraces), Roosevelt Lodge and just south of Canyon Junction (along the west side of Grand Loop Rd) offer guided one-hour ($20) and two-hour ($30) horseback rides, which depart every couple of hours 8 am to 7 pm daily mid-May to late September.

Fishing Seven pan-fryable fish species swim Yellowstone's waters: cutthroat, rainbow, brown, brook and lake trout; Arctic grayling; and mountain whitefish. The useful 'Fishing Regulations' pamphlet details the park's complex rules and regulations. The fishing season is usually from the first Saturday of Memorial Day weekend to the first Sunday in November, except for streams flowing into Yellowstone Lake and some tributaries of the Yellowstone River, which open July 15. The Yellowstone River through Hayden Valley and some other rivers are closed to fishing; others may close during the season due to bear activity.

A fishing permit is required for anglers age 16 and older. It costs $10 for 10 days or $20 for the season; nonfee permits are required for anglers ages 12 to 15. Permits are available from ranger stations, visitors centers and general stores. A boating permit (see below) is required for float tubes, which are allowed only on the Lewis River between Lewis and Shoshone Lakes. These permits are available from the South Entrance, Lewis Lake Campground, Grant Village Backcountry Office, Bridge Bay Marina and Lake Ranger Station.

Boating Boating is permitted May 1 to November 1, although some areas may close during the season. Motorized vessels are allowed only on Lewis Lake and parts of Yellowstone Lake. (Unpredictable weather and high wind on Yellowstone Lake's open water can capsize a small vessel: Be cautious and recognize that hypothermia sets in quickly in the lake's 45°F waters.) Sylvan, Eleanor and Twin Lakes and Beach Springs Lagoon are closed to boating. All streams in the park and the Yellowstone River are also closed to boating, except on the Lewis River between Lewis and Shoshone Lakes, where hand-propelled vessels are allowed. Launching is permitted only at these designated sites: Bridge Bay, Grant Village (opens mid-June) and Lewis Lake. Hand-carried vessels may launch at Sedge Bay.

Study the 'Briefed Boating Regulations' pamphlet before embarking.

A boating permit is required for all vessels, including float tubes (see Fishing, above). Permits for motorized vessels cost $10/week or $20/year and are available from Canyon Visitors Center, Bridge Bay Marina, Grant Village Visitors Center, Lewis Lake Campground and the South Entrance. Permits for nonmotorized vessels cost $10/year or $5/week and are available from Albright Visitors Center, the Northeast Entrance and Bechler Ranger Station.

Bicycling Bicycling is possible year-round, but late April to October is when the park's roads, which range from 5300 feet to 8860 feet, are usually snow-free. Cyclists may ride on all public roads and a few designated service roads but are banned from trails and backcountry areas. Most roads are rough and narrow and do not have shoulders: Expect careless drivers and wide RVs. Snowbanks cover many roadsides through June, making cycling more challenging.

The 'Bicycling in Yellowstone National Park' brochure has a map showing suggested routes, such as the 3-mile unpaved climb from the Chittenden Rd trailhead to Mt Washburn's summit (10,243 feet). Bicycle repairs, parts and rentals are not available inside the park; it's typically 20 to 30 miles between services.

Skiing & Snowmobiling Most park trails are not groomed, but unplowed roads and trails are open for cross-country skiing. Some roads are groomed for snowmobiles and other snow vehicles. A backcountry use permit (see Backpacking, earlier) is required for overnight trips. Such trips require extra caution, as streams and geothermal areas can be hidden by snow: Carry a map and compass when you venture off designated trails or roads.

More than a dozen outfitters offer ski trips, and another 20 outfitters rent snowmobiles and offer guided tours. Most are based in Moran, Cody, Jackson or Tetonia, ID, and Bozeman or West Yellowstone, MT.

WYOMING

Organized Tours

Guided bus tours operate in summer on Grand Loop Rd. Amfac (tel 307-344-7311) runs three daily tours: the ambitious 10-hour **Yellowstone in a Day** from Gardiner, MT, or Mammoth Hot Springs ($35/18 adults/children 12 to 16) early June to late September; the 8-hour **Washburn Expedition**, departing Lake Yellowstone Hotel and Fishing Bridge RV Park ($30/16) or Canyon Lodge ($25/13) mid-June to late September; and the 8-hour **Circle of Fire** ($32/17), departing Old Faithful Inn, Grant Village, Lake Yellowstone Hotel, Fishing Bridge RV Park and Canyon Lodge, mid-May to mid-October. Less-grueling three- to four-hour Lamar Valley **wildlife excursions** ($22/11) and **photo safaris** ($32) depart daily from several locations. Independent outfitters offer similar tours at slightly higher rates:

Buffalo Bus Co
(☎ 406-646-9353, 800-426-7669)
415 Yellowstone Ave, West Yellowstone, MT
Web site: www.yellowstonevacations.com/
buffalo

Gray Line of Yellowstone
(☎ 307-733-4325, 800-443-6133 in summer,
☎ 406-646-9374, 800-523-3102 in winter)
1580 W Martin Lane, Jackson, WY
Web site: www.graylineyellowstone.com

Greyhound Bus Lines
Bozeman, MT (☎ 406-587-3110)
Livingston, MT (☎ 406-222-2231)
Idaho Falls, ID (☎ 208-522-0912)
West Yellowstone, MT (☎ 406-646-7666)
Web site: www.greyhound.com

Mammoth Country

Mammoth Country is renowned for its geothermal areas, Mammoth Hot Springs and Norris Geyser Basin, its fossil forests and its numerous lakes and creeks, towered over by the Gallatin Range.

Orientation Mammoth Country is in Yellowstone's northwest corner. The North Entrance Rd meets the Grand Loop Rd at Mammoth Junction, just beyond Mammoth Hot Springs; the Grand Loop Rd leads east to Tower-Roosevelt Junction and south to Norris Junction. From Norris Junction, the

Norris-Canyon Rd goes east to Canyon Junction, and the Grand Loop Rd continues southwest through the Gibbon Canyon to Madison Junction.

Fort Yellowstone Mammoth Hot Springs was known as Fort Yellowstone from 1886 to 1918, when the US Army managed the park. The Mammoth Visitors Center Museum (☎ 307-344-2263), adjacent to Albright Visitors Center, features 19th-century watercolors by Thomas Moran and B&W photographs by William Henry Jackson, both of whom accompanied the 1871 Hayden expedition, and exhibits from the park's prehistory to the present.

Mammoth Hot Springs The imposing Lower and Upper Terraces of Mammoth Hot Springs (elevation 6239 feet) are the product of dissolved subterranean limestone deposited when the spring waters cooled on contact with the atmosphere. The terraces owe their colors to the bacteria and algae that flourish in the warm waters. Rangers lead area hikes and give natural-history talks.

Two hours worth of boardwalks wend their way around the Lower Terraces and connect to the Upper Terrace Loop. The rutting Rocky Mountain elks that sometimes lounge on expanding Opal Terrace are quite a curious site. Ornate travertine formations characterize colorful Minerva Spring. Nearby is the phallic, dormant hot-spring cone called Liberty Cap.

A less stimulating 1½-mile paved one-way road loops counterclockwise around the Upper Terrace; no vehicles longer than 25 feet are permitted. The Overlook affords impressive views of the Lower Terraces and Fort Yellowstone. A 500-foot boardwalk leads past Canary Spring, yellowed by sulfur-depositing bacteria. All other features are visible from the road.

Blacktail Plateau Drive This scenic 7-mile detour provides good glimpses of wildflowers (in June and July), the 1988 wildfire aftermath and, in September, fall color. The rough, unpaved road begins south of Grand

Million-Dollar Microbes

In 1966 microbiologist Dr Thomas D Brock discovered *Thermus aquaticus*, or 'Taq,' the hot-water microbe that creates an enzyme commonly used in DNA fingerprinting. The discovery of this microbe in the hot springs at Yellowstone National Park began an ongoing debate about 'bioprospecting' and the commercial use of national-park resources. The NPS has customarily issued free permits for scientific research teams, but microbes harvested for free have generated millions of dollars of revenue for the biotechnology industry. The Taq enzyme alone generates over $100 million a year. Until recently, no legal mechanism existed for the NPS or the park to receive royalty payments for such scientific discoveries, but in 1997 a California-based biotechnology firm made the first royalty agreement with the park for harvesting microbes. Experts acknowledge that as much as 99% of Yellowstone's microbes have yet to be discovered.

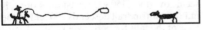

Loop Rd between Mammoth and Tower-Roosevelt junctions; it is passable by all vehicles.

Norris Junction The Norris area was a former US Army outpost. The historic log Norris Soldier Station (1908) houses the Museum of the National Park Ranger (☎ 307-344-7353). Exhibits detail the evolution of the ranger's profession from its military origins. The Gibbon River flows through meadows in front of the building, making it a pleasant place to look for wildlife. The museum is open 9 am to 5 pm in summer.

Norris Geyser Basin North and west of Norris Junction, the Norris Geyser Basin is North America's most volatile and oldest continuously active geothermal area. It's also the site of Yellowstone's hottest recorded temperatures, as three intersecting faults underlain by magma come within 2

miles of the surface. Its geothermal features change seasonally: Clear pools transform into spouting geysers or mud pots and vice versa. Barely 1000 feet below the surface, scientific instruments have recorded temperatures as high as 459°F.

Norris Geyser Basin has two distinct areas: Porcelain Basin and Back Basin. Overlooking Porcelain Basin is the **Norris Museum** (☎ 307-344-2812), which became the park's first in 1930. Open 9 am to 5 pm mid-May to early June, 8 am to 8 pm in summer and 9 am to 5 pm through September. One mile of boardwalks loops through the open Porcelain Basin, the park's hottest exposed basin, past the Crackling Lake and Whirligig Geysers. Two miles of boardwalks and gentle trails snake through forested Back Basin. Here **Steamboat Geyser**, the world's tallest active geyser, skyrockets infrequently up to 400 feet. Dramatic **Echinus Geyser**, the largest acidic geyser, erupts regularly (every 35 to 75 minutes), with eruptions reaching up to 60 feet and sometimes continuing for more than an hour. Rangers lead walks of Norris Geyser Basin that depart the Norris Museum several times daily.

Hiking & Backpacking The **Beaver Ponds Trail**, a 5-mile loop with gentle climbs and considerable wildlife, begins near Liberty Cap at Mammoth Hot Springs, ascends north through the fir and spruce forests along Clematis Creek and in 2½ miles reaches beaver ponds in meadows, where beavers are usually active in the morning and evening.

West of Mammoth is Sepulcher Mountain (9652 feet). The loop-hike via **Howard Eaton Trail** climbs 3400 feet to its summit and returns via Snow Pass.

The **Wraith Falls Trail** begins at the pullout east of Lava Creek Picnic Area, east of Mammoth Junction on the Grand Loop Rd, then follows Lupine Creek to the base of 79-foot Wraith Falls, a 1-mile hike.

The **Bunsen Peak Trail** leads to the summit of Bunsen Peak (8564 feet), south of Mammoth, offering outstanding panoramas of the Gallatin Mountains, Blacktail

Plateau, Swan Lake Flats and the Yellowstone River valley. From Mammoth, go 5 miles south on Grand Loop Rd and turn east onto Old Bunsen Peak Rd to the trailhead. (The road is closed to vehicles, but open to cyclists.) The trail climbs 1300 feet over 2 miles on the Old Bunsen Peak Rd to the top. Return by the same route. If it's not closed because of grizzly bear activity, you can also return via the **Osprey Falls Trail**, which drops 500 feet into the unique rock formations of Sheepwater Canyon, then follows Gardiner River to the base of the 150-foot Osprey Falls.

An appealing longer hike is the 12½-mile **Blacktail Deer Creek Trail**, 7 miles east of Mammoth. It descends 1100 feet from the trailhead north into the Black Canyon of the Yellowstone. After crossing the river, it continues downstream (northwest) to Gardiner, MT, necessitating a vehicle shuttle.

Three longer east-west backpacking routes begin west of Mammoth and lead to US 191 in Montana: The **Bighorn Pass Trail** begins from Indian Creek Campground, while the **Fawn Pass Trail** and **Sportsmen Lake Trail** to its north both begin west of Mammoth. The **Mount Holmes Trail** (10,336 feet) begins south of Indian Creek and heads west to the summit.

Two short trails are near Norris. A 2-mile trail connects Norris Geyser Basin to Norris Campground. A 1-mile trail through open forest leads to Artist Paint Pot, another geothermal area; the trailhead is 4½ miles south of Norris Junction on the Grand Loop Rd.

Roosevelt Country

President Theodore Roosevelt visited this area in 1903 and established the rustic Roosevelt Lodge near Tower-Roosevelt Junction (elevation 6278 feet) in 1906. Visitors wanting a real Wild West experience can still find it here. Fossil forests, the commanding Lamar River Valley and its tributary trout streams and the Absaroka Mountains' craggy peaks are the highlights of the park's most remote, scenic and undeveloped region.

Orientation Roosevelt Country is in the park's northeast corner. The Northeast Entrance Rd, which passes through the Lamar Valley, meets the Grand Loop Rd at Tower-Roosevelt Junction (6278 feet), which then leads west to Mammoth Hot Springs and south to Tower Falls and Canyon Junction. Tower Ranger Station is just west of Tower-Roosevelt Junction. Lamar Ranger Station is at Buffalo Ranch, just off Northeast Entrance Rd. The Yellowstone Institute (see below) and Expedition Yellowstone! are also headquartered here.

Calcite Springs Overlook This worthwhile overlook, 1½ miles south of Tower-Roosevelt Junction, offers vertiginous views of the abysmal Grand Canyon of the Yellowstone (see later).

Tower Falls Two and a half miles south of Tower-Roosevelt Junction, Tower Creek plunges over the 132-foot Tower Fall before joining the Yellowstone River. From a scenic overlook 150 yards past the store, a 1-mile roundtrip trail descends 200 feet to the base of the falls for better views. Stop for ice cream at the top on the way back.

Lamar Valley Elks and bison make the broad Lamar Valley their winter range; it is covered by mixed sage and grasslands, surrounded by rolling hills and guarded by granitic bluffs to the west. Roadside turnouts between Pebble and Slough Creek Campgrounds are also prime wolf-watching spots.

Established in 1907, the nonprofit **Yellowstone Institute** (☎ 307-344-2294) is an educational field program offering one- to five-day outdoor courses in the humanities and cultural and natural history. The historic Buffalo Ranch is the institute's headquarters, where most courses are held from late May to late September (some in January and February). Courses start at $50 to $60 per day, excluding food and accommodations. Buffalo Ranch's log-cabin bunkhouses start at $12. The institute's Web site is at www.yellowstoneassociation.org/institute.

Hiking & Backpacking The 4-mile **Lost Lake Loop** trail begins behind Roosevelt Lodge, passing Lost Lake en route to the petrified tree, from where it descends to the Tower Ranger Station.

From the stagecoach road near Tower-Roosevelt Junction, the **Garnet Hill Trail** is an easy two- to three-hour loop north of the Grand Loop Rd, with a possible extension up Hellroaring Creek. The trailhead can also be reached from the Gravel Pit parking area 3½ miles west of Tower-Roosevelt Junction.

The **Yellowstone River Picnic Area Trail** leads south 2 miles to The Narrows, an area offering spectacular views of the northernmost portion of the Grand Canyon of the Yellowstone. The trailhead is on the Northeast Entrance Rd, 1½ miles east of Tower-Roosevelt Junction. Cross to the south side of the river and follow the trail south past interesting features like Overhanging Cliff and the Basalt Columns. Retrace your steps, or continue east to a petrified forest at Specimen Ridge, making a full-day trip. Alternatively, the **Fossil Forest Trail** leads to Specimen Ridge along an unmaintained route; this trailhead is 4 miles east of Tower-Roosevelt Junction on the Northeast Entrance Rd.

The **Slough Creek Trail**, which begins 0.4 miles before the Slough Creek Campground, is a pleasant hike along a popular fishing stream. It's possible to head east up Elk Tongue Creek, cross Bliss Pass and descend along Pebble Creek to the Pebble Creek Campground. Fording Pebble Creek can be tricky early in the season. Another trailhead from a pullout on the Northeast Entrance Rd 1½ miles south of the Pebble Creek Campground leads 0.6 miles through fir forest to Trout Lake.

An extensive trail network branches off the upper Lamar Valley. The **Lamar River Trail** leaves the Northeast Entrance Rd along Soda Butte Creek, above its confluence with the Lamar River. Other trails lead off this one, heading east to Cache Creek and west to traverse Specimen Ridge and rejoin the trail from The Narrows. The main trail continues south along the Lamar River, ultimately leading toward the Wapiti Valley.

Stagecoach Rides & Cookouts Daily stagecoach rides ($6/5 adults/children) depart mid-June to early September. Old West dinner cookout trips depart via horseback ($50) or horse-drawn wagon ($32) nightly mid-June to mid-September ($28/17); reservations required.

Canyon Country
A series of scenic overlooks and a network of trails along the canyons' rims and interiors highlight the beauty of the Grand Canyon of the Yellowstone. The park's most impressive panoramas extend north from Canyon Junction (elevation 7918 feet) to Tower-Roosevelt Junction. Mud Volcano is Canyon Country's primary geothermal area.

Orientation Canyon Country is in the central part of the park. From Canyon Junction, the cliff-hanging Grand Loop Rd leads 14 miles north over Dunraven Pass (8895 feet) to Tower Falls and Tower-Roosevelt Junction, and 17 miles south through Hayden Valley to Fishing Bridge Junction and Yellowstone Lake. Canyon Village and Canyon Ranger Station are just east of Canyon Junction along North Rim Dr. The Norris-Canyon Rd goes west 12 miles from Canyon Junction over the Central Plateau to Norris Junction.

Grand Canyon of the Yellowstone The Yellowstone River flows north from Yellowstone Lake through Hayden Valley, tumbling over Upper Falls (109 feet) and Lower Falls (308 feet) before dropping into the Grand Canyon of the Yellowstone. Rangers lead excursions and hikes along the North and South Canyon Rims, departing from the Canyon Visitors Center. Bring binoculars to spot osprey that nest in the canyon from late spring until September.

Three scenic overlooks are along the 2½-mile North Rim Dr (one-way beyond Canyon Village): Inspiration, Grandview and Lookout Points. From Glacial Boulder

The Name 'Yellowstone'

Heated water reacting with volcanic rock in the Grand Canyon of the Yellowstone produced the beautifully colored canyon walls. The name 'Yellowstone,' however, did not originate from this canyon, but from the yellow-colored riverbanks near the confluence of the Yellowstone and Missouri Rivers in Montana. It was here that in 1797–98 British fur trader David Thompson used the term 'yellow stone' to describe the area near the Mandan villages of the upper Missouri.

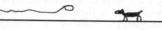

near the Inspiration Point parking lot, the **Cascade Overlook Trail** leads northeast to the Silver Cord Cascade Overlook. Lookout Point offers the best views of the Lower Falls, and an adjacent 0.4-mile trail drops 500 feet to Red Rock for even closer views. A lush three-quarter-mile trail begins at the southernmost parking lot beyond Lookout Point and descends 600 feet to the Brink of the Lower Falls. The **North Rim Trail** links Inspiration Point to the Chittenden Bridge on South Rim Dr. From Inspiration Point the walk is 2½ miles to the Upper Falls Overlook and 3/4 mile farther to the bridge. Upper Falls Overlook is also accessible by road: The turnoff is south of Canyon Junction and Cascade Creek on the Grand Loop Rd.

South Rim Dr leads to the canyon's most spectacular overlook, at Artist Point, passing the Upper Falls Viewpoint en route. **Uncle Tom's Trail**, which begins near the Upper Falls Viewpoint, is a steep route that descends 500 feet to the base of the Lower Falls. The 3¼-mile **South Rim Trail** follows the canyon rim from Chittenden Bridge to Point Sublime via Artist Point, just beyond the halfway point.

Two trails meander through meadows and forests past several small lakes southeast of the South Rim. The **Clear Lake Trail** begins at the parking lot near Upper Falls Viewpoint and skirts Clear Lake before joining the **Ribbon Lake Trail**, which leads to Ribbon Lake and the Silver Cord Cascade.

Hayden Valley The Yellowstone River is broad and shallow as it meanders through the vast grasslands of Hayden Valley. This old lake bed was formed in the last ice age when a glacial outburst flooded the valley. The former lake bed's silt-and-clay soil supports the rich shrubs and grasses favored by bison, but are impermeable to most trees. Trout swim the waters where aquatic vegetation thrives, and geese, white pelicans, ospreys and bald eagles fly overhead. This picturesque, treeless valley is excellent for birdwatching and roadside wildlife viewing but is closed to fishing except for two short catch-and-release stretches. Rangers lead excursions, departing from Canyon Visitors Center.

Mud Volcano Ten miles south of Canyon Junction and 6 miles north of Fishing Bridge Junction, this area contains an assortment of mud pots and other gurgling sulfurous features. A 1-mile boardwalk loop passes Mud Cauldron (whose bubbles indicate escaping gases rather than boiling water), Mud Geyser, Sour Lake (whose foul water is a function of sulfuric acid produced by bacteria), Mud Volcano and the consistently violent Dragon's Mouth. During a series of 1979 earthquakes, the mud pots developed enough heat and gases literally to cook lodgepoles and grasses on some hillsides. Mud Volcano, however, has not erupted since it was first seen by the 1871 USGS expedition. Across the road Sulfur Cauldron has a 1.2 pH level, roughly the equivalent of battery acid. Grizzly bears and bison frequent the area, especially in spring. Rangers lead excursions to Mud Volcano, departing from the Fishing Bridge Visitors Center.

Hiking & Backpacking The descent of **Seven Mile Hole Trail**, on the north side of the Grand Canyon of the Yellowstone, begins off North Rim Dr at Glacial Boulder just before Inspiration Point. The trail follows the canyon rim, offering spectacular views for a few miles before plunging into the canyon. Steep sections of the trail are slippery even when they are dry.

Two trails lead to the summit of Mt Washburn (10,243 feet), northeast of Dunraven Pass. One trailhead is at the parking lot at the end of the unpaved Chittenden Rd, which leaves the Grand Loop Rd north of the pass. Whitebark pine and fir give away quickly to alpine tundra as the trail ascends more than 1000 feet over 2.8 miles to the summit. Return the same way or traverse the peak by descending 3.2 miles to the Dunraven Pass Picnic Area, necessitating a vehicle shuttle. At Mt Washburn's summit are a fire lookout (closed to the public) and a shelter with a telescope. The summit view includes three mountain ranges: Beartooth, Absaroka and Teton. Bighorn sheep roam the hillsides, as do marmots. Allow three to five hours roundtrip. Mt Washburn can also be approached from the east via the longer Seven Mile Hole Trail.

The easy **Cascade Lake Trail** begins from the picnic area of the same name on the Grand Loop Rd 1½ miles north of Canyon Junction. Follow the right fork 2½ miles from the trailhead, which leads steeply through meadows and whitebark pines to Observation Peak (9397 feet). The trail continues past Cascade Lake, where it joins the **Grebe Lake Trail**, which passes Grebe and Wolf Lakes; these are also accessible from trailheads on the Norris-Canyon Rd.

The east-west **Mary Mountain Trail** traverses the Central Plateau, connecting Hayden Valley to Lower Geyser Basin. The trailhead is north of Alum Creek. The **Plateau Trail** traverses the Central Plateau north-south, from the trailhead on Canyon/Norris Rd west of Canyon Junction, and joins the Mary Mountain Trail at Mary Lake.

Lake Country

Yellowstone Lake (7733 feet), the centerpiece of Lake Country, is one of the world's largest alpine lakes, and home to the country's largest inland population of cutthroat trout. The Upper Yellowstone River flows north from the lake through the Hayden Valley to the Grand Canyon of the Yellowstone. In the mountains south of Yellowstone Lake, the mighty Snake River begins its long journey through Wyoming and Idaho to Oregon and the Columbia River. The often Alp-like Absaroka Mountains rise dramatically east and southeast of the lake.

Orientation Lake Country is in the southeast corner of the park. A 22-mile section of the Grand Loop Rd hugs Yellowstone Lake's north and west shoreline between Fishing Bridge Junction at its north end and West Thumb Junction at its west. Fishing Bridge is immediately east of Fishing Bridge Junction along the East Entrance Rd. Lake Village and Bridge Bay are off the Grand Loop Rd just south of Fishing Bridge Junction along Bridge Bay itself. Grant Village, on the lake's West Thumb Bay, is off South Entrance Rd, 2 miles south of the West Thumb Junction. Snake River Ranger Station is adjacent to the South Entrance; there's another ranger station at Bridge Bay.

Yellowstone Lake There's excellent fishing and boating, and the lake is a prime bird and wildlife habitat. Lake Village's Lake Yellowstone Hotel (1890) is on the National Register of Historic Places. Gull Point Dr is a scenic picnic spot and popular fishing area. See native cutthroat trout spawn at the north end of the lake from Fishing Bridge and 3 miles north of the bridge at Le Hardy Rapids. Rangers lead tours of Yellowstone Lake's shoreline from Fishing Bridge Visitors Center.

Bridge Bay Marina The marina offers dock rentals and hourly boat rentals ($6/30 row/outboard). One-hour sightseeing cruises ($9/5 adults/children) of northern Yellowstone Lake operate daily early June to late September. Guided Yellowstone Lake fishing trips ($55/hr with a two-hour minimum) depart from Bridge Bay Marina mid-June to mid-September. The marina area is closed to fishing.

WYOMING

West Thumb Geyser Basin West Thumb is a small volcanic caldera created some 150,000 years ago inside the much larger Yellowstone caldera. Waters from Yellowstone Lake filled it, creating West Thumb Bay, a circular inlet on the lake's western end. West Thumb Geyser Basin, near the West Thumb Junction, has a half-mile shoreline boardwalk loop with a shorter inner loop that passes more than a dozen geothermal features. At Fishing Cone, along the lakeshore, anglers used the infamous 'hook 'n' cook' method to prepare their catch. Abyss Pool is one of the park's deepest springs, while the Thumb Paint Pots are struggling to regain the energy that once catapulted boiling mud 25 feet into the air.

Rangers lead excursions to West Thumb Geyser Basin, departing from Grant Village Visitors Center; the village hugs the south shore of West Thumb Bay and has a boat launch. Nearby are five spawning streams for cutthroat trout that often close in late spring and early summer because of ravenous-bear activity.

Hiking & Backpacking A section of the 150-mile **Howard Eaton Trail** follows the Yellowstone River north from the parking lot east of Fishing Bridge. The **Pelican Creek Trail**, which departs Pelican Creek Bridge 1 mile east of Fishing Bridge Visitors Center, is an easy 1-mile loop through lodgepole forest and across wetlands. Storm Point juts into the northern end of the lake. The 2-mile walk around the point begins near Indian Pond: Here you can look for bison, moose, marmots and waterfowl. For the best views in the area, hike the 3-mile roundtrip **Elephant Back Mountain Trail**. The 800-foot climb begins from the trailhead 1 mile west of Fishing Bridge Junction. The 3-mile **Natural Bridge Trail** starts at the Bridge Bay Marina parking lot; a bicycle path also leads to this feature, which was carved by Bridge Creek. A few miles west of Yellowstone Lake and north of the East Entrance Rd is the **Avalanche Peak Trail**. This steep, unmarked trail climbs more than 2000 feet to Avalanche Peak (10,565 feet), affording excellent lake views.

A 2-mile roundtrip walk climbs 400 feet through meadows to the Yellowstone Lake Overlook with outstanding views of the lake and the Absaroka Mountains. The trailhead, south of West Thumb Junction near the entrance to West Thumb Geyser Basin, heads west off the South Entrance Rd. At the pullout just west of West Thumb Junction is the trailhead for the **Duck Lake Trail**. The half-mile walk to Duck Lake demonstrates the effects of the 1988 fires and offers views of Yellowstone Lake.

South of Grant Village, marshy meadows surround Riddle Lake, a favorite of moose. The trailhead is 3 miles south of Grant Village on the South Entrance Rd, just south of the Continental Divide sign. The 5-mile roundtrip trail traverses the Continental Divide and drops down to the lake.

Geyser Country
Geyser Country has the most geothermal features in the park, concentrated in several adjacent basins. The Firehole River and its tributaries flow through the area, containing 21 of the park's 110 waterfalls. Anticipated eruption times of several geysers are posted at Old Faithful Visitors Center, Old Faithful Lodge and Old Faithful Inn. The Firehole and Madison Rivers offer superb fly-fishing, and the meadows along them support large wildlife populations.

Orientation Geyser Country is in the park's southwest corner. From West Thumb Junction, the Grand Loop Rd goes west 18 miles over Craig Pass (8262 feet) to the Old Faithful area, crossing the Continental Divide twice en route. It then continues along the Firehole River to Madison Junction, from where it heads northeast along the Gibbon River. The West Entrance Rd meets the Grand Loop Rd at Madison Junction.

Upper Geyser Basin This heavily visited basin contains 180 of the park's 200 to 250 geysers, the most famous being geriatric **Old Faithful**. Boardwalks, footpaths and a cycling path along the Firehole River link the five distinct geyser groups, the farthest of which is only 1½ miles from Old Faithful. Historian Daniel Boorstin has suggested that the park's enormous appeal is 'due to the fact that its natural phenomena, which erupt on schedule, come closest to the artificiality of "regular" tourist performances.' Grab some popcorn and check estimated show times on the visitors center board or join a ranger-led interpretive walk in Upper Geyser Basin.

Erupting every 79 minutes or so to impatient (hand clapping is not uncommon) visitors' delight, Old Faithful spouts more than 8000 gallons of water up to 180 feet in the air, but the last time we checked, the old salt was in need of a dose of Viagra. Consistent seepage from neighboring Giantess Geyser (known for infrequent, but violent spurts) and Vault Geyser have created deposits of sinter (geyserite) terraces that look like scaled relief maps. Aurum Geyser resembles a human ear in outline. A short trail goes up to Observation Point on Geyser Hill, looping back to the boardwalks.

Next is Grand Geyser, one of the world's tallest predictable geysers. It spews in bursts every 8 to 12 hours and lasts about 12 minutes. It will often pause after 9 minutes and then restart after a minute or so; the subsequent bursts are typically the most spectacular. Across the river is the less reliable Castle Geyser, which yields ebullitions every 12 to 22 hours.

Boardwalks pass Beauty Pool en route to Giant Geyser, which produces stupendous 250-foot eruptions but may be dormant for years. Nearby Grotto Geyser has smaller but extended emissions, lasting up to 10 hours.

The predictable Daisy Geyser lets loose every 90 to 125 minutes (up to 75 feet), except when nearby Splendid Geyser erupts.

The picturesque Riverside Geyser puts on an amazing show: 20-minute outpourings occur about every six hours. A steamy favorite, well worth the walk, is beautiful Morning Glory Pool.

Old Faithful Inn Seattle architect Robert C Reamer designed the enchanting Old Faithful Inn (1904), a national historic landmark. The log rafters of its lobby rise nearly 90 feet, while the main fireplace chimney contains more than 500 tons of rock. The 2nd-floor observation deck provides views of Old Faithful geyser. It's definitely a worthwhile visit, even for nonguests. Free 45-minute Historic Inn tours depart from the fireplace at 9:30 and 11 am and 2 and 3:30 pm.

Black Sand & Biscuit Basins Black Sand Basin, 1 mile northwest of Old Faithful, and Biscuit Basin, 2 miles farther north, are two interesting roadside thermal areas. The black sand at the former is derived from volcanic glass (obsidian). The latter is best known for biscuitlike deposits surrounding Sapphire Pool, which were destroyed during eruptions after a 1959 earthquake. Trails, each a half-mile long, link Upper Geyser Basin's Daisy Group to both basins; cycling is allowed on the trail to Biscuit Basin.

Firehole Lake Drive Firehole Lake Dr is a one-way, 3-mile road starting 2 miles north of Midway Geyser Basin and about 1 mile south of the Fountain Paint Pot parking lot. It passes several large geysers, including Great Fountain Geyser, which soars up to 200 feet every 11 hours or so, and Firehole Lake, a large hot spring with an average temperature of 158°F.

Midway Geyser Basin Two miles south of the south entrance to Firehole Lake Dr is Midway Geyser Basin. The algae-created indigo waters of the 370-foot-wide Grand Prismatic Spring, the park's largest hot spring, are the key geothermal feature.

Lower Geyser Basin Roughly midway between Madison Junction and Old Faithful, Fountain Paint Pot offers a popular half-mile loop boardwalk through the hot springs and mud pots, which vary in color depending on the presence of bacteria and algae as well as the composition of the surrounding rock. The grassy basin supports the park's largest bison herd.

WYOMING

Firehole Canyon Drive The one-way Firehole Canyon Dr leaves the Grand Loop Rd south of Madison Junction. Dark rhyolite cliffs tower above the free **Firehole Swimming Area**, one of the few locations in the park that's open for swimming.

Hiking & Backpacking Two trailheads lead to 200-foot Fairy Falls, northwest of Midway Geyser Basin, and the popular **Fairy Creek Trail**. First is the Steel Bridge trailhead, 1 mile south of Midway Geyser Basin, which leads 2.6 miles one-way through burned lodgepole pine forest to the falls. Alternatively, follow Fountain Flat Dr, which leaves the Grand Loop Rd at Lower Geyser Basin, to the barricade. Continue walking on the road to its end and then head west to the falls. Retrace your steps from here or continue to Imperial Geyser. Beyond Imperial Geyser, the Fairy Creek Trail heads southwest to meet the Little Firehole River, from where the trail turns sharply east and heads to Biscuit Basin on the Grand Loop Rd. A vehicle shuttle is necessary unless you walk north on another trail along the west side of the Grand Loop Rd back to either trailhead. It's about 10 miles between Imperial Geyser and Biscuit Basin.

The **Mystic Falls Trail** begins at the west end of Biscuit Basin near Avoca Spring and parallels the Little Firehole River. Switchbacks lead to the top of the 70-foot falls, where you can continue to the **Little Firehole Meadows Trail**. To return to Biscuit Basin, take the right fork and descend to an overlook of Upper Geyser Basin; bring binoculars. The loop is about 2½ miles.

The trailhead to Lone Star Geyser is on the Grand Loop Rd 3½ miles east of Old Faithful, near the Kepler Cascades pullout. The trail follows the Firehole River 2½ miles to the 9-foot-high cone-shaped Lone Star Geyser, which erupts every three hours. Bicycles are permitted to the geyser but not beyond.

The **DeLacy Creek Trail** leads to Shoshone Lake, the park's largest backcountry lake. The trailhead is on the Grand Loop Rd, east of Craig Pass near the DeLacy Creek Picnic Area about 9 miles west of West Thumb Junction. The trail is 3 miles one-way to the lake. Alternatively, longer trails lead from Lone Star Geyser to Shoshone Geyser Basin at the west end of the lake, where routes circle the lake.

From the trailhead north of Lewis Lake, about 5 miles south of Grant Village, a 7-mile loop follows the Lewis River Channel between Lewis and Shoshone Lakes. It also links up with the DeLacy Creek and Shoshone Lake trails.

Fishing The Firehole (between Biscuit and Midway Geyser basins), Madison and Gibbon (downstream from Gibbon Falls) Rivers are open only for fly-fishing. (See Activities earlier in the Yellowstone section.)

Places to Stay NPS and private campgrounds, cabins, lodges and hotels are in the park, but in summer high demand for all types of accommodations makes it difficult to find any place to stay without a reservation despite there being 2175 rooms; call Amfac Parks & Resorts (☎ 307-344-7311). Most hotels and cabins are open mid-May to early October, but dates can vary depending on weather.

Camping inside the park is permitted only in 12 designated campgrounds, and is limited to 14 days from June 15 to Labor Day, and 30 days the rest of the year. Checkout time is 10 am, and quiet hours are 8 pm to 8 am. Each campground usually holds a nightly campfire program in its amphitheater. (See Backpacking, earlier, for regulations on backcountry camping.)

Late June to mid-August, it's best to have a reservation or to secure a campsite early in the morning, as all campgrounds are typically full by 11 am. Signboards at park entrances list campground availability; 'full' does not necessarily mean full. Check at the campground for availability or dial ☎ 307-344-2114 for recorded campground info. If, however, you arrive late in the day without a reservation, you are unlikely to find a spot inside the park. Some campsites ($4) are reserved for backpackers and cyclists (without vehicles) at all campgrounds except Slough Creek and Canyon. Alternative USFS campgrounds outside the park also fill up early each day; those nearest to the park fill up first and require driving many miles.

Five of the park's twelve campgrounds ($15/23 tents/RVs) accept reservations:

Bridge Bay Campground (7735 feet) – This is largely an open, shadeless and grassy area surrounded by forest, with 429 sites. Its more desirable and remote tent-only loops (E, F) have a few more trees and offer lovely lake views. Adjacent to the Bridge Bay Marina, it appeals largely to those interested in fishing and boating. Lake Country, along the northwest shore of Yellowstone Lake 3 miles southwest of Lake Village; open late May to late September.

Canyon Campground (7734 feet) – With 271 sites, Canyon offers the most tent-only sites and is also the most densely forested. Its high elevation makes it colder than many other campgrounds. Canyon Country, near Canyon Village and the center of the park; open early June to the middle of September.

Fishing Bridge RV Park (7792 feet) – Only hard-shelled RVs (341 sites) are allowed to camp here because of heavy bear activity. Lake Country, along the north shore of Yellowstone Lake 1 mile east of Fishing Bridge Junction; open mid-May to late September ($25).

Grant Village Campground (7770 feet) – This forested campground (425 sites) is the only one on Yellowstone Lake and has a nearby boat launch. Lake Country, along the west shore of Yellowstone Lake 22 miles north of the South Entrance; open late May to late September.

Madison Campground (6806 feet) – In a sunny, open forest in a broad meadow, Madison has 280 sites. Bison herds and the park's largest elk herd frequent the meadows to its west. Above the banks of the Madison River, it's a good fly-fishing base. Tent-only sites are ideally placed along the river. Geyser Country, west of Madison Junction along the Madison River 14 miles east of the West Entrance, 16 miles north of Old Faithful; open early May to early November.

Seven campgrounds ($10 to $12/23) are available on a first-come, first-served basis:

Indian Creek Campground (7300 feet) – This spot features 75 sites surrounded by moose territory, sparse and somewhat desolate in open forest on a low rise. Generators are not allowed. Mammoth Country, 8 miles south of Mammoth Junction; open early June to mid-September.

Lewis Lake Campground (7779 feet) – Lewis Lake offers 85 sites on a forested rise above the lake. Boat launch provides easy access to Lewis Lake and the Lewis River. Snow often remains here through June because of its high elevation and shaded location, so it may not be the best early-season campground. A few walk-in and tent-only sites are available, generators are not allowed. Geyser Country, about 10 miles north of the South Entrance at the south end of Lewis Lake; open mid-June to early November.

Mammoth Campground (6239 feet) – The park's least attractive campground, this is a barren, dusty sagebrush-covered area with sparse shade. In a hairpin bend in the road below Mammoth Hot Springs, its 85 sites get a lot of road noise, but its relatively low elevation makes it the warmest campground and a good choice for late-season visits. Mammoth Country, near the North Entrance, Mammoth Hot Springs; open early May to mid-October.

Norris Campground (7484 feet) – Here 116 sites nestle in scenic open forest on an idyllic, sunny hill overlooking the Gibbon River and bordering meadows. Nearby are fishing and wildlife-viewing opportunities. Mammoth Country, along Gibbon River north of Norris Junction; open mid-May to late September.

Pebble Creek Campground (6800 feet) – At this spot, 36 remote sites are surrounded on three sides by the distinctive rock faces and rugged cliffs of the Absaroka Mountains, the most dramatic physical setting of the park's campgrounds. It's along the banks of a creek in an open forest in grizzly habitat. Generators are not allowed. Roosevelt Country, near the Northeast Entrance at the lower end of Icebox Canyon; open mid-June to late September.

Slough Creek Campground (6400 feet) – Here, 29 remote sites lie 2.2 miles up an unpaved road in grizzly habitat along a peaceful fishing stream adjacent to meadows. A couple of walk-in sites and easy access to the Slough Creek Trail are available. Generators are not allowed. Roosevelt Country, 10 miles northeast of Tower-Roosevelt Junction; open late May to late November.

Tower Fall Campground (6650 feet) – This spot features 32 sites high above Tower Creek in an open pine forest, at the edge of burned forest. Generators are not allowed. Roosevelt Country, 3 miles southeast of Tower-Roosevelt Junction; open mid-May to late September.

WYOMING

Of the cabin options, the rustic Lake Lodge is the most peaceful. The Roosevelt Lodge offers the most authentic Western experience. The Lake Yellowstone Hotel is grand, but its cabins are, like most others in the park, tiny boxes scattered in a shadeless area near ye olde parking lot.

Simple *cabins with shared bathroom* are the park's least expensive places: Old Faithful Lodge Cabins ($35), Mammoth Hot Springs Cabins ($50) and the rustic Roosevelt Lodge Cabins ($43 to $57). The *most affordable cabins with bathrooms* are the centrally located Old Faithful Cabins ($43 to $63), Lake Lodge Cabins ($49 to $106) and Canyon Lodge & Cabins ($54 to $106). Cabins with bath cost $83 at Mammoth Hot Springs Hotel, Roosevelt Lodge, Lake Yellowstone Hotel and Old Faithful Snow Lodge. *Deluxe cabins with bathroom* cost $85 to $115 at Canyon Lodge, Lake Lodge and Old Faithful Snow Lodge.

Hotels in the park's older properties are grand reminders of a bygone era: *Mammoth Hot Springs Hotel, Lake Yellowstone Hotel* and *Old Faithful Inn*. Not all rooms are equal, however, and the best, of course, require many dead presidents. Their other accommodations are less distinctive and more modern. *Grant Village*'s clusters of condolike boxes called 'lodges' have been dismissed by author Alston Chase as 'an inner-city project in the heart of primitive America, a wilderness ghetto,' the architecture of which is 'a curious mixture of Cape Cod and Star Wars.' Think Ice Cube meets Martha Stewart meets Han Solo – ugghleeh.

Mammoth Hot Springs Hotel has the least expensive hotel rooms ($87); those at Grant Village and Old Faithful Inn are $90 to $120. Old Faithful Snow Lodge charges $125. Mammoth Hot Springs Hotel, Old Faithful Inn and Old Faithful Snow Lodge have rooms with shared bathroom from $65. Top-end rooms fetch around $100 at Lake Yellowstone Hotel, Grant Village and Old Faithful Inn. Deluxe rooms at Canyon Lodge are $120. Premium rooms range from $99 to $155 at Lake Yellowstone Hotel and $90 to $155 at Old Faithful Inn. Honeymoon-worthy suites are available at Mammoth Hot Springs Hotel ($265), Old Faithful Inn ($329) and Lake Yellowstone Hotel ($389).

Places to Eat Snack bars, delis and grocery stores are in several locations in the park. Moderately priced *cafeteria-style meals* are served at Canyon Lodge Cafeteria, Lake Lodge Cafeteria and Old Faithful Lodge Cafeteria. Other possibilities are the Mammoth Hot Springs Terrace Grill, Grant Village Lake House Restaurant and Old Faithful Snow Lodge Restaurant. The Roosevelt Lodge Dining Room requires reservations (☎ 307-344-7311 central reservations).

More elaborate meals are served at dining rooms in Mammoth Hot Springs Hotel (☎ 307-344-5314), Canyon Lodge (☎ 307-242-3999), Lake Yellowstone Hotel (☎ 307-242-3899), Grant Village (☎ 307-242-3499) and Old Faithful Inn (☎ 307-545-4999). Lunches are reasonably priced but can be crowded. Dinners are more expensive and require reservations, especially in summer.

Getting There & Away Year-round airports nearest to Yellowstone National Park are in Jackson (56 miles), Cody (52 miles), Bozeman, MT (65 miles; see Yellowstone Country in the Montana chapter), Billings, MT (129 miles; see Montana Plains in the Montana chapter) and Idaho Falls, ID (107 miles; see the Snake River Plain section of the Idaho chapter). The airport in West Yellowstone, MT, is usually open June to early September. It can be cheaper to land in Salt Lake City, UT (390 miles), or Denver, CO (563 miles), and rent a car there.

No public transport exists to or within Yellowstone National Park. In summer, commercial buses to the park operate from Jackson and Cody. Buses operate to West Yellowstone, MT, and Gardiner, MT, from Bozeman, MT, year-round. Greyhound operates daily buses between Idaho Falls, ID, and Bozeman via West Yellowstone in summer. Gray Line of Yellowstone runs tour buses from West Yellowstone and

Jackson to Old Faithful daily in summer (see Organized Tours earlier in this chapter).

John D Rockefeller Jr Memorial Parkway

This NPS-managed parkway is a 7½-mile corridor linking Yellowstone and Grand Teton National Parks. The US Congress recognized Rockefeller's contribution to the creation of Grand Teton National Park by designating this 24,000-acre parkway in his honor in 1972. Activities focus around historic Flagg Ranch, which became a US Cavalry post in 1872 and later a private guest ranch in 1910.

Orientation & Information North-south US 89/191/287 is the main road through the parkway. The turnoff to Flagg Ranch Rd is 2 miles south of the South Entrance to Yellowstone National Park and 15 miles north of Colter Bay Village. The turnoff to Grassy Lake Rd, which leads west to Ashton, ID, is immediately to the right off Flagg Ranch Rd. To reach Flagg Ranch Resort continue straight for about half a mile.

The Rockefeller Pkwy Visitor Information Station, near the Grassy Lake Rd turnoff, is open 9 am to 6 pm daily June to early September. Contact Flagg Ranch Resort (☎ 307-543-2861, 800-443-2311), which has an NPS concession, to book parkway accommodations and activities; www.flaggranch.com.

Activities Flagg Ranch Rafting, at Flagg Ranch Resort (see above), offers three-hour floating trips ($35/22 adults/children) mid-June to early September. A hiking trail runs beside the volcanic walls of Flagg Canyon, which was carved by the Snake River. In winter Flagg Ranch Resort rents snowmobiles (starting at $140/day), cross-country skis ($10/15 half/full day) and snowshoes ($7/12).

The east-west Grassy Lake Rd links US 89/191/287 to US 20 at Ashton, ID, offering an infrequently used 'back way' into the national parks. Numerous lakes and streams –

and endless fishing, hiking and camping options – are in the Jedediah Smith Wilderness Area south of Grassy Lake Rd and in the Winegar Hole Wilderness Area north of it. Grassy Lake Rd is also a good route for mountain biking.

Places to Stay & Eat When national-park campgrounds are full, try the lesser-known and free USFS *Sheffield Creek Campground* on the east side of US 89/191/287 just south of Flagg Ranch Rd. *Flagg Ranch Village* is open mid-May to mid-October and mid-December to late February. *Flagg Ranch Campground* has tent and RV hookups ($20/30), laundry and a nightly campfire program; it's open May to early October. Its *Motel* ($75 to $100) is along the banks of the Snake River. Cabins fetch $100 to $135; open mid-May to mid-October and mid-December to mid-March. The restaurant serves breakfast and dinner in summer and all meals in winter. Shuttles go to Jackson and the Jackson Hole Airport.

GRAND TETON NATIONAL PARK

The Teton Mountains' jagged, granitic spires are the centerpiece of spectacular Grand Teton National Park. Twelve glacier-carved summits rise above 12,000 feet, crowned by the singular Grand Teton (13,770 feet). This 40-mile-long range towers above Jackson Hole, where lakes and streams, including the nascent Snake River, mirror the soaring peaks.

Grand Teton National Park is south of Yellowstone National Park between the Targhee and Bridger-Teton National Forests (to the west and east, respectively). The abrupt eastern side of the Teton Range overlooks the Snake River and Jackson Hole, while the gentler west side slopes away toward Idaho's Teton Valley. Much of the national park lies within the valley of Jackson Hole, where Jackson Lake, a natural body of water raised an additional 65 feet by a dam, catches the Snake River as it flows south from its source in Yellowstone National Park, ultimately to feed Idaho farms.

WYOMING

The fault-block Teton Mountains, which still support a dozen relict glaciers, are the Rocky Mountains' youngest range. Between 5 million and 9 million years ago, sedimentary rocks west of the north-south Teton Fault rose along a 40-mile front, building a new mountain range 10 to 15 miles wide, 7000 feet above the subsiding land to the east. At the highest elevations, the relatively soft sandstone, shale and other sediments eroded, leaving resistant granite exposed to the elements. Freezing ice wedged and shattered this crystalline rock along its weakest joints, creating impressive pinnacles; then slow-moving alpine glaciers ground other areas into submission, leaving a legacy of sharp ridges, cirques and mountainside lakes confined by glacial debris dams known as moraines.

The area east of the fault filled with sediments, creating the broad Jackson Hole. South of Jackson Lake and east of Jenny Lake are depressions in the ground known as the Potholes, formed by huge blocks of melting glacial ice. Jackson Lake itself is a remnant of the Yellowstone ice sheet, whose broad moraines trapped the melted ice before the Snake cut a channel through them.

History

At least 12,000 years ago, people hunted and gathered in Jackson Hole and the Tetons. When Europeans first reached the area in the early 19th century, Blackfeet, Crow, Shoshone and Gros Ventre tribes all frequented the valley. The Shoshonean Snake Indians referred to the high peaks as *teewinot* (many pinnacles). John Colter, having split off from the Lewis and Clark Expedition, ventured here in 1807–08. Trappers like Colter and Davey Jackson made their living in the Tetons, but it was raffish French-speaking trappers who dubbed the three most prominent peaks Les Trois Tetons for their ostensible resemblance to female breasts. Jackson, in partnership with Jedediah Smith and William Sublette, acquired the Mountain Fur Company in 1826. A cousin of President Andrew Jackson, Davey Jackson claimed the low-lying Snake

River drainage as his informal trapping territory, and so lent his name to the expansive valley. Not until the 1880s did permanent settlers inhabit the area, and by the early 20th century dude ranching was proving more profitable than cattle ranching.

Still, transformation of the Tetons into a national park was no foregone conclusion, as commercial ranching and hunting interests resisted attempts to transfer USFS and private lands to the NPS. At its creation in 1929, Grand Teton National Park included only the main part of the Teton Range and the lakes immediately below. Distressed at Jackson Hole's commercial development, John D Rockefeller Jr purchased more than 55 sq miles of land to donate to the park (but retained rights to all park concessions!), but Congress repeatedly refused the cunning philanthropist's tax write-off until President Franklin D Roosevelt interceded.

Rockefeller's 32,000-acre bequest finally came under NPS jurisdiction when Roosevelt declared Jackson Hole a national monument in 1943. With post-WWII tourism booming in 1950, legislation conferred national-park status and expanded the boundaries to include most of Jackson Hole. Today, the Rockefeller-owned Grand Teton Lodge Company is the park's major concessionaire, and the curious park is the only one outside Alaska that permits hunting and the only one with a commercial airport.

Flora & Fauna

The wildlife of the Tetons strongly correlates with elevation. The Snake River floodplain of permanent and seasonal wetlands above 6000 feet is an exceptionally productive environment, though winters are severe. Moose, elks, mule deer and bison forage these bottomlands, where beavers, black bears and coyotes are also occasionally seen. Bears are less common here than in Yellowstone National Park. Bald eagles and ospreys fish the rivers and creeks, while migratory wildfowl like Canada geese and mallards rest among the beaver ponds and riparian wetlands. Trumpeter swans, North America's largest waterfowl, have 17 nesting sites. In the higher and drier sagebrush flats, pronghorn antelopes join the elks and bison.

On the mountain slopes between 7000 feet and 10,000 feet, thinner soils support less-diverse vegetation, though coniferous lodgepole pine, sub-alpine fir and spruce forests grow to surprising heights. The well-watered mountain canyons are occasionally visited by bighorn sheep, which prefer open alpine areas where their agility makes them less vulnerable to predators.

Summer is brief above 10,000 feet, when the clearings and meadows explode with colorful wildflowers like lupine, Indian paintbrush and alpine forget-me-nots. Chirping yellow-bellied marmots occasionally peek out of their hillside rookeries at passing hikers, and smaller rodents like pikas thrive even higher up. On the summits of the highest peaks, lichens and other tiny plants take advantage of the brief summer.

Orientation

Three roads lead to the park: US 26/89/191 from Jackson to the south; US 26/287 from Dubois to the east; and US 89/191/287 from Yellowstone National Park to the north.

US 26/89/191, contiguous along the east bank of the Snake River between Jackson and Moran Junction, constitutes the main north-south route through the park. At Moran Junction US 89/191 joins US 287 heading north along the shore of Jackson Lake to the John D Rockefeller Memorial Pkwy; US 26 joins US 287 heading east to Dubois via Togwotee Pass.

Teton Park Rd links Moose Junction to Jackson Lake Junction and US 89/191/287 via Jenny and Jackson Lakes. A 5-mile scenic Jenny Lake Loop Rd connects North Jenny Lake and South Jenny Lake junctions; the road is two-way to Jenny Lake Lodge and one-way south of it. Gros Ventre Rd heads east from US 26/89/191 at the southern end of the park to Kelly and the Gros Ventre Valley. Antelope Flats Rd is 1 mile north of Moose Junction east of US 89/191/26. The park has two entrance stations: Moose (south) on Teton Park Rd west of Moose Junction, and Moran (east) on US 89/191/287 north of Moran Junction.

USGS topographical maps, 1:62,500 and 7.5-minute quadrangles are widely available. Hikers may prefer Trails Illustrated's *Grand Teton National Park* (1:78,000 of the entire park, with the Grand Teton climbing area at 1:24,000) or the 1:48,000 Earthwalk Press *Hiking Map & Guide: Grand Teton National Park,* which covers only the southwest portion of the park but includes most of the key hiking areas.

Information

Tourist Offices Grand Teton National Park headquarters (☎ 307-739-3600), Box 170, Moose, WY 83012, shares the building with Moose Visitors Center. Its Web site is at www.nps.gov/grte. The Grand Teton Natural History Association (☎ 307-739-3403) sells books and maps at the following visitors centers:

Colter Bay Visitors Center
(☎ 307-739-3594), US 89/191/287, 6 miles north of Jackson Lake Lodge

Jenny Lake Visitors Center
(☎ 307-739-3343), Teton Park Rd, 8 miles north of Moose Junction

Moose Visitors Center
(☎ 307-739-3399, 307-739-3309, fax 307-739-3438 for backcountry permits), Teton Park Rd, half a mile west of Moose Junction

Colter Bay Visitors Center is open 8 am to 8 pm daily June to early October. (Colter Bay's **Indian Arts Museum** has an appealing selection of artifacts, some for sale, which gives background information on the area.) Jenny Lake Visitors Center is open 8 am to 7 pm daily June to September. Moose Visitors Center is open 8 am to 5 pm daily year-round, with extended summer hours to 7 pm.

Fees & Permits The park is open year-round, although some roads and entrances close in winter. Visitors must purchase a park entrance permit, which is valid for seven days for entry into both Grand Teton and Yellowstone National Parks. The

GRAND TETON NATIONAL PARK

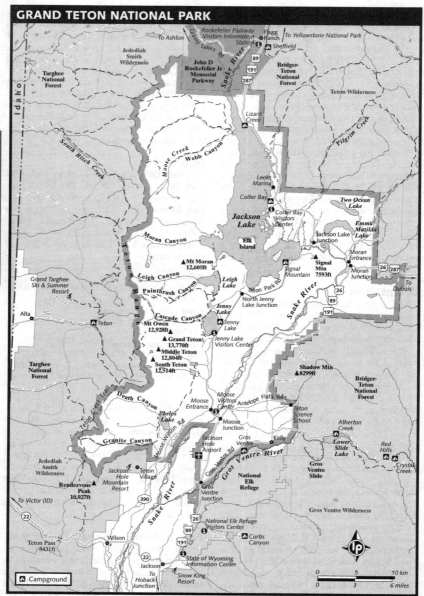

entrance fee is $20/vehicle, $15/person for individuals entering by motorcycle or snowmobile and $10/person for individuals entering by bicycle, skis or on foot. An annual pass costs $40. Visitors receive a free copy of the park newspaper *Teewinot*, which details the extensive program of ranger-led activities, and a brochure containing a good orientation map.

Concessionaires Three park concessionaires operate various accommodations, restaurants, marinas and activities:

Dornan's
(☎ 307-733-2522), Web site: www.dornans.com

Grand Teton Lodge Company
(☎ 307-543-3100, 800-628-9988),
Web site: www.gtlc.com

Signal Mountain Lodge
(☎ 307-543-2831),
Web site: www.signalmtnlodge.com

ATMs are at Dornan's and Jackson Lake Lodge. Post offices are at Colter Bay (zip code 83001, summer only), Kelly (83011), Moose (83012) and Moran (83013). Showers are $2 at Colter Bay Village, which also has a laundry.

Grand Teton Medical Clinic (☎ 307-543-2514) is opposite Jackson Lake Lodge.

Dangers & Annoyances Black bears and, to a much lesser extent, grizzly bears are present in Grand Teton National Park (for cautionary advice see Yellowstone National Park, earlier). Areas east of US 26/89/191, the region west of US 26/89/191 along the Snake River between Moose and Moran junctions and the John D Rockefeller Jr Memorial Pkwy are open to elk hunting mid-October to early December. The NPS 'Elk Ecology & Management' pamphlet has more details and a map. If you must, exercise caution (and don a bright orange vest!) when venturing into these areas in hunting season.

Teton Science School
The highly regarded Teton Science School (☎ 307-733-4765), in Kelly, offers lectures ($5) and natural-history seminars (from $50/day) for children and adults. It also houses the free Murie Natural History Museum; call for an appointment to visit. Web site: www.tetonscience.org

Historic Buildings
Half a mile north of Moose Village, a paved road leads to a short trail and William Menor's homestead cabin on the Snake River's west bank, which today you can cross in a restored version of **Menor's Ferry**. The nearby **Chapel of the Transfiguration** (1924) has a superb view of the Tetons through the altar window.

East of Blacktail Butte, an unpaved road connects Antelope Flats Rd on the north with Gros Ventre Rd to the south (when not washed over), passing **Mormon Row**, a series of pioneer barns and cabins. A nearby bison herd and the Teton backdrop makes this area exceptionally popular with photographers.

Rancher Pierce Cunningham, an early major supporter of Grand Teton National Park, lived at **Cunningham Cabin**, 6 miles south of Moran Junction; a short trail elucidates local homesteading.

Signal Mountain Summit Road
This 5-mile paved road east of Teton Park Rd goes to Signal Mountain's summit for a panoramic view. A 6-mile roundtrip hiking trail also leads to the summit from Signal Mountain Campground.

Hiking & Backpacking
The park has 200 miles of hiking trails, but higher elevations often remain snow-covered until late July. Obtain the NPS brochures 'Day Hikes' or 'Backcountry Camping' to plan your tramp. A free backcountry use permit, available at Moose or Colter Bay Visitor Centers or Jenny Lake Ranger Station, is required for overnight trips. Backcountry reservations can be made in advance by fax (faster) or mail January to mid-May (see Information, earlier).

The north-south **Teton Crest Trail**, which runs just west of the main summits, can be accessed from the east by several steep canyons. The main trailheads, south to

WYOMING

north, are Granite Canyon, south of Moose Visitors Center on the Moose-Wilson Rd; Death Canyon, south of Moose Visitors Center at the end of an unpaved road off the Moose-Wilson Rd; Taggart Lake, north of Moose Visitors Center on Teton Park Rd; Lupine Meadows, south of Jenny Lake at the end of an unpaved road off Teton Park Rd; Jenny Lake, off Teton Park Rd; and String Lake/Leigh Lake on Jenny Lake Loop Rd.

Day Hikes Hikes around Jenny Lake, Hidden Falls and Inspiration Point start from **String Lake trailhead**. Walk along the northwest shore of lovely Jenny Lake to Hidden Falls. Inspiration Point, a steep half-mile farther, is the start of the popular and more level **Cascade Canyon Trail**. Continue back around the south shore of Jenny Lake to the **Jenny Lake trailhead**, one of the most popular Teton day hikes; many people take the shuttle boat across Jenny Lake (see Boating & Floating, below). String Lake is the most popular picnic area, with dramatic views of the north face of Teewinot Mountain and Grand Teton from the sandy beaches along the east side.

Bradley and Taggart Lakes have a self-guiding trail, less heavily used than Jenny Lake, offering several easy loop options ranging from 3 to 5 miles total. A classic 10-mile roundtrip hike to Surprise and Amphitheater Lakes begins at **Lupine Meadows trailhead**. The strenuous trail climbs 3000 feet to the lakes, high on Disappointment Peak with Grand Teton in the background.

Two lakes, Ocean and Emma Matilda, are east of Jackson Lake. Turn north onto Pacific Creek Rd 1 mile west of Moran Junction and drive 4 miles to the parking area. A mostly flat 6-mile hike starting from the east end circles Two Ocean Lake with fine Teton views. It's a 13-mile loop to circle both lakes via panoramic Grand View Point.

Overnight Hikes From **Granite Creek trailhead**, a one-night 19-mile loop on the Valley Trail goes up Open Canyon and

down Granite Canyon. A two- to three-night 26-mile loop goes through Granite Canyon and Death Canyon via the **Teton Crest Trail**. A 38-mile trip up Granite Canyon, along the Teton Crest Trail and down Paintbrush Canyon to the String Lake trailhead takes four nights. The classic 20-mile **Cascade-Paintbrush loop**, one of the most popular, can be done as an overnight trip or a long day hike, starting from the String Lake trailhead.

Rock Climbing & Mountaineering

The Tetons are a favorite destination for rock climbers and mountaineers. Excellent short routes abound, as well as the classic longer summits like Grand Teton, Mt Moran and Mt Owen. The Jenny Lake Ranger Station (☎ 307-739-3343), open 8 am to 6 pm June to September, is ground zero for climbing information. All climbers staying overnight need a backcountry use permit (see Hiking & Backpacking, above) and must register at the Jenny Lake Ranger Station in summer or at Moose Visitors Center the rest of the year. Call ☎ 307-739-3604 for recorded climbing information.

The American Alpine Club's Climbers Ranch (☎ 307-733-7271), Teton Park Rd just south of the Teton Glacier turnout, operates an inexpensive summer *dormitory* ($7 bunks) with cooking facilities and showers; open to climbers only, from mid-June to mid-September (reservations advised).

For instruction and guided climbs, contact Exum Mountain Guides (☎ 307-733-2297), Web site: www.exumguides.com; or Jackson Hole Mountain Guides (☎ 307-733-4979, 800-239-7642), Web site: www.jhmg.com. Exum runs climbing schools at Hidden Falls on Jenny Lake's west shore and at the upper cliffs at the Jackson Hole Mountain Resort, accessed by the aerial tram, and has a base camp at Grand Teton's Lower Saddle (11,600 feet).

Boating & Floating

All private craft must obtain a permit, which costs $10 for motorized and $5 for nonmotorized craft (rafts, canoes or kayaks) and is issued at the Moose and Colter Bay Visitors Centers. Motorized craft (maximum 7½ horsepower) are allowed only on Jackson, Jenny and Phelps Lakes. Lakes permitting hand-propelled nonmotorized craft are Jackson, Two Ocean, Emma Matilda, Bearpaw, Leigh, String, Jenny, Bradley, Taggart and Phelps. Sailboats are permitted only on Jackson Lake.

The park has three marinas. Signal Mountain Marina (☎ 307-733-5470) rents all manner of floating vessels. Its scenic float trips cost $35/18 adults/children; half-day guided fishing trips start at $165. Colter Bay Marina (☎ 307-543-2811) handles fishing gear and licenses as well as motorboat, rowboat and canoe rentals. It also arranges lake cruises. Leek's Marina (☎ 307-543-2494), north of Colter Bay Junction, has a gas dock and overnight buoys.

Teton Boating Company (☎ 307-733-2703) runs shuttles and cruises and rents fishing boats. Shuttles cross Jenny Lake between the east-shore boat dock near Jenny Lake Visitors Center and the west-shore boat dock, offering quick (12-minute) access to Inspiration Point and the Cascade Canyon Trail ($5/2.50 roundtrip). Shuttles run every 20 minutes, 8 am to 6 pm, but expect long waits for return shuttles between 4 and 6 pm. Scenic Jenny Lake cruises are $8/5.

Several outfitters run leisurely Snake River float trips ($35/25). Two launch sites, north of the Snake River Overlook (2½ hours) and south of Teton Point Turnout (1½ hours), are north of Moose Junction on US 26/US 89/US 191. To book a float trip contact Barker-Ewing Float Trips (☎ 307-733-1800), in Moose (Web site: www.barker-ewing.com); Fort Jackson River Trips (☎ 307-733-2583, 800-735-8430), 135 N Cache Dr, Jackson; or National Park Float Trips (☎ 307-733-6445), in Moose.

Other Activities
Fishing Whitefish as well as cutthroat, lake and brown trout abound in park rivers and lakes. Fishing is subject to NPS and Wyoming state regulations, available at visitors centers. Licenses are issued at Moose Village store, Signal Mountain Lodge and Colter Bay Marina. Grand Teton Lodge Company offers guided Jackson Lake fly-fishing trips.

Horseback Riding Jackson Lake Lodge Corral and Colter Bay Village Corral offer guided horseback rides for $18/hour or $40/half-day; breakfast and evening rides, either on horseback or by wagon, are also available.

Bicycling Among the recommended rides from Moose Junction are the wide-shouldered Teton Park Rd north to Jackson Lake Junction, the Teton Village Rd south to Teton Village, and the Mormon Row/Kelly Loop via Antelope Flats Rd and the Gros Ventre Junction. Adventure Sports (☎ 307-733-3307), at Dornan's Market in Moose Village, rents bikes and provides a map of Jackson area cycling routes.

Places to Stay
NPS campgrounds and privately run cabins, lodges and motels are in Grand Teton National Park. Most campgrounds and accommodations are open early May to early October, depending on weather.

Camping Camping inside the park is permitted in designated campgrounds only and is limited to 14 days (seven days at Jenny Lake). Campgrounds usually hold a nightly campfire program in their amphitheater. Days, times and topics are prominently posted. The NPS (☎ 307-739-3603 for recorded info) operates the park's five campgrounds (ranging from 6600 feet to 6900 feet; $12) on a first-come, first-served basis. Demand for campsites is high early July to Labor Day, and most campgrounds fill by 11 am. Jenny Lake fills first and much earlier; Gros Ventre fills last. Colter Bay and Jenny Lake have tent-only sites reserved for backpackers and cyclists.

Colter Bay Campground – More than 300 large, wooded sites dot the east shore of Jackson Lake, with a separate RV park. US 89/191/287, 3 miles north of Jackson Lake Junction.

Gros Ventre Campground – This campground features 360 sprawling sites (more than 100 tent-only) surrounded by sagebrush and shaded by cottonwoods near the Gros Ventre River. It's closer to the Teton Science School (see above) and the Gros Ventre Mountains than most of the park's lakes, rivers and trails. Gros Ventre Rd, 4½ miles northeast of US 26/89/191/287 at Gros Ventre Junction.

Jenny Lake Campground – This very congenial and popular tent-only (49 sites) campground is convenient to many trailheads. Teton Park Rd, 8 miles north of Moose Junction.

Lizard Creek Campground – On a forested peninsula along the north shore of Jackson Lake, Lizard Creek Campground has 60 sites, including several walk-in sites. US 89/191/287, about 8 miles north of Colter Bay Junction.

Signal Mountain Campground – Sparse lodgepole pines dot Signal Mountain Campground (86 sites) along the southeast shore of Jackson Lake. Some sites farther away from the lake offer more privacy. Teton Park Rd, 5 miles south of Jackson Lake Junction.

Lodges & Cabins Grand Teton Lodge Company operates Colter Bay Village, Jackson Lake Lodge and Jenny Lake Lodge. Signal Mountain Lodge operates a property of the same name. Dornan's in Moose operates the Spur Ranch Log Cabins. Contact the appropriate park concessionaire (see Information earlier in this section) for reservations.

Call ☎ 307-543-3100 or ☎ 800-628-9988 or visit www.gtlc.com to make reservations for any of the places in this paragraph. *Colter Bay Village* (☎ 307-543-2828), half a mile west of Colter Bay Junction, offers two types of accommodations: tent village ($35) and cabins (semiprivate bathroom $32; one room with private bathroom $70 to $100; and two-room, four-person cabins $125). The tent village comprises tent cabins, simple log and canvas structures with two bunk beds (without bedding), a wood-burning stove, a table and benches and an outdoor barbecue. *Jackson Lake Lodge*, 1 mile north of Jackson Lake Junction, offers motel rooms (standard rooms $115, lakeview rooms $200) and cottages ($135 to $200). All-inclusive rooms at exclusive *Jenny Lake Lodge* (☎ 307-733-4647), off

Teton Park Rd, are $325/400; suites range from $550 to $600. Rates include some meals, bicycle use and guided horseback riding.

Lakeside *Signal Mountain Lodge* (☎ 307-733-5470), on Teton Park Rd 2 miles southwest of Jackson Lake Junction, has three types of accommodations: cabins (one-room cabins start at $80, two rooms at $100), motel rooms (standard rooms range from $100 to $150; lakefront rooms start at $155) and bungalows ($175). Web site: www.signalmtnlodge.com

In Moose, Dornan's *Spur Ranch Log Cabins* (☎ 307-733-2522) are open year-round. One-bedroom, four-person cabins range from $140 to $170 June to September, $35 to $60 lower in the off-season. Two-bedroom, six-person cabins are $210 in high season, $150 off-peak. Web site: www.dornans.com

Places to Eat

The Restaurant at Leek's Marina (☎ 307-733-5470), north of Colter Bay Village, is open for lunch and dinner and serves sandwiches, soups, salads, burgers and pizza. Colter Bay Village's *John Colter Chuckwagon* is open 7:30 am to 9 pm daily for moderately priced breakfast, lunch and dinner buffets in a relaxed atmosphere. Nearby, the *John Colter Cafe Court Pizza & Deli* serves sandwiches, salads, pizza, and rotisserie chicken and is a good place for a quick meal or to provision calories for a day trip. A snack bar is next to the grocery store.

Jackson Lake Lodge's *Mural Room* (☎ 307-543-3100), featuring 'Rocky Mountain cuisine,' serves breakfast, lunch and dinner; dinner reservations are recommended. The more casual *Pioneer Grill* at Jackson Lake Lodge, open 6 am to 10:30 pm daily, also offers box lunches and fills thermoses for day trips. Signal Mountain Lodge's *Aspens* has a coffee shop, lounge and dining room specializing in seafood. The upscale *Jenny Lake Lodge Dining Room* (☎ 307-733-4647) requires dinner reservations and expects men to wear jackets. The Sunday evening buffet's juice is worth the squeeze.

Dornan's *Original Moose Chuckwagon* (☎ 307-733-2415), in Moose Village, is an open-air restaurant with Teton views; some tables are inside tepees. They serve pancake-and-egg breakfasts ($7), sandwiches and salads for lunch, and steak and $15 all-you-can-eat prime rib dinners. Pizza, pasta and subs are served from noon to 8 pm in the lounge at *Dornan's Pizza & Pasta Company*. There's a deli and espresso counter in the nearby grocery store.

Jackson Hole

Early European visitors coined the term 'hole' to describe an open valley surrounded by mountains. Jackson Hole is such a place, bounded by the Gros Ventre ('GROW-vant') and Teton ranges to the east and west, respectively, and the Yellowstone lava flows and the Hoback and Wyoming ranges to the north and south. The communities of Jackson, Teton Village and Wilson and much of the Grand Teton National Park lie within this broad valley. In Hollywood parlance, Jackson is either Wyoming's tititllating establishing shot or its 'scenic climax.'

Jackson Hole and the Tetons are home to three resorts: the world-class Jackson Hole Mountain, Snow King and Grand Targhee Ski & Summer (the latter in Alta, WY, on the west side of the Teton Range; see the Snake River Plain section in the Idaho chapter). Moose, elks and bison roam the valley floor against the backdrop of the snowcapped Tetons, making Jackson Hole one of Wyoming's most breathtaking destinations. But recreation is what drives Jackson's popularity, making it Wyoming's most expensive destination. Downhill skiing is the primary activity, but summer visitors find no shortage of things to do, including hiking, biking, rafting, fishing and fauxcowboying.

JACKSON

Jackson (population 6000; elevation 6234 feet), the valley's commercial heart, can induce sensory overload. Diehard Wyomingites disparage it as a tourist enclave where jet-set celebrities frequent fancy restaurants, rapacious realtors push overpriced timeshares and fatuous shoppers swarm kitschy boutiques. Jackson has more than 2000 motel rooms, Wyoming's worst traffic and a petty-theft problem. However, the town also supports a vigorous cultural life and is the hub of a truly world-class ski resort.

Orientation
The main drag (US 89/26/191) follows eastwest Broadway into downtown, where it turns north onto Cache Dr. The pedestrian-oriented commercial district centers on the Town Square, at Broadway and Cache Dr. The exclusive community of Wilson is on Hwy 22, 5 miles west of Jackson, just west of the junction of Hwy 390 leading north to Teton Village.

Information
The helpful Wyoming Information Center (☎ 307-733-3316), 532 N Cache Dr, has an ATM and restrooms and is open 8 am to 7 pm daily in summer, 8 am to 5 pm in winter; visit www.jacksonholechamber.com. The USFS Bridger-Teton National Forest headquarters (☎ 307-739-5500) and Jackson Ranger District (☎ 307-739-5400), 340 N Cache Dr, are open 8 am to 4:30 pm weekdays. The Jackson Hole Conservation Alliance (☎ 307-733-9417), 40 E Simpson St, lobbies for biodiversity protection in the Greater Yellowstone Ecosystem; visit www.jhalliance.com for more. The Snake River Institute (☎ 307-733-2214), 5450 W Hwy 22 in Wilson, sponsors lectures and field trips.

Bank of Jackson Hole ATMs are at 990 W Broadway and at the corner of Broadway and Cache Dr. The post office is at 220 W Pearl Ave. Tune into 90.3 FM (NPR) or 96.9 KMTN for the local lowdown. Free newspapers include the *Jackson Hole Daily* (liberal) and the *Daily Guide* (conservative). Valley Bookstore (☎ 307-733-4533, 800-647-4111), in Gaslight Alley at the corner of N Cache Dr and Deloney Ave, is the best in town. Teton Bookshop

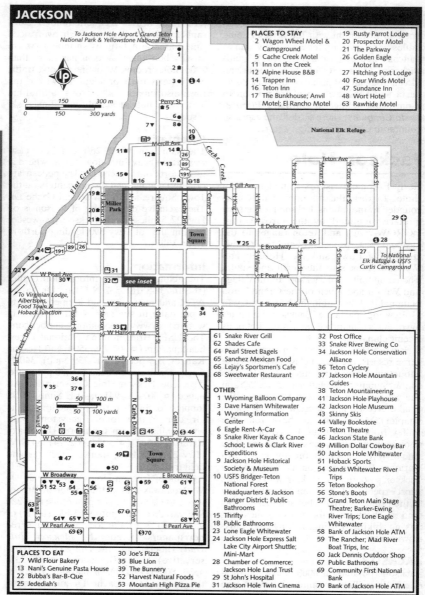

JACKSON

To Jackson Hole Airport, Grand Teton
National Park & Yellowstone National Park

National Elk Refuge

Perry St

Merill Ave

Cache Creek

Teton Ave

E Gill Ave

Miller
Park

E Deloney Ave

Town
Square

E Broadway

To National
Elk Refuge & USFS
Curtis Campground

W Pearl Ave

E Pearl Ave

see inset

To Virginian Lodge,
Albertsons,
Food Town &
Hoback Junction

W Simpson Ave

E Simpson Ave

W Hansen Ave

W Kelly Ave

Town
Square

E Deloney Ave

W Broadway

E Broadway

W Pearl Ave

E Pearl Ave

PLACES TO STAY
2 Wagon Wheel Motel &
    Campground
5 Cache Creek Motel
11 Inn on the Creek
12 Alpine House B&B
14 Trapper Inn
16 Teton Inn
17 The Bunkhouse; Anvil
    Motel; El Rancho Motel
19 Rusty Parrot Lodge
20 Prospector Motel
21 The Parkway
26 Golden Eagle
    Motor Inn
27 Hitching Post Motel
40 Four Winds Motel
47 Sundance Inn
48 Wort Hotel
63 Rawhide Motel

PLACES TO EAT
7 Wild Flour Bakery
13 Nani's Genuine Pasta House
22 Bubba's Bar-B-Que
25 Jedediah's
30 Joe's Pizza
35 Blue Lion
39 The Bunnery
52 Harvest Natural Foods
53 Mountain High Pizza Pie

61 Snake River Grill
62 Shades Cafe
64 Pearl Street Bagels
65 Sanchez Mexican Food
66 Lejay's Sportsmen's Cafe
68 Sweetwater Restaurant

OTHER
1 Wyoming Balloon Company
3 Dave Hansen Whitewater
4 Wyoming Information
   Center
6 Eagle Rent-A-Car
8 Snake River Kayak & Canoe
   School; Lewis & Clark River
   Expeditions
9 Jackson Hole Historical
   Society & Museum
10 USFS Bridger-Teton
   National Forest
   Headquarters & Jackson
   Ranger District; Public
   Bathrooms
15 Thrifty
18 Public Bathrooms
23 Lone Eagle Whitewater
24 Jackson Hole Express Salt
   Lake City Airport Shuttle;
   Mini-Mart
28 Chamber of Commerce;
   Jackson Hole Land Trust
29 St John's Hospital
31 Jackson Hole Twin Cinema

32 Post Office
33 Snake River Brewing Co
34 Jackson Hole Conservation
   Alliance
36 Teton Cyclery
37 Jackson Hole Mountain
   Guides
38 Teton Mountaineering
41 Jackson Hole Playhouse
42 Jackson Hole Museum
43 Skinny Skis
44 Valley Bookstore
45 Teton Theatre
46 Jackson State Bank
49 Million Dollar Cowboy Bar
50 Jackson Hole Whitewater
51 Hoback Sports
54 Sands Whitewater River
   Trips
55 Teton Bookshop
56 Stone's Boots
57 Grand Teton Main Stage
   Theatre; Barker-Ewing
   River Trips; Lone Eagle
   Whitewater
58 Bank of Jackson Hole ATM
59 The Rancher; Mad River
   Boat Trips, Inc
60 Jack Dennis Outdoor Shop
69 Public Bathrooms
69 Community First National
   Bank
70 Bank of Jackson Hole ATM

WYOMING

(☎ 307-733-9220), 25 S Glenwood St, has a fine Western selection. Clean up for a song at Soap Opera Laundromat (☎ 307-733-5584), 835 W Broadway. St John's Hospital (☎ 307-733-3636), 625 E Broadway, is the major medical facility.

Historic Buildings

The immediate downtown area retains a handful of noteworthy landmarks. The Jackson Hole Museum (see below) was originally **Deloney's General Merchandise** (1906). While here, check out the panoramic mural in the alley across from the Jackson Hole Playhouse between Deloney Ave and Broadway, behind the Sundance Inn. West and one block north of the museum, the dignified log cabin **St John's Episcopal Church** (1911–15) has a unique stockade-type bell tower. The log building at 132 N Cache Dr was once the studio of local artist Archie Teater; some of his work still adorns the walls of 15 Deloney Ave at N Cache Dr.

Jackson's **Town Square**, once the local rubbish dump, became a federal landmark in 1932. The popular Town Square Shootout reenactment occurs 6:30 pm nightly in summer. At its southeast corner, the early-1900s **Wort Winter Cabin** is a shoot-out prop that once belonged to the family that built the Wort Hotel. The **Van Vleck Cabin** (1910), 135 E Broadway, belonged to a local pioneer family. The **Miller House** (1921), 211 E Broadway, belonged to a usurious banker.

Museums

The **Jackson Hole Museum** (☎ 307-733-2414), 105 N Glenwood St, reviews local history from hunter-gatherers to the present epoch. Open 9:30 am to 6 pm Monday to Saturday and 10 am to 5 pm Sunday from Memorial Day to October 1; $3/2/1 or $6 for families. The museum director conducts one-hour Jackson walking tours ($2/1, $5 for families) 10 am Tuesday, Thursday and Saturday.

The free **Jackson Hole Historical Society & Museum** (☎ 307-733-9605), 105 Mercill Ave, focuses on Plains Indians, early Jackson Hole settlement and the creation of Grand Teton National Park, and maintains an extensive research library. It is open 8 am to 5 pm weekdays.

The **National Museum of Wildlife Art** (☎ 307-733-5771), 2820 Rungius Rd, 3 miles north of Jackson, displays paintings and sculptures by George Catlin, Albert Bierstadt, Karl Bodmer and Carl Rungius. An historic photographic exhibit covers cowboy culture. On permanent display is the recreation of John Clymer's Teton Village studio. The 51,000-sq-ft Arizona sandstone facility blends into the landscape overlooking the National Elk Refuge. The on-site Rising Sage Cafe is superb. Open 8 am to 5 pm daily in summer, 9 am to 5 pm daily in winter, 9 am to 5 pm Monday to Saturday and 1 to 5 pm Sunday in spring and fall; $6/5 or $14 per family.

National Elk Refuge

More than 8000 Rocky Mountain elks winter at the USFWS-administered, 39-sq-mile National Elk Refuge (☎ 307-733-9212), northeast of Jackson via Elk Refuge Rd, an extension of E Broadway. It was established in 1912 after Jackson Hole development disrupted seasonal elk migration routes. When snow covers the native grasses, the elks are fed pelleted alfalfa hay. The refuge offers winter sleigh rides, departing from the National Museum of Wildlife Art. Also in the refuge is the **Jackson National Fish Hatchery** (☎ 307-733-2510), 1500 Fish Hatchery Rd, reached from US 89 N, open for free tours 8 am to 4 pm daily.

Skiing

Jackson Central Reservations sells a Ski Three Multi Area Lift Voucher ($220 for five vouchers) good at Snow King, Jackson Hole Mountain Resort and Grand Targhee. See individual resorts later in this chapter for details.

Other Activities

Singles seeking **climbing** partners swear by the bulletin board at Teton Mountaineering (☎ 307-733-3595), 170 N Cache Dr. Teton Rock Gym (☎ 307-733-0707), 1116 Maple

Way, offers sport climbs of all levels and difficulty ($12/day).

The Jackson Hole Land Trust (☎ 307-733-4707), 555 E Broadway, is a private organization that manages more than 11,000 acres in and around Jackson Hole. It protects vital habitats by purchasing key properties or persuading ranchers to grant conservation easements in exchange for tax advantages. It encourages **hiking**, **horseback riding** and **mountain biking** on a few of its properties. Web site: www.jhlandtrust.org

Special Events

Jackson Hole hosts many events: Check local newspaper listings to see what's on. The **Elk Antler Auction** takes place every spring in the Town Square. The **Teton County Fair** (☎ 307-733-0658) takes over the Teton County Fairgrounds (Snow King Ave and Flat Creek Rd) in late July. The summertime **Jackson Hole Rodeo** (☎ 307-733-2805) takes place at the fairgrounds at 8 pm Wednesday and Saturday. Mid-September's **Jackson Hole Fall Arts Festival** lasts nearly three weeks.

Places to Stay

Summer and winter high-season rates are at least 30% higher than – and sometimes double – the low-season prices quoted here. Reservations are essential in peak periods. Cheaper weekly rates are available October 1 until the first big snowfall and after the snow melts until Memorial Day.

Budget Cramped *Wagon Wheel Campground* (☎ 307-733-4588, 435 N Cache Dr) is popular with climbers ($15/32 tent/full hook-up). Grassy *Snake River KOA* (☎ 307-733-7078, 800-562-1878) is 12 miles south of town off US 26/89/191 near Hoback Junction ($27/36). For cheaper public USFS campgrounds see Around Jackson Hole later in this chapter; the closest is *Curtis*, just east of the Elk Refuge off USFS Rd 30440.

At the Anvil and El Rancho motels (see below), *The Bunkhouse* (☎ 307-733-3668, 215 N Cache Dr) has $18 beds with a modicum of privacy in modest basement cubicles with kitchen access. Nonguests can shower here for $5.

In Jackson, 'budget' means $70 off-peak doubles and high-season rates pushing $100. Within walking distance of downtown are the friendly *Teton Inn* (☎ 307-733-3883, 800-851-0070, 165 W Gill Ave), the best of the lot (from $40); sprawling *Virginian Lodge* (☎ 307-733-2792, 800-262-4999, 750 W Broadway), from $45; *Rawhide Motel* (☎ 307-733-1216, 800-835-2999, 75 S Millward St), from $60; hospitable *Sundance Inn* (☎ 307-733-3444, 888-478-6326, 135 W Broadway), with a hot tub, afternoon snacks and a generous breakfast (from $50); and *El Rancho Motel* (☎ 307-733-3668, 800-234-4507, 215 N Cache Dr), from $65. North of town, convenient to the National Elk Refuge, are comparably priced *Elk Refuge Inn* (☎ 307-733-3582, 800-544-3582, 1755 N US 89) and *Flat Creek Motel* (☎ 307-733-5276, 800-438-9338, 1935 N US 89) (both from $60). South of downtown along US 89 are *Days Inn* (☎ 307-733-0033, 350 S US 89), from $70; *Motel 6* (☎ 307-733-1620, 600 S US 89), from $70/75; and *Super 8* (☎ 307-733-6833, 750 S US 89), from $65/75.

Mid-Range Moderately priced downtown motels starting between $75 and $100 are:

Anvil Motel
    (☎ 307-733-3368, 800-234-4507, 215 N Cache Dr)
Buckrail Lodge
    (☎ 307-733-2079, 110 E Karns Ave)
Cache Creek Motel
    (☎ 307-733-7781, 390 N Glenwood St)
Four Winds Motel
    (☎ 307-733-2474, 800-228-6461, 150 N Millward St)
Golden Eagle Motor Inn
    (☎ 307-733-2042, 325 E Broadway)
Hitching Post Lodge
    (☎ 307-733-2606, 800-821-8351, 460 E Broadway)
The Parkway
    (☎ 307-733-3143, 800-247-8390, 125 N Jackson St)
Prospector Motel
    (☎ 307-733-4858, 800-851-0070, 155 N Jackson St)
Trapper Inn
    (☎ 307-733-2648, 800-341-8000, 235 N Cache Dr)
Wagon Wheel Motel
    (☎ 307-733-2357, 800-323-9279, 435 N Cache Dr)

Top End Several B&Bs are within walking distance of downtown: *Alpine House* (☎ *307-739-1570, 800-753-1421, 285 N Glenwood St*) asks $80 to 130 and is run by Olympic skiers; and *Nowlin Creek Inn* (☎ *307-733-0882, 800-533-0882, 660 E Broadway*) charges $105 to $210. The *Jackson Hole B&B Association* (☎ *307-734-1999, 800-542-2632*) has photos and more information; visit its Web site at www.jacksonholebus.com/bbindex.html.

Rusty Parrot Lodge (☎ *307-733-2000, 800-458-2004, 175 N Jackson Ave*) has rooms that start at $100. The venerable *Wort Hotel* (☎ *307-733-2190, 800-322-2727, 50 N Glenwood St*) starts at $115. Intimate *Inn on the Creek* (☎ *307-739-1565, 800-669-9534, 295 N Millward St*) is the place to splurge (from $149).

Places to Eat

Jackson is home to Wyoming's most sophisticated grub. Plenty of places are unconscionably pretentious and expensive, but many offer good values, especially (but not exclusively) lunch specials. The free annual 'Jackson Hole Dining Guide' includes menus from around 75 eateries. Budget-conscious folks should shop *Food Town* (cheapest) or *Albertsons* (fancier) grocery stores, both at the west end of town off Broadway.

Harvest Natural Foods (☎ *307-733-5418, 130 W Broadway*) is the best healthy-vegan-soup-and-salad option, with groceries, a bakery and wheat grass juicery. *The Bunnery* (☎ *307-733-5474, 130 N Cache Dr*) has a wide breakfast, lunch and veggie selection and superb baked goods. *Jedediah's* (☎ *307-733-5671, 135 E Broadway*) is popular for cheap breakfast and also serves lunch and dinner (summer only). Pancakes, eggs, biscuits and gravy are their specialties. *Pearl Street Bagels* (☎ *307-739-1218, 145 W Pearl Ave*) also crafts sandwiches and steams espresso. Recommended *Shades Cafe* (☎ *307-733-2015, 82 S King St*) is a crowded breakfast alternative, with panini sandwiches and gourmet burritos after noon. The retail *Wild Flour Bakery* (☎ *307-734-2455, 345 N Glenwood St*) supplies many local restaurants and makes good sweet treats.

Get credible Philly cheesesteaks at the tiny chop shop inside the *Million Dollar Cowboy Bar*. Humble *Sanchez Mexican Food* (☎ *307-732-2326, 65 S Glenwood St*) rolls boffo burritos. Popular BYOB *Bubba's Bar-B-Que* (☎ *307-733-2288, 515 W Broadway*) features pork ribs and a decent salad bar. *Mountain High Pizza Pie* (☎ *307-733-3646, 120 W Broadway*) and *Joe's Pizza* (☎ *307-734-5637, 410 W Pearl St*) both deliver good pies. *Sweetwater Restaurant* (☎ *307-733-3553, 85 S King St*) dishes out creative lunches ($7 to $10) and bistro dinners (entrees $15 to $23).

Homey *Nani's Genuine Pasta House* (☎ *307-733-3888, 240 N Glenwood St*) is the best upmarket Italian option. French *Blue Lion* (☎ *307-733-3912, 160 N Millward St*) prepares excellent seafood and wild game. Mandarin Chinese *Lame Duck* (☎ *307-733-4311, 680 E Broadway*) also serves sushi. Moderately priced *Chinatown* (☎ *307-733-8856, 850 W Broadway*) prepares various provincial specialties. Beefeaters powwow at 24-hour *Lejay's Sportsmen's Cafe* (☎ *307-733-3110, 72 S Glenwood St*) or *Gun Barrel Steakhouse* (☎ *307-733-3287, 862 W Broadway*), which turns out Jackson's best steak. Upscale *Snake River Grill* (☎ *307-733-0557, 84 E Broadway*) is often recommended for its elaborate dinners. One of the Hole's better restaurants happens to be in Wilson: *Nora's Fish Creek Inn* (☎ *307-733-8288, 5600 W Hwy 22*) pulls 'em in from far and wide for breakfast and great prime rib.

Entertainment

The free *Jackson Hole Weekend Guide* appears Friday and reviews local entertainment possibilities, as does the *Stepping Out* insert.

Jackson's nightlife landmark is the touristy *Million Dollar Cowboy Bar* (☎ *307-733-2207, 25 N Cache Dr*). *The Rancher* pool hall (☎ *307-733-3886, 20 E Broadway*) is a local happy-hour favorite. The beer's better than the pub grub at the popular *Snake River Brewing Co*

(☎ 307-739-2337, 265 S Millward St). **Virginian Saloon** (☎ 307-733-2792, 750 W Broadway) has a daily happy hour (4 to 7 pm) and a big-screen TV. Wilson's **Stagecoach Bar** (☎ 307-733-4407, 5755 W Hwy 22) is worth the short drive: 'Mon-day' means reggae, Thursday is disco night and every Sunday the famous (and aging – they've been playing here for 30 years) Stagecoach Band recites country & western favorites until 10 pm. Herb tokers and cowpokers mingle here more than any other place in the West.

Local theater troupes stage Broadway-style musical comedies at **Jackson Hole Playhouse** (☎ 307-733-6994, 145 W Deloney Ave) and **Main Stage Theatre** (☎ 307-733-3670), Broadway & Cache Dr. The 1941 sandstone **Teton Theatre** (120 N Cache Dr) is the best place to catch a flick; the Jackson Movieline (☎ 307-733-4939) lists what's on at all three movie houses in town.

Shopping
Bogus false-front arcades, more befitting Disney's Frontierland, overwhelm Jackson's once-picturesque center, and prohibitive prices encourage window shopping. Reputable Western-wear outfitters include Corral West Ranchwear (☎ 307-733-0247), 840 W Broadway, and Stone's Boots (☎ 307-733-3392), 80 W Broadway. There are more than 40 commercial art galleries, a few of which handle local work. The Jackson Hole Gallery Association (☎ 307-739-8911) publishes the useful free 'Art Gallery Guide.' For one-stop (but costly) shopping, ring Jackson Hole Central Reservations (☎ 307-733-4005, 800-443-6931) and request its summer or winter vacation planner. Its Web site is at www.jacksonholeresort.com.

Getting There & Away
Jackson Hole Airport (☎ 307-733-5454) is 7 miles north of Jackson off US 26/89/191 within Grand Teton National Park. Delta (☎ 307-733-7920) flies daily between Jackson Hole and Salt Lake City, but note that it may be more affordable to land in Salt Lake City and rent a car there. Daily United flights link Jackson and Denver,

while weekend American Airlines flights connect Jackson with Chicago. Jackson Hole Express (☎ 307-733-1719, 800-652-9510) buses shuttle daily between Salt Lake City and Jackson, via Idaho Falls ($47 one-way, 5½ hours). The Jackson depot is the Mini-Mart at 395 W Broadway near Burger King.

Jackson is bisected by US 26/89/191, south of Grand Teton National Park. US 26/89/191 leads north to Moran Junction (31 miles), where US 89/191/287 continues north to Yellowstone's South Entrance (57 miles). US 26 leads north and east over Togwotee Pass (9658 feet) to Riverton (168 miles) via Dubois and the Wind River Indian Reservation, and south to Alpine (35 miles) at the Wyoming-Idaho state line. US 89 leads north through Grand Teton and Yellowstone National Parks to Gardiner, MT, and southwest to Salt Lake City (270 miles), the nearest metropolitan area. US 191 leads south to Hoback Junction (12 miles) and Rock Springs (178 miles). Idaho Falls–based bus company CART operates as needed between Jackson and Idaho Falls, ID, via Idaho's Teton Valley.

Getting Around
Southern Teton Area Rapid Transit (START; ☎ 307-733-4521) runs three color-coded routes between Jackson and Teton Village. START operates 6 am to 8 pm weekdays, April to November every two to three hours, and December to March every 20 minutes.

Alamo (☎ 307-733-0671), Avis (☎ 307-733-3422), Budget (☎ 307-733-2206, 800-533-6100) and Hertz (☎ 307-733-2272) are at the airport. In town are Eagle Rent-A-Car (☎ 307-739-9999, 800-582-2128), 375 N Cache Dr; National (☎ 307-733-0735), 345 W Broadway; Rent-A-Wreck (☎ 307-733-5014), 1050 US 89 S; and Thrifty (☎ 307-739-9300), 220 N Millward St.

Call All-Star Taxi (☎ 307-733-2888, 800-378-2944), AllTrans Inc (☎ 307-733-3135) or Buckboard Cab (☎ 307-733-1112) for a lift. A trip between the airport and downtown costs $20.

SNOW KING RESORT

The year-round, 400-acre Snow King Resort (☎ 307-733-5200, 800-522-5464), 400 E Snow King Ave, lies on Jackson's southern edge at a base elevation of 6237 feet. It offers downhill skiing, ice skating in an indoor rink, horseback riding and mountain biking, as well as restaurants and accommodations.

Three lifts serve various downhill ski runs with a maximum vertical drop of 1571 feet (15% beginner, 25% intermediate, 60% advanced). Full-day lift tickets are $30/20 adults/children, half-day tickets (after 1 pm) are $20/12. The ski season is Thanksgiving to March. Night skiing (Monday to Saturday 4:30 to 8:30 pm) is popular. This north-facing slope catches less snow than other resorts but is well suited for children and families.

In summer, scenic rides on the Snow King Chair Lift ($7/6/5) offer views of five mountain ranges. A ticket with lunch at Panorama House, the restaurant at the top, costs $10. When you hike to the summit, a chairlift ride down only costs $1. The lift operates 9 am to 6 pm daily mid-May to early September, with extended summer hours.

The meandering 2500-foot Alpine Slide of Jackson Hole (☎ 307-733-7680), behind the resort, is open late May to mid-September. Horseback rides depart from nearby Snow King Stables (☎ 307-733-5781).

The resort offers hotel rooms (from $200), suites (from $235) and condominiums (from $250). Its popular *Shady Lady Saloon* often features live jazz.
Web site: www.snowking.com

JACKSON HOLE MOUNTAIN RESORT

From the 6311-foot base at Teton Village (see below) to the summit of Rendezvous Mountain (10,450 feet), the greatest continuous vertical rise in the United States makes this one of the country's top ski destinations. Jackson Hole Mountain Resort draws skiers from around the world with its awesome 4139-foot vertical drop, long runs and deep powder. The resort is active year-round with hiking, mountain biking

and horseback riding once the snow has melted.

Information

Jackson Hole Mountain Resort (☎ 307-733-2292, 888-333-7766) is at Teton Village. The Jackson Hole Guest Service Center (☎ 307-739-2753, 800-450-0477) is in the Clock Tower building. The resort office (☎ 307-733-4005) is at 140 E Broadway, Jackson. Visit www.jacksonhole.com for more information.

Jackson Hole Aerial Tram

This scenic tram ($16/13/6 adults/seniors/children) rises 2½ miles to the top of Rendezvous Mountain, offering great views of Jackson Hole and providing quick access to Grand Teton National Park high-country trails. Hikers who take the Granite Canyon Trail to Rendezvous Mountain can ride the tram free down to Teton Village. Tram arrivals can either hike down Granite Canyon Trail or choose from a series of shorter trails: half-mile Summit Nature Loop, 3-mile Cody Bowl Trail or 4.2-mile Rock Springs Bowl. The tram is open 9 am to 5 pm late May to late September, and often to 7 pm when demand is high. Hiking boot rentals cost $5; sack lunches $8.

Skiing

Revered by experts and enthusiasts the world over, the resort's 2500 acres of skiable terrain are blessed by 380-plus inches of snow annually. The runs (10% beginner, 40% intermediate, 50% advanced) are served by nine lifts, an aerial tram, a new high-speed quad and the Bridger gondola. Full-day lift tickets are $54/27 adults/children, half-day tickets (after 12:30 pm) are $30/20. The ski season is usually Thanksgiving to early April. The 'Jackson Hole Mountain Map & Skiers Guide,' available at the resort and guest service center, diagrams Teton Village.

Former Olympic skier Pepi Stiegler operates the Jackson Hole Ski School (☎ 307-733-4505). Jackson Hole Nordic Center (☎ 307-739-2629) offers 20 miles of groomed track and wide skating lanes with rentals and instruction. High Mountain Heli-Skiing (☎ 307-733-3274) delivers skiers to the fluffy powder in the surrounding mountains; it maintains a Web site at www.skitvs.com.

There are several Teton Village shops that rent or sell downhill gear: Jack Dennis Outdoor Shop (☎ 307-733-6838), Jackson Hole Sports (☎ 307-739-2623), Teton Village Sports (☎ 307-733-2181) and Wilderness Sports (☎ 307-733-4297). For Nordic, look in Jackson: Skinny Skis (☎ 307-733-6094), 65 W Deloney Ave; Teton Mountaineering (☎ 307-733-3595), 170 N Cache Dr; and Jack Dennis Outdoor Shop (☎ 307-733-3270, 800-570-3270), 50 E Broadway. Boardroom of Jackson Hole (☎ 307-733-8327), on W Broadway in Jackson, is the nonskiers' alternative.

Places to Stay & Eat
There are three restaurants on the mountain: *Corbet's Cabin*, at the top of the tram, *Casper Restaurant*, at the base of the Casper lift and *Shades of Thunder*, for quick lunches or snacks at the base of the Thunder lift. (For accommodations, see Teton Village & Around, below, and Jackson, above.)

Getting There & Away
Jackson Hole Mountain Resort and Teton Village are west of Hwy 390 (also called Teton Village Rd and Moose-Wilson Rd), 6 miles west of Jackson via Hwy 22 and then 6 miles north of Wilson on Hwy 390, 1 mile south of the Grand Teton National Park boundary and 20 miles from the Jackson Hole Airport.

TETON VILLAGE & AROUND
Teton Village is a Bavarian-style development of hotels, restaurants and shops at the base of Rendezvous Mountain and Jackson Hole Mountain Resort. Teton Village hotels, restaurants and a Jackson State Bank (with ATM) are clustered in a semicircle along W McCollister Dr. Jackson Hole Trail Rides (☎ 307-733-6992) offers guided **horseback rides** ($20/hour, $75 full-day). Teton Village hosts the **Grand Teton Music Festival**

(☎ 307-733-3050) in Walk Festival Hall July to August; its Web site is at www.gtmf.com.

Places to Stay
The *Teton Village KOA* (☎ 307-733-5354, 800-562-9043, 2780 N Moose-Wilson Rd) is on Hwy 390 south of Teton Village and 1½ miles north of Hwy 22. Tent/RV sites are $26/36, kabins $43.

Seasonal rates vary widely and frequently. Some hotels also charge a 'resort fee.' Bargain-basement *Hostel X* (☎ 307-733-3415) has double-occupancy rooms with private bath from $45 in summer and $50 in winter (five-night minimum, book ahead); www.hostelx.com. Starting around $100 are the rooms at the *Crystal Springs Inn* (☎ 307-733-4423), above Teton Village Sports, and *Village Center Inn* (☎ 307-733-3155, 800-735-8342). Starting around $150 are *Alpenhof Lodge* (☎ 307-733-3242, 800-732-3244), *Sojourner Inn* (☎ 307-733-3657, 800-445-4655) and *Best Western The Inn* (☎ 307-733-2311, 800-842-7666).

Places to Eat
In Teton Village, the well-established *Mangy Moose Saloon* (☎ 307-733-9779) is a steak and seafood restaurant (entrees start at $12) and spirited nightspot with live music. Downstairs is *The Rocky Mountain Oyster* (☎ 307-733-5525), serving moderately priced breakfasts, burgers, pizza, soups and sandwiches. The *Alpenhof Dining Room* (☎ 307-733-3462) has a cosmopolitan dinner menu; reservations are advised. Entrees range from $17 to $30. A good value with an attractive outdoor summer deck, the *Alpenhof Bistro* (☎ 307-733-3242) serves wild game, seafood and prime rib. South of Teton Village, *Vista Grande* (☎ 307-733-6964), on Hwy 390 south of the Teton Village KOA, is the area's best Mexican restaurant. *Calico Italian Restaurant* (☎ 307-733-2460), north of Vista Grande, is also popular.

AROUND JACKSON HOLE
Mountain Biking
Some of the more popular mountain bike rides include Cache Creek, southeast of

Jackson into the Gros Ventre; Game Creek, along USFS Rd 30455 east off US 26/89/191 south of Jackson; Spring Gulch Rd, west off and parallel to US 26/89/191 between Hwy 22 and Gros Ventre Junction; and Shadow Mountain, along USFS Rd 30340 northeast of Antelope Flats at the eastern edge of Grand Teton National Park. Hard-core riders can try Old Pass Rd, the old way to Teton Pass, south of the current Hwy 22.

Teton Cyclery (☎ 307-733-4386), 175 N Glenwood St, Jackson, is an excellent bike shop with friendly, knowledgeable service and rentals. Hoback Sports (☎ 307-733-5335), 40 S Millward St, Jackson, has a good map of area bike trails.

Horseback Riding
Bar-T-5 Corral (☎ 307-733-5386, 800-772-5386), 790 Cache Creek Dr, offers guided rides in Cache Creek, east of Jackson. The A-OK Corral (☎ 307-733-6556), US 26/189/191 just north of Hoback Junction, offers guided hourly rides and full-day excursions. Both offer evening excursions and cookouts.

Rafting & Floating
White-water rafting is popular through the Class III Snake River canyon, south of Jackson along US 89/26 between Hoback Junction and Alpine. Ospreys and eagles nest in trees along the river, and wildlife viewing is possible. Half-day trips (from $30) put in at West Table Creek; they take out at Sheep Gulch (8 miles). Full-day trips (from $55) put in at Pritchard Creek, upstream from West Table Creek, take a break at Pine Creek campsite and take out at Sheep Gulch (16 miles). The rafting season is May to Labor Day. It can get crowded on the river in July and August; reserve ahead. Costs typically include transportation to and from Jackson.

Half-day scenic float trips (from $35/25 adults/children) on a 13-mile section of the swift-flowing Snake River put in south of Grand Teton National Park and take out north of Hoback Junction. Passing through Jackson Hole wetlands offers opportunities for birdwatching and wildlife viewing.

Reputable Jackson-based outfitters include:

Barker-Ewing River Trips
(☎ 307-733-1000, 800-448-4202),
45 W Broadway
Web site: www.barker-ewing.com

Dave Hansen Whitewater
(☎ 307-733-6295, 800-732-6295),
455 N Cache Dr
Web site: ww.davehansenwhitewater.com

Jackson Hole Whitewater
(☎ 307-733-1007, 800-700-7238),
650 W Broadway
Web site: www.jhwhitewater.com

Lewis & Clark River Expeditions
(☎ 307-733-4022, 800-824-5375),
335 N Cache Dr
Web site: www.lewisandclarkexped.com

Lone Eagle Whitewater
(☎ 307-733-1090, 800-321-3800),
455 W Broadway
Web site: ww.loneeagleresort.com

Mad River Boat Trips
(☎ 307-733-6203, 800-458-7238),
60 E Broadway
Web site: www.mad-river.com

Sands Wildwater River Trips
(☎ 307-733-7078, 800-358-8184),
110 W Broadway
Web site: www.sandswhitewater.com

Canoeing & Kayaking
Rendezvous River Sports & Jackson Hole Kayak School (☎ 307-733-2471, 800-733-2471) offers instruction; for details visit www.jhkayakschool.com. So does Snake River Kayak & Canoe School (☎ 307-733-9999, 800-529-2501), 365 N Cache; visit www.snakeriverkayak.com. For rig rentals, try Leisure Sports (☎ 307-733-3040), 1075 S US 89.

Hot-Air Ballooning
Rainbow Balloon Flights (☎ 307-733-0470, 800-378-0470) and Wyoming Balloon Co (☎ 307-739-0900), 450 E Sagebrush, Jackson, offer hour-long flights over the Tetons if you can afford the $175/person fee. The season runs from early June to mid-September. Balloon flights are dependent upon the weather.

WYOMING

GROS VENTRE MOUNTAINS

The Gros Ventre Mountains ('big belly' in French) east of Jackson Hole are bounded on three sides by rivers: the Snake to the west, Hoback to the south and Gros Ventre to the north. The Continental Divide forms their eastern boundary and the upper Gros Ventre Valley accesses the Wind River Mountains east of the Continental Divide. The most impressive views of the Gros Ventre are from Hoback Canyon (along US 189/US 191), looking at its rocky south face. A vast slide in 1925 dammed the Gros Ventre River, causing a huge flood. Today the forested north-facing slopes above Gros Ventre River, along Gros Ventre Rd east of Kelly, are called the **Gros Ventre Slide Geological Area**; a half-mile interpretive trail offers views. The resulting Upper Slide and Lower Slide lakes attract anglers. The Gros Ventre Wilderness Area and part of the Bridger-Teton National Forest cover its slopes.

Hiking

The Gros Ventre offer superb day hikes with big views and wildlife. Herds of bighorns wander the rocky slopes of **Sheep Mountain** (10,755 feet), also called Sleeping Indian, the most prominent peak east of Jackson Hole. Access to the trailhead for Sheep Mountain is via Flat Creek Rd from the south or Gros Ventre Rd to the north; 4WD is necessary. East of Snow King Mountain and southwest of Sheep Mountain is **Jackson Peak** (10,741 feet), another great hike. Head up from either Elk Refuge Rd, which becomes USFS Rd 30440 (take the right fork from the north) or the longer route via USFS Rd 30450 (Cache Creek Rd) from the south. **Goodwin Lake** is 2½ miles beyond the northern trailhead (at 8000 feet). From Hoback Canyon, other routes into the Gros Ventre Wilderness

Area begin along USFS Rd 30500 and Granite Creek.

Places to Stay

USFS campgrounds along Gros Ventre Rd (beyond the Antelope Flats Rd turnoff and north of Kelly) are **Atherton Creek**, 5½ miles; **Red Hills**, 10 miles; and **Crystal Creek**, 10½ miles. **Curtis Canyon Campground** is off USFS Rd 30440, off Elk Refuge Rd east of Jackson. **Granite Creek Campground** is off USFS Rd 30500 north of Hoback Canyon. All charge around $10.

MORAN JUNCTION TO TOGWOTEE PASS

US 26/287 climbs east from Grand Teton National Park's Moran Junction through the slopes of the Bridger-Teton National Forest to Togwotee Pass (9658 feet). The pass, named for a Shoshone guide who led the US Army Corps of Engineers here in 1873, is on the Continental Divide. North of US 26/287 is the 914-sq-mile Teton Wilderness Area, and to the south is the more distant Gros Ventre Wilderness Area.

The USFS Bridger-Teton National Forest (Buffalo Ranger District) Blackrock Ranger Station (☎ 307-543-2386, 307-739-5600) is on US 26/287, 8 miles east of Moran Junction. Paved Buffalo Valley Rd (USFS Rd 30050), which heads northeast from US 26/287 east of Moran Junction, leads to part of the Turpin Meadow Recreation Area. The Teton views from the Togwotee Overlook along US 26/287 are memorable.

The USFS campgrounds on US 26/287 are nice. **Hatchet Campground** ($5) is a quarter-mile west of Blackrock Ranger Station. Half a mile north of Buffalo Valley Rd is **Box Creek Campground** (free), with corrals, but no potable water. **Turpin Meadows Campground** ($5), on USFS Rd 30050, 4 miles north of US 26/87, is near several trailheads.

Montana

Montana

Facts about Montana

Although its name means 'mountain' in Spanish, Montana is best described by its nicknames. Historically (and now officially) the 'Treasure State,' Montana owes its foundation to gold and copper mining interests and, more recently – in the 1920s – the discovery of oil. Dubbed 'Big Sky Country' after AB Guthrie Jr's novel *The Big Sky* (1947), Montana indeed has an ever-changing and infinitely vast sky that dominates any view. The sky is also important for the precipitation it brings (or doesn't bring) in this land of ranchers, farmers and outdoor types. And since the publication of Montana's definitive literary anthology *The Last Best Place* (1988), which, perhaps not coincidentally, came out during a real-estate boom fueled by out-of-state buyers, Montana has come to represent in popular imagination a place that remains the way the 'Old West' once was.

Sparsely populated, the state offers plenty of wild territory to explore. The remote badlands of Makoshika State Park offer a delicate yet harsh landscape that few people take time to visit. On the other side of the Rockies – and Montana's tourist spectrum – Glacier National Park and Flathead Lake offer classic alpine beauty and solitude for those willing to hike a bit.

Famous, trout-filled rivers flow from Yellowstone National Park toward Bozeman (mecca for many skiers and climbers) through mountain ranges – Gallatin, Madison, Absaroka – that are wonderful for backcountry exploration. Slightly east, the high alpine tundra atop the Beartooth Plateau is unique in its geology and its accessibility to motorists – via the highest road in the USA. And then there's the state's history – from the wide-open prairies, irrigated by the Missouri River and explored by Lewis and Clark, to Old West mining towns like Dillon, Virginia City and

Highlights

- Glacier National Park – home to Montana's most picturesque scenery and abundant wildlife
- Big Hole Valley – a vast and lonely high-altitude valley, about as off the beaten track as you can get and still find some good bars and accommodations
- Bob Marshall Wilderness – a sprawling 3200 miles of trails and inspiring scenery
- Gates of the Mountain Wilderness – a remarkable limestone canyon that once played visual tricks on Lewis and Clark
- Beartooth Hwy – one of the few highways to go through alpine tundra – at an elevation of 12,000 feet
- Livingston – a charming town with vintage neon bar signs, new but tasteful galleries and good restaurants
- Big Sky – a favorite ski destination and Montana's largest year-round resort
- Makoshika State Park – a little-visited park with spectacular rock formations and seemingly endless badlands

MONTANA

Bannock, to battlefields where historic skirmishes such as the battles of the Little Bighorn, Big Hole and Rosebud took place. Home to the University of Montana and an energetic student population, Missoula is arguably Montana's most enjoyable town and is a good starting point for most itineraries.

INFORMATION
State Tourist Offices

Montana's statewide tourist board, Travel Montana (☎ 406-444-2654, 800-847-4868), 1424 9th Ave, PO Box 200533, Helena, MT 59620, has a Web site at www.visitmt.com and offers free publications, available throughout the state, including a state road map and the *Montana Vacation Guide*. Also free, but usually only available by contacting Travel Montana, are the *Montana Travel Planner,* which has details on accommodations and outfitters, and the *Montana Winter Guide*.

Travel Montana divides the state into six 'tourist zones' and publishes detailed guides for each one, available from Travel Montana or the chamber of commerce/visitors information center of the largest city within each zone: Kalispell or Missoula for 'Glacier Country'; Butte, Helena or Dillon for 'Gold West Country'; Great Falls for 'Russell Country'; Bozeman, Gardiner or West Yellowstone for 'Yellowstone Country'; Fort Peck or Malta for 'Missouri River Country'; and Billings or Miles City for 'Custer Country.'

See the Activities chapter for a list of the state's national parks, national monuments, national recreation areas and national historic sites.

Useful Organizations

Most environmental and conservation organizations belong to the Montana Environmental Information Center (☎ 406-443-2520), PO Box 1184, Helena, MT 59624. Their Web page (http://meic.org) has links to such groups as: Montana Department of Environmental Quality (www.deq .state.mt.us) and Rock Creek Alliance (www.sandpoint.org/rockcreek), which was

formed in 1987 to protect Rock Creek from mining interests and now fights numerous anti-mining battles across the state.

The Greater Yellowstone Coalition (www.greateryellowstone.org) monitors environmental issues in areas around the park and offers educational backcountry trips year-round (the winter Wolf Watching trip is said to be superb!). Volunteer with Buffalo Nations' Field Campaign (☎ 406-646-0070, buffalo@wildrockies.org Attn: Brandon), PO Box 957, West Yellowstone, MT 59758, www.wildrockies.org/buffalo, and you get to patrol for Yellowstone bison that wander out of national park boundaries onto private land in search of food during winter. Bring your own personal gear; food and lodging are provided.

The Montana Outfitters and Guides Association (☎ 406-449-3578), www.moga-montana.org/districts.html, provides contact information for all of the state's licensed outfitters.

Pride, the national gay and lesbian organization, has offices in Helena (☎ 406-442-9322, 800-610-9322 within Montana), PO Box 755, Helena, MT 59624, and a Web site at www.gaymontana.com/pride.

Area Code

Montana's telephone area code is 406.

Road Rules

After years of having no speed limit, and a few years of having a speed limit of 'reasonable and prudent,' Montana has enacted numerical speed limits: 75mph on interstates, 70mph on other highways during the day (65mph at night) and 65mph at all times on Hwy 93.

Seatbelts are required for the driver and front-seat passenger and for all passengers on highways and interstates. The fine for not wearing one is $60 per person. On motorcycles, helmets are required for anyone under 18.

A person with a blood alcohol content of 0.04% to 0.10% *may* be charged with drunk driving if there is evidence of drinking or reckless driving. Anyone with a blood alcohol level of 0.10% or greater *will* be

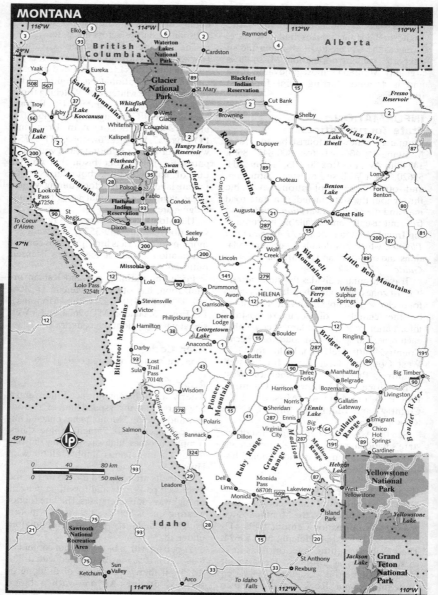

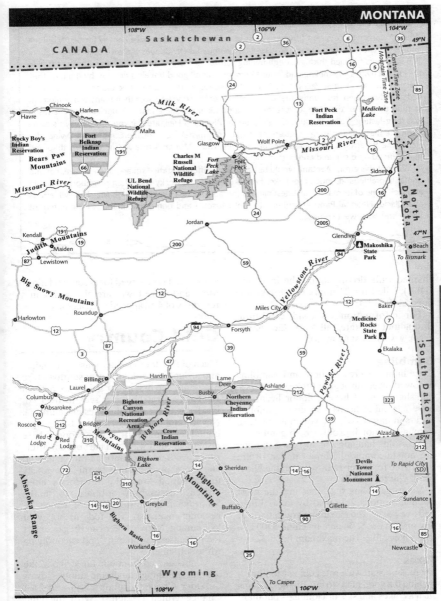

How Montana Took a Bite out of Idaho

When Abraham Lincoln sent surveyors west to define the border between newly formed Montana and the already existing Idaho Territory, the Continental Divide was the proposed demarcation. The surveyors traveled through rough mining camps like Helena and Bannack and participated in the local activities – gambling and 'entertainment' – as all good travelers do. But, by the time they reached the Deer Lodge Valley, they found themselves short on cash. Little did they suspect they had already crossed the Continental Divide. Whether the surveyors sold their maps and equipment to fund the rest of their trip, or lost them in a drunken gambling match, is unclear, but the result was long-lasting: Following an old trail through Missoula's Hellgate Canyon, the surveyors came upon the massive and rugged Bitterroot Range and, mistaking it for the Continental Divide, declared the Bitterroots Montana's western border. Thus, Montana received its western third and Idaho ended up disfigured and bottom-heavy.

Without this error, Montana would be an entirely different state – square, average size, flat and primarily prairie land, much more like the Dakotas than its Rocky Mountain neighbors. It would also lack some of its main tourist destinations (notably Flathead Lake, the Bob Marshall Wilderness and Glacier National Park), its cultural hub of Missoula and prime timberlands in the Bitterroot Valley and northwest corner.

charged with 'driving under the influence' (DUI), jailed for 24 hours to 60 days and fined $100 to $500.

For information on road conditions throughout the state, call ☎ 800-226-7623 or check www.mdt.state.mt.us.

Gambling

Once limited to reservation land, gambling is now allowed throughout the state. An establishment must have a liquor license to have a gaming license, so most gambling occurs in bars. Ironically, you must be 21 to purchase liquor but only 18 to gamble, so 19-year-olds hanging out in bars gambling are not uncommon! Minors under 18 are fined $100 for trying to buy liquor; the fine is $50 if you're 18 to 21.

Video gambling machines are the most popular options, followed by keno, bingo and live poker. The maximum you can win at any one time is $800 on a machine, $300 at a live poker table. The maximum bet is $2.

Taxes

There is no statewide sales tax in Montana – making it a good place to buy big-ticket items such as bikes and skis or clothing – but there is a 4% bed tax charged for accommodations. More and more towns are also voting in a resort tax of 4%, applied as a sales tax.

Gold Country

Much of the state's modern history began in and around the gold mines of southwestern Montana. The first major gold discovery, on Bannack's Grasshopper Creek in 1863, coincided with the end of rushes in California, Nevada and Colorado. Thousands of people bound for points farther west stopped here instead, in what was then part of Idaho Territory. As Bannack continued to yield gold and more people came to this previously undeveloped land, the territory's chief justice successfully lobbied to make Montana a separate state (of which he became governor). The federal policy of 'containing' Native Americans began under the pretense of protecting and encouraging white settlement.

Miners moved from one big strike to the next, establishing rough-and-tumble towns in Alder Creek (Virginia City) and Last Chance Gulch (Helena). With the land

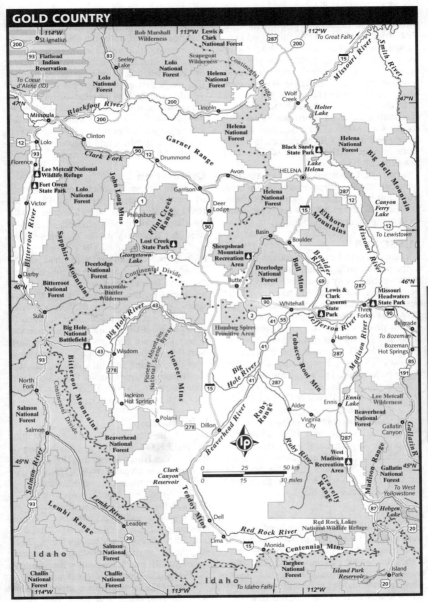

GOLD COUNTRY

MONTANA

cleared of Native American settlements, ranchers and cattlemen poured into the Bitterroot, Big Hole, Beaverhead and Deer Lodge Valleys. Businessmen who recognized that exploiting miners was generally more profitable than exploiting mineral deposits set up service and trade towns such as Missoula, Dillon and Deer Lodge.

In the 1870s and 1880s, as the advent of electricity created an enormous demand for copper wire, Marcus Daly struck the world's largest and purest vein of copper, thrusting Butte into the limelight as one of the richest towns in the USA.

Towns that endured the boom-and-bust cycle became the urban centers of this area, while mining camps and ghost towns scattered around the mountains are some of the most compelling destinations.

MISSOULA

Global import shops, vegetarian restaurants, people with dreadlocks and pierced parts – is this really Montana? The University of Montana (U of M) has one of the best creative writing departments in the USA and a similarly strong environmental studies program; together they attract students and faculty that make Missoula (population 58,460; elevation 3200 feet) a bastion of diversity compared to the rest of the state. Missoula's more traditional population of ranchers and mill workers has generally resigned itself to this liberal identity, while still fighting for logging rights and private land protection initiatives.

The Rattlesnake and Blue Mountain Wilderness Areas are spittin' distance from town, the Bitterroot Range spans its western edge, and the Clark Fork River courses right through it all – no wonder the traffic profile here looks increasingly like LA's.

History

The Salish, Blackfeet and Flathead Indians were the first inhabitants of Missoula, which takes its name from the Salish word *Im-i-sul-a,* meaning 'by the chilling waters.' The Salish regularly passed through Hellgate Canyon (the gap between Mt Jumbo and Mt Sentinel) on their way to hunt buffalo; the Blackfeet

would trap them in the narrow gorge and attack them from above. Lewis and Clark traveled through this same gorge in 1804, as did trappers and hunters in the 1820s.

In the 1840s Jesuit missionaries established St Mary's Mission 30 miles south and planted the area's first crops. Entrepreneurs Frank Worden and CP Higgins constructed the Missoula Mills near the Mullan Rd, which was replaced by railroads in 1893. Missoula's history as a mill town had begun. In 1895 the university was established, and Missoula has been western Montana's hub ever since.

Orientation

Missoula sits in the cradle of five valleys where the Bitterroot River, the Blackfoot River and Rattlesnake Creek converge with the Clark Fork of the Columbia River. I-90 runs past the north side of downtown Missoula. US 93 becomes US 12 coming into town, passes the airport, then turns into W Broadway. Orange St and Van Buren St are the main freeway exits off I-90, the latter leading straight to the university. Modern sprawl congests Reserve St, which creates Missoula's western and southern parameters.

A good way to explore is to park near the university, walk through the campus, turn west (left) onto the riverside path and cross over the Higgins St bridge into downtown. Downtown, Higgins Ave is the main street going north-south, with Front St and Broadway as the east-west arteries.

Information

Stop by the chamber of commerce (☎ 406-543-6623, 800-526-3465), one block south of the I-90 Van Buren St exit at 825 E Front St, or Adventure Cycling (☎ 406-721-8791), at 150 E Pine St, for maps and information.

The University Bookstore (☎ 406-243-4921), in the U of M student center, has regional guides and contemporary Montana literature. Fact and Fiction (☎ 406-721-2881) is at 220 N Higgins. Garden City News, 329 N Higgins Ave, carries out-of-state newspapers; open until 10 pm. Missoula's public library, 301 E Main St, has free Internet access.

Most banks are downtown, along Higgins Ave. The post office is at 200 E Broadway;

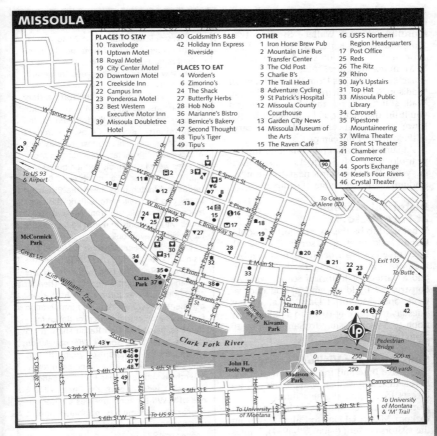

MISSOULA

PLACES TO STAY
10 Travelodge
11 Uptown Motel
18 Royal Motel
19 City Center Motel
20 Downtown Motel
21 Creekside Inn
22 Campus Inn
23 Ponderosa Motel
32 Best Western Executive Motor Inn
39 Missoula Doubletree Hotel
40 Goldsmith's B&B
42 Holiday Inn Express Riverside

PLACES TO EAT
4 Worden's
6 Zimorino's
24 The Shack
27 Butterfly Herbs
28 Hob Nob
36 Marianne's Bistro
43 Bernice's Bakery
47 Second Thought
48 Tipu's Tiger
49 Tipu's

OTHER
1 Iron Horse Brew Pub
2 Mountain Line Bus Transfer Center
3 The Old Post
5 Charlie B's
7 The Trail Head
8 Adventure Cycling
9 St Patrick's Hospital
12 Missoula County Courthouse
13 Garden City News
14 Missoula Museum of the Arts
15 The Raven Café
16 USFS Northern Region Headquarters
17 Post Office
25 Reds
26 The Ritz
29 Rhino
30 Jay's Upstairs
31 Top Hat
33 Missoula Public Library
34 Carousel
35 Pipestone Mountaineering
37 Wilma Theater
38 Front St Theater
41 Chamber of Commerce
44 Sports Exchange
45 Kesel's Four Rivers
46 Crystal Theater

MONTANA

postal code 59801. Medical help is available at Missoula's Community Medical Center (☎ 406-728-4100), on Fort Rd, just west of Reserve St, and St Patrick's Hospital (☎ 406-543-7271), 500 W Broadway.

Museums & Galleries

An art tour would visit the murals by artist Edgar Samuel Paxon at the Missoula County Courthouse, 220 W Broadway , and look at the contemporary exhibits and installations at the Missoula Museum of the Arts, 335 N Pattee St; open noon to 5 pm Monday to Saturday, $2 (free on Tuesday).

Missoula's Carousel

Missoulians talk passionately about their hand-carved carousel, in Caras Park near the river, that took five years to build. Local organizations and businesses sponsored the creation of the individual horses, which were carved primarily by local volunteers. Ride the carousel for 50¢, 11 am to 5:30 pm daily.

University of Montana

Since its inception in 1893, the U of M has grown from a refurbished schoolhouse on 40 acres and a student body of 50 to a 640-acre campus with 600 undergraduates and

2800 graduate students. Among its illustrious creative writing department grads are Dorothy Johnson, Wallace Stegner, Ivan Doig and William Kittredge, coeditor of *The Last Best Place*, an outstanding anthology of Montana literature.

Enter the campus from the south end of Madison St where there is a pay parking lot. Walk south towards the clock tower and you'll hit the main quad (bordered by the tower, the student center and main library) at the center of the campus.

At sunset, join the pilgrimage to the 84-year-old 'M' on Mt Sentinel for a spectacular view. The trail starts near the football stadium on the east edge of campus.

Historical Museum at Fort Missoula

What used to be the core of Fort Missoula, three blocks west of Reserve St on South Ave (take bus No 1 or No 9), now exhibits memorabilia of Missoula's development and a variety of historical scenes with reconstructed buildings and period decorations; open Memorial Day to Labor Day, Tuesday to Saturday 10 am to 5 pm, Sunday noon to 5 pm; Tuesday to Sunday noon to 5 pm the rest of the year; $3.

Smokejumper Visitors Center

The active base and training center for the heroic men and women who parachute into forests to combat raging wildfires is well worth a visit. Free tours begin hourly, 10 am to 4 pm, Memorial Day to Labor Day, from the visitors center (☎ 406-329-4934), 7 miles west of downtown on W Broadway (take bus No 10).

Rocky Mountain Elk Foundation & Wildlife Visitors Center

The RMEF, 2291 W Broadway (take bus No 2 or 10), is the fastest-growing conservation organization in the country and home to a large collection of stuffed North American big-game animals and related art. Somewhat ironically, most RMEF members are avid hunters, so their interest in conserving animals is primarily for recreational purposes (ie, hunting). It's open 8 am to 6 pm daily; free.

Fort Missoula

Fort Missoula was built in 1877 to provide fearful settlers a sense of protection from the neighboring Flathead Indians. The fort itself never saw any conflict between the settlers and Indians.

The quirkiest period in the fort's history (and the most indicative of Missoula's future) came in the 1890s with the formation of the 25th Infantry Bicycle Corps, Lieutenant James Moss' brainchild to test the feasibility of bicycles in the military. According to Moss, bicycles were less expensive than horses and didn't require nearly as much care. Besides frequent dispatch trips down the Bitterroot Valley and into Yellowstone Park, the corps made a 1900-mile trip from Missoula to St Louis, Missouri, only to return by train as the bicycle idea never took.

During WWI Fort Missoula was used as a training center, and in 1933 it became the Northwest Regional Headquarters for the Civilian Conservation Corps (CCC). Then, in 1941, the fort was turned over to the Department of Naturalization and Immigration for use as a detention center for Italian merchant seamen seized on Italian ships in US harbors. Some of Missoula's older population remembers the 'invasion' of young Italians who stole the hearts of the women in town. After the bombing of Pearl Harbor, Japanese-Americans were also interned here. At the end of WWII the fort served as a prison for court-martialed military personnel until it was decommissioned in 1947. The museum opened in 1975.

Rattlesnake National Recreation Area & Wilderness

Six miles north of Missoula, the Rattlesnake NRA covers 95 sq miles of the upper Rattlesnake Valley drainage. It's easy to do a day hike or bike trip within the 3-mile 'South Zone' radius of the main entrance, but getting to the more remote areas requires at least 11 miles of hiking (one-way). Camping is allowed only beyond the South

Zone. Bicycles are allowed on most trails that border the wilderness area.

Maps are posted at the entrance, 6 miles north of town via Van Buren St (which becomes Rattlesnake Dr). Anyone venturing beyond the South Zone should pick up a map at an outdoors store (see below) or the USFS headquarters (☎ 406-329-3511) downtown at the corner of Pine and Pattee Sts.

Bus No 5 gets you to within 2 miles of the entrance, but you must walk or hitch (especially easy on weekends) from there.

Activities

Ask at the chamber of commerce or one of the outdoors stores for a copy of the free 'Trails Missoula' guide, last published in 1998. One of the most accessible **hikes** is along the south side of the Clark Fork from McCormick Park (west of the Orange St bridge) back into Hellgate Canyon. Ascend the steep Mt Sentinel Trail (about a mile past the university) to reach Mt Sentinel's 5158-foot summit above the university.

Advanced skiers like **Snowbowl Ski Area** (☎ 406-549-9777), 17 miles north of Missoula, for its 2600-foot vertical drop (the biggest in Montana). There's a free shuttle on weekends and holidays that leaves from the Buttrey's supermarket on Broadway, east of Van Buren St; call the mountain for departure times. Families and beginners prefer **Marshall Mountain** (☎ 406-258-6000), 7 miles east of Missoula, which also has night skiing.

The Rattlesnake NRA (see above) is the best destination for backcountry skiers; inquire at the Trail Head for information and ski rentals.

The company 10,000 Waves (☎ 406-549-6670, 800-537-8315), with a Web site at www.10000waves.com, offers two-hour ($30), half-day ($47) and full day ($72) **rafting** and **kayaking** trips on the Class III and IV rapids of Alberton Gorge, or on the gentler Blackfoot River.

Anglers should stop in at Kesel's Four Rivers (☎ 406-721-4796), 501 S Higgins, for all things related to **fishing**, including gear and guided trips. The Trail Head (☎ 406-543-8440), www.trailheadmontana.com, on the

corner of Higgins and Pine Sts, rents skis, rafts, canoes, kayaks, backpacks, stoves and sleeping bags. Pipestone Mountaineering (☎ 406-721-1670), 101 S Higgins Ave, has climbing information, guides and equipment. The selection of used gear at Sports Exchange, 111 S Third St, yields great finds.

Special Events

On summer Wednesdays the whole town goes **Out to Lunch in Caras Park**, from 11:30 am to 1 pm at the north end of the Higgins Ave bridge. Local restaurants sell food and musicians play at this citywide picnic. The **Missoula Farmer's Market**, held Tuesday evenings and Saturday mornings between Higgins and Pattee Sts, is a lively event with music and vendors of produce, flowers, baked goods and crafts. The first week of April brings wildlife biologists, filmmakers and environmentalists together for the widely acclaimed **International Wildlife Film Festival**, begun in 1977. Participants include the BBC and National Geographic.

Places to Stay

Accommodations fill up quickly in late August and early September when students head back to school, and in May during graduation. Missoula's one urban camping option is the **Missoula/El-Mar KOA** (☎ 406-549-0881), three miles west of downtown at 3695 Tina Ave (well signed off W Broadway); tent/RV sites are $18/26.

The best budget motels are the **Downtown Motel** (☎ 406-549-5191, 502 E Broadway), the **City Center Motel** (☎ 406-543-3193, 338 E Broadway) and the **Ponderosa Motel** (☎ 406-543-3102, 800 E Broadway), which offer dated, no-frills rooms for around $45. The **Royal Motel** (☎ 406-542-2184, 388 Washington St), one block north of Broadway, and the **Uptown Motel** (☎ 406-549-5141, 800-315-5141, 329 Woody St), near the courthouse, have quieter locations and more modern rooms for about $48; the Uptown Motel also has one three-bed room that sleeps six for $70.

In the next price range up, your best bets are the **Creekside Inn** (☎ 406-549-2387, 800-551-2387, 630 E Broadway) and the

Campus Inn (☎ 406-549-5134, 800-232-8013), both with continental breakfast and rooms for $52/68. The *Holiday Inn Express Riverside* (☎ 406-549-7600, 1021 E Broadway) has $85 rooms, free breakfast and guest laundry. There's also the *Travelodge* (☎ 406-728-4500, 800-578-7878, 420 W Broadway) and the *Best Western Executive Motor Inn* (☎ 406-543-7221, 201 E Main St) in the heart of downtown.

For upscale accommodations, try the *Missoula Doubletree Hotel* (☎ 406-728-3100, 100 Madison St), two blocks south of E Broadway, which offers inexpensive off-season packages; rooms start at $95.

Goldsmith's B&B (☎ 406-728-1585, 809 E Front St) has a porch overlooking the river, a lovely reading room and a small refrigerator and microwave for guest use. Rooms cost $70/80, plus $15 for each additional person.

Places to Eat

There are supermarkets on the east and west ends of Broadway. The *Good Food Store* (☎ 406-728-5823, 920 Kensington St), one block west of Brooks St, has a great selection of organic produce, bulk foods and healthcare products. *Butterfly Herbs* (232 N Higgins Ave) makes teas that are famous throughout the state.

Missoula's student-oriented cafes, where you order at the counter, offer great food at good prices. Best of the bunch is *Food For Thought*, across from the university at the corner of Arthur Ave and Daly St, where breakfasts, sandwiches and salads cost around $5, pasta and stir-fry (served after 4 pm) are $8. *Second Thought* (529 S Higgins) is their smaller version with a condensed menu. *Worden's* (451 N Higgins), on the corner of Higgins and Spruce Sts, has imported deli items and makes a mean muffuletta sandwich. *Bernice's Bakery*, south of the river at 190 S 3rd St, is a mainstay for pastries, bread and strong coffee. There are good eats in several bars too (see Entertainment, below) if you don't mind the cigarette smoke.

For dinner you can't beat the *Hob Nob*, a cozy restaurant tucked in the back of the Union Club at 208 E Main St. Burgers (salmon, beef or several types of veggie), served with sweet potato fries, are $5, the steak sandwich is $8 and daily specials are $10 to $13; live jazz bands play Thursday through Saturday nights. *Tipu's* (115½ S 4th St) and the slightly fancier *Tipu's Tiger* (531 S Higgins) are the only Indian restaurants in Montana. Both do a fine job of creating tasty vegetarian dishes ($6 to $8) using lentils, garbanzos, seasonal vegetables and lots of spices; their chai tea is as good as it gets this side of Delhi.

The Shack (222 W Main) is a good choice for breakfast, while *Zimorino's* (424 N Higgins Ave) is the place for traditional pizzas and Italian fare. *Marianne's Bistro*, below the Wilma Theater at 131 S Higgins, is Missoula's finest dining option, with a large menu that covers the full spectrum of prices.

Entertainment

Pick up a copy of the *Independent* or look in the Entertainment section of Friday's *Missoulian* for what's going on around town.

The *Wilma Theater* (☎ 406-543-4166, 131 S Higgins) and the *Crystal Theater*, on the south side of the bridge at 515 S Higgins, show foreign and alternative films, as well as the occasional Hollywood blockbuster. The Wilma is also home to the noteworthy Missoula Symphony Orchestra and Chorale, whose season runs from October to May.

The *Front St Theater* (☎ 406-728-1911, 221 E Front St), Missoula's main live performance venue, is home to the Montana Repertory Theater group and the Montana Players Inc.

The Raven Café (130 E Broadway) has several pool tables, comfy chairs and shelves of books; no smoking or alcohol.

Barhopping is a favorite pastime among U of M students. Start with a homebrew, maybe something from their extensive food menu, at the *Iron Horse Brew Pub* (501 N Higgins) then venture over to *Charlie B's*, a Missoula institution where ranchers in hats drink Bud next to rasta-capped rock climbers drinking India Pale Ale. A pool table and small food counter that serves righteous Creole grub (shrimp po'boys, gumbo, jambalaya) until 2 am complete the scene. Next try the Ryman St trio of *The Ritz*, *Reds* and the *Rhino*, all with nightly drink specials and extensive selections of tap beer.

For live music try the *Top Hat (134 W Front)*, **Jay's Upstairs** *(119 W Main)* or Missoula's best jazz spot, *The Old Post (103 W Spruce),* which also serves Southwest-style food until midnight.

Getting There & Away
The Missoula County International Airport (☎ 406-728-4381) is 5 miles west of Missoula on US 12 W. Delta, Horizon Air, Northwest Airlines and United fly to and from Kalispell; Seattle, Washington; Salt Lake City, Utah; and Minneapolis, Minnesota.

All bus lines arrive and depart from the slightly run-down Greyhound bus depot (☎ 406-549-2339), 1 mile west of town at 1660 W Broadway. Daily departures go to Great Falls ($25), Whitefish ($24) via Polson, Bigfork and Kalispell, Helena ($14), and Billings ($47) via Butte ($15) and Bozeman ($31). A Greyhound bus departs once daily for long-distance trips to San Francisco ($122), Seattle ($61) and Denver ($105).

Getting Around
To/From the Airport There is an airport shuttle (☎ 406-543-9416, or call from the white courtesy phone in the baggage claim area) that charges $11 per person. Yellow Cab (☎ 406-543-6644) charges $10 for one person plus $1 for each additional person.

Going to the airport you can take Mountain Line (see below) bus No 10 and ask the driver to go to the airport (85¢).

Bus The free Emerald Line Trolley makes a full loop of downtown every 20 minutes, weekdays until 4 pm. Mountain Line Buses (☎ 406-721-3333) radiate from the transfer center on Pine St, between Woody and Ryman Sts, Monday to Saturday until 6 pm. Individual rides are 85¢, an unlimited day-pass is $1.75. Bus No 10 goes to the Greyhound station and, upon request, the airport. Schedules are available online

(www.mountainline.com) or from the transfer center and the chamber of commerce.

Car Hertz, Avis, Budget and National have counters in the airport. Less expensive options are Rent-a-Wreck (☎ 406-721-3838), Thrifty Car Rental (☎ 406-542-1540), Ugly Duckling (☎ 406-542-8459) and (usually the cheapest) Enterprise Rent-a-Car (☎ 406-721-1888), which all have pickup services.

BITTERROOT VALLEY
A drive-by view of the Bitterroot Valley (population 33,820; elevation 3400 feet) might cause wonder as to what all the fuss is about. But past the service centers and log home manufacturers along Hwy 93 are tons of opportunities for hiking, fishing and skiing. Parallel to Hwy 93, Eastside Hwy offers a glimpse of the Bitterroot's agricultural soul, which is quickly being lost to communities tied to the dot-com economy.

Hamilton, the valley's hub, is developing the most rapidly. The main streets of Stevensville, Corvallis and Darby are still pretty authentic to the 19th century, when Marcus Daly built the first of the valley's lumber mills, established Hamilton as the county seat and set up a 2000-acre horse ranch. The name 'Daly' appears around the valley only slightly more than the name 'Tammany,' Daly's most prized horse.

The valley is named after the elusive bitterroot plant, characterized by its showy pink or whitish flowers and a white, forked root. It only grows on dry hillsides and flowers on average just six weeks of the year. The Salish Indians used the plant's bitter root to flavor stews and sauces. Luckily, early settlers referred to the plant by its Salish name instead of its Latin name, or this would be 'Lewisia Rediviva Valley.'

History
The Bitterroot Salish Indians' interest in the 'magical' powers of the black-robed clergy brought Father Pierre De Smet to the area and helped establish St Mary's Mission near Stevensville in 1841. In 1850, John Owen, a trader with the US Army, bought the

MONTANA

BITTERROOT VALLEY

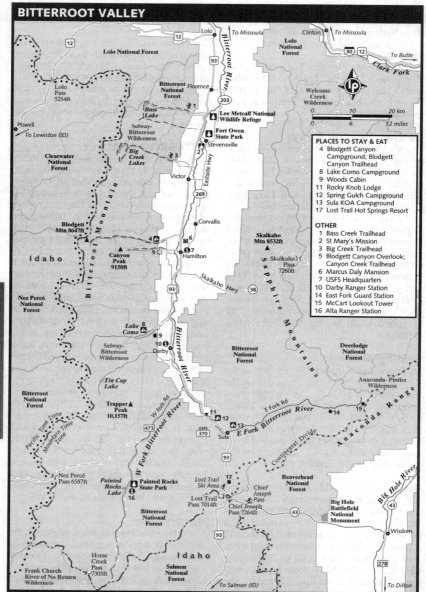

PLACES TO STAY & EAT
4   Blodgett Canyon
    Campground; Blodgett
    Canyon Trailhead
8   Lake Como Campground
9   Woods Cabin
11 Rocky Knob Lodge
12 Spring Gulch Campground
13 Sula KOA Campground
17 Lost Trail Hot Springs Resort

OTHER
1   Bass Creek Trailhead
2   St Mary's Mission
3   Big Creek Trailhead
5   Blodgett Canyon Overlook;
    Canyon Creek Trailhead
6   Marcus Daly Mansion
7   USFS Headquarters
10 Darby Ranger Station
14 East Fork Guard Station
15 McCart Lookout Tower
16 Alta Ranger Station

mission property and turned it into a trading post that thrived as a hub of activity for 22 years.

Under the Hellgate Treaty of 1855, the US government was supposed to survey the Bitterroot Valley to determine if it was a better site for the Salish than the proposed Flathead Reservation in the Mission and Jocko Valleys. By the time the survey started, the valley had so many white settlements that the government succumbed to economic pressure and decided (without ever completing the survey) that the Salish needed to move. Half the tribe moved immediately under a war chief named Arlee, but the other half remained with their tribal chief Victor and his son Charlo until they were escorted out by the army in 1891.

Orientation & Information

Stevensville (population 2187), Hamilton (population 4829) and Darby (population 1089) are the valley's main towns, each with gas stations, a bank, market, post office, Laundromat and a Bitterroot National Forest ranger station on its main street. The Forest Supervisor's office (☎ 406-363-7117), in Hamilton at 1801 N 1st St, has the widest selection of maps and literature for surrounding wilderness areas. The Bitterroot Chamber of Commerce (☎ 406-363-2400), www.bvchamber.com, on the corner of

Main St and US 93 in Hamilton, makes hotel reservations and has maps.

Things to See & Do

Footpaths meander through the **Lee Metcalf National Wildlife Refuge**, where pileated woodpeckers, ospreys, heron, geese, otter, muskrat, beaver and white-tailed deer make their homes. Exciting battles occur during peak migration periods (fall and early spring), when the ospreys return to their nests and have to evacuate the geese who have occupied the nests in their absence. Access to the refuge is from Wildfowl Lane which cuts west from Eastside Rd 4 miles north of Stevensville, then rejoins Eastside Rd a half mile north of town (from Stevensville turn east, off Main St, onto Eastside Rd then north on Wildfowl Lane).

The west end of what is now 4th St in Stevensville is where Father Pierre De Smet founded **St Mary's Mission** in 1841. Explore the grounds any time, or visit its original structures and graveyard on a guided tour 10 am to 5 pm (last tour leaves at 4 pm) from April to October; $3/1 adults/children.

The 24-bedroom, 15-bathroom **Marcus Daly Mansion** has sheltered, among others, Theodore Roosevelt, Will Rogers and artist Charles Russell. Built in 1890 as Marcus Daly's summer house, it remains an exquisite estate. You can roam the grounds for

MONTANA

'Black Robes' Bring Powerful Medicine

Christianized Iroquois who came from the northeast with trappers and traders brought stories of great men in black robes who wielded powerful medicine and had strong connections to the land beyond. Interested in obtaining some of this power to help them with their farming and their battles, the Bitterroot Salish sent a messenger to St Louis to ask the Catholic Church to send a 'Black Robe' (priest) to the West. But the church declined the request: The journey from St Louis was long and hard, and the West was considered dangerous and full of savages. Refusing to give up, the Salish (also known as the Flathead Indians) made three more separate entreaties until the church sent Father Pierre De Smet in 1841.

When Father De Smet expressed his desire to share his medicine with (or, convert) the Blackfeet – the Flatheads' most feared and hated enemy – the Flathead people became suspicious and angry with him. Two seasons of drought followed, and the relationship between the tribe and the missionaries rapidly deteriorated. Many Indians continued to worship as Catholics, but in the past 20 years or so, there has been a strong revival of traditional ceremonies as well.

Paramilitary Groups

Montanans have long felt a great attachment to their land and to their rights of stewardship. The vast expanse of the area enabled early settlers to acquire large acreage, and their exploitation of natural resources through mining, logging and raising livestock led to increasing industrial development.

As the state grew, ranchers developed an unwritten code of conduct – in essence: 'Do your own thing, as long as you don't hurt anybody,' and 'Don't mess with someone else's water or land.' But the decline of the mining industry and the growth of tourism are changing the face of Montana.

In 1972, a new state constitution was drafted that reflected contemporary environmental concerns. Meanwhile, increased federal oversight in the form of clean water and wetlands preservation acts, the Brady Law (which imposes a waiting period for gun purchases) and the growing authority of the Bureau of Land Management have threatened the locals' long-cherished autonomy.

To protect themselves from what they feel is the usurpation of their rights 'by the tyranny of a runaway, out-of-control government' (in the words of the Militia of Montana), some angry citizens have formed paramilitary groups. Made up of primarily white, right-wing conservatives from the Bitterroot Valley, the groups claim legitimacy through their interpretation of the US Constitution's Second Amendment – namely, their right to form militias and bear arms. But some also believe in 'Christian Identity,' a doctrine developed by a former Ku Klux Klansman that claims (among other things) that present-day Jews are 'the race of Cain' and that 'racial purity' is God's plan. Some groups have set up 'common law' courts that deny government authority, evade taxes and even issue their own checks.

Many militia members also belong to the Patriots, a decentralized movement that includes Christian Identity churches, Aryan Nation members, pro-gun groups and constitutionalists, and taps into an anti-Semitic and bigoted vein not unique to Montana. (In fact, in 1999, the Southern Poverty Law Center identified 217 anti-government Patriot organizations, including 68 militias, across the US.) Some Patriot groups only adhere to the Bill of Rights, denying the freedoms for African-Americans and women that were recognized in later amendments, while others are known for their tactics of intimidation and violence toward law enforcement officials.

On March 25, 1996, a militia group associated with the Patriot movement known as the Freemen began an 81-day standoff with the FBI at their ranch in Jordan, Montana. The group holed up on the estate when the FBI arrested two of their leaders for fraud and tax evasion. This standoff, along with the bombing of the Alfred P Murrah Federal Building in Oklahoma City, Oklahoma, the previous year, helped to bring nationwide attention to the militia movement. Timothy McVeigh, who was convicted of the bombing, had ties to a religious militant organization and had apparently acted in retaliation for the deaths caused by earlier FBI standoffs in Waco, Texas, and Ruby Ridge, Idaho.

To some extent, the Oklahoma City bombing discredited the militia movement – the American public was horrified by this act of homegrown terrorism. These groups remain on the fringes of society. Their anger toward the government notwithstanding, they now rely more on the media than violence as a tool to achieve their aims. When actor Steven Segal was filming *The Patriot* in Ennis, for example, he received threats from persons identifying themselves as militia members. The Militia of Montana quickly denied involvement and offered to act as movie consultants to present a fair portrayal of their kind. John Trochmann, head of the group, seized this opportunity to publicize one of his group's positions (fear of a United Nations-led conspiracy to form a New World Order), stating: 'I hope he (Segal) will come to the rescue of America, to stop the encroachment of global government.'

– Joslyn Leve

free, 10 am to 5 pm, though the tour given Tuesday to Sunday, 11 am to 4 pm, is well worth the $5; closed October 15th to April 30th. The mansion (☎ 406-363-6004) is 2 miles north of Hamilton on Eastside Rd; turn east on A St from US 93. Wheelchair access to the 1st floor only.

At the south end of the valley, **Darby** is worth a visit. The original town square, flanked by the public library (in the old firehouse) and a Pioneer Memorial Museum (housed in an old chicken coop), is the main attraction. Of equal interest is the Darby Historical Ranger Station, on the north end of town where Main St is again called US 93, built by the CCC in 1937–39; open daily, 9 am to 5 pm.

Down in Sula, **Lost Trails Hot Springs Resort** (☎ 406-821-3574) charges $4.50 for a soak in its hot outdoor pool; 8 am to 10 pm daily, to 6 pm on Tuesday.

Hiking

There are 29 drainages that cut east-west through the Bitterroot Range, creating dramatic canyons and epic hiking possibilities. Trailheads are well signed off US 93, usually 2 to 8 miles west via maintained roads. The 7-mile **Lake Como National Recreation Loop Trail** begins 4 miles west of US 93, where there is a swimming beach, boat launch and picnic area. The trail encircles the lake, crossing the **Rock Creek Trail,** which leads to the Selway-Bitterroot Wilderness Area.

Popular day hikes include the nontechnical but steep trail to the lookout tower atop St Mary's Peak (near Stevensville), the easy 1½-mile jaunt to the Blodgett Canyon Overlook (near Hamilton) and the 7-mile trip to Bass Lake at the south side of St Joseph's Peak (near Stevensville).

With more effort you can get to the top of stately Trapper Peak or into the Selway-Bitterroot Wilderness Area along the Big Creek and Storm Creek trails (both near Darby).

South of Darby by 28 miles (turn southwest off US 93 on West Fork Rd and continue 24 miles), Painted Rocks State Park has the wheelchair-accessible **Alta Pine Interpretive Trail**, plus a boat launch, fishing dock, potable water and campground. At the north end of the lake is the Alta Ranger Station, one of the first USFS ranger stations in the USA, built in 1899.

You can buy maps and other camping and hiking supplies at Bob Ward's & Sons (☎ 406-363-6204), 1120 N 1st St (US 93) in Hamilton.

Fishing

Most fishing access points (well signed off US 93) are in the north end of the valley between Victor and Hamilton, or south of Darby. For lake fishing, try Lake Como or Painted Rocks Lake (see Hiking, above).

Stop at the Fishaus (☎ 406-363-6158), 702 N 1st St (US 93) in Hamilton, for gear and information.

Skiing

One of Montana's best ski deals is the $20 lift ticket at Lost Trail Ski Area (☎ 406-821-3211), 13 miles south of Sula on US 93. The place is small (a 2400-foot vertical drop covered by two chairlifts and two surface lifts) but gets an average of 300 inches of light, dusty powder per year. You also have the thrill of carving turns across the Continental Divide and the Montana-Idaho border.

Cross-country skiers should turn east on Hwy 43 (towards Wisdom), before reaching Lost Trail, to access a vast network of trails at Chief Joseph Pass. The Darby and Sula ranger stations have trail maps. Another good cross-country destination is the unplowed Skalkaho Hwy (Hwy 38), which turns east 3 miles south of Hamilton and heads into the Sapphire Mountains.

Places to Stay

Camping For an atypical camping experience, inquire about renting the *East Fork Guard Station Cabin* or *McCart Lookout Tower;* reservations (☎ 406-363-3131) are usually required well in advance. Similar is the historic *Woods Cabin,* on the east end of Lake Como, that sleeps 15 people for $50 a night; you supply food and bedding.

MONTANA

The largest concentration of *USFS campgrounds* are south of Darby on US 93, and on Spring Gulch, West Fork and East Fork Rds. Most have toilets, water and fire rings and cost $6 to $9. The *Sula KOA Campground* (☎ 406-821-3364) charges $18 per tent, $24 for RVs.

Motels & Hotels In Hamilton try *Deffy's Motel* (☎ 406-363-1244, 321 S 1st St) or the *City Center Motel* (☎ 406-363-1651, 415 W Main St), both with rooms for $35/40. Chains like *Comfort Inn* (☎ 406-363-6600), *Super 8* (☎ 406-363-2940), and *Best Western Hamilton Inn* (☎ 406-363-2142), all on US 93, range in price from $45 to $95.

Good choices on Darby's Main St (US 93), include the *Wilderness Motel* (☎ 406-821-3405), at the south end of town, with rooms for $35/45, tent/RV sites for $6/18; and *Bud & Shirley's* (☎ 406-821-3401), with a popular restaurant and rooms for $50/60.

Lost Trail Hot Springs Resort (☎ 406-821-3574), 6 miles north of the US 93/Hwy 43 junction, is a quiet, woodsy resort with a bar and restaurant, log cabins ($63), a few motel rooms ($53) and naturally heated outdoor pool (free admission for guests).

Places to Eat

There are supermarkets on US 93 in Hamilton and Darby and a slew of fast-food restaurants near Hamilton.

In downtown Hamilton, *Wild Oats*, upstairs at 217 Main St, serves breakfast and lunch for under $6 and has good vegetarian options. *Nap's*, on Second St two blocks north of Main St, is the place for huge $5 burgers. Locals like *The Banque*, 225 Main St, for a steak, or its upstairs bar the *Exchange* for beer, burgers and a game of pool.

All-purpose *Trapper's*, 516 Main St in Darby, has a huge menu for breakfast, lunch and dinner. Also on Main St, the *Darmont Hotel* is Darby's original drinking establishment and a colorful spot for burgers, steaks, pizza and fried shrimp; the kitchen is open until 11 pm.

The *Rocky Knob Lodge* (☎ 406-821-3520), 12 miles south of Darby on US 93, is

famous for its hickory-smoked ribs, trout and roasted chicken. Dinner is $9 to $16, lunch around $7.

Entertainment

In Hamilton, the Shantilly Theater Group and Hamilton Players perform in a restored schoolhouse. Tickets and information are available at Chapter One Bookshop (☎ 406-363-5220) at 252 Main St.

People venture great distances for the English pints and pub atmosphere of *The Hamilton*, half a block west of US 93 in the small town of Victor. The owner wears a kilt, pulls a perfect Guinness and makes excellent fish and chips. For a totally different scene, make the rounds in Darby. The *Valley Bar*, *Darmont Hotel* (also known as The Sawmill) and *Dotson's*, all on Main St, are classic western gems with darts, pool tables and live music most weekends. The Darmont has a great collection of old saws hanging (yikes!) from the ceiling.

BIG HOLE VALLEY

The Big Hole River flows north from its source in the Bitterroot Range to meet the Jefferson River and eventually become part of the Missouri. Its wide course between the Bitterroot and Pioneer Mountains is entirely above 6000 feet, fitting the term 'hole' used by Native Americans to describe high mountain valleys. Montanans like to say that the Big Hole is 'uphill from everywhere.'

Most activity in the area centers around Dillon, but the small towns and wide-open spaces along Hwy 43 and County Rd 278 – where one person acts as the gas station attendant, bartender and undertaker – are where the real flavor of this sparsely populated and infrequently visited place lies. It's been said that Montana's best fishing is on the stretch of the Big Hole River between the Wise and the Beaverhead Rivers, north of Dillon off I-15.

History

Because of its elevation, the Big Hole only sees summer from about mid-July to September and thus remained a wilderness long after surrounding valleys were settled. Flathead Indians, who called the area the 'Land of the Big Snows,' came up from the Bitterroot Valley to gather camas bulbs, and trappers came through hunting buffalo, elk, deer and antelope. But settlement didn't come until ranchers discovered the valley's rich grass supply in the 1890s. Since then, the Big Hole has been serious ranch country with most ranches holding 2000 to 5000 acres. But even this remote spot is feeling the winds of change as parcels are divided into smaller holdings and recreation becomes increasingly important as a soft industry.

General George Custer's defeat in the **Battle of the Little Bighorn** in 1876 intensified fear among white settlers and prompted further demands that the government 'contain' the Nez Percé (see 'The Battle of the Little Bighorn'). Government officials instructed the US Army to move all remaining Nez Percé to the reservation in northern Idaho and made it clear to the Indians that the only alternative was war.

After three young Nez Percé braves went on a raid killing several whites, war became inevitable. Thunder Comes Rolling over the Mountains (better known as Chief Joseph) realized that the only hope of survival for his people lay in heading across Montana towards Canada, where Chief Sitting Bull and his people had found refuge. The Battle of the Big Hole was the first indication to the Nez Percé that they would not be permitted to peacefully go on their way.

Believing that General Howard's army was several days away and, more importantly, unaware that a second military force – 162 men under Colonel John Gibbon's 7th Cavalry – had joined the chase, Chief Looking Glass chose to set up camp beside the Big Hole River. Gibbon's scouts spotted the Nez Percé the following afternoon (August 8, 1877), and the next morning before dawn, the soldiers and 34 volunteers situated themselves across the river on 'Battle Hill,' 200 yards west of the camp. As dawn broke, a Nez Percé accidentally stumbled onto the concealed soldiers and the skirmish began with a chaotic volley of gun and cannon fire.

The battle lasted two days, until both sides had suffered so many casualties that caring for the dead and injured took precedence over continuing battle. If any victory was won, it was by the Nez Percé, who captured and disassembled the army's howitzer and put Gibbon's command out of action. Nonetheless, the Nez Percé lost 90 members of their tribe – the greatest loss of life during their extraordinary 1800-mile journey which finally ended in defeat at the Bear's Paw Battlefield.

Big Hole National Battlefield

Because of its semi-remote location, just west of Wisdom, Big Hole Battlefield National Monument (☎ 406-689-3155) is much less visited than Montana's other battlefield sites, but it's worth the detour. From the excellent museum and visitors center, open 8 am to 6 pm daily, a road leads to the Big Hole battlefield itself, half a mile away. Four different trails lead to key battle sites with wooden markers shaped like hats (blue for soldiers, beige for volunteers) and feathers marking where people fell.

Sioux chief Sitting Bull

MONTANA

Jackson Hot Springs

Halfway between Bannack and Wisdom, Jackson Hot Springs (☎ 406-834-3151, 888-438-6938) was discovered in 1806 by Lewis and Clark, who used its 104°F pool to boil meat and 'restore' themselves. Nowadays it's a good place to stop for a drink and some local atmosphere or to stay a few days and experience the valley's solitude. The large knotty pine lodge has a cozy dining room, TV area and a bar where live bands perform on weekend nights. Cabins are $75, economy cabins with shared bath are $40. A plunge in the pool is $5.

Wisdom

At the junction of Hwy 43 and County Rd 278, Wisdom (population 180) consists of two bars, two restaurants, a motel and a gas station. Despite its proximity to Butte (74 miles) and Dillon (64 miles), the town's unpaved streets, dilapidated wooden buildings and sagebrush-covered surroundings feel more like the 19th century than the 21st. It's the hub for local cattle ranchers and a good place to stop for a few minutes, even if only to poke your head in the bar and inquire how the fishing is (always a good question, even if you don't fish). *Fetty's Café* serves heaping open-faced sandwiches and good burgers, and the *Big Hole Crossing* has steak, chicken, fish and heavenly pie. If the gas station appears closed, ask for help at the bar across the street next to Fetty's. The *Nez Percé Motel* (☎ *406-689-3254*), on the east side of the Hwy 43 junction, charges $33/40 for nice rooms with a bath and TV.

Bannack Historic State Park

Bannack was the site of Montana's first gold strike, gold rush, school, frame house, Freemason lodge and territorial legislature. Today it stands out as the Grand Ghoul of ghost towns, preserved in its natural state as if the gold-seekers will return at any moment. State park rangers lead tours of the town and mine, or you can wander around on your own or with the self-guided tour map (free at the entrance). In either case, spend a few minutes at the visitors center (☎ 406-834-3413) to get a sense of what Bannack was like in its heyday. The public campground adjacent to the park has toilets, potable water, picnic tables and fire rings where rangers give campfire talks. Sites cost $11 per night.

Bannack Days, held the third weekend in July, attempt to reenact Bannack's gold rush period with costumed performers, wagon rides and the like. The park, 25 miles west of Dillon on County Rd 278 and another 4 miles south from its unmarked turnoff, is open year-round during daylight hours; $3 per vehicle.

Pioneer Mountains National Scenic Byway

The 35-mile, roller-coaster road between the towns of Wise River and Polaris cuts right through the middle of the Pioneer Range alongside the Wise River. This is a scenic alternative to I-15 (which runs parallel, east of the Pioneers) that takes about an hour longer to drive, without any stops. In winter the road is plowed from the south to Elkhorn Hot Springs and from the north to Crystal Park, but there is no through access.

Crystal Park About 2 miles south of Wise River, what looks like an abandoned battlefield is actually a 68-million-year-old granodiorite intrusion – rich with quartz amethyst crystals – that has been worked over by recreational diggers. The best bet is to find a relatively deep hole and dig in sideways beneath the sandlike granodiorite; crumbly reddish-brown zones mark traces of veins that might contain crystal pockets. It's helpful to have a shovel, some sort of prying tool (a crowbar works well) and a screen to sift dirt. Elkhorn Hot Springs (see below) rents equipment for a small fee, but just digging with a stick will usually yield at least a few pieces.

Elkhorn Hot Springs As rustic as they come, the 'resort' at Elkhorn Hot Springs (☎ 406-834-3434, 800-722-8978), 13 miles north of County Rd 278, used to be *the* place for local ranchers to soak their weary bones and drown their sorrows on a Saturday

The Vigilantes

A rough, self-serving man in a town of rough, self-serving men, Henry Plummer stands out as the man who made Bannack famous. Educated in the east, charismatic and poised, Plummer came to Bannack in 1863 and was elected sheriff one year later. Within eight months of public 'service,' Plummer and his gang of road agents, the 'Innocents,' had killed 102 people. Mainly they were after gold (supposedly they acquired $6 million worth in all), but they readily killed anyone deemed inadequately cooperative. Their favorite route was the stage between Bannack and Virginia City. One agent in Virginia City owned a business right next to the stage loading dock, where he would watch goods being loaded and then mark the stage with the gang's code numbers if it was worth robbing.

When the citizens of Bannack and Virginia City caught on that it was the sheriff who was responsible for most of the killing and robbery in the area, they were at first cowed; people cleared the streets when Plummer came riding into town and went silent when he walked in a room. But a group of citizens, most of them Freemasons sworn to secrecy under oath, formed a vigilance group, the infamous 'Vigilantes.' In a two-day swoop, the Vigilantes hunted down and hanged – from gallows that Plummer himself had built – 28 of the Innocents, including Plummer, whom they surprised during Sunday dinner at his in-laws' house. Most of the Innocents were buried in Virginia City, but Plummer's grave was laid separate from the rest of the cemetery. It has been dug up so many times now that nothing is left.

Even after the Innocents were gone, the Vigilantes continued their righteous yet bloody activities. Rarely asking questions, let alone trying offenders in a courtroom, they killed so many lawbreakers that even innocent men began to fear for their lives. Thomas Dimsdale published his *Vigilantes of Montana* as a newspaper series in 1865 and as a book one year later; this firsthand account is considered fundamental reading on the subject. RE Mather and FE Boswell argue, in *Hanging the Sheriff* (Historic Montana Publishing, 1999) and *Vigilante Victims: Montana's 1864 Hanging Spree* (Historical West Publishing Company, San Jose, 1991), that Plummer and others were unjustly hanged without trial.

night. The clientele is still local, interspersed with out-of-state snowmobilers and cross-country skiers during the winter.

A plunge in the pools (one hot, one extra-hot) costs $4 for nonguests. Log cabins (each with its own outhouse) and rooms in the lodge sleep two to six people for $45 to $105, meals in the knotty-pine dining room cost $5 to $12.

North of Elkhorn by 7 miles, Maverick Mountain is a small and steep downhill ski area – not worth a detour but not a bad place to recreate if you're in the area during winter.

Places to Stay & Eat Camping is available at seven public campgrounds (well marked off the road); each has pit toilets, fire rings, picnic tables and $10 sites. The ***Grasshopper Inn*** (☎ 406-834-3456), about 4 miles north of Polaris, is a full-service lodge whose restaurant and bar act as the area's main watering hole and weekend entertainment venue; single/double rooms cost $48/60. The ornate mahogany back bar sailed around Cape Horn from England to San Francisco, made its way by wagon to Bannack and then Dillon and finally found a home at the Grasshopper.

DILLON

Once the terminus of the Utah & Northern Railroad and the main supply station for Bannack's gold miners, Dillon (population 4342; elevation 5096 feet) is a rip-roarin' rancher's town that welcomes tourists but

MONTANA

doesn't depend on them. Feed and fertilizer industry lines the railway on the edges of town, but the downtown is small and charming in an unpretentious way. It's the seat of Beaverhead County, home of Western Montana College (which educates about 80% of the state's teachers) and one of the more lively overnight stops in the Big Hole. Lewis and Clark traded their canoes for horses in this region, returning several times to the 'Beaver's head' rock that watches over its namesake river north of town.

Orientation & Information
Dillon lies just east of the Beaverhead River and I-15, 65 miles south of Butte. Hwy 41 heads northeast from I-15 at the south edge of town and zigzags through Dillon along Atlantic, Helena and Montana Sts.

The Chamber of Commerce and Visitors Center (☎ 406-683-5511), in the old railroad depot on S Montana St between Sebree and Glendale Sts, provides a good walking tour map. The Beaverhead National Forest Headquarters (☎ 406-683-3900) is at 420 Barrett St. Banks with ATMs are located on Idaho and Montana Sts. Sagebrush Outdoor Gear (☎ 406-683-2329), 36 N Idaho St, is the best resource for recreation information.

Things to See & Do
The Patagonia Outlet (☎ 406-683-2580), 34 N Idaho St, is probably Dillon's hottest attraction. More educational is the Beaverhead County Museum, adjacent to the Visitors Center in the old railroad depot. It has a wealth of mining articles found at Bannack and a fireplace made of petrified wood and geodes; open 10 am to 8 pm weekdays, 1 to 5 pm weekends, June to August (10 am to 5 pm weekdays the rest of the year), free.

The Chamber of Commerce has a list of public access sites for fishing. Fishing Headquarters (☎ 406-683-6660), 610 N Montana St, offers guided float and walk-in trips on the Beaverhead and Jefferson Rivers for $150 per person. Tim Tollett's Frontier Angler (☎ 406-683-5276), 680 N Montana St, rents rafts and offers a shuttle service to people with their own gear.

Places to Stay
Dillon's KOA (☎ 406-683-2749, 735 Park St) sits beside the river; tent/RV sites are $23/35. Rooms atop a rowdy bar at the Dillon Hotel (☎ 406-683-9973, 24 E Center St) aren't bad for $14 (shared bath). A single/double with similarly shabby decor costs $16/18 at the once grand Hotel Metlen (☎ 406-683-2335, 5 S Railroad Ave), across the tracks from the railroad depot. The Sundowner Motel (☎ 406-683-2375, 800-524-9746, 500 N Montana St), at Franklin Ave, has singles/doubles for $40/42. The $31 rooms at the Sacajawea Motel (☎ 406-683-2381, 775 N Montana St) are an excellent value.

Chain-owned options on the edge of town include the Super 8 (☎ 406-683-4280, 550 N Montana St) and the Paradise Inn Best Western (☎ 406-683-4214, 650 N Montana St), both with rooms for $45 to $60. A better choice is the Guest House Inn (☎ 406-683-3636, 800-214-8378, 580 Sinclair St), off I-15, with snazzy rooms and breakfast for $44/53.

Places to Eat
Join locals at the Lion's Den (725 N Montana St) for an enormous prime rib dinner ($11), or try the reputable pizza at Papa T's (10 N Montana St), a less-than-intimate bar with a very intimate past (the 2nd floor used to be a brothel). The Western-Wok (17 E Bannack St), lives up to its name with Western decor and Chinese food for $6 to $9. The Sweetwater Coffee Co (26 E Bannack St) has comfortable atmosphere and good breakfast/lunch items for under $5.

Entertainment
Bar touring in Dillon's historic downtown is entertaining even for teetotalers. Shooters (31 E Bannack St) is a good place to start with the post-work crowd who comes in around 5 pm. Of interest on N Montana St, between Bannack and Center Sts, are the Moose Bar and Longhorn Saloon, with pool tables and microbrews on tap, and Papa T's, with a dance floor and live music on weekends. The most character of all is

across the railroad tracks at the ***Hotel Metlen***, especially on weekend nights when live bands play to a denim-clad, two-steppin' dance crowd.

DILLON TO THE IDAHO BORDER

What is now Clark Canyon Reservoir (see below) was the Corps of Discovery's 'Camp Fortunate,' where they finally met a group of Shoshone who provided them with horses and a guide that enabled them to cross the Bitterroot Range. Sacagawea recognized the Shoshone chief as the brother she had been separated from at birth, a chapter that reigns as one of the most emotional in the Lewis and Clark story.

Clark Canyon Reservoir

A popular weekend destination for boaters, Jet-skiers and anglers, this 'lake' is 18 miles south of Dillon and easily reached from I-15. **Hunter's Beaverhead Marina** (☎ 406-683-5556) sells fishing licenses, gas and a limited selection of groceries, and is the best place for local information.

About 20 miles south of the reservoir, the once-lively railroad town of Dell now owes its existence to ***Yesterday's Calf-A***, a 1903 schoolhouse turned eatery. Read the history of the place (printed on the menu) while waiting for a hot turkey sandwich or piece of homemade pie ($3).

Italian Peaks

West of I-15 from Dell, Big Sheep Creek Rd parallels the interstate then heads southwest for 19 miles to Nichola Creek Rd in the foothills of the Continental Divide, below the Italian Peaks. The **Continental Divide National Scenic Trail** stretches for 50 miles along the Montana-Idaho border here and crosses the highest point on Montana's portion of the Divide – Eighteenmile Peak (11,141 feet). Multi-day backpacking trips are the norm here, since a day or so is

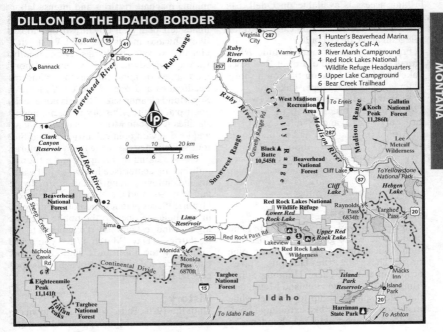

required to reach the elevations where you can see down into both states. The best access is via the Bear Creek trailhead: at Nichola Creek Rd turn west and go another 7 miles to Bear Creek Rd. The trailhead is 1½ miles farther, but cars can make the trip only in good weather.

Red Rock Lakes National Wildlife Refuge

In 1935, when plumes were at their height of popularity in women's fashions, the government established this refuge to protect the trumpeter swan. Currently there are about 110 trumpeters in the surrounding valley, along with sandhill cranes, Barrow's goldeneyes and great blue herons.

Canoeing the refuge's interwoven streams, marshes and lakes is an extremely pleasant way to see the wildlife. Lower Red Rock Lake is open in the fall, and Upper Red Rock Lake and Red Rock Creek are open from July 15 until the first freeze. Fishing access is available on Odell, Elk Springs and Red Rock Creeks, and at the east end of the refuge off Culver Rd, on Widgeon and Culver Ponds.

Free campgrounds here include *River Marsh* on the east end of Lower Red Rock Lake and *Upper Lake* on the south shore; water is available at Upper Lake only.

Visit the refuge headquarters (☎ 406-276-3536), 28 miles west of Hwy 87 (at Henry's Lake) and 28 miles east of I-15 (at Monida), for a map and guide (closed weekends), or visit their Web site, www.r6.fws.gov/redrocks. Interpretive displays, which also hold copies of the map and guide, are at various well-marked points throughout the refuge.

HUMBUG SPIRES

Roughly halfway between Butte and Dillon, nine white granite spires rise like mythological figures above a dense pine forest. These are the Humbug Spires, located in the 7000-acre Humbug Spires Primitive Area in the Highland Mountains. The tallest spires rise up to 600 feet while smaller ones just look like extra-large boulders. Rock climbers extol the abundance of

vertical crack climbs and 5.5- to 5.7-rated routes.

The one developed hiking trail follows Moose Creek for 1½ miles before cresting a ridge and encountering numerous game trails that make good backpacking routes if you're carrying a map and compass. The main trail leads another 1½ miles to an abandoned miner's cabin and a magnificent outcropping called the Wedge.

Reach the trailhead parking lot by exiting I-15 at Moose Creek Rd and heading east 3 miles up an improved dirt road; there's a registration box, maps and an outhouse at the parking lot.

BUTTE

In the late 1800s and early 1900s, mines around Butte (population 35,000; elevation 5549 feet) produced record amounts of silver and copper. Such intense mining created a dramatic existence for the locals, marked by erratic employment spurts, mining magnate rivalries and intense labor fights. Today the drama lies in what the mines left behind: a downtown that looks like Chicago meets the Wild West with elegant, ornate buildings lying totally vacant, gouged-out hillsides next to enormous piles of mine tailings, a skyline of headframes and one of the USA's largest Superfund cleanup sites. Butte is not a feel-good place, but its history is fascinating – significant beyond Montana's development and loaded with political intrigue – and the tourism industry has made it fun to explore.

Get a walking-tour map from the tourist information center (see below) or just walk around uptown, along Granite, Broadway and Park Sts, read the National Register of Historic Places plaques and poke your nose in any building open to the public (including bars and restaurants). If it happens to be St Patrick's Day (March 17th), you'll be joined by the thousands who come for parades, corned beef and cabbage feeds and general merrymaking.

History

Until the 1920s, Butte was the only town of any size between Minneapolis and Seattle,

The Copper Kings

At age 15, Marcus Daly left Ireland and arrived in New York with 'nothing in his pocket…save his Irish smile.' He made his way West to where people were making great fortunes in mining and went to work on Nevada's Comstock Lode. He emerged as a shrewd judge of silver properties with the reputation of being able to 'sniff the earth and find metals in it.' He landed in Butte in 1876, but disappointed the Salt Lake City bankers he was working for when he found more copper in the earth than silver. Taking a chance on instinct, he severed his ties to his employers and sank a few shafts of his own. Shortly afterwards electric lighting systems and motors, both heavily reliant on copper, became commercially available and Daly found himself sitting on an enormous fortune.

Simultaneously, William Andrews Clark came to Montana, from Pennsylvania, with three books: one on geology, one on law and *Poems by Burns* for 'recreational reading.' With money he acquired as a shipping agent in Missoula and Deer Lodge, he began buying mining properties in Butte in 1872. Clark had always dreamed of a political career and, at a time when politics and business went hand in glove, believed that industrial clout would gain him a seat in the US Congress. He challenged Marcus Daly's stronghold on Butte's copper market and, by 1880, was embroiled in battle for the 'wealthiest hill on earth' (Butte).

Each man owned a newspaper, had strong political ties (Daly to the Republicans, Clark to the Democrats), a stream of capital from banking connections on both coasts and a profound hate for the other. The multi-million-dollar mud-slinging between Daly men and Clark supporters reached every corner of the state, from the mines to the bars to the courtrooms and newspapers.

Third on this scene was Frederick Augustus Heinze who, in 1889, left Brooklyn to work as a mining engineer in Butte. Familiar with the law and 'stealth' in all business dealings, he soon set out on his own to organize the Montana Ore Purchasing Company. He challenged Daly's Anaconda Company and quickly gained favor with Clark.

If intent decides outcome, each man got what he deserved. Daly's true drive was business and in 1899 he sold his Anaconda Company to Standard Oil to create the Amalgamated Copper Company (AMC Co), which dominated the industry until the 1980s. Clark won the democratic nomination in 1889, only to find, upon arriving in Washington, that he had been defeated by an unknown republican backed by Daly. Then in 1899 he won a seat in the senate but resigned after he was charged with bribery. Finally, in 1901, he was appointed to the senate by the Lieutenant Governor, while the Governor was away on business, and served until 1907. The AMC acquired most of Clark's holdings in 1910.

Heinze made his most significant mark in 1903 when he challenged Daly to several court battles that effectively shut down the AMC, and Montana's economy, for several weeks. He sold the Montana Ore Purchasing Company and United Copper Company to AMC for $12 million in 1906 and returned to the East to buy a chain of banks and trust companies. His Knickerbocker Trust was the primary target of bankers who wanted to sway public and Congressional opinion away from trust companies. In 1907 "silent runs" began on Knickerbocker Trust and, after Heinze made faulty loans to his brothers (who were trying to corner the copper market on the stock exchange) the trust folded, ushering in the Panic of 1907.

and it was home to some of the richest, most powerful men in the country. In 1864 GO Humphrey and William Allison arrived from Virginia City's gold camp and found placer deposits in Silverbow Creek. Ten years later, William L Farlin laid claim to several outcrops of quartz, which turned out to be rich with silver. In 1878, two years after the town incorporated, the Utah & Northern Railroad linked Butte to the

Union Pacific's main line; the rush turned into a boom. By 1885, Butte had a population of 14,000.

The 1870s to the 1880s saw Montana's most intense period of mining. The enormous demand for copper wire created the wealth and fame of both Marcus Daly, who struck the world's largest and purest vein of copper, and William Andrews Clark. By the turn of the century both were equally powerful figures. These two 'Copper Kings' were both business and political rivals who changed the course and character of Montana politics for many years (see 'The Copper Kings').

Accounts of Butte's early days are bittersweet. When smoke rose from the mine stacks, all of Butte was employed, well paid and eager to spend. When no smoke bloomed from the stacks – either due to a labor strike or panic on the market – the entire town fell into a slump. Even during such periods of inactivity, Butte's air remained so thick with rank gas and acidic smoke that plants could only survive indoors and streetlights had to be left on during the day.

Neighbors bonded together in times of disaster or unemployment, but divisions among workers were pronounced: Irish, Welsh and Cornish miners enjoyed privileged status (Irish mine operators wrote their help wanted ads in Gaelic so only fellow Irish could apply), while Italian, German and Finnish miners, if only because they lacked strength in numbers, generally worked the night shift or held more dangerous positions. Chinese settlers, with whom the white settlers refused to work in the mines, were given the lowest paying jobs, usually cooking, doing laundry or dumping garbage.

Unlike the decline of so many other mining communities, Butte's was not due to the total depletion of its mineral resources – the copper veins could have produced ore for an estimated 200 years to come. It was more a case of big business (the mining companies) and big labor (the unions), in their efforts to do each other in, unwittingly contributing to their own demise. The

drastic drop in copper prices during the Great Depression didn't exactly help the situation.

In 1980, Atlantic-Richfield bought the Anaconda Company, which at one time practically ran the state and was known in Butte simply as 'The Company.' Two years later, the last pump shut down – the first time in a century that Butte's mines were totally silent. The population declined steadily until 1986, when the mine reopened (on a smaller scale, with a Canadian holding company) and several small environmental firms moved in to aid in the cleanup.

Orientation

I-90 and I-15 run through Butte together, cutting the city into 'uptown' (on the hill to the north) and 'the flats' (along Harrison Ave south of I-90/I-15). Uptown, where the mining took place, remains the heart of Butte where the historic district and most tourist sights are. The flats is essentially post-1960s Butte, consisting of motels, fast-food chains and the Butte Plaza Mall.

Information

You can get good maps and regional information from Butte's tourist information center and chamber of commerce (☎ 406-723-3177, 800-735-6814), at 1000 George St, north of I-15/I-90. The Old No 1 Trolley Tour covers all of Butte's major sights in 1½ hours for $5. Tours leave from the chamber of commerce five times daily between Memorial Day and Labor Day, with a limited schedule in September; reservations are a good idea.

ATMs are downtown along Harrison Ave and uptown on the corner of Park and Main Sts. The post office is at 60 W Galena.

Books & Books (☎ 406-782-9520), 206 W Park St, has a wide variety of books about Butte plus a good selection of national newspapers. For medical care, go to St James Community Hospital (☎ 406-782-8361), 400 S Clark St.

Things to See & Do

Arts Chateau Among the notable structures of uptown, the Arts Chateau

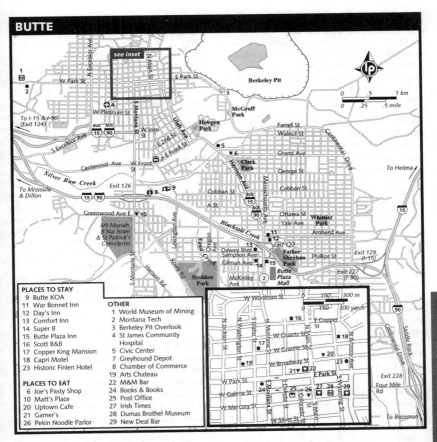

BUTTE

PLACES TO STAY
9 Butte KOA
11 War Bonnet Inn
12 Day's Inn
13 Comfort Inn
14 Super 8
15 Butte Plaza Inn
16 Scott B&B
17 Copper King Mansion
18 Capri Motel
23 Historic Finlen Hotel

PLACES TO EAT
6 Joe's Pasty Shop
10 Matt's Place
20 Uptown Cafe
21 Gamer's
26 Pekin Noodle Parlor

OTHER
1 World Museum of Mining
2 Montana Tech
3 Berkeley Pit Overlook
4 St James Community Hospital
5 Civic Center
7 Greyhound Depot
8 Chamber of Commerce
19 Arts Chateau
22 M&M Bar
24 Books & Books
25 Post Office
27 Irish Times
28 Dumas Brothel Museum
29 New Deal Bar

(☎ 406-723-7600), 321 W Broadway, built in 1898, is the only one functioning as a museum. Three stories exhibit art shows, period furniture and clothing; open noon to 5 pm, Monday to Saturday (10 am to 5 pm in summer); $5.

Copper King Mansion In what must surely disgust Marcus Daly's ghost, William Andrew Clark's former residence is billed as the Copper King Mansion (☎ 406-782-7580), 219 W Granite St. Restored in somewhat garish fashion as a B&B, the 36-room mansion is worth paying $3 to tour; 9 am to

5 pm daily from May to September, weekends only in April and October.

Berkeley Pit When the pumps shut down in 1980 and water collected in this 950-foot pit, it went from being the largest copper mine in the USA to the nation's deepest body of toxic water. Check it out from the viewing platform on the east side of Continental Dr.

World Museum of Mining It takes a good hour to explore the extensive collection of Butte's mining history at this museum (☎ 406-723-7211), built on an old silver and zinc mine at the west end of Park St (behind the Montana Tech campus). From here, catch a ride on the *Orphan Girl Express* ($1) for a 15-minute train tour of the mine sights atop Butte Hill; 9 am to 6 pm daily, April through October; $4.

Mineral Museum In Main Hall on the Montana Tech campus, the Mineral Museum (☎ 406-496-4414) has a world-class collection of rare gems and minerals, plus a working seismology center; open daily, 9 am to 6 pm from June to September, 9 am to 4 pm the rest of the year, and 1 pm to 5 pm on weekends in May, September and October; free admission.

Our Lady of the Rockies If the French reclaim the Statue of Liberty, this oversized icon of kitsch will become the USA's tallest statue. Its construction, came when thanks from a nearly widowed miner coincided with a major layoff in the mines, so the original height grew from 5 to 90 feet. You can see the statue from just about anywhere in town but to go there you must join the 2½-hour, $10 tour (☎ 406-782-1221), which leaves from the Butte Plaza Mall at 3100 Harrison Ave.

Dumas Brothel Museum A trip to the Dumas House (☎ 406-723-6128), 45 E Mercury St, used to be worth much more than the $4 charged to tour it nowadays, especially when the mines were in full operation. At the center of what used to be Butte's huge red-light district, the Dumas claims to be the only building in the USA that was originally constructed as a brothel and never used as anything else. Closed in 1986, it's been left 'as is' by the owner who gives tours daily from 9 am to 5 pm.

Places to Stay

The *Butte KOA* (☎ 406-782-0663), one block north and one block east of I-90 exit 126, charges $18/23 for tent/RV sites.

Good options uptown include the budget *Capri Motel* (☎ 406-723-4391, 220 N Wyoming St), with rooms starting at $36, and the *Historic Finlen Hotel* (☎ 406-723-5461), 100 E Broadway at Arizona Ave, whose rooms cost $50/55.

Chain accommodations, where the going rate for a standard room is around $65/70, are near the I-90/I-15 on Harrison Ave. These include *Days Inn* (☎ 406-494-7000), *Comfort Inn* (☎ 406-494-8850), Best Western's *Butte Plaza Inn* (☎ 406-494-3500), the *Ramada Copper King Inn* (☎ 406-494-6666, 800-332-8600) and *War Bonnet Inn* (☎ 406-494-7800, 800-443-1806). *Super 8* (☎ 406-494-6000) is $15 to $20 cheaper and does not have a pool, as the other ones do.

It's worth paying a little extra to stay in one of Butte's B&Bs, both uptown within walking distance of most sights. The *Scott B&B* (☎ 406-723-7030, 800-844-2952, scottinn@mcn.net, 15 W Copper St) is especially nice and has friendly owners and a small balcony overlooking the town. Rooms start at $68. The *Copper King Mansion* (☎ 406-782-7580, 219 W Granite St), in William A Clark's former mansion, has five rooms for $65 to $95.

Places to Eat

Butte's culinary specialty is the pasty, a compact yet hearty pie native to Cornwall, England, that resembles a turnover or calzone and is filled with meat, onions and potatoes or turnips. Arguments about who makes the best pasty are not to be taken lightly; two old reliables are *Gamer's* (see below) and *Joe's Pasty Shop* (1641 Grande Ave), near the Civic Center.

At one time, Butte's restaurants deserved a detour in themselves, and a few 'institutions' from better times remain. Among the best are *Gamer's* (15 W Park St), where a standard American breakfast or lunch costs under $5, and the *Pekin Noodle Parlor*, upstairs on Main St between Park and Galena Sts, whose individual 'dining cabins' and Pepto-Bismol pink walls show grease from years of lively activity; open 5 pm to midnight, to 3 am Friday and Saturday. Worth a drive to the flats are the burgers and shakes served from a drive-up window (or at the counter inside) at *Matt's*

Place, south of I-15 at the corner of Montana St and Rowe Rd.

For fancier fare try the *Uptown Cafe* (☎ *406-723-4735, 47 E Broadway)*, whose four-course menu changes daily and features seasonal specialties; dinner costs $15 to $20, lunch around $7.

Entertainment
Butte's bars deserve museum status. Though lacking the crowded, vigorous atmosphere of yore, they still have a gritty and authentic feel. Highlights are the *M&M Bar (9 N Main St)*, the *New Deal Bar (333 S Arizona St)* and the *Irish Times*, at the corner of Main and Galena Sts, which has Guinness on tap and live music most weekends.

The accomplished *Butte Symphony Orchestra* (☎ *406-723-5590)* performs a full schedule from October to April; tickets are available at the door for $8. The *Mother Lode Theater* (☎ *406-723-3602, 316 W Park St)*, built in 1920 as a Masonic Temple, hosts film festivals, live music and stage productions year-round.

Getting There & Around
Greyhound and Rimrock Bus lines have daily service to Dillon ($12.50), Missoula ($13.50), Helena ($12.50), Bozeman ($15.50) and Billings ($28). Both use Butte's Greyhound depot (☎ 406-723-3287) at 101 E Front St.

Mining City Taxi (☎ 406-723-6511) is Butte's one and only.

BUTTE TO MISSOULA
Decisions, decisions. Both I-90 and the Anaconda Pintler Scenic Loop (Hwy 1) offer beautiful ways to travel the 120 miles between Butte and Missoula. Lovers of picturesque roads might drive the loop as a day trip, though time to visit the sites in and around Philipsburg and Deer Lodge would be tight.

Pintler Scenic Highway
The Pintler route (Hwy 1) courses along Flint Creek, past large holdings of sheep and cattle ranches in the Flint Creek Valley. **Philipsburg**, the valley's hub and seat of Granite County, yielded silver in the early 1800s and provided manganese for use in WWII. Along its three paved streets is an interesting museum dedicated to ghost towns, stores that offer recreational sapphire digging and places to stop for ice cream or a beer with local ranchers. Leaving town, take Sansome St south from Main St and follow the well-signed dirt road to **Granite**, whose mines yielded $45 million worth of silver ore over an 11-year period. At its peak, Granite had a grand hotel, 18 saloons, and an aerial tramway that transported raw ore from the mines to the stamp mills. Most of the town burned down over the years, but there are still plenty of old structures left to see; a box of information sheets is at the site.

The other ghost town of interest is **Southern Cross**, north of Hwy 1 off the road to Discovery Basin Ski Area and behind the nondenominational St Timothy's Church. The view from here is as beautiful as the dilapidated old structures, worth the drive in itself.

The south shore of **Georgetown Lake** butts up against the Anaconda-Pintler Wilderness Area near access points to the Continental Divide National Scenic Trail. Campgrounds on the lake's west shore make it a good destination for hikers and swimmers, though fishing and hunting (in the fall) are what attract area locals.

The *Flint Creek Campground*, 8 miles south of Philipsburg off Hwy 1, has free, first-come first-served sites with toilets and potable water. USFS campgrounds at Georgetown Lake include *Philipsburg Bay* and *Piney*, both signed off Hwy 1. Each has toilets, potable water and a boat launch, and cost $10 per night. Two miles off Hwy 1 on Denton's Point Rd, *Georgetown Lake Lodge* (☎ *406-563-7020)* has a general store, big lodge with a bar and restaurant, and a large deck overlooking the lake. Rooms cost $75 in summer, $40 the rest of the year; sites at their *campground* (☎ *406-563-6030)* cost $10/17 for tents/RVs.

Philipsburg has the *Blue Heron B&B* (☎ *406-859-3856, 138 W Broadway St)*, where a well-stocked library and gourmet

MONTANA

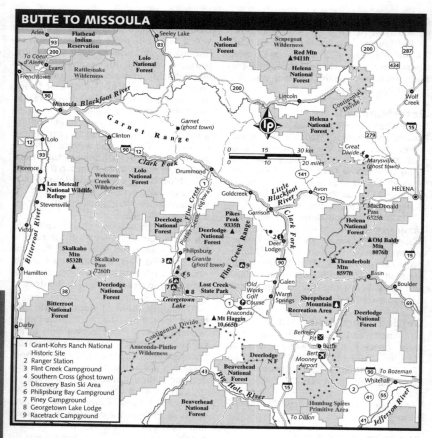

BUTTE TO MISSOULA

1 Grant-Kohrs Ranch National Historic Site
2 Ranger Station
3 Flint Creek Campground
4 Southern Cross (ghost town)
5 Discovery Basin Ski Area
6 Philipsburg Bay Campground
7 Piney Campground
8 Georgetown Lake Lodge
9 Racetrack Campground

breakfast make the $65 to $90 rooms a great value.

Deer Lodge Valley

A bit faster than the Pintler Scenic Hwy, I-90 follows the Clark Fork River through the Deer Lodge Valley, between the Continental Divide and the Flint Creek Range capped by Montana's own Pike's Peak (9335 feet). Once called 'Oregon country' in reference to the destination of passers-through, the area's abundant water and vegetation offered such welcome relief from the dusty prairies that many who came with

intentions of continuing west ended up staying.

Grant-Kohrs Ranch National Historic Site When John Grant saw that the valley was a natural stopping point for people coming over the Continental Divide, he came up with a scheme in which he traded one of his fat, healthy cows fed on rich Montana grass for two of the bony, sickly cows that accompanied most people on their westward journey. The Grants then fattened these cows and traded them for better quality stock. In 1862 they built a ranch, near present-day Deer Lodge. German-born Conrad Kohrs bought Grant's ranch and expanded it to become one of the country's largest ranches, extending into four states and encompassing over a million acres. A fraction of its former self but still worth a visit, the site (☎ 406-846-3388) is maintained as a working ranch with stables, ranchhands' barracks, carriage house, barn and a 23-room house open daily from 8 am to 5:30 pm June 1st to Labor Day, 9 am to 4:30 pm the rest of the year; free admission.

Deer Lodge Deer Lodge (population 3655; elevation 4736 feet) thrived as the nearest town to the Grant-Kohrs Ranch, and grew further with the establishment of the Montana Territorial Prison in 1871. It occasionally makes the news when things go awry at one of its state correctional facilities or sanitariums, but generally exists as 'town' for surrounding agricultural communities. The **Old Montana Prison Complex** (☎ 406-846-3111), on Main St, draws visitors on their way to/from the Grant Kohrs Ranch and is worth a look if you're interested in antique cars, antique dolls or old prison architecture and lore. The $8 admission includes all parts of the complex, with a less expensive ticket for individual exhibits; open 8 am to 9 pm daily in summer, limited hours from October to June.

The Old Prison Players stage off-Broadway musicals in the old prison recreation center. Performances, amateur but still entertaining, run Wednesday to Sunday nights from June through August. Tickets ($8) and schedules are available inside the Old Montana Prison Complex.

Places to Stay Free campgrounds in the Deer Lodge National Forest include **Orofino Campground**, 12 miles south of town (take Milwaukee Ave east from downtown, cross I-90 and turn south to FS Rd No 82), and **Racetrack Campground**, 12 miles southwest of the Racetrack exit off I-90 (go west 1 mile then south to FS Rd No 169). North of town, the **Deer Lodge KOA** (☎ 406-846-1629, 413 Park St) charges $15/18 for tent/RV sites.

In town are the **Western Big Sky Inn** (☎ 406-846-2590, 210 Main St), **Scharf's Motor Inn** (☎ 406-846-2810, 819 Main St) and, a block off Main St, the **Downtowner Motel** (☎ 406-846-1021, 500 4th St), all with rooms from $35 to $55.

Anaconda

Marcus Daly's original company town, Anaconda (population 9721; elevation 5265 feet) was aptly named after the serpent that allegedly strangles any competition that gets in its way. In the late 1880s the Anaconda Company was the world's largest producer of copper and the town was home to the largest copper reduction plant, tallest freestanding masonry structure and only newspaper to have color illustrations in the world.

Decreasing demand and increasing foreign competition led to a slow death, and in 1980 Atlantic-Richfield, the parent company, shut down the operation. A mid-1970s urban renewal plan demolished most of the buildings of Anaconda's golden (or, more appropriately, 'copper') era, leaving it the unsightly town that remains.

Most recently, one of the nation's largest Superfund cleanup efforts took the tailings and slag heaps left on site of the old copper smelter and used them to build the Old Works Golf Course (☎ 406-563-5989), designed by Jack Nicklaus. An **interpretive trail** that begins at the north end of Cedar St winds up past the smelter remnants and offers a great view of the town and golf course. For a good glimpse of the town's past, stop in at the **Historical Museum**, in the basement of Copper Village Arts Center at the corner of Commercial and Cedar Sts.

Orientation & Information Hwy 1 runs west through Anaconda as Park St, the main thoroughfare. Commercial St parallels Park St, and Main St crosses the two of them midway through town. Anaconda's visitors center (☎ 406-563-2400) is housed in the old railroad depot on Cherry St, between Park and Commercial Sts; open 8 am to 6 pm weekdays, and 9 am to 5 pm weekends. The main post office is at 218

MONTANA

Main St. Both Bank of Montana and Norwest Bank, on Park St, have ATMs.

Places to Stay Both the *Marcus Daly Motel* (☎ 406-563-3411, 800-535-6528, 119 W Park St) and the *Trade Wind Motel* (☎ 406-563-3428, 800-248-3428, 1600 E Commercial St) charge around $45/58 for a single/double. For local color, try the $25 rooms atop the *Harp & Thistle Pub* (☎ 406-563-2372, 23 Main St); they also have a terrific tap beer selection and live music most weekends.

HELENA

Montana's capital city is as good a place as any to spend a few days. Its sights are free, there's a lively arts scene and the downtown is charming and walkable. In fact, Helena (population 29,081; elevation 4090 feet) feels just sophisticated enough that you may forget you're in Montana. You need only venture to the nearby mountains, scattered with old mining camps and 'Lewis and Clark Were Here' markers, to remember.

History

When John Cowan, DJ Miller, Reginald Stanley and John Crab (subsequently known as the Four Georgians) left the gold-fields of Virginia City to explore Kootenai Creek, they met discouraged miners coming from that direction and decided to return to Georgia. Crossing over Prickly Pear Creek, one of the four joked 'OK boys, this is the last chance,' and thrust his pan into the creek. Enough gold came up that soon the word was out that Last Chance Gulch was paying off.

When Montana became a state in 1889, the two favorite capital city candidates were Anaconda, owned by Marcus Daly, and Helena, backed by Daly's rival WA Clark. Helena won by a slim majority, but a new twist to the story surfaced in 1989, when the house where the votes were counted was gutted for renovation. Adjacent to the ballot-counting room, a secret room was discovered, along with documents thought to be phony tally sheets giving Helena twice the amount of votes actually cast for the

town. All is speculation, but Anaconda's citizens like to claim that the capital should have been theirs.

Orientation

Helena sits east of the Continental Divide, west of the Big Belt Mountains. I-15 skirts the east side of town, intersected by US 12 which jogs through town as Euclid, Lyndale, Montana and Eleventh Aves.

Cedar St and Eleventh Ave are the two main exits off of I-15. Both lead to Last Chance Gulch, central Helena's main artery.

Information

Helena's chamber of commerce (☎ 406-442-4120, 800-743-5362), 225 Cruse Ave, is online at www.helenachamber.com, and is home to Travel Montana, a source of statewide information. In summer, the Visitors Center (☎ 406-447-1540), just east of I-15 at 2003 Cedar St, is open 9 am to 7 pm daily.

The Helena National Forest Office (☎ 406-449-5201), across from the Helena Regional Airport at 2880 Skyway Dr, has topographical maps and recreation information. The Montana Book Co (☎ 406-443-0260), 331 N Last Chance Gulch, has a good selection of regional guidebooks.

Downtown you'll find banks and the central post office in the City County Building at 301 S Park. St Peter's Community Hospital (☎ 406-444-2480) is east of downtown at 2475 Broadway.

Things to See & Do

In summer a **tour train** ($5) leaves from the corner of 6th Ave and Roberts St (in front of the capitol) hourly from 9 am to 6 pm (except at noon and 5 pm) and circles the Last Chance Gulch area, allowing you to get on and off.

First stop for most visitors is the **State Capitol Building**, 1301 6th Ave, built in 1899 and crowned with a 165-foot copper-faced dome. You're free to roam the building on a self-guided tour (pick up a map at the information desk just inside the front entrance) though the free docent-led tours (hourly from 10 am to 4 pm Monday to Saturday,

HELENA

PLACES TO STAY
1 Helena Inn
7 The Sanders B&B
8 The Barrister B&B
9 Jorgensen's Holiday Motel
17 Budget Inn
19 Iron Front Hotel

PLACES TO EAT
10 Miller's Crossing
11 On Broadway
15 The Real Foods Store
16 Morning Lights
18 No Sweat Café
20 Toi's Thai
22 Bert & Ernie's
24 Benny's

OTHER
2 Civic Center
3 Post Office
4 Grandstreet Theater
5 Chamber of Commerce
6 Original Governor's Mansion
12 Lewis & Clark County
   Courthouse
13 Myrna Loy Center for the
   Performing Arts
14 Montana Historical Society
   Museum
21 Holter Museum of Art
23 The Base Camp
25 Montana Book Co
26 Great Divide Cyclery

MONTANA

plus 11 am to 3 pm Sunday from Memorial Day to Labor Day) are worthwhile. Inside are Charlie Russell's painting *Lewis & Clark Meet the Flathead at Ross's Hole* (1911) and a noteworthy statue of Montanan Jeannette Rankin, the first woman elected to Congress and the only person to vote against entering both World Wars.

Across the street, the **Montana Historical Society Museum** houses a large collection of Charlie Russell's work, photographs by F Jay Haynes (the Ansel Adams of Yellowstone National Park), a comprehensive Montana history exhibit and temporary contemporary exhibitions; 8 am to 6 pm weekdays, 9 am to 5 pm weekends and holidays.

The **Holter Museum of Art**, 12 E Lawrence St, has an excellent new gallery space with changing exhibits of contemporary work; 10 am to 5 pm Tuesday to Saturday, noon to 5 pm Sunday.

One of the foremost schools of pottery in USA, the **Archie Bray Foundation** (☎ 406-443-3502), 4 miles west of downtown at 2915 Country Club Ave (take Euclid to Joslyn and turn right), is a magical place where pottery is scattered irreverently across the landscape, and artists in residence are busy sculpting, throwing and firing their latest works. A self-guided tour (available from the small visitors center) leads you around the old brickworks grounds (once owned by Bray's father) past site-specific sculptures and beehive-like kilns. The gallery is open from 10 am to 5 pm Monday to Saturday, but you can roam around the grounds at any time.

Prickly Pear Creek, long ago dried up and paved over, now winds its way through **Last Chance Gulch** (Helena's main business district) as an historic pedestrian mall. Pick up a walking tour map at the Helena Visitors Center and check out the often comic details of these elegant old buildings.

Just east of Last Chance Gulch, Ewing St is lined with stately homes, including the **Original Governor's Mansion**, 304 N Ewing St, built in 1888. Its symmetrical exterior hides a quirky but well decked-out interior; tours hourly from noon to 5 pm, Tuesday to Saturday. North on Ewing is **St Helena Cathedral**, whose twin spires, 218 feet high and topped with 12-foot-tall gold crosses, are probably the most recognizable architectural feature in the state.

Activities

Mount Helena City Park has **hiking** and **mountain biking** trails that wind around the base and to the summit of 5460-foot Mount Helena, an epic spot from which to take in views of the town and the Big Belt Mountains (ask someone to point out the 'Sleeping Giant' mountain). The trails begin at a parking lot at the end of Reeder's Village Dr, which connects to Main St just south of Reeder's Alley. A large, detailed map gives a description of each trail. From the southwest side of the park, the Mount Helena Ridge National Recreation Trail gives access to hundreds of miles of trails in the Helena National Forest.

The best **fishing** near Helena is at Holter, Hauser and Canyon Ferry Lakes, northeast of town. Trophy-size brown trout, weighing in at over 15 pounds, make regular appearances in the Missouri River below Hauser Dam. In the fall anglers come to fish for kokanee salmon. The best access sites are along Prickly Pear and Wolf Creeks, 20 to 35 miles north of Helena west of I-15.

The Great Divide Ski Area (☎ 406-449-3746), 20 miles northwest of Helena in Marysville (see Around Helena, later in this section), has decent downhill **skiing**; closed Tuesday. Cross-country skiers go to the Continental Divide National Scenic Trail at MacDonald Pass, 20 miles west of Helena on US 12 (there's a signed pull-out off US 12 where the trails begin), or Stemple Pass, 30 miles northwest of Helena on Hwy 279.

Find **equipment rentals,** topo maps and friendly advice at the Base Camp (☎ 406-443-5360), 333 N Last Chance Gulch, closed Sunday. Next door to its entrance on Jackson St is the Great Divide Cyclery (☎ 406-443-5188), which rents mountain bikes for $10 a day.

Places to Stay

The best camping around is on Holter Lake (see Around Helena, below) or at MacDonald Pass, 20 miles west of town on US 12, where the USFS *Cromwell-Dixon Campground* has $8 campsites, potable water and pit toilets.

The *Iron Front Hotel* (☎ 406-443-2400, 415 N Last Chance Gulch) has two rooms that rent nightly (the rest rent weekly or monthly) for $29 without bath.

Motels close to downtown include the *Helena Inn* (☎ 406-442-6080, 877-387-0102, 910 Last Chance Gulch) and *Budget Inn* (☎ 406-442-0600, 800-862-1334, 524 N Last Chance Gulch), both with rooms for $45/$50.

Most other accommodations are in chain motels, near I-15, where discount packages, Continental breakfast, pool, Jacuzzi and fitness center are the norm; rooms are $58 to $85. The best are the *Shilo Inn* (☎ 406-442-0320, 800-222-2244), *Best Western Colonial Inn* (☎ 406-443-2100) and *Holiday Inn Express* (☎ 406-449-4000). Popular with politicians, *Jorgensen's Holiday Motel* (☎ 406-442-1770, 800-272-1770, 1714 11th Ave) has $50 to $70 rooms.

Helena's B&Bs are well worth the splurge. If you stay in one B&B in Montana, try *The Sanders* (☎ *406-442-330, 328 N Ewing*), at 7th Ave. The house was built in 1875 and has elegant decor, friendly staff and excellent food; rooms are $90 to $105. One block north, across from the cathedral, *The Barrister* (☎ *406-443-7330, 416 N Ewing*) is an 1874 Victorian originally built as priests' quarters. Rooms cost $95 to $115; children under 10 are not allowed.

Places to Eat

Helena's restaurants cater to the working crowd: the same meal that fetches $15 at dinner costs $7 at lunch, and most places close on Sunday.

At the corner of Fuller and Placer Aves is *The Real Foods Store*, which has an outstanding deli and natural foods, and *Morning Lights*, the place to go for coffee and pastries.

Rootsy beyond its location, the *No Sweat Café* (*427 N Last Chance Gulch*) uses mostly organic ingredients in its hearty egg dishes, sandwiches and Mexican fare; open daily, 7 am to 3 pm. On weekdays, *Benny's* (*305 Fuller Ave*) is popular for salads and sandwiches.

Tiny *Toi's Thai* (☎ *406-443-6656, 423 N Last Chance Gulch*) has first-rate Thai dinners (probably Montana's best) for around $12. Reservations are required (a few hours before you want to eat is usually OK).

Miller's Crossing (*52 S Park Ave*) is more of a bar than a restaurant, but they do a good job on pastas and burgers for under $10 (open daily). Similar but nonsmoking is *Bert & Ernie's*, on the corner of Last Chance Gulch and Lawrence St.

For fancier dining try the seafood and house-made pasta at *On Broadway* (*106 Broadway*), or the steaks and seafood at the *River Grille* (☎ *406-442-1075, 1225 Custer Ave*), north of downtown near the corner of Montana Ave.

Entertainment

Helena's active theater scene revolves around the *Myrna Loy Center for the Performing Arts* (☎ *406-443-0287, 15 N Ewing St*), which shows films nightly and hosts live music most weekends.

Other performance venues include the *Grandstreet Theater* (☎ *406-443-3311*), at the corner of Park Ave and Lawrence St, which produces off-Broadway comedies and musicals. Pick up a copy of the *Lively Times* at cafes, the Visitors Center or the Myrna Loy Center for current performance listings.

Getting There & Around

Helena Regional Airport (☎ 406-442-2821) is at 2850 Skyway Dr, 2 miles north of downtown Helena and a half mile east of I-15. Big Sky connects Helena to most other airports in Montana; Delta services Salt Lake City, via Great Falls, and Horizon Air goes to Spokane, Washington, via Billings.

Rimrock Stages service Helena's bus depot (☎ 406-442-5860), 7 miles east of town on US 12. Daily buses go to Great Falls ($13), Butte ($13), Missoula ($19), Billings ($31) and Bozeman ($15). Taxi fare (☎ 406-449-5525) from the depot to downtown is $7.

U-Save Auto Rental (☎ 406-439-7283), 1018 W Custer Ave, is the cheapest in town. Others include National and Hertz, both at the airport.

AROUND HELENA
Gates of the Mountains Wilderness Area

Less than 20 miles from Helena, this is the least-used wilderness area in Montana. Its name comes from Gates of the Mountains Canyon, which Lewis and Clark mistook for a dead end until they discovered it to 'open like a gateway.'

The best way to get this perspective is on the Gates of the Mountains **tour boat** (☎ 406-458-5241) that departs from the south shore of Holter Lake, 18 miles north of Helena on I-15. It's a scenic trip through the canyon's 1000-foot limestone walls, and the captain gives a good historical narration. Boats stop at the Merriwether Picnic Area (where Lewis and Clark camped); you can disembark and catch a later boat back to the dock. Hiking trails from the picnic area lead to Vista Point, Colter Campground and Mann Gulch, famous site of a 1949 fire that killed 13 smokejumpers. Boats

MONTANA

depart at 11 am and 2 pm weekdays, with an additional boat at noon on weekends. In July and August trips are added at 1 and 3 pm weekdays, 4 pm Saturday and hourly between 10 am and 5 pm Sunday; $8.50.

The rest of the 44-sq-mile Gates of the Mountains Wilderness Area is relatively unused but offers excellent hiking and backpacking. Some trail suggestions are the dramatic but easy **Refrigerator Canyon Trail**, the lush but longer **Hanging Valley Trail** and the easy-to-access **River Trail**; pick up a map ($4.50) at the Helena National Forest Office or The Base Camp in Helena.

Holter, Hauser & Canyon Ferry Lakes

These 'lakes' are really Missouri River reservoirs dammed by concrete gravity structures that generate electricity for the greater Helena area. Holter Lake, the northernmost reservoir (43 miles north of Helena via I-15/US 287) is the most scenic, bordered by Gates of the Mountains Wilderness Area. Three USFS campgrounds on the lake's eastern shore, accessible off I-15 (turn east on Rec Rd, 3 miles north of Wolf Creek, then turn southeast on the well-signed county road), are nestled between the lake and the rugged cliffs of the Beartooth Wildlife Management Area, home to mountain goats, bighorn sheep and waterfowl. Campsites ($14) have access to pit toilets, potable water and fire rings. The Helena National Forest Office (☎ 406-449-5201) can provide information.

The forested eastern shore of Hauser and Canyon Ferry Lakes was badly burned in 2000. It's uncertain when the campgrounds and resorts there will reopen. Check with Lakeside Resort (☎ 406-227-6076), 12 miles from Helena on the south side of York Rd, or Kim's Marina (☎ 406-475-3723), 2½ miles past the Canyon Ferry Dam on the lake's east shore, for updated information.

Rogers Pass

Most Montanans know Rogers Pass, about 40 miles north of Helena on Hwy 200, for the afternoon of January 20, 1954, when it set a record for the lowest temperature ever

recorded in the state (-70°F). Birders, however, know it as a fantastic locale on a migratory corridor used by bald and golden eagles and a variety of hawks each November, and tundra swans and snow geese in the spring. Check with Helena's National Forest Office or the Department of Fish, Wildlife & Parks (☎ 406-444-2535) for information.

Ghost Towns

The town of **Marysville**, 20 miles northwest of Helena on Hwy 279, was the country's leading gold producer in the 1890s, but as the mine reached poorer ore quality Marysville's boom turned to bust and miners were forced to seek their fortunes elsewhere. Today, Marysville is a picturesque jumble of old wooden structures, rusty mining equipment and underground tunnels where Chinese miners drove away evil spirits with food offerings (small white mice dipped in honey) and incantations.

Southeast of Helena, between US 12 and I-15, rise the rugged limestone peaks of the Elkhorn Mountains. The abandoned town of **Elkhorn**, 11 miles north of Hwy 69 on USFS Rd 258, is an archetypal ghost town. Scenes from the movie *The Real West* were filmed here, making good use of the well-preserved cemetery, two-story Fraternity Hall and old signs that still line the dusty wooden sidewalks. A $14-million silver strike and minor discoveries of gold and lead gave Elkhorn its economic lifeblood, but in 1888 production began to slow, and a serious diphtheria epidemic the next year put the town permanently out of operation.

'Health Mines'

Forty-five miles south of Helena, signs lining I-15 advertise 'health mines,' old uranium mines whose radioactive radon emissions are touted by some (namely the folks who own them) as a cure for bursitis, arthritis, emphysema, multiple sclerosis and just about any other ailment. Apparently radon's beneficial effects were 'discovered' by owners of the Free Enterprise Health Mine, 2 miles south of where Hwy 69 meets I-15 at Boulder, who were entertaining a guest from Los Angeles who was cured of bursitis after visiting the mine. Cure-seekers are welcome to the underground tunnels from 8 am to 6 pm daily between March and November. Be aware that this is *not* a standard treatment in the USA, and people are advised to consult a physician before and after (to ensure that the radon hasn't done any harm) trying this.

Most people will prefer to take the cure at **Boulder Hot Springs** (☎ 406-225-4339) with a soak in the 104°F pools. Its elegant old lodge is frequented by visitors who come for retreats, self-help classes and weekend brunch. Lovely single/double guest rooms cost $55/70, including breakfast and access to the pools; just a soak is $5.

The town of **Boulder** (population 1689), originally a stage stop between Fort Benton and Helena, became a town after the hot springs started attracting wealthy guests to its spa facilities in the 1880s. Now the hub of the Boulder River Valley, its main street is lined with brick storefronts and crowned with the gargoyle-studded 1889 Jefferson County Courthouse. Nearby **Basin**, an old mining camp, is known for the beautiful works sold at Basin Creek Pottery (☎ 406-225-3218), just north of I-15 at 82 Basin St.

Glacier Country

Montana's northwest corner contains some of its most visited tourist attractions. Glacier National Park encompasses the northernmost section of Montana's portion of the Rocky Mountains, bordered by the Bob Marshall Wilderness Complex, which extends south through the Rockies almost to Helena. These are the best destinations for hiking, backpacking, camping or backcountry skiing in the state.

From west of the Rockies to where Montana meets Idaho is a growing tourist region centered around Whitefish and Flathead Lake. In contrast, the farthest northwest corner remains some of the least-visited land in Montana.

Any portion of the area offers a scenic drive. US 2 affords the most direct route from Seattle to Glacier National Park and is paralleled by train tracks, which once helped drive the area's economy and now provide a novel mode of transportation.

THE MISSION VALLEY

Named for the Jesuit mission in St Ignatius, the Mission Valley has good wildlife viewing areas, has been richly influenced by Native American culture and has a string of funky antique stores along US 93. The knife-like ridges of the Mission Mountains, which look much higher than they are because they rise straight up from the valley floor, make a scenic backdrop to the valley's farms, ranches and small reservation towns. Most land here is part of the Flathead Indian Reservation, but the only time people make a distinction between towns that are on the 'res' and those that aren't is when they go to buy cigarettes – tobacco isn't taxed on reservation land.

The Mission Mountains Tribal Wilderness, on the west side of the range, was the first tribal land to be put aside by an Indian nation as a wilderness preserve. Off limits to most nontribal members, the area is famous for its bear population, which hangs out around McDonald Peak from mid-July to October.

Orientation & Information

Most communities in the valley are scattered along US 93, with the exception of Charlo and Moiese, which are on Hwy 212. St Ignatius (population 921), Ronan (population 1980) and Pablo (population 300) are the largest towns in the valley, each with a gas station, post office and laundry; Ronan also has a bank.

Coming from the south, the best place to stop for information is Doug Allard's Trading Post (☎ 406-745-2951), on US 93 in St Ignatius. From the north, stop at The People's Center (☎ 406-675-0160), 2 miles north of Pablo on US 93, or, in summer, the Mission Valley Visitors Center (☎ 406-676-8300), on US 93 in Ronan, housed in a 100-year-old log cabin.

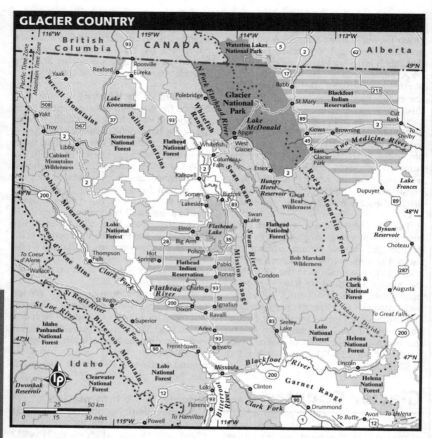

St Ignatius Mission

Built in 1854 by Jesuit missionaries, this was Montana's second mission and a teaching center for the Pend d'Oreille and Kootenai tribes. Within 35 years a boys' school, sawmill, flour mill, printing press and hospital grew up around the mission, with much help from the Sisters of Providence, the first women of European descent to cross the Rocky Mountains. The mission church, east of Hwy 93 in the town of St Ignatius, is decorated with colorful murals painted by the mission cook, Brother Joseph Carignano, depicting New Testament scenes. Next door is an excellent, if small, museum with memorabilia from the mission's past; open 9 am to 5 pm daily.

National Bison Range

Started in 1908 with the progeny of Montana's few surviving buffalo, the National Bison Range is the closest thing to an overland safari Montana has to offer. Pronghorn, elk, mountain goats and bighorn sheep share the 129-sq-mile range, which encompasses the thick-forested Red Sleep Mountain, wetlands and prairie grasslands.

There are two driving tours: a 19-mile, two-hour journey to the top of Red Sleep Mountain and a 3-mile, 20-minute jaunt that keeps to the lowlands. There is also a picnic area, short interpretive hike and excellent visitors center inside the entrance, which is about 20 miles from St Ignatius via Hwys 200 and 212, or 16 miles from Ronan on Hwy 212. Roads are open dawn to dusk and the visitors center (☎ 406-644-2211) is open daily from 8 am to 8 pm, to 4:30 pm in the winter. A 10-mile and a 2-mile drive stay open most of the winter; $4 admission from May to October.

Ninepipe & Pablo Reservoirs

Both designated National Wildlife Refuges, Ninepipe Reservoir, 5 miles south of Ronan, and Pablo Reservoir, 3 miles northwest of Ronan, cover 4500 acres of water, marsh and upland grasses – prime waterfowl habitat. The most numerous nesting birds are Canada geese, mallards, pintails, American widgeons, shovelers, ruddy ducks, gadwalls and mergansers. Fall is the main migrating season when the birds number over 80,000 (they've actually been known to pass the 200,000 mark).

After turning west off US 93 onto Hwy 212 towards Ninepipe, you can park at marked trailheads and set out on foot. Dawn and dusk are the best viewing times. Ninepipe has good fishing for yellow perch and largemouth bass, Pablo is known for rainbow trout. No boats or flotation devices are allowed and a joint state-tribal permit (available at Doug Allard's Trading Post in St Ignatius) is required. Camping is not an option at either one, though picnicking is.

The People's Center (Sqelixw/Aqtsmakni*K)

The Mission Valley's pride and joy is The People's Center (a mile north of Pablo on US 93), translated as 'Sqelixw' in Salish and 'Aqtsmakni*K' in Kootenai, both nearly impossible to pronounce unless you've grown up speaking the dialect. If you want to have a go at it, try something like 'ske-LEE-ef' and 'ackt-s-MUK-nik,'

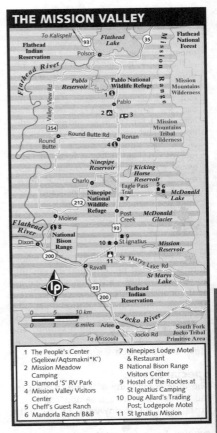

THE MISSION VALLEY

1 The People's Center (Sqelixw/Aqtsmakni*K')
2 Mission Meadow Camping
3 Diamond 'S' RV Park
4 Mission Valley Visitors Center
5 Cheff's Guest Ranch
6 Mandorla Ranch B&B
7 Ninepipes Lodge Motel & Restaurant
8 National Bison Range Visitors Center
9 Hostel of the Rockies at St Ignatius Camping
10 Doug Allard's Trading Post; Lodgepole Motel
11 St Ignatius Mission

then watch those around you try to figure out if you're choking or just trying to sneeze.

The building's architecture and its hands-on museum are meant to convey the message that the Native American culture is very much alive with traditions and ceremonies as important today as they were 500 years ago. One of the highlights is a free audio tour with an elder's voice speaking either Salish or Kootenai in the background. The gift shop has a good selection of books and local artwork; open daily from 9 am to 9 pm, $2.

MONTANA

The People's Building

Dominating the Sqelixw/Aqtsmakni*K is a rotunda, symbolizing a drum – the heartbeat of the people. It is made of three kinds of stone to represent the three major cultures on the reservation: granite from the Bitterroot, the traditional homeland of the Salish; flagstones from the Perma area, which is the home of the Pend d'Oreille; and gray argillite from the northern part of the reservation, where the Kootenai people live. The rotunda's skylight ceiling is made of patterned glass with triangles of blue (representing the water and mountains), green (vegetation), red (Native Americans) and white (the wisdom of the people).

Nearby is Salish Kootenai College, whose library is a great place to find information about local tribes and often used for genealogical and anthropological research. Traditional and not-so-traditional art (like Dwight Billedeaux's eagle sculpture made of old car parts) is found around the campus. For a tour, stop by the admissions office weekdays from 8 am to 4:30 pm.

Special Events

The little community of Arlee (named for the Salish Chief Arlee, meaning 'red night') hosts the biggest **powwow** in the state, which is also one of the biggest in the country. For a full week, culminating the first weekend in July, dancers come from all over the USA and Canada to compete for over $20,000 in prize money. Their families, supporters and spectators bring jewelry, arts and crafts, and food carts to round out the entertainment – a rollicking time where all are welcome.

Those of open mind and iron stomach might want to investigate the **Mission Mountain Testicle Festival** (a 'Rocky Mountain oyster' fry) that features a local delicacy harvested from hapless bulls. The festivities around the feed, welcome even to those who opt for a less adventurous lunch, include a wine-tasting and live bands. The whole affair takes place in early June at the Branding Iron Bar & Grill (☎ 406-644-9493), on Main St in Charlo, west of US 93.

Places to Stay & Eat

There are some good nontraditional places to stay in the valley; for chain motels, head north to Polson or south to Missoula.

Just north of St Ignatius at the corner of US 93 and Airport Rd, *Hostel of the Rockies at St Ignatius Camping* (☎ 406-745-3959) offers $10 tent spots, $20 RV spots and beds in an 'earthship,' a partially subterranean structure, for $13 per person. In addition to use of kitchen and laundry facilities, there's a communal living room and an equipment rental shop that has everything from backpacks to rain jackets to cross-country skis. The helpful owner guides trips and can make recommendations about exploring the nearby mountains and wilderness.

North of Ronan, the *Diamond 'S' RV Park* (☎ 406-676-3641) and *Mission Meadow Camping* (☎ 406-676-5182) both cater to RVs ($25) but have some tent sites for around $12.

The *Lodgepole Motel* (☎ 406-745-9192), part of Doug Allard's Trading Post in St Ignatius, has standard rooms for around $40. On US 93 in Charlo, the *Ninepipes Lodge Motel & Restaurant* (☎ 406-644-2588) has a popular restaurant and rooms for $60.

The *Mandorla Ranch B&B* (☎ 406-745-4500, 800-852-6668, 6873 Allard Rd), 4 miles south of Ronan off Eagle Pass Trail, is the valley's most established bed and breakfast, offering five rooms for around $125. At the end of Eagle Pass Trail, *Cheff's Guest Ranch* (☎ 406-644-2557) has swimming, horseback riding ($15 per hour) and pack trips into the Bob Marshall and Mission Mountain Wilderness Areas. Occasionally (and you're in luck if it's the occasion) they rent rooms by the night for around $75; otherwise it costs about $600 per week.

FLATHEAD LAKE

With 128 miles of wooded shoreline, picturesque bays and a large population of fish, Flathead Lake is one of Montana's most popular destinations. It is also the largest body of fresh water west of the Mississippi. It started forming about 10,000 years ago when moraines built up around the edge of lingering glacial ice. As the ice melted, the bed filled with water to form the lake.

It's a good day trip from Missoula, Kalispell/Whitefish, or Glacier National Park, and an excellent place to spend a few days camping, swimming or, in winter, skiing. The Flathead Lake Marine Trail makes paddling from one access point to another a fun way to explore. You can easily drive around the lake in four hours, but should plan for stops along the way.

At the south end of the lake, **Polson** (population 5033) is the area's service center, with an historic main street and the biggest concentration of motels, restaurants and gas stations. Its funky Miracle of America Museum, 2 miles south of town on US 93, is definitely worth a stop, exhibiting of all kinds of Americana, from dollhouses to guns used in the Vietnam War. Polson's other 'tourist attraction,' Kerr Dam (8 miles southwest of town via 7th Ave), can be skipped in good conscience.

At the lake's opposite end, **Bigfork** is a quaint tourist village with artsy shops, good restaurants and an excellent live performance theater along Electric Ave, its main drag. The first weekend in August brings artists, art and plenty of visitors to downtown Bigfork for the August Festival of the Arts, installed outside on the main street. Between Polson and Bigfork you've got campgrounds, summer-camp-style resorts and, on the lake's east side, cherry orchards that produce fat, mahogany-red cherries.

In either town you can catch a boat tour to **Wild Horse Island**, where wild horses thought to be descendants of Pend d'Oreille and Flathead horses roam, and **Painted Rock**, a large outcropping with ancient pictographs on it. Keep a lookout for Flathead Nessie, a distant cousin to the Loch Ness

Monster who has been lurking in the lake since the 1930s.

Orientation & Information

An informative, all-purpose Web site is www.gonorthwest.com/Montana/northwest/Flathead-Lake.htm. The Polson Chamber of Commerce (☎ 406-883-5969), part of Sailmaker Realty at 302 Main St, has information about accommodations, while Bear Dance (☎ 406-883-1700), on US 93 at 1st St, has information on outdoor activities and sells maps, guide services and tribal permits (needed for some paddling and hiking trips).

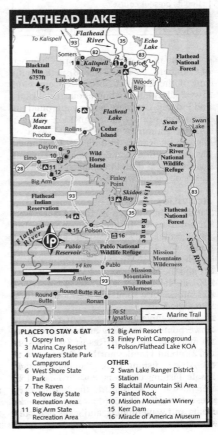

FLATHEAD LAKE

PLACES TO STAY & EAT
1 Osprey Inn
3 Marina Cay Resort
4 Wayfarers State Park Campground
6 West Shore State Park
7 The Raven
8 Yellow Bay State Recreation Area
11 Big Arm State Recreation Area
12 Big Arm Resort
13 Finley Point Campground
14 Polson/Flathead Lake KOA

OTHER
2 Swan Lake Ranger District Station
5 Blacktail Mountain Ski Area
9 Painted Rock
10 Mission Mountain Winery
15 Kerr Dam
16 Miracle of America Museum

MONTANA

Giant vs Geologist

According to legend, Paul Bunyan, the folk-loric giant lumberjack, had such an affinity for Polson that during one hard year he decided to help the economy by moving the outlet of the lake from Elmo to Polson. The story goes, he dug a channel out of the lake, past the west side of town, diverting the path of the water from its natural glacial outlet (the Big Draw) to the Flathead River.

According to geologists, however, it was a glacial moraine that blocked the old valley of Flathead River near Elmo and forced it to find its present course.

On the north end, the Bigfork Chamber of Commerce (☎ 406-837-5888), in the south end of the Lakehill Shopping Center on Hwy 35, has information about restaurants and lodging. For maps and campground information, stop by the Swan Lake Ranger District Station (☎ 406-837-5081), west of Bigfork on Ranger Station Dr. Each town has a post office, laundry, supermarket and gas stations, as does the small community of Lakeside on the west shore.

Activities

Paddlers should stop at Bear Dance (see Orientation & Information, above) for kayak rentals ($45 per day) and information about the Flathead Lake Marine Trail, which traces 30 miles of paddling routes around the lake. Montana FWP (☎ 406-752-5501 in Kalispell, ☎ 406-726-3344 in Arlee) has information about the marine campsites along the trail.

The cheapest place to rent rowboats, powerboats, waterskiing and fishing equipment is the Big Arm Resort (☎ 406-849-5622), about 11 miles north of Polson on US 93. All-day **fishing** trips, available through Eagle Fishing Charters, cost about $150 per person. Near Bigfork, the Marina Cay Resort (☎ 406-837-5861) rents **water-ski boats** and **waverunners**, and gives **parasailing** flights.

Hikers should continue on to Glacier or Jewel Basin, but **skiers** should look no further than Blacktail Mountain Ski Area (☎ 406-844-0999), a new downhill ski area at Lakeside (on the west shore) that is drawing people from all over western Montana. It's mostly intermediate, with a 1440-foot vertical drop; lift tickets are $24. There's a vast cross-country network at the base of the mountain.

Web site: www.blacktailmountain.com

Places to Stay

Camping The lake's best camping is on its east side. A quarter mile south of Bigfork, the *Wayfarers State Park Campground* has shady sites for $9; *Finley Point Campground*, on a picturesque promontory among fir and pine trees, has $11 sites and $3 day-use facilities; prettiest of all is the *Yellow Bay State Recreation Area* with $11 sites, pit toilets, fire rings and a swimming beach. Next door is U of M's biological research station which studies the life of lakes, ponds and streams; tours are available in the summer, weekdays from 8 am to 5 pm.

On the lake's west side, choose from *West Shore State Park*, with $8 sites, a day-use picnic area and boat launch (the campsites away from the lake are peaceful and uncrowded, those on the lake are a bit hectic); or *Big Arm State Recreation Area*, arguably the most crowded campground and day-use area on the lake, with $11 sites and a $3 day-use fee.

The *Polson/Flathead Lake KOA* (☎ 406-883-2151), 1 mile north of Polson on US 93, has $18/23 tent/RV sites.

Motels & Hotels Good values in Polson include the *Cherry Hill Motel* (☎ 406-883-2737, 1810 US 93), with rooms for $55/65 single/double, and the *Port Polson Inn* (☎ 406-883-5385, 800-654-0682, 502 US 93) with lake-front rooms starting at $77/87.

All the accommodations in Lakeside are on US 93 and have lake access. The *Sunrise Vista Inn* (☎ 406-844-3864) has a nice lawn overlooking the lake and $65 rooms. Rooms at the *Bayshore Resort Motel* (☎ 406-844-3131, 800-844-3132) have small kitchens and cost $85; they're open year-round and offer specials in the off season. Next door, the *Lakeside Resort Motel* (☎ 406-844-3570, 800-348-4822) has log cabins and smallish rooms for $50 to $95, depending on the view.

The *Hotel Bigfork* (☎ 406-837-7377, 425 Grand Dr) is the only motel in the heart of Bigfork. Rooms are above a lively restaurant-bar and cost $75/80 for a single/double. To check in or inquire about rooms talk to the bartender.

B&Bs & Resorts One of the best values is the *Osprey Inn* (☎ 406-857-2042, 800-258-2042), on the north end of the lake in Somers. This beautiful B&B has a hot tub, dock and view of Mission Mountains. Rooms start at $85, with a two-night minimum in July and August.

Marina Cay Resort (☎ 406-837-5861, 800-433-6516), off Hwy 35 N, is Bigfork's all-purpose, year-round resort that has everything from convention facilities to fishing charters. Accommodations range from hotel suites to family condos, for $80/85 single/double to $215 for a unit that sleeps four. More quaint is the *Swan River Inn* (☎ 406-837-2220, 360 Grand Dr), with plush rooms starting at $75.

Central to Polson is the *KwaTaqNuk Resort* (☎ 406-883-3636, 800-882-6363), owned by the Confederated Salish and Kootenai Tribes and operated by Best Western. There are indoor and outdoor pools, a hot tub, sauna and lakeside restaurant and bar; rooms start at $100.

Places to Eat

Two old favorites in Polson are the *Sunflower Bakery* (201 Main St) for coffee, pastries and sandwiches and *Price's Good Food* (110 2nd Ave E) for straightforward breakfast or lunch under $6. The *Watusi Cafe* (318 Main St) has interesting salads and sandwiches and a host of vegetarian options for around $7. *Buddeez Pizza* (11 3rd Ave W) is nothing to look at but makes great pizza, salads and subs for $6 to $10.

Bigfork is the lake's uncontested fancy dining destination. There's excellent, reasonably priced cuisine and an elegant atmosphere at *Showthyme* (548 Electric Ave). Locals go to *The Village Well*, one block east of Electric Ave, for microbrews, pizza, salads and grilled sandwiches under $10, and to *El Topo Cantina*, north of downtown on Hwy 35, for margaritas and Mexican fare. *Brookie's Cookies*, on the south end of Electric Ave, will satisfy any sweet tooth.

South of Bigfork, near Woods Bay, *The Sitting Duck* has one of the best views of the lake and good food for $9 to $14. South of Woods Bay, *The Raven* is the lake's best pub, with a deck overlooking the lake, live music and a great beer and wine selection; appetizers, sandwiches and burgers are $5 to $8.

Entertainment

Friday and Saturday nights swing dancing at the rustic *Bigfork Inn*, at the corner of Electric and Grand Aves, attracts folks from all over the valley. The *Bigfork Summer Playhouse* (☎ 406-837-4886), on Electric Ave, hosts Broadway musicals or off-Broadway comedies with actors from all over the Northwest. Performances are Monday to Saturday nights, with matinees on weekends; tickets cost around $15.

WHITEFISH

Once a major hub for the Great Northern Railroad, Whitefish (population 6292; elevation 3036 feet) has an Old West ambiance with new West restaurants, shops and bars. It sits in the shadow of Big Mountain, one of Montana's premiere year-round resorts (known mostly for downhill skiing) and is spittin' distance from Whitefish Lake. In summer and winter there's an influx of seasonal workers from all over the USA, so the nightlife rollicks. More sedate are the families who come to visit Glacier National Park and second-home owners that come to ski and golf. From October to December and April to June the locals reclaim their town, and many accommodations close for a rest.

Orientation & Information

US 93 goes through town as Spokane Ave (north-south) and 2nd St (east-west), connecting to Kalispell, 13 miles south, and to

MONTANA

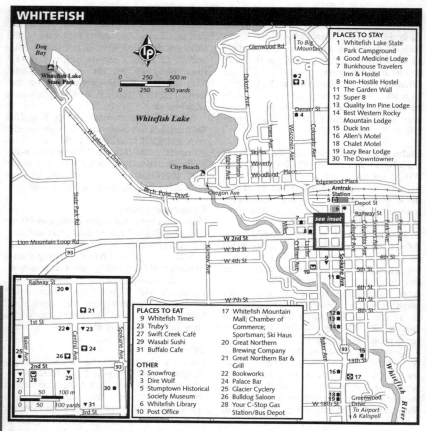

WHITEFISH

PLACES TO STAY
1 Whitefish Lake State Park Campground
4 Good Medicine Lodge
7 Bunkhouse Travelers Inn & Hostel
8 Non-Hostile Hostel
11 The Garden Wall
12 Super 8
13 Quality Inn Pine Lodge
14 Best Western Rocky Mountain Lodge
15 Duck Inn
16 Allen's Motel
18 Chalet Motel
19 Lazy Bear Lodge
30 The Downtowner

PLACES TO EAT
9 Whitefish Times
23 Truby's
27 Swift Creek Café
29 Wasabi Sushi
31 Buffalo Cafe
17 Whitefish Mountain Mall; Chamber of Commerce; Sportsman; Ski Haus
20 Great Northern Brewing Company
21 Great Northern Bar & Grill
22 Bookworks
24 Palace Bar
25 Glacier Cyclery
26 Bulldog Saloon
28 Your C-Stop Gas Station/Bus Depot

OTHER
2 Snowfrog
3 Dire Wolf
5 Stumptown Historical Society Museum
6 Whitefish Library
10 Post Office

US 2; Glacier National Park is 24 miles west via US 2. Wisconsin Ave goes north from downtown to Big Mountain. Check out www.whitefishmt.com for local weather and a variety of useful links.

The Whitefish Chamber of Commerce (☎ 406-862-3501, 877-862-3548), in the Whitefish Mountain Mall at 6475 US 93 S, is helpful in answering questions about the area or accommodations. The Tally Lake Ranger Station (☎ 406-862-2508) is 1 mile west of Whitefish on US 93 W.

Bookworks, at the corner of Central Ave and 1st St, has guidebooks and a good se-

lection of maps. Connect to the Web for free at the Whitefish Library (☎ 406-862-6657), 9 Spokane Ave.

Things to See & Do

The area's biggest attraction is undoubtedly **Big Mountain** (☎ 406-862-2900, 800-858-5439), www.bigmtn.com, which has 3000 acres of skiable terrain, a 2500-foot vertical drop and eleven lifts; tickets are $44, night skiing (December to March) is $12. In the summer the resort is a quiet, self-contained recreation area (good for families) and host of the acclaimed **Flathead Valley Music**

Festival which takes place near the end of July. A **gondola** to the top of the mountain offers incredible views of Flathead Valley and the peaks of Glacier National Park. It costs $9 to ride up once ($14 for unlimited rides); get yourself to the top and you can ride down for free. At the summit is a cafeteria, bar and a nature center, plus hiking and mountain-biking trails that wind through wildflowers, beargrass and, in July, huckleberries.

Stop in at the **Stumptown Historical Society Museum**, housed in the old Great Northern Railroad Depot at the north end of Spokane Ave, to see train memorabilia and photographs of Hell Roaring Ski Course where the Big Mountain ski area was born. The sexy architecture of the **Great Northern Brewing Company** (☎ 406-863-1000), 2 Central Ave, might catch your eye (it's visible from the railroad depot) – go have a look: the free tasting room is open daily and has a great view.

The roasting room and headquarters of **Montana Coffee Traders** is on the west side of US 93 at its junction with Hwy 40 (about 3 miles south of town). They do a good informational tour and sell Montana-made items, including their own whimsical merchandise.

Sportsman & Ski Haus (☎ 406-862-3111), in the Whitefish Mountain Mall at 6475 US 93 S, is an all-purpose **outdoors store** with a big rental department. Snowfrog (☎ 406-862-7547), on the way to Big Mountain at 903 Wisconsin Ave, is run by friendly folks and has the cheapest **ski rentals** in town. Glacier Cyclery (☎ 406-862-6446), west of Baker Ave at 336 2nd St, has maps and guided rides and rents **bikes** for $15/20 for a half-day/full day.

Places to Stay
Prices are generally 20% lower from Labor Day to mid-December and mid-March to Memorial Day, and you can often negotiate even lower rates if you stay at one place for three or more nights. For information and reservations contact Big Mountain's central reservation service (☎ 406-862-1900, 800-858-4152); they have excellent ski packages and allow children under 12 to stay for free.

Camping The *Whitefish Lake State Park* campground, on the southwest edge of the lake, has pit toilets, fire rings, potable water and $6 first-come, first-served sites. The *Whitefish KOA & Buffalo Bobs Pizza* (☎ 406-862-4242), 4 miles south of Whitefish on US 93, caters to RVs and has 15 tent sites ($18) a store, laundry and hot showers; its barbecues attract loads of people not staying at the campground.

Hostels The centrally located HI *Bunkhouse Travelers Inn & Hostel* (☎ 406-862-3377, 217 Railway St), charges $13 for a bunk and $30 for a private room. The tidy operation has a laundry room, communal kitchen and dining room, friendly owners and no curfew. Just up the street, the *Non-Hostile Hostel* (☎ 406-862-7447, 300 W 2nd St) claims that their title makes no reference to the Bunkhouse. It's a large place with a laundry room, guest computer and restaurant, but only sleeps six people ($15 each) at a time; reservations are accepted.

Motels & Hotels You pay for location rather than aesthetics at *The Downtowner* (☎ 406-862-2535, 224 Spokane Ave), where $60 to $95 rooms include use of the adjacent gym.

South of Whitefish on US 93 you'll find the *Chalet Motel* (☎ 406-862-2548, 800-462-3266) with a pool, hot tub and $60 to $80 rooms year-round (kids under 12 stay free); and *Allen's Motel* (☎ 406-862-3995, 6540 US 93 S), a value with singles/doubles for $45/63 and rooms that sleep up to four for $80. Near these but off the highway, the *Duck Inn* (☎ 406-862-3825, 800-344-2377) charges $60 to $85 year-round; rooms are quiet and each has a deck, fireplace, view and access to a TV room and Jacuzzi.

Chain-owned motels along US 93 S include the *Lazy Bear Lodge* (☎ 406-862-4020, 800-888-4479), *Best Western Rocky Mountain Lodge* (☎ 406-862-2569) and *Quality Inn Pine Lodge* (☎ 406-862-7600), each with a pool, Jacuzzi, fitness center and offering Continental breakfast. Prices are $95 to $110 in peak season and around $65 in the off-season. With a Jacuzzi only, *Super*

8 (☎ 406-862-8255) charges $83 peak season and $43 off-season.

B&Bs Whitefish's B&Bs are good values when compared with similarly priced motels. A few blocks from downtown, *The Garden Wall (☎ 406-862-3440, 888-530-1700, 504 Spokane Ave)* is a picture of elegance and grace with rooms for $70 to $105. More casual and outdoorsy, the *Good Medicine Lodge (☎ 406-862-5488, 800-860-5488, 537 Wisconsin Ave)*, north of town, has a hot tub, easy access to Big Mountain and rooms for $85 to $135.

Places to Eat
If you can stand the smoke, the bars on Central Ave in Whitefish serve good, cheap food until late. Also on Central is *Truby's*, a local favorite for wood-fired pizza, salads and pasta. The *Buffalo Cafe*, on 3rd St between Central and Spokane Aves, is one of those great breakfast spots that you hear about all over the state; most things are under $6. Also good for breakfast and really nice lunches under $10 is the *Swift Creek Café (307 E 2nd St)*. For coffee, pastries and reading material, head to the *Whitefish Times* on 4th St.

Sushi snobs will be surprised to find excellent sushi served in an upbeat atmosphere at *Wasabi Sushi (419 2nd St E)*; plan on spending at least $15 per person. For steak and (cooked) seafood, locals like the woodsy *Whitefish Lake Restaurant (☎ 406-862-5285)* at the Whitefish Lake Golf Club; reservations are recommended. The *Hellroaring Saloon & Eatery*, in the original

1940s lodge on Big Mountain, is crammed with ski memorabilia and usually crammed with people eating hearty appetizers ($6), burgers ($7) and dinner specials ($8 to $11).

Entertainment
Along Central Ave in Whitefish you'll find some classic old watering holes, including the *Palace Bar*, *Bulldog Saloon* and the *Great Northern Bar and Grill*, loved for its collection of old signs, pool and Ping-Pong tables and 4 to 6 pm happy hour. The *Dire Wolf*, north of town on Wisconsin Ave, is a popular spot for live bands on weekends; it's a smoke-free establishment that serves food as well.

Getting There & Away
Glacier Park International Airport (☎ 406-257-5994), halfway between Whitefish and Kalispell on US 2, is proof positive that the Flathead Valley is under siege from out-of-state home buyers: you can shop real estate listings (with pictures!) and choose the outside finish, tile and home spa for your new pad without even leaving the airport. The buyers come to town on Delta Airlines, Big Sky Airlines (☎ 800-237-7788), Horizon Air and United Express by way of Missoula, Salt Lake City, and Spokane and Seattle, Washington.

Intermountain Transport (☎ 406-755-4011) connects Whitefish to Kalispell ($7.50), Missoula ($24), Helena ($33), Bozeman ($45) and Seattle ($81). Buses stop at the Your C-Stop gas station, 403 2nd St, in Whitefish, and the bus depot, 15 13th St E, in Kalispell.

Travel to Glacier National Park on Amtrak's 7:35 am eastbound train, bound for Chicago, and return on the nightly westbound train that stops in Whitefish around 7:45 pm before continuing to Portland, Oregon, and Seattle, Washington. A round-trip ticket to West Glacier is around $15. The ticket office and depot (☎ 406-862-2268) are at the north end of Central Ave.

Getting Around
The Airport Shuttle Service (☎ 406-752-2842) charges $15 per person for trips

between the airport and Whitefish or Kalispell.

Avis (☎ 406-257-2727), Budget (☎ 406-755-7500), Hertz (☎ 406-257-1266) and National (☎ 406-257-7144) all have booths at Glacier Park International Airport. For cheaper rates, try the Duck Inn (see Places to Stay, above) or Rent-A-Wreck (☎ 406-755-4555, 800-654-4642), 2622 Hwy 2 E.

The Shuttle Network Of Whitefish (SNOW) bus runs between downtown Whitefish and Big Mountain from 6 am to around 10 pm during ski season; free. Bus schedules are available at most accommodations, or by calling the chamber of commerce or Big Mountain (see above).

KALISPELL

Kalispell (population 17,149; elevation 2989 feet) is Flathead Valley's commercial center. It's not a particularly charming city, but it's home to several worthwhile sights and the valley's concentration of budget lodging

and fast food. Glacier National Park is about an hour's drive northeast (via US 2). Flathead Lake is 15 to 20 minutes south by way of US 93.

History

The little settlements at Demersville, a steamboat landing on the Flathead River, 4½ miles southeast, and Ashley, half a mile west, were moved here piece by piece and became Kalispell in the 1870s. The name, given to the town by local businessman Charles Conrad, is a Blackfeet word that means 'grassy land above the lake.'

Born in Virginia, Charles Conrad fought in the Civil War on the Confederate side, but became disillusioned with the politics of the 'states' so he traveled to Fort Benton. There he married a Blackfeet woman, and together they moved west to Kalispell with the IG Baker Company to settle (and profit from) the Great Northern Railroad route. Under her guidance,

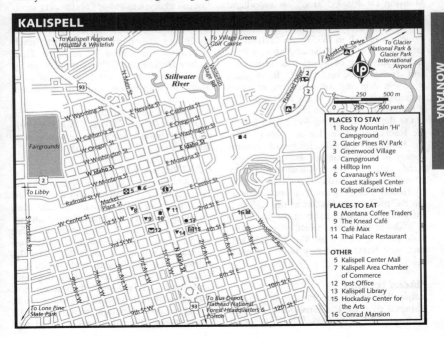

KALISPELL

To Kalispell Regional Hospital & Whitefish
To Village Greens Golf Course
To Glacier National Park & Glacier Park International Airport
Montclair Drive
Stillwater River
Whitefish Stage Rd
Flathead Drive

0   250   500 m
0   250   500 yards

N Main St
N Meridian Rd
93
W Wyoming St
E Nevada St
E California St
E Oregon St
E Washington St
W California St
W Oregon St
W Washington St
E Idaho St
W Idaho St
E Montana St
W Montana St
Fairgrounds
2
To Libby
Railroad St W
Market Place St
Center St
1st St W
W Center St
3rd St W
To Lone Pine State Park
S Meridian Rd
1st Ave E
2nd Ave E
2nd St E
3rd Ave E
4th St E
5th Ave E
4th Ave E
8th St E
Main St S
6th Ave E
Woodland Ave
16th St
9th St W
To Bus Depot Flathead National Forest Headquarters & Polson
10th St E
12th St E
93

PLACES TO STAY
1 Rocky Mountain 'Hi' Campground
2 Glacier Pines RV Park
3 Greenwood Village Campground
4 Hilltop Inn
6 Cavanaugh's West Coast Kalispell Center
10 Kalispell Grand Hotel

PLACES TO EAT
8 Montana Coffee Traders
9 The Knead Café
11 Café Max
14 Thai Palace Restaurant

OTHER
5 Kalispell Center Mall
7 Kalispell Area Chamber of Commerce
12 Post Office
13 Kalispell Library
15 Hockaday Center for the Arts
16 Conrad Mansion

MONTANA

Conrad acted as representative to the Blackfeet Nation in several land negotiations and was a staunch defender of Native American land rights.

Information

The Kalispell Area Chamber of Commerce (☎ 406-752-6166) has its office in an old railroad administration building on the corner of Center and Main Sts. Flathead National Forest Headquarters (☎ 406-758-5204), south of downtown and half a block east of Hwy 93 at 1935 3rd Ave E, has maps, trail guides and information on the flora and fauna of the Bob Marshall Wilderness and Glacier National Park. Check out Books West (☎ 406-752-6956) at 101 Main St. The Kalispell Library (☎ 406-758-5819), 247 1st Ave E, offers free internet access.

Things to See & Do

It's definitely worth the $6 ticket to tour the completely restored Norman-style **Conrad Mansion** (☎ 406-755-2166), on Woodland Ave between 3rd and 4th Sts E. The home of businessman extraordinaire Charles Conrad was built in 1895 by the architect of St Mary's Lodge in Glacier National Park and retains most of its original furnishings and decorations, including Tiffany glass windows, drinking fountains, an intercom system and elevator; 9 am to 8 pm daily from May 15 to October 15.

On the corner of 2nd Ave E and 3rd St, the **Hockaday Center for the Arts** (☎ 406-755-5268) gets a good selection of contemporary work by Montana artists and has a terrific gift shop; open Tuesday to Friday 10 am to 5 pm, Saturday 10 am to 3 pm, free admission. People gather on weekends at the **Kalispell Open Market** at the Kalispell Fairgrounds, west of town at the corner of W Idaho St and Meridian Rd (entrance and main parking lot are on Meridian), to sift, sort, sell, barter and buy new and used 'stuff.'

Places to Stay

Kalispell is an RV mecca. On US 2 from Kalispell east are the *Greenwood Village Campground* (☎ 406-257-7719) with

$13/$20 tent/RV sites, the *Glacier Pines RV Park* (☎ 800-533-4029) with $19 sites and the *Rocky Mountain 'Hi' Campground* (☎ 406-755-9573) with $14/18 tent/RV sites, a large playground and small 'lake.'

The best deal downtown is the *Kalispell Grand Hotel* (☎ 406-755-8100, 800-858-7422, 100 Main St), which charges $68 to $81, including breakfast. Of Kalispell's chain and budget motels, on US 93 south of town and US 2 east of town, the *Hilltop Inn* (☎ 406-755-4455, 801 E Idaho St) has well-kept rooms for $52/60. Part of the Kalispell Center Mall downtown, *Cavanaugh's West Coast Kalispell Center* (☎ 406-752-6660, 800-843-4667) is a hub of activity and a stopping point for tour groups; they have a pool, restaurant and $100 rooms.

Places to Eat

The two places not to miss in Kalispell are *Montana Coffee Traders*, across from the mall at 328 W Center St, which has an in-house bakery, fresh soups and hearty sandwiches; and *The Knead Café* (25 2nd Ave) whose 'Mediterranean-style' food includes excellent salads, pasta and fresh fish (lunch is around $6, dinner $7 to $11). *Thai Palace Restaurant* (319 Main St) is run by an adorable family that makes great soup and a mix of Chinese and Thai dishes for $7 to $10.

Kalispell's upper-end dining venue is *Café Max* (☎ 406-755-7687, 121 Main St), with an intimate atmosphere and a superb selection of food and wines ($9 to $15).

COLUMBIA FALLS

CF Aluminum Company, Plum Creek Timber and FH Stoltze Land & Lumber give Columbia Falls (population 4293; elevation 3068 feet) its distinctive (fresh-cut wood and processed pulp) smell, but the town is a mere shadow of the bustling industrial town it was in the 1940s. Roughly halfway between Whitefish and Glacier National Park, the town acts as a pit stop and occasional overnight stop when accommodations in other towns are full. There are a few chain-owned budget motels, a bank, sports stores, a big supermarket and plenty of fast-food restaurants along US 2, the town's main thoroughfare.

The *fishing access site* on the Flathead River, which is a half mile east of town, has no developed campsites or facilities but you can set up a tent as long as you take it down by 9 am.

At the junction of US 2 and US 206, *Glacier Mountain Shadows Resort (☎ 406-892-7686, 800-766-1137)* has a pool, hot tub, restaurant, store and laundry. Tent sites are $10, RV spots $16 for two people ($2 each additional person) and motel rooms are $67/78 single/double in summer, around $45 the rest of the year.

The *Glacier Inn Motel (☎ 406-892-4341)* is on the east edge of town, south of US 2. Rooms cost $52/62 for a single/double from Memorial Day to Labor Day, $36/40 the rest of the year. The *Old River Bridge Inn (☎ 406-892-2182)*, 2 miles north of town on US 2, is Columbia Falls' weekend entertainment center with a restaurant, bar and casino. All rooms have double beds and cost $65 in summer, $35 the rest of the year.

Consider a splurge at the *Bad Rock Country B&B (☎ 406-892-2829, 888-892-2829)*, which has a 5 pm social hour and rooms with fireplace for $110 to $155 in summer, $98 to $136 the rest of the year. No pets or children under 10. Take Hwy 206 south of the US 2/Hwy 206 intersection. After 2½ miles, turn right at Badrock Rd and continue for three-quarters of a mile.

NORTHWEST CORNER

Between US 93 and the Montana-Idaho border is territory that even most Montanans haven't explored. The area is similar to the Pacific Northwest in climate, vegetation and its reliance on the timber industry, and has more interaction with Canada and Idaho (in terms of commerce and tourism) than it does with the rest of the state. The Clark Fork and Kootenai Rivers, which drain the Cabinet, Purcell, Salish and Whitefish ranges, are perhaps the main link between the northwest corner and the rest of Montana.

Hwy 200, US 2 and US 93 are the travel arteries through here, each one as scenic as the others. US 93 gets the least use from American visitors but offers access to rugged and wonderful hiking destinations near Eureka, undeniably the most charming town in the region. Lake Koocanusa, formed by the Libby Dam on the Kootenai River, snakes its way up to Canada and offers a plethora of fishing and camping spots.

As growing environmental concerns decrease the lumber industry's activity up here, locals are becoming more vocal about protecting their livelihood. It's probably not a good idea to wear a 'Gore 2000' shirt around these parts. Mining will never compete with the timber industry, but some does occur on a small scale, and rumor has it that prospectors have their eyes on the rich silver and copper deposits beneath the Cabinet Mountain Wilderness.

History

David Thompson, the area's first documented explorer, navigated the Kootenai River in 1808 and then sent explorer and furrier Finan McDonald to set up a fur-trading post near the site of present-day Libby. Other than the trappers and traders who frequented the post, the area remained unsettled until placer gold and silver were found in local creeks in 1869. But the mining population was just a drop in the bucket compared to the influx of settlers brought by the Great Northern Railroad in 1893. With the iron horse's arrival, Montana's northwest corner became prime timber country and Libby became an important lumber town.

Eureka

At the northeast end of Lake Koocanusa, 8 miles from the Canadian border and 50 miles north of Whitefish by US 93, Eureka (population 1105) is a funky town that acts as social and commercial hub of the Tobacco Valley. It's both a lumber and a tourist town, and is increasingly important for its Christmas tree farms. There's a bounty of good hiking in the surrounding

NORTHWEST CORNER

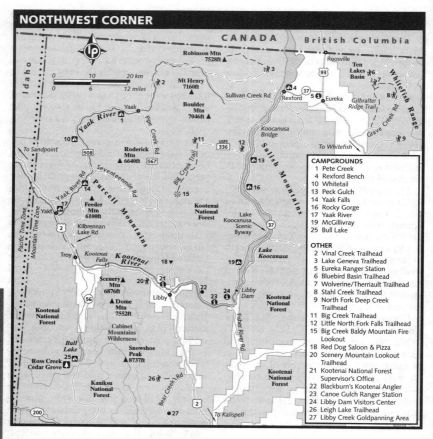

CANADA   British Columbia

Idaho

Robinson Mtn
7528ft ▲

Roosville

Ten
Lakes
Basin

Whitefish Range

0   10   20 km
0   6   12 miles

Mt Henry
7160ft
▲

Sullivan Creek Rd

Rexford

Eureka

Gilbralter
Ridge Trail

Yaak
River

Boulder
Mtn
7046ft ▲

Koocanusa
Bridge

Grave Creek Rd

To Whitefish

Roderick
Mtn
▲ 6640ft

USFS
336

Salish Mountains

To Sandpoint

Seventeenmile Rd

Big Creek Trail

Kootenai
National
Forest

Lake
Koocanusa
Scenic
Byway

Purcell Mountains

Feeder
Mtn
6100ft

Kilbrennan
Lake Rd

Lake
Koocanusa

Troy

Kootenai
Falls

Kootenai River

Scenery
Mtn
6876ft

Libby

Libby
Dam

Kootenai
National
Forest

▲ Dome
Mtn
7552ft

Fisher River Rd

Kootenai
National
Forest

Cabinet
Mountains
Wilderness

Snowshoe
Peak
▲ 8737ft

Bull
Lake

Ross Creek
Cedar Grove

Kaniksu
National
Forest

Bear Creek Rd

To Kalispell

CAMPGROUNDS
1 Pete Creek
4 Rexford Bench
10 Whitetail
13 Peck Gulch
14 Yaak Falls
16 Rocky Gorge
17 Yaak River
19 McGillivray
25 Bull Lake

OTHER
2 Vinal Creek Trailhead
3 Lake Geneva Trailhead
5 Eureka Ranger Station
6 Bluebird Basin Trailhead
7 Wolverine/Therriault Trailhead
8 Stahl Creek Trailhead
9 North Fork Deep Creek Trailhead
11 Big Creek Trailhead
12 Little North Fork Falls Trailhead
15 Big Creek Baldy Mountain Fire Lookout
18 Red Dog Saloon & Pizza
20 Scenery Mountain Lookout Trailhead
21 Kootenai National Forest Supervisor's Office
22 Blackburn's Kootenai Angler
23 Canoe Gulch Ranger Station
24 Libby Dam Visitors Center
26 Leigh Lake Trailhead
27 Libby Creek Goldpanning Area

MONTANA

forest, representing a third tree-based asset to the local economy. Locals up here are exceptionally friendly, and the drive between Eureka and Whitefish along US 93 makes an excellent day trip.

Downtown you'll find an array of nice gift shops (the local pottery is especially good) and, on the south edge of town, the rustic **Tobacco Valley Historic Village** where several of the town's original buildings are open for exploration.

Orientation & Information US 93 goes north to Canada and south to Whitefish and

runs through town as Dewey Ave, where you'll find a grocery store, a bank with an ATM and most businesses. The Eureka Ranger Station (☎ 406-296-2536) is on the north end of town where Hwy 37 turns west off US 93 towards Lake Koocanusa.

Hiking The Whitefish Range, east of Eureka, has seen less logging than other ranges in the area and thus offers some of the best hiking. The 3-mile **North Fork Deep Creek Trail** is an easy climb to a ridge overlooking the Williams Creek drainage that can be done in a few hours. The trailhead is

6 miles east of US 93 on Deep Creek Rd 368 (turn left at the trailhead sign just before the Deep Creek Bridge).

Even easier is the 1½-mile **Bluebird Basin Trail**, which leads to Paradise and Bluebird lakes. It starts at the same trailhead as the **Wolverine/Therriault Trail** which has multiple-day and loop options that pass by backcountry campgrounds. Reach the trailhead by turning east off of US 93 onto Grave Creek Rd 114 and continuing 14 miles to Forest Rd 319; turn left and continue another 14 miles to the trailhead at road's end. At the end of Stahl Creek Rd 7021, also off Grave Creek Rd 114 (10 miles from US 93), the **Stahl Creek Trail** climbs 3 miles to Stahl Peak Lookout from where you have terrific views into Glacier National Park.

A popular backpacking and backcountry ski destination is **Ten Lakes Basin**, a pocket of dazzling glacial lakes on the east side of the Whitefish Range's westernmost ridge. You can access the basin on a vigorous day hike along the **Gibralter Ridge Trail**, which connects to several long-distance trails. The trailhead is also on Grave Creek Rd 114, 5 miles east of US 93.

Places to Stay & Eat Choices here are the *Silverado Motel* (☎ 406-297-7777), with $52 rooms, or the *Ksanka Motor Inn* (☎ 406-296-3127), with rooms for $47; both are at the US 93/Hwy 37 junction north of downtown Eureka. *Huckleberry Hannah's B&B* (☎ 406-889-3381, 888-889-3381, huckhana@libby.org) has friendly owners, $55 to $100 rooms and acres of surrounding woods; call for reservations and the owners will give you directions.

There's a grocery store and natural foods store on Dewey Ave in the heart of town. The *Sunflower Bakery and Coffeehouse*, behind the natural foods store, has terrific baked goods and lunches for under $5. Locals also like *Sophie's Emporium* (205 Dewey Ave) for lunch and *Four Corners*, north of town at the US 93/Hwy 37 junction, for dinner. *Carmen's Little Kitchen*, north of 8th St on US 93, has simple but tasty Mexican fare for under $10.

Lake Koocanusa & Libby Dam

The name 'Koocanusa' is an amalgam of Kootenai, Canada and USA – the three nations meant to benefit from the reservoir's hydroelectric power and flood-control capabilities. The Kootenai, who live south on the Flathead Reservation, hardly feel any practical effects. Flanked by the Salish and Purcell mountains, the slim 90-mile-long reservoir is in fact a beautiful site despite its controversial birth: shackling the river to feed the Columbia River farther south depleted wildlife habitat, flooded productive land and altered the river's natural flow. Hwy 37 skirts the reservoir's east side for about 65 miles between US 93 and US 2.

Built in 1972, Libby Dam is a straight-axis, concrete gravity dam 17 miles east of Libby off Hwy 37. Free guided tours are offered from the visitors center (☎ 406-293-5577) on the west side of the dam, hourly from 10 am to 4 pm daily, Memorial Day to Labor Day; the center is open daily from 9:30 am to 6 pm.

There are numerous **bald eagle nests** between the dam and Libby. The raptors are abundant during the migration period from October to mid-November, especially below the dam where they catch kokanee salmon. A good viewing point is the east side of the David Thompson Bridge, just below the dam's powerhouse.

Hiking The best hiking is on the west side of the lake, accessible by crossing the Koocanusa Bridge, 15 miles south of Eureka and 50 miles north of Libby. The **Lake Geneva Trail** climbs 2 miles through an area of newly planted trees to a small lake with primitive camping and good fishing. The trailhead is 10 miles north of the bridge via USFS Rd 470 then 2½ miles northeast to the end of Young Creek Rd 303.

An easy creek-bottom hike is along the **Big Creek Trail**, which follows Big Creek for 4 miles and then climbs to a fire road (and another trailhead) where you have good views of the water. The trailhead is 8 miles south of the bridge on USFS Rd 228, then 6 miles east on Big Creek Rd 336 to where it branches off (just before North Big Creek

MONTANA

Bridge) and ends at the trailhead. A shorter hike is the half-mile jaunt to **Little North Fork Falls**, off Big Creek Rd 336, 2 miles east of USFS Rd 228.

Fishing The best place to find fishing information, guides and equipment is at Blackburn's Kootenai Angler (☎ 406-293-7578), www.montana-flyfishing.com, on Hwy 37 between the dam and Libby.

Places to Stay USFS campgrounds in the area tend to be large and filled with a fishing/motorized boating crowd in summer. North of the Koocanusa Bridge near the small community of Rexford, *Rexford Bench* has 106 sites, showers and a boat launch and takes reservations *(☎ 800-280-2267)*. South of the bridge on the east side of the lake, *Peck Gulch* has 75 sites and lake access while *Rocky Gorge* has 120 sites (most of them paved) but gets the least amount of traffic.

The west side of the reservoir is more primitive. USFS Rd 228 (the Lake Koocanusa Scenic Byway) starts on the west side of the Koocanusa Bridge (15 miles south of Eureka on Hwy 37) and heads south to where it meets Hwy 37 at the Libby Dam. The *McGillivray campground*, on the southern portion of the road, gets relatively little use.

Libby

Under the J Niel Lumber Company's direction, Libby (population 2948) thrived and promised a limitless future in the timber industry – the deep, dense and massive forest would never run out of trees, or so everyone thought. Since then other companies have bought and sold the mill, continually exploiting the forests. The present-day owner is Stinson Lumber Company, employing 63% of the town's population. With logging on the decline, Libby's new economic 'hope' is mining – the town's original industry – silver, lead and gold from the Cabinet and Purcell Mountains.

You'll see stickers declaring 'This family is supported by the timber industry' plastered on everything from house windows to car bumpers to baby carriers. Less politically loaded are the antics of **Libby Logger Days**, held in mid-July, when professional loggers compete for prizes with chain saws, cross-cut saws, axes and sheer strength.

Orientation & Information Libby sits at the junction of US 2 and Hwy 37, 89 miles from Kalispell, 190 miles from Missoula and 31 miles from the Idaho border.

Find camping, hiking and fishing information at the Kootenai National Forest Supervisor's Office (☎ 406-293-6211), on US 2 in Libby, or at the smaller Canoe Gulch Ranger Station (☎ 406-293-7773), 13 miles east of Libby on Hwy 37. The Libby Area Chamber of Commerce (☎ 406-293-4167), www.libby.org/libbyacc/index.html, downtown on 9th St, can answer questions about accommodations. Downtown on US 2 are the post office and a bank with an ATM.

Things to See & Do In Libby proper there's the **Heritage Museum,** with a collection of musical instruments, logging equipment and mining tools (open from Memorial Day to Labor Day, daily from 10 am to 6 pm; free).

Three miles north of Libby on Hwy 37, **Wildlife Recapture and Raft Rental** (☎ 406-293-7878) leads wildlife photo safaris ($100 per person) and guided raft trips on the Kootenai River ($100 for up to 6 people).

Eight miles northwest of Libby on the north side of US 2, the Kootenai River drops 200 feet with a powerful, breathtaking roar at **Kootenai Falls** – the largest undammed falls in the northern Rockies and one of the largest in the USA.

If you go south from Libby on US 2 and turn west down Bear Creek Rd for 18 miles, the USFS allows recreational gold panning along a quarter-mile stretch of Libby Creek. Old pie tins, hats and Frisbees work well as gold pans if you happened to leave yours at home. There is usually a ranger at the parking lot during summer months.

Places to Stay & Eat Pitch a tent in *Firemen's Park*, behind the chamber of commerce, for $2 per night. North of town on the west shore of the lake, the *Koocanusa Resort* (☎ *406-293-7548, 23911 Hwy 37)* has a gas station, lodge, horseback riding and boat rentals. Campsites cost $16 and cabins start at $45.

The *Pioneer Junction Motel* (☎ *406-293-3781)* has rooms for $40. The *Evergreen Motel* (☎ *406-293-4178)* charges $50 for slightly nicer rooms with cable TV. The *Venture Motor Inn* (☎ *406-293-7711, 800-221-0166)*, on US 2 W, has a pool, hot tub and restaurant; rooms start at $72.

Libby's best food is served at its bars. The favorites of the old guard are the 'buckburgers' ($1 each) at the *Pastime Saloon (216 Mineral Ave)*, an institution since 1916. The *Red Dog Saloon & Pizza*, 8 miles north of Libby on Pipe Creek Rd, has vegetarian options and a good selection of microbrews. The *Ho Wun Chinese Restaurant (1141 US 2 W)* does a good job with basic Chinese dishes like cashew chicken ($7) and wonton soup ($2).

There's a *Rosauer's* supermarket west of town on US 2 and, across the street, the *Caboose Restaurant & Lounge* which serves full dinners. The *Libby Cafe (411 Mineral St)*, near City Hall, is a good choice for breakfast.

Getting There & Away Libby's link to the outside world is Amtrak. The eastbound train comes by at 5:41 am and the westbound at 10:59 pm; a one-way ticket to Seattle, Washington, costs $67, to Whitefish $14. Libby's train depot is downtown at E 1st and Main Sts.

Bull River Valley
Northwest of Libby, Bull Lake Rd (Hwy 56) heads south from US 2 into the Bull River Valley and the heart of the Cabinet Mountains. After 22 miles it passes **Bull Lake**, known for its excellent trout fishing. The campground on the southern edge has pit toilets, a picnic area, fire rings and potable water; sites cost $10 per night.

South of the lake, USFS Rd 398 heads west to the valley's main attraction – the **Ross Creek Cedar Grove**. A short self-guided nature trail leads through the 100-acre preserve of towering western red cedars that average 175 feet in height, eight feet in diameter and date back 500 years.

Troy & Yaak River Valley
Sixteen miles northwest of Libby and 14 miles from the Idaho border on US 2, Troy (population 1124) is at the southern foot of the Yaak River Valley, the lowest point in Montana at 1892 feet. Immortalized by author Rick Bass in *Winter Notes* and *The Book of Yaak*, the lonely and beautiful valley is one of the most important biological corridors between the Canadian Rockies and the Cabinet Mountain Wilderness Area. Environmental groups like Rock Creek Alliance and the Clark Fork Pend d'Oreille Coalition are continually fighting for measures that will keep the land and water fit for species that use this area. A state restoration plan for the nearly extinct bull trout has put a halt to some extractive industry (long the area's economic backbone), but much of the land is still owned by lumber companies and the Sterling Mining Company.

Troy is the area's service center and has a bank, supermarket and gas station. From Troy the Kilbrennan Lake Rd heads north to where it joins the Yaak River Rd and continues north to the most remote settlement in Montana's northwest – the 'town' of Yaak, consisting of the Dirty Shame Saloon and the Yaak Mercantile.

A good way to explore the old-growth larch and red cedar forests around Yaak, and possibly see some elk, is by foot or skis along the **Vinal Creek Trail**. From town, take USFS Rd 68 3 miles north, then follow USFS Rd 746 along the Yaak River for 5 miles to the trailhead near Vinal Creek (look for the bridge).

USFS campgrounds around Troy have pit toilets, potable water, fire rings and picnic areas and charge $6 to $11 per night. The easiest to find is the *Yaak River Campground*, 7 miles northwest on US 2, which has 44 sites. Smaller and more remote are those on Yaak River Rd, which begins at US 2, 10 miles northwest of Troy. *Yaak Falls Campground* has seven sites, *Whitetail* has

12 sites and the **Pete Creek Campground** with 12 sites is northeast of Yaak along USFS Rd 92.

On US 2 in Troy, the **Holiday Motel** (☎ 406-295-4117) and **Ranch Motel** (☎ 406-295-4332) both charge around $40/45 for a single/double. The IGA Supermarket is open daily from 8 am until 9 pm. **Jack's Café** *(711 E Missoula Ave)* and the **Silver Spur Restaurant** on US 2 are both good spots for a meal.

Cabinet Mountains Wilderness Area

Southwest of Libby, bordered by US 2 and Hwy 56, the Cabinet Mountains Wilderness encompasses 148 sq miles of deep canyons, small lakes, waterfalls and snowcapped peaks in the Kootenai National Forest. The steep **Leigh Lake Trail**, at the end of USFS Rd 4786 (take Bear Creek Rd to access road), offers good views of Mt Snowy (8712 feet), the forest's highest peak, and access to longer trails that would be great for extended backcountry trips. Information and maps are available from the Kootenai National Forest Supervisor's Office (see Libby, earlier).

BOB MARSHALL COUNTRY

The Bob Marshall Wilderness Complex, affectionately called 'the Bob,' runs roughly from the southern boundary of Glacier National Park in the north to Rogers Pass (on Hwy 200) in the south. Within the complex are three designated wilderness areas that are separate only because they were designated at different times. These are (unbroken from north to south): the Great Bear Wilderness Area, the Bob Marshall Wilderness Area and the Scapegoat Wilderness Area. National Forest lands surround most of the complex, offering developed campgrounds, road access to trailheads and quieter country when the Bob gets loaded with hunters in autumn.

The sheer enormity of this wilderness is one of its biggest attractions. The core lands (not including the surrounding 1563 sq miles of National Forest) encompass 2344 sq miles, 3200 miles of trails and sections

that are more than 40 miles from the nearest road. The chances of finding total solitude here are very good, and the diversity of geology, plants and wildlife is incredibly rich.

None of the Bob's peaks reach above 10,000 feet – the highest is Red Mountain (9411 feet) – but the relief is such that they appear much higher than they are. The Rocky Mountain Front in the east rises straight up out of the plains in a limestone wall that is often likened to the top half of the Grand Canyon. Between this and the Swan Range, in the west, lies the Continental Divide Range, which contains the Bob's most famous feature – the 13-mile-long Chinese Wall.

These ranges run northwest-southeast and are separated from each other by the large valleys of the Two Medicine, Sun, Dearborn, and South and Middle Forks of the Flathead Rivers. It is these waterways, plus Birch and Badger Creeks, that act as main navigation and penetration routes into the Bob.

One of the most important wildlife features of this area is the Sun River Game Preserve, set aside in 1912, which protects the Sun River elk herd on the Rocky Mountain Front between Choteau and Augusta.

Orientation

You can access the Bob from the Seeley-Swan Valley in the west, Hungry Horse Reservoir in the north, the Rocky Mountain Front in the east and off Hwy 200 in the south. The easiest (and thus, most popular) access routes are from the Benchmark and Gibson Reservoir trailheads in the Rocky Mountain Front. Roads to these trailheads are plowed and well marked.

Other good access points are the Holland Lake and Pyramid Pass trailheads on the Seeley-Swan side. Trails in this range generally start very steeply, reaching the wilderness boundary after about 7 miles. It takes another 10 miles or so to really get into the heart of the Bob. There are good day hikes from all sides.

No permits are necessary to travel in the Bob, though fishing and hunting licenses are

Bob: The Man, the Myth, the Legend

The most important passion of life is the overpowering desire to escape periodically from the strangling clutch of mechanistic civilization. To us the enjoyment of solitude, complete independence, and the beauty of undefiled panoramas is absolutely essential to happiness...a person might die spiritually if he could not sometimes forsake all contact with his gregarious fellowmen, and the machines which they have created, and retreat to an environment where there was no remote trace of humanity.

– Bob Marshall, from *Impressions from the Wilderness*
(The Living Wilderness Journal, autumn 1937), written
in Montana and Idaho's Selway-Bitterroot Wilderness.

It is very fitting that one of the USA's most-beloved wilderness areas is named after one of its most renowned preservationists – Bob Marshall, who inspired friends, students and government officials with his love for the wild. Born in New York in 1901, Marshall grew up in an urban environment but constantly dreamed of adventures. In his early teens he began to explore the Adirondacks, and by age 21 he had published a book chronicling his climbs to 42 of the region's 46 peaks over 4000 feet (he eventually climbed all 46).

After receiving his master's degree in forestry from Harvard and his PhD from Johns Hopkins University, Bob wrote books on forest preservation, including *The People's Forest* (Harrison Smith & Robert Haas, New York, 1933), in which he writes:

Under their present management, the American forests are drifting into constantly expanding ruin....The time has come when we must discard the unsocial view that our woods are the lumberman's and substitute the broader ideal that every acre of the woodland in the country is rightly a part of the people's forest.

These principles were the foundation for *A National Plan for American Forestry*, a collaborative report written by Marshall and his fellow foresters, which set the groundwork for the wilderness preservation movement in Washington, DC, and led to the organization of the Wilderness Society. Bob Marshall died at the young age of 39 when he suffered a heart attack while traveling by train from Washington, DC, to New York.

MONTANA

required. Group size is limited to 15 people, and you may camp in one location for 14 days, after which you must move at least 5 miles to another campsite.

Information

For an extended backcountry trip it's best to consult maps well in advance. The USGS 'Bob Marshall, Great Bear, and Scapegoat Wilderness Complex' map is the best topo-trail map and shows access roads from the west (Seeley-Swan) and north (Hungry Horse); the 'Lewis and Clark National Forest – Rocky Mountain Division' map shows trailheads and access roads on the east (Rocky Mountain Front) side a little

better. Both maps are available ($5 each) by mail from the USGS or the ranger stations listed below, or can be bought at most book, sporting goods and hardware stores in the region. The ranger stations that tend to the Bob include:

Augusta Information Station
(☎ 406-562-3247), 405 Manix St, Augusta

Flathead National Forest Headquarters
(☎ 406-758-5204), 1935 3rd Ave E, Kalispell

Hungry Horse Ranger Station
(☎ 406-387-3000), on Hwy 2 in Hungry Horse

Lewis & Clark National Forest
Supervisors Office
(☎ 406-791-7700), 1101 15th St N, No 401, Great Falls

Rocky Mountain Ranger District
(☎ 406-466-5341), 1102 Main Ave NW, Choteau

Seeley Lake Ranger Station
(☎ 406-677-2233), 3 miles north of Seeley Lake on Hwy 83

Spotted Bear Ranger District
(☎ 406-758-5376), 55 miles south of Hungry Horse; open in summer only

Swan Lake Ranger District
(☎ 406-837-7500), in Bigfork

Outfitters

Because of its size, many people choose to explore the Bob on horseback. You can hire an outfitter to pack in your gear, allowing the luxury of setting up a well-stocked base camp; the outfitter can then pick you up at an agreed-upon location several days or weeks later, or simply let you pack yourself out. You can also hire an outfitter to act as cook, trip-planner and guide for multiple-day trips, or sign up for a trip that the outfitter has prearranged. Prices vary according to the level of service and length of trip desired.

There are many outfitters, especially around Choteau, Augusta and Seeley Lake. Cheff's Guest Ranch (☎ 406-644-2557), based in the Mission Valley, has an excellent reputation and has been leading Bob Marshall trips for over 50 years. Prices are about $195 per person, per day, with a week costing $1400. The Great Northern Llama Co (☎ 406-755-9044), www.gnllama.com, uses llamas in place of horses and has good rates for guide and pack-in/pack-out services.

Rocky Mountain Front

This eastern boundary of the Bob – called the Front Range or Front – is where the prairie meets the Rocky Mountains in one 100-mile-long, 1000-foot-high swoop. Many experienced outdoors folks consider this their favorite part of the Bob (if not their favorite chunk of wilderness in the USA). Sitting east of the Continental Divide, the Front's climate is dry, windy and colder than the terrain to the west. In early spring when areas west of the Divide are still under snow the Front Range is often covered with wildflowers. Vegetation on the mountain sides is relatively sparse, which makes for great views of the reefs, mesas and peaks which lie between the Front Range and the Continental Divide.

Blackfeet Indian Reservation The Blackfeet Reservation sits in the shortgrass prairies to the east of Glacier National Park. The Blackfeet Nation includes the Northern Piegan, Southern Piegan (Blackfeet) and Blood tribes that came south from the Alberta area in the 1700s. Originally an agrarian people, the Blackfeet took quickly to horses and guns, which helped them tremendously on buffalo hunts, and they developed a reputation as the fiercest warriors in the West. By the 1800s, when trappers and explorers arrived, the Blackfeet controlled the northern plains and the western mountain passes along the Front Range. Today the Blackfeet control their destiny through oil drilling, ranching, farming and manufacturing pencils.

The **Museum of the Plains Indians** (☎ 406-338-2230), 18 miles east of Glacier Park in Browning (at the intersection of US 2 and US 89), is one of Montana's better Native American museums. A highlight of the museum is *Winds of Change*, a multimedia presentation, narrated by Vincent Price, about the evolution of Indian cultures on the northern plains; open daily from 9 am to 5 pm from June to October, weekdays the rest of the year; $2. During July, **North American Indian Days** (☎ 406-338-7406 for information) takes place on the Tribal Fairgrounds adjacent to the museum. The four-day program, which includes dancing, games, parades and many encampments, is one of the largest gatherings of US and Canadian tribes in the Northwest.

The **Scriver Museum of Montana Wildlife and Bronze** (☎ 406-338-5425) might interest those who like bronze sculpture; open June to October, closed Monday.

Badger-Two Medicine The Two Medicine River and Badger Creek drain the Front's northern section (from US 2 to where Birch Creek crosses US 89), an important biological corridor between Glacier National

Park, the Bob and the Blackfeet Indian Reservation. Peaks here are less rugged or dramatic than in other parts of the Front Range, but as a result they see less traffic from people and pack animals. **Walling Reef** is the awesome escarpment on the south side of Swift Reservoir, 18 miles west of US 89, where most trails into this area begin; the turnoff is at a well-marked rest area half a mile north of Dupuyer. Suggested one-day climbs from here include Family Peak and Morningstar Mountain.

Teton River Drainage South of Badger-Two Medicine is the Teton River Drainage, whose main access routes are along the North, West and South Forks of the Teton River. The road that leads to these trailheads turns west off US 89 about 2½ miles north of Choteau and is marked by 'Ski Area' and 'Eureka Recreation Area' signs. About 16 miles from the highway, the road splits north and south. The North Fork Rd leads to the **Teton Pass Ski Area**, a friendly little mountain with three lifts and $20 tickets; the road is plowed all winter, making it the best access for ski touring in the Bob. Three miles past the ski area, at road's end, is the West Fork Ranger Station and a USFS campground. Popular destinations from this trailhead are Teton Pass and Mount Patrick Pass, from where you have a spectacular view of the Continental Divide Range.

The South Fork Rd passes a USFS campground and ends at a trailhead that is very popular for accessing the Chinese Wall via Headquarters Pass. There's also a great day hike from here to the beautiful alpine Our Lake near Rocky Mountain Peak, the highest peak in the Front Range.

Choteau Choteau (population 1893) is essentially a farm town with one main street – called Main St, of course. At its south end, where US 89 splits to go southeast to Great Falls and southwest as US 287 to Helena, there's a three-story sandstone courthouse and the *Big Sky Motel* (☎ 406-466-5318) with $48 rooms. On the north end is the Rocky Mountain Ranger District office

(☎ 406-466-5341) and the *Bella Vista Motel* (☎ 406-466-5711) whose single/double rooms cost $36/40. Between these two are a few bars and gift shops, a great *coffeehouse* and the **Old Trail Museum**, 823 N Main, famous for its involvement in paleontological digs that discovered Maiasaur nests and eggs on nearby Egg Mountain; open daily from 10 am to 5 pm from May to September.

A block east of Main St on First Ave NE, *Rex's Food Farm* has an ATM and is the best place in the area for groceries and supplies; open Monday to Saturday 7 am to 9 pm, Sunday until 5 pm. The *Choteau KOA* (☎ 406-466-2615), a mile east of town on Hwy 221, has tent/RV sites for $16/23.

Augusta South of Choteau on US 287, Augusta (population 300) is a picturesque Western town with raised sidewalks along its one main street and a disproportionate number of bars. The two shops in town are worth stopping for: Latigo and Lace has local handcrafted goods of exceptional quality and Allen's Manix Store (called the 'market' or 'general store') has everything from hunting licenses to gourmet chocolates on its well-worn shelves.

Most traffic comes through Augusta en route to/from the Gibson Reservoir and Benchmark trailhead, main access points to the Sun River Area (see below). The Augusta Information Station (☎ 406-562-3247), 1 block west of Main St on Manix St, has good maps and guidebooks to the Bob.

The *Bunkhouse Inn* (☎ 406-562-3387, 122 Main St) has rooms for $40 to $65 with shared bath and a light breakfast; closed mid-October to June.

Sun River Area The North and South Forks of the Sun River are some of the most heavily used access routes into the Bob, and with good reason: there are large elk and bighorn sheep herds in the area, access is easy via the roads from Augusta and trailheads here put you within 5 miles of the Continental Divide.

The North Fork is dammed by Gibson Dam to form the **Gibson Reservoir**, a 5-mile-long body of water with a USFS campground on its east end and a hiking trail along its north side. The road from Augusta to the reservoir is well marked starting from near the Augusta Information Station on Manix St.

Trails through Deep Creek Canyon, Hannan Gulch and Mortimer Gulch head north from the east end of the reservoir to intersect trails that head west into the heart of the Sun River Game Preserve. Another popular route is from the west end of the reservoir along the South Fork trail to Prairie Reef. A 6-mile uphill climb to the top of Prairie Reef is rewarded with awesome views of the Chinese Wall.

Augusta's Main St turns into Benchmark Road, which goes through Ford and Wood Creek Canyons, past the Nilan Reservoir and ends at the **Benchmark Trailhead** where there are two USFS campgrounds. This trailhead is heavily used by outfitters and thus has plenty of horse and hunting traffic. The trail's big attraction is the excellent access to the Chinese Wall along the west branch of the Sun River's South Fork and over White River Pass. Renshaw Mountain, a good climb with excellent views from its peak, is also accessed from here.

Seely-Swan Valley

Swan River flows north from the Mission Mountains into Flathead Lake, and the Clearwater River flows south from the Missions to the Blackfoot River. They meet here in the Seely-Swan Valley, between the Mission Range in the west and Swan Range in the east. Hwy 83 runs the length of the valley, from Seely Lake in the south to Swan Lake in the north.

The rugged Mission Range is split between the **Mission Mountains Wilderness** and **Mission Mountains Tribal Wilderness**, both for experienced hikers and climbers who can handle map-and-compass navigation over steep terrain. A tribal permit ($7 per day, available at sporting goods and grocery stores in the area) is required for the Tribal Wilderness.

The valley's hub is **Seeley Lake**, 27 miles north of the Hwy 83/Hwy 200 junction, where you'll find the valley's only concen-

tration of motels, a post office, gas station, visitors information center (in a small log cabin on the west side of Hwy 83) and **The Washouse**, which has public showers and a coin-op laundry. Maps, books and current trail, road and wildlife information are available from the Seeley Lake Ranger Station (☎ 406-677-2233), 3 miles north of Seeley Lake on the west side of Hwy 83.

Activities Just north of the services at Seely Lake, Morrell Creek Rd heads east 9 miles to where it splits to go north (left) toward the **Morrell Falls National Recreation Trail** trailhead and south (right) to the **Pyramid Pass** trailhead. Morrell Falls is a popular day hike destination, 2½ miles from the trailhead. The Pyramid Pass trail is popular with pack outfitters headed for the Bob, whose boundary is 4 miles from the trailhead. A network of **cross-country ski trails** begin a mile east of Hwy 83, alongside Morrell Creek Rd; trail maps and equipment rentals are available at Seely Lake Fun Center (☎ 406-677-3692).

Another favorite trailhead is at **Holland Lake**, 3 miles east of Hwy 83 via Holland Lake Rd, near one of the only breaks in the massive west face of the Swan Range. The 7-mile **Upper Holland Lake-Sapphire Lake** loop is a good day hike and gives access to the Necklace Lakes, scenic overnight destinations.

At the north end of the Swan Range, 32 miles east of Kalispell, the **Jewel Basin Hiking Area** encompasses 27 lakes and 35 miles of maintained trails in the Flathead National Forest. The area is mostly used for day hikes, but the upper lakes in the basin's interior are perfectly suited for camping. Reach the main parking lot by taking Hwy 83 east to Echo Lake Rd then to Foothills Rd, which connects with Jewel Basin Rd No 5392 (all are signed). Stop at the ranger station in Bigfork for maps and information.

The Double Arrow Resort (see below) in Seely Lake offers horseback riding for $15 an hour.

Places to Stay The USFS campgrounds around Seeley Lake charge $9. Right between Hwy 83 and Seeley Lake, *Big Larch* fills up quickly with the weekend party types and large groups. A bit more remote are the *River Point Campground*, 2½ miles northwest of Seeley Lake on Boy Scout Rd, and the *Seeley Lake Campground*, 1 mile farther north on the same road, which has a boat launch and swimming beach.

Two miles south of Seeley Lake on the east side of Hwy 83, *Double Arrow Resort* (☎ 406-677-2777, 800-468-0777) is the valley's premiere resort with a big lodge, log cabins ($70 to $115), a 9-hole golf course, spa, pool and good dining room.

One mile north of Seeley Lake, the *Montana Pines Hideaway* (☎ 406-677-2775, 800-867-5678) has quiet lakeside cabins for $98 and motel rooms for $50. One mile farther north, the *Tamaracks Resort* (☎ 406-677-2433, 800-477-7216) is a mellow cluster of old cabins ($85 to $205 for two to ten people), RV ($25) and tent spots ($13). In the heart of Seely Lake you'll find charmless but adequate rooms ($45/55) at the *Duck Inn Motel* (☎ 406-677-2335, 800-237-9978).

The rustic *Holland Lake Lodge* (☎ 406-754-2282, 800-648-8859), at the end of Holland Lake Rd, is a worthy diversion, complete with a sauna, game room, lounge, restaurant and equipment rentals. Rooms and cabins cost $55 to $110, tent sites are $10 and RV hookups $16.

Places to Eat The only supermarket in the valley is *Ward's Food Farm*, on Hwy 83 at the south end of town; it's open from 7 am to 9 pm (until 7 pm on Sunday). The two most popular grub stations in Seeley Lake are *The Ice Cream Place*, on the east side of Hwy 83, for burgers, shakes and fries, and the *Filling Station* for family-style breakfasts, sandwiches and dinners. For a steak dinner and local color, try *Lindley's Steak House* (☎ 406-677-9229), on the south edge of town just off Hwy 87 (well signed).

HIGHWAY 200

Heading into the Scapegoat Wilderness portion of the Bob from the south, off Hwy 200, is a good option for anyone with time constraints. There are plenty of good day hike destinations, and trailheads are easy to get to because of the many logging roads in the area. Even if you don't venture into the backcountry, Hwy 200 through the Blackfoot Valley is a scenic route between Missoula and Great Falls or Helena. **Lincoln**, the only real town along the highway, used to bill itself as a 'Gateway to the Wilderness' but is now better known as home of Theodore Kaczynski, the infamous Unabomber. Most residents appreciate it if you are more interested in the nearby mountains than in seeing where Kaczynski did his errands. The one-street town has a supermarket (open daily until 9 pm) with an ATM, gas station and a handful of restaurants.

The best wilderness access from Hwy 200 is 6 miles east of Lincoln, up the Landers Fork of the Blackfoot River via USFS Rd 330 (well marked opposite USFS Aspen Grove Campground). The road goes 8 miles north to popular Copper Creek Campground and on another mile and a half to the Indian Meadows trailhead. **Heart Lake**, 5 miles from the trailhead in the Helena National Forest, is the starting point for several trails that head north into the Bob.

GLACIER NATIONAL PARK

When the Rockies were being formed about 100 million years ago, a 30-mile-wide, 2-mile-thick slab (called the Lewis Overthrust) of ancient rock shifted up and moved from west to east about 50 miles. This shift left 2-billion-year-old rock sitting atop 100-million-year-old rock in the area that is now Glacier National Park (or simply 'Glacier'). More importantly, it brought Pacific Northwest ecosystems to within 30 miles of the plains, a phenomena that hasn't occurred anywhere else in the world. The biological diversity is thus totally unique, but it's Glacier's more obvious scenery – glacial peaks, horns and lakes – that visitors tend to remember.

As in most national parks, visitation is high in July and August, but the majority of visitors stick close to roads, developed areas and short hiking trails. Head into the backcountry, to the northwest corner or up into

MONTANA

Waterton Lakes, the park's Canadian extension, and you'll have the place to yourself (in a relative sense). Even those who don't have the time or desire to explore the remote reaches will likely be satisfied with a drive over Going-to-the-Sun Rd, from where you can see tremendous examples of glacial activity and, often, mountain goats and bighorn sheep. In winter, when Going-to-the-Sun Rd and most services are closed, the park is left to cross-country skiers, snow-shoers and the wildlife.

History

James Willard Shultz lived for months at a time among the Blackfeet people whom he considered his relatives and closest friends, and was among the men who first laid eyes on much of Glacier's interior. He introduced the area to Dr George Bird Grinnell, editor of the popular *Forest & Stream* magazine, and together with their Blackfeet friends, they explored the area and named many of its mountains, rivers and lakes. Grinnell dubbed the area the 'Crown of the Continent' and lobbied Congress for 10 years until, in 1910, President Taft signed the bill creating Glacier National Park.

In his lobbying efforts, Grinnell had much contact with the Canadian government which, in 1895, had designated the northern extension of Glacier as Kootenay Lakes Forest Park. After Glacier National Park was officially dedicated, Canada expanded Kootenay Lake Park and boosted its status to create Waterton Lakes National Park. The two national governments, along with Rotary International, declared the two parks an International Peace Park to signify harmonious relations between the two countries (preserving the parks' unique biological corridor was a backseat issue at that point).

As the parks' surroundings continued to develop, the biological riches preserved within became more and more valuable and were increasingly studied. In 1995 Waterton/Glacier International Peace Park was designated a World Heritage Site for its vast cross section of plant and animal species. Basically the equivalent of a Nobel prize,

this designation is given to sites of 'outstanding universal value to all the citizens of the world, not just the countries in which they may be located' and must be ratified by 147 nations.

Tourism is now an integral part of Glacier's economy, but visitors did not come regularly to the park until around 1912 when the Great Northern Railroad's James J Hill instigated an intense building phase to promote his Empire Builder line. Railway employees built grand hotels and a network of tent camps and mountain chalets each a day's horseback ride from the next. Visitors would come for several weeks at a time, touring by horse or foot, and stay in these elegant but rustic and rather isolated accommodations.

WWII forced the closure of almost all hotel services in the park, and many buildings fell into disrepair and were eventually demolished. The grand old lodges still standing – Glacier Park Lodge, Lake McDonald Lodge, Sperry Chalet, Granite Park Chalet and, in Canada, the much-photographed Prince of Wales Hotel – have been updated and are used for accommodations.

The popularity of motorized transport came quickly, and in 1921 federal funds were appropriated to connect the east and west sides of Glacier National Park by building the Going-to-the-Sun Rd. Continually repaired, improved and expanded, the 50-mile scenic road is the primary travel artery and, for many, the park's highlight.

Geography & Geology

From two million to 12,000 years ago, repeated episodes of ice created huge valley glaciers (like those in the Himalayas) that covered much of the park's surface. These gargantuan rivers of ice flowed like spike-covered conveyor belts through the previously V-shaped valleys, carving them into wide U-shaped valleys with steep, scoured cliffs forming their sides. Somewhat resembling an elongated half pipe, good examples of this feature are visible from the Going-to-the-Sun Rd, looking west toward the upper end of St Mary Lake and looking southwest from near Haystack Creek towards the west end of Lake McDonald.

At the head of most U-shaped valleys (especially in the Many Glacier and Belly River areas), cirques resemble massive amphitheaters and are often filled with lakes (called tarns). Can you think of a better camping destination? Most of the park's waterfalls, including Birdwoman Falls on the Going-to-the-Sun Rd, originate in hanging valleys, which are produced when main-valley glaciers cut down into their canyons more rapidly than smaller glaciers from tributary valleys.

Perhaps the park's most identifiable glacial feature, familiar to those who have seen pictures of Switzerland's famous Matterhorn (or have been to Disneyland and seen the replica), are glacial horns – sheer mountain peaks eroded on three or four sides. These are not to be confused with thin-walled arêtes formed by glaciers cutting away at the walls of adjoining cirques leaving a near-vertical, razor-thin ridge. The Highline Trail crosses the park's most visible arête – the Garden Wall – west of Logan Pass on the Going-to-the-Sun Rd.

The glaciers that carved the park's landscape melted approximately 10,000 years ago, allowing humans to appear on the scene. Between about 9000 and 5000 years ago, the glaciers, which once measured 3000 feet thick, disappeared for the most part. The 'Little Ice Age,' a period of global cooling in the 1700s, rebuilt many of the area's glaciers, and by the mid-1800s the glaciers were the largest they had been since the Pleistocene era. Over the past 100 years, however, the glaciers have been rapidly retreating. Highway-like glaciers no longer exist in the park, but there are 50 or so small alpine glaciers around. Grinnell Glacier is certainly impressive and relatively easy to access (see Hiking & Backpacking, later).

Flora & Fauna

The west and east sides of the park are like two different worlds as a result of the Lewis Overthrust shift. On the west side are small temperate rainforests typical of the Pacific Northwest; a good example is reached by the Trail of the Cedars, off Going-to-the-Sun Rd near Lake McDonald. On the east, especially around the border town of East Glacier, you'll find sage and jackrabbits that belong to a prairie landscape and climate. In between are typical Rocky Mountains flora and fauna. But because all of these microecosystems are concentrated in a relatively small area, crossbreeding has produced a wealth of unique species. Besides the 1200 plant species known to exist in the park, others that are not yet classified are continually discovered and researched.

On the larger scale, Glacier's variation in landscape correlates with changes of altitude and adheres to the rule that the farther up the side of the mountain you go, the tougher it is for plants to grow and large animals to survive. Elk, moose, whitetail and mule deer flourish in the forests on valley floors, while mountain goats, bighorn sheep, marmots and pikas (small members of the rabbit family who scurry about on the rocky slopes making bird calls that confuse hikers) live amongst mountain ridges above 6000 feet.

Wildflowers begin to appear at lower elevations around mid-May (depending on snowmelt) and can last into August at high elevations. Some of the most prolific wildflowers are bright pink fireweed, purple harebells, broad-leafed cow's parsnip, spiky-stocked devil's club and the ever-present beargrass – fist-size bunches of white flowers clustered at the end of large stalks that look like giant cotton swabs (despite the name, bears don't have much interest in the plant, though moose and elk like to munch the stalks). In the fall, especially on the east side around Two Medicine Lake, green forests are sprinkled with the bright gold of western larch, one of the world's few deciduous conifers, which are common in the Swiss Alps.

Canada is much less developed and populated than the USA and as a result has larger predator populations. Because Glacier and Waterton are protected as a contiguous biological corridor, Glacier has a link to relatively undeveloped land. Glacier is the only place in the lower 48 states where wolves, mountain lions and grizzlies have maintained continuous existence.

Unfortunately, one of the best places to see mountain goats is in the parking lot of the Logan Pass visitors center, where the animals come to lick sodium-rich antifreeze off the ground.

Orientation

The delineators of Glacier's 1562 sq miles are the North Fork of the Flathead River (west), US 2 (south), US 89 and the Blackfeet Reservation (east) and the Canadian border (north). Waterton Lakes National Park extends north into the Canadian province of Alberta.

The National Park Service (NPS) divides Glacier into five regions, each revolving around a ranger station: Polebridge encompasses the park's northwest corner; Lake McDonald, the West Entrance and Apgar Village are in the Lake McDonald area; Two Medicine, 12 miles northwest of East Glacier and US 89, envelops the Two Medicine Valley and its lakes; St Mary is the eastern end of the Going-to-the-Sun Rd, north of East Glacier on US 89; in the northeast corner, Many Glacier is 13 miles west of US 89 by way of Many Glacier Rd. Hiking trails connect all of these regions, but the Going-to-the-Sun Rd is the only paved road that directly cuts across the park.

Information

Tourist Offices It's worthwhile to write (Glacier National Park, West Glacier, MT 59936), call (☎ 406-888-7800) or check online (www.nps.gov/glac/home.htm or www.parkscanada.pch.gc.ca/waterton/) before your trip to receive the free 'Glacier National Park Trip Planner,' which has maps and information on camping, accommodations, activities and seasonal programs in the park. Upon entering the park you'll receive the quarterly *Waterton – Glacier Guide* newspaper which details opening hours and activities for that particular season.

Once in the park, visitors centers and ranger stations sell field guides and hand out hiking maps and reams of brochures on things to do in and near the park. Those at Apgar, Logan Pass and St Mary are open daily from late May to mid-October; the Many Glacier, Two Medicine and Polebridge Ranger Stations close at the end of September. Park headquarters (☎ 406-888-7800, TTY 406-888-7806), in West Glacier between US 2 and Apgar, takes care of administrative chores and provides visitor information year-round. In Waterton, the Visitors Reception Center (☎ 403-859-5133), opposite the Prince of Wales Hotel, is open from mid-May to October.

A recording of current park events (☎ 406-888-5551) tells of ranger-led hikes, programs and special events going on in the park and mentions any unique conditions (storm threats, fire danger) that visitors should be aware of.

The Glacier Natural History Association (☎ 406-888-5756), in West Glacier's Belton railroad station, is an excellent resource for field guides, books, maps and information on volunteer opportunities or interpretive programs.

The Glacier Institute (☎ 406-756-1211), PO Box 7457, Kalispell, MT 59904, offers afternoon to week-long field classes that range from Blackfeet History to Insect Ecology to the Art of Fly-Fishing. Web site: www.nps.gov/glac/inst.htm

Central Reservations (☎ 406-226-5551) makes reservations at any of the park's lodges or motels.

Fees & Permits A seven-day pass for anyone arriving by car, motorcycle or RV is $10. Those coming on foot or by bicycle pay $5. Remember that this fee does not include entrance to Waterton Lakes National Park. A one-year Glacier National Park Pass costs $20.

Day hikers do not need permits, but backpackers staying overnight in the park do. Permits cost $4 per person per day and are available at the Apgar Backcountry Permit Center from May 1st to October 31st; the St Mary's Visitors Center from late June to the end of September; and at the Many Glacier, Two Medicine and Polebridge Ranger Stations from the end of

GLACIER NATIONAL PARK

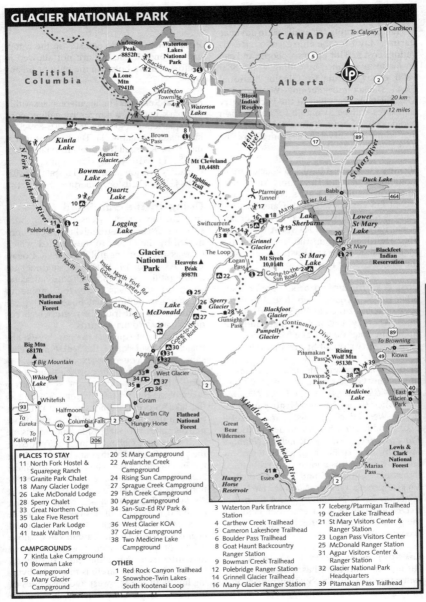

CANADA

To Calgary | Cardston

British Columbia

Anderson Peak – 8852ft ▲

▲Lone Mtn 7941ft

Kananga Pkwy

Blackiston Creek Rd

Waterton Lakes National Park

Waterton Townsite

Waterton Lakes

Alberta

Blood Indian Reserve

Brown Pass

Agassiz Glacier

Kintla Lake

Bowman Lake

Quartz Lake

Mt Cleveland 10,448ft ▲

Continental Divide

Highline Trail

Belly River

Ptarmigan Tunnel

Many Glacier Rd

Babb

Duck Lake

St Mary River

Lake Sherburne

Lower St Mary Lake

North Fork Flathead River

Logging Lake

Swiftcurrent Pass

Grinnell Glacier

St Mary

St Mary Lake

Blackfeet Indian Reservation

Polebridge

Outside North Fork Rd

The Loop

Logan Pass

Mt Siyeh 10,014ft

Going-to-the-Sun Road

Glacier National Park

Heavens Peak 8987ft ▲

Inside North Fork Rd (Closed in winter)

Camas Rd

Lake McDonald

Sperry Glacier

Gunsight Pass

Blackfoot Glacier

Continental Divide

Pumpelly Glacier

To Browning

Flathead National Forest

Going-to-the-Sun Road

Big Mtn 6817ft

Big Mountain

Whitefish Lake

Apgar

West Glacier

Pitamakan Pass

Rising Wolf Mtn 9513ft

Dawson Pass

Two Medicine Lake

Kiowa

Whitefish

Halfmoon

Coram

Martin City

Hungry Horse

Flathead National Forest

Great Bear Wilderness

Middle Fork Flathead River

East Glacier Park

Columbia Falls

To Eureka

To Kalispell

Hungry Horse Reservoir

Essex

Lewis & Clark National Forest

Marias Pass

MONTANA

0   10   20 km
0   6   12 miles

PLACES TO STAY
- 11 North Fork Hostel & Squarepeg Ranch
- 13 Granite Park Chalet
- 18 Many Glacier Lodge
- 26 Lake McDonald Lodge
- 28 Sperry Chalet
- 33 Great Northern Chalets
- 35 Lake Five Resort
- 40 Glacier Park Lodge
- 41 Izaak Walton Inn

CAMPGROUNDS
- 7 Kintla Lake Campground
- 10 Bowman Lake Campground
- 15 Many Glacier Campground
- 20 St Mary Campground
- 22 Avalanche Creek Campground
- 24 Rising Sun Campground
- 27 Sprague Creek Campground
- 29 Fish Creek Campground
- 30 Apgar Campground
- 34 San-Suz-Ed RV Park & Campground
- 36 West Glacier KOA
- 37 Glacier Campground
- 38 Two Medicine Lake Campground

OTHER
- 1 Red Rock Canyon Trailhead
- 2 Snowshoe-Twin Lakes South Kootenai Loop
- 3 Waterton Park Entrance Station
- 4 Carthew Creek Trailhead
- 5 Cameron Lakeshore Trailhead
- 6 Boulder Pass Trailhead
- 8 Goat Haunt Backcountry Ranger Station
- 9 Bowman Creek Trailhead
- 12 Polebridge Ranger Station
- 14 Grinnell Glacier Trailhead
- 16 Many Glacier Ranger Station
- 17 Iceberg/Ptarmigan Trailhead
- 19 Cracker Lake Trailhead
- 21 St Mary Visitors Center & Ranger Station
- 23 Logan Pass Visitors Center
- 25 McDonald Ranger Station
- 31 Apgar Visitors Center & Ranger Station
- 32 Glacier National Park Headquarters
- 39 Pitamakan Pass Trailhead

May to mid-September. No permit is needed from November to May.

Half the permits are available in advance starting May 1 for the entire season. Reservations cost $20 for up to six people and can be made in advance by calling ☎ 406-888-7800, or by writing to 'Glacier National Park – Backcountry Permits,' West Glacier, MT 59936. At least half of the backcountry campsites will be available for reservation two days to 24 hours before departure on a first-come, first-served basis from a park visitors center.

Money The nearest banks to Glacier are in Columbia Falls and Browning. Most merchants in Waterton Lakes National Park accept US currency, though Canadian currency is not widely accepted in Glacier National Park. There are ATMs at the Cedar Tree Deli in Apgar, in the lodges at Lake McDonald, St Mary and East Glacier and at the Many Glacier Hotel.

Post & Communications There are post offices in West Glacier (zip code 59936) and East Glacier (zip code 59434), and substations where you can post mail and buy stamps in Polebridge, Lake McDonald and in the grocery store at St Mary's Lodge.

Books An excellent historical account of life in the Glacier area is James Willard Shultz's *Blackfeet Tales of Glacier National Park*. The Glacier Natural History Association in West Glacier publishes many useful books and natural history guides, including *Place Names of Glacier/Waterton National Parks* by Jack Holterman, which tells how and why mountains and rivers were named things like 'Gunsight' and 'Two Medicine.' Vicky Spring's *Glacier National Park and Waterton Lakes National Park: A Complete Recreation Guide* is an excellent guide to the park's natural features, hiking trails and accommodations.

Laundry & Showers In the park, the Rising Sun Motor Inn has showers and the campstore next to the Swiftcurrent Motor Inn has showers and laundry facilities. The

KOA and the Glacier Campground, both in West Glacier, are other options.

Pets Fluffy and Fido can stay in the campground on a leash, but are not allowed in visitors centers, hotels in the park or on any trails.

Medical Services For all emergencies within the park contact a ranger by calling park headquarters (☎ 406-888-7800, 403-859-5133 in Canada) or dial ☎ 911. The best hospital in the area is Kalispell Regional Hospital (☎ 406-752-5111), 310 Sunnyview Lane, or, in Canada, Cardston Municipal Hospital (☎ 403-653-4411) in Cardston, Alberta.

Going-to-the-Sun Road

In 1927, the various access roads on both sides of Glacier National Park were connected by the Going-to-the-Sun Rd, which crosses the Continental Divide at Logan Pass. As proof of American engineering ability (still new on the international scene when the road was built) the engineers spurned the multiple switchbacks of typical alpine roads and found a route which required only two major turns.

Beginning at Apgar at the park's west entrance, the road skirts Lake McDonald's east shore, where you have excellent views of Stanton Mountain at the northeast end of the lake. Glacier Park 'cover shots' are often taken along this part of the road. Starting at the lake's northeast end, the road parallels the clear-flowing McDonald Creek through a narrow valley with steep-sided mountains on both sides. An excellent chance to experience the park's Pacific Northwest climate is along the **Trail of the Cedars**, a half-mile wheelchair-accessible loop that begins from the well-marked Avalanche Creek parking lot. Avalanche Lake, which is 2 miles from the trailhead, is a good half-day hike destination.

North of Avalanche Creek, the road begins to approach the **Garden Wall**, whose 9000-foot spine runs from Logan Pass north to Swiftcurrent Pass along the Continental Divide. This granite arête is the main dividing line between the west and east sides of the park. As the road ascends the Garden

Wall it offers fantastic views of McDonald Creek and the park's westernmost clump of glacial peaks. The **Loop**, a parking lot at the road's major hairpin turn, has an interpretive map that show the peaks' names.

Between the Loop and Logan Pass, Going-to-the-Sun Rd traverses the Garden Wall, passing the Weeping Wall and Bird Woman Falls, which vary from dripping to gushing throughout the year.

At **Logan Pass** there's an excellent visitors center with natural history displays, ranger talks and a good bookstore; open daily from mid-June to October. A popular trail from the upper level of the visitors center leads along the 1½-mile boardwalk to the **Hidden Lake Overlook**; the trail crosses the Continental Divide, passes hanging gardens and climbs (about 500 feet) to a basin lake at the foot of Reynolds Mountain (9125 feet).

At the west end of Saint Mary Lake, Going-to-the-Sun Mountain (9642 feet) stands guard over its namesake road. This easternmost part of the road is where you can best see Glacier's connection to the plains that stretch east from St Mary to the Dakotas. The St Mary Visitors Center, on the lake's east end, is the main visitors center in the east side of the park and has good geology exhibits (open daily from May to mid-October).

Without stopping, the drive from Apgar to St Mary takes about an hour and a half. Most people, however, take at least three hours to complete the picturesque trip. To make a loop trip, drive one-way on Going-to-the-Sun Rd then back along US 2 on the park's southern border.

From mid-October to mid-June, the road is closed from the Loop to St Mary. This is a good time to walk, run, bike or ski (depending on conditions) along the road.

Hiking & Backpacking

Visitors centers give out excellent hiking maps (divided into Lake McDonald, Logan Pass/St Mary, Many Glacier and Two Medicine areas) that have a map on one side and a spreadsheet – which tells the length, elevation gain, special features and trailhead locations – on the other. Each one covers 12 to 15 hikes.

Glacier Wilderness Guides (☎ 406-387-5555, 800-521-7238), www.glacierguides.com, is the only hiking and backpacking guide service licensed to operate in the park. Overnight trips to Granite Park Chalet cost $60, custom trips are around $95 per person per day with a four-person minimum; it's an additional $10 for equipment rental.

Two favorite overnight destinations are Sperry Chalet and Granite Park Chalet (see Places to Stay, later).

Many Glacier Three trailheads start hikers into the Many Glacier Valley from the end of Many Glacier Rd (Glacier Route Three), which runs west from US 89. The 5-mile **Grinnell Glacier Trail** starts at the picnic area half a mile before road's end and climbs 1600 feet, past Swiftcurrent and Josephine Lakes, to the base of the park's most visible and famous glacier. Taking the boat from the Many Glacier Hotel to the southwest end of Swiftcurrent Lake shortens the hike by 1½ miles.

From Swiftcurrent Motor Inn, the **Iceberg/Ptarmigan Trail** climbs 2300 feet in 5 miles to the Ptarmigan Tunnel, past Ptarmigan Falls and Ptarmigan Lake. Just west of the falls is a spur trail that heads south 2 miles to Iceberg Lake, an icy-blue cirque lake at the base of a sheer 3000-foot cliff; a flotilla of icebergs usually remains in the lake into July and August.

The 183-foot-long Ptarmigan Tunnel is the park's only tunnel constructed for hikers. Passing solo through it without encountering anyone (or anything) else on the way is supposedly a harbinger of good luck.

If you can do only one hike, make it the 6-mile **Cracker Lake Trail** which, over its 1400-foot gain, offers some of the most dramatic scenery a day hike can. It starts at the south end of the Many Glacier Hotel parking area, follows Cracker Creek through its canyon where 4100-foot cliffs rise up on both sides and ends at Cracker Lake in a cirque capped by 10,014-foot Mt Siyeh.

MONTANA

Two Medicine Valley Most trails in the Two Medicine Valley begin at the north end of Two Medicine Campground, or a half mile south at the east end of Two Medicine Lake, just past the boat dock. Taking the boat across the lake shaves almost 3 miles off any trail that passes the west end of the lake.

The **No Name Lake/Upper Two Medicine Lake Trail** rambles along the north shore of Two Medicine Lake and splits at mile 3½ to head either northwest another 1½ miles to No Name Lake and on through Bighorn Basin to Dawson Pass (3 miles beyond the split), or southwest to Upper Two Medicine Lake (1½ miles past the split), which rests in a cirque below Lone Walker Mountain. **Twin Falls**, a quarter-mile spur from the Upper Two Medicine Lake Trail, should not be missed.

The 7-mile **Pitamakan Pass Trail** heads northeast from Two Medicine Campground, around the east side of Rising Wolf Mountain and then west along the Dry Fork (which is very wet in the spring) of the Two Medicine River. Pitamakan Pass and Dawson Pass can be combined to make a 16.9-mile loop, a favorite route for backpackers with only a few days to spend in the backcountry.

Polebridge Glacier's northwest corner is the least visited part of the park. Most trails up here follow a creek through a thick pine forest to a southwest-northeast trending lake, such as Lake McDonald, which is the southernmost and largest on this side of the park. Dutch Creek, Logging Creek and Quartz Creek are all trails of this sort and can be reached off Polebridge Rd (Glacier Route Seven).

The most variety for hiking (and skiing) is found near **Bowman Lake**, accessible by car from the Polebridge Ranger Station. At the lake's south end is a campground, small ranger station and trails that extend in all directions. The Bowman Creek trail skirts the lake's northwest shore and continues to Brown Pass, surrounded by spectacular peaks and glaciers. Here the Boulder Pass Trail heads west to Upper Kintla and Kintla lakes (near the Agassiz Glacier, one of the

biggest in the park) and east to the Goat Haunt backcountry ranger station and Waterton Lake (a popular route into Canada).

Waterton North of the Canadian border, the approaches to spectacular hikes are much shorter since roads penetrate quite far into the 'backcountry.' South of Waterton Park's entrance station (at the junction of Canadian Hwys 5 and 6) the Akamina Pkwy heads south and west, past Waterton Townsite, Upper Waterton, Middle Waterton and Waterton Lakes. From the Townsite, where the park's headquarters and services are, the **Carthew Creek Trail** heads west along the base of Buchanan Ridge and ends at Cameron Lake (at the end of the Akamina Pkwy); this is a great overnight point-to-point hike for parties with two cars. Also starting at the Townsite is the primary route into Glacier National Park, along the west side of Waterton Lake.

For a hair-raising hike, step from Waterton Town's boat landing onto one of the boats that stops at the **Crypt Lake** trailhead. The 5½-mile hike from the trailhead up to Crypt Lake requires you to go through a glacial cirque by way of a natural tunnel and use a cable to traverse a sheer rock face.

In the north part of Waterton, at the end of Blackiston Creek Rd, the **Red Rock Canyon Trail** is a great day hike through a steep-walled canyon. Popular with backpackers is the **Snowshoe-Twin Lakes-South Kootenai Pass Loop**, which circles Anderson Peak (8852 feet).

Rafting

Glacier Raft Co (☎ 406-888-5454, 800-235-6781), www.glacierraftco.com, is the oldest and arguably most reputable raft company in the area. Trips down the North Fork and Middle Fork of the Flathead River cost $38 for a half-day, $71 for a full day including lunch (reservations recommended). They'll also rent you a two-person kayak ($79) or raft ($95), including a wetsuit and helmet, give some instruction and send you on down from West Glacier to Glacier River Ranch (12 miles). Rafting/accommodations packages are available at discounted price.

Also reputable is Great Northern White-water (☎ 406-387-5340, 800-735-7897), www.gnwhitewater.com, which has similar prices.

Bicycling

Glacier keeps its hiking trails off-limits to cyclists, so there is no mountain biking allowed. The closest thing to it is riding along the Polebridge Rd (Glacier Route Seven), which goes from the Fish Creek Campground near Apgar to the Polebridge Ranger Station and on to Bowman Lake or up to the Canadian Border along the North Fork of the Flathead River. This road is mostly dirt, gets relatively light traffic and is surrounded by thick forests.

Good road biking near the park is along its eastern boundary on Hwys 49 and 89, which parallel the Continental Divide for 31 miles between East Glacier and St Mary. From East Glacier the 8-mile side trip to Two Medicine Lake (the cutoff is 4 miles north of East Glacier) is beautiful, but very steep in some parts.

From mid-June to Labor Day (unless otherwise posted), cyclists are not allowed to ride from Apgar to Sprague Creek Campground in either direction or from Logan Creek to Logan Pass uphill (down-hill is OK) from 11 am to 4 pm. There are hiker/biker campsites ($3) at all campgrounds except Bowman and Kintla Lakes in the northwest corner. Spaces are first-come first-served for cyclists until 9 pm; sites at Fish Creek and St Mary campgrounds can be reserved (☎ 800-365-2267). Bike rentals are available in Apgar, at Mountain Mikes Rental Bikes (☎ 406-837-2453) in Bigfork and at Pat's Cycle Rentals (☎ 403-859-2266) in Waterton.

Fishing

No permit is required to fish Glacier's lakes and rivers. The North Fork and Middle Fork of the Flathead River are subject to Montana state fishing regulations (and thus require a fishing license) outside the park, but not within it. Fishing regulations and area restrictions are available at visitors centers. Favorite fishing spots among park

rangers are Lake McDonald, Glenns Lake, Bowman Lake and Kennedy Creek. Cut-throat trout dominate Glacier's waters, but brook trout, whitefish, kokanee salmon and Arctic grayling also live in the park.

Glacier Park Boat Co (☎ 406-226-4467) rents rowboats, canoes, kayaks, motor boats and fishing equipment from docks at Apgar, Lake McDonald, Two Medicine Lake and the Many Glacier Hotel (nonmotorized boats only).

Horseback Riding

Riders may bring their own horses into the park, but no stable rentals are available. A free brochure, available at visitors centers, explains the restrictions and regulations concerning horseback riding in the park.

Guided horseback trips, lasting from one hour to all day, are available at Lake McDonald Corral (☎ 406-888-5121), Many Glacier Corral (☎ 406732-4203) and the Alpine Stables (☎ 403-859-2462) in Waterton.

Winter Activities

Winter weather on the western side of the Continental Divide is generally snowy and overcast, while the eastern side of the divide tends to be windy and sunny. Going-to-the-Sun Rd from West Glacier to the head of Lake McDonald is plowed all winter, as are US 89 and US 2, which allow some access to Glacier's southern boundary, St Mary Valley and Many Glacier Valley. Roads into the eastern interior may be open depending on conditions.

All of Glacier's trails and roads are open for **snowshoeing** and cross-country or back-country **skiing** (snowmobiles are prohibited). The NPS 'Glacier Cross-Country Skiing' and 'Glacier Backcountry Winter Camping' brochures, available year-round from park headquarters and seasonally from ranger stations and visitors centers, outline trails in the Apgar, Marias Pass (on US 2), St Mary, Two Medicine Valley and Polebridge areas.

Guided cross-country trips and a network of groomed trails are available from the Izaak Walton Inn (☎ 406-888-5700) in Essex (on US 2). The North Fork Hostel

MONTANA

(☎ 406-888-5241, 800-775-2938) in Pole-bridge is open year-round and has cross-country ski and snowshoe rentals (free for guests).

The Apgar Visitors Center is open on weekends and has information on current road, weather and camping conditions for the entire park. East Glacier, West Glacier and Essex have accommodations during the winter months when all hotels inside the park are closed.

Ranger-Led Activities

Rangers lead a variety of summer activities, including morning strolls, day hikes, junior ranger programs and campfire talks. Sched-ules and activities vary from year to year, but always center around the Apgar Visitors Center, Logan Pass Visitors Center, St Mary's Lodge, Many Glacier Campground and Goat Haunt Ranger Station. Current schedules and topics are listed in the 'Nature with a Naturalist' insert in the *Waterton–Glacier Guide* newspaper given to people upon entering the park and avail-able at park ranger stations.

Even non-group-activity types might like to join an 8½-mile International Peace Park Hike from Canada to the USA. The hikes, held on Saturdays from the first of July to early September, begin at the Bertha Trail-head in Waterton Park and cruise back into Canada on Waterton Lake.

Organized Tours

Glacier Park Inc's fleet of historic 'jammer' buses (named for the days when the coaches did not have automatic transmis-sion and drivers ground and jammed the gears) are currently out of service but are supposed to be spruced up and reinstated in the future. For now they use regular buses for their four different tours (☎ 406-226-5666), which range from a 2½-hour trip between Lake McDonald Lodge and Logan Pass ($21) to an 8-hour journey that circles the park via US 2 ($61). You can also pur-chase a one-way 'shuttle' ticket between Many Glacier ($17), St Mary ($8) or West Glacier ($8) and Logan Pass (in either direction).

Blackfeet tribal members give interpre-tive **bus tours** of Going-to-the-Sun Rd through Sun Tours (☎ 406-226-9220, 800-786-9220), which leave from various points in East Glacier and St Mary; approximately six hours.

Glacier Park Boat Co (☎ 406-226-4467) offers **boat tours** ($11) on Lake McDonald (from the dock at Lake McDonald Lodge), St Mary Lake (from the Rising Sun boat dock), Two Medicine Lake (from the Two Medicine boat dock) and Swiftcurrent and Josephine Lakes (from the dock at the Many Glacier Hotel). The historic *International* has plied the waters of Waterton Lake between Waterton Marina (Canada) and Goat Haunt (USA) since 1927. The two-hour trip (☎ 403-859-2362) costs $18 roundtrip.

Places to Stay – Camping & Cabins

Glacier National Park The park has 13 campgrounds; call ☎ 406-888-7800 for camp-site availability information. Sites at *Fish Creek* and *St Mary* campgrounds (☎ 800-365-2267, *www.reservations.nps.gov*) can be reserved up to five months in advance and cost $17. All other sites are available on a first-come, first-served basis for $14. Sites fill up by mid-morning, particularly in July and August. Campfires are allowed in desig-nated fire rings, though are generally dis-couraged and often prohibited when fire conditions are hazardous. Year-round prim-itive camping is available at Apgar, Avalanche and St Mary and no fees are col-lected after October 1.

Often dictated by what's available, some favorite campground choices are: touristy *Apgar Campground*, on the southwest end of Lake McDonald near Apgar Village, convenient for campfire programs and ranger-led activities; lakeside *Sprague Creek Campground*, 1 mile south of Lake McDonald Lodge; unprotected *Rising Sun Campground*, 10 miles west of St Mary on the north shore of St Mary Lake, popular with travelers approaching the park from the east; and *Many Glacier Campground*, surrounded by peaks and popular with hikers.

Twelve miles north of East Glacier, *Two Medicine Lake Campground*, at the southern foot of Rising Wolf Mountain, is busy in the daytime due to boat tours on the lake and the historic Two Medicine Camp Store, but relatively uncrowded at night.

Built by the Great Northern Railroad in 1911 to accommodate saddle horse travelers, the Two Medicine Camp originally consisted of a large dormitory, dining hall and five cabins. When Going-to-the-Sun Rd increased auto traffic through the park, Two Medicine was sold to the government and taken over by the Civilian Conservation Corps. Franklin D Roosevelt was inducted into the Blackfeet Tribe at Two Medicine in 1934 and afterwards held one of his famous fireside chats in front of its grand hearth. The Two Medicine chalets have since been destroyed, leaving only what is now the camp store.

In the park's northwest corner are its two most remote campgrounds: *Kintla Lake Campground* and *Bowman Lake Campground*, both north of the Polebridge entrance and accessible via dirt roads. These campgrounds do not reserve spaces for hikers or cyclists.

Hike 6½ miles from Lake McDonald Lodge to stay at the historic *Sperry Chalet*, built by the Great Northern Railroad in 1914. A bed, family-style dinner, breakfast and lunch (or trail lunch) costs $100, plus $50 if you want a private room. The original publicity declared that all you need to bring is a 'toothbrush and a smile,' but a flashlight is helpful for midnight trips to the outhouse, and warm sleeping clothes could make up for the lack of heating. There are some good side trails from the chalet, worth exploring between lunch and dinner or breakfast and lunch, depending on when you arrive. Reservations can be made (☎ 888-345-2649, www.ptinet.net/sperrychalet) with a $40 deposit.

Sperry's sister, the *Granite Park Chalet*, is operated as a hikers' shelter. Stop in and have your lunch there, or make a reservation to spend the night ($60) through Glacier Wilderness Guides (see Hiking & Backpacking, earlier).

Waterton Lakes The *Townsite Campground* is closest to the services and action of Waterton Townsite. It's open from May to mid-October, with tent/RV sites for $16/$23. Sites at the *Crandell Campground*, alongside Blackiston Creek off Red Rock Parkway, cost $13 from June to September (closed the rest of the year). The *Belly River Campground*, off Chief Mountain Hwy near the USA border, are $10. Backcountry campers pay $6 per person per night and must register at the Visitors Reception Center in Waterton Townsite, across from the Prince of Wales Hotel.

West Glacier Campgrounds and cabins in West Glacier are generally open from May 1 to September 30. San-Suz-Ed and Great Northern Chalets are open year-round.

Three miles west of the park entrance and a half mile north of US 2, the *Lake Five Resort* (☎ 406-387-5601) has a summer-camp atmosphere. Cabins with four beds, a bathroom and kitchenette cost $92 per night, tent sites are $14 and RV sites are $18. Families return annually and often stay for at least a week, so reservations are highly recommended.

Next to the Lake Five turnoff, 2½ miles west of the park on US 2, is the *San-Suz-Ed RV Park & Campground* (☎ 406-387-5280), with tent sites ($17) and RV sites ($23) that are protected from US 2 by a thick stand of pine and fir trees; shower and laundry facilities are exceptionally clean.

The *West Glacier KOA* (☎ 406-387-5341), 2½ miles west of the park entrance and 1 mile south of US 2, has 42 tent sites ($22) and 106 RV sites ($30), cabins ($55), a store, laundry facilities, horseshoe court, breakfast, barbecue and nightly slide shows. Very similar is the *Glacier Campground* (☎ 406-387-5689) on the south side of US 2, 1 mile west of the park's entrance, which has $17 tent sites and $22 RV sites.

Cabins at the *Glacier Raft Co* (☎ 406-888-5454, 800 235-6781), on US 2, cost $175 for up to four people, less if you stay three or more nights.

Great Northern Chalets (☎ 406-387-5340, 800-735-7897), part of Great Northern

Whitewater, on US 2, offers deluxe cabins that sleep up to six for $179/$286 (off-season/peak-season); in July they require a minimum three-night stay.

East Glacier The *Firebrand Campground* (☎ 406-226-5573) is in a shadeless grass field 2 blocks south of US 2 on Lindhe Ave. It has 10 tent sites ($13) and 30 RV sites ($20), clean restrooms, showers and laundry facilities. All sites have unobstructed views of the surrounding peaks. Also in town are *Three Forks Campground* (☎ 406-226-4479), with similar prices; and the *Sears Motel & Campground* (see below), which has $11/18 tent/RV sites behind the motel. All are open from June to late September.

One mile west of St Mary is a *KOA* (☎ 406-732-4122) with $21/29 tent/RV sites, and $50 cabins.

Places to Stay – Hostels

The HI-AYH hostel *Brownie's* (☎ 406-727-4448), on the 2nd story of Brownie's Grocery & Deli on the east side of Hwy 49, is usually packed with young travelers and is consequently a great place to find hiking or backpacking partners. Accommodations are in crowded eight-bed, single-sex dorm rooms ($12) or, if you call early enough, private rooms with double beds ($30). The common room and kitchen are both clean and well stocked (there's a huge record collection). The hostel is locked from 9:30 am to 5 pm, except when the weather is bad; no curfew. Sleeping bags are not allowed; sheets, blankets and pillows are provided free of charge. It's open May to mid-September.

Also in East Glacier, the *Backpacker's Inn* (☎ 406-862-5600), behind Serrano's Mexican Restaurant on Dawson Ave, offers a quiet alternative to Brownie's. There are three dorm rooms (two single-sex and one coed), each with three bunk beds. Rooms tend to be on the chilly side and a large shady yard acts as the hostel's only common area, so think twice before staying here when the weather is bad. Beds cost $10 per person, $12 if you don't have your own sleeping bag. The hostel is locked from

10 am to 5 pm; the restaurant is open 5 pm to 9 pm and handles check-in; there are no kitchen facilities.

One of the best places to stay if you have some time is the ultrarustic and charming *Northfork Hostel & Squarepeg Ranch* (☎ 406-888-5241), www.nfhostel.com, in Polebridge. Bunk space is $13 ($10 after the first two nights), small and large cabins are $30/65, including the use of a kitchen, cozy reading area, mountain bikes, cross-country skis and snowshoes. It's open year-round, though the adjacent store and cafe close from mid-September to May. Reservations are a good idea, especially in winter. They'll pick you up at the Amtrak station in West Glacier for $25.

Places to Stay – Motels

West Glacier The *Vista Motel* (☎ 406-888-5311, 800-831-7101), on a hillside above US 2, 2 miles west of the park entrance, has 26 rooms for $55/59 single/double and an outdoor pool.

The *Glacier Highland Resort Motel* (☎ 406-888-5427, 800-766-0811) is at the turnoff to the park's west entrance on US 2, across from the train station. Above the rest of the complex are 33 motel units that cost $65/75 single/double May 15 to September 15 and $40/65 the rest of the year.

The closest motel to the park entrance is the *West Glacier Motel* (☎ 406-888-5662), on the north side of the railroad tracks and US 2. Rooms, a bit on the shabby side, go for around $65.

East Glacier All rooms and cottages in East Glacier are within a half mile of the junction of US 2 and Hwy 49. Most places are open from May to October.

The *East Glacier Motel* (☎ 406-226-5593), on the west side of Hwy 49, has cute cottages with double beds that cost $78 in July and August; $55 in May, June, September and October. Motel units with kitchenettes cost $98 and $75 in high/low season.

The *Mountain Pine Motel* (☎ 406-226-4403), on the west side of Hwy 49, has rooms and a few free-standing cabins for around $70.

The *Sears Motel & Campground* (☎ 406-226-4432), on the west side of Hwy 49, and the *Whistling Swan Motel* (☎ 406-226-4412), on US 2, have similar rooms for around $55. One block south of US 2, *Dancing Bears Inn* (☎ 406-226-4402) has rooms (which share a covered entry) for $80, and one cabin for $135.

Places to Stay – National Park Lodges

In the early 1910s James Hill's Great Northern Railroad built a series of grand hotels to entice wealthy travelers to visit Glacier National Park. Guests arrived by train and were transported by 'jammer' bus or horse-drawn carriage to their lodge of choice, often staying several weeks at a time or journeying from one lodge to the next. The *lodges* and *motels* are now operated by Glacier Park Inc (☎ 406-756-2444, 602-207-6000 for advanced reservations), open from mid-May to September and cost around $88 to $135 per room; cheapest are the $41 cottages (no bath) at the *Swiftcurrent Motor Inn*. Most places have a restaurant or coffee shop, laundry facilities, showers and general store, and are close to hiking trails.

The *Glacier Park Lodge* (☎ 406-226-9311), in East Glacier, is undoubtedly the flagship of Glacier's grand hotels. Blackfeet Indians called the lodge 'Oom-Coo-La-Mush-Taw,' or 'Big Tree Lodge': sixty Douglas fir timbers (estimated to be 500 to 800 years old) support interior balconies surrounding the lobby and a 65-foot ceiling with two skylights and two massive iron chandeliers. Rooms are modern and elegant, and the lodge has an outdoor pool, pitch-and-putt and nine-hole golf courses.

In the heart of the park on the north shore of Swiftcurrent Lake, surrounded by dramatic peaks, the chalet-esque *Many Glacier Lodge* (☎ 406-732-4411) is the largest hotel inside the park. Its remote location has made Many Glacier a bit precarious at times: in the spring of 1964 a major flood trapped the general manager, chef and 75 employees in the hotel for 10 days without electricity or heat.

Blackfeet Indians call the lake and river that pass in front of the *Swiftcurrent Motor Inn* (☎ 406-732-5531) 'Ixikuoyi-Yetahtai' which means 'swift-flowing stream.' Once employee dormitories for the Great Northern Railroad, the inn has the lowest rates of any park lodge.

The *Rising Sun Motor Inn* (☎ 406-732-5532), on the upper north shore of St Mary Lake, 6 miles from St Mary Village, was constructed in 1940 as a resting point for motorists making the (at that time) grueling Going-to-the-Sun Rd drive.

At the other end of the drive is *Lake McDonald Lodge* (☎ 406-888-5431), with its cozy hunting-lodge atmosphere and many rooms facing the lake, and the *Apgar Village Inn* (☎ 406-888-5632), which sits at the southern end of Lake McDonald in Apgar Village, near restaurants, gift shops and ranger activities.

It might be worth venturing across the border to stay in the seven-story *Prince of Wales Hotel* (☎ 403-859-2231), which sits on a pile of glacial till overlooking icy-blue Waterton Lake. The hotel has 81 rooms, a restaurant, lounge, tea room, gift shop, boat tours of Waterton Lake and a nearby golf course.

The *Izaak Walton Inn* (☎ 406-888-5700), in Essex halfway between East Glacier and West Glacier and a half mile north of US 2, is a popular cross-country ski destination. Decorated with old railroad memorabilia, including four cabooses that have been converted into charming rooms, the inn is worth a stop for travelers skirting the park's southern border. Amenities include a good but overpriced restaurant, rustic bar and access to hiking and cross-country ski trails. Rooms cost $98 to $140, and there are $350 ski packages that include lodging, all meals and equipment for three days.

Places to Eat

Unlike the accommodations around the park, most restaurants are open year-round. In summer, there are grocery stores with an array of camping supplies in Apgar, Lake McDonald Lodge, Rising Sun and at the Swiftcurrent Motor Inn.

MONTANA

In East Glacier, *Serrano's Mexican Restaurant* serves up good Mexican food and margaritas for under $10. *Brownie's Grocery & Deli* has a well-rounded grocery supply and makes all its own breads, cookies, pastries and bagels – and always has a pot of strong coffee on the stove.

Your best bet around West Glacier is to head to Hungry Horse, Columbia Falls or (better yet) Whitefish.

The dining room in *Waterton's Prince of Wales Hotel* is perfect for a nice meal and has a great view.

Getting There & Away

Air The closest airport to Glacier National Park is the Glacier International, 20 miles southeast of the park's west entrance. Delta, Big Sky Airlines, Horizon Air and United Express fly into this airport, but more airlines service the airport in Great Falls, 158 miles from East Glacier. Travelers flying to Canada land at either Lethbridge, Alberta, 80 miles northeast of the Waterton Lakes entrance, or Calgary, 165 miles to the north.

Train Amtrak's *Empire Builder* follows the southern border of Glacier National Park with stops at East Glacier (Glacier Park Station) and West Glacier (Belton Station). Eastbound trains stop at both stations in the morning (around 8 am) and westbound trains stop in the evening (around 8 pm). Riding time between East Glacier and West Glacier is approximately 30 minutes. Tickets are available at East Glacier's station from 6 am to 11:30 am and 6 to 7:30 pm. Travelers boarding the train in West Glacier must buy tickets onboard. A one-way ticket from either station to Whitefish is $4, to Havre is $32 and to Seattle, Washington, is $112.

Getting Around

The speed limit is 45mph on all Glacier National Park roads unless otherwise posted. Vehicle restrictions are imposed on the Going-to-the-Sun Rd only. Vehicles or combinations wider than 8 feet or longer than 21 feet are prohibited between Avalanche Creek Campground and the Sun Point picnic area. Trailers may be parked temporarily at campgrounds, or at Sun Point on the east side of the park.

Bus Glacier Park Inc's transportation office (☎ 406-888-9187) runs a shuttle service on Going-to-the-Sun Rd to cope with traffic and increasingly strict size restrictions for recreational vehicles. Hopefully Glacier will eventually limit all transportation to shuttle service. The Hikers Express leaves from Many Glacier Hotel in the morning and drops passengers off at three trailheads: Siyeh Bend, Logan Pass and The Loop (for $13, $17 and $20 respectively, per person each way; park entrance fees are not included).

Car In West Glacier rental cars are available from the Glacier Highland Resort (☎ 406-888-5427, 800-766-0811). In East Glacier the Glacier Park Trading Co (☎ 406-226-4433, 800-331-1212) handles Avis car rentals, and the Whistling Swan Motel (☎ 406-226-4412) works with U Save Car Rentals. In St Mary, U Save cars are available through the KOA Campground (☎ 406-732-4122). All car-rental companies offer vans and 4WD vehicles.

Yellowstone Country

'Yellowstone Country' refers to the part of Montana directly north and west of Yellowstone National Park. This section covers the three rivers that feed into the park, including the Yellowstone River, running through the Paradise Valley, and the Madison and Gallatin Rivers – both tributaries of the Missouri River. Bozeman is the area's 'urban' hub. With Yellowstone as a magnet, these valleys (which run north-south between I-90 and Yellowstone) have always been heavily traveled, but the past decade has brought unprecedented development. There's still plenty of open space here, however, alongside some of the USA's best fishing and skiing.

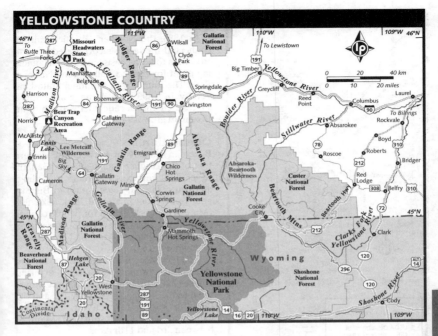

YELLOWSTONE COUNTRY

The area around Red Lodge is harder to get to (Billings is the largest gateway town) and thus less traveled than other parts around Yellowstone with Bozeman. It's an especially great destination in summer, when you can drive from Red Lodge to Yellowstone on the Beartooth Hwy.

BOZEMAN

To the surprise of native Montanans, 'Bozeman' is synonymous with 'Montana' for many travelers. Its arrival as an important town is relatively recent, and has more to do with the influx of Californians fed up with traffic and Coloradans fed up with Californians than with its place in the state's history or economy. Of course Montana State University (MSU) has long attracted students to its science and business schools, and ranchers have come to buy equipment or services for years. But students and ranchers are not the ones who keep the spe-

cialty boutiques and high end restaurants on Main St in business.

One common thread that runs through old and new populations is the love of recreation. Drive 20 minutes in any direction and you'll find world-class skiing, hiking, climbing (Heard of Alex Lowe? He lived here until his death.), mountain biking and fly-fishing; drive an hour and you're in Yellowstone National Park.

Bozeman (population 30,723; elevation 4754 feet) was developed as a rest area for travelers, and ever since it's been a place where people stay longer than they had planned. Tourists stick around for the shops, live music and diversity of good food that doesn't exist in such abundance elsewhere in Montana; college students stay well beyond the four-year mark; and skiers often arrive for a job at Bridger Bowl and find that they are still here in the summer, three years later, leading climbing trips in Hyalite Canyon.

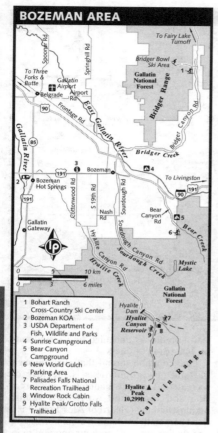

BOZEMAN AREA

To Fairy Lake
Turnoff

Bridger Bowl
Ski Area

Gallatin
National
Forest

Bridger Range

To Three
Forks &
Butte

Gallatin
Airport

Airport
Rd

Belgrade

Spooml Rd

Springhill Rd

East Gallatin River

Frontage Rd

Bridger Canyon Rd

Bridger Creek

Gallatin River

Bozeman

Bozeman
Hot Springs

To Livingston

Cottonwood Rd

S 19th Rd

Nash
Rd

Sourdough Canyon Rd

Bear
Canyon
Rd

Bear Creek

Gallatin
Gateway

Hyalite
Canyon Rd

Sourdough Creek

Mystic
Lake

Gallatin
National
Forest

Hyalite
Dam

Hyalite
Canyon
Reservoir

Gallatin Range

Hyalite
Peak
10,299ft

1 Bohart Ranch
   Cross-Country Ski Center
2 Bozeman KOA
3 USDA Department of
   Fish, Wildlife and Parks
4 Sunrise Campground
5 Bear Canyon
   Campground
6 New World Gulch
   Parking Area
7 Palisades Falls National
   Recreation Trailhead
8 Window Rock Cabin
9 Hyalite Peak/Grotto Falls
   Trailhead

0   5   10 km
0   3   6 miles

History

Bozeman has always been a natural stopping point for people traveling over the Bozeman Pass, the easiest route through the Bridger Mountains. Traders and trappers came looking for beaver in the wake of the Lewis and Clark Expedition, and miners flooded through in the mid 1800s.

John Bozeman landed here in 1863. He opened a spur of the Oregon Trail that crossed the area to meet the Overland Trail in Laramie, WY. The initially successful Bozeman Trail eventually met its fate at the hands of the Sioux, but by then the area was established as a crossroads and trade center.

In 1883, the Northern Pacific Railroad connected the newly incorporated town of Bozeman to both coasts, making it a launching point for trips to Yellowstone National Park. The founding of Montana State University in 1893 sealed the community's success. In the decade of its 100th year, Bozeman grew 35%.

Orientation

Bozeman sits halfway between the western foot of the Bridger Range and the Gallatin River. I-90 connects Bozeman to Billings and Butte; Hwy 191 goes south to Big Sky and Yellowstone National Park. Exit 308 (Main St), off I-90, is best for people coming from the east; exit 306 (7th Ave) puts you on 7th Ave, which meets Main St 2 blocks west of downtown.

College, Main and Mendenhall Sts are Bozeman's primary east-west arteries. Rouse, 7th and 19th Aves connect downtown to the Bridgers, I-90/Hwy 191 and the Gallatin Valley, respectively. The MSU campus is 10 blocks south of Main St between 3rd and 11th Aves.

Information

Bozeman's chamber of commerce (☎ 406-586-5421, 800-228-4224) puts out a helpful visitors guide and maintains a useful Web site (www.bozeman.avicom.net). In summer they staff a small Visitors Information Center, 1001 N 7th Ave, between downtown and I-90. A 24-hour recreation recording (☎ 406-587-9784) has current trail, road and weather conditions for the area.

Banks, bookstores and newsstands are found along Main St. The MSU bookstore (☎ 406-994-2811), in the basement of Strand Student Union, has an excellent selection. Country Bookshelf (☎ 406-587-0166) is at 28 W Main. Bozeman's post office (☎ 406-586-1508) is on Babcock St between Tracy and Black Aves; postal code 59715.

The Bozeman Public Library (☎ 406-582-2400), 220 E Lamme St, offers free Internet access. Medical help is available at Bozeman

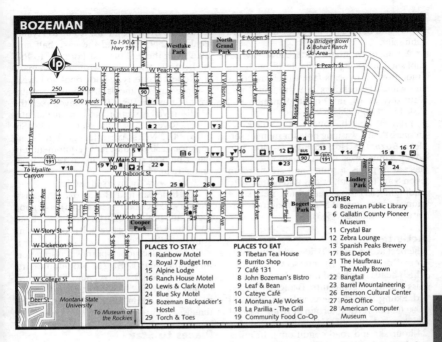

BOZEMAN

PLACES TO STAY	PLACES TO EAT	OTHER
1 Rainbow Motel	3 Tibetan Tea House	4 Bozeman Public Library
2 Royal 7 Budget Inn	5 Burrito Shop	6 Gallatin County Pioneer
15 Alpine Lodge	7 Café 131	Museum
16 Ranch House Motel	8 John Bozeman's Bistro	11 Crystal Bar
20 Lewis & Clark Motel	9 Leaf & Bean	12 Zebra Lounge
24 Blue Sky Motel	10 Cateye Café	13 Spanish Peaks Brewery
25 Bozeman Backpacker's	14 Montana Ale Works	17 Bus Depot
Hostel	18 La Parilla - The Grill	21 The Haufbrau;
29 Torch & Toes	19 Community Food Co-op	The Molly Brown
		22 Bangtail
		23 Barrel Mountaineering
		26 Emerson Cultural Center
		27 Post Office
		28 American Computer
		Museum

Deaconess Hospital (☎ 406-585-1000), 915 Highland Blvd.

Things to See & Do

Arguably Montana's most entertaining museum, MSU's **Museum of the Rockies** (☎ 406-994-3466), at the corner of S 7th Ave and Kagy Blvd, traces Montana's history from a few billion years ago to the 19th century. Exceptional are the exhibits of Ice Age fossils and native cultures of the Northern Rockies. The Taylor Planetarium (☎ 406-994-2251) has daily planetarium and laser shows ($5). A $9 combo ticket allows entry to the museum and planetarium; otherwise museum entry is $7, planetarium entry $3. Hours are 8 am to 8 pm Memorial Day to Labor Day; Monday to Saturday from 9 am to 6 pm, Sunday from 12:30 to 5 pm, the rest of the year.

Known around town as 'the Emerson,' the nonprofit **Emerson Cultural Center** (☎ 406-587-9797), 111 S Grand Ave, was once an elementary school doomed for demolition. Now it's the hub of Bozeman's art scene, with retail galleries, artists studios and changing exhibits of local artists work. Most galleries are open Tuesday to Saturday, 10 am to 5 pm. You can wander the halls and look at current exhibits any time.

The **Gallatin County Pioneer Museum** (☎ 406-582-3195), in the old jail building at 317 W Main St, does a good job portraying local history. Its library has extensive photo archives, including a fantastic collection documenting cowgirls of the 1920s; closed Sunday, free admission.

Every year the calculating 'dinosaurs' (slide rules, room-sized electronic computers, key punch machines) on display at the **American Computer Museum** (☎ 406-587-7545), 234 E Babcock St, seem more comic. Try your hand at an ancient typewriter in the 'hands on' section, or check out the prototypes of first-run video games. Hours are daily from 10 am to 4 pm June to August, from noon to 4 pm Tuesday, Wednesday, Friday and Saturday the rest of the year; $3 admission.

A tour of **Montana State University**, established in 1893, is available through the student-run Advocats (the MSU mascot is the wildcat) weekdays at 9 am and 2 pm, Saturday at 10 am. For information call Ask-Us (☎ 406-994-4636).

First a health source for Blackfeet Indians, then a washing hole for pioneer settlers, **Bozeman Hot Springs** (☎ 406-586-6492), 8 miles west of Bozeman off US 191, has seven pools, a sauna and steam room open 8 am to 10 pm, Friday and Saturday to midnight ($5). Spa treatments, new since pioneer days, start at $45 and require reservations (☎ 406-522-9563).

Activities

The best access to the Bridger Mountains is from Rouse Ave S (it intersects Main St), which heads north and under the I-90 overpass before veering into Bridger Canyon Rd. **Skiing** is prime here, with six lifts and 2000 feet of vertical terrain at Bridger Bowl Ski Area (☎ 406-587-2111, 406-586-2389 for 24-hour ski and road conditions), 16 miles northeast of town, and 18-miles of groomed cross-country trails at Bohart Ranch Cross-Country Ski Center (☎ 406-586-9070), half a mile from Bridger Bowl (both on Bridger Canyon Rd).

The Hyalite Canyon area, south of Bozeman via 19th Ave, is Bozeman's other playground. A 5½-mile ski-mountaineering route begins at the New World Gulch Parking Area, accessible via Bear Canyon Rd (take I-90 4½ miles west to the Bear Canyon Rd exit and head south past the Bear Canyon Campground). Hyalite is also considered one of the best ice-climbing spots in the USA.

In summer, both the Bridgers and Hyalite offer excellent **hiking**. A trailhead for the 3-mile hike to the top of Sacajawea Peak, the Bridgers' highest at 9665 feet, is at Fairy Lake, 6 miles past Bridger Bowl then 9 miles west of Bridger Canyon Rd (it's well signed). At the south end of Hyalite Canyon, 200-acre Hyalite Reservoir is the starting point for many hikes, including a 7-mile climb from West Fork Rd up to Hyalite Peak (10,299 feet), and the easy, half-mile hike from the end of East Fork Rd to Palisades Falls. 'Dayhikes Around Bozeman,' by Robert Stone, is a handy book to have.

Bozeman's prime **fishing** spots are southwest of town in Bear Trap Canyon (see the Madison Valley section) and on the Gallatin River. Rivers Edge Outfitters (☎ 406-586-5373), 2012 N 7th Ave, offers guided fishing trips for $230 per day, rents equipment and has a helpful staff. Pick up a free map of area streams here.
Web site: www.theriversedge.com

The little cabin at Bohart Ranch Cross-Country Ski Center (see above) is a good mountain biking departure point and has an 18-hole 'folf' (Frisbee golf) course; bring your own discs.

The best place for all-purpose information, maps and gear is Barrel Mountaineering (☎ 406-582-1335), 240 E Main St. Bangtail (☎ 406-587-4905), 500 W Main, is a good place to find mountain bike information and rentals.

Places to Stay

Camping Three campgrounds at *Hyalite Canyon Recreation Area*, 11 to 18 miles from Bozeman on Hyalite Canyon Rd, have wheelchair-accessible facilities and charge $11 per site. The *Window Rock Cabin*, 1 mile south of the reservoir, is a small field station built in the 1940s that sleeps six people (wheelchair accessible) for $23 a night. It's equipped with wood stoves, tables and chairs, an ax, shovel, bucket and cleaning supplies. For reservations contact the Bozeman Ranger Station (☎ 406-587-6920).

Bozeman KOA (☎ 406-587-3030), 8 miles west of Bozeman off I-90 (next to Bozeman Hot Springs), is the only campground in the area open year-round. Tent sites cost $24, RV sites cost $32.

In view of the Bridger Mountains, *Bear Canyon Campground* (☎ 406-587-1575), 3 miles east of Bozeman, off I-90 exit 313, has a heated pool, laundry facilities and store. Tent sites cost $12, RV hookups cost $17; open May 1 to October 31.

The **Sunrise Campground** (☎ 406-587-4797, 31842 Frontage Rd) is about 2 miles east of Bozeman off I-90 exit 309. Easy access to Bozeman is the selling point of this clean and lively site. Tent sites cost $12, and RV hookups cost $22; open April 15 to November 15.

Hostels The **Bozeman Backpacker's Hostel** (☎ 406-586-4659, 405 W Olive St), 2 blocks south of Main St, is an independent hostel that serves a young, international, active clientele. The house is clean, has a full kitchen and laundry, no curfew or lock-out. A bunk or spot in a double costs $14. In summer, there's a hostel-to-hostel shuttle ($28) to Cooke City, over the Beartooth Pass Hwy (see Red Lodge, later in this chapter).

Motels & Hotels The full gamut of chain motels can be found north of downtown on 7th Ave, near I-90. Better for the budget are independent places like the **Rainbow Motel** (☎ 406-587-4201, 510 N 7th Ave) and **Royal 7 Budget Inn** (☎ 800-587-3103, 310 N 7th Ave), both with rooms for $45 to $70.

A half mile east of downtown, near the bus depot, are three good choices. The **Blue Sky Motel** (☎ 406-587-2311, 800-845-9032, 1010 E Main St) has clean rooms for $58; the **Alpine Lodge** (☎ 888-922-5746, 1017 E Main) has rooms for $45 and suites that sleep six with a kitchen for $68; the **Ranch House Motel** (☎ 406-587-4278, 1201 E Main St) charges around $43/37 for a double/single.

Closer to downtown, the **Lewis & Clark Motel** (☎ 406-586-3341, 800-332-7666, 824 W Main St) is a glitzy affair with three stories of rooms, a pool, sauna, hot tub and sundeck. June to September prices are around $80, the rest of the year they drop to $55.

B&Bs There are literally dozens of B&Bs in the greater Bozeman area. Many of them are 10 to 20 miles out of town on Bridger Canyon Rd, or on US 191 near Gallatin Gateway. For a full listing, ask for an accommodations list from the chamber of commerce.

The **Torch & Toes** (☎ 406-586-7285, 309 S 3rd Ave) is in an elegant brick house in central Bozeman with lace curtains, a hot tub and three rooms with private bath for $110 per night. Behind the main house is a carriage house that sleeps six and has a kitchenette for $135 per night.

Places to Eat

Every town should have a market like Bozeman's **Community Food Co-Op** (908 W Main St). The store has a fantastic deli, salad bar, juice bar, bakery and a wide selection of bulk foods. Eat at the small tables inside or out on the grass.

The **Leaf & Bean** (35 W Main St) is Bozeman's primary caffeine merchant, busy from 7 am to 10 pm daily. **Café 131**, at the corner of Main St and Grand Ave, is another java joint that serves a full breakfast and lunch menu (closed Monday).

For around $5 you can stuff yourself on traditional Mexican fare at the **Burrito Shop** (203 N 7th Ave), try a Thai or Cajun wrap at **La Parillia – The Grill** (1533 W Babcock) or eat Asian at the **Tibetan Tea House** (122 W Lamme St).

For dinner try the cozy **Cateye Café** (23 N Tracy Ave), whose large menu includes chicken pot pie ($7), a grilled tuna sandwich ($6) and nightly specials ($10 to $13). Want to splurge? **John Bozeman's Bistro** (☎ 406-587-4100, 125 W Main St) has held its place as Bozeman's best restaurant despite the influx of nouveau gourmet eateries; expect to spend $25 per person.

A catch-all for food, beer, pool and people-watching is **Montana Ale Works** (611 E Main St), where a variety of pastas, salads, hearty appetizers and grilled meats run from $6 to $18. The chicken quesadilla ($5) is a favorite.

Entertainment

Pick up a free copy of the *BoZone* at a cafe or market for the latest entertainment calendars. The **Bozeman Symphony** (☎ 406-585-9774) performs monthly from February to May at the Willson School Auditorium, 2 blocks south of Main St on Willson Ave. **MSU Plays** (☎ 406-994-3904) performs alternative or little-known contemporary plays in the Strand Union Theater on the MSU campus.

MONTANA

Most nights bring live music – be it rock, funk, soul or reggae – to the *Zebra Lounge*, half a block north of Main on Rouse Ave S; shows start around 10 pm. For straightforward drinking, the *Crystal Bar (123 E Main St)* welcomes students, ranchers and tourists alike. In summer you'll find its clientele on the rooftop deck.

No beer lover should leave without a trip to *Spanish Peaks Brewery*, at the corner of Main St and Church Ave, made famous by Black Dog Ale and Spanish Peaks Porter. *Montana Ale Works* (see Places to Eat, above) is the Peaks' new rival.

Students seem to like the MSU class shields hanging on the walls and ceilings at the *Haufbrau (22 S 8th Ave)*, or maybe it's the $1.50 pints and $6 pitchers? Behind the Haufbrau, the *Molly Brown* is big, noisy and stocked with eight pool tables and 20 beers on tap.

Getting There & Away

Air Ever-expanding service to the Gallatin airport (☎ 406-388-6632), 8 miles northwest of downtown near the town of Belgrade, currently includes Delta, Northwest, United Express, Horizon Air and Big Sky.

A taxi from the airport to downtown costs around $12.

Bus The bus depot (☎ 406-587-3110) is half a mile from downtown at 1205 E Main St. Greyhound and Rimrock Trailways service all Montana towns along I-90 and go west through Idaho to Seattle, south to Salt Lake City and east through South Dakota to Minneapolis. Tickets cost $31 to Missoula, $15.50 to Helena and $24 to Billings.

Karst Stages (☎ 406-388-9923, 800-287-4759) runs five buses per day from the airport to Big Sky ($18) and two to West Yellowstone ($25). Service is limited from November to June.

Getting Around

Car rental agencies in the Gallatin airport include Budget (☎ 406-388-4091), Avis (☎ 406-388-6414), Hertz (☎ 406-388-6939) and National (☎ 406-388-6694). Rent-a-Wreck (☎ 406-587-4551, 800-344-4551),

5 E Mendenhall St, has slightly lower prices and arranges airport pick-up. All car-rental agencies have 4WD vehicles available, as well as ski racks.

In winter, the Bridger Bowl Ski Bus (☎ 406-586-8567) runs continuously on weekends and holidays from various locations in Bozeman; tickets cost $4 one-way, $5 roundtrip.

MISSOURI HEADWATERS

The Madison, Jefferson and Gallatin Rivers converge here, forming the headwaters of the Missouri-Mississippi River drainage (the largest in North America) 2464 miles above its mouth. Before Lewis and Clark arrived in 1805, explorers looking for the headwaters could practically smell the saltwater from here, believing the mighty river was part of a northwest passage leading to the Pacific Ocean and the exotic 'Orient' beyond. Competition to control such a route began in 1541 when Spanish explorer Francisco Vásquez de Coronado first heard of a 'mighty river to the north,' and ended in an American victory when Napoleon sold the Louisiana Territory in 1803.

Lewis and Clark arrived at the confluence July 25, 1805, and after several days' exploration determined that none of the tributaries was the Missouri itself, and that each was a separate fork. Lewis wrote, 'Both Captain Clark and myself corresponded in opinion with respect to the impropriety of calling either of these streams the Missouri and accordingly agreed to name them after the President of the US and Secretaries of the Treasury and State' – hence the names Jefferson, Madison and Gallatin.

Four miles northeast of I-90 a trail and road stretch the 1½-mile length of **Missouri Headwaters State Park,** giving an up-close-and-personal view of the riparian convergence. At the park's north end is a boat dock and picnic area, while the south end has a shadeless *campground* ($12 per night) and a visitors information area flanked by the remnants of Gallatin City. Day use costs $4 (free for Montana residents).

Across I-90 from the state park, Three Forks (population 1513) is the town that

Gallatin City would have become had the Milwaukee Railroad chosen a route 2 miles north. The one thing worth visiting here is the ***Sacajawea Inn*** (☎ *406-285-6515, 800-821-7326, 5 N Main St),* which was moved to its present location from Gallatin City in 1908. It has an Arts and Crafts–style interior, mahogany floors, high wood-trimmed ceilings and a large porch with wooden rocking chairs. Rooms, $75 to $105, include breakfast; the dining room has meals for $8 to $15.

A local miner named Dan Morrison led tours down into 'Morrison's limestone caves' before they were designated **Lewis & Clark Caverns State Park** in 1930. His tours directly defied an ordinance that prohibited trespassing on railroad-owned land, but apparently the $1 per person he made from each 12-hour tour was worth the risk. The formations within the caves are absolutely spectacular. Besides the stalagmites, stalactites and columns typically found in limestone caves, two erratic growths – helectites and globulites (cave popcorn) – bending upwards in gravity-defying formations are present. Two-hour tours (which can get chilly even in midsummer) leave every 20 to 30 minutes from the visitors center (☎ 406-287-3541), 3 miles inside the park from the highway; 9 am to 7 pm May to October.

MADISON VALLEY

Hardly visible to passers-through, mining in the Madison Valley began with gold finds around Pony in the 1860s and continues today with the world's largest talc-producing district in the Gravelly Range. In terms of scenery, the Madison is neither as rugged as the Gallatin Valley or as colorful as the Paradise Valley, but its high, wide valley bordered by the majestic Madison Range reminds some travelers of places in the Patagonian Andes or Mongolia.

More important to most people is that the Madison River from Ennis south to West Yellowstone has some of the finest 'blue ribbon' fishing in the USA. The best fishing is said to be between Ennis and Quake Lake, accessible from six sites along US 287. Ennis is a good stop for supplies, guides and information.

MISSOURI HEADWATERS & NORTH MADISON VALLEY

1 Red Mountain Campground
2 Potosi Campground; Potosi Peak Trailhead
3 Norris Hot Springs
4 Bear Claw Bar & Supper Club
5 Valley Garden Campground
6 Diamond J Ranch
7 Varney Bridge Campground

MONTANA

Buffalo Jumps

Buffalo jumps, or *pishkun*, were used by many Indian tribes as mass hunting tools. In the fall, when bison cows were fat, tribes journeyed to their pishkun site, where they camped and performed sacred dances and rituals to ensure a successful task. The site had to be a flat, wide expanse with a long, sheer cliff of at least 30 feet on one side.

Pishkun, the buffalo's dramatic destiny

Runners, chosen for their speed and agility, purified themselves in the sweat lodge to rid themselves of human odor, then put on buffalo, antelope or wolf skins. In disguise they coaxed a bison herd into a roundup area that led to a drive lane marked by large decorated cairns called 'dead men.' The head runner, dressed in a full buffalo robe with head and horns still attached (imagine the weight of this!), would then catch the attention of the lead bison and begin to run towards the cliff. The trick was to run at a pace fast enough that the bison had too much momentum when they reached the cliff's edge, but slow enough that they wouldn't get spooked and escape the herd.

Other people hiding behind the dead men kept the bison within the drive lanes – by spooking or swatting them – and when the herd reached the cliff the head runner jumped out of the way, usually into a hole that had been dug by the cliff's edge. The bison that survived the fall were killed by hunters waiting near the bottom of the fall.

Pony

If you're looking to see an authentic outpost of a mining town, head 6 miles west of US 287 to the town of Pony (population 80), where glorious old brick buildings – the bank, public school and Masons Hall – stand among unpaved streets at the foot of the Tobacco Root Mountains. These days the only businesses in what was Montana's largest gold mining town during the 1880s, are the post office and the Pony Bar, which has a good photograph collection on the wall.

A maintained dirt road on the east edge of Pony leads 6 miles to Potosi Campground, from where you can access the Potosi Peak and Louise Lake National Recreation Trails, good day hikes into the high, lake-studded plateau of the Tobacco Roots.

Ennis

If fishing is Montana's religion, then Ennis (population 1039 people, 110,000 fish) is its mecca. On the west bank of the Madison River, at the junction of US 287 and Hwy 287, Ennis is flanked by the Madison Range to the east, the Tobacco Root Mountains and Gravelly Ranges to the north and west. But the town's focus is undeniably the river. Since the filming of *A River Runs Through It*, the Madison has become the armchair angler's dream, and Ennis has become the natural hub for anglers who don't have their own vacation homes; you will see more out-of-state license plates in Ennis than in any other town its size.

Still charming in a 'Western outdoorsman' way, Ennis has a one-street downtown lined with fly shops, Western-wear stores, real estate offices, a movie theater and chamber of commerce (☎ 406-682-4388). More out of the ordinary are Jim Dolan's sculptures of cowboys and fishermen that appear along the Main St strip. The **Blue Heron**, 101 Main St, has an exceptional collection of antique fishing rods and reels, used cowboy boots and hats, sculpted silver cowboy spurs and local guidebooks.

Fishing Few people come to Ennis without casting a line at some point in their stay. The Madison River from Hebgen Lake north to Varney Bridge (11 miles south of Ennis) is open to fishing year-round. Ennis' fly shops all have good reputations and, for the most part, use the same pool of guides. The rule of thumb is to make sure you get a guide with at least four years of experience. The Tackle Shop (☎ 406-682-4263, 800-808-2832), 127 Main St, www.thetackleshop.com, offers guided trips for $275 to $500 per day for two people, including lunch. Madison River Fishing Company (☎ 406-682-4293, 800-227-7127), 109 Main St, www.mrfc.com, has similar rates and also offers half-day packages ($195) and a three-day fly-fishing school ($745 per person).

Places to Stay USFS campgrounds, most coupled with fishing access sites, are plentiful around Ennis. These all have fire rings,

The Politics of Fishing

In conducting the state's most definitive study on catch-and-release fishing, Dick Vincent did more for Montana's fishing populace than even Robert Redford and Brad Pitt. Catch-and-release fishing, which allows anglers to fish for sport rather than for dinner, dictates that all fish caught have to be returned to the river so that their stock won't be depleted. Using Ennis as his base, Vincent proved that a fishery could be sustained at the same level if catch-and-release fishing were practiced as if no fishing were allowed and hatchery fish were introduced. This refuted the 'no fishing' laws that Montana had imposed on some fished-out rivers, notably the upper Madison and Gallatin. As a result, the Dept of Fish, Wildlife & Parks eliminated state hatcheries and now uses the excess money to buy private land and signs for fishing-access sites, thereby decreasing fishing traffic. National hatcheries, like the one just east of Ennis, still operate to produce lake stock.

picnic tables and pit toilets, and cost $7 to $11 per night: ***Ennis Fishing Access Campground***, half a mile east of town on the Madison River's east bank; ***Valley Garden Campground*** , 2½ miles northeast of town (turn east on Jeffers Rd from US 287, a mile east of Ennis); and ***Varney Bridge Campground***, 12 miles south of town off Hwy 287.

Ennis' motels can be expensive and fill up quickly in summer. The two 'budget' motels are a few doors away from each other on the south end of US 287. The ***Riverside Motel*** (☎ 406-682-4240, 800-535-4139) has a range of rooms starting at $45. The ***Silvertip Lodge*** (☎ 406-682-4384) has cozy rooms with small kitchens for $50.

Just north of town on US 287, the ***Sportsman's Lodge*** (☎ 406-682-4242, 800-220-1690) has a lively lounge and restaurant, wood cabins for $60 and motel rooms from $55.

A mile south of town on US 287, *El Western* (☎ 406-682-4217) rarely has a vacancy due to anglers who come for weeks at a time; rooms cost $68 and log cabin cottages with full kitchens start at $95. Next door, the *Rainbow Valley Motel* (☎ 406-682-4264, 800-452-8254) is the same type of operation with singles/doubles for $55/65.

In the Madison Range's foothills, within 20 miles of Ennis, there are some notable guest ranches. Ten miles east of Ennis up Hammond Creek Rd (known locally as Jack Creek Rd), the *Diamond J Ranch* (☎ 406-682-4867, 877-929-4867), www.ranchweb.com/diamondj, is the Madison Valley's most complete family dude ranch. A one-week minimum stay is required ($1,150), and it includes all of the horseback riding, fishing, swimming, tennis and skeet shooting one can handle. Three meals a day are provided in the camp-style dining room. Most of their clients return year after year.

Places to Eat Largely supported by tourist dollars, Ennis' restaurants are surprisingly good (and pricey) for a town this size. The *Economy IGA Food Market* on Main St has a great deli; open until 9 pm.

Good casual choices on Main St include *Yesterday's Cafe* for breakfast and lunch and *Madison River Bakery and Pizza* for lunch and take-out. For fine dining, try the highly touted *Continental Divide* (☎ 406-682-7600, 315 E Main St). The *Silver Dollar Saloon* (133 Main St) has a good dining room with dinners for $7 to $11. The *Bear Claw Bar and Supper Club* (☎ 406-682-4619), 7 miles north of Ennis on US 287 in McAllister, has steak, chicken and seafood dinners for around $10.

Highway 84

This scenic farm road traverses the northern end of the Madison and Gallatin Valleys, connecting US 287 to Bozeman. A quarter mile east of its junction with US 287, at Norris, are **Norris Hot Springs** (☎ 406-686-3303), which come to the surface at 117°F to 124°F and get cooled to around 105°F by a recirculating fountain. The pool is not particularly pretty, but a $5 dunk may be good for weary travelers; campsites cost $35, including use of the pool.

At the heart of the BLM's first wilderness area, **Bear Trap Canyon** offers 9 miles of scenic hiking and fishing along a steep-sided gorge. Numerous pull-outs give access from along Hwy 84, as does the *Red Mountain Campground*, which has water, toilets and $9 sites.

Virginia City

An historical amusement park in the beautiful Tobacco Root Mountains, Virginia City is a touristy old mining town that serves as a popular stop along Hwy 287 between Dillon and Ennis. Born in 1863, when Bill Fairweather and his companions struck gold in Alder Gulch, the town was home to Henry Plummer's notorious road gang and hotbed of vigilante activity. More recently, it's been featured in Hollywood Westerns and all of Norman Fox's novels, including *Gunsmoke* and *Roughshod*.

It's worth a few hours of exploration for its wealth of historic buildings, the **Virginia City/Madison County Historic Museum** ($2) and **Boot Hill Cemetery**, where most of Plummer's road gang are buried. A short-line railroad ($5 roundtrip) at the west edge of town links Virginia City to neighboring **Nevada City**, site of the first vigilante execution and filming location of nine movies, including *Little Big Man, Missouri Breaks* and *Return to Lonesome Dove*. A $4 ticket allows access to the town's unrestored buildings, an outstanding train museum and a music hall with dozens of operable old music machines.

Places to Stay & Eat It's fun to spend the night here and nose around in the evening or early morning when most visitors are gone. The nearest camping is at *Alder KOA* (☎ 406-842-5677), 4 miles west on Hwy 287, where tent/RV sites cost $20/25. Central to Virginia City activity is the *Fairweather Inn* (☎ 406-843-5377, 800-648-7588), where $40 rooms have shared bath and $55 rooms have private bath.

The Fairweather also runs the *Nevada City Hotel & Cabins* in Nevada City, with 'Old West' rooms for $60 and restored 1860s cabins for $55; all have private baths. Rooms at the *Bennett House Country Inn* (☎ 406-843-5220, 877-843-5220, 115 E Idaho St) are good values at $65, including a big breakfast. The *Stonehouse Inn* (☎ 406-843-5504, 306 E Idaho St), Virginia City's first house to have electricity, has $70 rooms.

Entertainment Virginia City's garish stage shows are integral to its existence. The *Brewery Follies* (☎ 406-843-5218) is a slightly off-color song-and-dance comedy staged in the old Gilbert Brewery; tickets cost $9. The *Virginia City Opera House* stages three 19th-century melodramas each year; tickets cost $10 (☎ 406-843-5314 for ticket reservations). Reservations are recommended for all shows.

Quake & Hebgen Lakes

Just before midnight on August 17, 1959, an earthquake measuring 7.1 on the Richter scale shook the earth, drastically changing the landscape of the upper Madison River Canyon. Two large fault blocks in the Hebgen Lake area tilted and dropped. The lake's north shore dropped 18 feet, and parts of US 287 dropped into the water, taking several lodges along with it. A massive landslide buried two campsites and blocked the Madison River, forming Quake Lake in the process. The same quake caused major changes in the thermal features of Yellowstone National Park, especially around the Mud Volcano area.

Built atop part of the landslide, the **Madison River Canyon Earthquake Area Visitors Center** (☎ 406-646-7369) has a working seismograph, photographs from the quake and a half-mile interpretive trail that leads to a vista of the area; the center is open daily from 8:30 am to 6 pm, Memorial Day to Labor Day.

Hebgen Lake, connected to Quake Lake by a scenic stretch of river, has a dam that amazingly withstood the earthquake's rocking activity. Between the visitors center and the dam, **Beaver Creek Rd** turns north off the highway. The road follows Beaver Creek, through an area notorious for grizzly sightings, 3 miles to the Avalanche Lake/ Blue Danube Lake trailhead. Both lakes make excellent day hike destinations. One-eighth of a mile past the trailhead parking lot a side road branches off to the right and leads 200 yards to the USFS Beaver Creek cabin, which you can rent year-round ($30 per night). It has bunk beds to sleep six, a cookstove and utensils, firewood and an ax; contact the Ranger Station in West Yellowstone for reservations.

The Cabin Creek area, on US 287 a mile past Beaver Creek Rd, has a USFS campground, a trailhead with more good day hike possibilities and a 'scarp area' that offers a good view of the land shift that occurred during the earthquake. Across US 287, the *Campfire Lodge Resort* (☎ 406-646-7258) is a good place for breakfast and rents cabins for $40 to $90.

Instead of taking US 287 along Quake and Hebgen lakes, it's possible to reach West Yellowstone via US 87, which turns south of US 287 just west of Quake Lake. This route skirts the southwest base of the Lions Head area of the Madison Range then intersects with Hwy 20, which goes east over Targhee Pass to West Yellowstone. This route gives access to some wild and beautiful backcountry that often gets overlooked by people making a beeline for Yellowstone.

On the south side of Hebgen Lake (opposite the Quake Lake area) are three remote USFS campgrounds with pit toilets, potable water and fire rings. Reach these by turning north on Denny Creek Rd (USFS Rd 176), just east of the Super 8 Motel on Hwy 20 (about halfway between Targhee Pass and West Yellowstone); there's a big power transmitter and a wooden 'Gallatin National Forest Recreation Area' sign at the turnoff.

Two good hikes that give access to the Continental Divide National Scenic Trail are Mile Creek Trail, well signed off Hwy 87, 9 miles south of US 287, and, better suited to day hikes, Targhee Creek Trail, which starts 1 mile off Hwy 20.

WEST YELLOWSTONE

If not a particularly attractive town, West Yellowstone (population 1222; elevation 6600 feet) is well equipped to lodge, feed and briefly entertain visitors headed to Yellowstone National Park, a quarter mile from the town center. What's most redeeming to West Yellowstone residents is that within a bike ride, ski or long run from town, wilderness abounds outside of the park and it's free and often uncrowded even in the height of tourist season. The town thrives during the high seasons (June to September and mid-December to mid-

March) and resembles a ghost town at other times of the year.

A new NPS winter management plan will phase snowmobiling out of the park over a four-year span (beginning in 2001) and increase the number of 10-passenger snow coaches that tour the backcountry. Snowmobilers, who need fuel, lodging and plenty of food and drink, generate big profits for the town, so most locals fought to keep the park open to snowmobiling despite the known environmental damage it brings. Ski touring seems to be a great alternative future enterprise.

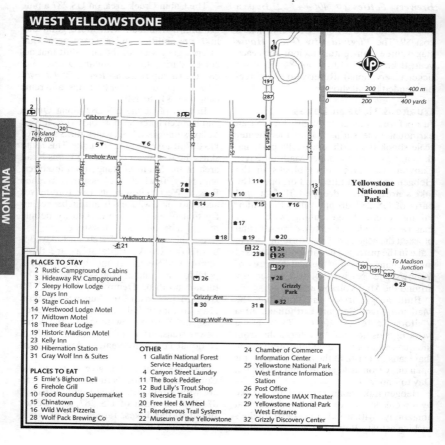

WEST YELLOWSTONE

PLACES TO STAY
2 Rustic Campground & Cabins
3 Hideaway RV Campground
7 Sleepy Hollow Lodge
8 Days Inn
9 Stage Coach Inn
14 Westwood Lodge Motel
17 Midtown Motel
18 Three Bear Lodge
19 Historic Madison Motel
23 Kelly Inn
30 Hibernation Station
31 Gray Wolf Inn & Suites

PLACES TO EAT
5 Ernie's Bighorn Deli
6 Firehole Grill
10 Food Roundup Supermarket
15 Chinatown
16 Wild West Pizzeria
28 Wolf Pack Brewing Co

OTHER
1 Gallatin National Forest Service Headquarters
4 Canyon Street Laundry
11 The Book Peddler
12 Bud Lilly's Trout Shop
13 Riverside Trails
20 Free Heel & Wheel
21 Rendezvous Trail System
22 Museum of the Yellowstone

24 Chamber of Commerce Information Center
25 Yellowstone National Park West Entrance Information Station
26 Post Office
27 Yellowstone IMAX Theater
29 Yellowstone National Park West Entrance
32 Grizzly Discovery Center

MONTANA

History

In 1908, the town of Riverside opened its post office at the end of the Union Pacific Railroad track. One year later, Dick Murray opened Murray's Yellowstone Hotel (still standing as the Madison Motel), and Sam and Ida Eagle opened a general store on Yellowstone Ave that is still in operation (as Eagle's Store) and thus Yellowstone (renamed the same year) began as a town welcoming travelers. The Union Pacific Complex, consisting of the depot, a dining hall (or 'beanery') and lodge, was the hub of activity and the community's major employer. Each afternoon, a line of 'beanery queens,' dressed in formal servants' attire, would meet arriving trains and escort travelers to the dining hall for a welcome dinner and park orientation.

Yellowstone National Park's popularity brought enough visitors to support service businesses besides those of Union Pacific, and with the growth of automobile travel, independent operations grew to overshadow the railroad's. In 1920 the community changed its name from simply Yellowstone to West Yellowstone in order to define itself geographically and avoid confusion between the town and the park.

Orientation & Information

US 191 and US 287 meet 8 miles north and run through town as Canyon St (West Yellowstone's main drag) then turn east at Yellowstone Ave to enter the park. US 20 heads west towards Idaho as Firehole Ave.

West Yellowstone's Chamber of Commerce Information Center (☎ 406-646-7701) is in Grizzly Park on Canyon St, one block south of Yellowstone Ave.

Web site: www.westyellowstonechamber.com

One building south, the Yellowstone National Park West Entrance Information Station (☎ 406-646-7332) has information specifically concerning the park, including campground availability. The Gallatin National Forest Service Headquarters (☎ 406-646-7369) is on Canyon St, 2 blocks north of Firehole Ave.

On Electric St, 1 block south of Yellowstone Ave, is a bank and the spiffy new post office; postal code 59758. Canyon Street

Laundry, 312 Canyon St, has coin-operated machines, drop-off service and public showers. For topo maps, natural history guides and a good general selection, stop at the Book Peddler (☎ 406-646-9358), 106 Canyon St.

Things to See

Five bears (Kodiak and grizzly) and nine gray wolves are kept in a pseudonatural setting at the **Grizzly Discovery Center** in Grizzly Park (in the southeast corner of town off Yellowstone Ave and Canyon St). Why keep live animals in captivity a quarter mile from one of the largest natural habitats in the lower 48 states? The concept is to educate travelers about the nature of bears, while protecting 'problem bears' – repeat offenders of garbage bin raids or harmful people encounters; open daily from 9 am to dusk, $8.

Next door, the **Yellowstone IMAX Theater** may be the only way for summer travelers to see Yellowstone in the winter or without crowds – all on a screen six stories high. Hourly showings from 9 am to 9 pm May to September, and from 1 to 9 pm October to April; $7.50.

The **Museum of the Yellowstone** (☎ 406-646-7814), housed in the 1909 UP railroad depot at 124 Yellowstone Ave, covers all aspects of West Yellowstone's and Yellowstone National Park's existence – from drawings and sculptures by Donald Clarke (a Blackfeet Indian from East Glacier) to three full-sized stuffed bison that were part of the last plains herd; open 8 am to 9 pm, $5.

Activities

The park is closed to vehicles from mid-October to December and mid-April to mid-May, but open to bikes or skis (depending on the weather).

The 30 miles of trails in the Rendezvous Trail System, just off Yellowstone Ave at Geyser St, are training ground for US Olympic cross-country ski teams. Less developed and more scenic are the Riverside Trails, which start on the east side of Boundary St between Madison and Firehole Aves. The main trail cuts through 1½ miles of fir and pine and comes out near the Madison

River, where there are old NPS roads and other trails that meander along the Madison River. Both of these trail systems offer great **mountain biking** and **trail running** when the snow melts.

Free Heel and Wheel (☎ 406-646-7744), just east of Canyon St on Yellowstone Ave, is the place to stop for maps, bike and ski rentals, friendly trail advice and free group activities (trail runs, mountain bike rides, etc) five days a week. Bud Lilly's Trout Shop (☎ 406-646-7801), 39 Madison Ave, rents fishing equipment and offers one-day float and walk trips for $175 per person.

Organized Tours

Gray Line Tours (☎ 406-646-9374, 800-523-3102), 555 Yellowstone Ave, runs eight-hour bus tours of the park daily the summer; $42 per person. In winter they team up with Yellowstone Alpine Guides (☎ 406-646-9591) to take people on snowcoach tours to Old Faithful ($90 per person) and the Grand Canyon of the Yellowstone ($100). They provide a picnic lunch and stop at the more famous geyser basins for short walking tours.

Skiers and snowboarders shouldn't miss a backcountry trip with Hellroaring Ski Adventures (☎ 406-646-4571). For $80 to $150 per person you get a shuttle, guide, meals, avalanche rescue equipment, climbing skins, hut accommodations and some fine terrain in the Centennial Mountains. Hut rental, for a minimum of four experienced people, costs $25 per person per night.
Web site: www.skihellroaring.com

Places to Stay

Considering the number of motel signs, the lack of variety in accommodations is surprising. During the off-season (October, November and mid-March to June) the few places that remain open, including the Stagecoach Inn, Days Inn and Kelly Inn, offer superlow rates. Reservations fill up two to six months in advance for high-season periods.

Camping The nicest tent campgrounds are *Bakers Hole Campground*, 3 miles north of

town on US 191, and *Lonesomehurst Campground*, 8 miles west on Hwy 20 and 4 miles north on Hebgen Lake Rd. Both are operated by the USFS, with water, flush toilets and sites for $12.

Most other campgrounds are clustered on US 20 at the west end of town and charge around $18/32 for tent/RV sites.

The *Hideaway RV Campground* (☎ 406-646-9049), 2 blocks west of Canyon St at the corner of Gibbon Ave and Electric St, is one of the smaller, quieter options. *Rustic Campground & Cabins* (☎ 406-646-7387, 624 US 20), at the corner of Gibbon Ave, has four RV sites for every tent and five cabins with two bunk beds (cabins cost $45 per night). The *Madison Arm Resort & Marina* (☎ 406-646-9328), 3 miles north of town and 5 miles west of US 191/US 287, would be a nice destination even if it wasn't so close to Yellowstone. The campground is well-suited to tenters, and there's a marina with swimming beach and boat rentals. Lack of shade is the main drawback.

The *Yellowstone Park KOA* (☎ 406-646-7606), 6 miles west of town on US 20, is a huge facility with a pool, hot tub, game room and nightly barbecue. The passing traffic on US 20 can be annoying.

Hostels The *Historic Madison Motel* (see below) has hostel rooms on its 2nd floor, each with three beds and a sink; beds cost $20 per person. There is no curfew and no kitchen.

Motels & Hotels Built in 1909 as Murray's Yellowstone Hotel, the *Historic Madison Motel* (☎ 406-646-7745, 800-838-7745, 139 Yellowstone Ave) has rooms for $35 to $42 with private bath, $30 without. In back, the Madison's modern motel rooms run $53 to $79.

The *Three Bear Lodge* (☎ 406-646-7353, 800-646-7353, 217 Yellowstone Ave) is decked out in pine logs from the lobby to the hot-tub room and motel corridors. Rooms start at $80. The nearby *Midtown Motel* on Dunraven Ave is owned by the Three Bear Lodge and shares its pool and hot tub. Rooms are $58 to $78.

A real gem, the ***Sleepy Hollow Lodge*** (☎ 406-646-7707, 124 Electric St) has small log cabins with kitchens for around $70. A bit cheaper but not as charming are rooms at the ***Westwood Lodge Motel*** (☎ 406-646-7713, 238 Madison Ave).

A longtime hub of West Yellowstone activity, the ***Stage Coach Inn*** (☎ 406-646-7381, 800-842-2882, 209 Madison Ave) has a comfortable reading area, hot tub and good restaurant. Rooms (some with refrigerators) start at $45 in the off-season, $80 in high-season.

The ***Days Inn*** (☎ 406-646-7656, 800-548-9551, 118 Electric St) here is pretty good, with an indoor pool, hot tub, sauna and free coffee and pastries. Rooms cost $70 to $100 year-round.

Similar are the ***Kelly Inn*** (☎ 406-646-4544, 800-259-4672) and ***Gray Wolf Inn & Suites*** (☎ 406-646-0000, 800-852-8602), next to each other on Canyon St across from Grizzly Park. Both have a pool, spa, free Continental breakfast and rooms in the $65 to $95 range. The new ***Hibernation Station*** (☎ 646-4200, 800-580-3557, 212 Gray Wolf Ave) has cozy cabins starting at $85.

Places to Eat

The ***Food Roundup Supermarket***, at the corner of Madison Ave and Dunraven St, is open daily from 7 am to 9 pm year-round.

The Book Peddler (106 Canyon St) has good coffee and pastries, plus a few lunch items, but seating is limited. A big ol' sandwich from ***Ernie's Bighorn Deli***, on Hwy 20 between Geyser and Hayden Sts, is sure to fill you for under $5.

There's a good local scene and great pizza at ***Wild West Pizzeria***, adjacent to Strozzi's Bar at 14 Madison Ave. The ***Wolf Pack Brewing Co*** (111 Canyon St), next to the IMAX theater, serves home-brewed beer, hearty appetizers and sandwiches for $5 to $8 in a smoke-free environment.

The ***Firehole Grill***, on US 20 at Firehole Ave, does great barbecue and is a lively place to be on weekend nights. For good Chinese food under $10 head to ***Chinatown***

on Madison Ave between Canyon and Dunraven Sts; ask for extra spice or no MSG if you desire.

GALLATIN VALLEY

US 191 hugs the Gallatin River from its headwaters in the northwest corner of Yellowstone National Park to where it meets the Madison and Jefferson Rivers and their master, the Missouri River, at Three Forks. Scenically sandwiched between the Madison and Gallatin Ranges, the route is peppered with enough trailheads to keep hikers and skiers busy for years.

Due to its narrow configuration, development in the valley itself is limited to occasional tourist services – guest ranches, lodges, outfitters – spread out every 10 miles or so. The exception is around the turn-off to **Big Sky**, the valley's foremost destination 36 miles south of Bozeman. As a world-class winter (and increasingly summer) resort, Big Sky attracts a full spectrum of seasonal workers and clientele that make it a tad more sophisticated (and expensive) than most other parts of Montana.

On a clear day you can see a distinct cluster of peaks (25 of which are over 10,000 feet) rising sharply out of the general profile of the Gallatin Range, west of US 191. These are the **Spanish Peaks**, the valley's premier hiking and backcountry ski destination and part of the Lee Metcalf Wilderness Complex.

Information & Orientation

The best place for trail maps of the area is Barrel Mountaineering (☎ 406-582-1335), with a Web site at www.barrelmtn.com, or the Gallatin National Forest Headquarters (☎ 406-522-2520), both in Bozeman. For information about Big Sky, contact Big Sky Chamber of Commerce (☎ 406-995-3000, 800-943-4111), on the Web at www.bigskychamber.com, or Big Sky Resort (☎ 800-548-4486).

Big Sky spreads from US 191 to the base of Lone Mountain in four parts – Gallatin Canyon, Westfork Meadows, Meadow Village and Mountain Village. Meadow Village and Westfork Meadows have the bulk of services;

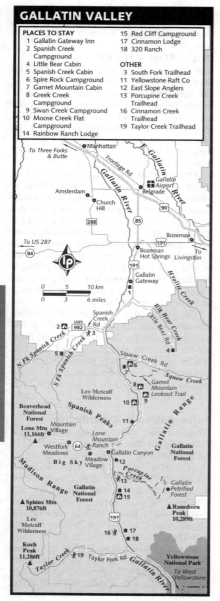

GALLATIN VALLEY

PLACES TO STAY
1 Gallatin Gateway Inn
2 Spanish Creek Campground
4 Little Bear Cabin
5 Spanish Creek Cabin
6 Spire Rock Campground
7 Garnet Mountain Cabin
8 Greek Creek Campground
9 Swan Creek Campground
10 Moose Creek Flat Campground
14 Rainbow Ranch Lodge
15 Red Cliff Campground
17 Cinnamon Lodge
18 320 Ranch

OTHER
3 South Fork Trailhead
11 Yellowstone Raft Co
12 East Slope Anglers
13 Porcupine Creek Trailhead
16 Cinnamon Creek Trailhead
19 Taylor Creek Trailhead

all are connected by a free shuttle service in summer and winter.

Hiking & Mountain Biking

Hiking trails – all open to mountain biking – head into the mountains along numerous creek drainages from both sides of US 191. Maps of the area are available through the Big Sky Chamber of Commerce or local sports stores. The trails in the southern half of the valley are part of Yellowstone National Park (marked by roadside signs), well maintained and marked with distance indicators – good for people who have no intention of buying a map.

A great destination on the eastern side of the valley is the Gallatin Petrified Forest. Access is actually easier from Tom Miner Basin on the eastern side of the mountains (off US 89), but the **Porcupine Creek Trail**, about 4 miles south of the Big Sky turnoff, makes a 22-mile loop to the forest; Portal Creek (4 miles from the trailhead) is a good day hike destination on this same trail. The 1½-mile climb to the top of the **Storm Castle Trail** offers great views; the last quarter mile, across loose scree, is especially strenuous and tricky. A favorite hike/post-hike combo is to hike up to the fire lookout at the top of the **Cinnamon Creek Trail**, then have lunch or dinner at the Cinnamon Lodge, near the trailhead on US 191.

A gondola shuttles people and bikes to the top of Big Sky's ski terrain at 10,000 feet, 9:30 am to 4:30 pm daily (June to October) for $12 ($20 for unlimited use); buy tickets at Big Sky Sports at the base of the mountain. Serious hikers can reach the peak of Lone Mountain (11,166 feet) from here.

Longer trails to the Spanish Peaks area start from the **Taylor Creek Trail**, 10 miles southwest of US 191 on the Taylor Fork Rd (around 56 miles south of Bozeman). Another popular access point is the USFS Spanish Creek Campground at the end of USFS Rd 982, about 22 miles south of Bozeman.

Skiing

Big Sky is comprised of Andesite Mountain (8800 feet) and Lone Mountain (11,166 feet), with a 4350-foot vertical drop and 3600 acres of skiable terrain, a 15-passenger tram, gondola, three high-speed detachable quads and 13 other lifts. The north side of Lone Mountain has some fantastic double-diamond chutes and bowls, accessible by the tram and limited to expert skiers only. Andesite Mountain caters more to intermediates, and beginners will find plenty of easy terrain off the Explorer lift (next to the main parking lot) and gondola.

Lifts operate 9 am to 4 pm. Tickets are $54/42 full-day/half-day; children under 10 ski free. Among the many rental shops around Big Sky, Mad Wolf Ski and Sport Shop (☎ 406-995-4369), 100 yards south of the Big Sky turnoff on US 191, tends to have the best prices. For snow conditions, call ☎ 406-995-2526.

Down near Westfork Village, spectacular Lone Mountain Ranch (☎ 406-995-4670, 800-514-4644) has 75km of groomed cross-country trails and a full-service lodge; day passes cost $15.

Fishing

There are fishing access sites at Greek Creek, Moose Creek Flat and Red Cliff campgrounds, but local anglers swear that anywhere you cast a line in the Gallatin is bound to be good.

East Slope Anglers (☎ 406-995-4369), 100 yards south of the Big Sky turnoff, has a store full of equipment for rent or sale and offers guided fly-fishing trips with instruction (if needed), as does Gallatin River-guides (☎ 406-995-2290), another mile south.

Other Activities

Geyser Whitewater Expeditions (☎ 406-995-4989), on US 191 at the Big Sky turnoff, has **white-water rafting** trips ($39/77 for a half/full day) and **kayak trips** ($59). Yellowstone Raft Company (☎ 406-995-4613), 7 miles north of the turnoff, has similar prices and services.

Horseback riding can be arranged through a number of outfitters, including Jake's Horses (☎ 406-995-4630), Diamond K Outfitters (☎ 406-587-0448) and Big Sky Stables (☎ 406-995-2972); cost is about $25

per hour, $65 for a half-day and $125 for a full day including lunch.

Places to Stay

Camping & Cabins Numerous USFS campgrounds snuggle up to the base of the Gallatin Range along US 191. Away from the road are *Spire Rock Campground*, 26 miles south of Bozeman, then 2 miles east on Squaw Creek Rd No 1321, and *Swan Creek Campground*, 32 miles south of Bozeman and a mile east on Rd No 481; at the turnoff for the latter is *Moose Creek Flat Campground* on the east side of the road. A mile north, *Greek Creek Campground* doubles as a fishing access site. The *Red Cliff Campground*, 48 miles south of Bozeman, has 68 sites, which means there's almost always space available. All of these have potable water, flush toilets and a fee around $10 per night.

Plan ahead and stay at one of the USFS cabins in the valley: *Little Bear Cabin*, 26 miles south of Bozeman off Little Bear Rd, is reached by a 10-mile hike; *Spanish Creek Cabin*, 7½ miles west of US 191 via Spanish Creek Rd, is a 3½-mile hike or ski from the trailhead; *Garnet Mountain Cabin*, an old fire lookout tower with fantastic views, is at the end of the popular 10-mile Garnet Mountain Lookout Trail. Most cabins are available year-round for $30 per night and are equipped with wood stoves, firewood, cooking supplies and blankets; contact Gallatin National Forest Headquarters (☎ 406-522-2520), in Bozeman, for information.

Lodges & Guest Ranches Most of the following are destinations in and of themselves; if you're pinching pennies (or dollars) stay in Bozeman or West Yellowstone.

At the valley's north end, 13 miles south of Bozeman, the *Gallatin Gateway Inn* (☎ 406-763-4672) was built by the Milwaukee Railroad in 1927 to act as the terminus for the Yellowstone line, and thus became a gateway to the park. Gourmet food and a beautifully appointed dining room attract both tourists and locals, mostly for 'special occasion' meals. Rooms start at $85. The bar has live music on weekends and is a favorite

MONTANA

watering hole for Bozeman's outdoorsy thirty-something crowd.

The ***Rainbow Ranch Lodge*** (☎ *406-995-4132*), 5 miles south of the Big Sky turnoff, has rooms ($140 to $250) with views of either the mountains or the river, five acres of Gallatin River frontage, an outdoor Jacuzzi and a great fireplace. Its restaurant is a favorite splurge for valley locals.

The ***Cinnamon Lodge*** (☎ *406-995-4253*), on the Gallatin River about 10 miles south of the Big Sky turnoff, gets everyone from seniors in RVs to families overloaded with sports equipment to groups of serious hunters and fly fishers. Accommodations include cabins with kitchens ($118), and a few basic motel rooms ($45). Its Western-feeling bar and cafe serves excellent Mexican food from 7 am to 9 pm. The ***320 Ranch*** (☎ *406-995-4283, 800-243-0320*), 12 miles south of Big Sky, has cozy log cabins starting at $89, a fishing shop, restaurant and saloon.

Inquire about condominium, cabin or house rentals in Big Sky through East West Resorts (☎ 877-845-9817), Golden Eagle Management (☎ 800-548-4488) or Big Sky Central Reservations (☎ 800-548-8846); ski packages are available throughout the winter season.

LIVINGSTON

In the late 1880s the Northern Pacific Railroad laid tracks across the Yellowstone River and began building Livingston (population 7626; elevation 4503 feet) as the primary jumping-off point for Yellowstone National Park. Since then, Livingston has grown as a departure point for rafting and fly-fishing trips on the Yellowstone River. Anyone even remotely interested in fly-fishing should stop in at the fly-fishing museum and make a pilgrimage to Dan Bailey's Fly Shop (see below).

Some of Bozeman's 'overflow' has brought upscale restaurants, antique shops and art galleries to Livingston's picturesque old buildings, but generally the town retains its rough-and-tumble, small-town feel. The saloons that Calamity Jane and Kitty O'Leary frequented remain relatively unchanged.

Orientation & Information

Livingston is at the north end of Paradise Valley, where I-90 meets US 89; the latter heads north to Great Falls (170 miles away) and south to Gardiner and Yellowstone National Park (53 miles away). Main St runs north to south and separates numbered streets (to the west) from lettered streets. Park St parallels the railroad tracks at the north end of town; Livingston's chamber of commerce (☎ 406-222-0850) is at 303 E Park St.

Things to See & Do

The **Federation of Fly Fishers Fly Fishing Museum** (☎ 406-222-9369), 215 E Lewis St, has beautiful displays of hand-tied flies, rod and reel prototypes and aquatic habitats; open 10 am to 6 pm Monday to Saturday and Sunday noon to four from Memorial Day to Labor Day, 10 am to 4 pm Monday to Friday the rest of the year, $3. On Tuesday evenings they give casting lessons free of charge.

Built on a legacy of Goofus Bugs, Humpy Flies, Trudes, Green Drakes and Hair Wing Rubber Legs (to name but a few), **Dan Bailey's Fly Shop** (☎ 406-222-1673, 800-356-4052), 209 W Park St, is known as one of the world's best. Fly-tying demonstrations occur regularly, and the shop arranges fly-fishing trips on the Yellowstone; prices start at $32 per hour for a basic clinic.

Across Park St is the original Northern Pacific Railroad Depot, built in 1902. It's now home to a railroad history and arts museum, called the **Depot Center** (☎ 406-222-2300); open from 9 am to 5 pm daily, May to October, $2. From June to August, the **Park County Museum**, 118 W Chinook St, displays local treasures in an old schoolhouse.

Places to Stay

There's a beautifully situated ***KOA*** (☎ *406-222-0992*) between US 89 and the East River Rd, 10 miles south of Livingston, charging $17 for tents, $25 for RVs; open May to October.

Two miles farther south, on East River Rd, ***Pine Creek Lodge & Cabins***

(☎ 406-222-3628), on East River Rd, has nice cabins for $60 and a cozy bar and restaurant (open from 7 am to 9 pm daily) with a big outside patio.

About 2 miles farther south on East River Rd, Lucckock Park Rd goes 3 miles east to the USFS *Pine Creek Campground*, which has $11 sites and pit toilets.

Central to Livingston's history, the *Murray Hotel* (☎ 406-222-1350, 201 W Park St) has rooms starting at $50. Also downtown, the *Guest House Motel* (☎ 406-222-1460, 800-222-1460, 105 W Park St) has a restaurant, lounge and rooms for $43/48 single/double. A half-mile north of downtown, the *Parkway Motel* (☎ 406-222-3840, 1124 W Park St) has double rooms for $42 in winter, $65 in summer.

The *Greystone Inn B&B* (☎ 406-222-8319, 122 S Yellowstone St) charges $65 to $95 for elegant rooms and a hearty breakfast. Four miles south of Livingston off Hwy 89, *The River Inn* (☎ 406-222-2429, riverinn@ wtp.net) lodges people in cabins or a sheepherder's wagon on the west bank of the Yellowstone for $95 to $125, including breakfast. The owners also guide hikes, mountain bike rides and canoe and fishing trips.

Places to Eat

There's a large *Albertson's* supermarket west of town; take Park St west towards the I-90/US 191 junction.

The cozy *Beartooth Bakery*, on Main St, makes wonderful cookies and brownies and has a full breakfast and lunch menu ($5 to $7). *Rumors*, at the corner of 2nd and Callender Sts, has a sophisticated flair to its ambiance and highly touted food; breakfast and lunch are under $10, dinners are $10 to $13.

The Sport (114 S Main St) has been running strong since 1909. It's a fun place to go for hot sandwiches ($6), steaks and Mexican food (around $10). For a first-rate wine list and reasonably priced fine dining, try Russell Chatham's *Livingston Bar and Grille* (☎ 406-222-7909, 130 N Main St), which has a back bar that came from San Francisco by wagon train around 1910 and got considerable use from Calamity Jane.

Getting There & Away

Greyhound (☎ 406-222-1460) leaves from 107 W Park St, next to the Guest House Motel; buses take I-90 to Billings, Butte, Helena and Missoula.

PARADISE VALLEY

With Livingston as a railroad stop, the Paradise Valley became the first travel corridor to Yellowstone National Park. Gardiner, 50 miles south of Livingston and just north of the Mammoth Hot Springs entrance to Yellowstone, is still one of the park's most popular entry points.

US 89 follows the Yellowstone River through this broad valley, flanked by the Gallatin Range to the west and the Absaroka Range to the east. The East River Rd offers a parallel alternative to US 89 and gets a bit less traffic, though it is narrower and rough in parts.

Chico Hot Springs

At the mouth of Emigrant Canyon, 22 miles south of Livingston and 30 miles from Yellowstone National Park, Chico Hot Springs (☎ 406-333-4933) was established in 1900 as a luxurious getaway for local cattle barons and a side trip for Yellowstone National Park visitors. The resort captured nearby hot springs in a large concrete pool and built an elegant lodge and stables around them. The place is unpretentiously elegant and has been restored with great attention to rustic detail, worth a visit just to poke around. A plunge in the large outdoor pool costs $5 for nonguests.

Accommodations come in a variety of sizes and prices (rooms in the main lodge with shared bath are $45, chalets that sleep up to 12 with a kitchen start at $149) but are very reasonable for what you get. Chico's 'activity center' offers horseback riding, raft trips down the Yellowstone and dogsled treks (in winter), and rents mountain bikes and cross-country skis.

The *Chico Inn Restaurant* is known throughout Montana and northern Wyoming; dinner will cost around $35 per person, including wine.

MONTANA

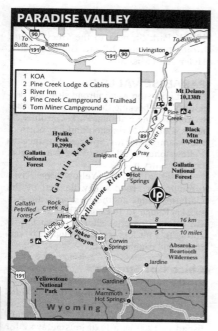

PARADISE VALLEY

1 KOA
2 Pine Creek Lodge & Cabins
3 River Inn
4 Pine Creek Campground & Trailhead
5 Tom Miner Campground

Tom Miner Basin

Tom Miner Rd heads west of US 89, 17 miles north of Gardiner and 35 miles south of Livingston, into one of the prettiest pockets of land in the area. Following Tom Miner Creek up towards its origin in a high basin of the Absarokas, the washboard road ends 12 miles west of the highway at USFS *Tom Miner Campground*, which has potable water, toilets and $7 sites. There are several trails that start at the campground, including a 3-mile loop through the **Gallatin Petrified Forest**, where remnants of wood and fossils between 35 million and 55 million years old stand upright among the Absaroka's volcanic rocks. Some of the logs are remains of trees buried where they grew, but most are deposits of a great mud flow activated when volcanoes erupted in the area about 50 million years ago.

South of the Tom Miner turnoff, US 89 winds through Yankee Jim Canyon, a narrow gorge cut through folded bands of extremely old rock (mostly gneiss) that look like marble cake. The Yankee Jim river access and picnic point is a good place to watch people float the river.

GARDINER

A quintessential gateway town founded and fed on tourism, Gardiner (population 120; elevation 5134 feet) is the only entrance to Yellowstone National Park open to automobile traffic year-round. Park St is the dividing line between Park County and Yellowstone National Park, and Mammoth Hot Springs is 5 miles south. The only real points of interest here, aside from the abundant food and lodging, are the Roosevelt Arch, dedicated by Teddy Roosevelt himself in 1903, and Kellem's Montana Saddlery, at the corner of 2nd and Main Sts, which produces beautiful custom-made saddles. The town is friendly though, and makes a good base from which to explore the northern reaches of the park.

Orientation

Gardiner is 53 miles south of Livingston via US 89, which is known as Scott St where it parallels the Yellowstone River and 2nd St where it turns south to cross the river. Note that most locals still simply say 'highway 89,' as street names are a recent phenomenon in town.

The Yellowstone River, which flows east to west through town, divides Gardiner into two distinct sections: the older grid to the south, bordering the national park, and the newer strip along Scott St, where most tourist services now operate. A short distance east of the bridge is the confluence of the Yellowstone and Gardiner Rivers.

Information

The chamber of commerce (☎ 406-848-7971) is at the corner of Main and 3rd Sts. There's an unattended information kiosk at the corner of 3rd and Park Sts.

The USFS Gallatin National Forest's Gardiner District Office (☎ 406-848-7375) is on Scott St, just west of Yellowstone St and north of the river. First National Park Bank on Scott St has an ATM. The post

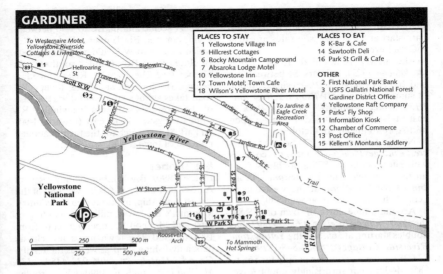

GARDINER

To Westernaire Motel,
Yellowstone Riverside
Cottages & Livingston

PLACES TO STAY
1 Yellowstone Village Inn
5 Hillcrest Cottages
6 Rocky Mountain Campground
7 Absaroka Lodge Motel
10 Yellowstone Inn
17 Town Motel; Town Cafe
18 Wilson's Yellowstone River Motel

PLACES TO EAT
8 K-Bar & Cafe
14 Sawtooth Deli
16 Park St Grill & Cafe

OTHER
2 First National Park Bank
3 USFS Gallatin National Forest
    Gardiner District Office
4 Yellowstone Raft Company
9 Parks' Fly Shop
11 Information Kiosk
12 Chamber of Commerce
13 Post Office
15 Kellem's Montana Saddlery

Yellowstone National Park

To Jardine & Eagle Creek Recreation Area

To Mammoth Hot Springs

office is on Main St between 2nd and 3rd Sts; postal code 59030. The nearest medical facility is the Mammoth Clinic (☎ 307-344-7965) at Mammoth Hot Springs in Yellowstone National Park, open 8:30 am to noon and 2 to 5 pm.

Activities
On the Yellowstone River, **river rafting** trips often run through Yankee Jim Canyon, one of Montana's more famous white-water spots. The Yellowstone Raft Company (☎ 406-848-7777), at 406 Scott St, runs half-day trips for $45, full-day for $90 including lunch. They also have **kayaking** lessons on the river for $65. Headwaters Angler (☎ 406-848-7110), in the Yellowstone Outpost mall near the west end of Scott St, does similar floats.

Several outfitters run **fishing** trips and **horseback riding** into Yellowstone and other nearby mountain areas, including Wilderness Connection (☎ 406-848-7287), Hell's A-Roarin' Outfitters (☎ 406-848-7578) and North Yellowstone Outfitters (☎ 406-848-7651). Rides start at around $12 per hour, $55 per half day and $95 per full day. Parks' Fly Shop (☎ 406-848-7314), on

2nd St between Stone and Main Sts, publishes an angler's map of Yellowstone National Park and surrounding areas, including the Gallatin and Missouri Rivers to the west. Prices are around $115 per person (including lunch and equipment), less with three or more people.

Places to Stay
Accommodations are abundant, but summer prices are often double what they are the rest of the year. Reservations are advisable because of Gardiner's proximity to Yellowstone National Park.

The woodsy USFS *Eagle Creek Recreation Area*, 2 miles northeast of Gardiner on Jardine Rd, has water and pit toilets but no hookups. Sites are $7 per vehicle.

Friendly *Rocky Mountain Campground* (☎ 406-848-7251), overlooking the river from Jardine Rd, has a store and excellent panoramas of Yellowstone but very little shade. Tent sites cost $18, sites with water and electricity cost $22 and those with full hookups are $24. A two-person tent cabin is available for $22; another four-person cabin costs $36.

The *Yellowstone Inn* (☎ 406-848-7000), at the corner of Main and 2nd Sts, is a pic-

MONTANA

turesque Victorian where rooms with shared bath cost $60 and rooms with private bath start at $98; off-season rates are 10% to 20% lower.

The newly remodeled *Town Motel* (☎ *406-848-7322*), on Park St between 1st and 2nd Sts, charges $52/60 a single/double in summer. Rates at *Wilson's Yellowstone River Motel* (☎ *406-848-7303*), on Park St east of 1st St, start at $55 a double; open mid-April to the end of October.

North of the river at 200 Scott St, *Hillcrest Cottages* (☎ *406-848-7353*) has cottages with kitchenettes for $75 a double, $95 for up to six people. The *Yellowstone Village Inn* (☎ *800-228-8158*), at the west end of Scott St, has doubles for around $80.

Around a mile north of town on US 89, the *Westernaire Motel* (☎ *406-848-7397*) has doubles starting at $65, and the *Yellowstone Riverside Cottages* (☎ *406-848-7719, 877-774-2836*) sleep two to six people for $65 to $85. Modern but surprisingly unobtrusive, the *Absaroka Lodge* (☎ *406-848-7414, 800-755-7414*) overlooks the river just north of the Yellowstone Bridge. All rooms have good views of the north entrance of Yellowstone National Park; they start at $90 and go to $115.

Places to Eat

Locals like the *Park St Grill & Cafe*, at the corner of Park and 2nd Sts, for its pasta and seafood ($9 to $14). The *Town Cafe*, next to the Town Motel on Park St, is a good family-style spot with breakfast, lunch and dinner year-round; their upstairs dining room (open in summer for dinner) has an excellent view into the park. Also open year-round is the *K-Bar & Cafe*, at the corner of 2nd and Main Sts, with pizza and daily lunch specials.

In summer, try the *Sawtooth Deli* (*220 W Park St*), which serves hot and cold subs and a nice selection of salads.

BIG TIMBER AREA

East of Livingston, I-90 leaves the mountains and enters the open ranges and prairies of eastern Montana. But south of the highway are some beautiful and accessible

parts of the Absaroka-Beartooth Wilderness Area. A scenic alternative to I-90 between Livingston and Big Timber is Swingley Rd, which turns into W Boulder Rd and meets Boulder River Rd 16 miles south of Big Timber (see The Boulder River Corridor, below). The journey, along a well-kept dirt road, takes about an hour and skirts the base of the Absarokas. To reach Swingley Rd from Livingston, head east (towards I-90) on Park St and watch for the turnoff about a mile out of town.

Big Timber

In the 1890s Big Timber (called 'Rivers Across' by Lewis and Clark) was one of the largest wool-shipping centers in the country. Montana's first wool mill, still standing at First and McLeod Sts, operated here from 1901 to 1930. The town has a few classic bars, a fly-fishing shop, as well as the terrific *Grand Hotel* (☎ *406-932-4459, 139 McCloud St*), built in 1890, where rooms cost $60 to $110 including breakfast. The *Big Timber KOA* (☎ *406-932-6569*), 6 miles west of town on I-90, has tent sites for $19, RV spaces for $25.

The Boulder River Corridor

The Boulder River flows from the upper reaches of the Absarokas to where it meets the Yellowstone River at Big Timber. To reach it, take McCleod St (Big Timber's main drag that runs south from I-90) south until it becomes Boulder River Rd. The pavement ends about 20 miles south of town, though the dirt road is generally well maintained.

There are numerous hiking trails along the river's tributaries, including the **Big Creek Trail** and the **Great Falls Creek Trail**, which make good day hikes or can be combined with other trails for multiple-day loops. The **Natural Bridge and Falls** viewing point and loop trail, about 25 miles south of Big Timber, is a worthwhile destination and good side trip when traveling along I-90. Stop at the Big Timber Ranger District Office (☎ *406-932-5155*), next to Frosty Freeze on the east side of I-90, for maps and information.

The Crazy Mountains

North of I-90, the Crazy Mountains are one of Montana's undiscovered gems. Accessible by only a few roads and having only one developed campground, the area is relatively unused, even by locals. The **Big Creek Trail** is the highlight of the area, starting off along a series of gentle cascades then passing through spectacular scenery up to Twin Lakes, set amongst dramatic cirques. From the lakes you can continue up to Conical Pass and make a nontechnical climb up to 10,737-foot Conical Peak. On the south side of the pass, Crazy Peak rises to 11,178 feet.

The trail starts at the east side of the *Half Moon Campground*, which has water, pit toilets and $7 sites. To get to the campground, drive 11 miles north of Big Timber on US 191 and turn west at the sign reading Big Timber Canyon; 3 miles west is another signed turnoff from where a bumpy country road winds 12 miles past a gated ranch and then continues 3 miles before it dead-ends at the campground.

The gated ranch through which you must pass to reach the campground is the *Lazy K Bar Ranch* (☎ 406-537-4404), a working cattle ranch (and childhood home to cowboy poet Spike Van Cleve) that welcomes guests each summer. The $1100 per-person, per-week price tag includes a horse, planned rides, hikes, campfires, three meals a day and a chance to pitch in with ranch chores.

Web site: www.mcn.net/~kirby/lazykbar.htm

Greycliff Prairie Dog Town

Seven miles east of Big Timber off of I-90, Greycliff Prairie Dog Town is an entertaining diversion. The little critters, part of the ground squirrel family and unique to North America, peek their heads out of the ground, look around, give a few 'yeep yeep' warnings to their friends and retreat back down into the earth. As soon as one comes into focus, it disappears and another one pops up somewhere else. Prairie dogs are some of the only vegetarians in Montana: they feed off grasses, roots and bulbs. In their highly organized social system, each

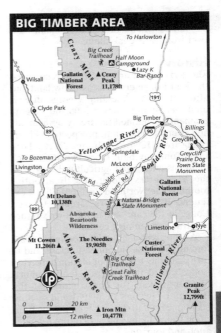

BIG TIMBER AREA

'town' consists of neighborhoods that house one or two adult males and two to four adult females. Their young are born in early spring and can be seen by mid-May. The crater-shaped mounds are back doors, dome-shaped ones are front doors. Almost as fun as watching the animals themselves is watching people watch the animals.

RED LODGE

A quaint old mining town with fun bars and more restaurants per capita than any other community in Montana, Red Lodge (population 2278; elevation 5555 feet) has long been the departure point for the Beartooth Hwy (the scenic 'high road' to Yellowstone National Park). It's really a destination in its own right, however, with a wealth of great hiking (see Around Red Lodge, below) and decent skiing nearby, plus a fun bunch of shops downtown. Despite the many newcomers to the area, the majority of Red Lodge's residents would never go hiking on

MONTANA

a rodeo day, and still refer to neighborhoods as Finn Town and Little Italy – names left over from early coal-mining days.

History
The 1851 Fort Laramie Treaty recognized the Red Lodge environs as Crow land, but after James 'Yankee Jim' George discovered coal outcroppings in 1866, the US government abandoned the treaty agreements and opened the area to prospecting. Flourishing from 1896 to 1910, the Rocky Fork Coal Company built fancy two-story brick buildings and began agricultural forays on the rich grass along the Beartooth's foothills. The Northern Pacific Railroad extended its Rocky Fork Branch to Red Lodge in 1889 and sealed the town's future as a trade and mining center.

A depression hit Red Lodge in 1924, forcing the West Side mine to close, and in turn half the town's population left. Red Lodge's hard times were relatively short-lived, however, for construction of the Beartooth Hwy began in 1931 and secured economic revitalization, beginning the transition from mining and agriculture to recreation and tourism.

Orientation
On the west bank of Rock Creek, Red Lodge is 60 miles south of Billings and 80 miles northeast of Cooke City (and the north entrance to Yellowstone National Park). US 212 runs north-south through town as Broadway Ave, the main street, and becomes the Beartooth Hwy south of town. With the exception of Red Lodge Mountain, 6 miles southwest of town, all of Red Lodge's attractions, accommodations and restaurants are within walking distance of each other.

Information
The Red Lodge Chamber of Commerce (☎ 406-446-1718), 601 N Broadway Ave, has accommodations information, while the Beartooth Ranger Station (☎ 406-446-2103), 3 miles south of Red Lodge on US 212, is the best resource for maps and information on the Absaroka-Beartooth Wilderness Area, Beartooth Mountains and Beartooth Hwy;

Early Red Lodge
Calling Red Lodge's history 'rough' is a considerable understatement. So many new buildings went up that there was no wood left to build sidewalks; people waded through streets of knee-deep mud as they passed between two dozen bars and a row of brothels known as 'the Castles.' Ambivalent laws failed at keeping peace and justice among the diversity of immigrant and US-born miners: Little Italy, Finn Town and Highburg (where rich mining executives lived) each had its own set of culturally designated rules. In the absence of a common language to solve misunderstandings, guns and fists became the major tools of communication.

John 'liver-eating' Johnson was an old frontiersman who was the only man in town tough and large enough to enforce law and order without words, and thus was appointed the first town constable in 1881.

There are plenty of stories of how he got his nickname: Some say he killed a man and ate pieces of the man's liver; others contend that during a fight with some Sioux, Johnson ripped open a calf and ate its liver. Still others claim he killed, scalped and ate the livers of Crow Indians as revenge for killing his wife, and others say he merely threatened to eat the liver of any Indian that came too close. Whatever the story, he was made all the more notorious by the Robert Redford movie *Jeremiah Johnson*.

closed from noon to 1 pm on weekends. There's a large topo map posted out front.

You'll find the bank, hardware store (which sells maps and fishing licenses) and bookstores along Broadway. The post office is on W 13th St at the corner of S Hauser Ave. The Carbon County Memorial Hospital (☎ 406-446-2345), 600 W 20th St, has a 24-hour emergency facility.

Things to See & Do
Set aside a few hours for browsing the shops and galleries along Broadway Ave,

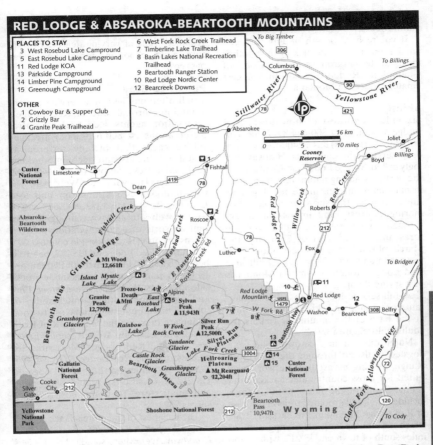

RED LODGE & ABSAROKA-BEARTOOTH MOUNTAINS

PLACES TO STAY
3 West Rosebud Lake Campround
5 East Rosebud Lake Campground
11 Red Lodge KOA
13 Parkside Campground
14 Limber Pine Campground
15 Greenough Campground

OTHER
1 Cowboy Bar & Supper Club
2 Grizzly Bar
4 Granite Peak Trailhead

6 West Fork Rock Creek Trailhead
7 Timberline Lake Trailhead
8 Basin Lakes National Recreation Trailhead
9 Beartooth Ranger Station
10 Red Lodge Nordic Center
12 Bearcreek Downs

making sure to stop in at **Red Lodge Ales**, 11 N Broadway Ave, for a tasting and brewery 'tour' (it's a small operation). Other artisan shops include Sylvan Peak, 9 S Broadway Ave, which makes outdoor clothing, and Magpie Toymakers, 115 N Broadway Ave.

The **Carbon County Museum** (☎ 406-446-3667), 224 N Broadway, has a terrific antique gun collection but is better known for its coverage of local rodeo lore. Alice Greenough, the first woman named to the Cowgirl Hall of Fame and one of the few women honored in the Cowboy Hall of Fame, started the

museum as a tribute to her father Ben 'Pack-Saddle' Greenough, who, among other things, won the first professional bronco-busting contest in the state and chopped wood for Calamity Jane. Part of the gallery displays costumes used at the Festival of Nations, held the second week in August, which celebrates Red Lodge's multi-cultural past with food, drink, dancing and traditional contests. Open daily from 10 am to 6 pm Memorial Day to Labor Day, $3.

The old railroad depot on Eighth St, 1 block west of Broadway Ave, is now the **Carbon County Arts Guild Gallery** where

MONTANA

local artists display their weavings, pottery, paintings, etc.

If you're here on 4th of July weekend and have an interest in bucking bulls, follow locals to the fairgrounds for the Home of Champions Rodeo, one of the biggest amateur rodeos in Montana.

Skiing

Six miles southwest of downtown, Red Lodge Mountain (☎ 800-444-8977, 406-446-2610 for ski reports) has a 2400-foot vertical drop serviced by eight lifts. Halfway jokingly called 'Sludge Lodge' or 'Crud Lodge,' the northeast-facing mountain gets most of its midwinter sunshine in the morning, so by the afternoon the snow resembles stale meringue, crusty and impossible to get through. By contrast, the higher temperatures and longer days of February and March, plus a higher base elevation (7400 feet) than any other Montana ski hill, give Red Lodge Mountain some of Montana's best spring skiing.

A full-service lodge with a bar, restaurant, rental shop and ski-school program is at the base of the mountain. Tickets for adults/children are $35/17.

Numerous hiking, snowmobile and dogsled trails cut through the Beartooth Range, making a vast trail network well suited for cross-country and backcountry skiing. Some of the more popular trails include: 6 miles of groomed trails at the base of Red Lodge Mountain; the Parkside Trail, which starts at the Parkside Campground 11 miles south of town on US 212, with 3- and 6-mile loops and access to the Absaroka-Beartooth Wilderness Area; the Basin Lakes National Recreation Trail, which has 3-, 5- and 7-mile loops, 5 miles southwest of town, up West Fork Rd; and the Palisades Trail, which traverses 2 miles between Red Lodge Mountain and Palisades Campground and offers consistently good wildlife viewing in the Willow Creek Valley. For more suggestions, see Around Red Lodge (below).

The Red Lodge Nordic Center (☎ 406-425-1070), 2 miles west of Red Lodge on Hwy 78, is Red Lodge's top cross-country resource and a good place for beginning skiers or those who want to ski on well-maintained tracks. The center has 6 miles of groomed trails of varying degrees of difficulty, a ski school and rental shop; a day pass costs $8.

Places to Stay

You'll often pay less by reserving accommodations through one of Red Lodge's reservation agents. Red Lodge Central Reservations (☎ 800-673-3563) arranges ski packages that include airfare, car rental, lift tickets and accommodations. Red Lodge Reservations (☎ 406-446-3942, 877-733-5634), with a Web site at www.redlodgereservations.com, and Red Lodging (☎ 406-446-1272, 800-673-3563), with a Web site at www.redlodging.com, rent all sorts of accommodations – from cabins to cottages to slopeside condos.

South of Red Lodge on US 212, before it begins to ascend the Beartooth Plateau, are 10 USFS campgrounds. With shady creekside locations, the nicest are *Limber Pine* and *Greenough*, both 10 miles south of town. A bit more remote and close to good hiking are those on the West Fork of Rock Creek and East and West Rosebud Lakes (see Around Red Lodge). Most sites are creekside at the *Red Lodge KOA* (☎ 406-446-2364), 4 miles north of Red Lodge on US 212, which also has a pool, playground and small store. Tent sites cost $20, RV spaces $32.

The cheapest of the motels is the family-owned *Eagle's Nest* (☎ 406-446-2312, 702 S Broadway Ave), where standard rooms cost $38/42 for a single/double, and 'pre-remodel' rooms (not much different from the others) are a bargain at $26.

The *Red Lodge Inn* (☎ 406-446-2030, 811 S Broadway Ave) has frilly rooms for $46/52. The *Yodeler Motel* (☎ 406-446-1435, 601 S Broadway Ave), at the corner of 17th St, charges $45/55 for subterranean rooms. Upper-level rooms with balconies and in-room Jacuzzis cost $68. Best Western's *Lu Pine Inn* (☎ 406-446-1321), a block west of Broadway Ave at the corner of 18th St and S Hauser St, has a pool and Jacuzzi and rooms starting at $65.

A fun and elegant place to stay is the old *Pollard Hotel* (☎ 406-446-0001, 2 N Broadway Ave), Red Lodge's first brick building. Its cozy lobby and restaurant are hubs of local activity and there's a nice health club with racquetball courts. Prices start at $90. The most upscale of Red Lodge's accommodations is the *Rock Creek Resort* (☎ 406-446-1111), 4½ miles south of town off US 212. Rooms start at $95 and condos are available for around $200.

Places to Eat

Self-caterers have the choice of *IGA Supermarket*, 2 blocks west of Broadway at the north end of town, and *Genesis Natural Food Store* on 13th St, 1 block west of Broadway Ave. A favorite pastime of locals is driving up to the Grizzly Bar (in Roscoe) for lunch or dinner.

The unexciting beige exterior makes *PD McKinneys*, on the corner of 15th St and Broadway Ave, look more like an old postal building than Red Lodge's favorite breakfast spot; closes at 2 pm. Get an hour of internet access with any purchase at *Red Lodge Coffee Roasters* (6½ S Broadway Ave), which has a smorgasbord of caffeinated goodies and fine pastries.

Bogart's Restaurant (11 S Broadway Ave) is popular for margaritas and Mexican food, while *Red Lodge Pizza Co* (115 S Broadway) makes excellent pies and calzones for way under market value. *Greenlee's*, at the Pollard Hotel (see Places to Stay, above), has won national acclaim for its wine list, fresh fish and creative pasta dishes ($9 to $14).

Entertainment

Many a moonlighting ski instructor fortifies Red Lodge's boisterous bar scene. A young, outdoorsy crowd congregates for drinking and dancing (to live bands on weekends) at the *Snowcreek Saloon* (124 S Broadway Ave), while the *Snag Bar* (107 S Broadway Ave) entertains a leather-faced crowd wearing cowboy hats and boots. *Natali's Front Bar*, next to the Red Lodge Pizza Co, has local beers on tap, a dartboard and big screen TV.

Getting Around

The Red Lodge Shuttle (☎ 406-446-2257) charges $46 per person, $70 per couple (less per person for larger groups) between Red Lodge and Billings.

During the winter a free ski shuttle connects accommodations in town to Red Lodge Mountain, daily from 9 am to around 4 pm; contact the mountain or any motel for information.

AROUND RED LODGE

Hwy 78 turns southwest off I-90 at Columbus and briefly follows the Stillwater River before turning south and then east to meet US 212 in Red Lodge. Besides being the best route between Red Lodge and the Bozeman area, the highway leads through some scenic one-bar towns and gives access to the Absaroka-Beartooth Wilderness Area.

Absarokee

Primarily a wilderness gateway, Absarokee (pronounced 'apsorkee') is the put-in point for raft trips on the Stillwater River. Depending on the snowmelt, most trips run from early June to mid-July. Beartooth Whitewater (☎ 406-446-3142) runs half-day/full-day trips for $30/60.

Paintbrush Adventure Trails (☎ 406-328-4158) offers one-hour ($15), half-day ($45), and all-day ($100) trail rides, plus overnight pack trips starting at $400.

Fishtail

Four miles southwest of Hwy 78 on Nye Rd, Fishtail is home of the *Cowboy Bar and Supper Club* (☎ 406-328-4288). The bar's trademark 'Chickenshit Game' is a pretty hilarious sight, whether you're sober or not. Two chickens share a large cage with a numbered grid painted on the bottom. People pick numbers (which correspond to grid numbers) out of a hat, and whichever numbers the chickens grace with their droppings are the lucky winners. Watching the crowd encourage defecation is about as good as it gets. The games start at 1 pm on Sunday (post-church entertainment?) and last until the chickens are pooped-out.

Bearcreek Downs

Imagine pigs with names like Oscar Mayer, Hot Links and Jimmy Dean wearing little numbered jackets and racing around a mud track to a food-laden finish line. Then imagine a crowd of full-grown adults, some of them sober, screaming and cursing over the $3 they won or lost on their porker. Surreal as it sounds, the scene portrays a normal weekend night at the Bearcreek Downs, directly behind the Bearcreek Saloon (☎ 406-446-3481), 7 miles southeast of Red Lodge. In a stroke of Montana genius, bar owners Pit and Lynn DeArmond ditched traditional mariachi band entertainment and began the 'Swine Sweepstakes' as a sideline attraction to their homemade margaritas and Mexican food. The food and drink is as good as ever but definitely takes a back seat to the pig track, which has attracted journalists and television crews from 'Good Morning America' and Japan's Fuji TV.

In 1984, the state declared the races illegal and refused to issue a license that would allow pari-mutuel betting to continue. To remedy the problem, Bearcreek adopted a 'spots pool' method and contributes half of each pool to a local scholarship fund. Races begin at 7 pm on Saturdays and Sundays Memorial Day to Labor Day.

Roscoe

Halfway between Absarokee and Red Lodge at a bend in Hwy 78, Roscoe (population 22) has a statewide reputation as home of the *Grizzly Bar* (☎ 406-328-6789). Not quite as rough and tumble as its name implies (although there is a giant stuffed grizzly above the entrance), the bar is a favorite with anglers, backpackers and hunters who make the bar their first re-entry destination upon leaving the backcountry, as well as locals and tourists. Basically its reputation rests on fantastic food, strong cocktails and an outdoor beer garden that is extremely lively in the summer months.

East Rosebud Lake

A drainage basin for several high lakes and East Rosebud Creek, this lake sits at the northern butt of the East Rosebud Plateau (a small extension of the Beartooth Plateau), with Sylvan Peak (to the southeast) and Mt Hole-in-the-Wall (southwest) visible on either side. On its northern shore, at the end of East Rosebud Creek Rd 14 miles south of Hwy 78 from Roscoe, is a small USFS campground with fire rings and pit toilets. From the campground trails, head south along the east side of the lake and East Rosebud Creek, into the heart of the wilderness area, and east to Sylvan and Crow lakes and eventually to the West Fork of Rock Creek near Red Lodge. Rainbow Lake, about 4 miles south along the **East Rosebud Creek Trail,** is a good day hike destination.

West Rosebud Lake

Created by the Mystic Lake hydroelectric dam, West Rosebud Lake is a favorite among anglers and day-hikers. The lake is the westernmost of a three-lake chain connected by a 7-mile hiking trail that begins from the parking lot on the lake's north shore. On the south side of West Rosebud Creek is a large campground with fire rings and pit toilets. The lake is 17 miles south of Fishtail at the end of West Rosebud Creek Rd. People with two vehicles can hike from East to West Rosebud Lake (17 miles), across the northern foothills of Mt Hole-in-the-Wall and Froze-to-Death Mountain; this route gives access to a nontechnical route up Granite Peak (12,799 feet), Montana's highest.

West Fork Rock Creek

A mile south of Red Lodge, just north of the Ranger Station, West Fork Rd turns southwest off US 212. The road passes the turnoff to Red Lodge Mountain and several USFS campgrounds along Rock Creek and continues 12 miles to the West Fork Rock Creek trailhead at road's end. The West Fork trail follows the creek 4 miles to Quinnebaugh Meadows, a popular day hike picnic spot, good for wildflower viewing in early July. From here you can take a steep 1-mile trail up to Lake Mary (where unmarked trails continue over to Sylvan, Crow and East Rosebud Lakes), or continue along the main trail to Sundance Lake and Sundance Pass, a good multiple-day option which takes you into some very rugged country and has the potential for a loop trip.

Another good day hike is up the Timberline Lake Trail, which starts on the south side of West Fork Rd, 2 miles before road's end. This trail climbs 4½ miles along Timberline Creek to Gertrude and Timberline lakes, both good for trout fishing.

West Fork Rd is only plowed to the Red Lodge Mountain turnoff in winter, making it a good backcountry ski route. The terrain is gentle and part of the road passes through deer and elk winter range.

Hellroaring Lakes

On a spur ridge of the Beartooth Plateau, the Hellroaring Lakes area is good for viewing rugged glacial features. A USFS road climbs from the Parkside Campground (well marked off US 212) to a trailhead on the Absaroka-Beartooth Wilderness boundary at 9840 feet. From here, a trail climbs southwest across rock slopes to Sliderock Lake, at the foot of Mt Rearguard. The fish-laden Hellroaring Lakes are half a mile north via an unmarked trail. The access road requires a high-clearance vehicle year-round. In winter it's popular with serious backcountry skiers.

BEARTOOTH HIGHWAY

The Beartooth Hwy (US 212) connects Red Lodge to Cooke City and Yellowstone's north entrance by an incredible 68-mile road that was built in 1932 for $2.5 million. An engineering feat, and the 'most beautiful drive in America' according to the late TV journalist Charles Kuralt, this road is a destination as well as a travel corridor.

From its northern starting point at Red Lodge, the highway climbs Rock Creek Canyon's glaciated walls via a series of gnarled switchbacks, crosses the Wyoming border with a fanfare of billboards and reaches the plateau's twin summits (and the only public toilets along the route) at

an elevation of 10,350 feet. Alpine tundra vegetation is the only thing that grows up here (where snow can last from October to mid-July), giving the landscape a desolate, otherworldly look. In fact, unless you are an outdoorsy type who makes frequent forays above 10,000 feet, it probably *is* another world – you can't usually reach this kind of terrain by car. There are turquoise blue tarns (glacial lakes), mini glaciers and jagged ridgelines visible on all sides of the highway, but to really experience the surroundings you must get out of the car, even if it's just for a few minutes to breathe the thin, cold air. The birdlike chirps of marmots signal their ubiquity in this terrain.

The grade is gradual from Cooke City to the summit and accessible lakes and trailheads are frequent. A detailed, turn-by-turn Beartooth Hwy map that highlights several hiking trails is available at the Beartooth Ranger District (☎ 406-446-2103), 3 miles south of Red Lodge, before the highway begins to climb.

Hiking & Backpacking

You can gain about 3000 feet of elevation by car and begin your hike from the Beartooth Hwy, but it's very important to allow a day or two to acclimatize. Also be aware that the barren terrain offers little shade, shelter or wood. With proper preparation, however, it's a stunning place to explore. Backpackers should inquire at the ranger station in Red Lodge about the three- to four-day **Spogen Lake Loop**, which traverses classic Beartooth Plateau scenery – glacial lakes, peaks and knife-edged ridges. An easy day hike is the 3-mile ramble to **Rock Island Lake**, which begins from a trailhead marker on USFS Rd 306 and meets the Beartooth Hwy about 2 miles east of Cooke City. An excellent book to have is *Hiking the Beartooths,* available at the grocery store and bookstores in Red Lodge.

Cooke City

Set between two forested ridges of the Beartooths, this one-street town (population 85 in winter, 350 in summer) on the northern edge of Yellowstone National Park gets a steady flow of summer visitors passing through en route to Red Lodge and the park. In winter, the road from Yellowstone is only plowed as far as Cooke City, so visitors – mostly backcountry skiers and snowmobilers – tend to check in and stay awhile. There's not much here in the way of shops, sights or even trailheads, but the town's got a backwoods feel and a year-round population that's as rugged as the surrounding peaks.

The tiny Cooke City Bike Shack (☎ 406-838-2412) is a good stop for anyone who wants to hike, bike or ski in the immediate area. They have a good inventory of equipment (from skis to freeze-dried food) and maps, and the owner is a longtime local who is tremendously helpful with trail suggestions. The historic Cooke City Mercantile is a fun browse and has some interesting history on the walls. They also have a good supply of groceries, beer and wine.

If it's not too far out, the ***Yellowstone Yurt Hostel*** (☎ *406-586-4659, 800-364-6242*) offers 'yurt-style' accommodations in a big round tent with hot showers and cooking facilities for $14 a person. The hostel is 3 blocks north of the main street from the west end of town (it's well marked from the road). On Main St you'll find rooms for $40 to $65 at the ***High Country Motel*** (☎ *406-838-2272*), ***Alpine Motel*** (☎ *406-838-2262*) and ***Elkhorn Lodge*** (☎ *406-838-2332*).

Montana Plains

In short, Eastern Montana, from the Rocky Mountains to the North Dakota border, is much more 'Midwest' than 'Rocky Mountains.' The big sky abounds, but it generally stretches from one flat horizon to another, only occasionally punctuated by mountains and big, sluggish rivers. Strip farms sprawl across the northern prairies along US2, interrupted every hundred miles or so by water towers, grain elevators and their accompanying towns. Around Billings, cattle ranches and oil deposits occupy the wealthy if aesthetically barren landscape north of the Crow and Northern Cheyenne Indian Reservations. Lewis and Clark traveled

along the Missouri River in 1805 and had to portage around the Great Falls of the Missouri, now a major stopping point for anyone retracing Lewis and Clark's itinerary. The isolated mountain ranges near Lewistown and breathtaking badlands in Makoshika State Park, on the North Dakota border, are the region's most compelling recreation destinations, both of them relatively 'undiscovered.'

Choosing a travel route through this area should be easy as there are only two. US 2 traverses Montana's northern tier along the Hi-Line, well serviced by small agricultural communities every 40 miles or so; Hwy 200 cuts across the very middle of the state, remote territory where Lewistown stands lonely watch. Indecisive types can bridge the two via US 191, roughly midway between Great Falls – the region's largest city – and the North Dakota border.

GREAT FALLS
Straddling the Missouri River, Great Falls (population 56,340; elevation 3334 feet) remains the agricultural and commercial center that it was meant to be when entrepreneur Paris Gibson laid the plans for the city in 1885. Home to large grain companies such as Purina and General Mills, major hydroelectric plants run by Montana Power Co, and Maelstrom Airforce Base, which has long-term NASA and defense contracts, the town is unquestionably the hub of Montana's northern plains. Though decidedly drab (and terribly cold in winter), it's a good stopping point between Glacier and Yellowstone National Parks, if only for its selection of cheap accommodations and food that lie near I-15 and Hwy 200.

Anyone interested in Lewis and Clark's journey should plan on spending a day along the River's Edge Trail, which skirts the southern flank of the Missouri. Here the Corps of Discovery was forced to portage 18 miles around the five waterfalls that make the river unnavigable by boat, a journey that took more than a month and had its fair share of high drama. Charlie Russell fans should also plan to spend an afternoon in Great Falls, where the artist

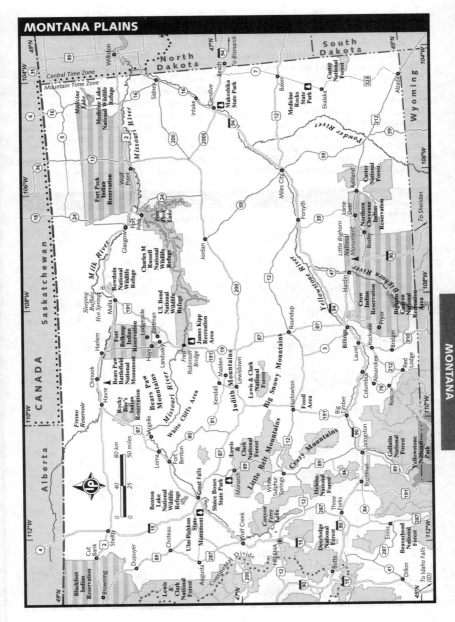

spent the last 24 years of his life. During the Lewis and Clark Festival on the last weekend in June, the city swells with people who come for historical plays, dugout canoe races, nature walks and reenactments of Lewis and Clark's portage.

History

The Blackfeet and Gros Ventre Indians had the Great Falls area to themselves until 1743, when French-Canadian trappers discovered the rich supply of beaver along the Missouri River. After the 1805–06 Lewis and Clark expedition, explorer Jim Bridger passed through on a solo trip up the Missouri River, followed 10 years later by a flood of trappers and traders who did business with the Blackfeet. Smallpox and the US government finally overcame the Blackfeet who, in 1855, reluctantly signed a treaty ceding their homeland to settlers. Blackfeet resentment erupted in several attacks on new settlements. The government responded by building Fort Shaw on the Sun River and, in 1879, Fort Assiniboine on the Milk River.

Paris Gibson came to the area in 1883, having made a fortune on the East Coast

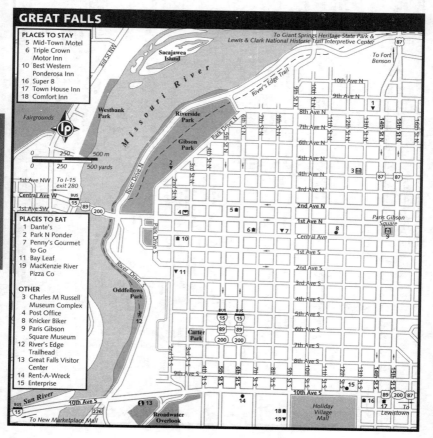

GREAT FALLS

PLACES TO STAY
5 Mid-Town Motel
6 Triple Crown Motor Inn
10 Best Western Ponderosa Inn
16 Super 8
17 Town House Inn
18 Comfort Inn

PLACES TO EAT
1 Dante's
2 Park N Ponder
7 Penny's Gourmet to Go
11 Bay Leaf
19 MacKenzie River Pizza Co

OTHER
3 Charles M Russell Museum Complex
4 Post Office
8 Knicker Biker
9 Paris Gibson Square Museum
12 River's Edge Trailhead
13 Great Falls Visitor Center
14 Rent-A-Wreck
15 Enterprise

producing woolen blankets. He bought thousands of acres of prairie land, contacted his friend James J Hill, owner of the Great Northern Railroad, and incorporated a town which became, by 1887, a major railroad hub (Gibson later became a US senator). As railroads replaced river transport, Great Falls replaced Fort Benton as the link that joined the mining communities of the gold country to the rest of the nation. A meat-packing plant, a copper reduction plant, silver smelters and hydroelectric dams further boosted Great Falls' importance.

Orientation

The Missouri River wraps around the west and north sides of downtown Great Falls, separating it from newer development across the river. Tenth Ave S is the major thoroughfare and commercial strip connecting to highways outside of town. Central Ave runs through the heart of downtown, between the river and 10th Ave S.

Information

Get help reserving accommodations and a good view of the city from the Great Falls Visitors Center (☎ 406-771-0885), well signed off I-15 and 10th Ave S (look for the large US flag), open daily from 9 am to 6 pm. The Chamber of Commerce Web site, www.greatfallschamber.org/visitor.htm, has useful links to accommodations, museums and city government offices.

You'll find ATMs downtown and in the commercial centers on 10th Ave S. The main post office (☎ 406-761-4894) is at the corner of 3rd St and 1st Ave N; postal code 59401.

The New Marketplace Mall, west of the bridge off I-15 exit 0, has a Barnes & Noble and other giant stores. For free Internet access, go to the public library, 301 2nd Ave N, open 10 am to 6 pm, until 8 pm Tuesday to Thursday, from 1 to 5 pm Sunday.

Benefits Health Care (☎ 406-761-1200), 1101 26th St S, has a 24-hour emergency room.

Things To See & Do

The best place to start an exploration of Lewis and Clark history is at the **Lewis and**

Charles M Russell

Born in 1864 to an upper-crust, Yale-educated St Louis family, young Charles whiled away his classroom hours drawing scenes inspired by the exploits of his great-uncle, William Bent, who founded Bent's Fort, CO. Convinced that a trip would cure his boyish daydreams, Russell's parents sent him west for his 16th birthday. Hardly disappointed, Charles took to the cowboy life and spent the next 10 years on the open range learning every aspect of cowpunching, from curing saddle sores to blowing paychecks on whiskey.

During that time, he spent a winter in Canada with the Blood Indians – a time that greatly influenced his painting. He came to know their language and culture, and emerged disillusioned about what the government had done to the Indians and buffalo. Besides being a painter, Russell was also a humorist and storyteller. Historians debate whether his poor grammar and misspelled words were intentional – to perpetuate his 'old cowboy' image – but, contrived or not, they were effective.

Clark National Historic Trail Interpretive Center (☎ 406-761-4434), 6 miles north of downtown via River Dr. It's one of the most balanced and complete interpretations of this chapter in United States history, with interactive exhibits, lectures and film explaining the parallel and interwoven histories of Native Americans and the Corps of Discovery; open Memorial Day to September 30th from 9 am to 6 pm, from 9 am to 5 pm Tuesday to Saturday the rest of the year, $5.

From here, walk along the **River's Edge Trail** – which begins at Oddfellows Park (downtown at 3rd Ave S and River Dr) – to **Giant Springs Heritage State Park,** where one of the world's largest freshwater springs pumps out 134,000 gallons of water per minute. The 201-foot stretch between the springs and the Missouri River is dubbed

MONTANA

the Roe River, the shortest river in the world. Walk to the park and pay 50¢, or drive (via River Dr) and pay $3. A visitors center (☎ 406-454-5840), a quarter mile north of the springs on the River's Edge Trail, has books, natural history exhibits and a great three-dimensional map of the Missouri River.

If you're at all inclined to physical activity, pick up the free 'A Guide to the River's Edge Trail' from the visitors center, rent a bike from Knicker Biker (☎ 406-454-2912), 1123 Central Ave, and ride to these sights from downtown. The trail passes Black Eagle and Rainbow Falls and continues north to the 'Great Falls of the Missouri' at Ryan Dam.

Downtown, at 400 13th St N, the **Charles M Russell Museum Complex** (☎ 406-727-8787) holds Montana's largest collection of the acclaimed artist's work and personal memorabilia. Visitors may be more acquainted with Charles Russell's paintings than they realize - his images of Native Americans, buffalo and the prairies can be seen on everything from coffee cups and greeting cards to the State Capitol in Helena; open Sunday from 1 to 5 pm year-round, Monday to Saturday from 9 am to 6 pm May to October, and Tuesday to Saturday from 10 am to 5 pm the rest of the year, $5.

Five blocks away at 1400 1st Ave N, the **Paris Gibson Square Museum** (☎ 406-727-8255) has contemporary exhibits, historic memorabilia and an excellent gift shop; open Tuesday to Friday from 10 am to 5 pm, weekends from noon to 5 pm from Memorial Day to Labor Day, $2.

Places to Stay

Accommodations downtown are handy for people who enjoy exploring on foot, while 10th Ave S motels (most of them chain-owned) offer proximity to highways and shopping malls.

For urban camping year-round, head to the *Great Falls KOA* (☎ 406-727-3191), on the eastern end of 10th Ave S at 1500 S 51st St, where grassy tent sites cost $24 and RV spaces are $35.

Cheapest along 10th Ave S is the Highwood *Village Motel* (☎ 406-452-8505, 800-253-8505, 4009 10th Ave S), which charges $25/30 a single/double. Others along 10th Ave S, with rooms starting at $34/37, include the *Rendezvous Suites Inn* (☎ 406-452-9525), 10th Ave S and Fox Farm Rd; the *Sahara Motel* (☎ 406-761-6150, 800-772-1330, 3466 10th Ave S); and the *Wagon Wheel Kanga Inn* (☎ 406-761-1300, 2620 10th Ave S), which is kid-friendly and has a swimming pool. Chain-owned motels on this strip – *Comfort Inn* (☎ 406-454-2727), *Town House Inn* (☎ 406-761-4600, 800-442-4667) and *Super 8* (☎ 406-727-7600) – charge around $50/60.

Downtown alternatives are the *Mid-Town Motel* (☎ 406-453-2411, 800-457-2411), at the corner of 6th St and 2nd Ave N, which shares lobby space with Perkins restaurant and has $55/60 rooms; *Triple*

Big Bellies or Waterfalls?

The name 'Gros Ventre,' French for 'Big Belly,' has nothing to do with physical appearance. It's not known exactly how the name came into use, but one version of the story has it that French trappers encountered members of the tribe along the Missouri River and tried to find out what lay ahead on their journey upriver. Familiar with the waterfalls near present-day Great Falls, the Indians made the hand signal for waterfall – palms toward them and raised eye-level, then brought down to their chests and, just above the belly, outwards in a circular motion. The trappers didn't know what to make of this, but ever afterwards called the tribe Gros Ventre.

The Gros Ventre have their roots in a branch of the Arapahoe, who came to Montana in the early 19th century and lived along the north bank of the Missouri River until the Cree drove them across to the south bank in 1872. The Assiniboine tribe originated in the Dakotas as a mountain-dwelling branch of the Sioux.

Crown Motor Inn (☎ *406-727-8300, 621 Central Ave*), with $35/40 rooms; and the *Best Western Ponderosa Inn* (☎ *406-761-3410, 220 Central Ave*), with rooms for $55/70.

Places to Eat

For breakfast and lunch, try one of the restaurants along Central Ave between 2nd St N, or go to *Bay Leaf (202 2nd Ave S)*, which serves elephantine pastries and sandwiches on homemade bread ($3 to $6). Watch the ducks and eat a full breakfast, soup or a burger for around $5 at the *Park N Ponder*, in Gibson Park at the end of 4th Ave N and 2nd St N. *Penny's Gourmet to Go (815 Central Ave)* has excellent salads, hot lunch specials and many vegetarian options (closed Sunday).

Locals are unanimous that *Eddie's Supper Club (3725 2nd Ave N)* serves the best steak in town ($9 to $14); open 5 to 11 pm. The best non-meat-intensive meal you'll find may be at *MacKenzie River Pizza Co*, next to the Comfort Inn at 1220 9th St, which has a wide variety of pizzas and copious salads. The adjoining bar has regional microbrews on tap and broadcasts sporting events. *Dante's* (☎ *406-453-9599, 1325 8th Ave N*) is *the* hip new fine dining spot, with a reputation for wonderful seafood, pastas and desserts; expect to spend $20 per person.

Getting There & Away

Great Falls International Airport (☎ 406-727-3404), 3 miles southwest of downtown on I-15, is serviced by Big Sky Airlines, Northwest, Delta and Horizon Air, which routes many of its flights through Missoula. A taxi (☎ 406-453-3241) from the airport will cost around $7 to 10th Ave S, $9 to downtown.

Near the airport baggage claim is Great Falls' bus terminal (☎ 406-454-1541), from where Greyhound and Rimrock buses service Helena ($11) and Butte ($18) twice daily, Missoula ($25) and Billings ($34) once a day, as well as Seattle ($91/59 standard/advance purchase), Chicago ($132/79), New York City ($152/89) and Salt Lake City ($72/59).

Getting Around

Car rental agencies at the airport include Hertz (☎ 406-761-6641), Avis (☎ 406-761-7610) and National (☎ 406-453-4386). Less expensive are Rent-a-Wreck (☎ 406-761-0722), 617 10th Ave S, Enterprise (☎ 406-761-1600), 1201 10th Ave S, and Allstar/Practical Rent a Car (☎ 406-727-1711), which offer pick-up service.

AROUND GREAT FALLS
Ulm Pishkun State Monument

About 12 miles south of Great Falls on I-15 and then west from the Ulm exit on a gravel road, steep cliffs rise above the golden prairie grass. Before they had horses to give them enough speed to hunt buffalo at close range, Assiniboine and Gros Ventre hunters used cliffs or *pishkun* to kill large numbers of buffalo. Hunters made a V-shaped formation behind the herd and drove it toward the steep cliffs; animals that did not die from the fall were immediately dispatched by tribesmen waiting at the bottom. Panels at the top of the cliffs describe the process in detail and map out a trail to follow around the site. There's an adjacent picnic area with an expansive view but no shade, and pit toilets.

Benton Lake National Wildlife Refuge

About 12 miles north of Great Falls, 5000 acres of Missouri River marshlands constitute the Benton Lake National Wildlife Refuge. Spring and fall migration periods are the most exciting times to visit, as tundra swans and snow geese pass en route to and from Canada. Other times of year you'll see a variety of waterfowl, especially in early morning and late afternoon. **Prairie Marsh Dr** makes a 9-mile loop through the refuge and is lined with site markers that correspond to an informative brochure available at the NWR headquarters (☎ 406-727-7400) at the refuge's entrance. To reach the refuge, take US 87 north to Bootlegger Trail (well signed), which jogs to the left of the highway and leads to the entrance. The refuge is open year-round, daily from dawn to dusk; the headquarters

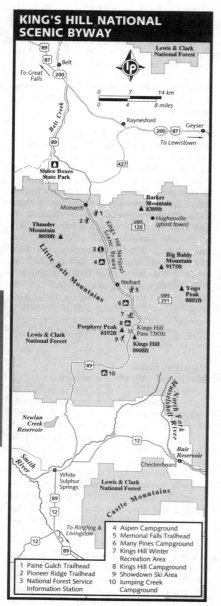

KING'S HILL NATIONAL SCENIC BYWAY

1 Paine Gulch Trailhead
2 Pioneer Ridge Trailhead
3 National Forest Service Information Station
4 Aspen Campground
5 Memorial Falls Trailhead
6 Many Pines Campground
7 Kings Hill Winter Recreation Area
8 Kings Hill Campground
9 Showdown Ski Area
10 Jumping Creek Campground

are open Monday to Friday from 7:30 am to 4:30 pm.

KING'S HILL NATIONAL SCENIC BYWAY

Between Great Falls and Livingston, US 89 follows a beautiful route through the Little Belt Mountains and over King's Hill Pass, Montana's highest at 7393 feet. The 71-mile stretch north of White Sulphur Springs is designated the King's Hill National Scenic Byway.

About 12 miles south of where US 89 turns south from US 87, **Sluice Boxes State Park** extends along an old rail line through a canyon bottom where Don Bosco, a Catholic missionary and philosopher, spent several years. From the parking lot (well signed off US 89) a trail runs along Belt Creek to his cabin and continues (another mile) to where the creek becomes a deep, narrow channel that flows through dramatically steep limestone walls, or 'sluice boxes.' The trail can be brushy after the first half mile, and wading may be necessary to reach Don Bosco's cabin and the sluice boxes, but the trip is well worth it. As a 'primitive' state park, there's no fee and no running water, just a pit toilet.

South of Sluices Boxes, US 89 ascends into the Little Belts, where the old mining camp of **Monarch** is now home to the ***Cub's Den*** (☎ 406-236-5922), a motel/lodge that serves as the area's most popular watering hole and only motel; rooms are $45.

Stop by the National Forest Service Information Station, south of Monarch, for maps and information on the numerous **hiking** and **mountain biking** trails in the area. Two recommended day hikes are the **Paine Gulch Trail**, which starts across from National Forest Service Rd 737, and the more rugged **Pioneer Ridge Trail**, 2 miles south off Rd 734.

Approaching **Neihart** from either direction you are greeted by huge old wooden mine shafts and gouged-out mountain sides, testimony to the town's once booming silver industry. The dilapidated old houses and sheds along the highway support one small grocery store and (of course) a bar. One-and-a-half miles south is a well-marked half-mile trail to **Memorial Falls**, a double waterfall in a narrow limestone canyon. Foot traffic gets heavy in summer, but it's still a nice little jaunt.

Snowmobile and cross-country ski trails radiate from the **Kings Hill Winter Recreation Area**, 14 miles south of Neihart, while downhill runs are at the adjacent **Showdown Ski Area** (☎ 406-236-5522). The lodge at Showdown has the area's only facilities – a sport shop, restaurant and equipment rental (closed in summer).

The natural 115°F hot springs that surface in **White Sulphur Springs** were used by the Crow and Gros Ventre, and later by weary stagecoach passengers, for medicinal purposes. They're now 'owned' by the *Spa Hot Springs Motel* (☎ 406-547-3366, 202 W Main St), which charges $4 for use of the pool and grounds and $1 for swimsuit and towel rental; rooms start at $45. The town's bars and graceful old homes – mostly from the 1880s – are worth a look, as is the **Meagher County Historical Museum** (☎ 406-547-2324), housed in an 1892 granite building called 'the castle,' 2 blocks north of Main St (turn up the hill at the Mint bar).

Campgrounds along US 89 include four USFS (Aspen, Many Pines, Kings Hill and Jumping Creek) with potable water and $7 to $11 sites, and *Rocking J Cabins & Campground* (☎ 406-236-5535), in Monarch, with $14 campsites and creekside cabins for $50.

MISSOURI RIVER

From Great Falls the Missouri River flows north and east through vast agricultural expanses to where it meets the Yellowstone River near the North Dakota border. Called 'Old Muddy' because of its coffee-with-cream color and languorous pace, the Missouri is generally more interesting for its history than its white-water opportunities. The river was the navigation artery for Lewis and Clark, fur traders and, starting in 1831, steamboats that brought people and supplies to Fort Benton, where overland travel to the West began.

In 1976 the 149-mile stretch of river between Fort Benton and the Fred Robinson

Bridge was designated a National Wild and Scenic River, thus preserved for ecological and historical reasons in its natural free-flowing state. Because its banks are so steep and high, the river is hard to explore at any length unless you embark on a multiple-day float trip (see below). There are, however, a few good river access roads that cross US 87, which runs between Great Falls and Havre.

Fort Benton & Around

As the terminus of steamboat travel, this sleepy riverside town (population 1581) was the jumping-off point for just about all homesteaders, prospectors and traders headed west. In the mid-1800s Front St was home to 150 saloons and deemed the 'roughest block in the West.' Nowadays it's a pleasant place to spend a few hours, along the riverfront walk or among the historical artifacts in its two noteworthy regional museums. The newly restored *Grand Union Hotel* (☎ 406-622-1882, 800-838-1882), on Front St, is an elegant place to stay ($78) or have a meal ($15).

North 12 miles is **Loma**, where you can cross the Missouri on the Loma Bridge (turn east at the Red Rose Inn, just before the Loma Bridge fishing access point). From the north side of the bridge improved gravel roads wind for about 22 miles through farm and ranch land to the Virgelle Ferry crossing. Here you press a sound signal and wait for the ferry guard to motor across on a large, cable-controlled platform to pick you up and take you across to the small homestead town of Virgelle; ferry service ends when the river starts to freeze, usually in November. You can also get to Virgelle from US 87 (the turnoff is well signed, 25 miles north of Fort Benton).

The **Virgelle Mercantile** (☎ 406-378-3110, 800-426-2926) was built in 1885 as a river outpost and homestead supplier, and is now run by two creative fellows who restore and sell antiques and operate the Missouri River Canoe Company (see below). Restored cabins and beautifully decorated rooms are available starting at $80, including breakfast.

Floating the Missouri

Travelers who have the time and money should consider a float trip along the Missouri River, through what's known as the 'Missouri River Breaks,' to see the steep white cliffs, caves, pillars and funky rock formations of shale and sandstone that are only accessible by boat. The BLM Upper Missouri Wild and Scenic Visitors Center (☎ 406-622-5185), closed October to May, in Fort Benton has all the information necessary for experienced floaters to plan their own trip and a list of outfitters offering guided trips. The BLM maintains a useful Web site, www.mt.blm.gov/ldo/missflt.html, and publishes the *Upper Missouri National Wild and Scenic River Floater's Guide,* a four-map set ($8) available at the visitors center or through the mail.

There are no permits or reservations required to float the river, but the BLM has registration boxes at the major launches, including Fort Benton, Loma and the James Kipp Recreation Area. Designated campsites are marked on the Floater's Guide, but primitive camping is allowed anywhere (except the islands) on federal land on a first-come, first-served basis.

The very reputable Missouri River Canoe Company (☎ 406-378-3110, 800-426-2926) offers fully guided four- to seven-day trips, including meals, accommodations and shuttles to and from Great Falls or Havre for about $300 per person, per day. They also have canoe rentals ($45) and van shuttles for do-it-yourselfers. Check out their Web site, www.canoemontana.com, and make reservations early in the season. Adventure Bound Canoe (☎ 877-538-4890), on Front St in Fort Benton, offers similar services and also rents out camping equipment.

THE HI-LINE

Paralleling the Great Northern Railroad's tracks and the Missouri River, US 2 crosses Montana's northern tier along a transportation corridor traditionally known as the 'Hi-Line.' Travelers accustomed to western Montana's dramatic mountains, forests and rivers are likely to find this portion of the state dry, desolate and even boring. Green for just two short months during spring, parched brown from June to October and white with snowdrifts the rest of the year, it consists of vast expanses of farm, ranch and reservation land mirrored in the boundless sky overhead.

The few towns that do exist along the Hi-Line are trade and service centers for surrounding agricultural communities, county seats and highway crossroads. These towns may not offer obvious tourist attractions (often they have little more than a gas station, cafe and grain elevator), but they embody a spirit and way of life which has all but vanished from more cosmopolitan areas.

Havre

Largest of the towns along the Hi-Line and the seat of Hill County, Havre (population 10,425; elevation 2494 feet) is a good stopping point, if only for its cheap accommodations and movie theater. The Bears Paw Mountains to the south offer a nice diversion for car-weary travelers who need some fresh air, though the Holiday Village Shopping Mall is a more popular playground among locals. Havre's location between the Milk River, which provides irrigation for wheat and hay fields, and the rich grazing lands of the Bears Paw foothills has created a stable and unique economic environment in which many people are both ranchers and farmers. Great Northern officials named the town after the French port Le Havre, but citizens have always pronounced it 'hav-er.'

Orientation & Information Sites and services are concentrated along Havre's 4-mile strip of US 2, which is called 1st St within the city limits. US 87 goes southwest to Great Falls 153 miles away, and Route 232 goes north 38 miles to the Canadian port of Wild Horse.

The chamber of commerce (☎ 406-265-4383), 518 1st St, or the Heritage Center (see below) provide maps and information about the area. The post office and banks with ATMs are on 3rd Ave.

Montana Immigrants & a Hill of Dreams

Following Montana's 1880s gold strikes, railroad companies began vying for land rights, knowing they stood to make a fortune carrying passengers to and from the gold fields. James J Hill, a Canadian who owned a route between St Paul, Minnesota, and Winnipeg, Canada, had dreams of building a northern railroad to the Pacific coast in order to compete with the powerful Union Pacific Railroad Company.

Initially, Hill faced a problem the UP had never encountered: Much of his Great Northern route passed through reservation land. President Grover Cleveland had qualms about infringing any more on Native American lands but, facing economic and political pressure, he legislated a 75-foot right of way – and the use of all adjacent stone and timber for construction purposes – to Hill's Great Northern Railroad in 1887.

Over the following six years, as the railroad crept west towards Everett, WA, Hill did everything he could to ensure that the railcars would be full. In a monumental campaign, he financed immigrant passage from Europe, offered free transportation west, and assaulted the Midwest and the East with Montana products and propaganda. Whether his tales of Montana's rich soil and mild climate were hopeful conjectures or just plain old lies is debatable, but in any case they worked. By 1910, new settlers – many of them Slavic and Scandinavian – had filed claims on five million Montana acres.

Between 1910 and 1917, the weather was unusually mild, farms flourished, wheat prices were high and James J Hill was a national hero. Bustling towns, named after unlikely European cities, sprang up in a matter of weeks. By 1925 however, Montana's climate was back to its old self and even harsher than average. Drought, wind and grasshoppers swept Montana's northern tier, forcing the foreclosure of 20,000 farms, and settlers who had once praised the name of James J Hill now cursed it, even as they rode his trains away from the scene of their ruin. Those who stuck it out, however, learned from their mistakes. Rust- and drought-resistant wheat and strip-farming – in which alternating strips of crops and fallow land conserve moisture and protect against wind – were the main inventions born of the experience and are still in use today. In fact, Montana is the most strip-farmed state in the country.

Things to See & Do There's no need to make Havre a destination, but its old downtown and surrounding sights provide good excuses to get out of the car and stretch your legs.

The **Heritage Center** (☎ 406-265-4000), 306 3rd Ave, is tourist central. Its Earl H Clack Museum and Gallery focuses on Fort Assiniboine, a 'peace-keeping unit' 6 miles southwest of Havre. In summer, daily tours ($5) leave the center to visit the fort's weathered remains.

Behind the Holiday Village Shopping Mall, on US 2, is the **Wahkpa Chu'qn Archaeological Site** (☎ 406-265-6417), a pishkun used to kill buffalo about 200 years ago. Visit the active excavation of the site on a guided tour ($5), hourly from 10 am to 5 pm Tuesday to Sunday and at 7 pm Tuesday to Saturday. Tours leave from a booth just inside the mall's south entrance.

One of Montana's more unusual tours is **Havre Beneath the Streets** (☎ 406-265-8888), 120 3rd Ave: a one-hour trip below ground, past Havre's old saloons, brothels and opium dens. In July and August tours ($6) leave hourly from 9 am to 5 pm, and at 7 pm Tuesday to Saturday; times are limited the rest of the year.

South of Havre, the **Bears Paw Mountains** – a scattering of dark buttes between 4000 and 5000 feet high – are used for religious ceremonies and vision quests by descendants of the Cree, Chippewa and Metis (a half-Chippewa, half-French tribe) that live on the Rocky Boy's Reservation. These

Indians came to Montana, led by Stone Child (called Rocky Boy), in the 1880s after a futile rebellion against the Canadian government. The only public access to the mountains is at the Bears Paw Ski Bowl, about 25 miles south of Havre, a beginner hill with one chairlift and an 875-foot vertical drop – as exciting to hike as it is to ski.

Places to Stay & Eat Chain motels and restaurants line US 2 west of downtown. Havre's most prominent lodging and dining facility is the *Duck Inn* (☎ *406-265-9615, 1300 1st St)*, on the eastern edge of town, which charges $55/58 for single/double rooms. The complex has three restaurants, a lounge and casino, and manages the Conoco gas station and general store across the highway.

The *Havre Budget Inn* (☎ *406-265-8625, 115 9th Ave)*, south of 1st St, has rooms for $37/42. The *Park Hotel* (☎ *406-265-7891, 335 1st St)* sits atop a decent cafe and has $36/42 rooms. Havre's deluxe (in the most relative sense) accommodations are at the *El Toro Inn* (☎ *406-265-5414, 800-422-5414, 521 1st St)*, which charges $43/50.

Getting There & Away Havre is on Amtrak's Empire Builder line which runs from Seattle to Chicago. One train in each direction stops daily in Havre – eastbound at 1:32 pm and westbound at 3:43 pm. The station is at 235 Main St, at the north end of 3rd St.

Bears Paw Battlefield

Part of the Nez Perce National Historical Park, the Bears Paw Battlefield (also called Chief Joseph Battlefield) marks the tragic end of the Nez Percé 1800-mile flight toward freedom (see 'The Battle of the Little Bighorn'). Believing US soldiers to be several days behind them, the Nez Percé stopped in this grassy coulee to rest for a day before their final push towards freedom in Canada, 40 miles away. The rub was that General Miles of Fort Keogh had learned of their location and decided to head them off in the Bears Paw Mountains. Without warning, US troops descended on

the camp and inflicted tremendous damage before the tribe had time to resist. Four days later, on October 5, 1877, after the fierce battle which claimed the lives of chiefs Sitting Bull and Looking Glass, Chief Joseph surrendered to General Nelson A Miles with these famous words:

It is cold and we have no blankets. The little children are freezing to death. My people, some of them, have run away to the hills, and have no blankets, no food; no one knows where they are – perhaps freezing to death. I want to have time to look for my children and see how many I can find. Maybe I shall find them among the dead.

Hear me, my chiefs. I am tired; my heart is sick and sad.

From where the sun now stands, I will fight no more forever.

The site has changed little since then, except for the addition of interpretive panels marking significant points on the battlefield, two pit toilets and a parking lot.

The park office (☎ 406-357-3130) is 16 miles north of the site, in Chinook at the corner of US 2 and Indiana St. Nine miles south of the Bears Paw Battlefield, the *Cleveland Bar* is a rough-edged watering hole (a favorite among hunters in the fall) with legendary burgers and baked beans.

Chinook

'Chinook' is the Indian name for the warm winds that blow off the eastern Rocky Mountain slopes, similar to France's mistral or Switzerland's foehn. By melting the snow and allowing cattle to access the rich bunchgrass pasture, these winds have been the saving grace of many a Hi-Line ranch. The town of Chinook is little more than a service center, good for resting and refueling en route to Bears Paw Battlefield. The **Blaine County Museum**, 501 Indiana St, has a good multimedia presentation on the Battle of the Bears Paw. Accommodations at both the *Chinook Motor Inn* (☎ *406-357-2548, 100 Indiana St)* and *Bear Paw Court* (☎ *406-357-2221)* on US 2 at the east edge of town, are quiet and clean; rooms are $35 to $45.

Fort Belknap Indian Reservation

Named after US Secretary of War William Belknap, the 1000-sq-mile Fort Belknap Reservation is home to the Assiniboine and Gros Ventre tribes. Once bitter enemies, the two tribes joined in alliance against the Canadian Bloods, with whom they eventually made peace in 1887.

Tribal Headquarters and a tourism office are at the Fort Belknap Agency (☎ 406-353-2205), 8 miles south of Harlem on Hwy 66. South of Harlem by 30 miles, Hays is home to **St Paul's Mission**, established in 1887 by Jesuit priests, and its shrine to the Virgin Mary, erected in 1931 by a German immigrant; its centerpiece is a replica of a holy statue in Einseldn, Switzerland. From the mission a road leads 1 mile south into **Mission Canyon**, a rock gorge cut into the Little Rocky Mountains by fast-flowing Little Peoples Creek.

Little Rocky Mountains

Accessible from Hwy 66, the arduous route between US 2 and US 191, the Little Rocky Mountains are a hotbed of mining activity. Gold strikes in 1884 brought the first rush of prospectors to the Little Rocky Mountains, but these early miners were 'get rich quick' types who extracted placer gold for a few months and then left. In the 1970s, the Pegasus Mining Company (originally on the scene as the Zortman Mining Company) revitalized the area's mines, pumping tons of toxic chemicals into the surrounding environment to extract gold and various semiprecious metals. After numerous legal battles with local Native Americans and environmental agencies, the mining activity is coming to a halt.

The only real reason to explore the area is its odd landscape of terraced pit mines and abandoned miners' sheds. **Zortman** has the most activity, centered in the *Kalamity Kafe* (☎ 406-673-3883) and the *Buckhorn Store & Cabins* (☎ 406-673-3162), which charges $10 for a tent site, $41 for a cabin with bathroom and kitchen. Once the livelier of the two towns, **Landusky** has a remote campground with fire rings and tables (no toilets), but otherwise has no businesses or houses, and usually no people.

Bowdoin National Wildlife Refuge

The 15-mile loop road that encircles Lake Bowdoin, centerpiece of this wildlife refuge, provides excellent opportunities to see pelicans, double-crested cormorants and great blue herons. Pick up a free driving tour map at the NWR Headquarters (☎ 406-654-2863), near the refuge's entrance, southeast off US 2, half a mile east of Malta.

Malta bears absolutely no resemblance to its Mediterranean namesake and gives no hint of its glory days as center of a cattle empire that stretched from Havre to Glasgow and from the Missouri River to the Canadian border. It does offer good lodging, though: The *Edgewater Inn & Campground* (☎ 406-654-1302, 101 W Hwy 2) charges $43/55 for single/double rooms and $12/21 for tent/RV sites, including a dunk in their indoor pool and spa (nonguests pay $2); the *Sportsman Motel* (☎ 406-654-2300, 231 N 1st St E) has $42/47 rooms; and the *Great Northern Hotel* (☎ 406-654-2100, 2 S 1st St E) has a lounge, steakhouse, coffee shop and rooms starting at $49.

Glasgow

Glasgow's Pioneer Museum (marked by an F-101 fighter plane on US 2) has some terrific photos of the construction of Fort Peck Dam, worth a stop if you're headed towards the dam. The buildings along 2nd Ave are decorated with colorful Art Deco tile while those along 1st Ave are home to some historic but still lively drinking establishments (notably the Montana Bar). Otherwise, there's not much to this agricultural town that owes its existence to the railroad line that arrived back in 1893.

People like to stay at the *Cottonwood Inn* (☎ 406-228-8213, 800-321-8213), on US 2, for its swimming pool, restaurant and lounge; rooms start at $52/63. The old *Roosevelt Hotel* (☎ 406-228-4341, 412 3rd Ave), between 4th and 5th Sts, is a bit of a relic but the cheapest sleep around with $35 rooms.

MONTANA

Fort Peck Dam & Reservoir

Established as a trading fort in 1863, the original Fort Peck now lies submerged beneath the waters of Montana's largest 'lake,' created by Fort Peck Dam. Completed in 1937 as a Public Works Administration project, the dam's construction took four years and was a tremendous boost to Montana's Depression-era economy. Fort Peck Dam's original functions were to control floods and make the Missouri River navigable; the dam's 165,000-kilowatt power-making capacity, somewhat of an afterthought, was not utilized until 1939.

An oasis in the middle of northeastern Montana's naturally arid prairie, Fort Peck Lake's 1600 miles of shoreline and fish-filled waters are popular for motorized watercraft sports and fishing. Tourist services and designated attractions are concentrated on the reservoir's northern shore, around the junction of Hwys 24 and 117. Adventurous types and fossil hounds with a good car (or boat) and a few days to kill will find the lake's more remote reaches worth exploring.

Orientation & Information The information booth at Fort Peck's entrance, 20 miles south of Glasgow via Hwy 24, is open weekends in summer. The town of Fort Peck (population 220), 2 miles south of the entrance via Missouri Rd, has a bank, post office and well-stocked market. Get a map of the sights, recreation areas and campsites listed below from the Corps of Engineers (☎ 406-526-3411), next to the Fort Peck Hotel in Fort Peck, open weekdays from 8:30 am to 4:30 pm.

Things to See & Do Free tours of Fort Peck's massive **power plant** leave from inside its front doors hourly from 10 am to 4 pm between Memorial Day and Labor Day. In addition to the magnificent bowels of the plant, the tour visits the power plant's museum, whose major contributors were amateur photographers and rock hounds who worked on the dam's construction. Four-mile-long **Fort Peck Dam** is the area's centerpiece. Three miles east of the dam, the **spillway** regulates and discharges overflow,

and divides Fort Peck Reservoir from the Missouri River basin. A side road at the spillway's west end leads to an overlook with a great view.

Built as construction and dam operation headquarters, the 'town' of Fort Peck is a picturesque cluster of woodsy buildings whose crown jewel is the **Fort Peck Theater** (☎ 406-228-9219). Stage productions, performed weekends from June to August, have an excellent reputation statewide; tickets are $9.

Arrange guided fishing trips ($125 per day) and boat rentals ($85 per day) at the **Fort Peck Marina** (☎ 406-526-3442), west of the north Hwy 24 entrance. South of Fort Peck, Hwy 24 undulates through ruggedly beautiful badlands, giving access to the ultraremote Bear Creek, Rock Creek, McGuire Creek and Nelson Creek **recreation areas**. The only services – a small campground and store – are at **Rock Creek Marina** (☎ 406-485-2560), open from April to October.

Places to Stay & Eat Campgrounds near Fort Peck include *West End Campground*, 2 miles west on Hwy 24, and *Downstream Camp* (☎ 406-526-3224), half a mile south, which takes reservations. Both have showers, picnic shelters, electricity and water hookups; sites are $12/16 for tents/RVs. Of the primitive campgrounds around the lake, the *The Pines*, 11 miles west of Fort Peck and 12 miles south of Hwy 24, is recommended for its shade; sites here include pit toilets and potable water for $9.

Built in 1934 as a guesthouse/construction-crew dormitory, the *Fort Peck Hotel* (☎ 406-526-3266, 800-560-4931), central to the town, looks like an upscale summer-camp lodge; rooms start at $60. Its woodsy dining room is a popular destination for this part of Montana. Breakfast or lunch is a good, under-$10 option but dinners ($11 to $17) are overpriced.

The *Gateway Inn*, on Hwy 24 near the entrance station, is a fun weekend hangout with live bands, a much-used dance floor and meals like home-fried chicken and barbecue beef sandwiches for under $10.

Wolf Point

This bicultural community is hub of the Fort Peck (Indian) Reservation, home to Assiniboine and Yanktonai Sioux tribes. The town was centered on the north bank of the Missouri River, a mile away, until 1912 when the railroad arrived and lured business away from steamboat trade.

Wolf Point's accommodations are among the cheapest on the Hi-Line. On US 2 at the east edge of town, the *Big Sky Motel* (☎ 406-653-2300) has rooms with coffeemakers and refrigerators for $34/40. One block west, the *Homestead Inn* (☎ 406-653-1300, 800-231-0986) offers coffee and pastries with their $32/38 rooms. The fanciest restaurant in town is at the *Sherman Motor Inn* (☎ 406-653-1100, 800-952-1100), where rooms start at $46. Advanced reservations are necessary around the second weekend in July, during the **Wild Horse Stampede**, Wolf Point's claim to fame. Besides being Montana's oldest continuous rodeo, it is one of the few that features Indian dance and drum competitions along with regular rodeo events.

LEWISTOWN

If you were to arrive directly from New York or even Portland, you'd probably view Lewistown as a small agricultural town with an hour's worth of attractions and nothing to do at night. If, however, you've been traveling in Montana awhile or live in one of the even smaller towns in the area, Lewistown (population 6380; elevation 3963 feet) appears a bustling bastion of civilization.

During the cattle-rustling and mining days of the 1880s, Lewistown was the place where men armed with Winchesters came to spend their loot on Saturday night. Nowadays people from the Eastern Plains come to shop, eat in restaurants and attend to medical needs. Folks from all over the West come the third weekend in August during the increasingly popular **Montana Cowboy Poetry Gathering**.

History

The Metis (a half-French, half-Chippewa tribe from Canada) settled what is now Lewistown in the 1880s, around the same time that gold was discovered in the nearby Judith Mountains. There are still names like Juneaux, LaFontaine and LeGrand in the phonebook. At the turn of the century, rustlers and outlaws found the Lewistown area much to their liking – few people, abundant cattle and just two days journey to the Canadian border.

Croatian immigrants arrived with the Central Montana Railroad in 1903 and built many of the structures along Main St (you can often spot the artisan's name somewhere near the door).

Orientation & Information

US 87 runs through town as Main St, intersected by numbered avenues that begin at the north end of town. Lewistown's Chamber of Commerce (☎ 406-538-5436) shares the address 408 NE Main St with the Central Montana Museum (see below). Recreation information is available at the BLM office (☎ 406-538-7462) and CM Russell NWR Headquarters (☎ 406-538-7461), next to each other on Airport Rd, off Main St on the west side of town. The main post office is at 204 3rd Ave N.

Things to See & Do

The **Lewistown Art Center** (☎ 406-538-8278), 1 block north of Main St at 801 W Broadway, was built with the same local sandstone as other buildings around town, but boards from local farms have been added to it and decorated with wrought-iron fixtures from the old high school. The pottery sold in the gift shop may be of more interest than the exhibits of local artists' work; open Tuesday through Sunday, free admission.

The **Central Montana Museum** (☎ 406-538-5436), 408 NE Main St, has the requisite collection of local memorabilia and relics focusing on homesteaders, Native Americans and ranchers; closed weekends from September to June, free admission.

Places to Stay

Camping is free at *Kiwanis Park*, 2 miles south of town on US 87/US 191, which has

MONTANA

bathrooms and running water but is not green, shady or quiet.

Lewistown's motels are concentrated at the ends of Main St. Neither quality (adequate) nor prices ($40 to $50) vary greatly; choices include the **Sunset Motel** (☎ *406-538-8741, 115 NE Main St*), **Trail's End Motel** (☎ *406-538-5468, 216 NE Main St*) and **B&B Motel** (☎ *406-538-5496, 800-341-8000, 520 E Main St*). The exception is the historic **Calvert Hotel** (☎ *406-538-5411*), 2 blocks from Main St at 216 7th Ave S, whose single/double rooms cost $23/30.

Places to Eat

The **Albertson's** on the corner of Juneaux St and 1st Ave has a full deli and bakery. Among the choices on Main St, locals like the **Whole Famdamily** (*206 W Main St*) for sandwiches, soups and dinner specials ($5 to $8) and **Java Bette's** (*618 Main St*) for coffee and morning chatter. A great spot for dinner is the **The Mint**, on the corner of Juneaux and 4th Ave, which serves fresh fish, steaks and pasta ($6 to $12) in a relaxed, sophisticated setting.

AROUND LEWISTOWN

The Big Open region, east of Lewistown, is just that – big and open. Its economy relies on oil production from the Cat Creek Anticline, Central Montana's richest concentration of 'black gold,' and open-range cattle ranching, started by Granville Stuart in the 1880s.

Of the old mining towns in the Judith Mountains, north of Lewistown, **Kendall** is the best kept and most accessible: take US 191 north for about 9½ miles from Lewistown, turn west on Hwy 81, then go 2½ miles to the gravel road marked 'KLM Scout Camp,' which leads straight to Kendall.

About 30 miles southwest of Lewistown in the west end of the Big Snowy Mountains, **Crystal Lake** is popular for fishing (no motorized boats allowed) and hiking; good hiking trails include the easy Crystal Lake Shoreline Trail and the 6½-mile Crystal Cascades Trail to Cascade Falls. Trails are well marked, but a useful map is available at the entrance to **Crystal Lake Campground**, at the lake's south end, which has pit toilets and first-come, first-served sites for $10.

Rugged and remote, the **Charles M Russell National Wildlife Refuge** technically has over 700 miles of roads, but less than 100 miles are paved. As a result, you'll need an off-road vehicle, a willingness to get lost and a full tank of gas to journey into its wilds. The 73-mile **Missouri Breaks Byway** begins 1 mile south of the Fred Robinson Bridge, 76 miles north of Lewistown on US 191. Camping is permitted anywhere along the route, but water is generally unavailable. More cautious travelers should stick to the area around the Fred Robinson Bridge. Even though this is the most traveled part of the refuge, you still have a good chance of viewing elk (reintroduced from Yellowstone National Park in 1951), pronghorn and bighorn sheep, and in spring (roughly from May to early June), sharp-tailed grouse courtship rituals.

On the south side of the bridge, the **James Kipp State Recreation Area** has a boat launch, picnic facilities and campground with pit toilets, potable water and $5 sites. A map of the area is posted at the campground, and some information is available from a small DFWP field station just south, but it's best to stop at the refuge headquarters (☎ 406-538-7461) in Lewistown before venturing out here.

On the north bank of the Musselshell River at the junction of US 12 and US 191, **Harlowton** (population 1075) has a wonderfully intact downtown of local sandstone buildings carved by immigrant stonecutters (most are listed on the National Register of Historic Places). Architecture aside, the only real reason to stop here is for food or fuel. The real attraction is 14 miles south of Harlowton, where a **fossil area**, well marked on US 191, contains pockets of 'gizzard stones' – rocks polished by the digestive process of dinosaurs millions of years ago. This is where, in 1908, Albert Siberling of Harlowton found the remains of a Paleocene mammal *Ptilodus montanus*, now at the American Museum of Natural History in New York.

BILLINGS

Montana's largest city, Billings (population 92,988; elevation 3300 feet) is a ranching and oil town, representative of eastern Montana and more akin to large cities in the Dakotas than to Missoula or even Bozeman (142 miles away). It shouldn't be priority on a Montana itinerary, but it's not a bad place to stay while visiting Little Bighorn Battlefield or heading to Yellowstone National Park. Billings' airport is one of Montana's best served, there is a myriad of accommodations and a day could be spent exploring the town itself.

Sandstone cliffs, known as the rimrocks or 'rims,' were carved by the Yellowstone River which brushes the east side of town. These physical boundaries used to define the city's limits, but an oil boom in the 1950s started a growth trend that has pushed the city edge out in all directions.

Ernest Hemingway brought excitement to Billings in November 1930 when he, John Dos Passos and a local cowboy crashed their car on the way home from Yellowstone Park. Hemingway broke his right arm and had to spend seven weeks at St Vincent's Hospital.

History

In 1881 Northern Pacific Railroad surveyors bypassed the one-horse town of Coulson and set up their construction headquarters on the site of modern Billings (named after the Northern Pacific president Frederick Billings). The town grew steadily until 1886, when three large fires and a disastrous winter wiped out most of what was built.

During reconstruction, irrigation was introduced to agriculture and local politicians insured Billings' place at the head of this new field. Following experiments in raising sugar beets with the new technique, PB Moss gathered enough investments to construct a sugar refinery – still the only refinery in the state.

Orientation

Billings sits at the junction of US 87 and I-90, 8 miles west of where I-94 splits off toward Miles City and 16 miles east of where US 212 goes south to Red Lodge and Yellowstone National Park.

Downtown, numbered streets run perpendicular to numbered avenues (28th St is named Broadway). The city center is where 27th St (which runs from I-90 exit 450 through downtown to the airport) crosses Montana Ave (which begins as Laurel Rd from I-90 exit 446 and crosses downtown perpendicular to 27th St). Shopping malls and hotel/motel chains are west of downtown, along 24th St W, off I-90 exit 466.

Information

Billings' visitors center (☎ 406-245-4111, 800-711-2630), half a mile north of I-90 at 815 S 27th St, has reams of local information and will help with hotel reservations; open daily May to September from 8:30 am to 7:30 pm, Monday to Friday to 5 pm the rest of the year.

You'll find banks clustered on N Broadway and the post office next to the Sheraton on 1st Ave N; postal code 59107.

Parmly Billings Library, on 4th Ave N between 28th and 29th Sts, has a Montana Room filled with books, videos, periodicals, maps and exploration charts, plus free internet access and local calls; open Tuesday to Thursday from 10 am to 9 pm, Friday to 5 pm and Saturday 1 to 5 pm. Thomas Books (☎ 406-245-6754) is at 209 N 29th St.

Deaconess Medical Center (☎ 406-657-4000), 2800 10th Ave N, is Montana's largest.

The Great Hog Debate

In 1882 hogs were set loose in the streets of Billings to devour excess garbage. Soon out of control, the hogs busted into several kegs of oysters – neither cheap nor easy to come by – that were sitting on a hotel's back steps. Within a week the hogs were bacon and their owner irate. Throughout the following year, the *Billings Gazette* ran articles on who was 'for' and who was 'against' the hogs, creating a political division in the city.

Things to See & Do

Most of Billings' sights are within walking distance of one another downtown. In summer the Billings Trolley has ongoing two-hour tours ($10) that cover everything you'd ever want to see; find out about pick-up and departure points from the visitors center.

As far as must-sees go, the two that stand out are the **Western Heritage Center** (☎ 406-256-6809), 2822 Montana Ave, which has changing exhibits and an outstanding artifact collection representing various cultural traditions – Crow, Northern Cheyenne, Hispanic, Japanese, Chinese, Volga German –

integral to Yellowstone Valley life, and the newly renovated **Yellowstone Art Center** (☎ 406-256-6804), on the site of the 1916 Yellowstone County Jail at 401 N 27th St. Both museums are free, and closed Monday.

Also worth seeing is the **Moss Mansion** (☎ 406-256-5100), 914 Division St at the corner of 2nd Ave N, designed by New York architect RJ Hardenbergh, noted for his work on the Waldorf Astoria Hotel in Manhattan. Docents lead tours of the 28-room, red sandstone mansion from 10 am to 4 pm Monday to Saturday and 1 to 3 pm Sunday from June to August, $5.

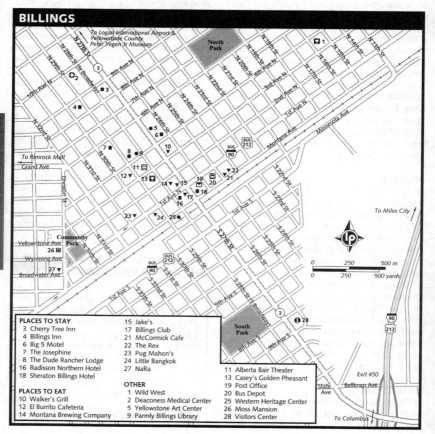

BILLINGS

PLACES TO STAY
3 Cherry Tree Inn
4 Billings Inn
6 Big 5 Motel
7 The Josephine
8 The Dude Rancher Lodge
16 Radisson Northern Hotel
18 Sheraton Billings Hotel

PLACES TO EAT
10 Walker's Grill
12 El Burrito Cafeteria
14 Montana Brewing Company

15 Jake's
17 Billings Club
21 McCormick Cafe
22 The Rex
23 Pug Mahon's
24 Little Bangkok
27 NaRa

OTHER
1 Wild West
2 Deaconess Medical Center
5 Yellowstone Art Center
9 Parmly Billings Library

11 Alberta Bair Theater
13 Casey's Golden Pheasant
19 Post Office
20 Bus Depot
25 Western Heritage Center
26 Moss Mansion
28 Visitors Center

The **Yellowstone County Peter Yegen Jr Museum** (☎ 406-256-6811), at the entrance to Logan International Airport, is good if you like 'old west' artifacts: guns, rodeo memorabilia, a late-19th-century chuckwagon, etc; open weekdays from 10:30 am to 5 pm, weekends from 2 to 5 pm, free admission.

Branching off from Hwy 318 near the airport, **Black Otter Trail** skirts the top edge of the rims, giving an expansive view of Billings and, on clear days, the Bighorn, Pryor, Crazy, Beartooth and Snowy Mountains. Black Otter was a Crow chief killed here by a Sioux war party and then given a treetop burial. The trail passes by the grave of Luther S 'Yellowstone' Kelly, one of those classic frontiersmen who left the comforts of the East Coast to live out west the wild way, learning Crow and Sioux languages. Farther along the trail is **Boothill Cemetery**, where lies Sheriff 'Muggins' Taylor, who let the world know of Custer's defeat.

Above the Yellowstone River and across from Black Otter Trail is **Sacrifice Cliff**. Crow legend has it that two brothers returned from a battle to find their camp (at the top of the cliff) infested with smallpox. To appease the gods, whom they believed were not happy with their acts in battle, the brothers blindfolded themselves, climbed on their best horse together and rode off the cliff.

A number of old hotels on Montana Ave, between S 27th St and N 23rd St, once serviced Billings' railroad depot (now a restaurant) and now house **antique shops** and junk boutiques.

The state's only zoo, **Zoo Montana** (☎ 406-652-8100), 2100 S Shiloh Rd at the west end of Billings, opened in 1997. It's nice as far as zoos go, with a petting zoo, nature trails and a sensory garden; open 10 am to 5 pm April 15 to October 15, $5/2 adults/children.

Places to Stay

Stay at one of chain motels near I-90 (exit 446) if you're just passing through. Downtown accommodations are better for airport arrivals and seeing the sights.

Camping Billings boasts America's first KOA, now called the ***Billings KOA*** (☎ 406-252-3104), started by two brothers to accommodate people traveling to the World's Fair. It's in a beautiful spot next to the Yellowstone River, half a mile south of I-90 (well signed off the interstate). Tent sites are $23, RV sites $34.

Motels & Hotels Nonchain motels near the freeway include the ***Picture Court Motel*** (☎ 406-252-8478, 800-523-7379, 5146 Laurel Rd) and, a quarter mile north along Laurel Rd, the ***Parkway Motel*** (☎ 406-245-3044, 4808 Underpass Ave), both with rooms for $55/40 single/double.

The best buys downtown are $31/36 rooms at ***Big 5 Motel*** (☎ 406-245-6646, 888-544-9358, 2601 4th Ave N) and $38/45 rooms at the ***Cherry Tree Inn*** (☎ 406-252-5603, 800-237-5882, 823 N Broadway).

For $46 to $70 you can stay at the ***Dude Rancher Lodge*** (☎ 406-259-5561, 800-221-3302, 415 N 29th St), whose groovy oak ranch oak furniture dates back to the 1940s. Rooms at the ***Billings Inn*** (☎ 406-252-6800, 800-231-7782, 880 N 29th St) include a microwave, refrigerator and breakfast for $55/59.

Catering to the convention crowd, the ***Radisson Northern Hotel*** (☎ 406-245-5121, 19 N 28th St) and the ***Sheraton Billings Hotel*** (☎ 406-252-7400, 800-325-3535, 27 N 27th St) have rooms with views starting at $85.

B&Bs *The Josephine* (☎ 406-248-5898, 514 N 29th St) has a computer for guest use and lavishly decorated rooms for $75 to $95.

Places to Eat

Besides offering the usual meat and potatoes, Billings has some well-trained, innovative chefs and good ethnic restaurants. Most pubs serve good food and offer happy hour specials until 6:30 pm. For coffee, pastries, lunch and lively atmosphere, stop by the ***McCormick Cafe*** (2419 Montana Ave).

A good Mexican choice is ***El Burrito Cafeteria*** (310 N 29th St), open until 8 pm, Korean-Japanese **NaRa**, on the corner of

Division St and 1st Ave N, or *Little Bangkok (2916 1st Ave)*. You can get a great meal at any of these little places for less than $10.

Popular with the thirty-something crowd, the *Montana Brewing Company (113 N Broadway)* brews its own beer, uses it to make crust for wood-fired pizzas and serves a big menu of salads, burgers and appetizers. An older local crowd likes the *Billings Club (2702 1st Ave N)* for beer, burgers and lunch specials. *Pug Mahon's (3011 1st Ave N)* is a friendly Irish bar with darts, cribbage, a great beer list and good food (Irish stew, sandwiches) to match. On Sundays people line up for Pug's brunch, complete with champagne.

Some locals claim that *The Rex (☎ 406-245-7477, 2401 Montana Ave)* serves the best steak in town, while others only eat beef at *Jake's (☎ 406-259-9375, 2701 1st Ave N)*. But if $40 is too much for a meal, head to *Walker's Grill (☎ 406-245-9291, 301 N 27th St)* where $20 will buy an excellent meal in a cosmopolitan bistro setting. Specialties include roast lamb, fresh fish and a variety of pastas.

Entertainment

Casey's Golden Pheasant (222 N Broadway) has live jazz and blues performances nightly. Weeknight shows are usually mellow affairs, while weekends draw a crowd and demand a cover charge of $4 to $10. Get a glimpse of modern American cowboy culture at the *Wild West*, at the corner of 4th Ave N and N 16th St. Tight jeans, boots, hats and the two-step dominate the dance floor, with Bud as the thirst-quencher of choice. Men pay $5 at the door, women are admitted *gratis*. (For Billings' other bars, see Places to Eat, above.)

A magnet for all of eastern Montana, the *Alberta Bair Theater (☎ 406-256-6052, 2801 3rd Ave N)* is Billings' cultural jewel. Productions range from country music to symphony concerts, and from children's theater to musicals. The extensive program ensures there will be entertainment available at least once a week all year long.

Getting There & Away

Air Logan International Airport, atop the rims, 2 miles north of downtown, is served primarily by Delta Airlines, which flies through Salt Lake City and is generally the cheapest to the West Coast. Continental and United Airlines both have three flights daily to Denver. Northwest Airlines flies to Minneapolis and the West Coast. Horizon Air flies to/from points west, and Big Sky Airlines flies within Montana.

Bus Between Greyhound and Rimrock Stages, there are three buses daily to Bozeman, Butte, Missoula, Portland and Seattle, and three to Miles City, Glendive, Minneapolis, Chicago and New York. One daily goes south through Wyoming to Denver. The bus depot (☎ 406-245-5116) is at 2502 1st Ave N.

Getting Around

Bus Billings' efficient bus system, the Billings Metropolitan Transit System (☎ 406-657-8218), runs Monday to Friday from 6 am to 7 pm, and Saturday from 10:30 am to 3:45 pm. The green and white buses stop at most corners and any of the blue and green MET signs around town. Buy tickets (75¢) from the driver.

Car Major car rental agencies, including Hertz (☎ 406-248-9151), Avis (☎ 406-252-8007), Budget (☎ 406-259-4168) and National (☎ 406-252-7626), are at the airport. Thrifty (☎ 406-259-1025) or Enterprise (☎ 406-652-2000) are cheaper alternatives.

Taxi Billings Area City Cab (☎ 406-252-8700) and Billings Area Yellow Cab (☎ 406-245-3033) run 24 hours.

AROUND BILLINGS

Five miles south of I-90 exit 452 on Coburn Rd, the three caves – Pictograph, Ghost and Middle – of **Pictograph Cave State Monument** have yielded over 30,000 Paleo-Indian artifacts left by a succession of cultures that inhabited the area over a period of 10,000 years. What remains now are pictographs, made of ground flowers, roots, bark, clay,

Going-to-the-Sun Rd, Glacier National Park, MT

JOHN ELK III

Sacagawea shows the way. Ft Benton, MT

MARISA GIERLICH

Custer's last lie, MT

ROB BLAKERS

Barely a ripple, Flathead Lake, MT

MARISA GIERLICH

They don't make 'em like they used to. Agricultural architecture, MT

Missoula, MT, from above the 'M' on Mt Sentinel

You'd think they would put up a sign. Augusta, MT

charcoal and animal fat, and applied with fingers, twigs, bones and tufts of hair attached to sticks. A quarter mile trail leads from the parking lot to the caves; open from 8 am to 8 pm daily April 15 to October 15.

Northeast of Billings off I-94, the massive sandstone butte of **Pompey's Pillar** is where William Clark (of Lewis and Clark) etched his signature on July 25, 1806. Clark is not the only graffiti artist to have scrawled upon the rock: Crow Indians before him, homesteaders after him and modern-day tourists have all left their mark. Clark named the rock after Sacagawea's son, who was nicknamed 'Pomp,' which, in Shoshone, means 'little chief.' A wooden walkway leads to the visitors center (open from 8 am to 8 pm daily in summer) and continues to the pillar's summit.

LITTLE BIGHORN BATTLEFIELD

The Crow Indian Reservation (Montana's largest) and the Northern Cheyenne Indian Reservation constitute the bulk of rolling prairies and low pine-covered hills where General George Custer made his famous 'last stand.' It's also where several Indian Nations converge the third weekend in August for the Crow Fair & Rodeo. Non-natives are also welcome to watch the rodeo and ceremonial dance competitions, eat fry bread and buy jewelry and handicrafts.

The Little Bighorn National Monument (called Custer Battlefield until 1993) is undeniably one of Montana's most popular attractions. As such, it has a wonderful visitors center with multimedia displays, an excellent book shop and knowledgeable rangers who give lectures and guided tours that focus on various aspects of the battle and its encompassing history.

Tour schedules are posted at the visitors center information desk. The handbook that is passed out at the entrance is also a good information source.

Beyond the visitors center, the battlefield is best suited for visiting by car: a 4½-mile tour begins at the center and winds around the area in a chronological order.

Entrance to the battlefield is 1 mile east of I-90 on US 212. It's open mid-April to Memorial Day from 8 am to 6 pm, Memorial Day to Labor Day to 8 pm, and the rest of the year to 4:30 pm. The entrance fee is $6 per vehicle, $3 per walk-in. For information, contact Little Bighorn Battlefield National Monument (☎ 406-638-2621), www.nps.gov/libi/index.htm.

AROUND LITTLE BIGHORN BATTLEFIELD

Near the Little Bighorn site are a few less-developed monuments and battlefields that better represent what the landscape was like at the time of conflict, and round out the story of why the Battle of the Little Bighorn occurred. **Rosebud Battlefield State Park**, 23 miles south of Busby on County Rd 314, then 3 miles west on a well-signed dirt road, is where General George Crook's troops did battle with Sioux and Cheyenne eight days before the Battle of the Little Bighorn. There was no real 'winner' in this bloody, six-day conflict, but Crook's unit was knocked out of commission and unable to support Custer's troops as planned. Significant sites are marked and there is historical information posted around the battlefield.

In 1936 an Indian trader by the name of Monicure built the **Chief Two Moon Monument** in memory of this Crow chief's participation in the Battle of the Little Bighorn. The simple stone monument sat quietly on US 212 near Busby until 1993 when the remains of 17 tribal members were returned for reburial. The people died around 120 years ago, and their remains sat in various museums until 1990.

In 1884, Bishop Brondel purchased land in the Tongue River valley (the Northern Cheyenne's original homeland) and founded the St Labre Mission. Visit the large collection of beadwork, clothing, religious and ceremonial artifacts at the **Northern Cheyenne Museum**, next to the teepee-shaped stone church in the small community of Ashland (well signed off US 212); June to September daily from 8 am to 4:30 pm, closed weekends September to May.

Inspired by Mt Vernon on a trip to Washington, DC, Crow chief Aleck-chea-ahoosh –

MONTANA

or Chief Plenty Coups – preserved his home as a memorial, **Chief Plenty Coups State Park**, to the Crow Nation. A small museum is the only alteration to the house since Chief Plenty Coups lived there. A nice picnic facility sits on the bank of Pryor Creek which runs alongside the park, a mile west of Pryor off Hwy 416; open daily May to September, $3 per vehicle, $1 per pedestrian or cyclist.

HARDIN

On the Crow Reservation's northern border and 18 miles northwest of Little Bighorn Battlefield National Monument, Hardin (population 3385; elevation 2902 feet) is the largest center of commerce in the area. The town really comes to life during Little Bighorn Days, held the last Wednesday to Sunday of June, when totally irrelevant activities – a professional rodeo, carnival, arts and crafts fair, antique show, street dancing, a Scandinavian feast and parade – attract throngs of people who seem oblivious to the area's history. The culmination and feature attraction of Little Bighorn Days is **Custer's Last Stand Reenactment**, an hour-long narrated spectacle with a cast of 300 horses, Indians and soldiers. The **Little Big Horn**

The Battle of the Little Bighorn

With the discovery of gold in the Black Hills, President Ulysses S Grant decided that a full attack on the Sioux would be the only way to get the Indians out of the newly prized area. The most famous of all the battles is Custer's Last Stand, more appropriately called the Battle of the Little Bighorn.

On March 17, 1876, Colonel Joseph J Reynolds, under command of General George Crook, attacked a Sioux camp on the Powder River. The surprised Sioux rallied and counterattacked, causing the soldiers to return to Fort Fetterman. The Oglala, Miniconjou and Cheyenne who fought Reynolds and his men set forth to the East Fork of the Little Powder River to unite with Crazy Horse, and then 60 miles on to another branch of the Powder River to find Sitting Bull. By early spring, 400 lodges including about 3000 people were joined together.

General Alfred H Terry led an expedition westward from Fort Abraham Lincoln (near present-day Mandan, North Dakota) toward the Yellowstone River. At the mouth of the Rosebud he sent one of his staff officers, General George Armstrong Custer, with the Seventh Cavalry forward to find the Sioux encampment believed to be in the Little Bighorn Valley. Terry would then continue up the Yellowstone to meet up with Colonel John Gibbon's forces in order to attack from the north.

On the morning of June 24, Custer's troops encountered a fresh Indian trail, and at the midday stop scouts reported that the Sioux were camped on the lower Little Bighorn. Not aware of the incredible size of the encampment that had formed over the weeks, Custer divided his Seventh Cavalry into three parts to form a three-prong attack. Two columns worked their way upstream to the west, and though Custer was to stay back, he changed his mind and went north. Dust from the running of cavalry horses alerted the Indians and they attacked Reno's troops (one of the two columns). Custer watched the fight, ordered reinforcements, then charged ahead into the encampment. Over 2000 warriors attacked the cavalry head on, causing the soldiers to flee in pure chaos. Not a single soldier survived.

Word reached the general public of the defeat on July 4, 1876 – the day that marked the centennial of the Declaration of Independence. The annihilation of a unit of the US Army by a force of so-called 'savages' shocked the country and placed the concept of the USA into question – it was clear the government lacked effective control over large sections of territory that it claimed. Only by devoting enormous resources to the defeat of the Sioux and their allies was the government able to overcome such a damaging blow to its prestige.

Symposium adds an academic side to the Hollywood-esque antics.

The **Bighorn Valley KOA** (☎ *406-665-1635*), half a mile north of I-90 on Hwy 47, is surrounded by cottonwood trees and has tent sites for $15, RV spaces for $24; closed October to April.

The **American Inn** (☎ *406-665-1870*), 1324 N Crawford Ave one block south of I-90 exit 495, has an outdoor pool and $51/65 rooms. Next door, **Super 8** (☎ *406-665-1700*) has $55 rooms.

A great mom-and-pop operation, the **Lariat Motel** (☎ *406-665-2683, 709 N Center Ave*) has homemade cookies and coffee on hand and cozy rooms starting at $45.

BIGHORN CANYON NATIONAL RECREATION AREA – NORTH UNIT

Robert Yellowtail, an interpreter for Chief Plenty Coups and the first Native American superintendent of his own reservation, fought the US government for 10 years to keep a dam from being built on the Bighorn River. It's obvious who won: Yellowtail Dam backs up the Bighorn River 71 miles into Wyoming. The so-called Bighorn Lake is a popular fishing and boating destination for this part of Montana and Wyoming. (For more on the Bighorn Canyon NRA, see Bighorn Country in the Wyoming chapter.)

Fort Smith Village, 42 miles southwest of Hardin by way of Hwy 313, is the area's service center. There's a store, cafe, gas station and several **fly-fishing** shops that offer guided trips; the Bighorn Angler (☎ 406-666-2233) has a long history here, running all-inclusive trips for around $300 per day (two people). Ok-A-Beh Marina, 10 miles south of Fort Smith Village, rents boats for $45 per day and has a small store.

The **Yellowtail Dam Visitors Center** (☎ 406-666-3234), on the northeast side of the dam, 6 miles from Fort Smith Village, has maps and recreation information, plus displays about the construction and engineering of Yellowtail Dam; open Memorial Day to Labor Day daily from 9 am to 6 pm.

Sites are free at **Afterbay Campground**, 1 mile northeast of Yellowtail Dam, but each vehicle must pay $5 for overnight use. All the northern unit's motels are operated by fly shops in Fort Smith Village. The **Bighorn Angler Motel** (☎ *406-666-2233*) charges $60/72 for motel units, $85 to $135 (three to five people) for a two-room cabin with a bathroom and kitchen. The **Bighorn Trout Shop** has units for $52/67 and rooms in an old cabin with a shared bath for $25/40. **Quill Gordon Fly Fisher's Motel** (☎ *406-666-2253*) has rooms for $60 to $85.

Polly's Place serves diner-style breakfast, lunch and dinner for under $10.

MILES CITY

Except for the fast-food restaurants and chain motels near the highway, Miles City (population 8698; elevation 2358 feet) hasn't changed much in the past 80 years. Two-story brick facades with bright neon bar signs stand face to face along Main St, sprawling gnarled oaks shade streets of elegantly restored houses with leaded-glass windows and deep porches, and steep bluffs rise above the Yellowstone River on the north side of town. Just outside the town limits the prairie stretches as far as the eye can see.

After the Battle of the Little Bighorn, General Nelson Miles commanded Fort Keogh, from where he continued to launch campaigns to force the Sioux onto reservations. The post grew rapidly into a town sustained by hunters, traders, miners and prospectors on their way to and from gold strikes in the Black Hills. Cattle drives through Montana stopped in Miles City and established the town's position as eastern Montana's primary horse and cattle market.

Orientation & Information

Travelers to Miles City used to know it as the point where the Tongue River meets the Yellowstone, but now it's better known as the halfway point on I-94 between Billings and the North Dakota border. Haynes Ave (Hwy 312) connects US 12 and I-94. Main St runs west from Haynes Ave, passes beneath the railroad tracks, cuts through the heart of downtown, bridges the Tongue River and becomes I-94/US 12 as it leaves Miles City to the southwest.

MONTANA

Plenty Coups

Crow chief Aleck-chea-ahoosh, which translates to 'Many Achievements' or 'Plenty Coups,' was the last Crow chief to earn his title by 'counting coups,' or earning war honors. After completing the four requisite acts to be considered for chieftainship – being the first to touch an enemy during battle, taking an enemy's weapon without killing him, 'cutting horse' (stealing a horse from the enemy camp) and leading a successful raid or war party – Plenty Coups 'counted coup' at least 80 times until the federal government prohibited 'violent warring activity' on reservation land, thus prohibiting counting coups.

As last warrior chief, Plenty Coups could have left a bitter legacy for generations prohibited from following in his footsteps. Instead, he was a model of transition and a wise leader for the Crow. For practicality's sake, Plenty Coups told his people not to wage war on new settlers, but to accept them; white culture was coming to stay, and the only way for the Crow to survive was to make peace with the settlers. Realizing that education would be his people's most powerful tool, he warned the Crow that 'with education you will be the white man's equal, without it you will be the white man's victim.'

As a spokesman for his people, Plenty Coups traveled frequently to Washington, DC, and was invited to the 1921 dedication of the Tomb of the Unknown Soldier.

You need not look farther than Main St for most things, including banks, a laundromat and the chamber of commerce (☎ 406-232-2890), www.mcchamber.com, which has local maps and visitors information. The main post office is at 196 N 7th St.

Things to See & Do

If you're in town on Tuesday, there's no better place to witness modern Western culture than at the **live cattle auction** at the Sales Yard, on W Main St just past Gerryowen Rd. The **Miles City Bucking Horse Sale**, held the third weekend of May, is the biggest such event in the USA.

The **Range Riders Museum** (☎ 406-232-6146), west of the Tongue River Bridge on Main St, has an excellent collection of spurs and tack, Native American photos and the reconstructed officers' quarters from Fort Keogh; open April to October daily from 8 am to 8 pm, $3.50.

More contemporary are the shows at the **Custer County Art Center** (☎ 406-232-0635), next to the Miles City Waterplant on the west end of Main St, which features regional multimedia art. The 'North American Indian' series of Edward S Curtis, who spent his professional life photographing tribes of the world, can be viewed on demand; open Tuesday to Sunday 1 to 5 pm (closed January), free.

Occupying 269 cottonwood-covered acres in the middle of the Yellowstone River is **Pirogue Island State Park**, 1 mile north of Miles City on Hwy 22, then 2 miles east on Kinsey Rd, a good spot for fishing, agate hunting, picnicking and spotting bald eagles and white-tailed and mule deer.

Places to Stay

A few mom-and-pop operations still stand among the chain-owned motels along the highways. There's a *KOA* (☎ 406-232-3991) at 1 Palmer St, walking distance to downtown, with $17/24 tent/RV sites; closed November to April.

Four miles northeast of downtown on US 10, the *Star Motel* (☎ 406-232-4473) offers dim but comfortable rooms starting at $29/36 a single/double. Tucked among the motels on Haynes Ave, *Custer's Inn* (☎ 406-232-5170, 800-456-5026, 1209 S Haynes Ave) has an indoor pool and rooms for $42/48. Across the street, the *Days Inn* (☎ 406-232-3550, 800-525-6303, 1006 S Haynes Ave) charges around $50.

The orange brick *Olive Hotel* (☎ 406-232-2450, 501 Main St) is a Miles City landmark, the hub of summer activity and undeniably the best place to stay for a dose of Old West ambiance. Rooms start at $45.

Places to Eat

If you're going to eat one steak in Montana, Miles City is the place to do it. One of the best options is *Louie's Steakhouse & Lounge* (☎ 406-232-7288), which got its start in the Olive Hotel and is now in a bigger space at 1111 S Haynes Ave. Downtown, the *Hole in the Wall (600 Main St)* and adjacent *600 Cafe* work in conjunction to serve salads, homemade soups, big sandwiches, hot lunch and dinner specials and breakfast all day. The bar and tin ceiling here date back to 1883.

A good alternative to meat and potatoes is *New Hunan (1710 S Haynes Ave)*, whose dinner buffet ($9.50) includes soup and four entrees. Individual dishes are better prepared and cost $6 to $11. For a quick caffeine fix, try *Montana Cactus Juice Espresso (1308 S Haynes Ave)*.

Entertainment

One of Miles City's most endearing attributes is its concentration of old bars. Lining Main St, the *Trails Inn*, *Montana Bar* and *Range Riders Bar* stand as they have for the past 50 years and serve much the same type of crowd. The Montana Bar *(612 Main St)* is the best of the bunch with its original 1902 tile floor, printed tin ceiling, carved mahogany back bar and not a Bud Light poster to be seen.

GLENDIVE

Glendive (population 4340; elevation 2078 feet) is the undisputed 'Paddlefish Capital of Montana,' and the base for exploring Makoshika State Park.

The Merrill Ave Historic District, along Merrill Ave between Douglas and Clement Sts, encompasses most of Glendive's downtown, built during prosperous railroad days in the early 1900s. The chamber of commerce has a detailed walking-tour map for real history hounds.

The Frontier Gateway Museum, 1 mile from downtown on Belle Frontage Rd off I-94 exit 215, has an exceptional agate collection, found locally on the Yellowstone River, and fossils and dinosaur bones, also found in the immediate area.

Bighorn Canyon

Crow legend tells of a young boy who lived with his stepfather near Bighorn Canyon. The stepfather was afraid that the boy's mother loved her son more than she loved him, so he took the boy hunting near the canyon and pushed him over the edge. Miraculously, the boy landed on a ledge and was saved by a herd of bighorn sheep.

The herd's leader, called 'Big Metal' because his hooves and horns glistened like steel, gave the boy his wisdom, surefootedness, sharp vision, strong heart and the honorable name of Big Metal on the condition that he return to his tribe and name the canyon and river 'Bighorn.'

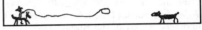

Orientation & Information

Glendive straddles the Yellowstone River just south of the Hwy 16 and I-94 intersection. Two auto bridges span the river: the northern one connects Glendive to I-94 via Merrill Ave (Glendive's main thoroughfare); the southern one hooks up with Hwy 16.

Banks, shops and the Glendive Tourist Information Office (☎ 406-365-5601) are found on Merrill Ave. The post office is at 221 N Kendrick Ave.

Paddlefishing

In May and June, the Intake fishing access site, 17 miles north of Glendive on Hwy 16, attracts curious tourists and anglers. Intake continually yields more paddlefish than any other spot in the country. Since catching – or rather, snagging – a paddlefish involves no serious skill, paddlefishing is popular with armchair anglers as well as experts. A heavy line is dropped to the bottom and jerked along until, with some luck, it snags one of these big creatures. Reeling in the fish is the hard part since they're known to put up a good fight.

In order to participate you'll need a fishing license (sold at the site) and a 'tag' (which costs $8). The paddlefish limit is one per person (hard-core anglers can cross into

North Dakota, which has a two-fish limit). The chamber of commerce processes the fish roe and sells it as 'Yellowstone Caviar' to fund local nonprofit organizations.

Places to Stay

The *Green Valley Campground* (☎ 406-359-9944), a half mile north of Hwy 16 off I-94 exit 213, is dominated by RVs, which pay $14, though there are a few grassy tent spots for $12.

The motels downtown are a bit more ragged than those near the highways, but are convenient to restaurants and shopping. The *Parkwood Motel* (☎ 406-377-8221, 1002 W Bell), next to Eyer Park, is the best deal in town, with rooms starting at $35. The *Riverside Inn* (☎ 406-365-2349, 800-283-4678), just north of the junction of Hwy 16 and I-94, is part of the Budget Host chain and charges $42/45.

The *Hostetler House B&B* (☎ 406-377-4505, 113 N Douglas), downtown, has two rooms, which cost $45/55 a single/double, in a restored 1912 house. Guests are welcome to use the hot tub, TV and sitting room.

Charley Montana (☎ 888-395-3207, 103 N Douglas) is the newest place to stay in Glendive – and the oldest. The innkeepers bought this 100-year-old house from the children of its original owner, rancher Charles Krug, and converted it to a B&B, retaining much of the original flavor – and furnishings. The owners are historians of the area, and guests are welcome to browse the collections of Western art and books. Rooms with private baths are $80 for one or two people, and activities from horseback riding to rock hunting can be arranged.

MAKOSHIKA STATE PARK

The Sioux called the land 'Ma-ko-shi-ka,' which roughly means 'badlands.' Makoshika State Park, Montana's largest, encompasses 8100 acres of hogback ridges, fluted hillsides, stratified canyons, pinnacles, caprocks and unique gumbo knobs, which extend east to the Dakotas. Because of its remote location, few tourists visit, but its odd and intriguing landscape thrills photographers, naturalists and hikers.

With the erosion of the Hell Creek Formation, fossils from the Cretaceous period – 'the age of reptiles' – have been unearthed. The park's largest discovery came in 1991, when archaeologists found a *Triceratops* skull in the southeastern corner. The skull is now on view in the park visitors center. Other fossils have been found of *Tyrannosaurus rex*, crocodiles and turtles.

Vegetation is sparse on the badlands' southern slopes, but those facing north abound with juniper and ponderosa pine, jackrabbits, mule deer, bobcats and coyotes. Prairie falcons, golden eagles and turkey vultures are also common – so common, in fact, that there's an annual **Buzzard Days** festival held in spring to honor the turkey vultures.

Orientation & Information

The park entrance is 2 miles southwest of downtown Glendive at the end of a route marked with green and yellow dinosaur footprints that begins where southern Merrill Ave veers left onto Barry St. The day-use fee is $4, while campers pay $10; there's one campground, with water and flush toilets, a mile from the visitors center.

An unpaved road loops through the park, giving access to the campground and several picnic areas. The most scenic viewpoints and the real heart of Makoshika, however, are reached by hiking trails and dirt roads that become impassable with the least bit of rain. The park headquarters and visitors center (☎ 406-365-6256) is open

---

Prehistoric Paddlefish

There are only two places in the world where you'll find paddlefish – in the Yangtze River in China and in the Missouri and Yellowstone Rivers in the USA. According to fossil evidence these unique fish have been around for 70 million years. And prehistoric they do look, with a paddle-shaped snout measuring up to 2 feet that helps the fish navigate through the murky rivers. An adult paddlefish can weigh from 50 to 160lb.

daily from 9 am to 5 pm. A park guidebook is available for $2.

Hiking & Backpacking

Hiking Makoshika is rewarding but somewhat risky. Water (not enough) and sun (too much), plus the occasional rattlesnake require hikers to be prepared and aware. The **Caprock Nature Trail** is a half-mile loop that skirts canyon walls and passes one exceptionally magnificent natural bridge.

For a good view of all that lies east, hike the first half-mile of the **Kinney Coulee Trail**, which descends 300 feet to the badlands bottom. The short descent is a fine hike in itself and good entry route for extended backcountry trips into the seemingly endless maze of canyons and gullies.

Both of these trails begin from the park's main road and are shown on the visitors center map.

EKALAKA & MEDICINE ROCKS

About 30 miles south of Baker, Ekalaka is the end of the road, in this case Hwy 7. Claude Carter, a buffalo hunter and bartender, was en route to a site near the railroads to set up a saloon when his wagon got stuck in the mud. 'Hell,' he said, 'any place in Montana is a good place to build a saloon.' So without traveling any farther, he built the Old Stand Saloon, still in business today.

David Harrison Russell homesteaded here in 1881 and married Sitting Bull's niece, Ijkalaka – Sioux for 'swift one'; when the post office was established he gave it that name, thus naming the town.

Ekalaka is not on the way to anywhere else: to come this far, you really have to want to be here, whether to visit nearby Medicine Rocks State Park or to view the dinosaur collection at the Carter County Museum. Virtually unchanged in appearance and mentality since the 1930s, Ekalaka embodies all that is lost to modernity – a slow gait, community pride and people who take time to visit.

Carter County Museum

Somewhat improbably, the Carter County Museum (☎ 406-775-6886) houses a world-renowned collection of dinosaur remains, including the world's only known remains of a *Pachycephalosaurus*. The museum curator is a touted authority on US paleontology and plains archaeology. The museum is open Tuesday to Friday from 9 am to noon and 1 to 5 pm, weekends from 1 to 5 pm; free admission.

Medicine Rocks State Park

Theodore Roosevelt wrote of what is now Medicine Rocks State Park:

> Over an irregular tract of gently rolling sandy hills, perhaps about three quarters of a mile square, were scattered several hundred detached and isolated buttes or cliffs of sandstone, each butte from 15 to 50 feet high, and from 30 to a couple of 100 feet across. Some of them rose as sharp peaks or ridges or as connected chains, but much the greater number had flat tops like little table lands. The sides were cut and channeled by the weather into the most extraordinary forms; caves, columns, battlements, spires, and flying buttresses were mingled in the strangest confusion…altogether it was as fantastically beautiful a place as I had ever seen.

These 60-foot cryptic sandstone formations that rise out of southeastern Montana's rolling prairie like fingers clutching for the sky were sacred to Native Americans for their spiritual power and protection or 'big medicine.' Though the rocks are scribbled over by modern graffiti artists, it is still possible to make out engravings from as early as 1889.

Some geologists contend that the Medicine Rocks are sand dunes which turned to stone under their own weight. The most accepted idea, however, is that they are sandstone deposits left by ancient seas and estuaries. Over the past 50 million years, the uplifted rocks have been worn down – by wind, heat, the freeze-thaw cycle, intrusive tree roots – at a slower rate than the rock that has become the surrounding prairie.

From the entrance gate (on Hwy 7, 25 miles south of Baker), a dirt road, impassable after rain, goes west 4 miles past several picnic areas to the park's western boundary. There's no camping permitted, and no developed hiking trails exist, but the land surrounding the formations is flat, open and easy to navigate.

Places to Stay & Eat

Camping is free at the USFS *Ekalaka Park* campground, 3 miles southeast of Ekalaka on US 323, which has flush toilets and potable water. Ekalaka is primarily just a wa-tering hole, but the *Guest House Inn* (☎ 406-775-6337) and *Midway Motel* (☎ 406-775-6619) have rooms for around $40. The *Old Stand Grill*, behind the Old Stand Bar, has good food for under $10 and is open until 10 pm. Across the street, the *Wagon Wheel Café* serves breakfast all day. A small *general store* has limited groceries and sundries.

Idaho

Idaho

Facts about Idaho

Idaho is synonymous with wilderness. The state has more than 18 million acres of federally protected national forests and wilderness areas – only Alaska has more. Idaho's 3100 runnable white-water miles are more than any other state; names like the River of No Return and Hells Canyon elicit yips of joy from river rats worldwide. And, not surprisingly, much rare wildlife – grizzly bears, woodland caribou, wolves and wolverines – is still found here.

Idaho's backcountry may be protected from further exploitation, but the adventure tourism boom – and the state's aggressive marketing of its natural beauty – threaten the wilderness ethos just as surely. The woods of central and northern Idaho attract legions of hikers, mountain bikers, hunters, snowmobilers and skiers. The state's arid southern half remains a major agricultural area. Idaho's most famous product is the potato and cattle are the biggest moneymaker, but many irrigated crops (from melons to marigolds) grow in the Snake River Plain.

Idaho's physical contrasts are mirrored in its disparate population. Social cohesion and a unified sense of purpose often seem absent. People can be suspicious of outsiders and indifferent to issues beyond their community. From Boise's trendy city slickers to insular Mormon farming communities to the Panhandle's ostracized white supremacist minority, there are few common ideals that tie the topographically diverse state together.

Idaho is not particularly destination-driven. Most visitors travel I-84 and US 95, the main east-west and north-south corridors. Those who escape the interstate are quickly rewarded. Travelers enjoy unlimited recreational opportunities here, and outfitters and guides to get you outdoors and 'up a crick,' through the rapids or down the

Highlights

- Boise – a lively city with an amiable mix of nightlife and cultural activity
- Harriman State Park – the state's most accessible wildlife viewing area
- Sun Valley – a touch of old-world grandeur meets new-world glitter in the guise of a world-class resort with some of the country's fluffiest, deepest powder for great skiing
- Salmon River – the 'River of No Return,' the longest undammed US river and a top white-water course
- Sawtooth National Recreation Area – boundless recreation among mountains, rivers, 1000 lakes, 100 miles of streams and 700 miles of trails
- Silver Mountain Resort – an ideal place to ski the powder in winter or kick back at an outdoor concert in summer
- Panhandle Lakes – activities galore at Lake Coeur d'Alene complement the perfect forest hideaway at Lake Pend Oreille

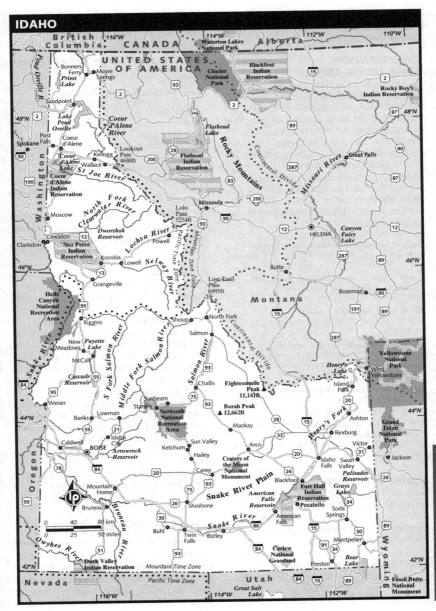

IDAHO

slopes are everywhere. The kaleidoscopic scenery is spectacular, and the cost of travel comparatively low.

INFORMATION
State Tourist Offices
The Idaho Travel Council (☎ 208-334-2470, 800-635-7820), 700 W State St, represents several state organizations. Request the 'Official Idaho State Travel Guide,' a state highway map, 'Idaho State Park Guide,' the useful 'Idaho RV & Campground Directory' and either a summer or winter activity package; See www.visitid.org for more information. Idaho's state welcome centers are on I-15 near Malad City, I-84 near Payette and I-90 near Post Falls. Several regional travel bureaus provide detailed information:

Eastern Idaho Visitors Information Center
(☎ 208-523-3278, 800-634-3246), 505 Lindsay Blvd, Box 50498, Idaho Falls, ID 83405-0498

North Central Idaho Travel Association c/o Lewiston Chamber of Commerce
(☎ 208-743-3531, 800-473-3543)

North Idaho Travel Committee
(☎ 208-769-1537), Box 877, Coeur d'Alene, ID 83814

South Central Idaho Travel Committee
(☎ 208-733-3974, 800-255-8946), 858 Blue Lakes Blvd N, Twin Falls, ID 83301
Web site: www.rideidaho.com

Southeastern Idaho c/o Lava Hot Springs
(☎ 208-776-5221, 800-423-8597), 430 E Main St, Box 668, Lava Hot Springs, ID 83246

Southwest Idaho Travel Association c/o Boise Convention & Visitors Bureau
(☎ 208-344-7777, 800-635-5240), 168 N 9th St, suite 200, Box 2106, Boise, ID 83701

Useful Organizations
Since Idaho is heavily visited by wilderness travelers, there are many public agencies and private organizations that provide information for exploring and preserving the backcountry. These include:

Idaho Dept of Fish & Game
(☎ 208-334-3700, 800-635-7820), 600 S Walnut, Box 25, Boise, ID 83707-0025
Web site: www.state.id.us/fishgame

Idaho Dept of Parks & Recreation
(☎ 208-334-4199), 5657 Warm Springs Ave, Box 83720, Boise, ID 83720-0065
Web site: www.idahoparks.org

Idaho Department of Water Resources River Information Line
(☎ 208-327-7865)

Idaho Outfitters & Guides Association
(☎ 208-342-1919, 800-494-3246), 711 N 5th St, Box 95, Boise, ID 83701
Web site: www.ioga.org

Idaho State BLM
(☎ 208-373-4000), 1387 S Vinnell Way, Boise, ID 83709-1657
Web site: www.id.blm.gov

Nature Conservancy
(☎ 208-726-3007), Box 165, Sun Valley, ID 83353
Web site: www.tnc.org

See the Activities chapter for a list of the state's national parks, national monuments, national recreation areas and national historic sites.

Area Code
Idaho's only area code is 208, but many intrastate calls incur toll charges.

Road Rules
Speed limits range from 45 to 65mph on state highways, and up to 75mph on interstate highways. Seatbelts are required for all passengers on highways and interstates. Motorcycle helmets are required for riders under 18. A person driving with a blood alcohol limit of 0.08% or greater is classified as driving under the influence. For statewide road condition reports, dial ☎ 208-336-6600 or ☎ 888-432-7623 (in Idaho only).

Taxes
State sales tax is 5%. The state bed tax is a minimum of 6%; some cities add 1% to 3% more.

Snake River Plain

Southwestern Idaho is a patchwork of desert, rivers and mountains. The Treasure Valley, known for its aromatic hops and sugar beets, extends east from Ontario, Oregon, to Mountain Home with Boise at

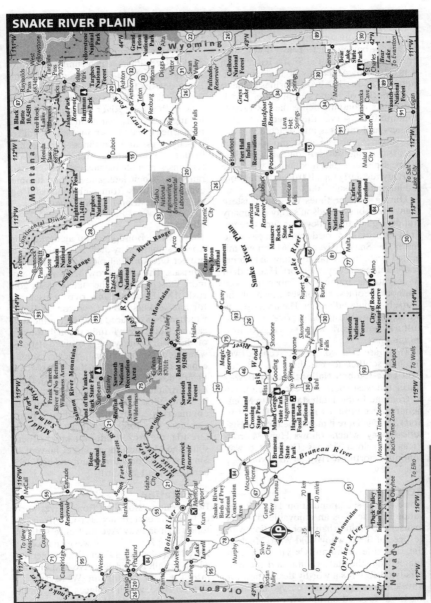

its center. The region's rivers are a world-class whitewater runners' wet dream and blue-ribbon trout lurk in its stocked lakes.

Once a barren tract of lava flows, sagebrush and scorpions, the Snake River Plain is now one of America's preeminent agricultural regions. The broad basin is home to the majority of Idaho's population and is the state's economic bellwether. Riverside communities serve the needs of area farmers and ranchers and welcome travelers with inexpensive rooms and wary courtesy. Traversing southern Idaho is a grueling affair, especially during summer when the mercury regularly tops 100°F and irrigation-fed humidity pushes 100%.

During frontier times the southeastern region was busy: Hudson's Bay Company trappers plied the valleys for furs, Oregon Trail pioneers traversed mountain passes to reach the Snake River and Mormons migrated north from Utah to establish farming communities. Today the Fort Hall Indian Reservation, home to Shoshone and Bannock peoples, comprises much of the sparsely populated region. The area's prime attractions are the appealing riverfront agricultural patchwork and the rugged, arid mountains.

There are two worthwhile scenic drives through southeastern Idaho. The 113-mile **Bear Lake-Caribou National Scenic Byway** traces the west shore of Bear Lake on US 89 from the Idaho-Utah state line to Montpelier and continues north on US 30 to Soda Springs. Here it meets the **Pioneer Historic Byway**, which follows Hwy 34 from Preston to Soda Springs. The joint byway continues north on Hwy 34 to Wyoming's Star Valley.

BOISE

Boise ('BOY-see'; population 170,000; elevation 2842 feet) is an enjoyable city that manages to meld urban sophistication with vestiges of the cowboy Wild West. Much of the riverside community's vibrancy emanates from the state capital and the university (BSU). It's a worthy destination for travelers who enjoy a hip, easygoing 'small big town' focused on the out of doors. It's

estimated that one in four residents of the greater metropolitan area has relocated here since 1995.

Boise sits at the western end of the vast Snake River Plain, which rumps up against the foothills of the Boise Front. The name Boise derives from the French word *boisé* for 'wooded.' The Boise River Greenbelt follows the Boise River the length of town, linking many city parks and civic institutions. The city center is noticeably devoid of big-city stress and scruffiness and much of its late 19th-century architectural core remains. Street life bustles: cafes and restaurants stay open late, and on hot summer evenings crowds from nightspots spill out into the pedestrian-friendly streets.

History

The town of Boise grew up alongside Fort Boise, established by the US army in 1863 to protect Oregon Trail pioneers from native reprisals. The city's growth, however, was more closely tied to the state's 1860s gold rush. The Boise Basin's rich veins lured fortune-seekers from Lewiston to Boise, which in 1865 replaced Lewiston as the state capital. Boise grew fitfully through the rest of the 19th century, but received a boost when federal irrigation projects created canals and reservoirs on the Snake River Plain's desert plateau. More recently, Boise has attracted several major corporate headquarters: Morrison Knudsen, the engineering-construction titan; Boise Cascade, the forest-products behemoth; Ore-Ida, the frozen tater-tot king; Albertson's, the Mormon supermarket maven; JR Simplot, the agricultural giant; and high-tech herald Hewlett Packard.

Orientation

Boise centers along the Boise River north of I-84. The eastern access route from I-84 follows Broadway Ave and enters downtown along Front St. The western access is Hwy 184 (I-84 exit 49), or 'the Connector,' which parallels Fairview Ave and empties into the city center on W Myrtle St. Capitol Blvd, which replaces 7th St, is the main north-south artery. It runs south from the Idaho State Capitol across the Boise River to the base of the hill dominated by the Depot (see below). Front St divides north-south addresses and 1st St divides east-west addresses. The main business district is bounded by State, Grove, 4th and 9th Sts.

Information

Facing the Grove in Boise Centre, the Information Center (☎ 208-344-5338), 850 Front St, has comprehensive tourist information. It's run by the Boise Convention & Visitors Bureau (☎ 208-344-7777, 800-635-5240), 168 N 9th St at Idaho St, open 8:30 am to 5 pm weekdays. It has brochures on several interesting walking tours. Request the 'Downtown Boise Map & Directory' or see www.downtownboise.org. Visitor Information on the 1st-floor rotunda of the Idaho State Capitol is also helpful. The city's Web site (www.boise.org) is useful and easy to navigate.

Boise Parks & Recreation (☎ 208-384-4240), 1104 Royal Blvd, produces a free *Boise River Greenbelt* map. The USFS Boise National Forest (☎ 208-373-4100), 1249 S Vinnell Way, and the Idaho State BLM (☎ 208-373-4000), 1387 S Vinnell Way, are off Overland Rd west of Cole Rd. Their shared Interagency Visitors Center (☎ 208-384-3200) is open 7:30 am to 4:30 pm weekdays.

The USFS Boise National Forest Boise Front-Mountain Home District (☎ 208-343-2527), 5493 Warm Springs Ave, is open 7:30 am to 4:30 pm weekdays. There you can pick up two useful maps: *Ridge to Rivers Trail System* and *Boise National Forest,* and excellent camping and hiking handouts. The BLM Boise District (☎ 208-384-3300) is at 3948 Development Ave. Dial ☎ 208-342-6559 for a regional weather forecast.

ATMs are everywhere downtown. The main post office is located in the US Federal Building at 8th and Bannock Sts. Since the untimely demise of the venerable Book Shop in August 2000, Vista Book Gallery (☎ 208-336-3011), 890 S Vista Ave in the Vista Village shopping center, is Boise's last independent bookseller.

There are scads of free papers, the most prominent being the lively *Boise Weekly* (www.boiseweekly.com), the best source for arts and entertainment listings. Another good source for listings and community features is the *Arbiter* (www.arbiteronline.com), BSU's student weekly. Look for queer news in *Diversity* (www.tcc-diversity.com/diversityhome.htm). Current political issues are parodied monthly in the wry *Idaho Comic News.*

The lively 16th Street Coin-Op Laundry (☎ 208-345-3958), 215 N 16th St, is open long hours, has large machines and is a great place to plot your next misadventure.

St Luke's Regional Medical Center (☎ 208-381-2269), 190 E Bannock St, is downtown. St Alphonsus Regional Medical Center (☎ 208-367-2121), 1055 N Curtis Rd, is west of downtown off I-84.

Idaho State Capitol

The state's domed capitol (1920) was modeled after the USA's capitol in Washington, DC. On Jefferson St at Capitol Blvd, it was built with convict-quarried sandstone from nearby Table Rock. The dowdy exterior belies its handsome interior, faced with four different colors of marble and embellished with mahogany woodwork. The 1st floor of this 200,000 sq foot building contains epic sculptures and a display of rare Idaho gemstones. The rotunda dome rises nearly 200 feet to end in a patch of sky blue emblazoned with 43 stars (Idaho was the Union's 43rd state). This is the nation's only geothermally heated statehouse. Open for self-guided tours 8 am to 5 pm weekdays and 9 am to 5 pm weekends; free guided tours (☎ 208-334-2470) by appointment only, 10 am to 1:30 pm weekdays during summer.

The Grove

Named for the street it interrupts, this brick-lined pedestrian plaza, centered on 8th and Grove Sts, is Boise's unofficial city center. Enjoying free live music during Alive After Five (5 to 8 pm Wednesday mid-May to mid-September), sunbathing and playing hackey-sack is the regular order of business. The

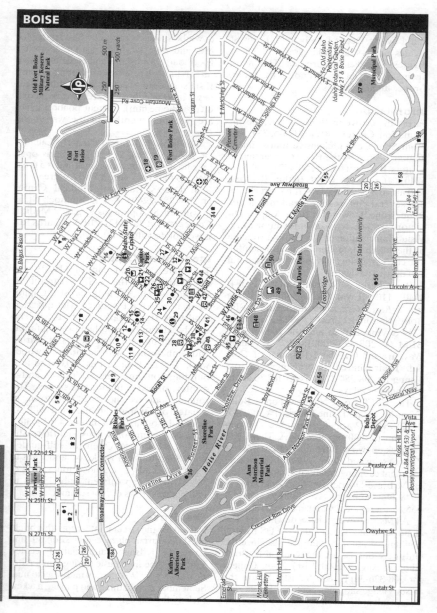

BOISE

PLACES TO STAY
2 Budget Inn
3 Doubletree Downtown
4 Cabana Inn
7 Sands Motel
9 Boise Centre GuestLodge
11 Owyhee Plaza Hotel;
    Gamekeeper Restaurant
13 Best Western Safari Inn
23 Statehouse Inn
34 Idaho Heritage Inn B&B
53 Boulevard Motel
54 University Inn
59 Boise River Inn

PLACES TO EAT
8 Boise Co-Op
22 Pollo Rey; BUS Transit Mall
24 Brick Oven Beanery
27 Flying M Coffeehouse
32 Moxie Java
38 Milford's Fish House
39 Kulture Klatsch
41 Cafe Ole
51 Aladdin's Egyptian Restaurant
55 The Ram
58 Flying Pie Pizzeria

OTHER
1 Practical Rent-A-Car
5 16th St Coin-Op Laundry
6 Greyhound Bus Depot
10 Neurolux Lounge
12 Blues Bouquet
14 Idanha Hotel
15 Boise Convention & Visitors
    Bureau
16 Idaho Travel Council
17 Visitor Information
18 Hospital
19 Boise Little Theatre
20 Post Office
21 Bitter Creek Ale House
25 Piper Pub & Grill
26 Egyptian Theatre
28 Knock 'Em Dead Dinner
    Theatre
29 Boise Centre; Information
    Center
30 The Grove; Bank of America
    Centre
31 Tom Grainey's Sporting Pub;
    TJ Toad's Lounge
33 Pengilly's Saloon

35 St Luke's Regional Medical
    Center
36 Wheels R Fun
37 Emerald City Club
40 Esther Simplot Performing
    Arts Academy
42 8th St Market Place Theatre
43 Basque Block; Basque
    Museum & Cultural Center;
    Cyrus Jacobs-Uberuaga
    House; Gernika
44 Boise Area Chamber of
    Commerce
45 Tablerock Brewpub & Grill
46 The Flicks
47 Idaho Historical Museum;
    Black History Museum
48 Boise Art Museum
49 Zoo Boise
50 Discovery Center of Idaho
52 Morrison Center for the
    Performing Arts
56 BSU Pavilion
57 Morrison Knudsen Nature
    Center; Idaho Dept of Fish
    & Game

Bank of America Centre (☎ 208-424-2200), Boise Centre (☎ 208-336-8900) and several restaurants face onto the Grove.

Eighth Street Marketplace
This gentrified area at 8th and Broad Sts houses produce, seafood, wine, cheese, crafts and clothing purveyors. It's the center of what used to be Boise's warehouse district. The marketplace extends south to the Boise River, east to Capitol Blvd and west to 9th St.

Old Boise
East of downtown is a district of fine old buildings, many transformed into shops, restaurants and bars, recalling Boise's bygone opulence. Centered around 6th and Main Sts, Old Boise extends east to 3rd St.

Julia Davis Park
This lovely park located right on the Boise River and contains several important museums and a floriferous **rose garden**. The **Bandstand** is a popular free concert venue.

The state's premier museum is the free **Idaho Historical Museum** (☎ 208-334-2120), 610 N Julia Davis Dr. Displays include good coverage of the region's Native Americans, Oregon Trail pioneers and Idaho's mining heritage; open 9 am to 5 pm Monday to Saturday and 1 to 5 pm Sunday. Adjacent to the museum is the new **Black History Museum** (☎ 208-433-0017), open 10 am to 5 pm Tuesday to Saturday, 1 to 5 pm Sunday; admission $2/1.

Boise Art Museum (☎ 208-345-8330), 670 S Julia Davis Dr, features permanent and traveling exhibits of visual arts, including an American Realism collection. The museum is open from 10 am to 5 pm Tuesday to Friday, from noon to 5 pm weekends; admission $4/2/1, free the first Thursday each month, when the museum stays open until 9 pm.

IDAHO

In the middle of the park is **Zoo Boise** (☎ 208-384-4260), 355 N Julia Davis Dr, which boasts a large display of birds of prey as well as moose, elk and Bighorn sheep. In addition to traditional African zoo favorites, there's a children's petting zoo. Open 10 am to 5 pm daily, and until 9 pm Thursday (half-price day) Memorial Day to Labor Day; admission $4/2/1.75 adults/children/seniors.

The **Discovery Center of Idaho** (☎ 208-343-9895), 131 Myrtle St, is a hands-on science museum that's popular with children. Don't miss the magnetic sand. Open 10 am to 5 pm Tuesday to Saturday and noon to 5 pm Sunday; admission $4/3/2.50.

The **Boise Tour Train** (☎ 208-342-4796) operates city tours in the open-air 'Tootin Tater' from Julia Davis Park daily during summer, Wednesday to Sunday in September, and weekends only October and May; call for departure times. Admission $7/6/4.50.

Boise State University

Idaho's largest university is across a footbridge from Julia Davis Park. Founded in 1932, BSU joined the state university system only in 1974. There's little notable architecture on the 110-acre campus, but its setting along the Boise River Greenbelt makes for a nice stroll.

Basque Block

Along Grove St between 6th St and Capitol Blvd, several sites commemorate Idaho's Basque pioneers. The entire block was rebuilt to resemble one from Euzkadi (the traditional Basque homeland) just in time for Jaialdi 2000 – don't miss this fantastic once-every-five-years celebration in 2005 if you're in town. The **Basque Museum & Cultural Center** (☎ 208-343-2671), 611 Grove St, tells the story of these Pyrenean people who settled in Idaho from the late 19th century onward; southwestern Idaho has one of the largest Basque populations outside of Europe. The adjacent **Cyrus Jacobs-Uberuaga House**, 607 Grove St, built (Boise's first brick building), is part of the museum. Both sites are open 10 am to 4 pm Tuesday to Friday and 11 am to 3 pm Saturday; admission $3/1.

Morrison Knudsen Nature Center

Behind the Fish & Game Dept, this free environmental education center (☎ 208-334-2225), 600 S Walnut St, has a large outdoor wetlands area and habitat exhibits – check out the underwater stream viewing windows. The wetlands and adjacent museum are open 9 am to 4 pm Tuesday to Friday and 11 am to 5 pm Saturday and noon to 4 pm Sunday. The stream area is open daily sunrise to sunset.

Boise Depot

The grand Union Pacific Railroad (UP) depot, 2603 Eastover Terrace off Crescent Rim, lords over Boise from Rose Hill. Built in 1925, the Spanish colonial building was mothballed when Amtrak discontinued its passenger service in 1997. The depot is closed indefinitely, but the city hopes to reopen it as a museum. The surrounding Platt Gardens are a nice shady spot for a quiet picnic.

Old Idaho Penitentiary

Idaho's first jail (☎ 208-368-6080), 2445 N Penitentiary Rd, was built in 1870 and used until 1974, when it was replaced by a new hoosegow and mutated into a museum. On the National Register of Historic Places, this creepy, fascinating and well-curated expokey (Idaho's number one tourist attraction) shows how incarceration facilities reflect changing cultural notions of punishment and criminality.

The Old Pen is open 10 am to 5 pm daily during summer, otherwise noon to 5 pm daily. A brochure describes a 90-minute self-guided tour; call for the guided tour schedule. Admission is $4/3. From Broadway Ave, follow Warm Springs Rd east 1½ miles to Penitentiary Rd.

Idaho Botanical Garden

This expansive garden (☎ 208-343-8649), 2373 N Penitentiary Rd, has numerous theme collections, including Basque, Heirloom rose and butterfly gardens. The Meditation Garden seems an odd place, backed up against the walls of the Old Pen. Open 9 am to 5 pm weekdays (Friday until 8 pm) and 10 am to 6 pm weekends mid-April to mid-October; admission $3.50/3.

Boise River Greenbelt

This 20-mile paved hiking, jogging and biking path paralleling Boise River links 12 of Boise's open spaces including Kathryn Albertson, Shoreline, Ann Morrison Memorial, Julia Davis, and Municipal parks; the BSU campus; Warm Springs Golf Course; and Discovery State Park (outside of Boise). The **Pioneer Walk** near Ann Morrison Memorial Park connects the Greenbelt with downtown's Front St. Waters at the **Natatorium and Hydrotube** (☎ 208-345-9270), 1811 Warm Springs Ave in Municipal Park, flow from nearby hot springs. Get a free map from Boise Parks & Recreation (see Information, earlier).

Activities

Wheels R Fun (☎ 208-343-8228), on Shoreline Dr at S 13th St in Shoreline Park, rents bicycles and in-line skates ($5/hour), rafts ($24/four hours) and sells inner tubes. Boise River Tours (☎ 208-333-0003) runs half-day rafting trips ($40/25) – 300,000 people float the river every year; its Web site is at www.boiserivertours.com.

Just minutes from downtown, the Boise River has a popular fly-fishing stretch. Favorite holes within an easy drive of downtown include: South Fork of the Boise River for rainbow trout; South Fork of the Snake River for cutthroat and brown trout; and Silver Creek for rainbow and brown trout. Contact Idaho Angler (☎ 208-389-9957, 800-787-9957), 1682 S Vista Ave, for tips, gear and guided trips.

Special Events

The **Boise River Festival** (☎ 208-338-8887), in late June, is one of the biggest community events of the year, featuring free headliner concerts, fireworks, parades and more. Get details at www.boiseriverfestival.org. The **San Inazio Basque Festival** (☎ 208-343-2671), the last weekend of July, celebrates Boise's Basque heritage with folk dancing, music and garlicky eats. The popular **Western Idaho Fair** (☎ 208-376-3247), in late August at the fairgrounds west of downtown, celebrates the spud state's agricultural bounty with a carnival, rodeo, cotton candy and many competitions; specifics are available at www.idahofair.com. September's **City Arts Celebration** (☎ 208-336-4936) brims with special performances, films and exhibits. **Art in the Park** (☎ 208-345-8330) is yet another fun annual arts and crafts festival held in Julia Davis Memorial Park in early September.

Places to Stay

There's a good selection of moderately priced accommodations. Stay close to downtown to enjoy the evening street life. Even with more than 3000 rooms, reservations are useful, especially when conventions are in town. Boise's grand dame, the regal *Idanha Hotel (928 Main St)* is closed indefinitely for renovation. Boise's bed tax is 11%.

Camping Swimming and fishing in the Boise River are offered by *On the River RV Park (☎ 208-375-7432, 800-375-7432, 6000 N Glenwood St)*. Tent sites cost $15; RV hookups $20. Head north 4 miles from I-84 exit 46, then east (right) on US 20/26 another 4 miles and turn left (north) onto Glenwood St. Near the same exit is *Fiesta RV Park (☎ 208-375-8207, 1101 Fairview Ave)*. Tent sites are $20; full hookups $25. The closest public campsites are off Hwy 21 in the Boise National Forest (see Around Boise, later).

Hotels & Motels Older motor lodges west of downtown include: *Sands Motel (☎ 208-343-2533, 1111 W State St)*, which has singles/doubles for $35/40; the similarly priced *Cabana Inn (☎ 208-343-6000, 1600 Main St)*; and the remodeled *Budget Inn (☎ 208-344-8617, 2600 Fairview Ave)*, with a sauna and restaurant ($40/45). There's another budget area along Capitol Blvd

IDAHO

near BSU. *University Inn (☎ 208-345-7170, 800-345-7170, 2360 University Dr)* has a restaurant and pool ($50 to $80). Across the street, *Boulevard Motel* has similar rates.

Downtown, the clean *Boise Centre Guest Lodge (☎ 208-342-9351, 1314 Grove St)* has a pool and nonsmoking rooms ($45/50). An original Boise hotel (1910), the fully renovated *Owyhee Plaza Hotel (☎ 208-343-4611, 800-233-4611, 1109 Main St)* has a good restaurant and pool (from $90/100). *Doubletree Downtown (☎ 208-344-7691, 1800 Fairview Ave)* is not as close to the city center as it claims but nonetheless its restaurant, pool and fitness center attract harried business travelers (from $70 weekdays, $100 weekends).

Boise River Inn (☎ 208-344-9988, 1140 S Colorado Ave), near the east end of BSU, has a pool and some rooms have kitchenettes ($55/60). *Best Western Safari Inn (☎ 208-344-6556, 800-541-6556, 1070 Grove St)* has a pool, sauna and hot tub ($60/75). Near the airport (I-84 exit 53) is *Best Western Vista Inn (☎ 208-336-8100, 800-727-5006, 2645 Airport Way)*; rooms start at $80. It caters to rafters and other backcountry travelers. Airport parking is $4.25/day.

Statehouse Inn (☎ 208-342-4622, 800-243-4622, 981 Grove St) is convenient to downtown and has a spa ($85/95). *Doubletree Riverside (☎ 208-343-1871, 2900 Chinden Blvd)*, west of downtown along the Boise River, has a restaurant, pool and fitness center (from $90). *West Coast Park Center Suites (☎ 208-342-1044, 800-342-1044, 424 E Park Center Blvd)* also caters to working stiffs (from $70).

B&Bs A former governor's mansion on the National Register of Historic Places, *Idaho Heritage Inn B&B (☎ 208-342-8066, 109 W Idaho St)* is within walking distance of downtown ($70 to $100). The antique *Robin's Nest B&B (☎ 208-336-9551, 800-717-9551, 2389 W Boise Ave)* is a 19th-century Victorian home ($75 to $100).

Places to Eat

The *Boise Co-op (☎ 208-472-4500, 888 W Fort St)* is Idaho's largest natural foods store; open 9 am to 9 pm daily (until 8 pm Sunday).

The *Brick Oven Beanery (☎ 208-342-3456)*, near 8th and Main Sts, offers outdoor seating facing the Grove. The food is inexpensive (most dishes under $7), hearty and quite good, featuring salads to burgers. In the 8th St Market Place, *Cafe Ole (☎ 208-344-3222, 404 S 8th St)* serves good, if a bit blase, Mexican food (most dishes less than $10). Downtown, *Pollo Rey (☎ 208-345-0323, 222 N 8th St)*, at Idaho St, rolls quick burritos (around $5). Friendly *Gernika (☎ 208-344-2175, 202 S Capitol)* has Boise's best beef tongue (Saturday only from 11:30 am for $6), solomo pork tenderloin sandwiches and other piquant Basque specialties (everything is less than $8), as well as a full complement of draught beers and Basque wine. Enjoy the sunset at a sidewalk table.

Kulture Klatsch (☎ 208-345-0452, 409 S 8th St) is a friendly caffeine-lovers' haven, with live music six nights a week and an eclectic light menu. Both artsy and homey, *Flying M Coffeehouse (☎ 208-345-4320, 500 W Idaho St)* serves pastries, espresso drinks and light lunches on mismatched thrift-store dinette sets. There's acoustic music in the evening and folk art for sale. Old Boise's *Moxie Java (☎ 208-343-9033, 570 W Main St)*, part of a ubiquitous chain, is another popular gathering place.

The Ram (☎ 208-345-2929, 709 E Park Blvd), near Broadway Ave in the Bighorn Brewing Company, is popular with families; try the fajitas. *Aladdin's Egyptian Restaurant (☎ 208-368-0880, 111 Broadway Ave)* offers Mediterranean cuisine and belly dancing Thursday through Saturday evenings. *Flying Pie Pizzaria (☎ 208-384-0000, 1016 Broadway)* delivers Boise's best pies – tear out a yellow pages 'Pizza' section and you get $2 off!

In the 8th St Marketplace, *Milford's Fish House (☎ 208-342-8382, 405 S 8th St)* serves a good selection of deep-sea creatures, including fresh Pacific oysters. *Gamekeeper Restaurant*, in the Owyhee Plaza Hotel, is a bastion of traditional American dining, with feats of carving presented in a stately 1920s dining room.

Entertainment

Cinemas Recline in the lap of the mummy and enjoy first-run releases at Old Boise's *Egyptian Theatre* (☎ 208-342-1441, 700 W Main St). Nearby is the mainstream *8th St Market Place Theatre* (☎ 208-342-0299), at 8th and Front Sts. For independent and foreign hits, head to *The Flicks* (☎ 208-342-4222, 646 Fulton St).

Theaters The *Idaho Shakespeare Festival* (☎ 208-336-9221, 408 S 9th St) performs al fresco in Park Center Park (3150 Park Center Blvd) mid-June to early September. *Boise Little Theatre* (☎ 208-342-5104, 100 E Fort St), *Stage Coach Theatre* (☎ 208-342-2000) and chop-sockey *Knock 'Em Dead Dinner Theatre* (☎ 208-385-0021, 333 S 9th St) are noteworthy regional troupes.

Performing Arts Select-A-Seat (☎ 208-426-3535, 426-1494) hawks tickets for many events; look on www.idahotickets.com. Most of the following companies perform on the BSU campus at either the *Morrison Center for the Performing Arts* (☎ 208-426-1110, 1910 Campus Dr) or at the *BSU Pavilion* (☎ 208-426-1766, 1800 University Dr). *Boise Master Chorale* (☎ 208-344-7901) holds concerts in October, December, March and May. The internationally acclaimed *Oinkari Basque Dancers* (☎ 208-336-8219) perform at festivals and cultural events throughout the year. The *Esther Simplot Performing Arts Academy* (☎ 208-345-9116, 516 S 9th St) is home to *Ballet Idaho* (☎ 208-343-0556), Boise's professional dance troupe; *Boise Opera* (☎ 208-345-3531); and the *Boise Philharmonic* (☎ 208-344-7849), which accompanies most of the above and has its own concert series.

Live Music Eclectic bands perform upstairs and downstairs at *Tom Grainey's Sporting Pub* (☎ 208-345-2505) and *JT Toad's Lounge* (☎ 208-345-2955, 107–109 S 6th St). For a head-on collision with Boise's punk scene, dive into *Neurolux Lounge* (☎ 208-343-0886, 111 N 11th St). Drown your sorrows at *Blues Bouquet* (☎ 208-345-6605, 1010 Main St). Boise's oldest watering hole, *Pengilly's*

Saloon (☎ 208-345-6344, 513 Main St), still rocks out several times a week.

Pubs & Bars On a balcony above this busy downtown intersection, *Piper Pub & Grill* (☎ 208-343-2444), at 8th and Main Sts, has a happening happy hour. A few blocks away is Boise's best microbrewery, *Tablerock Brewpub & Grill* (☎ 208-342-0944, 705 Fulton St), with German-style beers and the best wursts. *Bitter Creek Ale House* (☎ 208-345-1813, 246 N 8th St) serves local ales and decent pub grub. *Harrison Hollow Brew House* (☎ 208-343-6820, 2455 Bogus Basin Rd), on the way to the ski resort, is a favorite for aprés-ski quaffing. *Emerald City Club* (☎ 208-342-5446, 415 S 9th St) is Boise's cruisiest gay bar. A happy mix of gay and straight people mix and mingle here and get down to disco hits.

Getting There & Away

Boise Municipal Airport (BOI, ☎ 208-383-3110), I-84 exit 53, 3½ miles southwest of downtown ($10 taxi), is served by six major carriers: America West, Delta/SkyWest, Horizon, Northwest, Southwest and United. Delta serves Boise with a dozen daily flights from Salt Lake City, UT. Horizon has several daily flights to Boise from Pocatello, Idaho Falls and Hailey; Seattle and Spokane, WA; and Portland, OR. Northwest runs nonstop flights to Minneapolis, MN, while Southwest has several daily flights to Salt Lake City; Portland; Spokane; Las Vegas, NV; Phoenix, AZ; and St Louis, MO. United flies daily to Denver. A planned 20-year expansion starting in 2000 will double the size of the airport. Sun Valley Stages (☎ 208-733-3921, 800-574-8661) operates winter shuttles between and the Boise Municipal Airport and Sun Valley (see Ketchum & Sun Valley, later).

Greyhound (☎ 208-343-3681), 1212 W Bannock St, plies three principal routes: I-84 between Salt Lake City and Portland via Boise; I-15/US 20/287/191 between Salt Lake City and Bozeman, MT, via Pocatello; and US 95 between Reno, NV, and Spokane. Buses depart Boise three times daily for Salt Lake City and Portland.

IDAHO

Northwestern Trailways (☎ 208-336-3300, 800-366-3830) serves Seattle daily via Spokane. Idaho stops along this route include: Boise (departs Greyhound depot at 9:15 am), McCall, Riggins, White Bird, Grangeville, Lewiston and Moscow.

Boise is just north of I-84, which traverses southwestern and south-central Idaho, linking Salt Lake City to eastern Oregon via Twin Falls and Boise. US 95 snakes north-south along the length of western Idaho linking Reno to British Columbia via Boise, Lewiston and Coeur d'Alene. Hwy 55, a shorter route, heads north from Boise to New Meadows via McCall, where it joins US 95.

Getting Around

Boise Urban Stages (the BUS; ☎ 208-336-1010) numbered bus shelters are easy to spot, but those numbers don't correspond to numbered bus routes. The BUS Transit Mall is at Main and Idaho Sts between 9th St and Capitol Blvd. Not all routes run Saturday and some route numbers are reassigned. Buses do not operate Sunday. Schedules are available onboard, at the BUS office, tourist offices and local businesses.

The usual suspects – Avis (☎ 208-383-3350), Budget (☎ 208-383-3090), Hertz (383-3100) and National (☎ 208-383-3210) – await at the airport. Thrifty (☎ 208-336-1904), 2770 S Orchard St, is near the airport. Idaho Car Rental (☎ 208-342-7795, 800-634-6539), 2393 Airport Way, has cars, vans and 4WD vehicles. Beg Dollar (☎ 208-345-9727), in the terminal at 3201 Airport Way, or Practical Rent-a-Car (344-3732), 2565 W Main St, for cheaper rates. Enterprise (☎ 208-345-0004, 800-736-8222) will pick you up from your hotel.

Boise City Taxi (☎ 208-377-3333) and Yellow Cab (☎ 208-345-5555) are both on call 24-7.

AROUND BOISE
Boise Front

Northeast of Boise, trails network the mountains offering many **hikes**, typically up barren gulches. An easily accessible trail begins behind the Old Idaho Penitentiary

(see above). The Front, however, is usually too hot during summer for midday hiking. A short **scenic drive** up Table Rock Rd leads to the distinctive mesa overlooking Boise called **Table Rock** (3658 feet). Roads and trails also reach **Boise Peak** (6525 feet). The area is popular for **mountain biking**. Bogus Basin Rd continues behind Bogus Basin Resort (see below) to the *USFS Shafer Butte Campground*, the area's only campground. A good topo map for any activity is *Off-Road Vehicles on the Boise Front*, available from Boise's BLM office.

Bogus Basin Resort

Sixteen miles north of Boise, Bogus Basin (☎ 208-332-5100 ski area, ☎ 800-367-4397 reservations, ☎ 208-342-2100 ski report) offers downhill and cross-country skiing from mid-November to mid-April. The resort (base elevation 6000 feet) has two downhill areas, Bogus Creek and Pioneer, with 45 runs and a maximum vertical drop of 1800 feet. Bogus Creek has restaurants, lifts up Deer Point (7070 feet) and services at the Bogus Creek Lodge.

Pioneer offers lifts up Shafer Butte (7590 feet) and lodging (from $70) and restaurants at the *Pioneer Inn Condominiums* (☎ 208-332-5224). The resort has 17 miles of Nordic trails, night skiing, sleigh rides, instruction and rentals. It's open 10 am to 10 pm weekdays and 9 am to 10 pm weekends. Full-day lift tickets cost $35/8; half-day tickets are $20. During summer, the resort offers lift-served mountain biking and miles of hiking trails.

From downtown Boise, take Hays St north to Harrison Blvd, which leads directly onto Bogus Basin Rd.
Web site: www.bogusbasin.com

World Center for Birds of Prey

Primarily a rehabilitation facility, this center (☎ 208-362-8687), 5666 W Flying Hawk Lane, also contains fine educational displays. Its three sections include an interpretive center, the California Condor Facility and the Tropical Raptor Building. There are also 90-minute tours of the nursery (where rare birds such as the peregrine falcon are incubated) and the rehab center. The outdoor flight display stars trained falcons and an adult harpy eagle, one of the world's largest raptors. Open 9 am to 5 pm daily March to October, 10 am to 4 pm November to February; admission $4/3/2.

Follow S Cole Rd (I-84 exit 50) 6 miles to W Flying Hawk Lane.

BLM Snake River Birds of Prey National Conservation Area

This 755-sq-mile refuge encompasses North America's densest concentration of nesting birds of prey. Stretching along 80 miles of the basalt cliff–lined Snake River, the desert refuge is home to many pairs of majestic raptors, as well as red-tailed hawk, golden eagle, prairie falcon and great horned owl. Mid-March to late June is the best viewing season.

Access to the refuge is via Kuna, south of Boise, or Grand View. Take Hwy 69 (I-84 exit 44) south 8 miles to Kuna, and follow signs 5 miles south on Swan Falls Rd. The visitors center beyond Kuna and the BLM Boise District (☎ 208-384-3300) has an area map and brochure, which suggests a three- to four-hour 56-mile **driving tour** of the refuge. A 10-mile **hiking** trail follows the north side of the Snake River between Swan Falls Dam and Celebration Park. This section of river is popular for **floating**; contact MacKay Wilderness River Trips (☎ 800-635-5336), www.mackayriver.com, or Birds of Prey Expeditions (☎ 208-327-8903).

Three Island Crossing State Park

This state park (☎ 208-366-2394) is where the main branch of the Oregon Trail crossed the Snake River. Three islands divide the wide river into smaller, more easily fordable segments. Pioneers who forded here continued along the more hospitable north bank of the Snake River. Those who did not were consigned to the southern cutoff, a barren and dangerous trail through blistering desert.

The visitors center (open daily 10 am to 4 pm) provides a good overview of the history and hardships of the Oregon Trail, but is overshadowed by a shiny new inter-pretive center and movie theater (open 10 am to 4 pm Sunday to Friday, 9 am to 5 pm Saturday) in the day-use area; admission $3/1.50. A Conestoga wagon is on display in front of the visitors center, and it's hard to believe that people would attempt to cross the Snake – let alone the continent – in such an unwieldy contraption. 'Rut nuts' enjoy retracing a portion of the Oregon Trail that winds off through the park but disappears in the sagebrush; the easily visible remnants of the trail descend the steep hill across the Snake River from the park, where the crossing began.

A lovely *picnic area* (open sunrise to sunset) overlooks the islands and quiet *campground* ($12/16 for tents/RVs) has showers. Day-use is $2 per vehicle. Three Island Crossing (2482 feet) is 26 miles southeast of Mountain Home (I-84 exit 121), 2 miles southeast of Glenns Ferry.

Cambridge

Unassuming Cambridge (population 500; elevation 3840 feet) is at the junction of US 95 and Hwy 71, which is the only road leading to Hells Canyon Dam (see Hells Canyon National Recreation Area in the Central Idaho Rockies section). When traveling north on US 95, Cambridge offers more comfortable and cheaper places than does the often-scorching Weiser.

Indian Hot Springs (☎ *208-549-0070, 914 Hot Springs Rd),* 6 miles northwest of Weiser, has tent sites ($8) and RV hookups ($12) with a mineral-water pool (open to nonguests), a hot tub and showers. At *Frontier Motel & RV Park* (☎ *208-257-3851, 240 S Superior St)* sites cost $12 and rooms start at $28. *Hunters Inn* (☎ *208-257-3325)* and historic *Cambridge House B&B (same ☎),* along with a bistro and espresso shop, are on Superior St. Rooms start at $35 at the hotel; B&B rooms range from $40 to $70. *Kay's Cafe* (☎ *208-257-3561),* on Superior St, serves breakfast all day. Its steak and homemade pies are excellent.

New Meadows

At the important US 95/Hwy 55 junction (and on the 45th parallel, the halfway

IDAHO

Fiddle Fest

Fiddle-happy Weiser is known nationwide for its **National Old Time Fiddlers Contest**, which is held the third week of June and attracts folk musicians of all ages from across North America. A crafts fair, a parade, a rodeo and a cowboy-poet gathering are held in conjunction with the festival.

mark between the equator and the North Pole), New Meadows (population 550) is a good, cheap town in which to spend the night. The helpful USFS Payette National Forest New Meadows Ranger Station, on Hwy 55, is open 7:30 am to 4:30 pm weekdays.

Places to Stay & Eat

Popular with cyclists, *Zim's Hot Springs* (☎ *208-347-2686*), 4 miles north of New Meadows west of US 95, has grassy but shadeless tent sites ($8) and hookups ($13). Soaks are $4/6 for guests/nonguests. The *Heartland Inn* (☎ *208-347-2114, 888-509-7400*), on US 95 at Hwy 55, has basic rooms for $45/50, new suites with kitchenettes ($60), B&B rooms from $75 and a hot tub.

Campsites are $10 to $15 at *Givens Hot Springs* (☎ *208-495-2000*), 12 miles south of Marsing on Hwy 78. It offers mineral waters in a pool ($5 for nonguests), private baths and small cabins. It's a long but worthwhile drive to Silver City for the antediluvian *Idaho Hotel* (☎ *208-583-4104, 326-5051 in winter, PO Box 75, Murphy, ID 83650-0075*), presided over by amiable Ed Jagels. Historic rooms start at $20 and a six-room apartment ($50) sleeps up to eight. There's also a free primitive *BLM campground* in Silver City.

Two good restaurants feed this unlikely corner of Idaho. The *Sandbar* (☎ *208-896-4124, 18 1st St E*), on Hwy 78 a block east of Marsing from the junction with US 95, is a lounge and supper club overlooking the Snake River. The steak, fresh seafood and

prime rib are all excellent. (The prime rib is served weekends only.) Ten miles northwest of Murphy is the *Blue Canoe* (☎ *208-495-2269*), another popular surf-and-turf dinner house with a Cajun flair. Both are open for lunch and dinner; reservations advised.

BOISE BASIN

The timbered Boise Mountains and the Boise Basin's crystal-clear streams are bounded on the west by Hwy 55 between Boise and Banks, on the north by the beautiful South Fork of the Payette River, and on the east by Hwy 21 between Boise and Lowman. If you have the inclination, two scenic routes lead out of Boise through the Boise Basin: The **Payette River Scenic Byway** follows Hwy 55 between Boise and New Meadows, via the Long Valley and McCall; and the **Ponderosa Pine Scenic Byway** (Hwy 21) climbs northeast from Boise to Lowman, continuing on to the Sawtooth National Recreation Area (see the Central Idaho Rockies section, later in this chapter).

Information

Contact the USFS Boise National Forest for outdoors information; rafters should request their 'Payette River Whitewater' brochure. The USFS Boise National Forest Lowman Ranger Station (☎ 208-259-3361), Hwy 21 east of Lowman, is open 8 am to 4:30 pm daily.

Idaho City

Quirky Idaho City (population around 500), along Hwy 21, 38 miles northeast of Boise, was founded in 1862 after a large gold strike. Today the town has many well-preserved nineteenth-century buildings and two museums worthy of a visit: the Boise Basin Museum and a gold rush museum. The town is experiencing another mini–population boom, as its rustic charm seduces more Boise-employed commuters. The scenic Boise Basin loop drive leads through the tailings to the historic mining camps of Centerville, Placerville and Pioneerville.

Activities

The Payette River is the closest river to Boise with challenging **kayaking** and **white-water rafting** (see 'Recommended River Trips & Outfitters'). Enjoy the hot springs with nearby USFS campgrounds along the South Fork Payette River. **Pine Flats Hot Springs** are 6 miles west of Lowman on Hwy 17, ¼-mile from the campground. The popular riverside **Kirkham Hot Springs** are 3 miles east of Lowman near the campground. **Bonneville Hot Springs** are 18 miles east of Lowman along Warm Springs Creek. **Sacajawea Hot Springs**, near Grandjean Campground and the rustic Sawtooth Lodge (☎ 208-259-3331, 344-2437 in Boise), are 22 miles east of Lowman; go 5 miles down USFS Rd 524 to Wapiti Creek.

Places to Stay & Eat

There are three *USFS campgrounds* off Hwy 55 between Banks and the USFS High Valley Ranger Station. Idaho City's smoky *Calamity Janes Cafe*, just off Hwy 21 on Main St, serves up one hell of a 'sobbing omelet' for breakfast and lunch. Alternatively, just down the road, smoke-free *Trudy's Kitchen* offers prime rib and finer dining.

Getting There & Away

Northwestern Trailways (☎ 208-336-3300, 800-366-3830) stops on Hwy 55 in Horseshoe Bend. Daily buses go northbound to Spokane, WA, at 9:45 am; southbound buses go to Boise at 7:05 pm. It's 35 miles from Boise to Banks on Hwy 55, 35 miles between Banks and Lowman, and 71 miles from Lowman to Boise on Hwy 21.

McCALL

At the northern end of the deceptively long Long Valley, McCall (population 3200; elevation 5037 feet) sits along Payette Lake's southern shore, where the Payette River begins its journey south to the Snake River. This year-round resort community – unlike others in Idaho – tries to minimize hype and glitz and maintain a relaxing pace of life, while offering water sports, great winter skiing and good restaurants and lodging.

The outdoor decks at the lakefront marina's bars and restaurants offer views of distant forested mountains. Public access to the lake is largely limited to Ponderosa State Park (see below).

Orientation

Hwy 55 enters town from the northwest and becomes east-west Lake St as it follows Payette Lake's south shore. Restaurants and stores are diffused along Lake St. Downtown, Hwy 55 turns south and becomes N 3rd St.

Information

The USFS Payette National Forest headquarters (☎ 208-634-0700), 804 W Lakeside Ave, is open 7:30 am to 4:30 pm weekdays. Detailed recreation information is more readily available from the two USFS Payette National Forest offices: McCall Ranger District (☎ 208-634-0400), 102 W Lake St at Mission St; and forest Krassel Ranger District (☎ 208-634-0600), 500 N Mission St. The Idaho Dept of Fish & Game (☎ 208-634-8137) is at 555 Deinhard Lane. The post office is on the corner of Hwy 55 and Deinhard Lane. Blue Grouse Bookshop (☎ 208-634-2434), in McCall Drug at 2nd and Lenora Sts, is a good source for Idahoana. The McCall Memorial Hospital (☎ 208-634-2221) is at 1000 State St.

Ponderosa State Park

This lakeside park (☎ 208-634-2164) has two units: Main and North Beach. The day-use fee is $3 per vehicle. The Main Unit, on a peninsula extending into Payette Lake, is 2 miles east of McCall near the end of Davis Ave. Boating, fishing and swimming are popular summer pastimes. In winter, people flock here to build ice sculptures, which are showcased during the February **Annual Winter Carnival**, and to cross-country ski. A graveled loop road crowns the peninsula, leading to great view points and forest hiking trails. Wildlife is abundant – deer make themselves at home in the campground, while beavers, fox and elk roam the meadows and marshes. Tent sites ($12), hookups ($16) and showers are available year-round. The North

IDAHO

Beach Unit, at the north end of Payette Lake, is a summertime, day-use only area. Its sandy beach is a favorite with swimmers and nonmotorized boaters. Follow Warren Wagon Rd north from Hwy 55 along Payette Lake's western shore.

Activities

Canyons Inc (☎ 208-634-4303) provides floating and fishing trips, and offers boating and kayaking trips on Payette Lake. Sports Marina (☎ 208-634-8361), 1300 E Lake St, also rents boats. Gravity Sports (☎ 208-634-8530), 503 Pine St, sells and rents gear, including bicycles, kayaks and canoes. Mountain Cycle & Snowboard (☎ 208-634-6333), 212 N 3rd St, rents mountain bikes. Ya-Hoo Corrals (☎ 208-634-3360, 888-562-5772), Warren Wagon Rd, and Epley's Horse Rides (☎ 208-634-5173), Lick Creek Rd, offer guided horseback rides ($15/hour) with views of Payette Lake. Little Ski Hill (5324 feet), 3 miles northwest of McCall on Hwy 55, is run by the Payette Lakes Ski Club (☎ 208-634-5691). Its 405 feet of vertical terrain are ideal for Alpine and telemark skiers. The ski area features 25km of groomed Nordic trails ($6) and a snowboard park ($12). Also see Brundage Mountain, below.

Places to Stay

McCall Campground (☎ 208-634-5165, 190 Krahn Lane) is 1 mile south of McCall off Hwy 55. Tent sites ($7/person), RV hookups ($14) and showers ($4) are available year-round. On McCall's western end is the charming and well-run *Brundage Inn* (☎ 208-634-2344, 800-643-2009, 1005 W Lake St). Some of its clean rooms (from $45) have kitchenettes. The attractive *Riverside Motel Condominiums* (☎ 208-634-5610, 800-326-5610, 400 W Lake St) front the Payette River. Some rooms ($40/45) have kitchenettes and condos start at $75. *Brundage Bungalows* (☎ 208-634-8573, 308 W Lake St) are refurbished kitchenette cabins set among trees ($60 to $100). The friendly *Scandia Inn Motel* (☎ 208-634-7394, 401 N 3rd St) charges $45/50. *Hotel McCall* (☎ 208-634-8105, 1101 N 3rd St) is a remodeled property with a great

downtown lakefront location and individually decorated rooms from $70. Nestled amid pines two minutes west of town, *Northwest Passage B&B* (☎ 208-634-5349, 800-597-6658, 201 Rio Vista Blvd) is a modern home ($70 to $100). The peaceful *Bear Creek Lodge* (☎ 208-634-3551, 800-634-2327), 4 miles north of McCall at Hwy 55 milepost 149, has fully equipped lodge rooms and cabins ($125 to $150).

Places to Eat

Start the day with espresso and pastries at *Mountain Java* (☎ 208-634-2027, 501 Pine St) or ubiquitous *Moxie Java* (☎ 208-632-3607, 312 E Lake St). For something heartier, try *The Pancake House* (☎ 208-634-5849, 209 N 3rd St). The *Heartland Deli*, E Lake St in the McCall Mall, serves muffins, bagels and sandwiches on its sunny lakefront terrace. Watch smokejumpers land over quiche and soup on the sunny deck at *Mountain Juice & Coffee Co* (337 Deinhard Lane), near the airport.

Fort Boise Cafe (☎ 208-634-8551, 406 W Lake St) has homestyle family dining. *Lardo Grill & Saloon* (☎ 208-634-8191, 600 Lake St) serves pasta, steak and hamburgers ($8 to $12); the bar is the local favorite. *The Yacht Club* (☎ 208-634-5649, 203 E Lake St) is home to *Romano's Ristorante*, featuring a substantial American and Italian menu served in a lakefront dining room. Most pasta dishes are less than $10. *Si Bueno* (☎ 208-634-2128, 335 Deinhard Lane) yes, is good…Mexican. *McCall Brewing Company* (☎ 208-634-2333, 809 N 3rd St) serves handcrafted ales, homemade soup and tasty burgers and sandwiches. *The Mill Steak & Spirits* (☎ 208-634-7683), Hwy 55 at Stibnite St, is the premier steak house with prices to match.

Getting There & Away

Just south of town off Hwy 55, the McCall Airport is home to the USFS Smokejumpers Base. Private companies operate one- to eight-passenger, nonscheduled intercity and charter flights from McCall throughout central Idaho. Most charge an hourly rate for backcountry charter flights.

IDAHO

Many, however, offer a fixed per-seat fare with a two-passenger minimum on certain intercity routes. McCall Air (☎ 208-634-7137, 800-992-6559) flies Boise-McCall ($75); charter flights cost around $225/hour. Boise-based Access Air (☎ 800-307-4984) also has fixed per-seat fares for Boise-McCall. Pioneer Air Service (☎ 208-634-5445, 634-7127) operates Boise-McCall charter flights.

Northwestern Trailways (☎ 208-634-2340, 800-366-3830) stops at Bill's Grocery at 147 N 3rd St. Daily buses go northbound (11:45 am) to Spokane, Washington, via Riggins, Grangeville, Lewiston and Moscow; southbound buses (5:15 pm) go to Boise via Cascade and Horseshoe Bend. McCall is 28 miles north of Cascade and 12 miles southeast of New Meadows at the junction of Hwy 55 and US 95.

BRUNDAGE MOUNTAIN

Known for producing Olympic skiers, Brundage Mountain (☎ 208-634-4151, 800-888-7544 office, ☎ 208-634-7462 ski area) has 38 runs with a maximum vertical drop of 1800 feet over 2 miles. Base elevation is 5840 feet. Full-day lift tickets cost $32 for adults; $26 after 1 pm. Full-day tickets cost $24/17 for teens/children (seven to 11); $18/14 after 1 pm. Children under the age of seven always ski free. Brundage Mountain Ski Cats (☎ 800-888-7544) offers guided backcountry skiing. The Brundage Mountain Ski School and Brundage Mountain Rental & Ski Shop offer equipment rentals, instruction and a new snowshoe program. The ski season is mid-November to mid-April. Dial ☎ 208-634-7669 or ☎ 888-255-7669 for a snow report.
Web site: www.brundage.com

Brundage is also popular during summer for its outdoor concerts, hiking and biking. It has 15 miles of single-track mountain bike trails as well as several lift-served mountain biking areas. The resort is open 9:30 am to 4:30 pm daily. It's 4 miles east of Hwy 55 and 4 miles north of McCall. In the day lodge, the *Brundage Mountain Restaurant (☎ 208-634-7462)* serves breakfast and lunch.

TWIN FALLS

A sprawling agricultural service center, Twin Falls is affectionately known as 'Twin.' Along the Snake River, which forms the city's northern border, are two spectacular waterfalls: Shoshone Falls, and to the east the city's namesake, Twin Falls. The walkway on the 1500-foot-long and 486-foot-high Perrine Bridge is the best place to view the impressive Snake River Canyon.

Daredevil Evel Knievel's aborted attempt to leap the canyon aboard a rocket-powered motorcycle propelled Twin to cartographic fame in 1974. Twin Falls (population 35,000; elevation 3747 feet) is a convenient jumping-off point for nearby destinations, as well as the out-of-this-world Craters of the Moon National Monument, the Sun Valley Resort and the Sawtooth National Recreation Area (see the Central Idaho Rockies section, later in this chapter).

Orientation

Twin Falls is 3 miles south of I-84 exit 173 along US 93, just south of the Snake River. In town, US 93 becomes Blue Lakes Blvd and turns west onto Addison Ave (US 30). Twin Falls' easily overlooked quaint downtown grid, which is removed from these two commercial strips, diagonally follows Shoshone St from the junction of Blue Lakes Blvd and Addison Ave. Shoshone St replaces 1st St downtown. Southwest of downtown is the newly redeveloped Old Towne district. Washington St (Hwy 74) leads south across Rock Creek to the airport.

Information

The Buzz Langdon Visitors Center (☎ 208-734-9531), on the west side of US 93 south of Perrine Bridge at the Snake River Canyon viewing area, is open 8 am to 8 pm daily in the summer months, weekends only in winter. The USFS Sawtooth National Forest office (☎ 208-737-3200) is at 2647 Kimberly Rd E. Nearby is the BLM Jarbidge Resource Area office (☎ 208-736-2350), 2620 Kimberly Rd E.

IDAHO

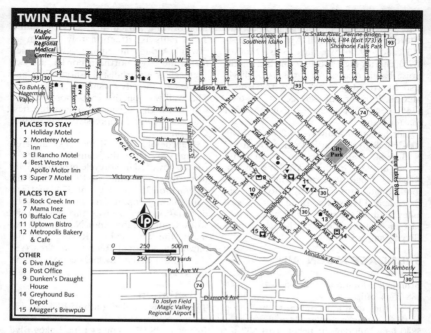

TWIN FALLS

PLACES TO STAY
1 Holiday Motel
2 Monterey Motor Inn
3 El Rancho Motel
4 Best Western Apollo Motor Inn
13 Super 7 Motel

PLACES TO EAT
5 Rock Creek Inn
7 Mama Inez
10 Buffalo Cafe
11 Uptown Bistro
12 Metropolis Bakery & Cafe

OTHER
6 Dive Magic
8 Post Office
9 Dunken's Draught House
14 Greyhound Bus Depot
15 Mugger's Brewpub

Herrett Center for Arts & Science

The free Herrett Center (☎ 208-736-3059), 315 Falls Ave on the College of Southern Idaho campus, displays an impressive collection of Pacific Northwest and pre-Columbian Central and South American artifacts. There's also a gallery of contemporary art and a planetarium ($4/3/2 or $9 per family). The center is open 1 to 9 pm Tuesday to Saturday in summer, 9:30 am to 8 pm Tuesday, 9:30 am to 4:30 pm Wednesday to Friday and 1 to 4:30 pm Saturday when school is in session.

Shoshone Falls Park

The 212-foot **Shoshone Falls** is nicknamed 'the Niagara of the West,' although it's more than 50 feet higher than Niagara Falls and once carried more water. Shoshone Falls may be dry, depending on when water from the Snake River is diverted about 20 miles upstream at Milner Dam for irrigation; flow

is highest March through May. The park's shaded lawns are a scenic picnic spot beneath the dramatic canyon walls. Nearby **Dierkes Lake** is a good place to swim, hike and dive.

Access to Shoshone Falls is only on the south side of the Snake River Canyon through the park. Take US 93 (I-84 exit 173) south 3 miles to Falls Ave (off Blue Lakes Blvd), head east 3 miles to a well-signed 3300 East Rd, and continue north 2 miles to the park. Day use is $3 per vehicle. There's a free overlook halfway to the park at a turnout beneath the power poles.

Places to Stay

Most places are clustered along Blue Lakes Blvd N and Addison Ave W; the latter is less expensive.

East of Twin Falls, ***Andersons Campground*** (☎ 208-825-9800), a half-mile east of I-84 exit 182, has a pool, laundry and showers ($17/23). The ***Twin Falls/Jerome***

KOA (☎ *208-324-4169, 800-562-4169*), 1 mile north of I-84 exit 173, has a laundry and a pool. Tent sites/RV hookups are $18/24.

Clean, nonsmoking rooms merit $27/30 at the friendly *El Rancho Motel* (☎ *208-733-4021, 380 Addison Ave W*). Other budget options include the *Holiday Motel* (☎ *208-733-4330, 615 Addison Ave W*) for $29/32 and *Monterey Motor Inn* (☎ *208-733-5151, 433 Addison Ave W*) for $30/35. The only reputable downtown property is the faded but acceptable *Super 7 Motel* (☎ *208-733-8770, 320 Main Ave S*), with rooms starting at $30.

Motel 6 (☎ *208-734-3993, 1472 Blue Lakes Blvd N*) charges $40/45. Comparably priced are the older *Weston Inn* (☎ *208-733-6095, 906 Blue Lakes Blvd N*) and the duper *Super 8 Motel* (☎ *208-734-5801, 1260 Blue Lakes Blvd N*). Rooms start at $45 at the *Best Western Apollo Motor Inn* (☎ *208-733-2010, 296 Addison Ave W*) and *Comfort Inn* (☎ *208-734-7494, 800-228-5150, 1893 Canyon Springs Rd*). Most have a pool.

All of Twin Falls' higher end hotels have pools, including the flashy *AmeriTel Inn* (☎ *208-736-8000, 800-822-8946, 1377 Blue Lakes Blvd N*), which charges $70/80; staid *Best Western Cavanaughs* (☎ *208-734-5000, 800-325-4000, 1357 Blue Lakes Blvd N*) at $80/90; and newer *Shilo Inn* (☎ *208-733-7545, 800-222-2244, 1586 Blue Lakes Blvd N*) for $75/85.

Places to Eat

Blue Lakes Blvd is chockablock with fast-food chains. Several locally owned restaurants downtown serve better food in friendly surroundings. Join ranchers at the *Buffalo Cafe* (☎ *208-734-0271, 218 4th Ave W*) for a hearty breakfast of buffalo chips, or fried potatoes smothered with gravy. Home to Twin's slightly alternative crowd, *Metropolis Bakery & Cafe* (☎ *208-734-4457, 125 Main Ave E*) is a great downtown bakery and espresso bar specializing in light lunches and decadent desserts. Next door, the *Uptown Bistro* (☎ *208-733-0900, 117 Main Ave E*) is a local lunch favorite where casual Cajun and Creole dinners are also a big draw. Southwestern *Mama Inez* (☎ *208-*

734-0733, 164 Main Ave N) serves interesting Mexican dishes like crab tacos. The area's best steak house is *Rock Creek* (☎ *208-734-4151, 200 Addison Ave W*), with good $15 prime rib dinners.

Entertainment

Dunken's Draught House (☎ *208-733-8114, 102 Main Ave N*) pours 21 draft beers, including cask-conditioned ales. The old bar is a friendly place to sup suds on a hot summer afternoon. Old Towne's lively *Muggers Brewpub* (☎ *208-733-2322, 516 2nd St S*), home of the Twin Falls Brewing Company, is Twin's newest dining and drinking hot spot; call to arrange a free brewery tour.

Getting There & Around

SkyWest/Delta (☎ *208-734-6232*) takes off daily for Salt Lake City, UT, out of the Joslyn Field Magic Valley Regional Airport (☎ 208-733-5215). Greyhound (☎ *208-733-3002*), 461 2nd Ave S, departs Twin Falls three times daily for Salt Lake City, Utah, and Portland, Oregon. There's also a daily bus to Pocatello. Sun Valley Stages (☎ *800-574-8661*) runs a winter charter service between Twin Falls and Ketchum.

Avis (☎ *208-733-5527*), Budget (☎ *208-734-4067*) and National (☎ *208-733-3646*) are at the airport. Hertz (☎ *208-733-2668*) is at 210 Shoshone St W. Used-A-Car Rental (☎ *208-733-2298*), 1654 Blue Lakes Blvd N, is cheaper.

AROUND TWIN FALLS
South Hills

About 25 miles southeast of Twin Falls in the Sawtooth National Forest (☎ *208-737-3200*) are the South Hills, a range of 7000-foot mountains with **hiking**, **horseback riding**, moderate to difficult **mountain biking** and camping. Take Hwy 50 east of Kimberly and head south on Rock Creek Rd (G3 or 3800 East Rd) up Rock Creek Canyon. Third Fork and Harrington For are popular trailheads. Family-run Mountain Magic Ski Area (☎ *208-423-6221*), with downhill and cross-country **skiing**, is at the end of the paved road.

IDAHO

Shoshone

Attention amateur spelunkers and Roadside America fans! Feeling touristy? The sleepy town of Shoshone (population 1385), 21 miles north of Twin Falls at the junction of US 26/93 and Hwy 75, is notable for nearby caves. **Mammoth Cave**, 10 miles north of Shoshone, 1½ miles west of Hwy 75, is actually a mile-long volcanic lava tube. The self-guided tour (admission $4/2) takes half an hour and the neglected museum above the entrance has a decaying taxidermy display. Seven miles farther north are the more touristy and inviting **Shoshone Indian Ice Caves** (☎ 886-2058), a glacier beneath lava flows 90 feet below ground. The largest cave is 1000 feet long, 30 feet wide and 40 feet high. Forty-minute tours ($5) depart 8 am to 7:15 pm May to September. Admission to the adjacent museum is free. Temperatures in the caves stay below freezing, so dress warmly, wear sturdy shoes and bring a flashlight. Contact the BLM Shoshone District office (☎ 886-2206) for more cave information.

City of Rocks National Reserve

The reserve(☎ 208-824-5519) is a jumble of granite towers, cliffs and pinnacles in a pinyon pine and juniper forest and contains some of the oldest exposed rock in North America. The California Cutoff of the Oregon Trail passed through the City of Rocks; on Register Rock, the names and initials of travelers, written with axle grease on the rock face, are still visible. The site offers world-class rock climbing with hundreds of short, mostly single-pitch, routes ranging from 5.4 to 5.14. *Campgrounds* ($8), open April to November, are primitive.

To reach the City of Rocks National Reserve from Twin Falls, head east on I-80 to Burley, then take Hwy 27 south for 17 miles to Oakley and follow the signs on a paved, then maintained-gravel, road 19 miles to the park.

Rafting & Kayaking

The 15-mile Murtaugh Section of the Snake River begins near the town of Murtaugh, southeast of Twin Falls, and ends at the eastern end of Twin Falls. This is an excellent Class III-IV day trip. To book a full-day white-water trip ($150), contact High Adventure River Tours (☎ 208-733-0123, 800-286-4123), 1211 E 2350 S, Hagerman, ID 83332.

East of Twin Falls (south of I-84 exit 188 at the end of Murtaugh Rd) the Snake River narrows to 40 feet. The resulting swirling waterfalls forced many explorers to abandon their boats and continue on foot. Downriver from here, the 14-mile whitewater Murtaugh Section is a kayaker's wet dream during springtime runoff.

Diving

Surprise! The deserts of Idaho may seem an unlikely place for scuba diving, but Dive Magic (☎ 208-733-8203), 236 Main Ave N, Twin Falls, offers lessons and rentals for use in nearby lakes.

HAGERMAN VALLEY

The well-irrigated Hagerman Valley (elevation 2959 feet) parallels a stretch of the Snake River Canyon that contains renowned fossils and Thousand Springs. The **Thousand Springs Scenic Byway** includes 48 miles on US 30 between Twin Falls and Bliss; the byway continues on Hwy 50 east of Twin Falls. Pleasant campgrounds with hot springs make this scenic area appealing. Fishing and birdwatching are excellent throughout the valley.

To reach the Hagerman Valley, follow US 30 west from Twin Falls or Buhl (US 30 drops into the valley 8 miles north of Buhl), or follow US 30 south (I-84 exit 141) from Bliss.

Hagerman

US 30 becomes north-south State St in Hagerman (population 850; elevation 2960 feet). The free **Hagerman Valley Historical Society Museum** on State St at Main St, open 1 to 5 pm Wednesday to Sunday, has a complete *Equus simplicidens* skeleton. See below for area lodging and restaurant information.

Thousand Springs

Rocky Mountain streams and rivers plunge underneath the basalt, lava-clogged Snake River Plain's porous surface and flow through subterranean aquifers as underground rivers. The Snake River's 400-foot canyon exposes these aquifers, which pour down its walls. The aptly named Thousand Springs are in all likelihood fed by the Lost River, which drains a large valley north of Arco only to disappear beneath the lava flows at Craters of the Moon National Monument. US 30 runs along the stretch of the Snake River where cascades of water gush out of the northern canyon walls, feeding a lush green valley. Much of the water is diverted directly into fish hatcheries and trout farms (producing 90% of the nation's farm-raised filets), and the rest is used for irrigation.

The Nature Conservancy (☎ 208-536-6797) owns the **Thousand Springs Preserve**, which includes 2 miles of springs and 3 miles of Snake River frontage and is open to visitors Friday to Monday afternoons, Memorial Day to Labor Day. To reach the preserve, turn off I-84 exit 155 at Wendell and follow signs toward Hagerman. After 3 miles, turn south at the sign for Buhl. Follow this road for 2½ miles and turn west at Rd 3200 S. After 2 miles the road comes to a T-junction; turn left onto Thousand Springs Grade. From the south, the site can be reached from US 30 via Clearlakes Rd at Buhl.

Malad Gorge State Park

The dramatic 250-foot Malad Gorge forms the core of Malad Gorge State Park (☎ 208-837-4505). The river crosses a lava plateau and plunges over a 60-foot waterfall into a narrow gorge, cutting its course 2½ miles downstream to its confluence with the Snake River. The best view of the waterfall and the springs gushing out of the canyon walls is from the Devil's Wash Bowl Overlook (3260 feet). The nearby steel footbridge spans the chasm leading to a 1-mile trail along the gorge's north rim. A road follows the gorge's south rim with stunning views overlooking the Snake River Canyon. The park has a picnic area, but camping is not allowed. To reach the park, take I-84 exit 147 and follow the signs 1 mile to the park. Alternatively from Hagerman, turn east on the small road immediately north of the Rock Lodge, which climbs 5 miles to the park.

A separate unit of the park, **Niagara Springs** is part of the Thousand Springs area and a national natural landmark. At this major waterfowl wintering site, a huge spring pours from the cliffs at 250 cubic feet per second to fill fishing-friendly Crystal Springs Lake. Take I-84 exit 157 and follow Rex Leland Hwy south 9 miles. From the south, take US 30 to Clearlakes Rd in Buhl.

Rafting & River Cruises

The Snake River through Hagerman Valley is a popular Class I-III rafting trip, not for white-water, but for exploration of canyon wildlife and geology. Most full-day trips put in below Lower Salmon Falls Dam, north of Hagerman, and take out 10 miles downstream near Bliss. Half/full-day dinner trips cost $50/60. Outfitters include High Adventure River Tours (☎ 208-733-0123, 800-286-4123) and Hagerman Valley Outfitters (☎ 208-837-6100), Box 245, Hagerman, ID 83332. 1000 Springs Tours (☎ 208-837-9006), US 30 at Sligars Springs (see below), operates scenic cruises from three launch sites: Hagerman's Bell Rapids Dock, Sligar's 1000 Springs Resort and Twin Falls. Trips ($25/18) depart according to demand, so phone ahead.

Places to Stay

Three hot springs south of Hagerman offer shady camping and riverside lazing. Isolated and peaceful ***Banbury Hot Springs*** *(☎ 208-543-4098),* off US 30 10 miles north of Buhl and then 2 miles east (follow the signs), has sites ($10 to $15) and a laundry. Neighboring ***Miracle Hot Springs*** *(☎ 208-543-6002),* off US 30 across from Banbury Hot Springs, has private baths and is OK in a pinch for camping, although it's sites are close to the road. Forlorn ***Sligar's 1000 Springs Resort*** *(☎ 208-837-4987),* 5 miles south of Hagerman on US 30, has a pool and riverside tent sites ($9) and RV hookups ($14).

IDAHO

At the north end of town, the ***Hagerman RV Village*** (*☎ 208-837-4906, 18049 US 30*) has shadeless but grassy tent sites ($15) with laundry and showers ($3.50 for nonguests). ***The Rock Lodge*** (see below) has a few grassy but cramped sites ($10). The inviting ***Gooding Hotel B&B*** (*☎ 208-934-4374, 888-260-6656, 112 Main St*) is north of the Hagerman Valley at the junction of Hwys 26 and 46 (I-84 exit 157 or 141). Rooms range from $40 to $60.

One mile north of Hagerman, ***the Rock Lodge*** (*☎ 208-837-4822, 17940 US 30*) has creekside rooms and cabins for $45 to $75. The bland ***Hagerman Valley Inn*** (*☎ 208-837-6196*), at Frog's Landing in Hagerman, asks $40/50.

Places to Eat

Half a mile north of Hagerman, the ***Emerald Valley Produce Stand*** is a must-stop during summer months for fresh-picked sweet corn and local peaches. In Hagerman, conspicuous ***Larry & Mary's Restaurant & Laundramat*** (*160 S State St*) is the best place to kill time over pizza or steak while waiting for the spin cycle to end. At the south end of town, the ***Snake River Grill*** (*☎ 208-837-6227*) at Frog's Landing boasts hearty country cooking, including local catfish and wild game. Grab an other-worldly potato ice cream milk shake *before* dinner at ***Smith's Dairy*** (*☎ 208-543-4272, 205 S Broadway*) in Buhl, where there are more than 31 seasonal flavors and the moo juice is still delivered to the door in glass bottles.

HAGERMAN FOSSIL BEDS NATIONAL MONUMENT

On a bluff above the Snake River, the free Hagerman Fossil Beds National Monument (*☎ 208-837-4793*) has the world's best Upper Pliocene terrestrial fossil beds. The fossil beds were created 2 to 3½ million years ago, when this desert canyon was a grassland dotted with lakes and marshes. First excavated by the Smithsonian Institute in 1929, these renowned beds, dubbed the 'horse quarry,' yielded hundreds of skeletons of prehistoric

horses, or *Equus simplicidens,* and more than 140 other fossilized species, including ancient camels and eight species found nowhere else.

The visitors center in Hagerman, 221 N State St, is open 9 am to 5 pm daily during summer, 10 am to 4 pm Thursday to Sunday in winter, and has informative displays on prehistoric life. Pick up the comprehensive self-guided tour handout. NPS rangers conduct natural history and guided site tours weekends June to September; call for the schedule. The site is also visible across the river from the Bell Rapids Dock just south of Hagerman off US 30.

To reach the fossil beds, go south 3 miles on US 30 from Hagerman and cross the bridge over the Snake River. Turn west onto an unmarked paved road that follows the river's true left bank. Continue about 12 miles and then follow signs to the monument.

POCATELLO

Gritty, blue-collar Pocatello (population 53,000; elevation 4454 feet) is the center of Idaho's third-largest metropolitan area. Greater Pocatello includes churlish Chubbuck, a suburb to its north. Both towns were carved out of the Fort Hall Indian Reservation in the 1880s. Pocatello was established as a rail junction in 1884, when the north-south railroads between Montana's gold fields and Salt Lake City were joined with the east-west UP. Pocatello thrived as the center of a vast agricultural area, including Idaho's noted potato fields. Present-day Pocatello, however, is not immediately appealing. The city center is in a decrepit state and the rest of the city sprawls along suburban streets. The Idaho State University (ISU; www.isu.edu) campus, home to nearly 13,000 students, with a curriculum emphasizing science and technology, is one of the few bright spots in an otherwise bleak picture.

Orientation

Two roads lead to Pocatello's city center south of the railroad tracks: the underpass at Center St and the overpass at Benton St.

IDAHO

...or they will get the last laugh. ID

Hope you like mash!

Future breakfast cereal, Palouse Hills, ID

Be Neil Armstrong for a day at Craters of the Moon National Park, ID.

Summertime and the living is easy. Lake Coeur d'Alene, ID

Nuggets galore, Boise, ID

So where's the gold? Kellogg, ID

Sierra Silver Mine tour, Wallace, ID

National Historic District, Wallace, ID

Newer businesses serve the I-15 and I-86 corridors, which intersect here. The main road is Yellowstone Ave/US 91 (I-86 exit 61), which turns into the one-way S 4th and S 5th Aves (US 91/US 30) and connects downtown and ISU.

Information

The USFS Caribou National Forest Pocatello Ranger District (☎ 208-236-7500), 250 S 4th Ave, is in the US Federal Building. The Idaho Dept of Fish & Game (☎ 208-232-4703) is at 1345 Barton Rd. The Pocatello Regional Medical Center (☎ 208-234-0777) is at 777 Hospital Way (I-15 exit 69).

Pocatello's farmers' markets (☎ 208-233-9192) are Idaho's biggest; they're staged in Centennial Plaza in front of city hall on the corner of E Oak St and Yellowstone Ave every Wednesday and Saturday, May to October.

Bannock County Museum & Fort Hall Replica

This museum (☎ 208-233-0434) contains displays about railroads and Native American history. Built in 1963, the Fort Hall Replica (☎ 208-234-6238) in Ross Park, near S 5th Ave and Barton Rd, is probably Pocatello's main tourist attraction. This replica of the Hudson's Bay Company's Fort Hall depicts the fort's history. The museum and fort are open 10 am to 6 pm daily late May to early September; $2.50/1.75/1.

Idaho Museum of Natural History

Near S 5th Ave and E Dillon St on the ISU campus, this museum (☎ 208-282-3317) is largely a paean to prehistoric reptiles. Children love the life-size movable dinosaurs. Open 9 am to 4 pm Monday to Saturday; admission $2.50/1.50.

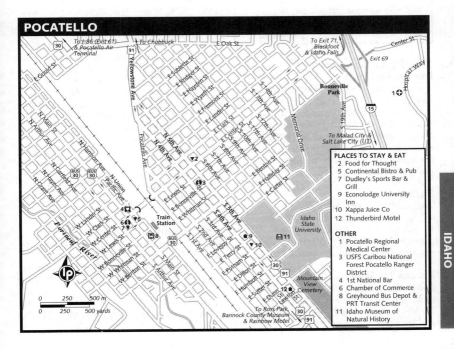

POCATELLO

PLACES TO STAY & EAT
2 Food for Thought
5 Continental Bistro & Pub
7 Dudley's Sports Bar & Grill
9 Econolodge University Inn
10 Xappa Juice Co
12 Thunderbird Motel

OTHER
1 Pocatello Regional Medical Center
3 USFS Caribou National Forest Pocatello Ranger District
4 1st National Bar
6 Chamber of Commerce
8 Greyhound Bus Depot & PRT Transit Center
11 Idaho Museum of Natural History

IDAHO

Lava Hot Springs

Modern chemical- and sulphur-stink–free facilities enable bathers to enjoy these soothing hot pools year-round. They're fed by several springs (102°–110°F). The complex (☎ 208-776-5221, 800-423-8597) is 35 miles southeast of Pocatello, off I-15 exit 47 in downtown Lava Hot Springs. The adjacent Idaho's Olympic Swimming Complex, 430 E Main St, is open early May to early September, featuring two huge pools, one 50m Olympic-size and the other a 25-yard lap pool, plus a vertigo-inducing 33-foot (10m) diving tower with three platforms. Open 11 am to 9 pm weekdays, 10 am to 9 pm weekends and holidays. Admission is $4.50 for adults; $4 for seniors and kids four to twelve; $1.50 for kids three and younger. Monday through Thursday are family days with reduced admission, and entrance to both facilities is $8 for everyone age 4 and older.

Web site: www.lavahotsprings.com

Shoshone-Bannock Indian Festival

Festivities are held the second weekend of August on the Fort Hall Indian Reservation. The 'Sho-Ban Festival' (☎ 208-238-3700) is known for its rodeo, dancing and dance competitions. About half of the reservation's original 525,000 acres between Pocatello and Blackfoot are still owned by the two tribes.

Skiing

The **Pebble Creek Ski Area** (☎ 208-775-4452), 3340 E Green Canyon Rd, Inkom, is 15 miles south of Pocatello off I-15. From Bonneville Peak (9271 feet), 24 runs plunge a maximum of 2000 feet vertical drop.

Places to Stay

Pocatello KOA (☎ 208-233-6851, 800-562-9175, 9815 W Pocatello Creek Rd), I-15 exit 71, has tent sites ($19), RV hookups ($26) and laundry.

Most lodgings are near I-15 and I-86. The best deals, however, are along S 5th Ave near ISU; most have a pool. They include the pot-o-gold **Rainbow Motel** (☎ 208-232-1451, 3020 S 5th Ave), with rates of $30 to $45; clean **Thunderbird Motel** (☎ 208-232-6330, 888-978-2473, 1415 S 5th Ave), with non-smoking rooms ($36 to $50); and **Econolodge University Inn** (☎ 208-233-5530, 800-377-0451, 835 S 5th Ave), with rooms from $45.

At I-86 exit 61 in Chubbuck are **Days Inn** (☎ 208-237-0020, 800-329-7466, 133 W Burnside Ave), ranging from $45 to $60, and **Motel 6** (☎ 208-237-7880, 291 W Burnside Ave), from $40 to $55. Near I-15 exit 71 are the **Best Western Cotton Tree Inn** (☎ 208-237-7650, 800-662-6886, 1415 Bench Rd) from $65, and **West Coast Pocatello** (☎ 208-233-2200, 800-527-5202, 1555 Pocatello Creek Rd) from $90.

Places to Eat

Feed your brain with soups, salads and sandwiches at healthy **Food for Thought** (☎ 208-233-7267, 504 E Center). Leafless **Bamboo Garden** (☎ 208-238-2331, 1200 Yellowstone Ave) dishes good Hunan and Szechuan food, while the matriarchal chain **Mama Inez** (☎ 208-234-7674, 390 Yellowstone Ave) serves decent Tex-Mex food.

Visit **Xappa Juice Co** (☎ 208-233-2752, 904 S 4th Ave) for superb smoothies. **Dudley's Sports Bar & Grill** (☎ 208-232-3541, 150 S Arthur Ave) is the spot for microbrews. Top-drawer **Continental Bistro & Pub** (☎ 208-233-4433, 140 S Main St), with a handsome old bar serving regional microbrews, features an ambitious menu with daily seafood and steak specials and a good wine list.

Entertainment

On Friday and Saturday nights, local bands jam at **1st National Bar** (☎ 208-233-1516, 232 W Center St). For information about concerts and other ISU events dial ☎ 208-282-2831 or ☎ 208-282-3662.

Sadly, only the sidewalk tile mosaic remains from the Chief Theatre, 215 N Main St.

Blackfoot's World Potato Expo

Hard-working Blackfoot is Idaho's potato capital. Irrigated fields stretch off in all directions; if you're in the area during harvest season (September to mid-October) pull off the interstate to admire the spud-filled railroad cars. The homegrown **Idaho's World Potato Exposition** (☎ 208-785-2517), 130 NW Main St in the former railroad depot (I-15 exit 93), is devoted to potato history and horticulture. The museum and adjoining gift shop are open 10 am to 7 pm Monday to Saturday and 10 am to 5 pm Sunday from May to October and promise 'free taters for out-of-staters.' Admission is $3/2.50/1 for adults/seniors/children.

Getting There & Away

The Pocatello Air Terminal, 5 miles west of town (I-86 exit 56), is served by Horizon Air and SkyWest/Delta. Daily Horizon flights connect Pocatello with Boise, while SkyWest/Delta wings it daily to Salt Lake City, UT. It may be cheaper to land in Salt Lake City and rent a car or take the shuttle (see below).

Trailways Salt Lake Express (☎ 208-656-8824) connects Salt Lake City and Pocatello (three hours one-way). Pick ups are at Texaco, 1527 Pocatello Creek Rd. The fare is $33 each way; call for departure times.

Greyhound (☎ 208-232-5365), 215 W Bonneville, dashes twice daily along I-15 northbound to Bozeman, MT, and twice daily southbound to Salt Lake City. Another daily bus darts west to Burley. Pocatello is on north-south I-15, which links Salt Lake City to Butte, MT, via Pocatello and Idaho Falls, at the junction of I-86.

Getting Around

The Pocatello Regional Transport (PRT) Transit Center (☎ 208-234-2287) shares the Art Deco Greyhound depot (1946); buses run 8 am to 5 pm weekdays and 10 am to 5 pm Saturday.

Avis (☎ 208-232-3244) and Hertz (☎ 208-233-2970) are at the airport. U-Save Auto Rental (☎ 208-237-9010, 800-426-5299) undercuts the competition at 1407 Yellowstone Ave.

Taxi connoisseurs recommend Pocatello Cab (☎ 208-232-1115).

IDAHO FALLS

Alpine lakes surrounded by meadows, untamed rivers, waterfalls, wildlife, rugged mountains and the backdrop of the Teton Range dazzle Eastern Idaho visitors. Idaho Falls (population 50,000; elevation 4600 feet) is the gateway to this inviting region.

Dominated by the **Mormon temple**, increasingly white-collar Idaho Falls' roots are as an archetypal agricultural center. Originally called Taylor Bridge, the city sprang to life in the 1860s as a Snake River crossing. In 1872 the railroad arrived and the community changed its name to Eagle Rock. A group of forward-thinking Chicago investors attempting to woo settlers with something snappier renamed the town Idaho Falls in 1891. In 1911, the erection of a hydroelectric diversion weir created a 20-foot-tall cataract that's best viewed from the Broadway Bridge. The **Snake River Greenbelt** connects the town's riverside parks. Craters of the Moon National Monument (see the Central Idaho Rockies section), Yellowstone and Grand Teton National Parks (see the Wyoming chapter) and southwestern Montana are all within a day's drive. It's worth noting that virtually the entire town shuts down on Sunday.

Orientation

Downtown has declined in favor of commercial strips leading out to suburbs. The old city center, however, retains some charming architecture, and a few mom-and-pop businesses persist. To reach downtown, take I-15 exit 118 and follow Broadway across the Snake River to Yellowstone Ave (US 26). The city center is wedged between the Snake River and Yellowstone Ave. The historic district centers on Ridge Ave, three blocks east of and parallel to Yellowstone Ave, between Pine and Birch Sts.

IDAHO

Information

The city's official visitors information center (☎ 208-523-3278, 800-634-3246 outside Idaho), 505 Lindsay Blvd, is open 8 am to 5 pm Monday to Saturday and has extensive regional travel information. The USFS Targhee National Forest Palisades Ranger Station (☎ 208-523-1412), on US 26, is just east of Idaho Falls. The BLM Idaho Falls District office (☎ 208-524-7500) is at 1405 Hollipark Dr. The Idaho Dept of Fish & Game (☎ 208-525-7290) is at 1515 E Lincoln Rd. The post office is at 605 4th St. The Eastern Idaho Regional Medical Center (☎ 208-529-6111) is at 3100 Channing Way.

Bonneville County Historical Museum

In the handsome old Carnegie Library, this museum (☎ 208-522-1400), 200 N Eastern Ave at Elm St, preserves the history of the original settlement of Eagle Rock, including a re-created main street and Native American artifacts. Another display explains the development of nuclear energy at the Idaho National Engineering & Environmental Laboratory (aka 'the Site'; see INEEL in the Central Idaho section). Open 10 am to 5 pm weekdays and 1 to 5 pm Saturday; admission $1/50¢.

Places to Stay

One night of free camping is allowed at the grassy, city-run *North Tourist Park*, at the corner of US 26 and S Anderson St, adjacent Pinecrest municipal golf course, and also at the less appealing *South Tourist Park*, on the south bank of the Snake River off S Yellowstone Ave near W 25th St. *Idaho Falls KOA* (☎ 208-523-3362, 1440 Lindsay Blvd) has a pool and laundry. Tent sites run $22, RV hookups $28, cabins $35. *Shady Rest Campground* (☎ 208-524-0010, 2200 N Yellowstone Hwy) has $13 full RV hookups and cheap tent sites.

Rooms (some with kitchenettes) start under $40 at the *Evergreen Motel* (☎ 208-522-5410, 3130 S Yellowstone Hwy). The older *Towne Lodge* (☎ 208-523-2960, 255 E St) has clean, comfortable singles/doubles for $39/50. The acceptable *Little-tree Inn* (☎ 208-523-5993, 888 N Holmes Ave) is near the municipal golf course ($35/42).

Most mid-range places are on the west bank of the Snake River, north of W Broadway St, and have pools and spas. *Super 8 Motel* (☎ 208-522-8880, 701 Lindsay Blvd) starts the bidding at $50. Rooms at the *Best Western Stardust Motor Lodge* (☎ 208-522-2910, 700 Lindsay Blvd) fetch $55/65. *Hampton Inn* (☎ 208-529-9800, 2500 Channing Way) and *Quality Inn* (☎ 208-523-6260, 850 Lindsay Blvd) both expect at least $65. The *Best Western Driftwood Inn* (☎ 208-523-2242, 575 River Pkwy) and *Shilo Inn* (☎ 208-523-0088, 780 Lindsay Blvd) begin at $75.

Luxurious digs at the revamped *West Coast Hotel* (☎ 208-523-8000, 800-432-1005, 475 River Pkwy) go for $85 to $125. Shelter starts at $90 at the *Best Western Cotton Tree*

Who Invented the Boob Tube?

The Philo Farnsworth TV Pioneer Museum (☎ 208-745-8423), 118 W 1st St in Rigby, 12 miles north of Idaho Falls off US 20, presents a well-curated collection that features several of television inventor Philo Farnsworth's earliest contraptions. Born in Rigby in 1906, Philo showed a remarkable talent for science and physics. At the age of 19 he formulated the technical theory behind the cathode-ray tube. In 1934, a London-based company hired Farnsworth to design the prototype of the modern TV. Philo licensed his product with Philco, RCA and later NBC, helping to usher in the age of television. The museum maintains a collection of early TVs and charts the history of the broadcast image. It's open 1 to 5 pm Tuesday to Saturday and by appointment. Admission is by donation.

Inn (☎ *208-523-6000, 900 Lindsay Blvd)* and $100 at *AmeriTel Inn* (☎ *208-523-1400, 645 Lindsay Blvd)*.

Places to Eat
Caffeine fiends rejoice! The *DD Mudd* (☎ *208-535-9088, 401 A St)* espresso bar and cafe serves sandwiches, light meals and a good cuppa joe in inviting modern surrounds. Pig out on pad Thai or a pork sandwich at the superb *Barbeque Pit & Thai Kitchen* (☎ *208-523-0255, 235 E St)*, which juggles both genres with admirable aplomb and out-smokes nearby chain outlet *Bubba's Bar-B-Que* (☎ *208-523-2822, 118 E 1st St)*, on the other side of the tracks. There are several conspicuous Chinese joints around the city center. A night out on the town means *Jaker's Steak, Ribs & Fish House* (☎ *208-524-5240, 851 Lindsay Blvd)*, featuring an eclectic menu of Western favorites. Rigby's salt-of-the-earth *The Loft* (☎ *208-523-1977)*, at N County Line Rd and US 20, is an old-fashioned log cabin steak house and cocktail lounge. Housed in a prefabbed storage shed, the funky *Hawg Smoke Cafe* (☎ *208-523-4804, 4330 N Yellowstone Hwy)* is Idaho's only gourmet biker bistro; reservations are essential at this five-table wonder. It's well worth a drive out to *Reed's Dairy* (☎ *208-522-0123, 2660 W Broadway)* for huge $1 scoops of huckleberry ice cream; support the local cows and ask about dairy tours – they still deliver door-to-door.

Getting There & Away
Air Idaho Falls is served by Horizon Air, SkyWest and Delta out of Fanning Field Municipal Airport (☎ 208-529-1221), I-15 exit 119. Daily Horizon Air flights connect Idaho Falls with Boise. SkyWest and Delta offer nine daily flights between Idaho Falls and Salt Lake City, UT. It's often cheaper to fly into Salt Lake City and rent a car or take a shuttle (see below).

Salt Lake City Airport Shuttle Trailways Salt Lake Express (☎ 208-656-8824) shuttles between Salt Lake City and Idaho Falls (4 hours, $35 one-way) thrice daily. Pickup is at

Kicks 66 (old Boozer's), 1300 W Broadway, west of I-15.

Bus Greyhound (☎ 208-522-0912), 850 Denver St, 1 block north of W Broadway, runs daily buses along I-15 to Bozeman, MT, and Salt Lake City. The Idaho Falls–based Community and Rural Transport (CART; ☎ 208-522-2278, 800-657-7439), 850 Denver St, offers Idaho Falls-Arco-Mackay-Challis-Salmon service on Tuesday and Friday. Another CART route goes twice daily to Teton Valley (via Rexburg); buses go to Jackson, WY, as needed.

Car & Motorcycle Idaho Falls is on I-15 at the junction of US 20 and US 26: I-15 continues north to Butte, MT; US 20 heads northeast to West Yellowstone, MT; and US 26 heads southeast to Jackson, via Alpine, WY. Dial ☎ 208-745-7278 for regional road conditions.

Getting Around
Avis (522-4225), Budget (☎ 208-522-8800), Hertz (☎ 208-529-3101) and National (☎ 208-522-5276) await at the airport. Enterprise (☎ 208-523-8111, 800-736-8222), 1626 Hollipark Dr, and U-Save Auto Rental (☎ 208-522-0695), 401 Northgate Mile, are in town.

Rouse Easy-Way Taxi (☎ 208-525-8344) for a cab.

CAMAS NATIONAL WILDLIFE REFUGE
Marshland, ponds and lakes comprise the Camas National Wildlife Refuge (☎ 208-662-5423), 36 miles north of Idaho Falls (I-15 exit 150 at Hamer). Spring and fall migrations bring more than 100,000 ducks and 3000 geese. Other waterfowl, birds, raptors and wildlife are easily spotted year-round. Pick up a brochure and map at the refuge.

SWAN VALLEY
The Snake River, coursing between the Caribou and Snake Mountains, enters eastern Idaho and fills the Palisades Reservoir. The verdant Swan Valley flows 60 miles northwest from Palisades Dam to the

confluence with Henry's Fork, just north of Idaho Falls in Menan. The Snake River downstream from Palisades Dam is a noted fly-fishing stream for cutthroat, rainbow and German brown trout. For guided fly-fishing trips, contact Drifter's of the South Fork (☎ 208-483-2722) in Swan Valley or the South Fork Lodge (see Places to Stay & Eat, below). Trout fishing is the main pastime, and river and lake access is abundant along US 26, which runs the length of this lovely rural valley. Most amenities are designed with anglers in mind – cafes often double as bait shops. If you're near Idaho Falls on US 20 and headed toward Yellowstone National Park, detour through Swan Valley and join the 108-mile **Teton Scenic Byway** through Teton Valley (see below) en route to Henry's Fork and West Yellowstone, MT, which ends in Afton, WY.

Orientation & Information
The three small burghs of Swan Valley, Irwin and Palisades line US 26 north to south. USFS campgrounds ring the reservoir. Free self-issuing permits are required for boaters and floaters along the South Fork of the Snake River at six designated launch sites (see Idaho Falls for the nearest USFS and BLM offices). The day use fee is $3.

Places to Stay & Eat
Try any of Palisade's competitive campgrounds, including hidden *Husky's*, popular *Palisades Pines* (☎ *208-483-4485*) and quirky *dot E dot*, each asking around $15 for RV hookups, a bit less for tents. USFS campgrounds along the reservoir include: *Big Elk Creek* ($8), north of US 26 on USFS Rd 262; *Blowout* ($5), with a boat launch; and *Alpine* ($8), at the west end of Alpine, WY. Swan Valley's rejigged *South Fork Lodge* (☎ *208-483-2112, 877-347-4735*) is the valley's best place to eat and nicest place to stay, but rates are steep. In Irwin are *McBride's B&B* and *Swan Valley B&B* (☎ *208-483-4663, 800-241-7926*), which has a spa. Nearby is the *Sandy Mite Fly Shop & Cafe* (☎ *208-*

483-2609), with locally tied flies and good bites.

Getting There & Away
From Swan Valley, Hwy 31 leads north over Pine Creek Pass (6764 feet) to Victor in the Teton Valley. US 26 continues 28 miles along the Snake River from Swan Valley to Alpine in Wyoming's Star Valley.

TETON VALLEY
John Colter stumbled upon the Teton Valley (elevation 6200 feet) in 1808 while hunting for beaver. The valley soon became a favored mountain man rendezvous, where trapper Jim Bridger and his ilk gathered to trade with natives. Farming has remained the valley's mainstay since Mormon families settled here in the late 19th century, but these once-sleepy ranching towns are now a year-round mecca for outdoor adventure and summer music festivals, with fabulous skiing, hiking, mountaineering and mountain biking.

The Teton River descends the west side of the Teton Range and flows northwest into the Henry's Fork of the Snake River near Rexburg. The valley is surrounded on three sides by the Targhee National Forest mountain ranges: the Teton Range to the west, the Snake River Range to the south and the Big Hole Mountains to the southwest. The west face of the mighty Teton Range soars above this broad, scenic valley, which is warmer, sunnier and more peaceful than its well-known Wyoming neighbor, Jackson Hole.

Orientation
Teton Valley's main towns from south to north along Hwy 33 are Victor (population 600), home to many Jackson Hole commuters; rapidly growing Driggs (population 1000), 9 miles north; and tiny Tetonia (population 155), 7 miles north of Driggs. Most of the valley lies in Teton County, ID, though a small portion (up to the Teton crest) is in Teton County, WY. Unassuming Alta, WY, the base village for Grand Targhee Ski & Summer Resort (see below) is 4 winding miles east of Driggs.

Information

Travelers will find essential services in Driggs. The USFS Targhee National Forest Teton Basin Ranger District (☎ 208-354-2312), 525 S Main St, has information on area trails and campgrounds. The post office is on S Main St. Dark Horse Books (☎ 208-354-8882, 888-434-8882), 76 N Main St, stocks an excellent selection of books and maps. Teton Valley Hospital (☎ 208-354-2383) is at 283 N 1st St E. On Hwy 33 between Victor and Driggs, the Spud Drive-In (☎ 208-354-2727), www.spuddrivein.com, is a classic 1950s outdoor theater.

Activities

Fishing in the Teton River is superb. In Driggs, Basin Travel Stop (☎ 208-354-2787), 111 N Main St, and Ye Old Spirits & Beverage Shoppe (☎ 208-354-8414), 52 N Main St, sell fishing licenses. Trails crisscrossing the Big Hole Mountains are excellent for **mountain biking**. Nearby **hiking** trails head east up Darby and Teton canyons on the west side of the Tetons. The area around Teton Pass on Hwy 33 is great for **backcountry skiing**. Teton Aviation (☎ 208-354-3100, 800-472-6382) at the Driggs Airport offers scenic **glider rides**. Several outdoors stores offer advice and rent all manner of gear.

About 8 miles east of Victor on the Idaho-Wyoming state line, Rendezvous Ski Tours (☎ 208-787-2906, 877-754-4887) operates three huts for rent while you're **backcountry cross-country skiing**. The huts sleep up to eight people and rent for $165 per night. Rendezvous also runs all-inclusive guided trips that start at $175 per person, per night. The huts fill quickly on weekends and holidays, so make reservations at least one month ahead; see www.skithetetons.com for details.

Places to Stay

The well-maintained *Teton Valley Campground* (☎ 208-787-2647), 1 mile south of Victor on Hwy 31, has a pool, showers and a laundry. Shaded tent sites are $19, RV hookups $26. There are several USFS campgrounds (starting at $5) nearby: *Pine Creek Campground* is 5 miles east of Victor on

Hwy 31 and *Trail Creek Campground* is 6 miles southeast of Victor on Hwy 33. *Reunion Flat Campground* (7500 feet) and *Teton Canyon Campground* (7200 feet) are 10 miles east of Driggs in the forested Teton Canyon; take USFS Rd 025 east past Alta, WY, and turn right onto USFS Rd 009.

Driggs' *Pines Motel Guest Haus* (☎ 208-354-2774, 800-354-2778, 105 S Main St) has rooms with shared bath ($35/40) and private bath ($40/50); breakfast is $10 extra. Alta's *Teton Tepee Lodge & Ski Shop* (☎ 307-353-8176) has basic rooms for $60. At Driggs' north end, *Super 8* (☎ 208-354-8888, 133 S Hwy 33) also starts at $60. *Intermountain Lodge* (☎ 208-354-8153, 34 E Ski Hill Rd), 1 mile east of Driggs, has two-bed log cabins with kitchens ($65). Driggs' *Best Western Teton West* (☎ 208-354-2363, 800-252-2363, 476 N Main St) has an indoor pool and rooms for $60 to $75. Tetonia's *Teton Mountain View Lodge* (☎ 208-456-2741, 800-625-2232, 510 Egbert Ave) charges $65 to $85. (Also see Grand Targhee Ski & Summer Resort, below.)

Teton Creek B&B (☎ 208-354-2584, 41 S Baseline Rd), a half-mile south of Driggs, charges $55 to $75. Teton-view rooms at Alta's homey *Wilson Creekside Inn B&B* (☎ 307-353-2409) fetch $70 to $80. Rooms at the modern *Alta Lodge B&B* (☎ 307-353-2582, 590 Targhee Towne Rd) are $65 to $85.

Places to Eat

Driggs has several good restaurants. The *Breakfast Shoppe* (☎ 208-354-8294, 95 S Main St) serves hearty fare. Diminutive *Java the Hut* is waiting to perk you up next-door. *Mike's Diner & Eats* (☎ 208-354-2797, 10 N Main St) does breakfast, pizza and BBQ 'buf' burgers. *Tony's Pizza & Pasta* (☎ 208-354-8829, 364 N Main St) is another good option. *Barrels & Bins* (☎ 208-354-2307, 36 S Main St) is a natural-foods gold mine.

Victor's *Old Dewey House Restaurant* (☎ 208-787-2092, 37 S Main St) offers fine dining. Victor's casual *Knotty Pine Supper Club* (☎ 208-787-2866, 58 S Main St) is a good place for baby back ribs, steak and seafood, with live music on weekends. Don't miss the huckleberry shakes at Victor's old-fashioned

IDAHO

Emporium soda fountain (☎ *208-787-2221, 45 N Main St*). In Tetonia, try the *Trails End Cafe* (☎ *208-456-2202, 110 N Main St*) for homestyle fare.

Getting There & Away

CART (☎ 208-354-2240) buses stop at 47 S Main St in Driggs. Buses depart twice daily for Idaho Falls via Rexburg ($7.50 one-way). Buses go to Jackson, WY, as needed ($13 one-way).

Hwy 33 parallels the Idaho-Wyoming border; Victor is 23 miles west of Jackson, WY. The Teton Scenic Byway follows Hwy 33 north from Victor through Driggs and Tetonia, where Hwy 33 veers west, then joins Hwy 32 and continues north to Ashton. Hwy 31 heads 21 miles southwest from Victor to Swan Valley. Hwy 33/22 between Victor and Jackson crosses Teton Pass (8429 feet), which has a 10% grade (plowed during winter) for several miles and is a major commuter route.

GRAND TARGHEE SKI & SUMMER RESORT

On the west side of the Teton Range, Grand Targhee Ski & Summer Resort (☎ 307-353-2300, 800-827-4433), Alta, WY, is worshiped for its incredible depth of powder (more than 500 inches of snow falls each winter!), its high-mountain location and its easygoing but professional service and amenities. Base elevation is 8100 feet, and four high-speed lifts to the top of Fred's Mountain (10,200 feet) access 1500 acres of runs, with a total vertical drop of 2200 feet in 3.2 miles. The runs are suited for families and intermediate-level skiers. Full-day lift tickets are $44/27; half-day tickets are $32. Seniors (62–69) pay $27 for a full-day ticket and tickets are free to folks over 70 – respect your elders.

Web site: www.grandtarghee.com

Adjacent Peaked Mountain (10,230 feet) is reserved for wilderness **snowcat powder skiing**. Half/full-day powder skiing costs $175/240. Grand Targhee offers a full range of rentals and instruction. Ten miles of groomed Nordic trails await ($8/5 day passes). Snowboards are welcome on all slopes. The ski season is mid-November to mid-April. Other winter activities include snowshoeing and dog sledding.

Targhee, as it's often called, is a year-round resort with summer hiking, climbing, horseback riding and lift-served mountain biking. A one-hour hike affords a spectacular vista of the Grand Teton itself; ride the lift down for free. Its summer **music festival** series includes Rockin' the Tetons in mid-July, the Blues & Microbrew Fest in late July and the Grand Targhee Bluegrass Music Festival in early August.

Places to Stay & Eat

Lodgings, based on a minimum double occupancy, include *Targhee* (standard room from $65/85 summer/winter), *Teewinot* (deluxe room with hot tub from $125/150) or the *Sioux Condominiums*. Sioux Lodge has four-person studios ($150/180) and eight-person two-bedroom units ($240/350). Rates vary; inquire about package deals. (Also see Teton Valley, above.)

Getting There & Away

Driggs is the closest 'town' to Targhee. Head 4 miles east on USFS Rd 025 (toward Alta) to the Idaho-Wyoming state line, and in Wyoming continue east 8 miles to Targhee. From the second switchback en route to the resort is the first glimpse of the Grand Teton and an overlook of the Teton Basin.

Resort shuttles between Targhee and airports in Idaho Falls and Jackson, WY, cost $30 per person for two or more people (reservations required). Targhee Express (☎ 800-443-6133) operates once-daily winter bus service between Jackson, Teton Village (☎ 307-733-3101) and Targhee. Roundtrip fare is $14 (reservations required).

HENRY'S FORK

North of Ashton, US 20 climbs steadily out of the potato-rich plains and onto a forested lodgepole pine plateau. Here one of Idaho's best trout streams, the Henry's Fork of the Snake, hurries purposefully through meadows and open forests.

Along Henry's Fork on US 20 are the small towns of Last Chance and Island

Park, and the privately owned 'resort' of Macks Inn. West of Island Park, the large **Island Park Reservoir** is popular for fishing, kayaking and camping. Several fly-fishing outfitters are based in the area. The helpful USFS Targhee National Forest Island Park Ranger Station (☎ 208-558-7301) is off US 20 on the towns' southern outskirts.

Mesa Falls Scenic Byway

The paved 25-mile Mesa Falls Scenic Byway (Hwy 47) begins at US 20 just east of Ashton and rejoins US 20 ¾-mile north of the Harriman State Park entrance. Lower (65 feet) and Upper Mesa Falls (114 feet) and views of the distant Teton Mountains are the drive's highlights.

Harriman State Park

In 1902 UP investors bought a 4500-acre ranch on the banks of Henry's Fork. Railroad Ranch, as the holding was known, became a getaway for the wealthy UP shareholders. The ranch was deeded to the state in 1961. The elaborate old ranch buildings are open to the public, and 16,000 acres around the ranch are designated the **Harriman Wildlife Refuge** (☎ 208-558-7368). More than 5000 trumpeter swans winter on the broad spring-fed Henry's Fork. The park is one of Idaho's best wildlife viewing areas, with abundant elk, deer, moose, black bear, beaver, otter, eagles, osprey, duck and sandhill cranes. The legendary Henry's Fork rainbow trout lures anglers. The park offers more than 20 miles of trails for hiking, cycling, horseback riding and cross-country skiing.

Camping is not allowed. The park is west of US 20, 19 miles north of Ashton and 8 miles south of Island Park. The day use fee is $3.

Henry's Lake State Park

Fishing is the main attraction in the Henry's Lake basin (6596 feet), centered around Henry's Lake State Park (☎ 208-558-7532), 14 miles southwest of West Yellowstone, MT. The park is open Memorial Day through October, weather permitting.

Hiking

Sawtell Peak (9866 feet) is northwest of Macks Inn. The trail crosses the Continental Divide and offers views of the Yellowstone caldera, then drops into the Rock Creek Basin. Head west from US 20 on USFS Rd 024 to the trailhead.

Places to Stay & Eat

Several private campgrounds (starting at $10) line US 20, but a few USFS campgrounds ($8 to $16) are lovely and worth the short drive. There are attractive USFS *campgrounds* at Warm River and Lower Falls. The USFS *West End Campground* is 9 miles west of the Harriman State Park entrance. In Henry's Lake State Park, campsites are $12 to $16.

Also try the USFS *Box Canyon Campground*, 1½ miles up USFS Rd 134 north of Last Chance, and *Upper Coffee Pot*, on unpaved USFS Rd 311, 2 miles west of US 20 south of Macks Inn, with a lovely riverside hiking trail.

Macks Inn (☎ 208-558-7272) has RV sites ($18) and rooms for $44 to $115. *Pond's Lodge* (☎ 208-558-7221) in Island Park has rooms in an attractive log lodge or riverside cabins ranging from $40 to $180.

For good clean fun, visit *Big Jud's Country Diner* (☎ 208-652-7806), on US 20 in Ashton, and order the 1lb burger and ice cream 'Big Deal' ($12); if you eat the whole thing, they take your picture and hang it on the wall. The friendly *Chalet* (☎ 208-558-9953) in Last Chance serves up hashbrowns and homemade pies.

Getting There & Away

Greyhound buses stop at Macks Inn daily en route to Salt Lake City, Utah, and Bozeman, MT. Island Park is on US 20, 49 miles north of Rexburg and 29 miles southwest of West Yellowstone, MT, via Targhee Pass (7072 feet) and the Idaho-Montana border. US 20 can be congested during summer. The scenic Ashton-Flagg Ranch Rd (USFS Rd 261) leads 45 miles east from Ashton to the John D Rockefeller Jr Memorial Parkway (see the Wyoming chapter).

IDAHO

Central Idaho Rockies

Powerful rivers carving through mountainous terrain characterize this scenic region, which contains the largest contiguous wilderness in the lower 48 states. The Salmon River, the USA's longest undammed river, runs 425 miles across central Idaho, beginning in the heart of the Sawtooth National Recreation Area (8000 feet) and ending at its confluence with the Snake River (905 feet) in Hells Canyon National Recreation Area south of Lewiston. The Continental Divide to the east follows the incised ridges of the Bitterroot Mountains along the Idaho-Montana state line. Take your time navigating the few two-lane, winding roads that penetrate this vast wilderness. Much of the region is accessible only by hiking, rafting, horsepacking or driving for miles along rough USFS roads. Many recreation enthusiasts opt to fly into the region's numerous remote airstrips. To see this region's vast wilds and wilderness requires some planning and initiative. Innumerable outfitters and guide services eagerly await to assist on your journey.

The aptly named Sawtooth Mountains, towering above the broad Stanley Basin's numerous lakes and tarns, are Idaho's most dramatic range. The Salmon River flows gently north through this valley before coursing northeast toward the town of Salmon. North of Salmon, the river pivots to the west and begins its descent through North America's second deepest gorge – a wild section nicknamed the River of No Return. To the south, world-renowned Sun Valley Resort nestles in the Big Wood River Valley between the Smoky and Pioneer Mountains.

ARCO & LOST RIVER VALLEY

Glowing Arco (population 1100; elevation 5328 feet), at the northern edge of the Snake River Plain, promotes itself as 'the first in the world lighted by atomic power,' and is the gateway to the Pioneer, Lost River and Lemhi Mountains. The Big Lost River flows through the desolate valley only to disappear south of Arco beneath the lava flows of the Craters of the Moon National Monument (see below).

US 93 runs north from Arco along the Big Lost River past Mackay (population 575), the valley's only other town, traverses Willow Creek Summit (7160 feet) and descends to Challis. The Lost River Range's **Borah Peak** (12,662 feet) is Idaho's highest. There are numerous campgrounds in the region.

Two interesting hikes are near Arco. The 80-foot limestone span of **Natural Bridge** is a shoulder of King's Mountain, north of Arco; a strenuous hike up nearby Bridge Canyon leads to the arch. Rising 2500 feet above the Snake River Plain is the 300,000-year-old **Big Southern Butte National Natural Landmark**, 15 miles southeast of Arco. Once an Oregon Trail landmark, hikers make the steep 2000-foot climb to its summit for panoramic views of immense lava flows.

Rooms at Arco's ***Riverside Motel*** (☎ 208-527-895, 800-229-8954) start around $20. The ***Lost River Motel*** (☎ 208-527-3600), ***DK Motel*** (☎ 208-527-8282, 800-231-0134) and ***Arco Inn*** (☎ 208-527-3100) all start around $30. Friendly ***Grandpa's Southern Bar-B-Q*** (☎ 208-527-3362, 434 W Grand Ave) is a welcome surprise, serving finger-lickin' lunch and dinner.

Community and Rural Transport (CART; ☎ 208-527-9944) runs two buses Tuesday and Friday from Pickles Place ('Home of the Atomic Burger') on Hwy 93 to Idaho Falls and north to Salmon via Mackay and Challis. Arco is on US 20/26 at the junction of US 93, which leads north to Mackay (27 miles) and Challis (54 miles northwest of Mackay). Arco is 67 miles west of Idaho Falls and 18 miles northeast of Craters of the Moon National Monument.

IDAHO NATIONAL ENGINEERING & ENVIRONMENTAL LABORATORY

In a barren swath of desert, this laboratory (known as INEEL) established in 1949 is one of the US government's primary atomic

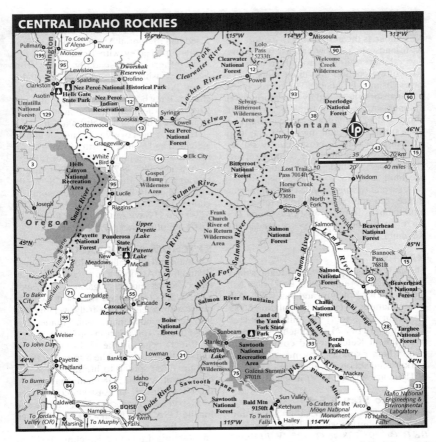

CENTRAL IDAHO ROCKIES

energy test sites. The first electrical generation using nuclear fission took place here in 1951. The world's first nuclear power plant, known as **EBR-1**, is a national historic landmark. This long-ago mothballed breeder reactor now serves as a visitors center (☎ 208-526-2331, 526-0050 for guided tours) for the 890-sq-mile nuclear reservation. The reservation is still the site of major Pentagon-sponsored nuclear R&D. Aircraft manufacturing giant Lockheed manages the reservation for the US Dept of Energy and employs 6700 people. To reach INEEL, take US 26 east of Arco for 20 miles or US 20 west of Idaho Falls for 46

miles. Open 8 am to 4 pm daily Memorial Day to Labor Day; free.

CRATERS OF THE MOON NATIONAL MONUMENT

Established in 1924, Craters of the Moon National Monument (☎ 208-527-3257) is an 83-sq-mile showcase of volcanism; the monument's size may increase tenfold in the near future. Uncanny lava flows, cinder cones and spatter cones offer glimpses of past volcanic activity. The visitors center (open 8 am to 6 pm daily Memorial Day to Labor Day, otherwise 8 am to 4:30 pm) has interesting exhibits. The 7-mile **Crater Loop Rd**, open 24 hours daily late April to mid-November, is the easiest way to explore the sci-fi landscape – allow at least two hours. Several short trails lead from the road to the edge of craters and into undeveloped lava caves (bring a flashlight). The barren black basalt absorbs heat, and by mid-morning on a sunny summer day temperatures soar above 100°F. The volcanic rock is sharp, so wear sturdy shoes. During winter, the loop road offers excellent **cross-country skiing**; call the visitors center for a snow report. Day use is $5/vehicle and includes a park brochure and map.

A surreal *campground* ($10) near the entrance station is open May to October. The monument is 18 miles west of Arco on US 20/26, or a one-hour drive southeast of Ketchum.

HAILEY

The early stomping grounds of Idaho's poet laureate Ezra Pound (born 1902) also has the airport for Ketchum and Sun Valley. Accommodations in Hailey (population 5600; elevation 5342 feet), 12 miles south of Ketchum on Hwy 75, are much less expensive than in Ketchum and commuting is easy, which explains why most seasonal workers and ski bums hang here.

There are several ATMs along Main St.

Places to Stay & Eat

Reservations are advisable July and August and during winter. *Povey Pensione B&B* (☎ *208-788-4682, 128 W Bullion*) charges $45/55. Hard-to-come-by rooms at the *Hailey Hotel Bar & Grill* (☎ *208-788-3140, 201 S Main St*) start at $50. Rooms at humble *Hitchrack Motel & Grocery Store* (☎ *208-788-1696, 619 S Main St*) are $50 to $70.

Near the airport, rooms at the *Airport Inn* (☎ *208-788-2477, 820 4th Ave S*) are $60 to $75.

For espresso it's *Wake Up and Live* (☎ *208-788-2444, 310 N Main St*). The *Sun Valley Brewing Co* (☎ *208-788-5777, 202 N Main St*) offers burgers to buffer its noted ales.

Getting There & Around

Horizon Air and SkyWest/Delta fly out of Friedman Memorial Airport. Daily Horizon flights link Hailey with Boise, and during winter there are also daily flights from Seattle, Washington, and weekend flights from Portland, Oregon. SkyWest/Delta shuttles daily between Hailey and Salt Lake City, Utah. The nearest major airports are in Boise (see earlier) and Salt Lake City.

Hailey is on Hwy 75, 12 miles south of Ketchum and 69 miles north of Twin Falls. It is a 2½- to three-hour drive east of Boise.

Avis (☎ 208-788-2382) can be found at the airport and Budget (☎ 208-788-3660), 118 N Main, Bellevue, is 3 miles south of Hailey. Practical Rent-A-Car (☎ 208-788-3224) and U-Save Auto Rental (☎ 208-788-9707) are often cheaper.

KETCHUM & SUN VALLEY

Ketchum and Sun Valley are Idaho's premier destinations. According to *Conde Nast Traveler*, *Gourmet* and *Ski* magazines, Sun Valley is the USA's top-ranked ski resort. Synonymous with celebrity, the truly wealthy live here year-round in their 'trophy' homes.

Ketchum (population 3875; elevation 5750 feet) began in the 1880s as a mining and smelting center, while Sun Valley (population 1025) sprang to life in 1936 as the creation of Averell Harriman, chairman of the UP Railroad. An Austrian count hired by Harriman selected Sun Valley as the site for the USA's first luxury ski resort, which quickly became a playground for the rich and famous. Longtime Ketchum resident Ernest Hemingway ended his life with a bullet here in 1961; there's a touching memorial to Hemingway in a grove of cottonwoods above Ketchum.

Today the area is no longer just a place to ski but a year-round destination, surpassing even Wyoming's Jackson Hole in its finery. Buffalo-skin jackets, turquoise-banded cowboy hats and buckskin skirts are in keeping with life here, the make-believe 'big hat, no cattle' world of an idealized Wild West. The summer season runs late June to Labor Day and the winter season December to March, weather depending.

IDAHO

Orientation

Hwy 75 bisects the narrow Big Wood River Valley, passing through the discrete communities of Ketchum, Sun Valley and Elkhorn. Ketchum's Main St is the area's main commercial district. Sun Valley is a mile northeast of Ketchum on Trail Creek Rd. Bald Mountain, the primary downhill skiing area, is west of Ketchum. Elkhorn is south of Sun Valley, adjacent Dollar Mountain.

Information

The Sun Valley/Ketchum Chamber of Commerce (☎ 208-726-3423, 800-634-3347), at 4th and Main Sts in Ketchum, runs a useful visitors center and a 24-hour recorded events line; www.visitsunvalley.com. Dial ☎ 208-622-8027 December to April for avalanche and weather information or ☎ 800-635-4150 for a ski report. For information about hiking, biking or camping, contact the USFS Sawtooth National Forest Ketchum Ranger Station (☎ 208-622-5371), 206 Sun Valley Rd, Sun Valley, open 7:30 am to 5 pm daily. Ketchum has most practicalities, including an ATM at First Security Bank of Idaho, 600 Sun Valley Rd; a post office at 301 1st Ave N; and Chapter One Bookstore (☎ 208-726-5425), 160 N Main St at 2nd St.

Activities

The impressive Wood River Trail System (WRTS) winds more than 20 miles through Ketchum and Sun Valley. The Sun Valley Trail is good for at least 10 miles of Class I **mountain biking** and connects to the WRTS. An **equestrian** lane also runs alongside the WRTS. During winter, trails are groomed daily for **ski skating**.

Several other excellent **hiking** trails are near town and bikes are permitted on many of them. Adams Gulch is a 5½-mile loop in a sunny canyon with four other nearby trails. Fox Creek, a 5-mile loop, has mountain views and connects with three other trails. The four Trail Creek Area trails, which

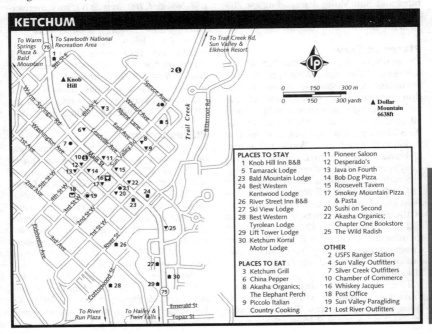

KETCHUM

PLACES TO STAY
1 Knob Hill Inn B&B
5 Tamarack Lodge
23 Bald Mountain Lodge
24 Best Western Kentwood Lodge
26 River Street Inn B&B
27 Ski View Lodge
28 Best Western Tyrolean Lodge
29 Lift Tower Lodge
30 Ketchum Korral Motor Lodge

PLACES TO EAT
3 Ketchum Grill
6 China Pepper
8 Akasha Organics; The Elephant Perch
9 Piccolo Italian Country Cooking
11 Pioneer Saloon
12 Desperado's
13 Java on Fourth
14 Bob Dog Pizza
15 Roosevelt Tavern
17 Smokey Mountain Pizza & Pasta
20 Sushi on Second
22 Akasha Organics; Chapter One Bookstore
25 The Wild Radish

OTHER
2 USFS Ranger Station
4 Sun Valley Outfitters
7 Silver Creek Outfitters
10 Chamber of Commerce
16 Whiskey Jacques
18 Post Office
19 Sun Valley Paragliding
21 Lost River Outfitters

IDAHO

include Aspen Loop (1¾ miles) and Proctor Mountain (6 miles roundtrip), offer views of Bald Mountain and Sun Valley. Pick up the 'Trails Around Town' brochure for details. For mountain biking tours and instruction, contact Sun Valley Singletrack (☎ 208-622-8687) or Trail Quest Mountain Bike School (☎ 208-726-7401), 122 Black Bean St, Ketchum.

The Big and Little Wood Rivers and Silver Creek are popular trout streams, most stretches of which are limited to catch-and-release **fly-fishing**. For a guide or rentals, contact, in Ketchum: Sun Valley Outfitters (☎ 208-622-3400), 651 Sun Valley Rd; Silver Creek Outfitters (☎ 208-726-5282, 800-732-5687), 500 N Main St; or Lost River Outfitters (☎ 208-726-1706), 171 N Main St.

Those interested in aerial activities should contact Mulligan Aviation (☎ 208-726-7261) for **hot-air balloon rides**, Sun Valley Soaring (☎ 208-788-3054) for **glider rides** and Sun Valley Paragliding (☎ 208-726-3332), 260 1st Ave N, for **paragliding** off Bald Mountain.

Places to Stay

The Sun Valley/Ketchum Chamber of Commerce (see Information, above) provides an invaluable, free accommodations reservation service. Reservations are recommended during peak seasons; budget places fill quickly year-round. Most accommodations have a pool and hot tub. Seasonal rate variation is considerable. Winter has its own high and low season; high season begins in early February. The bed tax is 9%.

South of Ketchum, the riverside **Sun Valley Camping & RV Resort** (☎ 208-726-3429, 106 Meadow Circle), off Hwy 75 north of the Elkhorn Rd junction, has a Jacuzzi and pool. Sites start at $20. Showers are $5 for nonguests. The free **USFS Boundary Campground**, off Trail Creek Rd 3 miles east of the USFS Ketchum Ranger Station, fills quickly.

There are several motel options along Ketchum's S Main St within walking distance of downtown. The **Ski View Lodge** (☎ 208-726-3441, 409 S Main St) has rustic

two-bed log cabins ($65 to $90). **Lift Tower Lodge** (☎ 208-726-5163, 800-462-8646, 703 S Main St), facing Bald Mountain, charges $56 to $80. **Ketchum Korral Motor Lodge** (☎ 208-726-3510, 800-657-2657, 310 S Main St) has nice older log cabins ($60 to $125). Rooms at the slightly faded **Bald Mountain Lodge** (☎ 208-726-9963, 800-892-7407, 151 S Main St) run $50 to $90.

The European-style **Tamarack Lodge** (☎ 208-726-3344, 800-521-5379, 500 E Sun Valley Rd) has a pool and rooms with fireplaces for $96 to $130. The **Best Western Tyrolean Lodge** (☎ 208-726-5336, 800-333-7912, 308 3rd Ave S) has beautiful views of Bald Mountain and is within walking distance of River Run Plaza. It has a spa and exercise room ($75 to $135). The modern **Best Western Kentwood Lodge** (☎ 208-726-4114, 800-805-1001, 180 S Main St) charges $109 to $169.

Large, comfortable rooms start at $140 at **The River Street Inn B&B** (☎ 208-726-3611, 888-746-3611, 100 River St W); www.theriverstreetinn.com. The luxurious **Idaho Country Inn** (☎ 208-727-4000, 800-635-4444, 134 Latigo Lane) has hot tubs, outstanding views and 11 sunny B&B rooms for $150 to $205. The attractive European-style **Knob Hill Inn B&B** (☎ 208-726-8010, 800-526-8010, 960 N Main St) has sumptuous rooms, a pool, a spa, a sauna and two restaurants. Rates are $185 to $375; www.knobhillinn.com.

Places to Eat

Ketchum has more than 80 restaurants and offers several good values. **Java on Fourth** (☎ 208-726-2882, 191 4th St) has espresso and homemade pastries. **Big Wood Bread** (☎ 208-726-2034, 270 Northwood Way) bakes organic, naturally leavened bread and operates a good cafe. Try **Akasha Organics** at The Elephant Perch on Sun Valley Rd and downstairs in Chapter One Bookstore (☎ 208-726-4777, 160 N Main St) for vegetarian soups and organic juices.

Bob Dog Pizza (☎ 208-726-2358, 380 Washington Ave N) and **Smokey Mountain Pizza & Pasta** (☎ 208-622-5625, 200 Sun Valley Rd) both deliver and are good bets for carbo-loading. **Sushi on Second**

(☎ *208-726-5181, 260 2nd St*) serves traditional raw fish dishes. ***Desperado's*** *(☎ 208-726-3068)*, at 4th St and Washington Ave, serves inexpensive Mexican food on its outdoor deck.

You needn't dress up or spend a lot here to dine in style. ***Piccolo Italian Country Cooking*** *(☎ 208-726-9251, 220 East Ave N)* has good three-course Italian meals ($15). In a converted old home, the friendly ***Ketchum Grill*** *(☎ 208-726-4460, 520 East Ave)* serves creative modern American cuisine, including game and fresh seafood, and always has a veggie option. ***The Wild Radish*** *(☎ 208-726-8468, 200 S Main St)* prepares 'international and alpine cuisine' for lunch and dinner (entrees start at $10). For superior Asian food, visit ***China Pepper*** *(☎ 208-726-0959, 511 Leadville Ave)*. ***Roosevelt Tavern*** *(☎ 208-726-0051, 280 N Main St)* serves sushi and bistro fare and often has live music. ***Pioneer Saloon*** *(☎ 208-726-3139, 308 N Main St)* is the best choice for prime rib, steak and seafood, and attracts a social crowd after hours.

Entertainment

A steady stream of musicians passes through the area. Most bars and lounges have music on weekends. ***Whiskey Jacques*** *(☎ 208-726-5297, 215 N Main St)* is a good place to sample the local scene.

Getting There & Around

See Hailey, earlier, for local air service. Boise Municipal Airport and Salt Lake City International Airport are the nearest major airports. Sun Valley Stages (☎ 208-733-3921, 800-574-8661) operates winter shuttles between Sun Valley and the Boise Municipal Airport, with stops at the Sun Valley Inn, the Chamber of Commerce and Hailey's Chevron station (three hours; $45/75 one-way/roundtrip).

Ketchum is 12 miles north of Hailey and 61 miles south of Stanley.

Ketchum Area Rapid Transit (KART; ☎ 208-726-7140) provides free daily bus service to River Run Plaza, Warm Springs Plaza, Ketchum, Sun Valley and Elkhorn, 7:30 am until midnight. U-Save Auto Rental

(☎ 208-622-9312) and Practical Rent-A-Car (☎ 208-622-4525), 512 N Main St, are in Ketchum. Other car rental companies are at the airport in Hailey. Ring A-1 (☎ 208-726-9351) or Bald Mountain Taxi (☎ 208-726-2650) for a ride.

SUN VALLEY RESORT

The doyen of Ketchum and Sun Valley is undoubtedly the Sun Valley Resort. The grand old Sun Valley Lodge has a princely lobby with a photographic display of the glitterati on skis – from Mary Pickford to Gary Cooper, Lucille Ball, the Kennedys and Marilyn Monroe.

Web site: www.sunvalley.com

Orientation & Information

The resort, a mile northeast of Ketchum, operates separate facilities at Bald Mountain, west of Ketchum, and Dollar Mountain, south of Sun Valley. Within the resort is the Sun Valley Mall with several restaurants, outfitters and other stores, a movie theater and a post office along an outdoor pedestrian boardwalk.

Contact the Sun Valley Resort (☎ 208-622-4111, 800-786-8259) for accommodations and Bald Mountain reservations; request a resort recreation guide. Call the Sun Valley Sports Information Line (☎ 208-622-2231) for information on all resort activities and for Dollar Mountain reservations. First Security Bank of Idaho has an ATM here. Wood River Medical Center (Moritz Hospital; ☎ 208-622-3333) is adjacent to the resort.

Bald Mountain

The forested slopes of Bald Mountain (9150 feet), known locally as 'Baldy,' catch tons of dry powdery snow, making this a world-class downhill skiing mountain. From the summit, 64 diverse runs served by 13 lifts plunge a maximum of 3400 vertical feet; almost two-thirds of the runs are advanced and snowboarding is welcomed. Bald Mountain has two lift areas, each with a day lodge, restaurant and ski school: **River Run Plaza**, south of Ketchum off 3rd St, and **Warm Springs Plaza**, northwest of

IDAHO

Ketchum on Warm Springs Rd. A day lodge, also with a restaurant, is on Seattle Ridge (8600 feet). There are two other lift-served restaurants on the mountain, Lookout and Roundhouse. Peak season full-day lift tickets are $59/33 for adults/ children; half-day $43/26.

Lifts operate 9 am to 4 pm ($15/7) mid-June to mid-September. The **Bald Mountain Trail** has great views; take the lift one way, walk the other. Trails criss-cross the mountain; Broadway Trail connects the summit to Seattle Ridge, and the Cold Springs Trail links with the WRTS and the Warm Springs Trail. Lifts from River Run Plaza are open for lift-served mountain biking. Pick up the Sun Valley 'Mountain Biking, Hiking, Sightseeing Trail Map' for details. The 8-mile **Baldy Perimeter Trail** is the ultimate for experienced mountain bikers.

Dollar Mountain

Sun Valley's original ski area is Dollar Mountain (6638 feet). Its arid, sage-covered slopes contrast dramatically with Baldy's higher, forested slopes. Dollar Mountain has five lifts serving 13 easy runs with a 628-foot maximum vertical drop, making it a family favorite. Snowboarding is welcomed. Peak season full-day lift tickets are $22/16; half-day $16/9. Mountain biking and horseback riding are popular during summer.

Sports Complex

The resort's Sports Complex (☎ 208-622-2231) offers almost every activity imaginable. The Nordic center provides ski rentals, instruction and access to 25 miles of groomed trails, and the resort has one of the USA's 50 best golf courses (reservations essential). Tennis, year-round ice skating, winter sleigh rides and guided horseback rides (☎ 208-622-2387) on Dollar Mountain are popular non-snow activities.

Places to Stay

Sun Valley Resort has four accommodations: *Sun Valley Lodge*, where rooms are $159 to $229 and suites start at $309; *Sun Valley Inn*, with $99 to $189 rooms; *Lodge Apartments*, offering one- to three-bedroom units for $149 to $439; and *Sun Valley Condominiums*, which has studio to four-bedroom units for $129 to $319.

Places to Eat

Try *The Konditorei* (☎ 208-622-2235) for European-style grilled breakfasts and lunch sandwiches like bratwurst and chicken schnitzel ($10). *The Ram Restaurant* (☎ 208-622-2225), at Sun Valley Inn, serves steak, pasta and seafood; entrees are $15 to $25. *Gretchen's* (☎ 208-622-2144), at the Sun Valley Lodge, serves American breakfast, lunch and dinner. The *Lodge Dining Room* (☎ 208-622-2150) is the area's most exclusive restaurant, serving traditional French cuisine accompanied by live music; the Sunday brunch is popular.

Entertainment

Internationally renowned figure skaters perform in the popular *Sun Valley Ice Show*, summer Saturday evenings at the outdoor ice arena (☎ 208-622-2288) behind Sun Valley Lodge. The *Sun Valley Opera House* (☎ 208-622-2244) screens films and hosts musical events.

AROUND KETCHUM & SUN VALLEY

A mile south of Sun Valley on Elkhorn Rd, the newly renovated *Elkhorn Resort* (☎ 208-622-4511, 800-355-4676) has a golf course, sports facilities and restaurants. 'Elkhorn,' as it is commonly called, also offers groomed cross-country trails, instruction and rentals. Rack rates are $88 to $138 off-season, $128 to $178 peak season and suites are $169 to $299. Web site: www.elkhornresort.com

East of Ketchum is **Hyndman Peak** (12,000 feet), the focus of a popular, stiff 5000-foot cross-country climb. Access is from USFS Rd 203; from Ketchum, go south on Hwy 75 to Gimlet and turn east onto Fork Wood River Rd, which connects with USFS Rd 203. Sun Valley Heli*Ski (☎ 208-622-3108, 800-872-3108), 260 1st Ave N, Ketchum, offers **backcountry skiing** trips mid-December to April.

SAWTOOTH NATIONAL RECREATION AREA

Established in 1972, the 756,000-acre USFS-administered SNRA spans parts of the Sawtooth, Smoky, Boulder and Salmon River Mountains. These timbered slopes, with 42 peaks over 10,000 feet, are home to four major rivers (Salmon, South Fork Payette, Boise and Big Wood), 1000 lakes, 100 miles of streams, 700 miles of trails and 217,000 acres of wilderness. The broad spring-fed meadows beneath these peaks are collectively known as the **Stanley Basin**. The adjacent 340-sq-mile **Sawtooth Wilderness Area** centers around the rugged Sawtooth Range. Pockets of privately owned land, including the town of **Stanley**, dot the area, primarily along Hwy 75. The region, visited by more than 1½ million people annually, offers easy access to endless recreational activities and supports commercial timber harvesting, grazing and mining.

Recreation in the SNRA and Stanley has two short seasons: winter and July through August (although some residents argue it is only July). It can snow any time. Summer activities include hiking, fishing, rafting, horseback riding and boating. Snowmobiling, hunting and cross-country skiing are the most popular winter activities.

Orientation

North-south Hwy 75 follows the Salmon River through the SNRA and provides access to most of the lakes, trailheads and campgrounds. Alturas, Pettit and Redfish Lakes, all west of Hwy 75, are popular activity centers. At Stanley, Hwy 75 veers east toward Challis, and Hwy 21 branches northwest. The only western access to the SNRA is from the sleepy hamlet of Grandjean off Hwy 21 via rugged USFS Rd 524.

Information

All SNRA and Sawtooth National Forest visitors must carry a Trailhead Parking Pass ($5/day or $15/year). Vendors include the SNRA headquarters, USFS Stanley and Lowman Ranger Stations and many local businesses.

The info-rich SNRA headquarters (☎ 208-727-5013, 800-260-5970), Hwy 75 (Star Route), 8½ miles north of Ketchum, is open 8:30 am to 5 pm daily and 9 am to 4:30 pm daily during winter (closed Sunday in spring and fall). The SNRA Stanley Ranger Station (☎ 208-774-3681) on Hwy 75, 3 miles south of Stanley, is open daily mid-June to Labor Day and weekdays the rest of the year. The Redfish Lake visitors center (☎ 208-774-3376) is open 9 am to 5 pm Wednesday to Sunday mid-June to Labor Day. There are laundry and showers at Redfish Lake near the gas station. Hot showers are also available at Easley Hot Springs and at the laundry in Stanley.

The Sawtooth Wildlife Council (☎ 208-774-3426) works to protect wildlife habitat, emphasizing education and recovery of salmon populations, and publishes a quarterly newsletter. The nonpartisan Sawtooth Society (☎ 208-387-0852), also works to preserve and protect the Sawtooth National Recreation Area; www.sawtoothsociety.org.

Galena Summit

Galena Summit (8701 feet), on Hwy 75 north of SNRA headquarters, divides the Salmon and Big Wood River watersheds. At the southern base of Galena Summit is the old silver and lead mining town of Galena, founded in 1879, and the Galena Lodge (see Places to Stay & Eat, below).

Sunbeam Dam & Hot Springs

Remnants of Sunbeam Dam, the only barrier ever imposed on the Salmon River, are visible from Hwy 75, 11 miles east of Lower Stanley. The hot springs are a favorite stop for rafters, drivers along Hwy 75 and visitors heading to or from the Land of the Yankee Fork State Park (see Challis & Around later in this chapter).

Sawtooth Fish Hatchery

Self-guided tours of the Sawtooth Fish Hatchery (☎ 208-774-3684), just south of Stanley on Hwy 21, are possible 8 am to 5 pm daily during summer. The hatchery works to restore salmon and steelhead trout populations.

IDAHO

Rafting

Half-day rafting trips on the Upper Main Salmon River (Class II-III) are ideal for beginners and families. Half-day trips start at around $70; trips with a riverside meal start at around $90. From June to mid-July the put-in is usually Basin Creek, which is 8½ miles east of Stanley and offers a longer run with two Class IV rapids. Mid-July to August the put-in is Elk Creek, 13½ miles east of Stanley. The take-out is near Torrey's Hole, 21½ miles east of Stanley. Independent rafters need self-issuing permits. Controlled launch times are usually 9 am to 3 pm daily. Mid-August to mid-September, rafters must portage the salmon spawning nests (called 'redd') at Indian Riffles and Torrey's Hole. See 'Recommended River Trips & Outfitters.'

Hiking & Backpacking

The SNRA trails offer great day hikes and backpacking trips. The most popular trails lead into the Sawtooth Wilderness Area. The Sawtooth National Forest provides free brochures describing most hikes.

For hikes into the Boulder Mountains, turn north off Hwy 75 at the SNRA headquarters onto USFS Rd 146 (North Fork Rd), and proceed 5.2 miles to the North Fork trailhead. For nice lake hikes, turn west off Hwy 75 onto Prairie Creek Rd, 10 miles north of the SNRA headquarters, and drive 2½ miles to the Prairie and Miner Lakes trailhead.

For hikes into the very popular Sawtooth Valley and Sawtooth Wilderness Area, turn west off Hwy 75 at milepost 170.3 onto Pettit Lake Rd and drive 2 miles to the Tin Cup trailhead. To hike into the White Cloud Mountains, Hwy 75 at milepost 174.6, turn east onto unpaved 4th of July Creek Rd. Champion Creek trailhead is 5 miles east, and 4th of July Lake trailhead is 10 miles east. Hikes in the Redfish Lake Area lead into the Sawtooth Wilderness Area. Turn southwest off Hwy 75 at milepost 185.1 onto Redfish Lake Rd and go 2 miles to the Redfish Lake trailhead. Most hikers then take the shuttle boat across the lake (see Boating, below). To reach Sawtooth Lake, turn off Hwy 21 at milepost 128.4, west of

Stanley, and go south on unpaved Iron Creek Rd 4 miles to the Iron Creek trailhead. The very popular 5-mile hike to Sawtooth Lake beneath Mt Regan (10,190 feet) climbs 1700 feet.

Mountain Biking

Trail riding is very popular. Easy rides are on Decker Flat Rd, west of Hwy 75 at milepost 174.7; and Nip and Tuck Rd, half a mile up Valley Creek Rd, north of Hwy 21 at milepost 125.9. More difficult rides are the Galena Loop, starting from Galena Lodge, and the Fisher Creek-Williams Creek Loop, starting at Fisher Creek Rd east of Hwy 75 at milepost 176.3. Galena Lodge has 25 miles of dirt and single-track trails. Mountain bikes are for rent at the gas station near Redfish Corrals.

Climbing & Mountaineering

The White Cloud and Boulder Mountains, east of Hwy 75, offer many nontechnical mountaineering routes. The granite Sawtooth Range, west of Hwy 75, offers fine wilderness Alpine climbs. Idaho's finest high-standard long routes (grade III-V, rated 5.8 to 5.11) are on Elephant Perch, west of Redfish Lake, as is popular Mt Heyburn. The Redfish Lake Lodge serves as the area's climbing information hub.

Other Activities

South of Galena Summit are the two **cross-country skiing** areas of Prairie Creek, west of Hwy 75, and Galena Lodge (☎ 208-726-4010), east of Hwy 75. Galena Lodge offers full-service, world-class Nordic skiing. Backcountry **ski touring** is possible throughout the SNRA.

Shuttle boats cross Redfish Lake with a minimum of four passengers, departing the far end of the lake four times daily ($5/2.50). Lady of the Lake offers one-hour **scenic tours** ($8/5).

Trout fishing is seasonally good in stocked Redfish, Stanley, Pettit and Alturas Lakes. Visit McCoy's Tackle & Gift Shop (☎ 208-774-3377), on Niece Ave at Ace of Diamonds Ave, Stanley, to find out what lures are working where.

Galena Stage Stop Corrals (☎ 208-726-1735), at the southern base of Galena Summit, and Redfish Corrals (☎ 208-774-3311), near Redfish Lake, offer 1½-hour ($32), half-day ($62) and full-day ($95) **horseback rides** mid-June to Labor Day.

Places to Stay & Eat

The SNRA has 33 campgrounds (10 reservable at ☎ 208-877-444-6777) or on its Web site at www.reserveusa.com in five regions: Wood River corridor, south of Galena Summit; Alturas Lake area, on Hwy 75 north of Galena Summit; Redfish Lake area, south of Stanley; Stanley Lake area, off Hwy 21 west of Stanley; and Salmon River Canyon, on Hwy 75 east of Stanley. Reservations (made at least five days in advance) are possible at the following *campgrounds*: Easley in the Wood River corridor; Point and Glacier View in the Redfish Lake area; and Elk Creek, Sheep Trail and Trap Creek in the Stanley Lake area.

Sites at other campgrounds are on a first-come, first-served basis; most are less than $10. The popular *Easley Campground*, 12 miles north of SNRA headquarters, has hot springs. Three miles south of Stanley, Redfish Lake, on Redfish Rd west of Hwy 75, has six campgrounds; *Sockeye*, is the most secluded. Along Stanley Lake, on USFS Rd 455, 4 miles west of Stanley and 3½ miles off Hwy 21, are the picturesque *Stanley Lake* and *Lakeview* campgrounds.

The rustic *Galena Lodge* serves breakfast and lunch daily and dinner on weekends. North of Galena Summit, year-round *Smiley Creek Lodge* (☎ 208-774-3547), has tent sites ($12), RV hookups ($22), tepees ($35), cabins ($40) and lodge rooms (from $50). Food is mediocre, but its ice cream parlor is good. The delightful *Redfish Lake Lodge* (☎ 208-774-3536), on Redfish Lake, has lodge rooms with shared bathroom (from $55), cabins ($115 to $150), motel rooms ($90) and a restaurant; open Memorial Day to Labor Day. (Also see Stanley, below.)

Getting There & Away

Three scenic byways penetrate the pristine SNRA. From the south, the 116-mile Saw-tooth Scenic Byway follows Hwy 75 between Shoshone and Stanley. Like a wicked witch from the west, the 131-mile Ponderosa Pine Scenic Byway follows Hwy 21 between Stanley and Boise. Like a snag-gletooth witch from the east, the 162-mile Salmon River National Scenic Byway follows Hwy 75 between Stanley and Challis, and continues on US 93 between Challis and Salmon.

STANLEY

The old ranching and mining community of Stanley (population around 96; elevation 6300 feet) sits amid breathtaking scenery. The first gold strike in the Stanley Basin was in 1863, and mining continued until 1879. Today Stanley survives as a private enclave within the SNRA (see above) and an excellent base for exploring the area. Tourism is well established, but out-of-the-way Stanley retains a low-key demeanor.

Orientation & Information

Upper Stanley sprawls along Hwy 21, while Lower Stanley is on Hwy 75, a mile north of the Hwy 21/75 junction. The rustic old town at the northern end of the SNRA is along the unpaved Ace of Diamonds Ave, a block south of and parallel to Hwy 21.

The friendly Stanley-Sawtooth Chamber of Commerce (☎ 208-774-3411, 800-878-7950), in the community building on Hwy 21, is open 9 am to 5 pm daily, with abbreviated winter hours; its Web site is at www.stanleycc.org. Jerry's Country Store and the Mountain Village 'Merc' have ATMs. The Sawtooth Hotel has a nice bookstore.

Things to See & Do

The tiny **Stanley Museum** (☎ 208-774-3517), Hwy 75 a half-mile north of the Hwy 21 junction, is in a former ranger station. On the National Register of Historic Places, the museum recounts Stanley Basin history and is open 11 am to 5 pm daily late May to Labor Day.

The Merc issues fishing licenses. Contact Sawtooth Guide Service (☎ 208-774-9947) for chaperoned **steelhead fishing**. Sawtooth

Rentals (☎ 208-774-3409) gives **snowmobiling lessons** during winter and rents summer adventure gear.

Places to Stay

Most places are Lincoln log cabin–style and have kitchenettes. Rates are highest July to August (reservations recommended). Spring and fall are the least expensive seasons.

Open May to mid-October, the no-nonsense **Elk Mountain RV Resort** (☎ 208-774-2202, 800-428-9203), 4 miles west of Stanley on Hwy 21, has a few tent sites ($15), RV hookups ($30), laundry, showers and a cafe (known for its BBQ chicken and ribs).

The charming **Cole's Sawtooth Hotel & Cafe** (☎ 208-774-2282), at the west end of Ace of Diamonds Ave, is the best deal in town. Rooms are $45/50 ($27/30 with shared bath). All other Stanley accommodations are along Hwy 21 west of the Hwy 75 junction. The well-maintained **Valley Creek Motel** (☎ 208-774-3606) has spectacular Sawtooth-view rooms with kitchenettes ($50 to $90) and a few RV sites – its friendly owner is a welcoming host. The cute **Stanley Outpost** (☎ 208-774-3646) starts at $80. Rustic **Danner's Log Cabin Motel** (☎ 208-774-3539) has rooms with one bed ($45) and two beds ($60). Rooms with private decks at the **Creek Side Lodge** (☎ 208-774-2213, 800-523-0733) start at $60. **Triangle C Ranch** (☎ 208-774-2266, 800-303-6258) has small log cabins ($75 to $100). Attractive rooms at **Mountain Village Lodge** (☎ 208-774-3661, 800-843-5475), with a natural hot spring, start at $65/75.

All Lower Stanley accommodations are on Hwy 75 north of the Hwy 21 junction. **Salmon River Lodge** (☎ 208-774-3422), off Hwy 75 east of the Salmon River, offers privacy and panoramic views ($55 to $70). **Sawtooth Rentals & Motel** (☎ 208-774-3409, 800-284-3185) has roadside rooms for around $65; riverfront rooms with private decks start at $85. **Jerry's Motel** (☎ 208-774-3566, 800-972-4627), at Jerry's Country Store, has clean riverfront rooms from $55. **Gunter's Salmon River Cabins** (☎ 208-774-2290, 888-574-2290) has rooms without

kitchenettes ($60) and riverfront rooms ($105).

Places to Eat

Sawtooth Hotel & Cafe (☎ 208-774-9947) is open for breakfast and lunch; try the homemade soup. Lower Stanley's **Peaks & Perks** has espresso, homebaked goods and ice cream. **Sawtooth Luce's Pizza & Suds** (☎ 208-774-3361) lives up to its billing. **Mountain Village Restaurant & Saloon** (☎ 208-774-3317) features homestyle ranch cooking for breakfast, lunch and dinner.

The **Baking Co** (☎ 208-774-2981) on Wall St also serves lunch, beer and wine. **Kasino Club** (☎ 208-774-3516, 21 Ace of Diamonds Ave) is open for drinks and dinner (all-you-can-eat soup and salad for $12), prime rib specials and promises 'service with a snarl.' It's got the town's only stoplight, and claims to be the Sawtooth's only gay bar. The rowdier **Rod N Gun Club** is always open late, as is the **Mountain Saloon** on some nights. Keep an eye out for **roadside taco and burger trucks** in summer for quick cheap eats.

Getting There & Around

Stanley Airport is south of Hwy 21. Private airlines operate nonscheduled intercity and charter flights from Stanley throughout central Idaho. Most charge an hourly rate for backcountry charter flights. Many, however, offer a fixed per-seat fare with a two-passenger minimum for certain intercity flights. Experienced Stanley Air (☎ 208-774-2276, 800-228-2236) is at the airport. McCall & Wilderness Air (☎ 208-774-2221 summer only; ☎ 208-634-7137, 800-992-6559 in McCall, ☎ 208-756-4713, 800-235-4713 in Salmon) has fixed per-seat/charter fares between Boise and Stanley (35 minutes; call for rates).

Stanley is 61 miles north of Ketchum, 52 miles southwest of Challis and 129 miles northeast of Boise. Contact the Mountain Village Lodge (see above) for car rental.

River Rat Express (☎ 208-774-2265 in summer, ☎ 800-831-8942 year-round) operates a shuttle service for rafters. Rates vary widely depending on individual needs; call for details.

MIDDLE FORK SALMON NATIONAL WILD & SCENIC RIVER

Ranked one of the world's top 10 whitewater rivers, the Middle Fork Salmon River has more than 100 Class III-IV rapids in less than 100 miles. The river can be run May to September in four to eight days; most rafters do it in six. Bounded by Frank Church River of No Return Wilderness Area, it boasts hot springs, waterfalls, pictographs and riverside ranches and lodges. The Middle Fork combined with Main Fork Salmon makes an 11- to 12-day trip (see Main Fork Salmon National Wild & Scenic River later in this chapter). A launch reservation is required June to September for rafting its 96 miles (see 'Launch Reservations for Access-Controlled Rivers' under Main Fork Salmon National Wild & Scenic River, later). Permits ($5/person per day) are still required for launch dates outside

the controlled-access period. Daily commercial rates start around $200/185 for adults/children and go up to $300/day, not including permits and taxes. See 'Recommended River Trips & Outfitters.'

At high water, the put-in is Boundary Creek (5640 feet), a two-hour drive northwest of Stanley. Take Hwy 21 northwest of Stanley to Bear Valley Rd (USFS Rd 198, which turns into USFS Rd 579). Head west to Dagger Falls Rd and continue north to the river.

During early June when snow blocks access and late August when water is low, rafters put in downstream of Boundary Creek. The intermediate put-in, Indian Creek (4662 feet), 20 miles downstream, requires flying in. (See Stanley, earlier, for the nearest airport to the put-ins and for information about vehicle shuttles.)

The take-out is at Cache Bar (3000 feet) on the Main Fork Salmon, 5 miles upstream from Corn Creek, the Main Fork Salmon put-in. (See Salmon, later, for the nearest airport to the Cache Bar take-out.)

Salmon of the Salmon River

Three species of salmon participate in one of the world's longest-known fish migrations, the 900-mile eight-month journey between the Upper Salmon River spawning beds and the Pacific Ocean. As of 2000 only a few hundred threatened Chinook, or king, salmon (*Oncorhynchus tschawytscha*) and even fewer endangered bright-red sockeye salmon (*Oncorhynchus nerka*) remain, along with a few thousand steelhead (*Oncorhynchus mykiss gairdncri*), the ocean-going rainbow trout. Eight huge hydropower dams on the Lower Snake and Columbia Rivers block the

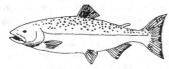

KING (CHINOOK) SALMON

SOCKEYE (RED) SALMON

route between the spawning beds and ocean and are the greatest factor in the decline of these once abundant fish. None of the proposed solutions – barging fish around the dams or the large hatchery program – has halted the steady decline in the fish run. It now appears that unless the dams are removed the salmon of the Salmon River will vanish.

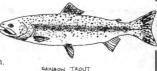

RAINBOW TROUT

IDAHO

Recommended River Trips & Outfitters

Rafting and kayaking are big business in Idaho, and with good reason: The state is blessed with some of the world's best river trips, offering ample opportunities to paddle your way to white-water heaven. The best way to enjoy these is to try an overnight or multiple-day trip. Some of the best options and reputable outfitters are listed below.

Bruneau River The 25-mile Class III-VI section from Indian Hot Springs (3790 feet) to Indian Bathtub (2580 feet) can be rafted in four or five days April to June. Contact **Hughes River Expeditions** (☎ 800-262-1882), www.hughesriver.com or **Wilderness River Outfitters** (☎ 800-252-6581), www.wildernessriver.com.

Middle Fork Clearwater National Wild & Scenic River The Selway and Lochsa Rivers, tributaries of the Middle Fork Clearwater National Wild & Scenic River, meet below the town of Lowell. Here they become known as the Middle Fork Clearwater, which flows west to Kooskia to join the Clearwater River.

The upper Selway River, known for its big Class III-V whitewater, is usually run in three to five days May to June. Launch reservations are required mid-May to July for rafting the 46 miles between Paradise Guard Station (3050 feet) and Meadow Creek (1720 feet) above Selway Falls (see 'Launch Reservations for Access-Controlled Rivers').

Lochsa River's 26-mile Class III-V section has more than 50 rapids between Grave Creek (2500 feet) and Split Creek (1720 feet), usually run in two or three days mid-May to mid-July. Daily commercial rafting rates start at $100.

Contact **River Odysseys West** (ROW; ☎ 800-451-6034), www.rowinc.com or **Three Rivers Rafting** (☎ 888-926-4430), www.threeriversrafting.com.

Moyie & Kootenai Rivers A 15-mile Class III stretch of the lower Moyie River is usually run May to June, and the enormous and powerful Kootenai River is run during summer. Day trips, including lunch, start at $55. Contact **Moyie River Outfitting Guide Service** (☎ 208-267-2108), **River Odysseys West** (see above) or **Twin Rivers Canyon Resort** (☎ 208-267-5932).

Owyhee River The river's many forks are run during April and May. Contact **Hughes River Expeditions** (see above), **Middle Fork River Expeditions** (☎ 800-801-5146), www.idahorivers.com, **River Odysseys West** (see above) or **Wilderness River Outfitters** (see above).

Payette River The South Fork sections can be combined for one- to three-day trips; otherwise all sections are run as day trips. The notoriously difficult North Fork below Smiths Ferry with its 1700-foot vertical drop is one of the world's finest advanced kayak runs; it is not offered commercially. The season is May to September, except on the Upper South Fork from Grandjean, where it is May to mid-July. Contact **Bear Valley River Company** (☎ 800-235-2327), www.webpak.net/~bvrc, **Cascade Raft & Kayak** (☎ 800-793-2221), www.cascaderaft.com, **Headwaters River Company** (☎ 800-800-7238), www.webpak.net/~rafting or **OARS** (☎ 800-328-0290, 800-346-6277), www.oars.com.

Main Fork Salmon National Wild & Scenic River The USA's largest undammed river is run June to September in five to seven days. A launch reservation is required from mid-June to mid-September if you want to raft the 79 miles between Corn Creek (2920 feet) and Vinegar Creek (1960 feet) near Long Tom Bar. There's a $5/day per-person fee. Daily commercial rates start around $175/160 for adults/children.

Recommended River Trips & Outfitters

For Upper Main Fork trips contact:
The River Company
(☎ 800-398-0346),
www.therivercompany.com
Triangle C Ranch Whitewater Expeditions
(☎ 800-303-6258),
www.worldoutfitters.com/outfitters/
trianglec

White Otter Outdoor Adventures
(☎ 800-438-4331), www.whiteotter.com

For Middle Main Fork trips contact:
Aggipah River Trips
(☎ 208-756-4167), www.aggipah.com
Echo:The Wilderness Company
(☎ 800-652-3246)
Holiday River Expeditions
(☎ 800-624-6323), www.bikeraft.com

Idaho Adventures River Trips
(☎ 800-789-9283),
www.idahoadventures.com
OARS (see above)
Warren River Expeditions
(☎ 800-765-0421), www.raftidaho.com
Wilderness River Outfitters (see above)

For Lower Main Fork trips contact:
Discovery River Expeditions
(☎ 800-755-8894),
www.idahodiscovery.com
Epley's Whitewater Adventures
(☎ 800-233-1813), www.epleys.com
Salmon River Challenge
(☎ 800-732-8574),
www.salmonriverchallenge.com

Salmon River Experience
(☎ 800-892-9223),
www.salmonriverexperience.com
Wapiti River Guides
(☎ 800-488-9872),
www.wapitiriverguides.com

Middle Fork Salmon National Wild & Scenic River The 3000-foot vertical drop offers more than 100 Class III-IV rapids. The Middle Fork is combinable with Main Fork Salmon River. Contact Aggipah River Trips (see above), Echo: The Wilderness Company (see above), Middle Fork Rapid Transit (☎ 888-433-5628), www.idahoraftadventure.com, Middle Fork River Expeditions (see above), OARS (see above), River Odysseys West (see above), Triangle C Ranch Whitewater Expeditions (see above).

Lower Fork Salmon River This fork passes through four gorges and is at lower elevations. It has fun Class III rapids, warmer water and great beaches, making it desirable for families. This can be done as an overnight trip. Contact **Aggipah River Trips** (see above), **Holiday River Expeditions** (see above), **Northwest Voyageurs** (☎ 800-727-9977), www.adventuresports.com/wwraft/northwest-voyageurs, **OARS** (see above) or **River Odysseys West** (see above).

Snake National Wild & Scenic River through Hells Canyon The classic Class III-IV river has all things big – waves, views, cliffs – as well as great wildlife viewing, fishing and swimming. Contact **Holiday River Expeditions** (see above), **Northwest Voyageurs** (see above), **OARS** (see above), **River Odysseys West** (see above), or **Salmon River Experience** (see above).

CHALLIS & AROUND

Challis (population 1075; elevation 5280 feet), along the Salmon River, is in the broad, agricultural Round Valley between the Salmon River Mountains and Lost River Mountains, and is the trade town for a widespread ranching and mining community. During the 1960s, a large open-pit molybdenum ('moly') mine opened southwest of town; other area diggins work tungsten, copper and cobalt veins.

Orientation & Information

Challis is on US 93 north of the US 93/75 junction, 52 miles northeast of Stanley, 81 miles north of Arco, and 55 miles southwest of Salmon. The USFS Challis National Forest Middle Fork Ranger District (☎ 208-879-4101) jointly administers parts of four major mountain ranges with the Mackay District: Pioneer, Salmon River, Lost River and Lemhi. The Land of the Yankee Fork is jointly administered by the USFS Yankee Fork Ranger District (☎ 208-838-2201) in Clayton and Idaho Dept of Parks & Recreation (☎ 208-879-5244). The Land of Yankee Fork Historic Area visitor center (☎ 208-879-5244) is at the Hwy 75/93 junction.

Land of the Yankee Fork State Park

Jordan Creek and the Yankee Fork were rich gold-mining centers in the 1870s, but by 1888 the General Custer mine closed. Nearby **Custer City** (6456 feet), now on the National Register of Historic Places, became a ghost town by 1910. Today, visitors can take a free self-guided tour of the town's many restored buildings and the interesting **Custer Museum**; open 10 am to 5:30 pm mid-June to Labor Day.

One mile west of Custer are the dilapidated remains of **Bonanza**, another former settlement. Nearby is the **Yankee Fork Gold Dredge**. Tours ($3) run from 10 am to 5 pm daily July to Labor Day. From Bonanza, USFS Rd 172 (Jordan Creek Rd) leads 9 miles north into the Frank Church River of No Return Wilderness Area.

Take Hwy 75 east of Stanley to Sunbeam, turn north onto paved USFS Rd 013 (Yankee Fork Rd), and continue 10 miles to Custer. Several campgrounds north of Sunbeam on USFS Rd 013 are along the river.

Places to Stay

South of Challis, family-oriented **Challis Hot Springs** (☎ 208-879-4442), 4½ miles west of US 93, has sites ($11 to $15) with year-round hot springs access. Several BLM campgrounds are on US 93 along the Salmon River between Challis and Salmon. The **Challis All Valley RV Park** (☎ 208-879-2393) has sites ($10 to $15), showers and a laundry. On US 93, **The Village Inn** (☎ 208-879-2239) has basic rooms ($40) and kitchenettes ($65). Comparably priced is the **Challis Lodge & Lounge** (☎ 208-879-2251), US 93 at Main St. Overlooking the river, the **Northgate Inn** (☎ 208-879-2490, 879-5767, 441 Main St) charges $37/40.

Antonio's Pizza & Pasta on Main St is the best eating option.

Getting There & Away

Challis is served by Challis Aviation (☎ 208-879-2372) out of Challis Municipal Airport. Community and Rural Transport (CART; ☎ 208-879-2448) operates twice-daily buses Tuesday and Friday southbound to Idaho Falls via Mackay and Arco and northbound to Salmon.

SALMON

When cash was scarce and the land was wild and free, Salmon (population 3500; elevation 4000 feet) was just another ranch and lumber town. Then tourism spurred new life. Today, Salmon caters to the throngs who come to raft the Salmon River, fish and hunt. Tune into the news on KSRA 960 AM or 92.3 FM for a soundbite of the local life.

The free **Lemhi County Historical Museum**, 210 Main St, is open 10 am to 5 pm daily. Salmon Air (see Getting There & Away, below) offers **scenic flights** around Salmon; call for prices. See 'Recommended River Trips & Outfitters' for information on half-day and full-day Salmon River rafting and fishing trips.

Dugout Dick's Ice Cave Ranch

Ever wanted to play homesteader for a day? Nineteen miles south of Salmon off US 93 just north of Elk Bend, across the bridge signed for Twin Peaks Ranch Resort, the antidote for the overcivilized world awaits. Dugout Dick's Ranch is a wonderful anachronism. Before Dick staked his claim in 1948, he busted sod, rode herd and rode the rails, and raised sheep and goats and hay, but now, as he explains with a sly grin, he's in the 'tourist business.' Personally guided tours of his unique ranch cost only a buck, and for another smackaroo you can take as many pictures as you please.

Dick claims he's never heard of Frank Lloyd Wright, but his architectural instincts epitomize 'organic.' Old age hasn't slowed thrifty Dick down, and you may find him hard at work refining his recycled 'rubber tire' building technique. Some of his spelunkable dwellings tunnel back into the hillside more than 100 feet. He claims that several of the dugouts that he rents for $25 a month cost him only $10 to build using driftwood salvaged from the riverbank and sundry scavenged materials, including $1 car hoods and double-thick windshields. He's quite proud of his wooden hinges and hand-hewn rock walls, which he rolled down the hill. He says he started building by digging out caves in riverbanks when he was knee-high to a grasshopper back in Indiana but refined his building techniques during his shepherding days and migrated to Idaho in the early 1940s to work on a dairy farm. His constructions have been studied and documented by *Smithsonian, National Geographic* and several universities.

Dick contemplates another architectural wonder.

If Dick's not around, check the orchard down by the river, or in the ice cave near the office, or just sit tight and wait a spell, he's probably in town checking his mail. If his cane is not by the 'cave tour' sign, he's most likely out on his bicycle. Conversely, if his bike's there, he's most likely in his home, the one with the small solar panel on the roof.

You're strongly encouraged to stick around long enough to find out why both the goats are nicknamed 'nuisance,' (the billy butted Dick and knocked him down the hill and broke his hip a few years back!), but don't stay next door to them unless you enjoy constant companionship. Rent is $2 to $5 a night (clean sheets graciously included), Dick's mood depending, and around $25 per month if you really get to feeling at home in the place. There's a choice of more than a dozen 'rubber tire houses,' including a few cavernous abodes that will sleep up to 12 folks comfortably, depending on your definition of 'comfort,' of course – check them all out, then decide which one meets your needs.

If it's available, shack up in the cabin farthest up the hill on the left-hand side. Or, in winter, bed down in the original homestead, in which Dick claims water won't freeze until it gets to be twenty below, which is more often than you might imagine. Bring a warm sleeping sack, matches for the stove and some grub, toilet paper and a flashlight to find your way to the outhouse, and don't forget your camera 'cause the folks back home might think you're pulling their legs. Don't expect Dick to leave the light on for you – there ain't one.

Orientation & Information

US 93 becomes Main St downtown. The USFS Salmon & Challis National Forest Ranger District (☎ 208-756-2215, 756-5100), and the BLM Salmon District office (☎ 208-756-5400, 756-2201) are adjacent to each other on US 93 just south of town. During the 2000 wildfires, a sign across the highway reading 'Welcome to Clinton & Gore Logging Headquarters – 1-800-LET-IT-BURN' pointed toward the complex. The no-less-controversial Dept of Fish & Game (☎ 208-756-2271) is at 1215 US 93 N.

Places to Stay

In a pinch, there's $5 drive-thru camping at **Shoup Bridge Recreation Site**, just south of the airport, right on US 93. The convenient **Salmon Meadows Campground** (☎ 208-756-2640, 400 N St Charles St), four blocks east of Main St, has tent sites ($15) and RV hookups ($20). **Century II Campground** (☎ 208-756-2063, 603 US 93 N) also has $15 sites. Both have laundry and showers. Five miles southeast of the airport off US 93, **Salmon Hot Springs** (☎ 208-756-4449) may have morphed into the **Wat-A-World** megaresort by the time you read this, but more likely it's still a low-key spot to while away the hours.

Basic rooms start at $35 at **Heritage Inn B&B** (☎ 208-756-3174, 510 Lena St) and **Solaas B&B** (☎ 208-756-3903, Hwy 28). At the south end of town, the clean **Suncrest Motel** (☎ 208-756-2294, 705 S Challis St) charges $37/48. Basic rooms at dubiously named **Motel DeLuxe** (☎ 208-756-2231, 112 Church St) are $40/45. Rooms at **Wagons West Motel** (☎ 208-756-4281, 800-756-4281, 503 US 93 N), two blocks north of the Salmon River Bridge, include use of a shared hot tub ($45/50).

Syringa Lodge B&B (☎ 208-756-4424, 2000 Syringa Dr) charges $40/60. North of the bridge, the inviting **Stagecoach Inn** (☎ 208-756-2919, 201 US 93 N) asks $55/65. It has a laundry and caters to rafters and other backcountry travelers. Anyone can park a vehicle here for free.

Places to Eat

Bertram's Salmon Valley Brewery, on Main St at S Andrew St, serves pub grub and local microbrews. **Bob's Food for Thought** (☎ 208-756-3950, 317B US 93 N), a block north of Stagecoach Inn, has the best vegetarian selection in this anti-herbivore town. The **Salmon River Coffee Shop** (☎ 208-756-3521, 606 Main St) serves well-prepared chops, steak, chicken and burgers, and has a salad bar.

For a bit of Italy, try **Garbonzo's Pizza** (☎ 208-756-4565), on Hwy 28 S. The company here is better than the food at the 24-hour **Smokehouse Cafe** (☎ 208-756-4334, 312 Main St). **Nature's Pantry** (☎ 208-756-6067), one block east of Main St on Center St, stocks natural and freeze-dried camping foods, so it's a good place to stock up. The Pantry plans to move to larger digs and add a cafe.

Getting There & Away

Salmon/Lemhi County Airport is 4 miles south on US 93. Private airlines operate nonscheduled intercity and charter flights throughout central Idaho. Most charge an hourly rate for charter backcountry flights. However, many offer a fixed per-seat fare with a two-passenger minimum for certain intercity flights.

Salmon Air (☎ 208-756-6211, 800-448-3413), has fixed per-seat fares from Salmon to Boise (around $125), Grangeville, Hailey, McCall and Stanley; call for fares and lift-off times or take a look at its Web site at www.salmonair.com. Wilderness & McCall Air (☎ 208-756-4713, 800-235-4713), also has fixed per-seat/charter fares for Boise-Salmon (from $125/500); go to www.mccallair.com.

Community and Rural Transport (CART; ☎ 208-756-2191, 800-258-4937), 206 S St Charles St, one block west of Main St, operates twice-daily buses Tuesday and Friday along the Salmon-Challis-Mackay-Arco-Idaho Falls route. Buses return to Salmon the same day. One-way/roundtrip Salmon-Idaho Falls fare is $22/40. Salmon is on US 93 at Hwy 28, 55 miles northeast of Challis.

NORTH FORK

The sleepy crossroads of North Fork is 21½ miles north of Salmon and 2½ hours south of Missoula, MT, on US 93. Here rafters head west on Salmon River Rd (FR 030) following the Main Fork Salmon River, and US 93 continues north 25 miles, where it crosses Lost Trail Pass (6995 feet) at the Idaho-Montana state line. Just over the border looms popular Lost Trail Ski Area (see Bitterroot Valley in the Montana chapter).

The USFS Salmon-Challis National Forest North Fork Ranger District (☎ 208-865-2700) is just north of town near the Shoup turnoff. The humble *North Fork* *Motel & Campground & Cafe & Store & Laundromat* (☎ *208-865-2412*) is a hive of activity, with tent sites ($8 to $15), motel rooms ($40 to $55) and hot showers. The nicer rooms ($50 to $65) and RV hookups ($18) at the recommended *River's Fork Inn* (☎ *208-865-2301*) are well worth the extra dough. Downstream, basic cabins behind the *Shoup Store* (☎ *208-394-2125*) cost $20/person.

MAIN FORK SALMON NATIONAL WILD & SCENIC RIVER

Bounded by five national forests, the Main Fork Salmon River flows through North

---

Launch Reservations for Access-Controlled Rivers

Private (noncommercial) rafters need to have launch reservations for access-controlled sections of four National Wild & Scenic Rivers:

Main Fork Salmon River
North Fork Ranger District
(☎ 208-865-2725 application requests, ☎ 208-865-2700 more info, fax 208-865-2739), 11 Casey Rd, Box 180, North Fork, ID 83466

Middle Fork Salmon River
Middle Fork Ranger District
(☎ 208-879-4112 application requests, ☎ 208-879-4101 more info, fax 208-879-4198), on US 93 N, PO Box 750, Challis, ID 83226

Selway River
West Fork Ranger District
(☎ 406-821-3269, fax 406-821-1211), 6735 West Fork Rd, Darby, MT 59829

Snake River
Hells Canyon NRA
(☎ 509-758-1957, 888-758-8037 October 1 to March 1, fax 509-758-1963), 2535 Riverside Dr, Box 699, Clarkston, WA 99403

Advance planning is required because more applications are submitted each year than there are permits to be allocated. Even though more than 1000 trip permits are issued annually for more than 10,000 rafters on these rivers, not everyone gets a launch reservation or receives a permit for their preferred river and launch date. Contact any of the above offices after October 1 for an information packet and application form for any of these rivers. They accept applications with a non-refundable $6 fee between December 1 and January 31 only. A February computer lottery determines who gets launch reservations. To inquire about unassigned, canceled or unconfirmed launches, which are reassigned on a first-come, first-served basis, call the above offices 8 am to 4:30 pm weekdays after March 1. On commercial rafting trips, the outfitter handles these details. Download the application online at www.fs.fed.us/r4/sc/recreation/4rivers.

IDAHO

America's second deepest canyon. The Class III-IV river is run June to September in five to seven days (also see Middle Fork Salmon National Wild & Scenic River, earlier). Along the river are hot springs, pictographs, historic sites and homesteads, including the interesting Buckskin Bill Museum at Five Mile Bar. Rafters camp on tranquil sandbars or stay at luxurious lodges.

A launch reservation is required from mid-June to mid-September for the 79 miles between Corn Creek (2920 feet) and Vinegar Creek (1960 feet) near Long Tom Bar. There's a $5/day per person fee. Daily commercial rates start around $200/175 for adults/children. See 'Recommended River Trips & Outfitters.'

The put-in is Corn Creek, 27 miles west of Shoup; Shoup is 19 miles west of North Fork. (See Salmon, earlier, for the nearest airport to the put-in.) The take-out is east of Riggins at Carey Creek boat ramp. See McCall, earlier, for the nearest airport to the take-out; see Stanley, earlier, for information about vehicle shuttles.

NEZ PERCÉ NATIONAL HISTORICAL PARK

This amorphous NPS-administered park is comprised of 24 distinct sites in four counties linked by 400 miles of road. The park brochure says it is 'as much an idea as it is actual physical property.' Sites are inside and outside the 137-sq-mile Nez Percé Indian Reservation (☎ 208-843-2253), established in 1855 and downsized in 1877. The **Nez Percé National Historic Trail**, which crosses Oregon, Idaho, Wyoming and Montana, passes many park sites. The park honors Nez Percé legend and battle sites, as well as locations significant to the history of pioneer exploration. Visiting more than a few of the widely scattered sites is time consuming.

The visitors center (☎ 208-843-2261) in Spalding, 11 miles east of Lewiston, houses an excellent museum; open 8 am to 5:30 pm daily in summer. Sites within 5 miles of the visitors center give a good sense of what the rest of the park is like. The scenic loop drive

---

Nez Percé Creation Myth

According to Nez Percé myth, Meadowlark told Coyote that a monster was devouring all the other creatures. Coyote put five knives and some fire-making tools in his pack, swung it over his back and set off to confront the monster. After exchanging challenges with each other, the monster inhaled Coyote, and Coyote tumbled inside the belly of the monster, where all the other animals were waiting. Coyote found the monster's heart, lit a fire and began to carve off portions. Finally, he cut the heart free and the monster died, allowing the captured animals to escape. Coyote butchered the monster and scattered all the parts of its body to the winds; the bits were transformed into various Native American tribes. Fox reminded Coyote that he had neglected to leave a portion of the body to create a tribe for the valleys of the Clearwater and Snake Rivers. Coyote washed his hands, and with the monster's blood created the Nee-Me-Poo, 'The People,' or the Nez Percé. **The Heart of the Monster**, a site on US 12 between Kamiah and Kooskia, is a stone mound that is believed to be the heart of the monster that died in the process of giving rise to this tribe.

---

along the **Clearwater Canyons Scenic Byway** (US 12), Hwy 13 and US 95 takes about three hours.

RIGGINS

Riggins (population 530; elevation 1800 feet) is a narrow strip of land in a deep canyon at the confluence of the Main Salmon and Little Salmon Rivers. Nestled along US 95 above the true left bank of the Salmon River, Riggins prides itself on being Idaho's whitewater capital and is the base for rafting on the Lower Salmon River and Snake River National Wild & Scenic River through Hells Canyon. Steelhead, trout and small-mouth bass attract many anglers. USFS roads west of Riggins offer limited access to the Hells Canyon National Recreation Area (see below).

Orientation & Information

Riggins is an animated one-raft town with businesses stretching along Main St (US 95) – street numbers are scarce. Contact the Salmon River Chamber of Commerce (☎ 208-628-3778) for a list of rafting, fishing and horsepacking outfitters. There's a helpful summer-only information kiosk (☎ 208-628-3440) in the center of town. Web site: www.rigginsidaho.com

Rafting

Refreshing half-day and full-day rafting trips on the Lower Salmon River (put in at or near Riggins and take out near Lucille) run May to September, when it's scorching hot. Half-day trips begin around $40/25 for adults/children. Full-day trips start at $65/50. See 'Recommended River Trips & Outfitters.'

Places to Stay & Eat

At the north end of Riggins is the small *River Village RV Park* (☎ 208-628-3441, 1434 N US 95), with laundry and shower. Grassy, shady tent sites above the river cost $10; RV hookups are $15. Quiet off-road rooms at the *Bruce Motel* (☎ 208-628-3005, N Main St) start at a negotiable $30. North of town, the clean *River View Motel* (☎ 208-628-3041, 888-256-2322, 708 N US 95) starts around $40. In town try the well-maintained older *Riggins Motel* (☎ 208-628-3001, 800-669-6739, 615 S Main St, rigmotel@micron.net) with a hot tub ($35/45); a $95 suite sleeps six. The remodeled *Salmon River Motel* (☎ 208-628-3231, 888-628-3025, 1203 S US 95) charges $35/40. You get a discount if you use its Web site: www.salmonrivermotel.com. The luxurious *Lodge at Riggins Hot Springs* (☎ 208-628-3785, escape@rhslodge.com) is 9 miles east of Riggins off Salmon River Rd. Rates ($150 to $350) include gourmet meals and access to the hot springs.

Cattlemen's Restaurant (☎ 208-628-3195, 601 S Main St) is the local favorite for breakfast and family-style lunch and dinner. The *Salmon River Inn* (☎ 208-628-3813), on Main St, serves good sub sandwiches, soups and salads. Five miles north of Riggins on US 95, the roadside *Fiddle Creek Fruit Stand* stocks fireworks and many fine provisions.

Getting There & Away

Riggins is on US 95, 44 miles south of Grangeville and 90 miles north of McCall. Northwestern Stagelines stops at city hall on US 95. Daily buses go northbound to Spokane, WA, via Grangeville, Lewiston and Moscow; southbound buses go to Boise via US 95 to New Meadows and then Hwy 55.

HELLS CANYON NATIONAL RECREATION AREA

As early as 1895, the term 'Hells Canyon' was applied to the Snake River's passage through North America's deepest gorge, thousands of feet deeper than the Grand Canyon. From He Devil Peak (9393 feet) on the east rim, the canyon drops 8913 feet to the Snake River at Granite Creek. The average depth is 6600 feet. Hat Point (6982 feet) in Oregon's Eagle Gap Mountains is the west rim's highest point. The remote 652,000-acre Hells Canyon NRA offers hiking, fishing, swimming, camping and dramatic views of the gorge and surrounding mountains.

Orientation

Hells Canyon NRA spans the Idaho-Oregon state line, but the park headquarters and Oregon section is not readily accessible from Idaho. From Cambridge (see Around Boise, earlier) Hwy 71 leads north to Hells Canyon Dam Rd and the dam at its south end. US 95 parallels its eastern boundary; a few unpaved roads lead from US 95 between Riggins and White Bird into Hells Canyon NRA, crossing parts of the Nez Percé National Forest and Hells Canyon Wilderness Area. Only one road leads from US 95 to the Snake River itself at Pittsburg Landing.

Information

The Hells Canyon NRA Riggins office (☎ 208-628-3916) has excellent information

IDAHO

and maps on campgrounds along the Snake and Salmon Rivers, as well as road, trail and fishing conditions in the Hells Canyon Wilderness Area. Located on US 95 in Riggins' southern outskirts, it's open 8 am to 5 pm weekdays. For river flows information, contact the USFS Hells Canyon NRA Wallowa-Whitman National Forest Snake River office (☎ 509-758-0616, 800-422-3143 for recorded information), at 2535 Riverside Dr, Clarkston, Washington, on Hwy 129 south of the Southway Bridge.

Hells Canyon Lookouts

Time-rich travelers drive to the canyon rim on unpaved fair-weather roads for dramatic views. The most popular drive is USFS Rd 517 (Seven Devils Rd). Go about a quarter-mile south of the Hells Canyon NRA Riggins office on US 95 and turn west on USFS Rd 517 (open July to mid-October). The gravel road (high clearance recommended) climbs steadily 17 miles, crossing Windy Saddle and arriving at the rim and Seven Devils Campground after about one hour. The road continues 2 miles north to **Heaven's Gate Lookout** (8430 feet), one of the area's most breathtaking view points.

4WD vehicles can follow the steep USFS Rd 241 (open mid-June to October) west from US 95, a quarter-mile north of Riggins, 15 miles to **Iron Phone Junction**. From Iron Phone Junction, USFS Rd 2060 continues west to **Sawpit Saddle** or USFS Rd 1819 to **Low Saddle**. A 17-mile loop trip along the rim follows other USFS roads before descending again on USFS Rd 241, or by continuing along the rim on dry weather–only USFS Rd 420 (USFS Rd 672 is the better choice in wet weather) for 25 miles to USFS Rd 493 (Deer Creek Rd).

The **Sheep Rock** promontory (6847 feet), on USFS Rd 106 at the NRA's south end, is a national natural landmark with outstanding views.

Seven Devils Mountains

The 8000-foot Seven Devils Mountains separate the Little Salmon River and Salmon River valleys from the Snake River canyon. Dozens of lakes brimming with brook trout

are east of the crest. Miles of spectacular **hiking** trails crisscross the slopes. One lovely trail follows the little-known Rapid National Wild & Scenic River, which tumbles down the eastern slopes. **Windy Saddle** is the main trailhead for the Seven Devils Mountains, Hells Canyon Wilderness Area and the Heavens Gate Scenic National Recreation Trail. Camping is free everywhere, but there is no piped water. Follow USFS Rd 517 west from Riggins to trailheads.

Lower Pittsburg Landing

The unpaved rough USFS Rd 493 (Deer Creek Rd) leaves US 95 at White Bird, heading west over Pittsburg Saddle to the Snake River at Lower Pittsburg Landing (17 miles, 1½ hours). Lower Pittsburg Landing has a boat launch, swimming beach, fishing area and campground (no potable water). The sandy terrain here was a longtime Nez Percé camp and was popular during the brief 1910s homesteading boom, when 21 homesteads clung to life along this precarious stretch of Hells Canyon.

Snake River National Recreation Trail

Upper Pittsburg Landing, 2 miles before Lower Pittsburg Landing, is the trailhead for the 30-mile Snake River National Recreation Trail, suited to **hiking** and **horseback riding** along the river to Hells Canyon Dam. A few walk-in campsites are at Upper Pittsburg Landing, but there's no drinking water.

SNAKE RIVER NATIONAL WILD & SCENIC RIVER

The stretch through Hells Canyon is popular with rafters and jet boaters. Rafters run this Class III-IV section May to September in three to five days. Known for all things big – waves, views, cliffs – the river is lined with historic homesteads, pictographs, hiking trails and wildlife such as bighorn sheep and mountain goats. Steelhead and sturgeon fishing begins in the fall. The warm waters are great for swimming.

The Mighty Snake River

The mighty Snake River flows into Idaho from Wyoming at the Palisades Reservoir, and then west through the scenic Swan Valley. The renowned Henry's Fork joins the Snake north of Idaho Falls. Here the Snake escapes eastern Idaho's forests and slithers through southern Idaho's arid plains, pausing at American Falls Reservoir near Pocatello. At Twin Falls, it plummets over Shoshone Falls into a dramatic canyon, then sidewinds through the verdant Hagerman Valley. South of Boise the river heads northward, forming the Idaho-Oregon border. The Snake ultimately merges with the Columbia River 1036 miles from its source in Yellowstone on the Continental Divide.

An Indian tribe in southern Idaho, now known as the Shoshone, used a hand signal resembling the motion of a snake to identify themselves. The term 'snake' became their tribal name and later the name for the river that flowed through their territory.

Rafting

A launch reservation is required late May to mid-September for rafting the designated 'wild' 31½ miles between Hells Canyon Dam and Pittsburg Landing (see 'Launch Reservations for Access-Controlled Rivers' under Main Fork Salmon National Wild & Scenic River, earlier). Self-issuing permits are required for launch dates outside the controlled-access period on this section and year-round for launches at or downstream of Pittsburg Landing, where the 36-mile designated 'scenic' section begins. Daily commercial rates are $175/145 to $225/195 for adults/children.

Jet Boat Trips

Half-day jet boat trips usually go to Dug Bar–Nez Percé Crossing (118 miles roundtrip). Half-day trips start at $50/35 for adults/children. Full-day jet boat trips go to: Rush Creek (182 miles roundtrip, $80/45); Granite Creek (200 miles, $100/55); or Hells Canyon Dam (216 miles, $150/80). Full-day trips usually include lunch. Dinner cruises to Hellar Bar Lodge (70 miles roundtrip) start at $42. The river is renowned for its white sturgeon, the world's largest freshwater fish, rainbow and steelhead trout and smallmouth bass. Full-day guided fishing trips are $125 to $150.

Two-day, one-night trips are $195 to $260; an additional day costs $125. Beamers Hells Canyon Tours (see below) is well-known for its historic 'mail run,' delivering the US mail to outlying canyon ranches. Two-day one-night fishing trips are $265 to $365; an additional day costs $185. Camping and lodging are available. To book a jet boat trip, contact:

Beamers Hells Canyon Tours
(☎ 509-758-4800, 800-522-6966), 1451 Bridge St, Clarkston, WA 99403
Web site: www.hellscanyontours.com

High Roller Excursions
(☎ 208-798-8178), 1030 Bryden St, Lewiston, ID 83501

River Quest Excursions
(☎ 208-746-8060, 800-589-1129), 1523 Powers Ave, Lewiston, ID 83501
Web site: www.riverquestexcursions.com

Snake Dancer Excursions
(☎ 509-758-8927, 800-234-1941), Box 318, Clarkston, WA 99403
Web site: www.snakedancerexcursions.com

Snake River Adventures
(☎ 208-746-6276, 800-262-8874), 227 Snake River Ave, Lewiston, ID
Web site: www.snakeriveradventures.com

To book a fishing-oriented jet boat trip, contact Scenic River Charters (☎ 208-746-6808), 1209 Main St, Lewiston or Mainstream Outdoor Adventures (☎ 208-743-0512, rapidrnr@aol.com), 5700 Tammany Creek Rd, Lewiston.

Getting There & Away

For rafters, the put-in is below the Hells Canyon Dam (1475 feet) in Oregon. The three-day take-out is Pittsburg Landing (1120 feet); the five-day at Hellar Bar (1080 feet). See McCall, earlier, for the nearest airport to both the put-in and Pittsburg Landing take-out. See Lewiston &

IDAHO

Jet Boats on National Wild & Scenic Rivers?

The 1976 Wild & Scenic Rivers Act gave federal protection to designated rivers. The Central Idaho Wilderness Act of 1980, however, stripped Idaho's National Wild & Scenic Rivers of basic protection conferred by the 1976 act as well as the more restrictive provisions of the Wilderness Act of 1964. How did this happen? Congress specifically directed that the requirements of the 1976 act would take precedence. But in the 1980 act Congress granted an allowance for jet boats, recognizing an 'historic use' of jet boats as an integral part of the transportation system on the Salmon River.

Today white-water rafters compete with jet boats on the Main Fork Salmon River and Snake River through Hells Canyon. Ironically, permits are required and access is controlled on National Wild & Scenic Rivers for rafters and kayakers, but not for jet boaters who have free rein to terrorize the waterways.

A 'jet back' is when a jet boat transports rafters back upstream after rafting, avoiding shuttles to return to their vehicles. Jet backs, however, are an intrusion whose frequency, especially on the Main Fork Salmon River, is escalating. Unfortunately jet boat use is not going to go away. Considered 'essential' to transport guests and supplies to private lodges along these rivers, their use is entrenched in local mentality. Rafters can avoid booking a trip with a company that uses jet backs or supports nonessential jet boat use, and so help preserve the wild and scenic nature of these amazing rivers.

Clarkston, earlier, for the nearest airport to the Hellar Bar take-out. See Stanley, earlier, for information about vehicle shuttles. Most jet boat trips depart from Lewiston's Hells Gate Marina or Clarkston's Swallows Crest Park boat launch.

LUCILE & AROUND

Lilliputian Lucile, 10 miles north of Riggins on US 95, has a few nice campgrounds. Northwest Voyageurs (☎ 208-628-3021, 800-727-9977) is one of only four businesses in town, with a trailer and RV park, a cafe and a handy shop. It rents rafts, kayaks, mountain bikes and other gear. It also offers steelhead trips. Along the true right bank of the Salmon River, the friendly ***Prospectors Gold RV & Campground*** (*☎ 208-628-3773*) offers shady tent sites ($5) and 50-amp RV hookups ($12), as well as gold panning.

LOWER FORK SALMON RIVER

About 15 million years ago, the Lower Fork Salmon River carved its canyon through Miocene lava flows. The Snake River created Hells Canyon, 8 miles to the west, in a similar way. The river has big sandy beaches for camping and warm water, great for swimming. Trails lead to nearby pictographs. Steelhead fishing begins in late September. This 40-mile Class III river is usually run in three to five days June to September. Its status as a National Wild & Scenic River is pending, meanwhile self-issuing permits are required year-round. Contact the BLM (☎ 208-962-3245) in Cottonwood for details. Daily commercial rates start around $175/160. See 'Recommended River Trips & Outfitters.'

The put-in is at Hammer Creek (1410 feet), adjacent to a BLM campground ($8), where US 95 leaves the valley at White Bird, about 28 miles north of Riggins. (See McCall, earlier, for the nearest airport to the put-in.) The take-out is at Hellar Bar (1080 feet) on the Snake River below the confluence of the Salmon and Snake Rivers, about 35 miles south of Lewiston. (See Lewiston & Clarkston, earlier, for the nearest airport to the take-out. See Stanley, earlier, for information about vehicle shuttles.)

IDAHO

WHITE BIRD & AROUND

Between Riggins and White Bird (population 120), US 95 follows the Salmon River through a narrow canyon. At White Bird, US 95 leaves the river and climbs White Bird Grade (4245 feet). The current US 95 was built in 1975, but history enthusiasts should take the winding 16-mile old highway. Built in 1915, it is designated the **White Bird Battlefield Auto Tour** after the first real battle of the so-called Nez Percé War, fought on this steep escarpment in 1877. Battle sites are keyed to a tour brochure available from the information post at the beginning of the route. It's on the National Register of Historic Places.

The USFS Nez Percé National Forest Salmon River Ranger District (☎ 208-839-2211), on US 95 near Slate Creek south of White Bird, is open 7 am to 4 pm weekdays. They sell excellent river guides and the 'Nez Percé National Forest' topo map. Ask for the free Clearwater Nez Percé Country Travel Planner. The site also houses the interesting **Forest Ranger Museum**.

GRANGEVILLE & AROUND

Surrounded by wheat farms and cattle ranches, Grangeville (population 3400) is an old agricultural trade town now changing to accommodate tourism. The Camas Prairie (elevation 3390 feet), a broad volcanic plateau cut on each side by deep canyons, sprawls northwest of Grangeville. The town is the gateway to Idaho's Northwest Passage and is a jumping-off point for the Gospel Hump and Selway-Bitterroot Wilderness Area.

Hwy 13 is Main St in town. Idaho Ave runs north-south and divides east-west street addresses. The USFS Nez Percé National Forest Clearwater Ranger Station (☎ 208-983-1950) is at 319 E Main St. The post office is on E Main St at Idaho Ave. Syringa General Hospital (☎ 208-983-1700) is at 607 W Main St.

Places to Stay & Eat

Harpster RV Park (☎ 208-983-2312), 13 miles east of town on Hwy 13, has tent/RV sites ($10/15). Clean *Monty's Motel* (☎ 208-983-2500, 700 W Main St) and *Elkhorn Lodge* (☎ 208-983-1500, 822 SW 1st), both with rooms starting at $35, are dwarfed by the fancy new *Super 8*. The Victorian *Meadows House B&B* (☎ 208-983-0718, 306 S Meadow) charges $65/75. On a 300-acre Camas Prairie farm in Cottonwood is *Mariel's B&B* (☎ 208-962-5927) with rooms for $40/50.

Grangeville has lots of flashy new eateries, but *Oscar's Restaurant* (☎ 208-983-2106, 101 E Main St), noted for its 12 different cuts of steak, still stands out. It also serves espresso, Mexican food, sandwiches, chicken and seafood. For organic groceries, visit *The Health Food Store* (☎ 208-873-1276, 709 W North St).

Getting There & Away

Grangeville is on US 95 at Hwy 13, 72 miles southeast of Lewiston and 44 miles

---

The Priory of St Gertrude & St Gertrude Museum

A satisfying side trip from the small town of Cottonwood, 14 miles north of Grangeville off US 95, leads to a Benedictine nunnery and an eclectic museum of early Idaho history; follow the signs from Cottonwood. Established in 1920, the Priory of St Gertrude, with its Romanesque-style stone chapel and convent, was completed in 1925; the nuns did much of the labor. The chapel, marked by twin 90-foot towers, is open to visitors. Next door, St Gertrude Museum (☎ 962-3224) began as a collection of relics gathered by Sister Alfreda Elsensohn, an expert in Idaho pioneer history. Highlights include the personal belongings of Main Salmon River homesteaders Sylvan Hart ('Buckskin Bill') and former Chinese slave Polly Bemis, Nez Percé artifacts. Open 9:30 am to 4:30 pm Monday to Saturday and 1:30 to 4:30 pm Sunday; or by appointment (☎ 962-7123).

IDAHO

north of Riggins. The **Clearwater Canyons Scenic Byway** heads east and north on Hwy 13 down Harpster Grade Rd to Kooskia. Hwy 14 leads southeast to Elk City, one of Idaho's most remote settlements; the town's year-round population is less than 20. From here more obscure USFS roads dead-end at distant wilderness trailheads.

Northwestern Stagelines stops on US 95 N at the Highway Station, the first easily visible gas station. Daily buses go northbound to Spokane, WA, via Lewiston and Moscow; southbound buses go to Boise via US 95 to New Meadows and then Hwy 55.

LOCHSA VALLEY

East-west trending US 12, locally known as the 'Lewis and Clark Highway,' was completed in 1962 and links Kooskia to Missoula, MT, via the Lochsa ('LOCK-saw') Valley. Lolo Pass (5235 feet) is at the head of the valley on the Idaho-Montana border, straddling the Continental Divide. This 99-mile stretch of US 12 mostly follows the Lochsa River, which originates in the Bitterroot Mountains and offers good fly-fishing. Footbridges provide access to the northern side of the 2095-sq-mile **Selway-Bitterroot Wilderness Area**, with 2000 miles of trails used primarily by horsepackers, snowmobilers and cross-country skiers. Except for the tiny settlements of Syringa (16 miles east of Kooskia), Lowell (7 miles east of Syringa at the confluence of the Lochsa and Selway Rivers) and Powell, near Lolo Pass, there are few signs of inhabitation.

Information

The informative kiosk at the US 12/13 junction is stocked with useful maps and brochures. The USFS Clearwater National Forest Lochsa Ranger District (☎ 208-926-4275) is south of the Clearwater Bridge at 502 Lowry St. Orofino's USFS Clearwater National Forest headquarters (☎ 208-476-4541), 12730 US 12, opens from 8 am to 4:30 pm weekdays and from 8:30 am to 5 pm weekends.

Hot Springs

The upper Lochsa River is fed by hot springs in the midst of green forested meadows. Short walks lead to two popular undeveloped soaking pools. **Weir Creek Hot Springs** is just east of milepost 142 at Weir Creek Bridge. Climb a steep half-mile trail up the crick's west bank to the pool. The popular **Jerry Johnson Hot Springs**, 10½ miles southwest of Powell, MT, has three sets of primitive pools. Head half a mile west of milepost 152 to the Warm Springs Pack Bridge turnout. Cross the bridge and hike one easy uphill mile to the springs. The free USFS-administered area is day-use (6 am to 8 pm daily) only.

Lochsa Historical Ranger Station

Twenty-four miles northwest of Lowell on US 12 near Boulder Creek is the Lochsa Historical Ranger Station, open 9 am to 5 pm daily Memorial Day to Labor Day. These 1920s log cabins pay tribute to the lives of firefighters who once inhabited this remote USFS station. The volunteer-administered site was converted into a museum in 1976.

Places to Stay & Eat

There are 12 USFS campgrounds off US 12; the best is *Wilderness Gateway*, 25 miles east of Lowell. The friendly, family-run, year-round *Three Rivers Resort* (☎ 208-926-4430, 888-926-4430), on US 12 in Lowell, has tent sites from $5/person, RV hookups ($18 to $25), motel rooms ($40/50), riverview cabins (from $79) and a delightful old forest service B&B cabin ($100), along with a pool and hot tubs. River outfitters set up camp here during highwater months. The rustic *Lochsa Lodge* (☎ 208-942-3405), 12 miles west of the Idaho-Montana state line, has unplumbed cabins ($35) and motel rooms ($45 to $70). Both have well-stocked restaurants and bars.

Folks trek all the way from Grangeville for the homecooked meals and huckleberry pie at the enduring *Middle Fork Cafe* (☎ 208-926-0169) and the newer *Clearwater Legacy Restaurant* (☎ 208-926-0874), both in Syringa.

Getting There & Away

Serpentine US 12 is heavily traveled during summer; allow sufficient time to reach your destination. Gas stations at Syringa, Lowell, Powell and Lolo Hot Springs (7 miles into Montana) close early in the evening. Lolo Pass gets mighty slippery during winter; dial ☎ 208-746-3005 for road conditions.

MIDDLE FORK CLEARWATER NATIONAL WILD & SCENIC RIVER

The Selway and Lochsa Rivers, tributaries of the Middle Fork Clearwater National Wild & Scenic River, flow through the Selway-Bitterroot Wilderness Area and meet below the town of Lowell. Here they become known as the Middle Fork Clearwater, which flows west to Kooskia to join the Clearwater River. See 'Recommended River Trips & Outfitters.'

Selway River Section

A pristine wilderness of fern-carpeted fir and cedar forests surrounds the upper Selway River. Known for its big Class III-V whitewater, the river is usually run in three to five days May to June. Launch reservations are required mid-May to July for rafting the 46 miles between Paradise Guard Station (3050 feet) and Meadow Creek (1720 feet) above Selway Falls (see 'Launch Reservations for Access-Controlled Rivers').

Lochsa River Section

The aptly named Lochsa (which means 'rough water' in Nez Percé) River is a challenging white-water run that is popular with kayakers. The 26-mile Class III-V section with more than 50 rapids between Grave Creek (2500 feet) and Split Creek (1720 feet) is usually run in two or three days from mid-May to mid-July. Wetsuits and helmets are recommended, as is prior white-water experience. No permit is necessary. Please note, bring your own gear as outfitters do not rent gear for use on this river. Rates for daily commercial rafting start at around $125.

Getting There & Away

Elk City, on Hwy 14 east of Grangeville, is the nearest town to the upper Selway's main put-in and take-out; from Elk City head north on USFS Rd 443, or from Lowell head southeast on USFS Rd 223. The Lochsa's 10 put-ins and take-outs are along US 12 east of Lowell. (See Lewiston & Clarkston, below, for the nearest airport to both put-ins and take-outs.)

LEWISTON & CLARKSTON

North-central Idaho is the state's mountainous midriff, cleaved by the Salmon, Clearwater and Snake Rivers to the south, north and west, respectively. The Snake River incises a deep gorge along the Idaho-Oregon state line. Few roads pass through this rugged area; US 95 and US 12 are the only paved north-south and east-west byways.

The twin hardworking commercial centers of Lewiston, ID, and Clarkston, Washington, sprawl across the flood plain at the Clearwater and Snake Rivers confluence. These friendly (but stinky) towns (population Lewiston 31,000; population Clarkston 7150; elevation 736 feet) are at the southern edge of the Palouse, a vast agricultural area producing peas, lentils, wheat and livestock. The Potlatch Lumber Mill on the Clearwater River is one of the state's largest timber-product facilities. Relatively new to the subtleties of tourism, Lewiston's and Clarkston's amenities are basic and inexpensive.

History

The towns' namesakes passed through here in 1805 and 1806 (see 'The Lewis & Clark Expedition' in Facts about the Rocky Mountains). The area, however, was first settled in 1860 at the beginning of Idaho's gold rush. The confluence was the head of steamboat navigation from Portland and the area boomed as a trade center, but the land was part of the Nez Percé Indian Reservation and the Indian Agent wouldn't allow permanent settlement. Thus, for two years Lewiston was a large tent settlement. In 1863, Lewiston, the first incorporated town, was named territorial capital. In 1865,

IDAHO

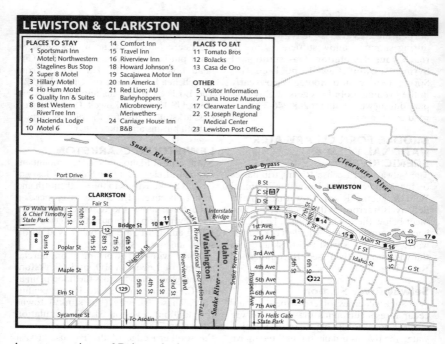

LEWISTON & CLARKSTON

PLACES TO STAY
1 Sportsman Inn
  Motel; Northwestern
  Stagelines Bus Stop
2 Super 8 Motel
3 Hillary Motel
4 Ho Hum Motel
6 Quality Inn & Suites
8 Best Western
  RiverTree Inn
9 Hacienda Lodge
10 Motel 6

14 Comfort Inn
15 Travel Inn
16 Riverview Inn
18 Howard Johnson's
19 Sacajawea Motor Inn
20 Inn America
21 Red Lion; MJ
  Barleyhoppers
  Microbrewery;
  Meriwethers
24 Carriage House Inn
  B&B

PLACES TO EAT
11 Tomato Bros
12 BoJacks
13 Casa de Oro

OTHER
5 Visitor Information
7 Luna House Museum
17 Clearwater Landing
22 St Joseph Regional
  Medical Center
23 Lewiston Post Office

however, partisans of Boise stole the state seal and decamped to the south. Lewiston filed suit to regain the capital, to no avail.

Lewiston and Clarkston continued to grow, especially as federal irrigation projects encouraged orchards along the temperate canyon bottoms. The biggest change for the area, however, came in 1955 when the US Army Corps of Engineers began to build Washington state's four Snake River dams, which brought slackwater to the port of Lewiston in 1975. Lewiston is the country's most inland port: Vessels drawing less than 14 feet and weighing less than 12,000 tons journey upriver 470 miles from the mouth of the Columbia River to Lewiston's loading docks.

Orientation

Lewiston is south of the Clearwater River and east of the Snake River; Clarkston is south and west. The effect is that of a huge T with a city tucked under each 'arm.' Two bridges span the Snake River linking Lewiston and Clarkston: Interstate Bridge (US 12) and Southway Bridge. US 95/12 crosses Memorial Bridge over the Clearwater River at Lewiston's northeast end. North of Lewiston, US 95 climbs the long 7.5% grade over Lewiston Hill.

Lewiston's downtown, below an imposing rock bluff, is along Main St between 1st and 9th Sts; US 12 bypasses downtown. Many newer businesses are along 21st St and Thain Rd, which lead south to the suburbs. US 12 E north of Memorial Bridge is also called North & South Hwy. Clarkston's downtown is along 5th and 6th Sts, although many businesses are on Bridge St (US 12). Hwy 129 (6th St) leads 5 miles south of Clarkston along Snake River past the basalt outcrop called Swallows Crest to Asotin, Washington.

Information

The Dept of Fish & Game (☎ 208-799-5010) is at 1540 Warner Ave, Lewiston. The

IDAHO

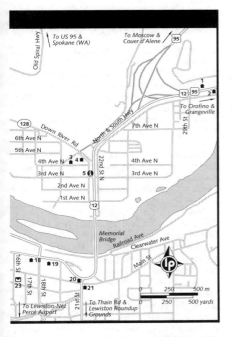

Lewiston post office is at 1613 Idaho St. Clarkston's is at 949 6th St. Kling's Book Store (☎ 208-743-8501), 704 Main St, Lewiston, has books and regional maps. St Joseph Regional Medical Center (☎ 208-743-2511) is at 415 6th St, Lewiston. Tri-State Memorial Hospital (☎ 509-758-5511), is at 1221 Highland Ave, Clarkston. Dial ☎ 208-743-3841 for a regional weather forecast.

Snake River National Recreation Trail

The 20-mile Levee Parkway runs along the Clearwater and Snake Rivers (the most heavily used portion is between the Interstate Bridge and Hells Gate State Park). **Clearwater Landing**, behind the Port of Lewiston, has displays on the history of Snake River navigation. In front of the interpretive center is the **Tsceminicum Sculpture** (si-min-eye-kum; Nez Percé for 'meeting of the waters'). To reach the center, follow D St or Levee Bypass between 1st and Levee Bypass and follow the signs.

Luna House Museum

Operated by the Nez Percé County Historical Society, this free museum (☎ 208-743-2535), 3rd and C Sts in Lewiston, displays pioneer and Nez Percé artifacts. Luna House is open 10 am to 4 pm Tuesday to Saturday.

Lewiston Roundup

This three-day event (☎ 208-746-6324) takes place the first weekend in September at the Lewiston Roundup Grounds, 7000 Tammany Creek Rd, south of Lewiston. It attracts top rodeo stars, and the community turns out for parades, carnivals and Nez Percé dancing.

Hells Gate State Park

Along the true right bank of the Snake River, 4 miles south of Lewiston, is the 960-acre Hells Gate State Park (☎ 208-799-5015). A popular antidote for scorching summer days, it offers a swimming beach, campground with showers and a picnic area (day use $2). Short hiking trails join the Levee Parkway. Hells Gate Marina (☎ 208-799-5016) is the departure point for most jet boat trips (see Snake River National Wild & Scenic River earlier in this chapter) and charter fishing trips. Displays at the Williams Memorial visitors center focus on Snake River geology and history and central Idaho's flora and fauna. Reservable tent sites are $12, RV hookups $16.

Places to Stay

Lewiston's budget motels are clustered north of Memorial Bridge. Try the **Hillary Motel** (☎ 208-743-8514, 2030 North & South Hwy) for $28/34; basic **Ho Hum Motel** (☎ 208-743-2978, 2015 North & South Hwy) at $25/29; or the slightly nicer **Sportsman Inn Motel** (☎ 208-743-9424, 877-240-1937, 3001 North & South Hwy). **Super 8** (☎ 208-743-8808, 3120 North & South Hwy) is another step up ($42/50).

There are several places along Lewiston's Main St, including: *Travel Inn* (☎ 208-743-4501, 1021 Main St), which asks $35/45; *Riverview Inn* (☎ 208-746-3311, 800-806-7666, 1325 Main St) for $40/50; *Sacajawea Motor Inn* (☎ 208-746-1393, 800-333-1393, 1824 Main St) for $45/55; and *Comfort Inn* (☎ 208-798-8090, 2128 8th Ave) with rooms for $55/65. *Howard Johnson's* (☎ 208-743-9526, 1716 Main St) starts at $65.

Patriotic *Inn America* (☎ 208-746-4600, 800-469-4667, 702 21st St) is a good value at $45/55. Across the street, Lewiston's charming *Carriage House Inn B&B* (☎ 208-746-4506, 504 6th Ave) has rooms for $80 to $100. Lewiston's best is the *Red Lion* (☎ 208-799-1000, 800-232-6730, 621 21st St), with river views and good restaurants ($80/90).

There are a few budget properties clustered along Bridge St in Clarkston, including the nice but older *Hacienda Lodge* (☎ 509-758-5583, 812 Bridge St) for $30/35 – ask for the 'biker rate' and watch out for feral dogs out front after dark! Several other cheap places on Bridge St, within stumbling distance of the casino, offer weekly rates.

Closer to the bridge, refurbished *Motel 6* (☎ 509-758-1631, 222 Bridge St) has a pool ($40/45). Across from the casino, *Best Western River Tree Inn* (☎ 509-758-9551, 800-597-3621, 1257 Bridge St) has some kitchenettes ($69/79). Next to the Budweiser warehouse, the newer *Quality Inn & Suites* (☎ 509-758-9500, 700 Port Dr) starts at $65/75.

Places to Eat
The choice of restaurants here is limited. For crazy burgers and a retro atmosphere, go to *Zany's* (☎ 208-746-8131), on 21st St at 19th Ave. *Thai Taste*, (☎ 208-746-6192, 1410 21st St) is a bit pricey but an authentic good change of pace. *BoJacks* (☎ 208-746-9532, 311 Main St) serves 'broiler-pit' steaks. The best Mexican food is at *Casa de Oro* (☎ 208-798-8681, 504 Main St). At the Red Lion, *MJ Barleyhoppers Microbrewery* and *Meriwethers* offer the best quality and selection in town. Clarkston's best choice is *Tomato Bros* (☎ 509-758-7902, 200 Bridge St), featuring wood-fired pizzas, pasta and salads.

Getting There & Around
Lewiston and Clarkston are connected to Seattle and Portland by Horizon Air (☎ 800-547-9308) out of the Lewiston-Nez Percé County Regional Airport (☎ 208-746-7962), the only airport in north-central Idaho with regularly scheduled flights. It's located off 17th St (which turns into 5th St) south of Lewiston.

Lewiston and Clarkston are 75 miles northwest of Grangeville and 110 miles south of Coeur d'Alene. US 12 leads east to Orofino (44 miles), and US 195 leads north to Spokane (89 miles).

Northwestern Stagelines (☎ 208-746-8108) stops at the Sportsman Inn Motel. Daily buses go northbound to Spokane, Washington ($24/39), via Moscow, and southbound to Boise ($38/59) via US 95 to New Meadows and Hwy 55.

Budget (☎ 208-746-0488), Hertz (☎ 208-746-0411) and National (☎ 208-743-0176) are at the airport. In Lewiston are Enterprise (☎ 208-746-2878), 1525 Idaho St; Rent-A-Wreck (☎ 208-746-9585), 3107 8th St; and Valley Car Rental (☎ 208-743-9371), at 18th and Main Sts.

MOSCOW & AROUND
The rolling soft white winter wheat fields of the stark windswept Palouse (pronounced 'pah-LOOSE') hill country span the Idaho-Washington state line, centering around Moscow ('MOS-coe'; population 20,000; elevation 2720 feet), home to the University of Idaho. During the academic year, the town's population is boosted by more than 11,000 students. Moscow has more of a liberal bent than does its academic sister-city and close-by western neighbor Pullman, WA, which is home to Washington State University. Downtown grain elevators and roadkill on campus help Moscow retain its rural feel.

Orientation
North-south US 95 (Main St) runs through downtown Moscow. For 10 blocks, however,

US 95 is divided into two one-way streets: northbound Washington St and southbound Jackson St. Hwy 8 is the main east-west road; west of Main St it is Pullman Rd, east of Main St it is Troy Hwy.

Information
The USFS Clearwater National Forest, Forest Service Information and Intermountain Research Station (☎ 208-882-3557) is at 1221 S Main St. The Latah County Historical Society (☎ 208-882-1004), 327 E 2nd St, publishes a walking tour brochure of historic Moscow homes. The post office is at 220 E 5th St; there's another branch at the university. Bookpeople of Moscow (☎ 208-882-7957), 512 S Main St, is a great place to browse. The University of Idaho bookstore (☎ 208-885-6469) is on Deakin St across from the student union. The Gritman Medical Center (☎ 208-882-4511) is at 700 S Main St.

Things to See & Do
The **University of Idaho** (UI), a land-grant university just west of downtown, has somewhat of a party school reputation – Go Vandals! Academically, natural resource fields are strong. The Shattuck Arboretum and Botanical Garden, along Nez Percé Dr behind the administration building, is a nice stop for the casual visitor. The visitors center (☎ 208-885-6424) is at 645 Pullman Rd. Web site: www.uidaho.edu

Stop by downtown's **Camus Winery** (☎ 208-882-0214), 110 S Main St, for a nip of its Hog Heaven Red (a sherry-grape blend) or Palouse Gold (a muscat-riesling blend). The tasting room is open noon to 6 pm Tuesday to Saturday. Upstairs is a wine bar, also pouring premium beers.

The free **Appaloosa Museum & Heritage Center**, 5070 Hwy 8 W, near the Idaho-Washington state line, details the interesting history of the horse breed developed by Nez Percé Indians. The Appaloosa Horse Club (☎ 208-882-5578) is also headquartered here; open 8 am to 5 pm weekdays and 9 am to 3 pm Saturday June to August.

An annual event, the **Lionel Hampon Jazz Festival** is hosted by vibraphone virtuoso Lionel Hampton and his New York Big Band. The festival brings many of the world's best players to UI's Kibbie Dome for four days in late February. Write to Box 444257, Moscow, ID 83844-4257, or phone (☎ 208-885-6765, 888-884-3246) for ticket information.
Web site: www.jazz.uidaho.edu

Places to Stay
Royal Motor Inn (☎ 208-882-2581, 120 W 6th St), charges $30/35. Sprawling *Mark IV Motor Inn* (☎ 208-882-7557, 800-833-4240, 414 N Main St) offers airport shuttles and has a pool and hot tub (from $35/40). *Hillcrest Motel* (☎ 208-882-7579, 800-368-6564, 706 N Main St), costs $45/50. All of the above have convenient downtown locations.

Off Pullman Rd west of the downtown area are *Palouse Inn* (☎ 208-882-5511, 101 Baker St) with rooms for $35/40; *Super 8* (☎ 208-883-1503, 175 Peterson Dr), at $35/42; and *Best Western University Inn* (☎ 208-882-0550, 1516 W Pullman Rd), at $75/85, which has a pool. Rates run higher during the academic year. Rooms are $75 to $105 at *Paradise Ridge B&B* (☎ 208-882-5292, 3377 Blaine Rd), a few miles south of town. *Peacock Hill B&B* (☎ 208-882-1423, 1245 Joyce Rd), 5 miles north of Moscow, looks down onto Moscow and the Palouse.

Places to Eat
Most eateries are on Main St between 1st and 6th Sts. Places along this strip seem to come and go faster even than the fickle students. The *Garden Lounge* (☎ 208-882-0743) and *West 4th Bar & Grill (same ☎)* are set in the atmospheric old Moscow Hotel, 313 S Main St. The *Moscow Food Co-op* (☎ 208-882-8537) is an excellent grocery store with a good deli.

Getting There & Away
Moscow is served by Horizon Air (☎ 800-547-9308) out of the Pullman-Moscow Regional Airport, off Hwy 270 in Pullman, Washington. Horizon has several daily flights from Seattle and Portland. Link Transportation (☎ 208-882-1223, 800-359-4541) provides airport transfers.

IDAHO

Moscow is 25 miles north of Lewiston and 85 miles south of Coeur d'Alene. Pullman is 10 miles west of Moscow.

Northwestern Stagelines (☎ 208-882-5521) stops at the Royal Motor Inn (see above). Two daily buses go northbound to Spokane, WA ($18/30 one-way/roundtrip). One daily bus goes southbound to Lewiston ($6/10); another goes to Boise ($40/69) via US 95 to New Meadows then on Hwy 55.

Getting Around
Moscow/Latah Public Transit (☎ 208-882-8313) runs buses 8 am to 4 pm weekdays, but not along any established route. Call at least 24 hours in advance to schedule a ride. Budget (☎ 509-332-3511) and Hertz (☎ 509-332-4485) are at the airport. Sears Rent-A-Car (☎ 509-332-5230) and U-Save Auto Rental (☎ 509-334-5195) may be cheaper.

Idaho Panhandle

Wedged between Washington, Montana and Canada, Idaho's largely unpopulated sliver evokes two images. Its dense forests, deep glacier-carved lakes and mighty rivers are where locals head for family vacations. But the Panhandle's remoteness has also attracted solitude-seeking survivalists and white supremacist groups. Though media coverage emphasizes their presence, few people are associated with these movements. The average traveler is more likely to encounter a moose than a militia in this beautiful, lake- and ore-rich region. Sixty lakes within 60 miles of Coeur d'Alene – including Priest, Pend Oreille and Coeur d'Alene – serve as playgrounds for residents of nearby Spokane, WA. Outdoor activities are everywhere; from white-water rafting near Bonners Ferry to water skiing on Coeur d'Alene Lake and steep-and-deep powder skiing at Schweitzer Mountain.

COEUR D'ALENE
At the head of a deep blue lake, Coeur d'Alene (population 34,000; elevation 2125 feet) has been a tourist destination since the 1910s. It began as a civilian community along-

Gettin' Hitched

Coeur d'Alene is the region's shotgun wedding capital and chapels abound. No blood test, witnesses or waiting are necessary. Some B&Bs and the resort host so many ceremonies that they have clergy on staff. You must be 18, or have a parent's permission; licenses cost $28 weekdays or $45 weekends and services at the Hitching Post (☎ 208-664-5510), conveniently located across the street from the courthouse at 524 Government Way, are $45 weekdays and $55 weekends.

side the US Army's Fort Sherman, which was founded in 1878 by Civil War general William Tecumseh Sherman. The area boomed when gold prospectors reached the South Fork Coeur d'Alene River. Steamboats provided transport and hauled freight until the 1920s. Today, Coeur d'Alene is the most popular of northern Idaho's lakefront resorts. Catering more to local residents looking to splurge than to jet-setters, Coeur d'Alene is a great place for family vacations. In summer, water-skiers and power boaters rule.

Orientation
Coeur d'Alene has two commercial districts. The newer strip, along US 95 north of I-90, is lined with chain hotels, fast-food emporia and shopping malls. Near the lake, the now-gentrified downtown harbors old storefronts that house restaurants and shops for vacationers. The most prominent shorefront building is the Coeur d'Alene Resort, known to most people simply as 'the resort.' The Coeur d'Alene Indian Reservation wraps around the lake's south end. Post Falls (population 17,000), 7 miles west on I-90, is a rapidly growing outlet shopping town that threatens to merge with Coeur d'Alene to form a greater metropolitan area.

Information
The USFS Idaho Panhandle National Forest office (☎ 208-765-7223) is at 3815

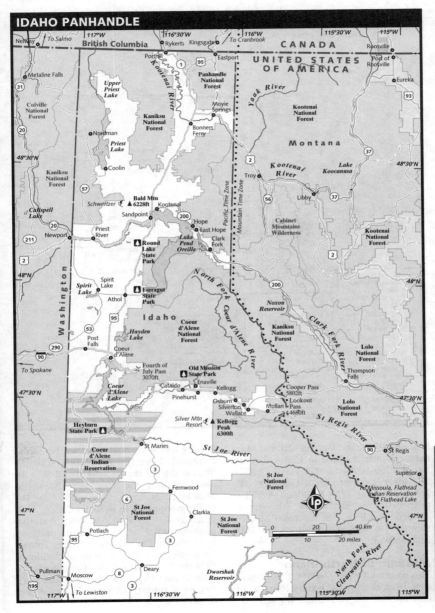

IDAHO PANHANDLE

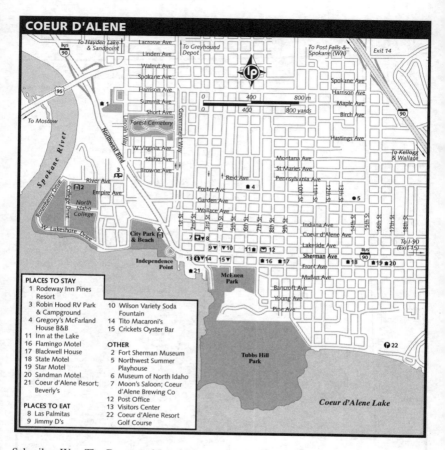

Schreiber Way. The Bureau of Land Management district office in Coeur d'Alene (☎ 208-769-5000) is at 1808 N 3rd St. The Idaho Dept of Fish & Game (☎ 208-769-1414) is at 2750 Kathleen Ave. The post office is at 111 N 7th St; the zip code is 83814. The Kootenai Medical Center (☎ 208-666-2000) is at 2003 Lincoln Way.

Museum of North Idaho

This museum (☎ 208-664-3448), 115 Northwest Blvd, charts local history from the indigenous Coeur d'Alenes through the logging and steamboat years to the establishment of the Farragut Naval Training Station during the Second World War. It also operates the free Fort Sherman Museum, near Empire Ave and College Dr on the grounds of North Idaho College. Not much is left of Fort Sherman, but the museum preserves many artifacts and historic photos. On the grounds are vintage forest-industry memorabilia, including a 1924 smoke-chaser's cabin. The museum is open 11 am to 5 pm Tuesday through Saturday, April through October; $1.50/50¢ ($4/family).

City Park & Beach

Coeur d'Alene's recreational heart is the popular lakeside park and beach on the west edge of downtown. During the summer, gaggles of folks flock here to swim, sail and sunbathe. Concessions and rental outfits operate at the park, Independence Point city dock and the nearby resort marina.

Activities

The 2-mile Tubbs Hill **hiking** loop starts from the resort's northernmost parking lot, crosses McEuen Park, then climbs through forested Tubbs Hill Park to a lakeside vista before looping back.

The 18-hole Coeur d'Alene Resort **golf course** (☎ 208-667-4653) features a floating green. Resort guests can reserve tee times on the spot; nonguests must call at least three days in advance. Summertime green fees are a steep $155.

Lake Coeur d'Alene Parasail (☎ 208-756-5367), at Independence Point, lifts people 500 feet above the lake for a quick **parasail**. Brooks Seaplane (☎ 208-664-2842), at Independence Point, offers **seaplane rides**. Flights cost $40/20 adults/children per twenty minutes.

Lake Coeur d'Alene Cruises (☎ 208-765-4000, 800-365-8338) offers a popular 90-minute **lake cruise** at least once daily early May to mid-October. Cruises depart the resort's marina and cost $14/13/9.

The three-day **Art on the Green** festival takes over the North Idaho College campus the first weekend of August.

Places to Stay

Camping Open April to November, the attractive *Wolf Lodge Campground (☎ 208-664-2812, 12425 E I-90)*, exit 22 east of town, sports grassy sites ($15 to $20) 1½ miles from the lake. Three blocks from the beach, the year-round *Robin Hood RV Park & Campground (☎ 208-664-2306, 703 Lincoln Way)* has grassy sites ($16 to $21).

The First Idaho Mission

In the early 1800s as the first European explorers and traders crossed the Rocky Mountains, Native Americans in Idaho and Montana began hearing about Christianity. The Flatheads, a Salish tribe living in western Montana and northern Idaho, became so intrigued by stories of the 'Black Robes' that in the 1830s four delegations of Flatheads journeyed to St Louis, MO, to ask for missionaries. In 1841, Father Pierre De Smet, a Jesuit, came west, establishing missions and farms among the Salish.

Father De Smet promised the Coeur d'Alene Indians their own mission and Black Robes, who in 1848 began building a mission on a bluff above the Coeur d'Alene River. In charge of construction was Father Anthony Ravalli, an Italian-born Jesuit who was also a physician, scientist, mechanic, artist, architect and sculptor. Using only local products, Ravalli, another Brother and the enthusiastic Coeur d'Alenes set to work.

The 3600-sq-foot church was built from a framework of mortised and tenoned beams, with dowels strung between. Straw and grass were woven through the dowels and then faced with river mud. The resulting walls were more than a foot thick; no nails were used in any part of the structure. In fact, the only tools available to the Brothers and the Indians at the time were an axe, pulleys, pocketknives and rope. To outfit the church, Ravalli turned to local goods: Old tin cans became chandelier sconces, the rough pine altar was faux painted to resemble marble and the walls were covered with newsprint, which was whitewashed and then painted with floral designs.

The mission remained in operation until 1924. The church and the parish house next door were declared a state park in 1974 and restored. Both can be visited at Old Mission State Park near Cataldo.

Coeur d'Alene KOA (☎ 208-664-4471, 800-562-2609), I-90 exit 22 off Hwy 97, has a pool (from $19).

Hotels & Motels Many properties are at I-90 exit 12 along US 95. If you plan to spend any time in Coeur d'Alene, bypass the commercial strip and head for the older, well-maintained motels downtown. They are convenient to beaches, recreation and shopping and differ little, except in price. ***Flamingo Motel*** (☎ 208-664-2159, 800-955-2159, 718 Sherman Ave) has a great location (from $65). Nearby is the ***Inn at the Lake*** (☎ 208-676-1225, 621 Sherman Ave) with rooms from $50. Farther up the street is the comparably priced ***State Motel*** (☎ 208-664-8239, 1314 Sherman Ave).

Closer to I-90 are the remodeled ***Star Motel*** (☎ 208-664-5035, 1516 Sherman Ave), with a pool (from $50), and the ***Sandman Motel*** (☎ 208-664-9119, 1620 Sherman Ave), with kitchenette rooms (from $65). Along the Spokane River a half-mile west of downtown is the more upscale ***Rodeway Inn Pines Resort*** (☎ 208-664-8244, 800-651-2510, 1422 Northwest Blvd), with a pool and spa ($50 to $90).

B&Bs & Resorts The ***Blackwell House*** (☎ 208-664-0656, 800-899-0656, 820 Sherman Ave) is a mansion built in 1904; rooms (some with shared bathroom) range from $75 to $125. ***Gregory's McFarland House B&B*** (☎ 208-667-1232, 800-335-1232, 601 Foster Ave), an old foursquare home with a wrap-around porch, has elegant rooms ($90 to $175) decorated with English antiques. The Coeur d'Alene B&B Association (☎ 208-664-6999, 800-773-0323) offers more information.

The four-star ***Coeur d'Alene Resort*** (☎ 208-765-4000, 800-688-5253), on Front Ave at 2nd St, put Coeur d'Alene on the tourist map. Among other luxuries, it has three lounges, two restaurants (one with an 18-foot salad bar) and recreation center, complete with a private bowling alley and racquetball court. The lakefront setting overlooks a marina and a floating boardwalk. During winter, the resort offers 'Ski &

Stay' packages in conjunction with Silver Mountain Resort (see Wallace, Kellogg & Silver Valley, later). Rooms start at $125; suites fetch up to $400.
Web site: www.cdaresort.com

Places to Eat
Coeur d'Alene has a lively restaurant scene. Prices are moderate; full dinners typically come in under $15.

Las Palmitas (☎ 208-664-0693, 201 3rd St) serves Mexican food in the former railroad depot. ***Tito Macaroni's*** (☎ 208-667-2782, 210 Sherman Ave) is a filling pasta house. For steak and Pacific coast bivalves head to ***Crickets Oyster Bar*** (☎ 208-765-1990, 424 Sherman Ave). For quality dining in a casual atmosphere, try the eclectic bistro menu at hometown favorite ***Jimmy D's*** (☎ 208-664-9774, 320 Sherman Ave). The Authentic ***Wilson Variety soda fountain*** (☎ 208-667-8138, 401 Sherman Ave) is in the drug store.

For fine dining and impressive views, ***Beverly's*** (☎ 208-765-4000), on the 7th floor of the resort, takes the cake; expect to drop around $25 for the catch of the day.

Entertainment
During their summer season, the ***Carrousel Players*** (☎ 208-667-0254) revive Broadway musicals at the North Idaho College Auditorium. The ***Northwest Summer Playhouse*** equity theater group (☎ 208-667-1323, 1320 E Garden Ave) mounts three shows each season, one of which is staged at the outdoor amphitheater at Silver Mountain Resort. ***Moon's Saloon*** (☎ 208-664-6747, 204 2nd St) serves pub grub to complement its fine selection of ales. Call to arrange a tour of its ***Coeur d'Alene Brewing Co***.

Getting There & Around
Spokane International Airport, 33 miles west of Coeur d'Alene, is the nearest major airport. Greyhound (☎ 208-664-3343), 137 E Spruce St, plies I-90 between Spokane and Missoula, MT (163 miles east) three times daily. North Idaho Community Express (NICE; ☎ 208-664-9769) runs four daily buses between Coeur d'Alene's Greyhound

bus depot and Sandpoint ($9/5 one-way). I-90 runs east-west along the northern edge of the lake. US 95 is the main north-south route: Sandpoint is 44 miles north and Lewiston is 121 miles south.

Auto Rental of Coeur d'Alene (☎ 208-667-4905), 120 Anton Ave, rents jalopies. Ring Sunset Taxi (☎ 208-664-8000) to order a cab.

AROUND COEUR D'ALENE
Silverwood Theme Park
This may not be the reason you came to Idaho, but Silverwood (☎ 208-683-3400), 15 miles north of Coeur d'Alene on US 95, will get the attention of any kids in your entourage. It features a full battery of amusement rides; an idealized re-creation of a mining camp, complete with sing-alongs, silent films and live stage shows; an authentic steam train that transports passengers around the 500-acre site and is menaced by desperadoes in the backwoods; and an air show. Admission is $25/15; open daily mid-June to Labor Day, weekends late May to mid-June and during September.

Emerald Creek Garnet Area
The star garnet gem, found only in Idaho and India, is accessible at one of the world's only public garnet-digging areas. The site, administered by the USFS St Maries Ranger District (☎ 208-245-2531), is south of Coeur d'Alene Lake and 5 miles south of Fernwood; take Hwy 3 to USFS Rd 447. Open Memorial Day to Labor Day. A $10 permit, available at the site, is required. Bring your own shovel, bucket and (ideally) a screen; be prepared to get muddy.

Hobo Cedar Grove Botanical Area
Northeast of Clarkia is the Hobo Cedar Grove Botanical Area, a national natural landmark. This 240-acre grove has old-growth western red cedar trees with trunks 5 to 8 feet in diameter. There's a self-guided nature trail and another trail that leads south up Marble Creek from St Joes Valley.

Rafting
Southeast of Coeur d'Alene, the **St Joe National Wild & Scenic River** flows into Coeur d'Alene Lake. This one-day Class III run of 12 to 14 miles is best done from May to June. Contact River Odysseys West (☎ 208-765-0841, 800-451-6034); its Web site is www.rowinc.com. Full-day trips start around $85.

WALLACE, KELLOGG & SILVER VALLEY
The world's richest silver and lead veins, along the upper reaches of the South Fork Coeur d'Alene River, have been the focus of intensive mining from the 1880s to the present. The well-preserved town center of Wallace (population 1000; elevation 2800 feet) will delight architecture enthusiasts. Quaint Kellogg (population 2500; elevation 2750 feet) is the basecamp for the superb Silver Mountain Resort. The area also has an interesting trail: Decades ago railroads snaked their ways around steep mountainsides and across narrow valleys to reach the Silver Valley mines, and today this engineering marvel – including the most expensive sections of rail line ever laid – is preserved as a rails-to-trails hiking and biking path (see below).

Orientation & Information
Wallace and Kellogg are 9 miles apart along I-90. Both ends of Silver Valley are mountain passes: Fourth of July Pass (3070 feet) above Coeur d'Alene Lake and Lookout Pass (4725 feet) at the Idaho-Montana state line bookend the Silver Valley. Both passes become icy during winter. Dial ☎ 208-772-0531 for a winter road report. Missoula, MT, is 121 miles to the east of Wallace, and Coeur d'Alene is 42 miles west of Kellogg.

The Wallace Visitors Center (I-90 exit 61) has bathrooms and good information. There's also a visitors center below the Silver Mountain gondola in Kellogg (☎ 208-784-0821). The USFS Panhandle National Forest Wallace Ranger District (☎ 208-752-1221), a couple of miles west of Wallace in Silverton, has hiking, camping and

IDAHO

mountain-biking information. The Wallace post office is at 403 Cedar St.

Greyhound runs three daily buses along the I-90 corridor between Spokane and Missoula.

Wallace National Historic District

Charming Wallace, a late 19th-century mining town, is on the National Register of Historic Places. The **Wallace District Mining Museum** (☎ 208-556-1592), 509 Bank St, chronicles the history of the area's silver and lead mines. Open 8 am to 8 pm daily July and August, shorter hours the rest of the year; $2/$1.50/50¢ (families $5).

At 6th and Bank Sts, **ornate buildings** house shops and businesses. Note the pressed-tin turrets on the White & Bender Building. A block north on 6th St at Cedar St, the Art Deco Civic Center Building is fronted with terra-cotta brick. Several old hotels, including The Jameson (1900), are on the next block north.

The **Northern Pacific Depot Railroad Museum** (☎ 208-752-0111) is at 219 6th St, below I-90. The 1st floor of this well-preserved Queen Anne is constructed of Chinese bricks, and the 3rd floor sports a chateauesque tower. Open 9 am to 7 pm daily Memorial Day to Labor Day, otherwise 10 am to 3 pm; admission $2/1.50/1.

The **Wallace District Arts Center** (☎ 208-753-8381), 610 Bank St, has an espresso bar and gallery featuring local artists.

Sierra Silver Mine Tour

From 420 5th St in Wallace, you can ride an open-air trolley to the abandoned mine entrance for an underground tour. Tours depart every 30 minutes 9 am to 4 pm mid-May to October; in June and July hours are extended to 6 pm; admission $9/8/7 – children under four are not allowed.

Silver Mountain Resort

Silver Mountain Resort (☎ 208-783-1111, 800-204-6428), sprawls across Kellogg (6300 feet) and Wardner (6200 feet) peaks. The centerpiece of winter and summer activities is the gondola, which goes from the valley floor to the Mountain Haus ski lodge (5700 feet). The impressive gondola is the world's longest single-stage carrier, transporting passengers 3.1 miles and gaining 3400 feet in 19 minutes. During winter the ski area offers lots of dry powder snow, 50 runs (including many black diamonds) and a maximum 2200-foot vertical drop. Weekend lift tickets are $32/26; midweek tickets are $25/23. Dial ☎ 208-666-8822 for a snow report.

During summer, the gondola carries passengers to the lodge. A series of outdoor concerts take place in the band shell. Hiking trails lead to remote meadows and overlooks, and a network of mountain bike trails ($11 day pass) leads back to Kellogg. The ski lifts continue to the top for panoramic views of three states and Canada. The gondola ($10/9/8) runs on weekends only from July 1 to September.

To reach Silver Mountain, take I-90 exit 49. Base Village is at 610 Bunker Ave, Kellogg.
Web site: www.silvermt.com

Old Mission State Park

The Mission of the Sacred Heart, now a state park (☎ 208-682-3814) in Cataldo (I-90 exit 39) is the state's oldest building. The park has a visitors center and picnic area, and guided tours are offered. A self-guided half-mile nature path leads to the river. The park is open from 8 am to 6 pm; day use is $3 per vehicle. Annually on August 15, members of the Coeur d'Alene tribe make a pilgrimage to the mission to celebrate the **Feast of the Assumption**. After Mass, members enact a pageant called 'The Coming of the Black Robes.'

Route of the Hiawatha Trail

The Taft Tunnel Preservation Society (☎ 208-744-1301) converted a mile of old Chicago, Milwaukee & St Paul Railroad track, tunnel and trestle into an exhilarating multi-use recreation trail. The centerpiece is the 8771-foot Taft Tunnel. The trail winds through nine tunnels and over seven wooden trestles before reaching the valley floor. Trail use requires a headlamp and helmet for bikers and flashlights for hikers; be prepared to get damp and chilly. The grade never exceeds 2%, but several vertigo-inducing trestles traverse sheer cliffs and steep rocky canyons.

To reach the trail, drive over Lookout Pass to Montana's I-90 exit 5 and head for the Taft Area. Turn south and follow Rainy Creek Rd 2 miles. At the Y-junction go toward East Portal. The trail follows the contours of Loop Creek until it meets Moon Pass Rd, which leads in 20 miles to Wallace (via Placer Creek Rd). This inventive privatization of public lands requires a $6/3 day-use fee from May 27 to October 6, when hunting season begins and paid trail marshals flee. Trailhead shuttle service costs another $9/6.

The Lookout Pass Ski Area (see below) and Excelsior Bikes (☎ 208-786-3751), 10 W Portland Ave, Kellogg, have route maps and rent mountain bikes.

Lookout Pass Ski Area
The family-oriented Lookout Pass Ski Area (☎ 208-744-1201), on the Idaho-Montana state line (I-90 exit 0), has a free Saturday ski school. Lift tickets are $10 to $20 full-day, including use of the new Buzzards Valley backcountry snowboarding area. No cross-country trails are groomed but USFS roads are popular for Nordic skiing.
Web site: www.skilookout.com

Places to Stay
Chain motels await near I-90 exits 49 in Kellogg and 61 in Wallace, but cheaper lodgings lining Cameron Ave between exits 49 and 54 have more character. Pinehurst's **Silver Valley KOA** (☎ 208-682-3612, 800-562-0799, 801 Division St), I-90 exit 45, has streamside sites ($20), full hookups ($25), a pool and laundry.

Wallace's historic **Brooks Hotel** (☎ 208-556-1571, 500 Cedar St) is one of northern Idaho's best lodging options ($35 to $65). Wallace's landmark **Jameson B&B** (☎ 208-556-6000, 304 6th St) charges $70 to $90. The upscale **Best Western Wallace Inn** (☎ 208-752-1252, 100 Front St) has a pool and spa

($70 to $100). The classy Victorian **Beale House B&B** (☎ 208-752-7151, 888-752-7151, 107 Cedar St) asks $75 to $100.

Kellogg's retro **McKinley Inn** (☎ 208-786-7771, 210 McKinley Ave) has comfortable rooms with double beds at an affordable $35 to $65.

A short walk from the gondola, the lovely uptown **Mansion on the Hill B&B** (☎ 208-786-4455, 877-943-4455, 105 S Division St) is perched atop Noah Kellogg's homestead in a refurbished home built in 1945. Smartly furnished suites cost between $115 and $135 and family-friendly cottages will set you back between $135 and $155, including full breakfast.
Web site: www.mansionBnB.com

The Reflections Day Spa (☎ 208-783-7032, 219 S Division St) is next door. **Kellogg Tourist Home Rentals** (☎ 208-786-4261, 800-435-2588) manages several Silver Valley properties.

Places to Eat
An abundance of roadside cafes and drive-ins ensures no one is ever going to 9starve in these old mining towns. The brass-and-wainscot–rich restaurant at **The Jameson** (see above) is a good choice for a midday burger or a steak dinner ($10 to $15). Next to Kellogg's City Hall, **Rancho Viejo** (☎ 208-783-4038, 319 Main St) offers a huge Mexican selection. **Grady's Bar & Grill** in the McKinley Inn (see above) does steaks, pizza and BBQ. **Wah Hing** on McKinley serves Vietnamese-tinged Chinese.

Entertainment
Towns on the National Register of Historic Places always seem to have a summer theater group specializing in melodrama, and Wallace is no exception. **Sixth St Melodrama** (☎ 208-752-8871, 212 6th St) performs campy theater from the first weekend of July to Labor Day. Shows happen in the Lux Building, one of Wallace's oldest structures.

As is true with any self-respecting mining town, there's no shortage of places to wet your whistle.

IDAHO

SANDPOINT & LAKE PEND OREILLE

Sandpoint (population 7500; elevation 2126 feet), with interesting shops and good restaurants, is the largest resort community on stunning Lake Pend Oreille ('POND-uhray'). Nestled between forested mountains, this beautiful 90,000-acre lake is the largest in Idaho and the second-deepest in the nation, next to Oregon's Crater Lake. During WWII the US Navy developed a huge base here that trained nearly 300,000 sailors. The navy still conducts acoustic and sonar research here. Winter brings abundant snow and energetic skiers to Schweitzer Mountain Resort, just north of town. A second resort area lies on the eastern lakeshore at Hope and East Hope. A profusion of campgrounds and marinas make it preferable for campers and boaters. The drive to Hope yields fantastic summer sunsets.

Orientation & Information

A one-way counterclockwise loop circles Sandpoint's downtown. First Ave parallels the waterfront; Bridge St turns off 1st Ave and leads to City Beach. Public parking is available on N 3rd Ave between Oak and Church Sts. East of Sandpoint on Hwy 200 is Ponderay, followed by Kootenai. Across the lake from Sandpoint are Hope and East Hope. At the south end of Lake Pend Oreille is Farragut State Park.

The Greater Sandpoint Chamber of Commerce (☎ 208-263-2161, 800-800-2106), 100 US 95 N, maintains a useful 24-hour information hotline. The USFS Idaho Panhandle National Forest office (☎ 208-263-5111) is at 1500 US 2. The post office is at 210 N 4th Ave. The Bonner General Hospital (☎ 208-263-1441) is at 520 N 3rd Ave.

City Beach

Take out your Speedos and head to where it's happening. The lake is the place to be in Sandpoint during summer. Most people make the easy stroll from downtown to City Beach for swimming and sunbathing. See Activities, below, for more information.

Farragut State Park

At the beginning of WWII, Eleanor Roosevelt, while flying across the northern USA, noted Lake Pend Oreille glimmering in the Idaho forests. She knew that the US Navy and her husband, President Franklin D Roosevelt, were looking for a large, remote inland lake to develop as a naval training camp. She reported back and, after a quick exploratory trip by the president, work commenced in 1942 on Farragut Naval Training Center, which for four years was the second-largest naval training base in the world.

It was decommissioned in 1946 and in 1964 became Farragut State Park (☎ 208-683-2425), E 13400 Ranger Rd. The 4000-acre park, at the south end of Lake Pend Oreille 4 miles east of Athol (which is 24 miles south of Sandpoint) and 18 miles north of Coeur d'Alene on US 95, is very popular. The $3 day-use fee per vehicle allows access to 16,000 feet of the Lake Pend Oreille shoreline, 32 miles of trails and a 9-mile designated mountain-bike path. (Also see Camping, below.)

Activities

Directly across from City Beach is Windbag Sailboat Rentals (☎ 208-263-7811). For **boating** and **water sports**, resorts along Lake Pend Oreille have marinas offering moorage, rental and charter services. In addition to the marina at City Beach in Sandpoint, there are East Hope Marina (☎ 208-263-3083) and the adjacent Holiday Shores Marina (☎ 208-264-5515). The best **fishing** access is along the eastern end of Lake Pend Oreille. Eagle Charters (☎ 208-264-5274) and Diamond Charters (☎ 208-264-5283) are the main charter outfits.

The nearby Clark Fork River is popular for **rafting**. To book a rafting trip, contact River Odysseys West (☎ 208-765-0841, 800-451-6034); its Web site is www.rowinc.com. The Alpine Boat & Ski Shop (☎ 208-263-5157), 213 Church St, does double duty as a ski shop and marina. Western Pleasure Inc (☎ 208-263-9066), 4675 Upper Gold Creek Rd, 4 miles outside Kootenai off Gold Creek Rd, offers guided **horseback rides**.

SANDPOINT

PLACES TO STAY
2 Quality Inn
3 K2 Inn
5 Page House B&B
6 Hawthorne Inn &
   Suites; Connie's Cafe
13 Best Western
   Edgewater Resort
15 Lakeside Inn

PLACES TO EAT
11 Truby's Health Mart
12 Bangkok Cuisine
17 Ivano's
18 Panhandler Pies
19 The Hydra Restaurant
20 Powerhouse Station
   Bar & Grill

OTHER
1 Chamber of Commerce
4 Bonner General
   Hospital
7 Kamloops Bar & Grill
8 Panida Theatre
9 Public Parking
10 Post Office
14 Alpine Boat & Ski Shop
16 Roxy's
21 Visitors Center

Lake Cruises

During summer, Lake Pend Oreille Cruises (☎ 208-263-4598) runs a two-hour boat tour ($13/11/8), departing from the boat ramp at the beach at 1:30 pm daily.

Festival at Sandpoint

Usually held the first two weeks in August, the festival (☎ 208-265-4554, 888-265-4554) presents music ranging from country to jazz and classical. The main stage is under the stars at Memorial Field; other festival events are held at the Schweitzer Mountain Resort.

Places to Stay

Camping The woods are full of campgrounds. West of Sandpoint along the Pend Oreille River is *Springy Point Recreation Area* (☎ 208-437-3133), with $12 tent sites, showers and river swimming. Take US 95 south across the bridge to Lakeshore Rd, the first road to the west, and continue 3 miles. There are several lovely campgrounds on the eastern lakeshore. The *USFS Samowen Campground* (☎ 208-263-5111), 2 miles west of Hwy 200 on Spring Creek Rd in East Hope, is a thrifty alternative to the area's expensive resorts. Sites are

IDAHO

on a peninsula and cost $12; reservations are recommended. For a more pampered experience try *Beyond Hope Resort* (☎ 208-264-5251), 3 miles down Samowen Rd off Hwy 200 E. Sites with RV hookups start at $23.

Farragut State Park (see above) has two campgrounds with showers and a swimming beach, which are favorites of vacationing families: *Whitetail Campground* has tent sites ($12), and *Snowberry Campground* has RV hookups ($16). Ten miles south of Sandpoint on Dufort Rd, year-round *Round Lake State Park* (☎ 208-263-3489) has sites starting at $11. During summer the small lake is popular for picnicking, swimming, fishing and hiking.

Hotels, Motels & B&Bs

Stay close enough to downtown to walk to shops and City Beach. Make reservations, as many places are booked months in advance, especially on weekends. The basic *K2 Inn* (☎ 208-263-3441, 501 N 4th Ave), charges $50/60. The remodeled *Hawthorne Inn & Suites* (☎ 208-282-0660, 415 Cedar St) is a large complex with a pool and spacious rooms ($90/100).

For comparatively inexpensive lake access, the *Lakeside Inn* (☎ 208-263-3717, 800-543-8126, 106 Bridge St) is unsurpassed ($70/85). Fronting Sand Creek, the upscale *Best Western Edgewater Resort* (☎ 208-263-3194, 800-635-2534, 56 Bridge St) is on the marina next to the beach ($110/125), with substantial off-season discounts.

Without reservations, you may end up staying farther from town – motels on US 95 north of town toward the ski area are often cheaper. *Quality Inn* (☎ 208-263-2111, 800-635-2534, 807 N 5th Ave) has good ski packages ($55/60). *Super 8* (☎ 208-263-2210, 3245 US 95 N), a couple of miles north of Sandpoint in Ponderay, starts around $55.

Downtown, the *Page House B&B* (☎ 208-263-6584, 800-500-6584, 506 N 2nd Ave) is an historic home built in 1918 by the town's first mayor. A room should cost you around $75.

Places to Eat

Sandpoint has many good restaurants. First Avenue is lined with espresso stands, pubs, bagel shops and various ethnic restaurants. *Connie's Cafe* is in the Hawthorne Inn & Suites. For wholesome organic treats, try *Truby's Health Mart* (☎ 208-263-6513, 113 Main St). *Panhandler Pies* (☎ 208-263-2912, 120 S 1st Ave) serves affordable homestyle cooking. The inviting *Hydra Restaurant* (☎ 208-263-7123, 115 Lake St) has a lunch buffet and good dinner values on everything from sandwiches to steak. Fine dining in Sandpoint means going Continental. *Ivano's* (☎ 208-263-0211, 124 S 2nd Ave) is the best northern Italian restaurant. *Powerhouse Station Bar & Grill* (☎ 208-265-2449, 120 E Lake St) is popular for fresh fish, pasta and sandwiches. *Bangkok Cuisine* (☎ 208-265-4149, 202 N 2nd Ave) bangs out excellent Thai food.

In Hope, *Tressle Creek Inn* (☎ 208-264-9017, 555 Hwy 200 E) is popular for pasta, steak and cocktails, and has a charming waterfront setting. The renowned *Floating Restaurant* (☎ 208-264-5311, 1250 Hwy 200), at Pend Oreille Shores Resort, offers a stunning pageant of color over the lake at sunset; the steak and fresh seafood are good, too.

Entertainment

On weekend nights, downtown bars offer live music, karaoke and dancing. Two of the best are *Roxy's* (☎ 208-263-6696, 215 Pine St) and *Kamloops Bar & Grill* (☎ 208-265-5453, 302 N 1st Ave).

Getting There & Away

North Idaho Community Express (NICE; ☎ 208-664-9769), which stops at Yokes Pac 'n Save, 3295 US 95 N, operates four daily buses between Sandpoint and Coeur d'Alene ($9/5). Amtrak's *Empire Builder* line goes daily between Chicago and Seattle. The depot is on Railroad St behind the Cedar St Public Market. East-west US 2 and Hwy 200 intersect at Sandpoint along US 95, which is 44 miles north of Coeur d'Alene and 64 miles south of the US-Canada border.

IDAHO

SCHWEITZER MOUNTAIN RESORT

Northern Idaho's best ski area is Schweitzer Mountain Resort (☎ 208-263-9555, 800-831-8810), 11 windy miles north of Sandpoint off US 2 and US 95, with downhill and cross-country skiing, and night skiing Thursday to Saturday. From a maximum elevation of 6400 feet, 48 runs drop a maximum of 2400 vertical feet. Annual snowfall usually exceeds 300 inches. Full-day lift tickets (including night skiing) start at $35/18. During summer, the chairlift provides rides for hikers and mountain bikers who want to explore the high country.

Web site: www.schweitzer.com

Accommodations are available, as are lessons and rentals. During ski season, rooms at *Selkirk Lodge* (☎ 208-263-0257, 800-831-8810) start at $129. Rates drop up to 50% during summer, when the lodge becomes the base for mountain biking, llama trekking, hiking and festival events.

BONNERS FERRY & AROUND

Bonners Ferry (population 2500; elevation 2180 feet) began as a ferry crossing on the Kootenai River during Canada's Wild Horse Creek gold rush in the 1860s. Since then, the town has gone through several incarnations, notably as a mill town. With lumbering on the skids, this town, situated in a deep canyon straddling the turbulent Kootenai River, is now trying to harvest tourist dollars. Recreation, such as great fishing and rafting, abounds, though it is the sometimes unsettlingly dense forests that most travelers recall.

Orientation & Information

Downtown Bonners Ferry is north of the Kootenai River, with newer development to its south. A cluster of businesses sits on the plateau above the canyon, near the junction of US 95 and US 2. The USFS Kaniksu National Forest Bonners Ferry Ranger Station (☎ 208-267-5561), is on US 95 just south of Bonners Ferry. The Boundary County Community Hospital (☎ 208-267-3141) is at 6640 Kaniksu St. The two US-Canada border crossings are 24-hour Eastport (☎ 208-267-

3966) on US 95 and Porthill (☎ 208-267-5309) on Hwy 1, open 7 am to 11 pm.

Bonners Ferry is truly in the boonies, on US 95, 32 miles north of Sandpoint and 32 miles south of Eastport.

Moyie Bridge & Falls

Eleven miles east of Bonners Ferry, the 1223-foot Moyie ('moy-yeah') Bridge carries US 2 at 450 feet above the Moyie River Canyon. For a closer look at the river and its impressive double-drop falls, turn toward Moyie Springs (population 600) at the west end of the bridge and follow the paved road south until a side road leads back under the bridge. This road overlooks the churning 100-foot and 40-foot falls.

Rafting

Two nearby rivers are popular for rafting: A 15-mile Class III stretch of the lower Moyie River is usually run May to June, and the powerful Kootenai River is run during summer. Day trips start at $55. See 'Recommended River Trips & Outfitters.'

Places to Stay

Bonners Ferry Resort (☎ 208-267-2422), south of town on US 95, has tent sites ($12), RV hookups ($16), motel rooms from $40, a pool and laundry. At the spectacular Moyie and Kootenai River confluence a mile east of Moyie Springs, the 160-acre *Twin Rivers Canyon Resort* (☎ 208-267-5932) has tent sites ($13), RV hookups ($21) and access to fishing, hiking trails and river swimming.

Kootenai Valley Motel (☎ 208-267-7567), US 95 just south of Bonners Ferry, is an attractive well-kept motel ($60 to $100). The newer *Bonners Ferry Log Inn* (☎ 208-267-3986), 2½ miles north of Bonners Ferry on US 95, has nicely furnished rooms ($55/72). *Best Western Kootenai River Inn* (☎ 208-267-8511), across from downtown in the Kootenai River Plaza, has dramatic riverfront rooms ($75 to $100) and a popular casino.

Places to Eat

Grab an early-morning espresso or sandwich at *Deli Delite* (☎ 208-267-2241, 1106 S

Main St). **Three Mile Junction Cafe** (☎ 208-267-3513), at the US 2/95 junction 3 miles north of Bonners Ferry, has great breakfasts and a daily sandwich-and-homemade-pie lunch special. **Alberto's** (☎ 208-267-7493, 222 E Riverside) serves the area's best Mexican food. In the Kootenai River Inn, the riverfront **Springs Restaurant** (☎ 208-267-8511) specializes in pasta, steak and fish.

Glossary

AAA – American Automobile Association, a private organization that provides information (including maps) and road services for motorists

acequia – Spanish word meaning 'irrigation ditch'

adobado – Marinated meat used in Mexican cooking

Anasazi – A group of Native Americans who inhabited southern Colorado and parts of Arizona, New Mexico and Utah from AD 100 to 1300

BIA – Bureau of Indian Affairs, an organization under the Dept of the Interior responsible for dealings with indigenous peoples in the continental USA

bison – A bovine (*Bison bison*) that once freely roamed North America's Great Plains but was hunted to near extinction; under federal protection, bison recovered slightly and are maintaining stable numbers in Montana and Wyoming, and have reached larger numbers in Colorado, where they are raised commercially; the term 'buffalo' is used interchangeably

BLM – Bureau of Land Management, an agency of the Dept of the Interior that controls portions of public lands in the Rocky Mountain states and elsewhere in the West

brown & white cooking – Slang for 'meat and potatoes'

buffalo – See *bison*

caldera – A giant, circular basin-like depression resulting from the cataclysmic explosion or collapse of the center of a volcano

C&W – Country & western music; an amalgamation of rock music and folk music of the southern and western USA; line dancing and the two-step are dances associated with C&W music

CB&Q – Chicago, Burlington & Quincy Railroad

chicken fried steak – a beef steak breaded (or battered) like a chicken breast and deep fried, served with white gravy

DOW – Colorado Dept of Wildlife

D&RG – Denver & Rio Grande Railroad

dude ranch – a vacation resort resembling a working ranch, offering horseback riding and other traditional Western leisure (or work) activities

14er or **fourteener** – Local Colorado term for a mountain whose elevation is 14,000 feet or more

full hookup – Facility equipped for the hookup of a recreational vehicle (see *RV*)

glacial erratic – A large rock fragment that has been transported by moving ice from its place of origin

Gold Medal streams – Waters designated by the Colorado Wildlife Commission for having a (naturally or artificially) high density of large trout

GOP – The 'Grand Old Party'; the Republican Party

hard-shell camping – Term for camping in an enclosed RV unit (excludes canvas pop-up trailers)

HI-AYH – Hostelling International-American Youth Hostels, a term given to hostels affiliated with Hostelling International, which is a member group of IYHF (International Youth Hostel Federation)

horno – A conical outdoor oven built of adobe

kiva – A subterranean circular room initially built by the Anasazi

KOA – Kampgrounds of America, a private RV-oriented organization that provides moderate- to high-priced camp sites with substantial amenities throughout the United States

krummholz – German for 'crooked wood,' referring to stunted trees, shaped by wind and snow, at mountainous treeline margins

Lakota – Plains Indians, also commonly known as Teton Sioux, who were the most effective opponents of the US army in the wars of the mid- to late-19th century

maverick – An unbranded calf; one who dissents from a group

mavericking – The unauthorized branding of calves, undertaken by cowboys trying to build their own herds on the open range; cattle barons considered such activities rustling and took both legal and illegal steps to eliminate the practice

metate – A stone with a concave indent used by Native Americans and Latin Americans to grind grain with a handheld 'mano' stone

moradas – Lodges in which the Penitente Brotherhoods of southern Colorado and New Mexico practiced their once secretive rites, including self-flagellation

NASTAR – National Standard Race, a recreational ski program created in 1969 that offers timed races at Alpine ski areas for amateurs

National Register of Historic Places – Listing of historic buildings, determined by the NPS based on supporting evidence supplied by owners and local authorities regarding a building's significance in the development of a community; restricts property owners from making major structural changes, but also provides tax incentives for preservation; often referred to as the 'National Register'

NPR – National Public Radio, a noncommercial listener-supported broadcast organization that produces and distributes news, public affairs and cultural programming via a network of loosely affiliated radio stations throughout the USA

NPS – National Park Service, a division of the Dept of the Interior that administers US national parks and monuments

NRA – National Recreation Area, a term used to describe National Park Service units in areas of considerable scenic or ecological importance that have been modified by human activity, most often major dam projects; some of these, like Flaming Gorge NRA in Utah and Wyoming, are now administered by the USFS

NRA – National Rifle Association, an influential Washington, DC–based organization that zealously lobbies against gun control of any kind and has many members in the West

PBS – Public Broadcasting System, a noncommercial television network that produces and distributes news, public affairs and cultural programming via a network of loosely affiliated television stations throughout the USA

Penitente Brotherhood – A Roman Catholic religious group with mainly Latino followers that formerly practiced such rites as self-flagellation and fasting

petroglyph – A carving or inscription on a rock

pictograph – A drawing or painting on a rock

Plains Indians – A group of native tribes, including the Lakota, Cheyenne, Arapaho, Comanche and Sioux, who were hostile to European settlement, and the Crow and Shoshone, who were cooperative with the US government

PRCA – Professional Rodeo Cowboys Association, an organization based in Colorado Springs that coordinates and sanctions rodeos throughout the West

res – slang for 'reservation,' frequently used by Native Americans

riparian – Relating to, living or located on a stream or river bank

rustler – One who steals stock, especially cattle

rut – The fall mating period for male moose, elk and bighorn sheep; comes from the Latin term for 'roar,' referring to the deep resonant sound made by the animals when they are 'in rut'

RV – Recreational vehicle; a large motorized object from which vacationers can see the USA in comfort akin to that enjoyed while staying home; also see *full hookup*

santos – Carved wooden religious figurines used in small Catholic shrines, including those of the Penitente; associated with these are *retablos* (altarpieces or religious pictures) and *bultos* (sculptures)

smokejumpers – Firefighters who parachute into forest fires

sopaipilla – A pillow-like flatbread often served with honey

Superfund sites – Toxic land sites identified and slated for federally funded cleanup

sutler – A civilian provisioner to an army post

SWA – State Wildlife Area designated in Colorado

TNM&O – Texas–New Mexico & Oklahoma Coaches, Inc

Uncle Pete – The Union Pacific Railroad, so nicknamed for the power it exercises in the towns of Wyoming's Southern Tier

UP – Union Pacific Railroad Corporation

USFS – United States Forest Service, a division of the Dept of Agriculture that implements policies on federal forest lands based on the principles of 'multiple use,' including timber-cutting, watershed management, wildlife management and camping and recreation

USFWS – United States Fish & Wildlife Service, an agency of the Dept of the Interior that has responsibility for fish and wildlife habitat and related matters

USGS – United States Geological Survey, an agency of the Dept of the Interior that is responsible for, among other things, detailed topographic maps of the entire country; widely available at outdoors-oriented businesses, USGS maps are particularly popular with hikers and backpackers

WPA – Works Progress Administration, a federal program established under Franklin Delano Roosevelt's administration during the Depression of the 1930s; throughout the country, WPA programs employed writers who produced guidebooks with great cultural and historical depth, and artists who left monuments like murals in federal government buildings

WSGA – The Wyoming Stock Growers Association

yurt system – A system of huts maintained for use in the summer by hikers and mountain bikers and in the winter by cross-country (Nordic) skiers; different systems maintain the huts for use from a simple stopover to overnight and weeklong stays

Acknowledgments

THANKS

Many thanks to the travelers who wrote to us with tips and information about this book.

Amanda Ayres, Andreas Berger, Mat Bowden, Julian & Louise Bradley, Jennifer Bray, Ron Casey, Carola Eder, Patricia Empsall, Samar Fay, Andrew Forshaw, Chris Gibb, Brendon Keane, Diana Korte, Barbara Kuemper, Paule Littlefair, Prue Lygo, Louise F Morgan, Julie Needham, Alan Sabatini, Christopher Sage, Jac Smeets, Anita Spencer, Britta Ulbrucht and Trevor Williams

LONELY PLANET

You already know that Lonely Planet produces more than this one guidebook, but you might not be aware of the other products we have on this region. Here is a selection of titles which you may want to check out as well:

USA
ISBN 1 86450 308 4
US$24.99 • UK£14.99

Hiking in the USA
ISBN 0 86442 600 3
US$24.99 • UK£14.99

Pacific Northwest
ISBN 0 86442 534 1
US$24.95 • UK£14.99

Canada
ISBN 0 86442 752 2
US$24.95 • UK£14.99

California & Nevada
ISBN 0 86442 644 5
US$19.95 • UK£12.99

Southwest
ISBN 0 86442 539 2
US$24.95 • UK£14.99

Available wherever books are sold.

Index

Abbreviations

Text

A

AAA 45, 67
Absaroka Mountains (WY)
  429–31
Absarokee (MT) 587
accidents 111
accommodations 74–7. *See
  also individual locations*
  B&Bs 75
  camping 74–5, 81, 88
  costs 53
  hostels 50, 75
  hotels 76
  lodges 77
  long-term 77
  motels 75–6
  reservations 77
activities 80–97. *See also
  individual activities*
acute mountain sickness (AMS)
  61–2
AIDS 63
Aikens, Thomas 146
air travel
  airlines 99–100
  airports 60, 99
  baggage 103
  buying tickets 100–2
  domestic 108
  glossary 101
  international 99–104
Alamosa (CO) 288–90
Alamosa National Wildlife
  Refuge (CO) 288
alcohol 79
Alliance for the Wild Rockies 33
Alpine Loop Byway (CO) 302–3
altitude sickness 61–2
American Automobile Association. *See* AAA

Anaconda (MT) 519–20, 520
Anasazi Heritage Center (CO)
  341
Ancestral Puebloans (Anasazi)
  19, 341–7, 349
Antonito (CO) 291–393
Apache 193, 351, 410
Arapaho 24, 120, 146, 351,
  364, 405, 426, 432, 440–2
Arapaho National Recreation
  Area (CO) 213
Arapaho National Wildlife
  Refuge (CO) 160
Arapahoe Basin Ski Area (CO)
  219
archaeological sites 19, 319,
  341, 346–7, 404, 599
Arco (ID) 650
Argo Gold Mill (CO) 142
Arkansas Headwaters Recre-
  ation Area (CO) 274
art galleries
  CO 197, 229, 262, 272, 327
  ID 636
  MT 497, 563
  WY 372, 399, 403, 420, 484
arts 40
Ashcroft (CO) 255
Aspen (CO) 252–63, **254**
  accommodations 257–60
  activities 255–7
  entertainment 261–2
  restaurants 260–1
  shopping 262
  transportation 262–3
Aspen Center for Environmen-
  tal Studies (CO) 253
Aspen Historical Society
  Museum (CO) 253
Assiniboine 594, 595, 601, 603

Astor House Hotel Museum
  (CO) 138
Atlantic City (WY) 439–40
ATMs 52
Augusta (MT) 545
Aultman, Oliver E 201
avalanches 70

B

B&Bs. *See* accommodations
Bachelor Historic Tour (CO)
  298–9
backcountry skiing 90, 91–2.
  See also skiing, cross-
  country
Bald Mountain (ID) 655–6
ballooning, hot-air 98, 433,
  487, 654
Bannack Historic State Park
  (MT) 508
Bannock 19, 23, 435, 622, 642
baseball 79, 134
basketball 79, 134
Basque pioneers 626, 627
Bear River State Park (WY) 395
Bearcreek Downs (MT) 588
bears 33, 34, 36, 68, 69, 457,
  573
Bears Paw Battlefield (MT) 600
Bears Paw Mountain (MT)
  599–600
Beartooth Highway (MT)
  589–90
Beartooth Range (WY) 431
Beaver Creek (CO) 247
beavers 21, 35, 376
Beckwourth, Jim 21, 23
Bedrock (CO) 338
Benton Lake National Wildlife
  Refuge (MT) 595–6

Bold indicates maps.

Bold indicates maps.

Bold indicates maps.

Bold indicates maps.

Bold indicates maps.

Boxed Text

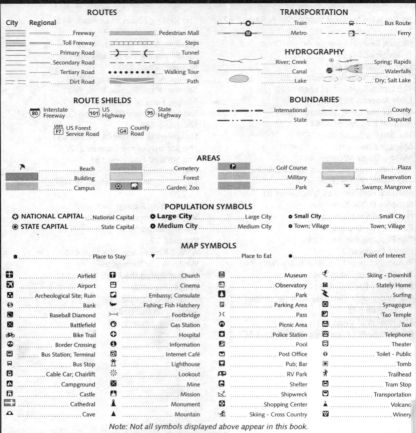

MAP LEGEND

ROUTES

City / Regional

- Freeway
- Toll Freeway
- Primary Road
- Secondary Road
- Tertiary Road
- Dirt Road
- Pedestrian Mall
- Steps
- Tunnel
- Trail
- Walking Tour
- Path

TRANSPORTATION

- Train
- Metro
- Bus Route
- Ferry

HYDROGRAPHY

- River; Creek
- Canal
- Lake
- Spring; Rapids
- Waterfalls
- Dry; Salt Lake

ROUTE SHIELDS

- (80) Interstate Freeway
- (101) US Highway
- (95) State Highway
- (F7) US Forest Service Road
- (G4) County Road

BOUNDARIES

- International
- State
- County
- Disputed

AREAS

- Beach
- Building
- Campus
- Cemetery
- Forest
- Garden; Zoo
- Golf Course
- Military
- Park
- Plaza
- Reservation
- Swamp; Mangrove

POPULATION SYMBOLS

- ◉ **NATIONAL CAPITAL** .... National Capital
- ◉ **STATE CAPITAL** .... State Capital
- ● **Large City** .... Large City
- ● **Medium City** .... Medium City
- ● Small City .... Small City
- ● Town; Village .... Town; Village

MAP SYMBOLS

- ● .... Place to Stay
- ▼ .... Place to Eat
- ● .... Point of Interest

Airfield	Church	Museum	Skiing - Downhill
Airport	Cinema	Observatory	Stately Home
Archeological Site; Ruin	Embassy; Consulate	Park	Surfing
Bank	Fishing; Fish Hatchery	Parking Area	Synagogue
Baseball Diamond	Footbridge	Pass	Tao Temple
Battlefield	Gas Station	Picnic Area	Taxi
Bike Trail	Hospital	Police Station	Telephone
Border Crossing	Information	Pool	Theater
Bus Station; Terminal	Internet Café	Post Office	Toilet - Public
Bus Stop	Lighthouse	Pub; Bar	Tomb
Cable Car; Chairlift	Lookout	RV Park	Trailhead
Campground	Mine	Shelter	Tram Stop
Castle	Mission	Shipwreck	Transportation
Cathedral	Monument	Shopping Center	Volcano
Cave	Mountain	Skiing - Cross Country	Winery

Note: Not all symbols displayed above appear in this book.

LONELY PLANET OFFICES

Australia
Locked Bag 1, Footscray, Victoria 3011
☎ 03 8379 8000 fax 03 8379 8111
email talk2us@lonelyplanet.com.au

USA
150 Linden Street, Oakland, California 94607
☎ 510 893 8555, TOLL FREE 800 275 8555
fax 510 893 8572
email info@lonelyplanet.com

UK
10a Spring Place, London NW5 3BH
☎ 020 7428 4800 fax 020 7428 4828
email go@lonelyplanet.co.uk

France
1 rue du Dahomey, 75011 Paris
☎ 01 55 25 33 00 fax 01 55 25 33 01
email bip@lonelyplanet.fr
www.lonelyplanet.fr

World Wide Web: www.lonelyplanet.com *or* AOL keyword: lp
Lonely Planet Images: lpi@lonelyplanet.com.au